Church of England Record Society
Volume 20

NATIONAL PRAYERS
SPECIAL WORSHIP SINCE THE REFORMATION

VOLUME 1

SPECIAL PRAYERS, FASTS AND THANKSGIVINGS
IN THE BRITISH ISLES
1533–1688

NATIONAL PRAYERS

SPECIAL WORSHIP SINCE THE REFORMATION

VOLUME 1

SPECIAL PRAYERS, FASTS AND THANKSGIVINGS IN THE BRITISH ISLES 1533–1688

EDITED BY
Natalie Mears, Alasdair Raffe,
Stephen Taylor and Philip Williamson
(with Lucy Bates)

THE BOYDELL PRESS

CHURCH OF ENGLAND RECORD SOCIETY

First published 2013

A Church of England Record Society publication
Published by The Boydell Press
an imprint of Boydell & Brewer Ltd
PO Box 9, Woodbridge, Suffolk IP12 3DF, UK
and of Boydell & Brewer Inc.
668 Mt Hope Avenue, Rochester, NY 14620–2731, USA
website: www.boydellandbrewer.com

ISBN 978–1–84383–868–5

ISSN 1351–3087

Series information is printed at the back of this volume

A CIP catalogue record for this book is available
from the British Library

The publisher has no responsibility for the continued existence or accuracy
of URLs for external or third-party internet websites referred to in this book,
and does not guarantee that any content on such websites is,
or will remain, accurate or appropriate.

Papers used by Boydell & Brewer Ltd are natural, recyclable products
made from wood grown in sustainable forests

Printed and bound in Great Britain by
TJ International Ltd, Padstow, Cornwall

Contents

VOLUME 2

GENERAL FASTS, THANKSGIVINGS AND SPECIAL PRAYERS
IN THE BRITISH ISLES, 1689–1870

EDITED BY

Alasdair Raffe, Stephen Taylor, Philip Williamson and Natalie Mears

VOLUME 3

WORSHIP FOR NATIONAL AND ROYAL OCCASIONS
IN THE UNITED KINGDOM, 1871–2012

EDITED BY

Philip Williamson, Stephen Taylor, Alasdair Raffe and Natalie Mears

Illustrations

Preface

This edition presents primary documents and historical explanations for a large number of special occasions of public worship in all or many localities in each kingdom of the British Isles over a span of almost 500 years, from the early sixteenth century to the early twenty-first century. The work on this edition originated in the Department of History at the University of Durham, from conversations between two historians whose research specialisms lay 400 years apart. Philip Williamson had noted the occurrence of 'national days of prayer' in publications on British politics and on the monarchy during the early twentieth century, without quite knowing what they were or being able to find out much about them. A two-page section in Owen Chadwick's history of the Victorian Church led to the realization that national days of prayer had links with special fast and thanksgiving days which had been ordered by the state not just during the mid-nineteenth century but also in earlier periods, and with annual religious commemorations which had been observed over several centuries. Meanwhile, Natalie Mears's research on political communication in Elizabethan England included examination of the 'special prayer books' or forms of prayer which had been used in churches for fast and thanksgiving days from the 1560s to the 1590s. Discussion during a departmental seminar in 2006 revealed not only a shared area of research interest between twentieth-century and sixteenth-century historians, but also the existence of a series of significant episodes, documents and historical issues extending over a very long period.

Subsequent searches in the Lambeth Palace Library catalogue, Early English Books Online (EEBO) and Eighteenth Century Collections Online (ECCO) showed that, in addition to the special services for fast and thanksgiving days and for the annual commemorations, a large number of special prayers had been added to the ordinary church services for specific days or specified periods. Occasions of special worship were also discovered in Scotland and Ireland as well as in England and Wales. Yet searches through bibliographies found only a small number of studies which mentioned the existence and considered the significance of these types of special worship. Valuable as these studies are, they dealt with only a few of these occasions, usually for only short periods. Most occasions of special worship were simply unknown. The significance of state or church decisions to order the observance of these occasions, the published documents that they produced, and the diverse and varying responses of the different churches and the mass of the people had been largely unconsidered. It was clear that these were materials and questions for a collaborative project, one which would reveal sources and new information for a very large number of religious occasions, would address significant issues in British religion, politics, culture and communication over the *longue durée*, and would advance studies across several fields of scholarship. Consultation with Stephen Taylor, then at the University of Reading, confirmed these early impressions. His expertise in religious and political history from the mid seventeenth to the early nineteenth centuries, and his experience as co-director of 'The Clergy of the Church of England Database 1540–1835' and as editor of series of texts and monographs in religious history brought the perspectives to complete our chronological and thematic approach.

The outcome was a successful application in 2006–7 to the Arts and Humanities Research Council, to which we are grateful for the award of a research grant for the project 'British state prayers, fasts and thanksgivings 1540s to the 1940s' (reference AH/E007481/1). This enabled the appointment as research associate of Alasdair Raffe, who provided expertise on early modern Scotland and also contributed research on special worship in Ireland, and of Lucy Bates as a doctoral student, who, in addition to her own research, assisted the project by bringing clarity to the considerable complexities of special worship in England from 1640 to 1660. The project was also assisted by a board of advisors, who particularly in the early stages but at numerous times since have offered valuable ideas, information and comment on drafts: Chris Brooks, Jay Brown, Arthur Burns, Jeremy Gregory, Matthew Grimley, David Hayton, Anthony Milton, Alec Ryrie, and John Wolffe.

This edition has expanded considerably in scope, chronological span and size from the original plan. In part, this was because our board of advisors confirmed our sense of the significance of the documents. They urged that versions of the complete texts rather than selections should be published, edited in order not just to print the formulae of orders, collects, psalms, biblical readings or addresses unique to particular occasions, but also to indicate the terminology and elements which became standard or which were repeated over the course of long periods. In part, expansion of the edition occurred due to the more detailed and wide-ranging research made possible by the project itself, and by the growing availability of searchable online sources. Many more occasions of special worship were found than had been expected: an initial list of around 450 occasions nearly doubled in number. It was decided to begin with a number of occasions in the 1530s which show the first effects of the Henrician reformation on special prayers and thanksgivings. Fixing a terminal date was less easy. Although, formally, the last national day of prayer was held in 1947, the established churches continued to order special prayers and services for particular matters. Remembrance Sunday had also to be included, as a twentieth-century revival of the tradition of annual commemorations, and which is still widely observed each year. Furthermore, special prayers and services issued for use in all churches to mark royal events had become more common from the late nineteenth century, and have continued into recent times. The edition therefore concludes with the prayers and services for the diamond jubilee of Queen Elizabeth II in 2012.

A project of this size and scope has required help and support from many individuals and organizations, in addition to members of its board of advisors. We especially thank Jacqui Fletcher and Christine Woodhead who assisted Alasdair Raffe in the considerable task of typing the texts of the documents, and have helped further in checking, formatting, proof-reading and advising on and indexing large parts of the text of all three volumes. Without their skill and patience this project would still be unfinished. Sharon Adams, Alex Barber, Melanie Barber, Rachel Cosgrave, Winifred Coutts, Elizabeth Evenden, Julie Farguson, Ken Fincham, Suzanne Forbes, Jo Fox, Richard Gameson, Raymond Gillespie, Julian Goodare, Margaret Harvey, Simon Healey, Richard Huzzey, Robert Ingram, Bill Jacob, Declan Kelly, James Kelly, Patrick Lynch, Alan MacDonald, Giles Mandelbrote, John Morrill, John Myerscough, Richard Palmer, Jason Peacey, Colin Podmore, Michael Prestwich, Nicole Reinhardt, Gabriel Sewell, Leona Skelton, David Smith, Laura Stewart,

Bernard Taylor, David Thompson, Kim Walker, John Walsh, Peter Webster, David Wykes, John Young and Aude Demezerac Zanetti assisted with specific enquiries. Rosalind Marshall facilitated access to the records of St Giles' Cathedral, Edinburgh. Christopher Wright at Cambridge University Press was especially helpful in finding forms of prayer and related records derived from Eyre and Spottiswoode and Cambridge University Press.

We are especially grateful to the staff of Lambeth Palace Library, where members of the project team have spent a great deal of time and have received assistance well beyond what a reader might normally expect. We also thank the staff of the many other archives and libraries we have visited to consult records, or who have supplied copies or information: Albert Sloman Library, University of Essex; Alexander Turnbull Library, Wellington, New Zealand; Armagh Public Library; Balliol College Library, Oxford; Bangor University Library; Beinecke Rare Book and Manuscript Library, Yale University; Berkshire Record Office; Berwick-upon-Tweed Record Office; Bodleian Library, Oxford; Borthwick Institute for Archives, University of York; Boston Public Library, Boston, MA; British Library; Buckinghamshire Record Office; Cambridge University Library; Canterbury Cathedral Library; Cashel Cathedral Library; Christ Church Library, Oxford; Clifton Diocesan Archives; Dublin (Roman Catholic) Diocesan Archives; Dr Williams's Library, London; Durham Cathedral Library; Durham University Library, Heritage Collections; East Riding Archives and Local Studies, Beverley Library; Emmanuel College Library, Cambridge; Folger Shakespeare Library, Washington, DC; Glasgow University Library; Guildhall Library, London; Harry Ransom Humanities Research Center, University of Texas at Austin; Hartley Library, University of Southampton; Robin Harcourt Williams, librarian and archivist to the marquess of Salisbury at Hatfield House, Hertfordshire; Hertfordshire Local Archives and Studies; Houghton Library, Harvard University; Hull History Centre; Institute of Historical Research, London; John Rylands University Library, University of Manchester; Keble College, Oxford; Lauinger Library, Georgetown University; Leicestershire, Leicester and Rutland Record Office; Liverpool Record Office; Liverpool University Library; London Metropolitan Archives; Marsh's Library, Dublin; National Archives, Kew; National Archives of Ireland; National Archives of Scotland; National Library of Ireland; National Library of Scotland; New College Library, Edinburgh; Norfolk Record Office; Parker Library, Corpus Christi College, Cambridge; Public Record Office of Northern Ireland; St Giles's Cathedral, Edinburgh; St John's College Library, Cambridge; St Paul's Cathedral Library; Representative Church Body Library, Dublin; the Royal Archives, Windsor; Society of Antiquaries; Trinity College Library, Dublin; University of East Anglia Library, Norwich; University of Missouri Library; Ushaw College Library, Durham; West Sussex Record Office, Chichester; West Yorkshire Archives Service, Wakefield; Westminster Abbey Library and Muniment Room; Westminster Diocesan Archives, including the Archives of the Archbishops of Westminster; Widener Library, Harvard University; York Minster Library; and Yale University Divinity School Library. Material from the Royal Archives is used with the permission of Her Majesty Queen Elizabeth II.

The scope and the detail of this project were made possible by access to a large number of online sources: library and archive catalogues from many parts of the world; EEBO, ECCO, The Cecil Papers, Medieval and Early Modern Sources Online (MEMSO), State Papers Online 1509–1782 and British History Online;

historical collections of newspapers and periodicals, particularly *The London Gazette*, *The Times*, *The Scotsman*, *The Glasgow Herald* and those made available from the British Library; Hansard 1803–2005 and the Cabinet Papers 1915–1982; and collections of newsreels and historical images. Some of these collections are freely available; for others, we are grateful for the access made possible by Durham University Library. We have also had considerable support from other resources and staff in the Department of History and more widely in the University of Durham.

Publication of this volume has been made possible thanks to a grant from the Scouloudi Foundation in association with the Institute of Historical Research.

The Project Group

Philip Williamson (principal investigator) is professor of history at the University of Durham, and author of *National crisis and national government. British politics, the economy and empire 1926–1932* (1992), and *Stanley Baldwin. Conservative leadership and national values* (1999). He has edited the private papers of William Bridgeman (1988) and, with Edward Baldwin, sources relating to Stanley Baldwin (2004). His further publications include essays and articles on twentieth-century British party politics, government and the monarchy, and more recently 'State prayers, fasts and thanksgivings: public worship in Britain 1830–1897', *Past and Present*, 200 (2008), and 'National days of prayer: the churches, the state and public worship in Britain 1899–1957', *English Historical Review*, 128 (2013).

Natalie Mears (co-investigator) is a senior lecturer in early modern English history at the University of Durham. She is the author of *Queenship and political discourse in the Elizabethan realms* (2005), and essays and articles on the Elizabethan court and political culture. Her recent publications include 'Public worship and political participation in Elizabethan England', *Journal of British Studies*, 51 (2012), and 'Special nationwide worship and the Book of Common Prayer in England, Wales and Ireland, 1533–1642', in *Worship and the parish church in early modern Britain*, ed. Natalie Mears and Alec Ryrie (2012).

Stephen Taylor (co-investigator), until 2012 professor of early modern history at the University of Reading, is now professor of history at the University of Durham. He is a director of *The Clergy of the Church of England Database* and honorary academic editor of the Royal Historical Society. He has published numerous essays, articles and co-edited volumes on the religious and political history of seventeenth- and eighteenth-century England. His editions and commentaries include *The entring book of Roger Morrice. Vol. 4: 1687–1689* (2007) and 'George III's recovery from madness celebrated: precedent and innovation in the observance of royal celebrations and commemorations', in *From the reformation to the permissive society*, ed. Melanie Barber and Stephen Taylor (Church of England Record Society, 18, 2010).

Alasdair Raffe (research associate), formerly lecturer at Northumbria University, is now chancellor's fellow in history at the University of Edinburgh. He is the author of *The culture of controversy: religious arguments in Scotland, 1660–1714* (2012), and his essays and articles include 'Nature's scourges: the natural world and special prayers, fasts and thanksgivings, 1543–1866', in *God's bounty? The churches and the natural world*, ed. Peter Clarke and Tony Claydon (Studies in Church History, 46, 2010).

Lucy Bates (doctoral student) is now director of studies at MPW college in Cambridge. Her doctoral thesis (Durham, 2012) is entitled 'Nationwide fast and thanksgiving days in England, 1640–1660'.

Advisory board

Professor Chris Brooks, University of Durham
Professor S. J. Brown, University of Edinburgh
Professor Arthur Burns, King's College, London
Professor Jeremy Gregory, University of Manchester
Dr Matthew Grimley, Merton College, Oxford
Professor David Hayton, Queen's University, Belfast
Professor Anthony Milton, University of Sheffield
Professor Alec Ryrie, University of Durham
Professor John Wolffe, The Open University

Summary List of Particular Occasions of Special Worship, 1533–1688

Key to codes

E	England and Wales
Ir	Ireland
S	Scotland
Number	added to letter codes when more than one occasion was ordered during a year
Number only	all three kingdoms
(P)	occasions ordered by parliament during the civil war, 1642–8
(R)	occasions ordered under the king's authority during the civil war

Notes

Occasions are listed in chronological order of observance.

Where occasions had several causes, only the principal ones are given here: for fuller details see 'Analytical list of occasions of special worship 1533–2012', pp. cxi–clvii, and the commentaries for each occasion in the main text.

'?' indicates where the cause of an occasion is unknown or uncertain.

Code	Description	Cause	Page
1533–E	thanksgiving service	birth of Princess Elizabeth	3
1535–E	procession	recovery from illness of Francis I of France	3
1537–E1	*Te Deums*	pregnancy of Queen Jane	4
1537–E2	processions, *Te Deums*	birth of Prince Edward	5
1537–E3	processions	health of Queen Jane and Prince Edward	6
1537–E4	dirges	death of Queen Jane	7
1540–E	prayers and processions	drought and disease	8
1541–E	prayers	severe drought	9
1543–E1	prayers	Ottoman invasion of Hungary	9
1543–E2	prayers and processions	wet weather and threats to the harvest	11
1544–E1	thanksgiving service	victories in Scotland	13
1544–E2	services and processions	military campaigns in France	14
1544–E3	thanksgiving services	victory at Boulogne	23
1544–E4	*Te Deums* and procession	Henry VIII's return from military campaign in France	24
1545–E1	processions	naval campaign against France	25
1545–E2	thanksgiving procession	victories in Scotland, relief of Boulogne	26
1546–E	thanksgiving procession	peace with France	27
1547–E	thanksgiving service, *Te Deums* and procession	battle of Pinkie	28
1548–E	prayers	victory and peace in the Scottish war	29
1549–E	service	Western and Kett's rebellions	31
1550–E	*Te Deums*	peace with France	34

Reader's Guide and Editorial Conventions

This edition brings together the core texts for all occasions of special national worship observed in the constituent parts of the British Isles from the beginning of the reformation in England to recent times, ending in 2012. It also provides commentaries and lists of sources for each occasion of special worship, together with related supplementary and contextual information, and a general explanatory Introduction.

The phrase 'special national worship' is used for editorial convenience. In strict terms, it is problematic for several reasons, not least the differences between an early modern kingdom and a modern nation; the changing relationships of the political units of England and Wales, Scotland and Ireland, and their incorporation in Great Britain and Ireland, and then the United Kingdom of Britain and Ireland (since 1921 Northern Ireland); and the varied and changing constitutional relationships between the governments and the established churches of the three kingdoms of the British Isles. It should particularly be noted that England and Wales was until recently a single political unit, and that until 1920 the Church of England included the anglican church in Wales: for this reason, 'England' is often used here as a shorthand for both England and Wales. In some periods, the English or British 'religious unit' was regarded as extending to the overseas plantations, colonies and dominions.

The term 'special worship' is taken to include both *particular* occasions of special worship, those appointed for one day or for short periods, and *anniversary* (or annual) religious commemorations, those appointed to be observed on a specific date each year.

These problems of definition and the principles for inclusion are discussed in detail in the Introduction. Essentially, however, the edition includes all those occasions on which the state and/or the established churches of England (and Wales), Scotland and Ireland, Great Britain and Ireland and the United Kingdom have ordered or requested special worship which either supplemented or replaced the normal patterns of daily and Sunday worship. The focus on the established churches means that orders for churches after they were disestablished – the Church of Ireland in 1871, the Church in Wales in 1920 – have not been included, nor have orders for dissenting, nonconformist or free churches, or the Roman catholic church.

The 'core texts' reproduced in the edition fall into two main groups – orders and forms of prayer – with a third group consisting of addresses. By 'orders' are meant the documents which were generated by the authorities in the state and/or the established church when arranging the occasions. In many cases, these are proclamations or orders in council issued by the crown, but orders could also take the form of parliamentary orders, resolutions of church assemblies, letters from monarchs, politicians or clergymen, or announcements in newspapers. Forms of prayer consist of the prayers and liturgies issued for use on most occasions of special worship by the Church of England and the Church of Ireland. Forms of prayer were not issued in England and Wales or in Ireland during the civil wars and Interregnum from 1642 to 1660 (with the exception of a few royalist forms published from 1642 to 1648). Nor, with the exception of the order of service for the first national fast in

1566, were forms of prayer issued by the Church of Scotland before the twentieth century. Instead, the revolutionary regimes from 1642 to 1660, and the Church of Scotland over four centuries tended to publish addresses – exhortations, admonitions, narratives, causes, letters – which were to be read out during church services. On a number of occasions, similar addresses were published within the forms of prayer for the Church of England.

The edition notes, where known, the observance of English, later British, occasions of special worship in the overseas colonies and other imperial or Commonwealth territories. This information is normally supplied just in the commentaries. The texts of a small number of orders or notices for overseas observances are printed, but only when these had a clear and general 'imperial' purpose – when issued by the crown or the sovereign from London to the governors or other presiding officials in *all or most* of the overseas territories, requiring or requesting observance throughout the colonies, protectorates, dominions, empire or Commonwealth. These orders or notices were usually for thanksgivings. Those orders or notices issued only on the 'local' initiative of overseas governors or officials – typically on receipt of news from the British Isles or (very often in the North American colonies before 1776) for 'local' colonial reasons – are not published here, because these strictly related only to the each particular colony or other territory. For the same reason, forms of prayers published by the authorities in the overseas territories are neither printed nor systematically recorded here.

CODES

Eight hundred and sixty-six *particular* occasions of special national worship have been identified. For ease of reference and cross-reference each *particular* occasion has been given an identification code in the format 1563–E1, or 1830–1, or 1643–E10(P).

Year This denotes the year during which the observance was marked. If the observance extended across two or more years, only the first year is given. Dates for the period before the calendar change in 1752 are in old style, but with the year taken to begin on 1 January.

Letter 'E', 'S' or 'Ir' indicate a *particular* occasion which took place in all (or, in some cases, some part) of England and Wales, or Scotland, or Ireland. When an occasion was observed in two, but not three, of these kingdoms, both geographical identifiers have been used, e.g. 1641–ES. It should be emphasized that the identifiers in the codes are simply geographical; they bear no relation to the changing constitutional relationships of the constituent parts of the British Isles across the last five centuries.

Letter and number Where more than one *particular* occasion in one or more geographical areas was ordered during the same year, a number is added to the code (e.g., 1651–E7 was the seventh occasion of special worship to be ordered for England and Wales during 1651). When several occasions took place in one year within a geographical area, these are numbered chronologically reckoned on the date of observance, rather than the date of order (see e.g. 1651–E1, 1651–E2 and 1651–E3).

Number only When an occasion took place in all three kingdoms, no letter is given but only a number, e.g. 1977–1.

(R) and (P) During the civil war from 1642 to 1648, occasions were ordered independently by the crown (the royalists) and by parliament. These are distinguished by the suffix (R) and (P) respectively.

In the index and in cross-references the suffix 'Ir' is occasionally added in brackets to distinguish the form of prayer used in Ireland from that used in England (e.g. 1739–1(Ir)).

Nine *anniversary commemorations* (AC) were at various periods appointed and observed in one or more kingdoms of the British Isles. These commemorations are as follows, giving the code by date in the year (where a set date was appointed) or by name of the commemoration (if the date in the year varied). In the list below – and in the section on Anniversary Commemorations in volume 3 – they are given in the order of their first appointment. The letters E, S and Ir in this list refer to England and Wales, Scotland and Ireland.

Special services for AC–Accession, AC–5 Nov., AC–29 May and AC–30 Jan. were annexed to the 1662 Book of Common Prayer at the start of each reign by a succession of royal warrants, and, together with the service for AC–23 Oct., to the Irish Book of Common Prayer. Except for the service for AC–Accession, all of these services were discontinued in 1859 (as, it appears, was that for AC–2 Sept. in most London churches).

Special services for AC–Accession and for AC–Remembrance remain available for use, and the service for AC–Accession has continued to be annexed to editions of the BCP.

AC–Accession	accession day of the sovereign E from 1576, Ir from 1686
AC–5 Aug.	failure of the Gowrie plot in 1600 S from 1601, E from 1603 (fell into disuse after 1625)
AC–5 Nov.	discovery of the gunpowder plot in 1605 E and S from 1606, Ir from ?1666 with addition of commemoration of the 1688 revolution E and Ir from 1689 (discontinued 1859)
AC–29 May	restoration of the monarchy in 1660 E and S from 1661, Ir from 1662 (discontinued in S 1690; in E and Ir 1859)
AC–30 Jan.	execution ('martyrdom') of King Charles I E from 1661, Ir from ?1666 (discontinued 1859)
AC–23 Oct.	discovery of the Irish rising in 1641 Ir from 1663 (discontinued 1859)
AC–2 Sept.	great fire of London London from 1667 (discontinued 1859)
AC–sovbirthday	birthday of the sovereign S from 1685 (fell into religious disuse after 1688)
AC–Remembrance	Remembrance Sunday churches in E, S, Ir from 1920, recognized by the UK government 1946

ORGANIZATION OF THE EDITION

Summary list

Each of the three volumes of the edition has a summary list of the *particular occasions* contained within each volume, giving code, a simple description and the opening page number for the commentary and texts for each occasion. This offers an easy finding aid.

Introduction

The Introductions in each volume have the purpose of providing readers with the general and contextual material necessary to use, understand and interpret the texts which follow. The Introduction in the first volume begins by outlining the significance of special national worship, and providing definitions of the types of occasions and documents. The second part of this Introduction – and the Introductions to the second and third volumes – describe the main phases and developments over the last five centuries and the reasons for the occasions, discuss some of the ambiguities and complexities of 'national' worship, analyse the process of ordering, printing and distribution and give an account of the sources. The Introductions do not, however, attempt to provide a full discussion of the purposes and meanings of these occasions. An interpretative and analytical monograph in which questions such as these will be discussed at length is planned. The Introductions may be read as introductory essays on the development of special national worship across five centuries. They are divided into sections and sub-sections in order to facilitate easy reference to a range of topics.

Analytical list

A complete 'analytical' list of all *particular occasions* from 1533 to 2012 follows the Introduction in the first volume. This longer list gives the date of observance and description of the type of occasion (fast day, thanksgiving day, special services, special prayers, national day of prayer, etc.); the day(s) of the week on which the observance took place, and an indication of whether it was observed once or on several days; the geographical area(s) within which observance took place; and a summary of the reason(s) for, or cause(s) of, the occasion. Fuller details under all of these headings are provided in the editorial apparatus which precedes the texts for each occasion in the three volumes.

Special worship and the Book of Common Prayer (BCP)

A guide to the BCP, printed in each volume, provides the reader with an outline of the structure of the three services (morning prayer, communion and evening prayer), together with the litany, in order to indicate the places in these standard services where changes were made on special occasions of worship in the Church of England and the Church of Ireland. The forms of prayer ordered for use on special occasions in both of these churches were, until the late nineteenth century, invariably based upon the successive versions of the BCP (1559, 1604, 1662), and the 1662 BCP remained a common point of reference for such forms of prayer well into the twentieth century. The guide provides an outline of the structure of the main services in the BCP, showing:

(a) the parts which were modified for the special services which were published for major occasions of special worship (typically fast days and thanksgiving days)

(b) the places where one or a small number of special prayers were inserted within the usual services for other special occasions.

Printers of official documents

This section gives the names of the printers of the chief documents published by government authority for occasions of special worship: the orders issued by the government itself (typically proclamations or orders in council), and the forms of prayer or other documents which were ordered by the government to be read in churches. These printers were usually the royal printers, though for short periods in the seventeenth century the printers were employed by parliament or the governments of the Republic. Royal printers in particular were usually appointed for long periods, and it is convenient as far as possible to list the names in this section, rather than to have many repetitions of the printers' names in the citations of sources. This section may also have value as a contribution to the history of printing by the government. From 1708, government orders were printed consistently in the official gazettes – the *London Gazette* (which normally printed not just the orders for England and Wales but also those for Scotland), and the *Dublin Gazette*. Hereafter, these are the preferred source, cited in the notes for each commentary. The effect is that from 1708, the list gives the names of the royal printers of forms of prayer in England and Wales and in Ireland.

Texts and commentaries

These are divided in two ways. First, the commentaries, notes and texts for the *particular* occasions of special worship, which form the bulk of the edition, and are divided as follows:

Volume 1	1533–1688
Volume 2	1689–1870
Volume 3	1871–2012

The dates at which the volumes are divided have some significance: the accession of William III (William II in Scotland) and the opening of the Nine Years War in 1689 were followed by the emergence of a series of annual fasts in time of war, while the illness of the prince of Wales in 1871 inaugurated a period of significant elaboration of special worship in royal occasions. But these dividing dates should not be invested with too much significance. Other dates are at least as important in the history of special national worship, and the division of the three volumes is primarily a matter of convenience.

Second, the commentaries, notes and texts for the anniversary commemorations from 1576 to 2012, printed in volume 3.

Appendices

Volume 3 contains a series of appendices, detailing, *inter alia*, omitted occasions, translations, forms of service from other religious bodies and broadcast services, together with the indices.

ORGANIZATION OF THE EDITORIAL APPARATUS AND TEXTS

The materials provided for each *particular* occasion are divided into two sections: the editorial apparatus and the texts. The format is standard for every occasion and consists of the following elements.

Editorial apparatus

The editorial apparatus is divided into four sub-sections.

Heading
A heading gives the identification code and a title, briefly describing the event and denoting what type of special worship was ordered (e.g. prayers, fast day, thanksgiving day, national day of prayer, etc.):

1533–E   Thanksgiving service for the birth of Princess Elizabeth

Sub-heading
A sub-heading summarizes the day(s) and date(s) on which the occasion was observed and the area within which observance took place, in the following format:

**Sunday 29 January 1626 (London, Westminster and adjacent places);
Sunday 19 February 1626 (elsewhere in England and Wales).**

Where the date of observance is not known – for instance, because the order does not survive – we place the projected dates in [square brackets]. For occasions when there were notable observances in the colonies or other territories, on different dates, this is indicated as follows: **various dates (colonies/empire).**

Commentary
A commentary is provided for each occasion, outlining its context, and further details when known: why, how and by whom the occasion was ordered; the ordering process; information about the form of prayer (if commissioned); and information, where extant, on observance. Attention is also drawn to significant developments in the types of occasion, the reasons for special worship, the ordering process, the format of liturgies etc. These commentaries vary substantially in length, depending on the context of the event, its complexity and the survival of evidence. Commentaries are intended to be self-contained, so that readers who are interested in only one occasion are provided with enough information to understand its context. But we are also aware that some readers may be interested in particular periods or types of occasion (e.g. those linked to the monarchy), and cross-references assist the reading of texts in sequence.

Bibliographical information
Unless otherwise stated, the place of publication is London.

Order(s): The type of order (proclamation, order in council, order of the general assembly, etc.) and the date of issue are given. The names of printers of most government orders before 1708 are given in the section on 'Printers of Official Documents' (consequently, where no publisher is given in these notes of bibliographical information, the name is to be found in the section on official printers). Orders published without an imprint are so identified. After 1708, the source for most government orders is the official *Gazette*. In cases of orders by other authorities, the names of the publishers are given in the source notes. The source of the text of the order is then given.

> 'Not known' indicates where it is not known whether a written or printed order was issued (some 'orders' were expressed verbally, at meetings).

> 'None found' indicates where it is known from other evidence that there was an order, but where there appears to be no extant copy.

When different orders were issued for different geographical areas, these are listed as follows: ENGLAND AND WALES: *Short title* … IRELAND: *Short title* … Notes regarding identical reprints are listed in [square brackets]. The few instances of 'imperial' orders from London to overseas territories are noted as COLONIAL: *Short title* …

For the period to 1800, orders, such as proclamations, which were published as broadsides and pamphlets are provided with the relevant number in the following bibliographical guides: STC, Thomason, Wing and ESTC.

An asterisk denotes that these items can be consulted in the main online digital collections: Early English Books Online (EEBO) and Eighteenth Century Collections Online (ECCO).

The term 'order' is for editorial convenience and is used liberally. For some occasions, and especially from the 1870s, the document might be an exhortation, a recommendation or a request. There are evident differences between a royal proclamation, enforceable by recourse to civil or ecclesiastical courts, and an announcement in a newspaper that an archbishop or church moderator suggests that special prayers should be said. But these varying types of document share the function that they publicly initiated an occasion of special worship.

Form(s) of prayer: The first edition of the form of prayer (if ordered and extant) is listed, followed by its page length and, in the case of forms printed before 1801, the STC, Wing, Thomason or ESTC number. An asterisk after this number indicates that the source text is the copy available on EEBO or ECCO during the preparation of this edition. For forms which were not available on EEBO or ECCO at the time of research, the library shelf-mark of the copy used in the edition is provided. Unless otherwise noted, the printer is the royal printer. Forms published without an imprint are so identified.

When different forms were ordered for different geographical areas, these are listed as follows: ENGLAND AND WALES: *title* … IRELAND: *title* … Notes regarding reprints – especially of sixteenth-century forms reproduced by W. K. Clay (*Liturgical services: liturgies and occasional forms of prayer set forth in the reign of Queen Elizabeth*) in 1847 – appear in [square brackets], as does a list of any variant editions of *official* forms of prayer. Thus, in the twentieth century, this list includes editions published by Cambridge University Press and Oxford University Press, as well as those of the royal printers.

'Not known' indicates when it is not known whether a form of prayer was published.

'None found' indicates where it is known from other evidence that a form was published, but no extant copy has been located.

Where a Welsh translation is extant, this is noted after the details of the English form. Most references to Welsh translations take the form '*LW*' and '*LWS*' followed by a number. These are cross-references to the standard bibliography of books in the Welsh language, as follows:

LW   *Libri Walliae. A catalogue of Welsh books and books printed in Wales 1546–1820*, ed. Eiluned Rees (Aberystwyth, 1987), vol. I.

LWS   *Libri Walliae ... Supplement*, ed. Charles Parry (Aberystwyth, 2001).

Only where a copy is not recorded in these volumes are fuller bibliographical details provided. An appendix in volume 3 comments further on these Welsh translations.

Official French translations (intended for the use of Huguenot congregations) are also noted, and discussed further in an appendix.

Where forms of prayer were not ordered (in Scotland and in England during the 1640s and 1650s), this item on 'Forms of prayer' is omitted from the list of Bibliographical Information

Forms of prayer (other editions): This lists versions of the standard Church of England or Church of Ireland form of prayer which were produced by printers other than the royal printer. In most cases, these were unofficial and unauthorized, indeed 'pirated', though in some cases they might represent some subcontracting by the royal printers. An attempt has been made to locate as many of these forms as possible, using searches in a number of libraries, archives and record offices and in online library catalogues and archive lists. But their survival and listing is haphazard, and the information provided here should be regarded as largely indicative.

If the title of such a form is essentially the same as the main form, only the place of publication, publisher and STC/Wing/ESTC number (or library location and shelf-mark) are given. If the title is significantly different, the title is given as well as the printer, place of publication and source/library information.

Address, Causes, Declaration, Letter: These headings are used in cases where, in addition to or instead of the order, a statement was published to be read in church. Most commonly, these were published by the Church of Scotland.

Additional sources: This lists the primary sources used in the writing of the commentary. Secondary historical writings are cited only if they contain primary evidence which was not otherwise available to the editors, or directly concerned with the particular occasion or series of occasions. Other secondary writings, such as monographs and articles, which refer to occasions as part of the discussion of other subjects, are not listed.

Printed sermons: An indicative list of printed sermons for each occasion is given. The list has been compiled primarily through searches of the standard bibliographies, notably STC and Wing before 1700, ESTC for the period from 1701

to 1801, and COPAC (www.copac.ac.uk) after 1801, supplemented by other sources, such as *Fast sermons to parliament*, ed. Robin Jeffs (34 vols., 1970–1). Sermons are organized by country, within which they are listed by surname of preacher (with initial if there were preachers with the same surname), followed by the place where the sermon was delivered and (up to 1801) the STC/Wing/ESTC reference. In the course of the nineteenth century, the earlier practice of publishing single sermons delivered on occasions such as this declined. It became common, however, for reports of major sermons to be published in the newspapers, and references are given to such reports in the chief national newspapers, typically *The Times* and *The Scotsman*. This practice of newspaper reports itself declined after 1945.

Texts

The texts are sub-divided into two sections.

Order(s)

A sub-heading gives details of the type of order, the issuing authority, and the date of issue. There might be several orders for the same occasion, for one or more reasons: separate orders for England and Wales, Scotland or Ireland (and occasionally for the colonies); separate orders by different authorities, most often in Scotland by the government and by the Church of Scotland; other supplementary orders by the government or the churches; from the late nineteenth century, separate orders appointing the worship and a public holiday.

A transcription is then provided of the order or orders. The orders for England and Wales, Scotland and Ireland are presented separately, in chronological order of ordering.

The main state orders – proclamations and orders in council – begin and end with standard formulations. For example, proclamations typically open with some such phrase as 'By the King a Proclamation [with title of occasion]', and ending with 'Given at Our Court at [place, date, regnal year]. God save the King.' In the transcriptions, these standard phrases are usually omitted. They are, however, usually added for Ireland (where a full text is extant), as the names of the lord lieutenant or lords justices and council members may be significant.

In many cases, a full transcription of the main text of the order is not provided. Instead, where sections of text have been repeated from an earlier order, these have been indicated by the use of catch-phrases, ellipses and a cross-reference to the earlier text within square brackets. This practice has been adopted partly for reasons of space, but also partly to alert the reader to the ways in which texts were either re-cycled or changed throughout the period. For some occasions, when there are only minor changes to an order – the date of the observance or the name of a royal child, for example – these are indicated in an editorial note in *[italics in square brackets]*.

In selecting the base texts for orders, contemporary printed sources have been preferred throughout, partly because these were the texts likely to have been most widely available. Until 1707, proclamations, declarations and ordinances printed as broadsides and pamphlets have been used whenever possible. From 1708, the copies of proclamations and orders in council for England and Wales and for Scotland which appeared in the *London Gazette* have been printed. For Ireland, the *Dublin*

Gazette has been used until these crown orders ceased in Ireland, following the disestablishment of the Church of Ireland in 1871. The *Edinburgh Gazette* normally reprinted verbatim the orders and notices from the *London Gazette*. It has been cited only when a special issue of the *London Gazette* seems not to be available, and when, for 1897–1, it alone published an order for Scotland.

For special worship ordered by parliament for which there is no separate printed order extant, the relevant entry/entries from the *Journals of the Houses of Commons* and the *Journals of the House of Lords* have been used.

For orders issued by the authorities of the Church of Scotland, printed broadsheets have been used where possible; otherwise Calderwood's *History*, the *Acts and proceedings of the general assemblies*, the *Records of the commissions of the general assemblies* or the *Principal acts of the general assembly* have usually been the source.

For other types of order, especially from the 1860s, the preferred source has been notices printed in *The Times*, *The Scotsman* or occasionally other newspapers.

Where contemporary printed orders are not available, we have used either manuscript letters or contemporary copies of manuscript letters from as close to the decision-maker as possible.

For general orders issued to overseas colonies, dominions and other territories, the text in the Colonial Office records is used.

Form(s) of prayer or Address, Causes, Declaration, Letter
A sub-heading gives the geographical area, where there is more than one form or address.

A transcription is then provided of the form or forms of prayer issued for each occasion, and any address, causes, declaration, exhortation or letter ordered to be read in church, most commonly by the Church of Scotland.

Where the occasion was observed in more than one geographical area, documents appear in chronological order.

In most cases, a full transcription is not provided. There are two reasons for this. As with the orders, it is partly because of the constraints of space, but the larger reason has been to indicate the material in particular forms of prayer which was derived from earlier sources.

First, where sections of text have been repeated from an earlier form of prayer or address (etc.), these have been indicated by the use of catch-phrases, ellipses and a cross-reference to the earlier form within square brackets. For some occasions, when there are only minor changes – the name of a royal child, for example – these are indicated in an editorial note in *[italics in square brackets]*. This practice also alerts the reader to the ways in which texts were re-cycled throughout the period.

Second, most forms of prayer for the Church of England and the Church of Ireland, certainly from the beginning of the seventeenth century until the mid-twentieth century, consisted of additions to or adaptations of the services printed in the BCP of 1559, 1604 and then 1662 and in Irish versions of the BCP. In these cases, the standard elements of the services have not been reproduced. Instead, they are indicated by square brackets in italics – e.g. *[Te Deum]*. The reader should be aware, however, that, over the centuries, practice varied in the printing of forms. Sometimes, elements of the service, such as the psalms and the epistle and gospel were printed in full, but sometimes they were just given as references. In this edition, no distinction has been made between these two practices, and, in all cases, the references only are printed (e.g. Ps. 30: 2), generally in square brackets, though occasionally such references and the accompanying rubrics are printed in full.

Rubrics have been retained where they are different from those in the BCP, where they provide additional information about the structure of the service or how it was celebrated, or when paraphrasing does not lead to a significant reduction in words.

Within orders of service, for ease of reference the headings for the different services have been standardized to 'Morning prayer', 'Litany', 'Communion' (or 'The second service' in some pre-civil war texts) and 'Evening prayer'.

Summary outlines of the liturgy from the BCPs of 1559 and 1662 are provided in the section on **Special worship and the Book of Common Prayer** in each volume. But any reader who wants to reconstruct *everything* that was said in a church service on any of these occasions will need to refer to the BCP, as, in fact, most ministers did when they used these forms of prayer.

Forms of prayer from other religious bodies
The scope of this edition is limited to occasions or worship ordered by the state or by the established churches of England and Wales, Scotland and Ireland, and to the documents published by the state and these established churches.

Other religious bodies outside the established churches may or may not have ordered special worship for their own congregations on the occasions appointed by the state or the established church. For some periods, they did not, but from the late nineteenth century many increasingly tended to do so. The orders issued by these churches are not easy to locate, but some forms of prayer are known to exist. Appendices in volume 3 provide information on the forms of prayer known to have been issued by other churches and religious groups, specifically the free churches, methodists, Roman catholics, the Episcopal Church of Scotland and the Jewish community. An attempt has been made to track down as many of these as possible, but their survival is haphazard and the information given here should be regarded as no more than indicative.

Descriptions of occasions
For a few, mainly sixteenth-century, occasions, when neither order nor form is extant, descriptions of the event have been printed, either from contemporary sources, such as *Wriothesley's chronicle* or from later antiquarian writings, whose authors had access to sources which are now lost.

TRANSCRIPTION

Most of the texts reproduced in this edition were printed, and the copy cited in the source notes has been used for the transcription.

Original spelling, capitalization and punctuation have been retained in the transcription of both printed and manuscript texts, except for common abbreviations such as the thorn (y^e, etc.), 'per', 'pro' and lines over vowels (such as 'Religiō'), which have been expanded silently. Thus, the use of 'u' for 'v' and 'v' for 'u' in sixteenth- and seventeenth-century texts has been retained. Any other expansions (e.g. 'm' overlined) appear in [square brackets].

Where printers have emphasized particular words of phrases of text by using a different font (e.g. roman type in a document printed primarily in black letter), this is denoted throughout by the use of *italics*.

The way in which psalms are presented has been standardized, as has the general layout of forms. Thus, in the case of the 'composite psalms' – that is, the 'psalms' composed for fast and thanksgiving days from a series of biblical verses – the references to each verse are consistently printed in brackets at the end of the verse; (round brackets) are used where the full references appear in the original texts, whether as marginal references, in-line references or footnotes, while [square brackets] have been used when part or all of the reference has been supplied by the editors and where an error in the original reference has been identified. In some cases, the authors of these 'psalms' loosely paraphrased the original, and it has not been possible to identify specific references.

Where documents have been damaged or the text is illegible, the missing text has either been supplied from another copy (as is explained in the commentary or footnotes) or projected in [square brackets].

It should be noted that from the sixteenth to the eighteenth centuries, minor differences of spelling, capitalization and punctuation sometimes occurred between different impressions of orders, forms of prayer and addresses, having been introduced by the use of several typesetters and printing frames. Consequently, when passages from one form have been reused in a later form, minor changes of spelling, capitalization and punctuation have been ignored.

In many respects, the editing of printed texts poses fewer problems of transcription and presentation than manuscript texts. However, compiling an edition containing printed texts through a period of almost five centuries presents some challenges. The tension between retaining the appearance and flavour of the original work and imposing consistency across the edition is much greater than when editing texts from a shorter period. Typographical practices changed significantly between the sixteenth and the twentieth centuries, most notably perhaps in the disappearance of black letter type, but also in a myriad of smaller ways. The editorial challenge is the greater because it is clear that the appearance of many forms of prayer was the product of much thought and discussion. It was decided, however, that while the history of the appearance of forms of prayer (and other documents such as proclamations and addresses) has much interest, it is not a subject that could be addressed in this edition. In the presentation of the texts, the edition therefore errs towards consistency of appearance, while enabling readers to obtain some sense of the appearance of the originals, and how these changed across the centuries, through the provision of a number of illustrations. Accordingly, in the transcribed materials the reader will see no difference between texts that were produced in black letter and those printed in roman type, though the transition is noted in the commentaries. The practice of early modern typesetters of printing the first couple of letters or first word of a document (or sometimes a paragraph) in capitals has not been replicated. Twentieth-century forms tend to include much more white space than early modern ones; again, this will not be apparent to readers.

LOCATION AND SURVIVAL OF SOURCES

The relevant major public and private libraries and archives – in England, Scotland and Ireland, and the USA – have been searched not just for the manuscript or printed texts, but also for sources to assist the writing of commentaries. The materials used have included the records of the established churches and the archbishops of

Canterbury, the state papers, the private papers of British government ministers and churchmen and, from the nineteenth century, records of government departments, the Royal Archives and archives of royal printers and the Society for Promoting Christian Knowledge. Searches have been undertaken in parish records in a number of local record offices in England, sufficient to indicate that further research in these records would be valuable. The major printed collections have been consulted, including the records of parliament, the works of early historians, compilers and anti-quarians, and editions of diaries, letters and historical texts. Extensive searches have been made in newspapers and periodical reviews, often using digital collections, and in the archives of particular newspapers. Much further evidence has become avail-able recently in the digitized and searchable online collections of printed material, including government and parliamentary publications, collections of older books and ephemeral and periodical literature in EEBO and ECCO. Limited searches have been undertaken in the archives of the Roman catholic and Free Churches to assist with the writing of commentaries.

It became clear during the research for this edition that the survival of orders and forms of prayer is haphazard for all periods from the sixteenth century to recent times. The following paragraphs indicate the problems and therefore offer explana-tions for some of the lacunae in texts and thinness of some commentaries.

England and Wales

For the earliest parts of the period, mandates and letters were not recorded system-atically in archi-episcopal and episcopal registers. For this reason, it is often unclear for the sixteenth century whether special worship ordered in Canterbury province of the Church of England was also ordered in York province. Successive archbishops – perhaps bizzarely, to the modern mind – do not appear to have kept a 'file copy' of the forms of prayer that were issued, and some of those who did, retained them as part of their personal libraries. For example, the forms of prayer collected by William Sancroft, archbishop of Canterbury 1677–91, are now located, along with much of the rest of his library, at Emmanuel College, Cambridge. Accordingly, while Lambeth Palace Library has provided copies of many of the texts used in the compilation of this edition, its collection of forms of prayer is not comprehensive. Parts of the Lambeth collection can be linked to individual archbishops – notably Thomas Tenison, archbishop of Canterbury 1694–1715 – but many of its forms have no obvious link with particular archbishops. A further extensive collection in the British Library supplied some further copies, but it too does not have a complete run of forms. A few parishes retained sequences of forms, generally for relatively short periods, and have deposited these in regional record offices. Some impor-tant collections were put together by antiquarians in the nineteenth and twentieth centuries, notably those of J. W. Niblock (at Dr Williams's Library in London) and the Josiah Benton collection (now in Boston Public Library, in the USA). But, in general, forms of prayer and, still more, the proclamations and orders in council that were sent to all parishes, were treated as ephemera, and the survival of copies does not reflect the large (from the nineteenth century, very large) numbers that were printed. This is true even of twentieth-century forms, which have not been routinely deposited in the copyright libraries.

Ireland

An explosion and fire at the Public Record Office in Dublin in June 1922 resulted in the destruction of the only substantial collection of Irish proclamations. Evidence for the existence of many proclamations can be found in lists of proclamations for all parts of the British Isles which had been compiled before this destruction (*A bibliography of royal proclamations of the Tudor and Stuart sovereigns and of others published under authority, 1485–1714*, compiled by Robert Steele (2 vols., Oxford, 1910) and *A handlist of proclamations issued by royal and other constitutional authorities, 1714–1910* ..., compiled by the earl of Crawford (Wigan, 1913)). But these did not calendar or transcribe the proclamations and other orders. For the period up to around 1700, therefore, there are significant gaps in our knowledge of the ordering of Irish fasts and thanksgivings, and often all that can be done is to cite 'Steele'. From the early eighteenth century the gaps can often be filled from the texts of proclamations published in the *Dublin Gazette*, though there are also significant gaps in the surviving holdings of that publication. Moreover, the explosion and fire in 1922 also destroyed much of the administrative record of the government in Dublin and of correspondence between Dublin and England, losses that may well have included records of the Irish privy council. Certainly, very little information has survived about the issuing of orders in council for special worship in Ireland, and it is often impossible to know whether there are gaps in the surviving evidence, or whether such orders were rarely issued for special worship in Ireland. More generally, much has been lost that would throw light on the reasons for special worship and on the ordering process in Ireland.

The survival of forms of prayer for the Church of Ireland is significantly more patchy than for the Church of England. This may be attributed to many of the same problems as in England and Wales. The forms were ephemera, of little interest to libraries or book collectors. The library of the Representative Church Body has not built up a collection of these liturgies, and there is no Church of Ireland equivalent to Lambeth Palace Library. Nor do parishes appear to have been any more concerned to keep these occasional forms among their records than in England. In Ireland, however, these problems are exacerbated by the fact that the Church of Ireland was a much smaller church, with far fewer parishes, so far fewer forms were published in the first place.

Scotland

A large number of special occasions of worship in Scotland were ordered by the Church of Scotland; indeed, before the 1660s, only a handful of occasions were ordered by the state. Most occasions of special worship were appointed by acts of the church's general assembly or, after 1642, by acts of its commission. The registers of the general assembly before 1638 have not survived, so it is not possible to give the text of the assembly's acts. Instead, descriptions of the ordering of fasts have been extracted from works by later authors and compilers who were able to use the registers and other documents which are now lost, or from the records of local presbyteries or regional synods. For the whole period up to modern times, very few relevant papers by leading members of the church have survived. One reason is that the chief office-holder, the moderator of the general assembly, was normally appointed just for one year. From the late eighteenth century, some of the instructions for special worship sent by the moderator of the general assembly to ministers were published as notices in newspapers, but these have not been easy to find.

The forms of prayer (more strictly, 'form and order of divine service') which the church periodically published in the twentieth century, beginning with *A form and order of divine service* in January 1915 (1915–1), have also been difficult to locate. As far as can be established, no file set of these forms seems to have been retained, or to have survived, either in the church's records or at William Blackwood & Sons, which printed and published the forms. Nor have systematic deposits been made at New College, Edinburgh (the principal location of surviving forms), with the Church of Scotland's records in the National Records of Scotland, or in the National Library of Scotland, and it has only been possible to identify one copy in a local record office. A good set of forms does survive at St Giles' Cathedral, but these are often different from the 'official' Church of Scotland form. As a result, for Scotland as for Ireland, for a number of occasions the form of prayer has not been found, paradoxically, perhaps, including the more recent occasions, from the 1960s. It is probable, however, that copies of 'missing' forms will in time appear in libraries.

Colonies and the empire

The texts of the orders or notices sent to overseas colonies and other territories from 1688 to 1763 are taken largely from the entry books of circular letters to 'Plantations general' in CO 324, supplemented where necessary by items in other colonial office series. After a re-organization of government departments in 1782, the main series of circulars was disrupted. When it resumed, for a long period no general orders or notifications for special worship appear. Specific orders may have been sent to particular colonies, or perhaps governors were now left to take their own initiative on the basis of receipt of copies of the *London Gazette* or other sources. From 1887 the circulars to governors about special worship, now in CO 854, consist for the most part of simple notifications of the orders issued in the British Isles (and often a copy of the English form of prayer), leaving any action to the discretion of individual governors.

Abbreviations

PUBLISHED SOURCES AND LOCATIONS OF UNPUBLISHED SOURCES

The place of publication of works listed here and elsewhere in this edition is, unless otherwise stated, London.

Aber. recs.	*Extracts from the council register of the burgh of Aberdeen* (4 vols., Scottish Burgh Records Society, 1844–72)
Add.	British Library, Additional Manuscripts
Alford exercise	*Records of the meeting of the exercise of Alford, 1662–1688*, ed. T. Bell (New Spalding Club, Aberdeen, 1897)
APC	*Acts of the privy council of England: new series*, ed. J. R. Dasent *et al.* (46 vols., 1890–1964)
Balfour	*The historical works of Sir James Balfour of Denmylne and Kinnaird* (4 vols., Edinburgh, 1825)
BCP	Book of Common Prayer
BL	British Library, London
Bod.	Bodleian Library, Oxford
BUK	*Acts and proceedings of the general assemblies of the Kirk of Scotland* (3 vols., Maitland Club, Edinburgh, 1839–45)
Burnet, *History*	Gilbert Burnet, *Bishop Burnet's history of his own time*, ed. Martin J. Routh (6 vols., Oxford, 1833)
Burton diary	*Diary of Thomas Burton, Esq. member in the parliaments of Oliver and Richard Cromwell, from 1656 to 1659 ... containing an account of the parliament of 1654; from the journal of Guibon Goddard*, ed. John Towill Rutt (4 vols., 1828)
Calderwood	David Calderwood, *The history of the Kirk of Scotland* [1678], ed. Thomas Thomson and David Laing (8 vols., Wodrow Society, Edinburgh, 1842–9)
CJ	*Journals of the House of Commons* (1803–)
Clay	*Liturgical services: liturgies and occasional forms of prayer set forth in the reign of Queen Elizabeth*, ed. William Keatinge Clay (Parker Society, Cambridge, 1847)
Clopton diary	Diary of [John] Clopton, Essex Record Office, D/DQs/18
CO	Colonial Office papers, The National Archives, Kew
Concilia	*Concilia Magnae Britanniae et Hiberniae, A Synodo Verolamiensi A.D. CCCCXLVI ad Londinensem A.D. MDCCXVII. Accedunt constitutiones et alia ad historiam Ecclesiae Anglicanae spectantia*, ed. David Wilkins (4 vols., 1737)

Craighall	*A diary of the public correspondence of Sir Thomas Hope of Craighall, Bart. 1633–1645* (Bannatyne Club, Edinburgh, 1843)
CSPC	*Calendar of state papers, colonial series*
CSPD	*Calendar of state papers, domestic series*
CSPI	*Calendar of state papers, relating to Ireland*
CSPSc	*Calendar of the state papers relating to Scotland and Mary, Queen of Scots, 1547–1603*, ed. Joseph Bain *et al.* (13 vols., Edinburgh, 1898–1969)
CSPSp	*Calendar of letters, despatches, and state papers relating to the negotiations between England and Spain*, ed. G. A. Bergenroth *et al.* (19 vols. in 13, 1862–1954) [continued by *Calendar of letters and state papers relating to English affairs, preserved principally in the archives of Simancas* (4 vols., 1892–9)]
CSPV	*Calendar of state papers and manuscripts, relating to English affairs, existing in the archives and collections of Venice, and in other libraries of northern Italy* (38 vols. in 40, 1864–1947)
ECCO	Eighteenth-Century Collections Online
EEBO	Early English Books Online
Edin. recs.	*Extracts from the records of the burgh of Edinburgh*, ed. Marguerite Wood and Helen Armet (Edinburgh, 1927–67)
ESTC	English Short Title Catalogue
EUL	Edinburgh University Library
Evelyn	*The diary of John Evelyn*, ed. E. S. de Beer (6 vols., Oxford, 1955)
FSP	*Fast sermons to parliament*, ed. Robin Jeffs (34 vols., 1970–1)
Grey Friars' chronicle	*Chronicle of the Grey Friars of London*, ed. J. G. Nichols (Camden Society, old ser., 53, 1852)
HALS, ASA	Hertfordshire Archives and Library Services, Hertford, Hertfordshire, Archdeaconry of St Albans
HH, CP	Hatfield House, Hertfordshire, Cecil Papers
HMC, *Second rep.*	*Second report of the Royal Commission on Historical Manuscripts* (1871)
HMC, *Fifth rep.*	*Fifth report of the Royal Commission on Historical Manuscripts* (1876)
HMC, *Seventh rep.*	*Seventh report of the Royal Commission on Historical Manuscripts* (1879)
HMC, *Eighth rep.*	*Eighth report of the Royal Commission on Historical Manuscripts* (1881)
HMC, *Thirteenth rep., app. IV*	*Thirteenth report, appendix IV. The manuscripts of Rye and Hereford corporations; Capt. Loder-Symonds, E. R. Wodehouse* (1892)
HMC, *Buccleuch, Drumlanrig*	*The manuscripts of his grace the duke of Buccleuch and Queensberry, K.G., K.T, preserved at Drumlanrig Castle* (Fifteenth report, appendix, part VIII) (2 vols., 1897–1903)

HMC, *Duke of Leeds etc.*	The manuscripts of the duke of Leeds, the Bridgewater Trust, Reading Corporation, the Inner Temple (Eleventh report, appendix 7) (1888)
HMC, *Leybourne-Popham*	Report of the manuscripts of F. W. Leybourne-Popham, of Littlecote, Co. Wilts., ed. S. C. Lomas (1899)
HMC, *Ormonde*	Calendar of the manuscripts of the marquess of Ormonde, K.P., preserved at Kilkenny Castle, new series (4 vols., 1902–6)
HMC, *Rutland*	The manuscripts of the duke of Rutland, preserved at Belvoir Castle (4 vols., 1888–1905)
Inverness and Dingwall records	Records of the presbyteries of Inverness and Dingwall, 1643–1688, ed. William Mackay (Scottish History Society, 24, Edinburgh, 1896)
Lambert, *Printing*	Printing for parliament, 1641–1700, ed. Sheila Lambert (List and Index Society, Special Series, 20, 1984)
Lamont	The diary of Mr John Lamont of Newton, 1649–1671 (Maitland Club, Edinburgh, 1830)
Lans.	BL, Lansdowne MS
Larkin	Stuart royal proclamations: royal proclamations of King Charles I, 1625–1646, ed. James F. Larkin (Oxford, 1983)
Larkham diary	The diary of Thomas Larkham, 1647–1669, ed. Susan Hardman Moore (Church of England Record Society, 17, Woodbridge, 2011)
Lauder, *Historical notices*	John Lauder, *Historical notices of Scotish affairs*, ed. David Laing (2 vols., Bannatyne Club, Edinburgh, 1848)
Lauder, *Historical observes*	John Lauder, *Historical observes of memorable occurrents in church and state from October 1680 to April 1686*, ed. Adam Urquhart and David Laing (Bannatyne Club, Edinburgh, 1840)
Life of Blair	The life of Mr Robert Blair, minister of St Andrews, containing his autobiography, from 1593 to 1636, with supplement to his life, and continuation of the history of the times to 1680, by his son-in-law, Mr William Row, minister of Ceres (Wodrow Society, Edinburgh, 1848)
LJ	Journals of the House of Lords (1846–)
LMA	London Metropolitan Archives
LPL	Lambeth Palace Library
Luttrell	Narcissus Luttrell, *A brief historical relation of state affairs from September 1678 to April 1714* (6 vols., Oxford, 1857)
LW	Libri Walliae. A catalogue of Welsh books and books printed in Wales 1546–1820, ed. Eiluned Rees (Aberystwyth, 1987), vol. I
LWS	Libri Walliae ... Supplement, ed. Charles Parry (Aberystwyth, 2001)
Machyn's diary	Diary of Henry Machyn, BL, Cotton MS Vitellius, F. V and available online at http://quod.lib.umich.edu/m/machyn/
MacLure	Millar MacLure, *Register of sermons preached at Paul's Cross, 1534–1642* (Ottawa, 1989)

Melvill	*The autobiography and diary of Mr James Melvill*, ed. Robert Pitcairn (Wodrow Society, Edinburgh, 1842)
Morrice	*The entring book of Roger Morrice, 1677–1691*, ed. Mark Goldie *et al.* (7 vols., Woodbridge, 2007)
Nicoll	John Nicoll, *A diary of public transactions and other occurrences, chiefly in Scotland, from January 1650 to June 1667* (Bannatyne Club, Edinburgh, 1836)
NLS	National Library of Scotland, Edinburgh
NRS	National Records of Scotland, Edinburgh
PC	Privy council papers, in The National Archives, Kew
Pepys	*The diary of Samuel Pepys*, ed. Robert Latham and William Matthews (11 vols., 1970–83)
PRO	Public Record Office: series of personal and miscellaneous papers, in The National Archives, Kew
RCGA	*Records of the commissions of the general assemblies of the Church of Scotland*, ed. Alexander F. Mitchell and James Christie (3 vols., Scottish History Society, 11, 25, 58, Edinburgh, 1892–1909)
Report of the deputy keeper	*Report of the deputy keeper of the records* [Public Record Office, Northern Ireland] (Belfast, 1925–90)
Row	John Row, *The history of the Kirk of Scotland* (Wodrow Society, Edinburgh, 1842)
RPC	*The register of the privy council of Scotland*, ed. John H. Burton (1st ser., 14 vols., Edinburgh, 1877–98), David Masson and P. Hume Brown (2nd ser., 8 vols., Edinburgh, 1899–1908), P. Hume Brown, Henry Paton and E. Balfour-Melville (3rd ser., 16 vols., Edinburgh, 1908–70)
RPS	*Records of the parliaments of Scotland to 1707*
Scot	William Scot, *An apologetical narration of the state and government of the Kirk of Scotland since the reformation* (Wodrow Society, Edinburgh, 1846)
SoA	Society of Antiquaries
SP	State Papers, unless otherwise indicated in The National Archives, Kew
SP Thurloe	*A collection of the state papers of John Thurloe, Esq., secretary, first, to the council of state, and afterwards to ... Oliver and Richard Cromwell ...*, ed. Thomas Birch (7 vols., 1742)
Spottiswoode	John Spottiswoode, *History of the Church of Scotland: beginning the year of our lord 203, and continued to the end of the reign of King James VI* [1625], ed. M. Russell (3 vols., Spottiswoode Society, Edinburgh, 1847–51)
STC	*A short-title catalogue of books printed in England, Scotland and Ireland and of English books printed abroad, 1475–1640*, first compiled by A. W. Pollard and G. R. Redgrave, ed. W. A. Jackson, F. S. Ferguson and K. F. Pantzer (3 vols., 1976–91)

Steele	Robert Steele, *A bibliography of royal proclamations of the Tudor and Stuart sovereigns, 1485–1714* (2 vols., Oxford, 1910) [continued by earl of Crawford, *Handlist of proclamations issued by royal and other constitutional authorities, 1714–1910* (Wigan, 1913)]
Stowe, 'Chronicle'	John Stowe, 'Two London chronicles from the collection of John Stowe', in *Camden miscellany 12*, ed. Charles L. Kingsford (Camden Society, 3rd ser., 18, 1910), pp. v–x, 1–57
Stowe, *Summarie*	John Stowe, *A summarie of Englyshe chronicles* ([1565]; STC 23319)
Stowe, *Chronicles*	John Stowe, *The chronicles of England* ([1580]; STC 23333)
Strathbogie presbytery	*Extracts from the presbytery book of Strathbogie AD. MDCXXXI–MDCLIV* (Spalding Club, Aberdeen, 1843)
Strype, *Annals*	John Strype, *Annals of the reformation and establishment of religion, and other various occurrences in the Church of England, during Queen Elizabeth's happy reign: together with an appendix of original papers of state, records, and letters* ([1709–31] 4 vols. in 7, Oxford, 1824)
Strype, *Ecclesiastical memorials*	John Strype, *Ecclesiastical memorials, relating chiefly to religion, and the reformation of it: and the emergencies of the Church of England, under King Henry VIII; King Edward VI; and Queen Mary I* ([1721] 3 vols. in 6; Oxford, 1822)
Strype, *Grindal*	John Strype, *The history of the life and acts of the most reverend father in God, Edmund Grindal, the first bishop of London, and the second archbishop of York and Canterbury successively in the reign of Queen Elizabeth* ([1710] Oxford, 1821)
Strype, *Parker*	John Strype, *The life and acts of Matthew Parker, the first archbishop of Canterbury, in the reign of Queen Elizabeth* ([1711] 3 vol., Oxford, 1821)
Strype, *Whitgift*	John Strype, *The life and acts of John Whitgift, D.D. the third and last lord archbishop of Canterbury in the reign of Queen Elizabeth* ([1718] 3 vols., Oxford, 1822)
Tanner	Tanner MSS, Bodleian Library, Oxford
Thomason	*Catalogue of the pamphlets, books, newspapers and manuscripts relating to the civil war, the Commonwealth, and restoration collected by George Thomason* (2 vols., 1908)
Two books of homilies	*The two books of homilies appointed to be read in churches*, ed. John Griffiths (Oxford, 1859)
Westminster assembly	*The minutes and papers of the Westminster assembly, 1642–1652*, ed. Chad van Dixhoorn (5 vols., Oxford, 2012)
Whitelocke diary	*The diary of Bulstrode Whitelocke, 1605–1675*, ed. Ruth Spalding (Records of Social and Economic History, new ser., 13, Oxford, 1990)

Wing	Donald Wing, *Short-title catalogue of books printed in England, Scotland, Ireland, Wales, and British America, and of English books printed in other countries, 1641–1700* (New York, 1994 edn)
Wodrow, *History*	Robert Wodrow, *The history of the sufferings of the Church of Scotland from the restoration to the revolution*, ed. Robert Burns (4 vols., Glasgow, 1828–30)
Wood	*The life and times of Anthony Wood, antiquary, of Oxford, 1632–1695, described by himself*, ed. Andrew Clark (5 vols., Oxford Historical Society, 19, 21, 26, 30, 40, 1891–1900)
Woodford diary	*The diary of Robert Woodford, 1637–1641*, ed. John Fielding (Camden Society, 5th ser., 42, Cambridge, 2012)
Wriothesley	*A chronicle of England during the reigns of the Tudors, from AD 1485 to 1559, by Charles Wriothesley, Windsor Herald*, ed. William Douglas Hamilton (2 vols., Camden Society, new ser., 11 and 20, Westminster, 1875–8)

BOOKS OF THE BIBLE

Old Testament

Gen.	Genesis	Eccles.	Ecclesiastes
Exod.	Exodus	S. of S.	Song of Solomon
Lev.	Leviticus	Isa.	Isaiah
Num.	Numbers	Jer.	Jeremiah
Deut.	Deuteronomy	Lam.	Lamentations
Josh.	Joshua	Ezek.	Ezekiel
Judg.	Judges	Dan.	Daniel
Ruth	Ruth	Hos.	Hosea
1 Sam.	1 Samuel	Joel	Joel
2 Sam.	2 Samuel	Amos	Amos
1 Kgs.	1 Kings	Obad.	Obadiah
2 Kgs.	2 Kings	Jonah	Jonah
1 Chr.	1 Chronicles	Mic.	Micah
2 Chr.	2 Chronicles	Nahum	Nahum
Ezra	Ezra	Hab.	Habakkuk
Neh.	Nehemiah	Zeph.	Zephaniah
Esther	Esther	Hag.	Haggai
Job	Job	Zech.	Zechariah
Ps.	Psalms	Mal.	Malachi
Prov.	Proverbs		

Apocrypha

1 Esdr.	1 Esdras	Judith	Judith
2 Esdr.	2 Esdras	Rest of Esth.	Rest of Esther
Tobit	Tobit	Wisdom	Wisdom

Ecclus.	Ecclesiasticus	Bel & Dr.	Bel and the Dragon
Bar.	Baruch	Pr. Of Man.	Prayer of Manasses
S. of III Ch.	Song of the Three	1 Macc.	1 Maccabees
	Children	2 Macc.	2 Maccabees
Sus.	Susanna		

New Testament

Matt.	Matthew	1 Tim.	1 Timothy
Mark	Mark	2 Tim.	2 Timothy
Luke	Luke	Titus	Titus
John	John	Philem.	Philemon
Acts	Acts of the Apostles	Heb.	Hebrews
Rom.	Romans	Jas.	James
1 Cor.	1 Corinthians	1 Pet.	1 Peter
2 Cor.	2 Corinthians	2 Pet.	2 Peter
Gal.	Galatians	1 John	1 John
Eph.	Ephesians	2 John	2 John
Phil.	Philippians	3 John	3 John
Col.	Colossians	Jude	Jude
1 Thess.	1 Thessalonians	Rev.	Revelation
2 Thess.	2 Thessalonians		

Introduction: General and 1533–1688

WHAT WAS SPECIAL WORSHIP?

In August 1563, the archbishops of Canterbury and York, acting on instructions from Queen Elizabeth I, issued an order for a public fast to take place every Wednesday during the outbreak of plague which was then afflicting London and much of the rest of the kingdom. Throughout the kingdom, all the queen's subjects were expected to suspend employment and entertainments for the day, to consume just one moderate and plain meal, and not only to attend church – where specially composed services were to be read – but also to spend the day in family or private prayer and study of scriptures and other religious works. Very nearly 450 years later, on 5 June 2012, public attention focused on a national service of thanksgiving at St Paul's Cathedral. This was the culmination of the celebrations of the diamond jubilee of Queen Elizabeth II, but it was not the only religious observance of that event. Services giving thanks for the queen's reign were also held in thousands of parish churches and other places of worship across England, Wales, Scotland and Northern Ireland. The transformation of British religious culture over 500 years and more has obscured the genealogy of the religious services for this jubilee. Yet, the 1563 fast days and the 2012 thanksgivings are both aspects of a continuous tradition of 'special worship' in Britain from the protestant reformation of the sixteenth century to the present.

'Special worship' is an awkward phrase, which was not used by contemporaries and for which there is no historical authority. It has been adopted as a generic term to describe the subject matter of these volumes for two reasons. First, it is a phrase which embraces the full range of occasions for which the civil and religious authorities in the British Isles ordered a departure from normal religious observance. These ranged from special services, such as those for the 1563 fast or the 2012 thanksgiving, to occasions when a single prayer was added to the normal daily liturgy. They also included annual religious commemorations such as the observance of the anniversary of the gunpowder plot on 5 November. Second, the phrase avoids the privileging of any of the terms used by contemporaries, whether fast and thanksgiving days, days of humiliation or intercession or national days of prayer, terms which have particular chronological associations and which often express important changes in the nature of these occasions across five centuries.

The main title of these volumes, '*national* prayers', raises almost as many problems as the term in the sub-title. First and foremost, it indicates the decision to restrict the contents to those occasions when all, most or many members of the kingdom or national community were expected or asked to join in an act of religious worship. This definition, however, immediately raises the question of what 'the kingdom or national community' was. In a territorial unit with a history as complex as that of the British Isles over the last five centuries, it is almost impossible to avoid an element of arbitrariness about what should and should not be included. A decision was taken to be broad and inclusive: for much of the period, the same occasions were observed in England and Wales, in Scotland and in Ireland, and occasionally also in the overseas empire; even in the sixteenth century, there is much to be learned from the parallel development of fast or thanksgiving days in England and Wales and in Scotland. Accordingly, this edition covers all occasions of special worship during the five centuries since the reformation for each kingdom in the British Isles – England and Wales, Scotland and Ireland – and later for the United Kingdom and the British Empire. It does so also for each established church: for the two anglican churches – the Church of England (which included Wales until the Church in Wales was disestablished in 1920) and the Church of Ireland (which were combined in 1801 as the United Church of England and Ireland, until the Church of Ireland was disestablished in 1871) – and for the presbyterian Church of Scotland. It includes too the occasions ordered during the civil wars and interregnum from 1642 to 1660 by parliamentary, commonwealth and protectorate governments, under which the established churches in England and Ireland were temporarily dismantled.

Second, a significant number of occasions included in this study were not, in fact, expected to be observed *throughout* the kingdoms in which they were ordered. In part, this was because during the 1640s the authority of the parliamentary and royalist regimes was limited to the parts of the country which they controlled. More significantly, fairly frequently during the early modern period and occasionally thereafter, prayers and services with national meaning and significance were ordered to take place only in a particular geographical area or in specific churches, generally in and around the national capitals.

The purpose of this edition is to bring together the surviving core texts, primarily orders and forms of prayer, for the 866 particular occasions of worship and the nine annual commemorations that have been identified for the period from 1533 to 2012. The number of particular occasions needs to be treated with some caution, as do discussions later in this introduction about the number of occasions during specific periods and for particular types of event. For some periods and for some areas, the nature and survival of evidence mean that it is unlikely that all occasions have been traced. This is certainly the case for England and Scotland in the sixteenth century, and it remains true for Ireland throughout the seventeenth and even into the eighteenth century. The period of the civil war presents problems of both evidence and definition, above all for royalist occasions, and it is sometimes unclear by whom a particular fast or thanksgiving was ordered and whether it was intended to be observed locally or more widely. Surprisingly, perhaps, both evidence and definition emerge as problems again in the twentieth century, a consequence of the growing marginalization of the established churches in the political and cultural life of the nation. Both the inter-war years and the decades since the 1970s witnessed a proliferation of calls to prayer by the church leaders. Many of these have been included, but some have been excluded on the grounds that they were directed towards groups *within* the churches rather than towards the nation more generally. It also becomes increasingly difficult to be confident that *all* such calls to prayer have been identified, since, in the years since the end of the second world war, the national press, often the best source of evidence, became less interested in religious affairs and less consistent in reporting them.

There is a further reason why counting occasions is potentially misleading. While it was common throughout the period for special prayers to be added to the normal Sunday or daily services for a period of weeks or even months, in the sixteenth and seventeenth centuries special services were sometimes ordered to be held regularly during a period of crisis. For example, the order for special worship in England and Wales during the plague in 1563 – just one 'occasion' in this edition – instituted a complex pattern of worship on Wednesdays, Fridays and Sundays, including a fast day every Wednesday. Consequently, perhaps twenty-five fast days and fifty further days of special services were observed in parish churches across the nation before the thanksgiving was held for the apparent passing of the epidemic at the end of January 1564. Fears in 1720–3 that a renewed epidemic of plague in Europe would spread to Britain generated three 'occasions' for this edition: an order for a prayer to be added to the normal daily services three times a week for the duration of the threat, a fast day in December 1720 and a second fast day in December 1721. In addition, for the anniversary commemorations, annual services were continued in some cases over many decades and for others for some 200 years. It is important to recognize that counting occasions offers at best a limited understanding of the patterns of special worship, and that attention also needs to be paid to the nature and frequency of the worship that was ordered.

The bulk of this edition is divided into two sections. The first and longest section, spread over three volumes, provides texts and commentaries for the 866 particular occasions. The second section, providing materials on the nine anniversary commemorations is published in volume 3. The first volume includes particular occasions for the period from 1533 to 1688, the second from 1689 to 1870, and the third from 1871 to the present. These divisions, while not entirely arbitrary, have been determined primarily by the desirability of creating volumes of approximately equal length. For each particular occasion and each anniversary commemoration, editorial *commentaries* explain the context, the decision to order special worship, the authority for the order and (where known) authorship of the texts, and any unusual details about the printing and distribution of documents and about the observance itself. Though presented as specific to the individual occasion, these commentaries may also be read *seriatim* in different ways – perhaps for special acts of worship in individual kingdoms, for certain periods or episodes, for particular sorts of events or for particular types of worship. Each commentary is accompanied by a list of the *sources*, both those for the texts printed for the occasion and those used in the writing of the commentary. The *texts* are divided into two groups. The first is the chief order or orders for the occasion, whether issued by government or by the church authorities. The second, when the order required or sanctioned these documents, is the prayer, service or address specially composed, published and distributed to the incumbent clergy for use in churches, chapels and cathedrals.

Recognizing that most readers are likely to be interested in particular chronological periods, separate **introductions** are provided for each of the three volumes. However, these introductions may also be read together to provide an overview of the nature of special national worship across five centuries, and particular emphasis is given in volumes 2 and 3 to issues of change and continuity. This overview may be especially useful because no other discussion exists of these occasions of special worship for the whole period, and only a few for more limited periods or even specific occasions.[1] More specifically, the introductions have several purposes. They

---

[1] The only modern work to consider any of these occasions over the *longue durée* is Roland Bartel, 'The story of public fast days in England', *Anglican Theological Review*, 37 (1955), 190–200. For works considering short periods or specific events, see the bibliographies appended to the introductions in this and subsequent volumes.

provide definitions of the different sorts of occasion of worship, the types of special acts of worship and the documents produced for them – the orders which appointed the special worship, and the texts which were read during church services. They consider what is meant in different periods by 'national' worship, exploring the implications of different conceptions of ecclesiastical authority, as well as the effects of political and ecclesiastical geography and of religious diversity. The origins of special worship are outlined in volume 1; the introductions to each volume then discuss the phases of change in the character of the occasions and their documents and texts. Finally, they describe the processes of ordering the occasions, and the printing and distribution of the documents, with other forms of dissemination. The introductions, therefore, focus on providing the information needed to understand and put in context the occasions and texts presented in the edition. What they do not attempt to do, more than in brief outline, is explore the character, meanings and reception of special occasions of worship, themes which are examined by the editors in other works.[2] Summary **lists** of the particular occasions of special worship contained in each volume help to reveal patterns in their incidence, as well as allowing the reader easily to identify a variety of different types of occasion.

THE SIGNIFICANCE OF SPECIAL WORSHIP

Special worship has been a recurrent feature of national life in the British Isles from the protestant reformations of the sixteenth century to the present. Across five centuries, governments and established churches have ordered special acts of public worship to be observed on a particular day or series of days in every parish in the realm, either separately for England and Wales, for Ireland and for Scotland, or co-ordinated between two or all three of the constituent parts of what, from 1707, has been called the United Kingdom. During periods of anxiety, strain, crisis and mourning, at times of relief and celebration, and for moments of commemoration, all members of the kingdom or national community were expected or asked to join in one or more acts of worship and religious reflection. Occasions of special worship were, therefore, revealing events, rich in meaning, purpose and consequence. They generated important documents and texts – the orders, prayers, services, acts, 'causes' and addresses circulated or published, and often read out in all churches – and have

---

[2] Natalie Mears, 'Special nationwide worship and the Book of Common Prayer in England, Wales and Ireland, 1533–1642', in *Worship and the parish church in early modern Britain*, ed. Natalie Mears and Alec Ryrie (Farnham, 2013), pp. 31–72; Natalie Mears, 'Public worship and political participation in Elizabethan England', *Journal of British Studies*, 51 (2012), 4–25; Natalie Mears, 'Brought to book: special book purchases in English parishes, 1558–1640', in *Negotiating the Jacobean printed book*, ed. Pete Langman (Farnham, 2011), pp. 29–44; Alasdair Raffe, 'Nature's scourges: the natural world and special prayers, fasts and thanksgivings, 1543–1866', in *God's bounty? The churches and the natural world*, ed. Peter Clarke and Tony Claydon (Studies in Church History, 46, Woodbridge, 2010), pp. 237–47; Stephen Taylor, 'George III's recovery from madness celebrated: precedent and innovation in the observance of royal celebrations and commemorations', in *From the reformation to the permissive society. A miscellany in celebration of the 400th anniversary of Lambeth Palace Library*, ed. Melanie Barber and Stephen Taylor with Gabriel Sewell (Church of England Record Society, 18, 2010), pp. 211–67; Philip Williamson, 'State prayers, fasts and thanksgivings: public worship in Britain, 1830–97', *Past and Present*, 200 (2008), 121–74; Philip Williamson, 'National days of prayer: the churches, the state and public worship in Britain, 1899–1957', *English Historical Review*, 128 (2013), 324–66.

considerable significance for historical understandings of religious, ecclesiastical, political, moral and social life, both for short episodes and over very long periods.

Special occasions of worship were of two main kinds. *Particular* occasions were usually ordered for one specific day, or sometimes for a number of specified days over periods of several weeks. Occasionally, as already noted, they were observed over several months, and in one case during the eighteenth century for as long as eleven years. These particular occasions marked such various events as extremes of weather, and bad or good harvests; earthquakes and epidemics, both human and animal; moral and economic anxieties; plots and rebellions; diplomatic endeavours; solidarity with co-religionists or political allies; military campaigns, naval expeditions, wars, battles and peace treaties; royal births, and the coronations, jubilees, illnesses and deaths of sovereigns. Some occasions involved no more than the addition of a prayer or prayers to the usual Sunday or daily services. But in many cases, new forms of service were issued, supplementing and frequently replacing the usual liturgical arrangements. Often, especially before the mid-nineteenth century, the orders 'set apart' a day in the middle of the week for special services and for further religious activities in the home and community, and accordingly these occasions required the suspension of public, legal and commercial business and a general cessation of work. These days of special worship have been given a variety of names – fast days, days of humiliation, days of intercession, thanksgiving days and national days of prayer – which reflect both their function and shifts in attitudes towards the nature and meaning of special worship.

The nine *annual* or *anniversary* commemorations, which were chiefly ordered and observed in England and Wales, may be sub-divided into three. The first, the celebration of the sovereign's accession day, was begun under Elizabeth I and continues for Elizabeth II. The second were days of protestant or anglican commemoration, all of which date from the seventeenth century. In chronological order of their creation, these were for the failure of the Gowrie plot (5 August), for the discovery of the gunpowder plot, later combined with celebration of the 1688 revolution (5 November), for the restoration of the monarchy (29 May), for the 'martyrdom' of Charles I (30 January) and for the beginning of the great fire of London (2 September). In Ireland, the discovery of the 1641 uprising was celebrated and in Scotland, for a short period, the sovereign's birthday. This type of annual religious commemoration was abolished in 1859. The third was the creation during the early twentieth century of a new anniversary occasion, for remembrance of the war dead.

Special occasions of worship are significant from numerous perspectives. The selection of occasions provides a register of what contemporaries considered to be important for the kingdom or the national community, in ways which are not always expected from later historical studies, still less from the 'national memory'. The ordering of special worship reveals much about church–state relations: the exercise of the royal supremacy over the established, episcopal churches in England and Wales and in Ireland, and the crown's relationship with the presbyterian Church of Scotland; the involvement of government ministers in decisions on religious matters; the *rôles* of the higher clergy or, in Scotland, the general assembly and its commission in public life. From the sixteenth to the nineteenth centuries, during successive periods of intense differences over these church–state relations and over forms of church government, worship and doctrine, decisions to appoint special worship were integral to the political and constitutional contentions between royal government and parliamentary groups or the general assembly of the Church of Scotland, and between political and religious factions within parliament and the churches. The importance of these occasions for government and church leaders is manifest in the extraordinary efforts taken to communicate their orders and to print and distribute the materials for use in church services to all parishes, however distant and scattered, usually within a short time, and so co-ordinated as to have simultaneous observance on specified days. Here, over a very long period, is evidence about the connexions between centre and localities, about the organization and reach of the government and churches, and about their ability to 'project' their purposes and messages throughout the kingdom or kingdoms. Here, too, is an aspect of the history of publication, in the rapid organization of texts, paper, ink, type, printing presses, skilled compositors, unskilled labourers and carriers in order to dispatch documents to every parish – numbering some 10,000 in England and Wales[3] – and, from the eighteenth century, to produce very large numbers for sale to members of their congregations and to the general public. By the end of the nineteenth century, millions of copies of forms of prayers were being produced and distributed within a matter of days.

Both the orders which appointed the occasions, and the prayers, services, acts, 'causes' or addresses which were read in churches, had several purposes and provide evidence for numerous aspects of religious, ecclesiastical, social, cultural and political history. They had considerable political and social significance in communicating news to local communities. Through the church services and associated penances or celebrations, they elicited officially sanctioned popular participation in public issues. They expressed official interpretations and religious beliefs about particular secular events and natural occurrences. They offer prime evidence on the changing meanings of prayer and worship – of the presumed relationship of the community and the individual with God – providing, in the words of one historian, 'a window into the nation's soul'.[4] More especially, into the twentieth century they show the force and persistence of an acknowledgment of divine superintendence over the English and Welsh, Scottish and Irish kingdoms and later the British nation and empire, and the belief in special providential interventions that could be assuaged or prompted by the united prayers of the whole people.[5] They provided the clergy with the biblical texts for the fast and thanksgiving sermons which, as historians have long appreciated, are a leading source for understanding public debate about religious and political ideas during periods of acute national crisis.[6] They had played

---

3   The number of parishes varied significantly across the period. Widely estimated at around 10,000 in the eighteenth century, the figure increased substantially in the nineteenth century with the creation of many new parishes, especially in urban areas. In 1761, Archbishop Secker calculated that 12,650 copies of order for single additional prayers were needed to supply parishes and at least some chapels in England and Wales. LPL, MS 1130, fo. 163.

4   C. J. Kitching, '"Prayers fit for the time": fasting and prayer in response to national crises in the reign of Elizabeth I', in *Monks, hermits and the ascetic tradition*, ed. W. J. Sheils (Studies in Church History, 22, Oxford, 1985), p. 243.

5   Williamson, 'State prayers, fasts and thanksgivings'; Williamson, 'National days of prayer'.

6   Wider historical awareness of fasts and thanksgivings is due almost entirely to work on sermons and preaching, rather than on their ordering and organization, and on the fundamental documents for these occasions. See H. R. Trevor-Roper, 'The fast sermons of the Long parliament', in *idem*, *Religion, the reformation and social change* (1967), pp. 294–344; Christopher Hill, *The English Bible and the seventeenth-century revolution* (1993), ch. 3; J. F. Wilson, *Pulpit in parliament. Puritanism during the English civil wars 1640–1648* (Princeton, 1969); Tom Webster, 'Preaching and

an important part in liturgical change during both the sixteenth and the twentieth centuries, and in the controversies over the appropriate types of worship during the seventeenth century, as they offered opportunities for experimentation and provide evidence of changing practice. They were central in shaping ideas of national identity in terms of protestantism, godliness and divine providence, and they helped to consolidate the idea of a British state. They also provide much material for understanding shifts in religious belief and in relations between the 'spiritual' and the 'secular', and for assessing the timing and character of 'secularization'.

As the 'theology' of these occasions stressed national sins and the consequent need for repentance and improved conduct, as much by the individual as by the community as a whole, they contributed to the shaping of moral attitudes. Both fast days and thanksgiving days required the attendance of everyone at church services, the main themes of which were dependence on God's providence and – even on thanksgiving days – on the need for repentance and reformation; both brought injunctions from church and civil authorities for weekday suspensions of ordinary work, and for almsgiving or other assistance from the rich and substantial to the poor or the wider community. Fasts involved modifications of diet and clothing, and limits on recreation; thanksgivings were marked by secular celebrations organized by the civil authorities and other leading personages. These 'days' were significant moments in social experience and social relations, bringing together communities across the nation in shared responses of penitence or thanksgiving at times of crisis or celebration. However, while days of special worship were given meanings in the

parliament, 1640–59', in *The Oxford handbook of the early modern sermon*, ed. Peter McCullough, Hugh Adlington and Emma Rhatigan (Oxford, 2011), pp. 404–22; Mary Ransome, 'The rise and fall of a martyrology: sermons on Charles I', *Huntington Library Quarterly*, 10 (1946–7), 135–67; Françoise Deconinck-Brossard, 'Sermons commémorant la mort de Charles Ier', *Confluences* (2000), 149–67; D. Napthine and W. A. Speck, 'Clergymen and conflict 1660–73', in *The church and war*, ed. W. J. Sheils (Studies in Church History, 20, 1983), pp. 231–51; Tony Claydon, 'The sermon culture of the Glorious Revolution: Williamite preaching and Jacobite anti-preaching, 1685–1702', in *Oxford handbook of the early modern sermon*, ed. McCullough, Adlington and Rhatigan, pp. 480–94; J. C. D. Clark, *English society 1688–1832. Ideology, social structure and political practice during the ancien regime* (Cambridge, 1985); Pasi Ihalainen, 'The political sermon in an age of party strife, 1700–20', in *Oxford handbook of the early modern sermon*, ed. McCullough, Adlington and Rhatigan, pp. 495–516; James Joseph Caudle, 'Measures of allegiance: sermon culture and the creation of a public discourse of obedience and resistance in Georgian Britain, 1714–60', Ph.D. dissertation, Yale University, 1996; Susannah Abbott, 'Clerical responses to the Jacobite rebellion in 1715', *Historical Research*, 76 (2003), 322–46; Françoise Deconinck-Brossard, *Vie politique, sociale et religieuse en Grande-Brétagne d'après les sermons prêchés ou publiés dans le nord d'Angleterre, 1738–60* (Paris, 1984); Françoise Deconinck-Brossard, 'The churches and the '45', in *The church and war*, ed. Sheils, pp. 253–62; S. J. C. Taylor, 'Church and state in England in the mid-eighteenth century: the Newcastle years 1742–62', Ph.D. dissertation, University of Cambridge, 1987, ch. 7; H. P. Ippel, 'Blow the trumpet, sanctify the fast', *Huntington Library Quarterly*, 44 (1980–1), 43–60; H. P. Ippel, 'British sermons and the American revolution', *Journal of Religious History*, 12 (1982), 191–205; James E. Bradley, 'The anglican pulpit, the social order and the resurgence of toryism during the American revolution', *Albion*, 21 (1989), 361–88; Paul Langford, 'The English clergy and the American revolution', in *The Transformation of Political Culture. England and Germany in the late Eighteenth Century*, ed. E. Hellmuth (Oxford, 1990), pp. 275–307; Nancy L. V. Murray, 'The influence of the French revolution on the Church of England and its rivals, 1789–1802', D.Phil. dissertation, University of Oxford, 1975; Robert Hole, 'English sermons and tracts as media of debate on the French revolution 1789–99', in *The French revolution and British popular politics*, ed. Mark Philp (Cambridge, 1991), pp. 18–37; Robert Hole, *Pulpits, politics and public order in England, 1760–1832* (Cambridge, 1989).

orders, prayers and other documents prepared by churchmen and politicians, those meanings were necessarily malleable and subject to re-interpretation. They could, therefore, also become occasions for the expression of political and religious dissent, or, alternatively, for religious dissenters to express loyalty to the civil authorities of sovereign or state. Having long provoked tensions between the established churches and various types of religious dissenters, during the twentieth century special days of prayer provided occasions for co-operation between the various churches and for the expression and development of ecumenical perspectives.

DEFINITIONS

The occasions addressed in this edition are generically simple to define: 'special occasions of public worship observed in all, or a significant number of, places of worship at the same or a similar time'. For all the occasions brought together in this edition, the intention was that all, most or many members of the realm should worship together and, as nearly as possible, simultaneously, in the belief that the realm or nation was an organic spiritual and moral unit.

As has already been noted, however, in specific terms definition is complicated. This is because occasions were ordered in or for the separate kingdoms of the British Isles – England and Wales, Ireland and Scotland – and later for the United Kingdom, and also for some occasions independently for England, Scotland and Ireland during the period when they were constituent parts of the United Kingdom. The three kingdoms had different constitutional and ecclesiastical arrangements, and in each of them the scattered parishes, often at considerable distances from the political and ecclesiastical centres, made co-ordination difficult. Definition is further complicated because these occasions persisted over a very long period and through considerable changes in political, religious and ecclesiastical conditions and in contemporary terminology and nomenclature.

As will be explained further in the next section, the complications include the definition of the terms 'national' and 'nationwide'. At various times, a number of national bodies ordered special worship, sometimes independently, sometimes in co-operation and sometimes as rivals – crown, parliament and church authorities. Particular occasions of special worship were not necessarily ordered in all kingdoms of the British Isles or constituent parts of the United Kingdom; nor were orders and observances necessarily co-ordinated for the same dates in all regions within a particular kingdom or a constituent part of the United Kingdom. For a number of reasons, certain occasions included in this edition were intended to have national significance even though they were observed in just particular regions and sometimes small areas, most often the capital cities. Increasingly from the mid-seventeenth century there were also the effects of religious pluralism, manifested in the existence of religious communities which did not accept the authority of the established churches and the crown in matters of worship, and which consequently faced a choice either to abstain, or to participate on their own terms.

This section addresses the problems of definition by considering the nomenclature used by contemporaries to describe both the various occasions of public worship and the types of documents associated with them. Like the rest of this introduction, it concentrates on the period from the reformation to the 1688 revolution.

Terms that were only used during the eighteenth, nineteenth and twentieth centuries are discussed in later volumes.

First, some preliminary definition is required of the phrase *England and Wales*. Wales had been officially incorporated into the English crown in 1284, at which point it became part of the ecclesiastical province of Canterbury, where it remained until the disestablishment of the anglican Church in Wales in 1920. English governmental and administrative structures were extended to Wales by the Henrician Acts of Union of 1536 and 1542. In the sixteenth and early seventeenth centuries, crown orders relating to England and Wales and the forms of prayer for the Church of England often referred to Wales vaguely ('our realm' or 'our realms') or implied its inclusion silently. From 1647, the orders and forms contained the formula 'England, [the Dominion of] Wales, and [Town of] Berwick upon Tweed'. Berwick had been a Scottish royal burgh but was made a county corporate of England in 1551. Scotland continued to dispute England's possession of the town until the Act of Union in 1707. Nevertheless, the peculiar status of Berwick-upon-Tweed continued to be acknowledged in state orders for special worship in England until 1919. For economy of space, in this edition references to Berwick are silently omitted in the headings for occasions from 1660 onwards (though retained in citations).

Occasions

(a) *special prayer or prayers*: one prayer or a small number of prayers ordered to be added to the ordinary church services, or to replace prayers normally prescribed for use in these services. These might be prayers of petition or thanksgiving: in this edition 'prayers' refers to petitionary prayers, while thanksgiving prayers are specified as such. Petitionary prayers were often ordered to be said during daily services for a period of time; thanksgiving prayers appear more commonly to have been said only on a single day.

(b) *special service or services*: complete services ordered to replace the ordinary church services, or substantial modification of the usual services, or further services which were added to the usual services. The services might be for penitence, petition or intercession, or for thanksgiving. Special services were also composed for anniversary commemorations.

(c) *fast day* (or general fast, or public fast, or day of humiliation): a day 'set apart' for – that is to say, a whole day dedicated to – religious penitence: acknowledgment of sins, repentance and petitions for God's mercies. In England and Wales and in Ireland these were invariably week days, though in Scotland they could also be appointed for Sundays. The principal feature was attendance at special services and sermons, but penitence was also to be shown by a limited and simple diet, modest clothing, almsgiving and private prayers and reflection on religious texts. When appointed for week days, secular employments and recreations were to be suspended. In the sixteenth and seventeenth centuries in England and Wales it was common for a fast day to be observed regularly, every month or even every week, during a period of crisis. In Scotland from 1566 to the early seventeenth century it was usual for fasts to be called for two successive Sundays, with fasting in the intervening week. Two anniversary commemorations, for 'the martyrdom of Charles I' and 'the dreadful fire of London', were observed as fast days.

(d) *day of thanksgiving* (or thanksgiving day): this usually followed one or a series of the petitionary fast days or days of humiliation or intercession. More rarely, it might follow a period of special prayers. A day of thanksgiving involved special services but also secular celebrations, often feasts, bonfires and 'treats' for the poor or other contributions to the community. These were often appointed as days 'set apart' during the week, but could be held on a Sunday. Most anniversary occasions were thanksgiving days: for Gowrie, gunpowder treason (and the 1688 revolution), the restoration and in Ireland for the 1641 rising.

Orders

As an editorial convenience, the citations for each occasion use a heading entitled 'order'. However, this embraces not only several different kinds of order by different authorities, but from the late nineteenth century certain notices or announcements which were more properly requests or recommendations rather than instructions. The chief document or documents appointing each occasion are printed in this edition, whether orders, notices or announcements.

By the sovereign or government

(a) *royal mandate* or other instruction: a letter from the king or queen to the archbishop of Canterbury ordering special prayers, fasts or thanksgiving. These appear to differ little from ordinary letters and the difference in nomenclature may only reflect later cataloguing practice. For the Church of England from 1662 to 1859 a *royal warrant*, renewed at the start of each reign, ordered the services for the annual commemorations to be printed and published, and (normally) annexed to the BCP.[7]

(b) *proclamation*: a decree issued and published by virtue of the royal prerogative, by the sovereign in privy council, or by the sovereign's deputies (lords justices or lord deputies) in council, or on exceptional occasions by the privy council alone. The first occasion of special worship to be ordered by proclamation was the thanksgiving for the reconciliation with Rome by Mary I in 1555. Thereafter, proclamations were not used until the beginning of the reign of Charles I. After 1625, proclamations were used to appoint both fast days and thanksgiving days, and, in England and Wales and in Ireland, to order the composition, distribution and use of the special services for these days. It is not clear why proclamations began to be used routinely from this time, but the immediate reason in the 1620s may have been a desire to assert the royal prerogative in response to parliament's request for a fast. Later, it came to be argued that a proclamation was necessary to authorize and enforce two aspects of fast and thanksgiving days: first, the temporary alteration or suspension of the BCP, the use of which had in England and Wales and in Ireland been required by statute, through successive Acts of Uniformity, and, second, in Scotland as well as in England and Wales and in Ireland the suspension of public and legal business and other secular activities, necessary for the observance of these days. In Scotland, special

---

[7] This point is discussed in detail in the commentaries on the anniversary occasions in volume 3.

worship was first ordered by proclamation in 1623. Because of the absence
of the sovereign in London, until the Act of Union in 1707 proclamations
were issued by the privy council, sometimes in the name of the monarch
and sometimes in its own name, though there is no obvious significance in
which of these two forms was used. The use of the royal prerogative to order
worship was, however, more controversial in Scotland than in England, as is
discussed below (p. lxiii).

(c) *order of council*, that is an order by the sovereign in privy council (or in
Ireland, by the lord lieutenant in council), or by lord justices or lord deputies in council, or by a committee of the privy council, the 'lords of the
council': a decree used occasionally in the sixteenth and seventeenth centuries to order special prayers for addition to ordinary church services. Orders
in council do not appear to have been used consistently for this purpose,
probably reflecting the greater informality of administrative processes, as
well as the survival of documentation. In Scotland, there is no evidence of
the use of orders by the sovereign in council for special worship before the
eighteenth century, except following the Gowrie conspiracy in 1600.

(d) *statute*: statute was used primarily for the establishment of annual fast and
thanksgiving days. It was first used by the Scottish parliament in 1600 to
create an annual thanksgiving for James VI's deliverance from the Gowrie
plot. Subsequently, the observation of 29 May was established by statute
in Scotland, though a royal warrant was used for 5 November. By contrast,
although a privy council order had established the observance of the Gowrie
thanksgiving in England, parliamentary statutes were passed to order the
observance of 5 November, 30 January and 29 May, and later for the fast
commemorating the great fire in London. In Ireland, statute was used to
establish the observance of 29 May and the anniversary of the 1641 Irish
rebellion, but not 5 November or 30 January.

(e) *ordinance*: ordinances were parliamentary statutes that lacked royal assent.
They were first used for 1641–ES to order the thanksgiving for the peace
between England and Scotland instead of a proclamation or parliamentary
act. After the establishment of the republic in 1649, ordinances, passed now
by the Commons alone, were styled as 'acts'.

(f) *parliamentary order*: parliamentary orders were used by parliament from
December 1642 to October 1648 and then by the parliamentary and interregnum governments from 1648 to 1653 and in 1659–60. These were initially
orders originating in the Commons but agreed to and issued by the Lords
(until its abolition in 1649). The Commons often issued further orders on its
own, adding additional causes to be remembered, usually military victories
which had occurred since a thanksgiving had been ordered. Their development is traced in the commentaries. Occasionally, they were referred to as
parliamentary *resolutions*. On some occasions, the House of Commons (e.g.
1644–E2(P), 1645–E17(P), 1645–E18(P)) alone ordered special worship.
Sometimes, this may have been a matter of convenience – on 2 February
1644, for example, when news arrived of the surrender of Nantwich and the
Commons ordered a thanksgiving, the House of Lords was not sitting – but
on other occasions it reflected differences between the houses.

(g) *declaration*: declarations were used principally by Oliver Cromwell as lord
protector, to encourage rather than to order people to observe special prayers,

fasts and thanksgivings, because he did not believe in ordering people to pray.

By the churches

(a) During the sixteenth and early seventeenth centuries, many prayers, fasts and thanksgivings in the Church of England and the Church of Ireland were ordered by *letters from archbishops* to other bishops. This does not necessarily imply that archbishops and bishops had authority to order special worship, nor that they thought they did. Rather it seems to reflect the personal nature of early modern monarchy – that monarchs or privy councils would write to archbishops and bishops to instruct them to organize special worship – and the survival of documentary evidence in this period.

(b) In the Church of Scotland, special worship could be ordered by the various church courts, from the general assembly, through the presbyteries to the kirk sessions. National special worship was ordered by *acts of the general assembly,* or of the *commission of the general assembly* (a standing committee that assumed most of the assembly's powers between full meetings), or of other church courts and national ecclesiastical conventions. Acts of the Scottish church courts were legislative resolutions, adopted unanimously or by majority vote, and were understood to have binding force for members of the church in the territory overseen by the court. In most cases, when the church ordered an occasion of special worship to be observed across Scotland, it did so by an act of the general assembly or of its commission, both of which had national jurisdiction. The nature of general assembly and commission acts varied immensely across the period, ranging from short orders to lengthy declarations, combining instructions with detailed justifications. In some cases, moreover, the church courts issued a separate document expounding the 'causes' for fasting (see below pp. lix–lx).

(c) Principally in the 1640s and early 1650s, the commission (or occasionally the general assembly of the Church of Scotland itself) sometimes issued a *letter*, directed to presbyteries or ministers more generally, in addition to its act appointing special worship. Letters provided further instructions about the observance of special occasions, and give some insight into the distribution of orders in Scotland.

Documents for church services

The reformations in England, Ireland and Scotland resulted in very different liturgical arrangements for the Churches of England and Ireland on the one hand, and the Church of Scotland on the other. In England, the BCP replaced the various uses of the medieval catholic church, imposing a single set liturgy, with prescribed readings, prayers and psalms for every day of the year, to be used throughout the nation. The first Edwardian prayer book, authorized by parliamentary statute in 1549, underwent major amendment in 1552. There were more minor changes in 1559 (following the brief restoration of catholicism under Mary I), 1604 (following the Hampton Court conference) and 1662, after its proscription by parliamentary ordinance in the period 1645–60. From 1645 to 1660 the Directory of Public Worship, composed by the Westminster assembly of English and Scottish divines, was widely though far from universally used. The 1549 BCP was used in English-speaking areas of Ireland.

Subsequently, the 1559 and 1662 prayer books were imposed on Ireland by Acts of Uniformity passed in the Irish parliament in 1560 and 1665.[8] In Scotland use of the second Edwardian prayer book was enjoined by the lords in council in 1557. But it was soon displaced by John Knox's Book of Common Order, first published for the English congregation in Geneva in 1556. The use of this book was enjoined in 1562 by the general assembly, which subsequently, in 1564, ordered the use of a revised edition by all ministers. In 1645, an act of the general assembly authorized the use of the Directory of Public Worship, produced by the Westminster Assembly of Divines. The Book of Common Order provided a structure for services and some prayers, but there was space for extempore prayer and there was no fixed lectionary. The Westminster Directory was a similar composition, providing a manual of directions rather than a set liturgy. Significantly, in the context of this volume, the prayers from Knox's *Ordour and doctrine of the generall faste* (see 1566–S1) were included in later editions of the Book of Common Order and then superseded in the Westminster Directory by sub-directories for thanksgivings and fasts (printed as an Appendix in volume 3 of this edition).

In the Churches of England and Ireland, therefore, except during the period of civil war and interregnum from 1641 to 1660, for occasions of special worship it was necessary to compose, authorize, print and distribute new texts – forms of prayer – which to a greater or lesser degree replaced those required by the BCP. By contrast, in the Church of Scotland from 1560 and in England and Ireland under parliament and the various republican regimes in the 1640s and 1650s, extempore prayers and sermons were expected to supplement the structures provided by the Book of Common Order and the Westminster Directory. Consequently, any texts read in these churches for special worship during these periods took the form of explanations of the reasons for the occasion, either contained in an extended church order (or act) or in a separate statement.

(a) *form of prayer*: the document which contained the text used in worship. For some occasions in the sixteenth and early seventeenth centuries these texts also included a preface or exhortation, to be read out in church, which explained the context of the occasion of special worship and was supposed to provide the basis for the sermon. The titles given to these documents varied, especially in the sixteenth century, but, by the reign of Charles I, the phrase 'form of prayer', adopted in this edition as a generic term, had become common. It then remained, throughout the period covered by volume 1 and well beyond, as the standard title for documents which contained either special prayers or special services; that is to say, a form of prayer might be either a very short document, with perhaps just one prayer, or a lengthy document containing as many as three services and perhaps an address.

(b) *causes, addresses and declarations*: these documents were occasionally issued by the general assembly, its commission, or other courts which appointed national worship in Scotland. 'Causes' provided detailed reasons (often in the form of a numbered list) for fasting (or, in the case of 1649–S2, giving thanks). The national church courts also produced 'declarations', a few of which related to occasions of special worship. These documents provide

---

8   Michael Kennedy, 'The first prayer books 1551–1666', in *The prayer books of the Church of Ireland 1551–2004*, ed. Brian Mayne (Blackrock, 2004), pp. 7–17.

additional information about the special occasions, and some (perhaps most) 'causes' and 'declarations' were to be read publicly in churches. Similar documents were issued from 1642 to 1660 by parliament and the protectorate in England and Wales, Ireland and latterly Scotland. Parliamentary statements, also sometimes intended to be read in churches, tended to be news of recent military victories and were composed by a committee of MPs using letters sent from the battlefield by army generals.

NATIONAL WORSHIP

As has been stated, this edition contains materials on all *particular* or *special* fasts, thanksgivings, prayers and services and all *anniversary religious commemorations* that were observed between the 1530s and 2012 on a *national* basis and by the *appointment* of the crown, state or one of the established churches, and which were normally conducted using special texts for prayers, services or explanation.

These occasions are distinguished from other fasts, festivals and special services observed regularly or predictably: fasts observed as part of the liturgical year and the feasts linked to saints' days observed by the anglican churches; sacramental fasts and thanksgivings observed before and after the administration of the eucharist in Scotland; and fasts held at the start of the Church of Scotland's general assembly in the town where it was meeting. They are distinguished also from certain observances which have sometimes been accorded 'national' significance, because kept by national authorities: in Scotland by commissioners to national church courts, and in England by the houses of parliament from 1642 to 1660 and by the Commonwealth and protectorate council of state from 1649 to 1660. These were observed on a semi-private basis within the assemblies, without the intention that the worship would be observed in parish churches.[9]

The ideal underpinning the concept of 'national worship' was that all members of the realm should worship together on the same dates, with the same purposes and the same texts – this was the nation conceived as a single spiritual and moral body, its members collectively expressing repentance and asking forgiveness for the nation's sins, appealing for God's mercy or striving to understand God's will, or expressing thankfulness for God's blessings. This collective, united and simultaneous effort was the explicit or implicit aim expressed in the orders and in the forms of prayer and addresses. But to a greater or lesser degree, the practice fell short of this ideal: 'national' worship, even when observed in all parishes in a kingdom or throughout the United Kingdom, was not always simultaneous, nor was it observed by all members of the nation.

Aside from the large but ultimately undefinable issue of abstention or dissent by individuals for any number of specific reasons, there were several general or structural reasons for practice diverging from the ideal. One set of differences, fundamental for all references to Britain and the United Kingdom, resulted from the distinction between the presbyterian Church of Scotland and the anglican estab-

---

[9] E.g. the parliamentary fast on 4 June 1651. *CJ*, VI, 581–2. These occasions are also distinguished from the 'special Sundays', such as Education Sunday and Mission Sunday, which developed as a feature of the Church of England's calendar in the late nineteenth and twentieth centuries.

lished churches in England and Wales and in Ireland. This section will explain the effects for special national worship, both of this difference between the established churches and of a further set of complications: different types of authority in matters of worship; regional differences, linked to matters of ordering, printing, distance and distribution; and the realities of a wider religious diversity. Like the rest of this introduction, it will focus on the period from the beginning of the reformation to the revolution of 1688, leaving developments in later periods, including the increasing convergence between religious groups in special worship during the twentieth century, to be examined in the introductions to volumes 2 and 3.

Authority

One defining characteristic of national occasions of special worship was order by legitimate national authority. While for much of the five centuries since the reformation special worship across all three kingdoms of the British Isles was commonly ordered by the crown, the nature and location of authority was contested, especially in Scotland, and shifted in ways that require further elucidation.

In *England and Wales* (and Berwick-upon-Tweed), throughout the period covered by this volume and, indeed, through to the 1860s, orders for special worship with national significance were made only by the public authority of the state.[10] Except for the periods from 1642 to 1649, when parliament contested the king's exercise of his prerogative powers, and from 1649 to 1660, when Commonwealth and protectorate regimes claimed forms of authority in religious matters, this meant the crown. The grounds and expression of the crown's authority over special worship, however, are not entirely clear, partly because they evolved through the period and partly because orders have not survived for several occasions. At the beginning of the reformation the role of the crown in the organization of special worship was already well established. (As early as 1009, religious observances had been ordered by Archbishop Wulfstan on the king's authority in the face of the Viking invasion.) After 1534, the king's authority was strengthened by the Act of Supremacy, declaring him 'supreme head in earth of the Church of England'.[11] Thus, during the reigns of Henry VIII and Edward VI most of the occasions of special worship for which evidence survives were ordered by royal mandate (1541–E1, 1543–E, 1544–E2). The exceptions were occasions in 1544 and 1545, which were ordered by the privy council while the king was absent on campaign, and a thanksgiving in 1547 for which Archbishop Cranmer's order survives but not the original royal order (1544–E3, 1545–E1 and 1547–E).

The situation was both clarified and complicated by the passage of successive Acts of Uniformity, in 1549, 1552, 1559 and 1662, which required all ministers to use the BCP and prohibited the use of any other services.[12] This was re-stated

---

[10] Partial exceptions occurred in the mid-nineteenth century, as ideas on ecclesiastical authority began to change: the organization of a day of humiliation by co-ordinated action of the Irish bishops for 1846–Ir (though this followed the appointment of special prayers by council order), and various days of humiliation authorized by the English bishops and by Scottish church courts for 1849–1, which were also held during a period of special prayers ordered by the privy council.

[11] 26 Hen. VIII, c. 1.

[12] According to 2 & 3 Ed. VI, c. 1 (1549): ministers were to use services and prayers 'in such order and form as is mentioned in the … [BCP] … and none other or otherwise'. This clause was confirmed by the provisions of 5 & 6 Ed. VI, c. 1 (1552) and repeated by 1 Eliz., c. 2 (1559).

and glossed in the clerical oath of subscription imposed by the church canons of 1604, requiring ministers to use the prayers and services prescribed in the BCP 'and none other, except so far as shall be ordered by lawful authority'.[13] Uniformity was required by law; but a 'lawful authority' had the power to order a temporary suspension of this statutory use of the BCP and to prescribe for a period the use of a replacement text. As canon 72 made clear, a lawful authority included the 'ordinary', that is (normally) the diocesan bishops, who could order special acts of worship and even fasts in parishes under their jurisdiction.[14] While this canon was new in 1604, it is clear that it did not claim for the bishops a power that they had not exercised during the reign of Elizabeth: in 1563, Edmund Grindal ordered prayers and composed a form of prayer for parish use in response to the plague in his diocese of London (1563–E), and one of his successors, John Aylmer, did the same in response to the earthquake in 1580 (1580–E). Bishop Laud of London interpreted the law in the same way in 1628: when Secretary Conway asked him to order the printing and distribution of a form of prayer in support of the English fleet's attack on La Rochelle (1628–E2), Laud replied, 'I cannot command the use of the prayer, further than in mine own diocese.'[15] However, before and after the canons of 1604, the legal position was uncertain, and Matthew Parker, archbishop of Canterbury, was doubtful whether even an archbishop could make orders throughout his diocese, still less for his province. In 1563, he was uncertain about the extent of his authority to order special prayers in response to the outbreak of plague (1563–E). He told William Cecil that 'we by our vocation shoulde haue speciall regarde of suche matter: yet because we be holden within certen lymitts by Statutes we maye stande in dowte howe it wilbe taken if we shoulde geue order therin'. He limited such prayers to the city of Canterbury and left ministers 'to ther owne libertie, to followe vs in the citie for common prayers, if they will'.[16] The situation is complicated further by the reproof sent by Archbishop Laud to the Archbishop of Cashel in 1636, informing him that the king took 'extremely ill' his order for a weekly fast throughout his province, 'the power only belonging to himself, and not to any Bishop whatsoever'.[17] Archbishop Spottiswood had been similarly censured, again by Laud on the instructions of the king, in December 1635.[18] The effect of this uncertainty was to shift authority for ordering nationwide special worship from the clergy to the crown. After the restoration in 1660, and probably by the 1630s (with the obvious exception of 1642–60), it had become accepted that crown orders were required for fasts, thanksgivings and prayers observed not just throughout the kingdom, but also in the ecclesiastical provinces, in dioceses, and in parishes.

---

[13] Canon 36, clauses 2–3, in *The Anglican canons 1529–1947*, ed. Gerald Bray (Church of England Record Society, 6, 1998), p. 321.
[14] See e.g. canon 72 of 1604 (if expressed negatively) in *ibid.*, p. 363: 'No minister or ministers shall, without the licence and direction of the bishop of the diocese ... appoint or keep solemn fasts ... other than such as by law are, or by public authority shall be appointed.'
[15] SP16/114/14, fo. 19r: Laud to Conway, 26 Aug. 1628.
[16] Lans. 6, fo. 154r: Archbishop Parker to Sir William Cecil, 23 July 1563.
[17] *The works of William Laud, DD sometime lord archbishop of Canterbury*, ed. J. Bliss and W. Scott (7 vols., Oxford, 1847–60), VII, 298: Laud to Wentworth, 20 Nov. 1636.
[18] SP16/303, fo. 17: Laud to Spottiswood, 1 Dec. 1635. The situation in Scotland was a little different, partly because of Laudian disapproval of the Church of Scotland's practice of fasting on Sundays – a practice 'contrary to the rules of Christianity and all the ancient canons of the Church' – and partly because the Scottish canons of 1636 (14.2) specifically laid down that fasts could only be 'appointed by his majesty'. *Anglican canons*, ed. Bray, p. 546.

Archbishops and bishops ceased to order special worship on their own authority for their provinces and dioceses; in England and Wales and in Ireland, these orders had become a crown monopoly.

In *Ireland*, the authority of the crown was exercised by the lord lieutenants, or lord deputies or lords justices. The evidence for special worship before the civil war is much thinner than in England, but what there is suggests a similar pattern. Of the four Irish occasions for which evidence survives, three were ordered either by the lord deputy or lords justices and council (1625–Ir, 1628–Ir and 1641–Ir). Only the first occasion, the thanksgiving for the defeat of the Spanish armada in 1589, seems to be an exception, in that the order appears to have come directly from England.

In *Scotland*, the nature of authority in matters of worship was debated and underwent more change. From its beginnings in 1560, the Scottish reformation was much more hostile to Erastianism than its English counterpart. Most of the reformed clergy drew a sharp distinction between church and state, denying the monarch all authority in the church and asserting the role of the general assembly as the supreme law-making body in religious matters. The appointment of special worship, therefore, was subject to ecclesiastical authority, part of the 'intrinsic right' of the church. Accordingly, in the period before 1660, most special worship observed in the whole of Scotland was ordered by national courts of the church: the general assembly, its commission and other conventions and commissions claiming to exercise national authority.[19]

Nonetheless, even before the restoration, some Scottish observances were appointed by the crown, the privy council or parliament. The growing participation of royal authority can be traced under James VI and Charles I, particularly with respect to thanksgivings.[20] Under the covenanters from 1638, parliament often consulted closely with the general assembly and its commissioners about special worship, and was wholly or partly responsible for appointing four occasions (1641–S, 1644–S4, 1645–S5, 1646–S4). At the restoration Charles II took advantage of divisions within the Kirk to restore episcopacy and to assert royal authority over the Church of Scotland. Nowhere, perhaps, was this more symbolically visible than in the ordering of special worship: all national fasts and thanksgivings in the Church of Scotland during the reigns of Charles II and James VII were ordered by royal or privy council proclamation, making Scottish practice more comparable with that in England and Ireland. However, whereas the patterns of ordering of special worship established in the 1660s remained fundamentally the same in England and Ireland for the next two centuries, the re-establishment of presbyterianism in Scotland following the revolution of 1688 brought renewed tensions between the civil and ecclesiastical authorities.

[19] Sometimes the authority of these meetings was challenged by the crown: see 1593–S2, 1596–S2, 1638–S2. In nine cases (1560–S, 1567–S1, 1588–S3, 1591–S, 1593–S1, 1596–S1, 1621–S, 1622–S, 1628–S), a shortage of information makes it is impossible to establish whether the worship was appointed by a national court. Yet national authority may have been involved in these fasts and thanksgivings, and they have been included. In another case that has been included (1640–S1), a local court, the presbytery of Edinburgh, claimed authority to appoint a day for the nation; its order seems to have been followed in other parts of Scotland. Another exceptional inclusion (1660–S) was appointed by the co-ordinated action of local ecclesiastical and civil authorities, in the absence of national government.

[20] See 1594–S1, 1600–S, 1623–S2, 1630–S, 1637–S, and also 1638–S1, a fast.

Geography

A second defining characteristic of national occasions of special worship was their observance across the kingdom; in principle, special prayers or services were to be held in all parishes in England and Wales, or Scotland, or Ireland, or the United Kingdom. However, in practice this did not necessarily mean that all parts of the British Isles or the United Kingdom, or even all areas within each kingdom or each constituent part of the United Kingdom, had the same occasions of special worship or observed them on the same dates. Indeed, in 1588–9 the thanksgiving day for the defeat of the Spanish armada occurred over two months later in Ireland than in England. This was exceptional, but even in the late seventeenth century fasts and thanksgivings in Ireland took place four or even six weeks after the observance of the same occasion in England and Wales.

Through the sixteenth century, England and Scotland were independent kingdoms with different rulers; each kingdom had separate national occasions ordered independently, by distinct authorities. Distinctive arrangements for special worship did not, however, cease with the union of the crowns in 1603, and there was relatively little co-ordination between observances in the two kingdoms before the eighteenth century. The only significant exception was the period of the Cromwellian union between 1654 and 1659, when, with only a few variations, the ordering of special worship was co-ordinated throughout Britain (and Ireland).[21] Another, unique, exception was the thanksgiving day for the conclusion of the peace between England and Scotland in September 1641 (1641–ES), provision for which was included in the peace treaty, though in England the thanksgiving was ordered by parliamentary ordinance. After the restoration there is some evidence for the co-ordination of occasions of special worship in the two countries, which is not altogether surprising given the assertion of crown authority over their ordering in this period. The thanksgivings for the Four Days' battle in August 1666 and for the pregnancy of Queen Mary in 1688 took place on the same day in most of England and in the Edinburgh area; similarly, the thanksgiving for the discovery of the Rye House plot took place across Britain on 9 September 1683. But such co-ordination was rare: occasions were observed in England but not in Scotland, and vice versa, and, when they were observed for the same reason in both countries, the dates could vary by up to two months.

As just noted, during the 1650s a number of occasions of special worship were ordered for Britain and Ireland together – the first was the thanksgiving for the victory at the battle of Worcester in 1651 (1651–1), though most occurred during the protectorate. It is difficult to say much about the period before 1640, as evidence only survives for three Irish occasions, all of which were organized and celebrated independently of any English occasions, even when the cause was the same (cf. 1588–E2 with 1589–Ir, and 1625–E with 1625–Ir). Harmonization between English and Irish observances seems to have begun in the restoration period. After 1661, all except two Irish fasts and thanksgivings were closely linked to English equivalents: if they were not held on the same day (as in 1683–1), either there is evidence of an order being sent from England to Ireland or the Irish proclamation was based closely on the English text (e.g. 1685–EIr).

---

[21] No occasions of special worship were ordered solely for Scotland during this period, though in 1658 thanksgiving days were ordered in both England and Scotland. See 1658–ES.

Even within kingdoms, it was common for special worship to be ordered for slightly different dates in different areas. The main reason for this was the pressure on printers and on the systems of communication and delivery. Given the nature of special worship, the notice was often short, because otherwise its purpose could be lost, and for some types of occasion the government evidently wanted to spread the news as soon as possible, either to preserve calm or to encourage celebrations. Yet, it was accepted that the orders and documents for worship could not always be printed and delivered at the same time for all places of worship in all areas, given their varying distances from the capital and its printing presses. It was therefore common for orders for nationwide observance either to specify different dates of observance for different areas, or to state that the observance should be held as soon as the order was received. Accordingly, it cannot be assumed that a fast, thanksgiving or special prayer held on a particular date in one location was being observed on that same date elsewhere.

For the first century after the reformation in England and Wales, it was common for special worship to be ordered to be observed as soon as parishes obtained the form of prayer; only the armada thanksgiving in 1588 and the fast for the plague in 1625 were observed on the same date across England and Wales. From 1626, however, it was usual for the dates of first observance in different areas to be specified in the order, with the kingdom being divided into, first, London, Westminster and the suburbs (sometimes defined as the bills of mortality[22]) and sometimes Southwark and then, secondly, the rest of England and Wales. This remained the pattern until the revolution of 1688, though increasingly through the restoration period fast and thanksgiving *days* were ordered for the same date across England and Wales. During the 1640s, the area within which occasions ordered by parliament were to be observed varied in a way which reflected how much of the country was under its control.[23]

Similar arrangements were made for special worship in Ireland, though it is difficult to discern a clear pattern. The fast for 1625–Ir was ordered to be observed across the kingdom, though no specific date for the beginning of the weekly fast was specified. Otherwise, the fragmentary evidence for occasions before the civil war makes it impossible to know whether observance extended much beyond Dublin (see 1589–Ir; 1630–Ir). From the 1650s through to 1688, special worship was normally ordered to be observed for the whole country on the same date, but for some occasions first in Dublin and then, one week later,[24] across the rest of the country.

The pattern in Scotland is much more confused. From the first fast day in reformation Scotland, appointed by the general assembly in December 1565, it was common for fasts to be appointed to be observed across the kingdom on two specific successive Sundays (1566–S1). However, throughout the later sixteenth and seventeenth centuries, other arrangements were common. Frequently, fast and thanksgiving days were ordered to be observed first in central Scotland and then in the rest of the kingdom. The definition of central Scotland varied: Edinburgh, Lothian and Fife,

---

[22] The area covered by the weekly printed broadsides listing the numbers of baptisms and deaths in the City of London, the City and Liberty of Westminster and parishes in Middlesex (including Spitalfields, St Giles in the Fields, Hackney, Islington, Shoreditch, Whitechapel and Bethnal Green) and Surrey (including the borough of Southwark and parishes in Lambeth, Rotherhithe and Bermondsey).

[23] For details, see below p. lxviii.

[24] Or, exceptionally, two weeks later (1660–Ir).

Edinburgh and Lothian, central Scotland,[25] or the Edinburgh diocese. Generally, as in 1566, the dates on which special worship was to be observed were specified, but, on some occasions in the sixteenth century, orders were deliberately vague: for example, the 1594 fast before the meeting of the parliament took place in Edinburgh 'and sick vther parts quher the samein may be conveniently had'.[26]

In addition to these occasions, which were certainly ordered for observance in all parts of each kingdom or part of the United Kingdom even if on different dates, a number of occasions, which were not ordered to be observed in all parishes, nonetheless had a 'national' character and are accordingly included in this edition. These may be divided into three groups:

(a) Some early special prayers and 'days' in England appear to have been observed in Canterbury province alone. This may be an impression resulting from an incomplete survival of orders and other evidence: there may have been observance in York province. But in some cases, observances do seem to have been ordered solely in Canterbury province, and this may be true of all of them.

(b) Some other special services in the early and mid-sixteenth century were held only in St Paul's Cathedral. Occasions of this type reflected the practice in France, which persisted up to the revolution of 1789,[27] and took place for events such as the queen's childbearing (1533–E, 1537–E1) the health of the monarch, their consort or foreign monarchs (1535–E, 1537–E4), victory in battle (1544–E1, 1545–E2, 1547–E, 1557–E1), and the suppression of rebellions (1549–E). In the 1530s and 1540s, and again during the reign of Mary I, services at St Paul's were often accompanied by processions attended by the city's parish clergy. No services of this kind were held after Mary's death, until the rather different case of the thanksgiving for the recovery of the prince of Wales in 1872 (1872–ES2).

(c) Various English, Scottish and Irish occasions across the period were appointed by the national authority but observed only in capital cities and sometimes their close vicinities. These were ordered at particularly short notice when urgent prayers were thought desirable in circumstances of national significance, and on an understanding that London, Edinburgh or Dublin could stand for the nation. They took place for events similar to the occasions at St Paul's Cathedral: the birth of the heir to the throne (1537–E2), the health of the monarch (1562–E2), victory in battle (1547–E, 1557–E2, 1596–E2), and the suppression of rebellions (1554–E1). In such cases, it was presumably expected that news of the observance would spread, and was likely to be mentioned by parish clergy elsewhere. During the later years of Elizabeth's reign in England and under the Stuart monarchs in England and Scotland up to 1688, this practice was much less common, and it is difficult to discern any pattern in the types of event which led to special worship in either London or Edinburgh.[28] During the Republic, however, there were thanksgiving days in London

---

[25] Defined as the dioceses of Edinburgh, Dunkeld, Brechin, Dunblane, Glasgow and St Andrews (1675–S), with the addition of the dioceses of Aberdeen and Galloway in 1684–S.

[26] *BUK*, III, 839 – see 1594–S2.

[27] Michèle Fogel, *Les ceremonies de l'information dans la France du XVIe au XVIIIe siècle* (Paris, 1989).

[28] In England, see 1666–E1, a thanksgiving day for the decline of the plague in London, and 1686–E, thanksgiving prayers for the capture of Buda from the Ottomans. The latter was one of the more exceptional cases of special worship. Not only was it highly unusual for thanksgivings to be ordered for the military victories of foreign powers, but services were, uniquely, ordered for St George's Chapel, Westminster Abbey and the church of St Mary-le-Bow, presumably to represent the court,

for a number of military victories (e.g. 1651–E4, 1657–E1), a practice which again became common in England and Ireland after the revolution of 1688.

(d) A substantial number of occasions during the 1640s and 1650s were not observed nationally because of the civil wars. From 1642 to 1646, both the English parliament and Charles I ordered rival fasts and thanksgivings, each claiming to exercise legitimate national authority. During the 1640s, the area within which occasions ordered by parliament were to be observed varied in a way that reflected how much of the country was under its control. In the first years of the war, it generally ordered prayers only for the London area (defined variously as the suburbs, the bills of mortality, the lines of communication[29] and ten or twenty miles from the city). From 1644, it increasingly ordered observance first in the London area and then across the rest of the country.[30] Sometimes, parliament stated explicitly that the occasion was for those parts of the country under its control (1645–E5(P) and 1645–E11(P)), but often it implicitly assumed jurisdiction across the whole of England and Wales, as did Charles I.

Uniformity and diversity

Although occasions of special worship were 'national' in the sense that they were ordered by a national authority and observed (in principle) in all parts of the realm, they were not necessarily observed by all religious groups or sections of the population, even before non-attendance at any form of religious worship emerged as a significant feature of British social life in the course of the eighteenth century. Non-observance of special worship was perhaps most noticeable during the civil war, when royalists and parliamentarians ordered separate days of prayer, fasting or thanksgiving, sometimes for the same event; for example when both sides claimed victory at the battle of Newbury, 1643–E9(P) and 1643–E10(R). In November 1643, the king ordered that the monthly fast, held on the last Wednesday of the month since early 1642, should be discontinued and replaced by a fast on the second Friday of every month. From this date, when parishes observed the fast became an indication of their political allegiance. There is also evidence that some royalists displayed their contempt for fasts ordered by parliament by feasting and drinking to the king's health.[31] In the 1650s, divisions among Scotland's presbyterians and opposition to the Cromwellian union led to systematic non-observance of several fasts and

---

Westminster and the City. In Scotland, there were only two occasions of special worship in Edinburgh alone in the seventeenth century: 1622–S ordered a week of fasts because of threats to the protestant cause, and 1623–S2 was a thanksgiving service following Prince Charles's return from Spain.

[29] A series of twenty-three fortifications that parliament ordered to be built to protect the City and its liberties from attack. They stretched from the Tower northwards to the Whitechapel Road, across to Hackney Road and Kingsland Road near Shoreditch, turning south-westwards to St John Street, Gray's Inn Lane and Oxford Road and then to Hyde Park Corner, Chelsea Turnpike and Tothill Fields. South of the river, the lines ran north-east from Vauxhall to St George's Fields, Borough Street, Kent Street, Deptford Street and to a point on the Thames opposite the Tower. The phrase was first used for 1644–E4(P).

[30] One of the early occasions on which parliament ordered observance across England and Wales (1644–E4) specified three dates: for the London area, then the area south of the Trent and finally the area north of the Trent.

[31] Lucy-Ann Bates, 'Nationwide fast and thanksgiving days in England, 1640–1660', Ph.D. dissertation, Durham University, 2012, pp. 223–7; *Quarter Sessions Records for County of Somerset (1646–1660)*, ed. E. H. Bates (1912), XXVIII, 135.

thanksgivings in Scotland (see e.g. 1656–2 and 1659–1). Similarly, in Ireland the thanksgiving for the defeat of the Spanish armada in 1589 was not widely observed in some areas because of opposition to the English regime. Archbishop Loftus complained to Burghley that 'verie fewe or none almost resorted thervnto but euen in Dublin it self the lawyers in terme time tooke occasion to leaue the towne, of purpose to absent them selves from that godlie exercise'.[32]

Until the passage of Toleration Acts in England in 1689 and in Scotland in 1712, it was assumed that all subjects in the two kingdoms were members of the established churches. Even after these (and subsequent) official adoptions of religious toleration – and well into the nineteenth century – both crown orders and orders by the churches continued to make this assumption. In Ireland, the situation was rather different, but there too neither Roman catholics nor presbyterians benefited from an *official* toleration, so both proclamations and privy council orders took very similar forms to those issued in England. In England and Wales, attendance at church on Sundays and holy days was required of the whole population not only by canon law but also by statute, as prescribed in successive Acts of Uniformity. In Scotland, a sixteenth-century statute allowed fines to be imposed for absence from church, and more severe legislation against nonconformity was passed in the restoration period.[33]

Evidence of observance or the lack of it is, however, limited for the sixteenth and seventeenth centuries. In the sixteenth century, there are cases of catholics being prosecuted for objecting to special worship. David Ramsey, an Essex labourer, for example, was prosecuted at the local assizes for saying that he was a 'papyste' and that he 'wolde praye for the pope', in response to the petitionary services for English success against the Spanish Armada on 11 August 1588.[34] Conversely, godly enthusiasm for, rather than abstention from, fasting was perceived as a problem both in the 1580s, by Archbishop Whitgift, and during the early Stuart period. These 'private' fasts, held in addition to the publicly ordered fasts, both supplemented official worship and often acted as a reproach to perceived failings or lack of interest of the authorities about the religious and political state of the nation. But, as Tom Webster has pointed out, in places like East Anglia and Dorchester 'discretion was often all that was required to maintain such exercises',[35] and few people seem to have been prosecuted for failing to observe special worship in the sixteenth century.

However, towards the end of Elizabeth's reign, there is some evidence that the authorities considered that the normal legal processes, laid down in the canons and the act of uniformity, were not enough to enforce observance of special worship. For 1586–E2, churchwardens and 'other discreete men of the Parish' were instructed to report negligent ministers to the ordinary. For 1596–E3, ministers and churchwardens were required to submit a certificate every month listing those who did not attend the services, and those who did not provide alms to the poor. In 1597,

---

32 SP63/154/37, fos. 129v–130r: Archbishop Adam Loftus of Dublin to Burghley, 22 Sept. 1590.
33 *RPS*, 1579/10/23; Alasdair Raffe, *The culture of controversy. Religious arguments in Scotland, 1660–1714* (Woodbridge, 2012), pp. 53–4.
34 *Calendar of Assize Records: Essex Indictments, Elizabeth I*, ed. J. S. Cockburn (1978), p. 331.
35 Tom Webster, *Godly clergy in early Stuart England. The Caroline puritan movement c. 1620–1643* (Cambridge, 1997), p. 67; *Conferences and combination lectures in the Elizabethan church. Dedham and Bury St Edmunds 1582–90*, ed. Patrick Collinson, John Craig and Brett Usher (Church of England Record Society 10, Woodbridge, 2003), p. lxxxiii. See order for 1596–E3.

some clergy were questioned for failing to observe special worship.[36] There was heightened concern under Charles I. The emergence of royal proclamation as the preferred means of ordering fast and thanksgiving days in 1625 possibly signalled a growing preoccupation with both the enforcement of uniformity in general and the observance of fasts and thanksgivings in particular. For 1625–E, Charles I required

> all Archbishops, and Bishops, in their seuerall Provinces, and Diocesses, and all Parsons, Vicars and Curats, within their seuerall Parishes and Charges, as also all Maiors, Sheriffes, Justices of Peace, and other Officers in their seuerall places, limits, and iurisdictions, respectively to take especiall care, that this His Maiesties Royall commandement be duly executed and obserued.

For 1626–E2, he enjoined that the requirements of the fasts during a plague outbreak

> shall be reverently and devoutly performed by all his loving subjects, as they tender the favour of Almighty God, and would avoide his just indignation against this Land; and upon paine of such punishments, as His Majestie can justly inflict upon all such, as shall conteme, or neglect, so religious a Worke.

Then, under Laud as archbishop of Canterbury in the 1630s, attempts by the ecclesiastical and civil authorities to prevent unlawful fasting intensified.[37]

From the 1660s through to the nineteenth century, proclamations for special worship continued include clauses that reinforced the existing law on attendance at church (legally new penalties could not be added in this way). This language emphasized the importance attached by the state to these occasions, and presumably had the effect of encouraging observance. After the restoration, however, religious nonconformity became a much more significant issue, although it is not clear to what extent – at least in the years before 1688 – this affected the observance of occasions of special worship. Some of the smaller groups of protestant dissenters, most notably the Quakers and perhaps also the baptists, would have refused to join in worship ordered by the state and may even have continued to open shops and businesses. In January 1688, Roger Morrice noted that the London dissenting ministers decided, as a body, to ignore the thanksgiving for the pregnancy of Mary of Modena, but the circumstances of the last months of James II's reign were extraordinary.[38] More commonly presbyterians and even some independents may well have participated in special worship. While many of them were uncomfortable with state orders, they tended to share the religious interpretation of events that prompted special worship. They also sympathized with the religious imperatives of special worship; indeed, in this period many presbyterians in particular were partial conformists who still regularly attended their parish church as well as the meeting house. In some cases, too, these groups were anxious to demonstrate their loyalty to the monarchy.

---

[36] *Diocese of Norwich. Bishop Redman's visitation, 1597: presentments in the archdeaconries of Norwich, Norfolk, and Suffolk*, ed. J. F. Williams (Norfolk Record Society, 18, 1946), pp. 7–8, 138, 147, 149, 151; Lans. 83/34, fo. 98r–v: Edward Phelippes to Lord Burghley, 20 Jan. 1597.

[37] SP 16/211, fo. 119r: additions made by Henry Alleyn to his examination, 22 Feb. 1632; SP16/261, fos 77r, 84–5: acts of court of high commission, Oct. 1634; SP 16/327, fo. 187r: Robert Aylett to Sir John Lambe, 29 June 1636; SP 16/406, fo. 175r: information by [Nicholas] Gare, [1638?]; SP 16/351, fo. 261v: metropolitical visitation of Nathaniel Brent, vicar-general, 28 Feb.–15 Mar. 1637; SP 16/362, fo. 214r: statement by John Sym, [June?] 1637, and see *Works of Laud*, ed. Bliss and Scott, VII, 299: Laud to Wentworth, 20 Nov. 1636.

[38] Morrice, IV, 213.

This is not to deny that occasions of special worship were sometimes the focus for partisan behaviour. The thanksgiving day for the discovery of the Rye House plot included celebrations in which bonfires consumed figures representing presbyterians and many sermons attacked dissenters, while some whigs and their sympathizers stayed away from the church services. The two thanksgivings in 1688, for the queen's pregnancy and the birth of the prince of Wales, were both held on Sundays (1688–EIr1 and 1688–EIr2), in the first case certainly and in the second probably in order to prevent widespread absenteeism. But this did not prevent widespread if silent protest, literally in the case of those congregations which did not answer the prayers for the prince. Nor, in January, did it prevent the London dissenting ministers from agreeing to take no notice of the queen's pregnancy.[39] But this behaviour was driven less by denominational distinctiveness than by politics, by the use of the occasions to demonstrate support for Charles II and, later, opposition to the catholicizing policies of James II. Even as late as 1688 the presbyterian lord mayor of London attended the service for the martyrdom of Charles I, long after many anglican preachers had turned it into an occasion for lambasting presbyterians of an earlier generation for their role in bringing the king to the executioner's block.[40]

As a result of the re-establishment of episcopacy in restoration Scotland, nonconformity was even more of a problem there than in England. As in England, opponents frequently asserted a link between political and religious dissent, though perhaps, in the light of presbyterian risings in 1666 and 1679, with more reason. Indeed, the royal proclamation for the fast in 1681 laid much of the blame for God's judgments on the extremist Cameronians, who had embraced 'sad, Blasphemous, Sanguinary and Treasonable Delusions' (1681–S). Even so, the evidence for presbyterian observance of fasts and thanksgivings is mixed. Early in the restoration, there is evidence that at least some dissenters did observe orders for fasts (e.g., 1665–S1). By contrast, at the end of Charles II's reign even some indulged presbyterian ministers (those who had been licensed to preach in churches) were prosecuted for not reading the royal declaration or observing the thanksgiving for the discovery of the Rye House plot (1683–S). Presbyterian meeting houses were not enjoined to observe the thanksgivings in 1688 for the queen's pregnancy and for the birth of the prince of Wales, and there is no evidence that any did so, despite the fact that they were benefiting from the toleration allowed under James VII's declaration of indulgence.

PHASES OF SPECIAL WORSHIP

As has been noted earlier, counting occasions of special worship is problematic and potentially misleading. Nonetheless, numbers, if interpreted with caution, do provide some guide to broad patterns of worship. In the almost five centuries since the reformation, if the nine anniversary commemorations are excluded, there have been 866 occasions of special worship. Of these, 187 took place only in Scotland and 33 only in Ireland.[41] The remaining 645 were observed either in England alone

---

[39] *Ibid*, IV, 213, 285.
[40] *Ibid.*, IV, 223; Andrew Lacey, *The cult of King Charles the martyr* (Woodbridge, 2003), pp. 154–5.
[41] Note that Irish occasions are only included up to 1871.

or in England and at least one of the other kingdoms. In all three countries, the seventeenth century accounts for the highest proportion of occasions[42] – well over one third, a figure that would be significantly higher if separate observances of occasions were counted. For instance, during the plague epidemic of 1625, the weekly fast ordered by Charles I (1625–E) should have taken place thirty-two times before the thanksgiving of January 1626.[43] Similarly, the monthly fast ordered at the beginning of the civil war should have been held on eighty-eight occasions before its repeal by the Rump parliament in 1649 (1641–E).

When examined more closely, however, other, perhaps more surprising, patterns emerge. A very large number of the seventeenth-century occasions took place during the mid-century years of civil war and interregnum – 119 in England from August 1642 to May 1660, 53 in Scotland from 1637 to 1660 and 13 in Ireland from 1642 to 1660.[44] The very high incidence of special worship during this period, even for a time of war, may reinforce the impression that there was a link between puritanism and special worship (or certainly between puritanism and fasting) in the early modern period. It also indicates that the Elizabethan and Stuart monarchies were less keen on special worship than might initially be assumed. In fact, during each of the periods 1588–1603, 1603–42 and 1660–88 there was, on average, less than one occasion of special worship annually in England and Wales, though it is important to bear in mind that four occasions were fasts ordered to be kept weekly during plague epidemics in 1563, 1593, 1603 and 1625. By contrast, during the reigns of William and Anne, there were three occasions per year, and, in the period between the accession of George I in 1714 and 1868, just over one. Even in the period between the middle of Victoria's reign and 2012, when the nature of special worship changed dramatically and the country underwent a process of secularization, there was, on average, slightly more than one occasion per year.[45]

The relatively high frequency of special worship during the reigns of William and Anne stands out and merits further attention, as it emphasizes another significant pattern. Britain was at war almost continuously during this period, and 99 of the 131 occasions of special worship across the three kingdoms from 1689 to 1713 were connected in some way with the conflict with France, while a number of those in the early years of William III's reign called for monthly fasts during the campaigning season. This reveals a broader pattern, as war, whether as the cause of petitionary and intercessionary prayer or to give thanks for victories and peace treaties, was the single most important cause of special worship throughout the period since the reformation, accounting for 378 of the 866 occasions. This pattern, moreover, has been broadly consistent right across the period: in every century, war was the single most important reason for the ordering of special worship, ranging from just under 30 per cent of occasions in the sixteenth century to just over 60 per cent in the eighteenth.

---

[42] The seventeenth century would not seem so unusual were it not for the incontinence in special worship between 1642 and 1660, and particularly during the 1640s.

[43] Visitations of plague almost invariably generated intense periods of special worship: in 1563, 1593, 1603, 1625 and 1636 weekly fasts were ordered, and in 1665 monthly.

[44] These figures are for England and England together with Scotland and/or Ireland, for Scotland only, and for Ireland only.

[45] The number of twentieth-century occasions is increased by the impact of war in 1914–18 and 1939–45. Non-royal occasions have not been included after c. 1973; on the reasons for this, see the introduction to volume 3.

The next most important group of occasions are those connected with the royal family, accounting for 147 occasions, though the nature of these changed significantly across the centuries. From the sixteenth century through to the end of the nineteenth almost all concerned the health of the king and queen and the birth of the monarch's children.[46] From the late nineteenth century, however, great royal commemorations and celebrations – jubilees, funerals and coronations – emerged as the most important occasions.

The third most important type of occasion related to natural occurrences: to plague and other diseases (both human and animal), to famine and harvest and to earthquake. These accounted for eighty-nine occasions of special worship, distributed relatively evenly across the period, though plague was the main focus of concern in the sixteenth and seventeenth centuries, cattle disease in the eighteenth and cholera in the nineteenth. This type of occasion last occurred in 1882 (prayers for the harvest in England), reflecting the declining impact of epidemic diseases and the weather on the lives of people, changing beliefs about God's agency in the world and the institution by the Church of England of the annual harvest thanksgiving service.

In order to assist the understanding of the material presented in this edition, this section – and its continuation in the introductions to volumes 2 and 3 – explores these themes in more detail, providing an overview of the successive chronological phases of special worship. The word, 'phases', has been chosen with some care. Each of the phases witnessed some significant change or development in the nature of special worship – in the types of occasion, in the nature of the observation, in the methods of ordering or the forms of worship, in the reasons for observance – but there was also, as will become apparent, much continuity between phases.

The medieval background

Special occasions of worship ordered for observance by a whole community were not the creations of the protestant reformations, nor has the practice been exclusively Christian. Probably all human societies have had similar types of worship during crises or as celebrations. For Christian societies, the model, the justification and in various senses the inspiration were provided by the Old Testament – Israel as God's chosen people, the 'elect nation', which at times of crisis prayed for God's assistance, which treated those crises as God's warnings and punishments, and which after repentance of sins seemed to receive God's mercies and blessings. Moses's prayers for an end to the plagues of Egypt, Helias's prayer for rain after years of drought, the successful prayers of Jehosaphat, Hezekiah and Judas Maccabeus for victory in battle, and the favour shown to Nineveh after its prayer and repentance were among the most popular Old Testament precedents cited in orders, forms of prayer and treatises on divine providence.[47]

For England, the earliest surviving order for special worship throughout the kingdom on particular dates is for (probably) 1009, when King Aethelred's Anglo-Saxon kingdom was threatened by a 'great army' of Danes and archbishop Wulfstan of York issued on the king's authority a set of directions for penance and supplica-

---

[46] The prayers ordered for the birth of the children of the prince of Wales in 1796 and 1864, and of the duke of York in 1894, were very unusual.

[47] Indices of the texts referred to in forms of prayer, whether in readings, psalms or 'composite' psalms are provided at the end of volume 3.

tion. On the first three days of the week before Michaelmas, all adults were required, with penalties for non-observance, to 'strive earnestly' to obtain God's 'mercy and compassion' against the enemy by fasting, by walking barefoot to church for confession, by hearing masses and collects 'against the heathen', by psalm-singing (especially Psalm 3, 'Why, O Lord, are they multiplied'), and by giving alms and food to the poor and infirm.[48] Little is known about medieval occasions of special worship in Wales, Scotland and Ireland. Special worship is likely to have begun in Wales shortly after the principality was incorporated into the English crown in 1284. In Scotland, it can certainly be traced to 1318, when St Andrews Cathedral was consecrated in a service of national thanksgiving for the victory at Bannockburn.[49] Special worship in Ireland may date from as early as c. 432 and the arrival of St Patrick.[50] Orders for special worship in England were issued more systematically in the 1290s in the context of Edward I's wars with Scotland and France. From this time onwards, and particularly during the Hundred Years War (1337–1453), worship for particular military expeditions, diplomatic negotiations and battles became more common, in some periods as often as once a year, and their organization was regularized. Requests for prayers and services – often in the form of lengthy explanatory writs – were sent from the king or the archbishops to the bishops (in Canterbury province sometimes through the bishop of London, in his capacity as dean of the province), who communicated them to heads of religious houses and to archdeacons, who passed them on to the parish clergy.

With no uniform liturgy, the structure and format of medieval special services varied, though many cathedrals and parishes would have followed the prescriptions of the dominant rite in England, the Sarum use.[51] Petitionary services (services *in causa necessitatis*) were similar to those conducted on rogation days and St Mark's day. They started at the choir step with the blessing of the salt and water, the asperges and the sprinkling of the high altar and worshippers. The choir sang an antiphon in the stalls, the priest sang a versicle and prayer and then the clergy and choir processed either to another altar in the church or to another church in the town. During the procession, the choir sang another antiphon or response and, when the procession reached the designated altar or church, the priest sang the versicle and prayer of the saint to whom the altar or church was dedicated. Prayers were recited in prostration (*preces in prostratione*) followed by the mass. After this, the litany was sung up to the 'Sancta Maria', at which point the procession returned to the choir stalls singing the remainder of the litany. When the procession had reached the choir step and the litany was finished, the priest sang another versicle and prayer.[52]

---

[48] *The laws of the kings of England from Edmund to Henry I*, ed. A. J. Robertson (Cambridge, 1925), pp. 114–17. Also printed with helpful annotation in *English historical documents I. c.500–1042*, ed. Dorothy Whitelock (2nd edn, 1961), pp. 447–8.

[49] Michael Lynch, 'Religious life in medieval Scotland', in *A history of religion in Britain. Practice and belief from pre-Roman times to the present*, ed. Sheridan Gilley and W. J. Sheils (Oxford, 1994), p. 106.

[50] 'The Book of Howth', in *Calendar of the Carew manuscripts preserved in the archiepiscopal library at Lambeth*, ed. J. S. Brewer and William Bullen (6 vols., 1867–71), VI, 16–17.

[51] Kenneth Stevenson, 'Worship by the book', in *The Oxford guide to the Book of Common Prayer: a worldwide survey*, ed. Charles C. Hefling and Cynthia L. Shattuck (Oxford, 2006), p. 10.

[52] Terence Bailey, *The processions of Sarum and the Western Church* (Pontifical Institute of Mediaeval Studies, Studies and Texts, 21, Toronto, 1971), pp. 12–14, 25–6; *Processionale ad usum insignis ac praeclarae ecclesiae Sarum*, ed. W. G. Henderson (Leeds, 1882), pp. 164–5.

The rite stipulated the texts to be used. The litany was that prescribed for the day, the versicles and prayer followed that for the matins memorial of All Saints, the antiphons were selected from a list in the rite and the *preces in prostratione* comprised Psalm 50, penitential versicles and a prayer, the latter two of which may have been unique to the occasion.[53] The seven penitential psalms were also recited.[54] Sermons (in English) were also preached on at least some occasions. The Sarum rite did not specify the format of thanksgiving services, but it is likely that they followed the pattern of those *in causa necessitatis*, not least because some of the texts prescribed for the latter were celebratory ones.[55] At Salisbury itself, the occasions were visually rich in ritual and the rite specified who attended the procession, their function (e.g. carrying the holy water), the order of precedence and what they wore. As perhaps befitted penitential and petitionary occasions, clothing on these occasions was more sombre than for the great festivals, with clergy usually dressed in plain copes and albs with amices.[56]

One obvious purpose of special worship in wartime was to appeal for the continuing support of all persons for the military effort and for the consequent taxes; this has been described by some historians as a form of 'propaganda' which assumed the existence of a 'public opinion'.[57] But, as is clear from use of the same types of penitential worship for episodes with no military or political causes – during epidemics, poor weather and poor harvests – special worship was driven by a fundamental underlying conception of the kingdom as a spiritual and moral community under an interventionist God. Calamities – war, disease and harvest failure were all equally calamities – were the result of divine displeasure at the collective sins of both subjects and rulers; repentance, prayer and reformation were the route to divine favour, and so to relief or victory. Appeals to God and analogies with Old Testament Israel were a commonplace in many royal as well as ecclesiastical documents, but some evidence, particularly after the great victories at Crécy (1346) and Poitiers (1356), suggests something more during these occasions of special worship: a sense of England as especially favoured by God, and perhaps, even before the reformation, an idea of it as *the* elect nation in succession to Israel. This, however, had a forbidding corollary, felt particularly after defeats later in the century: that the special favour of God was experienced as much in warning and punishment as in any blessings.[58]

This edition is concerned with the churches of England, Ireland and Scotland since the reformation, which is taken, in England, to date from the break with Rome in the early 1530s. (It also includes the brief return to catholicism under Mary I.)

---

[53] Bailey, *Processions of Sarum*, pp. 51 n. 2, 52–3, 128–32.

[54] *Ibid.*, pp. 52–3.

[55] *Ibid.*, pp. 128–32.

[56] *Ibid.*, pp. 12–14, 25–6.

[57] See, most usefully, W. R. Jones, 'The English church and royal propaganda during the hundred years war', *Journal of British Studies*, 19 (1979), 18–30; D. W. Burton, 'Requests for prayers and royal propaganda under Edward I', in *Thirteenth Century England III*, ed. P. R. Coss and S. D. Lloyd (Woodbridge, 1991), pp. 25–35; A. K. McHardy, 'Religious ritual and political persuasion: the case of England in the hundred years war', *International Journal of Moral and Social Studies*, 3 (1988), 41–57; *idem*, 'Some reflections on Edward III's use of propaganda', in *The age of Edward III*, ed. J. S. Bothwell (York, 2001), pp. 171–89.

[58] Andrea Ruddick, 'National sentiment and religious vocabulary in fourteenth-century England', *Journal of Ecclesiastical History*, 60 (2009), 1–18; John McKenna, 'How God became an Englishman', in *Tudor rule and rebellion*, ed. Delloyd Guth and John McKenna (Cambridge, 1982), pp. 25–43.

What, then, changed at the reformation in relation to special worship? In some key respects, the answer to this question is not much. Many of the late medieval practices and beliefs outlined above persisted in England after Henrician legislation had established a fully independent English church under the royal supremacy in ecclesiastical matters. Indeed, in some respects there are striking continuities from the thirteenth century through to at least the nineteenth century. As Alexandra Walsham has shown, ideas of divine providence remained as central to English protestantism – and counter-reformation catholicism – as they had been to the pre-reformation church,[59] and a number of scholars have argued that ideas of the English as God's chosen people strengthened after the reformation.[60] The causes for special worship were, therefore, much the same as they had been during earlier centuries: war, rebellion, bad weather, disease, the birth of royal children, the monarch's ill-health. Not only did the ideas that underpinned special worship survive the break with Rome little changed, but much of the process of ordering, organizing and communicating functioned much as it had done in the medieval kingdom. Special worship continued to be ordered by the crown, either through royal mandates or letters to the archbishop of Canterbury; on some occasions the texts of specially composed prayers were circulated with the orders; orders were still communicated to archbishops and bishops for dissemination to parish clergy, using administrative structures which survived the reformation largely unscathed and remained the basis for the government of the church well into the nineteenth century.

While there was considerable continuity over time, the reformation gradually coloured almost every aspect of special worship. Most striking were the liturgical changes brought about by the reformers, leading to the development of a set liturgy in the vernacular in England and in Ireland, and – in contrast – to the abandonment of set prayers in Scotland. Combined with the strengthening of the concept of the kingdom as a single spiritual and moral body standing before God, this contributed to the greater formalization of fasts and thanksgivings, which increasingly were ordered to be held on the same day (and thus often at around the same time), following, in England and Ireland, the same form of prayer. In both England and Scotland new forms of fasting were devised, self-consciously protestant to distinguish them from the superstition of catholic practices. As a result, 'fast days' emerged as perhaps the most characteristic form of special worship across the British Isles. In other respects, too, the reformation coloured the nature of special worship. In the Churches of England and Ireland, the assertion of the royal supremacy shifted notions of authority, though in Scotland this process was more contested. Increasingly, sovereigns and governments came to monopolize the process of ordering and to control the content of the worship; indeed, in England and Ireland the clergy came

---

[59] Alexandra Walsham, *Providence in early modern England* (Oxford, 1999).
[60] David Loades, 'The origins of English protestant nationalism', in *Religion and national identity*, ed. Stuart Mews (Studies in Church History, 18, 1982), pp. 297–307; Patrick Collinson, 'A chosen people? The English church and the reformation', *History Today*, 36:3 (1986), 14–20; *idem*, 'Biblical rhetoric: the English nation and national sentiment in the prophetic mode', in *Religion and Culture in Renaissance England*, ed. Claire McEachern and Debora Singer (Cambridge, 1997), pp. 15–45; Achsah Guibbory, 'Israel and English protestant nationalism: "fast sermons" during the English revolution', in *Early modern nationalism and Milton's England*, ed. David Loewenstein and Paul Stevens (Toronto, 2008), pp. 115–38.

to assume that neither individually nor collectively did they have authority to order special worship throughout the kingdom.[61]

England: Henry VIII to Mary I

Despite, or possibly because of, the vicissitudes in Henrician religious policy, the ways in which special worship was observed changed only slowly. Until the evangelical reforms of the 1540s, special worship was observed in a style similar to that of the pre-reformation church, with masses and processions; this style was briefly restored with the re-establishment of the Roman catholic church under Mary I (1553–8). For many occasions in this period, the evidence is fragmentary; sometimes all that exists is a brief reference in a chronicle. In particular, in some cases it is not known whether they were ordered or observed beyond London or certain dioceses, but they are included in this edition because it appears that special worship in the city or diocese of London or in the province of Canterbury was frequently used to represent the nation as a whole. In this respect, as in many others, Henrician worship continued earlier practices, and these early occasions therefore offer important indications of what came to be changed between the 1530s and 1560s, while also illuminating this process of change.

One of the most visible as well as most significant group of changes in special worship in the early decades of the reformation was liturgical.[62] These both reflected the major liturgical innovations of the period, with the authorization of the two Edwardian Books of Common Prayer in 1549 and 1552, and offer new insight into the broader process of liturgical change, as occasions of special worship appear to have offered some scope for experimentation. The Sarum and other medieval rites continued to be used until 1544, when the king commissioned a vernacular litany from Archbishop Cranmer, albeit based closely on the Sarum litany. Greater change occurred with the accession of the evangelical Edward VI. Initially, new, specially composed prayers were ordered to be inserted into the Henrician litany and then, from 1549, into the services in the BCP. These prayers either replaced one of the collects or were inserted between the collects and the communion service.[63] Then, in June 1551, a complete new liturgy, *A thankes geuing to God vsed in Christes churche*, was commissioned and authorized to be used for petitionary services during the outbreak of the 'sweating sickness' (1551–E). Effectively, this liturgy replaced the BCP services.[64] It conformed neither to the structure of services as defined by the BCP nor to the texts (prayers, psalms and readings) prescribed for daily services.[65] The psalms, for example, were printed in the metrical version of Sternhold and Hopkins, rather than the Coverdale version, familiar from the Bishops' Bible, that had been used in the 1549 BCP and was to be retained in 1552. Sternhold and Hopkins, published in 1549, had already firmly established its popularity in protestant circles for psalm singing, so this may have been an attempt

---

[61] See above, pp. lxi–lxiii.
[62] A fuller discussion of these themes may be found in Mears, 'Special nationwide worship'.
[63] LPL, Cranmer Register, I, fo. 55v: privy council to Cranmer, 6 May 1548; PRO, SP10/13/30, fo. 62r: Edward VI to the bishops, 18 June 1551; *A prayer for victorie and peace* (London, 1549; STC 16503); *Wriothesley*, II, 16–18, 20.
[64] It is not clear from the king's order whether it was intended to be used daily or only on Sundays.
[65] PRO, SP10/13/30, fo. 62r.

to encourage more congregational participation in the services. But while it is clear that the *Thankes geuing* was an exercise in liturgical experimentation, the purpose remains obscure. It may have been part of a process of review and revision of the BCP that culminated in the 1552 BCP. It may have been intended as a template for special worship during periods of disease and similar afflictions. If it was the latter, then the inclusion in the 1552 BCP of prayers to be used in times of famine, disease or war would suggest that it was an experiment that Cranmer decided not to pursue. In any event, the death of Edward VI in 1553 put an end to this period of liturgical innovation, and the Sternhold and Hopkins versions of the psalms were never used again in an official Church of England form of prayer.

The accession of Mary I brought the restoration of pre-reformation liturgical practices. However, this did not happen immediately, and the processions ordered in response to the bad weather in December 1553 (1553–E2) provided the crown and ecclesiastical authorities with the opportunity to signal official preferences and the direction of policy. When Mary had acceded to the throne in July 1553, the second Edwardian BCP remained the official liturgy of the church. Services in English were not banned until a royal proclamation of 20 December, and the parliamentary statute repealing both Edwardian Acts of Uniformity did not come into force until 30 December. Moreover, this statute re-established the liturgy from the last year of Henry VIII's reign, that is Cranmer's revised litany of 1544. So, technically, Mary's first occasion of special worship should initially have followed the litany as set out in the second BCP, and then, from 20 to 30 December, followed Cranmer's litany. The description, 'processions', however, suggests that the Sarum and other rites were used, as was also implied by the proclamation of 20 December.

Although pre-reformation liturgies were used for special worship throughout Mary's reign, the period was not without innovation, some of which drew on earlier Henrician or Edwardian practices. During the petitionary service organized at St Paul's Cathedral in response to the news that Mary was pregnant (1554–E3), William Chedsey, Chiswick prebendary of the cathedral, read out before the collation the council's order to Bishop Bonner ordering nationwide services. The December 1553 processions were ordered to take place thrice weekly – on Sundays, Wednesdays and Fridays – rather than on holy days and other festal days, a practice that was revived under Elizabeth I (1560–E2) and became common in English protestant worship into the early seventeenth century. More intriguing, perhaps, is the evidence of John Strype that the thanksgivings for England's reconciliation to Rome (1555–E1) were ordered by royal proclamation. This striking innovation may have been an attempt to secure uniformity of observance throughout the country; it may merely have been to order secular celebration with bonfires; or it may have been a demonstration of Mary's continued assertion of her prerogative in matters of religion.

England: Elizabeth I

The reign of Elizabeth was a crucial period in the development of special worship in England. In some respects, this might appear surprising, as the period was one of relatively few occasions (as defined in this edition) – well under one per annum. However, the intensity of special worship increased dramatically. As already noted, from August 1563 to January 1564 as many as twenty-five fasts took place in every parish across England and Wales as a response to the plague epidemic, with special prayers also said every Friday and Sunday through the same period. Most occasions of special worship during Elizabeth's reign similarly required repeated observance over a period of weeks or months: on Wednesdays and Fridays from May 1586 to January 1587, for example, during a period of dearth and war, or on Wednesdays, Fridays and Sundays during the expedition against Cadiz in 1596. Moreover, this was also the period during which the BCP became firmly established as the liturgy of the Church of England. Processions, the mass and the use of the Virgin Mary and the saints as intercessors had been dismantled during the 1540s and, after a brief revival under Mary, were banned once again under Elizabeth. By the time of the queen's death in 1603, most English men and women would have been familiar with no form of worship other than the Elizabethan BCP, a slightly modified version of the second Edwardian prayer book, imposed by the Act of Uniformity of 1559. As a result, in the course of Elizabeth's reign, it is possible to trace the emergence of patterns of special worship which were both distinctively protestant and distinctively English – were it not for the anachronism and the connotations of the word, it would be tempting to describe them as 'anglican'.

The most significant development in this period took place in the early years of the reign, from 1562 to 1564, when the main liturgical formats for special worship became firmly established. Following the practice of the Henrician and Edwardian regimes, individual prayers or collects were issued, as in October 1562 (1562–E1), to be included within the BCP services for morning and evening prayer. Numerous occasions of special worship continued to be observed in this way until the late twentieth century. But the regime also commissioned more extensive revisions of the BCP services, which were published as complete liturgies and distributed for use in cathedrals, parishes and chapels across the country. There were two distinct variants of this practice. First, the *Short fourme of thankesgeuyng* for the end of the plague issued in 1564 established a format which was used for the liturgies for most special services until the late nineteenth century (1564–E). It followed the structure of the BCP services, replacing the prescribed collects, psalms and readings with specially composed collects and with selected readings and psalms appropriate for the occasion. Psalm 95 (the *Venite*), said at the beginning of morning prayer, was often replaced by a special 'psalm', composed from a series of biblical verses.[66] Second, the form of prayer issued during the previous year for services during the plague (1563–E) went further, providing different services for different days of the week.[67] This format was used for some occasions until 1626, while the order of the fast, which was included in the 1563 form, established rules for the observance of national fasts during periods of plague which continued to be used until 1665. The development of these liturgical formats for special worship, moreover, reflects the emphasis of the Elizabethan church on uniformity in worship, in the sense that the same prayers and readings were required to be used in all places of worship across the country. There was clearly the expectation that the same texts would be read on the same days for special services across the realm, just as the BCP was used. In some respects, this could only have been an aspiration. Even assuming that enough

---

[66] This format was used for thirty-one occasions between 1564 and 1642.

[67] It is possible that this format may have been prefigured in 1560. The opening of the preface of the liturgy for 1560 is the same as the preface of the 1563 *Fourme to be vsed in common prayer twise a weeke* (STC 16505). But the liturgy for 1560 itself has not survived, and other evidence suggests that the 1563 liturgy was different. See 1560–E and 1563–E.

forms could be produced – and the organization of the press does appear to have been remarkably effective – forms could not be distributed so that they would arrive simultaneously in all parishes. Significantly, specific dates for the beginning of periods of special worship were not prescribed in orders. Churchwardens' accounts may also suggest that some parishes did not purchase the special prayer books, though the evidence is difficult to interpret.[68]

At the same time, there was a significant change in the way in which special worship was ordered, reflecting perhaps a subtle shift in attitudes towards the royal supremacy. Following the outbreak of plague in 1563, Archbishop Parker ordered prayers to be said within the city of Canterbury, as did Bishop Grindal for his diocese of London. However, as Parker later explained to William Cecil, the queen's principal secretary, he did not believe that he had the authority to make an order for worship outside his own diocese.[69] Cecil referred the matter to the queen, and, within days, prayers and fasts had been ordered for the whole of England and Wales. Thereafter, it was usually (and from 1603 to 1868 invariably) the government itself – not church leaders – which ordered special worship. The initiative might come from the archbishop or bishops, but equally it might come from the sovereign, or ministers, or, on a number of occasions from the 1620s to 1701, a parliamentary address. There was no requirement that any archbishop or bishop should be consulted in advance on whether special worship should be ordered or what form it should take, nor for any to be present at the council which made the order. The archbishop of Canterbury or other bishops were ordered to compose the actual prayers or services, but these texts for worship were subject to revision and acceptance by a council, consisting largely or wholly of lay persons, or by one or more of the leading ministers. This was not merely a technical point: sovereigns and ministers did read drafts of forms of prayer, and on occasion they suggested changes or deletions and even introduced their own text.[70] This was true of Cecil for 1563–E, 1564–E, 1585–E1 and 1596–E2, while in 1597 Elizabeth herself objected to the inclusion of one of her own prayers (probably 'O God, All-maker, Keeper, and Guider, inurement of Thy rare-seen unused and seld-heard-of goodness') in the form of prayer for the success of the English forces (1597–E). She ordered Whitgift to have it removed, even from those copies that had already been printed.[71]

During Elizabeth's reign, there was also an expansion of the reasons for which special worship was ordered, in ways which further reinforced the development of the distinctively protestant and English character of the church. After the break with Rome, special worship had continued to be ordered in support of Christians abroad, even as Europe became confessionally divided: in 1543, Henry VIII ordered prayers to be said in support of Ferdinand I during his war against the Ottomans in Hungary (1543–E1). Similar occasions continued under Elizabeth in response to the Ottoman invasions of Malta (1565–E1, 1565–E2) and Hungary (1566–E) and to

[68] Mears, 'Brought to book', pp. 29–44.
[69] Lans. 6/62, fo. 154r: Parker to Cecil, 23 July 1563.
[70] Lans. 6, fos. 156r–v, 192–3, 131r; Grindal to Cecil, 30 July, 15 Dec. 1563, 21 Jan. 1654; Lans. 116, fo. 73r: 'Thankes giving to god for withdrawing and ceasing the plage', 1563; Lans. 116, fos 77r–9r: 'A prayer of Thankesgivinge for the deliuerance of her maiestie from the murderous intentions of Dr Parry', 1585; Lans. 116, fos. 81r–82r: 'Forme of a prayer for the queene', 1596. For Whitgift's role in editing liturgies, see LPL, MS 113, fos. 1r–19v, referring to *Certaine prayers ... for the prosperous successe of her maiesties forces and navy* (1597; STC 16528).
[71] LPL, MS 3470, fo. 195r: Cecil to Whitgift, 11 July 1597.

the battle of Lepanto (1571–E). Special worship was also increasingly prompted by the plight of protestants at home and abroad, especially the Huguenots and Henry IV during the French wars of religion (1562–E1, 1572–E, 1590–E2).[72] In addition, it was ordered for new kinds of event which, like the support of foreign protestants, reflected growing confessionalization. From the 1580s, thanksgivings were ordered after the discovery of catholic plots against the monarch, including the Parry and Babington plots (1585–E1, 1586–E2, 1594–E, 1598–E). The language in the prayers, liturgies and accompanying sermons also became more stridently anti-catholic. The homily against disobedience, issued for use during special services after the failure of the Northern Rising (1570–E), argued that the rebellion had been organized by 'common enemies aswel to the trueth of thy eternall worde, as to their owne natural prince and countrey'. Prayers ordered for 1587–E stated that England was constantly 'vexed and tormented by the malice of Satan and his members, and at this time … inuironed on euery side, with strong and subtill aduersaries'.[73] These were the pope, the 'blood-sucking Romish Antichrist', and 'his creatures, the very loathsome *Locusts* that crawle out of the bottomlesse pitte', the Jesuit and seminary priests (1594–E, 1598–E).

England: James I and Charles I

At first sight, the pattern of special worship in Jacobean and Caroline England closely resembled what had been established under Elizabeth. A slight increase in the incidence of occasions is explained by the birth of children to both James I and Charles I, events which in this period normally generated both prayers for the queen during her pregnancy and then thanksgiving prayers after the birth. Otherwise, the main causes for worship remained, as they had been in the sixteenth century, those of war, plague and the weather. More significantly, the liturgies issued for special worship continued to follow the patterns established from 1562 to 1564, except that, from early in Charles I's reign, separate services for morning and evening prayer were produced (1626–E2).[74] On closer examination, however, a number of significant developments can be identified, at least some of which reflect the tensions over religious and constitutional issues that troubled both reigns and were in large part responsible for the collapse of royal authority during the crisis of 1640–2.

First, the opening years of James I's reign witnessed an innovation which was to have a significant influence on the nature and pattern of special worship right through to the mid-nineteenth century and, arguably, to the present: the institution of the first annual commemorations. The anniversary of the reigning monarch's accession had been observed since at least the late 1570s, perhaps by royal authority, though no official order survives until the canons of 1640, which were almost immediately a dead letter.[75] In 1603, however, the privy council ordered the observance of James I's deliverance from the Gowrie plot of 1600, extending to England a

---

[72] See also volume 3, Appendix: Omitted occasions, for 1589.

[73] See also *A prayer for the present estate* (STC 16504.3), sig. Aiii[r]; *A forme of prayer, thought fitte to be vsed in the English armie in France* (London, 1589; STC 16521), sig. Bii[r]; 1594–E.

[74] Before this, it seems likely that the prescribed collects, psalms and readings were intended to be used at both morning and evening prayer.

[75] The Elizabethan form of prayer for accession day was published by the royal printer, but there is no other evidence that it was an official occasion. See AC–Accession in volume 3.

thanksgiving which had been celebrated in Scotland since 1601. A special form of prayer was prepared by Archbishop Whitgift and reprinted on three occasions during James's reign, though there is no evidence that the day was observed thereafter. The Gowrie thanksgiving on 5 August, moreover, provided the precedent for the much more important and long-lasting celebration of 5 November, the thanksgiving for the discovery of the gunpowder plot, which was established as a 'perpetual Remembrance' by act of parliament in 1606. This was the most popular of the anniversary commemorations, perhaps not least because it became a focus both for the expression of English protestant identity and for partisan appropriation and re-appropriation, and it has continued as a day of secular celebration long after the abolition of the religious thanksgiving in 1859.[76]

Second, the first day of special worship of Charles I's reign, organized in July 1625 during both an outbreak of plague and the threat of war, was ordered by royal proclamation, the first for special worship since the thanksgiving for the reconciliation with Rome in the reign of Queen Mary (1555–E1) and the only one in the sixteenth century. From 1625, however, proclamations became the normal way of ordering *days* of special worship until the late nineteenth century. No contemporary comment appears to have survived about either this innovation or the reasons for it. It may simply have been a reflection of the new king's desire for greater order and regularity in government. Equally, it may have been a more deliberate decision to assert the royal supremacy in ecclesiastical matters, in reaction to a parliamentary petition for a general fast 'as a Thing most suitable to the present Times and Occasions'.[77] When Paul Wentworth made a motion in 1581 for a fast by members of the Commons to be held publicly in the Temple church, Elizabeth had responded angrily to what she described as the House of Commons' 'disorderly proceeding', asserting that 'Noe public fast could bee appointed but by her, and therefore [it] empeached her iurisdiction.'[78] Given that Charles I was prepared to conciliate the Commons by responding favourably to its initiative, in contrast not only to Elizabeth but also to his father when a similar motion had been made in 1624, it is not implausible that he should have at the same time found a way of reminding MPs of his prerogative powers.

The increasing role of parliament in the ordering of special worship is the third significant development during the early Stuart period, an expression of growing tension between king and parliament, which culminated in a direct challenge to the crown's monopoly over the ordering of fasts and thanksgivings. From 1624 to 1629, parliament regularly presented petitions, usually at the start of each session, asking the king for a general fast. MPs recognized that they did not have the authority to order a fast to be observed across the kingdom: Sir George More, speaking in support of the unsuccessful motion in 1624, stated that they had to petition James, 'this Motion being general, and not only for ourselves'.[79] They did, however, claim

---

[76] A fuller discussion is provided in the commentaries on the anniversary commemorations in volume 3. See also, especially, David Cressy, *Bonfires and bells. National memory and the protestant calendar in Elizabethan and Stuart England* (1989).

[77] *LJ*, III, 441.

[78] Cromwell's journal, in *Proceedings in the parliaments of Elizabeth I*, ed. T. E. Hartley (3 vols., Leicester and London, 1981–95), I, 527. See also *CJ*, I, 118–20; *The journals of all the parliaments during the reign of Queen Elizabeth*, ed. Sir Simonds D'Ewes (1682), pp. 277–90; J. E. Neale, *Elizabeth I and her parliaments. Vol. 1: 1559–81* (1953), pp. 378–82.

[79] *CJ*, I, 671.

the right, denied by Elizabeth, to order fasts for the Commons itself.[80] Charles I may have regarded the granting of these requests, when expressed by petition from the two houses, as a way of conciliating what Thomas Cogswell has called 'patriot' opinion in parliament, though by 1629 it is clear that he was losing patience with repeated fasting and argued that, at that particular time, 'fighting will do them [the reformed church abroad] much more good than fasting'.[81] When parliament was next summoned in the febrile atmosphere of 1640, after eleven years of the king's personal rule, a fast was again requested 'to beg the Divine Assistance … in all their Consultations', and Charles I, perhaps in an attempt to conciliate parliamentary opinion, not only conceded but also left the timing of it to the Lords and Commons.[82] The consequence, however, was to turn the ordering of special worship into a focus for tension between the two houses – the Lords was less hostile to the king's policies at this time – as well as between the king and parliament. The Commons agreed a motion appointing 2 May for parliament to observe the fast, but the Lords, apparently interpreting this action as an infringement of its privilege, refused to meet the Commons' delegation 'by reason of the very great and weighty Businesses they are now in, the King being there present'.[83] Indeed, the upper house refused to return to the issue and parliament was dissolved twelve days later, though some of the Lords believed that the Commons had observed the fast unofficially, 'because they sat so long' (on 2 May) and 'all day close'.[84] In April 1641, some unnamed MPs revived the question whether the Lords' support was needed for a fast petition, and a vote in favour of seeking the Lords' agreement was only won narrowly by 195 votes to 172.[85] Then, in September 1641, the thanksgiving for the conclusion of the peace treaty between England and Scotland was ordered by parliamentary ordinance, a remarkable demonstration of the extent to which the king's prerogative powers were being challenged by both houses. This challenge to the royal supremacy in ecclesiastical affairs was reinforced by the decision to issue no official form of prayer, reflecting the growing hostility of godly MPs towards the BCP and to set forms of prayer in general.[86] Moreover, the House of Commons ordered that John Williams, bishop of Lincoln and dean of Westminster, be prohibited from using the *Form of thanksgiving* which he had composed and had printed for use in his jurisdictions (1641–ES). After this episode, no further forms of prayer were issued until after the outbreak of the civil war, when the royalists issued forms (which followed the liturgical formats established under Elizabeth) to be used during the thanksgiving for their victory at the battle of Edgehill (1642–E1(R)), the fast for the success of

---

[80]   The Speaker, Sir Thomas Richardson, commented: 'We Power over ourselves only. The general, over the Kingdom, not in our Power.' *Ibid.*

[81]   *Commons debates for 1629 critically edited*, ed. Wallace Notestein and Frances Helen Relf (Minneapolis, 1921), pp. 28, 247.

[82]   *CJ*, II, 6; *LJ*, IV, 61, 63–4.

[83]   *CJ*, II, 9, 11; *Proceedings of the Short parliament of 1640*, ed. Esther S. Cope and Willson H. Coates (Camden Society, 4th ser., 19, 1977), pp. 169, 237, 241.

[84]   *CJ*, II, 17 (1 May); *Proceedings of the Short parliament*, ed. Cope and Willson, pp. 241–2.

[85]   *CJ*, II, 122 (17 Apr.); *Proceedings in the opening session of the Long parliament: House of Commons*, ed. Maija Jansson (7 vols., Rochester, NY, 2000–7), III, 604–5, 608. This proposal appears not to have been pursued further.

[86]   The holding of a thanksgiving was one of the provisions of the treaty of Ripon, but parliament took responsibility for ordering a date. *Proceedings of the Long parliament*, ed. Jansson, I, 17, 20–1, 29, 39, 45–6, 55–8, 64–9, 97, 100, 155, 161, III, 604–8, VI, 272, 370, 378, 387, 565–6, 570–3, 577, 591–2, 596, 607, 608, 612, 623, 626, 648–9.

the treaty negotiations at Uxbridge (1645–E1(R)) and, from October 1643, for a monthly general fast for God's protection for the king (1643–E10(R)).

Growing royal concern about the expression of puritan opinion before 1640 is also clear in further developments in special worship. Despite the reverses suffered by continental protestants during the Thirty Years War and the fact that James I's own daughter, the Electress Palatine, was at the centre of the conflict, the crown ordered far fewer occasions for foreign protestants than during Elizabeth's reign. Only three fasts in this period (1626–E3, 1628–E1 and 1629–E) were intended for the support of European protestantism; all were also motivated by other causes. In addition, concern about the 'abuse of Fasting' had led to the publication of a revised 'order for the fast' in 1603, which had limited both the number of sermons to a maximum of two on each fast day and their length to an hour (1603–E). While there appears to have been some anxiety about the transmission of plague within congregations, the main concern of the authorities was what they considered to be puritan abuse of fasting, in particular the holding of fasts 'without consent of Authority' and the transformation of the occasions into overt demonstrations of a distinctive piety by 'keeping the people together with ouermuch wearines and tediousnesse a whole day together'. Similar concerns can be detected in Archbishop Whitgift's instructions as early as 1588, but from the accession of James I to the outbreak of the civil war they feature repeatedly in the orders for fast days (1625–E, 1636–E3), prompting criticism from such puritans as William Prynne and Henry Burton, who denounced restrictions on preaching as an attack on the godly.

Scotland: 1560s–1630s

The development of national fasts and thanksgivings in Scotland in the decades after the reformation paralleled the experience of England and Wales, but there were several important differences. The most obvious, which determines the texts provided for Scottish occasions in this edition, is that the Church of Scotland never had the same degree of liturgical uniformity as the established churches of England and Ireland. For eight decades or more after 1560, most Scottish church services were conducted with some reference to the Book of Common Order, the liturgy developed by John Knox and other exiles in 1550s Geneva. But extempore prayer always had a role in Scottish protestant worship, and the riots provoked by Charles I's attempt to impose a version of the BCP in 1637 helped to crystallize an enduring opposition to liturgical forms among most Scots. These attitudes towards worship were reflected in the observance of national fasts. (As will be seen, national thanksgivings were much less common before the 1660s.) Worship during the early national fasts was structured by the order of worship published for 1566–S1, the first such occasion. This observance established the standard pattern for national fasts before the mid-seventeenth century: fasting on two successive Sundays, with worship on the intervening days in towns. But apart from the *Ordour and doctrine of the generall faste* of 1566, which was reprinted in successive editions of the Book of Common Order, no special services were produced until, in the early twentieth century, the general assembly's committee on aids to devotion produced a 'form and order of divine service' for the first national day of prayer (1915–1).

A further difference between Scottish days of national worship and those elsewhere in the British Isles lay in the ways in which the authority to appoint these occasions was understood. Especially in the sixteenth and seventeenth centuries, many Scottish protestants regarded the ordering of special days as a spiritual function, and accordingly the responsibility of the church rather than the civil magistrate. This understanding of the authority to call fasts and thanksgivings was a consequence of the nature of the Scottish reformation and the evolution of ecclesiastical structures in the century after 1560. Nevertheless, the influence of ecclesiastical and lay authorities over special worship was subject to change, and in the seventeenth century was increasingly contested.

The Scottish reformation resulted from a rebellion by protestant nobles, clergy and their followers against the Roman catholic queen regent, Mary of Guise. After the regent's death and the adoption of the reformation by parliament in 1560, the Church of Scotland established itself without much involvement by the crown. Mary queen of Scots did not attempt to suppress protestantism, but nor did she support the new church. After her deposition in 1567, the church developed amid the turmoil of civil war and the factional politics of a long royal minority; the protestant clergy received fluctuating levels of encouragement and support from Scotland's regents and other nobles. In this context, the church developed the practice of appointing special worship by the authority of its own courts. Parochial kirk sessions appointed special observances for individual congregations; after their establishment in the 1580s, presbyteries ordered occasions for the parishes in their districts. Synods did the same for larger regions. At the top of the ecclesiastical hierarchy, the general assembly called national occasions of special worship. The assembly was rarely free from royal influence, but it allowed Scottish churchmen more autonomy than was possessed by their English counterparts.

Consequently, from 1560 to the union of crowns in 1603 most occasions were ordered by acts of the general assembly, without any formal approval by the crown. Of the twenty-eight Scottish occasions in this period, at least fifteen were certainly appointed by the general assembly. Several others were probably ordered by the assembly, but this is unclear from the surviving evidence. A few other fasts (see especially 1592–S and 1596–S2) were appointed by conventions of ministers that were more autonomous of the crown than a general assembly. In the period between 1560 and 1603, fasts were more frequent than thanksgivings, accounting for twenty-four of the twenty-eight occasions. This suggests that Scotland's clergy thought that the usual purpose of special worship was fasting rather than thanksgiving. There is no doubt that fasting was as central a practice in the culture of Scottish protestants as for the godly in England, though the flexibility of Scottish worship allowed ministers to say prayers of thanksgiving when conducting normal Sunday services. With the exception of the thanksgiving worship for peace and for the success of the reformation in 1560, special thanksgivings before 1638 were prompted by events in the life of the royal family, and were ordered by the king or privy council (see 1594–S1, 1600–S, 1623–S2, 1630–S, 1637–S).

More than in England, early Scottish fasts were often justified with reference to perennial problems, such as widespread sinfulness or contempt of religion, as much as by specific crises. Certainly, it is not always clear why one general assembly chose to order a fast, while the next declined to do so. Nevertheless, the frequency of special worship in the sixteenth and seventeenth centuries is strongly linked to the regularity of meetings of the assembly. In the period from the accession of James VI to the English crown in 1603 to the outbreak of the Scottish revolution in 1637, during which the assembly met rarely, there were fewer occasions of special worship. Indeed, there were no occasions at all between 1601 and 1621. From 1621 to 1637, there were three thanksgivings, all ordered by the crown, and six fasts. No fast was definitely appointed by a general assembly; at least two were called by *ad hoc* ecclesiastical conventions more amenable than an assembly to royal direction; two were certainly ordered by the king (1625–S, 1638–S1). It is unclear whether the crown's appointment of thanksgivings from 1594 signalled a deliberate attempt by James VI to gain authority over special worship. But it is evident from the pattern of occasions in the 1620s and 1630s, and also from the lack of special observances for most of the two preceding decades, that the crown did stifle the autonomy which the Scottish clergy had previously possessed to appoint national fasts.

England: 1642–60

The period from the outbreak of civil war in 1642 to the execution of Charles I in 1649 was by far the most intensive period of special worship in England and Wales: in one year alone, 1645, nineteen occasions were ordered, to which should be added the monthly fasts established in 1641. It is hardly surprising that by 1649 there was evidence of fatigue, even in puritan circles.[87] One reason for the frequency of special worship during this period was its value as propaganda for both sides in the civil war. It was not simply that, as Hugh Trevor-Roper argued many years ago,[88] fast sermons offered a powerful tool for political persuasion, a fact recognized by Charles I when he issued a proclamation in November 1643 abolishing the 'Hypocriticall' monthly fast which had been abused by 'seditious' preachers 'to stirre up and continue the Rebellion raised against Us' (see 1643–E11(R)). In addition, the statements of causes accompanying parliament's orders for special worship were an effective way of ensuring the dispersal of the latest news of the war throughout the areas under its control. However, as Chris Durston has noted,[89] it is important to emphasize that these were religious occasions: fasting and humiliation were a Christian obligation, to remind men of their sinfulness and the justice of God's judgment, and to petition for his mercy, while thanksgivings were the responses of a dutiful people for mercies granted. The intensity of special worship in these years was largely a product of the intensity of the war, as both parliament and the king shared the assumption that victory was dependent on God's favour. The relatively small number of royalist occasions (in addition, it should be stressed, to a regular monthly fast, first on Wednesdays and then, from November 1643, on Fridays) may be partly a reflection of the survival of evidence. Once Charles had left London and the court had moved to Oxford, he had less access both to printing presses and to the main arterial road networks which emanated from London. Royalist orders for special worship sometimes appear to have been communicated by manuscript letter or word of mouth, and ministers were often expected to adapt earlier forms of prayer.[90] On both sides, 'national' fasts and thanksgivings were regularly supplemented by occasions organized locally. Nevertheless, the sheer number of occasions of special worship ordered by parliament was undoubtedly an expression of the centrality of fasting in godly culture.

---

[87] Clopton diary, 28 Feb., 19 Apr., 17 May 1649; act of parliament, 23 Apr. 1649 (1649–E2).

[88] Trevor-Roper, 'Fast sermons', p. 296.

[89] Christopher Durston, '"For the better humiliation of the people": public days of fasting and thanksgiving during the English revolution', *Seventeenth Century*, 7 (1992), 129–49.

[90] On royalist distribution, see Bates, 'Fast and thanksgiving days', pp. 183–94. See also 1645–E9(R).

Throughout the first civil war, Charles continued to use forms of prayer based on Elizabethan precedents, though only two liturgies were printed, both at Oxford (1643–E11(R) and 1645–E1(R)). In a change from pre-civil war practice which suggests the problems of printing and distribution facing the king, the thanksgiving service for the victory at Newark and the pregnancy of the queen (1644–E3(R)) was compressed on to a single sheet. This printed a single collect and merely listed the texts for the readings and psalms. Parliament, by contrast, had abandoned the use of set forms of prayer even before the outbreak of hostilities (see above), though use of the BCP was not officially proscribed until 1646. Instead, it often ordered that either the order itself or a specially commissioned account of 'causes' be read out during the service. For thanksgivings, the 'causes' were often composed by a committee of MPs, based on letters from the army's commanders on the battlefield. These 'causes' were sometimes extensive (e.g. 1644–E1(P)), and effective use was made of the press in London to produce copies for dissemination across the country.

Even after the execution of Charles I in January 1649, the intensity of special worship continued more or less unabated (though the monthly fast, inaugurated in 1641, was finally abolished in April 1649 on the grounds that it had become 'neglected' and 'prophaned'). The main explanation for this is that, for the first years of its existence, the Republic remained a state at war – in Ireland, against the Scots and royalists, and then, in 1652, against the Dutch. Through the 1640s and early 1650s, parliament and its supporters appear to have had few problems with the idea of 'state'-ordered worship, but, following the dissolution of the Rump in April 1653, there was a marked change in practice, reflecting the unease of the new authorities, and Cromwell in particular, with the role of the state in religious affairs. This was revealed clearly in the organization of the first occasion of special worship to take place after April 1653, the thanksgiving day for the English victory over the Dutch fleet which took place on 23 June 1653. Whereas, for the previous occasion on 12 April (1653–E3), parliament had 'resolved' that the day be 'set apart', Cromwell and the council of state 'thought fit to commend' the thanksgiving 'to all those, who are faithful in these Lands' (see 1653–E4) – that is to say, encouraging, rather than compelling or requiring, participation in prayers. During the next six years, war continued to be an important cause for special worship (1654–1, 1656–2, 1657–E1, 1657–E3), but other concerns, reflecting Elizabethan and early Stuart practice, also prompted observances: plague (1657–E2, 1657–E4, 1658–E), the persecution of protestants in Savoy (1655–E1r) and the failure of an assassination plot against Cromwell (1657–1). More unusually, given earlier English practice, there was a series of fasts in response to general concerns about the lack of godliness in the nation (1655–1, 1656–1, 1656–3) and, in 1657, in the closest that the protectorate came to ordering a day of worship, a commemoration of the battles of Dunbar and Worcester (1657–E3).

Scotland: 1638–60

The year of the National Covenant was a turning point for Scottish fasts and thanksgivings. The first occasion of 1638, a fast in November, was ordered by a royal declaration, reflecting the crown's recent control over special worship. But the second observance, a thanksgiving day kept variously in December 1638 and January 1639, was appointed by the closing session of the general assembly meeting in Glasgow, after it had disobeyed a royal command to dissolve. In the process of asserting its independence from the king and his commissioner, the assembly reclaimed its role as the main body with the authority to order days of special worship. Of the forty special observances appointed from 1639 to 1649, thirty-five were ordered by the assembly, its commission or, in one case, the presbytery of Edinburgh acting for the assembly. Of the other five observances, two were ordered by the Scottish parliament and the commission acting in co-ordination, two by parliament alone and one, in 1641, by the English and Scottish parliaments jointly. From 1639 to 1649, there were thirty-three fasts, six thanksgivings and one occasion combining fasting and thanksgiving. The thanksgivings were prompted by military victories or the conclusion of peace. Some fasts were justified partly with reference to military campaigns, forthcoming meetings of parliament or the assembly. But as with the earlier period, perennial sins were often stated as reasons for fasting.

The conquest of Scotland by Oliver Cromwell in 1650–2 and his suppression of the general assembly in 1653 explain why there were ten fasts and one thanksgiving in these years, but only twelve occasions over the following six years. These were appointed by the republican authorities, and with one exception were to be kept across the rest of Britain and Ireland.[91] The reality of the Cromwellian Union of Britain was demonstrated by the fact that these occasions were generally appointed by a single declaration issued in the name of the lord protector or the lord protector and parliament, though for reasons that are not clear the July 1653 thanksgiving was appointed separately by the Scottish council. In Scotland, however, hostility to the Cromwellian regime led to these occasions being widely disregarded.

Early Irish evidence

During the first century following the reformation, the evidence for occasions of special worship in Ireland is fragmentary. Only one occasion is known during the sixteenth century (1589–Ir), three in Charles I's reign before the meeting of the Long parliament, and two in 1641. It is possibly the case that there were other occasions for which no evidence has survived. Consequently, while special worship in Ireland might be expected to have developed broadly in parallel with England, the differences are perhaps more striking. Most notably, no forms of prayer were produced in Ireland; indeed, the instruction in the proclamation of October 1625 to the bishops to prepare 'a Prayer or prayers' for their own diocese, because 'some of the Cleargie cannot … make such forme of zealous prayer as the time requireth' suggests that extempore prayer was common.[92] Moreover, it is difficult to see any pattern in the events which prompted the ordering of special worship. Occasions were variously 'Irish', 'British' and 'English' events. They were responses to events in Ireland for which there was no parallel English occasion (1628–Ir), to issues which affected the Tudor and Stuart regimes as a whole for which there were parallel English occasions (the Spanish armada, 1589–Ir, and the birth of the future Charles II, 1630–Ir) and to events in England alone for which there were also parallel occasions (plague, 1625–Ir). Following the establishment of the Republic in 1649, as the frequency with

---

[91]   The exception, 1658–ES, a thanksgiving day for the discovery of a royalist conspiracy, the victory at the battle of the Dunes and the surrender of Dunkirk, appears to have been ordered only for England and Scotland.

[92]   SoA, Proclamations Ireland, fo. 42r: proclamation by the lord deputy and council, 13 Oct. 1625, STC 14202.

which special worship was ordered in Ireland rose, so too did the incidence of 'Irish' and 'British' contexts for special worship. Fasts and thanksgivings marked, on the one hand, the progress of the war and conquest of Ireland, plague and the death of the lord deputy (1651–Ir3) and, on the other, Britain's involvement in European wars and the interregnum regime's sense of widespread sinfulness threatening its political success. Where special worship was ordered for specifically 'English' interests – such as the success of parliament and a feared Scottish invasion of England (1651–Ir1) – these were combined with more local concerns, such as plague. It was also at this time that special worship was first ordered in Ireland in support of persecuted Christians abroad (1655–E1r), a reason that had stimulated special worship in England since the 1540s.

England: 1660–88

The re-emergence and consolidation of the characteristic styles of special worship under James I and Charles I is the most notable feature of the restoration period. Compared with the 1640s and 1650s, the frequency with which occasions were ordered declined markedly: between the return of the king in May 1660 and the flight of James II at the end of 1688 twenty-three occasions of special worship were ordered in England and Wales, a pattern which resembles that of the Elizabethan and early Stuart period and which can, to some extent, be explained by the relative peace of these years. The people's experience of fasting was, however, less intense than in the pre-civil war period, as only one monthly fast was ordered during this period, for the plague in July 1665, observance of which continued for nearly eighteen months until November 1666. This was not only the last outbreak of plague in England and Wales, but also the last occasion on which the Elizabethan order of the fast was issued. Five other developments in this period are worth emphasizing.

First, the observance of special worship provided one of the first indications that the worship and government of the pre-civil war Church of England were likely to be restored essentially unchanged. The royal proclamation for the thanksgiving day for the restoration, issued on 5 June, just a week after the king's triumphant return to London, made no reference to a form of prayer. But, shortly before the day itself, a form, based on the pre-civil war BCP, appeared 'by authority' from the king's printer. Thereafter, forms of prayer for fast and thanksgiving days followed the structure of the 1559 BCP (until 1662–E), and then the revised 1662 BCP (from 1665–E). The format, which had become increasingly standardized in the early seventeenth century, now took a form which remained more or less unchanged until the 1850s. The forms of prayer for fast days included services for morning prayer, the litany, ante-communion and evening prayer; most morning services would have included morning prayer, the litany, ante-communion and a sermon. Evening prayer, however, was not included in the forms produced for thanksgiving days.

Second, parliament continued to take an important part in proposing fasts and thanksgiving days. The thanksgiving for the restoration of the monarchy, ordered before the king's return by the convention on 26 April 1660 (1660–E2), continued the practice of the civil war and interregnum. In June the following year, however, returning to the practice of the 1620s, Lords and Commons joined in petitioning Charles II to appoint a fast in response to heavy rains and fear of famine. Thereafter, parliament played no part in the *ordering* of occasions, limiting its role to motions requesting the king to act. These parliamentary motions were a particularly notable feature of the politics of the mid- to late 1670s, when concerns about popery in general, and the revelation of the popish plot and attempts to exclude the duke of York from the succession in particular, led to a series of fast days (1674–E, 1678–E1, 1678–E2, 1679–EIr, 1680–E), all of which were initiated in this way. In the 1670s, as in the 1620s, therefore, fast days became part of the struggle between the royal government and opposition groups in parliament to mould the political agenda and to rally support across the country, as tensions grew over constitutional and religious issues. The long declaration, ordered to be read in all churches on the thanksgiving day for the discovery of the Rye House plot in 1683 (1683–EIr) – a striking innovation in the history of English special worship which was not repeated[93] – should also be seen in this context, as an opportunity for the court both to drive home and to celebrate the defeat of the campaign for exclusion.

Third, there was increasing co-ordination between the appointment of fasts and thanksgiving days in England and Wales and in Ireland. Evidence for the 1660s is patchy, and there was sometimes a delay of several weeks between observances in England and Ireland, but there were eleven occasions from 1665 to 1688 on which worship was co-ordinated between the two kingdoms, to which can be added the prayers ordered in October 1688 during the threat from invasion by William of Orange (see below).

Fourth, in 1685 special prayers based on the BCP order for the visitation of the sick were issued during Charles II's final illness, the first time that prayers for the recovery of the monarch had been ordered since they were used in the chapel royal for Edward VI in 1553 (1553–E1). This set a precedent for worship during the illness of the king or queen, which was repeated during the last days of Mary II (1694–E4), for Queen Caroline (1737–E), though she was only queen consort, and then through to the early twentieth century (1788–1, 1801–2, 1810–2, 1812–EIr, 1820–1, 1830–1, 1837–1, 1928–E, and see 1951–1).

Fifth, the restoration was the single most important period in the development of anniversary commemorations. Some occasions had been established informally during Elizabeth's reign, with the independent, *ad hoc* development of accession day, and then formally with the establishment of Gowrie day (5 August) and the thanksgiving for the failure of the gunpowder plot (5 November). Both parliament and the protectorate may have attempted to establish anniversary occasions of their own, for the failure of the Irish rebellion (1642–Ir) and for the battles of Dunbar and Worcester (1657–E3), though neither was as successful as the unofficial royalist observance of the 'martyrdom' of Charles I (30 January). After the restoration observance of 30 January was turned into an annual, 'perpetual' fast by act of parliament, which had already established an annual thanksgiving for the restoration (29 May) and then legislated further to create an anniversary fast commemorating the great fire of London in 1666 (2 September). The Cavalier parliament was therefore responsible for the creation or re-creation of most of a new liturgical calendar of state services (30 January, 29 May, and 5 November). These occasions persisted until their abolition in 1859. There were also new anniversary commemorations in Ireland for the discovery of the 1641 rising (23 October) and in Scotland for the king's birthday. On the other hand, the anniversary thanksgiving for the failure of

---

[93] No similar document was produced for any other Church of England occasion of special worship, though in some ways it resembles, and many have been suggested by, the 'causes' produced by the parliamentary and republican regimes in the 1640s and 1650s.

the Gowrie conspiracy was no longer observed in England and Wales. Moreover, because Charles II's accession day (30 January) was kept as a fast marking his father's execution, the anniversary of the monarch's accession was not itself celebrated again until it was revived by James II in 1686. In England the form of prayer for 5 November was revised by convocation and new forms were produced for 30 January and 29 May, though, until 1696, the great fire was observed using a form composed for a particular occasion, the fast of 10 October 1666 in response to the fire (1666–EIr3). The forms for 30 January, 29 May, 5 November and accession day were also, for the first time, annexed by royal warrant to the BCP.

Scotland: 1660–90

In Scotland, the restoration of the monarchy was marked by a day of thanksgiving, apparently appointed through the co-ordination of local church courts, in a period when no national civil or ecclesiastical bodies were functioning. After the re-establishment of episcopacy in 1661–2, the crown reasserted its power over special worship, appointing the remaining seven fasts and six thanksgiving days held during the reigns of Charles II and James VII. Because both English and Scottish observances were appointed by royal authority, there was greater co-ordination than previously between the kingdoms with respect to the events marked by special worship. There were, therefore, Scottish days prompted by the Anglo-Dutch war (1665–S1), the Rye House plot (1683–S) and Mary of Modena's pregnancy in 1688 (1688–S1). But it is important not to exaggerate the degree of co-ordination. In part, this can be explained by the decisions of the government. There was no Scottish fast after the great fire of London, presumably because this was viewed as a specifically English event, and, while the popish plot prompted a fast in Scotland, the fasts called under parliamentary pressure in England in 1674, 1678, 1679 and 1680 were not replicated in Scotland. A similar pattern can be observed in Ireland, revealing, probably in ways which alert contemporaries would have seen, the royal government's lukewarm support for these events. In part, however, it is a reflection of differences in ecclesiological principles and administrative practices. The court appears to have responded to pressure from Scotland, and probably from the clergy, in both 1675 and 1684 to order fasts for dearth and bad weather; certainly, the proclamations for these occasions echoed, in their detailed lists of the sins of the people, the reasons for Scottish fasts in the late sixteenth and early seventeenth centuries. Moreover, even when Scottish and English observances were called at similar times for the same reasons (1683–EIr and 1683–S are the best examples), the ordering processes were distinct: the Scottish proclamation was composed separately, by the Scottish bishops, and then issued by the Scottish privy council in Edinburgh.

Ireland: 1660–88

Following the restoration, in Ireland as in Scotland, greater co-ordination with England can be identified in the organization of special worship (though, as already noted, it is possible that lack of evidence may be obscuring patterns in the period before the civil war). Increasingly from 1665, fasts and thanksgivings which took place in England were paralleled by similar occasions in Ireland, and, conversely, there were only two occasions of special worship in Ireland which did not have English parallels, both in 1661. The first was a fast to mark the anniversary of the regicide on 30 January – the annual commemoration was not given a statutory basis in Ireland until 1666 – and the second was a fast before the meetings of the English, Irish and Scottish parliaments. After 1665, there were four occasions on which the Irish government failed to follow English practice in ordering fasts: in 1674, 1678 (twice) and 1680. Three of these were ordered by Charles II in response to parliamentary addresses at Westminster at times of heightened tension about popery; the fourth, in November 1678, was ordered by the king at the time of the popish plot and almost certainly in anticipation of a parliamentary address. It seems likely that on these occasions, all of which were attempts by critics of Charles II's government to shift the political agenda in England, the king's ministers failed, quite deliberately, to transmit the conventional instruction to the lord lieutenant to issue a similar proclamation in Ireland. Significantly, the only Irish fast during the period of the popish plot took place after the lord lieutenant and council, on hearing of the English fast of April 1679, took the initiative and themselves sought permission from England to order a fast.

Most fasts and thanksgivings in Ireland were ordered by proclamation of the lords justices or lord deputy and council on receipt of instructions from England. This was certainly the case for the thanksgivings for the defeat of the Rye House plot and of Monmouth's rebellion (1683–EIr and 1685–EIr), when the secretary of state sent copies of the English proclamations to Ireland with instructions to order similar events in Ireland. With the exception of 1683–EIr, when the thanksgiving took place on 9 September across England, Wales and Ireland, there was generally no attempt to co-ordinate dates. Irish occasions tended to take place three or four weeks – and, on one occasion, over six weeks (1679–EIr) – after those in England. However, the surviving evidence is fragmentary and it is possible that practices were only gradually becoming institutionalized. In 1672, for example, the Irish proclamation for a fast following the outbreak of the second Anglo-Dutch war was significantly different from the English one (1672–EIr), suggesting a certain independence of action. On the other hand, the fact that the lord lieutenant sought Charles II's permission to proclaim a fast in April 1679 (1679–EIr) might be taken to indicate that royal approval had come to be regarded as necessary for the ordering of special worship.

More puzzling is the absence of forms of prayer in Ireland until 1679. This cannot be explained by the fact that the Irish Act of Uniformity, requiring worship to follow the BCP, was not passed until 1666, as both a fast and a thanksgiving were ordered in 1666 after the passage of the act and another fast in 1672. Moreover, no form of prayer had been prescribed for the weekly fasts for the plague in 1625 (1625–EIr). Once forms of prayer began to be ordered, the normal practice until the 1688 revolution (it changed thereafter) appears to have been for the Irish proclamation to order the use of the form of prayer composed in England, though it was reprinted in Ireland with a title-page making clear that it was authorized for use by the Irish government.[94]

---

[94] It is not certain that this was the practice in 1679, as no copy of the Irish proclamation survives for 1679–EIr, though the Irish form of prayer is identical to the English. In June 1688, the Irish proclamation for the thanksgiving for the birth of the prince of Wales made no mention of the form of prayer, but the one issued was identical to the English form (1688–EIr2).

The colonies

As West Indian islands were occupied to establish trading posts, plantations and naval bases during the seventeenth century and as emigrant colonies developed along the Atlantic seaboard of North America, the religious ministers, public officials and assemblies in those settlements adopted English practices of special worship. In particular, the communities of godly 'puritans' in New England, released from the constraints of royal and episcopal authority, soon multiplied the occasions and numbers of fast and thanksgiving days. At first, these occasions of special worship in the colonies or other overseas territories were for particular causes relating to each colony, often including an annual appointment of a thanksgiving day in the autumn to mark the harvest and other notable events during the year.[95] This annual thanksgiving day became characteristic throughout the American colonies and was adopted by the United States from the 1770s. As other islands were occupied and further English colonies were established across the world during the next two centuries, the new authorities similarly appointed 'local' occasions of special worship. This edition does not consider this type of special worship, specific to each colony or overseas territory. It does refer in commentaries to a second type of colonial special worship – that appointed in response to events in the British Isles. The leaders of the colonies remained alert to political and religious developments in Britain and indeed in continental Europe, and periodically – with obvious delays due to distance and slow communications – they either added references to these events to the 'local' causes for their fast or thanksgiving days, or appointed special worship in solidarity with their co-religionists in what they often termed 'our native country'. In Massachusetts particularly, days of humiliation or thanksgiving were ordered during the 1640s and 1650s to pray for the causes of the parliamentarian and commonwealth regimes. During the late 1670s and early 1680s, a larger number of colonies appointed occasions of special worship on receiving news of political and religious crises in England. A few of these occasions were prompted by information about special worship in England, sent by the government in London, notably the commonwealth council of state's despatch to New England of copies of the narrative and order of thanksgiving for 1651–1.[96] Then, as royal authority was gradually asserted over the colonies, assisted by the creation of the Board of Trade of Plantations in 1675, a third type of colonial special worship emerged. This was the observance in the colonies of an English or British occasion of special worship, as a result of a general order from the government in London to the governors or other officials of all the colonies. This type of worship is treated as integral to the edition, which includes the texts of general orders from London to the colonies. No orders for the observance of fast days were sent to the colonies, largely because the circumstances in England or Britain and the long delays in communication meant that they were unlikely to have pressing relevance in the colonies. But certain days of thanksgiving ordered for England or Britain were ordered for the colonies, even though the colonial observance of these occasions would take place weeks or months after the date of the English or British observance. All the types of observances of English or British occasions of special worship in the overseas colonies and other territories

---

[95] The fullest account remains W. DeLoss Love, *The fast and thanksgiving days of New England* (Boston, MA, 1895).
[96] See *CSPC, 1574–1660*, p. 362.

will be considered more fully in the Introductions to volumes 2 and 3. But the first general order for a thanksgiving sent to colonial governors occurred in June 1688 and is included in this volume (see 1688–EIr2).

ORDERING, PRINTING AND DISTRIBUTION

Occasions of special worship observed throughout the nation required considerable organization. A decision to appoint special worship necessitated a series of wider decisions: about the reasons, the type of occasion and the dates for the observance. Then the making of the order had to be arranged. Orders were not just announcements of the occasion; they were authoritative instructions, which, depending on the body that issued them, carried the force of civil and/or ecclesiastical law.[97] Often, they also included a statement of the reasons for the occasion, expressed in terms of the relationship between worldly events and divine providence. Due process was required. After the relevant authority had made an order for the occasion and for the type of text to be distributed and read in churches, the prayers, services or any act or address had to be composed. The *order* had to be communicated to the church and civil bodies responsible for its implementation and to the printers charged with supplying both the order and the text for distribution to the churches. The order was then copied or printed in the numbers required to ensure observance in the localities. For all types of occasion the ecclesiastical hierarchy was used to send copies to the parish clergy; for 'days' of special worship, copies also had to be supplied to the civil authorities. In England and Wales and Ireland distribution to the parish clergy was undertaken by the bishops and their officials, and in Scotland by synods and presbyteries, until, from the late nineteenth century, copies were sent direct to the parish clergy themselves. In England and Wales and, from 1679, in Ireland, the *form of prayer* was printed for distribution to all places of worship across the country. In addition, from at least the early seventeenth century, the printers on their own initiative produced further copies for sale to individuals. The orders, forms of prayer and any act or address – and later any instructions on obtaining copies for congregational use – had then to be despatched to the localities, in such ways as to ensure timely delivery in each parish. Anniversary occasions were by their nature predictable: they could be prepared for well in advance, they became routine, and the liturgical documents had very long use. Indeed, forms of service for 30 January, 29 May, 5 November and accession day were printed as annexes to the BCP. Particular occasions, however, were by definition irregular and were ordered at short notice, placing much pressure on the processes of printing and distribution. Even once the custom of annual fast days during wartime had become established, the dates of ordering and observance were never certain and variations occurred in the texts of each year's orders, forms of prayer or acts or addresses.

This section discusses each stage of the process of ordering occasions and distributing the documents required for their observance. What follows includes some general comments, but concentrates particularly on practices in the period from

---

[97] There was occasional controversy about the legal force of these orders, notably the case of John Johnson in 1715–23, which is discussed in the introduction to volume 2. See John Johnson, *The case of occasional days and prayers, containing a defence for not solemnizing the accession day by reading the new form, and for not using occasional prayers* (Dublin, [1833]).

the reformation to the revolution of 1688. It should be emphasized at the outset, however, that the evidence for this period is often fragmentary and limited, and there are significant gaps in our knowledge. Developments after 1688, which can sometimes cast light on earlier practice, will be examined in the introductions to volumes 2 and 3; so too will descriptions of the distribution of orders and notices to overseas territories.

Decisions

As explained earlier, in England and Wales and in Ireland, except between 1642 and 1660, and then in the United Kingdom from 1707 until the 1860s, decisions about the appointment of special worship were made by the crown. Between 1642 and 1660 they were taken by those who assumed the exercise of royal prerogative powers during the civil war and interregnum, that is, parliament between 1642 and 1653 and again in 1659–60 and the lord protector from 1653 to 1659. In Scotland, the situation was more complex, and the anti-Erastianism of its reformed church meant that, before 1660 (except during the period of the Cromwellian Union of Britain), these decisions were in most cases taken by the general assembly and other church courts. But the growing influence of the crown can be detected in the early seventeenth century, and from 1660, as in England, decisions in Scotland were generally – though not invariably – made by the crown. In other words, from the reformation until the late nineteenth century the occasion, reason and explanation for special worship was normally determined not by those who were ordained clergymen, but by the civil authorities, and specifically by the crown. In practice, the crown meant the monarch, until, during the course of the eighteenth century, special worship came within the subjects on which by convention the monarch acted on government advice. Normally, the archbishop of Canterbury, as primate of all England, was involved in the decision, even when it related to Ireland (but the archbishops of Armagh and Dublin, the Irish primates, were not consulted) and occasionally when it related to Scotland. But it was not necessary for him, or for any other bishop or clergyman, either to initiate the proposal or to participate in the decision-making, or even be present at the meeting of the privy council which issued the order.[98] That said, proposals for special worship were often initiated by the higher clergy, either by direct suggestion to the monarch (e.g. 1543–E1) or when their own orders to organize worship in cities or their dioceses came to the notice of the crown or, more usually, a privy councillor (e.g. 1563–E). A further aspect of the decision-making process was the role of parliament. In England and Wales from the 1620s to 1641 and again from 1660 to 1680, parliament took a greater part in initiating special worship: parliamentary petitions, which invariably had their origins in the House of Commons, were presented to the king, requesting him to order fasts (e.g. 1625–E, 1626–E1, 1629–E1, 1640–E1, 1640–E3, 1641–ES, 1661–E, 1674–E, 1678–E1, 1679–E, 1680–E) and, on just one occasion at the restoration, a thanksgiving (1660–E2). Elizabeth I, however, had firmly resisted such initiatives, complaining that a motion by Paul Wentworth in 1581 'empeached her iurisdiction', and this view was reasserted in the eighteenth century, Lord North opposing a

---

[98] No bishops, for example, were present at the privy council on 13 Dec. 1779 or 3 Apr. 1789.

proposed address to the king for a day of thanksgiving in 1782 on the grounds that 'the appointment of fasts and thanksgivings should be left to the Crown'.[99]

Issue of orders

1530s to 1620s

In England and Wales from the reformation to 1625, when notices for fasts and thanksgivings began to be issued as proclamations, orders from the crown were normally sent to the archbishops of Canterbury and York.[100] They were then copied by hand for transmission to the diocesan bishops, and by them to their parish clergy, usually via archdeacons, ordinaries, apparitors and sumners. When time allowed, the parish clergy probably gave notice of the occasion during church services on the preceding Sunday; this certainly seems to have been customary during later periods. It seems likely that these orders were distributed along with forms of prayer on occasions when these were produced (see below). There were two exceptions to this pattern. The first was the letter from the privy council to Edmund Bonner, bishop of London, ordering prayers for the safety of Mary I in childbirth (1554–E3), a copy of which was printed; it is unclear why. Second, Elizabeth I's letter to the archbishops of Canterbury and York ordering prayers and a weekly fast in response to the plague in 1563 was printed within the form of prayer. Bishops not only gave directions to their clergy about the conduct of worship and the message to be conveyed in their sermons; on at least some occasions they also transmitted instructions to the local civil authorities about wider observance in the parishes. These included expectations on fasting and almsgiving for 1586–E1 and again at the end of 1596 (1596–E3), when ministers, churchwardens and 'other discreete men of the Parish' were required to ensure not only that services were held and well attended, but also that richer parishioners would be generous in almsgiving. Archbishop Whitgift's order to the bishops in 1596 further required that the civil authorities should assist church attendance by themselves leading the community in worship, arranging the suspension of secular activities and returning a monthly list of 'disobedient delinquentes' (1596–E3). For the English day of thanksgiving after the defeat of the Spanish armada (1588–E2), Bishop Chaderton of Chester informed the mayor of Chester that he had 'receyved speciall dyrection from her Majestie to appoynte generall prayers and thankesgeyynge to be made in every Churche throughout my dyocesse' on Tuesday, 19 November, and gave notice to him, to his 'Brethren' (the city's corporation members) and to 'other of your well affected cytizens' that they should prepare themselves to attend 'In your most comely and decent maner' the communion service for the day, and

> further that you wolde cause all shoppes, Tavernes, and Typlynge houses to bee shutte vp all that day (as they were and will be In London), lest throughe any worldly occasyon those who are not fully grounded in good heale myghte with-draw themselves from that most godly actyon.[101]

---

[99] *Proceedings in the parliaments of Elizabeth I*, ed. Hartley, I, 526; Parker's *General Advertiser and Morning Intelligencer*, 1754, 23 May 1782.

[100] The nature of the surviving evidence means that it is impossible to state definitely that crown orders were routinely sent to the two archbishops, but this conclusion is consistent with the evidence that we do possess.

[101] 11 Nov. 1588, in HMC, *Eighth rep.*, p. 374.

In Scotland, the process appears to have been similar. The general assembly or other body claiming authority in the church (the convention of ministers in 1592, for example, or the commissioners of the Kirk in 1596) issued instructions to the presbyteries which then passed them on to parish ministers. There is some evidence that members of the general assembly and the commission personally conveyed copies of acts appointing special worship to their presbyteries (see 1640–S2), though presumably this would only have happened when a fast was ordered towards the end of the assembly's proceedings. It is not clear whether these acts were printed, as the first surviving examples of acts and causes date from the 1640s (see 1643–S1, 1645–S2, 1646–S2 and 1646–S3). Very little evidence at all exists for Ireland, but in 1589 the queen's order for a thanksgiving appears to have been communicated by Lord Burghley to the lord deputy, and thence to the bishops, sheriffs and mayors or provosts of towns.

Proclamations of fast and thanksgiving days: from the 1620s
The manner in which fast and thanksgiving days were ordered in England and Wales changed significantly in 1625, when Charles I issued a proclamation for a series of prayers and fasts in response to plague and the war in Europe (1625–E). Only once had special worship been ordered by proclamation before this (1555–E1). After 1625, except during the period 1641–60,[102] fast and thanksgiving *days* were invariably ordered by royal proclamation until 1857.[103] The attorney-general would be ordered by the council (or asked in advance by the council clerk) to draft the proclamation; later he appears merely to have vouched for a draft which the council clerk had adapted from the proclamation for the previous fast or thanksgiving day.[104] The proclamation was then printed and distributed in the usual manner, read out and posted by the civil authorities in ways that sought to ensure that everyone was aware of the occasion. In addition, copies were sent to churchwardens in parishes throughout England and Wales along with the forms of prayer. Sometimes, as for the thanksgiving for the suppression of Monmouth's rebellion, the proclamation was ordered to be read out in church on the preceding Sunday (1685–EIr), but this was not routine (cf. e.g. 1678–E1). During the eighteenth and nineteenth centuries, proclamations were often displayed on the doors or boards of churches, and it is possible that this practice may have been common in the seventeenth century. During the

[102] Charles I continued to issue proclamations during the first civil war: for thanksgivings for the royalist victories at Edgehill and Newbury and the relief of Hereford (1642–E1(R), 1643–E10(R) and 1645–E9(R)), for a monthly fast during the war (1643–E11(R)) and a fast during the peace negotiations at Uxbridge (1645–E1(R)).
[103] The last in the continuous series of proclamations for days of fasting/humiliation and thanksgiving was for 1857–2, marking the 'Indian mutiny'. The next widespread days of humiliation in England and Wales were arranged by the bishops (see 1866–1), and church leaders were responsible for organizing the later equivalents, days of intercession or national days of prayer. The very last special worship ordered by proclamation was for the day of thanksgiving to mark the peace of Versailles (1919–1). Proclamations were used from 1872 to order public holidays for royal events which were also marked by special worship; but these proclamations did not contain orders for the special worship, which was organized by the church leaders. These developments are explored more fully in the introductions to volumes 2 and 3.
[104] See, e.g. TNA, PC2/46, fo. 432 for 1636–E3, PC2/58, fo. 100r for 1665–E3, PC2/97, fo. 115r for 1742–1.

restoration period they also began to be published in the *London Gazette*, though this was not done consistently until the early eighteenth century.[105]

The first evidence of the use of proclamations to order special worship in Ireland also dates from 1625, when, three months after the order for a fast in England, the lord deputy and council issued a proclamation for fast days on account of the plague in England. Thereafter, the surviving evidence, which is far from complete, suggests that fast and thanksgiving days were ordered by proclamation of the lord lieutenant (or lord deputy or lords justices) and council (see 1628–Ir and 1641–Ir). Moreover, the examples of 1683 and 1685, when the English proclamations were sent to Dublin with an instruction that a similar proclamation be issued by the Irish privy council, indicate that, under the Stuarts, special worship in Ireland was instigated by the English crown. This is supported by the fact that in April 1679 the duke of Ormonde, lord lieutenant of Ireland, explicitly sought the king's permission to hold a fast on the occasion of the popish plot (1679–EIr). As noted earlier, however, not all English occasions were observed in Ireland, and it is not until the eighteenth century that co-ordination of fast and thanksgiving days became routine.

In Scotland, the efforts of James VI and Charles I to assert greater royal influence over special worship can be traced in a series of privy council orders (1600–S, 1630–S, 1637–S), a proclamation by the privy council (1623–S2) and a royal declaration which was approved by the privy council (1638–S1). No royal proclamation was issued for any occasion of special worship until 1665, but thereafter proclamations became the usual means of ordering fast and thanksgiving days. Indeed, in striking contrast to pre-civil war practice, every occasion of special worship during the restoration was the subject of a royal proclamation, except the thanksgiving for the restoration of the king (1660–S), which was appointed before the reconstruction of monarchical government, and the two thanksgiving days in 1688 for Queen Mary's pregnancy (1688–S1) and the birth of the prince of Wales (1688–S2), which were ordered by privy council act. Royal proclamations were formally proclaimed at the mercat cross[106] in Edinburgh, and then distributed by royal messengers to the shires and stewartries, where sheriffs, stewarts and heralds were responsible for seeing that they were similarly proclaimed in the head burghs. After being read, proclamations were attached to the mercat crosses, allowing them to be inspected by persons absent from the public reading. The principle underlying this manner of publication was that, as the documents often stated, none should be able to 'pretend ignorance' of their contents. In addition, however, during the restoration proclamations for fasts and thanksgivings were sent to bishops who were instructed to ensure that they were read 'from the Pulpit' in every parish church, generally at the Sunday service before the fast or thanksgiving. There is some evidence that this happened at sessions of the church courts (see 1665–S1), though some proclamations were presumably distributed at times when the courts were not meeting.

The declarations issued by Oliver Cromwell and Richard Cromwell as lords protector from 1654 to 1659 in many ways resembled royal proclamations in form and purpose. While they were exhortatory, asking and calling on people to join in

---

[105] The first proclamation to be printed in the *London Gazette* was for 1672–EIr. *London Gazette*, 662, 21–5 Mar. 1672.

[106] The market cross. Originally, these crosses had symbolized the authority which gave permission for the holding of regular markets, but they came to be regarded as the more general symbol of royal or state authority.

worship on the prescribed days rather than ordering them to do so, ministers were still required to read the declarations in church on the Sunday before the fast or thanksgiving day, and the holding of markets and fairs was prohibited. When parliament was sitting, however, declarations were issued jointly by the lord protector and parliament (e.g. 1656–2 and 1657–1); what is less clear is why some declarations were issued jointly by the lord protector and privy council (e.g. 1657–E2).

Acts, orders and ordinances
Under the monarchy in all the British kingdoms, the only use of acts of parliament in relation to special worship was to institute anniversary occasions, though the observation of 5 November in Scotland was prescribed by the privy council and in Ireland both 30 January and 5 November were ordered by royal warrant, a bill to establish 30 January as a fast having failed in 1661. However, from the king's departure from London in 1641 through to the establishment of the protectorate and again following the collapse of the protectorate in 1659–60, parliamentary acts – or, more accurately, orders and ordinances – were the most common means by which special worship was ordered in England and Wales. The first occasion on which this happened was the thanksgiving for the peace between Scotland and England in 1641. A public thanksgiving had been one of the provisions of the treaty of Ripon and parliament merely acted to prescribe the date, but this was nonetheless a significant encroachment on the king's prerogative. Equally significant, perhaps, is that parliament, an overwhelmingly lay body, assumed exercise of the royal prerogative in the ordering of special worship during the rest of the 1640s; on the opening of the Westminster Assembly of Divines in 1643, MPs acted quickly to inform it that it had no independent authority to order fasts.[107] Before the abolition of the House of Lords in 1649, most orders for special worship were approved by both Commons and Lords, though proposals more commonly originated in the former, and occasionally orders were made by the Commons alone (e.g. 1644–E12(P) and 1645–E8(P)), reflecting moments of tension between the two houses.

Council orders for special prayers
After the revolution of 1688, privy council orders became a common way of ordering special prayers, a process which will be examined in the introduction to volume 2. The practice had its origins in the early seventeenth century, in a series of privy council orders, directed to the archbishops, for the preparation and circulation of prayers – for the fleet in 1628 (1628–E2), on the queen's pregnancy in 1633 (1633–E1) and for the expedition against the Scots in 1639 (1639–E). It is likely that there were others, as prayers were ordered for the queen's pregnancy and royal births on ten further occasions from 1628 to 1637, but no orders have survived. The Scottish privy council was also involved in ordering special worship during the reigns of James VI and Charles I, the first occasion being the order for thanksgiving days following the Gowrie plot (1600–S). However, while two thanksgivings were ordered in Scotland in 1688 by act of the privy council, there is no evidence that privy council orders for special prayers were revived in England and Wales after the restoration. Indeed, prayers were only ordered on two occasions between 1660 and 1688: during Charles II's final illness in 1685 and in response to the threatened

---

[107] *Westminster assembly*, V, 9–11.

invasion by William of Orange in 1688. No order survives for the former, and the prayers in 1688 were composed by the bishops after a direct request from James II on 8 October, approved by him on 10 October and ordered to be printed and distributed by the earl of Sunderland, as secretary of state, the following day.

Discontinuance of special worship

Many particular occasions of special worship were ordered for a specified date or duration, with the end of the observance inherent in the original order. But for some petitionary prayers and fasts the order gave just a starting date for an unspecified period of observance, with no indication of when it should cease. Only very rarely did a subsequent national order explicitly state that the observance should be 'discontinued'. The only case for which this happened before 1688 was the monthly Wednesday fast during the civil war which was first took place in January 1642 as a response to the Irish rebellion (1641–E). Charles I ordered its cessation and replacement by a monthly fast on Fridays in October 1643 (1643–E11(R)), and then parliament abolished it by act in April 1649 (1649–E2). In many cases, the discontinuance of special worship was implicit in one of two ways. It might occur due to the abrupt and obvious end of the reason for the occasion, most clearly when prayers during a sovereign's illness were followed by news of his or her recovery or death. Alternatively, it might be superseded by a later order: this was usually for a thanksgiving day or thanksgiving prayer (e.g. 1603–E and 1604–E), although in later periods it was sometimes for a replacement petitionary prayer when the anxiety intensified (e.g. cholera for 1832–1) or altered in character (e.g. cattle plague and cholera for 1866–2). In cases of disease, services were usually discontinued when the number of deaths per week dropped significantly enough to indicate that the crisis had passed. This proved problematic in 1564 when the thanksgivings for the diminution of the plague planned by Edmund Grindal, bishop of London, had to be abandoned when the city suffered an unexpected increase in deaths (Appendix, Omitted occasion, 1564). In some cases, however, the ending of fasts or prayers appears to have been left either to directions by the archbishop or more likely the individual bishops, or even to the judgment of individual clergymen.[108] Inevitably, the absence of clear instructions sometimes caused uncertainty for the clergy about how to act, never more, perhaps, than during the revolution of 1688 when, following James II's flight, the London clergy approached Archbishop Sancroft for instructions about whether they should continue to read the prayers ordered during the threat of invasion, only to meet with a deliberately evasive response (see 1688–EIr3).

Materials for church services

Forms of prayer

For occasions of special worship, the printed document most consistently sent to the clergy of England and Wales from the 1560s to recent times was the form of prayer, with interruption only from September 1641 (1641–ES) to May 1660 (with the exception of a small number of royalist occasions: 1643–E10(R), 1643–E11(R),

---

[108] In 1605, the bishop of London's chancellor told the archdeacon of St Albans that the prayers of thanksgiving for the birth of Princess Mary were to be used as long as was seen fit. HALS, ASA 5/4/181, p. 803.

1644–E3(R), 1645–E1(R), 1645–E10(R)). Until the 1620s, the form was probably
the only printed document received by clergymen. Once proclamations became the
public order for 'days', these invariably stated that the archbishops and bishops
had been directed to compose the form of prayer and, in the words of Charles I's
proclamation of 30 June 1626, 'to disperse the same throwout His whole Kingdome'. Council orders from 1626 consisted of orders to the archbishop of Canterbury to prepare the form; that it was to be printed and circulated was implicit in
the instruction that it be read in all churches. It can be assumed that successive
archbishops normally composed the drafts of forms of prayer themselves[109] – this
was too important a matter to be delegated to chaplains – though it is clear that,
on some occasions, a wider group of bishops was involved (e.g. 1625–E). When
special prayers were issued this meant the composition of one or two prayers, but
for fast and thanksgiving days it was a major task: two or three complete services
had to be produced, involving the writing of new prayers and collects, the selection
of others from earlier services, the choice of biblical readings, psalms and sentences
and the construction of a 'composite' psalm.[110] But it is worth emphasizing that,
even if bishops had suggested the holding of special worship, the instruction to
compose the form of prayer came from the crown and the choice of bishop was
the monarch's. In 1628, Charles I turned to Bishop Laud of London to prepare the
prayers for the fleet (1628–E2), and in December 1687 James II instructed Bishops
Crewe of Durham, Sprat of Rochester and White of Peterborough to compose the
thanksgiving for the pregnancy of Mary of Modena (1688–EIr1). Moreover, so long
as occasions were ordered by the crown, no clergyman had the final decision over
the words used in worship: this was a matter for the monarch and council. This was
a thoroughly Erastian supervision not just of the occasion, but of the very words
used in worship. It was not uncommon for the draft to be shown to and discussed
with the monarch or a leading minister; indeed, some monarchs, such as Charles I,
required it.[111] Monarchs and their ministers sometimes suggested changes, altered
the words of prayers or suggested the insertion of further prayers, as was done by
William Cecil for 1563–E, 1585–E1 and 1596–E1.

In Ireland, as has been noted, forms of prayer were not issued until 1679, and it
is possible that extempore prayer was used by the clergy on fast and thanksgiving
days before that date. For the one fast and the four thanksgiving days from 1679 to
1688 the English form of prayer was reprinted in Dublin for use in the Church of
Ireland, and on three of these occasions (1683–EIr, 1685–EIr, 1688–EIr1) its use
was specifically enjoined in the proclamation issued by the Irish executive.[112]

Printing

The history of the printing of the various documents produced for occasions of
special worship – orders, forms of prayers, acts, addresses and 'causes' – is compli-

---

[109] See, e.g. John Gutch, *Collectanea curiosa* (2 vols., Oxford, 1781), I, 414–18, for Sancroft's draft of
1688–EIr3.
[110] A psalm or 'hymn', composed of a series of biblical voices appropriate to the occasion, which
replaced the *Venite* (Ps. 95) in the order for morning prayer.
[111] SP16/158, fo. 7: Bishop Laud to Dorchester, 2 Jan. 1630.
[112] No copy of the proclamation for 1679–EIr has survived, and the proclamation for 1688–EIr2 makes
no mention of the form of prayer, though the form was printed in Dublin by the royal printer.

cated, reflecting changes not only in technologies of printing, publication and distribution across nearly five centuries, but also changes in the ordering, nature and purpose of the occasions. In the period between the reformation and the revolution of 1688, *orders* were not normally printed until fasts and thanksgivings began to be ordered by proclamation, in 1625 in England and Ireland and in 1665 in Scotland. Like other proclamations, these were printed by the royal printers in the various kingdoms. In Scotland, there is evidence from the 1640s that the acts and causes of the general assembly were printed (1643–S1, 1645–S2, 1646–S2) – by Evan Tyler, the king's printer – but few of these broadsides survive, and it is not clear whether they are representative of normal practice. From the mid-sixteenth century, the royal printers in England had already been deeply involved in occasions of special worship, assuming responsibility for printing the *forms of prayer* and other documents specified in the relevant orders. The exception to this pattern was during the civil war and interregnum. When Charles I abandoned London and occupied Oxford (1642), he lost access to the royal printer and so used the printer to the University, Leonard Lichfield, to print most of the king's proclamations, declarations and forms of prayer during the first civil war. At the same time, parliament had no official printer – in principle, parliamentary proceedings were not supposed to be publicized outside the two houses. Initially, therefore, during the early months of the civil war, parliament used the king's printer, Robert Barker and his assignees, as well as John Thomas or Joseph Hunscott (beadle of the Stationers' Company), to print their orders. From 1642 to 1660, parliament and the protectorate favoured particular printers who were responsible for printing, amongst other things, the orders and narratives for special worship. After the restoration, John Bill and Christopher Barker were granted a patent as king's printer and also successfully asserted their rights under that patent to print material from parliament.[113] The succession of royal printers of documents for special worship in England and Wales, in Ireland and in Scotland is listed on pp. clxvi–clxx.

By their 'letters patent' from the crown, the royal printers were required, and had the exclusive rights, not just to print but also to publish all official documents of the crown and parliament, and also a share of the rights to print and publish the Bible and, in England and Wales and in Ireland, the BCP. Consequently they, or at least those for England and Wales, considered themselves to be 'booksellers', and charged accordingly.[114] Two further aspects of their role in special worship will be considered below (see the section on distribution): their duties included delivery of the documents to designated individuals in the localities, and, in time, they also began to engage in a private trade in sales of forms, to members of congregations, to the general public and to other booksellers, making an already profitable official business still more valuable.

Occasions of special worship posed particular challenges for the royal printers because of their irregularity and the need for urgency. With little advance notification, large numbers of documents had to be printed, with great accuracy because these were official texts, and then delivered reliably to a large number of widely dispersed localities, all within a short period and for a stated deadline. The royal printers had

---

[113] *Printing for parliament, 1641–1700*, ed. Sheila Lambert (List and Index Society, Special Series, 20, 1984); Sheila Lambert, 'The beginning of printing for the House of Commons, 1640–42', *The Library*, 6th ser., 3 (1981), 43–61.

[114] *Ninth report from the committee on the public expenditure, parl. Papers*, 1810 (373), p. 183.

at short notice to command considerable resources of material, machinery, skilled workmen and manual labourers. This was especially the case for the English and the Irish printers, who had to print the sometimes lengthy and complicated forms of prayer in addition to the proclamations. In the early seventeenth century, the English printers could have orders and short forms (prayers alone) printed and delivered to clergy in the London area within twenty-hour hours.[115] Forms of prayer for fasts and thanksgivings, which were commonly around fifty pages in extent and sometimes much longer, required more time, and it was generally reckoned that six weeks were necessary for printing and distributing the proclamation and form of prayer throughout England and Wales. Certainly, attempts to shorten the period between order and observance suggested that the system could not cope. In 1685, when the thanksgiving for the defeat of Monmouth's rebellion was ordered to be held just over two weeks after the proclamation, Archbishop Dolben of York complained that his clergy did not receive the proclamation in time to announce the occasion.[116]

Quite how the royal printers coped with such unpredictable demands is not entirely clear. They were evidently substantial and efficient enterprises. For their official duties the English royal printers of 1583 had five printing presses, adding a sixth shortly afterwards; in 1620, following the increased work required to print the authorized edition of the Bible, they had expanded to perhaps seven or eight. In 1668, they were back to six presses; a hundred years later, they had nine.[117] These presses would have been sufficient for both the flow of government documents and the production of Bibles and prayer books. Production of proclamations, used for all kinds of government purposes, was largely a standard activity and for long periods contained consistent and formulaic terms, so the production of one-sheet proclamations for special worship fitted into regular patterns of work; indeed, the basic text and design may have been kept in type, with changes made as needed for the description and dates of the occasion.[118] The printing of forms of prayer was usually more demanding. The print runs for forms of prayers in the sixteenth and early seventeenth centuries are not known,[119] but around 10,000 copies were needed to supply one to every parish in England and Wales,[120] and in the 1670s almost 13,000 copies were being produced to the order of the archbishop of Canterbury for distribution across England and Wales.[121] Even in the seventeenth century it is likely that additional copies were produced for public sale. No doubt the English and Irish printers worked overtime, including through the night, to produce the docu-

---

[115]   Kitching, '"Prayers fit for the time"', p. 247.

[116]   Tanner 31, fo. 167: Dolben to Sancroft, 18 July 1685.

[117]   David Kathman, 'Christopher Barker (1528/9–1599)', and Patricia Hernlund, 'William Strahan (1715–85)', in *Oxford dictionary of national biography*; Graham Rees and Maria Wakely, *Publishing, politics and culture. The king's printers in the reign of James I and VI* (Oxford, 2009), pp. 52, 66, 138.

[118]   Rees and Wakely, *Publishing, politics and culture*, p. 140.

[119]   The first evidence for the number of copies of orders or forms printed (cited below, pp. civ–cv) relates to 1647–E3(P). But this evidence relates to an order; additional purchases were much more likely for forms of prayer. More evidence survives for the number of copies printed in later periods and it is discussed in the introductions to volumes 2 and 3.

[120]   The evidence of churchwardens' accounts, some of which is cited below, suggests that, in the sixteenth and seventeenth centuries, one copy was normally purchased by each parish. By the mid-eighteenth century, two copies were being sent to parishes, and by the mid-nineteenth century three copies (at least) seem to have been received.

[121]   Tanner 33, fos 28–9; 39, fo. 21; 141, fo. 83.

ments needed for occasions of special worship, but for fast and thanksgiving days they would have needed additional presses. Temporary suspension of other printing work (Bibles or prayer books) would have helped, but owners of the royal 'printing house' seem often to have had a further resource: they owned additional commercial businesses in further buildings, with additional presses.[122] So for instance, for 1708–1, at a period when (judging from the known numbers for 1668) the printers may have had six presses, the existence of ten different impressions suggests that further presses were used temporarily. In addition, royal (and parliamentary) printers may have subcontracted to other printers.

Distribution of forms and orders

During the sixteenth and seventeenth centuries, there were two methods for distributing forms of prayer to parishes in England and Wales. Occasionally, and perhaps only for short prayers intended for use by ministers as soon as they had been received, the higher clergy were expected to collect the forms directly from the royal printers. In 1605, for instance, the archdeacon of St Albans was informed that the prayers for Queen Anna's safe delivery in childbirth were being printed that night and would be available for collection from the royal printers by six o'clock the following morning.[123] More usually, however, the royal printers sent the forms of prayer in packages to each bishop. In 1563, Thomas Young, archbishop of York, received six copies of the form of prayer for 1563–E by post from Bishop Grindal of London with a note that 'the impression for his province shall followe with convenient spede'.[124] In 1596, Archbishop Whitgift, when asking Bishop Fletcher of London as dean of Canterbury province to arrange the use of a special prayer, added that

> there is Order given, that her Majesties Printer shall se a competent Number of them printed & sent downe to your Lordship, that every Parishe within your Dioces may have one of them at the least; the Price whereof he dothe sett downe unto your Lordship, which you must Cause to be collected by suche your Officers as dothe deliver them forthe, & to be returned upp unto the said Printer, in suche manner as he shall requier your Lordship by his Letters.[125]

Once in the diocese, forms of prayer were usually distributed to incumbent clergy or churchwardens by apparitors and sumners who toured the parishes and collected payment for remission to the printers. However, some parishes appear to have purchased texts directly from London or other towns, paying carriers or their own parishioners to collect them. In 1640, the churchwardens of Saffron Walden bought from Benjamin Newbolt two books of thanksgiving for the gunpowder plot as well

---

[122]   Rees and Wakely, *Publishing, politics and culture*, pp. 145–8, describes the rushed production of two official papers in 1618, when the royal printers not only worked overnight but were also able to use total of twenty presses. Henry Plomer, 'The king's printing house under the Stuarts', *The Library*, new ser., 2 (1901), 354, observes that it is probable that the office of king's printer 'brought with it a large amount of outside custom', and Hernland, 'Strahan', reports that in 1770 Strahan had three separate businesses in at least six buildings, with possibly more than twenty-five presses.

[123]   Kitching, '"Prayers fit for the time"', p. 247.

[124]   Lans. 6, fo. 166r: Grindal to Cecil, 21 Aug. 1563.

[125]   A postscript added to an order from Whitgift to Fletcher, 3 June 1596: for details see 1596–E1. A transcription of this letter is printed in T. Brooke, 'Queen Elizabeth's prayers', *Huntingdon Library Quarterly*, 2 (1938), 73–4.

as a service book, a book of homilies, two books of canons (1603 and 1640) and two books for the coronation, paying a porter 4*d* 'for bringing these bookes to the carier at the Bull' and another 6*d* to 'Thomas Parker for bringing them to Walden'.[126] The churchwardens of Loddon paid twelve pence to Robert Alling in 1625, 'for riding to Norwich and his horse hire for to by ii prayer bookes the 19th of Julii'.[127]

Churchwardens' accounts survive unevenly across England and Wales and favour richer parishes.[128] A survey shows that, before the outbreak of the civil war, these distribution networks were relatively effective: though by no means all parishes seem to have had copies of forms of prayer for all occasions, many parishes were able to obtain forms for many occasions, whether they were in London, the south-west or the north.[129] Nevertheless, in 1625 there were complaints in parliament that forms had not been distributed to all parishes, either through the failure of the bishops and their officers or because 'some particular Persons' had engrossed the copies and were profiteering, and that the cost to parishes was too high.[130] The price of forms does seem to have risen from an average of 3*d* or 4*d* for a copy of the form of prayer on the earthquake in 1580 (1580–E) to between 10*d* and 1*s* for forms between 1625 and 1636.[131] In the late sixteenth century, there is some evidence that the cost for parishes varied across the country, though the reasons for this are not clear. Distance from London does not seem to have been an obvious factor: the churchwardens of Prescot, Lancashire, bought five copies of the form for 1580–E for 20*d*, while those in Chagford in Devon were charged 10*d* for one.[132] It is also clear that, as the example of Prescot shows, some parishes purchased multiple copies which, along with purchases by individuals, meant that there were fewer copies for other parishes to have.[133] However, it is not until 1647–E3(P) that we have

---

126 Essex Record Office (Chelmsford), D/P 192/5/3, p. 102.

127 Norfolk Record Office, PD 595/19, [fo. 158r].

128 Andrew Foster, 'Churchwardens' accounts of early modern England and Wales: some problems to note, but much to be gained', in *The parish in English life, 1400–1600*, ed. Katherine L. French, Gary M. Gibbs and Beat A. Kumin (Manchester, 1997), pp. 74–93.

129 Mears, 'Brought to book', pp. 29–44.

130 *CJ*, I, 810.

131 For 1580 see LMA, MS 1013/1, fo. 36r (St Mary Woolchurch), MS 1002/1a, 211r (St Mary Woolnoth), MS 645/1, 105r (St Peter Westcheap); *St Martins-in-the-Fields: the accounts of the churchwardens, 1525–1603*, ed. John V. Kitto (1901), p. 319; H. B. Walters, 'The churchwardens' accounts of the parish of Worfield. Part VI: 1572–1603', *Transactions of the Shropshire Archaeological and Natural History Society*, 3rd ser., 10 (1910), 68; *The churchwardens' accounts of St Michael's in Bedwardine, Worcester, from 1539 to 1603*, ed. John Amphlett (Worcestershire Historical Society, Oxford, 1896), p. 81; J. R. Beresford, 'The churchwardens' accounts of Holy Trinity, Chester, 1532 to 1633', *Journal of the Chester and North Wales Archaeological, Architectural and Historical Society*, new ser., 38 (1951), 130; Thomas H. Baker, 'The churchwardens' accounts of Mere', *Wiltshire Archaeological and Natural History Magazine*, 35 (1907–8), 69. For the 1620s and 1630s, see Suffolk Record Office (Bury), FB 77/E2/3, pp. 77, 91; Essex Record Office (Chelmsford), D/P 94/5/1, fos. 193v, 198v, 208v, 284r; Essex Record Office (Chelmsford), D/P 115/5/1, pp. 119, 127; Essex Record Office (Chelmsford), D/P 128/5/1, fo. 62r; Essex Record Office (Chelmsford), D/P 16/5/5, unfol. (accounts for 1626 and 1636); Norfolk Record Office, PD 595/19, [fo. 159r]; Norfolk Record Office, PD 552/15, unfol. (microfilm MF 1839/137 and 167); Norfolk Record Office PD 111/69, 69r.

132 *The churchwardens' accounts of Prescot Lancashire 1523–1607*, ed. F. A. Bailey (Lancashire and Cheshire Record Society, 104, Preston, 1953), p. 84; *The churchwardens' accounts of St Michael's church, Chagford, 1480–1600*, ed. Francis Mardon Osborne (Chagford, 1979), p. 239.

133 For example of private purchases of forms and orders see 1625–E and 1626–E1.

the first evidence of how many copies of orders or forms of prayer were produced: ten quires for the City of London and 9,500 for the rest of England and Wales.

After the civil war, a similar procedure remained. For the fast day during the plague in 1665, the privy council issued a specific order to the royal printers about the distribution of forms of prayer. They were instructed to

> take Care to send the respectiue Numbers of Formes of Prayer imprinted for the Fasting & Humiliation wch are appointed for each Diocesse of this Kingdome, packt up directed to the respectiue Bishops and delivered to ye Carriers or such as driue the Stage Coaches, who go nearest to the Places where the said Bishops reside, to be safely deliuered unto them.[134]

No evidence, however, survives to indicate how forms of prayer were distributed in Ireland from 1679 to 1688.

As has been seen, orders for special worship in the sixteenth and seventeenth centuries were passed on to the clergy by the bishops using the same network of officials who distributed the forms of prayer. It seems likely that, from 1625, printed copies of the proclamations for fast and thanksgiving days were transmitted in the same way and perhaps together with the forms of prayer; certainly, churchwardens' accounts record purchases of proclamations as well as forms of prayer. But for proclamations there were also well-established processes for dissemination by the civil authorities, in Scotland as well as England. It is hardly surprising, therefore, that in the 1640s, with parliamentary attacks on the jurisdiction of the episcopate and the collapse of diocesan administration, secular officials took an increasingly important role in the distribution of orders for both parliamentarian and royalist occasions. In December 1641 (1641–E), the Commons ordered MPs in the City of London to 'take the best and speediest Course they can, for publishing through the City the Directions for the Fast to be observed on *Wednesday* next' (the royal proclamation, ordering the fast in the rest of England and Wales was not issued until 8 January 1642).[135] After this, parliament regularly required the lieutenant of the Tower of London, the mayor and aldermen of London, MPs, sheriffs and other secular officials to disseminate their orders. Similarly, though the evidence is much sketchier, Charles I appears to have relied increasingly on supporters and paid messengers to distribute orders to royalist supporters after he left London and lost control of both the main transport routes around England and Wales and the episcopal network (which was abolished in October 1646).[136] For 1650–E3, orders were distributed for the first time by post, though the regimes of the interregnum continued to prefer to use secular officers, such as the lord mayor of London, JPs and sheriffs (e.g. 1650–E5, 1651–E3). In Ireland, the interregnum government was following English practice by 1651, using secular officials – mayors, governors of garrisons, JPs, constables and others – to distribute orders and to ensure that special worship was observed (see 1651–Ir1, 1655–Ir1, 1658–EIr).

---

[134] PRO, PC2/58, fo. 101r: privy council order, 6 July 1665, for 1665–E3.
[135] *CJ*, II, 349.
[136] Bates, 'Fast and thanksgiving days', pp. 183–94.

Congregational provision

The duty of the privy council, archbishops and printers was to ensure the delivery of copies of the forms of prayer to the parishes in numbers sufficient to enable the clergy to obey the order to read the prayers or services on the appointed day or days. There was no official requirement for any of these bodies to supply members of the congregations. Yet from the reformation onwards, special worship expected congregational participation, giving responses and joining in prayers. Though it is clear from the examples of Loddon and Prescot that some parishes bought multiple copies of forms of prayers, in the sixteenth and seventeenth centuries they never acquired enough to provide one copy for each member of the congregation or even for each household. It is possible that the congregational responses were given through a process of 'lining out' in which the minister or, more likely, the curate or clerk read out the relevant parts line by line, for repetition by the congregation. However, no evidence of this practice has survived from the sixteenth and seventeenth centuries.[137] It is probable that the responses were given by the clerk alone; the rubrics for the form for 1563–E revealingly state that the responses should be made by the congregation *or* the clerk, while this and other forms defined parishioners' participation in the services in non-verbal terms – they were expected to pray 'with penitent hearts', 'devoutly give ear' to the sermons and, 'with mind' as well as with speech, assent to prayers.[138]

The obvious solution to the problem, at least in parishes with higher rates of literacy, was to have copies available for members of the congregation. The parochial records of Broadclyst in Devon contain handwritten extracts from three fast and thanksgiving services between 1704 and 1708; these may be a rare survival of a common seventeenth-century practice.[139] It is also clear that, from the early seventeenth century, private individuals were purchasing forms of prayer. The first evidence of this dates from 1625 (see 1625–E). By the later seventeenth century, the practice was common, at least in the richer urban parishes. When attending the thanksgiving for the pregnancy of the queen on 15 January 1688 the earl of Clarendon was sufficiently surprised that 'there were not above two or three in the church who brought the form of prayer with them' to note the fact in his diary.[140] As there is no evidence of pirated printing of forms of prayer in this period, this demand must have been met by the royal printers, who regarded their letters patent for producing official copies as giving them exclusive rights to print and sell further copies for general sale.

BIBLIOGRAPHY OF WORKS ON SPECIAL WORSHIP TO 1688

This bibliography is limited to works which relate directly to, and are primarily concerned with, occasions of special worship. Bibliographies for 1689–1870 and 1871–2012 are included in volumes 2 and 3.

---

[137] We would like to thank John Craig and Roger Bowers for discussing this point.
[138] *A fourme to be vsed in common prayer twise a weeke* (STC 16505), sig. Bi[r].
[139] Manuscript outlines for 1704–E1, 1705–E1 and 1708–E3, Devon Record Office, 3594A–99/PI/1–2, 3. We are grateful to Julie Farguson for this reference.
[140] *The correspondence of Henry Hyde, earl of Clarendon, and of his brother Laurence Hyde, earl of Rochester*, ed. S. W. Singer (2 vols., 1828), II, 156.

Early historical and antiquarian works, editions and lists

[Anon.], 'The history and authority of the state-prayers', *Christian Observer*, 42 (1843), 721–32

B[enham], W[illiam], *The prayer-book of Queen Elizabeth 1559 to which are appended some occasional forms of prayer issued in her reign* (1890)

Blunt, John Henry, *The annotated Book of Common Prayer* (1866), general appendix

Christian Guardian and Church of England Magazine for 1830, p. 160

Christian Observer, 30 (1830), 128

Clay, William Keating, 'A list of occasional forms of prayer and services, for the most part publicly and authoritatively used during the reign of Queen Elizabeth', *British Magazine*, 29 (1846), 121–9

Clay, William Keatinge (ed.), *Liturgical services: liturgies and occasional forms of prayer set forth in the reign of Queen Elizabeth* (Parker Society, Cambridge, 1847)

Cox, J. Charles, 'Special forms of prayer in the Church of England. Part 1 – sixteenth century', *Newbery House Magazine*, 6:5 (1892), 532–9

Cox, J. Charles, 'Special forms of prayer. No. II (James I and Charles I)', *Newbery House Magazine*, 7:3 (1892), 257–74

Cox, J. Charles, 'Special forms of prayer in the Church of England. Part III – Charles II, James II, William and Mary', *Newbery House Magazine*, 8:2 (1893), 129–39

Cox, J. Charles, 'Special forms of prayer in the Church of England. Part IV – Queen Anne', *Newbery House Magazine*, 8:4 (1893), 419–30

Cox, J. Charles [J.C.C.], 'Days of national humiliation', *Guardian*, 14 Feb. 1900, 239–40

Lathbury, Thomas, *Guy Fawkes; or, a complete history of the gunpowder treason* (1839)

Lathbury, Thomas, 'Occasional forms of prayer', *Notes and Queries*, 8 (1853), 53–7

Lathbury, Thomas, 'Form of prayer', *Notes and Queries*, 10 (1854), 341

Lathbury, Thomas, 'Occasional forms of prayer', *Notes and Queries*, 10 (1854), 439–40

Macray, John, 'Occasional forms of prayer', *Notes and Queries*, 9 (1854), 13

Mant, Richard, *History of the Church of Ireland* (2 vols., 1840), II, 251–9

Niblock, J. W. to the editor, Sept. 1826, *Christian Observer*, 26 (1826), 533–4

Niblock, J. W. to the editor, 23 July and 21 Nov. 1829, *Gentleman's Magazine*, 94 (1829), 31–2, 390

'Occasional forms of prayer', *Notes and Queries*, 9 (1854), 404–6

'Occasional forms of prayer', *Notes and Queries*, 10 (1854), 247

Percival, A. P., *The original services for the state holidays* (1838)

Taylor, E. S., 'Occasional forms of prayer', *Notes and Queries*, 13 (1856), 247–8

Pre-1500

Bachrach, David, 'The *Ecclesia Anglicana* goes to war: prayers, propaganda and conquest during the reign of Edward I of England, 1272–1307, *Albion*, 36 (2004), 393–406

Burton, D. W., 'Requests for prayers and royal propaganda under Edward I', in *Thirteenth-Century England III*, ed. P. R. Coss and S. D. Lloyd (Woodbridge, 1991), pp. 25–35

Jones, W. R., 'The English church and royal propaganda during the hundred years war', *Journal of British Studies*, 19 (1979), 18–30

McHardy, A. K, 'Liturgy and propaganda in the diocese of Lincoln during the hundred years war', in *Religion and national identity*, ed. Stuart Mews (Studies in Church History, 18, Oxford, 1982), pp. 215–27

McHardy, A. K., 'Religious ritual and political persuasion: the case of England in the hundred years war', *International Journal of Moral and Social Studies*, 3 (1988), 41–57

McHardy, A. K., 'Some reflections on Edward III's use of propaganda', in *The Age of Edward III*, ed. J. S. Bothwell (York, 2001), pp. 171–89

Moyes, Mgr., 'War prayers in medieval England', *The Tablet*, 2 Jan. 1915, 5–6

Ruddick, Andrea, 'National sentiment and religious vocabulary in fourteenth-century England', *Journal of Ecclesiastical History*, 60 (2009), 1–18

Wright, J. Robin, *The church and the English crown, 1305–1334: a study based on the register of Archbishop Walter Reynolds* (Toronto, 1980)

Reformation to 1688

Álvarez-Recio, Leticia, 'English protestant sermons at moments of crisis: the threat of the Spanish Armada', in *War sermons*, ed. Gilles Teulié and Lawrence Lux-Sterrit (Newcastle-upon-Tyne, 2009), pp. 31–52

Barnard, T. C., 'The uses of 23 October 1641 and Irish protestant celebrations', *English Historical Review*, 106 (1991), 799–920

Bartel, Roland, 'The story of public fast days in England', *Anglican Theological Review,* 37 (1955), 190–200

Bates, Lucy-Ann, 'Nationwide fast and thanksgiving days in England, 1640–1660', Ph.D. dissertation, Durham University, 2012

Callahan, William A., 'War, shame, and time: pastoral governance and national identity in England and America', *International Studies Quarterly*, 50 (2006), 395–419

Cooper, J. P. D., 'O Lorde save the kynge: Tudor royal propaganda and the power of prayer', in *Authority and consent in Tudor England*, ed. G. W. Bernard and S. J. Gunn (Aldershot, 2000), pp. 179–96

Cooper, J. P. D., *Propaganda and the Tudor state: political culture in the west country* (Oxford, 2003)

Cressy, David, *Bonfires and bells. National memory and the protestant calendar in Elizabethan and Stuart England* (1989)

Cressy, David, 'The protestant calendar and the vocabulary of celebration in early modern England', *Journal of British Studies*, 29 (1990), 31–52

Cressy, David, 'The fifth of November remembered', in *The myths of the English*, ed. Roy Porter (Cambridge, 1992), pp. 68–90

Cressy, David, 'National memory in early modern England', in *Commemoration. The politics of national identity*, ed. J. R. Gillies (Princeton, 1994), pp. 61–73

Cressy, David, 'God's time, Rome's time, and the calendar of the English Protestant regime', *Viator*, 34 (2003), 392–406

Deconinck-Brossard, Françoise, 'Sermons commémorant la mort de Charles Iᵉʳ', *Confluences* (2000), 149–67

Durston, Christopher, '"For the better humiliation of the people": public days of fasting and thanksgiving during the English revolution', *Seventeenth Century*, 7 (1992), 129–49

Durston, Christopher, 'By the book or with the spirit: the debate over liturgical prayer during the English revolution', *Historical Research*, 79 (2006), 50–73

Eeles, F. C., 'The English thanksgiving service for King James' delivery from the Gowrie conspiracy', *Scottish Historical Review*, 8 (1911), 366–76

Gibney, John, 'Protestant interests? The 1641 rebellion and state formation in early modern Ireland', *Historical Research*, 64 (2011), 67–86

Guibbory, Achsah, 'Israel and English protestant nationalism: "fast sermons" during the English revolution', in *Early modern nationalism and Milton's England*, ed. David Loewenstein and Paul Stevens (Toronto, 2008), pp. 115–38

Hazlett, W. I. P., 'Playing God's card: Knox and fasting 1565–6', in *John Knox and the British reformations*, ed. Roger A. Mason (Aldershot, 1998), pp, 176–98

Hill, Christopher, *The English Bible and the seventeenth-century revolution* (1993), ch. 3, 'Fast sermons and politics'

Hindle, Steve, 'Dearth, fasting and alms: the campaign for general hospitality in late Elizabethan England', *Past and Present*, 172 (2001), 44–86

Hindle, Steve, 'Dearth and the English revolution: the harvest crisis of 1647–50', *Economic History Review*, 61: supplement 1 (2008), 64–98

Hudson, Withrop S., 'Fast days and civil religion', in *Theology in sixteenth- and seventeenth-century England*, ed. W. S. Hudson and L. J. Trinterud (Los Angeles, 1971), pp. 3–23

Hutton, Ronald. *The rise and fall of merry England. The ritual year, 1400–1700* (Oxford, 1994)

Jorgenson, P. A., 'Elizabethan religious literature for time of war', *Huntington Library Quarterly*, 37 (1973), 1–17

Kelly, James, '"The glorious and immortal memory": commemoration and protestant identity in Ireland 1660–1800', *Proceedings of the Royal Irish Academy*, 94C (1994), 25–52

Kitching, C. J., '"Prayers fit for the time": fasting and prayer in response to national crises in the reign of Elizabeth I', in *Monks, hermits and the ascetic tradition*, ed. W. J. Sheils (Studies in Church History, 22, Oxford, 1985), pp. 241–50

Lacey, Andrew, 'The office for King Charles the martyr in the Book of Common Prayer, 1662–85', *Journal of Ecclesiastical History*, 53 (2002), 510–26

Lacey, Andrew, *The cult of King Charles the Martyr* (Woodbridge, 2003)

Lacey, Andrew, '"Charles the first and Christ the second": the creation of a political martyr', in *Martyrs and martyrdom in England c. 1400–1700*, ed. T. S. Freeman and T. F. Mayer (Woodbridge, 2007), pp. 203–20

Mears, Natalie, 'Brought to book: special book purchases in English parishes, 1558–1640', in *Negotiating the Jacobean printed book*, ed. Pete Langman (Farnham, 2011), pp. 29–44

Mears, Natalie, 'Public worship and political participation in Elizabethan England', *Journal of British Studies*, 51 (2012), 4–25

Mears, Natalie, 'Special nationwide worship and the Book of Common Prayer in England, Wales and Ireland, 1533–1642', in *Worship and the parish church in early modern Britain*, ed. Natalie Mears and Alec Ryrie (Farnham, 2013), pp. 31–72

Napthine, D. and W. A. Speck, 'Clergymen and conflict 1660–1763', in *The church and war*, ed. W. J. Shiels (Studies in Church History, 20, 1983), pp. 231–51

Nash, N. Frederick, 'Fast-day sermons for the House of Lords in the Long parliament', *Bulletin of Bibliography*, 42 (1985), 203–14

Neale, J. E., 'November 17th', in *idem, Essays in Elizabethan history* (1958), pp. 9–20

Potter, Lois, 'The royal martyr in the restoration: national grief and national sin', in *The royal image. Representations of Charles I*, ed. Thomas Corns (Cambridge, 1999), pp. 240–62

Prestige, G. L., 'November the fifth', *Theology*, 32 (1936), 357–66

Raffe, Alasdair, 'Nature's scourges: the natural world and special prayers, fasts and thanksgivings, 1543–1866', in *God's bounty? The churches and the natural world*, ed. Peter Clarke and Tony Claydon (Studies in Church History, 46, Woodbridge, 2010), pp. 237–47

Ryrie, Alec, 'The fall and rise of fasting in the British reformations', in *Worship and the parish church in early modern Britain*, ed. Natalie Mears and Alec Ryrie (Farnham, 2013), pp. 89–108

Sansom, Michael C., 'Liturgical responses to (natural) disaster in seventeenth-century England', *Studia Liturgica*, 19 (1989), 179–96

Stewart, Bryon S., 'The cult of the royal martyr', *Church History*, 38 (1969), 175–87

Streatfield, Frank, *The state prayers and other variations in the Book of Common Prayer* (London and Oxford, 1950)

Strong, Roy, 'The popular celebration of the accession day of Queen Elizabeth I,' *Journal of the Warburg and Courtauld Institutes*, 21 (1958), 86–103

Tomlinson, H., 'Commemorating Charles I – king and martyr?', *History Today*, 45:2 (1995), 11–18

Trevor-Roper, Hugh, 'The fast sermons of the Long parliament', in *idem, Religion, the reformation and social change* (1967), pp. 294–344

Walsham, Alexandra, *Providence in early modern England* (Oxford, 1999)

Wilson, J. F., *Pulpit in parliament. Puritanism during the English civil wars 1640–1648* (Princeton, 1969)

Analytical List of Particular Occasions of Special Worship, 1533–2012

KEY

? indicates unknown or uncertain matters, due to fragmentary or ambiguous evidence.

Code

See the Reader's Guide, pp. xxv–xxvi.

Date(s)

The date(s) of observance, with conventional abbreviations for months.

after: refers to the date of the order, indicating that the start of the observance is unknown

asap: as soon as possible

from: the date of the first known observance, indicating when the observance was to occur for a period or when the precise further dates of observance are uncertain

various: differing dates, decided upon by each regional or local authority (for example, in Scotland dates settled by individual presbyteries)

Day(s)

Days of the week: Mon., Tu., Wed., Th., Fr., Sat., Sun.

Area(s)

Canterbury	the province of Canterbury
E	England (used in this list only after the disestablishment of the Church in Wales in 1920)
E&W	England and Wales (used until the disestablishment of the Church in Wales in 1920)
Edinburgh	indicates observance within the burgh
Edinburgh area	'area' includes various contemporary formulations, e.g. 'Edinburgh and Lothian'; precise designations are given in the headings for relevant occasions
Dublin	refers to the city
Dublin area	'area' includes various contemporary formulations, e.g. 'Dublin, suburbs and adjoining liberties'; precise designations are given in the headings for relevant occasions

Ir	Ireland (used until the disestablishment of the Church of Ireland in 1871)
lines	'lines of communication': the area within a series of twenty-three fortifications which parliament ordered to be built during the civil wars of the 1640s to protect London and its environs from attack
London	refers to the City of London
London area	'area' includes various contemporary formulations, e.g. 'London and Westminster', 'London and within the bills of mortality'; precise designations are given in the headings for relevant occasions
S	Scotland
UK	the United Kingdom, used from 1915 for occasions arranged by co-ordination between leaders of the main churches (not just the established churches) both in England and Wales and in Scotland (and sometimes Ireland, and from 1921 Northern Ireland), and which were observed by all or nearly all churches, including those of Ireland, and from 1921 Northern Ireland

Description

The type of special worship. There was some variation in type and description, particularly before the 1560s, during the 1640s and 1650s, and during the twentieth century, but the principal types were as follows:

>   fast day/s
>   prayer/s
>   service/s (or thanksgiving service/s): used for occasions which were not ordered to be observed as special holy 'days', but when special services (in E&W and Ir with printed liturgies) were nevertheless to be held
>   thanksgiving day/s
>   thanksgiving prayer/s

A singular description (fast day, prayer, etc.) is used when the special occasion was ordered for one specified date and for all places of worship within one area (e.g. one date for the whole of E&W).

Plural descriptions (fast days, prayers, etc.) are used when the special occasion was to be repeated on successive specified dates; or for a specified or unspecified period (days, weeks, months); or when the occasion was to be held on different dates in different areas (e.g. one date for the London area, and a different date for elsewhere in E&W).

Cause

A summary description of the main cause or purpose of the appointment, given in a modernized form. The contemporary phrases (which typically contain much religious phraseology) will be found in the printed text of the orders (e.g., a proclamation).

CODE	DATE(S)	DAY(S)	AREA(S)	DESCRIPTION	CAUSE
1533–E	8 Sept.	Mon.	St Paul's Cathedral	thanksgiving service	birth of Princess Elizabeth
1535–E	12 Nov.	Fr.	St Paul's Cathedral	procession	recovery from illness of Francis I of France
1537–E1	27 May	Sun.	St Paul's Cathedral	*Te Deums*	pregnancy of Queen Jane
1537–E2	11 + 12 Oct.	Th. + Fr.	London	processions, *Te Deums*	birth of Prince Edward
1537–E3	19 Oct.	Fr.	London	processions	health of Queen Jane and Prince Edward
1537–E4	12 Nov.	Mon.	St Paul's Cathedral	dirges	death of Queen Jane
1540–E	from Sept.	weekly	E&W	prayers & processions	drought & disease
1541–E	after 20 May to Sept.	?	E&W	prayers	severe drought
1543–E1	after 19 July	?	Canterbury	prayers	Ottoman invasion of Hungary
1543–E2	after 23 Aug. to Sept.	?	Canterbury	prayers & processions	wet weather and threat to the harvest
1544–E1	23 May	Fr.	St Paul's Cathedral	thanksgiving service	victories in Scotland
1544–E2	after 8 June to Sept.	?	Canterbury	services & processions	military campaign in France
1544–E3	20 Sept. and after	Sat. +	E	thanksgiving services	victory at Boulogne
1544–E4	3 Oct.	Fr.	St Paul's Cathedral	*Te Deums* & procession	Henry VIII's return from military in France
1545–E1	after 10 Aug.	?	E&W	processions	naval campaign against France
1545–E2	23 or 24 Sept.	Wed. or Th.	St Paul's Cathedral	thanksgiving, procession	victories in Scotland and relief of Boulogne
1546–E	13 June	Sun.	St Paul's Cathedral	thanksgiving processions	peace with France
1547–E	20 Dec. after 20 Dec.	Tu. next holy day	St Paul's Cathedral Canterbury	thanksgiving service, *Te Deums* & procession	victory at the battle of Pinkie
1548–E	May, July	Sun. + holy days	E&W	prayers	victory and peace in the Scottish war
1549–E	21 July	Sun.	St Paul's Cathedral	service	Western and Kett's rebellions
1550–E	30 Mar.	Sun.	Paul's Cross	*Te Deums*	peace with France
1551–E	after 18 June–Oct.	?	E&W?	services	sweating sickness
1553–E1	June–July	?	Chapel Royal + possibly elsewhere	prayers	illness of Edward VI
1553–E2	8 Dec. after 8 Dec.	Fr. Wed., Fr., Sun.	St Paul's Cathedral London diocese	processions	bad weather

Code	Date	Days	Place	Type of service	Occasion
1554-E1	8 Feb.	?	London	*Te Deums*	failure of Wyatt's rebellion
1554-E2	22 + 23 July	Sun. + Mon.	London	*Te Deums* & processions	arrival of Prince Philip of Spain
1554-E3	27 Nov. to July 1555	?	E&W	services	Queen Mary's [supposed] pregnancy
1555-E1	25 Jan. / Jan. or Feb.?	Fri. / ?	St Paul's Cathedral / rest of E&W	thanksgiving services	reconciliation with the Church of Rome
1555-E2	after 23 May to June	?	Canterbury	prayers	for peace between France and the Empire, and for the election of the pope
1557-E1	c. 15 Aug.	Sun.	St Paul's Cathedral	thanksgiving service & procession	victory at St Quentin
1557-E2	19 Sept.	Sun.	London	*Te Deums* & procession	victory at Péronne
1560-E	after 8 July	daily, or three times a week	Canterbury	services & fast days	for better weather, and success in public affairs
1560-S	19 July?	Fr.?	St Giles's Church, Edinburgh	thanksgiving prayer	peace treaty of Edinburgh and success of the reformation
1562-E1	after 9 Oct.	?	E	prayers	military campaign in France, in support of the Huguenots
1562-E2	18 Oct.	Sun.	Paul's Cross, London	thanksgiving prayers	Elizabeth I's recovery from smallpox
1563-E	from Aug., during the epidemic	Wed., Fr., Sun.	E&W	services & weekly fast days	plague epidemic
1564-E	from 26 Jan.?	Wed., Fr., Sun.	London diocese & elsewhere	thanksgiving services	decline or end of the plague
1565-E1	July?	Wed., Fr.	London, Norwich & Salisbury dioceses	services	Ottoman siege of Malta
1565-E2	late Oct., for 6 weeks	Wed., Fr., Sun.	Canterbury	thanksgiving services	relief of Malta, and other Christian victories over the Ottomans
1566-S1	23 Feb.–3 Mar.	Sun. + week	S	fast days	perceived threats to the reformed church
1566-E	July–Aug.	Wed., Fr., Sun.	E&W	services	Ottoman invasion of Hungary
1566-S2	28 July–4 Aug.	Sun. + week	S	fast days	perceived threats to the reformed church
1567-S1	11–18 May	Sun. + week	S	fast days	[unknown]
1567-S2	13–20 July	Sun. + week	Edinburgh	fast days	consolidation of the reformation

ID	Date	Days	Region	Service	Occasion
1569-S	13–20 Mar.; when convenient	Sun. + week; Sun. + week	Lothian, Fife, &c; rest of S	fast days	[unknown]
1570-E	Jan. onwards?	?	E&W?	thanksgiving services	suppression of the Northern Rising
1571-E	9 Nov.	Fr.	London area	thanksgiving prayers	christian victory over the Ottoman fleet at the battle of Lepanto
1572-E	from 30 Oct.	Wed., Fr., Sun., holy days	Canterbury	services	catholic threat, after the St Bartholomew's day massacre
1572-S	23–30 Nov.	Sun. + week	S	fast days	catholic threat, after the St Bartholomew's day massacre
1577-S	9–16 July	Sun. + week	S	fast days	defence of protestantism across Europe, and in support of continued reformation
1578-S	1–8 June	Sun. + week	S	fast days	sinfulness, famine and threats to the church in Scotland, and to support good government
1580-E	after 23 Apr.	Wed., Fr., Sun.	E&W	services; prayers	London earthquake
1582-S	3–10 June	Sun. + week	S	fast days	catholic conspiracies, the church's financial difficulties, increasing sinfulness, fears about the king's religion, and oppression of the poor
1583-S	8–15 Dec.	Sun. + week	S	fast days	[unknown]
1585-E1	[Feb.–Mar.]	?	E&W?	thanksgiving services	failure of the Parry plot
1585-E2	unknown	Fr., Sun.	London diocese & possibly elsewhere	prayers	bad weather and sinfulness
1586-E1	[May–Jan. 1587?]	Wed., Fr.	E&W	services	dearth
1586-E2	after 24 Aug.	daily	E&W	thanksgiving services	failure of the Babington plot
1586-E3	after 3 Dec.	daily	E&W	prayers & fasting	dangers and plots
1587-S	Jan.–Feb.	daily	S?	prayers	safety of Queen Mary
1587-E	[Feb.–Aug.?]	daily	E&W	thanksgiving services	security of the church and realm
1588-S1	7–14 July	Sun. + week	S	fast days	catholic conspiracies, apostasy, the church's difficulties and sinfulness
1588-E1	after 10 July to Aug.	daily	E&W	services	threat of Spanish invasion
1588-S2	7–11 Aug.; 11 Aug.	Wed. – Sun.; Sun.	Edinburgh; S where possible	prayers & fast days	threat of Spanish invasion

Code	Date	Day	Location	Service	Occasion
1588–S3	19, 20, 27 Oct., 3 Nov.	Sat., then Sun.	S	thanksgiving days	defeat of the Spanish armada
1588–E2	19 Nov.	Tu.	E&W	thanksgiving day	defeat of the Spanish armada
1589–Ir	26 Jan.? before 12 Feb.	Wed. ?	Dublin elsewhere	thanksgiving days	defeat of the Spanish armada
1589–E	after 3 May	thrice weekly	E&W	prayers	naval expedition to Portugal and the Azores
1589–S	Oct.–Apr. 1590, weekly	Sun.	Edinburgh & probably elsewhere	weekly fast days	James VI's return from Denmark
1590–E1	after 6 Mar.	thrice weekly	Canterbury	services	threat of Spanish invasion
1590–E2	[Apr.–Aug.?]	?	E&W	prayers	for the success of Henry IV of France
1591–S	2 May	Sun.	Edinburgh & possibly elsewhere	fast day	alleged conspiracies of the earl of Bothwell and the North Berwick witches
1592–S	17 + 24 Dec.	Sun.	S	fast days	catholic conspiracies, religious indifference, apostasy and sinfulness
1593–S1	13 Feb.	Sun.	Edinburgh & possibly elsewhere	fast day	James VI's success against catholic conspiracies
1593–E	from July	Wed., Fr., Sun., holy days	London & probably elsewhere	services & weekly fast days	plague epidemic
1593–S2	21 Oct.	Sun.	S	fast day	threats to the reformed church and to James VI
1594–S1	19 Feb.	Tu.	Edinburgh & possibly elsewhere	thanksgiving service	birth of Prince Henry
1594–E	[Mar.]	?	E&W	thanksgiving services	failure of plots against Elizabeth I and her realm
1594–S2	26 May	Sun.	Edinburgh & if possible elsewhere	fast day	meeting of parliament
1594–S3	23–30 June	Sun. + week	S	fast days	[unknown]
1595–S	3–10 Aug.	Sun. + week	S	fast days	general troubles
1596–S1	1 + 3 Feb.	Sun. + Tu.	S	fast days	threats of Spanish invasion and continued dearth
1596–E1	June	Wed., Fr., Sun., festival days	Canterbury	prayers	naval and military campaign against Spain
1596–E2	Aug.	?	London	thanksgiving prayer	victories at Cadiz and Faro
1596–S2	5 Dec.	Sun.	S	fast day	religious tension

1596–E3	after 27 Dec.	Wed., Fr.	E&W	prayers & fasting	dearth
1597–E	after 11 July	?	E&W	prayers	naval expedition against Spain
1598–E	Nov.?	?	E&W	thanksgiving services	failure of plots against Elizabeth I and her realm
1599–E	after 2 Apr.	?	E&W	prayer	military campaign in Ireland
1600–S	30 Sept. + 5 Oct.	Tu. + Sun.	S	thanksgiving days	discovery of the Gowrie plot
1601–E	after 8 Feb.	?	E&W	thanksgiving prayers	failure of the earl of Essex's rebellion
1601–S	21–8 June	Sun. + week	S	fast days	general sinfulness
1602–E	Jan.	?	E&W	thanksgiving prayers	victory at the battle of Kinsale
1603–E	from Apr.?	Wed., Fr., Sun.	E&W	services & weekly fast days	plague epidemic
1604–E	late autumn/winter?	Wed., Fr., Sun.	E&W	thanksgiving services	decline of the plague
1605–E1	Jan.–Mar.?	?	E&W?	prayers	pregnancy of Queen Anna
1605–E2	after 8 Apr.	?	E&W?	thanksgiving prayers	birth of Princess Mary
1605–E3	after 8 Nov.	daily	E&W	thanksgiving services	discovery of the gunpowder plot
1606–E	Jan.–May?	?	E&W?	prayers	pregnancy of Queen Anna
1611–E	?	?	E&W?	services	drought
1613–E	?	?	E&W?	services	heavy rain and threats to the harvest
1621–S	24 June–1 July	Sun. + week	S	fast days	anxieties over contempt of religion, safety of the royal family, the Ottoman threat and persecution of German and French protestants
1622–S	12–19 May	Sun. + week	Edinburgh	fast days	anxieties over sinfulness, dearth, and threats to French, German and Bohemian protestants
1623–S1	29 June–6 July	Sun. + week	S	fast days	famine, and anxieties over idolatry and Prince Charles's proposed marriage
1623–S2	13 Oct.	Mon.	Edinburgh	thanksgiving service	Prince Charles's return from Spain
1625–E	20 July + weekly	Wed.	E&W	weekly fast days	plague epidemic, and for Charles I, his realm and their forces
1625–S	from July, weekly	Sun. + Wed.	S	weekly fast days	plague in London, the armed forces and an abundant harvest
1625–Ir	from Oct., weekly	Wed.	Ir	weekly fast days	plague in England

				thanksgiving days [& services?]	
1626-E1	29 Jan. + ?	Sun. [+ Wed., Fr.?]	London area	fast days	decline of the plague
	19 Feb. + ?	Sun. [+ Wed., Fr.?]	rest of E&W		
1626-E2	5 July	Wed.	London area	fast days	war with Spain, and continuing plague
	2 Aug.	Wed.	rest of E&W		
1626-E3	after 21 Sept.	?	Canterbury	prayers	war, plague and for Christian IV of Denmark
1627-E	June?	daily	E&W	prayers	English and allied military and naval campaigns against France
1627-S	8 + 12 Aug.	Wed. + Sun.	S	fast days	increasing popery, persecution of continental protestants, war against France and fears of famine
1628-E1	5 Apr.	Sat.	London area	fast days	war against France and persecution of protestants in Europe
	21 Apr.	Mon.	rest of E&W		
1628-S	18–25 May	Sun. + week	S	fast days	persecuted protestants in continental Europe, anxieties about general sinfulness and for success in the war against France
1628-Ir	May–July?	?	Ir?	weekly fast days	war, cattle disease and fears of famine and plague
1628-E2	after 22 Aug. to Sept.	?	E&W	prayers	naval expedition against France
1628-E3	autumn 1628–spring 1629	?	E&W	prayers	pregnancy of Queen Henrietta Maria
1629-E	18 Feb.	Wed.	London area	fast days	preservation of Charles I, his realm and his allies and the protestants of Europe
	20 Mar.	Fr.	rest of E&W		
1630-E1	after 2 Jan.	?	E&W	prayers	pregnancy of Queen Henrietta Maria
1630-E2	June	?	E&W	thanksgiving prayer	birth of Prince Charles
1630-S	June	?	S	thanksgiving prayer	birth of Prince Charles
1630-Ir	15 July	Th.	Dublin & possibly elsewhere Ir	thanksgiving day	birth of Prince Charles
1631-E1	?	?	E&W	prayers	pregnancy of Queen Henrietta Maria
1631-E2	Nov.	?	E&W	thanksgiving prayer	birth of Princess Mary
1632-E	Dec.	?	E&W	thanksgiving prayer	recovery of Charles I from illness
1633-E1	after 31 May	?	E&W	prayers	pregnancy of Queen Henrietta Maria
1633-E2	Oct.	?	E&W	thanksgiving prayer	birth of Prince James
1635-E	?	?	E&W	prayers	pregnancy of Queen Henrietta Maria

Code	Date	Day	Place	Type	Occasion
1636-E1	Jan.	?	E&W	thanksgiving prayer	birth of Princess Elizabeth
1636-E2	?	?	E&W	prayers	pregnancy of Queen Henrietta Maria
1636-E3	from Oct., weekly	Wed.	E&W	weekly fast days	plague epidemic
1637-S	Mar.	?	Edinburgh & possibly elsewhere	thanksgiving prayer	birth of Princess Anne
1638-S1	7 Nov.	Wed.	S	fast day	for success of the general assembly and an end to divisions
1638-S2	after 20 Dec.	Sun.	S	thanksgiving	achievements of the general assembly
1639-E	Apr.	?	E&W	prayers	Charles I's military campaign to Scotland
1639-S	10 Nov.	Sun.	S	fast day	general evils, and for the general assembly and parliament
1640-S1	10 + 12 Apr.	Fr. + Sun.	S	fast days	general evils, shortage of ministers and the failure of parliament and the peace negotiations
1640-E1	8 July	Wed.	E&W	fast day	to avert plague and war
1640-S2	23 + 27 Aug.	Sun. + Th.	S	fast days	preparations for war with England
1640-E2	after 8 July?	?	E&W	prayers	Charles I's military campaign against the Scottish covenanters
1640-E3	17 Nov.	Tu.	London area	fast days	plague, war and momentous public affairs
	8 Dec.	Tu.	rest of E&W		
1641-ES	7 Sept.	Tu.	E&W, S	thanksgiving day	peace treaty of London
1641-S	14 Nov.	Sun.	Edinburgh etc.	fast days	domestic divisions, the Irish rebellion and distress of continental protestants, for the success of the Scottish and English parliaments, and for the security of the church
	28 Nov.	Sun.	rest of S		
1641-Ir	from Dec., weekly	Fr.	Ir	weekly fast days	rebellion
1641-E	22 Dec.	Wed.	London	monthly fast days	Irish rebellion [continued after suppression of the rebellion: until Nov. 1643 in royalist areas – see 1643–E11(R); until Apr. 1649 in parliamentary areas – see 1649–E2]
	23 Dec.	Th.	Westminster		
	20 Jan. 1642	Th.	rest of E&W		
	23 Feb. + last Wed. each month	Wed.	E&W		
1642-Ir1	from May, each month	Fr.	Dublin area	monthly fast days	Irish rebellion

Code	Date	Day	Region	Type	Description
1642–S	11 + 14 Sept.	Sun. + Wed.	S	fast days	ignorance, wickedness, Irish rebellion, English divisions, and for religious unity and a good harvest
1642–E1(R)	[Nov.]	?	E&W	thanksgiving prayer	royalist victory at the battle of Edgehill
1642–Ir2	after 28 Oct. to Nov.	?	Ir	thanksgiving day	anniversary of failure of the Irish rebellion
1642–E2(P)	18 Dec.	Sun.	London area	thanksgiving prayers	parliamentarian victory at Winchester
1643–E1(P)	8 Jan.	Sun.	London area	thanksgiving prayers	parliamentarian victory at Chichester
1643–E2(P)	5 Feb.	Sun.	E&W	thanksgiving prayers	parliamentarian victory at Leeds
1643–S1	26 Feb. + 2 Mar.	Sun. + Th.	S	fast days	declining zeal, catholic threats, persecution of continental protestants, union between Scotland and England
1643–E3(P)	19 Mar.	Sun.	London area	thanksgiving prayers	failure of royalist plot in Bristol
1643–E4(P)	30 Apr.	Sun.	London area	thanksgiving prayers	parliamentarian capture of Reading
1643–E5(P)	28 May	Sun.	London area	thanksgiving prayers	parliamentarian capture of Wakefield
1643–S2	11 + 14 June	Sun. + Wed.	S	fast days	declining zeal, catholic threats, persecution of continental protestants, union between Scotland and England
1643–E6(P)	15 June	Th.	London area	thanksgiving days	discovery of plot against parliament
	11 July	Tu.	rest of E&W		
1643–E7(P)	21 July	Fr.	London area	day of humiliation	parliamentarian defeats in north and west
1643–E8(P)	17 Sept.	Sun.	London area	thanksgiving prayers	parliamentarian relief of Gloucester
1643–E9(P)	24 Sept.	Sun.	London area	thanksgiving prayers	parliamentarian successes at Gloucester and the first battle of Newbury
1643–E10(R)	after 9 Oct.	?	E&W?	thanksgiving prayer	royalist success at the first battle of Newbury
1643–S3	8 Oct.	Sun.	S	fast day	dangers to church and kingdom
1643–E11(R)	second Fr. every month from 10 Nov.	Fr.	E&W	monthly fast days	for success of the royalist cause
1644–S1	7 + 10 Jan.	Sun. + Wed.	S	fast days	ungodliness, dangers to church and kingdom and for success in England
1644–E1(P)	21 Jan.	Sun.	E&W	thanksgiving day	discovery of a plot against parliament and London
1644–E2(P)	4 Feb.	Sun.	London area	thanksgiving prayers	Scottish assistance, victory at Nantwich and relief of Nottingham
1644–S2	Feb.–Mar.	Wed.	S	fast day	poor condition of the Scottish army in England

ID	Date	?	E&W		Occasion
1644-E3(R)	[Mar.]	?	E&W	thanksgiving service	royalist victory at Newark and the queen's pregnancy
1644-E4(P)	9 Apr.	Tu.	London area	thanksgiving days	parliamentarian victory at the battle of Cheriton
	14 Apr.	Sun.	rest of E&W south of the Trent		
	28 Apr.	Sun.	rest of E&W north of the Trent		
1644-E5(P)	23 Apr.	Tu.	London area	thanksgiving day	parliamentarian victories at Selby, York and in Pembrokeshire
1644-E6(P)	23 June	Sun.	London area	thanksgiving prayers	parliamentarian relief of Lyme
1644-S3	7 + 11 July	Sun. + Th.	S	fast days	anxieties for the Scottish army in England
1644-E7(P)	18 July	Th.	London area	thanksgiving days	parliamentarian and Scottish victory at the battle of Marston Moor
	25 July	Th.	rest of E&W		
1644-S4	July	various	S	thanksgiving days	Scottish and parliamentarian victory at the battle of Marston Moor
1644-E8(P)	13 Aug.	Tu.	6 churches in London area	fast day	safety of the parliamentarian army in Cornwall
1644-E9(P)	12 Sept.	Th.	London area	fast & day of humiliation	parliamentarian defeat at Lostwithiel
1644-E10(P)	22 Oct.	Tu.	lines	fast & day of humiliation	for the parliamentarian armies
1644-E11(P)	27 Oct.	Sun.	London area	thanksgiving service	Scottish capture of Newcastle
1644-S5	27 + 30 Oct.	Sun. + Wed.	S	fast days	anxieties over the church, civil discord and military defeats
1644-E12(P)	30 Oct. + 5 Nov.	W + Tu.	lines	thanksgiving days	Scottish victory at Newcastle, parliamentarian victories at the second battle of Newbury, at Liverpool, in Lincolnshire and at Tynemouth
1644-S6	Nov.–Dec.	various	S	thanksgiving days	capture of Newcastle
1645-S1	5 Jan.	Sun.	S	fast day	for the meetings of parliament and the general assembly
1645-E1(R)	5 Feb.	Wed.	E&W	fast day	during peace negotiations at Uxbridge
1645-E2(P)	12 Mar.	Wed.	lines	thanksgiving day	parliamentarian victories at Weymouth, Shrewsbury, Scarborough, Plymouth and Lancaut
1645-S2	26 Mar.	Wed.	S	fast day	defeat by Montrose's forces
1645-E3(P)	20 Apr.	Sun.	lines	thanksgiving prayers	Montrose's retreat from Dundee

ID	Date	Day	Area	Type	Occasion
1645–E4(P)	18 May	Sun.	lines	thanksgiving prayers	parliamentarian success at Taunton
1645–S3	1 June	Sun.	S	fast day	Montrose's military advances
1645–E5(P)	19 June 27 June	Th. Fr.	London area counties under parliamentarian control	thanksgiving days	parliamentarian victory at the battle of Naseby
1645–S4	3 July	Th.	S	fast day	defeat at Auldearn, plague epidemic
1645–E6(P)	1 July	Tu.	London area	prayers	for parliamentarian forces in the south-west
1645–E7(P)	22 July	Tu.	E&W	thanksgiving day	parliamentarian victory at the battle of Langport, London's freedom from plague
1645–S5	26 + 27 July	Sat. + Sun.	S	fast days	gathering of the troops at Perth, and for the success of parliament
1645–E8(P)	27 July	Sun.	lines	thanksgiving prayers	parliamentarian victories at Bridgwater, Scarborough and Pontefract
1645–E9(P)	22 Aug.	Fr.	London area	thanksgiving day	parliamentarian victories, esp. at Bath, Bridgwater, Sherborne, in Pembrokeshire and Scottish victory at Canon Frome
1645–E10(R)	7 Sept.	Sun.	Hereford and possibly elsewhere	thanksgiving prayers	royalist relief of Hereford
1645–E11(P)	5 Sept. 19 Sept.	Fr. Fr.	lines 'parliament's quarters'	days of humiliation	Scottish defeats, Fairfax's army and cessation of plague
1645–E12(P)	21 Sept. 5 Oct.	Sun. Sun.	London area rest of E&W	thanksgiving prayers	parliamentarian victory at Bristol, Scottish victory at the battle of Philiphaugh
1645–S6	Sept.– Oct.	?	S	thanksgiving day	victory at the battle of Philiphaugh
1645–E13(P)	2 Oct. 16 Oct.	Th. Th.	London area rest of E&W	thanksgiving days	parliamentarian victories, esp. at Chester, Bristol, Devizes and in Pembrokeshire, Scottish victory at the battle of Philiphaugh
1645–E14(P)	19 Oct.	Sun.	London area	thanksgiving prayers	parliamentarian victories at Worcester, Basing House and Chepstow
1645–E15(P)	26 Oct. 9 Nov.	Sun. Sun.	lines rest of E&W	thanksgiving days	parliamentarian victories at Sherburn and Tiverton, and in Wales
1645–S7	Nov.		S	fast days	general sinfulness
1645–E16(P)	2 Nov.	Sun.	London area	thanksgiving prayers	parliamentarian victories at Carmarthen and Monmouth

Code	Date	Day	Location	Occasion	Cause
1645–E17(P)	5 Nov.	Wed.	London area	thanksgiving prayers	fifth anniversary of the Long parliament, and parliamentarian victories at Sherburn, Carlisle and Denbigh
1645–E18(P)	14 Dec.	Sun.	London area	thanksgiving prayers	parliamentarian victory at Lathom House
1645–E19(P)	28 Dec.	Sun.	lines	thanksgiving prayers	parliamentarian capture of Hereford
1646–E1(P)	5 Feb. / 12 Feb.	Th. / Th.	London area / rest of E&W	thanksgiving days	parliamentarian victory at Dartmouth
1646–S1	5 Feb.	Th.	S	fast day	measures against Montrose's supporters
1646–E2(P)	19 Feb. / 5 Mar.	Th. / Th.	London area / rest of E&W	thanksgiving days	parliamentarian victories at Chester and Torrington
1646–E3(P)	12 Mar.	Th.	London area	thanksgiving day	parliamentarian victories at Torrington and Cardiff
1646–E4(P)	2 Apr. / 16 Apr.	Th. / Th.	London area / rest of E&W	thanksgiving days	Fairfax's victories in the south-west, and the parliamentarian victory at Stow
1646–S2	30 Apr.	Th.	S	fast day	fears of continued rebellion
1646–E5(P)	12 May / 19 May	Tu. / Tu.	London area / rest of E&W	thanksgiving days	parliamentarian victories in the south-west and in Wales
1646–E6(P)	14 June	Sun.	London area	thanksgiving prayers	parliamentarian victories in the west
1646–S3	9 July	Th.	S	fast day	defeat of the Scottish army at the battle of Benburb in Ireland
1646–E7(P)	21 July	Tu.	London area	thanksgiving days	parliamentarian victories at Oxford, Farringdon, Anglesey and Lichfield
1646–E8(P)	8 Sept. / 22 Sept.	Tu. / Tu.	London area / rest of E&W	thanksgiving day	parliamentarian victories at Worcester, Wallingford, Ruthin, Raglan and Pendennis
1646–S4	20 Sept. or first Sunday	Sun.	S	fast day	general sinfulness, peace negotiations, Montrose's rising, defeat in Ireland and a for good harvest
1646–S5	13 Nov.	Fr.	Edinburgh	fast day	support for parliament
1646–E9(P)	9 Dec. / 23 Dec.	Wed. / Wed.	London area / rest of E&W	days of humiliation	heavy rain and floods
1647–E1(P)	10 Mar.	Wed.	E&W	day of humiliation	religious errors, heresies and blasphemies
1647–S1	4 Apr. or first Sun.	Sun.	S	fast day	campaign against royalists in northern Scotland
1647–S2	25 July	Sun.	S	fast day	for the general assembly, against English sectaries, for the king and for parliament

Code	Date	Day	Place	Type	Description
1647–E2(P)	31 Aug. 7 Sept.	Tu. Tu.	London area rest or E&W	thanksgiving days	victory at the battle of Dungan's Hill, Ireland
1647–S3	26 Sept.	Sun.	S	thanksgiving day	victory in Argyll, resistance to English religious independents, relief from plague
1647–S4	31 Oct.	Sun.	S	fast day	plague, English religious independents and other troubles
1647–E3(P)	5 Dec. 19 Dec.	Sun. Sun.	London area rest of E&W	thanksgiving prayers	parliamentarian victory in Munster
1648–S1	21 Feb.	Sun.	Edinburgh	fast day	negotiations over the Engagement with Charles I
1648–S2	12 Mar.	Sun.	Edinburgh area	fast day	parliament's consideration of the Engagement
1648–E1(P)	16 Apr.	Sun.	lines	thanksgiving prayers	end of London riots
1648–E2(P)	17 May	Wed.	London area	thanksgiving days	parliamentarian victory at the battle of St Fagan's
1648–S3	28 May	Sun.	S	fast day	divisions over the Engagement
1648–E3(P)	4 June	Sun.	London area	thanksgiving prayers	parliamentarian victory at Maidstone
1648–E4(P)	18 June	Sun.	London area	thanksgiving prayers	parliamentarian victories in Kent
1648–S4	29 June + 2 July	Th. + Sun.	S	fast days	protest against the Engagement and campaign against the English parliament
1648–E5(P)	9 July	Sun.	London area	thanksgiving prayers	parliamentarian victories at Cartington and Willoughby Field
1648–E6(P)	19 July	Wed.	London area	thanksgiving day	recent parliamentarian victories
1648–E7(P)	9 Aug.	Wed.	E&W	thanksgiving day	further parliamentarian victories
1648–E8(P)	10 Aug.	Th.	London area	day of humiliation	heavy rain and threats to the harvest
1648–E9(P)	7 Sept.	Th.	E&W	thanksgiving day	parliamentarian victories at the battle of Preston and at Colchester
1648–S5	10 Sept.	Sun.	S	fast day	general assembly protest against invasion of England
1648–E10(P)	12 Sept.	Tu.	London area	day of humiliation	peace negotiations between parliament and the king at Newport
1648–E11(P)	1 Oct.	Sun.	London area	thanksgiving prayers	parliamentarian victories at Carrickfergus, Belfast and Coleraine
1648–E12(P)	8 Oct.	Sun.	London area	thanksgiving prayers	parliamentarian victories in Anglesey
1648–S6	14 + 17 Dec.	Th. + Sun.	S	fast days	renewal of the Solemn League and Covenant
1649–S1	22 Feb.	Th.	S	fast day	execution of Charles I and accession of Charles II

Code	Date	Day	Location	Type	Description
1649–E1	19 Apr.	Th.	E&W	fast day	establishment of the Commonwealth
1649–E2	3 May	Th.	London area	fast days	end of monthly fasts, ending of divisions,
	17 May	Th.	rest of E&W		Commonwealth campaign in Ireland
1649–S2	25 May	Fr.	S	thanksgiving day	victory against royalists at Balvenie
1649–E3	7 June	Th.	London area	thanksgiving days	suppression of the Levellers, and naval success
	28 June	Th.	rest of E&W		
1649–E4	11 July	Wed.	London area	fast days	Commonwealth campaign in Ireland
	1 Aug.	Wed.	rest of E&W		
1649–S3	26 Aug.	Sun.	S	fast day	anxieties over witchcraft, threats in England and Ireland, Charles II's policies and the harvest
1649–E5	29 Aug.	Wed.	E&W	thanksgiving day	Commonwealth victory at the battle of Rathmines, Ireland
1649–E6	1 Nov.	Th.	E&W	thanksgiving day	Commonwealth victories in Ireland
1649–Ir	24 Nov.	Sat.	Ir	thanksgiving day	Commonwealth victories in Munster
1649–E7	16 Dec.	Sun.	London area	thanksgiving prayers	Commonwealth victories in Munster
1650–E1	28 Feb.	Th.	E&W	day of humiliation	anxieties for the Commonwealth government
1650–S1	Apr.	?	S	fast day	negotiations with Charles II
1650–S2	15 May or first convenient day	Wed.	S	thanksgiving day	victory over Montrose's forces at Carbisdale
1650–E2	13 June	Th.	E&W	fast day	royalist successes
1650–S3	30 June or first Sun.	Sun.	S	fast day	fears of invasion by English Commonwealth forces, and revival of Scottish royalists
1650–E3	26 July	Fr.	E&W	thanksgiving day	Commonwealth victories in Ireland
1650–S4	July–Aug.	?	S	fast days	Commonwealth invasion of Scotland
1650–Ir1	6 Aug.	Tu.	army camp, Clonmel, Youghal, Cork & where order received in time	fast days	plague epidemics
	13 + 20 Aug.	Tu.	whole of Ireland		
1650–E4	1 Sept.	Sun.	London area	thanksgiving prayers	Commonwealth victories at Carlow, Waterford and Duncannon
	15 Sept.	Sun.	rest of E&W		
1650–S5	Sept.	various	S	fast days	defeat at the battle of Dunbar
1650–E5	8 Sept.	Sun.	London area	thanksgiving prayers	Commonwealth victory at the battle of Dunbar

	Date	Day	Place	Type	Occasion
1650–E6	8 Oct.	Tu.	E&W	thanksgiving day	Commonwealth victory at the battle of Dunbar
1650–Ir2	7 Nov.	Th.	Ir	thanksgiving day	Commonwealth victory at the battle of Dunbar
1650–E7	1 Dec.	Sun.	London area	thanksgiving prayers	Commonwealth victory at Meelick Island, Ireland
1650–S6	22 + 26 Dec.	Sun. + Th.	S	fast days	before Charles II's Scottish coronation, for general sinfulness
1651–E1	30 Jan.	Th.	E&W	thanksgiving day	victories of Commonwealth army and navy
1651–E2	13 Mar. / 2 Apr.	Th. / Wed.	London area / rest of E&W	fast days	the Commonwealth's political, military and diplomatic anxieties
1651–S1	13 Apr.	Sun.	S	fast days	English occupation and domestic divisions
1651–S2	19 + 22 June	Th. + Sun.	S	fast days	for the army, Charles II and the reformed church
1651–E3	27 July	Sun.	London area	thanksgiving prayers	Commonwealth victory at Inverkeithing
1651–Ir1	28 Aug.	Th.	Ir	fast day	plague, Scottish invasion of England, English divisions
1651–E4	31 Aug.	Sun.	London area	thanksgiving prayers	Commonwealth victories at Wigan and in Scotland
1651–S3	31 Aug.	Sun.	S	fast day	domestic anxieties and divisions
1651–E5	7 Sept.	Sun.	London area	thanksgiving prayers	Commonwealth victory at the battle of Worcester
1651–1	24 Oct.	Fr.	E&W, Ir, S	thanksgiving day	British thanksgiving day for victory at the battle of Worcester
1651–E6	5 Nov.	Wed.	London area	thanksgiving day	Commonwealth victory in Jersey
1651–Ir2	26 Nov.	Wed.	Ir	thanksgiving day	Commonwealth victories at Limerick, Isle of Man, Guernsey, Jersey
1651–E7	7 Dec.	Sun.	London area	thanksgiving prayers	Commonwealth victories at Limerick. Jersey, Isle of Man
1651–Ir3	11 + 18 Dec.	Th.	Ir	days of humiliation	death of lord deputy, plague, storms
1652–EIr	9 June / 30 June	Wed. / Wed.	London area / rest of E&W, Ir	fast days	threat of conflict with the Dutch Republic
1652–S	12 + 19 Sept.	Sun.	S	fast days	anxieties about religion, the church and Charles II's policies
1652–E	13 Oct.	Wed.	E&W	fast day	first Anglo-Dutch war
1653–E1	27 Feb.	Sun.	London area	thanksgiving prayers	naval victory at battle of Portland
1653–E2	3 Mar.	Th.	E&W	fast day	for the Commonwealth government and forces during the first Dutch war
1653–S	27 Mar. + 3 Apr.	Sun.	S	fast days	domestic divisions and sinfulness

1653–E3	12 Apr.	Tu.	E&W	thanksgiving day	naval victory at the battle of Portland
1653–Ir	4 + 11 May	Wed.	Ir	fast days	change in the Commonwealth government
1653–E4	23 June	Th.	E&W	thanksgiving day	naval victory at the battle of the Gabbard
1653–E5	25 Aug.	Th.	E&W	thanksgiving day	naval victory at the battle of Scheveingen
1654–E	24 Mar.	Fr.	London area	fast days	drought
	7 Apr.	Fr.	rest of E&W		
1654–1	23 May	Tu.	E&W, S, Ir	thanksgiving day	peace treaty with Dutch Republic, end of drought
1654–Ir	21 Sept.	Th.	Ir	fast day	in support of new lord deputy
1654–2	11 Oct.	Wed.	E&W, S	days of humiliation	general sinfulness
	1 Nov.	Wed.	Ir		
1655–Ir1	3 May	Th.	Ir	fast day	plague epidemic
1655–EIr	14 June	Th.	E&W	fast days	in support of persecuted protestants in Savoy
	5 July	Th.	Ir		
1655–Ir2	8 Nov.	Th.	Ir	fast day	in support of protestants in Savoy and of the lord protector's policies
1655–1	6 Dec.	Th.	E&W, S, Ir	day of humiliation	general repentance of sins
1656–1	28 Mar.	Fr.	E&W, S	days of humiliation	general repentance of sins
	3 + 17 Apr.	Th.	Ir		
1656–2	8 Oct.	Wed.	London area	thanksgiving days	naval victory at the battle of Cadiz
	5 Nov.	Wed.	rest of E&W, S, Ir		
1656–3	30 Oct.	Th.	E&W, S, Ir	day of humiliation	general repentance of sins
1657–1	20 Feb.	Fr.	E&W, S, Dublin	thanksgiving days	discovery of assassination plot against Cromwell
	27 Feb.	Fr.	rest of Ir		
1657–E1	3 June	Wed.	London area	thanksgiving day	naval success at Santa Cruz
1657–E2	21 Aug.	Fr.	London area + where possible	fast day	severe sickness
1657–E3	3 Sept.	Th.	London area + where possible	thanksgiving day	anniversary of the battles of Dunbar and Worcester
1657–E4	30 Sept.	Wed.	E&W	fast day	severe sickness
1658–E	5 May	Wed.	London area	fast days	plague epidemic
	19 May	Wed.	rest of E&W		

Code	Date	Day	Region	Type	Description
1658–ES	21 July	Wed.	E&W	thanksgiving days	defeat of invasion attempts and plots, end of plague and good harvest
	29 July	Th.	Edinburgh area		
	19 Aug.	Th.	rest of S		
1658–EIr	13 Oct.	Wed.	E&W	fast days	death of Cromwell, plague epidemic
	14 Oct.	Th.	Ir		
1658–1	29 Dec.	Wed.	E&W	fast days	success of parliament and public affairs
	5 Jan.	Wed.	S, Ir		
1659–1	18 May	Wed.	E&W, S, Ir	fast day	general anxieties and for the success of parliament
1659–2	31 Aug.	Wed.	E[&W?], S, Ir	fast day	general anxieties and for success in public affairs
1659–3	6 Oct.	Th.	London area	thanksgiving days	defeat of royalist conspiracies and Booth's uprising
	3 Nov.	Th.	rest of E&W, S, Ir		
1660–Ir	3 Jan.	Th.	Dublin	thanksgiving days	Irish repudiation of the Commonwealth government
	17 Jan.	Th.	rest of Ir		
1660–1	6 Apr.	Fr.	E&W, S, Ir	fast day	for the success of the new parliament and restoration of stable government
1660–E1	10 May	Th.	London area	thanksgiving days	for the success of the dissolution of the Long parliament and restoration of the monarchy
	24 May	Th.	rest of E&W		
1660–S	19 June	Tu.	S	thanksgiving day	restoration of Charles II
1660–E2	28 June	Th.	E&W	thanksgiving day	restoration of Charles II
1661–Ir1	30 Jan.	Wed.	Ir	fast day	anniversary of the regicide of Charles I
1661–Ir2	2 May	Th.	Ir	fast day	for success of the parliaments
1661–E	12 June	Wed.	London area	fast days	heavy rain, fears of bad harvest and sickness
	19 June	Wed.	rest of E&W		
1662–E	15 Jan.	Wed.	London area	fast days	unseasonable weather and fear of scarcity and sickness
	22 Jan.	Wed.	rest of E&W		
1665–E	5 Apr.	Wed.	E&W	fast day	outbreak of second Anglo-Dutch war
1665–S1	7 June	Wed.	S	fast day	outbreak of second Anglo-Dutch war
1665–EIr1	20 June	Tu.	London area	thanksgiving days	naval victory at battle of Lowestoft
	4 July	Tu.	rest of E&W, Ir		

	date	day	London area / rest of E&W, Ir	monthly fast days & weekly prayers	during plague epidemic
1665–Elr2	12 July + first Wed. of month	Wed.	London area		during plague epidemic
	2 Aug. + first Wed. of month	Wed.	rest of E&W, Ir		
	prayers every Wed.	Wed.	E&W, Ir		
1665–S2	13 July	Th.	S	thanksgiving day	naval victory at the battle of Lowestoft
1665–S3	13 Sept.	Wed.	S	fast day	plague in England
1666–Elr1	31 May	Th.	London area	fast days	naval campaign against the Dutch; in Ireland, also for the government's direction of the war
	14 June	Th.	rest of E&W		
	20 June	Wed.	Dublin area		
	27 June	Wed.	rest of Ir		
1666–Ir1	after 20 June		Ir	thanksgiving day	naval victory in the Four Days battle
1666–S1	11 July	Wed.	south of S	fast days	naval campaign against the Dutch
	18 July	Wed.	north of S		
1666–Ir2	Aug.		Ir	thanksgiving day	naval victory in the Four Days battle
1666–Elr2	14 Aug.	Tu.	London area	thanksgiving days	naval victory in the battle of St James's day
	23 Aug.	Th.	rest of E&W		
	6 Sept.	Th.	Ir		
1666–S2	23 Aug.	Th.	Edinburgh & Lothian	thanksgiving days	naval victory in the battle of St James's day
	30 Aug.	Th.	rest of S		
1666–Elr3	10 Oct.	Wed.	E&W, Ir	fast day	great fire of London
1666–E	20 Nov.	Tu.	London area	thanksgiving day	decline of the plague in London
1672–Elr	27 Mar.	Wed.	London area	fast days	outbreak of the third Anglo-Dutch war
	17 Apr.	Wed.	rest of E&W, Ir		
1674–E	4 Feb.	Wed.	London area	fast days	divisions over catholic influences, and the third Anglo-Dutch war
	11 Feb.	Wed.	rest of E&W		
1675–S	28 July	Wed.	central S	fast days	dearth and drought
	4 Aug.	Wed.	rest of S		
1678–E1	10 Apr.	Wed.	London area	fast days	tensions between Charles II and the House of Commons
	24 Apr.	Wed.	rest of E&W		
1678–E2	13 Nov.	Wed.	E&W	fast day	the popish plot
1678–S	18 Dec.	Wed.	S	fast day	the popish plot

Ref	Date	Day	Place	Type	Occasion
1679–EIr	11 Apr.	Fr.	E&W	fast days	fears of catholic conspiracies
	28 May	Wed.	Ir		
1680–E	22 Dec.	Wed.	E&W	fast day	exclusion crisis
1681–S	29 June	Wed.	central S	fast days	drought, and support for parliament against catholic conspiracies
	6 July	Wed.	rest of S		
1683–EIr	9 Sept.	Sun.	E&W, Ir	thanksgiving day	discovery of Rye House plot
1683–S	9 Sept.	Sun.	S	thanksgiving day	discovery of Rye House plot
1684–S	7 May	Wed.	central S	fast days	bad weather and fears of famine
	28 May	Wed.	rest of S		
1685–E	from 5 Feb.	daily	E&W	prayers	illness of Charles II
1685–S	23 July	Th.	Edinburgh diocese	thanksgiving days	defeat of Monmouth and Argyll risings
	13 Aug.	Th.	rest of S		
1685–EIr	26 July	Sun.	E&W	thanksgiving days	defeat of Monmouth and Argyll risings
	23 Aug.	Sun.	Ir		
1686–E	12 Sept.	Sun.	Windsor, London	thanksgiving services	Christian capture of Buda from the Ottomans
1688–EIr1	15 Jan.	Sun.	London area	thanksgiving days	pregnancy of Queen Mary
	29 Jan.	Sun.	rest of E&W		
	19 Feb.	Sun.	Dublin area		
	26 Feb.	Sun.	rest of Ir		
1688–S1	29 Jan.	Sun.	Edinburgh diocese	thanksgiving days	pregnancy of Queen Mary
	19 Feb.	Sun.	rest of S		
1688–EIr2	17 June	Sun.	London area	thanksgiving days	birth of Prince James
	1 July	Sun.	rest of E&W, Dublin area		
	8 July	Sun.	rest of Ir		
1688–S2	21 June	Th.	Edinburgh & Lothian	thanksgiving days	birth of Prince James
	28 June	Th.	rest of S		
1688–EIr3	from 11 Oct.	daily	E&W	prayers	danger of invasion by William of Orange
	from 22 Oct.	daily	Ir		
1689–E1	31 Jan.	Th.	London area	thanksgiving days	William of Orange's intervention in defence of protestantism
	14 Feb.		rest of E&W		

ID	Date	Day	Area	Type	Description
1689–E2	28 Jan. to 16 Feb.	daily	E&W	prayers	for William of Orange
1689–S1	9 May / 16 May	Th. / Th.	south of S / north of S	thanksgiving days	William of Orange's intervention in defence of protestantism
1689–E3	5 June / 19 June	Wed. / Wed.	London area / rest of E&W	fast days	declaration of war against France
1689–S2	15 Sept. / 22 Sept.	Sun. / Sun.	south of S / north of S	fast days	military campaign in Ireland, defence of protestantism, good weather and a good harvest
1690–E1	12 Mar. + third Wed. monthly + daily prayers	Wed.	E&W	monthly fast days & daily prayers	William III's military campaign in Ireland
1690–S1	24 June or first Tu. after receipt / 1 July or first Tu. after receipt	Tu. / Tu.	south of S / north of S	fast days	William III's military campaign in Ireland
1690–Ir1	25 June + third Wed. monthly	Wed.	Ir	monthly fast days	William III's military campaign
1690–E2	after 11 July	daily	E&W	prayers	William III's military campaign in Ireland
1690–S2	5 Aug. / 12 Aug.	Tu. / Tu.	south of S / north of S	thanksgiving days	victory at the battle of the Boyne
1690–Ir2	15 Aug. + Fr. weekly	Fr.	Ir	weekly fast days	naval and military campaigns against the Jacobites
1690–S3	21 Sept. / 5 Oct.	Sun. / Sun.	Lothian / rest of S	thanksgiving days	victories in Ireland
1690–E3	19 Oct. / weekly	Sun. / Sun., Wed., Fr.	E&W	thanksgiving day / thanksgiving prayers	victories in Ireland / for William III during the war with France
1690–Ir3	16 Nov. / 23 Nov. / weekly	Sun. / Sun. / Sun., Wed., Fr.	Dublin area / rest of Ir / Ir	thanksgiving days / thanksgiving prayers	victories in Ireland / for William III during the war with France
1691–S1	8 Jan., or first convenient day	Th.	S	fast day	repentance following the restoration of presbyterianism
1691–E1	after 28 Mar. to ?2 May	daily	London area	thanksgiving prayers	after William III's return from Holland

	Date	Day	Region	Occasion	Event
1691–E2	29 Apr. + third Wed. monthly + daily prayers	Wed. / daily	E&W	monthly fast days & daily prayers	military campaigns against the Jacobites and France
1691–S2	27 May + last Wed. monthly	Wed.	S	monthly fast days	military campaigns against the Jacobites and France
1691–E3	after 27 May	daily	London area	prayers	the naval campaign against the French fleet
1691–Ir1	3 July + first Fr. monthly + daily prayers	Fr. / daily	Ir	monthly fast days / daily prayers	military campaigns against the Jacobites / for the navy
1691–Ir2	16 July	Th.	Dublin area	thanksgiving days	military victories against the Jacobites
	28 July	Tu.	rest of Ir		
1691–E4	after 17 Oct. to 26 Nov.	daily	London area	thanksgiving prayers	William III's return from the war in Flanders
1691–EIr	26 Nov.	Th.	E&W, Ir	thanksgiving day	William III's return from the war in Flanders, and victories in Ireland
1691–S3	26 Nov.	Th.	S	thanksgiving day	William II's return from the war in Flanders, and victories in Ireland
1692–E1	after 9 Mar. to Oct.	daily	E&W	prayer	William III's military campaign in Flanders
1692–EIr1	8 Apr. + second Wed. monthly	Wed.	E&W	monthly fast days & daily prayer	William III's military campaign in Flanders
	20 July + third Wed. monthly + daily prayers	Wed. / daily	Ir		
1692–E2	after 19 May to ?Sept.	daily / daily	E&W, Ir / E&W	prayer	naval campaign against the French fleet
1692–S1	25 May + last Wed. monthly	Wed.	S	monthly fast days	William II's military campaign in Flanders
1692–E3	after 26 May	daily	London area	thanksgiving prayers	naval victories at the battles of Barfleur and La Hogue
1692–S2	7 June	Tu.	Edinburgh area	thanksgiving days	naval victories at the battles of Barfleur and La Hogue
	14 June	Tu.	south of S		
	21 June	Tu.	north of S		
1692–E4	after 7 Oct. to 26 Oct.	daily	London area	thanksgiving prayers	discovery of a plot against William III, and his return from military campaign

Ref	Date	Day	Location	Type	Occasion
1692–EIr2	27 Oct.	Th.	London area	thanksgiving days	naval victories at Barfleur and La Hogue, discovery of a plot against William III, and his return from military campaign
	10 Nov.	Th.	E&W, Dublin		
	24 Nov.	Th.	rest of Ir		
1692–S3	10 Nov.	Th.	Edinburgh area	thanksgiving days	discovery of a plot against William II, and his return from military campaign
	24 Nov.	Th.	rest of S		
1693–EIr1	10 May + second Wed. monthly	Wed.	E&W, Dublin area	monthly fast days & daily prayer	William III's military campaign in Flanders
	17 May + second Wed. monthly + daily prayers	Wed.	rest of Ir		
1693–S1		daily	E&W, Ir	monthly fast days	William II's military campaign in Flanders
	18 May + third Th. monthly	Th.	S		
	[in June changed to 16th]	Fr.	Edinburgh area		
1693–E1	after 3 June to ?Sept.	daily	E&W	prayers	the naval campaign against the French fleet
1693–E2	6 Aug.	Sun.	London area	thanksgiving prayer	William III's safety during the battle of Landen
1693–EIr2	12 Nov.	Sun.	London area	thanksgiving days	William III's return from military campaign
	26 Nov.	Sun.	rest of E&W		
	3 Dec.	Sun.	Dublin area		
	10 Dec.	Sun.	rest of Ir		
1693–S2	16 Nov.	Th.	central S	thanksgiving days	William II's return from military campaign
	23 Nov.	Th.	rest of S		
1694–EIr	23 May	Wed.	London area	fast days & daily prayer	William III's military campaign in Flanders
	13 June	Wed.	rest of E&W		
	13 July	Fr.	Dublin area		
	27 July	Fr.	rest of Ir		
	+ daily prayer	daily	E&W, Ir		
1694–S1	31 May	Th.	S	fast day	lack of repentance, and William II's military campaign in Flanders
1694–E1	29 Aug.	Wed.	London area	fast days	William III's military campaign in Flanders
	19 Sept.	Wed.	rest of E&W		
1694–E2	after 18 Oct. to 2 Dec.	daily	London area	thanksgiving prayers	William III's return from military campaign

	Date	Day	Area	Type	Occasion
1694–S2	22 Nov.	Th.	Edinburgh area rest of S	thanksgiving days	William II's return from military campaign
1694–E3	6 Dec. 2 Dec. 16 Dec.	Th. Sun. Sun.	London area rest of E&W	thanksgiving days	William III's return from military campaign
1694–E4	late Dec.	daily	London area	prayers	illness of Mary II
1695–S1	8 Jan. 15 Jan. 22 Jan.	Tu. Tu. Tu.	Lothian south of S north of S	fast days	death of Mary II
1695–S2	13 June	Th.	S	fast day	war against France
1695–EIr1	19 June 12 July + daily prayer	Wed. Fr. daily	E&W Ir E&W, Ir	fast days & daily prayer	William III's military campaigns in Flanders
1695–EIr2	8 Sept. 22 Sept. 8 Oct. 27 Oct.	Sun. Sun. Tu. Sun.	London area rest of E&W Dublin area rest of Ir	thanksgiving days	victory at Namur
1695–S3	15 Sept. 22 Sept. 29 Sept.	Sun. Sun. Sun.	Edinburgh area south of Tay north of Tay	thanksgiving days	victory at Namur
1695–E2	after 11 Oct. to 28 Oct.	daily	London area	thanksgiving prayers	William III's return from military campaign
1695–E3	11 Dec. 18 Dec.	Wed. Wed.	London area rest of E&W	fast days	a new parliament
1696–S1	15 Mar. 22 Mar. 29 Mar.	Sun. Sun. Sun.	Edinburgh area south of S north of S	fast days	discovery of a plot against William II, and fear of French invasion
1696–EIr1	16 Apr. 23 Apr.	Th. Th.	E&W Ir	thanksgiving days	discovery of a plot against William III, and failure of intended French invasion
1696–E1	from May to Oct.	daily	E&W	prayers	William III's military campaign in Flanders
1696–S2	16 June 30 June	Tu. Tu.	south of S north of S	fast days	war against France
1696–EIr2	26 June 10 July + daily prayer	Fr. Fr.	E&W Ir	fast days & daily prayer	William III's military campaign in Flanders

ID	Date	Day	Region	Type	Description
1696-S3	25 Aug.	Tu.	south of S or as convenient	fast days	food shortages and bad weather
	8 Sept.	Tu.	north of S or as convenient		
1696-E2	after 28 Sept. to ?11 Nov.	daily	London area	thanksgiving prayers	William III's return from military campaign
1697-S1	21 Jan.	Th.	S	fast day	famine, mortality and threat of invasion
1697-E1	28 Apr.	Wed.	E&W	fast day	blessing on William III and his dominions
1697-E2	late Apr./May to Nov.	daily	E&W	prayers	William III's military campaign in Flanders
1697-S2	27 May	Th.	S	fast day	William II's military campaign and for the harvest
1697-E3	after 14 Nov. for two weeks	daily	London area	thanksgiving prayers	William III's return from military campaign, and the peace treaty of Ryswick
1697-EIr	2 Dec.	Th.	E&W	thanksgiving days	peace treaty of Ryswick
	12 Dec.	Sun.	Dublin area		
	19 Dec.	Sun.	rest of Ir		
1697-S3	16 Dec.	Th.	S	thanksgiving day	preservation of William II and the peace treaty of Ryswick
1698-S1	17 May	Tu.	Lothian & Tweeddale	fast days	bad weather, and fears of a poor harvest and famine
	25 May	Wed.	south of S		
	1 June	Wed.	north of S		
1698-S2	11 Sept.	Sun.	S	fast day	bad harvest and dearth
1699-S1	9 Mar.	Th.	S	fast day	continued dearth and the persecution of continental protestants
1699-EIr	5 Apr.	Wed.	E&W	fast days	blessing on William III and his dominions, and for persecuted continental protestants
	5 May	Fr.	Ir		
1699-S2	30 Nov.	Th.	S	thanksgiving day & prayers	good harvest and William II's return from Flanders, and in response to disease, sinfulness, disrupted trade and the persecution of continental protestants
1700-S1	28 Mar.	Th.	S	fast day	dearth, high mortality, commercial failures, fire in Edinburgh, and sinfulness
1700-S2	29 Aug.	Th.	S	fast day	failure of the Darien scheme

1701–EIr1	4 Apr. 2 May	Fr. Fr.	E&W Ir	fast days	a blessing on parliament, preservation of protestantism and peace
1701–S1	24 Apr.	Th.	S	fast day	dearth, failure of the Darien scheme, fire in Edinburgh and sinfulness
1701–S2	20 Nov.	Th.	Lothian & Tweeddale	fast day	fire in Edinburgh, and sinfulness
1701–EIr2	19 Dec. 16 Jan. 1702	Fr. Fr.	E&W Ir	fast days	French threats to the kingdoms and to protestantism, and for blessing on parliament
1702–E1	from ?May to ?1713	daily	E&W	prayers	during the war of Spanish succession
1702–EIr1	10 June 14 Aug.	Wed. Fr.	E&W Ir	fast days	after the outbreak of the war of Spanish succession
1702–S	9 July	Th.	S	fast days	war, drought and sinfulness
1702–EIr2	12 Nov. 3 Dec.	Th. Th.	London area rest of E&W, Dublin area rest of Ir	thanksgiving days & thanksgiving prayers	naval and military victories in Spain and the Low Countries, and recovery from illness of Prince George
1703–E1	17 Dec.	Th.	E&W	fast day	British and allied military and naval campaigns
1703–S	26 May	Wed.	S	fast day	lack of repentance for sins
1703–E2	26 Aug. ?Dec. 1703 to ?Jan. 1704	Th. daily	E&W	prayers	violent storms
1704–EIr1	19 Jan. 18 Feb.	Wed. Fr.	E&W Ir	fast days	violent storms, and military and naval campaigns
1704–S1	Apr. to May	various	S	fast days	bad weather and threats to the harvest
1704–E	9 July	Sun.	London area	thanksgiving prayer	victory at the battle of Donauwörth
1704–EIr2	7 Sept. 21 Sept.	Th. Th.	E&W, Dublin area rest of Ir	thanksgiving days	victory at the battle of Blenheim
1704–S2	5 Oct.	Th.	S	thanksgiving day	military victories
1705–EIr1	4 Apr. 11 May 25 May	Wed. Fr. Fr.	E&W Dublin area rest of Ir	fast days	British and allied military and naval campaigns
1705–S	after 12 Apr. to May	various	S	fast days	defence of protestantism, preservation of Queen Anne, conduct of the war and the session of parliament

	Date	Day	Area	Type	Occasion
1705–EIr2	23 Aug. 28 Aug. 6 Sept.	Th. Tu. Th.	E&W Dublin area rest of Ir	thanksgiving days	victories in the Low Countries
1706–E1	20 Mar.	Wed.	E&W	fast day	British and allied military and naval campaigns
1706–E2	19 May	Sun.	London area	thanksgiving prayer	victories at Ramillies and in Spain
1706–S1	23 May 6 June	Th. Th.	south of S north of S	fast days	defence of protestantism, preservation of Queen Anne, conduct of the war and negotiation for a treaty of union with England
1706–E3	26 May	Sun.	London area	thanksgiving prayer	victories in Brabant and Spain
1706–EIr1	27 June	Th.	E&W, Ir	thanksgiving day	victories at Ramillies and in Spain
1706–S2	9 July	Tu.	S	thanksgiving day	victories in the Low Countries and in Spain
1706–E4	22 Sept.	Sun.	London area	thanksgiving prayer	allied victory at the battle of Turin
1706–S3	after 22 Oct. to Nov.	various	S	fast days	parliamentary debates on the treaty of union
1706–EIr2	31 Dec.	Th.	E&W, Ir	thanksgiving day	British and allied victories during the year
1707–EIr1	9 Apr.	Wed.	E&W, Ir	fast day	British and allied military and naval campaigns
1707–EIr2	1 May	Th.	E&W, Ir	thanksgiving day & prayers	union of England and Scotland, and prayers for the British and allied naval campaigns
1708–1	14 Jan.	Wed.	E&W, S, Ir	fast day	British and allied military and naval campaigns
1708–S1	1 Apr.	Th.	S	fast day	threat of Jacobite and French invasion
1708–E1	18 Apr. 9 May	Sun.	London area rest of E&W	thanksgiving prayers	failure of attempted Jacobite and French invasion of Scotland
1708–S2	3 June	Th.	S	thanksgiving day	failure of attempted Jacobite and French invasion of Scotland
1708–Ir	27 June	Sun.	Ir	thanksgiving day	failure of attempted Jacobite and French invasion of Scotland
1708–E2	11 July	Sun.	London area	thanksgiving prayer	victory at the battle of Oudenarde
1708–EIr	19 Aug. 16 Sept.	Th. Th.	E&W Ir	thanksgiving days	failed Jacobite and French invasion attempt, and victory at the battle of Oudenarde
1708–S3	26 Aug.	Th.	S	thanksgiving day	failed Jacobite and French invasion attempt, and victory at the battle of Oudenarde
1708–E3	25 Dec.	Sat.	London area	thanksgiving prayer	British and allied victories during the year

Ref	Date	Day	Region	Type	Occasion
1709–1	17 Feb. / 17 Mar.	Th. / Th.	E&W, S / Ir	thanksgiving days	British and allied victories at Lille, Ghent and Bruges
1709–S	May	various	S	fast days	bad weather and dearth, and for success in the war
1709–E1	from 18 June	Sun., Wed., Fr.	E&W	prayers	British and allied forces
1709–E2	7, 9 + 11 Sept.	Wed., Fr., Sun.	London area	thanksgiving prayer	victory at the battle of Malplaquet
1709–2	22 Nov.	Tu.	E&W, S, Ir	thanksgiving day	victory at the battle of Malplaquet
1710–1	15 Mar. / 29 Mar.	Wed. / Wed.	E&W / S, Ir	fast days	British and allied military and naval campaigns
1710–S	13 July	Th.	S	fast day	sinfulness, and for success in the war
1710–E	17 Sept.	Sun.	London area	thanksgiving prayer	victory at the battles of Almenara and Saragossa
1710–ES	7 Nov.	Tu.	E&W, S	thanksgiving day	British and allied victories during the year
1711–S	after 6 Jan. to Feb.	various	S	fast days	war, fears of plague and sinfulness
1711–ES	28 Mar.	Wed.	E&W, S	fast day	British and allied military and naval campaigns
1712–ES	16 Jan. / 25 Jan.	Wed. / Fr.	E&W / S	fast days	peace negotiations, and British and allied military and naval campaigns
1713–1	16 June / 7 July	Tu. / Tu.	S, Ir / E&W	thanksgiving days	peace treaty of Utrecht
1715–1	20 Jan. / 1 Mar.	Th. / Tu.	E&W, S / Ir	thanksgiving days	accession of George I, and frustration of Jacobite hopes
1715–S	23 Aug. or asap	Tu. or asap	S	fast days	fears of a Jacobite invasion
1715–E	from Oct. 1715	Sun., Wed., Fr.	E&W	prayers	during the Jacobite rebellion
1716–1	7 June	Th.	E&W, S, Ir	thanksgiving day	suppression of the Jacobite rebellion
1717–S	Mar. to Apr.	various	S	fast days	threatened Jacobite invasion and rebellion
1720–EIr	from Nov. to Apr. 1723	Sun., Wed., Fr.	E&W, Ir	prayers	during the threat of plague
1720–1	16 Dec. / 23 Dec.	Fr. / Fr.	E&W, S / Ir	fast days	to avert the spread of plague from the continent
1721–1	8 Dec.	Fr.	E&W, S, Ir	fast day	to avert the spread of plague

ID	Date	Day	Region	Type	Description
1722–S	[June]	various	S	fast days	fears of Jacobite invasion
1723–1	25 Apr.	Th.	E&W, S, Ir	thanksgiving day	end of the threat of plague
1725–S	1 July, or 24 June or 8 July	Th.	S	fast days	persecution of continental protestants
1726–S	7 July	Th.	S	fast day	sinfulness, ingratitude for mercies, growth of catholicism and persecution of continental protestants
1734–S	7 Aug.	Wed.	S	fast day	sinfulness, secession in the church and possible British involvement in the war of Polish succession
1735–S	7 Aug.	Th.	S	fast day	sinfulness, and possible British involvement in the war of Polish succession
1737–E	from 18 Nov. [to 20 Nov.]	daily	London area	prayers	illness of Queen Caroline
1740–1	9 Jan.	Wed.	E&W, S, Ir	fast day	outbreak of war against Spain
1741–E	from Jan. 1741	daily	E&W	prayers	during war with Spain
1741–1	4 Feb.	Wed.	E&W, S, Ir	fast day	military and naval campaigns
1741–S	June	various	S	fast days	famine and war
1741–2	25 Nov.	Wed.	E&W, S, Ir	fast day	military and naval campaigns
1742–1	10 Nov.	Wed.	E&W, S, Ir	fast day	military and naval campaigns
1743–E	17 July	Sun.	London area	thanksgiving prayer	victory at the battle of Dettingen
1744–1	11 Apr.	Wed.	E&W, S, Ir	fast day	military and naval campaigns
1745–1	9 Jan.	Wed.	E&W, S, Ir	fast day	naval and military campaigns against Spain and France
1745–E	from Sept.	daily	E&W	prayers	during the Jacobite rebellion
1745–2	18 Dec.	Wed.	E&W, S, Ir	fast day	naval and military campaigns, and the Jacobite rebellion
1746–E	4 May / 25 May	Sun. / Sun.	London area / rest of E&W	thanksgiving prayers	victory at the battle of Culloden
1746–S	26 June	Th.	S	thanksgiving day	defeat of the Jacobite rebellion
1746–EIr	9 Oct.	Th.	E&W, Ir	thanksgiving day	defeat of the Jacobite rebellion

1747–1	7 Jan.	Wed.	E&W, S, Ir	fast day	naval and military campaigns against Spain and France
1748–1	17 Feb.	Wed.	E&W, S, Ir	fast day	naval and military campaigns against Spain and France
1748–E	from May 1748 to 18 Feb. 1759	daily	E&W	prayers	during the cattle plague
1749–1	25 Apr.	Tu.	E&W, S, Ir	thanksgiving day	peace treaty of Aix-la-Chapelle
1750–E	from 17 Mar., during Lent	daily	London area	prayers	earthquakes in London
1756–1	6 Feb.	Fr.	E&W, S, Ir	fast day	Lisbon earthquake, and for the fleets and armies during tensions with France
1756–S	22 July	Th.	S	fast day	outbreak of Seven Years War with France
1757–1	11 Feb.	Fr.	E&W, S, Ir	fast day	naval and military campaigns against France
1758–1	16 Feb.	Th.	S	fast days	naval and military campaigns against France
	17 Feb.	Fr.	E&W, Ir		
1758–E1	2 July	Sun.	London area	thanksgiving prayer	victory at the battle of Krefeld
1758–E2	20 Aug.	Sun.	London area	thanksgiving prayers	capture of Louisburg
	27 Aug.	Sun.	rest of E&W		
1758–Ir	3 Sept.	Sun.	Dublin area	thanksgiving prayer	victories
1758–S	from Oct. to Jan. 1759	various	S	thanksgiving days	good harvest and military victories
1759–1	15 Feb.	Th.	S	fast days	naval and military campaigns against France
	16 Feb.	Fr.	E&W, Ir		
1759–E1	18 Feb.	Sun.	E&W	thanksgiving prayer	end of cattle plague
1759–E2	12 Aug.	Sun.	London area	thanksgiving prayer	victory at the battle of Minden
1759–Ir1	26 Aug.	Sun.	Dublin area	thanksgiving prayer	victory at the battle of Minden
1759–E3	21 Oct. Sun. asap	Sun.	London area rest of E&W	thanksgiving prayers	capture of Quebec and other victories in Canada
1759–Ir2	28 Oct.	Sun.	Dublin area	thanksgiving prayer	capture of Quebec and other victories in Canada
1759–2	29 Nov.	Th.	E&W, S, Ir	thanksgiving day	capture of Quebec, other naval and military victories and an abundant harvest
1759–E4	9 Dec. Sun. asap	Sun.	London area rest of E&W	thanksgiving prayers	victory at the battle of Quiberon Bay

	Date	Day	Area	Occasion	Event
1760–1	13 Mar. / 14 Mar.	Th. / Fr.	S / E&W, Ir	fast days	naval and military campaigns against France
1760–EIr	12 Oct. / Sun. asap / 26 Oct.	Sun. / Sun. / Sun.	London area / rest of E&W / Dublin area	thanksgiving prayers	capture of Montreal and surrender of French forces in Canada
1761–1	12 Feb. / 13 Feb.	Th. / Fr.	S / E&W, Ir	fast days	naval and military campaigns against France
1761–E	26 July / Sun. asap	Sun. / Sun.	London area / rest of E&W	thanksgiving prayers	capture of Pondicherry, Belle Ile and Dominic, and victory at the battle of Villinghausen
1762–1	11 Mar. / 12 Mar.	Th. / Fr.	S / E&W, Ir	fast days	naval and military campaigns against France and Spain
1762–E1	28 Mar. / Sun. asap	Sun. / Sun.	London area / rest of E&W	thanksgiving prayers	capture of Martinique
1762–E2	15 Aug. / Sun. asap	Sun. / Sun.	London area / rest of E&W	thanksgiving prayers	birth of Prince George
1762–E3	3 Oct. / Sun. asap	Sun. / Sun.	London area / rest of E&W	thanksgiving prayers	capture of Havannah
1763–1	5 May	Th.	E&W, S, Ir	thanksgiving day	peace treaty of Paris
1763–E	21 Aug. / Sun. asap	Sun. / Sun.	London area / rest of E&W	thanksgiving prayers	birth of Prince Frederick
1765–E	25 Aug. / Sun. asap	Sun. / Sun.	London area / rest of E&W	thanksgiving prayers	birth of Prince William
1766–E	5 Oct. / Sun. asap	Sun. / Sun.	London area / rest of E&W	thanksgiving prayers	birth of Princess Charlotte
1767–E	8 Nov. / Sun. asap	Sun. / Sun.	London area / rest of E&W	thanksgiving prayers	birth of Prince Edward
1768–E	13 Nov. / Sun. asap	Sun. / Sun.	London area / rest of E&W	thanksgiving prayers	birth of Princess Augusta
1770–E	27 May / Sun. asap	Sun. / Sun.	London area / rest of E&W	thanksgiving prayers	birth of Princess Elizabeth
1771–E	9 June / Sun. asap	Sun. / Sun.	London area / rest of E&W	thanksgiving prayers	birth of Prince Ernest
1773–E	31 Jan. / Sun. asap	Sun. / Sun.	London area / rest of E&W	thanksgiving prayers	birth of Prince Augustus

Code	Date	Day	Location	Type	Occasion
1774-E	27 Feb. Sun. asap	Sun. Sun.	London area rest of E&W	thanksgiving prayers	birth of Prince Adolphus
1776-E	28 Apr. Sun. asap	Sun. Sun.	London area rest of E&W	thanksgiving prayers	birth of Princess Mary
1776-1	12 Dec. 13 Dec.	Th. Fr.	S E&W, Ir	fast days	naval and military campaigns in the War of American Independence
1777-E	9 Nov. Sun. asap	Sun. Sun.	London area rest of E&W	thanksgiving prayers	birth of Princess Sophia
1778-1	26 Feb. 27 Feb.	Th. Fr.	S E&W, Ir	fast days	naval and military campaigns in North America
1779-1	9 Feb. 10 Feb.	Tu. Wed.	S E&W, Ir	fast days	naval and military campaigns against France, and in North America
1779-E1	28 Feb. Sun. asap	Sun. Sun.	London area rest of E&W	thanksgiving prayers	birth of Prince Octavius
1779-E2	from 9 Aug.	daily	E&W	prayers	during the war
1780-1	3 Feb. 4 Feb.	Th. Fr.	S E&W, Ir	fast days	naval and military campaigns against France, and in North America
1780-E	1 Oct. Sun. asap	Sun. Sun.	London area rest of E&W	thanksgiving prayers	birth of Prince Alfred
1781-1	21 Feb. 22 Feb.	Wed. Th.	E&W, Ir S	fast days	naval and military campaigns against France, Spain and the Dutch Republic, and in North America
1781-E	?	daily	E&W	prayers	during the war
1782-1	7 Feb. 8 Feb.	Th. Fr.	S E&W, Ir	fast days	naval and military campaigns against France, Spain and the Dutch Republic, and in North America
1782-E	26 May Sun. asap	Sun.	London area rest of E&W	thanksgiving prayers	victory at the battle of the Saintes
1783-E	17 Aug. Sun. asap	Sun.	London area rest of E&W	thanksgiving prayers	birth of Princess Amelia
1784-1	29 July	Th.	E&W, S, Ir	thanksgiving day	peace treaty of Paris
1786-E	13 Aug. Sun. asap	Sun. Sun.	London area rest of E&W	thanksgiving prayers	failure of an attack on George III

ID	Date	Day	Region	Type	Occasion
1788-S	5 Nov.	Wed.	S	thanksgiving day	anniversary of the 1688 revolution
1788-1	from c. 15 Nov. / from late Nov.	daily / daily	E&W, S, / Ir	prayers	during George III's illness
1789-1	1 Mar. asap / from 7 Mar. / 8 Mar. asap	Sun. / Sun.	London area rest of E&W S / Dublin area rest of Ir	thanksgiving prayers	George III's recovery from illness
1789-2	23 Apr.	Th.	E&W, S, Ir	thanksgiving day	George III's recovery from illness
1793-1	18 Apr. / 19 Apr.	Th. / Fr.	S / E&W, Ir	fast days	naval and military campaigns in the French Revolutionary War
1794-1	27 Feb. / 28 Feb.	Th. / Fr.	S / E&W, Ir	fast days	naval and military campaigns against France
1795-1	25 Feb. / 26 Feb.	Wed. / Th.	E&W, Ir / S	fast days	naval and military campaigns against France
1795-2	after 15 Nov., asap + 14 days / from late Nov.	Sun. + 14 days / various	E&W, Ir / S	thanksgiving prayers	failure of an attack on George III
1796-ES	17 Jan. / Sun. asap / when appropriate	Sun. / Sun. / various	London area rest of E&W S	thanksgiving prayers	birth of Princess Charlotte, daughter of the prince of Wales
1796-1	9 Mar. / 10 Mar.	Wed. / Th.	E&W, Ir / S	fast days	naval and military campaigns against France
1796-E1	25 Sept. or Sun. asap	Sun. + 1 month	E&W	thanksgiving prayers	abundant harvest
1797-Ir	16 Feb.	Th.	Ir	thanksgiving day	failure of attempted French invasion
1797-1	8 Mar. / 9 Mar.	Wed. / Th.	E&W, Ir / S	fast days	naval and military campaigns against France
1797-E1	12 Mar. / Sun. asap	Sun. / Sun.	London area rest of E&W	thanksgiving prayers	naval victory at the battle of Cape St Vincent
1797-E2	29 Oct. / Sun. asap + next 2 Sun.	Sun. / Sun.	London area E&W	thanksgiving prayers	naval victory at the battle of Camperdown

	Date	Day	Region	Type	Description
1797–2	19 Dec. 16 Jan. 1798	Tu.	E&W, S Ir	thanksgiving days	naval victories
1798–1	7 Mar. 8 Mar.	Wed. Th.	E&W, Ir S	fast days	naval and military campaigns against France and its allies
1798–E	21 Oct. Sun. asap + next 2 Sun.	Sun. Sun.	London area E&W	thanksgiving prayers	naval victory at the battle of the Nile
1798–Ir	from late Oct., Sun. asap + next 2 Sun.	Sun.	Ir	thanksgiving prayers	naval victories at the battle of the Nile and the battle of Tory Island
1798–2	29 Nov.	Th.	E&W, S, Ir	thanksgiving day	victory at the battle of the Nile, and defeat of the attempted invasion and rebellion in Ireland
1799–1	27 Feb. 28 Feb. 13 Mar.	Wed. Th. Wed.	E&W S Ir	fast days	naval and military campaigns against France and its allies
1800–1	12 Mar. 13 Mar.	Wed. Th.	E&W, Ir S	fast days	naval and military campaigns against France and its allies
1800–EIr	from 18 May, Sun. asap + 30 days	Sun. + 30 days	E&W, Ir	thanksgiving prayers	failure of an attack on George III
1801–1	12 Feb. 13 Feb.	Th. Fr.	S E&W, Ir	fast days	dearth, and the naval and military campaigns against France and its allies
1801–2	19 Apr. + 7 days Sun. asap + 7 days Sun. asap	Sun. + 7 days	London area rest of E&W, Ir S	thanksgiving prayers	George III's recovery from illness
1801–EIr	from 13 Sept., Sun. asap + 1 month	Sun. + 1 month	E&W, Ir	thanksgiving prayers	abundant harvest
1802–1	1 June 17 June	Tu. Th.	E&W, Ir S	thanksgiving days	peace treaty of Amiens
1803–EIr1	27 Feb. or Sun. asap + 30 days	Sun. + 30 days	E&W, Ir	thanksgiving prayers	discovery of the Despard conspiracy
1803–EIr2	from 12 July	daily	E&W, Ir	prayers	during the Napoleonic war
1803–1	19 Oct. 20 Oct.	Wed. Th.	E&W, Ir S	fast days	naval and military campaigns against France
1804–EIr	26 Feb. Sun. asap + 20 days	Sun. Sun. + 20 days	London area E&W, Ir	thanksgiving prayers	George III's recovery from illness

Ref	Date(s)	Day(s)	Place	Type	Occasion
1804-1	25 May / 7 June	Fr. / Th.	E&W, Ir / S	fast days & thanksgiving prayers	naval and military campaigns against France, and George III's recovery from illness
1805-1	20 Feb. / 21 Feb.	Wed. / Th.	E&W, Ir / S	fast days	naval and military campaigns against France and its allies
1805-EIr	from early Mar.	daily	E&W, Ir	prayers	during the war
1805-2	5 Dec.	Th.	E&W, S, Ir	thanksgiving day	victory at the battle of Trafalgar
1806-1	26 Feb. / 27 Feb.	Wed. / Th.	E&W, Ir / S	fast days	naval and military campaigns against France and its allies
1807-1	25 Feb. / 26 Feb.	Wed. / Th.	E&W, Ir / S	fast days	naval and military campaigns against France and its allies
1808-1	17 Feb. / 18 Feb.	Wed. / Th.	E&W, Ir / S	fast days	naval and military campaigns against France and its allies
1809-1	8 Feb. / 9 Feb.	Wed. / Th.	E&W, Ir / S	fast days	naval and military campaigns against France and its allies
1809-2	25 Oct. / 29 Oct.	Wed. / Sun.	E&W, Ir / S	thanksgiving prayers	jubilee of George III
1810-1	28 Feb. / 1 Mar.	Wed. / Th.	E&W, Ir / S	fast days	naval and military campaigns against France and its allies
1810-2	from Nov.	daily	E&W, Ir, S	prayers	illness of George III
1810-3	18–25 Nov.	daily	E&W, Ir, S	thanksgiving prayers	abundant harvest
1811-1	20 Mar. / 21 Mar.	Wed. / Th.	E&W, Ir / S	fast days	naval and military campaigns against France and its allies
1812-1	5 Feb. / 6 Feb.	Wed. / Th.	E&W, Ir / S	fast days	naval and military campaigns against France and its allies
1812-EIr	from 6 Feb.	daily	E&W, Ir	prayers	illness of George III
1812-2	23 Aug. / Sun. asap / 30 Aug. or Sun. asap	Sun. / Sun. / Sun.	London area / rest of E&W, Ir / S	thanksgiving prayers	victories in Spain and Portugal, especially at the battle of Salamanca
1813-1	from late Feb.	daily	E&W, Ir, S	prayer	for the Prince Regent
1813-2	10 Mar. / 11 Mar.	Wed. / Th.	E&W, Ir / S	fast days	naval and military campaigns against France and its allies

1813–3	25 July Sun. asap 1 Aug.	Sun. Sun. Sun.	London area rest of E&W, Ir S	thanksgiving prayers	victories in Spain, especially at the battle of Vittoria
1813–4	10 + 17 Oct. 2 Sun. asap 10–17 Oct., or Sun. asap + week	Sun. Sun. Sun. + week	London area rest of E&W S	thanksgiving prayers	abundant harvest
1814–1	13 Jan.	Th.	E&W, Ir, S	thanksgiving day	British and allied victories against France
1814–2	7 July	Th.	E&W, Ir, S	thanksgiving day	peace treaty of Paris
1815–1	2 July Sun. asap 9 July or Sun. asap	Sun. Sun. Sun.	London area rest of E&W, Ir S	thanksgiving prayers	victory at the battle of Waterloo
1816–1	18 Jan.	Th.	E&W, Ir, S	thanksgiving day	peace treaty of Paris
1817–1	after 8 Feb., Sun. asap + 14 days after 8 Feb., Sun. asap	Sun. + 14 days Sun.	E&W, Ir S	thanksgiving prayers	failure of an attack on the prince regent
1820–1	after 17 Feb., Sun. asap + 14 days after 17 Feb., Sun. asap	Sun. + 14 days Sun.	E&W, Ir S	thanksgiving prayers	recovery of George IV from illness
1830–1	after 27 May	daily	E&W, Ir, S	prayers	illness of George IV
1830–2	after 24 Dec.	daily	E&W, Ir, S	prayers	popular disturbances
1831–1	after 2 Nov.	daily	E&W, Ir, S	prayers	threat of cholera
1832–1	after 6 Feb.	daily	E&W, Ir, S	prayers	cholera epidemic
1832–2	21 Mar. 22 Mar.	Wed. Th.	E&W, Ir S	fast days	cholera epidemic
1832–3	after 30 June	daily	E&W, Ir, S	thanksgiving prayers	for places free, or freed, from cholera
1832–EIr	from 11 Nov., 3 Sun.	Sun.	E&W, Ir	thanksgiving prayers	abundant harvest
1833–E	14 Apr.	Sun.	E&W	thanksgiving day	end of cholera outbreak

Ref	Date	Day	Nation	Type	Occasion
1835-S	23 July	Th.	S	day of humiliation	sinfulness and the shortcomings of the church
1837-1	after 16 June	daily	E&W, Ir	prayers	illness of William IV
1840-S	after 5 Mar.	a weekday	S	services of humiliation & prayer	divisions in the church
1840-1	21 June or asap + 30 days	Sun. + daily	E&W, Ir, S	thanksgiving prayers	failure of an attack on Queen Victoria
1840-2	29 Nov./Sun. asap after 21 Nov.	Sun. / not stated	E&W, Ir / S	thanksgiving prayers	birth of Princess Victoria
1841-S1	22 July	Th.	S	day of humiliation, thanksgiving & prayer	sinfulness, shortcomings, mercies and peace within the church
1841-S2	from 6 Sept. monthly	Mon.	S	monthly prayers	divisions within the church
1841-1	14 Nov./Sun. asap / not specified	Sun. / Sun.	E&W, Ir / S	thanksgiving prayers	birth of Prince Albert Edward
1842-1	5 June or asap + 30 days / 12 June or asap + 30 days	Sun. + daily / Sun. + daily	E&W, S / Ir	thanksgiving prayers	failure of an attack on Queen Victoria
1842-S	21 July	Th.	S	day of humiliation	divisions in the church and distress in the country
1842-2	2 Oct. / 2 Oct. or asap / 9 Oct. or asap	Sun. / Sun. or asap / Sun. or asap	E&W / S / Ir	thanksgiving prayers	abundant harvest
1843-1	30 Apr. or Sun. asap after 25 Apr. / 7 May or Sun. asap	Sun. / not specified / Sun.	E&W / S / Ir	thanksgiving prayers	birth of Princess Alice
1844-1	11 Aug. or Sun. asap / not specified / 18 Aug. or Sun. asap	Sun. / Sun.	E&W / S / Ir	thanksgiving prayers	birth of Prince Alfred
1846-1	12 Apr. or Sun. asap / 19 Apr. or Sun. asap	Sun. / Sun.	E&W, S / Ir	thanksgiving prayers	victories near the Sutlej river
1846-2	31 May or Sun. asap / 7 June or Sun. asap	Sun. / Sun.	E&W, S / Ir	thanksgiving prayers	birth of Princess Helena
1846-3	11 Oct. + 2 Sun. / 11 Oct. + rest of Oct.	Sun. / daily	E&W, S / Ir	prayers	famine in Ireland and Scotland

1846–Ir	20 Oct.–23 Nov. 20 Nov.	daily Fr.	Ir	prayers day of humiliation	famine
1847–1	24 Mar.	Wed.	E&W, Ir, S	fast day	famine in Ireland and Scotland
1847–S	after 31 May, esp. 4 July	daily	S	prayers	famine in Ireland and Scotland
1847–2	17 Oct. 17 Oct. or asap	Sun. Sun. or asap	E&W, Ir S	thanksgiving days	abundant harvest
1848–1	26 Mar. or Sun. asap 2 Apr. or Sun. asap	Sun. Sun.	E&W, Ir S	thanksgiving prayers	birth of Princess Louise
1848–2	21 Apr. + 4 Sun. 30 Apr. + 4 Sun.	Fr. + 4 Sun. Sun. + 4 Sun.	E&W, S Ir	prayers	Chartist demonstrations
1848–S	30 July or 6 Aug.	Sun.	S	days of humiliation	economic distress
1849–1	from 16 Sept. after 5 Sept. from 23 Sept.	Sun. + daily not specified Sun. + daily	E&W S Ir	prayers	cholera epidemic
1849–2	15 Nov.	Th.	E&W, Ir, S	thanksgiving day	end of the cholera epidemic
1850–1	5 May or Sun. asap 12 May or Sun. asap	Sun. Sun.	E&W, S Ir	thanksgiving prayers	birth of Prince Arthur
1853–1	10 Apr. or Sun. asap 17 Apr. or Sun. asap	Sun. Sun.	E&W, S Ir	thanksgiving prayers	birth of Prince Leopold
1854–S	19 Mar.	Sun.	S	prayers	likely war against Russia
1854–1	26 Apr.	Wed.	E&W, Ir, S	day of humiliation/fast day	military and naval campaigns in the Crimean war
1854–2	1 Oct. 8 Oct.	Sun. Sun.	E&W, S Ir	thanksgiving prayers	abundant harvest
1855–1	21 Mar.	Wed.	E&W, Ir, S	fast day/day of humiliation	military and naval campaigns in the Crimean war
1855–2	30 Sept. or Sun. asap 7 Oct.	Sun. Sun.	E&W, S Ir	thanksgiving prayers	British and allied victories in the Crimean, especially the capture of Sebastopol
1856–1	4 May	Sun.	E&W, Ir, S	thanksgiving day	peace treaty of Paris
1857–1	19 Apr. or Sun. asap 26 Apr. or Sun. asap	Sun. Sun.	E&W, S Ir	thanksgiving prayers	birth of Princess Beatrice
1857–S	after 12 Aug.	daily	S	prayers	revolt in India

	Date	Day	Region	Type	Occasion
1857–2	7 Oct.	Wed.	E&W, Ir, S	fast day	military campaign in India
1859–1	1 May	Sun.	E&W, Ir, S	thanksgiving prayers	suppression of the revolt in India
1860–S	20 Dec.	Th.	S	day of thanksgiving	third centenary of Scottish Reformation
1864–1	17 Jan. or Sun. asap not specified	Sun. S	E&W, Ir	thanksgiving prayers	birth of Prince Albert Victor, son of the prince of Wales
1865–1	from 8 Oct. / from 5 Nov.	Sun. + daily / Sun. + daily	E&W, S / Ir	prayers	cattle plague and to avert a cholera epidemic / to avert cattle plague and a cholera epidemic
1866–1	after 15 Feb. / 29 Mar.	various / Th.	E&W / S	days of humiliation	cattle plague
1866–2	from 12 Aug. / from 19 Aug.	Sun. + daily / Sun. + daily	E&W, S / Ir	prayers	averting a cholera epidemic, and cattle plague
1866–3	18 Nov.	Sun.	E&W, S / Ir	thanksgiving prayers	end of cholera and cattle plague / end of cattle plague
1868–1	28 June / 5 July	Sun. / Sun.	E&W, S / Ir	thanksgiving prayers	failure of an attack on the duke of Edinburgh, and success of Abyssinian expedition
1870–1	after 6 Aug.	daily	E&W	prayers	Franco-Prussian war
1871–1	10 Dec.–27 Dec.	Sun. + daily	E&W, S	prayers	illness of the prince of Wales
1872–1	21 Jan.	Sun.	E&W, S	thanksgiving prayers	recovery of the prince of Wales from illness
1872–2	27 Feb.	Tu.	St Paul's & elsewhere	thanksgiving services	recovery of the prince of Wales from illness
1875–E	after 11 Nov.	daily	E&W	prayers	visit of the prince of Wales to India
1876–E	after 12 May	various	E&W	thanksgiving prayers	return of the prince of Wales from India
1877–E	after 18 Sept.	daily	E&W	prayers	famine in India and war in the Near East
1881–E	after 23 Aug.	daily	Canterbury & elsewhere	prayers	better weather and a good harvest
1882–E1	18 May	daily	Canterbury & elsewhere	prayers	troubles and violence in Ireland
1882–E2	23 Aug.	daily	Canterbury & elsewhere	prayers	better weather and a good harvest
1882–E3	24 Sept.	Sun.	E&W	thanksgiving services	victories in Egypt
1883–S	10 or 11 Nov.	Sat. or Sun.	S	thanksgiving prayers	400th anniversary of the birth of Luther
1885–E1	after 13 Feb.	daily	E&W	prayers	military campaign in the Sudan

1885–E2	from 16 to 24 May	various	E&W	services	anxieties about imperial and domestic difficulties
1887–1	21 to 28 June	Tu. or later	E&W	thanksgiving services	golden jubilee of Queen Victoria
	21 to 26 June	Tu. or later	S		
1888–S	4 or 5 Nov.	Sun. or Mon.	S	thanksgiving days	commemoration of the revolution of 1688
1893–S	18 or 25 June	Sun.	S	day of humiliation	church defence
1894–1	1 July or Sun. asap	Sun.	E&W	thanksgiving prayers	birth of Prince Edward, son of the duke of York
	not specified	not stated	S		
1897–S	9 or 13 June	Wed. or Sun.	S	thanksgiving prayers	1300th anniversary of the death of St Columba
1897–1	20 June	Sun.	E&W, S	thanksgiving services	diamond jubilee of Queen Victoria
1898–E	after 1 Jan.	daily	E&W	prayers	dispute in engineering trades
1899–S	28 May	Sun.	S	thanksgiving prayers	80th birthday of Queen Victoria
1899–E	after 20 Oct.	daily	E&W	prayers	South African war
1900–S	21 Jan. or asap	Sun.	S	day of intercession	South African war
1900–E1	11 Feb. + wartime	Sun. + daily	E&W	day of intercession & wartime services	South African war
1900–E2	after 26 Sept.	daily	E&W	prayers	general election
1901–1	2 Feb. or to 9 Feb.	Sat. or various	E&W	day of mourning & services	commemoration of Queen Victoria
	2 Feb.	Sat.	S		
1902–1	8 June	Sun.	E&W, S	thanksgiving services	peace treaty of Vereeniging
1902–2	9 Aug.	Sat.	E&W, S	public holiday & services	coronation of Edward VII
1903–S	after 18 Nov.	daily	S	prayers	persecuted Christians in Macedonia
1905–E	after 14 Dec.	daily	E&W	prayers	general election
1909–E	after 4 Dec.	daily	E&W	prayers	general election
1910–1	20 May or to 27 May	Fr. or various	E&W	day of mourning & services	commemoration of Edward VII
	20 May	Fr.	S		
1910–E	after 18 Nov..	daily	E&W	prayers	general election
1911–1	22 June	Th.	E&W, S	public holiday & services	coronation of George V and Queen Mary
1911–E	after 9 Nov.	daily	E&W	prayers	visit of George V and Queen Mary to India

ID	Date	Day	Region	Service	Occasion
1912–E1	10 Feb.	Sun.	E&W	prayer	return of George V and Queen Mary from India
1912–E2	after 22 Feb.	daily	E&W	prayers	dispute in the coal industry
1912–1	17 Mar. + later from 20 Mar.	Sun. + daily daily	E&W S	day of prayer, services prayers	dispute in the coal industry
1913–E	27 Apr.	Sun.	E&W	prayers	Christians in China
1914–E1	4 Jan. + later	Sun. + various	E&W	prayers	peace in Ireland
1914–E2	12 June	Fr.	E&W	day of intercession	church in Wales
1914–E3	from 31 July	daily	E&W	prayers	peace in Europe and Ireland
1914–E4	from 4 Aug.	various	E&W	services of intercession	war against Germany
1914–S	from 6 Aug.	various	S	prayers	war against Germany
1914–E5	21 Aug. from 21 Aug.	Fr. various	E&W	day of prayer services	wartime
1915–1	3 Jan.	Sun.	UK	day of humble prayer & intercession	Great War
1916–1	from 3 Jan. 2 Jan. from 2 Jan.	various Sun. various	E&W UK S	services & prayers day of intercession services	wartime Great War wartime
1916–2	4 Aug.	Fr.	UK	day of humble prayer	second anniversary of the outbreak of the Great War
1916–3	31 Dec.	Sun.	UK	day of prayer	Great War
1917–1	29 July or 4 or 5 Aug. 4 + 5 Aug.	Sun. or Sat. or Sun. Sat., Sun.	S E&W	services	third anniversary of the outbreak of the Great War
1918–1	6 Jan.	Sun.	UK	day of prayer & thanksgiving	Great War
1918–2	4 Aug.	Sun.	UK	national day of prayer	fourth anniversary of the outbreak of the Great War
1918–E1	29 Sept.	Sun.	E&W	thanksgiving prayers	deliverance of the Holy Land from Ottoman rule
1918–3	from 11 Nov.	various	UK	thanksgiving prayers and services	armistice with Germany
1918–E2	after 21 Nov.	daily	E&W	prayers	general election

				days of commemoration & thanksgiving	
1918–E3	29 Dec. + 5 Jan. 1919	Sun.	E&W	prayers	aftermath of the Great War
1919–E1	from 11 Jan.	daily	E&W	prayers	for the Russian church and people
1919–E2	from 14 Jan.	daily	E&W	prayers	peace conference
1919–E3	from 16 Mar.	daily	E&W	prayers	dispute in coal mining industry
1919–1	6 July	Sun.	UK	thanksgiving day	peace treaty of Versailles
1919–2	28 Dec.	Sun.	E&W, S	prayer	famine victims in Europe and Near East
1920–E	from 28 Sept.	daily	E	prayers	crises in Ireland and in industrial relations
1920–1	14 Nov.	Sun.	E, S	prayer	first meeting of the League of Nations Assembly
1921–E1	17 Mar.	Th.	E	prayer	peace in Ireland
1921–E2	from 26 June	Sun. + various	E	prayers	for peace in industry, in Ireland, and in international relations
1921–E3	from 6 Nov.	Sun. + various	E	prayers	Washington disarmament conference
1922–E1	from 29 May	daily	Canterbury	prayers	Patriarch Tikhon and the Russian church
1922–E2	from 24 Sept.	Sun. + various	E	prayers	Chanak crisis
1922–E3	from late Oct.	daily	E	prayers	general election
1922–E4	24 Dec.	Sun.	E	prayer	international peace
1923–E	from 17 Nov.	daily	E	prayers	general election
1924–E	from 11 Oct.	daily	E	prayers	general election
1925–E1	from 24 July	daily	E	prayers	threat of national strikes
1925–E2	18 Oct.	Sun.	E	thanksgiving prayer	return of the prince of Wales from imperial tour
1926–E	from 16 Apr.	daily	E	prayers	threat of a general strike
1926–S	from 10 May	daily	S	prayers	General Strike
1928–1	26 or 27 Aug. 26 Aug.	Sun. or Mon. Sun.	E S	thanksgiving prayers	Peace Pact
1928–E	from 30 Nov.	daily	E	prayers	illness of George V
1929–E	from 16 May	daily	E	prayers	general election
1929–1	7 July	Sun.	UK	thanksgiving services	George V's recovery from illness

Code	Date	Frequency	Region	Service	Occasion
1929–S	6 Oct.	Sun.	S	thanksgiving services	re-union of the Church of Scotland
1930–1	12 + 19 Jan.	Sun.	S	prayers	London naval disarmament conference
	19 Jan.	Sun.	E	prayers	
1930–E1	16 Mar. + week	Sun. + daily	E	day of prayer & daily prayers	religious persecution in Russia
1930–E2	25–28 May	Sun. + 3 days	E	prayers	reconciliation in India
1930–E3	16 Nov. + during conference	Sun. + various	E	prayers	Indian round table conference
1930–E4	from 21 Dec.	Sun. + various	E	prayer	unemployment problem
1931–E	from 15 Oct.	daily	E	prayers	national crisis
1931–S	18 Oct.	Sun.	S	day of penitence & prayer	national crisis
1932–1	3 Jan.	Sun.	UK	day of prayer	national and international anxieties
1932–E	27 Nov.	Sun.	E	prayers	imperial, national and international problems
1933–E1	5 Feb.	Sun.	E	prayer	disarmament conference and meetings of the League of Nations
1933–E2	5 Mar.	Sun.	E	prayers	the Church of India, Burma and Ceylon
1933–E3	16 Apr.	Easter Sun.	E	prayers	troubles of the world
1933–1	11 June	Sun.	E, S	prayers	disarmament and economic conferences
1935–1	after 28 Feb.	daily	UK	prayers	reconciliation in India
1935–2	6 + 12 May	Mon. + Sun.	UK	thanksgiving day & services	silver jubilee of George V
1935–E1	6 June + week	Sun. + various	E	prayers	guidance for the statesmen of the world
1935–E2	1 Sept.	Sun.	E	prayer	council of the League of Nations
1936–1	26 + 28 Jan.	Sun. + Tu.	S	services	commemoration of George V
	28 Jan. to 4 Feb.	Tue. + various	E		
1936–E1	Sun. from 21 June	Sun.	E	prayer	League of Nations meetings
1936–E2	13 + 20 Sept.	Sun.	E	prayer	League of Nations meetings

Ref	Date	Day	Region	Type	Description
1937–1	9 + 12 May	Sun. + Wed.	E, S	services & public holiday	coronation of George VI and Queen Elizabeth
1938–E1	19 June	Sun.	E	thanksgiving day	400th anniversary of the English Bible
1938–E2	17 July	Sun.	E	prayer	persecuted Jews of Germany and Austria
1938–1	18 Sept.	Sun.	UK	day of national prayer	Czechoslovakian crisis
1938–2	2 Oct.	Sun.	UK	thanksgiving day	Munich agreement
1938–E3	from 13 Nov.	Sun. + various	E	prayers	Kristallnacht pogrom against German and Austrian Jews
1939–1	5 Feb.	Sun.	E	prayer	Palestine conference
	unspecified		S		
1939–2	28 May	Whit Sun.	E,S	prayer	for international peace
1939–3	27 Aug.	Sun.	E, S	prayer	prevention of war
1939–4	1 Oct. + various	Sun. + various	UK	day of national prayer & services	Second World War wartime
1940–1	12 May or asap	Sun. or Whitsuntide	E, S	prayers	against the rule of force and for lasting peace
1940–2	26 May	Sun.	UK	day of national prayer	for the British and allied cause
1940–3	9 June	Sun.	E	thanksgiving prayers	evacuation of British and allied forces from Dunkirk
	9 June or later	Sun or later	S		
1940–4	16 June	Sun.	E. S	prayer	for France
1940–E	from 1 July	daily	E	prayers	fears of invasion
1940–5	8 Sept.	Sun.	UK	day of national prayer	anniversary of the outbreak of the Second World War
1940–6	15 Dec.	Sun.	E, S	prayer	for Greece
1941–1	23 Mar.	Sun.	UK	national day of prayer	strength, guidance and thanksgivings in wartime
1941–2	7 Sept.	Sun.	UK	national day of prayer	second anniversary of the outbreak of the Second World War
1942–1	1 Jan.	Th.	E, S	prayer	association with day of prayer in the USA
1942–2	29 Mar.	Sun.	UK	national day of prayer	strength and guidance in wartime
1942–3	17 May	Sun.	E	prayer	the people of Norway
1942–E	21 June	Sun.	E	prayer	the nation and people of Russia

Code	Date	Day	Area	Type	Occasion
1942–4	3 Sept.	Sun. + Wed.	UK	national day of prayer & dedication	third anniversary of the outbreak of the Second World War
1942–5	25 + 28 Oct.	Sun.	E, S	prayers	the people of Czechoslovakia
1942–6	15 Nov.	Sun.	UK	prayers, & thanksgiving prayers	civil defence day, and victory at the battle of El-Alamein
1942–7	6 Dec.	Sun.	E, S	prayer	the people of Poland
1943–E1	3 Jan.	Sun.	E	prayer	the suffering Jews of Europe
1943–1	21 Feb.	Sun.	E, S	prayer	the people and Church of Russia
1943–E2	23 Apr.	Good Fr.	E	prayer	the suffering Jews of Europe
1943–2	16 May	Sun.	UK	thanksgiving prayers	British and allied victories in North Africa
1943–S	4 July	Sun.	S	thanksgiving day	tercentenary of the Westminster Assembly
1943–3	3 Sept.	Sun.	UK	national day of prayer & dedication	fourth anniversary of the outbreak of the Second World War
1943–4	12 Sept.	Sun.	UK	thanksgiving prayers	surrender of Italy
1943–5	10 Oct.	Sun.	E, S	prayers	for China
1943–6	28 Nov.	Sun.	E, S	prayer	for India
1944–E1	20 Feb.	Sun.	E	prayer	for British and Commonwealth prisoners of war
1944–E2	23 Apr.	Sun.	E	day of prayer & dedication	in preparation for the allied invasion of northern Europe
1944–1	from 6 June	daily	E	prayers	allied invasion of northern Europe
			S	services	
1944–2	11 June	Sun.	E, S	prayer	the united nations
1944–3	3 Sept.	Sun.	UK	national day of prayer	fifth anniversary of the outbreak of the Second World War
1944–4	from 15 Oct.	various	E	prayers	the people of Holland
	29 Oct.	Sun.	S		
1945–S	22 Apr.	Sun.	S	prayer	San Francisco conference
1945–1	from 8 May	various	UK	thanksgiving prayers	victory in Europe
	13 May	Sun.	UK	thanksgiving day	VE day
	from 13 May	various	E	prayers	continuing war in the Far East
1945–2	19 Aug.	Sun.	UK	thanksgiving day	victory over Japan

	Date	Day			
1946–1	from 29 July	daily	E, S	prayers	Paris peace conference
1947–E	from 14 Feb.	daily	E	prayers	severe winter weather, and the royal tour of South Africa
1947–1	6 July	Sun.	UK	national day of prayer	economic difficulties
1949–E	19 June	Sun.	E	thanksgiving services	400th anniversary of the first Book of Common Prayer
1950–E	from 31 Jan.	daily	E	prayers	general election
1950–S	30 Apr.	Sun.	S	commemoration services	tercentenary of the Scottish psalter of 1650
1950–1	29 Oct.	Sun.	UK	day of prayer	the United Nations and international peace
1951–E1	3 May to 30 Sept.	various	E	services	Festival of Britain
1951–E2	from 5 Oct.	daily	E	prayers	general election
1951–1	9 Dec.	Sun.	UK	thanksgiving prayers	recovery of George VI from illness
1952–1	10 + 15 to 22 Feb.	Sun., Fr. or various	E	prayers & services	commemoration of George VI
	10 + 15 Feb.	Sun., Fr.	S		
1953–S	29 Mar.	Sun.	S	prayers	commemoration of Queen Mary
1953–1	31 May + 2 June	Sun., Tu.	UK	services & public holiday	coronation of Elizabeth II (and I)
1954–E	16 May	Sun.	E	thanksgiving prayers	return of Elizabeth II from Commonwealth tour
1955–E	from 17 July	Sun. + various	E	prayers	Geneva conference and peace of the world
1956–S	24 June, or another Sun. in June	Sun.	S	services	400th anniversary of the first protestant sacrament in Scotland
1959–S	31 May	Sun.	S	day of prayer & dedication	anniversaries of the origins of Calvinism
1960–1	from 21 Feb.	Sun. + various	E	thanksgiving prayers	birth of Prince Andrew
	21 Feb.	Sun.	S		
1960–2	13 Mar.	Sun.	E, S	prayers	disarmament conference
1960–E	from 26 Mar., esp. 31 May	various	E	prayers	protest against apartheid in South Africa

ID	Date	Day	Region	Service	Occasion
1960–S	9 or 16 Oct.	Sun.	S	thanksgiving services & prayers	fourth centenary of the Scottish reformation
1963–S	9 June	Sun.	S	day of remembrance	1,400th anniversary of St Columba's arrival at Iona
1963–1	21 July	Sun.	E, S	prayers	protest against new apartheid laws in South Africa
1964–E	after 11 Mar.	various	E	thanksgiving prayers	birth of Prince Edward
1964–1	from 23 Dec.	daily	E, S	prayers	the peoples of the Congo and Vietnam
1965–1	19 Dec.	Sun.	E, S	day of prayer	crisis over Rhodesia
1971–1	26 Sept. – 3 Oct.	daily	UK	prayers	reconciliation in Northern Ireland
1972–E	17 + 19 Mar.	Fr., Sun.	E	prayers	peace in Northern Ireland
1973–E	30 Dec.	Sun.	E	prayers	national crisis
1977–1	22 May / 5 June	Sun. / Sun.	S / E	thanksgiving services	silver jubilee of Elizabeth II (and I)
1979–S	7 Oct.	Sun.	S	day of prayer	commemoration of the union of the Church of Scotland in 1929
1997–E1	from 4 Sept.	various	E	prayers	commemoration of Diana, princess of Wales
1997–E2	16, 20 or 23 Nov.	Sun.	E	thanksgiving prayers	50th wedding anniversary of Elizabeth II and the duke of Edinburgh
2002–E	from 1 Apr. / 2–8, 10–16 Apr.	various	E	prayers / services	commemoration of Queen Elizabeth the Queen Mother
2002–1	2 June	Sun.	UK	thanksgiving services	golden jubilee of Elizabeth II (and I)
2012–1	from 31 Jan. / 6 Feb. + 3 June + as desired / 3 June	various / Mon., Sun. + various / Sun.	E / E / rest of UK	thanksgiving prayers / thanksgiving services / thanksgiving prayers	diamond jubilee of Elizabeth II (and I)

Special Worship and the Book of Common Prayer

This section provides an outline of the structure of the main services in the BCP – morning prayer, the litany, communion (sometimes called the 'second service') and evening prayer – in order to indicate the parts which were typically modified by special services, and the places where particular prayers were to be added to, or to replace, the usual prayers in the services.

In the Church of England and the Church of Ireland, the forms of prayer for special occasions of worship were of two types: those which consisted of whole services, and those containing just one or more prayers. Both types were adaptations of the services in the BCP. Services involved significant alterations to the forms published in the BCP, commonly changing lessons and psalms, and adding or changing collects and prayers. When individual prayers were published on occasions of special worship, they were generally accompanied by instructions about where they should be inserted into the daily services as laid out in the BCP.

Before the introduction of the first BCP (1549), special liturgies were based either on medieval rites (such as the Sarum rite) or, after 1544, Archbishop Thomas Cranmer's revised English litany. During Edward VI's reign (1547–53), with the exception of services in response to the rebellions of 1549, there is no close link between forms of prayer for special worship and the BCPs of 1549 and 1552. Further editions of the BCP were published in 1559, 1604 and 1662. The Elizabethan Prayer Book of 1559 was imposed on the Church of Ireland by the Irish Act of Uniformity of 1560; the English BCP of 1662 was annexed to the Irish Act of Uniformity of 1665.

The editions on which special forms of prayer were principally based are those for 1559 and 1662; the 1604 BCP had only small additions, including further prayers for particular occasions such as rain, dearth, war and sickness, generally known as 'occasional prayers'. Accordingly, in the presentation of texts in this edition, it may be assumed that the 1559 BCP is the base text for forms published during the Elizabethan and early Stuart period up to the abolition of the BCP by parliament in 1645 and from the restoration in 1660 to 1662. The 1662 BCP, which has remained in use ever since, is the base text for special forms after 1662.

The Prayer Book Psalter is essentially the version of the psalms contained in the 'Great Bible' of 1539–41, translated by Miles Coverdale.

What follows consists of an outline of the structure for the 1559 BCP as modified in 1662. It is followed by a list of the occasional 'Prayers and Thanksgivings', printed at the end of the litany, many of which were incorporated in the liturgies ordered for occasions of special worship.

The best modern editions of the 1559 and 1662 Books of Common Prayer are:
The Book of Common Prayer 1559. The Elizabethan Prayer Book, ed. John E. Booty (Charlottesville, 1976; repr. 2005), and *The Book of Common Prayer. The texts of 1549, 1559, and 1662*, ed. Brian Cummings (Oxford, 2011).

Key to the outline below

Normal text indicates the unvarying parts of the service specified by the BCP throughout the entire period. Variations made in 1662 are indicated by the use of that date. Notes summarizing the BCP's rubrics are also given in normal text.

Italicised text in bold indicates those parts of the service which varied according to the minister's practice, or which changed from day to day following the BCP's calendar.

Fast days, days of humiliation, intercession or prayer, and days of thanksgiving
(a) usually the special services for these days made changes at the points of ***italicised text in bold*** in morning prayer, communion and evening prayers: so, in summary, to opening sentences, psalms, the lessons, collects, epistle, gospel, and offertory sentences
(b) further prayers were added, as follows:
     [*] indicates that material was added at this point across the period from 1625;
     [**] indicates that the addition of material at this point was common in a particular part of the period, as explained in the notes. Some additions and replacements consisted of one new prayer; others consisted of several.

Special prayers (in petition or thanksgiving)
The parts in the service where an individual prayer was added to the normal BCP service when special prayers were ordered or recommended are as follows:
     [+] indicates that an addition was common in different parts of the period
     [++] indicates that the addition of material at this point was unusual, or restricted to a specific part of the period, as explained in the notes.

MORNING PRAYER

Opening sentences [a choice of scriptural sentences, of which one (1559), or one or more (1662) is to be read by the minister]

Exhortation: 'Dearly beloved brethren, the Scripture moveth us' [spoken by the minister]

General confession: 'Almighty and most merciful Father' [the minister, followed by the congregation]

Absolution: 'Almighty God, the Father of our Lord Jesus Christ' [the minister]

The Lord's prayer [the minister; 1662: with the congregation]

The versicles: 'O Lord, open thou our lips', etc. [the minister, with responses from the congregation]

'Venite exultemus' (Psalm 95) [said or sung; 1662: except on Easter Day, and on the nineteenth of the month][1]

---

[1] Forms of prayer for fasts and thanksgiving days often specified a 'psalm' or 'hymn' in place of the *'Venite exultemus'*.

Proper psalms [as appointed for the day or by the special form of prayer]

First lesson [from the Old Testament, as appointed for the day or by the special form of prayer]

'*Te Deum laudamus*' or '*Benedicite*' [said or sung][2]

Second lesson [from the New Testament, as appointed for the day or by the special form of prayer]

[**][3]

'*Benedictus*' or '*Jubilate Deo*' (Ps. 100)

The Apostles' creed

'The Lord be with you', etc. [the minister, with responses from the congregation]

The Lord's prayer [the minister, clerks and congregation]

The suffrages: 'O Lord, shew thy mercy upon us', etc. [the minister, with responses from the congregation][4]

The collect for the day [the minister, as specified for the day by the calendar or varied by the special form of prayer]

The second collect, for peace: 'O God, who art the author of peace' [the minister]

The third collect, for grace: 'O Lord, our heavenly Father' [the minister]

[1662: Anthem, where a choir was present][5] [+] [**][6]

> [When the litany was read, morning prayer finished here. The sequence of prayers from the prayer for the monarch to the grace was read after the litany.]

Prayer for the monarch: 'O Lord our heavenly father'

Prayer for the royal family (when applicable[7]): 'Almighty God, the fountain of all goodness'

Prayer for the clergy and people: 'Almighty and everlasting God, who alone workest great marvels'

> **[BCP occasional 'prayers and thanksgivings' could be added here when the litany was not read.]**

---

2   1565–E1, 1566–E and 1572–E had a psalm in place of the *Te Deum*.
3   1604–E added a prayer here.
4   These suffrages were often altered in the forms of prayer for fast and thanksgiving days.
5   It seems that the anthem was omitted when a special prayer was to be used at this point.
6   1611–E and 1613–E added a prayer here.
7   It was first added in 1604.

Prayer of St Chrysostom

The grace (2 Cor. 13:14)

LITANY

[After morning prayer on Sundays, Wednesdays and Fridays, and when commanded by the ordinary]

'O God the Father of heaven', etc. [the minister, with responses from the congregation]

Kyrie eleison [in English]

The Lord's prayer

'O God merciful Father, that despisest not the sighing of a contrite heart' [the minister, with later sentences for the minister with the congregation]

[**]8

'We humbly beseech thee, O Father' [the minister]

[*]

Prayer for the monarch: 'O Lord our heavenly father'

Prayer for the royal family (when applicable): 'Almighty God, the fountain of all goodness'

Prayer for the clergy and people: 'Almighty and everlasting God, who alone workest great marvels'9

[+] [**]10

[BCP occasional 'prayers and thanksgivings' could be added here.]

[+]

Prayer of St Chrysostom

The grace (2 Cor. 13:14)

---

8 1603–E, 1625–E1, 1636–E3 and 1640–E added prayers here.
9 When prayers were added after 'We humbly beseech thee, O Father', the sequence of prayers from the prayer for the monarch to the prayer for the clergy and people was sometimes omitted.
10 1611–E and 1613–E added a special prayer after the prayer for the clergy and people here; various Elizabethan forms for days (e.g. 1563–E1, 1580–E, 1593–E) may have intended special prayers to be added here.

COMMUNION

The Lord's prayer [the minister]

Collect: 'Almighty God, unto whom all hearts are open'

The ten commandments [the minister, with responses from the congregation]

The collect for the monarch: 'Almighty God, whose kingdom is everlasting' OR 'Almighty and everlasting God' [the minister]

The collect for the day [the minister, as specified for the day by the calendar or vaired by the special form of prayer][11]

The epistle [or other portion of scripture]

The gospel

[**][12]

The Nicene creed

The sermon or homily

Offertory sentences [one or more scriptural sentences, from a specified selection, accompanying the collection of alms]

Prayer for the whole state of Christ's Church militant here in earth: 'Almighty and everliving God' [followed by the administration of communion, when applicable]

[*]

One or more collect(s) [from a selection of six]

Blessing: 'The peace of God, which passeth all understanding'

EVENING PRAYER

Opening sentences [a choice of scriptural sentences, of which one (1559), or one or more (1662) was to be read by the minister]

Exhortation: 'Dearly beloved brethren, the Scripture moveth us' [the minister]

General confession: 'Almighty and most merciful Father' [the minister, followed by the congregation]

---

[11] In the 1559 BCP, the collect for the day was placed before the collect for the monarch.
[12] 1628–E1 and 1629–E1 inserted a prayer here.

Absolution: 'Almighty God, the Father of our Lord Jesus Christ' [the minister]

The Lord's prayer [the minister; 1662: with the congregation]

The versicles: 'O Lord, open thou our lips' etc. [the minister, with responses from the congregation]

[*]¹³

Proper psalms [as appointed for the day or by the special form of prayer]

First lesson [from the Old Testament, as appointed for the day or by the special form of prayer]

'*Magnificat*' (Luke 1) or '*Cantate Domino*' (Ps. 98)

Second lesson [from the New Testament, as appointed for the day or by the special form of prayer]

'*Nunc dimittis*' or '*Deus misereatur*' (Ps. 67)

The Apostles' creed

'The Lord be with you', etc. [the minister, with responses from the congregation]

The Lord's prayer [the minister, clerks and congregation]

The suffrages: 'O Lord, shew thy mercy upon us', etc. [the minister, with responses from the congregation]¹⁴

The collect for the day [the minister, as specified for the day by the calendar or varied by the special form of prayer]

The second collect at evening prayer

[**]¹⁵

The third collect, for aid against all perils

[1662: Anthem, where a choir was present] [+] [*]¹⁶

[+]

Prayer for the monarch: 'O Lord our heavenly father'

---

¹³ If a prayer was specified for use in place of the '*Venite exultemus*' at morning prayer, it was often added here.
¹⁴ These suffrages were often altered in the forms of prayer for fast and thanksgiving days.
¹⁵ 1611–E and 1613–E added a prayer here.
¹⁶ Prayers inserted at the end of the litany were often read here as well.

Prayer for the royal family (when applicable): 'Almighty God, the fountain of all goodness'

Prayer for the clergy and people: 'Almighty and everlasting God, who alone workest great marvels' [*][17]

[BCP occasional 'prayers and thanksgivings' could be added here.]

Prayer of St Chrysostom

The grace (2 Cor. 13:14)[18]

PRAYERS AND THANKSGIVINGS UPON SEVERAL OCCASIONS[19]

* indicates those prayers added in 1604
** indicates those prayers added in 1662

Prayers

For rain
For fair weather
In the time of death and famine ['O God, heavenly Father, whose gift it is' or 'O God, merciful Father, who in the time of Elisha'**[20]]
In the time of war and tumults
In the time of any common plague or sickness
In the ember weeks, to be said every day, for those that are to be admitted to holy orders ['Almighty God, our heavenly Father, who hast purchased' or 'Almighty God, the giver of all good gifts']**
A prayer that may be said after any of the former
A prayer for the high court of parliament, to be read during their session**
A collect or prayer for all conditions of men, to be used at such times when the litany is not appointed to be said**

Thanksgivings

A general thanksgiving**
For rain*
For fair weather*
For plenty*
For peace and deliverance from our enemies*
For restoring public peace at home**

---

17 Prayers inserted at the end of the litany and the communion service were often read here as well.
18 1662 made clear, as 1559 had not, that evening prayer was to conclude with the sequence of prayers from the prayer for the monarch to the grace.
19 This title is taken from the 1662 BCP, and the section begins on a new page following 'Here endeth the Litany'. In 1559, however, the prayers are printed as a continuation of the litany.
20 'O God, merciful Father, who in the time of Elisha' first appeared in the 1552 BCP, but was left out in 1559 and only restored in 1662.

For deliverance from the plague, or other common sickness ['O Lord God, who has wounded us for our sins' or 'We humbly acknowledge before thee, O most merciful Father']*

Printers of Official Documents

For occasions ordered by the crown, the official documents – proclamations or other orders, forms of prayer and addresses – were normally printed and published by the royal printers, that is to say, depending on the sovereign, those described by some such formula as 'Printers to Her [the Queen's, or His or the King's] most excellent majesty', more simply termed 'the Queen's Printer' or 'the King's Printer', or more generally 'the royal printers'. Each of the three kingdoms of England and Wales, Ireland and Scotland had its own royal printers, and in each case this privileged position was over time granted to a succession of printing houses, designated by the name of their owner or that of a partnership.

For occasions ordered when the crown was in abeyance, official documents were not necessarily printed by the royal printers. These complications are explained below.

Printing houses could act as the official printers for prolonged periods, and therefore be responsible for long series of proclamations and other orders, and for forms of prayers or other documents read out in churches. Rather than have many repetitions of the names of printers in the citations for the source texts, in most cases it has seemed more economical to provide the names in summary form in this section.

The tables identify the printers of the official documents for the occasions of special acts of worship (whenever such documents were published, and copies are known to survive). Accordingly, the names of the printers are listed by the codes for these occasions. The years that are given (in the codes) are therefore distinct from the dates of their tenure of the position of royal printers, details of which may be found in the publications listed at the end of this section.

For anniversary commemorations, arrangements were rather different. The original orders and the separate forms of prayer for these commemorations were published by the royal printers; but thereafter in England and Wales and in Ireland the forms of prayer were appended by royal warrant to editions of the Book of Common Prayer, and it was in this form that clergy and congregations usually read the services. These issues are discussed further in the section on anniversary commemorations in volume 3.

ENGLAND AND WALES

Originally, the privilege to print official documents was regarded as belonging to the printer as an individual, rather than to the office of royal printer. Only from 1587 was the royal printing house established as a distinct set of works, with the privilege protected by royal 'letters patent'. Complex legal and financial arrangements enabled rights under these letters patent to be shared among sometimes anonymous financial partners – often, but not always, indicated by the terms 'assignees', 'assigns' or 'heirs' – and for some periods these rights were disputed.

During the civil war from 1642 to 1649, the king and parliament ordered rival occasions of special worship, using different printers to publish their documents;

for parliament, the House of Lords and the House of Commons often used different printers too. This explains the apparent chronological overlaps in printers' names for this period in the following table, but it will be apparent from the commentaries and notes which order was made by the crown, Lords or Commons. After 1649, the official printers worked for the Rump parliament, then the lord protector, and then, briefly, for parliament again, before the office of king's printer was restored in 1660.

After the revolution in 1688, the short-lived convention parliament employed several different printers, even for the order and form for the same occasion: their names are given after the titles of documents in the source notes for 1689–E1 and 1689–E2.

1544–E2 – 1545–E1	Thomas Berthelet
1548–E – 1551–E	Richard Grafton
1554–E3	John Cawood
1560–E	Richard Jugge
1562–E1 – 1570–E	Richard Jugge and John Cawood
1572–E	Richard Jugge
1580–E – 1587–E	Christopher Barker
1588–E1 – 1599–E	Deputies of Christopher Barker
1601–E – 1606–E	Robert Barker
1611–E – 1613–E	Robert Barker
1625–E – 1629–E	Bonham Norton and John Bill
1630–E1	Robert Barker and John Bill
1630–E2	Robert Barker
1631–E1 – 1641–E	Robert Barker [d. 1646] and assignees of John Bill
(1643–E11(R) – 1645–E9(R))	(Leonard Litchfield, Oxford, printer to the University printed all royalist forms)
(1644–E4(P) – 1649–E6)	(Edward Husband ['Printer to the Honorable House of Commons'])
(1646–E4(P) – 1648–E5(P))	(John Wright [printing for the House of Lords])
1649–E6 – 1649–E7	John Field for Edward Husband
1650–E1 – 1651–E1	Edward Husband and John Field
1651–E2 – 1653–E5	John Field
1654–E1 – 1654–2	Henry Hills and William Du Gard ('Printers to His Highness the Lord Protector')
1655–E1r – 1658–1	John Field and Henry Hills ('Printers to His Highness' or 'Printers to his Highness the Lord Protector')
1659–2 – 1659–3	John Field ('Printer to the Parliament')
1660–1	John Streater and John Macock ('Printers to the Parliament')
1660–E2	John Macock and Francis Tyton ('Printers to the House of Lords')
1660–E3 –1666–E1r3	John Bill and Christopher Barker
1666–E –1674–E	The assigns of John Bill and Christopher Barker
1678–E1 –1678–E2	John Bill, Christopher Barker, Thomas Newcomb and Henry Hills
1679–E1r –1680–E	John Bill, Thomas Newcomb and Henry Hills
1683–E1r – 1685–E1r	The assigns of John Bill deceased; and Henry Hills and Thomas Newcomb
1686–E –1688–E1r3	Charles Bill, Henry Hills and Thomas Newcomb
1689–E3 – 1691–E2	Charles Bill and Thomas Newcomb

1691–E3 – 1709–2	Charles Bill and executrix of Thomas Newcomb, deceas'd
1710–1 – 1712–1	Assigns of Thomas Newcomb, and Henry Hills deceas'd
1713–1 – 1723–E	John Baskett, and assigns of Thomas Newcomb, and Henry Hills deceas'd
1740–1 – 1741–2	John Baskett
1742–1 – 1761–1	Thomas Baskett, and the assigns of Robert Baskett
1761–E – 1768–4	Mark Baskett, and the assigns of Robert Baskett
1770–E –1784–1	Charles Eyre and William Strahan
1786–E	C. Eyre and the executors of W. Strahan
1781–1 – 1794–1	Charles Eyre and Andrew Strahan
1795–1 – 1830–2	George Eyre and Andrew Strahan
1831–1 – 1837–1	George Eyre and Andrew Spottiswoode
1840–1 – 1844–1	George E. Eyre and Andrew Spottiswoode
1846–1 – 1848–2	George E. Eyre and William Spottiswoode
1849–1 – 1872–2	George Edward Eyre and William Spottiswoode
1887–1 and certain further occasions	Eyre and Spottiswoode

From the 1870s, an increasing number of occasions of special worship were ordered by the archbishops (or sometimes the convocations) rather than the crown. They preferred to use the Society for Promoting Christian Knowledge (SPCK) as their main publishers for forms of prayer, although they also encouraged simultaneous publication of forms by the Cambridge University Press (CUP) and Oxford University Press (OUP), as well as by the royal printers, now Eyre and Spottiswoode. In time, this use of several printers influenced the arrangements for publishing forms of prayer for occasions which were ordered by the crown, with Eyre and Spottiswoode allowing simultaneous publication by the SPCK, CUP and OUP. In such cases, the names of the printers are given in the source notes for the relevant occasions, after the title of the document.

IRELAND

There was no formal designation of 'King's Printer in Ireland' until 1641, but before this date a number of individuals and, for some periods, the Stationers' Company held patents or were recognized as royal printer. Many proclamations from the 1650s survived into the twentieth century only in manuscript and the few that were printed have no imprint. It was not until 1658 that the name of the printer was more consistently recorded on official documents. As numerous orders and forms of prayer seem not to have survived, it is not always certain when particular printers started or ceased to print these documents.

1650–Ir1 – 1650–Ir2	Printed in Cork by unknown printer.
1658–EIr – 1661–Ir1	William Bladen
1665–EIr1– ?	John Crooke (to be sold by Samuel Dancer)
1672–Ir	Benjamin Took (to be sold by Joseph Wilde)
1679–EIr –1683–EIr	Benjamin Took and John Crook
1685–EIr	Benjamin Tooke (to be sold by John Crook and Samuel Helsham)
1688–EIr –?	Andrew Crook/e and Samuel Helsham, assigns of Benjamin Tooke (to be sold by Andrew Crook and Samuel Helsham)
1690–Ir2	Edward Jones

1690–Ir3 – 1693–EIr1	Andrew Crook, assignee of Benjamin Tooke
1693–EIr2 – 1723–1	Andrew Crook (from 1709 Crooke)
1740–1 – 1749–1	George Grierson
1756–1 – 1758–3	The executors of George Abraham Grierson
1758Ir – ?	Boutler Grierson
1779–1 – 1784–1	The executors of David Hay, assignee of the late Boulter Grierson
1788–1 – 1813–?	George Grierson
1814–1 – 1817–1	George Grierson and John Rowe Power
1820–1	George Grierson and Martin Keane
1830–2 – 1868–1	George and John Grierson

SCOTLAND

Many of the orders and the documents read in church services were issued by the Church of Scotland rather than the government, and for these the notes after the commentaries indicate the source and, where appropriate and known, the printer.

Before 1642, printed texts are known to have been issued for two occasions. The order and form of service for 1566–S1 was printed by the royal printer, Robert Lekpreuik; William Struther's *Scotlands warning* (1628), containing the order and causes for 1628–S, was printed by the heirs of Andro Hart. It is possible that other printed orders were issued in this period, but these have not survived.

From 1639 to 1653, appointment of special worship was largely controlled by the church. In the period to 1650, the few surviving texts issued for governments were printed by Evan Tyler, who had the designation of royal printer. From 1654 to 1660 Scotland was incorporated in the Cromwellian Commonwealth, and orders were mostly issued by the Protectorate government and its successor in London.

From the restoration to the Union, orders issued by the government were printed by the royal printer, as follows:

1665–S1 – 1666–S1	Evan Tyler
1675–S	Andrew Anderson
1678–S – 1693–S2	The heir of Andrew Anderson
1694–S1 – [1707]	The heirs and successors of Andrew Anderson

From 1708 onwards, the source for proclamations and other printed orders issued by the crown has been the *London Gazette*, and occasionally the *Edinburgh Gazette*.

BIBLIOGRAPHY

Aldis, Harry G., *A list of books printed in Scotland before 1700, including those printed furth of the realm for Scottish booksellers* (rev. edn, Edinburgh, 1970)

Haig, Robert, 'New light on the king's printing office 1680–1730', *Studies in Bibliography*, 8 (1956), 157–67

Hammond, Joseph, 'The king's printers in Ireland, 1551–1919', *Dublin Historical Record*, 2 (1950) 1: 29–31, 2: 58–64, 3: 88–96

Johnson, A. F., 'The king's printers 1660–1742', *The Library*, 5th ser., 3 (1948), 33–8

Lambert, Sheila, 'The beginning of printing for the House of Commons, 1640–2', *The Library*, 6th ser., 3 (1981), 43–61

Mann, Alastair J., *The Scottish book trade, 1500–1720: print commerce and print control in early modern Scotland* (East Linton, 2000)

Oxford dictionary of national biography

Plomer, Henry, 'The king's printing house under the Stuarts', *The Library*, new ser., 2 (1901), 353–75

Plomer, H. R., Bushnell, G. H. and McC. Dix, E. R., *A dictionary of the printers and booksellers who were at work in England, Scotland and Ireland from 1726 to 1775* (Oxford, 1932)

Printing for parliament, 1641–1700, ed. Sheila Lambert (List and Index Society, Special Series, 20, 1984)

Rees, Graham and Wakely, Maria, *Publishing, politics and culture. The king's printers in the reign of James I and VI* (Oxford, 2009)

A short-title catalogue of books printed in England, Scotland and Ireland and of English books printed abroad, 1475–1640, first compiled by A. W. Pollard and G. R. Redgrave, ed. W. A. Jackson, F. S. Ferguson and K. F. Pantzer (3 vols., 1976–91), III, 97–9

SPECIAL PRAYERS, FASTS AND THANKGIVINGS
IN THE BRITISH ISLES 1533–1688

TEXTS AND COMMENTARIES

1533–E   Thanksgiving service for the birth of Princess Elizabeth

Monday 8 September 1533 (St Paul's Cathedral, London)

This thanksgiving, the first since the passing of the Acts of Restraint of Appeals and of Supremacy which secured England's break from Rome, is known only from a brief note in the chronicle of Charles Wriothesley, Windsor Herald. Although Anne Boleyn's pregnancy by King Henry VIII had been privately known since January (and publicly from at least her coronation in March), it was probably not formally celebrated because her marriage (25 January) was not recognized until May, when Archbishop Thomas Cranmer was able to declare Henry VIII's marriage to Catherine of Aragon null and void. Anne gave birth to a daughter, the future Queen Elizabeth I, on 7 September. In the absence of evidence to the contrary, the service probably followed pre-reformation practice for thanksgivings laid out in the Sarum rite (the rite of St Paul's had been abolished in 1414 in favour of the more common Sarum use). Wriothesley noted that *Te Deum*s (the traditional hymn or psalm of thankgiving) were sung at St Paul's Cathedral in the presence of the mayor, the alderman and the heads of the livery companies and guilds. At this time, services at St Paul's appear to have been used regularly to represent the whole nation.

Order: none found.
Form of prayer: probably Sarum rite.
Source: *Wriothesley*, I, 22.

DESCRIPTION OF OCCASION

Wriothesley
Memorandum, the vii[th] daie of September, 1533, being Sonndaie, Queene Anne was brought to bedd of a faire daughter at three of the clocke in the after noune; and the morrowe after, being the daie of the Nativitie of Our Ladie, Te Deum was songe solempnlie at Powles, the Major [*sic*] and Aldermen being present, with the head craftes[1] of the Cittie of London.

1535–E   Procession for the recovery of Francis I of France from illness

Friday 12 November 1535 (St Paul's Cathedral, London)

The French king, Francis I, who was temporarily allied with Henry VIII against the Holy Roman Emperor Charles V in a dispute over the duchy of Milan, fell ill in Dijon while mustering troops in southern France. Processions for his recovery were

---

[1]   Livery companies.

held across France and at St Paul's Cathedral, the first time that public worship is known to have been ordered in England for the recovery from illness of a foreign monarch. The service at St Paul's probably followed the Sarum rite. It would have begun with antiphons and versicles sung by the choir in the stalls, but much of the service would have been said or sung as the priests and choir processed to other altars or churches. Wriothesley did not describe the route the procession took but emphasized the service's rich visual spectacle and the range of people who attended.

Order: none found.
Form of prayer: probably Sarum rite.
Sources: *Wriothesley*, I, 32; Viscount Hannaret to the Holy Roman Empress, Isabella of Portugal, 10 Nov. 1535, *CSPSp, 1534–1535*, p. 567; Dr Ortiz to the Holy Roman Empress, 1 Jan. 1536, *Letters and papers, foreign and domestic, of the reign of Henry VIII*, ed. J. S. Brewer *et al.* (23 vols. in 35, 1862–1932), X, 3; Stowe, 'Chronicle', pp. 11–12; Stowe, *Summarie*, fos. 189v–190r.

DESCRIPTION OF OCCASION

Wriothesley
This yeare, the 12th daie of November, was songe at Paules a masse of the Holie Ghost and Te Deum, first with the children of Paules schole, and then all the orders of fryars with copes on their backes, all the channons about London, the monkes of Tower Hill, Barmonsley, and Westminster, with all the priestes of everie parrishe in London, Poules quire going all in rytch robes of cloath of gould, and seaven abbotts and bishopps with myters on their heades, the Bishop of London bearing the sacramente of the aulter under a rich cannapie of gould with torches going about it, and then the batchles of the Majors craft following afore the Major and Aldermen, and after them all the craftes in London in their best liveries, which solemnitie was donne for the health of Frances the French Kinge, which was nighe dead, and so recovered againe by the goodnes of Almightie God.

1537–E1   *Te Deum*s for the pregnancy of Queen Jane

Sunday 27 May 1537 (St Paul's Cathedral, London)

Jane Seymour's pregnancy was publicly announced on 27 May when a *Te Deum* was sung at St Paul's. This was the first time that the pregnancy of a queen consort is known to have been celebrated. Unlike that of her predecessor, the news of Jane's pregnancy was uncontroversial. Both of Henry's previous wives were dead (Catherine of Aragon had died on 7 January 1536; Anne Boleyn had been executed on 19 May 1536), so the legality of his third marriage was undisputed. It was also hoped that Jane would produce Henry's long-awaited male heir. The service was well attended by a host of leading privy councillors, courtiers and higher clergy as well as City officials. The service probably followed the Sarum rite but Wriothesley's account indicates that Hugh Latimer, bishop of Worcester, added an oration 'shewinge the cause of their assemblye'. This was a device used in other Henrician services (e.g. 1541–E2), during Edward VI's reign (see 1544–E2) and, more regularly, during Elizabeth I's. In the evening, according to tradition, bonfires were lit across London and hogsheads of wine were provided for all to drink. It is unclear why Wriothesley's description of the occasion was more extensive than that for Anne (1533–E). He was an evangelical, who had benefited from the Boleyns' rise and began his chronicle with a lengthy account of Anne's coronation. It may have been because the service for Jane was better attended, less controversial or because Wriothesley invested more time in his writing.

Order: none found.
Form of prayer: probably Sarum rite.
Source: *Wriothesley*, I, 64.

DESCRIPTION OF OCCASION

Wriothesley
Alsoe, the 27 daye of Maye, 1537, being Trynytie Sondaye, there was Te Deum sounge in Powles for joye of the Queenes quickninge of childe, my Lord Chaunseler, Lord Privaye Seale, with diverse other lordes and bishopps, beinge then present; the mayre and aldermen with the beste craftes of the Cyttye beinge there in their lyveryes, all gevinge laude and prayse to God for joye of the same; wher the Bishopp of Worcester, called Docter Latymer, made an oration afore all the Lordes and Commons, after Te Deum was songe, shewinge the cause of their assemblye, which oration was mervelouse fruitefull to the hearers; and alsoe the same night was diverse greate fyers made in London, and a hogeshed of wine at everye fyer for poore people to drinke as longe as yt woulde laste; I praye Jesue, and it be his will, send us a prince.

1537–E2   Processions and *Te Deum*s for the birth of Prince Edward

Thursday 11 October–Friday 12 October 1537 (London)

On 11 October, there were solemn processions in London after Queen Jane went into labour. The following day, at two o'clock in the morning, the queen gave birth to a son, the future Edward VI. At eight o'clock, *Te Deum*s were sung in all parish churches in the capital and their bells rung. An hour later, a service was held at St Paul's Cathedral and guns were fired from the Tower. From five o'clock until ten, new fires were set up in every parish along with hogsheads of wine, and parish bells were rung. Guns were fired at the Tower.

Order: none found.
Form of prayer: Sarum rite or other use.
Source: *Wriothesley*, I, 65–8.

DESCRIPTION OF OCCASION

Wriothesley
This yeare, the 11th daie of October, Anno 1537, and the 29th yeare of the raigne of King Henrie the Eight, being Thursdaie, their was a solempne generall procession in London, with all the orders of friars, preistes, and clarkes going all in copes, the major and aldermen, with all the craftes of the cittie, following in their liveries, which was donne to pray for the Queene that was then in labour of chielde. And the morrowe after, being Fridaie and the eaven of Sainct Edward, sometime King of

Englande, at tow of the clocke in the morninge, the Queene [was] delivered of a man chielde at Hampton Court beside Kingston. And the same daie, at eight of the clocke in the morning, Te Deum was songe in everie parish church throughout London, with all the bells ringing in everie church, and great fiars made in everie street; and at 9 of the clocke their was assembled at Poules all the orders of friars, monkes, channons, priestes, and clarkes about London, standing all about Paules in rich copes, with the best crosses and candlestickes of everie parrishe church in London; the Bishopp of London, the Bishopp of Chichestre, Deane of Poules, and the Abbott of Westminster being mitred, the said Bishopp and Deane of Poules making a collation to the people at the quire dore of Poules, the French Kinges embassadour being present, the Lord Chauncelor of Englande, the Lord Privie Seale, the Lorde Marques Dorsett, with all the judges and serjeantes of the lawe; the Major of London, with the ordermen and sherives, with all the craftes of London, standing in their liveries; and after the said collation Poules quire song in attempne[2] of the Trinitie, with Te Deum, and the 9th responde of the Trinitie, with the colect of the same. Then the Kinges waites and the waites of London plaied with the shalmes; and after that a great peale of gonnes were shott at the Tower of London, all of which solempnitie was donne to give laude and prayse to God for joy of our prince.

Also, the same night, at five of the clocke, their was new fiers made in everie streete and lane, people sitting at them banquetting with fruites and wyne, the shalmes and waites playing in Cheepeside, and hogsheaddes of wyne sett in divers places of the Cittie for poore people to drinke as long as they listed; the major and aldermen riding about the cittie thancking the people, and praying them to give laude and praise to God for our prince; also their was shott at the Tower that night above tow thousand gonns, and all the bells ringing in everie parish church till it was tenne at the clocke at night; also the marchantes of the Styliard[3] made great fiers, and brent a hundred staffe torches at their place, and gave a hogeshed of wyne to poore people, and tow barrels of beare also.

1537–E3   Processions for the health of Queen Jane and Prince Edward

Friday 19 October 1537 (London)

Eight days after the birth of Prince Edward (see 1537–E2) a solemn procession was held for his and the queen's health. Although Edward's health was robust and Jane had initially recovered from a very long labour, the queen weakened at some point after Edward's christening on 15 October. Contemporaries reported that she suffered from septicaemia and delirium; this was probably caused by parts of the placenta being retained in her uterus. Despite the break with Rome, there had been relatively little theological change in the English church and Cranmer did not begin to reform the liturgy until the following year. Hence, the pre-reformation practices of

---

[2]   Anthem.
[3]   Steelyard. The 'merchants of the Steelyard' were from the Hanseatic League, formed *c.* 1320 by a group of northern German towns. The Steelyard was off Thames Street near Blackfriars.

petitioning for divine intervention, including processions, remained. Jane died before midnight on 24 October.

Order: none found.
Form of prayer: Sarum rite or other use.
Source: *Wriothesley*, I, 69.

DESCRIPTION OF OCCASION

Wriothesley
Also, the 19th daie of October, their was a solempne generall procession in London, with all the orders of friars and chanons, the monkes of Towre Hill, with all the priestes and clarkes of everie church in London, with Powles quire, and the best crosse of everie parish in London, with the baner for the same borne in the same procession, all the friars, monkes, canons, priestes, and clarkes, going in their best copes of everie church, the Bishop of London following Powles quire with his mitre, the major and aldermen, with all the craftes of the citie following in their lyveries, which procession was donne for the preservation and welfare of the Prince and the health of the Queene.

1537–E4   Dirges on the death of Queen Jane

Monday 12 November (St Paul's Cathedral, London)

Queen Jane died on 24 October and was buried at St George's Chapel, Windsor. As the first consort to die in 'good estate' since Henry VII's wife, Elizabeth of York, in 1503, elaborate, traditional rituals were followed for the preparation of Jane's body, lying in state and funeral. Tradition meant that Henry could not attend the funeral; he was represented by his elder daughter, Princess Mary, who had returned to court but was still excluded from the succession. Solemn dirges were sung at St Paul's Cathedral and knells rung in every parish church in London on 12 November, the day of Jane's funeral. The court was in mourning until Christmas, and Henry continued wearing black until February 1538.

Order: none found.
Form of prayer: probably Sarum rite.
Source: *Wriothesley*, I, 71–2.

DESCRIPTION OF OCCASION

Wriothesley
Allso, the sayde 12th of Novembre, at afternoone, there was a solemn herse made at Powles in London, and a solemne dirige done there by Powles queere, the Major of London beinge there present with the alldermen and sheriffes, and all the major's officers and the sheriffes sergeants, mourninge all in blacke gownes, and all the craftes of the cittie of London in their lyveries; also there was a knyll rongen in everie parishe churche in London, from 12 of the clocke at noone tyll six of the clocke at night, with all the bells ringinge in everye parishe churche solemne peales, from 3 of the clocke tyll the knylls ceased; and allso a solempne dirige songen in

everye parishe churche in London, and in everie churche of freeres, monkes, and chanons, about London; and, the morrowe after, a solemne masse of requiem in all the sayde churches, with all the bells ringinge, from 9 of the clocke in the morninge tyll noone; also there was a solemne masse of requiem done at Powles, and all Powles queere offeringe at the same masse, the major, aldermen, and sheriffes, and the wardeins of everie crafte of the cittie of London; and, after the sayde masse, the major and aldermen goeinge aboute the herse sayenge "De profundis," with all the craftes of the cittie followinge, everie one after their degrees, prayinge for the sowle of the sayde Queene.

1540–E   Prayers and processions during drought and disease

[From September? 1540] (England and Wales)

This occasion is only known through a reference in Wriothesley's *Chronicle*. Henry VIII's realms suffered hot dry summers from 1538. By 1540, Wriothesley reported, 'in divers partes of this realme the people carried their cattle six or seven miles to watter them'; many cattle died and people suffered from dysentery, agues and plague. So severe was the distress that the king commanded the organization of weekly prayers and processions in every parish. This was the first time since the break with Rome that special worship had been ordered throughout the kingdom. With no order extant, it is unclear when this order to the bishops was issued, but it was probably in late August or early September, because starting on Friday 17 September Bishop Bonner of London and the lord mayor arranged for a weekly procession through the City of London, preceded by a sermon in St Paul's Cathedral. The processions probably continued to use the Sarum or other rites.

Order: not extant.
Form of prayer: Sarum rite or other use.
Source: *Wriothesley*, I, 123.

DESCRIPTION OF OCCASION

Wriothesley

This yeare was a hott sommer and drie, so that no raine fell from June till eight daies after Michaelmas, so that in divers partes of this realme the people caried their cattle six of seven miles to watter them, and also much cattle died; and also their rayned strang sicknes among the people in this realme, as laskes [i.e. dysentery] and hot agues, and also pestilence, wherof many people died; wherfore the Kinges Majestie sent out commissions through this realme to everie par[ticular] bishopp to exhort the people to fall to prayer and to go in procession in everie parish in the hole realme; and also my Lord Mayer and the Bishopp of London caused generall procession to be once in the weeke through the cittie, which beganne the 17th daie of September, being Fridaie in the Ember weeke, and had a sermon made in Paules quire before the procession went, and used it so everie Fridaie, which as a godlie waie.

1541–E   Prayers during a severe drought

After 20 May–July 1541 (England and Wales)

Despite the rain that Wriothesley reported as falling after Michaelmas in 1540, the drought resumed during 1541. Rivers dried up, and the Thames was so low that seawater extended beyond London Bridge. In May, Cranmer was ordered by the king to organize public prayers in all cathedral, college and parish churches to petition for an end to the drought. In London, by order of Bishop Bonner, prayers and processions at St Paul's were organized every Friday from 29 July, with prayers said for the king, the queen (now Henry VIII's fifth wife, Katherine Howard), and for Prince Edward. It is not known for how long the prayers and processions were continued.

Order: royal mandate to Archbishop Thomas Cranmer, 20 May 1541, LPL, Cranmer Register, I, fo. 18r.
Form of prayer: Sarum rite or other use.
Additional sources: episcopal mandate from Bishop Edmund Bonner to [?], [n.d.], LMA, MS 9531/12: 1, fos. 24v–25r; *Wriothesley*, I, 125.

ORDER

Royal mandate to archbishop of Canterbury: 20 May 1541

Thomas etc dilecto nobis in Christo decano decanatus nostri de Archubus London nostre et ecclesie nostre Christi Cantuariensis iurisdictionis immediate seu eius Commissario vel deputato, salute. Breve & c Nos quatentus indilate post receptionem presentium dictum decretum cuius varia exmplaria in papiro inpresa vna cum presentibus vobis per latorem presentium transmittimus in omnibus et singulis ecclesijs Collegiatis parochialibus et Capellis ceterisque quibuscumque infra decanatum et iusidictionem predictos vbilibi constitutis ab omnibus et singulis Collegiorum ministris ecclesiarum parochillum Rectoribus vicararijs Curatis et plebanis in eisdem ecclesijs et Capellis ministrantibus diebus dominicis sine festivis & c vti in priori exemplari continetur. Et quid & c datus 20 maij 1541[.]

1543–E1   Prayers during the Ottoman invasion of Hungary

After Tuesday 19 July 1543 (Canterbury province)

The Ottoman sultan, Süleyman I, renewed his military campaign against the Habsburgs in Hungary in 1541. His aim was to secure control of the kingdom after the death of John Zápolyai, an Ottoman vassal who had contested the throne with the Holy Roman Emperor, Ferdinand I. In 1541 Süleyman conquered Buda, and during early 1543 he mounted a major campaign to conquer the rest of Hungary. These campaigns attracted the attention of much of christian Europe, protestant as well as catholic; Martin Luther published in 1541 an *Appeal for prayer against the Turk*. There was a long English tradition of special worship in support of foreign princes fighting 'infidels', reaching from 1252 to 1523, and this was continued during and after the Protestant reformation (see also 1565–E1, 1565–E2, 1566–E and 1571–E). In 1543 this was linked to Henry VIII's decision to send £10,000 to assist the Hapsburg forces, a sum he sought to recoup by voluntary collections from parishoners. Ostensibly on Cranmer's suggestion, in July the king appointed special prayers throughout Canterbury province to accompany this appeal for church collections. An 'exhortation' was circulated 'to put the people in Remembraunce to doo theire charytye', with a set of instructions on how churchwardens were to collect the 'benyvolences'. Through the mediation of Francis I of France, a truce was agreed between the Habsburgs and Ottomans in 1545, which enabling Süleyman to retain suzerainty over Hungary. From then until the mid-1560s he concentrated his military efforts elsewhere, on the other borders of his empire.

Order: Cranmer to Bonner [as bishop of London and dean of the province], 19 July [1543], LMA, MS 9531/12: 1, fo. 45v.
Exhortation and instruction: Ibid., fos. 45–6, printed in Paul Ayris, 'Preaching the last crusade: Thomas Cranmer and the "devotion" money of 1543', *Journal of Ecclesiastical History*, 49 (1998), 699–700.

ORDER

Archbishop of Canterbury to bishop of London: 19 July [1543]

After my hartye commendationes, ye shall vnderstande that vpon certayne Advertysmentes of the mayne Invasyon whiche the Turk makyeth this yere into hungarye and vpon suyte made by the kynge of Romannes to the kynges maiestye for ayde and succo' to withstande the same with Lamentable complaynte that chrestendome nowe troubled with warres the Turke taketh hys commodytye and oportunytie to oppresse and over throwe them. The kinges highnes moued with pitye and compassion of the State of thoose countreyes hathe of his mercyfull harte condescended agreed and promised to gyve a notable ayede and hathe of his treasure presentlye dysbursed a good parte thereof moche to the pleasure of god his maiestyes renowne and fame / And thonor of the Realme And forasmoche as I nothinge doubte but all goode chr[ist]en people will gladlye of their devocion not onely with theyr prayo' but also as they may spare with some parte of theire substaunce also shewe them selfes Ayders and succoroures in this case of calamytie thereby to be partakers of the meryte of so goode a dede I haue desyred the kinges maiestye to be contente that by his highnes auctorytye I mighte exhorte his people in this province to prayoure and charytable collation in this tyme of necessitie Accordynge wherevnto I directe vnto you theese my l[ett]res the effecte whereof I requyre you ye cause to be publysshed in youre dyocess and executed with speede And that for Receavinge the peoples devocions ye desyrethe churche wardens every sonday and holy daye bitwyxt this and myghelmasse to take the paynes eche daye ones in the tyme of service when the number of the people ys greatteste quyetely and charitably to Requyre benyvolence takynge in good parte what soever ys gyven more or lesse and the paryshe preeste to demaunde of the churche wardens everyday of gatherynge what some they haue collected and the monye to Remayne with the churchewardens vnto suche tyme as the kynges offycer shalbe appoynted to Receaue the same of them accordyng to suche Sommes as shall appeare be the Curattes or prieste certyficat to haue been gathered by them And in defaulte of Churche wardens the paryshe tappoynte some two honeste men in whose handes the monye may surelye Remayne to be holy Reserued to thuse yt ys gyvyn for forseynge allwayes that for thadvoydinge of all suspition of any Advauntage to growe to the Curate vs oure offycers that the Curate be onelye pryvye from tyme to tyme to the Some receaued and therof to certyfye you, every monyth and the money onelye to be towched by the churchewardens and suche other as shall receaue yt by appoyntemente of the kynges counsaile of them to be conveyed to his maiestyes handes I sende you also herewith an exhortation devised to be made to the people by the Curate ones and oftitener [*sic*] as shalbe thought Requysite to put the people in Remembraunce to doo theire charytye as apparteyneth[.]

1543–E2 Prayers and processions during persistent wet weather and threats to the harvest

After Thursday 23 August–September 1543 (Canterbury province)

The summer of 1543 was extremely wet and threatened the harvest. In August, Henry VIII ordered both private prayers and public prayers, rogations and processions to be conducted in all cathedral, town and parish churches in the province of Canterbury. These services probably followed the Sarum rite or other uses. Cranmer's second foray into liturgical reform – the litany – was not completed and authorized until 1544 (see 1544–E2).

Order: royal mandate to Cranmer, 23 Aug. 1543, LPL, Cranmer Register, I, fo. 22r.
Form of prayer: Sarum rite or other use.

ORDER

Royal mandate to the archbishop of Canterbury: 23 August 1543

Thomas etc Venerabili confratri nostro domino Edmundo eadem permissione London Episcopo vestro ve vicario in spiritualibus generali et officiali principali Salutem et fraternam in domino charitatem. Litteras supradicti Invictissimi domini nostri Regis nuper recepimus tenor subsequentem continentes. Moast Reuerend ffather in god right trustye & ryght entierly beloued we grete yow well / and for Asmuch as there hath ben now A late & still continuith muche Raine & other vnseasonable weder wherby is like to ensue grete hurt & damage to the corne and fructes nowe rype vppon grownde / Onles it shall plese god of his infinite goodnes to stretche forthe his holy hande over vs Considering by sundry examples heretofore / That god at the contemplation of ernest and devote prayers / oftymes extended his mercy and grace / And hath also assvredly promysed That whensoeuer we call vppon him for thinges mete for vs he will graunte vnto vs the same / We hauing the gouern[a]unce & charge of his people committed vnto vs / haue thoght good to cause the same to be exhorted by yow / and other the prelates of this o[ur] Realme with an ernest repentant harte for their Iniquit[i]es to call vnto god for m[er]cie and with devote and humble prayors / and supplicacions euery personne both by him selfe a parte / And also by commen prayour to beseche him to send vnto vs seasonable and temporate wedar to haue in thoes fructes and courne on the grownde / wich hetherto he hath caused so plentuously to groe / for the which purpose we requyre you and neuerthe lesse commaunde you to send vnto all your brotherne the Bysshoppes wyth in yo[r] province / to cause such generall Rogacions and processiones to be made incontynently w[t]in their dioc[ese] as in lyke case heretofore hath been accustomed / in this behaulf accordingly Yeuen vnder o[r] signet at o[r] man[or] of the Moore the xx[th] daye of August the xxxv[th] yere of our Raine. Quatenus attentis premissis sementis pestis / rigore et bellorum tumultibus quibus orbis Christianus in presentiarum x[?] pro dolor undique estuat omnibus et

1   An example of an early order for special worship: a royal mandate copied into
an archiepiscopal register, for 1543–E2. Royal mandate to Archbishop Thomas
Cranmer, 23 Aug. 1543, LPL, Cranmer Register, I, fo. 22r–v.

singulis confratibus nostris Coepiscopis nostris et ecclesie nostre Christi Cantuariensis suffraganeis, cum ea qua poteritis celeritate accomoda precipiatis vt ipsorum singuli in suis Cathedralibus et Civitatum ac diocesim suarum parochialibus Ecclesijs, exposito publice litterarum Regiarum huiusmodo xij° et Sancto tenore, Clericos / et laicos infra suas dioceses degentes sedulo et accurate moveant et Inducant aut moueri et Iuduci sanctis monitis et Salubribus preceptis faciant / Atque sic A vobis in Ciuitate et diocesi vestra London fieri volumus, qualibet quarta et Sexta ferijs publicis supplicaconibus, et Suffragijs altissimum deuote adorent eorumque precibus (vti fieri Assueuit suam immensam misericordiam impleret, Quantus in ira sua qua nostris malemeritis Juste provocauimus misericordie sue recordatus quibus offensus huiusmodi super nos merito imnisit afflictiones propitiatus misericorditer nobis recipiscentibus submoveat, Ab orationibus et suffragijs huiusmodi non cessantes donec aliud A nobis in hac parte habuerities in mandatis Dat in Manerio nostro de Croydon xxiij° die mensis Augusti Anno domini 1543 Et nostre Consecrationis Anno vndecimo.

1544–E1   Thanksgiving service for victories in Scotland

Friday 23 May 1544 (St Paul's Cathedral, London)

Henry VIII responded to the adultery and execution of his fifth wife, Catherine Howard, by attempting to bathe in military glory by enforcing the treaty of Greenwich with Scotland and by declaring war against France. Under the terms of a treaty agreed in 1543, England and Scotland were to be united with the marriage of Prince Edward to Mary Stuart, queen of Scots. The Scots' reluctance to honour the treaty led to Henry's campaign being called the 'rough wooings'. In the spring of 1544, as he prepared to go to France, Henry sent a force of 14,000 men under the earl of Hertford (maternal uncle of Prince Edward) against the Scots. Hertford pillaged Edinburgh for two days and captured a number of ships at Leith, but otherwise his campaign achieved little. This occasion is known only from descriptions by Wriothesley and in an anonymous chronicle contained in the register book of the Franciscan order of the Grey Friars in London. Contrary to tradition, on this occasion the secular celebrations were held on Ascension day, the day before the thanksgiving service, rather than on the same day. The thanksgiving service could not replace a major festival but it is unclear why the secular celebrations were not delayed, unless it was to mark the victory as soon as it was known. Cranmer's revised litany was not authorized for use until 27 May so this thanksgiving probably followed the Sarum rite. The identity of the preacher is unknown.

Order: none found.
Form of prayer: probably Sarum rite.
Sources: *Wriothesley*, I, 147; *Grey Friars' chronicle*, p. 47.

DESCRIPTIONS OF OCCASION

Wriothesley
This yeare the 22 day of May, beinge Assention day, there were great fyers made in the citye of London and the suburbes, and wine set in divers places of the citie, for the

victorie that the Kinges Majesties armie had in Scotland, and the morrowe after there was a sermon made in Pawles to the laude of God and prayse of the Kinges Majestie, with Te Deum songe, and after a generall procession.

Grey Friars' chronicle
Item, the xxij. day of May was the Assencion day, and at nyght was made grete bone-fyers thorrow all London, and grete chere in every parych at every bone-fyer, and grete melody with dyvers instrewmentes; and the mayer with the shreffes rydynge thorrow every warde of London to see how it was done, for the good tydynges that came owte of Scotland.

1544–E2   Services and processions during the military campaign in France

After Sunday 8 June–September 1544 (Canterbury province)

Henry's desire for military glory, the need to defend his realms and the longstanding rivalry between Francis I and Charles V led him to ally with the emperor against Francis in 1543 and to plan a joint attack on Paris in 1544. In June, Henry ordered Cranmer to organize public processions in all dioceses in the province of Canterbury; there is no extant evidence that orders were issued for York as well. The 'certayne godly prayers and suffrages in oure natiue englyshe tonge' specified were probably those in *An exhortation unto prayer*, Cranmer's new vernacular litany, which contained explicit references to Henry's campaign in France and was printed by the royal printer. *An exhortation* was the product of Cranmer's second attempt to provide a uniform and simpler liturgy for the Church in England (see 1537–E3 and 1541–E1) and provided a liturgical form for services of petition or intercession. Authorized on 27 May, it was heavily based on the Sarum rite, which Cranmer admired, and began with a lengthy exhortation explaining the need for common prayers (for similar devices used previously, see 1537–E1). After the exhortation, the procession began, during which the litany was said or sung in English. The litany opened with a series of suffrages and then prayers for the king, Queen Catherine (Parr), Prince Edward, the bishops and parish ministers, the privy council, the nobility, all magistrates and the people. There were further suffrages for peace, grace and mercy, followed by the Lord's prayer, and two sets of versicles and prayers. However, the penitential psalms and invocations to the saints were omitted. The choice of English was justified to encourage the attendance of those who 'have vsed to come very slackely to the procession' because 'they vnderstode no parte of soche prayers or suffrages as were vsed to be songe and sayde'. *An exhortation* also gave instructions on how the litany was to be used and the *rôle* of the congregation. The versicles were to be recited by the priest and choir. During the litany, those parishioners with personal copies could read quietly to themselves; those without their own copies should listen attentively to the priest. The mixture of private worship, vocal active participation and attentive listening during public services represents a combination of pre-reformation and post-reformation practices. It was common for parishioners to worship privately during pre-reformation services when they could not hear (or understand) the priests as they conducted the liturgy. Conversely, Elizabethan nationwide services comprised many 'composite psalms'made up from verses across the Bible, which were recited by the minister with a response from the clerk or congregation. There were also opportunities for silent meditation (see 1563–E). Though Henry had planned to attack Paris, in July 1544 he chose to lay siege to Boulogne and Montreuil instead, while Charles made a separate peace with Francis. It is unclear for how long prayers for the king's success were conducted, but they would have ended at the latest with news of Henry's victory at Boulogne in September (see 1544–E3). In 1545, Cranmer's litany was authorized for use in all services, though his attempts to reform the rest of the Sarum rite were unsuccessful.

Order: royal mandate to Cranmer, 8 June 1544, LPL, Cranmer Register, I, fos. 48v–49r [misdated to 1545 in *Miscellaneous writings and letters of Thomas Cranmer*, ed. John Edmund Cox (Parker Society, Cambridge, 1846), p. 495 n. 8; this part of the register is in chronological confusion].

Form of prayer: *An exhortation unto prayer, thoughte mete by the kinges maiestie, and his clergy, to be read to the people in euery church afore processyions. Also a letanie with suffrages to be said or song in the tyme of the said processyons* ([40] pp.; STC 10620)*; [later editions with the same title in 1544–5, often with music, STC 10621, 10621.5, 10621.7, 10622, 10623, 10623.3].

ORDER

Royal mandate to archbishop of Canterbury: 8 June 1544

… Moste reuerende father in god right trustie and right welbeloued we grete youe well / And let youe witte that callinge to oure remembraunce the miserable state of all Christendom beinge at this present besydes all other trobles so plaged wythe moste cruell warres hatreddes and discentions as no peace of the same almoste (beinge thole redused to a very narrowe corner) remaynethe in good peax agrement and concorde, thelpe and remedie whereof farre exceadinge the power of any man muste be called for of hym, whoo onely is able to graunte oure petitiones and never forsaketh ne repelleth any that firmely beleve and faythfully call on hym, vnto whome also thexamples of scripture encoragethe vs in all thies and other oure trobles and necessities to flie and to crye for ayde and succor beinge therefore resolued to have continually from hensforthe generall processiones in all cities townes churches and parishes of this oure realme sayde & songe wythe soche reverence and devotion as appertayneth forasmoche as heretofore the people partely for lacke of goode instruction and callinge on, partly for that they vnderstode no parte of soche prayers or suffrages as were vsed to be songe and sayde have vsed to come very slackely to the procession when the same have bene commaunded heretofore / Wee haue setforthe certayne godly prayers and suffrages in oure natiue englyshe tonge whiche we sende youe herewythe signifiynge vnto youe that for the speciall truste and confidence we have of oure godly mynde and earnest deasire to the settinge forwarde of the glorie of god and the true worshippinge of his most holy name, wythin that province committed by vs vnto youe We have sent vnto youe thies suffrages not to be for a monethe or twoo obserued, and after slenderly considered as other oure iniunctions, have, to oure no litle mervayle bene vsed but to thintent that aswell the same as other oure iniunctiones may earenestly be setforthe by preachinge goode exhortations and other wayes to the people in soche sorte as the fealinge the godly taste thereof may godly and ioyously wythe thankes, receyve embrace and frequent the same as apperteynethe / Wherefore we wyll and commaunde youe as youe wyll aunswere vnto vs for the contrary not onely to cause thies prayers and suffrages aforesayde to be publyshed frequented and openly vsed in all townes churches villages and parryshes of youre owne dioces but also to signifie this oure pleasure vnto all other bysshoppes of youre province, willinge and commaundinge them in oure name, and by vertue hereof to do and execute the same accordingly. Vnto whose procedinges in thexecution of this oure commaundement, we wyll that youe have a speciall respecte and make reporte vnto vs if any shall not wythe goode dexteritie accomplysshe the same …

FORM OF PRAYER

EXHORTATION TO PRAIER

FORASMVCHE as prayer is the veray true meane ordeyned of almightie god, and taught vs playnly in his holy word, wherby not onely we may, but also by gods holy commandement be bounden to haue a recourse and a refuge for helpe and ayde of almightie god our heauenly father, not onely in all our necessities, and tribulations of this world, but also vniuersally in all our affaires and businesses, what soeuer shalbe fall vnto vs, orels what soeuer thing we shall enterprise or take in hand. And forasmuch also as our father in heauen, of his mere mercie and infinite goodnes, hath bounden him self by his owne free promise, and certified vs of the same, by his owne sonne, our onely sauiour and lorde *CHRIST IESV,* in his gospel, that what soeuer we shall aske of him, we shall haue it, so that we aske such thinges, and in suche sorte, as we ought to doo. For these causes good christian people, beynge thus grounded vpon the sure foundation of goddis holie & blessed word, which can not deceiue vs, We are here at this time gathered togither, to make our comon prayer to our heauenly father. But nowe good christian people that by the true vse of praier we may obteine and enioye his gratious promise of aidé, comforte and consolation, in al our affayres and necessities, two thinges, concerning prayer, are specially to be learned. The first is, to knowe, for what thynges we ought to make our request and petition in our praier. The second is, in what wise we shuld make our prayer, in suche sorte as it may be acceptably hearde, and graciously graunted of our heauenly father.

As for the first, we ought instantly to aske of our heauenly father, his holy and blessid spirite, godly wisedome, faith, charitie, and to feare and dreade him, and that his holy name in al thingis, and euery where thorough al the hole world may be glorified, that his kyngedome maye come vnto vs, that is to saye, that here he may reigne in vs, by the faith of his welbeloued sonne our sauiour *IESV CHRIST,* and after this lyfe also to reigne in vs, and ouer vs euerlastingly in glorye.

We ought to pray, that his blessed wyl may be fulfylled here in this world emonges vs his mortall creatures, as it is of his immortall angels, and of al the holy company of the heauenly spirites. We muste pray for our dayly breade, that is, for our necessary fode and sustenance bothe of body and soule. Of body, as meate, drinke, and necessary apparaile, peace, helthe, and what soeuer god knoweth to be necessary for the behofe and conseruation of the same, that we may do to our lorde god true seruice therwith, euery man in his state and vocation, wherevnto god hath called hym. Of the soule, as the word of god, and the true knowledge of the same, the true conseruation of our heauenlye fathers holy and blessid commandementis, the liuely bread of the blessed body of our sauiour Iesu Christe, the holy and sacrate cuppe of the precious and blessed bludde, whiche was shed for vs vpon the Crosse, to purchase vs pardon and forgyuenes of our synnes. Furthermore we must pray for the forgiuenes of our synnes, that our heauenly father wyll be mercyfull vnto vs, and forgyue vs our synnes bothe many and great, wherby we offende against his infinite goodnes, as we do forgiue the offences of them that offend vs. whiche, howe great so euer they appere vnto vs, yet in comparison of the offences that we do against god, they be bothe small and fewe. We muste pray, that oure heauenly father suffre vs not to be ledde into temptation, for without his continuall aide and protection, we are but weke and soone ouerthrowen. Our gostely ennemy is stronge, violent, fierse, subtyll, and exceding cruell. And therfore we muste continually pray, with all instance that in al his assaultes we may be deliuered by the mighty hande of our heauenly father, from al euyll. Fynally, and before all thing, as saint Paule exhorteth vs in the fyrst epistle to Timothe, Let vs make our prayers, and supplycations, rendrynge and gyuyng of thankes for all men, and namely for kynges, princis, and al other set in chief dignitie and high roumes, that by theyr godly gouernance, their true faithfull and diligent execution of iustice and equitie vn to all their subiectes, our heauenly father may be gloryfied, the common welth may be daily promoted and increased, and that we al, that are theyr subiectes, may liue in peace and quietnes, with al godlines and vertue, and our christen princis & heades in vnitie and concorde emonges them selfes, euer callyng vppon theyr heauenly father, whiche is the king of all kynges, and the lorde of all lordes, which shall iudge without respecte of persone, accordynge to euery mans doing or workes, at whose hande the weake shall take no wronge, nor the myghty may not by any power escape his iuste iudgement. That our princes I say, thus calling vppon theyr heauenly father for grace, maye euer in all their affaires be directed and gouerned by the holie spirite of god, and bothe rule, and be ruled, by his holy feare, to their owne endles ioye, comforte, and conso-lation, and to theyr owne euerlastyng saluation, thorough our sauiour Iesus Christ.

And here specially let vs pray for our moste dere and soueraigne lorde the Kynges maiesty, who dothe not onely study and care dayly and hourely for our prosperitie and wealth, but also spareth not, to spende his substance and treasure, yea redye at all tymes to endaunger hym self for the tender loue and fatherly zeale, that he bereth towarde this his realme, and the subiectes of the same. Who at this present tyme hath taken vpon hym the great and dangerous affayres of warre. Lette vs praye, that it may please almghty god, lorde of hostes, in whose handes is onely wealthe and victorie, mercifully to assyst him, sending his holy angell, to be his succour, keper, & defender from all his aduersaries, and from all euyls. Let vs pray for our bretherne, that bende them selfes to batail for goddis cause and our defence, that god maye grant them prosperous successe, to our comfort, and the increase of his glory. Let vs praye for our selfes that remain at home, that almyghty god defende vs from synne, sickenes, derth, and all other aduersyties of bodye and soule.

The seconde thynge to be lerned, concernynge praier, is to know, howe we shal make true prayer, so that it may be graciousely harde, and mercyfully graunted of oure heauenly father. Fyrst of al we must, vpon consideration of our heauenly fathers mercy and goodnes towardes vs, and of his euerlastyng trueth, and free promyse made vnto vs in his owne holy worde, conceyue a full affiance hoope and trust: and that with out waueryng or doubtfull mistrustyng, eyther in his trueth, his goodnes, or in his almightie power, certainely assuring our selfe, that both of his omnipotencie, he may do what soeuer shall please his goodnes, and also for his infinite goodnes, and fatherlye affection towarde vs, that he woll both here and graunt al our lauful and godly requestes, after that measure, sort, and degree, as he of his infinite and incomprehensible wisdome knoweth the thynge to be moost mete, moost conuenient, and behofeful both for his own glorye and honour, and for the profit, behoufe, and commoditie of vs his children.

Furthermore also it is necessarily requyred to that, that our prayer may be accept-able vnto our heuenly father, to haue charitie, and brotherly loue betwixt neighbour and neighbour, and towarde all our euen christen. So *CHRISTE* him selfe teacheth vs, sayinge, whan you stande to praye, forgyue, if you haue any dyspleasure agaynste any personne: that your father, whiche is in heauen, maye forgiue you. It is a true saying that saint Augustine sayeth: There is no good fruicte, no good deede, no good woorke, whiche springeth not out of the roote of charitie. And saincte Paule teacheth plainely, that where as charitie lacketh, nothyng can auayle vs.

And moreouer we must in our prayer, be ware of vayne glory and prayse of man, outwardly shewing a great pretence of holynes, and being vayne of true godlynes inwardly, onely to haue the commendation of men before the world. for if we so do, we shall lose the reward and benefit of our prayer, as our sauiour *CHRIST* saieth his owne selfe. We must take hede also, that we thincke not the vertue of prayer, to consiste in multiplyeng of many wordes without faythe and godly deuo-tion, thynckyng as the heathen doth, that for our many wordes or moche speking, we shalbe herde of our heauenly father. Who so euer doth thinke so, he shall deceyue him selfe. for god doth not regarde neither the swete sound of our voice, nor the great number of our woordes, but the ernest feruentnes and true faythful deuotion of our hartes. Fynally we muste beware in our praier of that common pestilent infec-tion, and venemefull poyson of all good prayer, that is to say, when our mouthe prayeth, and our hartes praye not.

Of the whiche the prophete Esaie complayneth sore. And our sauyour in saynte Mathewes gospel rebuketh the pharisees, for the same, saying thus: O hipocrites, Esaie the prophet prophecied well vppon you, when he sayde thus: This people draweth nighe me with theyr lyppes, but their hartes are farre from me, that is to saye, they speake with their tongue and lippes, the wordes of praier, but in theyr harte, they mynde no thyng lesse then they speake, as that the goodnes of the prayer stode in the outwarde speking onely of the woorde, and not in the inwarde, true and faythfull request of the harte. And to the intent therfore your hartes and lyppes maye goo together in praier, it is verye conuenient, and moche acceptable to god, that you shuld vse your priuate prayer in your mother tongue, that you vnderstandyng what you aske of god, may more ernestly & feruently desyre the same your hartes & myndes agreing to your mouthe and woordes. Wherfore let vs eschewe (good people) in our prayers, al the afore rehersed vices, for elles we shall not obteine our petitions, and requestes, but contrarye wyse we shall hyghly displease god and greu-ously offende him. Therfore good Chrystian bretherne, seynge we are come togyther to praye, let vs do it accordyng to our bounden duetie, and as it ought to be done. Let vs truly praye with a faithfull harte, and a sure affiaunce of our heauenly fathers infi-nite mercy, grace, and goodnes? let vs make our prayers, beyng in loue and charitie with all and euery one of our neighbours, euer hauing in our herte an ernest request and desyre of those godly benefyttes, which are appointed in goddes worde, that we shulde pray for, and yet not prescribing vnto god, either the tyme, place, measure, or degree of his gracious benefittes, but holly committing our selues to his blessed wil and pleasure, receyuyng in good woorthe, and with thankes giuinge, what so euer, and when so euer, it shall please his gracious goodnes, to bestowe his gracious gyftes vpon vs. Let vs also fournishe and beautifie this our prayer, that it may plese god the better, and delite the eares of our heauenlie father, with fasting and holsome abstinence, not onely from all delicious liuing in voluptuouse fare, and from all excesses of meate and drinke, but also to chastyse and kylle the synfull lustes of the bodye, to make it bowe and redy to obey, vnto the spirituall mocions of the holye gooste. Let vs also furnish it with almes dede, and with the woorkes of mercie and charite. For praier is good and acceptable vnto god, when it is accompanied with almose dedes, & with the workes of mercy, as the holy man Thobye sayth, with the whiche, and vsyng the vertues afore rehersed, and also eschewyng dyligently the foresayde vices, our prayers shalbe of muche price and value, as was the prayers of Hely, Danyel, & Moyses, before our heauenly father, and that for our sauiour Jesus Chrystes sake, whiche hathe redemed vs with his preciouse bloude, and hathe signed & sealed vs vp to euerlasting life. To whom both now and euer, with his father and the holy goost, be glorie and honour without ende. *AMEN.*

AS THESE holye prayers and suffrages folowynge, are sette furthe of most godly zeale for edifying and stirring of deuotion of al true faythfull christen hartes: so it is thought conueniente in this commune prayer of procession to haue it set furthe and vsed in the vulgar tungue, for stirringe the people to more deuotion: and it shalbe euery christen mans part, reuerently to vse the same, to the honour and glory of almighty god, and the profit of their own soules. And such among the people, as haue bokes, and can reade, may reade them quietely and softly to them selfe, and suche as can not reade, let them quietly & attentifely gyue audience in tyme of the said prayers, hauynge their mindes erect to almighty god, & deuoutly praying in theyr hartes, the same petitions which do entre in at their eares, so that with one sounde of the hart, and one accord, God may be glorified in his churche.

And it is to be remembred, that that whiche is printed in blacke letters, is to be sayde or songe of the priest with an audible voice, that is to say, so loude and so playnly, that it maye well be vnderstande of the hearers: And that which is in the redde, is to be answered of the quiere sobrely and deuoutely.

THE LETANY AND SVFFRAGES

O god, the father of heauen, haue mercy vpon vs miserable sinners.
O god, the father of heauen, haue mercy vppon vs myserable synners.
O god, the son, redemer of the world, haue mercy vpon vs miserable sinners.
O god, the son, redemer of the world, haue mercie vpon vs miserable sinners.
O god, the holy goost, proceding from the father and the son, haue mercy vpon vs miserable sinners.
O god, the holy ghoste, procedyng from the father and the son, haue mercie vppon vs miserable synners.
O holye, blessed, and glorious trinitie, one God, haue mercy vpon vs miserable sinners,
O holy, blessed, and glorious trinitie, one god, haue mercy vppon vs myserable synners.
Saint Mary, mother of god our sauiour Iesu Christe,
Pray for vs.
All holy aungels and archangels, & all holy orders of blessed spirites,
Pray for vs.
All holy patriarkes, and prophetes, apostels, martyrs, confessours, and virgins, and all the blessed company of heauen,
Pray for vs.
Remembre not lorde, our offences, nor the offences of our forefathers, neyther take

thou vengeance of our sinnes, spare vs good lord, spare thy people, whom thou haste
redemed with thy most precious bloud, and be not angrye with vs for euer.
Spare vs good lorde.
From all euyll and mischief, from sinne, from the craftis and assautes of the deuyll,
from thy wrathe, and from euerlastynge damnation,
Good lord delyuer vs.
From blyndnes of hart, from pryde, vaynglory, and hypocrisy, frome enuy, hatred,
and malice, and all vncharitablenes,
Good lorde deliuer vs.
From fornication, & al deadly synne, and from all the deceites of the worlde, the
flesshe, and the deuil,
Good lorde deliuer vs.
From lightnyng and tempest, frome plage, pestilence, and famine, frome battayle and
murder, and frome sodayne deathe,
Good lorde deliuer vs.
From all sedition and priuey conspiracy, from the tyranny of the byshop of Rome,
and all his detestable enormities, from all false doctrine and heresy, from hardnes of
hart and contempte of thy word and commandement,
Good lorde delyuer vs.
By the mystery of thy holy incarnation, by thy holy natiuitie & circuncision, by thy
baptisme, fastyng, and temptation,
Good lorde delyuer vs.
By thyne agonie and bluddy sweat, by thy crosse and passion, by thy precious deathe
and buriall, by thy glorious resurrection and ascension, by the commyng of the holy
goste,
Good lorde deliuer vs.
In all time of our tribulation, in all tyme of our wealthe, in the houre of deth, in the
day of iugement,
Good lord delyuer vs.
We synners doo beseche the to heare vs, O lorde god, and that it may plese the to rule
and gouerne thy holy churche vnyuersall in the right way.
We beseche the to heare vs good lorde.
That it may plese the to kepe *HENRY* the. *VIII.* thy seruant & our kyng and gouernour,
We beseche the to here vs good lord.
That it may please the to rule his hart in thy faithe, feare, and hole, that he may euer
haue affiance in the, and euer seeke thy honour and glory,
We beseche the to heare vs good lorde.
That it maye please the to be his defendour and keeper, gyuyng hym the victorye ouer
all his ennemies,
We beseche the to here vs good lorde.
That it may please the to kepe our noble quene *CATHERINE* in thy feare and loue,
gyuynge her increase of all godlynes, honour, and children,
We beseche the to here vs good lorde.
That it may plese the to kepe and defende our noble prynce *EDVVARD,* and al the
kynges maiesties chyldren,
We beseche the to here vs good lorde.
That it may please the to illuminate all bishoppes pastours and minysters of the
churche, with true knowlege and vnderstandyng of thy word, and that both by theyr
preaching and lyuyng, they may set it forthe and shew it accordingly,

We beseche the to here vs good lorde.

That it maye please the to endue the lordes of the counsaile, and al the nobilitie, with grace, wysedom, & vnderstandyng,

We beseche the to here vs good lord.

That it maye plese the to blesse and keepe the magistrates, gyuyng them grace to execute iustice, and to maynteyne truthe,

We beseche the to heare vs good lorde.

That it may plese the to blesse and kepe all thy people,

We beseche the to heare vs good lorde.

That it may please the to gyue to all nations vnitie peace and concorde

we beseche yᵉ to here vs good lord.

That it may please the to giue vs an harte, to loue and dreade the, and diligently to lyue after thy commandementes,

We besech the to heare vs good lord.

That it may please the to giue all thy people increase of grace, to here mekely thy word, and to receyue it with pure affection, and to bring forthe the fruites of the spirite,

We beseche the to heare vs good lorde.

That it may plese the to bring into the way of truthe, all suche as haue erred & ar deceiued,

we beseche the to here vs good lord.

That it maye please the to strengthen suche as do stande, and to comforte and helpe the weake harted, and toraise vp them that fall, and fynally to beate downe Satan vnder our fete.

We beseche the to heare vs good lorde.

That it may please the, to succour helpe and comfort all that be in daunger necessitie and tribulation,

We beseche the to here vs good lorde.

That it may please the to preserue all that trauaile by lande or by water, all women labouryng of chyld, all sycke persons and yong children, and to shew thy pitie vpon al prisoners and captiues,

We beseche the to here vs good lord.

That it maye please the to defend & prouide for the fatherles children and wydowes, and all that be desolate & oppressed,

we beseche the to here vs good lord.

That it maye plese the to haue mercy vpon all men.

We beseche the to heare vs good lorde.

That it maye please the to forgiue our enemies, persecutours and sclanderours, and to turne their hertes,

We beseche the to heare vs good lorde.

That it may please yᵉ to giue to our vse the kindly fruites of the erthe, so as in due tyme we maye enioy them: & to preserue them.

We be seche the to here vs good lord.

That it may please the to giue vs true repentance, to forgyue vs all our sinnes, negligences and ignorances, and to endue vs with the grace of thy holy spirite, to amende our lyues according to thy holy word,

we beseche the to here vs good lorde.

Sonne of god, we beseche the to heare vs.

Sonne of god, we beseche the to heare vs.

O lambe of god, that takest awaye the synnes of the worlde,
Graunt vs thy peace.
O lambe of god, that takest away the synnes of the worlde.
Haue mercy vpon vs.
O Christ, heare vs.
O Christ he are vs.
Lorde haue mercy vpon vs.
Christe haue mercy vpon vs.
Lorde haue mercy vpon vs.
Our father whiche arte in heauen. *with the residue of the Pater noster.*
And suffer vs not to be ledde into temptation.
But delyuer vs from euyll. Amen.

The versicle.
lorde, deale not with vs after our synnes.
The answere.
Neyther rewarde vs after our iniquities.

Let vs pray.
   O *God,* mercyfull father, that dispisest not the sighing of a contrite harte, nor the desyre of suche as be sorowfull, mercifully assiste our prayers, that we make before the in all our troubles and aduersities, when so euer they oppresse vs.
And graciousely heare vs, that those euyls, which the craft and subtiltie of the deuyll or manne worketh against vs, be brought to nought, and by the prouidence of thy goodnes, they may be dispersed, that we thy seruauntes, being hurt by no persecutions, maye euermore gyue thankes vnto the, in thy holye churche, through Iesu Christ our lorde.
O lord, arise, helpe vs, and deliuer vs for thy honour.
O god, we haue hearde with our eares, & our fathers haue de clarid vnto vs the noble workis that thou diddest in their daies, and in tholde time before them.
O lord, arise, helpe vs, and deliuer vs for thy names sake.
Glory to the father, the sonne, and to the holy goste, as it hath ben from the beginning, is, and shalbe euer world without end. Amen.
From our enemies defend vs, O Christe.
Graciousely looke vppon oure afflictions.
Pitifully beholde the dolour of our harte.
Mercyfully forgyue the synnes of thy people.
Fauourably with mercy heare our prayers.
O sonne of Dauid haue mercy vppon vs.
Both nowe and euer vouchesaufe to here vs Christ.
Graciousely here vs, O Christ, Graciousely heare vs, O lorde Christe.

The versicle.
O lorde, let thy mercie be shewed vpon vs.
The answere.
As we do put our truste in the.

Let vs pray.
   We humbly beseche the, O father, mercifully to loke vpon our infirmities, & for

the glorie of thy name sake tourne from vs all those euilles, that we moost rightuously haue deserued. Graunt this o lord god, for our mediatour and aduocate Jesu Christes sake. Amen.

O God, whose nature & propertie is euer to haue mercy, and to forgyue, receyue our humble petition, & though we be tied and bounde with the chaine of our synnes: yet lette the pitifulnes of thy great mercye leuse vs, for the honour of Jesus Christes sake, ourmediatour and aduocate. Amen.

Almighty and euer lyuynge god, whyche onely workest great meruailes, sende downe vpon our bysshops and curates, and al congregations, commytted to their charge, the healthfull spirite of thy grace, and that they may truely please the: powre vpon them the contynuall dewe of thy blessynge. Graunte this (O lorde) for the honour of our aduocate & mediatour Jesu Christe. Amen.
We beseche the, O lorde, to shewe vpon vs thyne exceding great mercy, which no tongue can woorthily expresse, and that it may please the to deliuer vs from al our sinnes, and also from the paynes, that we haue for them deserued. Graunt this, o lord, thorough our mediatour & aduocate Jesu Christ. Amen.

Gravnt, we beseeche the, O almyghty god, that we, in our trouble put our hole confidence vpon thy mercy, that we may against al aduersitie be defended vnder thy protection. Grant this, O lord god, for our mediatour and aduocate Jesu Christis sake. Amen.

[4]*Almighty* god, whiche haste gyuen vs grace at this time with one accorde, to make our commune supplications vnto the, and dost promise, that whan two or thre be gathered in thy name, thou wilt graunt their requestes: fulfyll nowe, O lord, the desires and petitions of thy seruantes, as may be most expedient for them, graunting vs in this worlde knowledge of thy trueth, and in the world to come lyfe euerlasty ng. Amen.

1544–E3 Thanksgiving services for victory at Boulogne

Saturday 20 September 1544 and after (England)

Boulogne surrendered on 13–14 September and Henry VIII entered the city in triumph on the 18th (see 1544–E2). The only surviving official order for this occasion is a letter from Queen Catherine and the privy council to the earl of Shrewsbury, lieutenant-general in the north, which ordered 'devout and general processions' in all northern towns and villages. However, Wriothesley recorded that a general procession with *Te Deum*s was held at St Paul's Cathedral in London on 20 September, followed by bonfires across the city 'and so after in every part of the realme'. The precise format of these services is unclear. Cranmer's revised litany (see 1544–E2) was written specifically for the intercessory or petitionary services during Henry's campaign in France; it was thus inappropriate for use for a thanksgiving and, moreover, was not authorized for general use (i.e. all festival days) until 1545 when it officially replaced

---

4   In margin: 'A prayer of Chsostome.'

pre-reformation litanies. It is possible, therefore, that the Sarum or other rites were used for this occasion. The use of the lieutenant-general of the north to convey the council's orders to northern England was unusual: traditionally, orders were issued to the archbishops and bishops and distributed further by archdeacons.

Order: privy council and Queen Catherine to the earl of Shrewsbury, 19 Sept. 1544, LPL, MS 3192, p. 147 [also in *Letters and papers*, ed. Brewer *et al.*, XIX: 2, 130, and *Illustrations of British history*, ed. Edmund Lodge (3 vols., 1791), I, 65].
Form of prayer: none found; possibly Sarum rite or other use.
Additional source: *Wriothesley*, I, 149.

ORDER

Privy council and Queen Catherine to the earl of Shrewsbury: 19 September 1544

After our most harty commendacions vnto your good lordship The Quenes highnes having this night assured advertisment from the kinges maiestie by Sr Will[ia]m Herbert knight one of the gentlemen of his maiesties privie chamber that Bulloign is now in thandes and possession of his maiestie without effusion of Blood not doubting but that this tydinges will be Ioyfull to your and all others there; hath willed vs tadvertise your Lordship with spede of the same to thintent that your lordship yevinge thankes to almighty god and causyng the lyke to be donn by devout and generall processions in all the townes and villages of those north partes shuld also with spede signifie to all the wardens of the marches this great benefite of god heaped vpon vs in suche sort as we all ar most bounden to rendre most humble thankes vnto him, and pray for the long continnuaunce of our most puissant master whom almighty god long preserve. /…

1544–E4 *Te Deum*s and procession for Henry VIII's return from military campaign in France

Friday 3 October 1544 (St Paul's Cathedral, London)

Henry VIII returned from his campaign in France on 30 September, landing at Dover. According to Wriothesley, the only source for this occasion, a procession with *Te Deum*s was held in celebration on 3 October at St Paul's Cathedral, conducted by Bonner in his *pontificalibus* (clerical dress conferred by the pope). As with the thanksgiving for Henry's victory at Boulogne held a few days previously (1544–E3), it is unclear what liturgical form was used.

Order: none found.
Form of prayer: none found; possibly Sarum rite or other use.
Additional source: *Wriothesley*, I, 149.

DESCRIPTION OF OCCASION

Wriothesley

The last daye of September the Kinges Majestie landed at Dover at midnight; and the thirde daye of October the Bishop of London in his pontificalibus beganne Te Deum in Pawles, which was songe for the good returne of the Kinges Majestie, and generall procession after.

1545–E1 Processions during the naval campaigns against France

After Monday 10 August 1545 (England and Wales)

In 1545, Francis I retaliated against Henry's Scottish raids (see 1544–E1) and the capture of Boulogne (1544–E2, 1544–E3 and 1544–E4). In July, the French fleet attacked Portsmouth and the Isle of Wight by surprise; Henry VIII's warship, 'Mary Rose', listed and sank. In August, the privy council ordered processions on the 'accustomed days' (the holy and festal days, such as saints' days, which were subject to local variation) to be held throughout the land. The order did not state what liturgical form was to be used. Strype (*Ecclesiastical memorials*, II: 1, 205) suggested that Catherine Parr's *Prayers stirryng the mynd vnto heauenlye medytacions* (1545; STC 4818) was used, but there is no evidence for this. The reference in the order to 'the inglyshe tonge' suggests that Cranmer's revised litany of 1544 was used, though it was not authorized for general use (i.e. for all festival days, rather than just during Henry's campaign in France) until at least October 1545. The litany was reprinted several times in 1545, suggesting there was a demand for copies and that it was being used even though processions for Henry's campaign in France had long ended.

Order: privy council to Cranmer, 10 Aug. 1545, LPL, Cranmer Register, I, fos. 26v–27r [also in *Miscellaneous writings and letters of Thomas Cranmer*, ed. Cox, pp. 495–6; summarized in *APC*, I, 225; *Letters and papers*, ed. Brewer et al., XX: 2, 43].
Form of prayer: possibly reprinted versions of *An exhortation unto prayer* (see 1544–E2), including STC 10623.5, STC 10624.
Additional source: archiepiscopal mandate to Bonner, 11 Aug. 1545, LMA, MS 9531/12: 1, fos. 72r–v; Strype, *Ecclesiastical memorials*, II: 1, 205; Cranmer to Henry VIII, 7 Oct. 1545, SP1/208, fos. 166r–v.

ORDER

Privy council to archbishop of Canterbury: 10 August 1545

… After our ryght hartye commendationes to your good Lordeshype theis shalbe to sygnyfye vnto the same that the kynges hyghenes hauyng so prouyded for the saftye of his graces realme as the greate mallyce of his enemyes shall by grace of God take smale effecte / for the repulsynge of the whiche his hyghenes hathe in a redynes to sett abrode at the furtheste on wedynsdaye nexte suche A puyssaunt Navye as hath not ben seene assembled in the remembravnce of man Consyderynge neuertheles that all vyctoryes & good successes commythe onnly at the dyrectyon and appoyntement of god ffollowynge herein the trade of suche A Chrystyan prynce as he ys hath dyuysed to haue processyons throughe out the realme in suche sorte as in lyke casces hathe heretofore laudablye been accustomed. Requyrynge your Lordeshipe therfore to take ordre incontynentlye that from henceforthe thorowght your prouince the sayde processyones be kepte contynuallye apon the accustomed dayes and none otherwyse / and songe or sayde as the numbre of the quyer shall serue for the same in the inglyshe tonge to thentent that there maye be an vnyformyte in euery place / wherby yt maye please God at all tymes to prosper his Maiestye in all his affayres & the rather to haue regarde at this tyme vnto the vpryghtnes of his graces quarrell & to sende his highenes vyctoryous successe of the same / And thus we bydde yor good Lordeshype most hartely well to ffare.

1545–E2 Thanksgiving procession for victories in Scotland and the relief of Boulogne

Wednesday 23 or Thursday 24 September 1545 (St Paul's Cathedral, London)

Henry followed up the attacks on Edinburgh and Leith in 1544 with a second campaign in Scotland, led by Hertford (see 1544–E1); the Scots had received military reinforcements from France. In September, Hertford targeted Kelso and Jedburgh, destroying sixteen castles, seven monasteries, five towns and over 200 villages. Meanwhile, in France, the English continued to defend Boulogne (see 1544–E2, 1544–E3 and 1545–E1). This thanksgiving is known only from descriptions in Wriothesley's and the Grey Friars' chronicles, which record different dates: 23 September (Grey Friars) or 24 September (Wriothesley). The Grey Friars' author also omits the reason for the thanksgiving. As with the intercessory processions held in August (1545–E1), it is unclear whether the liturgical form used was Cranmer's revised litany or, possibly more likely, as it was a thanksgiving and not an intercessory service, the Sarum rite.

Order: none found.
Form of prayer: possibly the Sarum rite.
Source: *Wriothesley*, I, 161; *Grey Friars' chronicle*, pp. 49–50.

DESCRIPTIONS OF OCCASION

Wriothesley
The 24th daie of September there was a solempne generall procession kept at Powles with a sermon, the bishoppe of London in his pontificalibus singing Te Deum, and after the procession, with all the priestes and clarkes going in rytch copes, and 70 crosses of silver gilt of the parishes of the cittie borne before them, which procession was geaven to give laude and prayse to God for the victorie that God had sent the Kinges Majestie in Scotland, and that the French armie was departed from Bolleyne [Boulogne].

Grey Friars' chronicle
Item the 23. daye of the same monyth [September] was a gret generalle processione of alle parsons, vekeres, curattes, with alle other prestes in every church, clarkes alle in copys and a crosse of every churche, and soo went up un to Ledyne halle[5] one the onsyde, with alle Powles in their copys and the byshoppe in his myttor, with alle the crafftes in theire best lyverys, and soo downe one the other syde, and soo to Powlles agayne.

---

5   Leadenhall Street, one of the main thoroughfares in London.

1546–E   Thanksgiving procession for the peace with France

Sunday 13 June 1546 (St Paul's Cathedral, London)

Despite victories in both France and Scotland during the previous two years, in 1546 Henry's military efforts remained stretched and sources of revenue began to dry up. The king maintained the 'rough wooings' in Scotland, but he concluded peace with France in June. Under the terms of the Treaty of Camp (also known as the Treaty of Ardres), Henry agreed to restore Boulogne to the French king within eight years in return for a payment of 800,000 crowns. No orders for this thanksgiving are extant; it is known only from descriptions in Wriothesley's chronicle and in John Stowe's *Summarie of Englyshe chronicles*. As with other processions held in the 1540s it is unclear whether Cranmer's revised litany or the Sarum Rite was used, although as it was a thanksgiving the latter is more likely. Bonfires were lit in the evening, and Wriothesley noted that a dinner was held by the lord mayor on Whit Monday, to which the former French governor of Boulogne and some French captains were invited. According to Stowe, this was the last procession in which the rich crosses and copes were used; they were subsequently called in by the crown with other church plate.

Order: none found.
Form of prayer: possibly the Sarum rite.
Source: *Wriothesley*, I, 163–5.
Additional source: *Wriothesley*, I, 165–6; Stowe, *Summarie*, fos. 206v–7r.

DESCRIPTION OF OCCASION

Wriothesley

This yeare, the 13th daie of June, being Whitsoundaie, was a solempne peace proclaymed within the cittie of London, with other ceremonies as hereafter followeth; first, my lord major with his brethren the aldermen assembled in the cathedrall church of Paules, with all the citizens in their best lyveries; and, the high masse being ended, there was a sermon made in the upper quire, afore the highe aulter, exhorting the people to give laud and prayse to Almightie God for the contynuance of the same peace. The sermon ended, Te Deum was songen within the quire, the bishopp in his pontificalibus, with my lord major sitting in the deanes stall, and the bishopp next him. Then a solempne procession, with all their crosses and banners, of all the parish churches in London; the children of Paules schoule going formost with tow crosses afore them, then all the other crosses following theim. Then the clarkes of the parishes in rytch robes, all the priestes and curattes following them in rych copes also. Then the quire with their crosses and copes, the bishopp of London bearing the sacrament of the alter under a rych canopie, bareheaded, his crosse and miter borne afore him, with fower great branches of waxe and tow torches, going about the sacrament, my lord major and his brethren the aldermen, with their craftes of the cittie, following. The procession waie out at the north dore of Paules into Cheepe, by Sainct Michaells at the Querne, on the north side of Cheepe, and so by Stolkes[6] and Cornehill, on the same side of London, to Leadenhall corner, and so homewarde, on

---

6   i.e. the stock market at the corner of Lombard Street and Cornhill.

the south side, throughe Cheepe, and then through Paules churchyarde, and comming in againe at the west dore of Paules church.

First assembled at Saint Magnus in Fish Streate the haroldes and sherives of London, where was made the first proclamation [of the peace], then fower trumpettes riding in trump cowples, tow haroldes next in their cote armors, the serjeant-at-armes of the cittie riding betwene them with his masse. Then Wyndsor, an harold, in his cote armor following alone. Then Norrey and Clarentius Kinges-at-Armes, in their rych cotes of armes following; then the tow shrives in their scarlett gownes with white roddes in their handes following; and so rode in order to Leadenhall corner, where was made the second proclamation; and so from thence through Cornehill into Cheep beyond the Crosse, where was made the third proclamation before my lord major and his brethren; the procession standing still till the proclamation was made their. Then throughe Poules churchyeard, and out of Ludgate to the conduite in Fleete Streete, and their proclaymed last; Norrey Kinge-at-Armes reding the proclamation, and Rach [i.e. Rouge] Dragon the harold proclayming, a trumpett blowing first three tymes, and after proclamation all the trumpettes blowing in everie place, and so made an ende.

1547–E   **Thanksgiving service, *Te Deum*s and procession for victory at the battle of Pinkie**

Tuesday 20 December 1547 (St Paul's Cathedral, London); first possible holy day (rest of Canterbury province)

On the accession of Edward VI, the earl of Hertford (now duke of Somerset and lord protector) continued Henry VIII's campaign to assert suzerainty over Scotland and unite the realms by the new king's marriage to Mary (see 1544–E1 and 1545–E2). Somerset's army defeated a substantial Scottish force at Pinkie, near Edinburgh, on 10 September. The king and privy council ordered thanksgiving sermons to be preached at St Paul's Cathedral on 20 December, followed by a procession and *Te Deum*, with prayers said in English. Processions and *Te Deum*s were to be made in all churches in Canterbury province on the next holy day after the order. It is unclear why the thanksgivings were delayed for over three months. The battle was significant strategically – 10,000 Scots died (not 15,000, as alleged in the council's order) – and ideologically: English and anglophone/protestant Scottish writers made much of the victory as a stepping stone to a united protestant island. The order did not specify a liturgical form to be used for the thanksgiving, but references to the sermon being followed by the procession suggests that Cranmer's revised litany of 1544 (which had been authorized for use in the Edwardian church by royal injunctions in August 1547) was used with the sermon replacing the 'exhortation'. This was also the first time since the break with Rome that specific reference was made to the provision of a sermon. Sermons had been preached during pre-reformation intercessory and thanksgiving services, but they became a central part of post-reformation special worship.

Order: Cranmer to the dean and chapter of St Paul's Cathedral, 18 Dec. 1547, LPL, Cranmer Register, I, fo. 55r–v [described as a mandate to Bonner and with references to the bishop but clearly addressed to the dean and chapter of St Paul's; also in *Miscellaneous writings and letters of Thomas Cranmer*, ed. Edmund, pp. 417–18, and *Concilia*, IV, 18].

Form of prayer: possibly *An exhortation unto prayer* (see 1544–E2) though no copies were reprinted after 1546.

ORDER

Archbishop of Canterbury to the dean and chapter of St Paul's Cathedral, London: 18 December 1547

After oure right hartie commendations where it hathe pleased almightie godde to sende the kinges maiestie soche victorie against the Skottes as was almoste aboue thexpectation of manne, and soche as hathe not bene hoord of in anie partes of Christendomme this manie yeares. In whiche victorie aboue the nomber of fiftene thowsande scottes be slayne, twoo thowsande takenne prisoners and amonge theme manie noble menne and others of goode reputation, all there ordenaunce and baggage of theire campe also wonne frome theme / The kinges maiestie wythe the aduise of his highnesse privie counsaile presentlie attendinge vpon his maiesties moste Royall parsonne, well knowinge this as all other goodnesse to be the giftes of godde hathe and so dothe accompt it / And therefore renderithe vnto hym thonelie glorie and prayse for the same, and so hathe willed me not onelie in his maiesties cathedrall churche, and other churches of my diocese, to gyve thankes to almightie godde, but also to require in his name to require all other bysshopes of the province of Canterburie, to doo or cause to be done semblablie in there cures, whiche his maiesties pleasure I have thought goode to signifie vnto youe / Requiringe youe not onelie to cause a sermonne to be made in youre cathederall churche, the next hollydaye after receipte hereof, declaringe the goodnesse of godde, and exhorting the people to faythe and amendment of lyf, and to gyve thankes to godde for this victorie, but also at the same tyme immediatelie after the sermon and in presence of the Mayor, Aldermenne and other the citezynnes of the citie of Londonne to cause the precession in Englyshe, and Te deum to be openlie and devoutelie songe, and that youe do also cause the lyke ordre to be gyven in every parishe churche of your diocesse, vpon somme holliday whenne the paryshoners shalbe there present wythe as moche spede as youe may Not faylinge, as youe tender his maiesties pleasure / … The Counselles pleasure is youe shall see this executed on tuesday nexte /

1548–E   Prayers for victory and peace in the Scottish war

Sundays and holy days, May and July 1548 (England and Wales)

Protector Somerset sustained English garrisons in Scotland with difficulty in 1547–8 and failed to maintain the naval blockade of the Firth of Forth. In June, French forces landed at Leith to support the Scots, established their own garrisons and took some English posts. Somerset attacked them unsuccessfully in August and again in early 1549. The proposed marriage alliance between Mary and Edward was frustrated when the queen was taken to France. In May and July the privy council ordered prayers for victory and peace to be said on Sundays and holy days. They were supplemented in August by processions. The text of the prayer sent by the council to Cranmer in May was probably *A prayer for victorie and peace*. It was to replace one of the collects in the litany.

Order: privy council to Cranmer, 6 May 1548, LPL, Cranmer Register, I, fo. 55v [also in *Concilia*, IV, 26–7].
Form of prayer: *A prayer for victorie and peace* ([14] pp.; STC 16503)* [MS copy: SP10/2/6; misdated to [July?] 1547 in *CSPD, Edward VI*, p. 17].
Form of prayer (other editions): *A prayer for victory and peace* ([13] pp.; Richard Jugge, STC 16503.5).
Additional sources: Sir Thomas Smith, principal secretary to Matthew Parker, vice-chancellor of the University of Cambridge, 21 Aug. [1548], Corpus Christi College, Cambridge, MS 106, no. 183 (p. 493f); privy council to Thomas Thirlby, bishop of Westminster, May 1548, Strype, *Ecclesiastical memorials*, II: 1, 166–7.

ORDER

Privy council to archbishop of Canterbury: 6 May 1548

After our hartie commendations to your goode Lordshippe / Hearinge tell of greate preparation made of forayne princes, and otherwyse beinge enforsed for the procurement and continuaunce of peax to make preparation of warre for somoche as all power and aide valayble comithe of godde the whiche he grauntethe as he hathe promised by his holie worde by nothinge somoche as by hartie prayer of goode menne the whiche is also of more efficacie made of an hole congregation togither gathered in his holie name / Therefore this is to will and require youe to gyve aduertisement and commaundment to all the curates in youre diocese, that everie sonday and holy day in there commonne prayer they make deuoute and hartie intercession to almightie god for victorie and peace / And to thentente that youe sholde not be in doubte whatte sorte and manner thereof we do lyke we haue sent vnto youe one, the whiche we wolde that youe and they sholde folowe and rede it in stede of one of the collettes of the kinges maiesties procession / Thus wee pray youe not to fayle to do wythe all spede …

FORM OF PRAYER

A PRAIER FOR VICTORIE AND PEACE, SET FURTHE BY THE KYNGES MAIESTIE, BY THADUYSE OF HIS MOSTE DERE UNCLE, EDWARD DUKE OF SOMERSET, GONERNOR [*sic*] OF HIS MOSTE ROYALL PERSONE, AND PROTECTOR OF ALL HIS REALMES, DOMINIONS AND SUBIECTES, AND OTHERS OF HIS HIGHNES PRIUIE COUNSAILL, THE .X. OF MAIE, M.D.XL. VIII.

Moste mercifull God, the graunter of all peace and quietnes, the geuer of all good gyftes, the defender of al nacions: who hast willed al men, to bee accompted as our neighbors, and commaunded vs, to loue theim as oure selfe, and not to hate our enemies, but rather to wishe them, yea, and also to do them good. Bowe doune thy holy & mercifull iyes vpon vs, and looke vpon the small porcion of yearth, whiche professeth thy holy name and thy sonne Jesu Christ. Geue to all vs desire of peace, vnitie, and quietnes. And a spedy werysomnes, of all warre, hostilitie, and enemity to al them that be our enemies, that wee and thei maie in one harte, and charitable agrement, praise thy most holy name, and reforme oure lifes, to thy Godly commaundementes. And especially, haue an iye to this Isle of Britaigne: and that whiche was begonne, by thy greate and infinite mercie and loue, to the vnitie and concord of both the nacions, that the Scottishmenne and wee, might for euer liue herafter, in one loue and amitie knit into one nacion, by the moste happie and Godly mariage, of the Kynges maieste, our souereigne lorde, and the young Scottishe Quene whereunto promises and agrementes, haue been heretofore, moste firmely made by humayne ordre: Graunte, O Lorde, that the same may go forward and that our sonnes sonnes, and al our posteritie hereafter, maie fele the benefite and commoditie of thy greate gyft of unitie, graunted in our daies. Confounde all those that woorketh against it: Let not their counsaill preuail deminishe their strength: lay thy sworde of punishment vpon them, that interrupteth this godly peace: Or rather conuert their hartes to the better waie and make them to embrace that vnitie & peace, whiche shalbee moste for the glory and profite of bothe the realmes. Put awaie from vs all warre and hostilitie: and if we be driuen therto, hold thy holy and strong power and defence ouer vs: be our guarrison, oure shelde and buckler: and seyng wee seke but a perpetuall amitie and concord, and performaunce of quietnes, promised in thy name: Pursue the same with vs, and send thy holy Angelles to bee our aiders, that either none at all, or els so litle losse and effusion of christen bloud as can be, be made thereby. Looke not, O Lorde, vpon oure synnes, or the synnes of oure enemies, what thei deserue, but haue regard to thy moste plenteous & aboundaunt mercie, whiche passeth al thy workes, being so infinite and meruellous. Do this, O lorde, for thy sonnes sake Jesu Christe. Amen.

To bee saied to the people of hym that dooeth Preache when he moueth the people to praie.

You shall also make your hartie and effectual praier to almightie God, for the peace of all christian regions: and especially, that the mooste ioyfull & perpetuall peace and vnitie of this realme and Scotland, may shortly be perfited, & brought to passe by the moste Godly and happie mariage of the kynges maiestie, and the yong quene of Scotlande: And that it would please the almightie to aide with strength, wisedom, and power, and with his holy defence, all those who fauoreth and setteth forwarde the same: And weaken and confound al those, whiche laboreth or studieth, to the let and interrupcion of so Godly a quiet, wherof bothe these two realmes sholud [sic] take so greate a benefite and profite.

1549–E   Service during the Western and Kett's rebellions

Sunday 21 July (St Paul's Cathedral, London)

The Western rebellion (in Devon and Cornwall) and Kett's rebellion (in East Anglia) broke out in June and July respectively in response to the appointment of enclosure commissions. In the Western rebellion, there was also strong, conservative opposition to the new BCP and other religious changes, including those to baptism and confirmation. There were also demonstrations in other counties, including Oxfordshire, Lincolnshire and Yorkshire. The order for this occasion is not extant, but both Wriothesley's and the Grey Friars' chronicles describe the service held at St Paul's and it is possible that the occasion was limited to the cathedral and Paul's Cross, the country's leading public preaching place, situated in the cathedral yard. Certainly, Wriothesley implies that the service was not planned in advance: Cranmer came 'sodenly' to preach. The service followed the liturgy as set out in the new BCP. Cranmer made a lengthy exhortation at the beginning and recited an additional prayer (no longer extant), probably between the collects and the communion. His chaplain, John Joseph, preached at Paul's Cross on the text for the day, but added a summary of Cranmer's exhortation. Wriothesley summarized Cranmer's exhortation in his chronicle: the rebellions were the workings of the devil and a plague sent as punishment and warning to people for failing to listen to protestant preachers and reform their lives. Cranmer criticized the rebels for attempting to change the law and for ignoring royal authority. The full text of the exhortation may survive in manuscript at Corpus Christi College, Cambridge, though it is disputed whether this exhortation or sermon was written by Cranmer or Peter Martyr Vermigli, Regius Professor of Divinity at Oxford. Moreover, Burnet and Strype suggest that this text was preached at a fast day at court. Two further related services were held in St Paul's Cathedral. On 10 August, Cranmer preached to mark John, Lord Russell's taking of Exeter and, on 31 August Joseph preached in Cranmer's stead. Both of these sermons, directed at the Western rebels, argued that the Western rebellion was caused by 'popysse presttes'. Wriothesley's and the Grey Friars' accounts of the service on 21 July emphasized the changes in the officers who conducted the services (fewer of them), the less elaborate dress they wore (albs and tunicles) and how the communion was administered (by Cranmer himself to selected members of the church).

Order: none found.
Form of prayer: BCP (1549) with, on 21 July, an exhortation at the beginning and additional prayer (no longer extant).
Additional sources: *Wriothesley*, II, 16–18, 20; *Grey Friars' chronicle*, pp. 60–2; Gilbert Burnet, *The history of the reformation of the Church of England* (6 vols., Oxford, 1865), II, 213–14; John Strype, *Memorials of the most reverend father in God Thomas Cranmer, sometime Lord Archbishop of Canterbury* ([1694] Oxford, 1812), pp. 187, 248; *The remains of Thomas Cranmer*, ed. Henry Jenkyns (4 vols., Oxford, 1833), I, lxvi–lxvii, II, 245–73.
Sermon: Cranmer, St Paul's 21 July (summarized in *Wriothesley*, II, 16–18; full text possibly sermon on rebellion, Corpus Christi College, Cambridge, MS 102, pp. 411–99).

DESCRIPTIONS OF OCCASION

Wriothesley

The one and twentith daie of Julie, the sixth daie after Trinitie Soundaie, the Archbishopp of Canterburie came to Poules, and their in the quire after mattens in a cope with an aulble under it, and his crosse borne afore him with two priestes of Poules for deakin and sub-decon with aulbles and tuniceles,[7] the deane of Poules followinge him in his surples, came into the quire, my lord Maior with most part of the aldermen sitting their with him. And after certaine assembly of people gathered into the quire the said Bishopp made a certaine exhortation to the people to pray to almightie God for his grace and mercy to be shewed unto us. In the which exhortation he admonished the people of the great plague of God reigning ouer us now in this realme of Englande for our great sins and neglecting his worde and commandments, which plage is the commotion of the people in most parts of this realme now raigning among us speciallie against Godes commandmente and the true obedience to our most Christen king Edwarde the sixt, naturall, christian, and supream head of this realme of Englande and other his domynions, which plage of sedition and divicion amonge ourselues is the greatest plage, and not like heard of since the passion of Christ, which is come on us by the instigation of the Devill for our miserable sinnes

---

[7]   I.e. albs and tunicles.

and trespasses in that we have shewed us to be the professors and diligent hearers of his worde by his true preachers and our lives not amended, which godlie exhortation was so godlie sett fourth to the hearers with the true obedience also to our kinge and superiors and also to be the confutation of the rebellors, with also monition geauen to the people to fast and pray, putting all pride aside with other sinns and vices raigning amonge us, as delicious and superfluous feedinge and sumptuous apparell, that it would haue moued and stirred any christian hart to lament their offences and call to Almightie God for mercy and grace.

This daie procession was song according to the Kinges booke, my lord [arch-bishop] and the quire kneling, my lord singing the collectes and praying and adding one other prayer which he had written for this plage. This donne he went to the highe aulter with deacon and subdeacon, and their to celebrate the holie communion of the bodie and bloud of Christ, accordinge to the Kinges booke last sett fourth by Act of Perliament for the service and sacrafice of the church, he ministring the sacrament of the bodie of Christ himself to the deane and vii other, the deacons following with the chalice of the bloud of Christ.

The communion donne, Mr. Joseph, his chaplaine, went to Poules Crosse and made a sermon of the gospell of this Soundaie, breiflie and shortlie declaring in the same sermon parte of my lordes exhortation to the people, because all herde him not before, and so committed the people to God ...

... The tenth of August, beinge Saterday, the Archbishop of Canterbury made a colation in Pawles quire for the victory that the Lord Russell, Lord Privie Seale, had on Monday last past against the rebells in Devonshire, which had beseeged Exeter, and lyen in campe afore yt by the space of 3 weeks and like to have famished them in the towne, but the sayd monday the Lord Privye Seale entred the city and slewe, hurte, and tooke prisoners of the sayd rebells aboue iiii m[8] and after hanged divers of them in the towne and about the countrye.

Grey Friars' chronicle

Item the xxj. day of the same monyth [i.e. July], the wyche was sonday, the byshoppe of Cauntorbery came sodenly to Powlles, and there shoyd and made a narracyon of thoys that dyd rysse in dyvers places within the realme, and what rebellyous they were, and wolde take aponne them to reforme thynges befor the lawe, and to take the kynges power in honde. And soo was there at procession, and dyd the offes him selfe in a cope and no vestment, nor mytter, nor crosse, but a crose staffe; and soo dyd alle the offes, and hys sattene cappe on hys hede alle the tyme of the offes; and soo gave the communione hym selfe unto viij. persons of the sayd churche ...

... Item the x. day of the same monyth [i.e. August] the byshoppe of Cauntorbery came and preched at Powlles, the wych was sattorday, in the qwere in the byshoppes stalle that he was wonte to be stallyd in, for them that [rose] in the West contre of the comyns of Devynchere and Cornewalle, and there he shoyd that the occasyone cam of poppych prestes was the most part of alle hys sermond ...

... Item the last day of the same monyth [i.e. August] the byshoppe of Cauntor-bery shulde a come agayne to Powlles, and a preched agayne, but he send Josephe hys chaplyne, and he preched in the qwere of the subdewynge of them that dyd rysse in all iij. places, and how mysery they ware browte unto, and there he rehersyd as hys master dyd before that the occasyone came by popysse presttes.

---

8   I.e. 4,000.

1550–E   *Te Deum*s for peace with France

Sunday 30 March 1550 (Paul's Cross, London)

Though England and France had been formally at peace since the treaty of Camp (June 1546), France had continued to provide military aid to Scotland and to harry Boulogne, taking most of the outlying parts of the town in 1548. After the fall of Somerset (1549), John Dudley, duke of Northumberland and now president of the council, cut England's losses and sold Boulogne to Henry II of France for £180,000. This occasion is known only from Wriothesley's and the Grey Friars' chronicles, which recorded secular celebrations on 29 March and a thanksgiving held on 30 March (Palm Sunday). The thanksgiving was unusual. First, it was held at Paul's Cross, not in the cathedral. From Edward VI's reign, Paul's Cross became the principal public preaching place in London, where sermons ordered by the government in times of crisis were preached. However, it was rarely used alone as the forum for thanksgivings (see 1562–E2). Second, neither a full service nor a sermon was held; instead, the *Te Deum* was sung polyphonically in English. Though the opposition to polyphonic music – indeed to music and singing generally – by reformers in sixteenth-century England has been exaggerated, this occasion appears to have been unique in post-reformation special worship. The Grey Friars' chronicler stated that there were secular celebrations for the peace across England, but there is no evidence that there were also thanksgiving services or prayers.

Order: none found.
Form of prayer: *Te Deum*s only.
Source: *Wriothesley*, II, 35.
Additional sources: *Grey Friars' chronicle*, p. 66; Stowe, 'Chronicle', p. 21.

DESCRIPTION OF OCCASION

Wriothesley
[On 30 March] was a sermon made at Pawles Crosse to give laude to God for the peace, and, the sermon ended, the canons and clarkes of Pawles quire songe Te Deum in Englishe in partes, standinge before my Lord Mayor where he sitteth the sermon tymes in Pawles Churchyard, my Lord Mayor and all the aldermen wearing scarlett this day to the sermon.

1551–E   Services during the sweating sickness

After Thursday 18 June–October 1551 (England and Wales?)

The 'sweat' was a viral disease, with no modern equivalent, that first appeared in England in 1485. It was characterized by profuse sweating and prostration, and death or recovery occurred within twenty-four hours. Though it claimed fewer lives than plague, it struck without warning, spread more quickly and acted much faster: deaths in a town or village were concentrated in a period of days rather than spread over weeks or months. This fifth major outbreak of the disease began in March or April in Shrewsbury, spread to London in July, to the north and south west in August and ceased in October. Around 15,000 people died; the two most famous victims were Henry and Charles Brandon, the second and third dukes of Suffolk and nephews of Henry VIII. In June, Edward ordered the bishops to 'persuade the people to resort more diligently to common prayer'. However, it was not until 25 July that the order was communicated to the London diocese by Nicholas Ridley, who had succeeded as bishop of London after Bonner had been deprived for being too 'conservative'. At some point, a full liturgy, *A thankes geuing to God*, was issued, the first for special worship since Cranmer's revised litany in 1544 and the publication of the BCP in 1549. Of unknown authorship, it did not follow the services for morning or evening prayer as authorized in 1549. As on earlier Henrician and Edwardian occasions, the liturgy began with an exhortation (see 1544–E2 and 1549–E), followed by the apostles' creed, the Lord's prayer, the gloria, Ps. 25, 28, 30, the first lesson (Rom. 13), Ps. 6, the *Nunc dimittis*, the suffrages, a collect and an extended version of the second collect for the king. The psalms were taken, with only minor changes, from Thomas Sternhold's and John Hopkins's metrical version of the psalms, which had been published in December 1549. Sternhold was responsible for the paraphrases of Ps. 25 and 28, and Hopkins for Ps. 30. This appears to be the only time that this highly popular edition of the psalms, explicitly intended for congregational singing, was used in special worship; the reasons for this are not known. The exhortation emphasized the providential nature of the epidemic: it was a divine warning and punishment for the realms' sins. It reiterated not only the message of the king's order in June, which had identified the realm's sins specifically as the rejection of protestantism, but also of sermons, such as that by Thomas Hancock (who has not been identified).

Order: Edward VI to the bishops, 18 June 1551, SP10/13/30, fo. 62r–v.
Form of prayer: *A thankes geuing to God vsed in Christes churche on the Monday, Wednisday and Friday* (Richard Grafton; [24] pp.; STC 16504; Pepys Library, Cambridge, PL 228 (2)).
Additional sources: Bishop Nicholas Ridley to [?], 25 July 1551, LMA, MS 9531/12: 2, fo. 289v; Machyn's diary, fo. 3v; John Caius, *A boke or counseill against the disease commonly called the sweate* (1552; STC 4343); Strype, *Ecclesiastical memorials*, III: 1, 111–12; Stowe, 'Chronicle', p. 24; Thomas Sternhold [and John Hopkins], *Al such psalmes of Dauid as Thomas Sternehold late grome of [the] kings maiesties robes, didde in his life time draw into English metre* ([1549]; STC 2420).
Sermon: Thomas Hancock Preacher his relations, [n.d.], BL, Harleian MS 425, fo. 128v.

ORDER

Edward VI to the bishops: 18 June 1551

Right reuerend father in god right trustie and welbeloued we grete you well. And beinge not a litle disquieted to se the subiectes of our realme vexed w^t this extreme & suddayn plague that dayly encreaseth over all: we cann not but lament the peoples wyckednes thorough the wch the wrath of god hath byn thus mervelously provoked / ffor the more we study how to instructe them in the knowlege of god, & of his most holy woorde that consequently they might follow and observe his lawes and preceptes: So moche the more busie is the wicked spirite to alienate their hartes from all godlynes. and his malice hath so moche prevayled that bycause the people ar become as it wer open rebelles against the divine ma^{te} God after one plague hath sent an other and an other, encreasing it so from one to one till at length seing none other remedie he hath throwen furth this most extreme plague of sodden death / And bycause ther is no other way to pacifie his furie and to recover his grace & mercy but by prayer and amendment of lief: Considering the cure and charge committed vnto you we have thought good to call vpon you to vse all diligence possible thoroughout your hole diocese aswell by yourself as by good ministers to persuade the people to reasorte more diligently to common prayer then they have don and there not only to pray w^t all their hartes in the feare of god as good and faithfull men shuld do but also to have a better regarde vnto their lyvinges and specially to refrayne their gredy appetites from that insatiable serpent of covetousness wherw^t most men ar so infected that it semeth eche one woold devore an other w^tout charitie or any godly respect to the poore to their neighbours or to their common welth / for the wch god hath not only now poured out this plague vpon them but also prepared an other plague that after this lief shall plague them everlastingly. wherin you must vse those persuations that may engender a terro^r to reduce them from their corrupt naughtie and detestable vices but as the body and membres of a dull or sicke hed can not be lustie or apte to do well: So in many cures of this are realme aswell the chief as the particuler ministers of the churche have ben bothe so dull & so feble in discharging of their duties that it is no mervaill though their flockes wander, not knowing the voyce of their shepeharde / and moche lesse the voyce of their principall & souerryn m[aste]^r we trust ye ar none of those, but if ther have byn suche negligence w^tin your jurisdiction we exhorte and pray you and neverthelesse chardge and command you by thauctoritie given vs of god to se it refourmed, encreasing also amendment in that that alredy is well begon, in suche sorte as your diligence may declare you wourthy of your vocation and theffectes therof yelde vnto god an obedient faithfull and fearefull flocke wch we wisshe to god we may shortly see yeven vnder o^r signet at our honour of hamptoncourt the xviijth of July the fifte yere of our reign.

Form of prayer

The priest standing in the model of the churche, shal exhort the people as foloweth

Charitable and faithful Christians, Be this knowen vnto you, god so hathe loued the worlde that he hath geuen his owne sonne to the death of the crosse, for the sinnes of such as beleue, whiche only sonne, by his most holy and sacred worde, hathe made a fast promes, and sworne a greate othe, to perfourme our saluacion vnto all faithfull, saiyng, Verely verily I say vnto you, whosoeuer beleueth in me, shall haue euerlasting life, and farther he saith, aske and it shalbe geuen you: seke and ye shal finde, knocke & it shalbe opened vnto you. But if thou wilt know, how we shal ask, & how we shal obtein? Our sauior teacheth vs also saiyng, whatsoeuer ye aske the father in my name, he shall geue it you. S. James saith, aske in faith and doubt not, for he is faithfull that hath promised, & wil graunt your godly & faithful peticions. The holy Apostle s. Paul, declareth this maner of asking to be by prayer, & saith, pray continually, and in al your doings and supplications, geue thankes vnto the lorde by prayer, for so is the will of god, through Jesus Christ towards you. Forasmuch therfore, as it is the most blessed will of god that continually by prayer, wee should lift vp our hartes vnto him, and call for his godly help and succor, in all our necessitees, and yelde vnto him most harty thankes for all ye benefites that we haue receaued. I shal most hartely besech & exhort you, in the bowelles of Jesus Christ our sauior, to prepare now your mindes to praier, beseeching his deuine maieste, to extend his mercy vpon vs wretched sinners and not to enter into iudgement with vs, but that he wil behold vs with the eies of his great mercy, & take from vs these his plagues which our sinnes haue iustly deserued, and graunt vs of his grace, that we as repentaunt sinners, may bewayle the wickednes of our liues whiche hath prouoked his iust vengeance ouer vs, & let vs say & cry with yᵉ prodigal sonne, we haue sinned o lord we haue sined before heauen & the, & are no more worthy to be called thy sonnes, be merciful vnto vs and deale not with vs after our sinnes and deseruinges, but according to thy great mercy be merciful vnto vs. And let vs with one hart and minde sing and praise his moost holy name. To whome be all honour and glory, worlde without ende. Amen.

I beseche you al, to say with me the confession of the faithe, and the peticions of the Pater noster.

The priest kneling in the body of the churche the clerkes on either side, shal say
I beleue in god the father almighty, maker of heauen and earth. And in Jesus Christ his onely sonne our Lorde. Which was conceiued by the holy Ghoste, borne of the Virgin Mary. Suffred vnder Ponce Pilat, was crucified, dead, buried, descended into hell. And the thirde day he rose againe from deathe. He ascended into heauen, sitteth of the right hande of God the father almighty. From then he shall come to iudge the quick and the ded. I beleue in the holy ghost. The holy catholike churche, The communion of sainctes. the forgeuenes of sines. The resurrection of the body. And the life euerlasting. Amen.

[The Lord's prayer as in the BCP, 1549]

Then let the priest say in a higher voice.
O Lorde heare our praiers.
The Quere
    And let vs cry come to the.
Glory be to the father, to the sonne and to the holy ghost. As it was in the beginning, is now and euer shal be, worlde without ende. Amen.

Adte domine leuaui. Psal. xxv.
I Lift mine hart to the, my God & guide most iust:
Now suffer me to take no shame for in yᵉ do I trust,
    Let not my foes reioyce nor make a scorne of me:
    And let them not be ouerthrowen, that put their trust in the.
Confounded are al suche, whose doings are but vaine:
O lord therfore thy pathes & waies declare vnto me playne,
    Direct me in thy strength and teache me I the pray,
    Thou art my god and sauior that helpest me euery day.
Thy mercies manifolde I pray the Lord remember.
And eke thy pite plentiful, that doth endure for euer.
    Remember not the faultes, and frailty of my youth,
    Remember not how ignoraunt, I haue bene of thy truth.
Nor after my desertes, let me thy mercy finde:
But of thine owne benignite, Lorde haue me in thy minde.
    His mercy is ful swete, His truth the perfect way,
    Therfore the lord wil geue a law, to them that go astray,
For al the wayes of god, are truth and mercy bothe,
To them that seke his testament, the witnes of his troth,
    Now for thy holy name, o lord I the intrete:

To graunt me pardon for my sinne, for it is wonderous great.
Whoso doth feare the lord, the lord doth him direct,
To leade his life in such a waie, as he doth best accept.
    His soule shal euermore, in goodnes dwel and stand,
    His sede and his posterite, inherit shal he land,
To those that feare the lorde, he is a firmament.
And vnto them he doth declare, his will and testament.
    My eares and eke my hearte, to hym I will aduaunce:
    that pluckt my fete out of ye snare, of wilfull ignoraunce.
With mercy me beholde. to the I make my mone:
For I am poore and solitarie, comfortlesse alone.
    The troubles of myne heart, are multiplied in dede:
    Bringe me oute of this misery, necessitie and nede.
Beholde my pouertie. mine anguishe and my payne:
Remit my sinne and mine offence, and make me cleane agayne.
    O Lorde, beholde my foes, how they doe stil increase:
    Pursuyng me with deadly hate. that fayne would liue in peace.
Preseue and kepe my soule, and eke deliuer me:
And let now me be ouerthroen, because I trust in thee.
    The iuste and innocente, by me does sticke and stande:
    Because I loke for to receyue, my succour at thy hande.
Deliuer lorde the folke, that be of thy belefe.
Deliuer lorde thyne Israll, from all his payne and griefe.
    To the father, and the sonne, be all glory and prayse, and to the holy ghost,
    As was and is now, and shalbe always, thoroughout every coaste. Amen.

Ad te domine Psal, xxviii
O Lord I cal to thee for helpe and if thou me forsake
I shalbe likened vnto them that fall into the lake.
    The voice of thy suppliaunt here, that vnto thee doth crye:
    When I lyft vp my hearte and handes, vnto thy heauens hye.
Repute me not among the sorte of wicked and peruerte:
That speake right faire vnto their frendes & thynke full yll in hearte.
    According to their hanndy worke as they deserue in dede:
    And after their inuencions, let them receiue their mede.
They not regard the workes of god, his lawe ne yet his lore:
Therfore wil he their workes and them destroy for euermore.
    To render thankes vnto the Lorde. How great a cause haue I.
    My voice, my praier and my complaint That hard so willingly.
He is my shield and fortitude. My buckler in distresse.
My hope, my help, my hartes relief, My song shal him confesse.
    He is our strength and our defence, Our enemies to resist,
    The health and the saluacion. Of his elect by Christ.
Thy people and thyne heritage, Thy blessed word preserue,
Extoll thy flocke with faithful foode, That they may neuer swerue.
    To the father and the sonne, And to the holy ghost,
    Be laude and prayse, now and euer, Thorowghout euery coaste. Amen.

Exaltabo tc. Psal. xxx

All Laide, and praise w^t hart and voice, O Lord I geue to the,
which wil not se my foes reioyce Nor triumphe ouer me.
    O Lord my god to the I cried, In al my payne and grief,
    Thou gauest an eare & I diddest prouide To ease me with relief.
Of thy good wil those hast cald back My soule from hel to saue.
Thou dost releue when strength doeth lack To kepe me from the graue.
    Sing praise ye saintes y^t proue & see, The goodnes of the Lorde,
    In memory of his maieste, Reioyce with one accorde,
For why his anger but a space, Doth last and slake againe,
But yet the fauour of his grace, For euer doth remaine,
    Though gripes of grefe & panges ful sore, Do chaune vs ouer night,
    The Lord to ioy shal vs restore, Before the day be light.
When I enioyed the worlde at wil, Thus would I boast and say,
Tushe, I am sure to finde none yl, This welth shal not decay,
    For thou o Lord of thy good grace, Haddest sent me strength and ayde,
    But when thou turnedst away thi face My minde was sore dismaied,
Wherfore againe yet did I cry, To the o lord of might,
My god with plaints I did apply, And praied bothe day and night,
    What gaine is in my blud sayd I If death destroy my dayes,
    Doth dust declare thy maieste, Or yet thy truth doth praise,
Wherfore my god, some pitie take, O Lorde I the desier
Do not this simple soule forsake, Of helthe I the require.
    Then didst thou turn my grief & wo Unto a cheerful voice,
    the mourning wede thou tokest me fro, And madest me to reioice,
Wherfore my soule vncessauntly, Shal sing vnto thy praise,
My Lorde my god to the wil I Geue laude and thankes alwaies.
    To the father and the sonne, be all glory and praise, And to the holy ghost,
    As was, and is now, & shalbe alwayes, Thorowghout euery coast.

Lesson: Rom. 13

After the lesson sing this Psalm
Domin ne in furore. Psal. vi
Lord in thy wrath reproue mee not though I deserue thine Ice.
Ne yet corect me in thy rage. O lorde I the desier.
    For I am weake thefore o lorde Of mercy me forbeare,
    And heale me Lorde, for why thou knowest my bones do quake for feare.
My soule is troubled very sore, and vexed vehemently,
But lorde, how long wilt thou delay, to cure my mysery.
    Lorde turne the to thy wonted grace my selfe soule vp take,
    O saue me not for my desertes, but for they mercies sake,
For why no man among the dead, remembreth the one whit
Or who shal worship the o lord in the infernal pit.
    So greuous is my plaint and mone that I waxe wonderous faint:
    And washe my bed where as I couche, With teares of my complaint
My beaute fadeth cleane away, with anguishe of mine hart:
For feare of those that be my foes, and would my soule subuert.
    But now away from me al ye, that work iniquite,

For why, the lorde hath hard the voice, of my complaint and cry.
He hard not only the request and prayer of my hart
But it receiued at my hand and toke it in good parte.
    And now my foes that vexed me the lord wil sone defame,
    And sodeinly confounde them all, to their rebuke and shame,
To the father and the sonne, And to the holy ghost.
Be all laude and praise, now and euer. Throughout euery coast. Amen.

Nunc dimittis. Luc. i.
Lorde nowe lettest thou thy seruant depart in peace, according to thy worde.
For mine eies haue sene thy saluacion.
Which thou hast prepared before the face of all thy people.
To be a light to lighten the gentiles, and to be the glory of thy people Israel.
    To the father and the sonne, And to the holy ghost.
    Be all laude and praise, now and euer. Throughout euery coast. Amen.

Lorde haue mercy vpon vs, Christ haue mercy vpon vs. Lorde haue mercy vpon vs.

Priest: Deale fauourably with vs o mercifull Lorde.
Answer: And take from vs thy heuy displeasure.
Priest: Spare vs o lord, spare thy people.
Answer: For thou hast redeemed vs with thi most precious blood.
Priest: Strengthen our hartes with thy holy spirit.
Answer: And let the light of thy grace shine ouer vs.
Priest: In the O Lord we put our trust.
Answer: Therefore let vs not be confounded.
Priest: Heare vs o lorde, whiche cal vpon the.
Answer: And mercifully graunt our peticions.

Let vs pray.

Collect
    O Lorde GOD, and our sauiour Jesu Christ, whiche art the very true and euer-
lasting life, of al them that liue and die in the, we wretched sinners being sory for
our offences, wholly submit our selues, to thy mercifull will, & we moost hartely
thanke the good Lorde, that it hath pleased the to visit vs with sicknes which is
the rod wherewith thou correctest those whome thou louest: and who may doubt
in the (that art all in al, and when wee beyng enemies vnto the, disdaynedst not to
take our nature vpon the, and become man for vs, to pacifie the wrath of thy father
against vs) that thou wilte nowe lay this burthen of thy plague so vpon vs, but that
y^u wilt geue vnto vs strength to cal our sinnes to remembraunce, to reconcile our
selues to our neighbours, to make cleane the house of our soule, wherin thou hast
promised to dwell, saiyng, he that abideth in my worde, abideth in me, and I in
him, whiche request mooste humbly and hartely, we desire of the, and faithefully
beleue to obteine. We yelde vnto the o lorde most humble thankes for thy creacion,
redemption, and all the other giftes whiche we haue receaued of the, beseeching y^e
mercifully to pardon vs for the abusing of those thy precious giftes, in this mortall
life. And we beseche the o Lorde to make our soules strong against the assaultes of
the deuell that he ouerthrowe vs not by frailte of our flesh, neyther that we dispayer

in ye time of this thy visitacion, and graunt that the sweete Sacrifice of thy body and blood may nowe make the attonement betwixt the wrathe of thy father (which our sinnes haue deserued,) and vs. Let al the merites of thy passion be our saluacion, for in those we trust, and not in our selues, Graunt that this faithe and trust, which we haue in the, neuer decay in vs, but that so long as we liue, it mai waxe euer stronge and stronger, so that bothe liuing and diyng, we beyng repentaunt of our sinnes, may assuredly trust, that ye price of thy preciousbloud hathe pacified the wrath of god & purchased for vs the kingdom euerlasting, which he graunt vs that died for vs. To whome be al honor and praise, for euer and euer. Amen.

A collect for the king

[*The second collect for the king from the BCP communion service (1549)*: ... *committed to his charge*] in wealthe, peace and godlines. And as of thy greate mercy, notwithstanding thy Justice, in punishing the sinne of Dauid thy prophet by pestilence, yet thou diddest preserue him for that he was thine annointed king: So O mercifull and gracious lorde, preserue our souereine lord, thy true anointed & our most innocent king, from these thy plages which our sinnes haue iustly deserued. For it is we o lord, that haue offended, deale therfore fauourably with vs o merciful god, and we wil bewaile our offences and blesse and praise thy holy name, bothe now and for euer. Amen.

1553–E1 Prayers during the illness of Edward VI

June–July 1553 (Chapel Royal, and possibly elsewhere in England)

Edward was not the sickly boy he has often been portrayed as, but in February 1553 he contracted a feverish cold. He remained weak and declined further in June. This prayer was commanded to be said in the Chapel Royal by John Russell, the earl of Bedford, a privy councillor. Though no order exists for its public use, the form published on 19 June noted that it was 'mete to be used of all the Kinges trew Subiectes' and thus may have been used informally during the short period between its printing and Edward's death on 6 July. The copy of this prayer now in the Huntington Library in California was never sold, but was used as scrap by a bookseller to advertise the price of a more expensive book.

Order: none found.
Form of prayer: *A prayer sayd in the kinges chappell in the tyme of hys graces sicknes, for the restauracion of his helth, commaunded to be sayd there, by the right honorable erle of Bedford, and mete to be vsed of all the kinges trew subiectes. Set forthe the xix day of June MDLIII* (William Copland; [1] p.; STC 7508)*.

FORM OF PRAYER

Allmighty, and moste merciful Lorde, the onely lyfe and helth, of all theym that truste in thee, which workest saluacion in thy elect, as well by sicknes as other wise, and therfore bringest theim very lowe, and yet restorest to helth againe: looke downe wyth thy pytyfull Eies vpon thy seruaunt Edward our Kyng, and vpon this Realme of England, professing thi worde & holy name, and as thou didest moste fauorably deliuer King Ezechias from extreame sicknes, and prolongedst his lyfe for the saluegarde of thy people the Israelites, & defendedst theim and the Citie from the Tyranny of the Assyryans: so we moste entierlye appeale to thy great mercies, graciously to restore the helth and strength agayne of thy seru[an]t[9] Edward our Soueraine Lorde, that as [thou][10] haste begonne by him the rooting out of Errour, Idolatry & Supersticion, and the planting of trew Religion, trew worshippyng & veritie: so it may please thy mercyful goodnes, longe to preserue hym for the confyrmacyon & establishment of the same, and also for the saulfgarde and defence of this Realme, from al outward & inward Enemies, for the glorye of thy holye name. Looke not herin (O Lorde) upon our desertes, whyche for abusinge thy worde, and sinfulnes, deserue great punishmentes, but vpon thy plentyful mercyes, whyche reioycest to heale the greatest myseries. Be no lesse fauorable (O Lorde) at this present, to Edward our kyng, restorynge thy trew religion: then in times past to Ezechias refourmyng thy Religion. Be no lesse mercyfull to England thy Churche now: then in those dayes to Jury thy Churche than. But as thy heauenly grace hath ben more reueled in these dayes by the commyng of thy deare Sonne our Sauiour and mayster Chryste, and preachyng of the Gospell: so it may please thy fatherlye loue and goodnes, to bestow vpon vs more abundaunce of the same fauourable grace and mercy, according to thy wyl in this our humble request. Do thys O most mercyful Father for thy owne names sake, and for the merytes and death of thy Sonne our only medyator and redemer Jesus Christe. Amen.

1553–E2 Processions during bad weather

Friday 8 December 1553 (St Paul's Cathedral) and Wednesdays, Fridays and Sundays thereafter (diocese of London)

Edward VI's successor, his elder sister Mary, was intent on restoring catholicism in England and religious allegiance to the papacy. Although the Edwardian government had increasingly presented national disasters as divine warnings for failure to conform to the new religion, special worship in times of such crises was not a reformed monopoly but had long (Roman catholic) antecedents. The processions in December 1553 are known only through the diary of Henry Machyn, a merchant taylor from London. A procession for better weather was held at St Paul's Cathedral on 8 December. Edmund Bonner, reinstated by Queen Mary as bishop of London in August, then ordered parish processions every Wednesday, Friday and Sunday. The precise nature of these processions is unclear; no forms appear to have been issued. Services in English were only banned by a proclamation of the Marian regime on 20 December, and the parliamentary statute repealing the Edwardian acts of uniformity which had established the 1549 and 1552 BCPs as the authorized liturgy did not come into force until 30 December. Moreover, this statute restored the liturgy from the last year of Henry VIII's reign, i.e. Cranmer's litany of 1544. Technically, therefore, the processions should initially have followed the litany as set out by the second BCP; between 20 and 30 December, they would either have followed Cranmer's litany (as

---

9   Page damaged.
10 Page damaged.

prescribed by statute) or the Sarum or other rite (as implied by the proclamation). Though Mary's staunch commitment to catholicism might have been exaggerated and her relative sympathy to some Henrician reforms overlooked, it seems unlikely that either she or Bonner would have accepted any form of Edwardian service. The royal proclamation, and its issue before the statute, also suggests that the Sarum or other rite was used. Whatever the liturgical form of this occasion, however, there was one clear innovation: processions were held regularly, three times a week, rather than on holy days and other festal days (see 1545–E1). This not only created a uniform practice across the diocese but it was also the first time that thrice-weekly events (processions or services) are known. The practice was revived in 1560 (see 1560–E) and was common for petitionary services (especially for plague) until 1626.

Order: none found.
Form of prayer: none found; possibly the litany of 1544, Sarum rite or other use.
Additional sources: Machyn's diary, fo. 25v.

DESCRIPTION OF OCCASION

Machyn's diary
The viij day of desember was prossessyon at powll[s &] when all was don my lord of london commondyd y[t] e[very] paryche chyrche shuld provyd for a crosse & a staffe & a co[pe] for to go of pressessyon euere sonday & wedynsday & ffryday [to] pray vnto god for fayre weth thrug London[.]

1554–E1 *Te Deum*s for the failure of Wyatt's rebellion

8 February 1554 (London)

Machyn reported that Mary and Bonner ordered *Te Deum*s to be sung and parish bells rung on 8 February 1554 in celebration of the collapse of Wyatt's rebellion, led by Sir Thomas Wyatt. The *Te Deum* at the chapel royal followed a procession through the City of 'all the Queens hoste ... on goddlye araye'. No form of prayer appears to have been issued. As parliament had reinstated, in 1553, the rites and ceremonies of the last year of Henry VIII's reign, it seems most likely that this occasion followed the Sarum or other rite, as was probably the case for late Henrician thanksgivings (see, e.g., 1544–E3, 1544–E4 and 1545–E2). The rebellion had challenged Mary's projected marriage to Philip of Spain, tapping into a vein of general discontent about Philip's role as king consort, and anxiety that England would be drawn into the Habsburg–Valois war. The rebels marched from Kent to London at the end of January, but surrendered after a rousing speech by Mary garnered the City's support against them. Wyatt was arraigned on 15 March and executed on 11 April. The government tried unsuccessfully to make him implicate Princess Elizabeth, though she was confined to the Tower. Lady Jane Grey, who had held the crown briefly before Mary's accession, was now executed; although not involved in the rebellion, she posed a danger as a protestant claimant to the throne.

Order: none found.
Form of prayer: none found, possibly the Sarum rite or other use.
Additional sources: Machyn's diary, fo. 28v; *Wriothesley*, II, 111; *Grey Friars' chronicle*, p. 87.

DESCRIPTIONS OF OCCASION

Machyn's diary

The viij daie of feybruarij was commondyd by ye quene & ye bysshope of london y^t powll & evere paryche that they shuld syng te deum laudamus & ryngyng ffor ye good victory y^t ye quen grace had a ganst wyatt & ye rebellyous of kent ye wyche wher over come thankes be vnto god w^t lytyll blud shed & the reseduw taken & had to presun & after wher dyuers of them putt to deth in dyuers places in londun & kentt & processyon evere wher that day for joy.

Wriothesley

And then all the Queens hoste came throughe London in goodlye araye, and Te Deum was sunge in the Queens Chappell for ioye of the sayde victorie, and so few slayne.

Grey Friars' chronicle

… and that same day was Te Deum songe in the qwenes chapelle for joye of it.

1554–E2 *Te Deum*s and processions for the arrival of Philip of Spain

Sunday 22 July–Monday 23 July 1554 (London)

Philip of Spain's arrival in England, at Southampton, on 20 July (Grey Friars' reported this mistakenly as the 19th) was proclaimed the following day. Bonfires were lit and bells rung in the capital in celebration on 21 and 22 July. Mary ordered processions and *Te Deum*s on 23 July. The processions probably followed the Sarum or other rite. Her marriage to Philip took place on 25 July at Winchester Cathedral.

Order: none found.
Form of prayer: none found, possibly the Sarum rite or other use.
Sources: Machyn's diary, fo. 34v; *Grey Friars' chronicle*, pp. 90–1.
Additional sources: *Wriothesley*, II, 118; Stowe, 'Chronicle', pp. 36, 37.

DESCRIPTIONS OF OCCASION

Machyn's diary

The xxiij day of julij wher commondyd that ever[e parish in London] shuld goo a prossessyon & to syng Te deum landam [in] evere paryche in london & ryngyng of ye bell[s].

Grey Friars' chronicle

Item the x[ix] day of the same monyth [July] the prince of Spayne came in at Hamtone, and there was goodly resevyd. And the xxij^ti day of the same monyth, the wych was Mary Maudlyne day, at nyght was commandment gevyn in London to have bonfyers and belles ryngynge thorrow alle Londone. And the nexte day to have Te Deum in every church for joye of hym.

1554–E3 Services for the safety of Mary's [supposed] pregnancy

After Tuesday 27 November 1554 to July 1555 (England and Wales)

In November, Mary was thought to be pregnant and the privy council printed and distributed letters ordering the bishops to organize *Te Deum*s, masses and prayers for her safe delivery. Machyn reported that Bonner distributed these orders in London on 29 November but, according to Wriothesley and the Grey Friars' chronicler, a service was held at St Paul's at nine o'clock the day before, attended by ten bishops (including Bonner), the lord mayor and aldermen. This service appears to have followed the Sarum rite, with the anthem 'Ne timeas Maria' (Luke 1:30) after the collation and 'Salve, feste dies' sung during the procession around the circuit of the cathedral. A sermon was also preached by Dr William Chedsey, Chiswick prebendary of the cathedral. There was one innovation: before the collation Chedsey read out the council's order to Bonner. This seems to mimic the reading of exhortations in late Henrician and Edwardian services, as well as of royal statements in the thirteenth and fourteenth centuries about the purpose of nationwide prayers. In late December, a service was held at Canterbury Cathedral attended by Philip II (there are no references to Mary being present), the first time a monarch or royal consort is known to have attended a public special service since the break with Rome. This too seems to have departed from the official rite, as Stephen Gardiner, bishop of Winchester, recited prayers of his own composition, either instead of, or in addition to, the designated prayers. The Spanish ambassador reported that Gardiner's prayers are 'now said at every mass in the island'. Indeed, a number of prayers seem to have circulated in manuscript and print – including those said at Westminster School and one by Sir Thomas Smith – though it is unclear if they were for private or public use. Mary's delivery was falsely announced and celebrated in some places during April and May. Her delivery was still expected in July but, by the end of the month, Mary realized the pregnancy was false and the planned nursery was disbanded.

Order: privy council letter to Bonner, 27 Nov. 1554, STC 7753.6, Corpus Christi College, Cambridge, MS 106, no. 339 (p. 629) [also in [Henry Wharton], *A specimen of some errors and defects in the history of the reformation* (1693; Wing W1569), pp. 175–7].
Forms of prayer: probably Sarum rite or other use, with new prayers added to, or replacing, prescribed prayers in some services.
Additional sources: Machyn's diary, fos. 40r, 44v; *Wriothesley*, II, 123–4; *Grey Friars' chronicle*, p. 93; Stowe, *Chronicle*, p. 1094; *Calendar of the patent rolls, preserved in the Public Record Office ... Philip and Mary* (4 vols., 1937–9), III, 184–5; *A prayer made by the deane of Westminster* (John Cawood; 1 p.; STC 25291.5; Cambridge University Library, Peterborough W.9(2)); John Foxe, *Actes and monuments* (1563; STC 11222), pp. 1014–16; 'Nowe singe, nowe springe, oure care is exild' ([1554]; STC 17561); John Heywood, *A balade, specifienge partly the maner, partly the matter, in the mariage between our soueraigne lord, and our soueraigne lady* ([1554]; STC 13290.3); 'A ballad to Queen Mary by a protestant', [*c.*1553], BL, Harleian MS 424/15, fos. 58r–59v; John Foxe, *Actes and monuments* (1583; STC 11225), pp. 1596–7; [Wharton], *Specimen of some errors*, p. 141.

ORDER

Privy council to bishop of London: 27 November 1554

After our right hartie commendations vnto your good Lordship. Whereas it hathe pleased almightie God amonges other his infinite benefites of late moste gratiouslye powred vpon vs, and this whole realme to extende his benediction vpon the Quenes maiestie, in suche sorte, as she is conceaued, and quicke of childe. Wherby (her maiestie being our naturall liege ladye, quene, and vndoubted inheriter of this Imperial Crowne) good hope of certeyne succession in the Crowne is geuen vnto vs, & consequently the great calamities which (for wante of such succession might otherwise haue fallen vpon vs, and our posteritie) shall by Goddes grace be wel auoyded, yf we thankefullye acknowledge this benefite of almightie God, endeuourynge oure selfes with earneste repentaunce to thanke, honoure, and serue him, as we be most bounden. These be not only to aduertise you of these good newes, to be by you published in all places within youre diocese, but also to praye and require you, that bothe youre selfe do geue God thankes with vs, for this his especiall grace. & also geue ordre, that thankes maye be openlye geuen by syngynge of Te Deum in all the Churches within your sayd diocese. And that likewise all priestes, and other ecclesiasticall ministers in theyr Masses, and other diuine seruices maye continuallye praye to almightie God so to extende hys holye hande ouer her maiestie, the kynges hyghnes, and thys whole realme, as thys thyng being by hys omnipotente power graciouslye thus begonne, maye by the same be well continued and brought to good effect, to the glorye of hys name. Wherevnto albeit we doubte not, ye wold of your selfe haue had speciall regard without these oure letters, yet for the earnest desyre we haue, to haue this thinge done out of hande, and diligently continued, we haue also wrytten these our letters, to put you in remembraunce.

1555–E1   Thanksgiving services for England's reconciliation with the Church of Rome

Friday 25 January 1555 (St Paul's Cathedral, London); [January or February?] elsewhere in England and Wales

Negotiations to reconcile the Tudor realms to the Roman catholic church were slow and difficult, both at home and in Rome, not least because of the thorny issue of whether former monastic lands should be returned to the church. Cardinal Reginald Pole, the papal legate, absolved the nation of sin in November 1554, but an order for nationwide thanksgivings in all cathedral and parish churches does not seem to have been issued until January: Strype cited a proclamation dated January 1555 in a private collection which is now either untraceable or no longer extant. On 25 January, a procession was organized in London, beginning at St Paul's and proceeding up Leadenhall Street and back down the other side. The subsequent service was attended by Philip II and Pole. Bonfires were lit across the city that evening.

Order: royal proclamation, [blank] Jan. 1555 in Strype, *Ecclesiastical memorials*, III: 1, 264–6.
Form of prayer: Sarum rite or other use.
Additional sources: *Grey Friars' chronicle*, p. 94; *Wriothesley*, II, 126; Stowe, 'Chronicle', pp. 40–1; Machyn's diary, fo. 49v; MacLure, p. 37.

ORDER

Royal proclamation: [blank] January 1555

Trusty and welbeloved, wee grete you wel: And whereas by the especial favour of Almighty God, many and sundry great matters touching our Christian faith, and a godly concord with the rest of Christendom, have, in our late Parlament, with one consent of the Lords spiritual and temporal, and other our loving subjects, been agreed upon and established: wherby this our whole realm, and al our loving subjects of the same, being delivered, by authority of the Pope's Holiness, from al sentences of interdiction, and other censures of the Church, be now restored again into God's favour, and the unity of the mother holy Church, as by the buls of our dearest cousin, the most reverend father in God, Lord Cardinal Pole, legate *de latere* from the Pope's said holiness, fully appeareth: like as we, considering how much we both for these and other innumerable benefits of Almighty God abundantly powred upon us, do humbly acknowledge ourselves most bounden to thank, and praise, and serve him al the days of our life; so thinking good that al our subjects, of every degree, should in al places, with repentance of their former lives, both give thanks for these his great mercies, and to exercise themselves in prayer, fasting, and works of charity, as they may shew themselves true children of the holy Church, whereunto they be now thus reconciled; and that they take the same so thankfully as they have just cause to do: we have, by other our letters to the bishops of our realm, required them to cause solemn mass with Te Deum openly in al their cathedral churches to be sung, and the like to be sung and said openly in al other churches within their several dioceses: and to the intent the common people may likewise by some token declare joy and gladness which they ought justly to conceive for this reconciliation and uniting of the realm to the rest of Christendom, we have thought good to require you to give order throughout al your sheriffwick, for making of bonfires in al places, for some demonstration of rejoycing for the good success of the premisses accordingly. Wherefore we require you not to fail.

1555–E2 Prayers for peace between France and the Empire and for the election of the pope

After Thursday 23 May–June 1555 (Canterbury province)

During the spring of 1555 Queen Mary, assisted by Cardinal Pole, now one of her key advisers, promoted peace negotiations at Gravelines between France and the Empire. Then on 1 May Pope Marcellus II died, and Mary supported Pole as his replacement. The order for prayers for these two endeavours was issued by the privy council on behalf of Mary and Philip, and emphasized the providential nature of war as a punishment for the sins of the realm. On the day that the council's order was issued, Gian Pietro Carafa was elected in Rome as Pope Paul IV. Soon afterwards, the peace negotiations at Gravelines failed, although later, in February 1556, France and the Empire concluded a temporary peace by the Treaty of Vaucelles.

Order: privy council to Bonner, 23 May 1555, LMA, MS 9531/12: 2 fos. 363r–v [printed in *Concilia*, IV, 128].
Form of prayer: Sarum rite or other use.

ORDER

Privy council to bishop of London: 23 May 1555
After our righte hartye commendatyones vnto your good Lordshipp wheare it hathe pleased Allmighty god soo to directe the hartes of the highe and mighty princes,

Themporours maiesti, and the Frenche king towardes peace and concorde that they
have of late thoroughe the good medyacyon of the queenes maiestye appoynted
sondrye personages of honour to treate and conclude vpon some good meanes
of agrementes, and ende of theis longe and cruell warrs. Forasmuche as it is well
considered that theis and all other warrs be the iust punyshmentes and plagues sente
from Allmighty god to punysshe the syns and wyckednes of the worlde, lyke as the
kinges and Quenes maiestyes of there godly dysposytions have sente certayne greate
personages from hens, to be mediators in this treatye; so there maiestyes knowing that
the chieffe means to bring this medyatyon to a good end is to appease the wrathe and
displeasure of allmyghty god haue willed vs to require you not only to admonysshe,
and cause to be admonyshed all your diocesans to call to god for mercye, and praye
devoutlye that it may pleasse him of his infynyte goodnes so to inspire the hartes of
the saide princes and there Commyssyoners as of this meating the desired fruycte of
peace maye ensue to the common wealthe of Christendome, and to cause common
prayers to be vsed for this purpose, in all churches within your diocesse; but also
to wryte to all other bisshopeps and ordinaryes of the province of Canterbury to
doo the like in there dioces. And in the same there common prayers to praye also to
Allmightie god to governe the hartes of the colledge of Cardinalls now assembled
for the electyon of a pope, that they may in shorte tyme well agree for the choyse of
such one as maye be to thonor of allmyghty god and mete to restore the vnytie and
concorde of christes churche, which of late hathe beyn soo soore troubled In bothe
which cases their maiesties requireth your Lord to give order with diligence[.]

1557–E1   Thanksgiving service and procession for victory at St Quentin

c. Sunday 15 August 1557 (St Paul's Cathedral, London)

Fears that England might be dragged into the Habsburg–Valois war as a result
of Mary's marriage to Philip were realized in 1557 when Mary and some of her
councillors agreed to support her husband after France, backed by Paul IV, broke
the treaty of Vaucelles and invaded northern Italy. There was early success on 10
August with the earl of Pembroke's victory at St Quentin. On 15 August, all London
parishes were ordered to attend a procession and service at St Paul's, though it is
unclear whether this occurred on the 15th itself or later. After the service, Nicholas
Harpsfield (archdeacon of Canterbury and vicar-general of London) preached a
thanksgiving sermon at Paul's Cross.

Order: none found.
Form of prayer: Sarum rite.
Additional sources: Machyn's diary, fo. 77v.

DESCRIPTION OF OCCASION

Machyn's diary
[The] xv day of august cam a commondment to [all the churches of] london to go
to powll[s] all prest[s] in caps a pross[ession Before t]her whentt they of powll[s]
songe Te devm lawdam[us & after that] down they whent a prossessyon in to chepe

ron[d about y]ᵉ crosse syngyng salve ffesta dyes & my lord mayre [and aldermen in] skarlett rond a bowtt powll[s] wᵗ owtt & aft [to Paul's C]rosse to sermon & ther pryched yᵉ archedeken of lond[on, Doctor h]arpfeld & mad a godly sermon yᵉ wyche day was yᵉ [day of the As]sumsyon of owre blessyd lade yᵉ vyrgyn and in ys ser[mon he de]claryd how many wher taken & what nobullᵐᵉⁿ there w[ere].

1557–E2 *Te Deum*s and procession for the victory at Péronne

Sunday 19 September 1557 (London)

Machyn recorded that processions were held, *Te Deum*s sung and parish bells were rung across London on 19 September for a victory at Péronne, twenty miles away from St Quentin.

Order: none found.
Form of prayer: Sarum rite or other use.
Additional sources: Machyn's diary, fo. 79v.

DESCRIPTION OF OCCASION

Machyn's diary
The xix day of September cam a commondem[ent] downe to all paryche in london yᵗ they shuld g[o on] prossessyon at powll[s] & Te deum laudamus songe [in] all yᵉ chyrches in london to synge & rynge for [the] wynnyng of perron in ffransse & odur plases.

1560–E   Services and fast days for better weather and success in public affairs

Daily or three times per week, after Monday 8 July 1560 (Canterbury province)

The military victories of summer 1557 were followed by defeats and, in January 1558, by the loss of English control of Calais. Queen Mary died on 17 November 1558, bringing the end of the catholic regime and, under her successor Elizabeth I, a restoration of protestant religious arrangements. New acts of supremacy and uniformity imposed, from 1559, the use of a revised BCP. The reasons for the special worship ordered in July 1560 are not entirely clear. The surviving order by Edmund Grindal, the protestant replacement for Bonner as bishop of London, referred to the weather, and the title of the presumed form of prayer added a reference to the 'affayres of the realm'. No contemporary accounts of the weather in this year have survived, so it is not known whether it was unseasonably dry or wet. Concerns about public affairs may have centred on English military support for the protestant Lords of the Congregation in Scotland, which continued until the signing of the treaty of Edinburgh (6 July). Fears remained of a French invasion (to press the claims of Mary Stuart, wife of the Dauphin, to the English crown), together with increasingly tense relations with Spain over military support of the Scots and the Elizabethan regime's aggressive protestantism. Although the 1559 BCP included prayers to be said during periods of bad weather and war, Matthew Parker, the archbishop of Canterbury, prepared a full liturgy – probably *A short form and order* printed by the royal printer, Richard Jugge – which temporarily replaced services from the BCP. A letter of 1563 from Grindal to William Cecil, the queen's principal secretary, suggests that an order for a weekly fast was also issued. Why Parker wrote a full liturgy is unclear, though it might be explained by the need to explicate and justify a distinctively protestant form of fasting. Of Parker's liturgy and order for the fast, only the text for the beginning of the preface and some bibliographical details have survived. It is therefore impossible to know how extensively the service differed from the BCP, or how far it resembled *A fourme to be vsed in common prayer twise a weeke,* issued three years later during an outbreak of plague (1563–E). This later form copied the opening of Parker's preface from 1560, although it also had a further independent source. Without clear evidence about the structure and format of the 1560 *Short form and order*, it cannot be ascertained whether it was this form or the form for 1563 which established one of the three main liturgical formats used in special worship until 1641 (see 1562–E1, 1563–E and 1564–E). However, it appears that this occasion in 1560 was marked by the first fast days to be observed widely in England since the Reformation (it is unclear if fasts were held in 1550: see Appendix 1: Omitted occasions). On 7 July, Parker ordered Grindal, as dean of the province, to organize public prayers 'euery day' at morning service. Grindal conveyed these orders to the archdeacons of London, Essex, Middlesex, Colchester and St Albans on 8 July. However, the form only required observance three times a week and it is possible that Grindal's order superceded Parker's. The practice of observing special worship three times a week followed an earlier innovation by Mary (see 1553–E2) and became standard until 1626.

Order: Grindal to the archdeacon of London, 8 July 1560, LMA, MS 9531/13: 1, fo. 7r.
Form of prayer: *A short form and order to be vsed in common prayer thryse a Weeke, for seasonable wether, and good successe of the com[m]on affayres of the realme* (Richard Jugge; ?pp.), [fragment only], printed in Strype, *Parker*, I, 179 [see also Clay, p. 475].
Additional sources: Grindal to Cecil, 30 July 1563, Lans. 6, fo. 156v; Strype, *Parker*, I, 179; Clay, p. 458; Joseph Ames, *Typographical antiquities* (3 vols., 1785–90), II, 726.

ORDER

Bishop of London to the archdeacon of London, 8 July 1560

After my hartye commendacyons vnto you thees shalbe to certifie you that on sondaye beinge the vijth daye of Iulye I receaued a forme concerninge the establisshinge of the Wether hearein enclosed from my lorde of Canturburyes grace, Wherfore thees shalbe to charge and commaunde you that you immedyatlye vppon the sighte hereof doo giue commaundement to all Curates and ministers within yor Archdeaconrye that they and euerye of them obserue the forme of the sayde booke dewlye and beginne there seruyes at viij of the clocke in the morninge euery daye and that euerye of theim prouide the sayde booke at the coste and charges of the parisshe And faile not this to doo with all expedicyon …

FORM OF PRAYER

PREFACE
That we were taught by many and sundry examples of holy Scripture, that upon

occasion of particular punishments, afflictions, and perils, which God of his most just judgments hath sent among his people, to shew his wrath against sin, and to call his people to repentance, and to the redress of their lives, the godly have been provoked and stirred up to more fervency and diligence in prayer, fasting, and alms deeds; to a more deep consideration of their consciences, to ponder their unthankfulness &c.

1560–S   Thanksgiving prayer for the peace treaty of Edinburgh, and the success of the reformation in Scotland

[Friday 19?] July 1560 (St Giles's Church, Edinburgh)

This thanksgiving prayer, the first protestant observance of national significance in Scotland, marked the victory of the pro-reform Lords of the Congregation in their military struggle against the catholic queen regent, Mary of Guise. Instrumental in the Lords' success was the intervention of England, secured because Elizabeth I was persuaded of the threat posed by the French forces on Mary's side. Domestic strife reduced the ability of France to support the regent, and her death on 11 June 1560 made way for peace negotiations. Under the treaty of Edinburgh (6 July), French and English troops were removed from Scotland, and a meeting of parliament was called. Assembling in August, parliament ratified a reformed confession of faith, renounced papal authority and prohibited the celebration of the mass. This thanksgiving worship in St Giles's Church, Edinburgh, consisting of a sermon and the following prayer, was attended by many of the pro-reform nobles. The occasion is known only from John Knox's *History of the reformation*, which implies that the initiative for the worship came from the clergy.

Order: described in *The works of John Knox*, ed. David Laing (6 vols., Wodrow Society, 1846–64), II, 84 [Anglicized version in John Knox, *History of the reformation in Scotland*, ed. William Croft Dickinson (2 vols., Edinburgh, 1949), I, 332].
Form of prayer: *Works of Knox*, II, 84–7 [Anglicized version in Knox, *History*, I, 332–4]
Additional source: A. Ian Dunlop, *The Kirks of Edinburgh* (Scottish Record Society, new ser., 15 and 16, Edinburgh, 1989), p. 15.

DESCRIPTION OF ORDER

The works of John Knox
[T]he Preachouris exhortit thame, [i.e. the Lords of the Congregation] (for than in Edinburgh war the maist pairt of the cheif Ministeris of the Realme) to be thankfull unto God, and nixt to provyde, that the ministeris mycht be distributeit as the necessitie of the countrey requyreit. Ane day was statute, quhen the haill Nobilitie, and the greitest pairt of the Congregatioun assembillit in Sanct Geilis Kirk in Edinburgh, quhair, efter the sermond maid for that purpoise, publick thankis war gevin unto God for his mercifull deliverance, in forme as followis:–

FORM OF PRAYER

O Eternall and Everlasting God, Father of oure Lord Jesus Chryst, quha hes nocht onlie commandit us to pray, and promeisit to heir us, but alsua willis us to magnifie thy mercies, and to glorifie thy name quhen thou schawis thy self pitiefull and favorabill unto us, especiallie quhen thow delyveris us frome disperatt daingearis: ffor sa did thy servantis Abraham, David, Jehosaphatt, and Ezekias; yea, the haill pepill of Israell omittit nott the same, quhen thow by thy mychtie hand did confound thair ennemeis, and deliver thame frome feir and daingear of death intentit. We aucht not, nor can not forgett, O Lord, in how miserabill estait stude this poore countrey, and we the just inhabitants of the same, not many dayis past, quhen idolatrie was menteynit, quhen creuell straingearis did impyre, quhen virgennis war deflorit, matronis corruptit, mennis wyfeis violentlie and vylanouslie oppressit, the blud of innocentis sched without mercie; and finallie, quhen the unjust commandementis of proud tyrannis war obeyit as ane law. Out of thir miseries, O Lord, could nather our witt, policey, nor strength delyver us; yea [they] did schaw unto us how vayne was the help of man, quhair thy blessing gevis not victorie. In thir our anguischeis, O Lord, we suitit unto thee, we cryit for thy help, and we reclameit thy name, as thy trubillit flock, persecutit for thy treuth saik. Mercifullie hes thow hard us, O Lord, mercifullie, we say, becaus that neither in us, neither yitt in our confederatis was thair any caus quhy thou souldest have gevin unto us sa joyfull and suddane a delyverance: for neither of us bayth ceassit to do wickitlie, evin in the myddis of oure greitest trubillis. And yitt hes thow lukit upoun us sa pitifullie as that we haid gevin unto thee maist perfyte obedience, for thou hes disapoyntit the counsals of the crafty, thow hes brydillit the rage of the crewell; and thow hes of thy mercie sett this oure perisching Realme at ane reasonabill libertie. Oh, gif us hartis (thou, Lord, that onlie gifis all guid gyft), with reverence and feir, to meditat thy wondrouse warkis lait wrocht in oure eyes. Let not the remembrance of the same unthankfullie to slip frome oure wavering myndis. We grant and acknawlege, O Lord, that quhat soever we haif resavit sall fall in oblivioun with us, and so turne to oure condempnatioun, unless thou, by the power of thy Holie Spreit, keip and reteyne us in recent and perpetuall memorie of the same. We beseik thee thairfoir, O Father of mercyis, that as of thy undeservit grace thow hes partlie removit our darknes, suppressit idolatrie, and taikin frome above oure heidis the devouring sword of mercyless strangearis, that sa it wald pleise thee to proceid with us in this thy grace begune. And albeit that in us thair is nathing that may move thy Majestie to schaw us thy favour, O yit for Christ Jesus, thy onlie weilbelovit Sonis saik, quhais name we beir, and quhais doctrin we profess, we beseik thee never to suffer us to foirsaik or deny this thy veritie quhilk now we professe. Bot seing that thou hes mercifullie heard us, and hes caussit thy veritie to triumphe in us, sa we crave of thee continewance unto the end, that thy godlie name may be glorifeit in us thy creaturis. And seing that nathing is mair odiouse in thy presence, O Lord, than is ungratitud and violatioun of ane aith and convenant maid in thy name; and seing that thou hes maid our confederatis of Ingland the instrumentis by quhom we are now sett at this libertie, to quhom we in thy name have promeisit mutuall fayth agane; lett us never fall to that unkyndnes, O Lord, that ather we declair oure selfis unthankfull unto thame, or prophanaris of thy holie name. Confound thow the counsalls of thame that go about to brek that maist godlie liegue contractit in thy name, and reteyne thou us sa firmlie togidder by the power of thy Holie Spreit, that Sathan have never power to sett us agane at variance nor discord. Geve us thy grace to leif in that Christiane cheritie quhilk thy Sone, our Lord Jesus, hes sa earnestlie commandit to all the memberis of his body; that uther natiouns, provockit be our example, may sett asyde all ungodlie weir, contentioun, and stryff, and studie to leif in tranquilitie and peace, as it becumis the scheip of thy pasture, and the pepill that daylie luikis for our finall delyverance, by the cuming agane of oure Lord Jesus; to whom with Thee, and the Holie Spreit, be all honour, glorie, and prayse, now and ever. AMEN.

1562–E1   Prayers for the military campaign in France, in support of the Huguenots

After Friday 9 October 1562 (England)

On 20 September 1562, Elizabeth signed a treaty to provide military support to the French Huguenots besieged at Newhaven (Le Havre) in return for the promise of the restitution of Calais to English control; the Huguenots' catholic opponents were supported by the papacy and Philip II. Orders for public prayers for a successful campaign were issued on 9 October 1562, five days after English troops arrived in Normandy. Though prayers had previously been (and continued to be) ordered in support of foreign Christians threatened by 'infidels' (see 1541–E2, 1565–E1, 1565–E2, 1566–E and 1571–E), this was the first occasion when prayers were ordered throughout the kingdom in support of co-religionists abroad. There is no evidence to corroborate the arguments of John Strype and the liturgical scholar William Keatinge Clay – based on a passing reference to a 'comen prayer … apointed in the Gwises tyme' made by Parker in a letter to Cecil on 23 July 1563 – that prayers were issued in 1559 or 1560 in response to the threat posed by the duke of Guise's support for his niece, Mary queen of Scots' claim to the English throne (see Appendix 1: Omitted occasions).

Prayers for persecuted co-religionists abroad became common during Elizabeth's reign as England resumed its Edwardian *rôle* as a leader of the reformed church in Europe, despite Elizabeth's reluctance. Though the Elizabethan BCP included prayers to be said during times of war, a new prayer was commissioned for this occasion. This revived the practice established under Henry VIII and Edward, and was the first of three liturgical formats for special worship developed during Elizabeth's reign (see also 1563–E and 1564–E); this format continued to be used until the late twentieth century. There are two versions of the prayer extant: a manuscript version in Grindal's episcopal register and four imperfect printed copies at Hereford Cathedral. The printed copies are uncut and unbound, as they would have come off the printer's press. The prayer emphasized the providential nature of war and that military victory lay in God's hands. It justified English intervention in France because the French crown posed a danger both to the true faith and to the English crown, reflecting the beliefs of many in the Elizabethan regime that France, Spain and the papacy were conspiring to depose Elizabeth and put her cousin, Mary, on the English throne. In the absence of other evidence, it is likely that the prayer was inserted into the liturgy as prescribed by the BCP. The military campaign was a disaster. The Huguenots lost Rouen, and deaths amongst the leadership of both French forces led to a rapprochement between Huguenots and catholics. Grindal preached at Paul's Cross on 1 November on the divine punishment this rapprochement would provoke. The English troops continued to defend Newhaven against the French catholic forces until plague forced them to surrender during July and August 1563. England's rights to Calais were lost in the ensuing treaty of Troyes (April 1564). Machyn misdated his account of the prayers and of Grindal's sermons

(14 November and 26 December respectively). The prayer was not universally popular. Giles Fezard, from a prominent catholic yeomanry family in Downhead St Mary in Wiltshire, was prosecuted at the local assizes for complaining that the prayer was 'vngodly', 'vncharitable', 'not to be suffyrd' and 'meter to sett princes together by the eares'. He argued that 'the Duke of Guyes is a godly man and no tyrant or cruell person but a favourer and seker of godes glorye and suche a man as wolde be oure frende'. He also stated that Elizabeth 'had gon so farr in suche matters [i.e. the religious settlement] that nowe she wold torne agene if she wist howe'. After he was acquitted, the attorney-general sued the witnesses in Star Chamber for perjury and the jury for corruption.

Order: Grindal to Robert Horne, bishop of Winchester, 9 Oct. 1562, LMA, MS 9531/13: 1, fo. 26r.
Form of prayer: *A prayer for the present estate, to be used in churches at the end of the letanye, on Sundayes, Wednesdayes, and Fridayes, through the whole realme* (Richard Jugge and John Cawood; 8 pp.; STC 16504.3; Hereford Cathedral) [copy imperfect: missing sentences supplied from the manuscript version in Grindal to Horne, 9 Oct. 1562, LMA, MS 9531/13: 1, fos. 26r–v; complete text in Clay, pp. 476–7].
Additional sources: *A declaration of the quene's maiestie* (1562; STC 9187.3); *Expositio causarum quibus Angliae regina commouebatur* (1562; STC 9187); Machyn's diary, fos. 155v, 156v; MacLure, p. 46; Clay, pp. 458–9; Strype, *Annals*, I: 1, 422–4, 545 (which dates the order to 14 Nov. possibly on the evidence of Machyn); Strype, *Parker*, I, 179–80; Parker to Cecil, 23 July 1563, Lans. 6, fo. 154r; *Attorney-General* v. *Jury of Wiltshire*, 5 Elizabeth [1562–3], STAC5/A8/5, fos. 1r, 2r, 4r, 5r, 6r; Same vs Edward Bennett, 5 Elizabeth [1562–3], STAC5/A10/14; *Attorney-General* v. *Fessard and Sherwood*, n.d., STAC 5/A52/17; *Attorney-General* v. *Sherwood, Beacher and Bendbury*, n.d., STAC 5/A34/3; Interogatories to be ministred to Edward Bennet John Blacher and Thomas Bunter, [n.d.], STAC 3/10/73.

ORDER

Bishop of London to Bishop of Winchester: 9 October 1562

After my hartye commendacyons to your good lordeshipp I haue receaued order from my lorde of Canturburies his grace bothe to imparte vnto you the good newes enclosed and also to sende you a forme of prayor to be vsed in all your churches prayenge your L[ord] to make soo good meanes as ye cann for obteyninge suffycyente number of Copies with speade and also to see the saide prayor dewlie vsed as apperteyneth ...

FORM OF PRAYER

O Most myghtie Lord god, the Lorde of hoastes, the gouernour of all creatures, the only geuer of all victories, who alone art hable to strengthen the weake against the mightie, and to vanquyshe infinite multitudes of thine enemies with the countenaunce of a fewe of thy seruauntes, calling upon thy name and trusting in thee: Defende O Lorde, thy seruant and our gouernour under thee, our [Quene Elisabeth and all] thy people committed to her charge, and especially at this tyme, O Lorde, haue regarde to those her Subiectes which be sente ouer the seas, to the ayde of such as be persecuted for the profession of thy holye name, and to withstande the crueltie of those which be common ennemies as well to the trueth of thy eternal worde, as to theyr owne naturall Prince and countrie, & manifestly to this crowne and Realme of Englande, whiche thou hast of thy diuine prouidence assigned in [these our daies to the gouernemente of thy seruaunte our soueraigne and gracyous Quene, O mooste mer]cifull father (yf it be thy holy wyll) make softe and tender the stonye hartes of all those that exalt them selues agaynst thy trueth, and seke to oppresse this crowne and Realme of Englande, & conuert them to the knowledge of thy sonne the only sauiour of the worlde Jesus

Chryste, that wee and they maye ioyntlye glorifie thy mercies. Lighten we besech thee theyr ignoraunt harts to embrace the trueth of thy worde, or else so abate theyr crueltie (O moste myghtye Lorde) that this our Christian Region with others that confesse thy holye Gospell maye obteyne by thy [ayde and strengith suretie] from our enemies, without shedding of Christian and innocent bloud, whereby all they which be opressed with theyr tirannye, maye be relieued, and all whiche be in feare of theyr crueltie, maye be comforted: and finallye that all Christian Realmes and speciallye this Realme of Englande, may by thy defence and protection enioye perfite peace, quietnes, and securitee: and that we for these thy mercies, ioyntlye all together with one consonant hart and voyce, may thankefully render to thee all laude and prayse, and in one godly concord and vnitie emongst our selues, may [continuallie magnifie thi] glorious name, who with thy sonne our sauiour Jesus Chryste and the holye ghost, art one eternall, almyghtie, and most mercyfull God. To whom be all laude and prayse, worlde without ende. Amen.

1562–E2 Thanksgiving prayers for the recovery of Elizabeth I from smallpox

Sunday 18 October 1562 (Paul's Cross, London)

Elizabeth I contracted smallpox in early October and remained close to death for a week. The only account of her illness is by the Spanish ambassador, de Quadra. He stated that privy councillors had discussed who could succeed Elizabeth: they rejected Mary, queen of Scots' claims unanimously, but were divided between those of Catherine Grey and the earl of Huntingdon. The privy council ordered an announcement to be made of the queen's recovery at Paul's Cross on 18 October and prayers to be said in thanks to God. No official prayers or form are extant; there is no evidence that any were commissioned or ordered for use. The fears provoked by Elizabeth's illness prompted calls in parliament during 1563 for her to settle the succession.

Order: privy council to Grindal, 17 Oct. 1562, LMA, MS 9531/13: 1, fo. 26r [also in *Concilia*, IV, 243].
Form of prayer: none ordered or extant.
Additional sources: Alvarez de Quadra, bishop of Aquila and Spanish ambassador, to the duchess of Parma, 16, 17 Oct. 1562, and to Philip II, 25 Oct. 1562, Add. 26056a, fos. 187r–v, 189r–90v [letter of 16 Oct. in *Relations politiques des Pays-bas et de l'Angleterre, sous le règne de Philippe II*, ed. Kervyn de Lettenhove (11 vols., Brussels, 1882–1900), III, 164–5].

ORDER

Privy council to bishop of London: 17 October 1562
After our verie hartye comendacyons to your lordeshipp Wheare the Queenes maiestie is at this presente God be thancked after some extemitie of sicknes, verye well recouered because it maye happen that some vaine brutes maye be spread abroade of this matter especyallie in the cyttie of London, We haue thought good to signifie these ioyfull tydinges vnto your lordeshipp and praye you to tak order that the same maie be publysshed to morowe at Poules crosse and there thanckes to be

giuen to Almightie godd for this her maiestyes good recouerye and humblie to praise his blessed goodnes to contynewe the same …

1563–E   Services and weekly fast days during a plague epidemic

Wednesdays (services and fasting), Fridays and Sundays (services only), beginning August 1563, during plague (England and Wales)

The outbreak of plague in 1563 was the worst during Elizabeth's reign, claiming approximately 80,000 lives, with 20,000 in London alone. It began in July in larger, poorer parishes such as St Botolph Bishopsgate, before spreading to richer parishes and the rest of the realm. Grindal and Parker ordered services and sermons respectively for the diocese of London and the city of Canterbury. Grindal's were written by him and Alexander Nowell, dean of St Paul's and one of the bishop's chaplains; Parker's was probably based on the form for 1562–E1. Services for wider use in England were not available until the following month when Cecil, hearing of Parker's and Grindal's initiatives, persuaded Queen Elizabeth that she herself should order special services. Parker had explained to Cecil that he had not ordered special worship for other parts of the kingdom because he believed that archbishops did not have sufficient authority to do so.

Though the Elizabethan BCP, like the second Edwardian BCP (1552), included occasional prayers to be added to the litany in times of crisis – including during plague – Grindal and Nowell were commissioned to compose a complete liturgy for this occasion. Their form of prayer comprised the royal order, a preface, full service and order for fasting, and was based on their London form and the preface for 1560–E. In the original version, the authors, both former Marian exiles committed to reforming the Elizabethan church further, introduced 'Innovacions', specificially instructions for the whole service to be held in the nave, rather than having the litany read in the chancel. Parker changed this to make the service conform more closely to the conduct of BCP services, but refrained from editing the prayers, even though he considered them too long. The final version of the form required different liturgical formats to be used on different days of the week (Sundays, Wednesdays and Fridays, the days when the litany was usually prescribed to be read). Sunday services comprised the service for morning prayer, omitting the opening sentences and first prayer and changing the prescribed lessons, followed by the litany and new special prayers. Wednesday services comprised the service for morning prayer, followed by an exhortation for private prayer (usually a homily), fifteen minutes of silent private prayers and meditations, the litany and the new prayers, concluding with the communion. If there was no communion, the ten commandments, epistle and gospel were to be read, followed by a sermon or homily. The service ended with the prayer for the whole church and the prayers 'Almighty God the fountain of all wisdom' and 'Almighty God which hast promised'. Wednesdays were also designated fast days, on which everyone between the ages of sixteen and sixty (excluding the sick and labourers at harvest time) was ordered to eat only one moderate and plain meal and to spend time in reading the Bible as well as attending church. It is unclear why Wednesday was chosen as a fast day. It may have been to distinguish it from the traditional (Catholic) fast on Fridays, which had effectually been secularized since the homily on fasting (1547) had justified its continuance for the purpose of maintaining stocks of sheep and cattle and supporting the fishing industry. Alternatively, it may have been because Wednesday had commonly been observed as a voluntary fast day by the pious. Friday services were short, comprising only morning prayer, the litany and the special prayers. Characteristic of the liturgy, and of much early Elizabethan special worship, were the antiphonal psalms that were composed from verses scattered across the Bible and which were ordered to be recited as a call and response by the minister and the clerk or congregation. With parishes buying only two or three copies of the forms at most, and no evidence of 'lining out' in this period, it is most likely that these psalms were read only by the minister and clerk. On 1 August, the form was approved by Cecil and sent to the royal printer, Richard Jugge. Orders to Thomas Young, archbishop of York, were not sent until at least 21 August and copies of the form for general distribution appear to have been sent later. A form for private use (*A forme of meditation*, STC 16504.5) was also printed; it may have been written by Grindal though he did not claim authorship in a letter to Cecil (21 August), when commenting on the delay in its publication.

This occasion of special worship is significant for five reasons. First, this form established one of the three main liturgical formats for special worship (along with 1562–E1 and 1564–E), a format used until 1626–E2. Second, this was the first occasion for which an order of the fast is extant (cf. 1550–E and 1560–E); this order in basic outline established how national fasts during times of plague in England were to be conducted until 1665–EIr2. Third, the ordering of regular fasting represented a significant change in English attitudes towards the practice, and established one of the three ways in which fasting continued in protestant England and Wales (the others being private fasts and Friday 'fish days'). Fasting was controversial for early English protestants, because it was associated with Catholicism, works-righteousness and superstition. In the 1530s and 1540s, fast-breaking had become an important marker of evangelicalism, as well as a means to draw people into the new religion. However, some remained concerned that, in rejecting fasting, English protestants handed a propaganda victory to their Catholic opponents; as Grindal told Cecil in August 1563, 'my opinion hath ben longe that in no one thinge the Aduersarie hathe more advantage agaynste vs, then in the matter off faste, which we vtterly neglecte'. Indeed, by Elizabeth's reign, Protestant objections had largely been overcome, given the numerous biblical precedents which were now interpreted as justifying fasting as a central part of a godly life. Fourth, it is the first extant form to include a lengthy preface (see also 1560–E). These prefaces were important because they were used by the regime to outline the reasons for special worship, articulate widespread beliefs about divine providence, causation and national identity, and to convey factual information about the event at hand. Ministers were expected to use them as the basis of their weekly sermon. The regime thus attempted to use these prefaces to influence the way that people understood the events for which they were praying. Fifth, it was the first time that a royal order for prayers was printed in the form of prayer; this practice was not revived until 1689 (see 1689–E2) and became common in the reigns of William and Anne.

Orders: royal letter to the archbishop of Canterbury, 1 Aug. 1563, printed in editions of *A fourme to be vsed in common prayer twise a weeke* ... for the province of Canterbury (see below under Form of prayer); royal letter to the archbishop of York, 1 Aug. 1563, printed in editions of *A fourme to be vsed in common prayer twise a weeke* ... *for the province of York,* STC 16506.7, Emmanuel College Library, Cambridge (draft of letters in SP12/29/56).

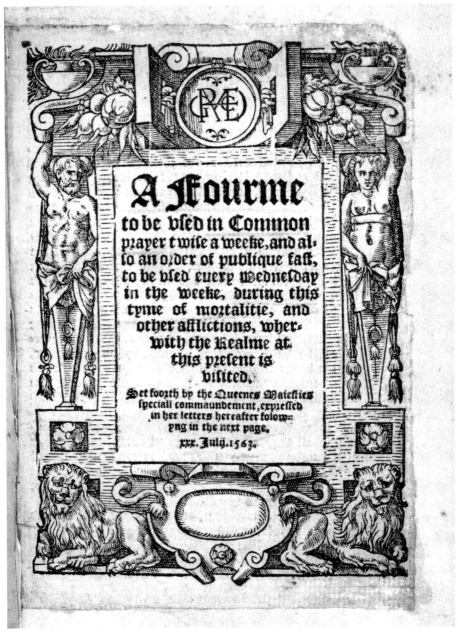

2 Title-page of the Elizabethan form for petitionary services and fasts during an
outbreak of plague, 1563–E. *A fourme to be vsed in common prayer twise a weeke,
and also an order of publique fast, to be vsed euery Wednesday in the weeke, during
this tyme of mortalitie ...* (4°, 1563; STC 16505); BL, 692.d.33, sig. Ai^r.

Form of prayer: *A fourme to be vsed in common prayer twise a weeke, and also an order of publique fast, to be vsed euery Wednesday in the weeke, during this tyme of mortalitie, and other afflictions, wherwith the realme at this present is visited* (edition for province of Canterbury [48] pp.; STC 16505) [also in Clay, pp. 478–502].

Form of prayer (other editions): STC 16506, 16506.3, 16506.7, 16506.9.

Additional sources: Parker to Cecil, 23 July, 6 Aug. 1563; Grindal to Cecil, 30 July, 1, 12, 21 Aug. 1563, Lans. 6, fos. 154r, 162r, 156r–157r, 160r, 168r, 166r–v; Strype, *Parker*, I, 259–69, III, 60–3; Strype, *Grindal*, pp. 104–9, 119–24, 473–5; *The remains of Edmund Grindal, D.D.*, ed. William Nicholson (Parker Society, Cambridge, 1843), pp. 78–9, 258–69; Clay, pp. 459, 503–7.

ORDER

Royal letter to archbishop of Canterbury: 1 August 1563

By the Queene

Most Reuerende father in GOD, ryght trustie, and right welbeloued, we greete you wel. Lyke as almyghtie God hath of his mere grace committed to vs next vnder him the chiefe gouernement of this Realme, and the people therein: so hath he of his lyke goodnes ordered vnder vs sundry principall ministers, to serue and assist vs in this burden. And therefore considering the state of this present tyme, wherein it hath pleased the most highest for thamendement of vs and our people, to visite certaine places of our Realme with more contagious sicknesse then lately hath ben: for remedie and mittigation thereof, we thinke it both necessarie and our bounden duetie, that vniuersall prayer and fasting be more effectually vsed in this our Realme. And vnderstandyng that you haue thought and considered vpon some good order to be prescribed therein, for the which ye require thapplication of our aucthoritie, for the better obseruation thereof amongst our people, we do not onlye commende and alowe your good zeale therein: but do also commaunde all maner our Ministers Ecclesiasticall or Ciuil, and all other our subiectes, to execute, folowe, and obey such godly and holsome orders, as you beyng Primate of all Englande, and Metropolitane of this prouince of Cantorbury, vpon godly aduise and consideration shall vniformely deuise, prescribe and publishe, for the vniuersall vsage of prayer, fastyng, and other good deedes, during the time of this visitation by sicknesse and other troubles …

To the most Reuerende father in GOD, our ryght trusty and ryght welbeloued Tharchbyshop of Cantorbury and Primate of all Englande [in STC 16506: Tharchbyshop of Yorko and Primate of Englande]

FORM OF PRAYER

[The order 'By the Queene' as above]

THE PREFACE

We be taught by many and sundry examples of holy Scriptures, that vppon occasion of particuler punishmentes, afflictions, and perils, which God of his most iust iudgement hath some tymes sent among his people, to shew his wrath agaynst sinne, and to call his people to repentaunce, and to the redresse of their lyues: the godly haue ben prouoked and styred vp to more feruencie and diligence in prayer, fasting, and almes deedes, to a more deepe consideration of their consciences, to ponder their vnthankfulnesse and forgetfulnesse of Gods mercifull benefites towardes them, with crauing of pardon for the time past, and to aske his asistaunce for the time to come to liue more godly, and so to be defended and deliuered from all further perils & daungers. So kyng Dauid in the tyme of plague and pestilence which ensued vppon

A Fourme of

the readyng of the Gospell, as hath ben accustomed, And so the minister commending the people to God with thaccustomed benediction, shall dimisse them.

If there be no Communion, then on euery of the sayde Wednesdayes after the Letanie, the .x. Comaundementes, the Epistle, the Gospell, the Sermon or Homilie done: the generall vsuall prayer for the state of the whole Churche shalbe read, as is set forth in the booke of Common prayer. After whiche shall folowe these two prayers:

Almightie God the fountayne of all wysdome. &c. And, Almightie God which hast promised. &c. With the accustomed benediction.

¶ The order for Frydayes.

On frydayes shalbe only the mornyng prayer, and the Letanie, with the prayers nowe appoynted to be annexed to the same.

❧ Homilies to be read in order
on wednesdayes.

1 First, an Homily intituled, an Homily concernyng the Justice of God in punishing of impenitent sinners. &c. Newly now set forth for that purpose.

2 The .viii. Homily of the first Tome of Homilies, entituled, Of the declynyng from God.

3 The .ix. Homily of the same Tome, entituled, An exhortation agaynst the feare of death.

4 The Homily of Fastyng, in the seconde Tome of Homilies.

5 The Homily of Prayer, in the same Tome.

6 The Homily of Almes deedes, in the same Tome.

7 The

3 Page from the 1563 form of prayer, showing the instructions for Friday services. *A fourme to be vsed in common prayer twise a weeke, and also an order of publique fast, to be vsed euery Wednesday in the weeke, during this tyme of mortalitie* (4°, 1563; STC 16505); BL, 692.d.33, sig. Aiii^v.

his vayne numbryng of the people, prayed vnto God with wonderfull feruencie, confessing his fault, desiring God to spare the people, and rather to turne his yre to himward, who had chiefly offended in that transgression. The lyke was done by the vertuous kynges Josaphat and Ezechias in their distresse of warres and forreyne inuasions. So dyd Judith and Esther fall to humble prayers in lyke perils of their people. So dyd Daniel in his captiuitie, and many other moe in their troubles. Nowe therefore callyng to mynde that God hath ben prouoked by vs to visite vs at this present with the plague and other greeuous diseases, and partly also with trouble of warres: It hath ben thought meete to set foorth by publique order, some occasion to excite and stirre vp all godly people within this Realme, to pray earnestly and hartyly to God to turne away his deserued wrath from vs, and to restore vs aswell to the health of our bodyes by the holsomnesse of the ayre, as also to godly and profitable peace and quietnesse. And although it is euery Christian mans duetie of his owne deuotion to pray at all tymes: yet for that the corrupt nature of man is so slouthful and negligent in this his dutie, he hath neede by often and sundry meanes to be styred vp and put in remembraunce of his duetie. For the effectuall accomplishment wherof, it is ordered and appoynted, as foloweth.

First, that all Curates and Pastours shall exhort their parishioners to endeuour them selues to come vnto the Churche, with so many of their families as may be spared from their necessary businesse, (hauing yet a prudent respect in such assemblyes to kepe the sicke from the whole, in places where the plague reigneth) and they to resort, not onlye on Sundayes and Holydayes: but also on Wednesdayes and Frydayes, during the tyme of these present afflictions, exhortyng them there reuerently and godly to behaue them selues, and with penitent heartes to pray vnto God to turne these plagues from vs, whiche we through our vnthankfulnesse and sinfull life haue deserued.

Secondly, that the said Curates shall then distinctly and plainely reade the general confession appointed in the booke of seruice, with the residue of the Morning prayer, vsing for both the Lessons the Chapters hereafter folowing. That is to say,

For the first Lesson, one of these Chapters, out of the olde Testament *[2 Kgs. 24, Lev. 26, Deut. 28, Jer. 1:1–18, and 22, 2 Chr. 34, Isa. 1, Ezek. 18 & 19, Joel 2, 2 Esdr. 9, Jonah 2 & 3 together]*. Whiche Chapters woulde be read orderly on Sundayes, Wednesdayes, and Frydayes.

And for the seconde Lesson, one of these Chapters, out of the newe Testament *[Matt. 3, 6, 7, 24, 25, Luke 13, Acts 2:22–47, Rom. 2, 6, 12, 13, Gal. 5, Eph. 4, 5, 1 Tim. 2, Rev. 2]*.

The order for the Wednesdayes.

On Wednesdayes (whiche be the dayes appointed for generall fast, in such fourme as shall hereafter be declared) after the Morning prayer ended, as is aforesayde, the sayde Curates and Ministers shall exhort the people assembled (with the Homyly therof made, or the like) to geue them selues to their priuate prayers and meditations: For whiche purpose, a pawse shalbe made of one quarter of an houre and more: by the discretion of the saide Curate. During whiche tyme, as good scilence shalbe kept as may be.

That done, the Letanie is to read in the middes of the people, with the additions of prayer hereafter mentioned.

Then shal folowe the ministration of the communion, so oft as a iust number of

Common prayer.

¶ The Homyly of repentaunce, in the same Tome alſo. When theſe Homylyes are once read ouer, then to begyn agayne, and ſo to continue them in ordcr.

After the ende of the collect in the Letanie, whiche begynneth with theſe wordes, We humbly beſeche thee O father. &c. ſhall folowe this Pſalme, to be ſayd of the Miniſter, with the aunſwere of the people.

¶ The Pſalme to be

ſayde in the Letanie befoze one of the prayers newly appoynted. Whereof one verſe to be ſayde of the Miniſter, and an other by the people, clarke, oz clarkes.

Come, let vs humble our ſelues, and fall downe befoze the Lozd with reuerence and feare: 1. Pſal. 95.

Foz he is the Lozde our God, and we are the people of his paſture, and the ſheepe of his handes   2.

Come therefoze, let vs turne agayne vnto our Lozd, foz he hath ſmitten vs, & he ſhal heale vs.   3. Oſee. 6.

Let vs repent, and turne from our wickednes: and our ſinnes ſhalbe fozgeuen vs.   4. Actes. 3.

Let vs turne, and the Lozde wil turne from his heauy wzath, and wyll pardon vs, and we ſhall not peryſhe,   5. Jonas. 3.

Foz we knowledge our faultes: and our ſinnes be euer befoze vs.   6. Pſal. 51.

We haue ſoze prouoked thine anger, O Lozde: thy   7. Lament. 3.

4 Page from the 1563 form of prayer, showing the opening of the 'composite' psalm. *A fourme to be vsed in common prayer twise a weeke, and also an order of publique fast, to be vsed euery Wednesday in the weeke, during this tyme of mortalitie* (4°, 1563; STC 16505); BL, 692.d.33, sig. Aiv[r].

Communicants shalbe therto disposed, with a sermon if it can be, to be made by such as be aucthorised by the Metropolitane or byshop of the diocesse, and they to entreate of such matters especially as be meete for this cause of publique prayer: or els for want of such preacher, to reade one of the homylyes hereafter appointed, after the readyng of the Gospell, as hath ben accustomed, And so the minister commending the people to God with thaccustomed benediction, shall dimisse them.

If there be no Communion, then on euery of the sayde Wednesdayes after the Letanie, the .x. Commaundementes, the Epistle, the Gospell, the Sermon or Homilie done: the generall vsuall prayer for the state of the whole Churche shalbe read, as is set forth in the booke of Common prayer. After whiche shall folowe these two prayers:

Almightie God the fountayne of all wysdome. &c. And,

Almightie God which hast promised. &c. With the accustomed benediction.

The order for Frydayes.

On frydayes shalbe only the mornyng prayer, and the Letanie, with the prayers nowe appoynted to be annexed to the same.

Homilies to be read in order on Wednesdayes

1 First, an Homily intituled, an Homily concernyng Justice of God in punishing of impenitent sinners, &c. Newly now set forth for that purpose.

2 The .viii Homily of the first Tome of Homilies, entituled, Of the declynyng from God.[11]

3 The .ix Homily of the same Tome, entituled, An exhortation against the feare of death.[12]

4 The Homily of Fastyng, in the seconde Tome of Homilies.[13]

5 The Homily of Prayer, in the same Tome.[14]

6 The Homily of Almes deedes, in the same Tome.[15]

7 The Homyly of repentaunce, in the same Tome also.[16]

When these Homylyes are once read ouer, then to begyn agayne, and so to continue them in order.

After the ende of the collect in the Letanie, whiche begynneth with these wordes, We humbly beseche thee O father .&c. shall folowe this Psalme, to be sayd of the Minister, with the aunswere of the people.

The Psalme to be sayde in the Letanie before one of the prayers newly appoynted. Whereof one verse to be sayde of the Minister, and an other by the people, clarke, or clarkes.

O Come, let vs humble our selues and fall downe before the Lord with reuerence and feare: (Ps. 95) [95:6]

---

11 *Two books of homilies*, pp. 81–90.
12 *Ibid.*, pp. 91–104.
13 *Ibid.*, pp. 279–96.
14 *Ibid.*, pp. 320–38.
15 *Ibid.*, pp. 382–99.
16 *Ibid.*, pp. 525–49.

For he is the Lorde our God: and we are the people of his pasture, and the sheepe of his handes [95:7]

Come therefore, let vs turne agayne vnto our Lord, for he hath smitten vs & he shal heale vs. (Hos. 6) [6:1]

Let vs repent, and turne from our wickednes: and our sinnes shalbe forgeuen vs. (Acts 3) [3:19]

Let vs turne, and the Lorde wil turne from his heauy wrath and wyll pardon vs, and we shall not peryshe, (Jonah 3) [3:8 & 9]

For we knowledge our faultes: and our sinnes be euer before vs. (Ps. 51) [51:3]

We haue sore prouoked thine anger, O Lorde: thy wrath is waxed hot, and thy heauy displeasure is sore kyndled agaynst vs. (Lam. 3) [3:42]

Thou hast made us heare of the noyse of warres, and hast troubled vs by the vexation of enemies. [?]

Thou hast in thine indignation striken vs with greeuous sicknes, and by and by we haue fallen as leaues beaten downe with a vehemente wynde. (Isa. 64) [? & 6]

In deede we acknowledge that all punyshmentes are lesse then our deseruynges: but yet of thy mercy Lorde correct vs to amendement, and plague vs not to our destruction. (Judith 8; Job 11; Sap. 11) [Job 11:6]

For thy hande is not shortened that thou canst not helpe, neither is thy goodnes abated that thou wylt not heare. [59:1]

Thou hast promised, O Lorde, that afore we crye thou wylt heare vs: whylest we yet speake thou wylt haue mercy vpon vs. (Esai. 65) [Isa. 65:24]

For none that trust in thee shalbe confounded: neither any that call vpon thee shalbe despised. [Ps. 25:1]

For thou art the only Lorde, who woundest, and doest heale agayne, who killest, and reuiuest, bryngest euen to hell, and bryngest backe agayne. (Tobit 3; Job 5; Hos. 6) [Job 5:18 & 20]

Our fathers hoped in thee, they trusted in thee, and thou dyddest delyuer them. (Ps. 22) [22:4]

They called vpon thee, and were helped: they put theyr trust in thee, and were not confounded. (Ps. 22) [22: 5]

O Lorde rebuke vs not in thyne indignation: neyther chasten vs in thy heauy displeasure. (Ps. 6) [6:1]

O remember not the sinnes and offences of our youth: but accordyng to thy mercie thynke thou vppon vs, O Lorde, for thy goodnes. (Ps. 25) [25:5 & 6]

Haue mercy vpon vs, O Lord, for we are weake: O Lorde heale vs, for our bones are vexed. [Ps. 6:2]

And nowe in the vexation of our spirites, and the anguysh of our soules, we remember thee, and we crye vnto thee: Heare Lorde, and haue mercie. (Baruch 3; Jonah 2) [Baruch 3:1]

For thyne owne sake, and for thy holy names sake, incline thine eare, and heare, O mercifull Lorde. (Dan. 9) [17 & 18]

For we do not powre out our prayers before thy face, trusting in our owne righteousnes: but in thy great and manyfolde mercies. [Dan. 9:18]

Washe vs throughly from our wickednesse: and cleanse vs from our sinnes. [Ps. 51:2]

Turne thy face from our sinnes, and put out all our misdeedes. [Ps. 51:9]

Make vs cleane heartes, O God: and renue a ryght spirite within vs. [Ps. 51:10]

Helpe vs, O God of our saluation, for the glorye of thy name: O delyuer vs, and be mercyfull vnto our sinnes for thy names sake. (Ps. 79) [79:9]

So we that be thy people, and sheepe of thy pasture, shall geue thee thankes for euer, and wyll alwayes be shewyng foorth thy prayse, from generation to generation. [Ps. 79:14]

After this Psalme, shalbe sayde by the Curate or Minister openly and with an hygh voyce, one of these three prayers folowyng: and after that, orderly the rest of the Collectes appoynted in the Letanie. At which tyme the people shall deuoutly geue eare, & shall both with mynds and speache to them selues assent to the same prayers.

A prayer, conteynyng also a confession of sinnes. Which is to be sayde after the Letanie, aswell vpon Sundayes, as Wednesdayes and Frydayes.

O Almightie, most iust and mercifull God, we here acknowledge our selues most vnworthye to lyft vp our eyes vnto heauen, for our conscience doth accuse vs, and our sinnes do reproue vs. We knowe also that thou Lorde, beyng a iust iudge, must needes punishe the sinnes of them which transgresse thy lawe. And when we consider and examine all our whole lyfe, we fynde nothyng in our selues that deserueth any other thyng but eternall dampnation. But because thou, O Lorde, of thy vnspeakeable mercie, hast commaunded vs in all our necessities to call onlye vpon thee, and hast also promised that thou wylt heare our prayers, not for any our desert (which is none) but for the merites of thy sonne our onely Sauiour Jesus Christe, whom thou hast ordeyned to be our onely mediatour and intercessour: we laye away all confidence in man, and do flee to the throne of thy onely mercie, by the intercession of thy onely sonne our Sauiour Jesus Christe. And first of all we do most lament and bewayle from the bottome of our heartes, our vnkindnesse and vnthankfulnesse towardes thee our Lorde, consideryng that besides those thy benefites which we enioy as thy creatures common with all mankynde, thou hast bestowed many and singuler speciall benefites vpon vs, which we are not able in heart to conceaue, much lesse in wordes worthyly to expresse. Thou hast called vs to the knowledge of thy Gospel. Thou hast releassed vs from the harde seruitude of Satan. Thou hast deliuered vs from all horrible and execrable idolatrie wherein we were vtterly drowned, and haste brought vs into the most cleare and comfortable lyght of thy blessed worde, by the which we are taught howe to serue and honour thee, and howe to lyue orderly with our neyghbours in trueth and veritie. But we most vnmyndefull in tymes of prosperitie of these thy great benefites, haue neglected thy commaundementes, haue abused the knowledge of thy Gospell, and haue folowed our carnall libertie, and serued our owne lustes, and through our sinfull lyfe haue not worshipped and honoured thee as we ought to haue done. And nowe, O Lorde, beyng euen compelled with thy correction, we do most humbly confesse that wee haue sinned, and haue most greeuously offended thee by many & sundry wayes. And yf thou, O Lorde, wouldest nowe beyng prouoked with our disobedience, so deale with vs as thou myght, & as we haue deserued, there remayneth nothing els to be loked for, but vniuersall & continuall plagues in this worlde, and hereafter eternal death and dampnation both of our bodyes and of our soules. For yf we shoulde excuse our selues, our owne consciences woulde accuse vs before thee, and our owne disobedience and wickednes would beare witnesse agaynst vs. Yea euen thy plagues and punishementes which thou doest nowe laye vpon vs in sundry places, do teache vs to acknowledge our sinnes. For seyng, O Lorde, that thou art iust, yea euen iustice it selfe, thou punishest no people without desert. Yea euen at this present O Lorde, we see thy hande terribly stretched out to plague vs, and punishe vs. But although thou shouldest punishe vs more greeuously then thou hast done, & for one plague sende an hundred, yf thou shouldest powre vpon vs all those the testimonies of thy most iust wrath, which in tymes passed thou powredst on thy owne chosen people of Israel: yet shouldest thou do vs no wronge, neither coulde we denie but we had iustly deserued the same. But yet O mercifull Lorde, thou art our God, and we nothyng but dust & ashes: thou art our creatour, and we the worke of thy handes: thou art our pastor, we are thy flocke: thou art our redeemer, & we thy people redeemed: thou art our heauenly father, we are thy children. Wherfore punishe vs not, O Lorde, in thyne anger, but chasten vs in thy mercie. Regarde not the horrour of our sinnes, but the repentaunce thereof. Perfect that worke whiche thou hast begunne in vs, that the whole worlde may know that thou art our God and merciful deliuerer. Thy people of Israel often tymes offended thee, & thou most iustly afflictedst them: but as oft as they returned to thee, thou diddest receaue them to mercie. And though their sinnes were neuer so great, yet thou alwayes turnedst away thy wrath from them, & the punishment prepared for them, and that for thy couenaunt sake, which thou madest with thy seruantes, Abraham, Isahac, and Jacob. Thou hast made the same couenaunt with vs (O heauenly father) or rather a couenaunt of more excellencie and efficacie, and that namely through the mediation of thy deare sonne Jesus Christe our Sauiour, with whose most precious blood it pleased thee that this couenant should be as it were written, sealed, and confirmed. Wherfore, O heauenly father, we nowe castyng away all confidence in our selues or anye other creature, do flee to this most holy couenaunt & testament, wherein our Lorde and Sauiour Jesus Christe once offeryng him selfe a sacrifice for vs on the crosse, hath reconciled vs to thee for euer. Loke therefore O mercifull God, not vppon the sinnes which we continually commit: but vppon our mediatour & peacemaker Jesus Christ, that by his intercession thy wrath may be pacified, & we agayne by thy fatherly countenaunce releeued & comforted. Receaue vs also into thy heauenly defence, and gouerne vs by thy holy spirite, to frame in vs a newnesse of lyfe, therin to laude and magnifie thy blessed name for euer, and to lyue euery of vs accordyng to the seueral state of life wherunto thou Lorde hast ordeyned vs. And although we are vnworthy (O heauenlye father) by meanes of our former foule life, to craue any thyng of thee: yet because thou hast commaunded vs to pray for all men, we moste humbly here vpon our knees beseche thee, saue and defende thy holy Churche, be mercifull, O Lorde, to all common weales, Countreis, Princes, and Magistrates, and especially to this our Realme, and to our most gracious Queene and gouernour Queene Elizabeth, increase the number of godly ministers, indue them with thy grace to be founde faythfull and prudent in their office, defende the Queenes Maiesties Counsell, and all that be in auctoritie vnder her, or that serue in any place by her commaundement for this Realme. We commende also to thy fatherly mercie, all those that be in pouertie, exile, imprison-ment, sicknesse, or any other kinde of aduersitie, and namely those whom thy hande nowe hath touched with any contagious and dangerous sicknesse, which we beseche thee, O Lorde, of thy mercie (when thy blessed wyll is) to remoue from vs, and in the meane tyme, graunt vs grace and true repentaunce, stedfast faith, and constant patience, that whether we lyue or dye, we may alwayes continue thyne, and euer praise thy holy name, and be brought to the fruition of thy Godhead. Graunt vs these and all other our humble petitions (O mercifull father) for thy deare sonnes sake Jesus Christe our Lorde. Amen.

Or els in the steade of the other, this prayer may be vsed, and so to vse the one one day, the other an other.

O Eternall and euerlyuyng God, most mercifull father, which of thy great long sufferyng and pacience hast hytherto suffered and borne with vs most miserable offenders, who haue so long strayed out of thy way, and broken al thy lawes and commaundementes, and haue neither by thy manifolde benefites bestowed vpon vs vnworthy & vnthankfull sinners, nor by the voyce of thy seruauntes and preachers, by continuall threatnynges out of thy holy worde, hytherto ben moued, either as thy children of loue to returne vnto thee our most gracious father, either for feare of thy iudgementes, as humble and lowely seruauntes to turne from our wickednesse. And therefore, most ryghteous iudge, thy patience beyng (as it were) ouercome at the last with our obstinate vnrepentaunce, thou hast most iustly executed those thy terrible threates nowe partly vpon vs, by plaguyng vs so (with most dreadfull and deadlye sicknesse) (with troubles of warres) (with penurie and scarcenesse of foode and vittell)[17] wherby great multitudes of vs are dayly afflicted and consumed. We beseche thee, O most merciful father, that in thy wrath thou wylt remember thy old great mercies, and to correct vs in thy iudgementes, and not in thy iust anger, lest we be all consumed and brought to naught. Loke not so much vpon vs & vpon our deseruynges, O most ryghteous iudge, to take iust vengeaunce on our sinnes: but rather remember thy infinite mercies, O moste mercifull father, promised to vs by thy dearely beloued sonne our Sauiour Jesus Christe, for whose sake, and in whose name we do earnestly and humbly craue mercie & forgeuenesse of our sinnes, and deliueraunce from this horrible sicknes, being thy iust punishment and plague for the same. And as thy holy worde doth testifie, that thy people of all ages, beyng iustly plagued for their sinnes, and yet in their distresse vnfaignedly turnyng vnto thee, and suyng for thy mercie, obtayned the same: So lykewyse we, most worthyly now afflicted with greeuous & dreadful plagues for our iniquities, pray thee, O most mercifull father, to graunt vs thy heauenly grace, that we may lykewyse both truely & vnfaignedly repent, and obtayne thy mercie, and delyueraunce from the same, which we beseche thee, O father of all mercies, and God of all consolation, to graunt vs, for the same Jesus Christes sake, our onlye Sauiour, mediatour and aduocate. Amen.

This Prayer may be sayde euery thirde day.

It had ben the best for vs O most ryghteous Judge, and our most mercyfull father, that in our wealthes and quietnes, & in the myddest of thy manifolde benefites continually bestowed vpon vs most vnworthy sinners, we had of loue hearkened to thy voyce, & turned vnto thee our most louing and gracious father: For in so doing, we had done the partes of good & obedient louyng children. It had also ben well, yf at thy dreadful threates out of thy holy worde continually pronounced vnto vs by thy seruauntes our preachers, we had of feare, as corrigible seruauntes, turned from our wickednes. But alas, we haue shewed hytherto our selues towardes thee, neyther as louyng chyldren (O moste mercifull father) neither as tollerable seruauntes, O Lorde most myghtie. Wherfore nowe we feele thy heauye wrath, O most ryghteous Judge, iustly punyshyng vs with greeuous and deadly sicknesse and plagues, we do nowe confesse and acknowledge, and to our most iust punyshment do fynde in deede, that to be most true, which we haue so often hard threatned to vs out of thy holy scrip-

---

[17] In margin: 'Note to pray agaynst any of these plages as they shall touche vs.'.

tures, the worde of thy eternall veritie: that thou art the same vnchaungeable God, of the same iustice that thou wilt, & of the same power that thou canst punyshe the lyke wickednes and obstinacie of vs impenitent sinners in these dayes, as thou hast done in all ages heretofore. But the same thy holy Scriptures the word of thy trueth do also testifie, that thy strength is not shortened but that thou canst, neyther thy goodnes abated but that thou wylt helpe those that in theyr distresse do flee vnto thy mercies, & that thou art the same God of all, riche in mercy towardes all that call vpon thy name, and that thou doest not intende to destroy vs vtterly, but fatherly to correct vs, who hast pitie vpon vs, euen when thou doest scourge vs, as by thy sayd holy worde, thy gracious promises, & the examples of thy saintes in thy holy scrip- tures expressed for our comfort, thou hast assured vs: Graunt vs, O moste mercifull father, that we fall not into the vttermoste of all mischiefes, to become worse vnder thy scourge, but that this thy rod may by thy heauenly grace speedily worke in vs the fruite and effect of true repentaunce, vnfained turning and conuerting vnto thee, & perfecte amendement of our whole lyues, that as we through our impenitencie do now most worthily feele thy iustice punishing vs: so by this thy correction we maye also feele the sweete comfort of thy mercies, graciously pardonyng our sinnes, & pitifully releassing these greeuous punishmentes and dreadfull plagues. This we craue at thy hande, O most mercifull father, for thy deare sonne our Sauiour Jesus Christes sake. Amen.

A Short meditation to be sayde of such as be touched in affliction.

    O Father, doubtlesse our owne wickednes do rewarde vs: but do thou, O Lorde, according to thy name. Our oft transgressions & sinnes be many. Agaynst thee haue we sinned, yet art thou the comforter and helper of thy humble subiectes, in the time of theyr trouble. For thou O Lorde, art in the myddes of vs, and thy name is called vpon vs. Forsake vs not O God, forsake vs not for the merites of thy only sonne our Sauiour Jesus Christ, to whom with thee and the holy ghost be all honour and glorye. Amen.

Psalmes which may be song or saide before the beginnyng, or after the endyng of Publique Prayer.
[1, 2, 3, 4, 5, 6, 13, 15, 25, 26, 30, 32, 46, 51, 67, 79, 84, 91, 102, 103, 107, 123, 130, 143, 147]

THE ORDER FOR THE GENERAL FAST

It is most euident to them that reade the scriptures, that both in the olde Church vnder the lawe, and in the Primitiue Churche vnder the Gospell, the people of God hath alwayes vsed generall Fasting, both in tymes of common calamities, as Warre, Famine, Pestilence. &c. and also when any waightie matter, touching the estate of the Churche or the common wealth, was begon or intended. And it can not be denyed, but that in this our tyme, wherein many thinges haue ben refourmed according to the doctrine and examples of Gods worde & the Primitiue Church, this part for Fastyng and abstinence, beyng alwayes in the scripture as a necessarie companion ioyned to feruent prayer, hath ben to much neclected.

    Wherefore, for some begynnyng of redresse herein, it hath ben thought meete to the Queenes Maiestie, that in this contagious tyme of sicknesse and other troubles and vnquietnesse, accordyng to the examples of the godly kyng Josaphat, and the kyng of Niniue, with others, a generall Fast should be ioyned with general Prayer throughout her whole Realme, and to be obserued of al her godly subiectes, in maner and fourme folowing.

1. First, it is ordayned that the Wednesday of euery weeke, shalbe the day appointed for this generall Fast.

2. Secondly, all persons betweene the age of .xvi. yeres and lx. (sicke folkes and labourers in haruest or other great labours only excepted) shall eate but one only competent and moderate meale vpon euery Wednesday. In whiche sayde meale shalbe vsed very sober and spare diet, without varietie of kindes of meate, disshes, spyces, confections, or wines, but only such as may serue for necessitie, comlynesse, and health.

3. Item, in that meale it shalbe indifferent to eate fleshe or fishe, so that the quantitie be smal, and no varitie or delicacie be sought. Wherein euery man hath to aunswere to God, if he in such godly exercises, eyther contempne Publique order, or dissemble with God, pretending abstinence, and doing nothing lesse.

4. Item, those that be of wealth and habilitie, ought that day to abate and diminishe the costlynesse and varietie of their fare, and encrease therwith their liberalitie and almes towardes the poore, that the same poore, whiche eyther in deede lacke foode, or els that whiche they haue is vnseasonable and cause of sicknesse, may therby be relieued and charitably succoured, to be maintayned in health.

5. Last of all, this day beyng in this maner appointed for a day of generall Prayer and Fasting, ought to be bestowed by them whiche may forbeare from bodyly labour, in Prayer, studie, reading or hearing of the scriptures, or good exhortations. &c. And when any dulnesse or werynesse shall arise, then to be occupied in other godly exercises: But no part therof to be spent in playes, pastimes, or ydlenesse, muche lesse in lewde, wicked, or wanton behauiour.

When there is a Sermon, or other iust occasion, one of the lessons may be omitted, and the shortest of the three prayers appoynted in the Letany by this order may be said, and the longest left of.

Forasmuch as diuers Homylyes appoynted before to be read in this fourme of common prayer, are conteyned in the seconde Tome of Homylyes nowe lately set foorth by the Queenes Maiesties aucthoritie: therefore it is ordered, that the Churchwardens of euery parishe shall prouide the same seconde Tome or booke of Homylyes with all speede, at the charges of the Paryshe.

AN HOMYLY, CONCERNING THE JUSTICE OF GOD, IN PUNYSHYNG OF IMPENITENT SYNNERS, AND OF HIS MERCIES TOWARDES AL SUCH AS IN THEIR AFFLICTIONS VNFAYNEDLY TURNE VNTO HYM. APPOYNTED TO BE READ IN THE TYME OF SYCKENES.

The moste ryghteous God, and the same our moste mercyfull father, abhorryng all wickednes and impietie, and delighting in all ryghteousnesse and innocencye, and wyllynge that we hys people and chyldren, shoulde herein be conformed, and become lyke to oure God and heauenly father, that we myghte be also partakers of hys inheritaunce and euerlastyng kyngdome: In his holye Scriptures, conteynyng the perfecte rule of ryghteousnes, and wrytten for our learnynge and directyon towardes hys sayde kyngdome, both by great threatninges doth continuallye feare vs from all impietie and wyckednes so displeasaunte to hym, and also by moste large and gentle promyses, like a louynge father, dothe prouoke and intyce vs to ryghteousnes and holynesse soo acceptable vnto him, and so leaueth nothyng vnassayed, no waye vnproued, whereby he myghte saue vs from perpetuall destruction, and brynge vs to lyfe euerlastynge. To this ende, all those threatnynges of temporall punyshmentes and plagues, whereof the Scryptures be so full, are to be referred, that we, for feare of temporall punyshementes,[18] refraynynge from all vnryghteousnes, mygh[t] also escape eternall payne and dampnation, wherevnto it woulde fynally brynge vs, if we shoulde not by repentaunce turne from the same, and returne vnto our God and moste mercifull father, who woulde not the destruction and, deathe of synners, but rather that they shoulde conuert and be saued.[19]

But when he perceaueth that neyther gentlenes can wynne, vs as hys louynge chyldren, neyther feare and threatnynges can amende vs, as beyng moste stubberne and rebellious seruauntes: at the laste he perfourmeth in dede that, whyche he hath so ofte threatned, and of fatherly sufferaunce and mercye so longe, vpon hope of amendemente, deferred, hys longanimitye and pacyence beynge nowe ouercome with oure stony hardenes and obstinate impenitencie. After thys sorte, we shall fynde by the holy Scriptures and hystoryes Ecclesiasticall, that he hathe dealte wyth hys people of all ages, namelye the Isralytes, whom in sundrye other places, but especially in the .26. of Leuiticus,[20] and .28. of Deuteronomium,[21] aswel by fayre promyses, as by menaces, he laboureth to bring to due obedience of his lawe, whyche is perfect ryghteousnes. If (sayth he) thou heare the voyce of the Lorde thy God, and kepe hys commaundementes, all these blessynges shall come vpon thee: Thou shalt be blessed in the Citye, and in the fielde. The seede of thy bodye, the fruite of thy earthe, the increase of thy cattell, shalbe blessed. &c. Thou shalte haue seasonable weather,[22] fruitefull grounde, victorye of thy enemyes, and after, quiet peace in thy costes, and I wyll be thy louyng Lorde & God, thy ayde and defender, and thou shalte be my beloued people. But yf thou wylte not heare the voyce of the Lorde thy God, nor kepe hys commaundementes, but despyse hys lawes, &c. all these curses shall come upon thee: Thou shalte be cursed in the Citye & in the fyelde, thy Barne, all thy storehouses shalbe cursed, the fruite of thy bodye, of thy cattell, & of thy grounde, shalbe cursed, thou shalte be cursed goyng out and commynge in. The Lorde shall sende thee famyne and necessitye, he shall stryke thee with agues, heates, and coldes, with pestilences, and all other euyll [d]iseases, yea, and with all the botches and plagues of Egipte. He shall make heauen ouer thee, as it were of brasse, and the earthe whyche thou treadest on, as it were Iron. He shall sende thee vnseasonable weather. &c. warres, and ouerthrowe thee at thyne enemyes handes, and thy carren shalbe a praye to the byrdes of the ayre, and the beastes of the earthe, and there shalbe no man to dryue them awaye: and so forth, many mo most horryble euyls and mischiefes, wrytten at large in those two Chapters,[23] where ye maye see howe louynglye on the one parte he promisethe to the obedient. and howe terryblye on the other parte he threatnethe the disobedyente, and howe largely and at lengthe he prosecuteth the matter, specially in the threatnynges and menaces, moste meete for the Jewes, a people euer styffe necked and rebellious. And in dede the hole wrytynges of the prophetes, & vniversallye of all the Scryp-tures, be nothinge els but lyke callynges to true obedyence, and to repentaunce from oure transgressions by lyke promyses & threatnynges, yea, and greater also, as by promyse of lyfe euerlastyng to the faythfull obedient, and penitente, and contraryly,

---

18 In margin: 'Gene. 12 Job, 36a, Psal, 7, 12, 119, Esa 26c Jer, 30b Job, 5, r,'.
19 In margin: 'Tob.3, c 2 Pe, 3 b'.
20 In margin: 'Leui, 26'.
21 In margin: 'Deu. 28'.
22 In margin: 'Leui, 26'.
23 In margin: 'Leui, 29 Deu, 28,'.

of euerlasting dampnation & deathe to the stubberne, rebellous, and impenitente synners. And to prosecute thys matter, when the Jewes were monyshed, remonyshed, prayed, threatned, so ofte by so manye prophetes, and all in vayne: Dyd not the Lorde at the laste brynge vpon them all those euyls whyche he had threatened, namely famine, warre, and pestylence, as yee maye reade at large in the bookes of Judges, Kynges, and Chronacles, in the lamentatyons of Jeremy, namelye the .2. 4. and .5. Chapters, and in other places of the Prophetes and the olde Testament, conteyninge the descriptions of extreme famines, horrible warres and captiuities, and dreadfull plagues, whereby God punyshed and afflicted hys people, for theyr synnes and rebellyon agaynst hym moste sharpely? Yea, and when all thys coulde not amende them, but that they waxed worse under the rodde and correction:[24] did he not at the last, which is most horryble, vtterlye destroy them with famine, warre, and pestylence, and caryed the rest into captiuitie, and destroyed vtterly theyr Cities and countryes, accordinge to the prophecy of Esay, and as our sauiour Chryst,[25] lykewyse in the Gospell foresheweth of the myserable destruction and ruyne of theyr Cities and temple,[26] so horryble, that one stone shoulde not be lefte upon another? In lyke maner, the same immutable GOD, proceaded aforetyme wyth the Chrystians of Asia, Affricke, and Grece; he sente them lyke Prophetes, learned doctours, and holy sayntes, Saint Clement, Ignatius, Tertullian, Ciprian, Origine, Gregorius, Basyll, Chrysostome, Augustine, and manye moo, who oute of holy Scriptures lykewyse warned and warned them agayne, to turne from theyr synnes, and to returne to God, vnto whome after, when they woulde not be warned with words, he sente them the swordes of the Gothes, Hunnes, Vandales,[27] Saracens, and Turkes, he sente them lykewyse famynes, and pestilences, and fynally, when neyther threates nor punyshmentes coulde amende them by those nations, & especiallye the Saracens & Turkes, he hath either vtterly destroyed them, or els made them most miserable captyues of the miscreantes Turkes, vnder them to be in all vnspeakeable slauery and misery: and that, whiche is most horrible of all, where theyr forefathers worshypped Christe the Sauioure of the worlde, to serue in his steade fylthye and dampned Machomet, the deceyuer of the worlde.

Nowe to come to our times (most dearelye beloued in our sauiour Chryst) hath not GOD likewyse begone thys order of proceadynge with vs Christians of thys age? hath he not sente amonges vs hys Prophetes and preachers, who out of Gods holye worde haue continuallye called vs to repentaunce, continuallye denounsed vnto vs, that he is the same immutable God, of the same iustice that he wyll, and of the same power, that he can, persecute the same wickednes and impenitency, wyth lyke punyshementes and plagues? In the whyche also he hath vsed hys wonted clemencye, in denouncynge euiles before he brynge them vpon vs, that by speedye repentaunce we myght auoyde and escape them. And hathe he not, I pray you, prosecuted the same hys proceadinges with vs also continuyng in impenytencye, by sendynge vs sundrye plagues at sundrye tymes, warres, famynes, exyles, horryble fyres? And hath he not nowe at the laste, after almoste xx. yeares pacience and forbearinge of vs, sent vs the pestilence, whiche of all sickenesses we moste feare and abhore, as in dede it is to be feared? Seyng we haue so longe despysed hys iustice, requirynge oure

---

[24] In margin: 'Jere. 20, f, and 5, a,'.
[25] In margin: 'Esay, 3, b,'.
[26] In margin: 'Math, 24, Marke, 13,'.
[27] In margin: 'Gothes'.

innocencye, he can not but vysyte wyth hys iustice, punyshynge oure iniquytye, and that, he dothe more iustly execute vpon vs, than he did vppon hys people of anye tyme before vs: for that we, besydes the warnyng of his Scriptures, and preachers of his worde, by so manye examples of the punyshmentes of all former ages for lyke vyces, haue not ben amended or moued to anye repentaunce. Wherefore nowe at the laste, he hathe sent to vs, that coulde neuer in healthe by anye meanes be brought to the obedience of hym, horrible sicknes, & the dreadfull feare of death present at oure dores, & before our eyes. We that could neuer skyll of compassion towardes the miserye of others, are nowe oure selues by hys iuste iudgementes fallen into extreme mysery. We that haue not visited and comforted the sicke, accordynge to Gods wyll, are nowe fallen into such sicknes, that the nearest of oure frendes refuse to visite vs. We that could neuer be brought from the loue of thys worlde, are nowe moste iustly brought in feare, sodenly to leaue and departe out of thys world. We that loued our wicked mammon so much, that we could not fynd in oure hartes to bestowe any part thereof vpon the reliefe of oure poore brethren and systers, are nowe brought in feare sodenly to lose it altogether, & oure selues also with it, by soden & dreadfull death of our bodyes, and for thabusyng of it, in daunger and dread to lose our soules also euerlastyngly. We that set all oure delyght in gatheryng together & heapyng of worldly mucke, in buylding of fayre houses, & purchasyng of landes, as though we should liue for euer, are nowe iustly put in feare of losse of lyfe, & all with it, as the short warnyng of .2. or .3. dayes, and often not many mo houres. All those doctrynes of the vanitye of thys transitory lyfe & world, set out in the Scryptures in so manye places, preached vnto vs in so manye sermons, whych we yet could neuer hytherto by hearynge beleue, are nowe put in practise in dede, and set before oure eyes, and all oure senses to see and perceaue most certaynely. Wherefore, vnlesse we nowe at the last repente, I see not what tyme is left for repentaunce. It hadde ben the best in dede, as we haue bene ofte forewarned, to haue turned to oure heauenly father in tyme of quyetness, for loue of oure father, rather than feare of the rodde, for that had bene in dede the part of louynge and good chyldren : but not to be mended with strypes, is nowe the part not of servauntes that be corrigible, but of indurate and desperate slaues. Let vs not (O dearelye beloued) fall into the vttermost of all myschyfes, that we shoulde be incorrigible with punyshmente also,[28] and worse under the scurge, as were those stiffnecked Jewes who, when fyrst after threatnynges, and then after plagues of warre, famine, and pestilence, they remayned indurate and incorrigible: Lastlye, as he by his holye Prophetes had threatned theim, he ouerthrewe them as a hyghe wall downe to the grounde,[29] and dashed them all to peeces as an earthen vessell, that theyr ruyne myghte be wythoute helpe, and theyr destructyon remedylesse. Whyche most horrible myschiefe that we maye auoyde, let vs auoyde the cause thereof: contempte, obstinacie, and hardnes of hart, in Gods most iust wrath and scourge nowe vsed for our correctyon. There is yet no cause for al this why we shoulde dyspayre or dystrust: but rather that we shoulde turne from our synnes, and returne to oure mercyfull father, crauyng pardon and delyueraunce at his hand. For the declaration whereof, it shalbe shewed out of the Scryptures: Fyrst,[30] that God doth not punyshe vs in this worlde, and sende vs these miseryes and sickenes, of hatred, to destroye vs, but of loue, mercyfully to correcte

---

[28] In margin: '2, Bar, 28 a Jerem, 2, f, and, 5, n, Ezech, 24, Agge, 2, Sopho, 3, Prou, 1, d, and 29, a,'.
[29] In margin: 'Esay, 30, c'.
[30] In margin: 'Leuit, 26, f, 30, g, Deut, 8 b Psa, 118 Jud, 8, d,'.

vs. And out of infinite places, it shall suffyce to rehearse a fewe notable, seruing for this purpose. And here the testimony of Job, a man both sore punyshed and most fauoured of God, hath a worthye place, who well vnderstandyng Gods goodness & mercye, euen in hys greuous punyshementes:[31] Blessed or happy (sayeth he) is the man whom GOD punysheth. Therefore refuse not thou the chastenyng of the almyghtye. For thoughe he make a wounde, he geueth a playster, thoughe he smyte, hys hand maketh whole agayne. He shall delyuer thee in syxe troubles, & in the seuenth there shal no euyll come vnto thee. In hunger, he shall feede thee from death, and in the warres, he shall delyuer thee from the power of the sworde: and so forth, howe GOD in dearth and destructyon wyll helpe and saue, and howe that suche correction kepeth vs from synnynge. And agayne, in the .36. Chapter,[32] God by punyshynge & nourtring of men, roundeth them (as it were) in the eares, warneth them to leane of theyr wyckednes, and to amende. If they now take heede and serue him they shal weare out theyr dayes in prosperytye, and theyr yeares in prosperitie & ioy. And Toby,[33] a man lykewyse exercysed in afflyctyons, sayth: Blessed is thy name, O God of oure fathers, who when thou art angry, shewest mercye, & in tyme of trouble forgeuest the synnes of them that call vpon thee. And by and by after: This may euery one that worshippeth thee, looke for of a certayntie, that yf hys lyfe be putte to tryall, he shalbe crowned, yf he be in trouble, he shalbe delyuered; yf he be under correctyon, he shall come to thy mercye. For thou delyghtest not in oure destruction, for after tempest thou sendest calme, and after mournyng and wepynge thou bringest ioy and reioysynge, thy name, O GOD of Israel, be blessed for euer. And[34] in the .6. Chapter of Osee God saith: In their aduersitie they shall seke me and saye: Come, let vs turne agayne vnto the Lorde, for he hath smytten, and he shall heale vs, he hath wounded vs, and he shall bynde vs vp agayne. After two dayes shall he quycken vs, and the third day shal he rayse vs vp, so that we shall lyue in hys syght. Then shall we haue vnderstandyng, and indeuour ourselves to knowe God.

And in the third Chapter of the Prouerbes:[35] My sonne (sayth Salomon) despyse not the chastenyng of the Lorde, neyther faynte when thou arte rebuked of hym, for whom the Lorde loueth, hym he chasteneth, yea, and delyghteth in hym, euen as a father in his owne sonne. The Apostle to the Hebrues[36] hath the lyke most comfortable doctryne, whych he yet amplyfyeth more, saying: Ye haue forgotten the exhortation whyche speaketh vnto you as vnto chyldren: My sonne despyse not thou the chastenynge of the Lorde, neyther faynte when thou art rebuked of him, for whom the Lord loueth, him he chasteneth, yea and scourgeth euery sonne that he receaueth. If ye endure chastenyng, God offereth himselfe vnto you as vnto sonnes. What sonne is he whom the father chasteneth not? If ye be not vnder correction, whereof all are partakers, then are ye bastardes and not sonnes. Therefore, seeyng we haue had our corporall fathers correcting vs, and we gaue them reuerence: shall we not much rather be in subiection vnto the father of spirites, and lyue? And they veryly for a fewe dayes nourtured vs after their owne pleasure: but he nourtureth vs for our profite, to the intent that he may minister of his holynes vnto vs. No maner

31 In margin: 'Job, 5, c'.
32 In margin: 'Job.36'.
33 In margin: 'Tob, 3, c'.
34 In margin: 'Osee. 6, a, Esay. 29'.
35 In margin: 'Pro. 3.b,'.
36 In margin: 'Hebr, 12. b,'.

chastening for the present tyme seemeth to be ioyous, but greeuous: Yet afterward it bringeth the quiet fruite of righteousnes vnto them which are exercised thereby.[37] And Christe sayth, As many as I loue, I rebuke and chasten: be zelous therefore and repent. And saint Paul declareth,[38] that neither trouble nor perill, neyther lyfe nor death, nor any other thing, can separate vs from the loue of God. And he teacheth,[39] that God doth punishe and correct vs in this wretched worlde, that we shoulde not be condempned with the wicked in the world to come, but rather by our repentaunce and obedience, be the children of God, and so made partakers of the kyngdome of heauen, through our Lorde and sauiour Jesus Christe, to whom with the father and the holy ghost be all honour and glory for euer. Amen.

The seconde part of the Homelie.

We haue (good people) in the former part of this exhortation (concernyng our turnyng to God) opened to you of the seueritie and iustice of God, and also declared howe God by his great goodnesse yet so tempereth his rod and punishment of iustice, that though the wicked by their obstinacie begin their hell here in such punishment: yet the godly by taking the rod of his iustice in repentaunce, haue such commoditie thereof, that it beginneth not onlye chyldelie and reuerent feare to his maiestie, but also strongly moueth vs to an earnest and stable purpose of lyuing, more agreeablie to his honour and our duetie. Nowe the more to recount this our duetie to our Lorde God, I wyll secondly in a fewe wordes set before you some part of gods mercifull promises towarde such (as with all their heart turne to him.) In the .4. of Deuteronomium[40] where God threatneth (for our example) to bring the Jewes into all miseries, yf they do disobey him: so sayth he agayne, If thou in thy great distresse do turne vnto the Lorde thy God, and heare his voyce, and seeke him, thou shalt finde him, yf thou seeke him with all thy heart & soule. For the Lorde thy God is a mercifull God, he wyl not forsake thee, nor destroy thee,[41] And in the .30. Chapter of the same booke, If (sayth the Lord) for thy sinnes the curses written in this booke do lyght vpon thee, and thou moued with repentaunce of thy heart turne vnto the Lorde, and obey his commaundementes with all thy hearte and with al thy soule: the Lord thy God shal bring thee agayne out of captiuitie, and wyll haue compassion vpon thee: and the Lord thy God wyll bryng thee into the lande whiche thy fathers possessed, and thou shalt enioye it, and he wyll shewe thee kyndnesse, and multiplie thee aboue thy fathers. And the Lorde thy God wyll circumcise thyne heart, and the heart of thy seede, that thou mayst loue the Lorde thy God with all thy heart, and with all thy soule, that thou mayst lyue. And the Lorde thy God wyll put all these curses vpon thine enemies, and on them that hate thee, and that perse-cute thee. But thou shalt turne and hearken vnto the voyce of the Lord, and do all his commaundementes which I commaunde thee this day, and the Lorde thy God wyll make thee plenteous in all the workes of thy handes, in the fruite of thy body, and in the fruite of thy cattel, and in the fruite of thy lande, for thy wealth. For the Lorde wyll turne againe and reioyce over thee to do thee all good, as he reioyced over thy fathers. The booke of psalmes is very plentifull of such comfortable prom-

37 In margin: 'Apoc. 3.b.'
38 In margin: 'Rom. viii. g.'.
39 In margin: 'i. Cor. xi. ?'.
40 In margin: 'Deut.4. e.'.
41 In margin: 'Deut.30.a.'.

ises. Psalm .50.[42] Call vpon me in the tyme of thy trouble, and I wyll deliuer thee (saith the Lorde) and thou shalt honour me. Psalm .86.[43] Thou Lorde art good and gracious, and of great mercie vnto all them that call upon thee. And by and by, In the tyme of my trouble I wyll call vpon thee, for thou hearest me. In the .91. Psalme[44] be large promises of God's helpe and deliueraunce, yea and that expressly from the plague and pestilence, and all other euyls. Psalm .145.[45] The Lorde is nygh to all them that call vpon him, yea, all such as call vpon him faythfully. And the Lorde by his prophete Jeremie saith,[46] If that people agaynst whom I haue thus deuised conuert from their wickednesse, I wyll repent of the plague that I deuised to bryng vpon them. Agayne, when I take in hande to builde or to plant a people or a king-dome, yf the same people do euyll before me, and heare not my voyce, I wyll repent of the good that I deuised to do for them. And in another place,[47] Ye shall cry vnto me, and I shall heare you, ye shall seke me, and fynde me: yea, yf so be that you seke me with your whole heart, I wyll be founde of you (saith the Lord) and wyll deliuer you. And againe in another place:[48] I hearde Ephraim that was led away captiue complayne on this maner, O Lorde, thou hast corrected me, and thy chas-tenyng haue I receaued. Conuert thou me, and I shalbe conuerted, for thou art my Lorde God: yea, assoone as thou turnest me, I shal refourme my selfe. And by his prophet Ezechiel he saith,[49] If the vngodlye wyll turne away from all his sinnes that he hath done, and kepe all my commaundementes, and do the thyng that is equall and ryght: doubtlesse he shall lyue, and not dye. As for all his sinnes that he dyd before, they shall not be thought vppon, but in his ryghteousnes that he hath done he shall lyue. For haue I any pleasure in the death of a synner (sayeth the Lorde GOD) but rather that he conuerte and lyue? And shortelye after agayne: When the wycked man turneth awaye from his wyckednes that he hath done, and doth the thing which is equall and righte, he shall saue hys soule alyue. For in soo muche as he remem-breth hymselfe, and turneth hym from all the vngodlynes that he hath vsed, he shall lyue and not dye. And agayne: Wherefore be conuerted, and turne you cleane from all youre wyckednes, soo shal there noo synne do the harme. Cast awaye from you al youre vngodlines that ye haue done, make you newe hartes, and a newe spirit. Wherefore wyll ye dye, O ye house of Israell? seynge I haue no pleasure in the death of hym that dyeth (sayeth the Lord God) turne you then and ye shal lyue. And lykewyse by hys Prophete Joell:[50] Although an horryble destruction be threatned to be at hande: yet (sayth the Lorde) turne vnto me with all your hartes, with fastynge, wepynge, and mournyng, rent youre hartes and not youre clothes, turne you vnto the Lorde youre God, for he is gracious and mercifull, & of greate compassion, and redy to pardon wyckednes. And anone: Euery one that calleth vppon the name of the Lorde shalbe saued. And the Lorde hym selfe testifyeth,[51] that he hath perfourmed these hys promyses accordyngly saying: Thou calledst vppon me in troubles, and I

---

[42] In margin: 'Psal.50. a.'.
[43] In margin: 'Psal.86. a.'.
[44] In margin: 'Psalm.91.a.'.
[45] In margin: 'Psalm. 145. d.'.
[46] In margin: 'Jere. 18. a.'.
[47] In margin: 'Jere. 19. e.'.
[48] In margin: 'Jere. 31. d.'.
[49] In margin: 'Ezech. 18. e.'.
[50] In margin: 'Joel.2. e,'.
[51] In margin: 'Psal, 83, c.'.

delyuered thee, and harde thee, what tyme as the storme fell vppon thee. Yea, and it is so accustomed vnto GOD to helpe those that in theyr troubles flye vnto hym for succoure, that he is, as it were, by a specyall name called in the Scryptures the helper and refuge[52] in the daye of trouble, the father of mersyes, the God of all comfort,[53] that therby we myght in oure dystresse be ye more encorraged to sue to the thron of hys heauenlye grace, whereunto our Sauyour[54] most louingly calleth all such as feele the burthen of aduersitie, and their synnes withal.

Nowe it remayneth, for the thyrde parte, rehersall be made of certayne examples of suche as beynge in trouble, and trustynge to Gods mercyfull promyses, called vppon hym, and were delyuered. And fyrst of Dauyd,[55] a man wonderfullye exersysed in worldelye troubles, to hys eternall health and saluation, who confesseth, that GOD was euer hys helper and delyuerer, when he called vpon hym, in trouble, syckenes, or anye other aduersitie, and that in verye manye places of the Psalter, a number whereof are noted in the margentes. Yea, when he was in desperate state concerning al worldely helpe,[56] cryinge oute, that the snares and sorowes of death had compassed hym rounde aboute, and that the paynes of hell hadde come vpon hym,[57] and taken holde of hym: that he woulde yet call vpon the name of the Lorde, besechyng hym to delyuer hys soule, and that God out of hys holy temple woulde not fayle to heare, and spedely to helpe and saue hym, and notablye and directly to this purpose,[58] the same kynge Dauid, as is testified in the 2. booke of kynges, and 24. Chapter, when .70. thousande were in three dayes slayne with the plague for hys and theyr synnes, makynge most humble confessyon of hys offence, and earnest prayer for mercye and pardon, obteyned the same, and the plague at Gods commaundement sodenly ceassed.[59] Ezechias, and the people wyth hym, in theyr greate dystresse, wherunto they were broughte for theyr synnes, called vppon the mercyfull Lorde, and he harde, and holpe them, not remembrynge theyr synnes. Jonas, when by dysobedyence he hadde offended God, and was swallowed vp of ye Whale:[60] yet by prayer, he was deliuered euen oute of the belly of hell, as he hymselfe speaketh, that none, euen in most desperate state should distrust in gods mercye and helpe. The Jewes also, euer mooste stubbourne and rebellious agaynste God: yet when they beyng afflicted most worthelye, dyd in theyr distresse, call vpon the Lorde for mercy and helpe, he harde and relieued them, as appeareth by all the scriptures of the olde testamente: But especiallye and notably the .107. Psalme,[61] whyche rehearseth the manyfoulde rebellions of that natyon agaynst theyr Lord and God, and the sundrye afflictions that he therfore sent vppon them. But euer this verse, as it were the burden of the Psalme or songe, is often tymes amonge rehearsed: But thei cryed to the Lorde in theyr trouble, and he delyuered them from theyr distresse. And in the ende of the Psalme is added, that they that be wyse wyll consider these examples, and thereby vnderstande the mercies of the Lorde, in lyke

---

52   In margin: 'Jrre. 24 [illegible] &.16.a'.
53   In margin: I. Cor.i a'.
54   In margin: Ma.11d'.
55   In margin: 'Psal. 4.a 31, c, 34. Ab.d. 77, a 86.b. a, 118.b. 142.a 143.c.'.
56   In margin: 'Psal, 8, 1 126, a.'.
57   In margin: '2 Re, 20, 1,'.
58   In margin: '2. Reg. 24.b,'.
59   In margin: 'Eccl, 48d'.
60   In margin: 'Jonas, 8'.
61   In margin: 'Psa. 107 a b c.'.

distresse to flye therevnto. The lyke rehearsal of Gods mercies[62] shewed vnto them when they in theyr troubles called vpon hym, is in the booke of Nehemias, or .2. of Esdras, and the .9. Chapter:[63] Howe mercifullye relieued God Ismaell and hys mother in theyr great distresse? What mercye was shewed to wycked Manasses, truelye repentynge?[64] Lykewyse to Nabuchodonosar, turnynge vnto the lorde in hys trouble?[65] Howe graciouslye is the prodigall sonne receaued of hys father in hys extreme misery,[66] procured by hys owne wyckednes? Howe mercifullye is the thiefe pardoned, euen in the myserable ende of hys moste wycked lyfe? Yea, all those diseases whyche the Gospell recordeth to be so miraculously cured by oure sauioure Chryste, in suche as sued to him for health, and by faythe trusted to obteine the same: what be they eles but testimonyes to vs of oure lyke reliefe in oure greuous sicknes, yf with lyke faythe we call to hym for helpe?[67] For it is the same Lorde of all, ryche in mercy towardes all that call vpon hym, Neyther is hys hande shortened or weakened, that he can not, nor hys goodnesse abated or diminysshed, that he wyll not, nowe helpe hys seruauntes that in theyr distresse do flye to hys mercye and goodnes. For it is nowe also trewe, as it was then, when it was wrytten of the sheepe and penye loste and founde agayne, & that there is more ioy in heauen vpon one synner repenting, than vpon .99. ryghteous.

I haue more largely prosecuted thys part, for that I thought it necessary that we shoulde be instructed by the doctryne of Gods word, hys mercifull promyses, and the comfortable examples of hys Saintes in theyr troubles: that God dothe punyshe vs in thys wretched worlde,[68] that we be not dampned with the wicked world, and that he wyll not refuse nor reiect suche, as beynge punyshed for theyr synnes, do vnfaynedlye in theyr distresse returne vnto hym. For where oure neglygence in comming to him heretofore in the time of our quietnes, myght nowe in the day of our trouble come into oure myndes, to the great dysquyetyng of oure fearefull consciences: I thoughte it expedient to styrre vp & erect our good hope in his mercies in the tyme of oure troubles by the manyfoulde, moste sweete, and assured comfortes of the holye Scriptures, wrytten for oure doctryne and consolation, both at all tymes, and speciallye in the tyme of affliction: for then is that heauenly mede-cine moste necessarye, when oure dysease doth most grieue & feare vs, which we should vndoubtedlye receiue at Godes mercifull hande to oure eternall health, if we accordyng to the aboue wrytten doctrynes, promyses, and examples, do vnfayn-edlye turne to the Lorde our God in these dayes of our afflyction.[69] Vnfaynedlye I saye, not for the tyme of afflyction onelye, as Maryners in the tempeste, neyther as dogges returnynge agayne to theyr vomytte: but to remaine suche in healthe and securitie,[70] as in syckenes and daunger we promysed to be, and all the dayes of our lyfe hereafter, being delyuered from feare of all plagues, to serue the LORD oure GOD sincerely and contynually in al holynes & ryghteousnesse acceptable to hym.[71]

[62] In margin: '1. Esd, 6,, b, c, d,'.
[63] In margin: 'Gene.21, c,'.
[64] In margin: '2, Par, 33, c'.
[65] In margin: 'Dani, 4,'.
[66] In margin: 'Luke, xv,'.
[67] In margin: 'Rom, 10,'.
[68] In margin: '1, Cor, 11'.
[69] In margin: 'Deu, 4, e, and, 30, a, Psal, 125, d Esay, 58, a,'.
[70] In margin: 'Jer. 19, c Eccle, 2 c'.
[71] In margin: '[illegible], I g'.

Wherfore I thought good to admonyshe vs, that we do not by dissemblynge with God, who can not be deceaued, deceaue our selues. But, that as the Lorde woulde haue thys plague not to be an vtter destruction vnto vs, but to be our fruitfull correction, as by the doctryne and examples aboue rehearsed appeareth: So we of this crosse myghte wyn that gayne, & gather that fruite, whyche may be helthfull vnto vs, as it was to those godlye Sayntes, whiche were before vnder lyke correctyon and chastisement of the Lorde. Therfore let vs learne by this affliction to mourne for oure synnes, to hate and forsake synne, for the whyche God dothe thus shewe hys anger & dyspleasure agaynst vs. For when shal we mourne for oure synnes, yf not nowe in the time of mourninge? When shall wee hate them, yf not nowe when they soo greuouslye wounde vs, and bryng vs to presente daunger of double death both of bodye and soule, yf we flye not from them: When shal we forsake synne in oure lyfe, yf we cleaue to it nowe when lyfe forsaketh, or is most lyke to forsake vs? And yf we shall enter into particularities: When wyll we forsake oure pryde, yf not nowe when all glorye is falling into the dust? When wyll we leaue oure enuye, malyce, hatred, and wrathe: yf not nowe when we are goynge to the graue, where all these thynges take an ende? When wyll we geue ouer oure gluttony: yf not nowe when we must forgoo the belly and whole body also? When wyll we leaue our fleshely lustes: yf not nowe when oure fleshe shall turne to dust? When wyll we geue over the cares of thys lyfe: yf not nowe when wee shall ceasse to lyue? When wyll we ceasse from oure vsurye: yf not nowe when we must loose both the increase and the stocke whollye? When shal we willingly geue ouer the loue of wicked mammon: yf not nowe when we canne not holde nor vse it, but wyll we nyl we, we must part from it? Wherfore, eyther nowe lette vs make vs frendes of it, who may receaue vs into the heauenlye tabernacles, or els there is no hope that we euer wyll.

When shal we relieue the poore in theyr neede: yf not nowe, thereby to prouoke the Lorde to succour vs in this our great distresse? When wyl we awake, that we slepe not in death: yf not nowe at the poynt of death? When shall we euer truelye remember the last times, thereby to auoide synne yf not nowe in the last tymes them selues? And as we ought now in affliction to flye all wyckednes: so oughte we to learne the loue of ryghteousnes, wherevnto of long by gentlenesse GOD hath drawen vs, and nowe by his iuste punyshement meaneth to dryue vs. Lette vs learne the feare of God nowe punyshynge vs, whych by his longe sufferaunce and pacience heretofore was almost cleane gone out of our heartes.[72] For there be speciall promyses that he wyll heare them that feare hym. And when wyll we feare hym: yf not nowe when he punysheth vs? Let vs learne pacience,[73] knowynge that afflyction in the chyldren of saluation worketh pacience, pacience bryngeth tryall, tryall hope, and hope shall not suffer vs to be confounded. For the shorte euyll of oure troubles in thys worlde, paciently taken, worketh in vs an exceadyng hygh & euerlastynge wayght of glory in the worlde to come. Let vs learne the contempt of this wretched life and wicked world, with all her tryflyng and vncertayne ioyes, and manyfoulde and horrible euyles.[74] For when shall we vnderstand that thys lyfe is as a vapoure, as a shadowe pashyng and fleyng away, as a fading flowre, as a bull rysynge on the water: yf not nowe in the decayinge, passyng, and vanyshynge away of it? When shall we forsake thys wycked worlde: yf not nowe when it forsaketh vs? Lette vs

[72] In margin: 'Psa, 105, d'.
[73] In margin: 'Roma 5, a, 2, Cor, I, v, Jaco, 1, a 2, Cor, 4. d,'.
[74] In margn: 'Jacob, 4. Job.'.

learne the desire of heauen, & the lyfe to come, where be both many and moste greate and certeyne ioyes, myngled with no euyls, no plagues of famyne, warre, pestylence, or other syckenesse and myseryes whereof thys wretched lyfe is full, as we nowe by experience proue.

To conclude, let vs, geuing over all wyckednesse,[75] now at the last, when we are in moste greatest daunger to geue ouer oure selues & helpynge the nedye and poore, that the Lorde in oure necessities maye relieue vs, Let vs, I saye, nowe at the last, turne vnto the Lorde oure God, and call for helpe and mercye, and we shalbe harde & relieued, accordynge to the doctrine of Gods worde, & hys mercyfull promyses made vnto vs, and after the examples foreshewed to vs out of the holye scryptures afore declared, and in infinite other places, to oure great comforte. For yf, as God by affliction goeth aboute as oure heauenlye scolemaster, to teache vs thus to flye from synne, and to folowe ryghteousnes, to contempne thys worlde, and do desyre the lyfe to come, wyth suche other Godly lessons: So we lyke hys good discyples do well learne the same, we shall not nede muche to feare thys plague as dreadfull and horryble, but with the blessed man of God Job,[76] to truste in hym, yea, thouge he shoulde kyll vs bodylye, and pacientlye to take our sicknes as Gods good visitation and fatherlye correction, and in it quietlye and costantlye to commyt oure selues whollye to the holy wyll of oure most mercifull father, by our Sauioure Chryste, whether it be to lyfe or death,[77] knowyng that he is the Lorde of lyfe and deathe, & that whether we lyue or dye, we be the Lordes, for it can not peryshe, whyche is committed vnto him. In whom they that beleue, though they dye, shall lyue, and in whom all that lyue and truste faythfully in hys mercye, shall not dye eternallye, and by whom, through oure Sauiour Christ, all that dye in hym haue lyfe euerlastynge, whiche I beseche the same oure moost mercyfull heauenlye father, for the death of oure Sauiour Jesus Chryst, to graunt vnto vs all: vnto whom with the father and the holy gost, one eternall maiestie of the most glorious God, be al honor, glorye, & dominion, world without ende. Amen.

1564–E   Thanksgiving services for the decline or end of the plague

Wednesdays, Fridays and Sundays [from Wednesday 26 January?] (diocese of London, and elsewhere in England and Wales at ministers' discretion)

The issue of when thanksgiving prayers were ordered for the end of the plague in 1564 is complicated. Four letters (dated 15 December 1563, 21 January, 22 February and 7 March 1564) in the Lansdowne collection in the British Library from Grindal to Cecil discuss the plague and the bishop's plans for thanksgivings for both the diminution of the plague and its cessation. There is a printed form, *A short fourme of thankesgeuyng to God for ceassing the contagious sicknes of the plague*, issued for the diocese of London and elsewhere. The title-page of the copy at Emmanuel College, Cambridge, has been annotated '22 January 1563' (i.e. 1564) in a contemporary hand; this date also appears, in a nineteenth-century hand, on the

---

[75] In margin: 'Esay. 58, d, Dani, 4, e'.
[76] In margin: 'Job, 13, [illegible]'.
[77] In margin: 'Deut, 31, [illegible] Sapien, 16 Rom, 14, Jhon, 18, d,'.

endorsement of a copy in the state papers. The form of prayer fits in with Grindal's letter of 21 January, in which he informed Cecil that 'The thankesgivinge for the qwenes Maiesties preseruation, I have inserted into the Collecte, which was apter place in my opinion then in the psalme': it offers thanks for God's deliverance of 'our moste gracious Quene and gouernour from all perylles and daungers, yea euen from the gates of death: but nowe also to preserue her from this late moste daungerous contagion and infection'. Finally, there are two sets of draft psalms and a draft prayer in the Lansdowne collection; both psalms are endorsed by the same contemporary hand as those composed for the end of the plague. One psalm has been placed after Grindal's letter of 15 December 1563, though catalogued as dating to [January 1564?]; the other psalm and the prayer follow the bishop's letter of 7 March. Another copy of the prayer, edited by Cecil, appears in another volume of the collection; it is endorsed in a contemporary hand as relating to the ceasing of the plague and dated (in a later hand) to 1563. Strype printed the first psalm and the psalm and prayer as attachments to Grindal's letters in December and March respectively (he seems to have been unaware of the prayer edited by Cecil), but they do not fit with Grindal's description of the material he had prepared and was sending to Cecil. On 15 December he enclosed a psalm and a prayer, not just a psalm. His letter of 7 March makes no mention of any thanksgiving, but refers to complaints that preachers were exhorting their parishioners 'to breake ye orders sett furthe' (it is not clear if this refers to the order for the fast, issued in 1563 or to orders about quarantining those suffering from plague etc.) and 'for setting furth an Admonition to be redde in Churches'. Neither can the psalm and prayer be related to Grindal's letter of 21 January, because the prayer contains no references to the queen. The psalms and prayer do not seem to be drafts for the printed form either, as there is no similarity in the verses selected for the psalms or the texts of the prayers. There are further complications to understanding this occasion. The plague itself ebbed and flowed: the numbers of deaths seemed to decline over the winter but then increased again during February – because, Grindal argued, the 'idle sort off people' (especially youths) gathered to watch plays. Grindal himself was also reluctant to initiate thanksgivings until, he supposed, 'ye number off the plage be vnder a hundreth a weeke'.

How do these materials and events fit together? It appears that, in December, Grindal discussed and planned thanksgivings for both the diminution of the plague and its cessation. He seems to have expected the first thanksgiving to be observed relatively soon and the second to occur some time later, as a much larger event, including the procession of the London Companies, in their liveries, to St Paul's. It is possible that one or both of the manuscript psalms were drafted for the former occasion but were subsequently discarded. The prayer, too, appears to have been drafted (and discarded) for this occasion: it offered thanks to God 'that it hathe please the ... partly to mytigate thy seuere rodde of this terrible plague' and it was clearly received, and edited, by Cecil. In January, *A short fourme of thankesgeuyng to God for ceassing the contagious sicknes of the plague* was probably issued for use in the diocese of London and, by implication, the form ordered the previous summer for use during the plague (1563–E) would have been replaced or altered. On 26 January, Thomas Cole, archdeacon of Essex, preached a sermon on the plague at Paul's Cross. Grindal also seems to have taken the unusual step of ordering the form to be used outside his own diocese at the discretion of parish ministers, rather than of diocesan bishops. Grindal was authorized to issue this order as dean of the province of Canterbury; it was probably designed to enable vicars and rectors to observe thanksgivings when the plague had receded from their parish. However, it is unclear why Parker, as archbishop, was not involved nor why the order was not issued to the bishops themselves, who could have commanded the thanksgivings to be observed in their dioceses. These thanksgivings, however, proved premature, even in London, and further secular measures for reducing the plague were instituted in March.

Although this seems the likeliest explanation, it is also possible that *A short fourme of thankesgeuyng* was issued later in 1564. We do not know if an order for a (co-ordinated, nationwide) thanksgiving for the end of the plague, as proposed by Grindal in December, was ever issued. Certainly, it seems unusual that the developing pattern of petitionary and thanksgiving prayers for major outbreaks of disease was not followed, especially as the outbreak of plague in 1563–4 was one of the most significant in the sixteenth century.

The format of *A short fourme of thankesgeuyng* had enduring significance, as the third liturgical format composed by Elizabethan bishops for special worship. Its style of variation of BCP services continued to be used for most special services until the late nineteenth century. The format followed the BCP service, but replaced the prescribed collects and psalms with specially composed or selected alternatives – or, often, selected verses from different psalms – which were more closely attuned to the current issues. Unlike the form published after the outbreak of plague during the previous year, the format of these 1564 services did not change according to the day of the week.

Order: none found.
Form of prayer: *A short fourme of thankesgeuyng to God for ceassing the contagious sicknes of the plague, to be vsed in common prayer, on Sundayes, Wednesdayes, and Frydayes, in steade of the common prayers, vsed in the time of mortalitie. Set forth by the byshop of London, to be vsed in the citie of London, and the rest of his diocesse, and in other places also at the discretion of the ordinary ministers of the churches* ([8] pp.; STC 16507) [also in Clay, pp. 513–18].
Form of prayer (other edition): STC 16507.5
Additional sources: Grindal to Cecil, 15 Dec. 1563, 21 Jan. 1564, 22 Feb. 1564, 7 Mar. 1564; Lans. 6, fos. 192r–193v, 194r–195v; Lans. 7, fos. 141r–v, 143r–v; draft antiphonal psalm, [Jan 1564?], Lans. 6, fos. 194r–195v (in Clay, pp. 508–12); The prayer or collect [n.d.], and [psalms] [n.d.], Lans. 7, fos. 144r, 145r–146r; Thankes giving to god for withdrawing and ceasing the plage [corrected by Cecil], 1563, Lans. 116, fo. 73r; *A short fourme of thankesgeuyng to God for ceassing the contagious sicknes of the plague ...* (1564; STC 16507; Emmanuel College, Cambridge); Strype, *Grindal*, pp. 119–24, 473–8; Clay, pp. 459–60; MacLure, p. 47.

FORM OF PRAYER

After the ende of the Collect in the Letanie which begynneth with these wordes: We humbly beseche thee O father. &c. shall folowe this Psalme to be sayde of the Minister, with the aunswere of the people.

Lorde thou art become gratious vnto thy lande, thou hast turned awaye the afflictions of thy seruauntes. (Ps. 85) [85:1]
Thou hast taken away all thy displeasure, and turned thy selfe from thy wrathfull indignation. [Ps. 85:3]
For yf thou Lorde hadst not helped vs, it had not fayled, but our soules had ben put to scilence. (Ps. 94) [94:17]
But when we sayde our feete haue slypped, thy mercy, O Lorde, helped vs vp. [Ps. 94:18]

In the multitude of the sorowes that we had in our hartes, thy comfortes haue refreshed our soules. [Ps. 94:19]

Our soules wayted styll vppon the Lorde, our soules hanged vpon his helpe, our hope was alwayes in hym. (Ps. 62) [62:5]

In the Lordes worde dyd we reioyce, in Gods worde did we comfort our selues. (Ps. 63) [?]

For the Lorde sayde: Call vpon me in the tyme of trouble, and I wyll heare thee, and thou shalt prayse me. (Ps. 50) [50:15]

So when we were poore, nedy, sickly, & in heauines, the Lord cared for vs: he was our helpe and our sauiour accordyng to his worde. (Ps. 40) [40:20 & 21]

In our aduersitie and distresse he hath lyft vp our heades, and saued vs from vtter destruction. (Ps. 27) [27:6]

He hath deliuered our soules from death, he hath fedde vs in the tyme of dearth, he hath saued vs from the noysome pestilence. (Ps. 33) [33:18]

Therfore wyll we offer in his holy Temple, the oblation of thankesgeuyng with great gladnes: we wyll syng and speake prayses vnto the Lorde our Sauiour. (Ps. 27) [27:7]

We wyll geue thankes vnto the Lorde, for he is gratious, and his mercy endureth for euer. (Ps. 106) [106:1]

The Lorde is full of compassion and mercy, long sufferyng, plenteous in goodnes and pitie. (Ps. 86, 103) [86:15 & 103:8]

His mercy is greater then the heauens, and his gratious goodnes reacheth vnto the cloudes. (Ps. 57, 108) [57:11 & 108:4]

Lyke as a father pitieth his owne chyldren: euen so is the Lorde mercyfull vnto them that feare hym. (Ps. 103) [103:13]

Therfore wyll we prayse thee and thy mercyes, O God, vnto thee wyll we syng, O thou holy one of Israell. (Ps. 71) [71:20]

We wyll syng a newe song vnto thee, O God, we wyll prayse the Lorde with Psalmes of thankesgeuyng. (Ps. 98) [98:6]

O syng prayses, syng prayses vnto our God: O syng prayses, syng prayses vnto our kyng. (Ps. 47) [47:6]

For God is the kyng of the earth, syng prayses with vnderstandyng. [Ps.47:7]

We wyll magnifie thee O God our kyng, we wyl prayse thy name for euer and euer. (Ps. 145) [145:1]

Euery day wyll we geue thankes vnto thee, and prayse thy name for euer and euer. [Ps.145:2]

Our mouth shall speake the prayses of the Lord, and let all fleshe geue thankes to his holy name for euer and euer. [Ps.145:21]

Blessed be the Lorde God of Israell for euer: and blessed be the name of his Maiestie world without ende. Amen. Amen. (Ps. 21, 72) [72:18 & 19]

After this Psalme, shalbe sayde by the Minister openly and with a hygh voyce, the Collect folowyng.

O heauenly & moste merciful father, what mynd or what tonge can conceiue or geue thee worthye thankes, for thy most great and infinite benefites, whiche thou hast bestowed, and doest dayly bestowe vpon vs, most vnworthy of this thy so great and continuall goodnes and fauour, though we shoulde bestowe all our lyfe, power, trauell, and vnderstandyng, thereaboutes only and wholly. When we were yet as clay is, in the potters handes, to be framed at his pleasure, vessels of honor or dishonor: of thy onlye goodnes without our deseruyng (for howe coulde we deserue any thyng, before we were any thyng?) thou hast created and made vs of nothyng, not dombe beastes voyde of reason, not vile vermins crepyng vpon the earth: but the noblest and most honorable of all thy worldly creatures, litle inferiour to thy heauenly Aungelles, indued with vnderstandyng, adourned with all excellente gyftes, both of body and of mynde, exalted to the dominion ouer all other thy earthlye creatures, yea the Sunne and the Moone with other heauenly lyghtes, appoynted to our seruice, enriched with the possession of al thinges, either necessary for our vse, or delectable for our comfort. And as thou hast made vs so excellente of nothyng, so hast thou restored vs beyng lost, by thy sonne our Sauiour Jesus Chryste, dying for vs vpon the crosse, both more marueylously & mercifully then thou dydst first create vs of nothyng, besydes that thou doest continually forgeue and pardon our synnes, into the whiche we do dayly and hourely fall most daungerously, yea deadlye also, dampnably, and desperately, were not this thy present and moste redye helpe of thy mercye. And what haue we, that we haue not by thee? or what be we, but by thee? All which vnspeakable benefites, thou hast lyke a moste louyng father, bestowed vppon vs, that we thereby prouoked, myght lyke louyng chyldren, humbly honor and obedientlye serue thee, our good and most gratious father. But forsomuch as we haue dishonored thee, by, and with the abusying of thy good gyftes, thou doest euen in this also lyke a father correctyng his chyldren whom he loueth, when they offende, no lesse mercifullye punyshe vs, for the sayde abuse of thy gyftes, then thou dyddest bounteously before geue them vnto vs, scourging vs sometyme with warres and troubles, sometymes with famyne and scarsitie, sometyme with sicknes and diseases, and sundrye other kyndes of plagues, for the abusyng of peace, quietnes, plentie, health, and suche other thy good gyftes, agaynst thy holy worde and wyll, and agaynst thy honor and our owne health, to thy great displeasure and hygh indignation: As thou now of late terribly, but most iustly and deseruedly, plaged vs with contagious, dreadful, & deadly sicknes, from the which yet thou hast most mercifully, & without all deseruynges on our parte, euen of thyne owne goodnes, nowe agayne delyuered vs, and saued vs. By the which thy most mercifull delyueraunce, and especially in that amonges other thy great and manyfolde benefites, it hath pleased thee of thyne eternall goodnes, most mercifullye and miraculously, not only heretofore to delyuer our moste gracious Quene and gouernour from all perylles and daungers, yea euen from the gates of death: but nowe also to preserue her from this late moste daungerous contagion and infection: lyke as thou hast exceadyngly comforted our sorowefull hartes: so we for the same do yelde vnto thee, as our bounden duetie is, our moste humble and hartie thankes, O moste mercifull father, by thy deare sonne our Sauiour Jesus Christe, in whose name we praye thee to continue this thy gracious fauour towardes vs, and staye vs in thy grace, defendyng vs agaynste the assaultes of Sathan, that we continuallye enioying thy fauour, with the health of our soules, whiche is the quietnes of our consciences, as a taste here in earth of thy heauenly ioyes, and as a pledge of thy eternall mercie, may alwayes in this lyfe render therefore all laude and honor to thee, and after this transitory and miserable lyfe, may euer lyue and ioye with thee, through the same our only sauiour and mediatour Jesus Chryst thy only sonne, who with thee and the holy ghoste, one immortall maiestie of the moste glorious God, is to be praysed and magnified, worlde without ende. Amen.

Psalmes whereof may be vsed in stede of the ordinary Psalmes in the Morning prayer, one, two, or three, in order, according to the length therof: And also one of the same, may be said or songe in the beginning or endyng of publique prayer.
[34, 95, 96, 100, 103, 107, 116, 118, 145, 146, 147, 148]

1565–E1 Services during the Ottoman siege of Malta

Wednesdays and Fridays [July?] 1565 (London, Norwich and Salisbury dioceses)

Malta, the base of the Knights of St John of Jerusalem (the Hospitallers), was besieged by Ottoman forces from 28 May 1565. The Knights repelled the attack on St Elmo (23 June), forcing the invaders to lay siege to the two other main fortresses, St Angelo and Il Burgo, and to bring in reinforcements from Algiers. In July, the Spanish ambassador, Guzman de Silva, reported to Philip II that Elizabeth had ordered public prayers for Malta, though no order is extant. This was the first time since 1541 that public prayers had been ordered on behalf of catholics abroad (see 1543–E1) and contrasted with the Elizabethan practice of organizing special worship in support of persecuted foreign protestants. Prayers were probably ordered because the Ottoman invasion was perceived as posing a new and serious threat to Europe and to Christendom after two decades of relative stability following the establishment of Ottoman hegemony in east-central Europe in 1541 and the redirection of Süleyman I's military campaigns towards Persia (Iran) and the Indian Ocean. The form of prayer followed the structure and format of that for plague in 1563, 1563–E. For the first time, separate editions are extant for London, Norwich and Salisbury dioceses; they follow the same title, format and text.

Order: none found.
Form of prayer: *A fourme to be vsed in common prayer euery Wednesdaye and Frydaye, within the cittie and dioces of London: to excite all godly people to praye vnto God for the deliuery of those Christians, that are now inuaded by the Turke* (William Seres; [8] pp.; STC 16508) [also in Clay, pp. 519–23].
Form of prayer (other editions): *A forme to bee vsed in common praier euery Wednesdaie and Fridaie, within the citie and dioces of Norwiche to excite all godlie people to praie vnto God for the deliuerie of those Christians, that are now inuaded by the Turke* (John Waley; STC 16508.3); *A forme to bee vsed in common praier euery Wednesdaie and Fridaie, within the cittie and dioces of Sarum* (John Waley; STC 16508.7).
Additional sources: Guzman de Silva to Philip II, 23 July 1565, *CSPSp, 1558–1567*, p. 455; Strype, *Grindal*, p. 152; Clay, pp. 460–1.

FORM OF PRAYER

THE PREFACE

For as much as the Isle of *Malta* (in olde tyme called *Melite*, where S. Paule arriued when he was sent to Roome)[78] lying nere vnto Sicilie and Italy, and beinge as it were the keye of that parte of Chrystendome, is presently inuaded wyth a great Armye and nauy of Turkes, Infydels & sworne enemies of Christian religion, not only to thextreme daunger and peryll of those Chrystians that are besieged, and daylye

---

[78] In margin: 'Act. 28.'.

assaulted in the holdes and fortes of the sayd Iland: but also of all the rest of the countreys of Chrystendome adioyning, it is our partes whych for dystance of place cannot succor them wyth temporall relief: to assyst them wyth spiritual ayde: that is to say, wyth earnest, hearty, and feruent prayer to almightye God for them, desyring him after thexamples of Moses, Josaphat, Ezechias, & other godly men,[79] in hys great mercy to defend and deliuer christians, professing his holy name, and in his iustyce to represse the rage and violence of Infydels, who by all tirrany and cruelty labour vtterly to rote out not only true religion: but also the very name and memory of Chryst our onelye sauiour, and al christianity, and if they shuld preuaile against the Ile of *Malta*, it is vncertain what furder peryll might folow to the rest of Christendome. And although it is euery christian mans duty *[as 1563–E: of his own devotion … ordered and appoynted]* as foloweth.

First that al Pastors & Curates shall exhort theyr parishioners to endeuor them-selues to come vnto the church, wyth as many of theyr family, as may be spared from their necessary busynesse, and they to resort thither, not only vpon Sundaies and holy dais, but also vppon Wednesdayes and Fridayes, duringe this daungerous and perillous time: exhorting them there reuerently and godly to behaue themselues, and with penitente myndes knelynge on theyr knees to lifte vp theyr heartes, and praye to the mercifull god to turne from vs, and al Christendome, those plagues and punishments: which we and they through oure vnthankfulnes and sinfull liues haue deserued.

Secondly that the said Pastors and Curates shal then distinctly and plainly read the general confession appointed in the booke of seruice, with the residue of the morning prayer vnto the first lesson.

Then for the fyrst lesson shalbe read one of the chapters hereafter folowyng, or so much thereof as is appoynted
[Exod. 14, Exod. 15:1–20, Exod. 17:8–15, Judg. 7, 1 Sam. 23:19–29, 2 Kgs. 7, 2 Kgs. 19, 2 Chr. 20]

After that in stead of Te deum laudamus, that is to saye, We prayse thee O God, shall be saide the li psalme. Haue mercy vpon me O God &c.

Then immediatly after shalbe saide the Crede: I beleue in God &c. and after that, the accustomed praiers folowyng vnto the end of the morning prayer.

That done, the Letanye shalbe sayd in the mids of the people, vnto thend of the Collect in the same Letany, which beginneth with these wordes: We humbly besech thee O father. &c. And then shall folowe thys Psalme to be said of the Minister wyth thaunswere of the people.

The Psalme
O God, the heathen are come into thyne enheritaunce: thyne aduersaryes roare in the myddes of thy congregations, & set vp their banners for tokens. (Ps. 79, 74) [79:1 & 74:5]
They haue set fyre vppon thy holy places, and haue defiled the dwellinge place of thy name, and destroyed them euen vnto the grounde. (Ps. 74) [74:8]

---

[79] In margin: 'Exod. 17. 2. Paral.20. 4.Regu. 19.'.

The dead bodies of thy seruauntes haue they geuen to be meate vnto the fowles of the ayre, and the fleshe of thy sainctes vnto the beastes of the lande. (Ps. 79) [79:2]

Their bloud haue they shed lyke water on euery side of Hierusalem, and there was no man to bury them. (Ps. 79) [79:3]

And so we are become an open shame to our ennemies, a very scorne and derision vnto them, that are rounde about vs? (Ps. 79) [79:4]

Lorde, howe longe wilte thou be angry? shall thy gelousie burne lyke fyer for euer. (Ps. 79) [79:5]

O God wherfore art thou absent from vs so long, why is thy wrathe suche agaynste the sheepe of thy pasture? (Ps. 74) [74:1]

Oh remember not our olde synnes, but haue mercye vpon vs, & that sone, for we are come to great misery. (Ps. 79) [79:8]

But thinke vppon the congregation, whom thou hast purchased, and redemed of olde. (Ps. 74) [74:2]

Helpe vs O god of our saluation, for the glory of thy name: Oh delyuer vs, & be mercifull vnto our sinnes for they names sake. (Ps. 79) [79:9]

Wherfore do the heathen say: where is now their God? (Ps. 79) [79:10]

Lyfte vppe thy feete, that thou mayst vtterly destroye euery enemie, which hath done euyll in thy sanctuary. (Ps. 74) [74:4]

Powre out thyne indignation vpon the heathen, that haue not knowen thee: & vpon the kyngdomes, that haue not called vpon thy name. (Ps. 79) [79:6]

Let the vengeaunce of thy seruauntes bloud, that is shed, be openly shewed vpon the heathen in our sight. (Ps. 79) [79:11]

Let the sorowfull sighynge of the prysoners come before thee, accordyng to the greatnes of thy power, preserue thou those that are appointed to dye. (Ps. 79) [79:12]

And as for the blasphemie (wherewith our ennemies haue blasphemed thee) rewarde thou them (O Lorde) seuen folde into their bosome. (Ps. 79) [79:13]

So we that be thy people, and shepe of thy pasture shall geue thee thankes for euer: and wyll alwaye be shewing forth thy praise from generation to generation. (Ps. 79) [79:14]

Glory be to the father &c.

As it was &c.

After the Psalme the prayer following shalbe saide by the minister alone with a high voice, at saying wherof the people shall deuoutly geue eare, & shall both with minde and speache to them selues assent to the same prayer.

The prayer.

  O Almightye and euerlyuyng God our heauenlye father, we thy disobedyent and rebellious chyldren, nowe by thy iuste iudgemente sore afflicted and in great daunger to be oppressed, by thine and our sworne and most deadlye enemyes the Turkes, Infidels, and Miscreantes, doe make humble sute to the throne of thy grace for thy mercye, and ayde agaynst the same our mortall enemyes: for though we do professe the name of thy only sonne Christ our sauiour, yet through our manyfolde synnes and wickednesse, we haue most iustlye deserued so muche of thy wrathe and indygnation: that we can not but say, O Lorde correct vs in thy mercy and not in thy furye. Better it is for vs to fall into thy handes, then into the handes of men, and especially into the handes of Turkes and Infydelles thy professed ennemyes, who nowe inuade thine inheritaunce. Agaynst thee O Lorde haue we synned, and

transgressed thy commaundementes. Againste Turkes, Infidelles, and other ennemies of the gospell of thy dere sonne Jesus Christ haue we not offended, but onely
in thys that we acknoweledge thee, the eternall father, and thy onely sonne our
redemer, with the holy ghost the comforter, to be one onelye true almighty and
euerliuyng God. For if we wolde denye and blaspheme thy most holy name, forsake
the gospel of thy dere sonne, embrace false religion, commit horrible Idolatries,
and geue our selues to all impure, wicked, and abhominable lyfe, as they doe: The
Deuill, the worlde, the Turke, and all other thine enemyes wolde be at peace with vs,
accordinge to the saying of thy sonne chryst: if you were of the worlde the worlde
wolde loue hys owne.[80] But therfore hate they vs, because we loue thee: therfore
persecute they vs, because we acknoweledge thee, god the father, and Jesus christ
thy sonne, whom thou hast sente. The Turke goeth aboute to set vp, to extoll, and to
magnify that wicked monster and damned soule Mahumet aboue thy derely beloued
sonne Jesus christ, whom we in hart beleue and with mouth confesse to be our
onelye sauior and redemer. Wherfore awake O lord our God and heauenly father,
loke vpon vs thy children and all such Christians as nowe be beseged and afflicted,
with thy fatherly & mercifull countenaunce: and ouerthrowe and destroy thine and
our enemies sanctify thy blessed name amonges vs, whych they blaspheme, esta-
blysh thy kyngdome, whych they labor to ouerthrow: suffer not thyne ennemyes to
preuayle agaynst those, that nowe call vpon thy name, and put their trust in thee,
least the Heathen and infydels say: where is now their god? but in thy great mercy
saue, defende, & deliuer all thy afflicted Christians in thys and all other inuasions of
these Infidels, that we and they that delyte to be named christians may continually
laud, praise and magnify thy holy name, wyth thy onely sonne Jesus Chryst, and the
holy ghost, to whom be al laud, prayse, glory, and Empyre for euer and euer. Amen.

Psalmes whych may be song or sayd before the beginning, or after the ending of
publique prayer.
[2, 3, 7, 10, 11, 14, 22, 27, 46, 52, 56, 70, 74, 83, 90, 94, 121, 123, 130, 140]

1565–E2 Thanksgiving services for the delivery of Malta and for other victories over the Ottomans

Wednesdays, Fridays and Sundays, [late October 1565 for six weeks from receipt] 1565 (Canterbury province)

The Hospitallers eventually repulsed the Ottoman assault (see 1565–E1) with
support from Habsburg imperial forces which arrived from Sicily in August; the
Ottoman fleet retreated on 11 September. In October, Cecil was keen to organize a
public thanksgiving but Grindal advised him to delay for eight days partly because
he believed nothing could be written and printed in less time, but mainly because he
considered it essential that news of the victory, received by Parker, was verified. He
drew Cecil's attention to the difficulties created by precipitate prayers for Mary I's
safe delivery (1554–E3). The form followed the format of the thanksgivings after

---

[80] In margin: 'John. 15.'.

plague (1564–E) in which new prayers, psalms and collects were added to the BCP service and the same service was followed on all days of observance.

Order: described in Grindal to Cecil, 12 Oct. 1565, SP12/37/54, fo. 159r.
Form of prayer: *A short forme of thankesgeuing to God for the delyuerie of the Isle of Malta from the inuasion and long siege therof by the great armie of the Turkes both by sea and lande, and for sundry other victories lately obteined by the Christians against the saide Turkes, to be vsed in the common prayer within the prouince of Canterburie on Sondayes, Wednesdaies, and Fridaies, for the space of syx weekes next ensuinge the receipt hereof. Set forthe by the most reuerend father in God, Matthew by Goddes prouidence archebyshop of Canturburie, primate of all Englande and metropolitane ... Psalme .50. Call vpon mee in the day of trouble, so will I deliuer thee, and tho shalte glorifie mee* (William Seres; [8] pp. STC 16509) [also in Clay, pp. 524–6].
Additional sources: Strype, *Grindal*, pp. 152–3; *The remains of Edmund Grindal*, ed. Nicholson, pp. 287–8; Strype, *Annals*, I: 1, 190–2; Clay, p. 461.

DESCRIPTION OF ORDER

Bishop of London to Sir William Cecil, 12 October 1565

S^r, I haue received frome my L. off Canterburie certeyn advertisementes concernynge Malta &c. /. I perceive yo wisshe some publicke thankes gevinge to be hadde on Sondaye nexte. / I am off opinion, y^t it wer good to differre it 8. dayes lenger, and thatt for 2. cawses. / one is, yt more certeyntie off the uetory maye be knowen, which by this advertisement semeth to me vncertaynn. / it were lesse inconvenience to differre a weeke, then to make solemne gratulations if the matter hereafter proove vntrue, as in this case off Malta, and the birthe off qwene Maries firste sonne hathe hertofore appeared. /. Another cause is, for y^t nothinge in this shorte tyme, I meane before Sondaye, cann be devised, and printed for thatt purpose. / yff ye resolue other wese with Mr Wattes the bringer, I wille doo whatt I cann, butt I distruste the newes.

FORM OF PRAYER

After the ende of the Collecte in the Letany which beginneth with these wordes: We humbly beseche thee O father .&c. shal followe this Psalme to be sayd of the mynister, with thaunswere of the people.

Wee prayse thee O Lorde with oure whole hartes, and wee wyll speake of thye marueylouse woorkes. (Ps. 9) [9:1]
Wee wyll be glad and reioyce in thee, we wyl sing praises vnto thye name O most highe. [Ps.9:2]
For that our enemies are turned back, are fallen and peryshed at thy presence. (Ps. 9) [9:3]
For that thou hast rebuked the heathen, and destroied the wicked, and brought theyr destruction to an ende. [Ps. 9:5]
Thou hast bene a refuge for the poore, a refuge in due tyme, euen in affliction. (Ps. 9) [9:9]
Thou hast delyuered vs from our stronge enemie, and from them that hated vs, for they were to stronge for vs. (Ps. 18) [18:17]
We haue sinned with our fathers, we haue committed iniquity, and done wickedly. (Ps. 108) [106:6]
Neuertheles the Lorde hath saued vs for hys names sake, that he myght make his power to be knowen. [Ps. 106:8]

O our deliuerer from our enemies, euen thou hast set vs vp from theym that rose against vs: thou haste deliuered vs from the cruell man. (Ps. 18) [18:49]

Greate delyueraunce hast thou geuen vs, and shewed vs great mercie in the day of our calamitie [?]

Though we saide in our hast, we were caste out of thy sighte, yet thou heardest the voice of our praier when we cried vnto thee. (Ps. 31) [31:24 & 25]

Thou remembredst vs in our base estate, and rescwedst vs from our oppressours. (Ps. 137) [136:23 & 24]

O God the proude were risen againste vs, and the assemblies of vyolente men sought our soules, and did not set thee before their eies. (Ps. 86) [86:14]

They saide in theyr hartes let vs destroy them altogether, there is no helpe for them in God. (Ps. 74, 3) [74:9]

If the Lorde had not bene on our side may we now say: if the lord had not bene on oure side, when Infidels rose vppe against vs. (Ps. 124) [124:1]

They had swallowed vs vp quick, when their wrathe was kindled against vs. [Ps. 124:2]

But praysed be the Lorde which hath not geuen vs as a praye vnto their teeth, nor suffred our enemies to triumph ouer vs (Ps. 124, 30) [124:5 & 30:1]

Let vs therefore confesse before the Lorde his louinge kindenes, and his wonderful workes before the sonnes of men. (Ps. 107) [107:31]

Let vs exalte him in the congregation of the people, and prayse him in the assembly of the Elders. (Ps. 107) [107:32]

Blessed be the Lorde God of Israell, whiche onely dothe wonderous thynges, and blessed be the name of his maiestie for euer. Amen. Amen. (Ps. 72) [72:18 & 19]

After this Psalme shalbe sayde by the mynister openly and with an high voice the Collecte followynge.

The Collecte

O heauenly and most mercifull father, the defender of those that put their truste in thee, the sure fortresse of al them that flee to thee for succoure: who of thye most iust iudgementes for our disobedience againste thy holy woorde, and for our synne-full and wycked lyuinge, nothinge answerynge to our holy profession, which hath bene an occasion that thy holy name hath bene blasphemed emonges the heathen, hast of late moste sharpely corrected and scourged our christian bretherne thy seru-antes with terrible warres and dreadful inuasions of most deadly and cruell enemies, Turkes, and Infidels: But now of thy fatherly pitie and merciful goodnes, without any desert of ours, even for thine owne names sake hast by thy assistence gyuen to dyuerse Chrystian prynces & potentates at lengthe, when all our hope was almost past, dispersed and put to confusion those Infidels being thyne and our mortall ennemies, and graciously delyuered thy afflycted and distressed christians in the Isle of *Malta* and sundry other places in chrystendom, to the glory & prayse of thy name, and to the excedynge comforte of all sorowfull Christian hartes: We render vnto thee most humble and hartye thanckes for these thy great mercies shewed to them that were thus afflycted and in daunger, we laude and praise thee, moste humbly beseching thee to graunt vnto all those that professe thy holy name, that we maye shewe our selues in our lyuinge thankfull to thee for these and all other thy benefites: Endue vs (O Lorde) and all other Christian people with thy heauenly grace, that we may truly knowe thee and obediently walke in thy holy commaunde-

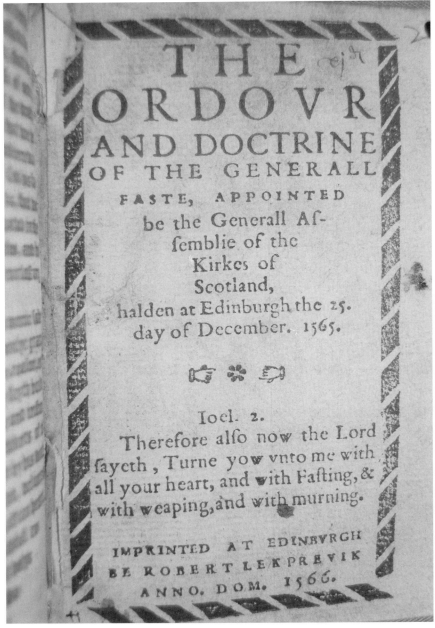

5 Title-page of the earliest extant order for special worship in Scotland. Compiled by John Craig and John Knox for 1566–S1, this was used for subsequent Scottish fast days and included from 1587 in editions of the Book of Common Order.
The ordour and doctrine of the generall faste (8°, Edinburgh, 1566; STC 22041); Emmanuel College, Cambridge, S10.5.81 (2).

mentes, leaste wee againe prouoke thy iuste wrathe againste vs: Continue thy great
mercies towardes vs, and as in this, so in all other inuasions of Turkes and Infidelles
saue and defende thy holy Churche, that all posterities ensuynge maye continually
confesse thy holy name, praising and magnifying thee with thy only sonne Jesus
Christ, and the holy ghost, to whom be all laude, prayse, glory and Empire for euer
and euer. Amen.

1566–S1   Fast days during perceived threats to the reformed church

Sunday 23 February – Sunday 3 March 1566 (Scotland)

This fast, the first in post-reformation Scotland, was appointed by the general
assembly of December 1565. The assembly instructed a group of men – John Craig
(Canongate), John Douglas (rector of St Andrews University), Robert Maitland
(dean of Aberdeen), William Christison (Dundee), David Lindsay (Leith), Gilbert
Garden (Monifeith), Thomas Maclean and John Majoribanks (both commissioners of
Edinburgh) – to consider the reasons for fasting. In the fourth session on 28 December,
they 'declared the necessitie of a publict fast', and the assembly appointed John
Knox and John Craig to compose a form of worship for the occasion. The resulting
work, *The ordour and doctrine of the generall faste*, also contained a lengthy order,
providing justifications for this new pattern of worship. It concluded with two letters
to ministers and users of the text; it is unclear whether the phrase 'Iohne Knox at
the command of the publict Assemblie' at the end of the second letter indicated
Knox's authorship of this letter or his contribution to the work as a whole. The form
of worship was used on subsequent Scottish fast days; the text of *The ordour and
doctrine of the generall faste* was included in editions of the Book of Common Order
from 1587. Although David Calderwood and other sources incorrectly dated the fast
as observed on 3–12 March, the Canongate Kirk session minutes confirm that it
was observed on the eight days specified in the order. National fasts held on two
successive Sundays and, at least in the burghs, the intervening weekdays were the
norm in Scotland until the 1630s.

Order: by the general assembly, 28 Dec. 1565, in *The ordour and doctrine of the generall faste, appointed
be the generall assemblie of the kirkes of Scotland, halden at Edinburgh the 25 day of December 1565*
(Edinburgh, Robert Lekpreuik; [110] pp.; STC 22041)*, sigs. A2r–E6v [two EEBO copies compared].
Instructions and order of service: *Ordour and doctrine of the generall faste*, sigs. E6v–F8v.
Letters: Superintendents, ministers and commissioners at the general assembly to the ministers of Scotland, *Ordour and doctrine of the generall faste*, sigs. G1r–G6r; 'to the faithfull reader', *Ordour and
doctrine of the generall faste*, sigs. G6r–G7v.
Additional sources: Calderwood, II, 303–6, 317; *BUK*, I, 76; *The buik of the Kirk of the Canagait,
1564–1567*, ed. Alma B. Calderwood (Scottish Record Society, 90, Edinburgh, 1961), p. 40.

ORDER

Order by the general assembly: 28 December 1565
The present troubles being somewhat considdered (but greater feared shortly to
follow) it wes thoght expedient (dearelie beloued in the Lord Iesus) that the whole
Faithfull Within this Realme, shuld together, and at one time prostrat them selues
before their God, crauing of him pardone and mercy for the great abuse of his former

benefites, and the assistance of his holy Spirite, by whose mightie operation we may yet so conuert to our God, that we prouoke him not to take from vs the lyght of his Euangle, which he of his mercie hath caused so clearly of laite dayes to shine within this realme. But because that suche publicte Supplicationes requyre alwayes Fasting to be ioyned therewith, And publict Fastynge craueth a certane time and certane exercises of godlynes then to be vsed with greater streatnes then at vther tymes. The whole Assemblie after deliberation hath appointed ye last Sonday of February, and the first Sonday of Marche nixt following the date of the said assemblie, to that moste necessare exercise (as tyme now standeth) of publict Fasting. And further, did require the same to be signified be all Ministers to their people the Sonday preceading the said last Sonday of Februarie. But lest that the Papistes shall think that now we begine to authorise and praise that which some tymes we haue reproued and dampned in them. Or els that the ignorant who knowe not the commoditie of this moste godlie exercise shall contempne ye same. We haue thoght expedient somewhat to speak to the one and to the vther. And vnto the Papistes first we say, that as in puritie of conscience, we haue refused their whole abhominationes, and amongest the rest, that their superticious and Pharisaicall maner of Fasting: So euen vnto this day do we continew in the same purpose, boldely affirming that their Fasting is no Fasting that euer God approued, but that it is a deceauing of the people, and a meare mocking of God, which moste euidentlie will appeare. If in the Scriptures we searche what is the ryght end of Fasting, what Fasting pleased God, and which is it that his soule abhoreth. Of Fasting in the Scriptures we finde two sortes, the one priuate, the vther publicte. The priuate is that which man or woman doeth in secrete, & before their God, for such causes as their owen conscience beareth record vnto them. As Dauid during the time that his Sone which wes begotten in adulterie, wes struken with mortall seickness, fasted, weapt, and lay vpon the ground, because that in the seicknes of the Chylde he did considder Godes displeasure agains him self for the remouing, whereof he fasted, murned, & prayed, vnto suche tyme as he saw Godes wil fulfilled by the awaytaking of the Chylde Priuatlie fasted Anna, wyfe to Alcana, euen in the verray Solempne Feastes, during the tyme of hir barrennes. For she weapt and eat nothing,[81] but in the bitternes of hir heart she prayed vnto the Lord, nether ceased she from sorow and murning, vnto suche tyme as Eli the hie Preist concurred with her in prayers, by whose mouth after that he had hard her petifull complaint, she receaued conforte. Of this Fasting speaketh oure Maister Iesus Christ in these wordes, when ye Fast, be not sowr as the Hypocretes, for they disfigure their faces,[82] that they may seme vnto men to Fast. But thow when thow Fastest, anoynt thy heade, and washe thy face, that thow seame not vnto men to Fast, but vnto thy Father which seeth in secrete, and will rewarde the opinly. Of the same no dout speaketh ye Apostle when that he sayeth, defraude not one another,[83] except it be with consent for a tyme, that ye may giue your selues to Fasting and prayer. To this priuate Fasting which standeth chiefly in a temperat, dyet, & in powring furthe of our secrete thoughtes and necessities before God, can be prescriued no certane rule, certane tyme, nor certane ceremonies, but as the causes and occasiones why that exercise is vsed are diuers (yea so diuers that seldome it is that many at ones are moued with one cause) so are diet, tyme, together with all vther circumstances requyred to suche Fasting, put in

81 In margin: '1. Sam. 1'.
82 In margin: 'Math. 6.'.
83 In margin: '1. Cor. 7.'.

the libertie of them that vse it. To this Fasting we haue bene faithfully and earnestly exhorted by oure Preachers, as oft as the Scriptures which they entreated offered vnto them occasion. And we dout not but the godlie within this Realme haue vsed the same as necessitie craued, albeit with the Papistes we blew no Trumpetes, to appoynt thereto certane dayes.

The vther kynde of Fasting is publict so called, because that it is openlie awowed, some tymes of a Realme, some tymes of a multitude, some tymes of a cietie, and some tymes of a meaner company, yea, some tymes of particulare persones, and yet publictlie vsed, and that for the wealth of a multitude. The causes thereof are also diuers,[84] for sometymes the feare of enimies, sometymes the angrie face of God punishing, sometymes his threatning to distroy, some tymes iniquitie deprehended that ryghtlie before wes not considered, and sometymes the earnest zeale that some beare for preseruation of Godes people, for aduancing of his glorie, & performing of his worke, according to his promes, moue men to publict Fasting, confession of their sinnes, & solempned prayers, for defence against their enimies, recouering of Godes fauoures, remouing of his plagues, preseruation of his people, & setting fordwarde of that worke, which he hath of his merce promised to finishe, as in the subsequent probations euidently shall appeare. When Messingers came to Iosaphat saying, there cometh a great multitude against thee from beyond the sea, out of Aram (that is Syria) &c. Iosaphat feared,[85] and set him self to seke the Lord, and proclamed a Faste throughout all Iuda. And Iuda gathered them selues together, to aske counsall of the Lord, they come euen out of all the cieties of Iuda to inquire of the Lord. And Iosaphat stoode in the Congregation of Iuda, and Ierusalem in the hous of the Lord, before the new court, And all Iuda stoode before the Lord with their yonge ones, their wyfes and their Chyldrene. And Iosaphat said, o Lord God of our Fathers, are not thow God in heauen, and reignest not thow in all Kingdomes of the Heathen? And in thy hand is power and myght,[86] and none is able to withstand thee. Haste not thow our God cast out the inhabitantes of this Land, before thy people Israell, and haste giuen it to the sead of Abraham thy freand for euer. &c. But now the Ammorytes, and Moabytes, & the Mont Seir ar come to cast vs out of thy possession? O Lord our God shall thow not iudge them? In vs there is no strengh to stand against this great multitude that commeth against vs, nether knowe we what to do, but vnto thee are our eyes bent. &c. Of this Historie we haue the first cause of publict Fasting, and the solempnitie thereof sufficiently prowen. For the feare of enimies compelled Iosaphat to seik the Lord, he knowing him selfe burdened with the care of the people, exhorted them to do the same. They fra all cieties and quarters repared to Ierusalem, whereupone a statute day the King and the people, yea, wyues and Childrene presented them selues before the Lord in his holy Temple,[87] exponed their necessitie, implored his helpe against that enraged multitude, that alwayes wes enimie to Godes people, & gaue open confession of their owen weaknes, leaning onely to the promes and protection of the omnipotent. Which exemple, we & euerie people likewyse assaulted, may and ought to follow in euerie poynt. This onely excepted, that we are not bound to conuene at any one appoynted place, as they did at Ierusalem. For to no one certane and seuerall place

---

[84] In margin: 'Causes that ought to moue men to publicte Fasting.'
[85] In margin: '2. Parali. 20' (i.e. 2. Chron. 20).
[86] In margin: 'The prayer of Iosaphat'.
[87] In margin: 'The ceremonie of publicte fasting'.

is that promes made, that then wes made to the Temple of Ierusalem,[88] which wes
that whatsoeuer men in their extremitie shuld ask of God in it, God shuld grant it
from his holie habitation in the heauen. Iesus the Messias then looked for,[89] whose
presence wes sought in the mercie seat, and betuix the Cherubinnes, is now entered
within the vale, that is in the heauen, and there abydeth onely Mediator for vs, vnto
whome from all the coastes of the earth, we may lift vp pure handes, direct our
prayers,[90] supplicationes, and complaintes, and be assured that they shalbe receaued,
in whatsoeuer place we conuene. And yet in tyme of suche publict exercyses, we
wold wishe that all men and wemen shuld repare to suche places as their conscience
may be best instructed, their Faith moste edified, repentance moste liuely sturred
vp in them, and they by Godes worde may be moste assured that their iust peticions shall not be repelled. Which thinges can not be done so liuely in secrete
and priuate meditation, as that they are in publict Assemblie, where Christ Iesus is
trewly preached, & this muche shortlie for the firste head. Of the second, to wit, that
the angrie face of God punishing, aught to dryue vs to publicte Fasting, & humiliation of our soules before our God, we haue two notable exemples, the one written
in Iosua, who hearing and vnderstanding, that Israell had turned the back before the
Cananite and the Elders of Israell rent their clothes,[91] fell vpone their faces before
the Arke of the Lord vnto the nyght, and caste dust vpone their heades, in signe of
their humiliation and deiection. The vther is expressed in the booke of the Iudges,
where Israell being commanded by God to fight against Beniamin,[92] because that
they menteaned wicked men that deserued death, loste the first day twentie two
thousand of their armie, and the second day eightene thousand. At the firste lose
they were lyghtlie touched, and asked counsall if they shulde renew, the battell, but
at the second ouerthrow, the whole people repared vnto the hous of the Lord, sat
there, weapt before the Lord, & Fasted that day vnto the night, for then began they
to considder Godes angrie face against them.

   In this last historie their appeareth iust cause why the people shulde haue rune to
the onely refuge of God, because that there first army of fourtie thousand men wes
vtterlie distroyed. But what iust occasion had Iosua so lamentablie to complaine,[93]
yea, so boldely as it were to accuse God, that he had deceaued him in that, that
against his promeis he had suffered Israell to fall before their ennimies. Wes the lose
of thrette men (no mo[re] fel that day in the edge of the sword) so great a mater
that he shuld dispare of any better successe, that he shulde accuse God that he had
brought them ouer Iordane, and that he shuld feare that the whole army of the Lord
shuld be inueroned aboute, and consumed in the rage of their ennimies, yea, if
Israell had onely looked no further then to the lose of the fourty thousand men, they
had bene but feable Soldioures, for they had sufficient strenth remaning behinde, for
what were fourtie thousand, in respect of all the trybes of Israel? Nay, nay (deare
brethren) it wes an vther thing then the present lose that terrified & effrayed their
consciences, and made them so effeminatlie (so wold fleshe iudge) to complaine,
weap, and owle before God, to wit, they saw his angrie face against them, they
saw his hand fortifie their ennimies, and to fight against them, whome both he had

---

88 In margin: 'The promeis made to the temple of Ierusalem is now to be soght in Christe Iesus.'
89 In margin: 'Hebr. 7.'.
90 In margin: '1. Time. 2.'.
91 In margin: 'Iosua. 7.'.
92 In margin: 'Iudi. 20.' (i.e. Judges 20).
93 In margin: 'Let his complaint be noted.'

commanded to fight, and had promised to giue them victorie.[94] For euerie commandement of God to do any thing against his ennimies, hath included within it a
secrete promes of his godly assistance, which they fand not in the beginning of
their interpryses, and therefore they did considder the fearcenes of his displeasure,
& did tremble before his angrie Face, whose myghtie hand they fand to fight against
them, and that wes the cause of their dolorous complaintes and fearfull crying before
their God. What wes the cause that God delt so framedly with the one, and with
the vther? we may perchance somewhat speak, when that we shall entreat of the
frutes of Fasting, and of those thinges that may holde back from vs the assistance
of God, euen when we prepare vs to put his commandement in execution. The
thride cause of publict Fasting, is Godes threatninges pronounced, ether against a
multitude, or against a persone in particulare. Of the former the exemple is Ni[n]iue,
vnto the which Ionas cryed, yet fourtie dayes, & Niniue shalbe distroyed, which
vnpleasing tydinges cumming to the eares of the King, he proclamed a Faste, he
humbled his owen soule, yea, euen to Sackcloth, and sitting in the duste, he straitlie
commanded reformation of maners in all estates, yea, and that signes of repentance,
of terrours, and feare shuld appeare, not onely in men & wemen, but also in the brute
beastes,[95] from whome wes all kynde of nurishement commanded to be withdrowen,
to witnes that they feared aswell Godes iudgementes to fall vpone the creatures that
serued them in their impietie, as vpone them selues that had prouoked God to that
hote displeasure. Of the vther the exemple is moste notable (moste notable we say)
because that it fell in a wicked man, to wit, in Achab, who by instigation of his
wicked wyfe Iesebell, saulde him self to do all iniquitie. And yet when that he hard
the fearefull threatninges of God pronounced by the Prophet Elias against him,[96]
against his wyfe and hous, he rent his royall garmentes, put on Sackcloth, sleipt
therein, fasted and yead baire footed, what ensewed the one and the vther, of these
we shall after heare.

The fourt cause of publict Fasting and murning (for they two muste euer be
ioyned) is iniquitie deprehended, that before wes not ryghtly considdered. The testimony whereof we haue in Esdras, after the reduction of the captiuitie, & that the
temple & the work of the Lordes hous wes stayed. It wes shawen vnto Esdras
that the people of Israell,[97] the Preistes and the Leuites were not seperat from the
people of the Nations, but that they did according to their abhominations, for they
maryed vnto them selues, and vnto their Sonnes, the doughters of the Cananites,
the Pherisites, Hithetes, Iebusites, Ammorites, Moabites, and Egiptiens, so that the
holy sead wes mixt with Prophane Idolateris, which thing being vnderstand, & more
deaply considdered, then it wes before, for then Esdras sawe iust cause why the
worke of the Lord prospered not in their handes. This considdered, we say Esdras
taking vpone him the sinne and offence of the whole people, rent his clothes, and
pulled furth the heares of his head and beard, sat as a man desolate of all conforte,
till the euening Sacrifice, and then rysing he bowed his kneis, and streached furth
his hande, before the Lord, and made a moste semple & humble confession of all
the enormities that were committed be the people, as well before the captiuitie as
after their returning, and ceased not his lamentable complaint, vnto suche tyme as

---

[94] In margin: 'Euerie commandement of god to do any thing, hes the secrete promes of his assistance.'
[95] In margin: 'what shall become of the hardnes of our heartes in these dayes.'
[96] In margin: '2. Reg. 21.' (i.e. 2 Kgs. 21).
[97] In margin: '1. Esdr. 9.'

a great multitude of men, wemen and childrene moued by his exemple,[98] weapt vehementlie, and promised redres of that present disordour and impietie.

Of the last cause of publict Fasting to wit, the zeale that certane persones beare for preseruation of Godes people, for aduancing of his glorie, and performing of his worke according to his promes.

We haue exemples in Mardocheus,[99] Daniell,[100] and in the faithfull assembled at Antioche,[101] for when that Mardocheus hard of that cruell sentence, which by the procurement of Haman, wes pronounced against his Nation. To wit, that vpone a day statute and affixed, shuld the Iewes in all the prouinces of the King Artaxarses be destroyed,[102] oulde and yong, men and wemen, and that their substance shuld be exponed in pray. This bloody sentence we say being hard, Mardocheus rent his clothes, put on Sackcloth and Ashes, past furth in the middest of the cietie, and cryed with a great and bitter crye, & coming to the Kinges gate, gaue knoweledge to Ester what crueltie wes decreed against the Nation of the Iewes, willing her to make intercession to the King, in the contrare, who efter certane excuses said. Go and gather all the Iewes that are in Susan,[103] and faste for me, eat not, nor drinke not, thre dayes and thre nyghtes, and I also, and my handmades shall likewyse faste, & then shall I enter vnto the King, although that I shuld perishe.

In this we may clearely se that the zeale that Mardocheus had to preserue the people of God, moued not onely him self to publict Fasting, but also Ester the Quene, her maides and the whole Iewes that hard of the murther intended, and moued Ester also to hasart her lyfe in going vnto the King without his commande-ment.

Of the uther, to wit, that the earnest desyre that Godes seruandes haue that God will performe his promes, & manteane the worke that he hath begune. Exemple we haue in Daniell,[104] and in the Actes of the Apostles. For Daniell vnderstanding the nomber of the yeares forespoken by the Prophet Ieremie, that Ierusalem shuld ly waist, to haue bene completit in the first yeare of the Reigne of Darius, turned him self vnto God, fasted, humbled him self in Sackcloth and Ashes, and with vnfeaned confession of his owen sinnes, and of the sinnes of the people, he vehe-mentlie prayed. That according to the promises sometymes made be Moyses, and after rehearsed by the Prophet Isay & Ieremie,[105] he wolde suddingly send them deliuerance,[106] and that he wolde not delay it for his owen Names sake.

When the Gentiles began to be illuminated,[107] and that Anteochia had so boldely receaued the Euangle of Iesus Christ, that the Disciples in it first of all tooke vpone them the name of Christianes.

The principall men of the same Church, thrusting no dout that the Kingdome of Iesus Christ shulde further be enlarged, and that the multitude of the gentiles shuld be instructed in the ryght way of Saluation,[108] Fasted and prayed, & whill that they

98   In margin: 'O that Scotland wolde follow this obedience.'
99   In margin: 'Ester. 4.'
100 In margin: 'Daniell. 9.'
101 In margin: 'Actes. 13.'
102 In margin: 'So intend the Papistes this day.'
103 In margin: 'Esdr. 4.'
104 In margin: 'Daniel [9].'
105 In margin: 'Deut. 30.'
106 In margin: 'Ierem. 31.'
107 In margin: 'Actes. 11.'
108 In margin: 'Act. 13.'

wer so exercised, charge wes giuen, that Paule and Barnabas shuld be seperated frome the rest, to the worke whereunto God had called them. &c. Of these former Histories and Scriptures, we may clearly se for what causes publict Fasting, and generall supplicationes haue bene made in the Church of God, and ought to be made when that euer the lyke necessities appeare, or occasions are offered. Now let vs shortly heare what conforte and frute ensewed the same. For the ennimie, yea, the murtherer of all godly exercise is disperation, for with what corage can any man with continuance call vpone God? If he shall disperatly dout: whether God shall accept his prayer or not? How shall he humble him self before his Throne? Or to what end shall he confesse his offence? If he be not perswaded, that there is mercy and good will in God to pardone his sinnes, to accept him in fauour, & to grant vnto him more then his owen heart, in the middest of his dolour can requyre or ymagine.

Trew it is, that this vennome of disperation, is neuer throughlie purged from our heartes, so long as we cary this mortall Carcasse.

But yet the constant promises of our God, and the manyfolde documentes of his mercy & help, showen vnto men in their greatest extremitie, ought to animat vs to follow their exemple, and to hope for the same successe that they haue gotten abufe mannes expectation. Iosaphat after his humiliation and prayer,[109] obtened the victorie, with out the lose of any of his Soldioures, for the Lord reased Ammon & Moab, against the inhabitantes of Mont Seir, who being vtterly destroyed,[110] euerie one of the ennimies of Godes people lift his sworde against another, till that, of that godles multitude, there wes not one left aliue, Iosua and the Israelites after their deiection, wer conforted againe. Niniue wes preserued, albeit that Ionas had cryed destruction, yea, Achab not withstanding all his vngodlynes,[111] loste not the frute of his humiliation, but wes recompensed with delay of the vttermoste of the plagues, during his lyfetyme. The murning of Esdras wes turned in ioy, when that he saw the people willing to obey God, and the worke of the hous of the Lord to go fordwart.

The bitter crying of Mardocheus, and the painefull Fasting of Ester were abound-antly rewarded, when not onely wes the people of God preserued, but Haman their mortall ennimie, wes hanged vpon the same gallous that he had prepared for Mardo-cheus.

Daniell after his Fasting, confession and prayer, gat moste notable reuelationes & assurance, that his people shuld be deliuered, yea, that in all extremities, they shuld be preserued, till that the Messias promysed vnto them shuld come, and manifestly showe him self.

And the godly of Anteochea wer not frustrate of their conforte, when that they hard how potently God had wrought amongst the Gentiles by the ministerie, of Barnabas & Paule, so that we may boldely conclude, that as God hath neuer dispysed the petitions of such as with vnfeaned heartes haue soght his comfort in their necessities, so will he not send vs away emptie & voyd, if with trew repentance we seak his face

If any wolde aske in what extremitie we finde our selues now to be, that hertofore we haue not sene. And what are the occasiones that shuld moue vs now to humble our selues before our God by publict Fasting, more then that we did in the begin-

---

[109] In margin: 'The frutes of trew Fasting, and vn feaned inuocation of god'.
[110] In margin: 'Let so thy ennimies perishe o lord.'
[111] In margin: 'Vnfeaned humiliation temporally profiteth the verray reprobate.'

ning? When this Euangile wes now last offered vnto vs, for then by all apperance, we and it in our persones stoode in greater danger, then we do yet,.

We answer, that the causes are mo[re] then for greif of haert we can expresse. First, because that in the beginning we had not refused godes graces, but contrariwyse with such feruencie we receaued them,[112] that we could beare with no kinde of impietie: but for the suppressing of the same, we nether had respect to frende, possession, land or lyfe, but all we put in hasard, that godes treuth myght be aduansed, and Idolatrie myght be suppressed.

And therefore did our God by the mouth of his Messingers, in all our aduersities, assure vs that our ennimies shuld not preuale against vs,[113] but that they shuld be subdewed vnder vs, that our God shuld be glorified in our semple & vpryght dealing. But now sence that carnall wisdome hath perswaded vs to beare with manifest Idolatrie, & to suffer this realme that God had ones purged, to be polluted againe with that abhomination, yea, allace, sence that some of vs that God made sometymes instrumentes to suppresse that impietie, haue bene the cheif men to conduct & conuoy that Idole throughout all the quarters of this Realme, yea, to the houses of them that sometymes detested the masse as the Deuill & his seruice. Sence that tyme we say, haue we funde the face of our God, angrie against vs, his threatninges haue bene sharpe in the mouthes of his Messingers, which albeit for the tyme, we dispysed & mocked, yet the iust experience conuicteth vs, that we were wicked, & that they in threatning vs,[114] did nothing but the dewtie of Godes trew Messingers.

And this is the second cause that moue vs to this publict humiliation, rather now then in the beginning, to wit, that then we followed god, and not carnall wisdome, & therefore made he few in nomber, feare full to many, fooles before the worlde to confound the wyse, and suche as before neuer had experience in armes, made God so bolde and so prosperous in all their interpryses, that the expertest Souldioures feared the poore plowmen, yea, our God faught for vs by sea, and by land, he moued the heartes of strangers to supporte vs, and to spend their liues for our releif.

But now allace we se no signe of his former fauour, for wisdome & manhead, strength and freindes, honour and blood ioyned with godlynes, are fallen before our eyes, to let vs vnderstand what shall be our distruction, if in time we turne not to our God, before that his wrathe be further kindled. But this is not the end. For esperance, (or at least some opinion) had men before, that God shulde moue the Quenis Maiesties heart, to heare ye blissed euangle of Iesus Christ trewlie preached, and so consequentlie that she shuld abandone all Idolatrie and fals Religion. But now she hath giuen answer in plaine wordes, that that Religion in whiche she hath bene nourished (and that is meare abhomination) she will manteane and defend. And in declaratioun thereof, of laite dayes there is erected a displayed baner against Iesus Christ, for corrupted Hypocrites, & suche as haue bene knowen deceauers of the people, are now authorised, to spew out their vennome against Iesus Christ his eternall treueth, and trew Messingers of the same. That Idole the Masse is now againe in diuers places erected. And what hereof may ensew, yea, or what we may looke, shalbe the end of suche vnhappy beginninges, we desyre the godly deaply to consider. But let it be granted, that we had not fallen back from our former feruencie, that we saw not Godes angrie face, threatning vs with more fear full plagues to follow, that the best

---

[112]   In margin: 'Causes that now moue vs to faste that moued vs not befor'.
[113]   In margin: 'Let the fathfull call to mynde.'
[114]   In margin: 'God grant that men may yet consider'.

parte of our nobilitie wer not exiled this Realme, nether yet that our Souerane were ennimie to our Religion, and that she bare no greater fauour to flattering freres, and to corrupted Papistes, then that she doeth to our poore Preachers.

Supponing we say that none of these foresaid causes we had to moue vs (as that we haue them all, and mo[re], if that we list to recompt them) yet is there one which if it moue vs not to humiliation, we showe our selues more then insensible. For now is Sathan so enraged against Iesus Christ,[115] and so odius is the light of his Euangile vnto that Romaine Antichrist, that to suppresse it in one prouince, Realme or Nation, he thinketh it nothing, vnles that in all Europe the godlie, and suche as abhorre the Papisticall impietie, be therewith also vtterly distroyed, and so rased from the face of the earth, that no memorie of them shal after remaine.

If any think that suche crueltie can not fall in the heartes of men, we send them to be resolued of those Fathers of the last counsall of Trent, who in one of their Sessions haue thus concluded. All Lutheriens,[116] Caluenistes and suche as are of the new Religion, shall vtterlie be exterminate, the beginning shalbe in France, by conducting of the Catholik Kinge, Philip of Spaine, and by some of the Nobilitie of France, which mater (say they) put to some stay the whole force of bothe, together with the Popes Army, and force of the Dukes of Sauoy, & farrar shall assault Geneua, and shall not leaue it, till that they haue put it to sack, sauing in it no leuing creature. And with the same mercy shal so many of France,[117] as haue taisted of the new Religion be saued. Frome thence expedition shalbe made against the Germaine, to reduce them to the obedience of the Apostelick seat. And so shal they proceed to vther Realmes & Nationes, neuer ceasing till that all be exterminate, that will not make homage to that Romaine Idole. How fearefull a beginning this conclusion and determination had, France will remember mo[re] ages then one. For how many abufe a hundreth thousand men, wemen, babes Virgines, Matrones, and aged Fathers suffered, some by sworde some by water, some by fyre, & vther tormentes. The verray ennimies them selues are compelled to acknoweledge. And albeit that God of his mercie in a part: disapoynted there cruell interpryses, yet let vs not thinke that their will is changed, or their malice asswaged. No let vs be assured that they abyde but oportunitie to finishe the worke that cruellie against God, against his treuth, and the trew professoures of the same, they haue begune. The whisperinges whereof are not secrete, nether yet the tokenes obscure. For the trafique of that dragone, now with the princes of the earth, his promyses and flattering entysementes tend to none vther end, but to inflambe them against Iesus Christ, and against the trew professoures of his Euangle. For who can think that the Pope, Cardinalles, and horned Bishopes, will offer the greatest portion of their Rentes for susteaning of a warre, whereof no commoditie shuld redound (as they suppose) to them selues. If any think that we accuse them without cause, let them heare their owen wordes,[118] for this they wrate neare the end of the same decre.

And to the end that the holy fathers on their parte, appeare not to be negligent, or vnwilling to giue their ayde and supporte vnto so holy a warre, or to spaire their owen rentes and money, haue added that the Cardinalles shall content them selues

---

[115] In margin: 'The suppressing of christes holy Euangle wes decried in the last counsall of Trent'.
[116] In margin: 'The Counsall of trent.'
[117] In margin: 'The mercie of the Fathers of trent.'
[118] In margin: 'The wordes of the counsall of trent.'

of the yearely Rent of 5. or 6. thousand Ducates,[119] and the rychest Bishope of 2. or 3. thousand at the moste. And to giue franckly ye rest of their Reueneues to the intertenement of the warre,[120] which is made for the extirpation of the Lutheriens and Caluinistes sect. And for reestablishing of the Romaine Churche, till suche tyme as the mater be conducted to a good & happy end. If these be not open declarationes, in what danger all faithfull stand, if they can bring their crueltie to passe, let verray Idiotes iudge, but let vs heare their conclusion. France and Germanie (say they) being by these meanes so chastised, abased & conducted to the obedience of the holy Romaine Churche, the Fathers dout not, but tyme shall prouide bothe counsal and commoditie, that the rest of the Realmes about may be reduced to one flok,[121] and one Apostolick gouernour & Pastour. &c. By this conclusion we thinke that the verray blinde may see what is purposed against the Saintes of God, in all Realmes and Nationes, to wit, distruction with crueltie, or els to make them to worship that blasphemous beast who being an Idole, vsurpeth to him selfe the Name of vniuersall Pastoure, and being knowen to be the man of sinne and perdition, will be holden for an Apostolick Gouernour. But some shall say they are yet fare from the end of their purpose, and therefore we neid not to be so fearefull, nor so sollist. We answer, the danger may be nerar, then we beleaue, yea, perchance a parte of it hath bene neirar to our neckes then we haue considdered. But how so euer it be, seing that God of his mercie hath brought furth to lyght their cruell and bloody counsall, in the which we nead not to dout, but still they continew. It becommeth vs not to be negligent nor sleuthfull, but we ought to follow the exemple of Ezechias, the King of Iuda, who receauing not onely the dispytefull answer,[122] but also the blasphemus and threatning letter of Sennaherib, first send vnto the Prophet Isayas, and pietifully compleaned of the instant troubles, willing him to make intercession vnto God, for the remanent that were left. Vnto whome albeit that the Prophet answered, confortablie assuring the King that the ennimie shuld not cume so neir as to shoote Darte or Arrow within Ierusalem. Yet ceased not the godlie King to present him self in the Temple of the Lord. And as a man dispared of all worldely conforte, spred abrod the letters that proud Sennaherib had sent vnto him and made vnto God his moste feruent prayer, as in the 37. Chapter of the Prophet Isayas we may read.

The ennimie had turned back,[123] and God had put a Brydle in his nosethirles, and so men myght haue thought that the King neded not to haue bene so solliste. But the Spirite of God instructed the heart of his seruand, to seak helpe where it wes onely to be found, and from the handes of God, who only wes able to put finall end to that tyrannie. The exemple (we say) of this approued seruand of God, we ought to follow now when the like distruction is intended against vs, yea, not against one Realme only, but against all that professe the Lord Iesus, as before we haue heard. Albeit that God of his mercy hath stayed the furie of the Papistes for a tyme, we ought not to think that their malice is changed, nether that suche as trewly professe the Lord Iesus, can be in securitie, so long as that Babiloniane hoore hath power to enchant the Princes of the earth. Let vs therefore vnderstanding that she being dronken with the blood of the Saintes, can neuer repent of crueltie & murther, vse against her the

---

[119] In margin: 'These are the successoures of the Apostles.'
[120] In margin: 'No man nedeth to dout of the liberalitie of those Fathers, so that Christ Iesus may be crucified, and his Euangle exiled.'
[121] In margin: 'Let Scotland aduert.'
[122] In margin: 'Isa. 36. & 37'.
[123] In margin: 'Isay. 37.'

spiritual weapones, to wit,[124] earnest inuocation of Gods Name, by the which we finde the proude tyrannes of the earth, in tymes past, to haue bene ouerthrowen. Abufe all these causes foresaid, we haue yet one that ought not to be omitted, to wit, the body of this Realme hath long enioyed quietnes, whill that vther nations about vs haue bene seueirly plagued. What thousandes dyed in the east cuntreyes, and in England of the pest? anno 1563. 1564. Their owen confessions beare record.

What crueltie hath bene executed in France? what townes spoyled, and murther committed, somewhat before we haue declared, & more we myght if that we had not respect to breuitie and tyme. And what trouble is presently, and long hath bene betuix Denmarke and Swaden, the posteritie of that cuntrie will after vnderstand. And in all this tyme now sex yeares, and more hath God spared vs, so that the publict estate hath alwayes remaned quyet, except within these few monethes. Ought not the deap consideration of this moue vs now to stoupe before our God?

For haue we bene spared because that our Rebellion to God is les, then is the Rebellion of those nations that we haue sene punished? If so we think, we are far deceaued. For in so great lyght of the Euangle, we think that greater inobedience wes neuer showen vnto God, nor greater ingratitude vnto his Messingers, sence the dayes of the Apostles, then of laite yeares hath bene (and yet is) within this Realme. Idolatrie is obstinatly menteaned, Huredome and adulterie are but pastyme of the flesh, slaugther and murther is esteamed small sinne, if any man haue freind in court, craftie dealing with the semple, disceat and oppression is compted gude conques, (yea allace almoste vniuersally) Parcialitie in iudgement, is but interpretation of Lawes, yea, delaying of Iustice, what mater is that? what reuerence is had to Godes Messingers, and what respect vnto the poore that now so multiplies within this Realme (that the lyke hath seldome bene sene) thought we will cease, the stones will crye, & condempne vs, and yet what supefluitie? what vanitie? what feasting? Ryotous Banckating? hath bene (& yet is) vsed in court, cuntrey and townes, although the tounges of men dar not speak, yet we think the purses of some do feal, and in their maner complaine. If these be not sinnes that craue plagues from God, we humblie desyre men to considder what are the sinnes that were layed to the charge of Sodome and Gomorha, by the Prophet Ezechiell.[125]

Now say we, God before our eyes hath punished vthers, and can he spaire vs? Being more cryminall then they were? Nay he can not. And therfore there restes nothing vnto vs but vtter exterminion,[126] if we vnfeanedly turne not vnto our God before that his wraithe be further kindled against vs. Iudgement is begune in his owen hous, for if within Scotland amonges men of their estate, there wes to be fund equetie, iustice, temperance, compassion vpone the poore and vpryght conscience, they did moste clearly shyne in them, whome God before oure eyes hath firste deiected. Therefore (yet agane) we say that onely repentance can saue vs from plagues more greuous then they haue felt, or that we haue sene of many yeares within this Realme.

But now we knowe, that suche as nether lufe God, nor trewly feare his Iudgementes (for mo[re] Atheistes we haue, nor consumate Papistes within this Realme)[127] shall grudge and crye, what new ceremone is this that now we here of? Wherefore

---

[124] In margin: 'what veapons weshall vse against the crueltie of the papistes.'
[125] In margin: 'Ezechi. 16.'
[126] In margin: 'O that we shold heare before God plages more'.
[127] In margin: 'That is men without god'.

shall we Faste? and who hath power to command vs so to do? A Feg for their Fasting, we will fill & farse our bellies vpone the oulde fassion. &c. Let not the godly be offended at the brocardes and lardons of such godles people, but let vs tremble before our God, and considder that suche hath bene the proude contempt of the wicked in all ages before vs, as in the Prophetes we may read. For Isay compleaneth, saying,[128] when the Lord calleth to Sackclothe and ashes, there is nothing heard, but let vs eat & drink kill the fat, and make Banket, let vs bring wyne in aboundance,[129] and more, and if we must dye, let vs departe in ioy, for so they ment, when that they said, let vs eat and drink, the morrow we shall dye.

But let vs consider, what answer they receaue. As I liue sayeth the Lord,[130] this your iniquitie shall not be forgiuen vnto the death, I shall take from yow the myrth of wyne and oyle,[131] your yong men shall fall by the sworde,[132] your aged men shal be led captiues, your delicate Dammes shall trote vpone their fete ouer the riuer (meaning Euphrates) their buttockes shalbe naked,[133] and their shame shall not be hid. &c.

Ieremie the Prophet preached and cryed euen to the King,[134] and to the Quene, and commanded them to walk in lowlynes, to do iustice. to represse impietie, and so he promised that they shoulde sit still vpone their Throne in ioy and quyetnes. But if they wolde not, he boldelie pronounced that their Carcasses shalbe cast to the heit of the Sone and to the frost,[135] and colde of the nyght.[136] Ezechiel in his age vseth the same ordour, and in his owen bodie showeth vnto them signes of humiliation, and of the plagues that shuld apprehend them for their Rebellion.

All their admonitions were dispysed we confesse, but thereto we shulde not looke, but vnto that which ensewed suche proude contempt.

Yf we wolde that our Palices shuld be so distroyed, that they shuld remaine desolate, and be dennes to Dragones.

Yf we wolde that our land shuld be laide waist and be a pray to our ennimies,[137] and if we wolde that the rest of the plagues, threatned by the Prophetes, and which haue apprehended the disobedient before vs, shuld come vpone vs in full perfection. Then we nede nether to faste nor pray, repent nor turne to God. But and if we desyre ether to finde mercy in this lyfe, or ioy & confort in the lyfe to come, we muste showe our selues vnfeanedly, sory for the abhominations that now vniuersally Reigne,[138] we muste be lyke Lothe in Sodome & Noha, in that Catholick defection from God, which wes into the first age. And by their exemples, and notable deliuerances,[139] ought we to be encoraged, to showe our selues sory for this present corruption, & to oppone our selues thereto, to the vttermoste of our powers, vnles that we wolde haue portion with the wicked. Nether ought we to be discoraged, because that the contemners, godles people, and mockers of all godlynes, shall

---

128   In margin: 'Isay. 22.'
129   In margin: 'Isay. 58.'
130   In margin: 'Isay. 22.'
131   In margin: 'Isay. 5. 6. 9.'
132   In margin: 'Isay. 20.'
133   In margin: 'Ierem. 13.'
134   In margin: 'Ierem. 13.'
135   In margin: 'Ier. 16 & 19.'
136   In margin: 'Ezech. 21.'
137   In margin: 'Leuit. 26.'
138   In margin: 'If we will not perishe with the worlde, we must be vnlike vnto it.'
139   In margin: 'Gen. 6. & 19'.

preuale vs in multitude. Their number (deare brethren) shal not hurt our innocencie, if that we with vnfeaned heartes turne vnto our God, for the promes of his mercy is not bound vnto the multitude, so that he will not heare but where the greatest parte is godly.[140] No deare brethrene, where soeuer two or thre be gathered in his name, there is he in the middest of them,[141] and againe, whosoeuer incalleth the name of the Lord, he shalbe saued, yea,[142] euen when in Godes displeasure the whole worlde shalbe plagued. And therefore let vs not follow the multitude in euil doing,[143] but let vs declyne from the wayes of their vanitie, and by vnfeaned humiliation of our selues. Let vs purches fauoure before that Gods vengeance brust out lyke a fyre.

The power that we haue to proclame this Fasting, is not of man, but of God, who by the mouth of his Prophet Ezechiell, pronounceth this sentence.[144] If the watcheman se the sworde, or any vther plague comming vpone the land, if he blowe not the trumpet, and plainely warne them to turne to God: and if the sword come & take any away,[145] the wicked shal perishe in their iniquitie: but their blood shalbe requyred from the handes of the watcheman. Now so it is, that God of his mercy hath rased vp amonges vs mo[re] wathemen then one or two, of whose mouthes we can not deny, but we haue hard fearefull threatninges of plagues, to follow vpone this proude contempt of all Godes graces.

And therefore we in the feare of our God. willing to avoyd the vttermoste of the Plagues, haue with one consent concluded this godly exercise to be vsed amonges vs, in signe of our vnfeaned humiliation, which albeit the godles shall mock yet are we assured, that he who ones pronounced this sentence.

The soule that shall not be afflicted that same day,[146] to wit, the day appointed to publict humiliation, shall perishe from amonges his people, yea, euerie soule that shall do any worke that day I shall distroye suche a soule frome the middest of his people. The ceremonie and the certane statute day we knowe to be abolished, at the comming of Christ Iesus, together with the rest of the figurall ceremonies, but the effect thereof shall abyde so long as their abydeth an trew Church vpon the face of the earth, into the which repentance and remission of sinnes are publictly preached. And therefore albeit we haue no corporall punishment, to inflict vpone the contemners of that Godly exercise, yet haue we the spiritual sword, which ones will stricke sorer then any materiall sword can or may.

The Iudgementes and iustice of our God are immutable,[147] he abydeth the same and one God that drowned the world by water,[148] that consumed Sodome and Gomorha,[149] with fyre from heauen,[150] that plagued Pharo, distroyed Ierusalem, and hath executed his fearce iudgementes in all ages, yea, and euen before our eyes. It is the same God (we say) that this day by his faithfull seruandes calleth vs to repentance, whose voces if we contompne, we declare our selues Rebellious to our God,

---

[140] In margin: 'The promes of gods mercy, and deliuerance, is not bounde to the multitude.'
[141] In margin: 'Math. 18.'
[142] In margin: 'Ioel. 2.'
[143] In margin: 'Exod. 23.'
[144] In margin: 'Ezech. 33.'
[145] In margin: 'The power that the Church hath to command publict Fasting.'
[146] In margin: 'Leuit 21.'
[147] In margin: 'Malach. 3.'
[148] In margin: 'Gene. 7.'
[149] In margin: 'Gene. 19.'
[150] In margin: 'Exod. 8. 9. 10. & 14.'

mockers of his threatninges,[151] and suche as sometymes in dispyte cryed,[152] we will walk according to the lust of our owen heartes, and let the counsal of the holy one of Israell cum as it list. &c.

And if so we do, then wo, yea, wo and double damnation vnto vs for then euen as assuredly as God liueth,[153] so assuredly shall the plagues that oure eares haue oft heard, be poured furth vpone vs, euen in the eyes of this same peruerst generation, with whome we contempne God, and before whome we are nether feared nor eshamed, stubburnlye to procead from sinne to contempt. Our hope is better of yow (deare brethrene) that haue professed the Lord Iesus with vs, within this Realme, albeit that this we speake to let yow vnderstand, what Rebellion hath bene in flesh before vs, and how it hath bene punished, that we may learne to stoupe before our God, by vnfeaned repentance, and then we shall be assured, that according to the promes made by the mouth of Ioel. Our God shall leaue vnto vs a benediction, albeit that the vehement fyre of his wrath shall consume the inobedient.

But now least that we shoulde thinke that the obseruation of the ceremonie is yneugh to please god we must vnderstand what thinges must be ioyned with fruetfull Fasting, and what thinges they are that may make our Fasting odious to our God. And first we haue to understand, that Fasting by it selfe considdered, is no suche thing as the Papistes heretofore have ymagined, to wit, that it is a worke meritorious,[154] and a satisfaction for the sinnes before committed, no all they that Faste with that intent, renounceth the merites of Christs death and passion, in so farre as they ascriue to Fasting (whiche is but an exercise vsed by man) that whiche is onely proper to Iesus Christ, which is, that he by offering vp him self ones for all, hath made perfyte for euer,[155] those that shalbe sanctified, we must further vnderstand, that as the Kingdome of God is nether meat nor drink, so is nether Fasting by it self semplie considered.[156] The cause why that Kingdome is granted to the chosen, nether yet eating (moderat we meane) any cause why the reprobate are frustrat thereof. But vnto Fasting there must be somewhat ioyned,[157] if that God shall looke vpone it at any tyme in his fauour. The Prophet Ioel is witnes hereof, who in the persone of God, said vnto suche as he had seueirly threatned, Turne vnto me in your whole heart,[158] in Fasting & murning, in which wordes the holie Ghoste first requyreth the conuersion of the heart vnto God, & thereto ioneth Fasting & murning as witnesses of the sorow that we haue for our former offences, and feare that we haue of his seueir iudgementes, the releif whereof we publictly professe, we can obteane by no vther meanes, but by Gods fre mercie, from whome we haue before declyned. So that the verray exercise of Fasting & the murning,[159] and prayer therewith annexed, do solempnedly protest, that by our Fasting we merite not, for he that still confesseth his offence, and in bitternes of heart cryeth for mercy, doeth not brage of his merites, if the Papistes reply, yet god looketh to the Fasting, and heareth

---

151 In margin: 'Isay. 22.'
152 In margin: 'Iere. 2. 5. 6.'
153 In margin: 'Let Scotland yet be forewairned.'
154 In margin: 'The opinion of Papistical fasting.'
155 In margin: 'Hebr 9. & 10'.
156 In margin: 'Rom. 14.'
157 In margin: 'Fasting by itself is but a dead and improfitible ceremonie'.
158 In margin: 'Ioel. 2.'
159 In margin: 'Let the papist considder'.

the prayers of suche as ryghtly humble them selues before him, we deny not,[160] but thereto we adde, that righly did neuer man humble him self before God, that trusted or glorified in the merites of his owen works, for without Faith it is vnpossible to please God, and faith dependeth vpone the promes of gods fre mercy through Iesus Christ, & not vpone the merites of any workes. The Pharise in braging wes reiected, but the Publican in denying him self,[161] and calling for mercie, wes iustified, not by his workes which he had not, but by grace and mercy, for the which he sobbed. Daniel Fasted, confessed his sinnes, and the sinnes of the people, and thereto he added moste earnest and feruent prayers. But doeth he allege any of them as a cause why God shuld ather be mercyfull to him, or to the people, nay we finde no suche thing, but the plaine contrarie, for thus he concludeth.[162] Now therefore our god heare the supplication and prayer of thy seruand, & showe thy pleasing visage vnto thy Sanctuary, that lyeth waiste for the Lordes saik. O my God giue thy eare that thow maiste heare, and open thyen eyes, that thow maiste see the waist places of the cietie which beareth thy name, for we alledge not our ryghteousnes in our prayers, that we poure furthe before thee: but thy moste abounding mercy. Lord heare, Lord be mercyfull, Lord take head, & helpe, & delay not for thy owen self my God.

We may plainely se whereupon this excellent seruand of God grounded him self to purches Godes fauour, to wit, vpone the Lord, that is vpone the Sauiour and Mediator promised, vpone the moste aboundant mercie of God, and vpone God him selfe, for he vnderstoode what God had promised, aswell by the mouth of Moyses as by the Prophet Isaias saying Beholde that I am, yea, euen I am the Lord, & there is no God but I. I kill and I giue lyfe againe. I giue the wound, and I shall heale.[163] For my owen names saike will I do it, sayeth the Eternall.

Apone these and the lyke promises we say, did all the Sainctes of God in all there extremities, depend and did looke to receaue comferte, without all respect to their owen workes, they dampned the best of their owen workes,[164] & called them nothing but filthynes before God. And therefore yet as of before, we boldely affirme, that the papisticall Fasting wes not onlie vaine (for what Fasting is it? to absteane from fleshe, and to fill the bellie with fishe, wyne, spyce, and [o]ther delicates) but also it wes odious vnto God,[165] and blasphemous to the death of Iesus Christ, for the causes forewritten. And this muche shortely for those thinges that must be ioyned with frutefull fasting.

Now we haue to consider, what thinges may make our Fasting odious, besydes this proude opinion of merite, whereof we haue spoken. It is no dout but that infidelitie maketh all the workes of the reprobate odious before God,[166] yea, euen when that they do the verray workes that God hath commanded, as we may read in Math. 5. 6. and 7. Isai. 1. and 66. &c. And diuers vther places, but because that infidelitie lurketh oft in the heart, and can not well be espyed, but by the bitter and rotten frutes that spring thereof. The Spirite of God hath painted furthe vnto vs in plaine wordes, what vices may make vs and all our workes odious before our God, so that nether will he heare our prayers, nor regarde our Fasting. Salomon sayeth, he that

---

[160]   In margin: 'Trew humiliation dependeth vpone mercy, & not vpone workes.'
[161]   In margin: 'Luc. 18.'
[162]   In margin: 'Daniel. 8.'
[163]   In margin: 'Deut. 32.'
[164]   In margin: 'Esay 64'.
[165]   In margin: 'The Papistes call Fasting, vaine and blasphemus.'
[166]   In margin: 'Infidelitie maketh all the workes of the reprobate odious before God.'

ditteth his eare from the crye of the poore,[167] his prayer shal be abhominable before God. And Isai in the persone of God sayeth. Albeit that ye shall stretche out your handes, and multiplie your prayers, yet will I not heare yow,[168] for your handes are full of blood. But most plainely to our purpose speaketh the same Prophet, saying. The hous of Iacob daylie seaketh me,[169] & they wolde knowe my wayes as a Nation that wrought iustice, and that had not left the iudgement of their God. They ask me iudgementes of iustice (that is they querrell with me) and they desyre that God shall drowe neare. Why haue we fasted (say they) and thou beholdest not? We haue afflicted our soules, and thow misknowest it. The Prophet answereth in the persone of God, and sayeth. Beholde in the day of your Faste, ye will seak your will, and require all your dettes, beholde ye Faste: to strife, and debaite, and to smyte with the fist of wickednes, Ye shall not Faste as they do to daye, to make your voice be heard aboue, that is to oppresse vthers, so that they are compelled to crye vnto God. Is it suche a Faste that I haue chosen? That a man shuld afflict his soule for a day, and to bow downe his head, as a bul rash, and to ly downe in Sackcloth and ashes. Wilt thow call this a Fasting, or an acceptable day vnto the Lord? Is not this the Fasting that I haue chosen, to louse the bondes of wickednes,[170] to take of the heauie burdinges, and to let the oppressed go fre, and that ye break euerie Yock? Is it not to deale thy bread vnto the hongrie? And that thow bring the poore that wandreth vnto thy hous? When thow seest the Nacked, that thow couer him? And hyde not thy self from thy owen fleshe. Then shall thy light break furth as the morning, and thy health shall growe spedelie, thy righteousnes shall go before thee, and the glorie of the Lord shall embrase thee. &c.

In these moste notable sentences, and in suche as follow in the same place, we haue to marck, what thinges may make our Fasting to be rec[eiv]ed of God, what he craueth of suche as Faste frutefullie, and what promes he maketh to such as obey him. This people externallie professed God, they daylie sought his face, by reparing to the Temple, hearing of the Law, and exercising of the Sacrifices, yet did God plague them in mo[re] sortes then one, as in the bookis of the Kinges & Cornickles we may read. In their extremitie they ran (as to them appeared) to the vttermoste refuge, they Fasted, and vnfeanedly humbled their bodies, for that the Prophet meaneth, when that he sayeth, that they Fasted till that their neckes were weakned and made faint as a bull rashe, for verray lack of corporall foode. They layed of their gorgious garmentes, and put on Sackcloth. &c. And yet wer their troubles nothing releued.

And that wes the cause why they querrelled with God, and said.

Why haue we Fasted, and thou hast not sene? &c. And in verray dead to the natural man it wes strange, for god had promised that he wolde conforte his people, whensoeuer they shuld humble them selues before him,[171] notwithstanding their former iniquitie.

In the externall ceremonies, nor in the corporall exercises, there could no fault be espyed. Why then doeth not God heare them? complaine they. God answereth that their outwarde profession wes but Hipocrisie, their Fasting wes but mocking of God,

167   In margin: 'Pro. 21.'
168   In margin: 'Isay. 1.'
169   In margin: 'Isay. 58.'
170   In margin: 'O that Scotland shulde vnderstand & follow.'
171   In margin: 'Deut. 3. 1. Reg. 8.'

and their prayers could do nothing but prouoke him to further displeasure. Because that albeit they reteaned the Name of God, and albeit that they appeared in his Temple, yet had they forsaken bothe his iudgementes, statutes, and holie ordinances. Albeit the bodie stouped, & wes afflicted by Fasting, yet remaned the heart proude and rebellious against God,[172] for they followed their owen corrupted wayes, they oppressed suche as were subiect vnto them, their heauie Yock lay vpone the neckes of suche as could not ridde them selues from their bondage. Amonges them were stryfe, debaite, whisperinges of malice, yea, open contention, and manifest violence, which all were euident declarations of proud heartes, and impenitent Soulles.

And therefore God giueth vnto them open defyance, in the tyme when they think that they seak his peace moste earnestly. And here to ought we this day that professe the Lord Iesus, & haue renounced abhominations of Papistrie within the Realme of Scotland, giue deligent head. For it is not the semple knoweledge of the trueth onelie, nor yet the externall profession of the same, that is acceptable before God. Nay nay deare brethrene,[173] he requireth the frutes of repentance,[174] and they are to declyne from euill, and to do good, as we may read in many places of the Scripture, Think we it a thing aggreable with the nature of the Eternall our God, that he shal receaue vs in fauour, after that we haue offended? And we will not for his saike remit the iniuries that are done to vs. Can we thinke to be at peace with him? When that we stubburnelie will continew in strife amonges our selues. Shal he releiue our greif, bondage, or Yock? And we will not releiue the burdinges that vniustly we lay vpone our brethrene. Shall he bestowe his vndeserued mercie vpone vs? And we can showe no bowels of mercie, to such as we se in miserie before our eyes. Let vs not be deceaued, God can not deny him self, murther, malice, hatrent, crueltie, oppression, stryfe, thift,[175] deceat, iniust dealing, couetousnes, auaritiousnes, and vnmercifulnes vnto the poore, besydes pryde, horedome, adulterie, vantones, and the rest of the workes of the flesh, are so odious before god, that whill that any of them reigneth in the heart of man, he and his whole workes are detestable before God. And therefore if we desyre that Gods fearefull iudgementes shalbe stayed, let vs (that knowe the trueth and say that we professe the same) vnfeanedlie returne vnto our God. Let vs not be inferioures to the King of Niniue, who commanded euerie man to turne from his wicked wayes, and from the iniquitie that wes in his handes. Let vs considder what our God craueth of vs, but especiallie let Earles, Lordes, Barrons, Burgesses, and Artificers considder by what meanes their substances are increassed.

It is not yneugh to iustifie vs before God,[176] that ciuile Lawes can not accuse vs. Nay brethrene, the eyes of our God pearseth deaper, then mannes Law can streache.

The Law of man can not conuict the Earle, the Lord, the Barrone, or Gentilman, for oppressing of the poore labourers of the ground, for his defence is ready.

I may do with my owen as best pleaseth me. The Merchand is iust yneugh in his owen conceat. If before men he can not be conuict of thift and deceat. The Artificer and Craftisman, thinketh him self fre before God, albeit that he nether worke sufficient stuffe, nor yet sell for reasonable price.

---

172 In margin: 'Let euerie man examin his owen conscience.'
173 In margin: 'Psalm. 34.'
174 In margin: '1. Pet. 3'.
175 In margin: 'The workes that may make oure fasting odious.'
176 In margin: 'Christiane iustice craueth more than ciuile Lawes.'

The worlde is euil (sayeth he) and how can men liue, if they do not as vther do. And thus doeth euerie man leane vpone the iniquitie of another, and thinketh him self sufficientlie excused, when that he meitteth Craft with Craft, & repulseth back violence, ether with deceat, or els with open iniurie. Let vs be assured deare brethrene, that these be the sinnes which heretofore haue prouoked God, not onlie to plague,[177] but also to distroy, and vtterlie ouerthrowe stronge Realmes, and flourishing common wealthes.

Now seing that the iustice, and Iudgementes of our God abyde for euer, and that he hath solempnedlie pronounced, that euerie Realme, Nation or Cietie, that sinneth as did Iuda and Ierasalem,[178] shalbe like wise punished. Let that fearefull distruction, that came vpone them, into the whiche after honger and pest, the sworde deuored without discretion,[179] the ryche and poore,[180] the Noble, and those that were of basse degre, the yong, and olde, the Preistes, and Prophetes, yea, the Matrones, & Virgines, eschaped not the day of that sharp visitation. Let their punishment (we say) prouoke vs to repentance, and so no dout, we shall finde fauour in the eyes of our God, albeit that he hath begune to showe vnto vs euident signes of his displeasure,[181] iustlie conceaued against vs. But (as God forbide) if we mocke his Messingers, and dispyse his wordes, till that their be no remeadie as they did. Then can we (whome God hath rased vp to instruct and forewarne yow) do nothing but take witnesse of heauen and earth, yea, and of your owen conscience, that we haue faithfullie instructed yow in the ryght way of God, aswell as concerning his trew worshipping, as in doing of your dewties one to another.

And also that we haue forewarned yow of the plagues to come, firste by our tounges, and now by our pen, for a perpetuall memoriall to the posteritie that shall follow.

Who shall glorifie God, ether for your conuersion, or els for your iust condemnation, and seueire punishementes, if ye continew inobedient.

To prescriue to euerie man his dewtie in particulare, we can not, because we knowe not whereintill euerie man, and euerie estate particularlie offendeth, but we must remit euerie estate, and euerie man in his vocation, to the examination of his owen conscience. And that according as God commandeth in his hole Law, and as Christ Iesus requireth, that suche as shall possesse the Kingdome, with him shall do.

Which is, whatsoeuer (sayeth he) that ye wolde men shulde do vnto yow,[182] do ye the lyke vnto them. By this reule whiche the Author of all equitie, iustice, and policie hath established. Send we the Earles, Lordes, Barrons, and gentilmen, to trye their owen consciences, whether that they wolde be content that they shuld be entreated (if God had made them huseband men, and laubowrers of the ground) as they haue entreated, and presentlie doeth entreat, suche as some tymes had a moderate and resonable life vnder their predecessours.

Whether we say that they wolde be content that their steadinges and malinges should be rased from male to ferme, from one ferme to two, & so going vpward, till that for pouertie, the Ancient laubourers are compelled to leaue the ground in the handes of the Lord. If with this entreatment they wolde be content, we appeale

---

177   In margin: 'Consulte with the 22. Chapter of the Prophet Ezechiell.'
178   In margin: 'Iere. 7.'
179   In margin: '2. Paral. 26.'
180   In margin: '2 Reg. 25.'
181   In margin: '2. Paral. 36'.
182   In margin: 'Math. 7.'

their owen conscience. And if they thinke that they wolde not, then in Godes Name we require them to begin to reforme them selues, and to remember that it is not we, but that it is Christ Iesus that so craueth of them. And vnto the same reule we send Iudges, Lawers, Merchandes, Artificers, and finallie, euen the verray laubourers of the ground them selues That euerie one in his vocation may trye how iustlie, vprightlie, & mercyfullie he dealeth with his Nighboure. And if he finde his conscience accused by the former sentence of our Master, let him cal for grace, that he may not onelie repent for the bypast, but also amend in tymes to cume, and so shall their Fasting, and prayers be acceptable vnto God.

If men think that we require the thing that is vn possible. For what were this els? But to reforme the face of the whole earth? Which neuer wes, nor yet shalbe, till that the righteous King and Iudge appeare, for the restauration of all thinges. We answer, that we speak not to the godles multitude, nether yet to suche as are mockers of Godes Iudgementes, whose portion is in this life, and for whome the fyre of hell (which now they mock) is assuredlie prepared.[183] But we speak to such as haue professed the Lord Iesus with vs, who haue communicated with his blissed Sacramentes, haue renounced Idolatrie, and haue awowed them selues to be new creatures in Iesus Christ, in whome they are ingrafted as liuelie branches,[184] apt to bring furth good frute. Now why it shuld be thought vnpossible, that these men (of what vocation that euer they be) shulde begin to expresse in their liues, that which in worde they haue publictlie professed. We se no good reasone, vnles that we wolde say that it is vnpossible that God shall now work in men of this age, as we read that he hath wrought in men before vs, and that were blasphemie.

Seing that the hand of our God is no more shortned towardes vs,[185] then that it hath bene towardes those that haue past before vs.

At Godes semple commandement Abraham left his Fathers hous & natiue countrie.[186] Moyses preferred the condition of the people of Israell,[187] euen in their greatest afliction, to the ryches and glorie of Pharose Courte. Dauid vpon the vnction of Samuell,[188] did pacientlie abyde the persecution of Saul many yeares. Zacheus at an dennar with Christ Iesus,[189] wes not onelie content to restore whatsoeuer he had before defrauded, but also to giue the half of all his substance to the sustentation of the poore. And the faithfull in the dayes of the Apostles, solde their possessions, and ministrat vnto the indigent.[190] None of these excellent workes craue we of the faithfull in our age, but onely those, without the which the Spirite of Sanctification can not be knowen to be in man, to wit, that euerie man speak the trueth with his brother,[191] that none oppresse nor defraude another in any busynes,[192] that the bowels of mercy may appeare amongs suche as God hath called to his knoweledge, and finally, that we altogether that professe the Lord Iesus, and do abhorre Idolatrie,

---

183   In margin: 'Math. 25.'
184   In margin: 'Ioan. 15.'
185   In margin: 'Isay. 50.'
186   In margin: 'Gene. 12.'
187   In margin: 'Exod. 2.'
188   In margin: '1. Samu. 16.'
189   In margin: 'Luc. 19.'
190   In margin: 'Act. 2.'
191   In margin: 'Ephes. 4.'
192   In margin: '1. Thess. 4.'

abhorre also all kynde of impietie,[193] studying to habound in all good workes, and
to shyne as lyghtes in the middest of this wicked generation.

Which if we do not, we declare no dout that Christ Iesus dwelleth not within vs,
but that we ar they that heare and knowe the will of our Lord but do not the same.
And vnto what curse and malidiction suche persones are subiect, the parable of the
Fegge tre whiche wes threatned to be cut downe, if it brought not furth frute,[194] the
curse giuen to it, vpon the which Christ Iesus being hongrie fand no frute: and his
last sentence against the reprobate, do sufficiently witnes.

In the which we haue to obserue, that the reprobate are adiudged to the fyre,
that neuer shalbe quenched, not onely because they committed iniquitie,[195] but also
because they were not found frutefull in good workes. Let euerie man therefore that
will avoyde plagues temporall and perpetuall, vnfeanedlie studie to accomplishe in
worke, that which in worde, and outwarde profession he doeth awowe, and vpone
suche no dout shall the benediction of God rest, when the manifest contempners,
and cloked Hypocrites shalbe rased from the face of the earth, and shalbe cast in
vttermoste darknes, where there shalbe weaping and gnasheing of teith without end,
whiche shalbe the rewarde of all their wicked workes.

Mo[re] thinges we wolde haue written, suche as the notes vpone the disconfiture
of Iosua at Hay, and of the Israelites fighting against Beniamin, together with the
foolishe opinion of the Papistes, who think them selues oblished to fast fourtie dayes
(whiche they call their Lent) because that Christ Iesus fasted fourtie dayes, immediatlie after his Baptisme. But these we are compelled for this present to pretermit,
be reason that the tyme appoynted to this present exercise of Fasting approcheth so
nye.

If God of his mercy shall please to continew the light of his Euangle amonges vs,
this argument will be enlarged and set furth with greter circumstances frome tyme
to tyme.

[Instructions and order of service]

Now to the ordour, exercise, & abstinence that is to be kept into this publict Fasting.
First it is to be obserued, that the two dayes before expressed, to wit, the last Sonday of
Februarie instant, and the first Sonday of Marche immediatly thereafter following,[196]
ar not appoynted for any Religion of tyme, nether yet that those precised dayes shalbe
obserued eurerie yeare following, but because that shortly thereafter are the Estates
of this Realme appoynted to conuene in Parliament. Therefore the whole Assemblie
thoght those dayes for the present necessitie moste meit, leauing in the libertie of the
Churche, what tyme they will appoynt to that exercise in all tymes to cum.

The Sondayes are appoynted not of superstition,[197] nether yet to bring in any
Schysme within the Church, but because that vpone the Sonday the people (especially that dwell a landwart) may best attend vpone prayer, and the rest of the exercises that ought to be ioyned with publict Fasting.

The abstinence is commanded to be from Setterday at eight houres at nyght, till
Sonday after the exercise at after none that is after 5. houres. And then onely bread

193   In margin: 'Colloss. 3.'
194   In margin: 'Math. 21.& 25.'
195   In margin: 'Everie tre that bringeth not furth good frute, shalbe cutte downe and cast in the fyre.'
196   In margin: 'The reason of the tyme.'
197   In margin: 'The reason of the Sondayes.'

& drinck to be vsed,[198] and that with great sobrietie, that the body crauing necessary food, the soule may be prouoked earnestly to craue of God that which it moste
neadeth, that is mercy for our former vnthanckfulnes, and the assistance of his holy
Spirite in tymes to cum.

Men that will obserue this exercise, may not any of the two dayes vse any kynde
of gammes,[199] but exercise them selues after the publict Assemblies in preuie meditation with their God.

Gorgious apparrell wolde be absteaned fra,[200] during the whole tyme of our
humiliation. Which is from the one Sonday in the morning till the nixt Sonday at
nyght. Albeit that the straitnes of abstinence is to be kept, but the two dayes onely.

We do not bind the conscience of persones that be vnable to the extremitie of
the abstinence,[201] and yet do we exhorte them to vse their libertie (if any they tak)
in secret, least that vthers ather follow their euill exemple, or els iudge them to be
dispysers of so necessarie an exercyse.

The tyme that shalbe spent, aswell before none as after, must be left to the
wisdome of the discrete Ministers, who best can iudge bothe what the auditore
may beare, and what them selues are able to sustene. But because that this exercise is extraordinary, the tyme thereof wolde be somewhat longer then it vsed to
be in the accustomed Assemblies. And yet we wolde not haue it so tedious, that it
shulde be noysome to the people.[202] And therfore we think that thre houres & les,
before noune, and two houres at after noune, shalbe sufficient for the whole exercyse publict. The rest to be spent in preuie meditation, euerie familie aparte.

The Sonday preceading the last Sonday of February as before is said, shall euerie
minister giue aduertisement to his flocke, of such thinges as are to be done the nixt
Sonday following, and of the causes of the same, with suche exhortation as God
shall put into their mouthes, to make the people to embrase the iust commandement
of the Churche with more glaide myndes.

In townes we think expedient that the exercise of the doctrine begine vpone the
Setterday at after noune,[203] immediatly preceading the first Sonday of abstinence,
that the people may be the better prepared Religiously to vse the obseruations of
the nixt day. But in landwart we think good that the doctrine begine the Sonstay
before. The argument of the Sermond and exhortation to be taken from some proper
place of the Prophetes,[204] as of Ioel the first, where he sayeth.[205] Sanctifie a Faste,
appoynt the Assemble. &c. Or of Ionas the thride, where Ionas cryed, and yet fourtie
dayes,[206] and Niniue shal be distroyed. &c. Or of Ieremia the seiuent. Where that
he sayeth, Heare the worde of the Lord all Iuda, and ye that enter in by these gates.
&c. Or of the threttene of Lucas,[207] vpone the declaration of them that shewe to
oure Master the crueltie of Pylate, and vpone his answer. Or vpone any vther proper
place within ye Scripture, that entreteth of repentance, of publict humiliation, of the

---

[198] In margin: 'The faste time.'
[199] In margin: 'No gammes may be vsed vpone the dayes of abstinence.'
[200] In margin: 'Gorgious apparel is to be left.'
[201] In margin: 'The seicke and weake are not bound to this exercyse.'
[202] In margin: 'what houres before none & what after none.'
[203] In margin: 'In townes the doctrine shall begine vpone the Setterday.'
[204] In margin: 'Places proper for the first sermon of Fasting.'
[205] In margin: 'Ioel. 1.'
[206] In margin: 'Ionas. 3.'
[207] In margin: 'Luc. 13.'

causes, and of the frutes of the same. This ended, as it were for preparation, the beginning shalbe vpone Sonday, from the Law of God, because that all that offendeth Gods Maiestie, proceadeth from the transgression thereof, and therefore after a shorte prayer, That God will please to make his holy word to fructifie amonges vs, this confession shalbe made.

The Confession that shal go before the reading of the Law, and before euerie exercyse.

It is of thy mercy o Lord, and not of our merites, that it hath pleased thee to showe thy self vnto the worlde, euer from the beginning, & vnto vs now in this last and moste corrupt age, yea, Lord we further confesse, that neither Law, nor Euangle, can profite vs to Saluation, except that thow of thy meare grace worke into vs abufe all power that is in this oure nature. For albeit thow teache, we shall remaine ignorant, albeit thow threaten, we shal contempne.[208] And albeit thow promes mercy & grace,[209] yet shall we dispaire and remaine in infidelitie: Onles that thow creat in vs new heartes, write thy Law into the same,[210] and seale into vs remission of our sinnes, and the sense and fealing of thy fatherlie mercy, by the power of thy holie Spirite. To the originall world thow spak by Noha.[211] To Pharo and his people, by thy seruand Moyses.[212] To all Israell by the fearfull Trumpet of thy Law.[213] To the Cietie of Ierusalem, by thy owen wisdome, our Lord Iesus Christ.[214] And to ye multitude, aswel of Iewes as Gentiles, by the preaching of thy holy Apostles.[215] But who gaue obedience? Who trembled, and constantly feared thy hote displeasure? Who did rightly acknowledge the tyme of their visitation? And who did embrase and kepe to the end, thy fatherly promises?

Onely they o Lord, to whome thy Spirite wes the inwarde teacher, whose heartes thow opened,[216] & from whome thow remoued Rebellion and infidelitie, the rest were externally called, but obeyed not, they heard aswel mercy offered, as threatninges pronounsed, but nether with the one nor with the vther were they affectually moued. We acknowledge o Lord that the same corruption lurcketh in vs, that budded furth in them to their distruction, and iust condemnation. And therefore we moste humbly beseak thee o Father of mercies, for Christ Iesus thy sones sake, that as thow hast caused the lyght of thy worde clearely to shyne amongs vs, and as thow hast plainely instructed vs by the external ministerie, in the ryght way of Saluation. So it will please thee inwardly to moue our dulle heartes, and by the power of thy holy Spirite, that thow will write and seale into them that holy fear and reuerence, which thow crauest of thy chosen childrene, and that faithfull obedience to thy holie will, together with the fealing and sence that our sinnes are fully purged & frely remitted by that only one Sacrifice, whiche onely by itself is acceptable vnto thee, to wit, the obedience, death, & mediation of thy onely Sone our Souerane Lord, onely Pastor[,]

---

208 In margin: 'Hebe. 8.'
209 In margin: 'Psal. 51.'
210 In margin: 'Iere. 31.'
211 In margin: 'Gene. 6.'
212 In margin: 'Exod. 2.3.4'.
213 In margin: 'Exod. 20.'
214 In margin: 'Mat. 20 &c. Ioan. 12.'
215 In margin: 'Act. 3.4.14 & 16.'
216 In margin: 'Ioan. 6.'

Mediator, and hie priest, our Lord Iesus Christ. To whome with thee, and with the holy Ghoste, be all honour and glore, worlde without end.

This Confession ended, the Minister or Reider shall distinctlie read the 27. and 28. of Deuteronomion, which ended, the Minister shall wishe euerie man to discend secretly into him self, to examine his owen concience, whereinto he findeth him selfe giltie before God. The Minister him self with the people shall prostrate them selues, & remaine in priuate meditation a reasonable space, as the quarter of an houre or more. Thereafter shal the Minister exhorte the people to confesse with him their sinnes and offences as followeth.

Iust and ryghteous art thow o Lord God, Father euerlasting, holy is thy Law, and moste iust are thy iudgementes, yea, euen when thow doest punishe in greatest seueritie, we do confesse as the treuth is, that we haue transgressed thy whole Law, and haue offended thy godly Maiestie, in breaking and violating euerie precept of the same. And so moste iustly may thow poure furth vpone vs all plagues that are threatned: and that we finde powred furth vpone the disobedient at any tyme from the beginning. And so muche the rather o Lord, because that so long we haue bene called, by thy holie worde to vnfeaned repentance, & newnes of lyfe: and yet haue we still remaned in our former Rebellion, and therefore if thow wilt enter in iudgement with vs, we can nether eschape confusion in this lyfe, nor iust condempnation in the lyfe to cum. But Lord thy mercy is without measure, and the treuth of thy promises abydeth for euer. Vnworthy are we that thow shuldest looke vpone vs, but Lord thow hast promised that thow wilt show mercy to the moste grieuous offenders, whensoeuer that they repent, And further, thow by the mouth of thy deare Sone our Lord Iesus Christ, hast promised that thow wilt giue thy holy Spirite to suche as humblie cal vnto thee. In boldnes of the whiche promes, we moste humbly beseak thee o Father of mercies, that it wold please thy godly Maiestie, to worke into our stubburne heartes, an vnfeaned dolour for our former offences, with some sense and fealing of thy grace and mercy, together with an earnest desyre of Iustice and righteousnes, in the which we are bound continually to walk. But because that nether we nor our prayers can stand before thee, be reason of that imperfectione which still remaneth in this oure corrupted nature. We fle to the obedience and perfite Iustice of Iesus Christ, our onely Mediator, in whome, and by whome, we call not onely for remission of our sinnes, and for assistance of thy holy Spirite, but also for all thinges that thy goldly wisdome knoweth to be expedient for vs, and for thy Church vniuersall. Praying as he hath taught vs saying.

   Our Father that art. &c.

This ended, the Minister shall read the Text whereupone he will ground his Sermon.

First he shal expone the dignitie and equitie of Gods law.[217] Secondly, the plagues and punishmentes that ensew the contempt thereof, together with the blessinges promised to the obedient obseruers of it. Thridly, he sall teache Christ Iesus to be the end and perfection of the Law,[218] who hath perfitely accomplished that whiche wes impossible to the Law to do.

---

[217] In margin: 'The heades of the first sermone.'
[218] In margin: 'Rom. 3.'

And so shall he exhorte euerie man to vnfeaned repentance, to steadfast faith in Christ Iesus, and to showe frutes of the same.

The Sermone ended, the commone prayer shalbe vsed that is conteaned in the Psalme booke, the 46. page thereof, beginning thus. God almyghtie and heauenly Father &c. Which ended, the 51. Psalme shalbe soung whole, & so with the benediction, the Assemble is to be demitted for that exercise.

[The prayer specified is in the Book of Common Order (1565; STC 16577a, first part, 46–53)]

At after noune.

Efter inuocation of Godes Name publictly by the Minister, and secretly by euery man for a reasonable space. The Minister may take the argument of his Sermone from the beginning of 119. Psalme, where the deligent Reader shall obserue the properties & conditions of suche, as in whose heartes God writeth his Law. Or if that be thought ouer hard, then may ye take the Text of Iohne.

God is lyght, and into him there is no darcknes,[219] if we say we haue fellowshipe with him. &c. The prayer is referred vnto the Minister, the 6. Psalme shalbe soung.

The benediction and exhortation, to call to mynde wherefore that exercise is vsed, being ended. The publict exercise shalbe put to end for that day.

Albeit that to landwart the people can not well conuene euerie day betuix the two Sondayes yet in Broughes & Townes we think they ought to conuene, an hour before none, and an houre & more at after none. The houre before none, to be the houre accustomed to the commone prayers. The houre at after none to be at 3. houres or after.

The exercise of the whole weke.

The beginning euer to be with Confession of our sinnes, and imploring of Godes graces. Then certane Psalmes, and certane Histories to be distinctly red, exhortation to be conceaued thereupon, and prayers lyke wise, as God shall instruct and inspyre the Minister or Reader.

[Monday forenoon: Ps. 2, 3, 10; Judg. 2
Monday afternoon: Ps. 12, 15, 17; Judg. 16
Tuesday forenoon: Ps. 25, 28; Judg. 7
Tuesday afternoon: Ps. 36, 40; Judg. 4
Wednesday forenoon: Ps. 14, 55; Judg. 19
Wednesday afternoon: Ps. 44, 56; Judg. 20
Thursday forenoon: Ps. 49, 57; Esther 3–4
Thursday afternoon: Psalm 37; Esther 5–7
Friday forenoon: Ps. 59, 61, 64; 2 Chron. 20
Friday afternoon: Psalm 69; Isa. 36
Saturday forenoon: Ps. 68, 70; Isa. 37
Saturday afternoon: Ps. 74, 77; Ezra 9–10]

---

219   In margin: '1. Ioan. 1.'

Sonday the last day of this publict exercise for this tyme, before none shalbe vsed in all thinges as the former Sonday, except that the 26. of Leuiticus may be red for the 28. of Deuteronomie, and for the prayer shal be vsed that which is to be found in the Psalme book, the 165. page, beginning. Eternall and euerlasting. &c.

[The prayer specified is in the Book of Common Order (1565; STC 16577a, third part, 165–74)]

[Sunday afternoon: Ps. 78; Dan. 9]

The exhortation and prayers ended, for the conclusion shalbe distinctly red the 80. Psal. And so with exhortation to euery man to considder to what end the whole exercise tendeth. With benediction the Assemblie shalbe demitted.

The exhortations and prayers of euerie seuerall exercise, we haue remitted to be gathered by the discrete Ministers, for tyme preassed vs so, that we coulde not frame them in suche ordour as was conuenient, nether yet thought we it so expedient to pen, prayers vnto men, as to teache them with what heart, and affection, and for what causes we shulde pray in this great calamitie, appearing shortlie to ouerwhelme this whole Realm, vnles god of his great mercy abufe mannes expectation finde the remeady. Before whome it is that we haue (and presently do) prostrate our selues, for obteaning of those thinges, without whiche the lyght of his Euangle, can not long continew with vs. And therfore yet ones againe we exhorte, & by the power committed vnto vs by God, charge all that professe the Lord Iesus, and the sinceritie of his Euangle, within this Realme, that euen as they loue the quyetnes of their common wealth, the continuance of Christ Iesus his holy Euangle within the same, and their owen Saluation, together with the Saluation of their posteritie, that vnfeanedly they prostrate them selues before the Throne of Godes Maiestie, & in bitternes of heart pray with vs.

Aryse o Lord, and let thyne ennimies be confounded. Let them fle from thy presence, that hate thy godly name. Let the grones of thy afflicted enter in before thee. And preserue thow by thy owen power suche as be appoynted to death. Let not thy ennimies thus triumph to the end: but let them vnderstand that against thee they fight. Preserue the wyne which thy ryght hand hath planted. Oppone thy power to the power of that Romaine Antichrist, and let the glorie of thyne annoynted Iesus Christ our Lord shyne before all Nations. So be it.

Hasten Lord and tary not.

LETTERS

The Svper Intendentes, Ministers, and Commissioners of Kirkes, Reformed within the Realme of Scotland, Assembled in Edinburgh the 25. day of December. 1565. To the Ministers of Iesus Christ, within the same Realme, desyre grace and peace from God the Father of our Lord Iesus Christ, with the perpetuall conforte of the holy Spirite.

    The present miserie, and greater troubles appearing shortly to follow, craue (deare brethrene) that euerie one of vs exhorte and admonishe another, that we recule not back in the beginning of this battel, which is cum vpon vs, vnlooked for of many. And therefore it is that we your brethrene, partakers with yow of the afflictions of Iesus Christ, vnderstanding the extremitie, wherein the whole Ministers within this Realme now stand, for sake of reasonable prouision, to them selues and poore families. Haue thought expedient to communicate with yow our myndes by this our letter. Which is, that firste we shall deligently marke those wordes of the Apostle saying, No man shalbe crouned, onles he striue laughfully,[220] and also that fearefull sentence of our Master Iesus Christ saying. No man putting his hand to the plough, and looking backe,[221] is apt to the Kingdome of God. We haue ones professed our selues warriours against Sathan, and laubourers in the husbandrie of the Lord our God, who of his mercy hathe opened oure mouthes to exhorte vthers to contempe this wicked worlde, and to contend to enter into that heauenly Ierusalem. God hath honored vs so, that men hath iudged vs the Messingers of the euerlasting, by vs hath he disclosed Idolatrie, by vs are the wicked of the worlde rebuked, and by vs hath our God comforted the consciences of many that were oppressed with ignorance and impietie. Consider then deare brethrene what sclander & offence shall we giue to the weak? What occasion of reioysing shall the ennimies haue? And to what ignominie shall we expone the glorious Euangle of Iesus Christ? If that we for any accasion shall desist and cease from publict preaching of the same.

We that admonishe yow are not ignorant, nether yet altogether without experience, how vehement a dart pouertie is, & what troublesome cogitations it is able to rase, yea, euen in men of greatest constancie. But yet deare brethrene, we ought earnestlie to considder with what conditiones we are entered, into this moste honorable vocation, and what we chiefly seake in the preaching of the Euangle. For if we lay before vs vther conditions, then Iesus Christ laide before his Apostles,[222] when he send them furth firste to preache the glaide tydinges of his Kingdome, & if we seake and ymagine to our selues, better entreatment of this wicked generation, then we find the derrest seruands of God haue gotten in the worlde, we ether deceaue our selues, or els declaire vs not to be trew successours of those, whose doctrine we propone to the people. They were send furth as sheape, amongs the middest of Wolfes, to them it wes pronounced. That they shuld be hated, they shuld be mocked, men shuld cursse and persecute them for the Testimonie of the treuth,[223] which threatnings we find not to haue bene vaine, but to haue fallen vpone the chiefest members of Iesus Christ, as the Actes of the Apostles beare testimonie. And think we that the same Euangle which they preached, can haue ane vther successe in oure Ministerie, then it had in theires? In giftes we muste confesse oure selues farre Inferioure to those lyghtes of the worlde, in deligence and painefull trauell we can not be compared, and yet we look to be partakers of the Kingdome, which god hath prepared for such as paciently abyde the gaine comming of the Lord Iesus. And shall we in nothing communicate with them? They were some tymes whipped, some tymes stoned, oft cast in preason, and the blood of many sealed vp their doctrine.

And shall we for pouertie leaue the flock of Iesus Christ, before that it vtterly refuse vs? God forbid deare brethrene, for what shall discerne vs from the Mercenaries and Hyrelings? If our constancie in aduersitie shal not do it The Hyrelings in

---

220   In margin: '2. Timet. 2.'
221   In margin: 'Luc. 9.'
222   In margin: 'Math. 10.'
223   In margin: 'Ioan. 16.'

tyme of quiet[n]es, teache the treuth as we do, in giftes and vtterance they commonlie excead vs, in lyfe and conuersation, they may for a season be irreprehensible. What is it then that maketh them Hyrelings? Our master & Sauiour Iesus Christ answereth saying. The mercenarie seeth the Wolfe comming, and fleeth, because he is a Mercenarie.[224] Then the leauing of the flock, when Wolfes come to inuade it, proueth suche as were holden Pastours, to be nothing but Hyrelings, we deny not, but if in one Cietie we be persecuted, we may laughfully flee vnto another, yea, if one Realme cast vs furth, we may receaue the benefite of another. But euer still with this condition, that we cast not from vs the profession that publictly we haue made, nether yet that we cease to fead the flock of Iesus Christ, and to gainestand the teachers of fals doctrine, so farre furth as in vs lyeth. But hereinto standeth the question, whether may we whome God hath called to this honour, that he hath made vs Ambassadoures of his good will, vnto this vnthankfull generation, desist frome our vocations? Because that we can not be prouided of Reasonable liuinges, as God hath Commanded, and our trauelles deserue.

The Spirite of God vniformlie through the Scriptures wil answer vs. That Helias wes send to be fed by the Rauens.[225] Elizeus and his Scollers were compelled to gather Herbes to make pottage.[226] Paule did oft liue by the worke of his owen handes, but we neuer finde that they receaued dimission from their vocations. Seing then dear brethrene, that God as yet hathe tempted none of vs with the extremitie that we finde vthers before vs, haue suffered and ouercome, let vs be ashamed so suddenly to faint, euen in the brunt of the battell The price of Christ Iesus his death and passion is committed to our Charge, the eyes of men are bent vpon vs, and we must answer before that Iudge, who will not admit euerie excuse that pleaseth vs, but will Iudge vpryghtly, as in his worde he hath before pronounced. Let vs therefore stand fast, not onely in the treuth, but also in defence and aduancing of the same, which we can not do, if we cease from our publict vocations. Let vs deare brethren stand fast in the fyre, & commit our bodies to the care of him who feadeth the foules of the aire, and hath promysed that he knoweth whereof we haue need. He preserued vs in the darkness of our Mothers bosome, he prouyded our foode in their breastes, and instructed vs to vse the same, when we knew him not, he hath nourished vs in the tyme of blyndnes and of impietie, and will he now dispyse vs? When we call vpone him, and preache the glorious gospell of his deare Sone our Lord Iesus. Nay deare brethrene, he nether will nor can, vnles that infidelitie cut vs of from his mercyfull prouidence. Let vs considder that the whole earth is the Lordes, and all the falnes of the same, that he is able to moue the heartes of men, as best pleaseth him. He is able to blisse and multiplie thinges that are nothing in the eyes of carnall men.[227] It is but pouertie that as yet doeth threaten vs, which if we be not able to contempne: how shall we abyde the furie and terroure of death? Which many thousandes before vs haue suffered for the testimonie of the same treuth, which we professe and teache, and dispysed all worldly redemption, as the Apostle speaketh.[228] This is but a gentill tryall which our Father taketh of our obedience, which if we willingly offer vnto him, the bowels of his Fatherly compassion, will rather cause the heauens, yea, the

---

[224]   In margin: 'Ioan. 10.'
[225]   In margin: '1. Reg. 17.'
[226]   In margin: '2. Reg. 4.'
[227]   In margin: '2. Reg. 4. Ioan. 6. Math. 14.'
[228]   In margin: 'Heb. 11.'

Rockes & Riuers to Minister vnto vs thinges necessarie to the bodie, then that he shall suffer vs to perishe, if we dedicate our whole liues vnto him. Let vs be frequent in reading (which allace ouer many dispise) earnest in prayer, deligent in watcheing ouer the flock, committed to our charge, and let our sobrietie and temperate lyfe, eshame the wicked, and be exemple to the godly. And then there is no dout, but the Eternall our God shall remeady this extremitie, he shall confound our ennimies, and shall shortly conuert our teares & murning, in ioy and myrth, to the glorie of his owen Name, and to the conforte of the posteritie to cum. Through the merites and intercession of Iesus Christ oure Lord, whose holy Spirite conforte yow and vs to the end. Of Edinburgh in our generall Assemblie, the last Session thereof. ANNO. 1565.

To the faithfull Reader.

Albeit that nether suche as did firste command, nether yet those that haue trauelled to set furthe this ordour of publict Fasting, and admonitions to the Ministers, haue impyre aboue the bodies of suche as vnto whome they wryte: yet haue they no dout power from God to rebuke sinne, & to craue repentance, especially of suche as God hath called to his knowledge, in the middest of this moste obstinate and corrupt generation. And therefore in the bowels of Iesus Christ, we requyre all men to ponder and wey, what is the estate of this Realme at this present, and if they se not clearely iust causes why that God shoulde punishe in his hote displeasure, then we can be content that men liue at their owen quyetnes. But if that iustice be vniuersally oppressed, & iniquitie so menteaned, that it ouerfloweth this whole realme, then dare we be bolde to cry with the Prophet Ezechiell,[229] that suche as murne not for the abhominations that now habound, shall perishe in the iniquitie of this moste stubburne generation. Whill that suche as semplie obey God, speaking by his moste dispysed Ministers, shall avoyde vengeance bothe temporall and eternall, we dout not but suche as think them selues more wyse, then they declaire them selues godly, shal ask wherefore shall we be subiect to the ordinances of men? Haue we not the Spirite of God to teache vs in all thinges? We answer, that if we as men command any thing, let it not be obeyed, but if we in this age command the same things which God in the ages before vs hath commanded by his seruands, let them beware, least that in dispysing of vs, they dispyse not also the Eternall God: whose holie worde is to vs assurance of euerie precept that we haue giuen. And further, we feare not to say that suche as murne not with Iacob in his affliction, shal not reioyse with him in the day of his deliuerance, but they shalbe compelled to murne and quaike with Pharo without end.

Many thinges we haue omitted to further oportunitie, and better occasion. God grant that things semplie spoken, & vprightly ment, may be interpret according to the reule of charitie, and obedientlie followed as God requyreth.

Iohne Knox at the command of the publict Assemblie.

---

229 In margin: 'Ezech. 9.'

1566–E   Services during the Ottoman invasion of Hungary

Wednesdays, Fridays and Sundays, July–August 1566 (England and Wales)

On 1 May 1566, Süleyman I renewed his campaign against the Habsburgs, leading a force of 200,000 towards Vienna. Strype attributed the initiative for these services to Parker, but there is no corroborating evidence. While the services were most evidently ordered because the Ottoman campaign once again threatened the safety of Europe and Christendom, it may be significant that the campaign coincided with the (ultimately unsuccessful) marriage negotiations between Queen Elizabeth and the Habsburg archduke of Austria, Charles: one of the prayers in the services praised the emperor, Charles's older brother. On 22 July, Parker sent a form to Cecil and Elizabeth for their approval and suggested that 'som pray^r of thankes be added, or ellys inserted in the preface som short advertisement to gyve god thankes for our so long restful peace'. This probably accounts for the long prayer in the evening service, preceded by the first inclusion of specific instructions in a special form of prayer on how the BCP service of evening prayer was to be modified. Otherwise, the form followed the format used during the outbreak of plague in 1563 (see 1563–E). Two extant copies have interesting additions. A prayer has been handwritten at the end of the copy in Lambeth Palace Library; this could either have been composed by a minister or it could be an official thanksgiving prayer (for which there is no extant order), circulated later as a printed broadside and then copied into the form (see appendix at the end of this entry). The British Library's copy of the form has 'Turk' and 'Turkes' changed to 'pope' and 'papistes' by hand in the margin, suggesting that this particular copy may have been re-used to pray against catholics.

Order: none found.
Form of prayer: *A fourme to be vsed in common prayer euery Sunday, Wednesday, and Fryday, through the whole realme: to excite and stirre all godly people to pray vnto God for the preseruation of those Christians and their countreys, that are nowe inuaded by the Turke in Hungary or elswhere. Set foorth by the most reuerende father in God, Mathewe archbyshop of Canterbury, by the aucthoritie of the queenes maiestie* ([22] pp.; STC 16510)*; manuscript prayer: LPL, G199 5.04, sig. Civ^v.
Additional sources: Parker to Cecil, 22 July 1566, SP12/40/34; Strype, *Parker*, I, 462–4.

FORM OF PRAYER

THE PREFACE
Where as the Turkes the last yere moste fiercely assaylyng the Isle of *Malta* with a great armie and nauye, by the grace and assistaunce of almightie God, (for the whiche we with other Christians at that tyme by our hartie prayers made moste humble sute) were from thence repelled and dryuen, with theyr great losse, shame, and confusion: they beyng inflamed with malice and desyre of vengeaunce, do nowe by lande inuade the kyngdome of Hungary (whiche hath of long tyme ben as a moste strong wall and defence to all Christendome) farre more terribly and dreadfully, and with greater force and violence, then they dyd eyther the last yere, or at any tyme within the remembraunce of man: It is our partes, whiche for distaunce of place, can not succour them with temporall ayde of men, to assist them at the least with spirituall ayde, that is to say, *[as 1565–E1:* wyth earnest, hearty, and feruent prayer … deliuer christians*]* professynge his holy name, & to geue sufficient myght and power to the Emperours exellent Maiestie, as Gods principall minister, to represse the rage *[as 1565–E1:* and violence … Chryst our onelye sauiour, and*]* all Christianitie. And for so much as if

the Infidels, who haue already a great part of that most goodly and strong kyngdome in theyr possession, shoulde preuayle wholly agaynst the same (whiche God forbyd) all the rest of Christendom should lye as it were naked and open to the incursions and inuasions of the sayde sauage and moste cruell enemyes the Turkes, to the moste dreadfull daunger of whole Christendome, all diligence, hartinesse, and feruencie is so muche the more now to be vsed in our prayers for Gods ayde, howe farre greater the daunger and peryll is nowe, then before it was. And although it is euery Christian mans duetie *[as 1563–E:* of his own devotion … ordered and appoynted as foloweth*]*.

Fyrst that al Parsons and Curates shall exhort theyr paryshyoners to endeuour them selues to come vnto the Church, with as many of their famyly, as maye be spared from theyr necessary business: And they to resort thyther, not only vppon Sundayes and holydayes, but also vpon Wednesdayes and Frydayes, duryng this daungerous & peryllous tyme: exhortyng them there reuerently & godly to behaue them selues, and with penitent myndes kneelyng on theyr knees to lyft vp theyr hartes, and pray to the mercyfull God to tourne from vs, and all Christendome, those plagues & punyshmentes: whiche we and they through oure vnthankfulnesse and sinnefull liues haue deserued.

Secondly, that the sayde Parsons and Curates shall then distinctly and playnely reade the generall confession appoynted in the booke of Seruice, with the residue of the Mornyng prayer vnto the first Lesson.

Then for the fyrst Lesson shalbe read one of the Chapters hereafter folowyng, or so muche thereof as is appoynted.

[Exod. 14; Exod. 17:8–15; Josh. 10:1–27; Judg. 7; 1 Sam. 17; 2 Kgs. 7; 2 Kgs. 19; 2 Chr. 20:1–30; Acts 12]

After that in stead of *Te Deum Laudamus*, that is to say: We prayse thee O God: shalbe saide the. li. Psalme: Haue mercy vpon me O God &c.

Then immediatly after, vpon Wednesdayes and Frydayes, shalbe sayde the Crede. I beleue in God &c. And after that the accustomed prayers folowyng, vnto the ende of the Mornyng prayer. And vpon Sundayes, the seconde Lesson shalbe read, as they are ordinarily appoynted, with the rest of the Mornyng prayer.

That done, the Letanie shalbe sayde in the myddes of the people, vnto the ende of the Collect in the same Letany, which begynneth with these wordes: *We humbly beseche thee O father. &c.* And then shall folowe one of these Psalmes in theyr order to be sayde of the Minister accordyng to the order of the dayes, with the aunswere of the people.

Heare our prayer O Lord, consider our desire: harken vnto vs for thy trueth & righteousnes sake. (Ps. 144) [144:1]

O harken then to the voyce of our callyng, our kyng and our God: for vnto thee wyll we make our prayer. (Ps. 5) [5:2]

O God, the Heathen are come into thine inheritaunce: thine aduersaries roare in the middes of thy congregations, & set vp theyr banners for tokens. (Ps. 79, 74) [79:1 & 74:5]

[then nine verses as 1565–E1: They haue set fyre … for they names sake. (Ps. 79)]

Wherefore doe the Heathen say: where is now their God? (Ps. 79) [79:10]

Make haste that thou mayest vtterly destroy euery enemie: whiche hath done euyll in thy sanctuarie. (Ps. 74) [74:4]

Aryse O GOD: mayntayne thyne owne cause: remember how the wicked man blasphemeth thee dayly. (Ps. 74) [74:23]

Powre out thyne indignation vppon the Heathen, that haue not knowen thee: and vppon the kyngdomes, that haue not called vppon thy name. (Ps. 79) [79:6]

O let the vengeaunce of thy seruauntes bloud that is shedde: be openly shewed vpon the Heathen in our syght. (Ps. 35) [79:11]

Deliver us from our enemyes, O God: defende vs from them that ryse vp agaynst vs. (Ps. 59) [59:1]

Lette them be confounded and put to shame: let them be tourned backe and brought to confusion that imagyne mischiefe against vs. (Ps. 79) [35:4]

So we that be thy people, and sheepe of thy pasture shal geue thee thankes for euer: and wyll alwaye be shewyng foorth thy prayse from generation to generation. (Ps. 79) [79:14]

Glory be to the father, and to the sonne, and to the holy ghost.

As it was in the begynnyng, is nowe, and euer shalbe, worlde without ende. Amen

Or this Psalme.

The Heathen do furiously rage together, and the Kynges of the earth stand vp, and rulers take councell together: agaynst the Lorde and agaynst his annoynted. (Ps. 2) [2:1 & 2]

The vngodly bende theyr bowes, & make redy theyr arrowes within the quyuer: that they may shoote at those that call vpon the name of the Lorde. (Ps. 11) [Ps. 11:2]

They smite downe thy people, O Lorde: and trouble thyne heritage. (Ps. 94) [94:5]

Lorde howe are they encreased that trouble vs? many are they that ryse agaynst vs. (Ps. 3) [3:1]

Many one ther be, that say of our soules: there is no helpe for them in their God. (Ps. 3) [3:2]

The vngodly are so proude, that they care not for God: neyther is God in al their thoughtes, nor his iudgementes in theyr sight. (Ps. 10) [10:4 & 5]

They haue sayde in theyr hartes tushe God hath forgotten: he hideth awaye his face, and he wyll neuer see it. (Ps. 10) [10:6]

For thy names sake, O Lorde, be mercyfull vnto our sinnes: for they are great. (Ps. 25) [25:10]

Turne thee vnto vs & haue mercye vpon v[s]: for we are desolate & in great misery. (Ps. 25) [25:15]

Stande not so farre of, O Lorde: neyther hyde thy face in the nedefull tyme of trouble. (Ps. 10) [10:1]

Harken vnto our voyce O Lorde, nowe when we crye vnto thee: aryse O Lorde God, and lyft vp thyne hande, and forget not thy people. (Ps. 27) [27:8 & 10:13]

Wherfore shoulde the wycked blaspheme God? whyle he doth say in his hart, tushe, thou God carest not for it. (Ps. 10) [10:14]

O take the matter into thy hande: thy people commit them selues vnto thee, for thou art their helper in their distresse. (Ps. 10) [10:16]

Breake thou the power of the wicked and malicious: smyte all our enemies vpon the cheeke bone, and breake the teeth of the vngodly. (Ps. 10, 3) [10:17, 3:7]

Rayne snares, fyre and brimstone, storme and tempest vpon them: and let this be theyr portion to drynke. (Ps. 11) [11:7]

Recompence thou theyr wickednesse, & destroy them in their owne malice: yea, the Lord our God shall destroy them, and deliuer vs. (Ps. 94) [94:23]

And we shal geue thankes vnto the Lord accordyng to his great mercyes: & wyll praise the name of the lord the most high. (Ps. 7) [7:18]

We wyll declare thy name vnto our brethren: in the myddes of the congregation wyll we prayse thee, and magnifie thy saluation worlde without ende. (Ps. 22) [22:22]

Glory be to the father &c.

As it was in the begynnyng &c.

Or this.

O Lord many dogges are come about vs: and the councell of the wicked layeth siege agaynst vs. (Ps. 22) [22:16]

Many Oxen do compasse vs: fat bulles of Basan close vs in on euery syde. (Ps. 22) [22:12]

They gape vpon vs with their mouthes: as it were rampyng & roaryng Lyons. (Ps. 22) [22:13]

Our enemyes are dayly in hande to swallowe vs vp: for they be exceedyng many that fight agaynst vs, O thou most hygh. (Ps. 56) [56:2]

O remember not the sinnes and offences of our youth and tymes past: but accordyng to thy mercy thynke vppon vs, O Lorde, for thy goodnes. (Ps. 25) [25:6]

For thou, O Lorde, art our defender: thou art our health, and our saluation. (Ps. 3) [3:3]

O Lord our God in thee haue we put our trust: saue vs from all them that persecute vs, and deliuer vs. (Ps. 7) [7:1]

Lest they deuour our soules like Lions, & teare them in peeces: whyles there is none to helpe. (Ps. 7) [7:2]

Saue vs from these Lyons mouthes: & from among the hornes of the Unicornes. (Ps. 22) [22:21]

O delyuer not the soule of thy turtle doue vnto the multitude of the enemyes: and forget not thy poore congregation for euer. (Ps. 74) [74: 20]

And our prayses shalbe of thee in the great congregation: our vowes wyll we perfourme in the syght of them that feare thee. (Ps. 22) [22:25]

And all the endes of the worlde shall remember them selues, and be turned vnto the Lorde: and all the kynredes of the nations shall worshyp before hym. (Ps. 22) [22:27]

Glory be to the father. &c.

As it were in the begynnyng. &c.

After the Psalme, the prayer folowyng shalbe sayde by the Minister alone, with a hygh voyce. At saying whereof, the people shall deuoutly geue eare, and shall both with mynde and speache to them selues assent to the same prayer.

The prayer

Almyghtie and euerlyuyng GOD our heauenly father *[as 1565–E1:* we thy disobedyent and rebellious chyldren ... our onelye sauior and redemer.*]* Wherfore awake O Lorde our God and heauenly father, and with thy fatherly and mercyfull countenaunce loke vpon vs thy chyldren, and all such Christians, as are now by those most cruell enemies inuaded and assaulted, ouerthrowe and destroye thyne and our enemyes, sanctifie thy blessed name amonge vs *[as 1565–E1:* whych they blaspheme ... all thy afflicted Christians*]* in this and all other inuasions of these infidels, & geue to the Emperour thy seruaunt, and all the Christian army now assembled with hym, thy comfortable myght and courage, that we and they that delyght to be named

Christians, may enioy both outwarde peace, & inwardlye laude, prayse, and magnifie thy holye name for euer, with thy onlye sonne *[as 1565–E1*: Jesus Chryst … Amen*]*.

This prayer to be sayd at Euenyng prayer, immediatly after the Collect of the daye.

O Lorde God of hostes most righteous iudge, and most mercyful Father: These dreadfull dangers and distresses wherin other Christian men our brethren and neyghbours doo now stande, by reason of the terrible inuasions of moste cruel and deadlye enemyes the Turkes, Infidels and miscreantes, do set before our eyes a terrible example of our owne worthy desertes, by our continuall sinnyng & offendyng against thy great maiestie and most seuere Iustice: and do also put vs in remembraunce, here in this our Realm of England, of our most deserued thankes for our great tranquillitie, peace, and quietnes, whiche we by thy hygh benefite, & preseruation of our peaceable Prince, whom thou hast geuen vs, do enioye: Whyles others in the lyke or lesse offences, then ours are against thy maiestie, are by thy righteous iudgementes so terribly scourged, this thy fatherly mercies, do set foorth thy vnspeakable pacience whiche thou vsest towardes vs thy ingrate chyldren, aswell in the same thy gratious benefites of suche our peace and tranquillitie, as in thy wholsome warninges of vs, by thy iuste punishments of others, lesse offenders then we be. For the whiche thy great benefytes bestowed vpon vs without al our derseruing, as we prayse thy Fatherlye goodnes towardes vs: so beyng stryken in our myndes with great dread of thy iuste vengeaunce, for that we do so lytle regarde the great ryches of thy Fatherly goodnes, and pacience towards vs: we moste humble beseche thee to graunt vs thy heauenlye grace, that we continue no longer in the takyng of thy manyfold graces and goodnes in vayne. And vppon deepe compassion of the dreadfull distresses of our brethren and neighbours the Christians, by the cruell and most terrible inuasions of these most deadlye enemies the Turkes: we do make and offer vp our moste humble and hartie prayers before the throne of thy grace, for the mitigation of thy wrath, and purchase of thy pitie and fatherly fauour towardes them: and not only towards them, but to vs also by them, for so much as our daunger or safetie doth folowe vppon successe of them. Graunt them and vs thy grace, O most mercyfull Father, that we may ryghtly vnderstande, and vnfaynedlye confesse our synnes agaynst thy maiestie, to be the very causes of this thy iust scourge, and our miserie: graunt vs true and hartie repentaunce of all our synnes agaynst thee, that the causes of thy iuste offence beyng remoued, the effectes of these our derserued miseries maye withall be taken awaye. Geue to thy poore Christians, O Lorde God of hostes, strength from heauen, that they, neyther respectynge theyr owne weakenes and paucitie, nor fearyng the multitude and fiercenes of theyr enemies, or theyr dreadfull crueltie, but settinge theyr eyes and only hope and truste vpon thee, and callynge vppon thy name, who arte the geuer of al victorie, maye by thy power obteyne victorie agaynst the infinite multitudes and fiercenes of thine enemies, that all men vnderstandynge the same to be the acte of thy grace, and not the deede of mans myght and power, maye geue vnto thee all the prayse and glory: and specially thy poore Christians (by thy strong hand) beyng deliuered out of the handes of theyr enemyes, we for theyr and our owne safetie with them, may yelde & render vnto thee all laudes, prayses, and thankes; through thy Sonne our Sauiour Iesus Christe, to whom with thee and the holy ghost, one eternall God, of most sacred maiestie, be all prayse, honour and glorie, world without ende. Amen.

Or this Colecte of the Letanye folowynge. [The collect in time of war from the BCP]

Psalmes which maye be songe or said before the begynnynge, or after the endynge of
publique prayer, or before and after Sermons. [2, 7, 10, 11, 22:1–22, 27, 46, 52, 56,
70, 74, 83, 91, 94, 121, 123, 140]

APPENDIX: MANUSCRIPT PRAYER OF THANKSGIVING

O Eternall god and moste mercifull father we geue thee hartie thankes for this thie
mightie woorkinge in ouerthrowinge That Cursed and cruell Turke the enemye of thie
deare sonne Christe Jehsus / and his deare Christians / And for relevinge his poore
afflicted members / in delyveringe them from his & there blouddy handes: Wherfore
(deare Father) we beseche thee to continewe in this thie mercifull defendinge them
And in overthrowinge his tyrannicall power that they thereby may well feelle &
knowe that ther is none other God besydes thee & thei sonne Jehsus Christe owr
savio^r Preserue (O Lord) Those godlie & christian Princes wich venter ther lyves
againste this *thie* Enemye as namely the Emperours magestie, with his too Brethren
and his whole nobilitie / geuinge them prosperous success and Victorious conquest.
Grant this O Father for thie deare sonnes sake Jehsus christe our Sauioure. Amen /

1566–S2   Fast days during perceived threats to the reformed church

Sunday 28 July – Sunday 4 August 1566 (Scotland)

This fast was ordered by the general assembly on 26 June 1566. The precise motives
for its appointment are unclear, but it followed a period in which Queen Mary had
reconciled pro-reform nobles to her court in the aftermath of the murder of her
servant David Riccio on 9 March. Mary's policy, together with the birth of her son,
the future James VI, on 19 June, seems to have raised fears among the clergy for the
future of the reformed church. The description in Calderwood's *History*, which is
more complete than that in the *Book of the universal Kirk*, suggests that the fast was
to be observed from 21 to 28 July, but the entry in the Canongate kirk session minutes
states that the fast was to begin on 28 July.

Order: by the general assembly, 26 June 1566, described in Calderwood, II, 324.
Additional sources: *BUK*, I, 78–9; *Buik of the Kirk of the Canagait*, ed. Calderwood, p. 48.

DESCRIPTION OF ORDER

Order by the general assembly: 26 June 1566
It was appointed a publick fast sould be holdin the two last Sabboth dayes of Julie, in
respect of the dangers imminent wherewith the Kirk is like to be assaulted; and that
the Lord's Supper be ministred upon the same day, if it can be done convenientlie.

1567–S1   Fast days [reasons unknown]

Sunday 11 May – Sunday 18 May 1567 (Scotland?)

This fast is known only from a brief description in Calderwood's *History*. This
account is difficult to interpret, but it may derive from a contemporary source that has

been lost. Extant contemporary sources covering this period concentrate on larger political events: the earl of Bothwell's abduction of Queen Mary on 24 April, the announcement of their intention to marry (8 May) and the wedding itself (15 May). In Edinburgh, John Craig, minister of St Giles, initially refused to read the banns, but later complied on the orders of the queen. When called to account for this action by the December 1567 general assembly, Craig made no reference to the fast, despite describing events in the week beginning 12 May. Nevertheless, this source does not rule out the possibility that a fast was kept by at least some congregations from 11 to 18 May. Calderwood's reference to chapters preached on during the fast is misleading. Some editions of the Book of Common Order, beginning with that of 1587, contained the text of *The ordour and doctrine of the generall faste*, together with a list of chapters used by the ministers of Edinburgh and Holyroodhouse in various circumstances in late 1566 and 1567 (this list appeared in 1574 in a reprint of *The ordour and doctrine of the generall faste* (STC 22043), sigs. Fiʳ–[Fii]ᵛ).

Order: none found.
Source: Calderwood, II, 358.
Additional sources: *BUK*, I, 114–16; Knox, *History*, II, 206–7; *The CL. psalmes of David in meter* (1587; STC 16582), pp. 243–5.

DESCRIPTION

Calderwood, *History*
What doctrine sounded in the pulpits in these times, may be easilie considered, by the chapters chosin for the fast, which was celebrated the secund and thrid Lord's day of May. The note of the chapters is extant in our Psalme-bookes, at the end of the treatise of Fasting.

1567–S2   Fast days for consolidation of the reformation in Scotland

Sunday 13 July – Sunday 20 July 1567 (Edinburgh)

Queen Mary's surrender to the confederate opposition at Carberry, on 15 June 1567, provided Scotland's protestants with an opportunity to consolidate the gains made in 1560, and to pursue further reformation. On 25 June, the general assembly met to discuss the threats to protestantism in Scotland and elsewhere, and the Kirk's lack of financial security, resolving to reconvene on 20 July. On 28 June, the meeting appointed this fast, to be kept in Edinburgh on the two Sundays preceding the next assembly. Presumably there was not thought to be sufficient time to order national observance of the fast. On Sunday 13 July, Sir Nicholas Throckmorton, Elizabeth I's ambassador in Scotland, initially failed to gain an audience with the confederate lords, who were observing the fast.

Order: by the general assembly, 28 June 1567, described in *BUK*, I, 99.
Additional sources: Row, pp. 32–3; Sir Nicholas Throckmorton to Elizabeth, 14 July 1567, SP52/14/24.

Order by the general assembly: 28 June 1567
The haill kirk thoght good that ane publick fast sould be proclaimed in the towne of Edinburgh only, to begin on Sonday the 13 of Julij nixt, and on Sonday the 20 of the same.

1569–S   Fast days [reasons unknown]

Sunday 13 March – Sunday 20 March 1569 (Lothian, Fife and where possible); when convenient (elsewhere in Scotland)

This fast was appointed in the context of deep social divisions following the deposition of Queen Mary in 1567, and her flight to and imprisonment in England. But in general, this was a period in which the reformed church benefited from the support of the Regent Moray. It is thus unclear why the general assembly of March 1569 chose to order a fast. Probably the assembly's act should be seen less as an order for a specific national fast, than as an attempt to encourage more frequent fasting in the provinces of the superintendents and commissioners who at this time administered the church. The act also described a standard pattern for such fasts, which were to be eight days long, and to be observed in accordance with the order of worship issued for 1566–S1.

Order: by the general assembly, 8 Mar. 1569, described in *BUK*, I, 138–9.
Additional sources: Calderwood, II, 486; Row, p. 39.

Order by the general assembly: 8 March 1569
It was concludit be the haill brethren assemblit, that ane generall fasting be proclaimit through all Scotland, and to begin in Lowthiane, Fyfe, and sick uther places as may receive advertisement, the 13 day of this instant. Thereafter the superintendents and commissioners of provinces to advertise and begin at sick tymes as they thinke most expedient, and to continue fra the first day to that day aught dayes inclusive; and in the meane tyme to use the exercise accustomeit in the kirk of the first institutioun, and els to use sobrietie in eating and drinking in tyme of the exercise. Moreover concludit that all Superintendents and Commissioners of provinces sall heirafter institute and use the same ordour of fasting, so oft as just occasioun sall serve and sall seime meit be ther godlie wisdome, without any further appointment be the Generall Assemblie.

1570–E   Thanksgiving services for the suppression of the Northern Rising

[January 1570 onwards?] (England and Wales?)

The Northern Rising was prompted in November 1569 by Elizabeth I's discovery of the duke of Norfolk's plan to resolve the succession issue by marrying Mary, queen of Scots, then imprisoned in Tutbury Castle in Staffordshire. The earls of Northumberland and Westmorland, Norfolk's supporters, were summoned to court for punishment, but went into revolt, supported by others who opposed the Elizabethan settlement. After seizing Hartlepool, the rebels moved on to Darlington and York but retreated on 24 November when a *c.* 7,000-strong royal army advanced from the south. No order for this occasion is extant and the precise nature of the thanksgivings, and their number, is unclear. *An homelie against disobedience and wylful rebellion* was published in 1570, attributed by Strype to Parker, to be read in all churches. It comprised a five-part homily with a prayer repeated at the end of the first four parts and a thanksgiving for the rebellion's suppression at the end. Clay argued that the prayer and thanksgiving were also used on separate occasions, though there is no evidence to support this from the printed text. A number of parishes, mainly in London, recorded purchases of 'prayer books' in 1570, which must relate to the rising (there being no evidence of other public prayers at this time) though 'prayer book' does not describe *An homelie* accurately and it was more usual for churchwardens to describe books of homilies as 'homilies'. It is possible that a form of prayer was issued in 1570 and is no longer extant. Whether there were one or two occasions of special worship in response to the rising, *An homelie* represented a new and different format for special worship: a designated homily read as part of the normal BCP service together with new prayers, rather than adopting a full liturgy or inserting new psalms and/or prayers into the daily service. This was not the first time that the Tudors had commissioned a homily on obedience – the first Book of Homilies (1547) included a homily on good order and obedience to rulers and magistrates – or had ordered nationwide thanksgivings after a domestic rebellion (see 1554–E1). However, it was the first time that they had mobilized the church and the homelitic genre to inculcate obedience in response to a specific domestic threat across the realms. This tactic was repeated in 1585 after the Parry plot (see 1585–E1). Thomas Drant, Grindal's chaplain, preached on the rising at court on 8 January 1570 but it is unclear whether this was part of the nationwide thanksgivings. Like the prayers in *An homelie*, Drant presented the rising as part of a general catholic conspiracy against England. *An homelie*, with its accompanying prayers, was reprinted in the second Book of Homilies from 1571 and, with the rest of the homilies, was ordered to be read in every parish church at least twice a year.

Order: none found.
Form of prayer: two prayers included in *An homelie against disobedience and wylful rebellion* ([80] pp.; STC 13679.2)*, sigs Ci^v–Cii^r, Kii^v–Kiii^r [also in Clay, pp. 536–9].
Additional sources: Strype, *Annals,* I: 2, 322–4; Clay, p. 462.
Printed sermon: Drant, court (STC 7171, sigs. Iir–Lviiir).

FORM OF PRAYER

[After each of the first four parts of the homily][230]
O most mightie God, the Lorde of hoastes, the gouernour of all creatures, the only geuer of all victories, who alone art hable to strengthen the weake against the mightie, and to vanquishe infinite multitudes of thyne enemies with the countenaunce of a fewe of thy seruauntes calling vpon thy name, and trusting in thee: Defende, O Lorde, thy seruaunt and our gouernour vnder thee, our Queene Elizabeth, and all thy people

---

[230] *Two books of homilies*, pp. 550–600.

committed to her charge, & especially at this tyme, O Lorde, withstande the crueltie of all those which be common enemies aswel to the trueth of thy eternall worde, as to their owne natural prince and countrey, and manifestly to this crowne and Realme of Englande, whiche thou hast of thy diuine prouidence assigned in these our dayes to the gouernement of thy seruaunt our soueraigne and gratious Queene. O most mercifull father (if it be thy holy wyll) make soft and tender the stonie heartes of all those that exalt them selues against thy trueth, and seeke eyther to trouble the quiet of this Realme of Englande, or to oppresse the crowne of the same, & conuert them to the knowledge of thy sonne the only sauiour of the worlde Jesus Christe, that we and they may ioyntly glorifie thy mercies. Lighten we besech thee their ignoraunt heartes to embrace the trueth of thy worde, or els so abate their crueltie (O most mightie Lorde) that this our Christian Region with others that confesse thy holy Gospel, may obtaine by thine ayde & strength suretie from al enemies, without shedding of Christian blood, wherby all they whiche be oppressed with their tyrannie, may be relieued, and they which be in feare of their crueltie, may be comforted: and finally that all Christian Realmes, and specially this Realme of Englande, may by thy defence and protection continue in the trueth of the Gospell, and enioy perfect peace, quietnesse, and securitie: and that we for these thy mercies, ioyntly altogether with one consonant heart & voyce, may thankfully render to thee all laude and prayse, that we knit in one godly concorde and vnitie amongst our selues, may continually magnifie thy glorious name, who with thy sonne our sauiour Jesus Christe, and the holy ghost, art one eternall, almightie, and most mercifull God. To whom be all laude and prayse, worlde without ende. Amen.

[After the fifth part of the homily]
A thankesgeuing for the suppression of the last rebellion.

O heauenly and most merciful father, the defendour of those that put their trust in thee, the sure fortresse of all them that flee to thee for succour: who of thy most iust iudgementes for our disobedience and rebellion against thy holy word, and for our sinfull and wicked liuing nothing aunswering to our holy profession, wherby we haue geuen an occasion that thy holye name hath ben blasphemed amongst the ignoraunt, hast of late both sore abashed the whole Realme and people of Englande with the terrour and daunger of rebellion, thereby to awake vs out of our dead sleepe or carelesse securitie: and hast yet by the miseries folowyng the same rebellion more sharply punished part of our countrey men, and Christian brethren, who haue more neerely felt the same: and most dreadfully hast scourged some of the seditious persons with terrible executions, iustly inflicted for their disobedience to thee, and to thy seruaunt their Soueraigne, to the example of vs all, and to the warnyng, correction, and amendement of thy seruauntes, of thyne accustomed goodnesse, turnyng alwayes the wickednesse of euill men to the profite of them that feare thee: who in thy iudgementes remembring thy mercie, hast by thy assistaunce geuen the victorye to thy seruaunt our Queene, her true nobilitie, and faithfull subiectes, with so little, or rather no effusion of Christian blood, as also myght iustlye haue ensued, to the exceedyng comfort of all sorowfull Christian heartes, and that of thy fatherly pitie, and mercifull goodnesse only, and euen for thyne owne names sake, without any our desert at all. Wherefore we render vnto thee most humble and hartie thankes for these thy great mercies shewed vnto vs, who had deserued sharper punishment, most humbly beseching thee to graunt vnto all vs that confesse thy holy name, and professe the true & perfect religion of thy holye Gospell, thy heauenly grace to shewe our selues in our liuing accordyng to our profession: that we truely knowyng thee in thy blessed word, may obediently walke in thy holy commaundementes, and that we being warned by this thy fatherly correction, do prouoke thy iust wrath agaynst vs no more: but may enioy the continuaunce of thy great mercies towarde vs, thy ryght hande, as in this, so in all other inuasions, rebellions, & daungers, continually sauing and defendyng our Churche, our Realme, our Queene and people of Englande, that all our posterities ensuing, confessing thy holy name, professing thy holy Gospell, and leadyng an holye lyfe, may perpetually prayse and magnifie thee, with thy onlye sonne Iesus Christe our sauiour, and the holy Ghost, to whom be all laude, prayse, glory, and Empyre for euer and euer. AMEN.

1571–E   Thanksgiving prayers for the victory against the Ottomans at Lepanto

Friday 9 November 1571 (London and suburbs)

Süleyman I died during the night of 6–7 September 1566, while the Ottoman armies were besieging Sziget in Hungary. Ottoman forces nevertheless continued to threaten Christendom, seizing Habsburg outposts in North Africa, notably Tunis in 1569, and taking Nicosia in Cyprus from Venice in 1570. In the face of this general threat and with the particular aim of relieving the besieged Venetian colony of Famagusta, during 1571 Pope Pius V drew together Spain, Venice, Genoa, Savoy, the Papal States, and the Knights Hospitaller from Malta into a Holy League. On 7 October the League's fleet, commanded by Philip II's illegitimate half-brother, Don John of Austria, encountered the Ottoman navy off Lepanto in the Gulf of Patras, off the Greek coast. Though numerically smaller, the greater firepower of Don John's navy secured a resounding victory, with the League losing only twelve galleys to the Ottomans' 200. The victory was widely celebrated throughout catholic Europe, and annual thanksgivings were appointed in Venice. The celebrations of the victory in England are known only through copies of documents that seem no longer to be extant, which were transcribed in 1703 for Archbishop Tenison and also published by John Strype in 1725 in his *Annals of the Reformation*. The thanksgiving was not noted by Clay, nor was the related sermon preached at St Paul's Cross recorded in MacLure's register of the Paul's Cross sermons. News of Don John's victory arrived in England at the beginning of November – according to Strype, communicated directly to Elizabeth by the Spanish governor of the Netherlands, the duke of Alva (or Alba) – and thanksgivings were reported to have been observed at court. Two orders for public celebrations in the City of London were issued by the privy council on 8 November. In the first, the lord mayor was ordered to organize bonfires in every ward and suburb of the city on the evening of the following day, Friday 9 November, together with other signs of 'joy and thankfulness to God, as hath been in such cases accustomed upon a victory, or any other benefit received'. These instructions were reported in the second order, written partly in Cecil's hand, which was sent to Edwin Sandys, bishop of London, and which directed him to arrange for thanksgiving prayers to be said during the Friday morning in St Paul's Cathedral and in parish churches in and around London. Sandys was also ordered to ensure that the minister preaching the regular Sunday sermon at St Paul's Cross should include some appropriate words of thanksgiving. Although the city was given only a short notice of the celebrations, churchwardens' accounts show that there were many bonfires and much bell-ringing. Several of these churchwardens' accounts record that Sandys issued special prayers for the occasion, although no copies have survived. He and the printers evidently acted very quickly, as the prayers were to be used on the day after the order was issued. The churchwardens of St Margaret Pattens paid 'the somner when he brought the prayer from the Byshop' on 9 November; those at All Hallows London Wall, All Hallows Staining, St Benet Gracechurch Street, St Mary Aldermanbury, St Mary Woolnoth and St Stephen Wallbrook noted purchases of 'a book of thanksgiving' for the victory against the Turks, prayers against the 'tyrannye of the Turke', or prayers 'that the bishop sent for the overthrow of the Turk'. It is not known why the thanksgiving prayers were ordered for use only in London, rather than more widely as were the prayers and services for 1565–E1, 1565–E2 and 1566–E; nor why the prayers were ordered at such short notice, and only for a Friday rather than for services on the following Sunday.

Important as the victory was for Christian Europe, it did little to halt the Ottoman threat in the Mediterranean because the Ottomans rebuilt their fleet within six months. Nevertheless, the danger of further land invasion into central Europe receded, and from the 1570s English relations with the Habsburgs deteriorated, resulting in wars with both the Empire and Spain. Special worship in support of catholics who were fighting against the Ottomans was not ordered again in England until 1686, when Vienna was threatened (see 1686–E).

Order: [privy council] to the bishop of London, 8 Nov. 1571, copy in LPL, MS 680, fos. 73r–v [also in Strype, *Annals*, II:1, 156–7].
Form of prayer: none found but referred to in GL, 5090/2, fos. 12v–13r; 4956/2, fo. 106v; 1432/2, unfol.; 1568/1:1, 218; 4524/1, fo. 11r; 4570/2, 75; 3556/1, fo. 17v; 1013/1, fo. 19v; 1002/1a, fo. 165r; 2895/1, fo. 197r; 593/2, fo. 60r.
Additional sources: [privy council] to the lord mayor of London, [Nov.] 1571, copy in LPL, MS 680, fos. 73v–74r [also in Strype, *Annals*, II:1, 157]; GL, 4241/1, pp. 4, 9; 4810/1, fo. 42r; 1016/1, fo. 51r; 2895/1, fo. 194v; 645/1, fos. 90v, 92v; *The accounts of the churchwardens of the parish of St Michael, Cornhill in the city of London, from 1456 to 1608*, ed. Alfred James Waterlow (n.p, 1883), p. 166.

ORDER

[Privy council] to the bishop of London, 8 November 1571

After our hartie commendations to yor good Lo^p: The Queens Matie hauing intelligence giuen her from ye Duke of Alua of a greate victorie lately giuen by Gods goodness to ye Christian Army seruing in the Levant Seas against the Turke to the Distruction and ruyne of many of their Gallyes and great numbers of their people. And being thankfull and joyfull therefore as for a singular great blessing sent by Almighty God to ye benefitt of ye uniuersall estate of Xρiandome hath thought it necessarie as well by common prayers, as otherwise to haue a publick Demonstration within her Highnes householde of ye Comfort that her Matie conceaueth of so generall a good turne. And haueing Commaunded to ye Lord Maior of London, that a like joyfull signification may be expressed throughout ye Cittie by common Bonfyres and other tokens of joy & thanksgiuing to Almightie God to morrow at night being Frydaie her Matie hath likewise thought convenient, and so her pleasure is that we should signifie unto you, that you giue order, not only within yor Cathedrall Church but in all other Churches throughout ye Cittie and neer about that ye people may be solemnly assembled at some common prayer of praise and thanksgiuinge at some conuenient time to morrow in the forenoon. And for that so great & beneficiall fauour of Almightie God ought to be deeplie impressed in the harts of the people to prouoke their thankfulness the more, to ye continewance of Gods great goodness towards us, the State of Christendome. It shall be uerie necessarie that he who shall preach at ye Crosse, on sunday next being prepared to say something on this behalfe. And ye same also being no lesse then her Maties pleasure is that we should signifie unto you wee doubt not but your Lo^p· will be carefull that euerie part thereof shall be effectuallie performed according to her Maties Godly intention. And so we bid your Lo^p right hartely farewell. From Greenw^ch·, the 8th day of November. 1571.

1572–E   Services during the catholic threat, after the St Bartholomew's day massacre

Wednesdays, Fridays, Sundays and holy days, from 30 October 1572 (Canterbury province)

The St Bartholomew's day massacre was ordered by Charles IX in Paris on the night of 23–4 August 1572. Its aim was to destroy the Huguenot leadership but it sparked more widespread attacks both in Paris and in provincial towns, leading to the deaths of around 13,000 people and precipitating the outbreak of the fourth French war of religion. In England, the massacres were regarded as proof of an international catholic conspiracy against protestantism and the need to support co-religionists abroad (see earlier occasions 1562–E1 and 1570–E), and they precipitated not only nationwide services in England, but also a fast in Scotland (1572–S). The massacres also had a lasting effect on the outlook of some of Elizabeth's advisors and were recalled, for instance, during the marriage negotiations between Elizabeth and Charles IX's brother, Francis, duke of Anjou, in 1579 as proof of the perfidy of the French. The form was dated 27 October 1572 and Parker issued orders to the bishops for its use on 29 October (in Latin because it was an archiepiscopal mandate). It is unclear why it took so long for this occasion to be ordered. The queen and members of the privy council and court received news of the massacre within days, but the continuing marriage negotiations between Elizabeth and Francis, then duke of Alençon, and the need of both sides for an alliance might have made an immediate, public reaction to events impolitic. By October, Elizabeth had cooled over the marriage and was carefully trying to put pressure on Charles to make peace with the Huguenots and not to send troops to Scotland, without driving the young king into Spanish arms. The form of prayer provided instructions and texts for full liturgical services for Sundays, Wednesdays, Fridays and holy days. Services on Wednesdays and Fridays were shorter than those on Sundays, omitting the second lesson. Parishioners were also expected to recite the prayer for the queen every day, as the second collect of the litany. Rhetorically, the message conveyed by the service was mixed, perhaps reflecting the complex diplomatic game that Elizabeth was playing. One the one hand, the prayers and texts presented the massacre politically as a divine punishment and warning to all Christians for their sinfulness. On the other, the unusual choice of the collect in time of war to be read during the litany underlined the regime's interpretation of the events in France as part of a longstanding catholic conspiracy against protestant England: the collect called on God to '[s]ave and deliver us …

from the hands of our enemies, abate their pride, assuage their malice, and confound their devices'.

Order: archiepiscopal mandate to Bishop Edwin Sandys, 29 Oct. 1572, LPL, Parker Register, II, fo. 73r [also in *Correspondence of Matthew Parker*, ed. John Bruce and Thomas Thomason Perowne, (Parker Society, XXXIII, Cambridge, 1853), 402; *Concilia*, IV, 272–3].
Form of prayer: *A fourme of common prayer to be vsed, and so commaunded by auctoritie of the queenes maiestie, and necessarie for the present tyme and state 1572. 27. Octob.* ([18] pp.; STC 16511)*.
Additional source: Strype, *Parker*, II, 131–3.

ORDER

Archiepiscopal mandate to bishop of London: 29 October 1572
Scriptum fuit maiestat per Reuerendissimmi patrem retroscriptum pro captione Corporis retrouoiati Thome Carden sub dato penultimo Novembris Anno domini Millimino Quingen^erno^ Septuage^quo^ secundo. Mattheus prouidentia diuina Cantuariensis Archiepiscopus totius Angliae primas et Metropolitanus, venerabili confratri nostro domino Edwino, eadem permissione diuina Londinensi, Episcopo, Salutem et fraternam in domino charitatem. Cum nos librum quendam precum publicarum intitulatum, A forme of comon prayer to be vsed, and soe commaunded by authorytie of the Queenes maiestie and necessary for the present tyme and state 1572 vicesimo Septimo Octobris de mandato Illustrissimae domine nostrae Reginae componi, ac imprimi et publicari fecimus; No igitu^r^ Librum praedictum in et per totam prouinciam Cantuariensem debitae exequtioni demandari volentes, librum ipsum praesentibus annexum vobis transmittimus publicandum volentes ac fraternitati vestrae firmiter iniungendo mandantes quatenus vera exemplaria libri praedicti vniuersis et singulis venerabilibus confratribus nostris dictae Prouinciae nostrae Cantuariensis cum ea qua fieri poterit matura celeritate transmittatis seu transmitti faciatis eisque ex parte nostra iniungatis quibus nos etiam tenore praesentium sic iniungimus quatenus eorum singuli in singulis dioecesibus eorundem coram decano et Capitulo cuiuslibet ecclesiae cathedra^lis^ ac Archidaconis et clero suae dioecesis prout ad eos et eoru^m^ quemlibet pertinet, librum praedictum debite publicent et ab omnibus quos concernit obseruari et debitae executioni demandari procurent siue sic publicari et obseruari faciant cum effectum Et praeterea fraternitati vestrae vt supra iniungimus quatenus librum praedictum in et per dioecesim vestram Londinensem prout ad vos attinet debite et effectualiter publicari et executioni demandari faciatis provt decet.

FORM OF PRAYER

THE PREFACE
Firste, that al Parsons & Curates shall euery sunday, at conuenient tymes exhort theyr parishioners to endeuor themselues to come to ye Churche, with as manye of their familie as may be spared from their necessary busines: and they to resorte thither, not onlye vpon Sundayes and Holydayes, but also vpon Wednesdayes, and Frydayes, specially in Cities and great Townes, during this daungerous and perillous tymes of the troubles in Christendome, exhorting them there reuerently and godly to behaue them selues, and with penitent myndes, kneelyng on theyr knees, to lift vp theyr hartes, and praye to the mercyfull God, to turne from vs of this Realme, and all the reast of Christendome, those plagues and punishmentes, which we and others through our vnthankefulnesse and sinfull lyues haue deserued.

Secondly, that the sayd Parsons and Curates, shall then distinctlye and plainely reade the generall confession appoynted in the booke of seruice, with the residue of the mornyng prayer, vnto the firste Lesson.

Then for the first Lesson shalbe read one of the Chapters hereafter folowyng, or so muche therof as is appoynted.

Any of these Chapters may be read for the firste Lesson, at the disposition of the Minister, in the weeke dayes: and vpon the Sunday or holy dayes for the seconde Lessons, [Matt. 3; Matt. 5:1–12; Matt. 6; Matt. 7; Matt. 10:16–42; Matt. 16; Matt. 24; Matt. 25; Luke 15; Luke 17:20–37; Luke 18:1–14; Luke 21; Acts 9:1–31; Rom. 2; Rom. 12; Rom. 13; Eph. 5:1–21; 1 Thess. 2:14–20; 1 Thess. 4:13–18; 1 Thess. 5; 1 Tim. 2]

[Then Psalm 51 in place of the Te Deum*]*

[On Wednesdays and Fridays, Psalm 51 to be followed by the Apostles' creed, the prayers to the end of morning prayer, and the litany. On Sundays, this to be followed by the second lesson, the prayers to the end of morning prayer, and the litany]

[After 'We humbly beseech thee' at the end of the litany, one of the following in daily rotation]

A prayer for the forgeuenesse of sinnes

O Come, let vs humble our selues: & fall downe before the Lorde our maker, with reuerence and feare. (Ps. 95) [95:6]

Let vs repent and turne from our wickednesse, and turne agayne vnto our Lorde: and our sinnes shalbe forgeuen vs (Hos. 6, Acts 3) [Acts 3:19?]

Let vs turne, and the Lorde wyl turne from vs his heauie wrath: he hath smitten vs, and he wyll heale vs, he wil pardon vs, and we shall not perishe. (Jon. 3, Hos. 6) [Jonah 3 and 9]

We acknowledge our faultes, O Lord: and our sinnes are euer before our syght. (Ps. 5) [51:3]

We haue sore prouoked thyne anger, O Lorde: thy wrath is waxed hot, and thy heauy displeasure is sore kindled against vs. (Lam. 51) [Lam. 4:11]

But rebuke vs not, O Lord, in thyne indignation: neyther chasten vs in thy heauie displeasure. (Ps. 6) [6:1]

In deede we acknowledge that all punishments are lesse then our deseruing: but yet of thy mercye Lorde, correct vs to amendement, and plague vs not to our destruction. (Jth. 8, Job 11, Zeph. 11) [Job. 11:6]

O remember not the sinnes and offences of our youth, & tymes past: but according to thy mercy thynke vpon vs, O Lorde, for thy goodnesse. (Ps. 25) [25:6]

Stand not so farre of, O Lord: neyther hyde thy face in the needefull tyme of trouble. (Ps. 10) [10:1]

Turne thee vnto vs, and haue mercy vpon vs: for we are desolate and in great miserie. (Ps. 25) [25:15]

And now in the vexation of our spirites, and the anguishe of our soules: we remember thee, & we crye vnto theee, heare Lorde, and haue mercie. (Bar. 3, Jon. 2) [Baruch 3:1]

For wee do not powre out our prayers before thy face, trustyng in our owne ryghteousnesse: but in thy great and manyfolde mercyes. (Dan. 9) [9:18]

For thyne owne sake, and for thy holye names sake, encline thyne eare, & heare: and be mercifull to our sinnes, for they are great. (Ps. 25) [25:10]

*Helpe vs, O God of our saluation, for the glory of thy name: O deliuer vs, and saue
vs for thy names sake.* (Ps. 79) [79:9]

So we that be thy people, and sheepe of thy pasture, shall geue thee thankes for ther:
and wil be alwayes shewing forth thy prayse from generation to generation. (Ps. 79)
[79:14]

Glory be to the father. &c. As it was in the .&c.

Prayers for true repentaunce and mercye.

Moste mercyfull father, who hast in thy holye worde, the worde of trueth,
promysed mercy vnto sinners that do repent and turne vnto thee, and haste by thy
terrible examples of thy iust anger, beyng executed vppon people and Countreyes
rounde about vs, called vs, and moste mercyfullye moued vs to repentaunce, and
by thy patience and long sufferyng of vs hytherto, haste gratiouslye graunted vs
tyme and space to repente: graunt also we beseeche thee, both to them and vs grace
truelye to repent, and vnfaignedly to turne vnto thee with amendment of life, and
to truste in thy mercyes, and safely to rest vnder thy continuall protection from all
enimies and euylles both bodyly and ghostly, through our sauiour Jesus Christe, who
with thee and the holy ghost, lyueth and raigneth one God worlde without ende.
Amen.

An other for the same.

We haue sinned Lorde, we haue sinned greeuously, we haue done vniustly, we
haue liued wickedly, we are sorye therefore, O Lorde, yea we are most sorie, that
we are no more sorie for our sinnes, but thou Lorde GOD, father of all mercies, we
humbly beseeche thee, be not angry with vs for euer for our great and manyfolde
sinnes, neither deale with vs according to our desertes, neither rewarde vs according
to our wickednesse, but euen for thy selfe, O Lorde God, and for thy holy names-
sake, for thy most gratious assured promises made vnto penitent sinners in thy holy
woorde, the woorde of trueth, for thy infinite mercies whiche are in thy dearely
beloued sonne Jesu Christe our Sauiour, for his sake, for his death and pretious
blood, be mercyfull vnto vs sinners, and so we who haue most greeuously offended
thy diuine maiestie, shal continually magnifie thy great and infinite mercie, through
our sauiour Jesus Christ, to whom with thee and the holy ghost be al honour and
glory world without ende. AMEN

A prayer to be deliuered from our enemies.

O Hearken to the voice of our prayer, our king & our God: for vnto thee doo we
make our complaint. (Ps. 5) [5:2]

*O Lorde, the counsayle of the wicked conspireth agaynst vs: and our enemies are
daylye in hande to swalowe vs vp.* (Ps. 22) [56:2]

They gape vpon vs with their mouthes: as it were ramping and roring lions. (Ps. 22)
[22:13]

But thou O Lorde art our defendour: thou art our health and our saluation. (Ps. 3)
[3:3]

We do put our trust in thee O God: saue vs from all them that persecute vs, and
deliuer vs. (Ps. 7) [7:1]

*O take the matter into thy hande, thy people commit them selues vnto thee: for thou
art their helper in their distresse.* (Ps. 10) [10:16]

Saue vs from the Lions mouthes, and from the hornes of the Vnicornes: leste they
deuoure vs, and teare vs in peeces, whyle there is none to helpe. (Ps. 7, 22) [7:2;
22:21]

O delyuer not the soule of thy Turtle doue vnto the multitude of the enemies: and
forget not thy poore congregation for euer. (Ps. 74) [74:20]

Deliuer vs from our enemies O God: defende and saue vs from them that imagine
mischeefe, and ryse vp agaynst vs. (Ps. 59) [59:1]

And we shall geue thankes vnto thee, O Lord, accordyng to thy great mercies: and
wyl praise the name of the Lorde most high. (Ps. 7) [7:18]

We wyll declare thy name vnto our brethren: in the middes of the congregation wil
we praise thee, and magnifie thy saluation worlde without ende. (Ps. 22) [22:22]

Glorye be to the father, and to the sonne: and to the holy ghost.

As it was in the beginnyng, is now, and euer shalbe: worlde without end. Amen

[The BCP special prayer in time of war]

The prayer folowyng for the Queene, must be sayde euery day for the seconde
Collecte after the Psalme.

A thankesgeuyng and prayer for the preseruation of the Queene, and the Realme.

   O God, moste mercyfull father, who in thy great mercies hast both geuen vnto vs
a peaceable princesse, and a gratious Queene, and also hast very often and miraculously saued her from sundry great perilles and daungers, and by her gouernment
haste preserued vs and the whole Realme from manifolde mischeefes, and dreadful
plagues, wherewith nations rounde about vs haue ben, and be moste greeuously
afflicted: haue mercy vpon them, O Lorde, and graunt vs grace we besehe thee,
for these thy great benefites, that we may be thankfull and obedient vnto thee, to
flie from all thynges that may offende thee, and prouoke thy wrath and indignation agaynst vs, and to order our lyues in all thynges that may please thee, that
thy seruaunt our soueraigne Ladye, and we thy people committed to her charge,
may by thy protection be continuallye preserued from all deceiptes and violences
of enimies, and from all other daungers and euylles both bodyly and ghostly, and
by thy goodnesse may be maynteyned in al peace and godlynesse: graunt this, O
mercyfull father, for thy deare sonnes sake our sauiour Jesus Christe, to whom with
thee, and the holy ghost, one God immortal, inuisible, and only wise, be all honour
and glorye for euer and euer. Amen.

A prayer for deliueraunce from enemies.

   Heare our prayer, O Lord, consyder our desyre: hearken vnto vs for thy trueth
and mercies sake. (Ps. 143) [143:1]

Lorde howe are they increased that trouble vs: many are they that ryse agaynst vs.
(Ps. 3) [3:1]

The vngodly bende their bowes, and make ready theyr arrowes within the quiuer: that
they may shoote at those that call vpon the name of the Lorde. (Ps. 11) [11:2]

They smyte downe thy people, O Lorde: and trouble thyne heritage. (Ps. 104) [94:5]

The dead bodyes of thy seruantes haue they geuen to be meate vnto the foules of the
ayre: and the fleshe of they saintes vnto the beastes of the lande. (Ps. 79) [79:2]

Their blood haue they shed lyke water on euery syde of Hierusalem: and there was
no man to burye them. (Ps. 79) [79:3]

And we that lyue are become an open shame to our enemies: a very scorne and derision vnto them that are rounde about vs. (Ps. 79) [79:4]

O Lorde, why is thy wrath suche agaynst the sheepe of thy pasture? howe long wylt thou be angry? shall thy gelousie burne lyke fyre for euer? (Ps. 74, 79) [74:1; 79:5]

Wherfore should the vngodly say, where is nowe their God: there is nowe no more helpe for them in their God. (Ps. 79) [79:10]

Oh remember not our olde synnes, but haue mercy vpon vs, and that soone; for we are come to great miserie. (Ps. 79) [79:8]

O let the sorowfull syghyng of the prysoners come before thee, according to the greatnesse of thy power: preserue thou those sely soules, that are appoynted to dye. (Ps. 79) [79:12]

O Lorde, thinke vpon the congregation of thy people, whom thou haste purchased and redeemed of olde: O deliuer vs, and saue vs, for the glory of thy name. (Ps. 74) [74:2]

And our prayses shalbe of thee in the great congregation: our vowes wyll we perfourme in the syght of them that feare thee. (Ps. 22) [22:25]

And all the endes of the worlde shal remember them selues, and be turned vnto the Lord: and all the kynredes of the nations shall worshippe before hym. (Ps. 22) [22:27]

Glorye be to the father. &c.

As it was in the begynnyng. &c.

A prayer.

O most ryghteous GOD, and most mercyfull father, who aswell by the dreadfull plagues, and afflictions of nations round about vs, as by long suffring and sauing of vs, and by manyfolde benefites bestowed vpon vs, hast shewed thy seueritie in punishing, or trying of them, and thy mercy in sparyng and blessyng of vs: we moste humblye and heartely beseeche thee, in thy iustice to remember thy mercy towardes them, and to saue them, and to graunt vnto vs grace not to dispise the rychesse of thy patience and goodnesse towards vs, neyther by hardnesse of heart and impeni-tencie to heape vpon our selues vengeaunce in the day of vengeaunce, but that we beyng taught by the example of their punishment to feare thy iustice, & moued by thy long sufferyng and blessyng of vs to loue thy goodnesse, may by true repent-ance for our sinnes, and with al our soules, heartes, & mindes, vnfaignedly turnyng vnto thee in newenesse of lyfe, both escape thy wrath and indignation, and enioy the continuaunce and increase of thy fauour, grace, & goodnes, through our sauiour Jesus Christ, thy only sonne, to whom with thee and the holy ghost, one God of most glorious maiestie, be al honour and glory worlde without ende. AMEN.

Or this.

O Lorde our God and heauenly father, loke downe, we besiche thee, with thy fatherlye and mercyfull countenaunce vpon vs thy people, and poore humble seru-auntes, and vppon all suche Christians as are any where persecuted, & sore afflicted for the true acknowledging of thee to be our God, and thy sonne Jesus Christe, whom thou hast sent to be the only sauiour of the world: saue them, O mercyfull Lorde, who are as sheepe appoynted to the slaughter, and by heartie prayer do call and crye vnto thee for thy helpe and defence, heare theyr crye, O Lorde, and our prayer for them, and for our selues, deliuer those that be oppressed, defende suche as are in feare of crueltie, releeue them that be in myserie, and comfort all that be in sorowe and heauinesse, that by thy ayde and strength, they and we may obtayne suertie from our enimies, without sheddyng of Christian & innocent blood. And for that, O Lorde, thou hast commaunded vs to pray for our enimies, we do beseche thee, not only to abate theyr pryde, & to stay the furie and crueltie of such as eyther of malice or ignoraunce do persecute them whiche put theyr trust in thee, and hate vs, but also to molifie theyr harde heartes, to open theyr blynded eyes, and to lyghten theyr ignoraunt myndes, that they may see and vnderstande, and truely turne vnto thee, and embrace thy holy worde, and vnfaygnedlye be conuerted vnto thy sonne Jesus Christe, the onely sauiour of the worlde, and beleeue and loue his Gospell, and so eternally to be saued. Finally, that all Christian Realmes, and specially this Realme of Englande, may by thy defence and protection, enioy perfite peace, quiet-nesse, and securitie, and all that desyre to be called and accompted Christians, may answere in deede and lyfe to so good & godly a name: and ioyntly al togeather in one godly concorde and vnitie, and with one consonant hart and minde, may render vnto thee al laude and prayse, continually magnifiyng thy glorious name, who with thy sonne our sauiour Jesus Christ, and the holy ghost, art one eternal, almightie, and most mercyfull God, to whom be all laude and prayse, worlde without ende. AMEN.

1572–S   Fast days during the catholic threat, after the St Bartholomew's day massacre

Sunday 23 November – Sunday 30 November 1572 (Scotland)

In response to reports of the St Bartholomew's day massacre in France (see 1572–E), a proclamation was issued in the name of King James VI on 3 October 1572, summoning commissioners from Scotland's churches to Edinburgh to discuss the catholic threat. This convention met on 20 October; Calderwood reported that it was thinly attended, perhaps reflecting the illness of the Regent Mar. On 22 October, the convention proposed various anti-catholic measures in a document directed to the regent and council, which also appointed this fast. Mar's death on 28 October may have led people to ignore the fast, which is not mentioned in other sources. It is conceivable that it was cancelled after a convention of the nobility was summoned to elect a new regent. This convention named the earl of Morton as regent on 24 November.

Order: by the convention of ministers and other commissioners, 22 Oct. 1572, Calderwood, III, 227.
Additional sources: *The copie of the proclamatioun set furth be the kingis maiestie and his counsall* (St Andrews, 1572; STC 21940); Calderwood, III, 225–30.

ORDER

Order by the convention of ministers and other commissioners: 22 October 1572

The Assemblie of the kirk conveened at Edinburgh, the 22d day of October 1572, according to the proclamation, first have thought expedient, so farre as present convention is instituted, to provide remeed against the treasonable crueltie of the Papists; and to resist the same. To mitigat the wrath and indignatioun of God, whereby they are stirred up against us for our sinnes, there sall be a publict humiliation of them that feare God, throughout the whole realme, to beginne the 23d of November nixt to come, and to end the last day of the same.

1577–S   Fast days for the defence of Protestantism across Europe, and in support of continued reformation

Sunday 9 July – Sunday 16 July 1577 (Scotland)

It is unclear whether this national fast was a response to any specific event, although it coincided with an upsurge of religious violence in France following the failure of the edict of Beaulieu of May 1576. For many Scottish clergy, however, the government of the Kirk, which was unstable and politically controversial in this period, was the focus of particular attention. In April 1576, the assembly had appointed a committee to make proposals for a permanent settlement of ecclesiastical polity (*BUK*, I, 362–3). This work, which was continuing at the time of the April 1577 assembly, produced the *Second book of discipline* in 1578 (see 1578–S).

Order: by the general assembly beginning 1 Apr. 1577, Calderwood, III, 384.
Additional sources: *BUK*, I, 390–1; Scot, p. 42.

ORDER

Order by the general assembly beginning 1 April 1577
The Generall Assemblie of this realme, considering the great abundance of iniquitie overflowing universallie the whole face of this commoun wealth, now, in so great light and revelatioun of the true and Christian religioun, justlie provoking and stirring up the justice and equitie of God to tak judgement and vengeance in this unworthie and unthankfull natioun; seing also the manie and perelous stormes and rage of persecutioun daylie invading the kirk and spous of Jesus Christ, the sore and extreme troubles of the true and zealous members therof in the parts of France and ellis where, professing our Saviour, Lord, and Messias; the worke also of establishing a perfyte order and policie within the kirk, being presentlie in hands; hath thought it good, meet, and expedient, for the same reasons and good causes, that earnest and speedie recourse sall be had to God, with commoun supplicatiouns and prayers: and to that effect, that a generall fast be observed and keeped universallie through all the kirks of this realme, with doctrine and instructioun to the people; to beginne the secund Sunday of Junie nixt to come, which is the nynth day therof, and to continue to the nixt Sunday therafter; using in the meane time exercise of doctrine, according to the accustomed order: and to that end, that intimation be made heerof by the commissioners of countreis, to the ministers within their bounds, as apperteaneth.

1578–S   Fast days against sinfulness, famine and threats to the Church in Scotland, and to support good government

Sunday 1 June – Sunday 8 June 1578 (Scotland)

This fast was appointed at a time of considerable tensions. On 15 March 1578, a convention of estates had declared James VI to be of age, ending Morton's regency. The ensuing factional struggle within the Scottish nobility resulted in a number of prominent murders, one of which was referred to in the fast act. Meanwhile, the *Second book of discipline*, the Kirk's blueprint for ecclesiastical government, had been completed. The general assembly of April 1578 arranged for copies to be given to the king and the privy council, and formed a committee of clerics to consult with the government on implementing the *Book*'s proposals. When parliament considered the *Book* in July, no decision on church polity was reached, reflecting the reluctance of many leading nobles to concede to the Kirk's requests for greater independence.

Order: by the general assembly beginning 24 Apr. 1578, Calderwood, III, 404–5.
Additional sources: *BUK*, II, 407, 409–11; Row, pp. 62–3; Scot, p. 43; Melvill, p. 62.

ORDER

Order by the general assembly beginning 24 April 1578
The Generall Assemblie finding the universall corruptioun of the whole estats of the bodie of this realme, the great coldnesse and slacknesse of a great part of the professors in religioun, the daylie increasse of all kinde of fearefull sinnes and enormiteis, as incest, adultereis, murthers, and, namelie, recentlie committed in Edinburgh; cursed sacriledge, ungodlie sedition and divisioun within the bowells of this realme, with all maner of disorders and ungodlie living, which justlie have moved and provoked our God, although long-suffering and patient, to stretche out his arme in his anger, to correct and visite the iniquitie of the land, and, namelie, by the present penurie and famine, joynned with the cruell and domestick seditions, wherupon doubtlesse greater judgements must succeed, if these corrections work not reformatioun or true amendement in men's hearts: seing also, the bloodie conclusions of the cruell councels of that Roman beast, tending to extermine and raze from the face of all Europ the true light of the blessed Word of salvatioun; for these causes, and that God of his mercie would blesse the king's Highnesse and his regiment, and make him to have a godlie and prosperous governement, as also, to putt in his Highnesse' heart, and in the hearts of his noble estats in parliament, not onlie to mak and establish good and politick lawes, for the weale and good governement of the realme, but also to sett and establishe suche a policie and discipline in the kirk, as is craved in the Word of God, and is conceaved and penned alreadie, to be presented to his Highnesse and counsell, that in the one and the other God may have his due praise, and the age to come an exemple of upright and godlie dealing; the Generall Assemblie, therefore, hath concluded that an universall fast sall be keeped throughout all the kirks of this realme, to beginne the first Sunday of Junie nixt to come, and to continue till the nixt Sunday therafter, inclusive, keeping the accustomed use of exercise according to the booke of publict fasting. And that this act be intimated to the king's Majestie and counsell, and his Grace and counsell humblie required to discharge, by proclamatiouns, all kinde of insolent playes, as Robin-hood, King of

May, and suche like, in all persons, als weill schollers as others, under suche paines as they sall thinke good.

1580–E   Services and prayers after the London earthquake

Wednesdays and Fridays, and a Sunday prayer [after Saturday 23 April to May] 1580 (England and Wales)

An earthquake in London at 6pm on 6 April 1580 lasted only a minute but caused considerable alarm, damaged buildings and killed two children; there were aftershocks the following night (in Kent) and in early May. The genesis of the form of prayer for this occasion is confused, probably because of the uncertain status of Edmund Grindal, now archbishop of Canterbury, who had been suspended in 1577 after the conflict with the queen over prophesyings but was still exercising some episcopal functions. John Aylmer, bishop of London, immediately wrote a form of prayer for the city. According to a letter sent by the privy council, Grindal may also have ordered prayers to be said in his diocese on Wednesdays and Fridays. On 22 April the privy council ordered Aylmer to prepare a form for the whole realm, but Aylmer told Burghley there was insufficient time to prepare a new form and suggested that his London form should be used instead. On 23 April (misdated by Strype as 12 April), the council told Grindal to order prayers across the realm. The prescribed services followed the liturgical format established in 1563, rather than adding individual prayers or psalms to the BCP service (e.g. 1562–E1). This probably reflected both the format of Aylmer's original form and the importance of the event itself. The adoption of the format from 1563 means that the liturgy should have been used on Sundays, Wednesdays and Fridays, but there is no explicit order to this effect in the privy council's letter. The earthquake was quickly and widely regarded as a divine omen that presaged greater punishments to come and immediately spawned a number of pamphlets to that effect. This view was reinforced by news of Laurence Chaderton's prophetic choice of text for his sermon in Debden, Essex, the day before the earthquake (Joel 3:16, 'The heaven and earth will shake, but the Lord will be the hope of His people') and of the inhabitants of Great Chart and Ashford, Kent, who refused to observe the national fast and found their parishes hit by aftershocks. Indeed, the earthquake continued to be cited in sermons and lectures until the 1620s, as well as in Shakespeare's *Romeo and Juliet* and a newspaper report in 1638. The form of prayer largely followed the liturgical format of 1563, except that the structure of the service for Sundays was not specified: only one prayer was stipulated for use on that day, which was to be recited after the creed, epistle and gospel. The services and texts were, however, not laid out as they were in 1563–E. Instead, the form began with lengthy instructions for the structure of the services on Wednesdays and Fridays, followed by the full texts of the prescribed psalm and lessons. Added to this were a prayer for household use in the evenings, the first time a text had been provided in this way for private worship; Psalm 46 with music (it is unclear when this was supposed to be said or sung); a prayer for use on Sundays; a report on the earthquake and a 'godlie admonition' which reiterated the message that the earthquake was a divine warning. Another edition printed a preface – arguing that the earthquake was a divine omen – after psalm 46 instead of the Sunday prayer, report and admonition (see Appendix at the end of this entry). The setting of both these copies is inconsistent and so it is difficult to tell if the form was hastily composed and printed or related texts, printed separately, have been bound together. The Sunday prayer and the admonition were reset and printed in Arthur Golding's *A discourse vpon the earthquake* (London, 1580; STC 11987); the prayer may also have been printed separately.

Order: privy council to Archbishop Grindal, 23 Apr. 1580, LPL, Grindal Register, I, fos. 198v–199r.
Form of prayer: *The order of prayer vpon Wednesdayes and Frydayes, to auert and turne Gods wrath from vs, threatned by the late terrible earthquake, to be vsed in all parish churches and housholdes throughout ye realme, by order giuen from the queenes maiesties most honourable priuie counsel* ([52] pp.; STC 16513)* [also in Clay, pp. 562–79].
Form of prayer (other edition): *The order of prayer vpon Wednesdayes and Frydayes, to auert and turne Gods wrath from vs, threatned by the late terrible earthquake, to be vsed in al parish churches. Set foorth by authoritie.* (Christopher Barker [and Henry Bynneman]; STC 16512).
Additional sources: Grindal to his officers, 30 Apr. 1580, LPL, Grindal Register, I, fo. 199r (also in *The remains of Edmund Grindal*, ed. Nicholson, pp. 415–17); Bishop John Aylmer to Lord Burghley, 22 Apr. 1580, Lans. 30, fo. 145r; *APC*, XI, 450; Ames, *Typographical antiquities*, II, 108; Strype, *Annals*, II: 2, 334–5, 396–7; Stowe, *Chronicles*, pp. 1210–11; Arthur Golding, *A discourse vpon the earthquake* (1580; STC 11987); Strype, *Grindal*, 368–70; John Strype, *Historical collections of the life and acts of the Right Reverend Father in God, John Aylmer, lord bishop of London in the reign of Queen Elizabeth* ([1701] Oxford, 1821), pp. 51–2; Clay, pp. 464–5.

ORDER

Privy council to archbishop of Canterbury: 23 April 1580

After our very hartie Comendacions vnto your Lordship considering the state of this presente tyme wherein it hath pleased the most highest for the Amendment of all Sortes of people aswell to vysite the moaste parte of this Realme with the late terrible earthquake as an extraordynary token of his wrath agaynst them and fatherly admonicion to turne them from their offences and contempte of his holly worde as also of his infynyte goodnes and mercy to deale more favourably with vs therein then he hath dealte with other Nacions in the like case: in that we thanckes be vnto his maiestie haue receyued no greate hurte therby in comparyson of that they have had sundry tymes heretofore by the like occasion wherby not onely their howses and Cyties have been overthrowen and destroyed but also many thowsandes of people haue pitifully perisshed And vnderstanding that you have consydered vppon and Appoynted a good and conveniente order of prayer and other exercyses to be vsed in all the parrysshe Churches of your dioces vppon Wennesdayes and Frydayes for the turning of god his wrath from vs threatned by the sayd Earthquake with a godly prayer for the like respect to be vsed of howsholders with their Famylies wee doo not onely comende and allowe your good zeale therein But also thincke the same very meete to be generally vsed in all other dioces of this Realme: Requyringe you to gyve order that in everye of the same the sayd holsom & godlye order of prayer may for the respect aforesayd be executed followed and obeyed during suche tyme as you thinck meete[.]

FORM OF PRAYER

THE ORDER OF PRAYER, AND OTHER EXERCISES VPON WEDNESDAYES AND FRYDAYES, TO BE VSED THROUGHOUT THE REALME BY ORDER AFORESAIDE.

First the Minister shall vse the order set downe in the booke of Common prayer, to the ende of *O Come, let vs sing vnto the Lord.*

Then shall followe these three Psalmes, the 30. 46. and 91.

Also for the first Lesson, some one of these three chapters, the 1. or 2. of Ioel, or the 58. of Isaiah, & after that, *Te Deum* or *Benedicite*, with a Chapter of the Newe Testament for the second Lesson, according to the booke afore sayde.

Then after the Letanie shalbe said this praier, *Oh eternal, mighty, and most louing father &c.*

Then shalbe read the Homilie of repentance, or a part thereof, as in the booke of homilies it is deuided, if there be no sermon.

Also after the sermon, or homilie, shalbe sung the 46. Psalme in Meter.

Moreouer, that the Preachers & Curates do exhort their flocke to refraine those ii. dayes weekely from one meale, and to bestow the value or some part thereof (as God shall stirre vp their deuotion) vpon the poore, teaching them that such almes is more acceptable to God, then that which commeth by constraint of Law.

Also that they call vpon their parishioners, to cause their family euery night, before their going to bed, al together to say the prayer set out for that purpose, meekely kneeling vpon their knees.

[MORNING PRAYER]

[Ps. 30, 46, 91]
[First lesson: Joel 1; Joel 2; or Isa. 58]

[LITANY]

[After 'we humbly beseech thee' at the end of the litany]

A prayer to be vsed of all housholders, with their whole familie, euery Euening before they go to bed, that it would please God to turne his wrath from vs, threatned in the last terrible earthquake. Set forth by authoritie.

Oh eternall, mighty, and most louing Father, which hast no desire of the death of a Sinner, but that he conuert and liue, & vnto whom nothing is so pleasant as the repentant, contrite and sorowfull heart of a penitent person: for thou art that kinde Father that fallest moste louinglie vpon the necke of the lost sonne, kyssest, imbracest and feastest him when he returneth from the puddle of pleasures, and swill of the swine, and disdaynest not the repentant prayer of thy poore and sinful seruants, when so euer with true faith they returne and call vpon thee, as we haue most comfortable examples in Dauid, Manasses, Magdalen, Peter, and the thiefe vpon the gibbet: we most hartily and humbly beseech thy Fatherly goodnesse, to looke downe from the throne of thy mercie seate vpon vs most miserable, and sinfull slaues of Sathan, which with fearefull and trembling heartes doe quake, and shake at the strange & terrible token of thy wrath and indignation appearing most euidently vnto vs, by thy shaking, and mouing of the earth, which is thy footestoole, whereby (if we be not vtterly destitute of grace) we be warned, that thy comming down amongst vs, to visite our sinnes in most terrible maner, can not bee farre off, seeing thou treadest so harde vpon this thy footestoole the earth, which wee most shamefully haue polluted and defiled with our most wicked, sinfull, and rebellious liues, notwithstanding thy continuall crying and calling vpon vs by thy seruantes, the Prophetes, and preachers, by whom we haue learned to knowe thy will, but haue not followed it: we haue heard much, and done litle, yea nothing at all, but like most peruerse and vnthankefull children, haue made a mocke of thy woorde, derided thy Ministers, and accompted thy threatninges trifles, and thy warninges, of no wayght or moment: wherefore wee haue iustly deserued to taste most deepely of the bitter cuppe of thy anger & vengeance, by warres, famine, pestilence, yea, and eternall death, if thou shouldest not temper the rigour of thy iustice with the mildnes of thy mercy: But such is thy fatherly affection towards vs, that thou shewest thy selfe slow to anger, long suffering, and of much pacience and mercie, Yea, thou art a thousand times more readie to forget and forgiue, then we to aske and require forgiuenesse. Therefore, though we be not woorthie of the least mite of thy mercie, yet gratious Lord, looke not vpon vs & our sinnes, but vpon thy owne selfe & thy Sonne Jesus Christ the fountaine of grace, the treasure of mercie, the salue of all sicknesse, the Jewel of ioy, and the onely hauen of succour and safetie: by him we come to thee, in him and for him we trust to finde that we haue lost, and gaine that he hath gotte: he is the seale of Jacob, by whom wee clime vp to thee, & thou by the Angels of thy mercie commest down to vs: him we present vnto thee, and not our selues, his death & not our doings, his bloudie wounds & not our detestable deseruings, whose merites are so great, as thy mercie can not bee litle, and our ransome so rich, that our beggerly and beastly sinnes are nothing in thy sight, for the great pleasure and satis- faction that thou takest of his paines and passion. Turne this Earthquake, oh Lorde, to be benefite of thine elect, as thou didst when thou shookest the prison, loosedst the locks, fetters and chaines of thy seruantes, Paul and Silas, and broughtest them out of prison, and conuerted their keeper: so gracious Lord, strike the heartes of tyrantes with the terror of this thy worke, that they may know that they are but men, and that thou art that Sampson, that for their mocking and spiting of thee and thy woorde canst shake the pillers of their palaces, and throwe them vpon the furious Philistines heades. Turne thy wrath, oh Lord, from thy children that call vpon thy Name, to the conuersion or confusion of thine enemies that defie & abhorre thy Name, and deface thy glory. Thou hast knocked long at theyr doores, but they will not open to let thee in: burst open therefore the brasen gates of their stonie hearts, thou that art able of stones to rayse vp children to Abraham: and finally, so touch our hearts with the finger of thy grace, that wee may deepely muse vpon our sinneful liues, to amend them, & call for thy mercie to forgiue & pardon them, through Christ our Lorde, who liueth with thee, and the holy Ghost, three persons and one eternall God, to whom be al dominion, and glorie, with praise and thankesgiuing, for euer and euer. Amen.

[Ps. 46, printed in full with musical annotation]

A PRAYER FOR THE ESTATE OF CHRISTES CHURCH TO BE VSED ON SUNDAYES
Gracious GOD and most merciful Father, thou that art the God of all comfort and consolation: wee poore and wretched sinners acknowledge against our selues, that we are vn worthie to lift vp our eyes to heauen: so horrible and great are the sinnes that we haue committed against thee, both in thought, word, and deede: But thou art that God whose propertie is alwayes to haue mercie and thou hast extended thy mercie vnto vs in thy beloued Sonne our Sauiour Christ Jesus, in whome thou hast loued vs, before the foundation of the world was layde: and to the ende thou mightest aduance thine owne mercie, in a good and happie time hast called vs, by the preaching of thy blessed and holie Gospel, to repentance, preferring vs before many and great nations (to be a people consecrate vnto thee,) to holde foorth thy righteousnes, and to

walke in obedience before thee all the dayes of our liues. In this perswasion of faith, and by him, good Father, we present our selues before thee, renouncing all our sinnes and corruptions, and trusting onely in him and his righteousnes, beseeching thee for his sake to heare vs, and to haue mercie vpon vs. Thou hast made an holie promise vnto vs, that shalbe performed, that at what time soeuer, a sinner doth repent him of his sinne from the bottome of his heart, thou wilt heare him: And that who soeuer calleth vpon thee in his Name, thou wilt grant all his requestes. Our sinnes therefore doe grieue vs at the very heart, and we are displeased with ourselues for them; yea we lothe our selues for the frailties and transgressions that cleaue so fast vnto vs. Wherefore, good Father, heare vs, and accept the sacrifice: of thy Sonne, as a most sufficient satisfaction for them, and beholde vs in his righteousnes. Goe forward with that excellent worke that thou hast begonne in vs, and neuer leaue vs, till thou haue made it perfect, till the day of Jesus Christ. Encrease our knowledge, and giue vs a liuely sense to discerne sweete from sowre, and sowre from sweete, good from euill, and euill from good, that sinne and superstition deceiue vs not vnder the cloke of religion and virtue. O Lorde, this must be thy worke: for wee confesse that our reason is blinde, our will is frowarde, but wittes craftie to deceiue ourselues, our vnderstanding and all our naturall powers quite alienated and estranged from thee. It must be the seede of thy word, by the quickening of thy Spirite, that must leade vs to newenes of life, that must worke in vs the excellent hope of immortalitie, and make vs to liue to righteousnes: and therefore put to thy helping hand: Let thy gratious goodnes neuer fayle vs, to the increase of all heauenly vertues, and continuall growth and gaine to godlines. And because the Ministerie of thy word is the ordinarie meane for the attayning of this vnspeakeable blessing we beseeche thee, Let vs neuer lacke that excellent helpe: Let our bodies rather famish then our soules, yea let vs rather lacke all worldly things than that most precious Jewell of thy holy word, and comfortable Gospel preached for our saluation. And therefore, thou that art the Lorde of the haruest; send foorth labourers into thy haruest and double thy Spirit vpon thy seruants, making them as brazen zealles against thine enemies, giuing them courage and boldnes to doe thy message, yea and that to Kings and Princes, that they being called and sent of thee, in the assured perswasion of their offices, may not feare the faces of any mortall creatures, nor be dismayed with any transitorie maiestie. Good Lord, make thy word sharpe in their mouthes to an effectuall operation, that sinne may be cut downe, and thy righteousnes may florish: Graunt to them the feare of thy Name: Let their lippes, O Lord, preserue knowledge, and their liues shine in holines to the stopping of the mouthes of their aduersaries, and drawing many by their example to thy blessed and holie religion. Bowe the heartes of all Kings and Princes of the earth, to the obedience of thy dearely beloued Sonne Christ Jesus: If otherwise they shewe by plaine effectes, that they belong not to thy folde, good Lorde let them feele thy hand, and finde against whome they set themselues: let the blood of thy Saints, which they shedde without mercie, make them drunken to perdition. In meane time assist those that thou callest to this triall, that they may feele thy helpe and comfort amidst al their sufferings; whilest they shal be assured to be blessed when they suffer for righteousnes sake, and to reigne with thy sonne, when they fulfill his sufferings in their flesh, & carie in their bodies the scarres and markes of his woundes. O Lord, sanctifie their blood, that it may water thy Church, & bring a mightie increase and gaine to thy self, and a decrease and losse to the kingdome of Antichrist, and to the Princes of the earth, who are become his slaues and butchers. And herein (good Lord) by special name we beseech thee for the Churches of Fraunce, Flaunders, and of such other places: helpe them after their long troubles, as thou shalt see to bee best for them, in the aduauncing of thine owne glorie. And now (Lord) particularly wee pray vnto thee for this Church of England, that thou wilt continue thy gracious fauour still towardes it, to maintaine thy Gospell still amongst vs, and to giue it a free passage. And to that ende saue thy seruant Elizabeth our Queene, graunt her wisdome to rule this mightie people, long life and quietnesse rounde about her, detect all the traiterous practises of her enemies deuised against her, & thy trueth. O Lorde, thou seeth the pride of thine enemies: and though by our sinnes we haue iustly deserued to fall into their handes, yet haue mercie vpon vs and saue thy litle flocke. Strengthen her hande, to strike the stroke of the ruine of all their superstition, to doubte into the bosome of that rose coloured whore, that which shee hath powred out against thy Saintes, that shee may giue that deadly wound not to one head, but to all the heads of that cruell beast: that the life that quiuereth in his dismembred members yet amongst vs may vtterly decay, & wee, through that wholesome discipline, easie yoke, & comfortable scepter of Jesus Christ, may inioy his great righteousnesse, that thy Church may florish, sinne may abate, wicked men may hang their heads, and all thy children be comforted. Strengthen her hande, and giue her a swift foote to hunt out the bulles of Basan, and the deuouring beastes that make hauocke of thy flocke. And because this worke is of great importance, assist her with all necessarie helpes, both in giuing her godly, wise, and faithfull counsellers, as also in ministring to her such inferior rulers and officers as may sincerely, vprightly and faithfully doe their dueties, seeking first thy honour and glory, then the common wealth and quiet of this realme: that we may long inioy thy trueth, with her, and all other thy good blessings that in so great mercie thou hast bestowed vpon vs, with growth in goodnesse, gaine in godlinesse, and dayly bettering in sincere obedience. Good Lorde, comfort those that feele the heauie burthen of their sinnes, and haue no assurance in present feeling of that blessed inheritance thou hast purchased for them. Blesse all such (if it bee thy good will) whom thou hast vnited and knitte vnto vs in any league of familiaritie or affinitie, that we may reioyce in the best bonde, and onely in this, that wee are made partakers of one inheritance. Be mercifull vnto thy people of England which confesse thy name, & make vs not a by worde among the heathen, as our sinnes haue deserued. Turne away thy wrath which thy terrible tokens do threaten toward vs, and turne vs vnto thy selfe, remoue vs not out of thy presence, but let thy fatherly warnings mooue us to repentance. And thus (good Lorde) commending our seuerall necessitites vnto thee, who best knowest both what we want, and what is meet for vs, with giuing thee humble and heartie thankes for all thy mercies and benefites: wee knit vp these our prayers with that prayer that Jesus Christ our Lord and master hath taught us. *Our Father which art in heauen, &c.*

This prayer may be vsed after the Creede which foloweth the Epistle and Gospel.

THE REPORT OF THE EARTHQUAKE

On Easter Wednesday being the sixt of Aprill. 1580. somewhat before six of the clock in the afternoone, happened this great Earthquake whereof this discourse treateth: I meane not greate in respect of long continuaunce of time, for (GOD be thanked) it continued litle aboue a minute of an houre, rather shaking Gods rod at vs, than smyting vs according to our deserts: Nor yet in respecte of any greate hurt done by it within this Realme: For although it shooke all houses, castles, churches, and buildings, euery where as it wente, and put them in danger of vtter ruine: yet within this Realme (praysed be our Sauior Chryst Iesus for it) it ouerthrewe fewe or none that I haue yet heard of, sauing certaine stones, chimneys, walles, & pinacles of high buildings, both in this Cittie and in diuers other places: Neyther do I heare of any Christen people that receyued bodylie hurt by it, sauing two children in London, a boy & a girle, the boy named THOMAS GRAY, was slain out of hand, with the fal of a stone shaken down from the roof of a Church: & the girle (whose name was MABEL EVERITE) being sore hurt there at the same present by like casualties, died within fewe dayes after: But I terme it great in respect of the vniuersalnesse therof almost at one instant, not only within this Realme, but also without, where it was much more violente and did farre more harme: and in respecte of the greate terror which it then strake into all mens hearts where it came, & yet stil striketh into such as duely consider how iustly GOD may be offended with al men for sin, and specially with this realme of England, which hath most abundantly tasted of Gods mercie, and most vnthankfully neglected his goodnes, which yet hee warneth vs by this terrible wonder, what far more terrible punishments are like to light vpon vs ere long, vnlesse we amend our sinfull conuersation betymes.

A GODLIE ADMONITION FOR THE TIME PRESENT

Many and wonderfull ways hathe God in all ages moste mercifullye called all men to the knowledge of themselues, and to the amendement of their Religion and conu-ersation, before he haue laid his heauy hand in wrathful displeasure vpon them. And this order of dealing he obserueth, not onely towardes his owne deare children, but also euen towardes the wicked and castawayes: to the intente, that the one sort tourning from their former sinnes, and becomming the warer all their life after, shold glorify him the more for his goodnesse in not suffring them to continue in their sinnes vnreformed, to their destruction: and that the other sort should be made vtterlye vnexcusable for their wilful persisting in the stubbornesse of their hard and forward heartes, against all his friendly and fatherly admonitions.

He called *Cayne* to repentaunce, before he punished hym for shedding his brothers bloud, and gave him a long tyme to haue bethought himselfe in.

He warned the old world a hundred yeare and more, before he brought the floud vpon the Earth.

He chastized the Children of *Israel* diuerse wayes, ere he destroyed them in the wildernesse.

He sent Hornets and wilde Beastes, as foregoers of his hoste, into the land of Canaan, before he rooted out the old inhabiters therof.

He punished not *Dauid* for his murder and aduoutrie, vntill he had first admon-ished him by his Prophet.

He remoued not the *Israelits* into captiuitie, vntil all the warnings of his Proph-etes, and all the former corrections which he had vsed in vaine to reforme them, did shew them to be vtterly past hope of amendment.

Before the last destruction of *Ierusalem*, there went innumerable signes, tokens, and wonders.

Finallye, God neuer powred out his grieuous displeasure & wrath vpon any Nation, Realme, Citie, Kingdome, State, or Country, but he gaue some notable fore-warning thereof by some dreadfull wonder.

To let passe the examples of forraine Nations, which are many and terrible: what plagues, pestilences, famins, dyseases, tempests, ouerflowing of waters both salt and fresh, and a number of other moste prodigeous tokens happened successiuely long time togither, before the displacing of the Britons by the hands of our auncestors, for their neglecting of Gods word preached and planted many hundred yeares among them? Likewise, what great warnings did GOD giue to our forefathers, in diuers Princes reignes, before the alteration of the State, both by the *Danes*, and also by *William* the Conqueror? Againe, euen in these our dayes, how manifestly hath God threatned, and stil doth threaten our contempt of his holie Religion, and our securitie & sound sleeping in sinne, shewing vs euident tokens of his iust displeasure neere at hande, both abroade and at home.

I will not speake of the great ciuill Warres, nor of the horrible and vnnaturall massacres of good men, betrayde vnder the holyest pretences, whiche haue bin of late yeares in the Countryes bordering vpon vs: bicause such dealings, being pleasaunt to suche as seeke bloude, are taken for no wonders. Neyther will I stande vpon the rehearsall of the straunge things that befell in the Realme of *Naples* in the yeare 1566: nor of the Earthquake, whereby a great part of the Citie *Ferrara* in *Italy* was destroyed in the yeare 1570: or of the miraculous sightes that were seene in *Fraunce* about *Mountpellier* the year 1573: or of the lyke terrible sighte that appeared little more than a yeare agoe at *Prage*, the chiefe Citye of *Boemia*: nor of diuerse other thyngs whyche haue happened in forraine Countryes within the compasse of these fewe yeares: bycause it will perchaunce bee thought, that those tokens concerne the Countries where they befell, and not vs.

Well, I will not saye. *That whatsoeuer things haue bene written aforetimes, were written for our learning, that wee myghte learne too beware by other mennes harmes.*

We haue signes and tokens ynow at home, if we can vse them to our benefite.

What shall we say to the sore Famine whiche happened in the time of our late soueraigne Ladye *Queene Marye*, which was so great, that men were fayne to make breade of Acornes, and food of Ferne rootes? or to the perticular Earthquake, in the time of our most gracious soueraigne Ladye that nowe is, which transposed the boundes of mens grounds, and turned a Church to the cleane contrarie situation? or to the monstrous birthes both of Children & Cattel? or to the vnseasonablenesse of the seasons of some years, altering (after a sort) Sommer into Winter, and Winter into Sommer? or to the wonderfull newe Starre so long time fixed in Heauen? or to the straunge appearings of Comets, the often Eclipses of Sunne and Moone, the great and straunge fashioned lightes seene in the firmamente in the night times, the sodaine falling, and vnwonted abiding of vnmeasurable abundaunce of Snowe, the excessiue and vntimely raines and ouerflowing of waters, the greatnesse and sharpe continuaunce of sore frostes, and manye other such wonderfull things, one following in anothers necke? Shall we saye that none of these also do concerne us? or rather more truelye, that bycause they bee gone and paste (Oh ouer great securitie and blindness of hearte) we haue cleane forgotten them, or at least wise make no greate accompte of them, according our common Prouerb, that a wonder lasteth with vs but nine dayes.

Therefore, least we should want eyther proofe of the certaintie of Gods irreuocable iudgments, or argument of his continuall mercifull dealing towards vs, or matter wherewith to conuict vs of our excessiue vnthankfulnesse: behold he sendeth vs now lastely this Earthquake that befell the sixt day of this Month, not so hurtful in present operation, as terrible in signification of things to come. For the tryed experience of al ages techeth vs, & the wrytings of the wise and learned (specially of holy Scripture) do assuredly witnesse vnto vs, that such tokens are infallible forewarnings of Gods sore displeasure for sinne, and of his iuste plagues for the same, where amendment of life ensueth not.

And althoughe there be peraduenture some, whiche (to keepe themselues and others from the due looking back into the time earst misspent, and to foade them still in the vanities of this worlde, leaste they shoulde see their owne wretchednesse, and seeke to shunne Gods vengeaunce at hande) will not sticke to deface the apparent working of God, by ascribing this miracle to some ordinarie causes in Nature: Yet notwithstandyng, to the godly and wel disposed whych looke aduisedly into the matter, pondering the manner of this Earthquake throughly, and considering the manner of our dealings from the late restitution of the Gospell vnto this daye, and conferring the same with the manner of Gods fauourable dealing with vs, & wyth his ordinary dealing in cases where his truthe hath bin planted, and growth to be contemned: it must needs appeare to be the very finger of God, and as a messenger of the miseries due to such desertes.

For, firste of all, whereas naturally Earthquakes are sayde to be engendered by winde goten into the bowels of the earth, or by vapors bred and enclosed wythin the hollowe caues of the earth, where by their striuing and struggling of themselues to get oute, or being haled outwarde by the heate and operation of the Sun, they shake the earthe for want of sufficient vent to issue out at: If this Erthquake had risen of such causes, it could not haue bin so vniuersall, bycause there are many places in this Realme, which by reson of their substancial soundnesse and massie firmenesse, are not to be pierced by any windes from without, nor haue any hollow-nesse wherein to conceiue and breede any suche aboundaunce of Vapors, specially in places far distant from the Sea, or from Riuers, moores, marishes, fennes, or light and open soyles.

Neyther could it haue bene in so many places vniuersally at one instant both by sea and land. For the striuing thereof within the grounde, taking his beginning at some certaine place, and proceeding forward to get a vent, would haue required some space of time to haue attained to so manye places so farre off, or else haue broken oute with greate furie in some place that had bin weakest.

Againe, wheras in Earthquakes that proceede of natural causes, certain signes and tokens are reported to go before them, as, a tempestuous working and raging of the sea, the weather being faire, temperate and vnwindie, calmenesse of the ayre matched with great cold: dimnesse of the Sunne for certaine dayes afore: long and thinne strakes of Clouds appearing after the setting of the Sun, and the weather being otherwise cleere: the troublednesse of water euen in the deepest welles, yeelding moreouer an infected and stinking sauour: and lastly, great and terrible soundes in the earth, like the noyse of gronings or thunderings, as wel as afore as after the quaking: We finde not that anye such foretoken happened against the comming of this Earthquake. And therefore we maye well conclude (though there were none other reason to moue vs) that this miracle proceeded not of the course of any natu-rall causes, but of Gods onely determinate purpose, who maketh euen the very foundations and pillers of the earth to shake, the mountaynes to melte like Warre, and the seas to dry vp, and to become as a drye fielde, when he listeth to shewe the greatenesse of hys glorious power, in vttering his heauy displeasure against sinne.

But put the case that some naturall causes or secreate influences had their ordi-narie operations in this Erthquake, whereof notwithstanding there is not any suffi-cient likelyhoode: shall we so gaze vpon the meane causes, that we shall forget or let slip the chief and principall causes? Know we not (after so long hearing and professing of the Gospel) that a Sparow lighteth not on the ground without Gods prouidence? That the neglecting of his louing kindenesse, and the continuing in sinne without amendment, prouoke his vengeance? And yet that he of his owne fatherlye free goodnesse, doth euer giue warning before he striketh? Surely, we can not but knowe it, yea, and see it to, vnlesse the God of this worlde hath so blinded our eyes, that we wyll not see it. For it is daylye and almoste hourly tolde vs by the Ministers of hys worde, and the Bible lyeth alwayes open for vs to reade it oure selues, that as the onely originall cause and Welspring of all plagues and punishments is Sin: so the plagues and punishements themselues, and the orderlie disposing, directing, and guiding of al causes to their due endes and effects, is the onely worke of God, who to make all offendors vnexcusable (as I sayd before) doth often cause euen the verye Elementes and senselesse creatures, to foreshewe in moste terrible maner euen by their naturall opetions, the approching of his iuste vengeance. And truely, as it is sayde in the Psalme: their speaking and talking vnto vs, is not softly and whisper-ingly, as that the voices of them cannot be hearde: but contrariwise, they be so loude in our eares, so manifest to our eyes, and so sensible to oure feeling: that (vnlesse we be stony and steelie hearted, or gyuen ouer to a leude minde,) they cannot but be greeuous to our heartes, and terrible to our consciences.

Nowe then, shal we thinke thys rare and vnaccustomed miracle, suche as no man lyuing, nor none of our forefathers haue euer seene or heard of, to be a thing of no importance, as happening by chaunce, or grounded vppon some natural cause, and not rather as a messenger & summoner of vs to the dreadefull Judgementseate of the almighty and euerliuing God?

Let vs enter into our selues, and examine our time past. Since the sharpe tryall which God made of vs in the raign of Queene *Marie*, (at whiche time we vowed all obedience to God, if he woulde vouchsafe to deliuer vs againe from the bondage of the Romishe Antichrist, into the libertie of the Gospell of his sonne Jesus Christe) hee hearkening effectually to our request, hath giuen vs a long resting and refreshing time, blessed with innumerable benefites both of body and soule: For peace, health, and plentie of al things necessarie for the lyfe of man, we haue had a golden world aboue all the residue of oure neighbours bordering rounde about vs.

The worde of truth hath bin preached vnto vs early and late without lette or disturbance. And bicause our prosperitie hathe made vs to playe the wanton children againste God, he hathe chastized vs in the meane season with many fatherly correc-tions.

We haue bene taught, instructed, exhorted, encouraged, allured, entreated, reprooued, rebuked, vpbrayded, warned, threatned, nurtured, and chastised. To be shorte, there is not that meane whereby we mighte be wonne to the obeying and louing of our God, whether it were by fauourable mildenesse or moderate rigor, but he hathe ministred the same most mercifully and seasonably vnto vs. And what are we the better for all this?

Haue we so profited in this Schoole, that of couetous we be become liberall? of Proude and Enuious, Meeke and Lowly? of Leacherous, Chaste? of Gluttons, Meas-urable feeders? of Drunkardes, Sober? of Wrathfull and testie, Milde and patient? of Cruell and hard harted, Pitifull and gentle? of Oppressors Releeuers? and of Irreligious, Seruiceable to God?

Haue we so put off the old man, and so clothed ourselues with the new, in lyuing sincerely according to the doctrine we professe, that neyther the enimies of Chrystes Church, nor oure owne consciences can reprooue vs? Then neede we not to be afraide of anye signes from the Heauen aboue, nor of any tokens from the earth beneath: for wee haue builded our houses wiselye vppon the rocke, whiche neither wind, water, nor Earthquake, no nor Sathan hymselfe wyth all his Feends can shake downe or empayre.

But alas, it is farre otherwise with vs: we haue growen in godlynesse as the Moone doth lighte when she is paste the full. For who seeth not the emulation that remayneth still among vs for excesse of apparel, fare, & building? Who perceyueth not the disdaine of superiors to their inferiors, the grudge and hart-burning of infe-riors towards their superiors, & the want of loue in al states one towards another?

Who complayneth not of corruption in Officers, yea, euen in Officers of Justice, and Ministers of the lawe? Is it not a common byword (but I hope not true though common) that *as a man is friended, so the lawe is ended?*

In Youth there was neuer like looceness and vntimely libertie, nor in Age like vnstayednesse and want of discretion, nor the like carelessnesse of duty in either towards other.

The Boye mateth the man of aged grauity, and is commended for that whyche he deserueth to be beaten for.

Seruants are become Maysterlike, and fellowes wyth Maysters: and Maysters vnable to mayster their owne affections, are become seruantes to other folkes seru-auntes, yea, and to their owne seruants too.

Men haue taken vp the garishe attyre, and nice behauior of Women: and Women transformed from their owne kinde, haue gotten vp the apparell and stomackes of men: & as for honest & modest Shamefastnesse the preferrer of all Vertues, it is so highly mislyked, that it is thought of some folkes scarce tollerable in children.

Hatred, Malice, Disdaine, and desire of Reuenge for the waighte of a feather, are the vertues of oure yong Gentlemen in commendation of their manhoode and valiantnesse.

Deepe Dissimulation and Flatterie are counted Courtly behauior: Might ouer-commeth Right: and Truth is troded vnder foote.

Idlenesse and Pride bring dayly infinite numbers to that point, that they had rather rob and be shamefully hanged, than labour and liue with honesty.

Usurie, the consumer of priuate states, and the confounder of Common weales, is become a common (and in some mens opinions commendable) trade to liue by.

Faithfulnesse is fled into exile, & Falshod vaunteth himselfe in his place, till he haue gotten great summes of money into his hande, that he may playe the Banker-oute, to the vndoing of such as truste him.

The Sabboth dayes and holy dayes ordained for the hearing of Gods word to the reformation of our liues, for the administration & receyuing of the Sacraments to our comfort, for the seeking of al things behouefull for bodye or soule at Gods hande by Prayer, for the minding of his benefites, and to yeelde prayse and thankes vnto him for the same, and finally, for the special occupying of ourselues in al spiritual exer-cises: is spent ful heathnishly, in tauerning, tipling, gaming, playing, and beholding of Bear-bayting and Stage-playes, to the vtter dishonour of God, impechment of al godlinesse, & vnnecessarie consuming of mens substances which ought to be better employed.

The wante of orderly Discipline and Catechizing, hath eyther sent great numbers both olde and yong backe again into Papistrie, or let them run loose into godlesse Atheisme.

And would God that we which cal others to obedience, shewing them the way, and rebuking their vices: mighte not be iustlye charged to bee as Trumpets, whiche wyth their sound encourage other men to the battel, but fight not themselues. Nay Woulde God, that in all degrees, some suche as ought to be Lanternes of Light and Ring leaders to Vertue, were not infecters of others by theyr euill example.

I feare me, that if the Prophet Esay were here aliue, hee woulde tell vs as hee sometime tolde the Jewes, that from the crowne of oure head to the sole of our foote, there is no whole or sounde parte in oure body, but that all is full of sores, blaineds, and botches. Thinke we then that such doing shal scape vnpunished, or such buildings stande vnshaken? Wel may we deceyue oure selues in so hoping: but God deceyueth not, neyther is deceyued.

It is written, that euery plant which our heauenly Father hathe not planted, shal be plucked vp by the rootes, and that euery tree whiche beareth not good fruite, shall bee cut downe, and caste into the fire.

The Axe is laide to the roote of the tree: and the longer that Gods vengeance is in comming, the sorer it smiteth when it is come.

Terrible, and most true is this saying of his by the mouth of Salomon: *For as muche as I haue called, and you haue refuzed: and I haue stretched out my hands, and you haue not regarded it: but haue despized al my counsel, and set my correc- tion at nought: therefore wil I also laughe at your destruction, and mock yee when the thing that yee feare cometh vpon you: euen when the thing that yee be afrayde of breaketh in vpon you like a storme, and your miserie like a tempest. When trouble and heauinesse come vpon you on all sides: then shall ye call vpon me, but I wil not aunswere you, yee shall seeke me early, but yee shall not finde me: euen bicause yee hated knowledge, and didde not chooze the feare of the Lorde. Ye would none of my counsell, but hated my correction: and therfore shal ye eat the fruit of your owne ways, and be filled with your own inuentions.*

Soothly it is a dreadfull thing to fall into the hands of the Lorde. For as he is mercyful, so is he also iust, and in al his determinations he is vtterly vnchaunge- able. And (as the Prophet Jeremie sayth) *When sentence is once gone forth of his presence, it shall not retourne without performance.*

Wherfore let vs not be as horses and Mules which haue no vnderstanding: neyther let vs tarrie til Judgement bee sent forth vnto victorie. But let vs consider the time of oure visitation, and while we haue time, let vs vse it to our benefit.

So long as God calleth vnto vs, so long as he entreateth vs, so long as he teacheth, allureth, exhorteth or warneth vs, yea so long as he doeth as yet but threaten vs: so long the gate is stil open for vs, so as he wil heare vs if we cal, and be found of vs if we seeke him. But if he once hold his peace, and begin to smite, then it is too late to cal back his hande, our crying wil not boote vs.

Therfore while we haue respite, and while it is called to day, let vs not harden our harts as in the prouocation, and as in the day of Temptation in the wildernesse, but let vs hearken to his voyce, and forsaking the lustes and the wicked imagina- tions and deuices of our owne hartes, let vs turne to the Lord our God with hartie repentance and vnfeined amendment of life, least (beside other meaner plagues both of bodie and mind) our Candlesticke be remoued, our light quenched, Christs Gospel taken from vs, and we for our vnthankefulnesse be cast out wyth our chil- dren into vtter darkenesse, and in the terrible daye of Judgement heare this dreadfull sentence of the iust Judge pronounced against vs: Depart from me yee workers of wickednesse, which hardened your hartes against me and made your faces as hard as brasse, at such time as my long sufferance wayted for you, prouoking you by mildenesse and patience to amendment. FINIS.

APPENDIX: PREFACE IN VARIANT EDITION

Wee be taught *[as 1563–E:* by many and sundry examples … to shew his*]* wrath against sinne, and to call them to repentance, and to the redresse of their liues, all men ought to be prouoked and stirred vp *[as 1563–*E: to more feruencie … Josaphat and Ezechias in their*]* distresse of warres and forreine inuasions. So did the King and people of Nineue, and *Hester*, fall to humble prayers *[as 1563–E:* in lyke perils … prouoked by vs to*]* visit vs at this present with the plague and other grieuous diseases: It hath beene thought meete to excite and stirre vp all godly people within this Realme, to pray earnestly and heartily to God to forgiue vs our sinnes, and consequently to turne away his deserued wrath from vs, and to restore vs to his gracious fauour, and to our bodily health. And although it is euery Christian mans duety, of his owne deuotion to pray at all times: yet for that the corrupt nature of man is so slothfull and negligent herein, hee hath neede by often and sundry meanes to be stirred vp and put in remembrance of his duety. For the effectuall accomplishment whereof, it is thought meete that this order of Prayer following should at this time be published, being such as shall be vsed by the Minister in the Church, and may by euery man in his priuate family.

1582–S Fast days in response to catholic conspiracies, the church's financial difficulties, increasing sinfulness, fears about the king's religion and oppression of the poor

Sunday 3 June – Sunday 10 June 1582 (Scotland)

This fast was a response to many of the late sixteenth-century Scottish clergy's perennial grievances, notably the perceived violence and conspiracies of the catholic reformation and the weak financial position of the Kirk. Domestically, catholicism seemed a threat in the royal court, particularly owing to the influence of the king's French-born cousin, the duke of Lennox. The church had not been granted the revenues envisaged in the *Second book of discipline*. The assembly's request for royal proclamations in support of the fast may be a further indication of the Kirk's uneasy position. Another contemporary difficulty was the nomination of Robert Montgomery as archbishop of Glasgow, which the king seemed determined to uphold in the face of presbyterian opposition, both to Montgomery and to the archiepiscopal office. According to Spottiswoode, the attempts of the provost of Glasgow to force Montgomery's admission as archbishop were seen by some as an additional reason for fasting, and 'furnished matter of long discourse to the preachers'.

Order: by the general assembly beginning 24 Apr. 1582, described in Calderwood, III, 615–16.
Additional sources: *BUK*, II, 569; Row, p. 95; Melvill, p. 128; Spottiswoode, II, 281–8; *Stirling presbytery records, 1581–1587*, ed. James Kirk (Scottish History Society, 4th ser., 17, Edinburgh, 1981), 44.

DESCRIPTION OF ORDER

Order by the general assembly beginning 24 April 1582

The Assemblie, understanding what are the universall conspiraceis of Papists, and enemeis of God in all countreis, against Christians, for executioun of the bloodie Councell of Trent – the oppressioun and thraldome of the Kirk of God, waisting of the rents therof, without remedie, falling from our former zeale; flocking home of Papists and Jesuits; bloodshed, incest, adultereis, and other suche horrible crimes defiling the land; the danger wherin the king's Majestie standeth, through evill companie conversing about him, by whom it is to be feared he may be corrupted in maners and religioun; universall oppressioun and contempt of the poore, – ordeaneth a fast to be observed and keeped universallie in all kirks of this realme, with teaching and instructioun of the people; and that it beginne the first Sabboth of Junie nixt to come, and continue till the nixt Lord's day theiafter, inclusive; the exercise of preaching used in the meane time according to the accustomed order; and that the king's Majestie be certified heerof by the commissioners directed to him, and requested to hold hand thereto, by setting furth of proclamatiouns to that effect.

1583–S   Fast days [reasons unknown]

Sunday 8 December – Sunday 15 December 1583 (Scotland)

There is no record of this fast in Calderwood or *BUK*, but it is mentioned in the register of Stirling's presbytery, the earliest extant records of this new form of church court. Its minutes of 22 October 1583 make clear that this was a national fast, appointed by the last general assembly (which met earlier in October), but give no sense of the reasons for the fast. The presbytery recorded its observance of the week's fasting, and later pursued two clerics who had celebrated weddings during it. The fast is also mentioned in the register of the St Andrews kirk session, which investigated the non-observance of the worship by a group of golfers.

Order: none found.
Sources: *Stirling presbytery records*, ed. Kirk, pp. 178, 190–2, 201; *Register of the minister, elders and deacons of the Christian congregation of St. Andrews*, ed. David Hay Fleming (2 vols., Scottish History Society, 1st ser., 4 and 7, Edinburgh, 1889–90), II, 515.

1585–E1   Thanksgiving services for the failure of the Parry plot

[February–March] 1585 (England and Wales?)

In February 1585, William Parry, newly elected MP for Queenborough, was denounced by his alleged co-conspirator, Edward Neville, for plotting to assassinate Elizabeth I; he was executed on 2 March. No order for the occasion exists but Ralph Newberry licensed the 'Orders for the Dyocesse of Wynchester with William Parries voluntarye confession' with the Stationers' Company on 24 February. Similarly, the only extant form of prayer was printed for the diocese of Winchester. Though Winchester had a strong tradition of recusancy, it is unlikely that special worship for such a significant event would have been ordered only in one diocese. It is more probable that orders were issued for the whole realm and that the printing of some orders and forms was contracted out by the royal printer, Christopher Barker. This had occurred in for 1565–E1 and, in late 1587, Barker delegated most of his day-to-day printing to Newberry and George Bishop. The hypothesis is strengthened by evidence in some London churchwardens' accounts which record in this year the purchase of prayer books which could relate to this occasion. In a change to usual practice, no special liturgy was commissioned for this thanksgiving. Instead, ministers were ordered to conduct the normal BCP service and to add a sermon on the authority of princes and obedience of subjects. They were also instructed to read out Parry's confession, followed by a special prayer. The format of these services, therefore, was close to those ordered after the Northern Rising (1570–E). The three additional prayers noted by Clay were printed in the pamphlet *A true and plaine declaration*, though they may have been issued separately for private use as they are paginated separately from the rest of the pamphlet.

Order: none found.
Form of prayer: *An order of praier and thankes-giving, for the preseruation of the queenes maiesties life and salfetie: to be vsed of the preachers and ministers of the dioces of Winchester. With a short extract of William Parries voluntarie confession, vvritten vvith his owne hand* ([Henry Denham for] Ralph Newberry; [8] pp.; STC 16516)* [also in Clay, pp. 583–90].
Additional sources: draft of prayer corrected by Burghley, Lans. 116/29, fos. 77r–79r [also in Strype, *Annals*, III: 2, 334–7]; *A transcript of the registers of the Company of Stationers of London, 1554–1640*, ed. Edward Arber (4 vols., 1875–7), II, 440; *A true and plaine declaration of the horrible treasons, practised by William Parry the traitor, against the queenes maiestie* (1585; STC 19342); Strype, *Annals*, III: 1, 360–82, III: 2, 330–7; Clay, pp. 465–6.

FORM OF PRAYER

The Direction how to vse this Order
    First, where anie Preacher is, the next Sonday after the receauing of this order, he shall make a Sermon of the authoritie and Maiestie of Princes, according to the worde of God, and how streight dutie of obedience is required of all good and Christian subiects, and what a greeuous and heynous thing it is both before God and man traiterouslie to seeke their destruction, and the shedding of their blood, which are the Anointed of God, set vp by him to be the Ministers of his iustice and mercie to his people. In the ende of which Sermon, he shall set forth and declare the briefe notes of the confession of the wicked purpose conceaued of late by Doctor Parry, to haue murdered the Queenes Maiestie, animated therevnto by the Pope and his Cardinals, as you maie see it set downe here following. Last of all he shall saie the praier here prescribed for that purpose, and desire the people to lift vp their harts to God together with him. After the praier, there shall be songe or said the xxj. Psalme, or some other Psalme to the like effect.

A short extract of a volvntarie confession made by William Parrie, written with his owne hand, the [blank] Februarie. 1584.
    William Parrie Doctor of Lawe, carieng an offensiue minde against the state, by reason of his conuiction, in a trial of life & death at Newgate, for the attempting of the murdering of one Hugh Hare, for the which notwithstanding he receaued her Maiesties most gracious pardon, and therevpon departing the Realme, in the yeare 1582. for that he conceaued no hope of aduancement here, because he was

in his owne opinion a pretended Catholique, and had not in 22. yeares receaued the Communion. At his being in the partes beyonde the seas, hauing first reconciled himselfe to the Church of Rome at Paris, and then at Millain, conceaud with himselfe a meane (as he pretended) to relieue the Catholiques of this Realme, which was by killing of the Queenes Maiestie.

And nothing staied him in this concept, but onlie to be assured in conscience, that it was lawfull and meritorious, and before the execution thereof to receaue absolution from the Pope. For his assurance, or rather setling of his conscience herein, he receaued ful satisfaction, first from an olde Iesuit in Venice: next from the Popes Ambassadour, resident there, then from other good fathers (as he termeth them) in Lyons and Paris, and lastlie was incouraged to proceede therein by the Nuntio to the Pope, resident at Paris, who promised him, after he assented to that wicked enterprise, to recommend him to the altar, and also to procure the like to be done generally through Paris, which was accordingly performed in generall termes, by *Recommending of one that had taken vpon him to doe some daungerous enterprise, tending greatly to the aduancement of the Catholique religion.* The saide Nuntio did also conueigh the said Parries letters directed to the Pope, and to the Cardinal by the which he did signifie to them his ful resolution to proceede in his enterprise, & for his better successe in the same, praied his benediction Aposticall, wherunto answer was made by letters written in Rome by the Cardinal dated the last of Ianuarie, which he receaued from him when the Court lay at Greenewich, in March last.

The tenor of those letters was a commendation of his enterprise, an allowance thereof, an absolution in his holines name of all his sinnes, and a request to go forward in it, in the name of God.

Which letters confirmed his resolution to kill her Maiestie, and made it cleare in his conscience, that it was lawfull and meritorious, as he setteth downe in his said confession. Wherevpon he insinuated himselfe into the Court, and by waies & meanes sought to winne credit, &c. to the entent to bring his wicked purpose to passe. Which at sondrie times he had done, had not the gracious prouidence of God, by strange meanes, interrupted his purpose.

A Praier for the Queene

O Eternall God and mercifull Father, with humble heartes we confesse that we are not hable, either by tounge to vtter, or in mind to conceaue, the exceeding measure of thine infinite goodnes and mercie towardes vs wretched sinners, and towards this our noble Realme and naturall contrey. Not many yeares since, when for our vnthankful receauing of the heauenly light and truth of thy Gospell, we were iustlie cast into thraldome and misery, and thrust again vnder the kingdome of darknes, so that our consciences lay groning vnder the heauie burdens of errour, superstition, and idolatry, euen then, euen then O Lord, thou didest vouchesafe of thy great goodnes, not only without our desert, but far beyond our hope & expectation, to preserue for vs thy faithfull seruant our gratious prince and Soueraigne Queene Elisabeth, and to saue hir from the iawes of the cruell Tigers, that then sought to sucke hir bloud and to worke to vs perpetuall tirannie, and bondage of conscience. This thou diddest, O gratious Lord vndoubtedly, that she might be to this thy church of England, a sweete and tender nurse, and that this realme vnder hir happie gouernement, might be a blessed Sanctuarie, and place of refuge for thy poore afflicted Saints, in these daungerous daies persecuted and troubled in many contreyes for the profession of thy Gospell: yea, and that this our benefit, and their comfort might be the more assured, thy diuine prouidence from time to time hath many wayes mightily and miraculously preserued and kept hir from the craiftie, cruell and traiterous deuises of hir bloudie aduersaries, and the deadly enimies of thy Gospell which with barberous crueltie haue sought to extinguish the light thereof, by sheading hir Maiesties most innocent bloud: but this thy gracious goodnes & mightie prouidence, neuer so apparently shewed it selfe, at any one time, as euen within these few dayes, when a traiterous subiect, neuer iniured or greeued by hir, but sundry times holpen, releeued, and countenanced far aboue his state and worthines had of long time retained a wicked and diuelish purpose and often sought occasion and oportunitie to lay violent hands vpon hir royall person, and to haue murdered her. But still the vigilant eye of thy blessed prouidence did ether preuent him by some sudden interruption of his indeuour, or by the Maiestie of her person and princely behauiour towards him, diddest strike him so abashed: that he could not performe his conceaued bloodie purpose. And at the last this wretched villanie was by thy meanes disclosed, and his owne tunge opened to confesse his detestable and wicked intent. For this thy inestimable goodnes towards vs (O heauenlie Father) with humble heartes and mindes we thanke thee: and blesse thy name for euer and euer. For assuredlie if thou haddest not bene now on our side (as the Prophet Dauid saith) the whole fluds and waues of wickednes had ouerwhelmed vs, and we had beene sunk into the bottomeles pit of infinite and vnspeakable miseries. We beseech thee therfore (O Lord) that thou wilt blesse vs so with thy grace, that we may be rightlie and trulie thankefull to thee: that is, not in word only, but in deede also, dailie studieng to frame our liues according to the direction of thy holie word, which thou hast sent among vs: And that hir Maiestie thus feeling the mightie hande of thy prouidence fighting for her salfetie, may more boldlie and constantlie with an heroicall spirite stand in the protection & defense of thy blessed Church, which by thy word thou hast planted among vs. And lastlie that ye cruel spirits of Antichrist that seeke the subuersion of the Gospel, maie by the hand of thy iustice, feele what it is to set to sale for money the innocent bloud of thine annointed Princes, which thou hast prepared and set vp, to be the nurses and protectors of thy truth: Grant this O heauenlie Father, for Jesus Christes sake thy onlie sonne our Sauiour, to whom with thee and the holie Ghost, be giuen all honor and glorie: world without ende.

1585–E2 Prayers in response to bad weather and sinfulness

Fridays and Sundays [month unknown] 1585 (London diocese; possibly elsewhere in England and Wales)

There are no extant contemporary accounts of the weather in 1585, but the title-page of this form indicates that it was unusually stormy and wet. The extant form was ordered for use by Aylmer in the diocese of London but, as its title-page makes clear, it was also to be used by householders across the realm. Thus, 'national' observance of this occasion may have been unofficial and private rather than official and public: there are no references to purchase of the form in printed churchwardens' accounts outside the diocese of London, no order for nationwide observance exists and Aylmer's authority to order private observance outside his diocese is doubtful. As Aylmer ordered the form to be used in London, it is possible that it was written by him. However, unlike previous forms composed by him (e.g. 1580–E), this one comprised only a very lengthy prayer (which would have been inserted into the BCP service, probably at the end of the litany) rather than a full liturgy. This format had been used earlier for special worship (e.g. 1562–E1) and became more common from the 1590s to the early 1640s without rivalling the regime's preference for complete liturgies, but why it was chosen for this occasion is unclear. It may reflect Aylmer's growing intolerance of puritanism in his diocese and his *rôle* in the (short-lived) campaign for conformity organized by the new archbishop of Canterbury, John Whitgift, in 1584–5. When obliging radical ministers to conform to the BCP, Aylmer may have been reluctant to diverge too far from its precepts. The prayer's emphasis on the sins of the nation was typical of special worship and the references to Marian persecution, Elizabeth's providential accession and the restoration of the true faith were characteristic of Elizabethan mainstream protestantism. However, the prayer's shrill, intemperate tone reflected growing clerical concern about ungodliness and sin, as well as anxiety about the possibility of an ideological war with Spain.

Order: none found.
Form of prayer: *A necessarie and godly prayer appoynted by the right reverend father in God Iohn, bishop of London to be vsed throughout all his dioces vpon Sondayes and Frydayes, for the turning away of Gods wrath. Aswell, conserning this vntemperate wether and raine, lately fallen vppon the earth, as also all other plagues and punishments, which for our manyfolde sinnes wee moste iustly deserve: moste needfull to be vsed of euerie housholder and his famely: throwout the realme of England.* 1585 (printer unknown; [8] pp.; STC 16515) reprinted in *Two forms of prayer of the time of Queen Elizabeth now first reprinted*, ed. Ayrton Chaplin (Cambridge, 1876), pp. 9–16.
Additional sources: Strype, *Historical collections of Aylmer*, pp. 80–1; Clay, pp. 466–7.

FORM OF PRAYER

O almightie GOD and most mercifull Father, we humbly prostrate our selues before thy mercy seat, with vnfeigned acknowledgment of our manyfolde sinnes, wherewith wee our Fathers, and our Children haue iustlye prouoked, thy Maiestie to wrath, and polluted this good Lande which thou hast of thy great goodnesse giuen vs to enioy. Wee willingly confesse moste righteous Lord, that our distruction proceedeth from our selues: and that thou hast shewed all maner of mercie, pacience and long sufferance to inuite vs to repentaunce. Thou hast not dealt so with any of the Nations rounde about vs: no, not with thy people Israell: for thy compassions haue not failed vs, but are renued euery day. Thou beheldest our miserable captiuitie bothe of body & soule vnder Antechrist, and didst consider our calamitie in the late dayes of persecution, when the bodies of the Sainctes were burned in our streates, and didst in a moment turne our mourning into mirth, our heauinesse into gladnesse: causedst the crueltie of the enemies to cease, their tyrannie to passe awaye as a Clowde: since which tyme thou hast giuen vs ioyfulnesse of heart, and plentie of peace, and all thinges as in the dayes of Salomon thy Seruant. Thou O Lord, didest also purge thy Sanctuarie, and Church from all the abhominations and Idolatrie of Antichriste, and haste placed thy Tabernacle, and thy glorious seat and rest among vs, and hast made vs an holy people vnto thy selfe. All thy blessinges O LORD, haue ouer taken vs, because thou louedst vs: Thou didest exalte thy Seruant Elizabeth, and deliueredst her from the mouth of the Lyon, to rule ouer vs with iustice and equitie, whose raigne hath beene peaceable, glorious and prosperous, that shee might buyld a Sanctuary vnto thy name. Thou hast moreouer raysed vs out of our loynes our owne Sonnes to bee witnesses vnto vs of thy mercy and fauour, and they haue brought peace to our houses, and the glade tydings of saluation to our doores. Finally, O moste mercyful Father, thou haste made vs plenteous in the frute of the Earth: wee haue sowne our Feeldes and reaped our corne in abundance: Thou hast blessed vs in the frute of our bodie, in the frute of our cattell and the in crease of all thinges: There hath no Famyne come neere vs: there hath beene no complaning in our streates: no noyse or terrour of war, but deep peace with in the walles of England, and plenteousnesse within her pallaces: neither yet doothe hee cease to doe vs good, but his mercies are increased day by day.

These benefites and many other, lyke as wee doe acknowledge to haue receiued at thy mercyful hands only, so doe wee with greefe and vnfeigned sorrow confesse that wee haue sundrie wayes abused thy Fatherly goodnesse, in multiplying our offences and fillyng and defilyng this good Land with all abhominations. All haue sinned from the least to the highest, there is no parte whole or free from greeuous enormities: Wee haue not obeyed thy Seruants and Ministers which haue spoken to vs in thy name, to our Princes, and to all the people of the Land, but haue despised and defiled thy ministrie, and powred the dung of contempt and reproche vpon their faces: Wickednesse hath proceeded from the mightie and all fleshe haue corrupted their way, and the Earth as in the dayes of Noe and Lot replenished and oppressed with the burthen of our iniquities crieth strongly and groneth for vengeance. There is no faith, no trueth, no knowledge of GOD in the Land, but lying, swearing and forswearing, whordome Adulterie, Treasons, and conspiracies, and blood toucheth blood. Wee haue flattered thee O LORD, with our tounges and dissembled in our double harts lyke the Isralites, whome thou hast fearfully punished in the sight of all the world, and saluted thee long with Judas kisse: to wit. with a vizard and shewe of Religion with the gloze of outward profession, drawing neere to thee with our lippes, but our hartes far from thee, and our woorkes against thee, hauing a shewe of godlynesse but denying the force thereof, and crusifying againe thy deer sonne, and treading the bloode of his Testament vnder our feete, and tearing in peeces his vnseamed Coate by dissention and deuision among our selues to our vtter confusion.

The Nations which call not vppon thy name are more righteous then wee, and we haue iustified the Jewes, Turkes, and all other Paynims: Our Idolatrous & ignorant fathers shall ryse in iudgment and condemne vs who followed that they knewe, but wee knowe thy will (O LORD) and followe it not: Therfore O righteous God, wee iustly feare thy fearefull hand, those stripes which wee deserue, and thy heauy iudgements which thou hast executed for sinne vppon all the sinfull Kingdomes of the earth.

The crye of our sinnnes so many and so monsterous is doubtlesse come vp before thee, as by many euydent signes thou declarest, and our owne consciences accuse vs and conuict vs to be worthie, that all thy curses and scourges shoulde light vppon vs. The fearfull translations and sundrie mutations of the Kingdomes of the earth, thy iudgements burning among our Neighbours round about, which might teach vs righteousnesse and thy feare: the swift running and preaching of thy woord, and so rare faith and repentaunce in the worlde, the corruptions incurable in all orders and degrees, the intollerable securitie, the monsterous pryde, and the insatiable couet-ousnesse of this Age, the rage and power of Antichrist, the wrath of the Deuill now fearcer toward the end of the world, the swarme of Heresies, fearefull signes bothe in heauen and earth, as before the ruine and desolation of Jerusalem, doe menace certaine and vndoubted destruction vnto vs if thou (O Lord) deale not mercifully with vs, and vppon our prayer and true repentaunce receiue vs to fauour againe. O righteous Lorde, many are the plagues which thou hast in store for the wicked and for vs wilfull sinners, they are of long continuance and sore.

For by thy word (O Lord) the Pestilence spreadeth in the darknesse, and the deadly plague that maketh such slaughter in the Noone day, and the fearefull diseases of Egipt, and euery sicknesse cleaueth, vnto vs till thou haue made vs of a populous nation fewe in number: At thy beck and call are the mightie Tyraunts of the earth, and thou canst send from farre Heathen and straunge nations to possesse our goodly houses, our Wheat, our honie, our wine, our Oyle, the encrease of our flockes, and our holy Temples & strong Citties, as thou hast done to Jerusalem, the Citties of Greece, Roome, and other places of the world: Sometime also thou canst arme thy sencelesse creatures against vs, turning the waters into blood and killing the Fyshes in the verry waters: At the voyce of thy Commaundement swarmes of Flyes & Lyce come foorth in our Coastes: Thou canst raine stones from heauen, and with horrible flames burne vp the Frute of the Earth: Thou canst open the Windowes of Heauen, and destroye euerye liuing thing, thou canst stir vp the Grashoppers and caterpillers to deuoure the greene herbe, and consume whatsoeuer groweth. With these and such like darts thou beatest down our pryde, our Uynes, our Figgetrees, and breakest the strength of bread, and causest vs to feede vppon the fleshe of our sonnes and daughters, of Rattes and Myce, and such lothsome and vnnaturall foode: Thou O Lord, openest thy good treasure, euen the heauen to giue Raine in due season and sealest vp the same when it pleaseth thee by thy terryble and glorious power, and these drops which thou hast appointed of thy mercie, to refresh and renue the face of the Earth, thou makest to choke and drowne the Creatures of the Earth, as thou dooest now moste fearfully and iustly threaten vs with vnseasonable weather, with immoderate and excessiue raine, by this thy loouing Rod threatning greatter vengeaunce to come, and by these black and heauie cloudes signifying the darck day of Gods wrathfull visitation, which doubtlesse is not farre of, except thou Lord stay thy holy hand, and yet loe for our repentance, haue mercy therfore vppon vs O LORD haue mercy vpon vs, and turne away this plague of raine and all other plagues from vs, and let vs not be confounded in the sight of our & thine enemies, least they blaspheme thy blessed name which is called vpon vs, thy treuth whiche is professed among vs: Powre out thyne indignatioun vppon the heathen which knowe thee not, and vpon that cursed sea and generation of Antichrist: who lyke to Antiochus seeketh by all meanes to extinguish the true seruice and Gospell of thy Sonne Jesus Christe. Let them know O LORD, against whome they raile, blaspheme, conspyre and whome they cursse with their tirannous interdictions and Bulles, that they may vnderstand that thou art a mighty Wariour for thy Church and that thy right hand will defend it. Remember O Lord, how many Aduersaries thy trueth hath, how the Turke in the east, Antichrist in the West doe persecute the same dayly and openly, and false bretheren within couertly, and that there are but fewe Ilands and Citties, and those scattered here & there that confesse thy name, and there enemies compasse and hemne them in round about. And bee mercyfull vnto vs O Lord, and leaue a seed and a remnant still among the people of the World to prayse & magnifie thy name. Thou hast no pleasure in the distruction of sinners, neither doest thou willingly punishe and aflict the Children of men. The dead that are in their graues giue vnto thee neither prayse nor righteousnes, but the soules that are vexed for the greatnes of their sinnes, the eyes that fayle, and the knees that faint, and the harts that mourne, and the wet faces of penitent Sinners yeelde prayse to thee, and cause thee indeede to be called mercyfull to many generations.

Forget not O Lord, how this land hath been a sanctuary to an infinit number of aflictted seruants to flee vnto in their extremities. Call to remembraunce the ashes and bloud of thy holy Martyres, which haue suffered for the testimonie of Jesu, and for the worde of thy sonne Christ, and write it vp in thy booke for euer and euer, that England was the mother and Nurce of so many thy blessed seruantes. Hearken moreouer to the continuall prayers of thy faithfull seruantes which stand in the gappe to intreate day and night before thy Throne for the peace of this Land, whose heades are full of water, & whose eyes are fountains of teares to bewaile and lament for the sinnes of the Land: Attend to their petitions as thou diddest to the praier of Moses, when thou wouldest haue destroyed the name of Israell from vnder Heauen: & as thou diddest in great mercie heare the crye of the Niniuites, and let not the righteous perish with the wicked. We do not require mercy (O Lord our God) for the righteousnes of our fathers, our princes, & ministers but for thy names & thy trueths sake: according to thy mercie therfore let thine anger cease and be turned away from vs: shut wee beseeche thee the Floodegates of Heauen, that it raine no more to hurt the frute and encrease of the earth: Giue vs such seasonable weather, that wee may reape the frutes of the earth in due season: and auert from vs all other thy plagues which wee most iustly haue deserued, & cause thy face still to shine vppon this thy Church of England: Exalt and aduance still the horne of thyne annoynted Seruant: sustaine the pillars theirof, thrust out labourers into the Haruest: procure still and maintaine the peace and wealth therof, that wee may prayse thy goodnesse for many Generations, through Jesus Christ our Lord. Amen.

1586–E1   Services during a time of dearth

Wednesdays and Fridays [May 1586–after January 1587] (England and Wales)

Following the bad weather and persistent rain that prompted the special prayers for 1585–E2, a succession of poor harvests into the late 1580s caused widespread dearth, high grain prices, and serious social distress, these at a time of mounting fears of war. In May 1586 Whitgift instructed his diocesan bishops to order licensed preachers in all their sermons to persuade parishioners to avert God's judgments through repentance of their sins and by prayers, fasting, amendment of their lives, and charity towards the poor, needy and afflicted. Where parishes had no preachers, ministers were to read out the homilies on repentance, fasting and almsgiving, as reprinted in a special form of prayer. This form also contained directions and texts for special morning and evening services every Wednesday and Friday: a selection of psalms and biblical readings, with the litany followed by the BCP prayers for the time of dearth and famine, and for the time of war. As with later occasions (see 1588–E2 and 1589–E), the text and date of Whitgift's order is known through its inclusion in a letter from Aylmer, who in the bishop of London's capacity as dean of the province was responsible for communicating the archbishop's orders to other bishops and senior clergy. Both Whitgift's order and Aylmer's letter made arrangements for ensuring that the form of prayer ('booke') was available in all parishes, and the form itself contained further orders to ensure observance: at least one member of every household was to attend each service, and churchwardens were to report to the bishops any ministers or parishioners who failed to fulfil their duties. It can be inferred that similar orders were issued in York province.

Whitgift's orders were renewed during the following winter, in support of an initiative in government social policies. At the end of December 1586 the privy council agreed to the issue of a 'book of orders' for the relief of the poor and regulation of the grain markets. These orders were sent in early January 1587 to justices of the peace, sheriffs and other government officials, alongside letters from the council to the archbishops of Canterbury and York. The archbishops were asked to instruct all clergy and preachers to urge the prosperous to give more in charity and to moderate their diets, and the poor to understand the need for repentance and patience, to appreciate the efforts now being made to assist them, and to report any profiteers to the JPs, rather than resorting to riots. In forwarding this council direction to Aylmer and the senior clergy, Whitgift's own letter added that they were to ensure that his directions of the previous May were being observed, including the provisions for Wednesday and Friday services and use of the form of prayer. His instructions were notable for two further features. He enjoined the bishops and the clergy to prevent a recurrence of 'disordered conventicles, or innovacons', the first expression on occasions of special worship of concern about the activities of zealous puritans. He also required the bishops to obtain a monthly report from each parish on the provision of charity and the condition of the poor, and to send summaries to himself whenever convenient. It is not clear how far these requirements were enforced, but this measure was revived for 1596–E3.

Orders: Aylmer to William Hutchinson, archdeacon of St Albans, 14 May 1586, HALS, ASA 5/2/54, pp. 329–30; Aylmer to Hutchinson or to Mr Williams, preacher of St Albans, 8 Jan. 1587, HALS, ASA 5/2/68, pp. 369–71.

Form of prayer: *An order for publike prayers to be vsed on Wednesdayes and Frydayes in euery parish church within the province of Canterburie, conuenient for this present time set forth by authoritie* ([48] pp.; STC 4587)*.

Form of prayer (other edition): STC 4587.3.

Additional sources: *CSPD, 1581–90*, p. 373; *APC*, XIV, 277–8, 279–80; Strype, *Whitgift*, II, 67–9 (misdating this occasion to 1590); Clay, pp. 467–8.

ORDERS

Bishop of London to archdeacon of St Albans: 14 May 1586

After my harty Commendacons to yow. Whereas I have receaved lettres from my Lordes grace of Canterbury whereby I am directed to give order generally throughout the whole province of Canterbury for publicacon of a forme of Common praiers appoynted to be vsed on wednesdaies and frydaies as may appeare by his graces said lettres the tenor whereof dothe hereafter ensewe viz:/

Salutem in Christo: Almightye god in greate mercye far above our desertes hathe for manye yeares past vnder the happie gouernment of our Soueraigne, powred the manifolde benefittes of the true prechinge [sic] of his worde of peace, of plentye, & suche like his riche blessinges vpon vs beyonde all example either of former ages or of this presente tyme in other Countries nere vnto vs, which his abundante mercye and vnspeakable kindenes because we have not bine thanckfull for (as we oughte) nor answered with true repentance humiliacon and due obedience, but rather by to lavishe excessive and riotouse spendinge have diversly abused his good Creatures provided for the necessarye sustentacon and Coveringe of our bodies, It is greately to be feared leaste as god hathe begun to shake his fatherly Rod already at vs by some scarsitye and dearthe of Victualles, and of other necessaries of this life, so likewise in his Justice he dothe proceede to power out the full measure of his wrathe and indignacon, vpon vs, and multiply not only this but other the plauges & Calamities of pestilence, Ware, and suche like wherewith other Contries have bine longe & lamentabye distressed: Vnles by vnfayned repentaunce and amendement of our life we prevent his grevous Judgmentes thus hanginge ouer our heades, Therefore for appeasinge his wrathe and displeasure iustly conceaved and for preventinge and divertinge his Judgmentes not obscurely threatned; It is thought verye mete and convenient that we fall to earneste repentaunce praiers fastinge and other dedes of Charitye; And to thintente that the people maye the rather be thereto perswaded & induced, I have thought good to will and require your Lordship not onlye to give order to the preachers of your owne Dioces <but> *and* specially to suche as occupie the Crosse that in all their Sermons and exhortacons they will earnestlye move and perswade the people to hartye repentaunce prayers fastinge and amendement of life and liberalitye to the pore, nedye, and afflicted members of Christe. whereby god maye the rather be moved to withdrawe from vs his indignaton and his heavye punishment but also to signifye the same to the rest of my brethren the Bisshoppes of <this> *my* province, requiringe them and euerye of them to doe the <same> *like* in their seuerall dioceses, And where there be no preachers that the parsons Vicar or Curate doe Reade to the people suche homilies as are sett forthe in the booke which herewithall I sende vnto yow together with the psalms, praiers, and lessons for the purpose therein noted requiringe the Churchwardens of euerye parishe to provide one of the said bookes for the vse of the parishe And so not doughting of your Lordships Care to performe the Contentes hereof with all Convenient spede: I Committ yow to the Tuicon of Almightye god From Lambethe the xiiii^th of Maye 1586 / Your Lordships lovinge brother in / Christe Jo: Cantuar

For the more spedye execution of so good & godlye an action I have herewith sent vnto yow one of the bookes whereof mention is made in his graces *saide* lettres, willinge and requiringe yow to cause his said graces lettres to be put in exequution throughoutt all your Archdeaconry as spedilye & effectually as yow cann And so I Commit yow to the tuicon of Almightye god from my howse at Fulham the xiiii^th of Maye 1586 / your lovinge frende in Christe/ John Lond.

Bishop of London to archdeacon of St Albans or Mr Williams, preacher of St Albans: 14 May 1586

After my hartie commendacons vnto yowe: Whereas of late I receiued letters from my Lord his grace of Cantorburye, with a copie of a letter from the lordes of her maiesties most honorable privie counsell therein enclosed the tenor*s* whereof hereafter en[s]ewethe. / . / viz. /

After our right hartie commendacons to your Lordship: Whereas the Queenes maiestye having a great and princelye care that some good order and provision might be made in this tyme of scarcitie and dearth, for the better maintenance, releife and sustentacon of the poore people of the Realme, hathe caused vs to advise and consider of those meanes that might seeme convenient to remedie this great necessitie, by cawsing the markettes to be dewlye served, and the people sett on worke: wherevpon we have by her maiesties commandemente divised certein orders to be generallie observed throughout the Realme whereby we hope the poore shall fynde great ease and comforte, if the same maye be dewlie executed: And for the better furtherance of this her maiesties charitable meaninge, and purpose we have thought good to praye your Lordship to direct your letters to all the Byshoppes and ordinaries with in your province, requiring them to instruct the Curates, and mynisters of the severall parrishes with in their dioces and especiallie the preachers of the worde, to exhorte in their sermons, and att tymes of common prayer, all persons of habilitie welth and calling, with such good reasons deduced out of the worde of god, as there of are plentie: to extend their benivolence and charitie in meat and drink, and in settinge of the poore people on worke and such other provision as god hathe blessed them withall, or els in monye, and almes to the succours and releefe of the poore sorte: And also to move the rytche to moderate theyr vnnecessarye spending of victualles in this tyme of dearth, and scarcitie, layeng a side all feasting banquitting and excesse of fare, and to converte all superfluous expenses to releife of the poore: Likewise that the poorer sorte maye be instructed by them to beare patientlye this manner of dearth, seing the same hathe proceded of godes visitacon, in sending vnseasonable wether as parte of punishement for our offences (thoughe this plauge of famine be farr greater in other countries of Europe, next adioyning vnto vs) neuertheless that there is great hope he will withdraw his heavie hand and send a plentifull harvest The rather if we turne to him by repentance and take this his visitacon with patience, and thankefullnes: And they may be given further to vnderstand (if it maye appeare that this scarcitie hathe growen and proceeded by the covetuousnes of cornemasters and Ingrossers, or by any other indirect meanes of anye evill desposed parsons) the providente and gratiouse care her maiestie hathe to see the same redressed, as may appeare by her proclamaton, and certen orders published by her highnes commaundement for the Iustices to see the furneshing of the markettes, and to the helpe of the poore: And therefore to advise them, if anye of them shall fynde greife, by reason theise orders are not dewlye observed: Then that they repaire to the Iustices to enforme them therof and open their greifes vnto them, and so seeke redresse: warning them to take heede they committ no disorders, or tumultes, synce her maiestie hathe so commended to the Iustices, the care to se the sayd orderes duelye observed, and the poore provided for, as we doubte nothing of their diligence, and fidelitie in that behalfe: So referring to your Lordships wisdome, and gravitie to giue therein such further direction for the Accomplishement of this godlie purpose as yow shall think convenient: we bidd your Lordship right hartilie fare well From Grenewitche the vth of Ianuarie 1586. /

Your Lordships assured lovinge freindes.

Will: Burleigh H: Derby R: Leycester
C: Howarde W: Cobham Tho: Buckhurst
F: Knollis James Croft W Davison J: Wolley. /

After my hartie commendacons to your Lordship: Wheare the Lords and other of her maiesties most honorable privie counsell have written to me theyr honorable letters (the copie whereof I have verbatim herein enclosed) and required me to write to the Byshoppes and all other having ordinarie Iurisson [i.e. jurisdiction] within this province dewlie, and effectuallie to accomplishe the contentes thereof. Theise are earnestlye to praye, and require your Lordship immediatly vpon receipt hereof in all diligent, and carefull sorte, to provide, and take order, that all parsons, vicars, Curates, and preachers with in your dioces, according to the Queenes maiesties most gratious care, and tenor of their Lordships letters, vse their best indeuoure in exhorting, and instruct[t]inge the people committed to their charge, to the charitable releiving of the poore (one of the chefest, and principall fruictes of the gospell) and to the performance of everie other pointe of their sayd Lordships letters, And to

thintent the same may be the better in everye place of your dioces executed, even
where there are no preachers: Theise are to require your Lordship to see that the
order heretofore taken for wensdaye and Frydaye duringe the tyme of this dearth be
dewlye observed, and the homilies there expressed read on sundayes, hollidayes and
att other tymes when there is no sermon: Furthermore that yow do giue iij charge
to the preachers and others to take more then ordinarie paines therein and to vse
that moderacon, and discretion, as in such a case is convenient, whereof I wolde
wishe your Lordship to have verie carefull consideracon, & that your Lordship also
call such as are not resident vpon theyr cures to be resident during this hard tyme,
and aswell your selfe to giue good example herein, as by all good meanes to move
the rest of the Clergie within your dioces, especiallie those of the welthier sorte to
do the same, that by your, and theyr examples others may be moved to the like,
for seing that there is no disordered conventicles, or innovacons, vnder pretence
hereof. such as were of late vsed in some places, tending rather to the offending
of manye, then the working of anye good, or charitable effect: And for the better
accomplishement of the premisses, it is convenient that your Lordship require a
certificate monethlye from everye parrishe of the dew execution of theyr Lordships
letters, and of the state, and behavioure of the poore, and how they be releiued
during this tyme of scarcitie and to send me worde by your letters, as often as youw
maye convenientlye of the procedinge of your Clergie, and your owne in this good
service. Alwayes provided that your sayd Clergie be nowaies burdened with anye
extra ordinarie fees in respect thereof, as heretofore in like cases they have byn in
some places to there charge, and to the no small offence of others: And that your
Lordship procure notice hereof to be given to your Clergie with as lytle trouble or
molestacon as maye be and in no case either churchwardenes or any other of the
laytie to be by coulor hereof assembled. Although there is no mention made in their
Lordships letters of anye Cathedrall, or Collegiate church within [your] Dioces, yet
your Lordship maye likewise give order to all members thereof to take care, vpon
all occasions in theyr preaching there, and in all other places, to theyr vttermoste
powres, to satisfie the contentes of their Lordships sayd letters, and by theyr good
example likewise in keping of hospitalitie and releiving the poore, to move and Firre
vpp others therevnto[.]

[in a different hand] Theise are therfore to will and require yow to have carefull
consideracon of the contentes of bothe the sayd letters and to see the same duelye
exequted within all the parishes of your Archdeaconrye, with as much speede as
maye be, and thereof to retourne me certificate in such convenient tymes, as certificate thereof may be made accordinglie: I have further received from his grace certen
orders for the encrease of learninge in the inferior sorte of mynisters, agreed vpon in
the last convocacon a copie whereof is enclosed herein, which yow muste likewise,
with all speede, see duelye putt in exequution, as the same letters do require[.]

FORM OF PRAYER

PREFACE

The fatherly care and goodnesse which Almightie God by his Prophetes in many
places declared vnto his people, neuer appeared more abundantly toward any nation,
then of late yeeres it hath done toward this Realme of England. For when we were in
thraldome and captiuitie vnder the tyrannie of Rome, & carried away with the false
worshipping of God, he, by our gracious Souereigne, deliuered vs: he planted the

elect & chosen vine of his gospel among vs, by law & authoritie: he raised vp seruants to digge & delue about this vineyard that it might prosper: he hath continually fenced vs from our enemies on all sides, by his gracious & mightie prouidence: beyond the reache of mans policie he hath reuealed their conspiracies, defeated their purposes, and made frustrate their counsels & deuises: he hath erected a watch tower of wise and godly gouernment: he hath shed downe from heauen, and blessed vs with his manifold graces, aswel of spirituall gifts, as of all plentie of earthly creatures. And for these his manifolde benefites, he hath looked for some fruites at our handes according to our dueties, that his name by our good doings might be glorified: but as the worlde seeth, & our owne consciences accuse vs, we haue yeelded little other then sower & vnsauorie grapes, vnpleasant vnto God, and mouing him to wrath towarde vs, that is, contempt of his word, worldly securitie, infidelitie, hipocrisie, vsing religion only for a shewe, and dishonoring the name of God and profession of the Gospell in deede, with the practise of all maner of wickednesse. Seeing therefore his mercie & goodnes wil not allure vs, the Arme of his iustice will be stretched out against vs: For he can abide nothing lesse then the contempt of his worde and mercifull calling. Remember the wordes of God vttered by Ieremie the Prophete in the 7. Chapter, *Because you haue done all these workes, and I rose vp early and spake vnto you, but when I spake, you woulde not heare, neither when I called, would ye answere: Therefore will I do vnto this house, whereupon my Name is called, wherein also ye trust, euen to the place which I gaue to you, and to your fathers, as I haue done to Silo, and I wil cast you out of my sight, as I haue cast out all your brethren, &c.* Let vs therefore remember our selues in time, & call vpon God with earnest repentance, before he turne his face cleane from vs: let vs followe the good counsell of the blessed Prophet Esay,[231] *Seeke the Lorde while he may be founde, call vpon him while he is nigh vs: let the wicked man forsake his wicked wayes, and the euill man his naughtie cogitations, and returne vnto the Lord, & he will haue mercie vpon vs. Let vs returne vnto God: for he is ready to forgiue.* Yea, God himselfe calleth vs by the prophet Ioel: *Turne vnto the Lorde* (saith he) *with all your heart, with fasting, with weeping, and with mourning, rent your hearts and not your clothes, & turne vnto the Lord your God: For he is gracious & merciful, slow to anger, and of great kindnes, & repenteth him of the euill that he hath purposed.* Let vs therefore imbrace the mercie of God while it is offred: he hath not yet stretched out his arme against vs: only as a merciful father he hath shaken the rod of his iustice toward vs, to wake vs out of the deepe slumber of our securitie. The Lord God graunt, that in time we may take warning thereby, and not harden our hearts, and make stiffe our neckes against our gracious God. These are therfore in the feare of God to charge the watchmen of the Lords citie, diligently & carefully to sounde the Trumpet in Sion, to gather the people together, to teach them in sackcloth & ashes to repent, to will them inwardly to rent their hearts and not outwardly their garments onely: sanctifie the congregation, assemble the elders, cal the yong ones, & euen those that sucke the breast. Let the bridegrome & his spouse, let them that liue in delicacie and pleasure of this life, in what state or condition soeuer they be, high or low, cast away their mirth & solace, and come and weepe & crie with bitter repentance before the mightie God, saying, Spare thy people (O Lord) and giue not thine heritage & beloued vineyard into reproch, that the wicked seed of Antichrist rule ouer it. Let not the enemies of thy truth, say among themselues, Where is now their God, in whom they haue put their trust? Then vndoubtedly wil

---

[231] In margin: 'Cap.55.'

the Lord be ielous ouer this land, and spare his people, yea the Lord will answere, and say vnto his people, Beholde I wil send you corne, and wine, and oyle, and you shall be satisfied therewith, and I wil no more make you a reproch among mine enemies, and I wil remoue farre from you the Northerne armie, that is, the Antichristian power, and I wil driue him into a land barren and desolate, with his face toward the East sea, and his ende to the vttermost sea, & his stinke shal come vp, and his corruption shall ascende, because he hath exalted himselfe against the truth of God. Feare not (O land) but be glad and reioyce, for the Lord wil doe great things for thee. This godly admonition was giuen to the prince, priests and people, with great zeale and earnestnes by Ioel the prophet in the dayes of that good king *Ezechiah*, and is the only way to turne away the wrath of God from vs, and to obtaine the continuance of his gracious goodnes toward vs, & his diuine protection ouer vs, in al our difficulties and distresses.

That therefore this admonition or exhortation may take the better effectes in mens heartes, it is ordered and streightly charged, that in euery parish where there is a preacher allowed by the Ordinarie, that euery Sunday in some publike Sermon, he shall put the people in remembrance of Gods exceeding benefites & blessings bestowed vpon vs these many yeres, & of our vnthankful receiuing & vsing of the same, & exhort them to sincere & true repentance, & that in such sort, as they declare the inward affection of their hearts, with the outward exercises of prayer, fasting, and almes deedes, that the world may testifie & see that they truely returne to their Lord God. In other places where such sufficient & discreete preachers be not, the Ministers vpon the same daies shal reade some part of these Homilies folowing, distinctly and reuerently, that the people may be moued thereby to the effect of that which is before mentioned. Moreouer, vpon the Wednesdayes and Frydayes, the Ministers in euery parish shal say Diuine seruice morning and euening in such sort, as hereafter foloweth. At which Seruice, one of euery house in the parish shall be present. And if either the Ministers shalbe negligent in doing their dueties appoynted vnto them in this seruice, or the people disobedient in comming or resorting to this godly exercise, the Churchwardens and other discreete men of the Parish are required to complaine thereof vnto the Ordinary, that the slacknesse of eche partie may be corrected. The people also at eche time of assemblie would be admonished, to make their charitable contribution to the reliefe of the poore, at the least according to the order of the Statute.

The order of this Booke.

First, the Confession, as it is in the Booke of Common prayer, with some one or two of the sentences of Scripture set before the same.

Then two or three of these Psalmes following in order. *[Ps. 6, 10, 25, 38, 41, 51; Ps. 31, 34, 37, 112, 143, 145]*

Then some one of these Chapters following. *[Isa. 5; Isa. 48; Isa. 59; Isa. 65; Ezek. 17; Zech. 7; Joel 1; Joel 2; Jonah 3; Luke 16; Luke 21; Matt. 25; 1 John 3]*

Then the Letanie, with the prayer appoynted to be sayde in the time of dearth and famine: and the next Prayer following for the time of Warre.

And if there be a conuenient nomber of hearers vpon any of the workedayes in the Church, then one of these Homilies may be read, if there be no Sermon. *[Homilies of repentance, fasting and almsgiving]*

1586–E2 Thanksgiving services for the failure of the Babington plot

After Wednesday 24 August 1586 (England and Wales)

In early August 1586, Anthony Babington and his confederates were arrested for plotting to assassinate Elizabeth, as a precursor to an invasion by Spain and the French Catholic League to place Mary, queen of Scots, on the throne and restore catholicism. On 24 August Whitgift issued orders for thanksgiving services, evidently to Aylmer as dean of the province, for communication to the other diocesan bishops. The form of prayer broadly followed the format of 1563–E and 1564–E, although the liturgy was not printed in full. Those who were licensed to preach were expected to preach a weekly sermon; those who were not were ordered to read a homily. In contrast to recent occasions of special worship, there was less emphasis on the realm's ungodliness. Instead, the form emphasized that England was subject to catholic conspiracy, reminded parishioners of the Marian persecution and Elizabeth's providential accession and, more briefly, characterized the realm as unworthy of God's protection. Babington and his co-conspirators were tried on 13–15 September and executed on 20–1 September at St Giles in the Fields. Mary's letters to Babington, conveyed in beer barrels, were intercepted by Elizabeth's principal secretary, Sir Francis Walsingham, and would lead to her trial for treason.

Order: Whitgift to [Aylmer], 24 Aug. 1586, LPL, Whitgift Register, I, fo. 126v [also in *Concilia*, IV, 319–20].
Form of prayer: *An order of prayer and thankesgiuing, for the preseruation of her maiestie and the realme, from the traiterous and bloodie practises of the pope, and his adherents: to be vsed at times appointed in the preface* [followed by texts from Eccles. 10:20 & 8 and Prov. 21:30–3]. *Published by authoritie* ([16] pp.; STC 16517)* [also in Clay, pp. 595–603].
Additional sources: Elizabeth to the lord mayor and aldermen of London, 18 Aug. 1586, in Strype, *Annals*, III: 1, 607–9, III: 2, 370–2; Aylmer to Hutchinson, 27 Aug. 1586, HALS, ASA 5/2/62, p. 351; Strype, *Whitgift*, I, 513–14; Clay, p. 468.
Printed sermon: Rainolds, Oxford (STC 20621, 20621.5).

ORDER

Archbishop of Canterbury to Bishop of London: 24 August 1586
Salutem in Ch[rist]o. Wheareas I haue caused to be sett forth in printe a booke conteyninge an order of prayer and thankesgiuinge for the preseruacion of her maiestie and the realme from the trayterouse and bluddy practizes of the Pope and his adherentes, to be vsed at tymes appoynted in the preface of the same booke the trewe trans[cri]pte whereof I send vnto your Lordship herewith in print. These are to praye and require your Lordship that with all convenient spede you do not onlie publishe and cause to be but [i.e. put] in execucion the said booke of prayer accordinge to the tenor thereof thorough out your owne Dioces but alsoe that you will send seuerall copies and trans[cri]ptes thereof togeather with Copies of these my lettres to all the rest of my brethren the Bushopps of my province willing and requiringe them and everie of them to do the like in there severall Dioces and Jurisdictions.

FORM OF PRAYER

THE PREFACE
Considering the great peace and quietnesse, wherewith God hath continually blessed this Noble Realme of England, since the time that it pleased him by the hand of her

Maiestie to haue the sincere trueth of the Gospel of our Sauiour planted among vs, and his great blessings of all sortes, wherewith he hath enriched vs, and giuen vs our heartes desires to our comfort, and the admiration of our neighbours rounde about vs: It were too great impietie, not to shewe our selues dayly thankefull for these great mercies, and not to craue the continuance of Gods holy hand ouer vs. But weighing further, with what perill of violent death, by meanes of wicked popish practises, our gracious soueraigne hath mainteined the trueth, which we professe, vpon whose life (next vnder God) the profession of the same in this land, and the continuance of the liues and welfare of vs her faithfull Subiects, doe depend: and knowing that the Almightie most miraculously hath preserued her highnesse, from al treason hitherto intended against her most Royall person, and kept our blood from flowing in euery streete like water, our Cities & Houses from sacking, and the whole Land from extreme ruine: with what zeale ought euery one of vs to be inflamed to prayse the Lord, for the detecting and confusion of our secrete foes, whom his right hand hath bruised? and howe ought we to detest that doctrine which bringeth foorth so traiterous and bloodie fruites? *Moses* and *Miriam*, and the whole hoste of Israel had neuer greater cause to sing vnto the Lorde for the ouerthrowe of *Pharao* and his armie: nor *Debora* and *Barac* for the victorie of *Sisera*: nor *Iudith*, and the Citizens of *Bethulia* for the end of *Holofernes*, and the flight of his hoste, then we haue for the wonderfull preseruation of the life of our most gracious *Queene*, and thereby for our owne safetie. Wherefore, let euery one that feareth the Lord among vs, not onely with the *Iewes* in the booke of *Esther* yeerely holde a memoriall with great ioy of so notable deliuerance, but dayly in common assemblies haue this great goodnesse in remembrance, and pray that God will not suffer the light of *Israel* to be quenched, but that it will still please him to preserue his annoynted from the perill of the sworde, and to giue her long and happie dayes, to the glorie of his Name, to the comfort of his chosen, & to the stablishing of his trueth in this Lande, till the comming of his Sonne in the cloudes of Heauen. That this may the better be accomplished, this litle booke is by authoritie published, dayly to be vsed in *Common prayer*, where any is, or otherwise at such times as are by lawe appointed for *Diuine Seruice: viz*, the Prayer, and one or two of the *Psalmes* following, according to the discretion of the Minister, and likewise to be adioyned vnto those prayers, that are alreadie of late set foorth, for turning from vs the scarcitie of victuall, and warre, at such times as they are appointed to be read in the Church.

THE PRAYER

O Eternall God and mercifull Father, we thy vnworthie creatures most humbly doe confesse, that we are not able with our tongues to vtter, nor in our heartes to conceiue, the exceeding measure of thine infinite goodnesse in this latter age shewed to this Noble Realme, in that thou (O Lord) hast in most dangerous times, by thy prouidence, beyond expectation of man, preserued the Noble person of our now Soueraigne Lady Elizabeth, by thy grace: First, according to her right to come to this kingdome and Royall seate of her Noble Father, and next, by her (being therein established) to deliuer vs thy people, that were as captiues of Babylon, out of thraldome of the enemies of thy true Church, and to restore vs agayne to the free fruition of the Gospel of thy Sonne our Sauiour Christ. For the enioying whereof now many yeeres, we doe confesse and acknowledge, that when wee by our daily vnthankefulnesse, and by our sinful liues, haue most iustly prouoked thee to withdrawe these thy fauours from vs, thou (O Lorde) with thy mightie power diddest strengthen thy seruant our most gracious Queene, constantly against the threatnings of the greatest of the world to persist, in maintenance of vs in all maner of prosperitie, peace and wealth: But most singularly in a peaceable freedome, to enioy the blessed benefites of thy holy worde against the mightie enemies of thy Church daily conspiring against this Realme, and especially against the Royall person of our gracious Queene, thy humble seruant and true handmayden, whose estate being in the opinion of a nomber of wicked persons many times in great and secret dangers, yet thou (O Lorde) of thy heauenly goodnesse hast alwayes preserued and defended her by many miraculous meanes, and (as we haue good cause to thinke) by many other meanes, and at many other times, then to vs are yet knowen. But yet, besides thy preseruation of her person from the attempt of two wicked persons, that suffered for the same of late yeeres, euen nowe in this present time, when we had no thought, that any woulde haue minded such a wicked fact, we haue fully felt the power of thy miraculous goodnesse, by the discouerie of sundry wicked Conspirators, very secretly bent and combyned to make desperate attempts against her life, and against the peaceable estate of thy Church and this Realme. The stay whereof onely hath proceeded (good Lord) by thy most continual, tender and fatherly care ouer her, in the strange discouering, and the maner of apprehending of the malefactors, being many, and not by the wit or strength of any worldly creature. For otherwise then by thy speciall goodnesse, we do nowe perceiue, and that with trembling of our hearts, that shee could not at sundry times haue escaped the danger of violent death, wickedly and resolutely against her intended, so that wee may truely say with *Dauid* in his Psalme, *That all men that see it, shal say, This hath God done: for they shall perceiue, that it is his worke.* Wherefore we now thy humble creatures, acknowledging our vnworthinesse of these great graces, beseech thee (O Lord) that thou wilt without regard of our former vnthankfulnesse, and contempt of thy worde, shewe thy mercie to vs, and continue thy blessings ouer vs, that we may, for these so vnspeakeable benefites, be more thankfull then wee haue bene, not onely in wordes, or as hearers, but in deedes also, as doers of thy will, according to the direction of thy holy word. And that it would please thee stil to holde this thy blessed hand ouer our *Queene Elizabeth*, and preserue her *Royall* person from all maner of open or secrete perils, whereby her yeeres may be prolonged, as farre as it may please thee to graunt, by the course of *Nature* for the maintenance of thy glory, and of thy sonne *Iesus Christ*, and of his *Gospel*, and for continuance of vs thy people her naturall subiects in the due feare and seruice of thee, and in our naturall obedience to her, whereby we and our posteritie may still inioy such peace, as wee haue had these many yeeres, vnder her Maiesties gouernement, farre aboue any like example in any age by past. Grant this (O heauenly Father) for *Iesus Christes* sake, thy onely sonne our Sauiour, to whome with thee and the holy Ghost be all honour and glorie, worlde without end. Amen.

The first Psalme.
We reioyce in thy strength, (O Lorde:) exceeding glad are we of thy saluation. (Ps. 21) [21:1–3]
Thou hast giuen vs our hearts desire: and hast not denyed the request of our lippes.
Thou hast preuented vs with the blessings of goodnesse: and hast made vs glad with the ioy of thy countenance.
For the vngodly had drawen out the sworde, and had bended their bowe: to cast downe the poore and needie, and to slay such as be of a right conuersation. (Ps. 37) [37:14–15]

Their sword shall goe through their owne heart: and their bow shall be broken.
All thine enemies shall feele thine hand: thy right hand shall finde out them that hate thee. (Ps. 22) [21:8–12]
Thou shalt make them like a fierie Ouen in the time of thy wrath: the Lorde shall destroy them in his displeasure, and the fire shal consume them.
Their fruite shalt thou roote out of the earth: and their seede from among the children of men.
For they intended mischiefe against thee: and imagined such a deuice, as they are not able to perfourme.
Therefore hast thou put them to flight: and the strings of thy bowe hast thou made readie against the face of them.
Thy mercy (O Lorde) reacheth vnto the heauens: and thy faithfulnesse vnto the cloudes. (Ps. 36) [36:5–7]
Thy righteousnes standeth like the strong mountaines: and thy iudgements are like the great deepe.
Thou Lord doest saue both man and beast: how excellent is thy mercie, O Lord? and the children of men shal put their trust vnder the shadow of thy wings.
O continue forth thy louing kindnesse vnto them that knowe thee: and thy righteousnesse vnto them that are true of heart.
O let not the foote of pride come against vs: and let not the hand of the vngodly cast vs downe.
Withdrawe not thou thy mercie from vs, O Lorde: let thy louing kindenesse and thy trueth alway preserue vs. [Ps. 40:14]
But let the vngodly perish, let thine enemies consume as the fat of lambes: yea, euen as the smoke let them consume away. [Ps. 37:20]
So wee that bee thy people, and sheepe of thy pasture shall giue thee thankes for euer: and will alway bee shewing forth thy prayse from generation to generation. (Ps. 79) [79:14]

The second Psalme.
Deliuer vs, O Lorde, from the euill men: and preserue vs from the wicked men. (Ps. 140) [140:1–2, 5]
Which imagine mischiefe in their hearts: and stirre vp strife all the day long.
The proud haue layed a snare for vs, and spred a net abroade with cordes: yea, and set trappes in our wayes.
They courage themselues in mischiefe: & common among themselues, how they may lay snares, and they say no man shal see them. (Ps. 64) [64:5–6]
They imagine wickednesse and practise it: that they keepe secret among themselues, euery man in the deepe of his heart.
But let not the vngodly haue their desire, O Lord: let not their mischieuous imaginations prosper, least they be too proude. (Ps. 140) [140:8]
Thou, O Lorde, shalt soddenly shoote at them with a swift arrowe: that they shallbe wounded. [Ps. 64:7]
And all men that see it, shall say, This hath God done: for they shall perceiue, that it is his worke. [Ps. 64:9]
Praysed be the Lorde dayly, euen the God that helpeth vs: and powreth his benefites vpon vs. (Ps. 68) [68:19–20]
Hee is our God, euen the God of whome commeth Saluation: *God is the Lord by whom we escape death.*

He hath giuen victorie vnto vs: and hath deliuered *Dauid* his seruant from the perill of the sword. (Ps. 144) [144:10]

O that men woulde therefore prayse the Lord for his goodnesse: and declare the wonders that he doth for the children of men. (Ps. 107) [107:21, 32, 22]

That they would exalt him in the congregation of the people: and prayse him in the seate of the Elders.

That they would offer vnto him the sacrifice of thankesgiuing: and tell out his works with gladnesse.

Then shall our sonnes growe vp as the yong plants: and our daughters be as the polished corners of the Temple. [Ps, 144:12]

Our garners shall bee full and plenteous with all maner of store: our sheepe shal bring forth thousandes, and tenne thousandes in our streetes. [Ps. 144:13]

Our Oxen shall be strong to labour, there shall be no decay: no leading into captiuitie, and no complaining in our streetes. [Ps. 144:14]

Happy are the people that be in such a case: yea blessed are the people, that haue the Lord for their God. [Ps. 144:15]

The third Psalme.

We will magnifie thee, O God our King: and will prayse thy Name for euer and euer. (Ps. 145) [145:1–4, 7, 18–20]

Euery day will wee giue thankes vnto thee: and prayse thy name for euer and euer.

Great is the Lorde, and marueilous worthy to be praysed: there is no end of his greatnesse.

One generation shall prayse thy workes vnto another: and declare thy power.

The memoriall of thine aboundant kindnesse shall be shewed: and men shall sing of thy righteousnesse.

The Lord is righteous in all his wayes: and holy in all his workes.

The Lorde is nigh vnto all that call vpon him: yea, all such as call vpon him faithfully.

He will fulfill the desire of them that feare him: hee also will heare their crye, and will helpe them.

The Lorde preserueth all them that loue him: but scattereth abroad all the vngodly.

Though wee walke in the middest of trouble, yet shall he refresh vs: hee shall stretche foorth his hand vpon the furiousnesse of our enemies, and his right hand shall saue vs. (Ps. 138) [138:7]

The snares of death compassed vs round about: & the paynes of hel gate hold vpon vs. (Ps. 116) [116:3, 8]

But thou, Lord, hast deliuered our soules from death: our eyes from teares, and our feete from falling.

Thou hast turned our heauinesse into ioy: thou hast put off our sackcloth, and girded vs with gladnesse. (Ps. 30) [30:12–13]

Therefore shall euery good man sing of thy praise without ceassing: O God, we wil giue thankes vnto thee for euer.

The fourth Psalme.

O Giue thanks vnto the Lord, for he is gracious: and his mercie endureth for euer. (Ps. 106) [106:1–2, 6–8]

Who can expresse the noble actes of the Lord: or shew forth all his prayse?

For wee haue sinned with our Fathers: we haue done amisse and dealt wickedly.

We haue not regarded thy wonders, nor kept thy great goodnesse in remembrance: but haue been disobedient to thy holy will.

Neuerthelesse, hee hath holpen vs for his names sake: that he might make his power to be knowen.

For loe, the vngodly had bent their bowe, and made ready their arrows within the quiuer: that they might priuily shoote at vs. (Ps. 11) [11:2]

Many Oxen purposed to haue come about vs: fat *Bulles* of *Basan* intended to close vs in on euery side. (Ps. 22) [22:12–13, 16]

They gaped vpon vs with their mouthes: as it were ramping and roaring Lions.

The counsell of the wicked layd siege against vs: they set trappes in our wayes.

They had priuily layd their net to destroy vs without a cause: yea, euen without a cause had they made a pit for our soule. (Ps. 35) [35:7]

But thou (O Lorde) hast deliuered our soule from the sworde: thy darling from the power of the dogge. (Ps. 22) [22:20–1]

Thou hast saued vs from ye Lions mouth: thou hast heard vs from amongst the hornes of the Vnicornes.

A sodaine destruction is come vpon them vnawares, and the net that they had layde priuily, hath catched themselues: they are fallen into their our [*sic*] owne mischiefe. (Ps. 35) [35:8, 4]

They are confounded and put to shame, that did seeke after our soule: they are turned backe & put to confusion that imagined mischiefe for vs.

Wherefore prayse the Lorde, yee that feare him: magnifie him al ye of the seede of *Iacob*, and feare him all ye of the seede of *Israel*. (Ps. 22) [22:23–5]

For he hath not despised, nor abhorred the lowe estate of the poore: hee hath not hid his face from him, but when we called vnto him, he heard vs.

Therefore our prayse is of thee in the great *Congregation*: our vowes will we performe in the sight of them that feare him.

Glory be to the Father, to the sonne &c.

Hereunto also may be added at the discretion of the Minister the lxxxiii. the Ciii. and the Cxxiiii. Psalmes. And for the first Lesson, when she shall see occasion, he may reade one of these Chapters: Viz. Exod.xv. Iudg.v. Esther.vi.vii.viii. and ix.

1586–E3 Prayer and fasting during dangers and plots

Daily after Saturday 3 December 1586 (England and Wales)

This occasion is known only from Aylmer's letter to William Hutchinson, archdeacon of St Albans, which included a verbatim copy of Whitgift's instruction to the bishop. Though the exact nature of 'the daungerousnes of the tyme and [the] extreame mallice the adversarye beareth to the trewe profession of the gospell' in unclear, it is likely to refer to the reverberations of the Babington plot (see 1586–E2). The plotters themselves were tried and executed in September. In October, Mary Stuart was tried and found guilty of complicity in the plot; later the same month, parliament petitioned Elizabeth for a guilty verdict. In fact, Elizabeth's privy council had persuaded the queen to call parliament in an attempt to put pressure on the queen to allow Mary's execution for treason. The guilty verdict was publicly announced on 4 December, the day after Aylmer's letter to Hutchinson. As the archbishop's order must have been decided upon a day or more earlier, it can be inferred that the intention of the prayers and fasting was to assist the reception of the verdict. No form of prayer was commissioned for this occasion: Whitgift instructed Aylmer that services should follow 'the order of the booke'. This presumably refers to the BCP and the prayers at the end of the litany: in contrast if a form was commissioned, the archbishop usually referred to it by its title. He also ordered the BCP to be used during the famine in 1596–7 (see 1596–E3). However, only the 'prayer in time of war' seems appropriate to this occasion: it petitioned God to 'saue and deliuer vs … from the handes of our enemies'. Moreover, the BCP did not include any order for fasting, an activity which Whitgift encouraged parishes to observe. For this, ministers would have had to consult the 1563–E form for plague. Why Whitgift chose not to issue a special liturgy or prayers is unclear, especially as the occasion may have provided opportunity for the puritan 'disordered conventicles, or innovacons' that the archbishop had warned bishops to prevent during special worship for dearth and war the previous year (see 1586–E1).

Order: Aylmer to Hutchinson, 3 Dec. 1586, HALS, ASA 5/2/70, p. 377.
Form of prayer: possibly BCP.

ORDER

Bishop of London to archdeacon of St Albans: 3 December 1586

After my hartye Commendacons vnto yow, Whereas of late I have rec[eived] a letter from my Lord his grace of Cant[erbury] the tenor whereof heareafter enseweth.

Salutem in Christo. In respecte of the daungerousnes of the tyme and extreame mallice the adversarye beareth to the trewe profession of the gospell and the daylye practises against the same: I thincke yt convenient that we shold resorte to the vsuall Weapons of good Christians in such Caseis, that is to prayers, Fastinge and other godlye exerciseis, Wherefore these are to requyre your Lordship (within your dioces) to take care for the same and that there may be daylye prayers in the seuerall parishes according to the order of the booke, and some extraordinarye paynes taken by the seuerall ministers of euerye Cure (licensed there unto) in instructinge the people Committed to theire Chardge, and exhortinge theim to repentance and the Fruictes thereof, a thing at all tymes requisit, but most of all at this instante, & in these our dayes, And so I Committ your Lordship to the tuicon of Almightie god From Lembeth the xxx^th of November 1587.

Your Lordships lovinge Frend & brother
Jo Cantuar

To my Vearye good Lord and brother the Bishop of London /

These are therefore to require you that yow give order to euerye minister within your Archdeaconrye or Iurisdiccon that the contents of his sayd graces lettre be put in due execucon consideringe the necessetye which yt requyreth …

1587–S   Prayers for the safety of Queen Mary

January–February 1587 (Scotland?)

Since fleeing to England in 1568, following her forced abdication as queen of Scots the previous year, Mary Stuart had been imprisoned, first at the Sheffield properties of the earl of Shrewsbury, and from 1585 at a series of other locations in the midlands. Until the mid-1580s, she was given considerable freedom, which allowed her to become involved in conspiracies against Elizabeth. Mary's position as catholic claimant to the English and Scottish thrones made her a focus of domestic and overseas catholic intrigue. In 1586, in the context of heightened Anglo-Spanish tensions, Anthony Babington had drawn Mary into a plot to murder Elizabeth. Deliberately manipulated by Sir Francis Walsingham, the plot gave him and Lord Burghley a means of persuading Elizabeth to bring Mary to trial. The trial took place in October 1586, and in the following month parliament petitioned the queen for Mary's execution (see 1586–E3). News of these events prompted James VI to attempt to intercede with Elizabeth on his mother's behalf, though his desire to preserve the Anglo-Scottish alliance and his hopes of succeeding to the English throne limited the force of his appeals. As well as writing letters and ordering his representatives at the English court to speak to the queen about Mary, James apparently asked Scottish clergy to pray for Mary's safety. The king's request is known only from Spottiswoode's *History*. It is interesting for several reasons. This was the first occasion on which the crown attempted to order special worship in Scotland. The king's request for prayers was largely resisted by the clergy, though Spottiswoode recorded that his father-in-law David Lindsay had complied. Moreover, Spottiswoode referred to the 'form prescribed', implying that a fixed prayer was given to the ministers. Apart from Spottiswoode's brief description, nothing is known of this prayer. It is unclear whether the ministers' refusal to comply with James's direction was a response to the content of the prayer and their disapproval of Mary, or because of the king's unprecedented attempt to command the clergy in matters of worship. Mary was executed on 7 February.

Source: Spottiswoode, II, 355–6.

DESCRIPTION

Spottiswoode, *History*

The king perceiving by all these letters that the death of his mother was determined, called back his ambassadors, and at home gave order to the ministers to remember her in their public prayers, which they denied to do, though the form prescribed was most christian and lawful; which was, that it might please God to illuminate her with the light of his truth, and save her from the apparent danger wherein she was cast. Upon their denial, charges were directed to command all bishops, ministers, and other office-bearers in the Church to make mention of her distress in their public prayers, and commend her to God in the form appointed. But of all the number only Mr David Lindsay at Leith and the king's own ministers gave obedience. At Edinburgh, where the disobedience was most public, the king purposing to have their fault amended, did appoint the third of February for solemn prayers to be made in her behalf, commanding the bishop of St Andrews to prepare himself for that day;

which when the ministers understood, they stirred up Mr John Cowper, a young man not entered as yet in the function, to take the pulpit before the time and exclude the bishop. The king coming at the hour appointed, and seeing him in the place, called to him from his seat, and said, 'Mr John, that place is destined for another; yet since you are there, if you will obey the charge that is given, and remember my mother in your prayers, you shall go on'. He replying, 'that he would do as the Spirit of God should direct him', was commanded to leave the place: and making as though he would stay, the captain of the guard went to pull him out; whereupon he burst forth in these speeches: 'This day shall be a witness against the king in the great day of the Lord': and then denouncing a wo to the inhabitants of Edinburgh, he went down, and the bishop of St Andrews entering the pulpit did perform the duty required.

1587–E   Thanksgiving services fit for the security of the church and realm

[February–August?] 1587 (England and Wales)

No orders are extant for this occasion. Clay linked it to Sir Francis Drake's successes against the Spanish fleet (April–May) which delayed the armada until 1588. However, the form focused on thanksgivings for God's protection of the queen and the dangers posed to the realm by their enemies, rather than a jubilant celebration of a particular success. Therefore, it may have been issued to seek divine assistance (and provide assurance to people) in the face of mounting catholic aggression as war with Spain became more likely in retaliation after the execution of Mary queen of Scots in February and an English military campaign in the Netherlands, led by the earl of Leicester. During June and July Spanish forces under the duke of Parma attacked Sluys and Ostend, the former surrendering on 26 July. These were key towns from which a Spanish invasion of England could be launched. As with the thanksgiving for the discovery of the Babington plot (1586–E2), the form provided a prayer, a list of suitable psalms, collects, readings and homilies for ministers and curates to add to the BCP service at their discretion, rather than a full special liturgy. The clergy were also encouraged to use prayers from earlier occasions of special worship; a weekly fast on Friday was 'very convenient, and to be wished' but was not ordered. This laissez-faire attitude was at odds with Whitgift's continuing campaign for conformity and may reflect the strength of opposition to it by courtiers, such as Burghley and Leicester, and how the catholic plots, Mary's execution and Leicester's campaign in the Netherlands diverted attention from domestic religion.

Order: none found.
Form of prayer: *A prayer and thanksgiuing fit for this present and to be vsed in the time of common prayer* ([6] pp.; STC 16518; BL, C.104.cc.9) [also in Clay, pp. 604–7].
Additional source: Clay, pp. 468–9.

Form of prayer

O Lorde God of hosts, most louing & mercifull Father, we thy humble seruants prostrate our selues before thy diuine Maiestie, instantly beseeching thee of thy gratious goodnesse to be mercifull to thy Church militant here vpon earth, many wayes vexed and tormented by the malice of Satan and his members, and at this time as it were inuironed on euery side, with strong and subtill aduersaries. Wee confesse and acknowledge O Lorde (with all humble and hearty thanks) the wonderfull and great benefites which thou hast bestowed vpon this thy Church and people of England, in giuing vnto vs not onely peace and quietnesse, but also in preseruing our most gratious Queene thy handmaid so myraculously from so many perils and dangers, and in granting her good successe against the attempts of her aduersaries: for the which so wonderfull and great benefites, we humbly beseech thee to stirre vp our dul mindes to such thankefulnesse and acknowledging of thy mercies as becommeth vs, and as may bee acceptable vnto thee. O Lord, let thine enemies know, and make them confesse, that thou hast receiued England into thine owne protection. Set (O Lord we pray thee) a hedge about it, and euermore mightily defend it. Let it be a comfort to the afflicted: a helpe to the oppressed: a defence to thy Church and people persecuted abroade. And forasmuch as thy cause is nowe in hande, we beseech thee to direct and goe before such as haue taken the same vpon them. Pitch thy tents about them, and graunt vnto them (O Lord) so good and honourable victories, as thou diddest to Abraham & his company, against the foure mightie kings: to Josua against the fiue kings, and against Amalech: and as thou vsest to doe to thy children when they please thee. We acknowledge all power, strength and victorie to come from thee. Some put their trust in Charets, and some in horses, but we will remember thy name, O Lord our God. Thou bringest the counsell of the heathen to nought, and makest the deuises of the people to bee of none effect. There is no king that can be saued by ye multitude of an host, neither is any mighty man deliuered by much strength: A horse is but a vaine thing to saue a man. Therefore we pray vnto thee, O Lord: thou art our helpe & our shield. And yt our prayers may be the more effectuall & acceptable vnto thee, graunt vnto vs, wee beseech thee, true repentance for our sinnes past, namely for our vnthankefulnesse, contempt of thy worde, lacke of compassion towards the affliected, enuie, malice, strife & contention among our selues, and for al other our iniquities. Lord deale not with vs as we haue deserued: but of thy great goodnesse and mercy doe away our offences. O Lord, giue good and prosperous successe to all those that fight thy battell against the enemies of thy Gospell: shewe some token continually for our good, that they which hate vs may see it and be confounded: and that wee thy litle and despised flocke may say with good King Dauid, *Blessed are the people whose God is the Lord Iehoua, and blessed are the folke that he hath chosen to be his inheritance.* These and all other graces necessary for vs, graunt (O heauenly Father) for Jesus Christs sake, our onely mediatour and redeemer. *Amen.*

Hereunto may be added the Collect of the Letanie appointed to be vsed in the time of warre. And other prayers heretofore published vpon the like occasions, according to the discretion of the Minister. And when there are no Sermons, then to reade one of the Homilies of repentance, fasting, and almes deedes, lately published.
Some of these psalms may be sayde or sung at the dayes and times before mentioned after the prayer [*Ps. 2, 20, 21, 33, 46, 56, 70, 83, 94, 140].*
One of these Chapters may be read on Wednesdayes and Fridayes at the discretion of the Curate [*Exod. 14; Exod. 17:8–16; Joshua 10:1–28; Judg. 7; 1 Sam. 17; 2 Kgs. 7; 2 Kgs. 19; 2 Chron. 20:1–30; Acts 12].*

It were very conuenient, and to be wished, that euery one shoulde forbeare one meale at the least euery weeke, ouer and aboue the ordinary appointed fasting dayes: to the ende they might bee more able to relieue the poore, and be more apt to prayer, hearing of the word, and other godly exercises.

1588–S1 Fast days in response to catholic conspiracies, apostasy, the church's difficulties and sinfulness

Sunday 7 July–Sunday 14 July 1588 (Scotland)

When the general assembly appointed this fast, the perceived catholic threat had apparently not yet taken the specific form of a Spanish invasion attempt (for which, see 1588–E1). The assembly compiled lists of grievances, which were submitted to the king, emphasizing the activities of Jesuits and seminary priests in Scotland, and complaining of catholicism's supporters among the nobility. These concerns, together with other causes reflected in 1582–S, were expressed in the fast act.

Order: by the general assembly beginning 8 Feb. 1588, described in Calderwood, IV, 676.
Additional sources: *BUK*, II, 727–8; Calderwood, IV, 654–66; Row, p. 137.

DESCRIPTION OF ORDER

Order by the general assembly beginning 8 February 1588
The nixt Generall Assemblie was appointed to be holdin at Edinburgh the first Tuisday of August, betuixt and which tyme a generall fast was appointed to be keeped universallie the first two Sundayes of Julie. The causes are these following: 1. The universall conspiraceis of the enemeis of the truthe against Christ's kirk, to putt in executioun the bloodie determinatioun of the Councell of Trent. 2. The flocking home of Jesuits and Papists to subvert the kirk within this countrie. 3. The defectioun of a great number frome the truthe. 4. The conspiraceis intended against the samine by great men, interteaners of Jesuits and Papists. 5. The coldnesse of professors. 6. The wracke of the patrimonie of the kirk, abundance of bloodshed, adultereis, incest, and all kinde of iniquitie.

1588–E1 Services during the threat of a Spanish invasion

After Wednesday 10 July–August 1588 (England and Wales)

The Spanish armada set sail from Lisbon on 30 May under the duke of Medina-Sidonia, aiming to join with the duke of Parma's troops in the Netherlands, invade England through Kent and capture Elizabeth. Simultaneous risings were planned for Ireland and the borders. Whitgift issued orders some time in June or early July to the bishops in his province for public prayers. He reiterated these instructions on 10 July and instructed the bishops to send for a form of prayer which he had commissioned; he also issued a set of articles to ministers to ensure conformity to the BCP and the new form. Whitgift may have been acting independently because the privy council did not order special prayers until 23 July 'upon new advertysment of the discovery again of the Spannisshe Fleet' (probably its sighting off the Scilly Isles on 19 July).

Strype recorded that London ministers were summoned to a special meeting to encourage observation of these orders. Whitgift's form of prayer borrowed heavily from the preface of the form for 1563–E (to emphasize man's sinfulness and how this provoked God's wrath) and, perhaps more appropriately, the prayers from the form for 1572–E and 1587–E ('O Lord God of hostes'). There was only one wholly new prayer. This might explain Aylmer's description of the form to the archdeacon of St Albans as 'a booke upon the lyke occasions penned to be newlye printed with some additions', though the plague and the St Bartholomew's day massacre were hardly 'lyke occasions', other than being signs of divine providence. No fast was ordered – indeed, Aylmer's instructions to Hutchinson stressed that fasts not sanctioned by the BCP were not to be allowed – though everyone was encouraged to be moderate in diet and to give alms to the poor. This probably reflected Whitgift's longstanding antipathy to, and actions against, the puritans, who believed that fasting was an important means of effecting individual and national repentance. Ministers were also instructed only to preach one sermon per day and were required to prevent parishioners from 'sermon-gadding' (travelling to other parishes to hear sermons). This was probably yet another attempt to restrict the activities of puritans (see 1586-E1) who had continued to attack the 'but halfly reformed' Elizabethan church in parliament (with bills to abolish the BCP and replace it with the Genevan Book of Discipline) and in print (the Martin Marprelate tracts which attacked, amongst other things, epsicopacy). 'Unofficial' prayers, as well as ballads and pamphlets, were printed, including *A godly prayer for the preseruation of the queenes maiestie* (STC 17489) by Anthony Marten, Sewer of the Royal Household, and Christopher Stile's *Psalms of inuocation* (STC 23266). It is unclear for how long petitionary services were continued, but after the flight of the Spanish fleet following the battle of Gravelines on 29 July, some thanksgiving sermons were preached (see 1588–E2).

Order: Archbishop Whitgift to the bishops, 10 July 1588, LPL, Whitgift Register, I, fo. 148r [also in Strype, *Whitgift*, I, 526–7, and *Concilia*, IV, 337–8].
Form of prayer: *A fourme of prayer, necessary for the present time and state* ([24] pp.; STC 16519)* [also in Clay, pp. 608–18].
Additional sources: privy council to Whitgift, 23 July 1588, *APC*, XVI, 172; Strype, *Whitgift*, I, 527; Strype, *Annals*, III: 2, 546–7; *A transcript of the registers of the Company of Stationers*, ed. Arber, II, 495–7; Aylmer to Hutchinson, 12 July 1588, HALS, ASA 5/2/78, pp. 421–2; Clay, p. 469.

ORDER

Archbishop of Canterbury, to the bishops: 10 July 1588

Salutem in Christo. Consideringe the daungerousnes of the tyme I thincke it convenient that you cause publique prayers to be had in everie severall parishes within your dioces accordinge to the lettres heretofore written vnto you,[232] fore seeinge that noe other order of fastinge or other exercise be vsed then such as you shall prescribe accordinge to the Lawes and orders of the church established I haue caused a booke vpon the like occacions penned, to be newlie printed with some additions, which you maye haue for your Dioces, yf you send for the same. And soe wishinge you to be carefull herein.

---

[232] These have not been identified or found.

Privy council to archbishop of Canterbury: 23 July 1588

A letter to the Archbisshop of Canterbury upon new advertysment of the discovery again of the Spannisshe Fleete, to pray his Lordship to give order to all the Bisshops and pastors in all the Dioces in his Lordship's Province to move their auditoryes and parishioners to joyne in publyke prayers to Almighty God, the giver of victoryes, to assiste us against the mallyce of our enemyes, &c; the copy remaynethe in the Counsell Chest.

FORM OF PRAYER

PREFACE

[As 1563–E: ... Nowe therefore callyng to mynde that*]* God hath bene prouoked by vs many and sundry wayes, and doth after a sort threaten vs with wars and inuasion: it behoueth vs to pray earnestly and hartily to God, to turne away his deserued wrath from vs, and as well to defend vs from the fiercenesse and furie of our enemies, (which combine and conspire together against vs) as also from all other plagues and punishments, which our vnthankfulnesse and contempt of his worde hath iustly deserued. And although it is euery Christian mans dutie *[as 1563–E*: of his owne deuotion ... by often and sundry meanes to be*]* stirred vp, and put in remembrance of the same.

It is therefore meete and requisite: First, that all Curates and Pastors should exhort their Parishioners *[as 1563–E*: to endeuour ... from their*]* necessary businesse, and they to resort not onely on Sundayes and Holidayes, but also on Wednesdayes and Fridayes, and at other times likewise during the time of these imminent dangers, exhorting them *[as 1563–E*: there reuerently ... with the*]* residue of the Morning prayer, vsing according to their discretion some of the Psalmes and prayers hereafter folowing, and for the first lesson some of these Chapters: Exodus 14. Exodus 17. begin at the 8. verse. Iosua 10 vntill the 28. verse. Iudges 7. 1. Samuel 17. 2. Kings 7. 2. Kings 19. 2. Chron. 20 vnto the verse 30.

Finally, it is very requisite, that in their Sermons and exhortations, they should mooue the people to abstinence and moderation in their diet, to the ende they might bee the more able to relieue the poore, to pray vnto God to heare his holy worde, and to doe other good and godly workes.

PRAYERS

['A prayer for forgiuenesse of sinnes'; 'A prayer to be deliuered from our enemies'; 'A prayer for deliueraunce from enemies'; 'For true repentaunce and mercye'; 'An other for the same': all as 1572–E]

An other prayer to be delivered from our enemies:

O Lorde God of hostes most louing and merciful father, we thy humble seruauntes prostrate our selues before thy diuine Maiestie: most heartily beseeching thee, to grant vnto vs true repentance for our sinnes past, namely for our vnthankfulnesse, contempt of thy word, lacke of compassion towards the afflicted, enuie, malice, strife and contention among our selues, and for all other our iniquities. Lord deale not with vs as we haue deserued, but of thy great goodnesse and mercy, doe away our offences, and giue vs grace to confesse and acknowledge, O Lord, with all humble and heartie thanks, the wonderfull and great benefits which thou hast bestowed vpon this thy Church and people of England, in giuing vnto vs without all desert of our part, not onely peace and quietnesse, but also in preseruing our most gracious Queene thine handmaid, so miraculously from so many conspiracies, perils and dangers, and in granting her good successe against the attempts of her aduersaries: for the which so wonderfull and great benefites, we humbly beseech thee to stirre vp our dull mindes to such thankfulnesse and acknowledging of thy mercies as becometh vs, and as may bee acceptable vnto thee. We doe instantly beseech thee of thy gracious goodnesse to be mercifull to thy Church militant here vpon earth, many wayes vexed and tormented by the malice of Satan and his members, and at this time as it were compassed about with strong and subtill aduersaries. And especially O Lord, let thine enemies know, and make them confesse that thou hast receiued England (which they most of all for thy gospell sake do maligne) into thine own protection. Set we pray thee (O Lord) a wall about it, & evermore mightily defend it. Let it bee a comfort to the afflicted, a helpe to the oppressed, a defence to thy Church and people persecuted abroad. And forasmuch as thy cause is now in hand, we beseech thee to direct and goe before our Armies both by sea and land, blesse and prosper them, and grant vnto them O Lord, so good and honorable successe & victories, as thou didst to Abraham and his company against the foure mightie kings, to Josua against the fiue kings and against Amalech, to Dauid against the strong and mightie armed giant Goliah, and as thou vsest to do to thy children when they please thee. Wee acknowledge all power, strength and victorie to come from thee: some put their trust in charets and some in horses, but we will remember thy name, O Lord our God. Thou bringest the counsell of the heathen to nought, and makest the deuises of the people to be of none effect. There is no king that can be saued by the multitude of an host, neither is any mightie man deliuered by much strength. A horse is but a vaine thing to saue a man, therefore wee pray vnto thee, O Lord, thou art our helpe and our shield, O Lord giue good and prosperous successe to all those that fight thy battell against the enemies of thy Gospell, shewe some token continually for our good, that they which hate vs may see it and bee confounded. And that we thy little and despised flocke may say with good King Dauid, Blessed are the people whose God is the Lorde Jehouah, and blessed are the folke that he hath chosen to be his inheritance. These and all other graces necessary for vs, graunt O heauenly Father, for Jesus Christes sake our onely mediatour and redeemer.

[The BCP collect in time of war; the prayers 'O most righteous God, and most mercifull Father' and 'O Lorde our God and heauenly father, looke down': both as 1572–E]

A prayer.
Be mercifull (O Father of all mercies) to thy Church vniuersall, dispersed throughout the whole world: and grant that all they that confesse thy holy name, may agree in the truth of thy holy worde, and liue in godly concord and vnitie. And specially bee mercifull to such as are vnder persecution for the testimonie of their conscience, and profession of the gospell of thy Sonne our Sauiour Jesus Christ. Represse (O Lord) the rage and tyrannie of such as are bent to bloodshed, and mind nothing but murther: and saue and deliuer those silly soules, which (as sheepe) are appointed to the shambles and slaughter. And namely, bee mercifull to thy Church and realme of England: to thy seruant our souereigne and gracious Queene ELIZABETH, whose life (O Lord) long and long preserue from all the conspiracies and euils, which the

craft and malice of the deuill, Antichrist, or other wicked men hath or can deuise against her (as hitherto most graciously thou hast done.) Bee mercifull (O Lorde) to the Queenes most honourable counsell, giuing them grace to counsel and to execute that which may be to thy honour and glory, to the edifying of the Church of thy sonne our Sauiour Jesus Christ, and to the benefit & safetie of the realme. Be mercifull also (O Lord) to the clergie, nobilitie, Judges, magistrates, people, and communaltie of this realme, granting to euery one thy heauenly grace, that they may in their vocation doe their dueties, to the honour and glory of thy name, the benefite of this church & realme, and to the saluation of their owne soules. Grant this (O Lord) to vs most vnworthy sinners for the worthines of thy deare sonne our Sauiour Jesus Christ, to whome with thee and the holy ghost, bee all honour and glory world without ende. *Amen.*

[*'A thankesgeuyng and prayer for the preseruation of the Queene, and the Realme': as 1572–E]*

1588–S2 Prayers and fast days during the threat of a Spanish invasion

Wednesday 7 August–Sunday 11 August 1588 (with fasting on Thursday 8 August and Sunday 11 August) (Edinburgh); Sunday 11 August 1588 (elsewhere in Scotland if possible)

The general assembly met on 6 August 1588, at the height of the armada invasion scare. In response to the emergency, the assembly appointed this observance to begin in Edinburgh on the following day. The northward flight of the armada after the battle of Gravelines (see 1588–E1) apparently increased fears in Scotland. According to Melvill, the tenor of the sermons and devotions in Edinburgh was heightened by reports of the Spanish fleet's progress, 'sum tymes of thair landing at Dumbar, sum tymes at St Androis, and in Tay, and now and then at Aberdein and Cromertie'.

Order: by the general assembly beginning 6 Aug. 1588, Calderwood, IV, 682–3.
Additional sources: *BUK*, II, 730; Row, p. 137; Melvill, p. 261.

ORDER

Order by the general assembly beginning 6 August 1588
Forasmuche as it is thought expedient, that in the frequencie of this Assemblie, the most necessar things be first handled; and that there are certane generalls, which, before all others, come to be resolved, namelie, concerning the present dangers imminent to the kirk of Christ within this realme, and to the commoun wealth therof, by the arrivall of forrane natiouns, as Spaniards and barbars: as also, the danger and decay of religioun, by the raritie and povertie of the ministers of the Evangell, occasiouned by the continuall spoilzie of the patrimonie of the kirk: For the first, the Assemblie hath thought, for their part and duetie in this behalfe, that a Fast be proclamed the morne, by the ordinar teacher in the Kirk of Edinburgh, to be continued in the said toun, with supplicatiouns to God, and continuall exhortatiouns to be used the whole weeke, by the brethrein underwrittin. The dayes of fasting to be,

the Thursday and Sunday nixt. And likewise, the samine Fast to be keeped upon the said Sunday, by so manie kirks about this toun as may have the opportunitie. And for using the said exhortatiouns in this meane tyme, appointeth the brethrein following, viz., Mr Walter Balcalquall upon Wedinsday after noone; and upon Thursday in the morning at seven houres, Mr Johne Craig; at five houres after noone, Mr Patrik Simsone. Upon Fryday, at eight houres, David Fergusone; and after noone, James Andersone. Saturday, before noone, Johne Durie, and Mr James Robertsone, after noone. On Sunday before noone, in the New Kirk, Mr James Balfour, incace of the absence of Mr Robert Bruce; and in the High Kirk, after noone, Mr Johne Knox: and these brethrein to lay out the dangers of the saids enemeis, and circumstances therof to the people, exhorting them to the defence of the true religioun, libertie of the countrie, and maintenance of the king's Majestie.

1588–S3   Thanksgiving days for the failure of the Spanish armada

Saturday 19 October, Sunday 20 October, Sunday 27 October, Sunday 3 November 1588 (Scotland)

Calderwood and Spottiswoode reported that special worship was arranged in response to the failure of the armada. No precisely contemporary sources mention the observance, and it is unclear whether it involved fasting, as Calderwood suggested. No record of a royal order has been found; but it is possible that the observance was appointed by the crown.

Order: none found.
Sources: Calderwood, IV, 696; Spottiswoode, II, 389.

DESCRIPTIONS

Calderwood, *History*
There was a fast keeped through the whole countrie for the notable deliverie God had givin from the invasioun attempted by the cruell Spaniard, which beganne upon Saturday, the nynteenth of October, and continued three Sabboth dayes, wherwith was joyned the celebratioun of the Lord's Supper.

Spottiswoode, *History*
The king caused solemn thanks for this deliverance to be given to God in all the churches of the kingdom, beginning in his own court for an ensample to others.

1588–E2   Thanksgiving day for the failure of the Spanish armada

Tuesday 19 November 1588 (England and Wales)

After the English success at Gravelines on 29 July 1588, celebrations and thanksgivings were initially slow and muted, probably because it was not clear how decisive the battle had been. Public thanksgiving sermons were not preached at Paul's Cross until 20 August (Nowell), 8 September (unknown; ensigns and banners taken from the

Spanish ships were displayed around the Cross and the cathedral) and 17 November (Cooper). On 30 September, the privy council wrote to William Wickham, bishop of Lincoln, and John Piers, bishop of Salisbury, asking them to come to court to discuss the preaching of further thanksgiving sermons, though the results of these meetings are not known. There was no official, nationwide thanksgiving until 19 November – a month after celebrations began in Scotland (see 1588–S3) – when celebrations were held in provincial cities and towns, including Chester, Norwich, Shrewsbury, Salisbury, as well as small parishes, such as Baldock (Hertfordshire) and Shillington (Bedfordshire). Elizabeth herself attended a thanksgiving service at St Paul's Cathedral on Sunday 24 November. This was the first time since the break with Rome that a sovereign had attended a major public service to mark a special occasion of 'national' worship (although Philip of Spain had done so as royal consort for 1554–E3). The queen processed from Somerset House to the cathedral, dressed in silver and white in a 'chariot throne, made with fower pillers' drawn by grey horses, preceded by the gentlemen of the privy chamber, the gentlemen pensioners and footmen carrying poleaxes. She was flanked by equerries and footmen and followed by the master of the horse (the earl of Essex) with the palfrey of honour and the chief lady of the honour for the train, the lord chamberlain (the earl of Oxford), vice-chamberlain (Sir Thomas Heneage), the ladies of the honour, the captain of the guard (Sir Walter Raleigh), further guards, the French ambassador, members of the nobility and privy council, judges and serjeants at law, all richly attired. She was met at Temple Bar by the lord mayor and the city aldermen where she was presented with a sword (to symbolize her authority over the city); in return, she presented the mayor with a sceptre (to symbolize the delegation of her authority to him during her visit). The mayor carried the sceptre before the queen in the procession; the sword was carried by the marquis of Winchester. Members of the London livery companies, led by the most senior company, the Drapers, lined the streets between Temple Bar and the cathedral. The queen was greeted by Bishop Aylmer of London, Alexander Nowell (dean of St Paul's) and other higher clergy (controversially robed in former catholic vestments) at the west door of St Paul's, where she knelt in prayer before being escorted, as the litany was sung, down the west aisle to a privy closet on the north wall. From here, she appears to have listened to the sermon preached at Paul's Cross by her almoner and bishop of Salisbury, John Piers. Elizabeth subsequently dined at Aylmer's palace in Fulham before returning to Somerset House. It is unclear when the form of prayer for parish use was issued; it must have been after 4 November because it was not mentioned in either Whitgift's letter of instruction to Aylmer, bishop of London, or in the bishop's own letter to the archdeacon of St Albans the following day. In contrast to earlier occasions, the form comprised only a psalm and a collect which would have been inserted into the BCP service. The collect would probably have been read at the end of the litany; it is unclear when the psalm would have been said or sung. A manuscript prayer, possibly written by Whitgift's secretary, Michael Murgatroyd, is extant; it is unclear when, where or if this was used.

Order: privy council to the archbishop of Canterbury, and to the dean and chapter of York, 3 Nov. 1588, described in *APC*, XVI, 334; Aylmer to Hutchinson, 5 Nov. 1588, HALS, ASA 5/2/84, pp. 441–2. **Form of prayer:** *A psalme and collect of thankesgiuing, not vnmeet for this present time: to be said or sung in churches* ([8] pp.; STC 16520)* [also in Clay, pp. 619–23]. **Additional sources:** privy council to the bishops of Salisbury and Lincoln, 30 Sept. 1588, *APC*, XVI, 292; Advices from England, 5 Nov. 1588, *CSPSp*, IV, 470–1; John Stowe, *The Annales of England* (1592; STC 23334), sigs. Ppppi^r–Ppppi^v; Huntington Library, California, MS EL 1118, fos. 17v–18r;

'A Joyfull newe ballad of the Royall entrance of Quene' and 'Gyve eare awhile good people all', Add. 82370, fos. 19r–22r, 23r–26v; Strype, *Annals*, III: 2, 27–31; *A transcript of the registers of the Company of Stationers*, ed. Arber, II, 508; Clay, pp. 469–70; MacLure, p. 66; manuscript copy of prayer made by Michael Murgatroyd, Whitgift's secretary, LPL, MS 178, fo. 40r.

ORDER

Privy council to archbishop of Canterbury, and to the dean and chapter of York: 3 November 1588

A letter to the Archbishop of Canterburye letting his Lordship to understande that her Majesties expresse pleasure and commaundement was that order should be given by his Lordship in all the Dioces under his Lordship's Province to the severall Bishoppes, Curates and Mynisters to appoint some speciall daye wherein all the Realme might concurr in givinge publique and generall thanckes unto God with all devocion and inward affection of harte and humblenesse for His gratyous favor extended towardes us in our deliveraunce and defence in the wonderfull overthrow [and] destruction shewed by His mighty hand on our malytious enemyes, the Spannyardes, whoe had sought to invade and make a conquest of the Realme.

The lyke letter wrytten unto the Deane and Chapter of the Bishoprick of Yorke to take the same order within the Dyocesse of that Bishoprick as was in all pointes specyfied in the former letter.

Bishop of London to archdeacon of St Albans: 5 November 1588

After my hartye Commendacons whereas of late I receaved a letter from my Lord of Canterburye his grace, the Tenor whereof heareafter enseweth. /

Salutem in Christo. whereas vpon Consideracon of the greate and spetiall favor of god, so mightelye and gratiouslye shewed in the overthrowe of greate preparacons and forces sett forthe by the King of Spayne this last Sommer with a most malicious entente to invade this Realme and to make a Conquest of the same, Her Maiestie hath fownd some Fawlte that there hath as yet bynn no publique prayer and generall thankesgevinge ordaynd for so rare benefittes and graces And therevppon hath signefyed vnto me by lettres from the Lords of her highnes most honorable privye counsell her expresse pleasure and Commandement for order to be given throughowt all the Province of Canterburye that vpon the xix[th] daye of this Instant monthe of November beinge Tewsedaye (as a speciall daye by her Maiestie for that purpose appoynted) there shulde be a generall concurrence of all the people of this Realme in repayringe to theire seuerall parishe churches and in givinge publique thanckes vnto god for his most gracious favor extended towardes vs in our deliverance and defence, and in the wonderfull overthrowe and destruction shewed by his mightie hand on our malicious enemyes, These are therefore to requyre your Lordship that with all expedicon possible yow give order to your Cathedrall churche, and all other the seuerall parishe churches within your dioces for the generall celebracon of the said xix[th] day according to her Maiesties good pleasure and entente. which that yt may be the better performed your Lordship shall do well to cause all such as are preachers within your dioces in there sermons vpon that daye aswell to declare vnto the people the wonderfull mercyes of god shewed vpon vs in the sayd overthrowe of our enemyes (the particulareties whereof they maye vnderstand by such pamphletts as have byn published of late touchinge the successe of the spannishe Navey) as also by all good meanes and exhortacons to incite and stirr vpp the myndes and hartes of the people with all devotion and inwarde affection to prayse god for the same And in those parisheis wherein there are no Preachers to provyde as much as may be for sermons to be had to that effecte by suche as your Lordship shall appoynte thereunto, Together with a generall ringinge of the bells, singinge of psallmes and all other externall Signs of ioye and thankesgivinge for so great and speciall benefittes as in such like caseis hath byn vsuallye accustomed, that yt may be done withall solemnetye, And so not dowbtinge but your Lordship will take speedye and speciall care for the accomplishement hereof accordinge to her maiesties expectacon and our bownden dutyes I Committ yow to the Tuicon of Almightie god, From Lambeth the fowrth of November 1588

            Your Lorshipps lovinge brother in Christ

            John Cantuar

    These are therefore to will and requyre yow to see the contentes of his sayd graces lettre dewlye within all Churches of your Archdeaconrie put in execution att the full, to the satisfaccon of the good expectacon thereof, aswell in places exempte as not exempte with all possible speede as may be, And that accordinge to his graces lettres in those parisheis where no preachers be, yow do drawe such preachers as have no speciall chardge to those parisheis whoe want preachers …

FORM OF PRAYER

A Psalme of thankesgiuing.

O Come hither, and hearken all yee that feare God, and we will tell you what he hath done for our soules. (Ps. 66.c.14) [66: 16]

For we may not hide his benefites from our children, and to the generation to come, and to all people we will shew the prayses of the Lord, his power also, and his wonderful workes, that he hath done for vs. (Ps. 78.a.4) [78:4]

When the Kings & Rulers of the earth, and Nations round about vs, furiously raged, and tooke counsell together, against God, and against his annoynted. (Ps. 2.a.1) [2: 1 & 2]

When men of an other deuotion then we be, (men bewitched by the Romish Antichrist,) *men drowned in idolatries and superstitions, hated vs deadly, and were maliciously set against vs, for our profession of the word of God, and the blessed Gospel of our Sauiour Christ.* (Ps. 144.b.7; Matt. 10.d.2; Matt. 24.b.9.10; Ps. 115.a.4; Ps. 55.a.3) [Ps. 144:7; Matt. 10:2; Matt. 24:9–10; Ps. 115:4; Ps. 55:3]

They cast their heads together with one consent, they tooke their common counsell, and were confederate, and imagined mischiefe, against thy people, O Lord God. (Ps. 83.a.3)[233] [83: 3]

They secretly layd wayte, they priuily set snares and nettes, they digged pittes for our soules, thinking that no man should see them. (Ps. 35.b.:7; Ps. 56.b.6; Ps. 64.a.5.6; Ps. 83.b.3) [35:7; 56:6; 64:5–6; 83:3]

They communed of peace, and prepared for most cruel warre, for they thinke that no faith, nor trueth is to be kept with vs, but that they may feine, dissemble, breake promise, sweare, and forsweare, so they may deceiue vs and take vs vnwares, and oppresse vs sudainely. (Ps. 12a.1.2; Ps. 14.b.5.6; Ps. 59.b.7.c.12 & 120.a.2.140 a.2.3.b.9) [12:1–2; 14:5–6; 59: 7, 12; 120:2; 140:2–3, 9]

---

[233] In the margin alongside the biblical reference: '*The counsell of Trent, and the holy league.*'

And in deede innumerable multitudes of these most subtil and cruell enemies, and too mightie for vs, came sudainely vpon vs, by sea, and by land, when we looked not for them. (Ps. 3.a.1.2.; Ps. 22.c.12.16 & 59.a.3 & 69.a.4) [3:1–2; 22:12, 16; 59:3; 69:4]

They came furiously vpon vs, as it were roaring and ramping Lions, purposing to deuoure vs, and to swallowe vs vp: they approched neare vnto vs, euen to eate vp our flesh. (Ps.17.b.12. Ps.22.c.13. & 56.a.1.2. Ps.27.a.2) [17:12; 22:13; 56:1–2; 27:2]

They sayd in their hearts, Let vs make hauocke of them altogether, let vs roote them out that they be no more a people, and that the name of England *may be no more had in remembrance.* (Ps. 74.b.8. 83.a.4)[234] [74:8; 83:4]

And surely their comming was so sudaine, their multitude, power, and crueltie so great, that had we not beleeued verely to see the goodnes of God, and put our trust in his defence and protection, they might haue vtterly destroyed vs. (Ps. 27.c.15. Ps.55.a.3. Ps.124.a.1.2. &c. Ps. 94.c.17) [?; 55:3; 124:1–2; 94:17]

But though we had great cause to be afrayd, yet we put our whole trust in God: we cryed vnto the Lord in our trouble and distresse, we sayd, Helpe vs O Lord our God, for vaine is the helpe of man. (Ps. 56.a.3. & 107.b.6, 108.c.12) [56:3; 107:6; 108:12]

We said, we commit our selues wholly vnto thee, according to the greatnes of thy power, preserue vs O Lord, who are appointed to die. (Ps. 60.c.11.12, 108.c.12.13) [60:11–12; 108:12–13]

And the Lord enclyned his eare and heard vs, and gaue courage to the hearts, and strength to the hands of our captaines and souldiers, and put the enemies in feare. (Ps. 81.b.7. & Ps. 34.35.37. Ps.48.a.5.6) [81:7; 34; 35, 37; 48:5–6]

The Lord arose, and tooke the cause (*which in deede was his owne*) into his owne hands, and fought against them, that fought against vs. (Ps. 10.c.12.14. Ps.35.a.1) [10: 12, 14; 35:1]

The Lorde scattered them with his windes, he confounded and disapointed their deuises and purposes of ioyning their powers together against vs. (Ps. 11.b.6 Ps.18.c.11.12.13) [11:6; 18:11–13]

The Angel of the Lord persecuted them, brought them into dangerous, darke, and slipperie places, where they wandering long to and fro, were consumed with hunger, thirst, colde, and sicknesse: the sea swalowed the greatest part of them. (Ps. 48.a.6. & 83.c.15. Ps.35.a.5.6. Ex.15.a.4.5) [Ps. 48:6; 83:15; 35:5–6; Exod. 15:4–5]

And so the Lord repressed the rage and furie of our cruel enemies, intending nothing but bloodshed and murther, and turned the mischiefe which they purposed against vs, vpon their owne heads: and deliuered and saued vs, who were as sheepe appointed to the shambles and slaughter. (Ps. 7.c.15.16. Ps.35.b.8. Ps.9.c.15.16.17.18. Ps.9.b.9. Ps.18.d.17. Ps. 44.b.12.d.22) [7:15–16; 35:8; 9:9, 15–18; 18:17; 44:12, 22]

This was the Lords doing, and it is marueilous in our, & in our enemies sight: and in the eyes of all people, and all that see it, shall say, This is the Lords worke. (Ps. 64.b.9. Ps.107.f.42.43. Ps.118.d.2) [64:9; 107:42–43; 118:2]

God is our king of olde: the helpe that is done by sea and by land, is his. (Ps.74.c.13. Ps.107.d.22.23.&c) [74:13; 107:22–3]

It is God that giueth deliuerance vnto Princes, and that rescueth our QVEENE from the hurtfull sword, and saueth her from all dangers and perils. (Ps. 144.b.10)[235] [144:10]

We will therefore giue thankes whom the Lord hath redeemed, and deliuered from the hand of the enemie. (Ps. 107.a.2) [107:2]

---

234 In the margin, opposite 'England': '*Israel* '.
235 In margin opposite 'QVEENE': '*Dauid*'.

We wil confesse before the Lord, and prayse him for his goodnes: and declare the woonders that he doth for the children of men. (Ps. 107.d.21) [107:21]

We will offer vnto him the sacrifice of thanksgiuing: and tell out his works with gladnesse. (d.22) [107:22]

We will exalt him also in the Congregation of the people, and prayse him in the presence of the Elders. (Ps. 107.e.50) [?]

O sing vnto the Lord a new song: for hee hath done marueilous things. (Ps. 98.a.1) [98:1]

With his owne right hand, & with his holy arme: hath he gotten himselfe the victorie. (a.2) [98:2]

O giue thanks vnto the Lorde, and call vpon his name: tell the people what things he hath done. (Ps. 105.a.1) [105:1]

O let your songes be of him, and prayse him: and let your talking be of all his wonderous workes. (a.2) [105:2]

Reioyce in his holy name: let the hearts of them reioyce that seeke the Lord. (a.3) [150:3]

And thou my soule, be ioyful in the Lord: let it reioyce in his saluation. (Ps. 35.b.9) [35:9]

All my bones shal say, Lord who is like vnto thee, which deliuerest the oppressed from them that be too strong for them: yea, and them that are in distresse, from them that seeke to spoyle them. (b.10) [35:10]

Blessed be the Lord God, euen the God of Israel: which onely doth wonderous things. (Ps. 72.c.18) [72:18]

And blessed be the name of his maiestie for euer and euer: and all the earth shall be filled with the glory of his maiestie. Amen. Amen. (c.19) [72:19]

Glorie be to the Father, and to the Sonne: and to the holy Ghost.

As it was in the beginning, is now, and euer shall be: world without end. Amen.

A Collect of thankesgiuing.

We cannot but confesse, O Lord God, that the late terrible intended inuasion of most cruell enemies, was sent from thee to the punishment of our sinnes, of our pride, our couetousnesse, our excesse in meats and drinks, our securitie, our ingratitude, and our vnthankefulnesse towards thee, for so long peace, and other thy infinite blessings continually powred vpon vs, and to the punishment of other our innumerable, and most greeuous offences continually committed against thy diuine maiestie. And in deed our guiltie consciences looked for (euen at that time) the execution of thy terrible iustice vpon vs, so by vs deserued. But thou O Lord God, who knowest all thinges, knowing that our enemies came not of iustice to punish vs for our sinnes committed against thy diuine maiestie (whom they by their excessiue wickednesse haue offended, and continually do offend, as much or more then we) but that they came with most cruell intent & purpose to destroy vs, our cities, townes, countrie and people, and vtterly to root out the memorie of our nation from off the earth for euer: and withall, wholly to suppresse thy holy word, & blessed gospell of thy deere sonne our Sauiour Jesus Christ, which they (being drowned in idolatries and superstitions) doe hate most deadly, and vs likewise, onely for the profession of the same, and not for any offences against thy diuine maiestie, or iniuries done to themselues. Wherefore it hath pleased thee, O heauenly father, in thy iustice to remember thy mercies towards vs, turning our enemies from vs, and that dreadfull execution which they intended towards vs, into a fatherly and most mercifull admonition s: and to execute iustice vpon our cruell enemi hey intended against vs, vpon their owne heads. st gracious protection of vs, and all other thy grace. nually, and most plenteously powred vpon our Church, our *QVEENE*, our Realme and people of England, we beseech thee adde, and powre also the grace of gratitude and thankefulnesse into our hearts: that we neuer forgetting, but bearing in perpetuall memorie, this thy mercifull protection, and deliuerance of vs, from the malice, force, fraud, and crueltie of our enemies, and all other thy benefits most plenteously powred vpon vs, may inioy the continuance of thy fatherly goodnes towards our Church, our *QVEENE*, our Realme and people of England, and continually magnifie thy holy, and most glorious name: which we doo beseech thee, O heauenly Father, to grant to vs most vnwoorthie sinners, for the woorthinesse of thy deere sonne our Sauior Jesus Christ, to whom with thee, and the Holy ghost, one God of most glorious maiestie, be all honour and glorie world without end. Amen.

1589–Ir   Thanksgiving days for the failure of the Spanish armada

[Wednesday 26 January 1589?] (Dublin); before Wednesday 12 February 1589 (elsewhere in Ireland)

This is the first known occasion of special worship in Ireland since the reformation. No order exists, but a request for thanksgivings appears to have been communicated by Lord Burghley to the bishops, sheriffs and 'Soveraignes' (i.e. the mayors or provosts of towns), on the queen's behalf. It is unclear whether Burghley was acting as a member of the privy council or informally as Elizabeth's secretary. Neither is it clear when the services took place. In a postscript to a letter to Burghley, the lord deputy, Sir William Fitzwilliam, implied that the thanksgivings may not have been observed in Dublin until 26 January 1589.[236] Services elsewhere were observed before 12 February, when Fitzwilliam reported to Burghley how well they were attended; it appears from this letter that the thanksgivings may have been ordered to be observed only in one principal church per county. The services comprised prayers and sermons but there is no evidence that a form of prayer was issued. For occasions of special worship in Ireland in the early seventeenth century, bishops were ordered to compose their own prayers for use in their dioceses (e.g. 1625–Ir) and this may have been the case here. Burghley appears to have asked the lord deputy and the Irish bishops to report the numbers and names of those who attended the services and how many of these took communion. The results were mixed. The lord deputy reported that the service in Dublin had been poorly attended

the people nere about vs here haue for the most part bene so farre off from performing the duties of good and Louing subiectes, as they haue rather seemed discontented & to repyne at her maiesties good successes then otherwise, shewing them selues as obstinate and backward in this accion of prayer & thancksgeuing, as they were last Somer (in the heate of all our troubles) to make any Musters.

236   The letter is dated 16 January but the lord deputy appears not to have been able to send it for several days because of bad weather.

This was confirmed by Archbishop Adam Loftus in a later report:

> notwithstanding the sheriffes of ech county did ther duties with all diligence, and warned all men to repaire to the principall church in euery county … yet verie fewe or none almost resorted thervnto but euen in Dublin it self the lawyers in terme time tooke occasion to leaue the towne, of purpose to absent them selves from that godlie exercise[.]

Attendance at the service at Youghal was similarly poor, though this was blamed on the churchwarden, Walley, who had refused to implement the bishop's orders. By contrast, 2,000 people attended the service and sermon given by William Lyon, bishop of Cork and Ross, in Cork; 600 attended the sermon preached by Lyon's chaplain at Ross, and 'great nombres' attended services in Carbery, Kinsale and Clony. Indeed, at Kinsale 'the churche was not hable to receue all the people that came thether, but that great nombres were inforced to stand with out who hong upon the walles & windowes to heare the sermon'.

Sources: Lord Deputy Fitzwilliam to Lord Burghley, 16 Jan. and 12 Feb. 1589, SP63/140/22, fo. 89r, SP63/141/21, fo. 54r; Archbishop Adam Loftus of Dublin to Burghley, 22 Sept. 1590, SP63/154/37, fos. 129v–130r.

DESCRIPTION

Lord Deputy Fitzwilliam to Lord Burghley: 16 January 1589
Post script
It may please your Lordship: the 25 of this instant (till which tyme this Letters attending wynd was no perclosed) being the .4th. day within the Terme, we celebrated here (according to her Maiesties pleasure) a generall thancksgeuing, hauing a sermon preached by the Lord Chauncellor & a commonyon: And albeit presentlie vpon the receipt of your Lordships letters in that behaulf, the day & tyme was published, yet was there not any of the Irishe Judges, Lawyers or learnyd that did commvnycate, & but very few of them, or noble men, or gentlemen that heard the Sermon: Whereby your Lordship may perceiue the miserable state of this Land & thereby the great necessitie it hath of godlie preachers, especiallie of such as haue Authorytie comyted to that function: And yet I thanck God ther was not a greater Commvnyon here sence my Last coming into Ireland.

Lord Deputy Fitzwilliam to Lord Burghley: 12 February 1589
And now hauing receaved severall Certificates from the Bushoppes, Shriefes & Soveraignes within the Pale, tutching the nombres & names of suche as assembled them selves to celebrate the generall thancksgeuing for her maiesties happie successe agaynst the Spa[nish], albeit it appeareth thereby that the people nere about vs here haue for the most part bene so farre off from performing the duties of good and Louing subiectes, as they haue rather seemed discontented & to repyne at her maiesties good successe then otherwise, shewing them selves as obstinate and backward in this accion of prayer & thancksgeuing, as they were the last Somer (in the heate of all our troubles) to make any Musters, & so vnwilling ether to fight or pray for her Maiestie: Yet hath it pleasid God for our comfortes so to counterpoyse the same with his exceeding blessinges vpon the people of the remote partes, as that at Carbery, Kinsale, and Clony they resorted in great nombres to their severall parish churches

where many of them did communicate and with earnest prayers & prayses to God for her maiesties happie victory and saulftie most ioyfullie & dutifullie behauid them selues, especially at Kinsale where the churche was not hable to receue all the people that came thether, but that great nombres were inforced to stand with out who hong vpon the walles & windowes to heare the sermon; which ended, the Soueraigne of the Towne, his brethren and Comons together with their wyves and servantes receavid the Commvnyon: Also at Cork (where the Bushop of that dyoces preached) there was congregated 2000 people to heare the sermon, of whom there was a great nombre of Communicantes: Likewise at Rosse there were assembled to heare the Bushops chaplen (who preached there) no lesse then 600 persons of whom .300. receaved the Commvnyon Howbeit at Youghil there was nothing done through the willfull asbsence of one Walley warden there, who notwithstanding notice geven him at Corck by the Bushop, of her maiesties pleasure, did not repayre to his charge, which vndutifullnes of his I haue the rather thought mete to signifie vnto your Lordship lest otherwise he (being now in England) might with his smoth & filed speaches induce your Lordship (who knoweth not his conversation) to thinck more honorablie of him then he deserveth, Being in truth of so bad a disposition, as that by report there lyveth not a man more lewd & wicked …

Archbishop of Dublin to Burghley: 22 September 1590

… But yet I assure your Lord ther obstinacy nowe is such, that vnlesse they be inforced, they will not once come to heare the word preached as by experience we observed, at the time appointed by the Lord Deputy and counsell for a generall assemblie of all the noble men, and gentlemen of ech county after her maiesties good successe against the Spaniardes, to give god thankes for the same: at which time notwithstanding the sheriffes of ech county did ther duties with all diligence, and warned all men to repaire to the principall church in euery county, where order was taken for publique prayers and thankesgivinges vnto god, together with a sermon to be preached by choise men in ech diocesse, yet verie fewe or none almost resorted thervnto but euen in Dublin it self the lawyers in terme time tooke occasion to leaue the towne, of purpose to absent them selues from that godlie exercise: so bewraying in them selves besides ther corruption in religion, great want of duty and loyaltie vnto her maiestie, and giving iust occasion vnto vs, to conceive doubtfull opinion of them …

1589–E   Prayers for the naval expedition to Portugal and the Azores

Three times a week after Sunday 3 May 1589 (England and Wales)

This occasion is known only from a letter from Aylmer to Hutchinson, the archdeacon of St Albans (in which Whitgift's order to the bishops is copied verbatim) and Hutchinson's mandate to his apparitor, John Grynsell. Sir John Norris and Sir Francis Drake commanded a naval and land force which aimed to place Dom Antonio on the Portuguese throne and to capture the Spanish treasure fleet off the Azores. Dom Antonio, the grandson of Manuel I, had disputed Philip II's claim to the Portuguese throne since the death, without issue and without designating a successor, of Henry 'the Cardinal-King' in January 1580, and he had received sporadic English support thereafter. The English fleet set sail on 18 April, so these prayers were ordered at the presumed time of its engagement with Spanish forces. As for 1586–E3, no form appears to have been commissioned; instead, ministers were instructed to conduct prayers according to 'the order of the booke and accordinge to former orders sett forthe by aucthoretye, at the leaste thrise in euerye weeke'. 'The order of the booke' probably referred to the prayers at the end of the litany in the BCP – Whitgift had used this formulation for 1586–E3 – but it is less clear what the 'former orders sett forthe by aucthoretye' were. This may refer to the format of thrice-weekly services established in 1563 during plague time (see 1563–E). Hutchinson's mandate to Grynsell provides an insight into the distribution and enforcement of orders for special worship, though care must be taken because St Albans was a peculiar and so might not represent accurately the practice in other parishes. Wishing to spare the churchwardens' 'travell and paynes' by commanding them to assemble together to hear the order, Hutchinson urged them 'to have due consideracon of your paynes and travell' (i.e. to pay Grynsell his expenses in travelling to the parish), stating that, if they did not, they would have to appear before one of his officials. The archdeacon also instructed Grynsell to ensure that the churchwardens reported to him whether or not ministers executed the orders. This reflected a growing concern to monitor the observance of special worship – a similar directive had been issued in 1586–7 (see 1586–E3) – though, once again, it is unclear whether this order was enforced. The naval expedition proceeded badly, and failed in both of its aims. The queen was annoyed at what she considered to be the disregard of her orders, and both Drake and Norris were summoned before the privy council to explain their actions.

Order: Aylmer to Hutchinson, 3 May 1589, HALS, ASA 5/2/89, p. 457.
Form of prayer: possibly BCP and/or following the format set down in 1563–E.
Additional source: Mandate from Hutchinson to John Grynsell, apparitor, 5 May 1589, HALS, ASA 5/2/99, p. 461.

ORDER

Bishop of London to archdeacon of St Albans: 3 May 1589
Salutem in Christo I have receaved Letters from my Lordes grace of Canterburye, the tenor whereof heareafter enseweth. /

Salutem in Christo. Your Lordshipp is not ignorant of the greate and worthie enterprise of Sir John Norrys and Sir Frauncys Drake nowe in Action the good successe whereof must needes tend to the glorye of god and to the singuler benefitt of his Churche, And for asmuche as all goodnes Commeth from above, and that god onelye givethe the victorye I thought yt good by these my lettres to move your Lordshipp to take diligent care that in euerye parrishe Churche within your dioces, publique prayers be had accordinge to the order of the booke and accordinge to former orders sett forthe by aucthoretye, at the leaste thrise in euerye weeke, which althoughe I do not dowbte yow have of your selfe remembred to performe, yett I thoughte itt not amisse to putt yow in mynde of the same att this tyme, And so with my hartye Commendacons I Committ yow to the Tuicon of Almightie god From Lambeth the second of Maye 1589

      Your lovinge brother and Freende
      Jo: Cantuar
I ame to requyer yow that forthe with vpon receipte heare of yow give present order to euerye parishe within your Iurisdiccon aswell to the minister as Churchwardens

that the order in his graceis lettres heare sett downe be observed that both the minister may vse his dilligence in publique prayers accordinge as is heare appoynted and the people give theire diligent attendance in ioyninge hartes and handes to god, for the prosperous successe of so good a service taken in hande for the benefitt of his Churche ...

[in a different hand]
yow shall also admonishe the ministers once in the weeke att the leaste to preache; that the people maye be stirred vpp to prayer and fastinge accordinge vnto their Christian devotion: /

1589–S   Weekly fast days for James VI's return from Denmark

Sundays, October 1589 – April 1590 (Edinburgh; and probably elsewhere in Scotland)

James VI married Anna of Denmark in a proxy ceremony conducted at Copenhagen on 20 August 1589. Storms delayed Anna's journey to Scotland, initially preventing her from travelling beyond Oslo, and James waited anxiously for his wife's arrival. It was reported that a fast was observed in Edinburgh on her account in September 1589; James was said to have requested further fasts and prayers. On 22 October, the king himself sailed for Norway, where he met Anna. Their departure was delayed by the weather, and the couple spent the first four months of 1590 in Denmark, before returning to Scotland on 1 May. On 24 October 1589, Edinburgh's town council issued a proclamation ordering observance of weekly fasts on Sundays until the king's return. On 30 October, William Asheby reported from Edinburgh that the clergy had initiated the weekly fasts. It is not known whether these fasts were kept throughout Scotland, although after the general assembly added its authority in March 1590, weekly fasting was presumably observed beyond the capital. On 24 May 1590, the king expressed his thanks for the ministers' appointment of the fasts.

Order: by the general assembly beginning 3 Mar. 1590, described in Calderwood, V, 86.
Additional sources: *BUK*, II, 747; James Hudson to Sir Francis Walsingham, 27 Sept. 1589, SP52/44/79; William Asheby to Walsingham, 8 Oct. 1589, SP52/44/82; William Asheby to Burghley, 8 Oct. 1589, same to same, 30 Oct. 1589, BL, Cotton Caligula D. I, fos. 407v, 414v; William Asheby to Burghley, 10 Nov. 1589, *CSPSc, 1589–95*, p. 192; *Edin. recs., 1589 to 1603*, p. 8; Calderwood, V, 98.

DESCRIPTION OF ORDER

Order by the general assembly beginning 3 March 1590
It was appointed that a fast sould be keeped everie Sabboth till the king's returne.

1590–E1   Services during the threat of a Spanish invasion

Three times a week after Friday 6 March 1590 (Canterbury province)

Philip II planned a second armada in 1589 and again in 1590; both came to nothing. In 1590, the blockade of Paris by the new protestant French king, Henry IV, and his defeat of catholic opponents at Ivry turned Philip's attention to France and support of the Catholic League. Fears of a Spanish invasion of England nevertheless remained high, and in March Whitgift ordered bishops in his province to organize public prayers. This order was given as a coda to a lengthy letter in which Whitgift, in response to a letter from the privy council, reminded the clergy of a requirement made by the council and parliament during the armada threat of 1588 – that they should ensure that sufficient horses, armour and other equipment was available in their districts, in case it was needed for defence against invasion. In ordering the prayers, Whitgift may have been acting independently as archbishop because the council's letter to him made no mention of special worship. This may explain why there is no evidence that prayers were ordered in the northern province, though it should be noted that orders for special worship are recorded inconsistently in episcopal registers, including those of York. As was becoming increasingly common, the form of prayer issued by Whitgift comprised a series of prayers and psalms to be inserted into the BCP service, rather than a full liturgy. There were no instructions on where in the service these texts should be read. The form primarily copied the prayers issued in for 1588–E1 (themselves copied from 1572–E). In addition, three prayers were copied from the form issued for use by the English armies in France in 1589 (see Appendix 1: Omitted occasions) and there were two new prayers.

Order: Whitgift to the bishops, 6 Mar. 1589/90 [i.e. 1590], LPL, Whitgift Register, I, fo. 163r–v.
Form of prayer: *A fourme of prayer, necessarie for the present time and state* ([32] pp.; STC 16522* [also in Clay, pp. 632–46].
Additional sources: privy council to Whitgift, 4 Mar. 1589/90 [i.e. 1590], LPL, Whitgift Register, I, fo. 163r; Strype, *Whitgift*, II, 67–9 (who mistakenly dated this occasion to 1586); mandate from Hutchinson to John Grynsell, apparitor, 13 Mar. 1590, HALS, ASA 5/2/100, p. 489; Hutchinson to Aylmer, 4 Apr. 1590, HALS, ASA 5/3/104, p. 497; Clay, pp. 470–1.

ORDER

Archbishop of Canterbury to the bishops: 6 March 1590

Salutem in Christo … And for asmuch as these meanes *[the provision of soldiers, horses and equipment by the clergy]* will profitt litle or nothinge vnlesse God be on our side, therefore I thincke it alsoe most requisite that you forth with cause publique prayers through out your whole Dioces to be vsed in everie severall parish Church thrice in the weeke at the least accordinge to such order as was taken at the last intended invasion vntill you shall receave further direction from me. /

FORM OF PRAYER

[The general confession and the absolution from the BCP; the Lord's prayer; 'A praier for the forgiuenesse of sinnes' and 'A prayer for deliuerance from our enemies' (beginning 'Heare our prayer, O Lorde'): both as 1572–E]

Psalmes.
[Ps. 44:1–9, and then]
Be not thou farre off, O Lord: put vs not to confusion, goe foorth with our Armies.
Make our enemies to turne their backes vpon vs.
Suffer vs not to be rebuked of our Neighbours: to be laughed to scorne, and had in derision of them, that are round about vs.

Make vs not a by worde among the heathen: vp, Lorde, and sleepe not, awake and be not absent from vs.
Hide not thy face from vs: forget not our trouble.
Arise and helpe vs: and deliuer vs for thy mercies sake. (Ps. 44)

Another Psalme
['O harken to the voyce of our prayer, our King and our God', as 1572–E]

[Ps. 115]

A prayer
  O Lorde God of Hostes most mightie and mercifull Father, who in thy vnspeak-able wisedome and mercie hast gathered vnto thy selfe a Church truely professing thine holy Name and Gospel: We doe here most humbly acknowledge, that through our manifolde sinnes and offences against thy heauenly Maiestie, committed by vnthankfull receiuing of thy holy worde, and by wicked ledde liues, wee haue made our selues vnworthy of the least of these and other thy singular blessings hitherto very aboundantly powred vpon vs. Neuerthelesse (O heauenly father) with an assured confidence relying vpon thy promises, we make bold to drawe neere vnto the throne of they grace, humbly crauing forgiuenesse of our sinnes, and the continuance of thy blessinges vpon vs, and vpon all Princes, Countries, and Common wealthes, that haue receyued and doe embrace thine holy Gospell. Therefore being cast downe in soule, we doe bewaile our iniquities, setting the bitter death and precious bloodshed of thy deare sonne Christ Jesus betwixt vs and thy iust wrath conceyued against vs. Turne (O Lord) thy wrathfull indignation from vs: And forasmuch as it is not for these our sinnes, that our enemyes in their purpose haue thus banded themselues against vs, but for the sincere profession of thy word and Gospell: with thy mighty arme confound and bring to nought the deuises, power, and strength of all such, as set themselues against the same. Thou knowest (O Lord) how the heathen and such as hold of superstitious vanities, doe euery where rush into thine inheritance, to make thy chosen Jerusalem, euen thy Church a desolate heape of stones, to lay wast thy holy Sanctuarie: yea, euen to giue vp the flesh of thy deare children to the birds of the aire, and the slaine carkeises of thy saints to the beastes of the field. Wherefore (most mightie God of Hostes) which art the Lorde of glorie and power, that canst arme the most base and meanest of thy creatures to the ouerthrowe of all the mightie of the world, that be enemies to vs for thy truthes sake: Auance thy selfe like a mighty Giant with a swift and terrible iudgement against them: frustrate the counsels of all their *Achitophels*: breake them downe with an iron rodde like an earthen vessel: send an host of Angels to scatter their armies both by sea and land: confound them as thou didst the host of the *Assyrians*: Let thine owne sword fight for vs and deuoure vp them: be thou as fire vnto them, and let them bee as stubble before thee. Finally, let them bee as *Oreb* and *Zeb*: yea like vnto *Zebah* and *Salmanah*, and be made as dung on the face of the earth. Send (good Lord) vpon them the spirit of feare and trembling, that they may flee before the host of thine Israel as chaffe before the winde, to the ende they may bee discomfited and ouerthrowen by thy mightye hande. Neither giue thou vs vp (O Lord) to be a pray to their teeth, or a by word and reproche to such as hate the true profession of the Gospel: For we doe onely rest assured vnder the shadowe of thy wings. Protect vs in mercy as the apple of thine eye, and mercifully powre vpon vs the spirit of

wisedome, foresight, counsell, strength and courage: that in full assurance of thine heauenly helpe fighting for vs, tenne of vs may chase an hundred, and an hundred of vs put to flight a thousand of them. Be thou (O Lord) our continuall refuge and strong rocke of defence: Let thine holy Angels pitch their Tents round about vs, that wee may knowe thine holy hand both stretched out for our help, and strongly set against them: teach our handes to warre, and our fingers to fight: prosper that wee shall take in hand, O prosper thou our handy worke, and make vs alwaies to reioice in thy saluation and deliuerance: that so all such, as loue not the truth of thy Gospell, hearing thereof, may bee discomforted: and that thy feare may fall vpon them, to the perpetuall glorye of thy holy name: That wee escaping the rage and furie of those, which seeke after our liues, may in thine holy Church here militant, and after in the Church triumphant in heauen, eternally sing praises to thee our heauenly father the onely giuer of all victorie. Graunt these thinges for thy sonne Christ Jesus sake: to whom with thee and the holy Ghost, three persons and one eternall, immortal, inuisible, and onely wise God be all honour, praise, glorie, and dominion now and for euer. Amen.

Another prayer

Most mightie God, and mercifull Father, Forasmuch as thou hast promised to mainteine and defend the cause of thy Church, so deerely purchased & redeemed, euen with the precious bloode of thy deerely beloued Sonne: wee, thy humble seruantes, confessing our owne vnworthinesse through the infinite nomber of our wilfull transgressions, doe at this time prostrate our selues here before thy diuine Maiestie, and wholy relying vpon thy promises, most heartily beseech thee through the merites of Jesus Christ our Sauiour, to protect vs this day and euer hereafter, from the furie of our enemies, to pardon our sinnes past, and to haue mercie vpon vs. Thou knowest, O Lord, how they that fight against vs, haue entred into a league, and combined themselues, neuer to desist, vntill they haue destroyed all such as professe thy Gospell, and layed the glory of *Sion* in the dust. And though our offences do most iustly deserue, that wee shoulde bee deliuered to the edges of their swordes: Yet seeing that they do hate vs onely for thy cause, and that wee are noted in the world for such as outwardly professe thy name, and the true doctrine of the Gospell of thy sonne our Sauiour Christ: saue vs in thy mercy (O heauenly Father) from the crueltie of these conspirators: cast a feare and trembling into their heartes, take our cause into thine owne handes, goe before our hoast, fight our battels, and subdue them: So shall they haue no cause to insulte ouer thy true Church, and ouer vs thy seruaunts, nor to say with the olde enemies, *Where is nowe their God?* And wee thy penitent and most humble suppliants will from henceforth declare thy Name with cheerefull heart vnto our brethren: In the midst of the Congregation we will euer praise thee, and magnifie thy saluation, worlde without ende.

Graunt this (O mercifull Father) not for our owne sakes, but for thy deare Sonnes sake, our Lord and Sauiour Jesus Christ: to whome with thee and the holie Ghost, three persons and one God, be all honour, glory, power, and dominion nowe and for euer. Amen.

[The BCP prayer for the Queen 'O Lord our heavenly Father, high and mighty'; the BCP collect in time of war; the prayers 'For true repentance and mercie' *and* 'An other for the same': *both as 1572–E]*

An other prayer to bee deliuered from our enemies.

O Lorde God of hostes, most louing & mercifull father, we thy humble seruauntes prostrate our selues before thy diuine Maiestie: most heartily beseeching thee, to grant vnto vs true repentance for our sinnes past, namely for our vnthankfulnesse, contempt of thy word, lacke of compassion towards the afflicted, enuie, malice, strife and contention among our selues, and for all other our iniquities. Lord deale not with vs as we haue deserued, but of thy great goodnesse and mercy, doe away our offences, and giue vs grace to confesse and acknowledge, O Lorde, with all humble and hearty thankes, the wonderfull and great benefites which thou hast bestowed vpon this thy Church and people of England, in giuing vnto vs without all desert of our part, not onely peace and quietnesse, but also in preseruing our most gracious Queene thine handmaide, so miraculously from so many conspiracies, perils and dangers, and in graunting her good successe against the attemptes of her aduersaries: for the which so woonderfull and great benefites, wee humbly beseech thee to stirre vp our dull mindes to such thankfulnesse and acknowledging of thy mercies as becommeth vs, and as may bee acceptable vnto thee. Wee doe instantly beseech thee of thy gracious goodnesse to bee mercifull to thy Church militant here vpon earth, many wayes vexed and tormented by the malice of Satan & his members, and at this time as it were compassed about with strong and subtill aduersaries. And especially O Lord, let thine enemies know, and make them confesse that thou hast receiued England (which they most of all for thy Gospel sake do maligne) into thine own protection. Set we pray thee (O Lorde) a wall about it, & euermore mightily defend it. Let it bee a comfort to the afflicted, a helpe to the oppressed, a defence to thy Church and people persecuted abroad. And forasmuch as thy cause is now in hand, we beseech thee to direct and go before our Armies both by sea and land, blesse and prosper them, and grant vnto them O Lorde, so good and honorable successe & victories, as thou didst to Abraham and his company against the foure mightie kinges, to Josua against the fiue kinges and against Amalech, to Dauid against the strong and mightie armed giant Goliah, and as thou vsest to doe to thy children when they please thee. Wee acknowledge all power, strength and victorie to come from thee: some put their trust in charets, and some in horses, but wee wil remember thy name, O Lord our God. Thou bringest the counsell of the heathen to nought, and makest the deuises of the people to bee of none effect. There is no king that can be saued by the multitude of an host, neither is any mightie man deliuered by much strength. A horse is but a vaine thing to saue a man, therefore wee pray vnto thee, O Lord, thou art our helpe and our shield, O Lord giue good and prosperous successe to all those that fight thy battell against the enemies of thy Gospell, shewe some token continually for our good, that they which hate vs may see it and be confounded: And that we thy little and despised flocke may say with good King Dauid, Blessed are the people whose God is the Lorde Jehouah, and blessed are the folke that hee hath chosen to be his inheritance. These and all other graces necessary for vs, graunt O heauenly father, for Jesus Christes sake our onely mediatour and redeemer.

['An other prayer for the same' beginning 'O Lord our God & heavenly Father, look down we beseech thee' (as 1572–E); 'A prayer' beginning 'Be merciful (O Father of all mercies)' (as 1588–E1); 'A thankesgiuing and prayer for the preseruation of the Queene and the Realme' *(as 1572–E)]*

A prayer.

O almightie God and heauenly Father, who for the great iniquitie which aboundeth in these latter dayes, art iustly prouoked to send foorth the heauie executioners of thy fearce wrath, the very fore-runners of the comming of thy sonne, these cruel, vnchristian, & vnnatural warres, which haue set the whole world out of course: Nation rising against nation, people against people, and the same people against it selfe: We giue thee (as we are bound) most heartie thankes, for that thou hast spared vs thine vnworthie seruantes so long, and not suffred vs as yet to feele the greeuousnesse of this vniuersal plague in that measure, that our neighbours haue done: but hast hitherto deliuered vs and blessed vs vnder the gouernement of our true, naturall, and gratious Queene with a long and wonderfull peace. Our sinnes (we confesse) are no lesse, if not greater then our neighbours: our vnthankfulnesse much more: so that we must needes acknowledge thine vndeserued mercy to be the greater in affording vs this vnspeakeable benefite. Neuerthelesse, because their enemies and ours are al one, and the chiefe cause of their malice the same: Wee together with them (as true members of the same Communion) most entierly beseech thy diuine Maiestie to forgiue our former transgressions and vnthankfulnes, and to be merciful vnto vs and them in asswaging the malice of our common enemies, confounding their blind & cruell deuises, and in deliuering of vs from their cruel and bloody designements. And that the rather, because they are confederate with Antichrist, and sworne against the trueth: and in the pride of their hart & confidence of their owne strength they seeke the suppression of thy Gospell, and the ouerthrow of all such, as doe professe it. Conuert them (O Lord) if it be thy wil: make them to see the madnesse and wickednes of their enterprise, and that they doe but kicke against the pricke: to the end they may giue ouer the pursuit of their badde cause, absteyne from shedding Christian blood, and in time kisse thy sonne in humilitie, whom in pride they haue hitherto so vnaduisedly impugned. Otherwise, if they goe on in their malicious wickednesse, and continue in their bloudie purposes: Wee beseech thee to weaken their hands, to astonish their harts, to infatuate their counsels, and to confound them: that they neuer be able to deuise or execute any thing preiudiciall to the cause of thy Gospel, or the weale of thy children. Establish (O Lord) in their harts and kingdomes all such Princes and Gouernours, as professe and fauour thy Gospel: and especially preserue in long life and prosperitie thy seruant our gratious Queene Elizabeth: that by her and them as thy ministers, thy truth may haue the vpper hand, thy Gospel florish, and all we with one voyce say: *Happie are the people, that bee in such a case: yea blessed are the people, vvhich haue the Lord for their God.* Graunt this (O heauenly Father) for thy sonne our Sauiour Jesus Christ his sake, Amen.

Another prayer.

O Most mightie Lord God, the Lorde of Hostes, the gouernour of all creatures, the only giuer of all victories, who alone art able to strengthen the weake against the mightie, and to vanquish infinite multitudes of thine enemies with the countenance of a few of thy seruants, calling vpon thy Name, and trusting in thee: Defend, O Lorde, thy Seruant and our Gouernour vnder thee, our Queene Elizabeth, and all thy people committed to her charge. And especially at this time, O Lord, haue regarde to those her Subiectes, which be sent to withstand the crueltie of those, which be common enemies aswel to the truth of thy eternall woorde, as to this Crowne and Realme of England, which thou hast of thy diuine prouidence assigned in these our dayes, to the gouernment of thy seruant, our soueraigne and gratious Queene. O most mercifull Father (if it be thy holy will) make soft and tender the stony harts of al those, that exalt themselues against thy truth, and seeke to oppresse this Crowne and Realme of England, and conuert them to the knowledge of thy sonne, the onely Sauiour of the world, Jesus Christ, that wee and they may ioyntly glorifie thy mercies. Lighten we beseech thee their ignorant harts to embrace the truth of thy word: Or els so abate their crueltie, (O most mightie Lord) that this our Christian Region with others that confesse thy holy Gospel, may obteine by thy ayd & strength, suretie from our enemies, without sheading of christian and innocent bloud: Whereby al they, which be oppressed with their tyrannie, may be releeued, and all which be in feare of their crueltie, may be comforted. And finally, that al christian Realmes, and especially this Realme of England, may by thy defence and protection enioy perfect peace, quietnesse, and securitie: And that wee, for these thy mercies, ioyntly all together, with one consonant heart and voyce, may thankfully render to thee all laude and praise, and in one godly concorde and vnitie amongst our selues, may continually magnifie thy glorious name, who with thy sonne our Sauiour Jesus Christ, and the holy ghost, art one eternall, almightie and most mercifull God. To whom be all laude and prayse, world without end. Amen.

1590–E2   Prayers for the success of Henry IV of France

[April–August?] 1590 (England and Wales)

Elizabeth continued to support the Huguenots during the 1590s (see 1562–E1 and 1586–E1), providing military and financial assistance to Henry of Navarre to secure his claim to the French crown after the assassination of Henry III (1–2 August 1589) in opposition to Charles, cardinal of Bourbon, the Catholic League's candidate. Henry was not only the rightful heir, but was protestant and his accession augured the conversion of France to the 'true faith'. The defeat of the Catholic League would also deny Philip II an ally against the Netherlands and England. No orders exist to date this occasion precisely, though the involvement of English troops in the siege of Paris might suggest April to August 1590. The form comprised three prayers that were probably inserted into the normal BCP service at the end of the litany. The first two prayers were very largely drawn from prayers in the form for 1590–E1; the third was largely derived from that for 1562–E1. Though the prayers mentioned Henry explicitly and the Catholic League obliquely, their tone was more muted than earlier prayers (e.g. 1585–E2, 1586–E1) and focused on petitioning for God's mercy and protection rather than on catholic conspiracy. This may have been because, although catholic conspiracy seemed a reality, the Elizabethan regime was becoming more conservative and authoritarian and did not want to give ideological ammunition to its puritan subjects. In addition to the two editions of the 'official' form, two other related single sheet folios were printed: the final prayer of the form, 'O Most mightie Lord God, the Lorde of hostes' and, in August, *A prayer vsed in the queens maiesties house and chappell.*

Order: none found.
Form of prayer: *Certaine praiers to be vsed at this present time for the good successe of the French king, against the enemies of Gods true religion and his state* ([8] pp.; STC 16523)* [also in Clay, pp. 647–51].

Form of prayer (other edition): STC 16523.3.

Additional sources: Clay, p. 471; *A prayer to be vsed in euery parish church at morning and euening prayer* ([1590?]; STC 16523.5); *A prayer vsed in the queens maiesties house and chappell* ([1590]; STC 16523.7).

FORM OF PRAYER

A prayer

   O Lord God of hostes, most mightie and merciful Father, who in thy vnspeake-able wisedom and mercie, hast gathered vnto thy selfe a Church truly professing thy holy name and Gospell: We doe here most humbly acknowledge that through our manifold sinnes and offences against thy heauenly maiestie, committed by vnthankfull receiuing of thy holy word, & by wicked led liues, we haue made our selues vnwoorthie of the least of these and other thy singular blessings hitherto very aboundantly powred vpon vs. Neuerthelesse (O heauenly Father) with an assured confidence, relying vpon thy promises, we make bold to draw neere vnto the throne of thy grace, humblie crauing forgiuenes of our sinnes, & the continuance of thy blessings vpon vs, and vpon all princes, countries and common wealths that haue receiued & do embrace thine holy Gospel, & that at this time fight thy battels against the aduersaries of thy Gospell, and those that vphold the kingdome of Antichrist. Therefore being cast downe in soule, we doe bewaile our iniquities, setting the bitter death and precious blood shed of thy deare sonne Christ Jesus, betwixt vs & thy iust wrath conceiued against vs & them. Turne (O Lord) thy wrathfull indignation from vs and them: And forasmuch as it is not for our sinnes that our enemies in their purpose haue thus banded themselues against vs, but for the sincere profession of thy word and Gospel: With thy mightie arme confound and bring to nought the deuises, power and strength of all such as set themselues against the same. Thou knowest (O Lord) how the heathen and such as hold of superstitious vanities, euen at this present in *France*, and elsewhere doe rushe into thine inheritance to make thy chosen Jerusalem, euen thy Church, a desolate heape of stones, to lay waste thy holy sanctuarie, yea euen to giue vp the flesh of thy deare children to the birdes of the aire, and the slaine carcasses of thy Saints to the beasts of the field. Wherefore (most mightie God of hostes) which art the Lord of glorie and power, that canst arme the most base & meanest of thy creatures to the ouerthrow of all the mightie of the world that bee enemies for thy truethes sake: aduance thy selfe like a mightie Giant with a swift and terrible iudgement against them, frustrate the counsels of all their Achitophels, breake them down with an iron rod like an earthen vessell, send an hoste of Angels to scatter their armies, confound them as thou diddest the host of the Assyrians, let thine owne sword fight for thy seruants, & deuoure vp their enemies: be thou as fire vnto them, and let them be as a stubble before thee. Finally, let them be as *Oreb* and *Zeb*, yea like vnto *Zebah* and *Salmanah*, and be made as dung on the face of the earth. Send (good Lord) vpon them the spirite of feare and trembling, that they may flee before the hoste of thine *Israel*, as chaffe before the wind, to the ende they may bee discomfited and ouerthrowen by thy mightie hand, neither giue thy seruants (O Lord) to be a praie vnto their teeth, or a by word and reproch to such as hate the true profession of thy Gospell: For we doe onely rest assured vnder the shadow of thy wings. Protect in mercy as the apple of thine eie, and mercifully powre vpon those armies that fight against ye enemies of the Gospell, the spirit of wisedom, foresight, counsel, strength and courage, that in full assurance of thine heauenly helpe fighting for them, ten of them may chase an hundred, & an hundred of them put to flight a thousand of their aduersaires. Be thou (O Lorde) their continuall refuge and strong rocke of defence, let thy holy Angels pitch their tents round about them, that they may know thy holy hand both stretched out for their helpe, and strongly set against their and our enemies. Teach their hands to warre, and their fingers to fight: prosper that which they take in hand, O prosper thou their handie worke, and make them alwaies to reioice in thy saluation and deliuerance, that so all such as loue not the trueth of thy Gospel, hearing thereof, may bee discomfited, and that thy feare may fall vpon thine enemies to the perpetuall glory of thy holy name, and that we escaping the rage and furie of those which seeke after our liues, and the ouerthrow of thy trueth, may in thy holy Church here militant, and after in the Church triumphant in heauen, eternally sing praises to thee our heauenly Father, the onely giuer of all victorie. Grant these things for thy Sonne Christ Jesus sake, to whom with thee and the holy Ghost, three persons and one eternall, immortall, inuincible, and onely wise God, bee all honour, prayse, glory and dominion, now and for euer. *Amen.*

A prayer

Most mightie God and mercifull Father, for so much as thou hast promised to maintaine and defend the cause of thy Church so deerely purchased and redeemed euen with the precious blood of thy deerely beloued Sonne: we thy humble seruants confessing our owne vnworthinesse, through the infinite number of our wilfull transgressions, doe at this time prostrate our selues here before thy diuine maiestie, and wholy relying vpon thy promises, most heartily beseech thee through the merites of Jesus Christ our Sauiour, to protect and strengthen thy Seruants our brethren in *France*, that are now readie to fight for the glory of thy name. Thou knowest (O Lord) how the aduersaries that come to fight against them, haue entred into a league and combined themselues together, neuer to desist vntill thy haue destroied all such as professe thy Gospell, and laid the glory of thy *Sion* and *Temple* in the dust. And although both our and their offences doe most iustly deserue, that both they and we should bee deliuered to the edge of the sword: yet seeing that these conspirators and rebellers doe hate thy seruants onely for the cause of thy trueth, and that they are noted in the world for such as outwardly professe thy name, & the true doctrine of the Gospell of thy Sonne our Sauiour Christ: Saue them in thy mercy (O heauenly Father) from the crueltie of their enemies, cast a feare and trembling into the hearts of their aduersaries, take the cause of thy Gospel into thine own hands: go before them, fight the battels of thy children, and subdue their enemies: so shal that proud generation haue no cause to insult ouer thy true Church, and ouer thy seruants, nor to say with thy old enemies, *Where is now their God?* And we thy penitent and most humble suppliants that doe here at this time make intercession both for our brethren and for our selues, will from henceforth declare thy name with cheerefull hearts in the midst of the congregation, we will euer praise thee and magnifie thy saluation, world without end. Graunt this (O mercifull Father) for thy deare sonnes sake our Lord and Sauiour Jesus Christ, to whom with thee and the holy Ghost, three persons and one God, bee all honour, glory, power and dominion, now and for euer. Amen.

Another.

O Most mightie Lord God *[as 1562–E1*: the Lorde of hoastes … Defende O Lorde,*]* thy seruant the *French King*, and especially at this time giue him power, to withstand the crueltie *[as 1562–E1*: of those which … as well to*]* to the trueth of thine eternall worde, as to his Crowne and Realme, which thou hast of thy diuine prouidence assigned vnto him in these our dayes. Most mercifull Father *[as 1562–E1:* (yf it be … and*]* seeke to oppresse the professours thereof. Conuert them to the knowledge *[as 1562–E1:* of thy sonne … abate theyr crueltie*]*/(O most mightie Lorde) that such Christian Regions as confesse the holy Gospell *[as 1562–E1:* maye obtayne … strength*]* surety from their enemies *[as 1562–E1:* without shedding … worlde without ende.*]* Amen.

1591–S   Fast day prompted by the alleged conspiracies of Bothwell and the North Berwick witches

Sunday 2 May 1591 (Edinburgh; and possibly elsewhere in Scotland)

In 1591, a witch-hunt centring on North Berwick, Haddingtonshire, became intertwined with court politics when the enigmatic Francis Stewart, earl of Bothwell, was accused of having consorted with witches to bring about the death of James VI during his return from Denmark the previous year (see 1589–S). Bothwell was warded (i.e. imprisoned) in Edinburgh Castle on 15 April, while James and the privy council investigated the allegations. This fast, which may have been limited to Edinburgh, is known only from the report of the English ambassador, Robert Bowes, to Lord Burghley, which implies that the king and council requested that the clergy appoint the observance.

Order: none found.
Source: Robert Bowes to Lord Burghley, 5 May 1591, SP52/47/46.
Description
Robert Bowes to Lord Burghley: 5 May 1591
… the kinge and Counsell have directed the Ministrie to ordeine a generall faste wth prayers for this discovery wch faste and excercise was solempnized wth greate devotion on sondaye laste the seconde herof.

1592–S   Fast days in response to catholic conspiracies, religious indifference, apostasy and sinfulness

Sunday 17 December and Sunday 24 December 1592 (Scotland)

This fast reflected the clergy's continuing fears of militant catholicism in Europe and frustration at prevalent sinfulness at home, expressed in formulaic terms similar to those used in earlier fast acts (see 1578–S, 1582–S, 1588–S1). The fast order also responded to a period of particular turbulence in Scottish politics. The catholic earl of Huntly had been involved in the murder of his rival, the earl of Moray, in February 1592, and was at feud with various other enemies in the north. Ministers worried about the Spanish contacts of such magnates as Huntly, and the influence of catholic nobles on the king. Although parliament had ratified presbyterian government in the so-called 'golden act' of June 1592, the Kirk's requests for the return of its pre-reformation landed property had not been satisfied. Moreover, the golden act had asserted the king's right to specify the time and place of general assemblies. After the dissolution of parliament, the privy council had issued an ordinance appointing a meeting of the general assembly, without indicating the time and place. The convention of ministers which met at Edinburgh in November was not a general assembly, but itself claimed the authority to summon a meeting of the assembly for January. The convention's appointment of a fast can be seen as part of its attempt to press the king to support the church and act against the catholic threat.

Order: by the convention of ministers beginning 15 Nov. 1592, described in Calderwood, V, 179–80 [Calderwood's source was Melvill, pp. 299–300].

DESCRIPTION OF ORDER

Order by the convention of ministers beginning 15 November 1592
… it is concluded, that there be a generall fast in all the kirks of this countrie, the 17th and 24th days of December nixt, that by true humiliatioun and unfained repentance, the fearefull judgements of God that hang over this land may be prevented.

THE CAUSES OF THE GENERALL FAST
1. The practises of the enemeis within and without the countrie intending to execute that bloodie decree of the Councell of Trent, against all that truelie professe the religioun of Christ, to the utter subversioun therof, and of the king's estate and persoun, whose standing and decay they acknowledge to be joynned with the standing and decay of religioun.
2. A miserable desolatioun of the greatest part of the countrie, perishing in ignorance through laike of pastors, and sufficient moyen to interteane the Word of God among them, with a carelessness of the magistrats to remeed these misereis.
3. A fearefull defectioun of a great number of all estats in this land to papistrie and atheisme, especiallie of the nobilitie, through the resorting and traffiquing of Jesuits, Seminarie preests, and other Papists, without executioun of anie law against them.
4. The generall disorder of the whole estate of the commoun wealth, overflowing with all kinde of impietie; as contempt of the Word, blasphemie of the name of God, contempt of the magistrat, treasoun, innocent bloodshed, adultereis, witchecrafts, and other abominable crymes.
These causes to be enlarged and eeked by the discretioun of everie brother, according as he sall have sure knowledge and sense of the premisses.

1593–S1   Fast day for James VI's success against catholic conspiracies

Sunday 13 February 1593 (Edinburgh; and possibly elsewhere in Scotland)

Although the earl of Huntly had withdrawn to his north-eastern estates in March 1592, his opponents continued to link him to catholic conspiracies, particularly when in December 1592 his signature was found among papers addressed to the king of Spain. This discovery encouraged James to pursue a more active policy against the earl. This fast for the king's success is known only from Robert Bowes's letter to Lord Burghley. It seems to have been appointed by the clergy in response to a royal request.

Order: none found.
Source: Robert Bowes to Burghley, 14 Feb. 1593, SP52/50, fo. 29r.

DESCRIPTION

Robert Bowes to Burghley: 14 February 1593

… the k[ing] hathe caused an inquest to be sommoned this daye to trye Fentrye & Ladylands to morrowe by assyse. and beinge found giltye (as it is verelye looked they shalbe) the k is presentlie resolued to command spedye & [illegible] execution. Yet I fynde that they have manye & great frinds willinge to deliver them from this shower. Wherin it appearethe that the k hathe earnestlie wrastled with all his Counsell to bringe them to this pointe, and it is fered that he shall hardlie gett his desyre. For the which he hath striven and labored mightelie in his owne person, sekinge bothe thadvyse & helpe of the ministers, and also that publick fast & prayer might be made for him & for his good successe in these Causes. which fast & prayers the people performed on Sondaye last with all humilitye.

1593–E   Services and weekly fast days during a plague epidemic

Wednesdays (fast days), Fridays, Sundays and holy days (services) [from July] 1593 (London, [England and Wales?])

The 1590s was a decade of economic crisis because of plague, bad weather, poor harvests and famine, exacerbated by war and high taxation. Elizabeth's realms had suffered localized outbreaks of plague since the first major epidemic in 1563. During 1593 the outbreaks were more general and more severe, especially in London and Staffordshire. Contemporary accounts put the death toll in the capital and its environs alone at 20,000. No orders are extant for this occasion. The only extant form of prayer is for the diocese of London, but because the outbreak of plague was so widespread it is likely that prayers were ordered throughout the kingdom. It is possible that editions were issued for different dioceses, as for 1565–E1. As its title indicates, the London form was based on that for the 1563–E, but in an abridged and shorter format. The homily printed in 1563 was omitted and the basic structure of the service for morning prayer was described in the 'Preface', specifying the psalms and lessons. The BCP collects in times of dearth and famine, of war and of plague were also added, as was increasingly common in special worship since the late 1580s. (In this edition the prose of the original form re-formatted to facilitate comparison with other forms.) The rest of the form consisted, again as the title indicated, of 'certaine prayers collected out' of the 1563 form to be said during and after the litany. The only part that was expanded was the 'order for the fast'. This was substantially revised, partly to achieve a more economical wording. Additions were made to the instructions for behaviour on fast days: 'instructing' children and 'reforming' families, were added to the appropriate activities; there was to be no 'common buying, and selling', as well as no bodily labour, and 'haunting' of taverns became another pleasure to be shunned. Time mis-spent on fast days was declared to be one of the sins for which God was punishing the nation. The main change was in a sixth clause – an admonition that only one sermon should be preached on fast days, lasting no more than an hour. Although this was explained in part as a means to reduce the risks of contagion, it was also explicitly a further instance of Whitgift's efforts to curtail the enthusiasm of godly puritans (see 1586–E1 and 1588–E10): excessive sermonizing was an 'abuse of fasting', making it the mark of 'action more than religion'.

Order: none found.
Form of prayer: *Certaine praiers collected out of a fourme of godly meditations, set foorth by her maiesties authoritie in the great mortalitie, in the fift yeere of her highnesse raigne, and most necessarie to be vsed at this time in the like present visitation of Gods heauie hand for our manifold sinnes, and commended vnto the ministers and people of London, by the reuerend father in God, Iohn bishop of London, &c. Iuly. 1593* ([16] pp.; STC 16524)*.
Additional source: Clay, p. 471.

FORM OF PRAYER

PREFACE
[As 1563–E: We be taught … with trouble of warres*]* It hath bene thought meete to excite and stirre up all godly people within this Realme *[as 1563–E:* to pray earnestly … shall then distinctly and plainely*]* reade the generall Confession appoynted in the booke of Seruice, and the Absolution following …

MORNING PRAYER

[Ps. 6, 39, 51, 90, 91, 94, 130]
[First lesson: 2 Sam. 24 or 2 Kgs. 24]
[Second lesson: Matt. 6:24]

LITANY

[After the litany, the BCP collects in time of dearth and famine, in time of war, and in time of common plague and sickness, then the psalm (as 1563–E); then one of the three following prayers in daily rotation]
    O Almightie, most iust and mercifull God *[as 1563–E]*
    O Eternall and euerliuing God *[as 1563–E:* most mercifull father … nowe partly upon us by*]* plaging vs so (with most dreadful & deadly sicknes) whereby great multitudes of vs *[as 1563–E:* are dayly afflicted … Amen*]*
    It had bene the best for vs *[as 1563–E]*

THE ORDER FOR THE GENERAL FAST
The godly vse of Fasting, in time of common calamitie, as warre, famine, pestilence, and also when any weighty matter was in hand, for the Church and common wealth, is euident in holy Scriptures. Wherefore it is necessarie in so contagious time of sickeness, and troublous state of the Realme, (our sinnes procuring iustly the wrath of God) that folowing the godly examples of king Iosaphat, and the King of Nineue, with others, fasting with prayer be commended to the people by their preachers, exhorting their audience chiefely to these points.
    1. That this fasting be euery weeke vpon the Wednesday.
    2. All persons betweene the age of 16. and 60. yeares, (sicke folkes, and haruest labourers, or the like excepted) shall on that day eate but one competent and moderate meale: obseruing sobrietie of diet, without superfluitie of riotous fare, respecting necessitie, and not voluptuousnes.

3. The quantitie being but sufficient, and without delicacie, it is indifferent to eate flesh or fish. Let no publike order be contemned herein, nor dissimulation with God committed, pretending like hypocrites godlie abstinence, but doing nothing lesse.

4. The wealthier sort, are to be mooued to giue of that they spare, and are besides able inough to giue, to releeue the poore, considering the misery and distresse, of a number of poore miserable soules, either staruing for lacke of foode, or being sicke with eating vnseasonable meats.

5. This day the people are to bee warned, to forebeare bodily working, and common buying, and selling, and to be exercised in holy prayer, deuout studie, reading the Scriptures, instructing their children, reforming all their familie: especially to take heede they spend it not in playes, pastimes, idlenes, haunting Tauernes, lasciuious wantonnes, surfeiting, and drunkennesse, for which sinnes (the proper sinnes of this nation) the heauy displeasure, and wrath of God is come vpon vs.

6. Admonition is heere lastly to be giuen, that on the fasting day they haue but one Sermon at Morning Prayer, and the same not aboue an houre long, to auoyde the inconuenience that may growe by abuse of fasting: as some make it a faction more then religion, and other with ouermuch wearines and tediousnesse, keepe the people a whole day together, which in this time of contagion, is more dangerous in so thicke and close assemblies of the multitudes. God giue vs grace to repent, and in his mercy turne away his punishments from vs. *Amen.*

1593–S2   Fast day during threats to the reformed church and to James VI

Sunday 21 October 1593 (Scotland)

Relations between the clergy and the crown were tense in autumn 1593, in large part because of continuing disagreements about the threat posed by catholic nobles. In September, the synod of Fife excommunicated the earls of Angus, Huntly and Erroll, and three other leading catholics. To give additional authority to this irregular sentence, which was opposed by the king, the synod called for a convention of ministers, barons and burgesses to meet at Edinburgh. The synod envisaged that the announcement of the excommunication should be accompanied by fasting, and the convention, which met on 17 October, appointed a fast day. Although commissioners from various parts of Scotland attended the convention, it was not an official assembly, and it cannot be established how widely its request for a fast was obeyed.

Order: by the convention of ministers, barons and burgesses, 17 Oct. 1593 [described in an account of the convention enclosed with Robert Bowes to Burghley, 18 Oct. 1593, SP52/51/46].
Additional sources: Calderwood, V, 261–8, 270–3; Bowes to Burghley, 22 Oct. 1593, SP52/51/48, fos. 165r–v.

DESCRIPTION

Order by the convention of ministers, barons and burgesses: 17 October 1593
Ordaines ane publick fast to be in all the kirks of this convention the next sabbothe. The causs the presente danger of religion, and the hazarde of the k ma^te person is presently into.

1594–S1   Thanksgiving service for the birth of Prince Henry

Tuesday 19 February 1594 (Edinburgh; and possibly elsewhere in Scotland)

Prince Henry, James VI's first child, was born at Stirling on 19 February 1594. On the king's request, a thanksgiving service was held at Edinburgh; the town treasurer's accounts show that bonfires were ordered in Leith. It is unclear whether the thanksgiving was observed elsewhere in Scotland. According to Calderwood, the Edinburgh minister Walter Balcanquhall used the occasion to preach against flattering courtiers who allegedly encouraged the king's hostility to the presbyterian clergy.

Order: by Edinburgh town council, 19 Feb. 1594, *Edin. recs., 1589 to 1603*, p. 109.
Sources: *Edin. recs., 1589 to 1603*, p. 109; Calderwood, V, 293–4; David Moysie, *Memoirs of the affairs of Scotland* (Bannatyne Club, Edinburgh, 1830), p. 113.

ORDER

Order by Edinburgh town council: 19 February 1594
Understanding that the Queynis Matie is delyverit this day in the morning in the castell of Stirling of ane young prince, prayset be God, and that the Kings Matie hes desyret the toun to be advertist thairof and to schaw all signes of joy, thairfore … fynds it expedient that the pepill be callet to the Kirk to gif God publick thanks, that the haill bellis of the stepill be rung at aynes and baynefyres sett furth throw the haill toun and publict proclamatioun to be maid thairof.

1594–E   Thanksgiving services for the failure of plots against Elizabeth I and her realm

[March] 1594 (England and Wales)

There were two alleged plots against Elizabeth in 1594: one by her Portuguese physician, Dr Roderigo Lopez, and another by Patrick O'Cullen. Lopez was tried in February and executed in June; O'Cullen was tried and hanged in March. Little is known about O'Cullen's plot, while the veracity of allegations against Lopez remains unclear. No order is extant, but the form must have been available by mid-March because a copy in the Huntington Library (STC 16525) has this handwritten note on the fly leaf: 'rec[eived] this book the 24 of Marche 1593' [i.e. 1594]. As had become common, the form comprised a selection of psalms and prayers which would have been inserted into the BCP service, probably at the end of the litany (the form contained no instructions). There was also an 'Admonition to the Reader', which criticized the conspirators (without naming them or giving details of the plots) and emphasized that England had more reason than other nations to thank God for his protection. It may have been designed to provide ministers with information on which to base their sermons, though sermons were not specifically ordered. At some point, either coterminously with the first edition or at a later date (possibly in June), the form was reset and the admonition extended to place the Lopez and O'Cullen plots in the context of other catholic conspirators from 1562 including John Felton, the duke of Norfolk, Francis Throckmorton and Anthony Babington. Launcelot Andrewes's Lent court sermon on 6 March ended with a thanksgiving for Elizabeth's reign which was unusual for such sermons; it is possible that he was responding to news of the plots.

Order: none found.

Form of prayer: *An order for prayer and thankes-giuing (necessary to be vsed in these dangerous times) for the safetie and preseruation of her majesty and this realme. Set forth by authoritie* ([32] pp.; STC 16525)* [also in Clay, pp. 654–64]. The extended 'admonition' included here comes from *An order for prayer and thankes-giuing (necessary to be vsed in these dangerous times)* ([24] pp.; STC 16525.7)*, sigs. A2r–A3v.

Form of prayer (other editions): STC 16525.3, 16525.7.

Additional sources: Aylmer to Hutchinson, 7 Mar. 1594, HALS, ASA 5/3/125, p. 581; Lancelot Andrewes, *XCVI sermons* (1629; STC 606), pp. 299–308 [also in Peter E. McCullough, *Lancelot Andrewes: selected sermons and lectures* (Oxford, 2005), pp. 108–21); Clay, p. 472. For the dating of Andrewes's sermon see the entry for 6 Mar. 1594 in the list of sermons appended to Peter E. McCullough, *Sermons at court: politics and religion in Elizabethan and Jacobean preaching* (Cambridge, 1998)].

FORM OF PRAYER

AN ADMONITION TO THE READER

There haue bene sundry, but *heathen men*, (as *Plato* and others) being no better instructed then the lame reache of reason coulde guide them, nor any clearer enlightened, then by the dimmed glimpse of nature, who neuertheles arriued thus farre, as to know and acknowledge that God, who is aboue all, extendeth his carefull prouidence ouer all, and especially in preseruation of kingdomes, and of other politique societies, and of their Gouernours and Rulers. *For that which may bee knowen of God, is manifest* (saieth Saint Paul)[237] *among them: for GOD hath opened it vnto them. For his inuisible thinges beeing vnderstoode by his woorkes through the creation of the worlde, are seene: that is, both his externall power and Godhead, so that they are without excuse.* Then howe much more must all *Christians*, to whome the *Day-starre* hath in greater brightnesse and measure appeared, and the treasures of *God* the *Father* in his sonne *Christ Iesu* bene opened, acknowledge this his prouidence, and reuerently adore and magnifie that good *God*, which to the heape of all other his mercies towardes them, addeth this blessing and protection of *Magistracie* and gouernment, whereby men liue peaceably with all honesty in this life?

But if euer any nation, yea if all the nations in the worlde besides, haue cause with thankefulnesse to acknowledge this kinde of benefite, surely, wee the people of *England* haue most iust and abundant occasion of all others, to performe this duetie vnto God. First, for placing ouer vs our most gratious dread Soueraigne Ladie *Queene Elizabeth*, by whose happie gouernement wee haue so long breathed from the burden of intolerable miseries of *scarcity*, *bloodshed*, and spirituall *bondage*, vnder which afore wee laye grouelong, and pitifully groned. Then, for preseruing these her Realmes and dominions so long in the true profession of the Gospel, and in peace and tranquillitie, notwithstanding the sundrie priuie conspiracies and open hostilities practised both inwarde and outwarde for the interruption of our quiet repose and holy profession. Thirdly, for protecting so long and so often her sacred royall person from the cruell and bloodie handes of such and so many seuerall

---

237   In margin: 'Rom.1.ver.19, 20.'

detestable and treacherous Conspirators. And likewise for the Lordes prouident and watchfull eye ouer her and vs, and for the woonderfull happie discoueries of so manifolde cruell designements so closely plotted against her innocent life, and so dangerously against her *Highneβe* Realmes and dominions. Which mischieuous deuises as they haue all flowed from none other fountaine, then from that citie of seuen hilles, the *See* of *Rome*, and seate of the *Beast*,[238] not in regarde of any desert of ours, but because wee haue abandoned the cuppe of spirituall abhominations, wherewith these haue long intoxicated the Kings of the earth: So haue they beene continually proiected, caried forwarde, and managed by idolatrous *Priestes* and *Iesuites* his creatures, the very loathsome *Locusts* that crawle out of the bottomlesse pitte. Howebeit they haue beene and are mightily seconded by certaine, who doe nothing els but serue themselues of that idolatrous *Romish religion*, as of a Maske and stalking horse, therewith to couer the vnsatiable ambition wherewith they are possessed of vsurping the *kingdoms* of other Princes.

Which their most dangerous and desperate plots and enterprises, God of his great mercie hath hitherto most happily discouered to his infinite glorie, and our vnspeakeable comfort. So that it may aptly bee verifed, that her Maiesties life hath all this while bene susteined *in manu altissimi*, and that vnder the shadowe of his wings shee hath not miscaried. Al which whosoeuer hee bee that will attentiuely weigh and consider, and can not see the very finger of God mightily working herein by his prouidence and mercy, no doubt, hee is insensible blockish: who seeth and will not acknowledge it, is wilfully malicious: but who acknowledgeth and also tasteth of the sweete blessings that are enioyed thereby, and is not most heartily thankefull to God therefore, is extremely impious, and doth but adde this vngratefulnes vnto the masse of all his other wickednes, euen vnto his owne greater damnation. Let euery of vs therfore who haue good will to the trueth of the Gospel, turne from our wicked waies, & from the euil that is betwixt our hands, and incessauntly with heart and voyce yeelde most humble and hearty thankes to God our deliuerer. But let it not be for a day or two onely, whiles the intended wound doeth (as it were) present it selfe fresh and greene before the eyes of our mindes; but continually, euen so long as wee may iustly imagine the same deuill in his impes still to rage and to bee prest to deuoure vs; so long as *our habitation is amongst the Tents of Mesech*, and our *soules amongst Lions, who hunt after our liues*, and doe greedily seeke to *giue our Dearling to the dogge, and to lay our honour in the dust*: to the intent, that (if it be so Gods good will) our ioy may long and long bee redoubled and trebled vnto vs vnder the happy gouernment of so gracious a *Soueraigne*. Which our bounden duetie that it may the more frequently and fruitfully be performed of vs; it hath bin thought meete to publish this forme of Praier for the continuance of Gods mercies towardes vs, and of thankesgiuing for his vnspeakable goodnesse in detecting so many conspiracies, and auerting so great mischiefes intended against vs. Which duetie of praying and thankesgiuing there is no doubt, but euery true hearted *English* man and faithfull *Subiect* will both priuatly and publikely from the bottome of his heart performe.

[STC 16525.7 has the same text until the end of para. 2 above, which it alters and adds to as follows] possessed of vsurping other mens *kingdoms*. For if we will first particularly cast our eyes vpon the variable conspiracies that haue bin entred into

---

[238]   In margin: 'Apocal.13.&17.'

but against her Highnes realmes: shal we not find yᵉ treason of the two *Pooles*, of *Felton*, & of the late Duke of *Northfolk*, of *Throgmorton*, of *Englefield*, of *Paget*, of *Shelley*, & *Stanley*, & *Yorke*, & of all the seminaries *Priests* and *Iesuites*, to haue bene tickled vp by Romish busses & practises, and to haue bin caried forward by their own grosse dotage vpon that absurd religion?

As for those other attempts against her dominions, which haue not stayed themselues in the bare termes of conspiracie onely, but haue also broken further into open rebellion & hostilitie: they likewise haue no lesse bin blown vp by that brood of *Maßing Priests* being vnnaturall subiects (for the most part) of these *kingdomes*. For was not *Moreton* a Priest sent from the *Popes* own side to stirre vp the two Earles & others vnto the Northren rebellion? Did not *Saunders* second his bookish treasons euen with banner displayed, and by commotion in *Ireland*? And doeth not that *carnall arch-traitour Allen* proclaime to the world vnto his owne euerlasting reproche, that hee and others excited the *King* of *Spaines* inuincible *Nauie* (vainly so surnamed) by inuasion to haue conquered his own natiue countrey, and to haue swallowed vs all vp? Yea, and in all those their latter hidden, hellish and damnable designes against her Maiesties owne person and life, such *Priestes* haue also beene the principall stirrers and agents vnder their vnholy father *Somerfield* and *Arden*, were not they drawn into that action by *Hall* the Priest? *Parry* by Cardinall *Como*, & by certaine English fugitiue Priests at *Millaine* and *Paris*, and also by *Allens* trayterous writings? *Babington* and all the other bloodie conspirators his complices by *Ballard* the Priest? So *Lopez* his late purposed empoisoniug [*sic*] is said to haue bin first plotted and set forward in *Spaine* by *Parsons* the Iesuit Frier. And *Patrick o Cullen, Laton Kale, Poule Wheele*, & sundry others very lately were animated by *Holt, Hart, Sherwood* & other priests the detestable instruments of the Bish. of *Rome*, and of the king of *Spaines* most dishonorable intended executions.

These & some other complots we see how desperatly they haue bin attempted, yet (thanked be God) are not atchieued: how perillously plotted, but are not perfected: how secretly deuised, yet most happily hitherto discouered to Gods infinit glory, & our vnspeakeable comfort. So that it may aptly be verified *[and as above, para. 3, l. 3].*

PRAYERS
[Ps. 20, 21, 27, 31, 33, 91]

Prayers for the preseruation of the Queenes Maiestie.

Almightie and euerlasting God, Creator and Gouernour of all the world, by whom *Kings* doe beare rule, and vnder whose prouidence they are woonderfully & mightily oftentimes protected from manie fearefull dangers, by which the malice of *Satan* & his wicked ympes doe seeke to intrappe them: We giue vnto thy heauenly maiestie most humble and heartie thanks, for that it hath pleased thee of thine infinite mercie and goodnesse in *Christ Iesu* so wonderfully to vpholde, deliuer and preserue thine *Hand-maid* our most dread & Soueraigne Queene *Elizabeth* so many and sundrie times from the cruell and bloody treacheries of desperate men, who addresse themselues to all wickednes, and at this time especially, wherein her innocent life was shotte at by diuers wicked designements of blood-thirstie wretches and traytors. And we doe most humbly and from the bottome of our hearts pray and beseech thee in *Christ Iesu*, to continue this thine vnspeakable goodnesse towardes her and this realme, and euermore to defend and protect them. O Lord, dissipate and confound al practises, conspiracies, and treasons against her, against this Realme of *England*, and against the trueth of thine *holy word* here taught and professed. Smite our enemies (good Lorde) vpon the cheeke-bone, breake the teeth of the vngodly, frustrate their counsels, and bring to nought all their deuises. Let them fall into the pitte, that they haue prepared for vs: Let a sudden destruction come vpon them vnawares: and the nette that they haue laide for others priuily, let it catch themselues, that they may fall into their owne mischiefe. Let them bee ashamed and confounded together, that seeke after her life to destroy it. Let them bee driuen backeward and put to rebuke, that wishe vs euill: so that the whole worlde and all posteritie may see and know howe mightily with thy fatherly care and prouidence thou watchest ouer and defendest those which put their trust in thee, and are in the hande of the most highest, and dwel vnder the shadow of the almighty: And that those which seeke thee, may bee ioyfull and glad in thee, and all such as loue thy *Saluation*, may say alway, *The Lord bee praised*. Graunt this (O most louing and mercifull father) for thy deare sonnes sake *Iesus Christ* our Lord and onely *Sauiour.* Amen.

Another.

O Almightie and eternal God, creator and gouernour of the whole world, vnto whome al power belongeth ouer all creatures both in heauen and earth, who spake the word, and they were made, commaunded and all thinges were created, and by whome alone it is, that not onely all *Kings* and *Princes* doe rule and gouerne the people committed to their charge, but are likewise by thy diuine prouidence and mightie protection (so long as it seemeth best to thy godly wisedome,) defended and deliuered euen in the middest of all their perilles and dangers, out of the handes of all their enemies: Wee yeelde vnto thee most humble and hearty thankes, for that it hath pleased thy gratious goodnes according to thine accustomed fauour towardes her, still to preserue and defend thy welbeloued *Handmaide* and our most gracious *Queene Elizabeth* from all the wicked conspiracies, traiterous attemptes, and deuilish deuises, which either the forreine and professed enemies abroade, or else her most vnloyall, desperate, and rebellious *Subiects* at home, were able at any time to deuise and practise against her. But especially (*O Lorde*) at this time, as iust occasion is offered vnto vs all, we al euen from the bottome of our hearts praise thy holy Name, and giue thee most hearty and vnfeined thankes for this thy late and most happy deliuery of her *Maiesties* most royall person from all those manifolde treasons which were most wickedly inuented and cruelly attempted against her: most humblie beseeching thee of thine infinite goodnesse and mercie, still to continue thy fatherly protection ouer her, daily to encrease and multiply thy heauenly blessings and graces vpon her. Be thou euer vnto her (*O Lorde God of hostes*) euen a strong rocke and tower of defence against the face of all her enemies, which eyther openly abroade, or secretely at home goe about to bring her life vnto the graue, and lay her honour in the dust. Disclose their wicked Counselles, and make frustrate all their deuillish practises in such sorte, as that all the worlde may learne and knowe, that there is no counsell, no wisedome, no pollicy against the Lorde. And if it be thy will (*O Lorde*) either giue them grace in time to see howe in vaine they stil kicke against the prickes, and doe seeke to depose her whome thou doest exalt, and so acknowledge and repent them of these their sinnes, and thus conuert them in thy mercie: or else in thy iust iudgements (if with the wilfull, obstinate, and reprobate sinners they still harden their hearts and wil not repent) let all the enemies (*O Lord*) let all the malicious and deadly enemies of thine annointed seruant & our most gracious Queene *Elizabeth* perish together. Let them fall into the ditch which they haue digged for others, and be taken in their owne nettes: but let her Maiestie (*O Lorde*) euer escape them, that all the worlde may see howe deare and precious in thy sight the life of this thine annointed is, who doeth not so much as imagine this euill against them that thus continuallie thirst after her blood. Wherfore (O Lord our God, King of kings and Lord of all lords, vnto whose eyes all thinges are open, and from whome no secretes are hidde, who onely knowest all the deuises and thoughts of men, & searchest out the depth of their hearts) thou knowest (*O Lord*) that nothing at any time hath been more deare vnto thine annoynted *Hand-maide Elizabeth* our Queene, then the publike good and benefite of thy Church, and the godly peace and vnity of all good *Christians* among themselues. Wee beseech thee therefore of thy great goodnes (*O Lord*) still to looke down from heauen, and behold her with thine eye of pitie and compassion, daily with thy mightie power and stretched out arme to saue and deliuer her from all her enemies, preserue and keepe her as the apple of thine own eie, and graunt vnto her (O most mercifull father) a long, prosperous, and happie reigne ouer vs, and prolong her daies as the daies of heauen heere vpon earth, that she may bee an olde mother in *Israel*, and see her desire vpon all thine and her enemies, though in number neuer so many, or in power neuer so mightie. And finally after this life, giue vnto her euerlasting life, through *Iesus Christ* thine onely sonne and our onely *Sauiour*.

Another.

O most gracious God and our most louing and merciful Father, which hast not onely created vs, and all thinges by thy power, but hast also continued our preseruation by thy holy prouidence, therein working wonderfully, reuealing things hidden and secret, as thou doest discouer the bottoms & foundations of the deepe: howe can wee worthily prayse thy goodnesse, or sufficiently declare thy louing kindenesse which thou hast at all times shewed vnto vs thy seruants in the land of the liuing? wee magnifie thy glorious name: thou hast a mighty arme, strong is thy hand, & high is thy right hand, yea thy wisedome is infinite. The prowd haue risen against thee, O Lorde, and against thine annointed our Soueraigne vnder thee, and against thy people that cal vpon thy Name: but thou hast cast them downe from time to time, and scattered them abroad, for thy mercie endureth for euer. They haue taken wicked counselles together, saying, None shall be able to espie it: but thou hast opened them, and brought them out of darknes into light, for thou art God alone which destroyest the wisedome of the wise, and castest away the vnderstanding of the prudent, therefore doe wee worship thee and praise thy holy Name, reioycing continually in thy strength and thy saluation, for thou art the glorie of our power, and by thy fauor and louing kindenesse are wee preserued. Our shield and defence belongeth to thee (O Lorde of hostes) and our gracious Prince to thee, O thou Holie one of Israel. And because thou hast loued her for thy names sake, and the glorie of thy kingdome vpon the earth, and vs also thy people to whome thou hast giuen her, and many excellent blessings together with her righteous gouernement, thou hast many times also preserued and kept her as the apple of thine eye, from the mischieuous imaginations, and cruell handes of thine and her enemies, and from the secrete practises of those that haue indeuored to rise vp against her. Thou (O Lorde) hast preserued her Honour from the ignominy, her life from the crueltie, and her Crowne from the tyranny of the wicked, her estate from ruine, her peace from disturbance, her kingdome and her people from beeing a pray to the malignant. The foote of pride hath come against vs, but the hand of iniquitie hath not cast vs downe: Therefore do wee reioyce before thee, and be glad in thee, yea our songs doe wee make of thy name, O thou most Highest, and will be euer setting foorth thy prayse and thy glorie, thy might, and thy mercie from one generation to another. Onely, O Lord, forsake vs not in this time of our age, vntil we haue shewed thy strength to this generation, and thy power to all that are yet for to come. And albeit if thou Lord in thy displeasure doe marke among vs all what is done amisse, there is none that can abide it, yet forsake vs not, nor leaue vs, O GOD of our saluation. Giue courage and constancy to our Soueraigne to perseuere in perilles: prudence, and wisedome to her Counsell, wisely to foresee and discouer the subtil sleights and dangers of all enemies: faithfulnesse and fortitude to the Nobles of the land: duety and obedience to vs all that are vnder her. Forgiue also wee most humbly pray thee thorow thy fatherly kindenesse in Jesus Christ, the multitude of our sinnes and transgressions against thy diuine Maiestie, and thy commaundements, and according to the multitude of thy mercies do away all our offences, that the light and candle of thy seruaunt *Elizabeth* our gracious Queene and Gouernour, which is our life in the light of thy countenaunce, and the breath of our nosethrilles, bee not put out, but may still shine and burne bright, illumined by the beames of thy heauenlie grace. Protect her (O Lorde) we still beseech thee in safetie, saue her in maiestie, keepe her in peace, guide her in counsell, and defend her in danger: blesse her, Lorde, in all temporall and celestiall blessinges in Christ, that shee may still blesse thee: for in death no man remembreth thee, and who shall giue thee thankes in the pitte? Detect and reueale still the foundations and buildings of all treasons and conspiracies both at home and abroade, and herein (O Lorde) either conuert the wicked hearts and secret conceites from their wicked imaginations, or confounde their deuises, and make them as the vntimely fruit that they neuer see the sunne. Say (O Lorde) to her soule as sometime thou diddest to *Abraham* the Father of the Faithfull, I am thy buckler and thy exceeding great reward: and as thou diddest sometime to the soule of thy seruaunt *Dauid*, I am thy saluation, with my holie oile haue I annointed thee. Therefore my hand shall holde thee fast, and mine arme shall stablish thee. The enemy shall not be able to doe thee violence, the sonne of wickednesse shall not hurt thee. I will beate downe thy foes before thy face, and plague them that hate thee. Heare, Lorde, and saue vs O King of heauen, when wee call vpon thee, and so shall we all both Prince and people dwell still vnder the shadowe of thy winges, protected by thy power, and preserued by thy prouidence, and ordered by thy gouernance, to thy euerlasting praise, and our vnspeakeable comforte in Jesus Christ, to whome with thee, O Father and God of all consolation, and the holy Spirite of sanctification, be all honor and glorie both nowe and for euer. Amen.

1594–S2   Fast day on the Sunday before the meeting of parliament

Sunday 26 May 1594 (presbytery of Edinburgh; and elsewhere in Scotland if possible)

The crown's continuing failure to resolve the threat posed by the catholic nobles was a principal matter of concern at the May 1594 general assembly. The clergy placed their hopes in the forthcoming meeting of the Scottish parliament, which duly forfeited the earls of Angus, Huntly and Erroll. The appointment of this fast reflected the importance of the parliament for the Kirk, but Bowes's letter suggested that some clergy were pessimistic about the prospects of 'reformation by the help and hand of man'.

Order: by the general assembly, 15 May 1594, *BUK*, III, 839.
Additional sources: Calderwood, V, 326–7; Robert Bowes to Burghley, 18 May 1594, SP52/53/56; Row, p. 159.

ORDER

Order by the general assembly: 15 May 1594
The Assemblie ordanes ane fast to be keipit within the Presbitrie of Edenburgh, and sick vther parts quher the samein may be conveniently had, vpon Sonday the 26 of this instant, immediatlie preceiding the Parliament; and his Majestie to be remembrit that ane exhortatioun may be had, according to the custome quhilk was keipit of befoir, the first day of the Parliament, and a thanksgiving at the conclusion therof be ane of the Ministrie; and also that his Majestie be put in mynd of the said fast appointit the foirsaid day, to the effect his Majestie and his house may keip the samein.

1594–S3   Fast days [reasons unknown]

Sunday 23 June–Sunday 30 June 1594 (Scotland)

The general assembly appointed this fast immediately after ordering 1594–S2, presumably in response to fears of domestic catholic conspiracies. The causes that James Melvill, Patrick Galloway and James Nicolson were ordered to prepare have not been found. By the time the fast was observed, the Scottish parliament had forfeited the catholic earls (see 1594–S2). There is evidence that some ministers used the fast to preach favourably on the king's apparent desire to resolve the crisis, but other clergy were sceptical of James's motives.

Order: by the general assembly, 15 May 1594, *BUK*, III, 839.
Additional sources: Calderwood, V, 327, 336–9; Row, p. 159.

ORDER

Order by the general assembly: 15 May 1594
In lyke maner it is ordanit, that a generall fast be observit [vniversallie][239] through the haill realme, the twa last Sondayis of Junij nixt to come, with exhortatiouns and prayers to be keipit betuixt the twa Sondayis on the weik dayes: The causes of the quhilk fast salbe intimat and presentit the morne in wryte be Mrs James Melvill, Patrick Galloway, and James Nicolsone.

---

[239] This word was added in the printed edition of *BUK* from Calderwood's equivalent text.

1595–S   Fast days in response to general troubles

Sunday 3 August – Sunday 10 August 1595 (Scotland)

By the end of March 1595, military action by the crown had forced the earls of Huntly and Erroll, together with the earl of Bothwell (who had sided with the catholic nobles since the previous autumn) to flee Scotland. This helped to reduce tensions between the Kirk and the king, and the June 1595 assembly was peaceful. The assembly appointed this fast, leaving the clergy to specify causes for fasting. *The cavses of this general fast*, published by the presbytery of Edinburgh for use in its own bounds, referred to a general increase in sinfulness, the threat of catholic conspiracies and signs of God's anger such as unseasonable weather and dearth. Looking back over the period since the reformation parliament of 1560, the presbytery complained of '36 yeares dissobedience to the Gospel' (sig. 4^r), while finding reasons to trust in divine providence, including the defeat of the Spanish armada and the failure of the catholic earls in Scotland.

Order: by the general assembly, 28 June 1595, *BUK*, III, 854.
Additional sources: Calderwood, V, 376; *The cavses of this general fast* (Edinburgh, 1595; STC 7485.5); George Nicolson to Robert Bowes, 4 Aug. 1595, SP52/56/74.

ORDER

Order by the general assembly: 28 June 1595

Forsameikle as ther is great cause of humiliatioun of vs befor God, whose visible anger appears on the heids of this land, yet be the most pairt little regairdit: The Kirk hes ordainit a generall fast and humiliatioun to be vniversallie observit in all the kirks within this realme, vpon the twa first Sondayis of August nixt to come: The causes therof to be led out gravelie be the Pastours, according to the grounds they sie and perceive.

1596–S1   Fast days during threats of Spanish invasion and continued dearth

Sunday 1 February and Tuesday 3 February 1596 (Scotland?)

This fast is known only through references in English diplomatic correspondence. It was not appointed by the general assembly, which did not meet until March, and observance may have been limited to Edinburgh. The early months of 1596 saw good relations between the Kirk and the crown, but fears of Spanish invasion were again high.

Order: described in George Nicolson to Robert Bowes, 16 Jan. 1596, SP52/58/8.
Additional source: same to same, 29 Jan. 1596, SP52/58/16.

DESCRIPTION OF ORDER

George Nicolson to Robert Bowes: 16 January 1596

The k. hathe him self willed the ministers to make a generall fast before the musters for calling to God to assist them against the Spanyards and the miserable dearthe here.

1596–E1 Prayers during a naval and military campaign against Spain

Wednesdays, Fridays, Sundays and festival days, June 1596 (Canterbury province)

In June 1596, Elizabeth financed an attack on Cadiz, commanded jointly by Lord Admiral Howard and the earl of Essex, with the aim of destroying the Spanish fleet. The force, comprising 150 ships (including eighteen royal navy ships and eighteen Dutch war ships) and 10,000 men, sailed from Plymouth on 3 June. The same day, Whitgift ordered Richard Fletcher, bishop of London, to organize days of prayer across the province and sent him a copy of the form of prayer to be used. This comprised one prayer, printed on a single sheet folio, the first time such a minimal format had been used. Ministers were expected to preach 'some breefe & pithie Exhortation … to stir them [parishioners] up to Repentance, to Amendment of there Lives, Fervencie in publique & privat Prayers for Victorye against our Enimyes', or, if unlicensed, to read a relevant homily; they were also ordered to exhort their parishioners to fast and give alms. However, bishops were warned not to allow any public assemblies, fasts or other actions 'tending towards Innovation', an admonition clearly directed at puritan nonconformists (see 1586–E1, 1588–E1 and 1593–E). Whitgift's order provides rare information on the production and distribution of official prayers. The royal printer was instructed to print sufficient copies for each parish to have at least one copy – an enormous task because there were more than 9,000 parishes in England and Wales. The printer set the price of forms; they had to be collected and distributed by episcopal officials, who were also expected to remit the money collected from parishes to the printer. It is unclear whether bishops from further afield were expected to send officials to collect forms: certainly for 1563–E, Burghley sent the archbishop of York copies of forms by carrier. Several manuscript copies of 'A prayer made by the queen at the departure of the fleet', dated to 1596, are extant but its relationship to this occasion is unknown.

Order: Whitgift to Fletcher, 3 June 1596, in Francis Peck, *Desiderata curiosa: or, a collection of divers scarse and curious pieces* (2 vols., 1732–5), I, book 5, no. 12, pp. 10–11.
Form of prayer: *A prayer set forth by authoritie to be vsed for the prosperous successe of her maiesties forces and nauie* (1 p.; STC 16526; BL, RB.23.b.1970(2)) [also in Clay, p. 665].
Additional sources: Fletcher to Bishop William Chaderton, 5 June 1596, in Peck, *Desiderata curiosa*, I, book 5, no. 13, pp. 11–12; 'A prayer made by the queen at the departure of the fleet' [1596], LPL, MS 250, fo. 338v [see *Elizabeth I: collected works*, ed. Leah S. Marcus *et al.* (Chicago and London, 2000), pp. 425–6]; Clay, pp. 472, 666.

ORDER

Archbishop of Canterbury to bishop of London: 3 June 1596

1. Salutem in Christo. Your Lordship shall receyve hereinclosed the Forme of a Prayer printed, which I thinke fitt to be sent unto every Bushopp & *Custos Spiritualitatis* in this Province; with Chardge, in her Majesties Name, that they geve present Order in there severall Jurisdictions, not only for reverent celebratinge & due frequentinge, in every parishe Churche, of publique Prayers upon *Wensdayes, Fridayes, Sondayes* & Festivall Dayes, according to the Booke of Common Prayer; but also that this Prayer be then & there devoutly used, for the prosperous Successe & victorious Returne of her Majesties Forces & Navie nowe imployed against the professed Enimyes of her Majestie & this Kingdome; whose Mallice is kindled against us for none other Cause more then for our Mayntenaunce of the syncere Profession & Preachinge of Christs Gospell.

2. And, where the Minister is a Preacher, our Bretheren the Bushops must also geve Order, that some breefe & pithie Exhortation be used unto the People, to stir them up to Repentance, to Amendment of there Lives, Fervencie in publique & privat Prayers for Victorye against our Enimyes, Fastinge, Abstinency & Humiliation with Allmesse-Deeds & other Works of Charitie.

3. And, where he is noe Preacher, to reade some of the Homilies heretofore sett out for those Purposes. But, in any wise, without anie Usinge or Proclaiminge of [any] other Assembly or publique Fastinge, or any other [Course] tending towards Innovation, or not receyved by publique Authorytie…

[Postscript] For the printed Prayer there is Order given, that her Majesties Printer shall se a competent Number of them printed & sent downe to your Lordship, that every Parishe within your Dioces may have one of them at the least; the Price whereof he dothe sett downe unto your Lordship, which you must Cause to be collected by suche your Officers as dothe deliver them forthe, & to be returned upp unto the said Printer, in suche manner as he shall requier your Lordship by his Letters.

FORM OF PRAYER

Not vnto vs (O Lorde) not vnto vs, but vnto thy name giue the glory by beholding of vs thy seruants graciously at this time, against whom the proude are risen vp, and the enemies haue conspired and banded themselues. It is thy might and Maiestie alone (O Lorde) that putteth downe all the vngodly of the earth like drosse, that stilleth the raging of the Sea, and the noyse of his waues, and the madnesse of the people, that breaketh the bow and knappeth the speare in sunder, and burneth the Chariots in the fire. Arise then (O Lorde) to our defence, and breake the power and counsels of thine and our enemies, and make them like those people that became as the chaffe before the wind, when they conspired and went out against those, whose shield and buckler, whose castle of defence, whose God and Sauiour thou wast from euerlasting. And blesse good Lorde, (wee most humbly beseech thee) the people of our land prouided to withstand their tyrannie, and to stand for the iust defence of thy seruaunts and people of this kingdome. Incourage all our heartes (O heauenly King and Prince of power) with ioy and gladnesse in thy sauing health: and the handes of our armies with strength and constancie. And as thou art the God of hosts, so blesse our hosts and companies by Sea and by land, by giuing them victory in battell and strength in conflict to ouercome. So shall wee confesse to the prayse of thy Name, that it is not our vowe nor our sword that hath saued vs, but thy holy hand and outstretched arme. And all the world shall know, that it is thy fauour that prospereth, and thy power that ouercommeth, and thy blessing that preserueth thy Church from hostilitie and tyranny, and vs thy people from destruction. Heare vs (O Lord our defendor) for the glory of thy holy Name, through Jesus Christ our blessed Sauiour and Redeemer. Amen.

1596–E2   Thanksgiving prayer for victories at Cadiz and Faro

August 1596 (London)

The attack on Cadiz by Howard and Essex was successful, and the port was pillaged for two weeks before being set on fire. Faro was also attacked on the return journey. However, the two men had failed to destroy the main Spanish fleet (harboured at Lisbon) and brought English ships home unfit to resail against the East and West Indies fleets as planned. No official order is extant for this occasion though there is no evidence to support Strype's comment that it was ordered by Essex. Rather, it appears to have been Whitgift's suggestion. A letter from Burghley to Matthew Hutton, archbishop of York, indicates that the thanksgiving was originally to be nationwide, but it was later limited to London by Elizabeth, possibly in order to curb Essex's growing popular support. Authorship of the form – which, like the previous occasion, comprised a single prayer – is also unknown, though Bughley and an unidentified person corrected a draft. William Barlow, Whitgift's chaplain, preached a thanksgiving sermon at Paul's Cross on 8 August; the text is no longer extant. Barlow was to be widely criticized in 1601 when he preached again at the Cross after Essex's rebellion (see 1601–E): he was accused of being a time-server who, having failed to win promotion from the earl in 1596, had turned against him in 1601.

Order: none found [but see Burghley to Matthew Hutton, archbishop of York, 2 Aug. 1596, in *The corre-spondence, with a selection from the letters, etc. of Sir Timothy Hutton* (Surtees Society, XVII, 1843), pp. 111–12, and Edward Reynoldes to Essex, 1596, LPL, MS 658, fos. 259r–260v].
Form of prayer: *A prayer of thanksgiuing, and for continuance of good successe to her maiesties forces* (1 p.; STC 16527)* [also in Clay, pp. 668–70].
Form of prayer (other edition): STC 16527.5
Additional sources: 'Forme of prayer for the Queene', Lans. 116, fos. 81r–82r; Strype, *Annals*, IV, 364–6; John Stowe, *The abridgement of the English chronicle ... by E. H. Gentleman* (London, 1618: STC 23332), p. 405; Clay, pp. 472–3; MacLure, pp. 72–3; William Barlow, *A sermon preached at Paules Crosse, on the first Sunday in Lent: Martij 1. 1600 With a short discourse of the late earle of Essex his confession, and penitence, before and at the time of his death ... Whereunto is annexed a true copie, in substance, of the behauiour, speache, and prayer of the said earle at the time of his execution* (1601; STC 1454).
Printed sermons: Barlow [Whitgift's chaplain], 8 Aug., Paul's Cross, London (STC 1454) (also noted in MacLure, pp. 72–3).

DESCRIPTIONS OF ORDERS

Burghley to archbishop of York: 2 August 1596

Maie it please your Grace … The good newes that are commonlie reported of the great victorie of hir Majestie's army and navy in Spayne is so certainlie confirmed by the generalls as it is ment that both in the province of Canterbury and of yours at York there should be publick prayer and thanksgiving for the same, whereof your Grace shall shortlie heare.

Edward Reynoldes to the earl of Essex: 1596
… I may not forgett to lett your lordship vnderstand how ho: my Lord Arch Bishop: hath carried himselfe towardes your lordship in procuring a thanksgiuing for this victory which once was graunted to be generall in all partes but afterwards restrayned by her maiesties commaundement for London only.

FORM OF PRAYER

O Lord God of Hostes, euerlasting and most mercifull Father, we thine vnworthy creatures doe yeeld vnto thy diuine Maiestie all possible prayse and humble thankes for thine infinite benefites, which thou hast of long time plentifully powred vpon thine Handmaiden, & humble seruant our Soueraigne Lady the Queene, and vpon her whole Realme, and vs her Subiects the people of this Kingdome. And namely, O Lord, for that graciously respecting vs in the merites of thy deere Sonne our Sauiour, and by his intercession passing ouer and forgiuing our manifold sinnes, thou hast this present Sommer so fauourably conducted the Royall Nauie and Armie sent to the Seas by our Gracious Queene (not for any other worldly respects, but onely for defence of this Realme, and vs thy people, against the mighty preparations of our Enemies threatning our ruine,) by safely directing them vnto places appointed, and by strengthening the Gouernours and Leaders of the same with counsell and resolution, and blessing them with notable victories both by Sea and Land, whereby the insolencies and pride of our Enemies, which sought our conquest and subuersion, is by these late victories notably daunted, repulsed, and abased. Graunt vnto vs (most mercifull Father) the grace, with due thankfulnesse to acknowledge thy fatherly goodnesse extended vpon vs, by the singular fauour shewed to thy Seruant and Minister our Soueraigne Lady and Queene. And for thy holy Name continue these thy wonderfull blessings still vpon vs, to defend vs against our Enemies, and blesse vs with thy gracefull hand to the endlesse prayse of thy holy Name, and to our lasting ioy. And direct our Armies by thy prouidence and fauourable support, to finish these late victories to the honour of our Soueraigne, and safetie of her Realme, that hath most carefully made the same able to ouermatch her Enemies: So as the Noble men, and all others seruing in the same Nauie and Armie vnder their charge may with much honour, triumph, and safetie returne home to their Countries, and to giue thee due thankes for thy speciall fauours merueilously shewed vnto them, in preseruing of them all this Sommer time from all contagion and mortalitie by sworde or sicknesse, notwithstanding their force and violence most manfully exercised against their Enemies, to the vanquishing of great numbers both by Sea & Land, and to the destruction of their most mighty Ships, that heretofore haue attempted to inuade this Realme, and of their Fortes and Castles, and waste of their notable substances of their riches, without hurting any person that did yeelde, or of any women or children, or Religious persons, to whom all fauour was shewed that they did require. All which prosperous successes we do most iustly acknowledge (O Lorde) to haue proceeded onely from thy speciall fauour, to whom with thy Sonne and holy Ghost be all honour and prayse. Amen.

1596–S2   Fast day due to religious tension

Sunday 5 December 1596 (Scotland)

This fast was appointed by commissioners of the Kirk, who met in Edinburgh on 20 October 1596. In effect, it served as the culmination of a programme of local fasts, started by the general assembly in March, which had been observed in various places as part of the ceremony of renewing the Covenant (the Negative Confession of 1581). By the autumn, tensions between the Kirk and the crown had re-emerged, stimulated by the return to Scotland of the earls of Huntly and Errol, and the seditious preaching of David Black, who declined the authority of the privy council with the support of other clergy. The meetings of the commissioners of the Kirk, which the king tried in vain to dissolve, were a further source of confrontation. In these circumstances, the fast was presumably not observed throughout Scotland.

Order: by the commissioners of the Kirk, 20 Oct. 1596, described in Scot, p. 69.
Additional sources: presbytery of Peebles minutes, 1596–1602, NRS, CH2/295/1, p. 6; Scot, pp. 65–6; Melvill, pp. 346, 353–67; Calderwood, V, 394–6, 400–1, 406–8, 433–7.

DESCRIPTION OF ORDER

Order by the commissioners of the Kirk: 20 October 1596

From this Convention likewise were sent to the Presbytries informations of the dangers arising from the returning and remaining of the forfaulted Earles; and for remedies, the ministers were desired to make the professors sensible of the danger, to keep a publick humiliation the first Sabbath of December, to urge an amendment in all estats, beginning at themselves[.]

1596–E3   Prayers and fasting during a time of dearth

Wednesdays and Fridays, after Monday 27 December 1596 (England and Wales)

Bad harvests in 1596 and 1597, caused by excessive rain, were some of the worst in the sixteenth century, leading to famine until 1598 and causing distress which was compounded by plague and high taxation. At some point during 1596, *Three sermons, or homilies, to mooue compassion towards the poore and needie in these times* were issued for parish use, presumably by order of the privy council. These homilies emphasized that dearth was a warning and punishment for the realm's greed and exhorted everyone to moderate their diets and give generously to the poor. In August, the queen and council reissued the Book of Common Orders (see 1586–E1) to regulate the sale of grain and Whitgift ordered bishops in their sermons to 'admonish the Farmors & Owners of Corne' in their sermons for hoarding and increasing grain prices. But not until December were public prayers, fasts and collections for the poor ordered to be organized in all parishes. No form was issued; instead, ministers were to use the BCP (probably meaning in particular the prayers 'In the time of dearth and famine' and 'For fair weather'). Ministers were expected to encourage their parishioners to abstain from supper on Wednesdays as well as on Fridays and other official fasting days. There was great emphasis in the order on strict observance of prayers and greater admonition to make people fast and give alms. Monthly reports made by the clergy on poor relief, almsgiving and hospitality, introduced in 1586–7 (see 1586–E1), were rigorously enforced for the first time. Whitgift also encouraged preachers to admonish grain-hoarding. This use of special worship to enforce social policy was new; it was probably a product of the severity of dearth and the regime's growing anxiety about unrest during wartime, caused by famine, plague, vagrancy and high taxation.

Order: Whitgift to the bishops, 27 Dec. 1596, LPL, Whitgift Register, II, fo. 149r–v [also in *Concilia*, IV, 351–2].

Form of prayer: none [prayers from the BCP were to be used].

Additional sources: Whitgift to Chaderton, 10 Aug. 1596, in Peck, *Desiderata curiosa*, I, book 5, no. 14, pp. 12–13; *Three sermons, or homelies* (1596; STC 13681).

ORDER

John Whitgift to the bishops: 27 December 1596

After my hartie Comendations to your Lordshipp. / Amongest all our sinnes wherbye we haue provoked God iustlie to plague vs with this dearth and scarsitie / It is to bee thought that none haue been more forceable therevnto, then our excesse and ryott in dyett and the wastfull consuminge of his good creatures, for supplie of which presente scarsitie towardes the poorer sorte the Queenes Maiestie hath everye waye shewed a most princelie Care and gratious tender affection, not onelye by causinge the marketts to be duelie served, and greate store of graine to be provided from forreine partes freelye without payinge anie Custome: but alsoe a most virtuous and Godlye Soveraigne dayelie studieth to quallifye the mischiefe, by takinge awaye the cause of yt. Therfore for redress of that abuse, and prevention of further punishement by like scarsitie, her maiestie hath straightlye commaunded mee to signifye by my letters, that it is her highnes expresse pleasure, and absolute commandement, that publique prayers, accordinge to the booke of common prayer in everye severall parishe Church and Chappell be on all wednesdaies and Fridaies hereafter devoutlie vsed, and diligentlye frequented that such as be of better abilitie, doe in the feare of god vse a greater moderation, then heretofore in their dyet: but namelye that by none of degree soever anie fleshe bee dressed or eaten one such daies, as by lawe stande alreadye prohibited, other than such as by reason of infirmitye be lawfullye therevnto licensed, and, that not onelye one Fridaies and other daies by lawe alreadye appointed for fastinge dayes noe suppers att all be provided or taken by anie, either for themselves or housholde: but alsoe that everie one not letted by greevous weekenes doe abstaine from suppers altogeather one each Wednesdaie at night, to the intent, that what is by forbearance of that meale, and att other meales by abstinencye from all superfluous fare, fruictfullie spared, maye presentlye, especiallie by the welthier sort be charitablie converted to the relief and comforte of the poore and needie, soe as notice thereof maye be taken, accordinge to her maiesties gratious expectacion, at the handes of all such her dutifull subiectes, as be respectiue of her Royall Commaundementes. In this behalf your Lordshipp is alsoe to geve speciall order that the collections for the poore in everie parishe maye be carefullye made and (in respect of the great want) charitablie by those whoe be of good habilitie increased and duelie and seasonablie bestowed for the succour of the most distressed: It is further likewise required by her maiestie, that those which haue housholdes, doe not for sparinge discharge anie of theire houshold to shifte for them selves, nor themselves to soiorne from their vsuall habitacion. And because the example of ecclesiasticall persons maye induce men as well as theire teachinge in this behalf; all such as haue benefices must be reioyned to reside on theire lyvinges to kepe hospitalitye and relieve theire neighboures: and such as haue pluralities in conscience ought to doe the like by theire Farmors and such as rent theire lyvinges at their handes: But there must a verye watchfull eye be caried by the minister and churchwardens in everye parishe or bye such charitable discreete men as they shall nominate and appoint, vnto all Inns, Tavernes, and victualinge howses: howe both the keepers of them with theire houshold, and, alsoe their gesse and resorters to their howses doe observe theis her Maiesties Commaundementes: Nowe for the better publishinge of her highnes gratious pleasure in the premisses; your Lordshipp must take precise order, that everie minister in the diocesses doe diligentlie recom [sic] the observation of them vnto the people in theire severall chardges And alsoe doe from tyme to tyme in their sermons and exhortacions earnestlie and pythelie exhorte and stirr vpp everie of them to fervent prayer both publique and priuate to abstinencye, fastinge, true humiliation, to forbeare all excesse to relieve the poore, and needie by good housekeepinge, by settinge them one worke, and by other deedes of Almes and brotherlie compassion. And consideringe the most princelie and gratious care her maiestie hath for their relief and that all good meanes should be vsed for the succour and helpe of them in theis tymes of dearth, the people must be duelie taught to endure this scarsitie with patience, and especiallie to beware howe they geve eare to anie persuasions, or practizes of disconted [sic] and idle braines, to move them to repine or swarue from the humblee duties of good subiectes to the further offence of God and discontentinge of her maiestie, that hath soo tender a care of theire wellfare / And for that her maiestye would be enformed, howe duelie theis orders shall be observed, as her speciall care is they should, your Lordshippe is therefore to procure a Certificate to be made vnto you monethlie, by everye the ministers and churchwardins conteynnge as well the names of disobedient delinquentes in anie the premisses as of those, well disposed persons, who haue had a dutifull regard of her Maiesties Commaundement, and a charitable compassion for the relief of the poore, to the entent, that once everye quarter the said certificates beinge transmitted over vnto mee I maye satisfie her Maiesties gratious expectacion touching the successe and fruicte arrisinge by theis godlye orders. But your Lordshipp is to foresee and to geve speciall direction that the prescript of theis letters, bee in everie severall parishe observed, without callinge or sufferinge persons of other parishes to assemble themselves, as some heretofore offensiuelie of their own headdes haue attempted vnder colloure of generall fastes[.]

1597–E   Prayers for a naval expedition against Spain

After Monday 11 July 1597 (England and Wales)

On 10 July, the earl of Essex set sail from Plymouth with a substantial fleet to attack the Spanish navy at Ferrol as it prepared to invade Ireland as a springboard into England. No order survives for this occasion, but copies of the form were printed in early July. They comprised seven prayers which, in the absence of instructions, were presumably to be inserted into the BCP service at the end of the litany. The author of the prayers is unknown, though it may have been Whitgift who made extensive corrections to the original drafts. Sir Robert Cecil (youngest son of Lord Burghley and recently appointed principal secretary) presented a copy of the form to Elizabeth before 11 July, and read out three or four of the prayers to her. She ordered some of them to be used in the Chapel Royal but objected to the inclusion of a prayer of her own. She requested Whitgift to 'make stay of it, and that the same may be taken out of all the books that are printed'. The queen's prayer is presumably 'O God, all maker, keeper, and guider', which is not present in some editions (STC 16528 and STC 16528.5). On this basis (*pace* STC), STC 16528a and STC 16528a.5, which include 'O God, all-maker, keeper, and guider', are the earlier editions. STC 16528a is transcribed below. Both the English and the Spanish fleets were driven back to port by storms.

Order: none found.
Form of prayer: *Certaine prayers set foorth by authoritie, to be vsed for the prosperous successe of her maiesties forces and nauy* ([24] pp.; STC 16528a)* [printed in Clay, pp. 671–8].
Form of prayer (other editions): STC 16528a.5, 16528 and 16528.5.
Additional sources: Whitgift's draft amendments of the prayers, LPL, MS 113; Cecil to Whitgift, 11 July 1597, LPL, MS 3470, fo. 195r; 'O God, All-maker, Keeper, and Guider', Harleian MS 6986/35, fo. 58r [also in *Elizabeth I: Collected works*, ed. Marcus *et al.*, pp. 426–7]; Clay, p. 473.

FORM OF PRAYER

O God all-maker, keeper, and guider: Inurement of they rare-seene, vnused, & seeld-heard-of goodnesse, powred in so plentiful sort vpon vs full oft, breeds now this boldnes, to craue with bowed knees, and hearts of humilitie, thy large hand of helping power, to assist with wonder our iust cause, not founded on Prides-motion, nor begun on Malice-stock; But as thou best knowest, to whom nought is hid, grounded on iust defence from wrongs, hate, and bloody desire of conquest. For since, meanes thou has imparted to saue that thou hast giuen, by enioying such a people, as scornes their bloodshed, where suretie ours is one: Fortifie (deare GOD) such hearts in such sort, as their best part may be worst, that to the truest part meant worst, with least losse to such a Nation, as despise their liues for their Countreys good. That all Forreine lands may laud & admire the Omnipotencie of thy worke: a fact alone for thee only to performe. So shall they Name be spread for wonders wrought, and the faithfull encouraged, to repose in thy vnfellowed Grace: And we that minded nought but right, inchained in thy bonds for perpetuall slauerie, and liue & die the sacrificers of our soules for such obteined fauour. Warrant, deare Lord, all this with thy command. AMEN.

Most mighty God and mercifull Father, as hitherto of thyne infinite goodnes thou hast very miraculously protected thy humble Seruant our Soueraigne Lady & Queene, and all vs her subiects the people of her Dominions, from many dangerous conspiracies, malicious attempts, and wicked designements of her and our very obstinate & implacable enemies: Forasmuch as they stil continewing their malice, & preparing their Forces to assaile vs both by Land & Sea, thou (O Lord) to withstand their furie, hast stirred vp the heart of thine Anoynted our Soueraigne, to send out some of her Forces for our defence: we thine vnworthy seruants doe most humbly beseech thee, through the merites of our Sauiour Christ, so to conduct them, encourage them, and defend them with thy strong and mightie arme, as that whatsoeuer they shall attempt and take in hand, for defence of this Realme against her enemies, may prosper and haue most happy successe. Direct & leade them (O Lord) in safetie, strengthen their Gouernours and Leaders with sound counsell and valiant resolution. Blesse their conflicts with notable victories both by Sea and Land: preserue them from all contagion and mortalitie, either by sworde or sicknesse, and giue vnto them (O Lord) if it be thy blessed will, such an honourable and happy returne, as may tend to our defence by the confusion of our enemies, to the renowme & comfort of our Soueraigne to the benefite of thy Church, to the good of this Kingdome, and to the prayse and glory of thy most mighty Name, through Jesu Christ our Lord: To whome with thee and the holy Ghost be ascribed all honour, power, and dominion, both nowe and for euer. Amen.

O most mightie GOD, and Lorde of Hostes, which reignest ouer all the Kingdomes of the world, who hast power in thine hand to saue thy chosen, & to iudge thine Enemies, and in all ages hast giuen great and glorious Victories vnto thy Church, with small handfuls ouerthrowing great multitudes and terrible Armies: Let thine eares be now attent vnto our prayers, and thy mercifull eye vpon this Realme & kingdome. And as of thine vnspeakeable goodnes, thou hast blessed vs with infinite and extraordinary blessings, all the yeres of her Maiesties most happy reigne ouer vs, and of late hast also myraculously deliuered vs from sundry the bloody practises of our very implacable enemies: So now, we humbly beseech thee (O mercifull Father) to ayde vs with thy mighty Arme in this our present iust cause, waging warre not in pride or ambition of mind, or any other worldly respect, but onely for the necessary defence of Religion, our liues, and Countrey. Be mercifull therefore, O Lord, to our present Forces, and passing ouer both their transgressions and ours, prosper them both by Sea and land. Giue our Leaders & companies, the strength of Unicornes, the hearts of Lyons, armes of steele, hands of iron, and feete of flint, to beate and tread downe all thine enemies and ours. Let thine helpe from aboue at this time strengthen our Nauy and Armie, thy mercie ouershadowe them, thy power as a wall of fire enuyron them, thy wisedome direct them, thy prouidence secure them, thine holy Angels garde them, thy Sonne our Lorde Jesus Christ stand vp for them, and thy Justice confound, and Maiestie ouerwhelme all aduersarie power exalting it selfe against this land and thy Gospel. That all the world may know, that it is thy fauour that prospereth, thy blessing that preserueth, and thine arme that ouercommeth in the day of battell. So we that be thy people and sheepe of thy folde, shall sing vnto thy glorie the songs of prayse and thankesgiuing, and magnifie thy goodnesse in the midst of thine holy Temple for euer, through Jesus Christ our Lord, our only Sauiour and Mediatour. Amen.

O almightie Lorde God of Hostes, it is thine owne gracious promise, that when thy people shall go out to battell against their enemies, by the way that thou shalt send them, & shall call vpon thee for thy holy helpe, that then thou (Lord) wilt heare their prayers in heauen, and iudge their cause: In assured trust of this thy good promise, we present this our supplication before thee. O Lorde iudge thou our cause, iudge thou betweene vs and our cruell enemies. Thou seest Lorde, that they first inuaded vs, and so doe still continue, and not wee them: that they first conspired to root vs out, that we might be no more a people of *English* birth, and that then though thou from heauen diddest shew thy selfe, in scattering their proud forces, to be displeased with their attempt, yet notwithstanding by mightie preparations at this present they seeke our ruine still. That which armeth vs, is neither desire of enlarging our owne borders, nor thirst of blood, nor rauine of spoyle, but onely our owne iust defence, onely to breake the power of our enemies, and to turne away the battell from our owne gates: For that if we sit still, and suffer them to gather strength, they will suddenly make a breach vpon vs, and destroy the mother with the children. This they seeke, O Lord, & as thou seest, that the heart of thine Anointed in all her actions is vpright before thee, so mainteine thou our right, & be enemie to our enemies. Great is their malice (as thou Lord seest) and great is the mischiefe they intend against vs. Let not the wicked haue their desire: O Lord, let not their mischieuous imaginations prosper, least they be too proude. And albeit our many and grieuous iniquities may testifie against vs, and iustly deserue, that thou shouldest make the enemies sword the auenger of thy couenant which wee haue broken; Yet deale thou with vs according to thy mercy, O Lord, We haue sinned, Lord, doe thou vnto vs what seemeth good in thine eyes: onely at this time wee pray thee to succour vs, and not make vs a scorne and derision to our oppressers. The rather O Lord, for that wee put not our trust in any strength of our owne, but our eyes looke onely to thee. We know, Lord, the battell is thine, and that with thee it is nothing to saue with many, or with few: For that except thou command the winds, we can not stirre, and except thou blesse with counsell and courage, wee shall not preuaile, and all these are in thine handes to giue or to withholde. Helpe vs, O Lord God, for we rest on thee, and in thy Name go we foorth against these mightie preparations. O Lorde thou art our God, let not man preuaile against thee: let thine arme rise vp, and put on strength to preserue vs nowe as of olde, euen the same arme that was mightie for vs and against them in their former pride and furie.

Wherefore from thy holy Sanctuarie, O Lorde, open thine eyes and behold, incline thine eare and heare the prayer of thy seruants. Goe foorth, O Lord, with our Hostes by Sea and by land. Send forth the windes out of thy treasures to bring them to the place appointed. Take all contagious sicknesse from the middest of them, O Lord the strength of our saluation. Couer their heads in the day of battell. Send thy feare before thy seruants, & make their enemies to flee and fal before them. Let thy faith (Lord) make them valiant in battell, and put to flight the Armies of Aliens. And by this shall we know, O Lorde, that thou fauourest vs, in that our enemie doeth not triumph ouer vs, and shall alwayes confesse to the prayse of thy Name, that it was thy hand, and that it was thou, Lord, the shield of our helpe, and sword of our glory, that hast done these great things for vs, and euermore say, Praysed be the Lorde, that hath pleasure in the prosperitie of his seruants. Heare vs, O Lord for the glorie of thy Name, for thy louing Mercie, and for thy trueth sake, euen for the merites and intercession of our Lord Jesus Christ. Amen.

O eternall GOD, in power most mighty, in strength most glorious, without whom the Horse & Chariot is in vaine prepared against the day of battell: vouchsafe (wee beseeche thee) from thy high throne of Maiestie, to heare and receiue the heartie & humble prayers, which on bended knees, wee the people of thy pasture and sheepe of thy handes, doe in an vnfayned acknowledgement of thy might and our owne weakenesse, powre out before thee on the behalfe of our gratious Soueraigne, and on the behalfe of her Armies, her Nobles, her Valiants, and men of warre: who by thee inspired haue put their liues in their hands, and at this time doe oppose themselues, against the malice and violence of such, as beare a mortall hate at thy Sion, and doe dayly conspire and rise vp against it, euen against the Church, thine Annointed, and the people of this her Land. Arise then (O Lord) and stand vp we pray thee, to helpe and defend them: be thou their Captaine to goe in and out before them, and to leade them in this iourney: teache their fingers to fight, and their hands to make battaile. The Generall and Cheiftaines blesse with the spirite of wisedome, counsell, and direction: the Souldiers with mindes ready to performe and execute. Gird them all with strength, and powre out vpon them the spirite of courage: giue them in the day of battell, heartes like the hearts of Lions, inuincible and fearelesse against euill, but terrible to such as come out against them. Where the enemie doeth rage, and danger approche, be thou (O Lord) a rocke of saluation, and a tower of defence vnto them. Breake the enemies weapons: As smoke vanisheth, so let their enemies be scattered, and such as hate them, flie before them. Thou seest (O Lord) the malice of our aduersaries, howe for thy Name which is called on ouer vs, and for the trueth of thy Gospell wherein wee reioyce; they beare a tyrannous hate against vs, continually vexing and troubling vs, that faine would liue in peace. Styrre vp therefore (O Lord) thy strength, and auenge our iust quarrell: turne the sword of our enemie vpon his owne head, and cause his delight in warre to become his owne destruction: As thou hast dealt with him heretofore, so now scatter his Forces, and spoile his mighty Ships, in which he trusteth. So shall we the people of thine inheritance, giue praise vnto thy Name, and for thy great mercy giue thankes vnto thee in the great Congregation: yea, the World shall know, and the Nations shall vnderstand to the praise of thy glory, that thou alone defendest them that trust in thee, and giuest victorie vnto Princes. Heare vs (O Lord our strength) in these our prayers for Jesus Christ his sake. Amen.

O almighty GOD, which onely doest great wonders, shewe foorth (wee pray thee) at this time the power of thy might, and the glorie of thy strength, by preseruing our Armies at Sea & Land, from death and sicknesse, and all perils on the Sea, and by helping them in the day of battell, against the rage and violence of the Aduersarie. Thou seest (O Lord) that not for any worldly respects, but for the defence of this Realme, and the peace of thy Churche in it, this iourney is vndertaken, to abate & withstand the pride, and to daunt the insolencies of our enemies, who conspire and bandie themselues against vs, breathing out wrath and vtter subuersion. Arise therefore wee pray thee (O Lord of Hostes) vnto our helpe, & let our enemies feele that thou still defendest our iust cause, and in the day of battell doest fight for vs. Not in our owne sword, nor in the arme of our owne flesh, doe we put our trust, but our trust is in the multitude of thy mercies, & in the strength of thy mightie Arme, who art God alone. Blesse therfore the Chieftaines & Leaders of our bands, with the spririt of wisedome, counsell, and magnanimitie, and the Souldiers with courage and fortitude, to stand vndaunted, & without feare in the day of battell. But as for their enemies, and such as come out against them, cast a feare & astonishment vpon them, that they may fal, and couer their faces with shame & confusion. That all the worlde may knowe, that thou (O God) resistest the proude and wicked men, and that thou auengest the cause of such, as put their trust in thee. Heare vs, O God of Hostes, euen for Christ his sake our only Sauiour and Redeemer. Amen.

O God most glorious, the shielde of al that trust in thee, who alone doest sende Peace to thy people, and causest Warre to cease in all the worlde, Consider the dayly troubles of thy seruants, & behold the malice of our Aduersaries, who for thy Names sake, which is called on ouer vs, and for the trueth of thy Gospel wherin we reioyce, doe conspire & band them selues against vs, breathing out wrath and vtter subuersion.

Many a time hath their wrath bene kindled, so that they would haue swallowed vs vp quicke: but by thy power their purpose hath bene frustrated, their counsels preuented, their preparations ouerthrowen, and we deliuered. Yet, O Lorde, their heart is set against vs, still to vexe & trouble vs that faine would liue in peace. But for the quiet of thy Church, and that thine enemies may knowe thee to be a God of mercy, cause them to returne at last, and not any longer to hate those whome thou hast loued: Make them to see that their plotts & designements are against thee, who for vs fightest against them, drowning their ships, & casting downe their strong holdes in which they doe trust: that thy Name may be glorified in the day of their conuersion. But if they shall still harden their hearts, and will not vnderstand either our defence, or their owne calamitie to come of thee: Make voyde their deuises, disclose their counsels, discouer their secret complots, that in the snare which they haue layd for vs, their owne feete may be taken. Finally, O Lord, whensoeuer they prepare them selues to battaile, take the defence of our iust cause into thine hand: Breake their Nauies, disperse their Armies, and cast vpon them a feare and astonishment, that they may tremble at thy presence, and flye before they be pursued: Graunt this O Lord our strength euen for Christ his sake. Amen.

O eternall God, Lord of the whole Worlde, and guide of Sea and Land, who by thy mightie power sortest to what effect thou wilt, the Councels and actions of all men: gratiously vouchsafe to blesse & order vnto happy issue, the late begunne worke of our gratious Soueraigne, in the hand of her Nobles and men of warre, nowe sent out by Seas, to withstande the Enemies of her life, her people, and thy Church. As Guide and Generall of the iourney, let it please thee (mightie Lorde of Hostes) to goe in and out before them, with best fore-windes and streightest course to speede and prosper them in the way. And when thou hast brought them to the appointed place, in a pillar of fire giue light to direct their steps, and in a pillar of a Cloude defend them. Put vpon them thy spirit of Counsell and fortitude, & vnder the banner of thy power and protection, let the worke be effected. Courage and imbolden them in the day of conflict, to stand vndaunted & without feare. Make way and opportunitie for them to attempt with aduantage, and for thy Names sake graunt (O glorious God) to their puissant attempts happy successe in battell, to their battell a ioyfull victorie, and to their victorie a safe and triumphant returne. So will we the people of thine inheritance, which nowe pray for the blessing of thy grace vpon them, praise thy Name for euer, & together with them ascribe both cause and glory of the worke, not to our owne strength, but vnto thy power, who alone giuest victory in the day of battell: and for thy great mercies will giue thankes vnto thee in the midst of the Congregation. Heare vs, O Father, euen for Christ his sake. Amen.

1598–E   Thanksgiving services for the plots against Elizabeth I and her realm

[November?] 1598 (England and Wales)

In 1598, Edward Squire, a scrivener who had worked in the royal stables since 1593, was arrested and tried for plotting to poison Queen Elizabeth and the earl of Essex, the former by poisoning her saddle. He was hung, drawn and quartered at Tyburn on

23 November. No orders for the occasion exist, though the plot fitted into an existing matrix of alleged catholic conspiracy that had prompted earlier public prayers and thanksgivings, notably 1585–E2, 1586–E2 and 1594–E. The form drew on 1594–E, copying the extended 'Admonition to the Reader' from the later edition (STC 16525.7), with a new paragraph on Squire and providing five prayers (some based on those from 1594) and a selection of psalms to be inserted into the BCP service.

Order: none found.

Form of prayer: *An order for prayer and thanksgiuing (necessary to bee vsed in these dangerous times) for the safetie and preseruation of her maiestie and this realme. Set foorth by authoritie anno 1594. And reuewed [sic] with some alterations vpon the present occasion* ([32] pp.; STC 16529)* [also in Clay, pp. 679–88].

Additional sources: *APC*, XXIX, 506; William Camden, *The history of the most renowned and victorious Princess Elizabeth* (4th edn, 1688; Wing C363), pp. 561–2; Clay, p. 473.

FORM OF PRAYER

An admonition to the Reader

[As 1594–E until the end of para. 2 where it follows the text of STC 16525.7 until] swalowed vs all vp? And those vnnaturall and disloyall defections in *Ireland*, which turned eftsoones into violent commotions, and in the ende brast out into open rebellion, and that cruell bloodshed wherewith that countrey is now so sorely afflicted and gored, arose they not from the irreption of those vndermining vermine the *Priests & Iesuites* couertly sent in, first alienating the minds of true subiects from their *Prince*, and the faith of sound professors from religion, and then inciting and perswading them to this open hostilitie and crueltie? *[As STC 16525.7*: Yea, and in all those … most dishonourable intended executions.*]*

Bvt that which passeth the rest & may be an effectuall motiue to worke in all Christian hearts, a sounder deuotion of thankfulnesse to our God, & a greater detestation of that blood-sucking *Romish Antichrist*, with his whole swarme of shauelings, was that dreadfull[240] attempt of *Squire*, being appointed not onely quite to extinguish one of the bright starres of our Nobilitie, the Erle of *Essex*, euen in the time of that his great imploiment for the Realme and State; but withall, which we her true subiects doe tremble at to remember, vtterly to quench the light of *Israel*, & by poison to make away our *Soueraign Prince*, both which, he to his power, executed aswel on her Maiesties Saddle, as the Erle his Chaire, by a confection so strong, that the very smell thereof did presently strike dead a Dog, vpon which he first had tried it. To which horrible practise, the sayd *Squire* in his voluntarie confession, without any torture at all, professed that he was first incited, and afterward at seuerall times perswaded, and appearing somewhat backward, at last encouraged by one *Walpoole* a cursed *Iebusite* (*Iesuite* I should say) both by a blasphemous application or rather detortion of that excellent Scripture, *Vnum necessarium*: One thing is necessarie, as if our Sauiour by that *One*, had ment the treasonable slaughter of his *Holy ones*: as also by a promise of a large Fee from D. *Bagshaw* the Popes *Iudas* or pursebearer as it seemeth, and withall the hope of eternall merite from God, as if with such bloody sacrifices of Christian princes, God were promerited, to vse their owne worde,[241] *Heb.13.16.* and in the end armed with the confection it selfe from *Walpoole* to effect

240   In margin: 'Octob. Anno 1598.'
241   In margin: 'Rhem.testa.'

it throughly, and adiured by receiuing the Sacrament, to performe it secretly. These and many other complots wee see how desperately they haue bene attempted, yet (thanked be God) are not atchieued: how perillously plotted, but are not perfected: how secretly deuised, yet most happily hitherto discouered, and this last attempt most strangely reuealed, their owne consciences, like the *Midianites*[242] swordes, mutually disbowelling their owne secret conspiracies. For *Walpoole* hauing receiued intelligence that *Squire* being in the Erles companie, had fit opportunitie to execute it, yet the purpose not effected; in an affrighted mind fearing that *Squire* had of himselfe reuealed it, and yet with a mischieuous deuise more diuelishly to acte it, addressed ouer one *Stanly* and others, to detect the plot and designment of *Squire*, by which maske of Discouerie an easier entrie being made for the sayd *Stanly* into the Erles affection and companie, hee might more safely and with lesse suspicion execute and effect the intended villanie. So that it may aptly bee verified, that her Maiesties life hath all this while bene sustained *in manu altissimi*, and that vnder the shadow of his wings she hath not miscaried:[243] & that the sacred oile wherewith he hath annointed her royall maiestie, is a soueraigne Antidote and preseruatiue against all the venemous infections, or empoisoning confections, whether *Romish* or *Spanish*.

All which whosoeuer hee bee that will attentiuely weigh and consider *[as 1594–E: and can not see … greater damnation.]* Let euery of vs therefore who haue good will to *Sion*, turne from our wicked wayes *[as 1594–E: and from the euil … Which]* our bounden duetie that it may the more frequently and fruitfully be performed of vs; it hath bene thought meete to publish this forme of prayer for the continuance of Gods mercies towards vs, and of thanksgiuing for his vnspeakable goodnesse in detecting so many conspiracies, and auerting so great mischiefes intended against vs. Which duetie of praying and thanksgiuing there is no doubt, but euery true hearted *English man* and faithfull *Subiect*, will both priuately and publikely from the bottome of his heart performe.

[Ps. 20, 21, 27, 31, 33, 91]

Prayers for the preseruation of the Queenes Maiestie.

[As 1594–E: Almightie and euerlasting God, … who addresse themselues to all wickednes,*]* and at this time especially, wherein her innocent life was not onely attempted, but had it not bene thy mercifull power to preuent it, much indangered by wretched traitors appointed to that purpose, who had performed as much as in them lay their wicked designements of impoisoning her sacred Maiestie, which notwithstanding it pleased thee most strangely to defeat, causing the authors thereof to be their owne betrayers, and killing the force of that strong confection prouided for her and applied. And what are we, that thou shouldest thus respect vs? or what may wee doe to requite these thy benefits, but still most humbly and from the bottome of our hearts pray and beseech thee in Christ Jesu *[as 1594–E: to continue … and against the]* truth of thine Holy word here taught & professed: so that the whole world and all posterity may see and know how mightily with thy fatherly care and prouidence thou watchest ouer and defendest those which put their trust in thee, and that we whom thou vouchsafest these thy fauours more then ordinary, may the

---

242 In margin: 'Iudg.7.22.'
243 This sentence copies that in the admonition in STC 16525.7 (see Clay, p. 659)

more deuoutly giue thanks vnto thee, and here-after more carefully labour to serue and please thee in newnesse of life and vprightnesse of heart. Grant this (O most louing and mercifull father) for thy deare sonnes sake Jesus Christ our Lord and onely Sauior. Amen.

Another.

O almighty and eternall God, Creator and gouernour of the whole world, vnto whom all power belongeth ouer all creatures both in heauen and earth, and by whom alone it is, that not onely all Kings and Princes do rule and gouerne the people committed to their charge, but are likewise by thy diuine prouidence and mighty protection defended and deliuered euen in the midst *[as 1594–E:* of all their perilles … most happy deliuery of*]* her Maiesties most royall person from those desperate treasons which were most wickedly inuented *[as 1594–E:* and cruelly attempted … no counsell, no wisedome,*]* no policy against the Lord. Let them fall into the ditch which they haue digged for others, and be taken in their owne nets: but let her Maiesty (O Lord) euer escape them, that al the world may see how deare and precious in thy sight the life of this thine anointed is, who doeth not so much as imagine this euill against them that thus continually thirst after her blood, and so behold her with thine eye of pity and compassion, dayly with thy mighty power and stretched out arme so saue and deliuer her from all her enemies, preserue and keepe her as the apple of thine owne eie, & graunt vnto her (O most mercifull father) a long, prosperous, and happy reigne ouer vs, and so prolong her dayes as the dayes of heauen heere vpon earth, that she may bee an olde mother in Israel, and see her desire vpon al thine & her enemies, though in number neuer so many, or in power neuer so mighty. And finally, after this life, giue vnto her euerlasting life, through Jesus Christ thine only sonne, & our onely sauior.

Another.

O most gracious God and our most louing and mercifull Father *[as 1594–E:* which hast … the bottoms &*]* foundations of the deepe: that though our foes haue taken wicked counsels together, saying, None shalbe able to espie it: yet thou hast opened *[as 1594–E:* them, and brought them … to thee,*]* O thou holy one of Israel. Thou (O Lord) hast preserued her honor from the ignominy *[as 1594–E:* her life … Onely, O Lord,*]* forsake vs not in this time of our age, but giue courage and constancie to our Soueraigne to perseuere in perils *[as 1594–E:* prudence, and wisedome … blessinges in Christ, that*]* shee may still blesse thee. Detect and reueale still the foundations and buildings of all treasons and conspiracies both at home and abroad, and heerein (O Lord) either conuert the wicked hearts and secret conceits from their wicked imaginations, or confound their deuices, and make them as the vntimely fruit that they neuer see the Sunne. Heare Lord, and saue vs, O King of heauen *[as 1594–E:* when wee call vpon thee … Amen*]*

Another.

Most gracious God, which by thy worde appoyntedst man to rule thy other creatures, but in wisdome hast lifted vp Kings and Princes to commaund and rule men in their seuerall places: We the people of thy choyse, and the subiects of this land, heartily acknowledge thy especiall prouidence in annoynting ouer vs so gracious a Princesse, so carefull of thy glory, so religious in thy feare, so tender of our good, and yet so maligned and shot at by the enemies of thy Gospel, both forreine professed rebels, and homeborne vnloyal and discontented runnagates, as were not thy mercy her shielde of defence, and thy power the sword of her reuenge, long since they had brought her life to the graue, and laid our honour in the dust: Of late especially hauing prepared and applied very neare the sacred body of her royall Maiestie a most deadly poyson, the purpose strangely thou didst reueale, and the practise mightily thou didst defeate: For which exceeding kindnesse, most louing Father, wee on our knees, and from our hearts doe giue thee thanks, and desire the assistance of thy grace for the amendment of our liues, and the repentance of our sinnes, which are more deadly then any poyson to infect vs, and more strong then any foe to ouerthrowe vs, and the only motiues of thy wrath against vs, which if thou canst not but execute vpon vs, our crying sinnes so calling for thy vengeance, yet gracious Lorde, enter not so farre in iust reuenge as to quench the light of our land, our most Soueraigne Queene, lest the enemies of thy Gospell, her prosperitie, and our welfare take occasion thereby to triumph and say that thou hast forsaken vs, but rather, wee humbly beseech thee prosper her dayes and prolng her life, and renew her yeeres to the aduancement of thy glory, the amazement of the foe, and the establishing of our peace by Jesus Christ thy onely Sonne and our onely Sauiour. To whom, &c.

Another.

Eternal God which createdst all men after thy likenesse, and hast aduanced Kings more like thy selfe in places of gouernment, and to that end hast both anoynted them with thy *Holy oyle* aboue others, and also layde a curse vpon them which touch thine anoynted: Wee render vnto thee, in all dutifull seruice most heartie thankes for thy continuall protection of our sacred Prince *Queene Elizabeth*, whom as thou hast many times heretofore preserued from dangerous attempts plotted against her by malignant wretches, either frustrating their counsels, or preuenting their execu-tions, or reueiling their intentions: so of late most strangely thou hast kept her from a danger not onely intended, but practised; from a poyson not onely confected, but applyed very neere her; wherein as thou didst manifest thy power in quelling the *Aspe* and the *Basiliske*, qualifying the deadly force of that dreadfull compound, so didst thou shewe thy mercie vnto vs of this land, who, if the *Sheepeheard* of Israel had bene stroken, might bee either confusedly scattered, or cruelly massacred. Good Lord strike a sence of this thy powerful mercy into our hearts, from thence to fetch a sorrowfull sighing for our sinnes, an earnest desire of amendment, and most intire vnfained thanks to thee our gracious Preseruer: But those priests of *Baal*, the hellish Chapleines of *Antechrist*, accursed runnagates from their God and Prince, the bellowes and fuell of these flagrant conspiracies, confound them in thy wrath, since thy Grace wil not conuert them, and that which thy power cannot worke on them in defeating their enterprises, let thy fury performe in reuenge vpon their persons, the rather, O Lord, because that most blasphemously they abuse thy holy Word for the furtherance of their deuilish complots: But let our gratious Queene still raigne and rule in despight of *Rome*, and *Rhemes*, and *Spaine* and Hell, Preserue her gouern-ment ouer vs, vnite our hearts to her, continue both her and our thankefulnesse to thy selfe, which blessest vs dayly with so many benefites. Heare vs O Lord for Jesus Christ his sake.

1599–E   Prayer for the military campaign in Ireland

[After Monday 2 April] 1599 (England and Wales)

Appointed lord lieutenant of Ireland on 30 December 1598, Essex left London on 27 March 1599 to quash the earl of Tyrone's rebellion in Ulster. Preparations for a form of prayer began a few days later when Whitgift sent a text to Cecil for the queen's approval. There was at least one 'unofficial' prayer produced: John Norden's *A prayer for the prosperous proceedings and good successe of the earle of Essex.* In addition, the 'stranger' (i.e. foreign) churches in London may also have organized prayers in support of the earl's campaign. Lacking sufficient resources to attack Tyrone directly, Essex led an initially successful campaign in Munster to secure southern Ireland from Spanish invasion. He took Cahir Castle on 30 May and relieved Askeaton in early June. However, spiralling costs, dwindling resources, and Essex's physical exhaustion brought the campaign to a halt and he secretly negotiated a peace with Tyrone (7 September) before returning, without permission, to England.

Order: none found.
Form of prayer: *A prayer for the good successe of her maiesties forces in Ireland* (1 p.; STC 16530)*.
Additional sources: Whitgift to Cecil, 2 Apr. 1599, HH, CP 69/43; Clay, pp. 473–4; John Norden, *A prayer for the prosperovs proceedings and good successe of the earle of Essex and his companies, in their present expedition to Irelande against Tyrone and his adherents, rebels there* (1599; STC 18632), reprinted in *Two forms of prayer of the time of Queen Elizabeth*, ed. Chaplin, pp. 3–8.

FORM OF PRAYER

Almightie God and most mercifull Father, which by thine holy Worde declarest thy selfe to be the first ordeiner and continuall vpholder of all Princely power and right, and by thy terrible iudgements against *Core*, *Dathan*, and *Abiram*, in opening the earth to swallow vp them and theirs, And with like vengeance powred vpon *Absalon*, *Achitophel*, *Adoniah*, and *Sheba*, diddest manifest to the whole world, how much thou hatest all resistance and rebellion against thy Diuine ordinance: Vouchsafe (wee humbly beseech thee) to strengthen and protect the Forces of thine anoynted our Queene and Souereigne, sent out to suppresse these wicked and vnnaturall Rebels. Be thou to our Armies a Captaine, Leader, and Defender. Let thine holy Angels pitch their Tents round about to guard them, and giue them victorie against all such as rise vp to withstand them. Let not our sinnes (O Lord) be an hinderance to thine accustomed mercies towards vs, neither punish our misdeeds by strengthening the handes of such, as despise thy Trueth, and haue wickedly cast off the rightfull yoke of their due allegiance: That so thy blessed Handmayde our dread Soueraigne, may alwayes reioyce in thy Saluation, And we her loyall Subiects still haue cause to magnifie thy glorious Name, and to offer to thee with ioy the sacrifices of praise and thankes-giuing in the middest of the great Congregation. Graunt this (O most righteous Lord God of Hosts) we beseech thee, through Jesus Christ our onely Sauiour and Redeemer. Amen.

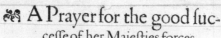

❧ A Prayer for the good suc-
cesse of her Maiesties forces
in Ireland.

A Lmightie God and most mercifull Father, which by thine holy worde declarest thy selfe to be the first ordeiner and continuall vpholder of all Princely power and right, and by thy terrible iudgements against Core, Dathan, and Abiram, in opening the earth to swallow vp them and theirs, And with like vengeance powred vpon Absalon, Achitophel, Adoniah, and Sheba, diddest manifest to the whole world, how much thou hatest all resistance and rebellion against thy Diuine ordinance : Vouchsafe (wee humbly beseech thee) to strengthen and protect the Forces of thine anoynted our Queene and Souereigne, sent out to suppresse these wicked and vnnaturall Rebels. Be thou to our Armies a Captaine, Leader, and Defender. Let thine holy Angels pitch their Tents round about to guard them, and giue them victorie against all such as rise vp to withstand them. Let not our sinnes (O Lord) be an hinderance to thine accustomed mercies towards vs, neither punish our misdeeds by strengthening the handes of such, as despise thy Trueth, and haue wickedly cast off the rightfull yoke of their due allegiance : That so thy blessed Handmayde our dread Souereigne, may alwayes reioyce in thy Saluation, And we her loyall Subiects still haue cause to magnifie thy glorious Name, and to offer to thee with ioy the sacrifices of praise and thankes-giuing in the middest of the great Congregation. Graunt this (O most righteous Lord God of Hosts) we beseech thee, through Iesus Christ our onely Sauiour and Redeemer. Amen.

❧ Imprinted at London by the Deputies of *Christopher Barker*, Printer to the Queenes most excellent Maiestie.

ANNO 1599.

6 For some occasions of special worship from 1596, individual or a small number of prayers were ordered to be read out during the usual services from the Book of Common Prayer. These prayers were printed and distributed as single folio sheets, as in this example for 1599–E. *A prayer for the good successe of her maiesties forces in Ireland* (1599; STC 16530), Folger Shakespeare Library, MS 362, fo. 450r.

1600–S   Thanksgiving days for the discovery of the Gowrie plot

Tuesday 30 September and Sunday 5 October 1600 (Scotland)

For an account of the Gowrie conspiracy, see the section on Anniversary commemorations in volume 3. A report of the events at Perth reached Edinburgh on the morning of 6 August. The privy council met, informed the burgh's ministers of the conspiracy, asking them to give public thanks for the king's delivery, and appointed bonfires and other celebrations that evening in Edinburgh, the Canongate and Leith. Five of Edinburgh's ministers initially refused to believe the reports of the plot, and failed to conduct thanksgiving worship. At the king's return to Edinburgh on 11 August, however, two other ministers made amends by preaching sermons of thanksgiving. On 21 August, the king and council ordered this national thanksgiving. James Melvill's account indicates that the provincial synods met as requested by the privy council order, and drew up suitable forms of worship for the occasion. No form has been traced, however.

Order: privy council order, 21 Aug. 1600, *RPC*, 1st ser., VI, 156–7.
Form of service: none found.
Additional sources: *RPC*, 1st ser., VI, 142–4, 147–9, 155–6, 158–9, 161–2; Melvill, pp. 485–8; Calderwood, VI, 45–6, 50–9; Spottiswoode, III, 89–90; George Nicolson to Sir Robert Cecil, 21 Aug. 1600, SP52/66/69.

ORDER

Order of the Scottish privy council: 21 August 1600

Forsameikill as the Kingis Majestie, with advyse of the commissioneris of the Generall Assemblie, hes appointit ane solemne and publict thanksgeving to be maid and keipit in all the kirkis of this realme, upoun the last Tuysday of September nixt and the Sabbothe nixt and immediatlie following thairefter, for his Hienes miraculous preservatioun and delyverie frome the treasonable and cruell invasioun of his Majesteis lyfe, attempted at Sanct Johnestoun be umquhill Johne, Erle of Gowrie, Maister Alexander Ruthven, his brother, and thair associattis: lyk as his Majestie and the saidis commissioneris hes fund guid and concludit that the haill Provinciall Assembleis salbe haldin in the thrid Tuysday of September, to the effect that the maist convenient forme for the honour of God and steiring up of his Majesteis subjectis to thankfulnes in everie province may be condiscendit upoun and keipit with uniformitie: thairfoir ordanis letteris to be direct to mak publict intimatioun heirof be oppin proclamatioun at the mercat croces of the heid burrowis of this realme, quhairthrow nane pretend ignorance, and to command and chairge the haill ministeris to keip the saidis Assembleis cairfullie, and all his Majesteis subjectis to convein the saidis dayis and keip the ordour to be prescryvit, as thay will ansuer to his Majestie upoun the contrarie, and will gif his Hienes a testimonie of thair trew affectioun to his Majestie and the quyetnes of his estait.

1601–E   Thanksgiving prayers for the failure of the earl of Essex's rebellion

[After Sunday 8 February] 1601 (England and Wales)

The earl of Essex fell from Elizabeth's favour after his precipitate return from Ireland in September 1599. This triggered a mental collapse which exacerbated the earl's existing fears that 'enemies' plotted against him. On 8 February 1601, supported by a group of disaffected nobles and gentry, he marched on the City of London. When prevented from entering the city, he returned to Essex House on the Strand and eventually surrendered at nine o'clock in the evening. No orders exist for this occasion. The form adopted recent practice, comprising several prayers which were probably inserted into the BCP service at the end of the litany. However, unlike earlier thanksgivings after the discovery of catholic plots (e.g. 1594–E, 1598–E), there was no lengthy 'Admonition' contextualizing the plot. This may have been because it was more difficult (and impolitic) to explain why one of the queen's closest advisors, who was popular with the London public, had rebelled. Essex was tried for treason on 19 February and executed at the Tower on 25 February; accounts of his death circulated widely. Sermons on the rebellion were preached at Paul's Cross on 15 February (John Hayward, St Mary Woolchurch), 22 February (unknown but from notes by Bancroft) and 1 March (William Barlow, St Dunstan-in-the-East and royal chaplain).

Order: none found.
Form of prayer: *Certaine prayers fit for the time. Set foorth by authoritie* (12 pp.; STC 16531) * [also in Clay, pp. 689–95].
Additional sources: Strype, *Annals*, IV, 495–7; Strype, *Whitgift*, II, 441; MacLure, pp. 75–6; Richard Bancroft to Sir Robert Cecil, 15 and 21 Feb. 1601, HH, CP76/75 and 180/27); Clay, p. 474.
Sermons: Hayward, 15 Feb., Paul's Cross, London (MacLure, p. 75; HH, CP76/75); unknown, 22 Feb., Paul's Cross, London (MacLure, p. 75; HH, CP180/27); Barlow, 1 Mar., Paul's Cross, London (STC 1454; MacLure, pp. 75–6).

FORM OF PRAYER

Almightie God and most merciful Father, who of thy inifinite goodnesse towards all Countreys and Nations, for the auoiding of confusion, hast appointed Kings and Princes as thine Angels and Lieutenants, & the Seales of thy similitude, full of wisedome and beauty, to rule and gouerne in thy Name the people on the earth committed to their charge: commanding all their Subiects to honour, and in no sort to resist them, but to obey them in thy feare, euen for conscience sake: and likewise to offer vnto thee for them, all Supplications, Prayers, Intercessions, and Thanksgiuing, as being the Lights, the preseruation, and the meanes vnder thy Diuine Maiestie of the Peace, the Health, Prosperitie and Glory of all their Subiectes and Kingdoms: We thy humble seruantes, bowing downe the knees of our heartes, & prostrating our selues before thy glorious Throne, doe render vnto thee all Praise, Power, Honour, and Thanksgiuing for thy most gracious fauour and mercifull deliuerance of our most dread *Souereigne Lady* (thy Vicegerent in her Dominions) QVEENE ELIZABETH, as euer heeretofore, so at this time, from the traitourous attempts and desperate designments of sundry most vnkinde and disloyall wicked persons: who forgetting their duety both towards thee (O Lord) and towards thine Anointed, haue in the height of their Pride, after a popular sort with diuers false pretences, and many slanderous calumniations, sought in open Rebellion, not only the destruction and extinguishing of thy Seruant, our Comfort, our Health, and our Glory: but the vtter ruine also and tragicall ouerthrow of this our natiue Countrey her Maiesties (through thy manifolde mercies) so worthy, so happy and so renowmed a Kingdome. This thy most mighty and Fatherly protection (O Lord God of hosts) we intirely beseech thee, with penitent hearts for our former offences, to continue ouer vs from age to age, by defending still the sacred person of our *Souereigne Lady*, from all such dangerous designments; her Kingdomes and Countreys, from all treacherous practises; and vs her Subiects, from the deceitfull baits and crafty allurements of all popular and ambitious dissembling *Absalons*: that so our heartes being still replenished with the ioy of thy Saluation, we may dayly present in all thankfulnesse before thy Fatherly goodnesse, the Freewill offerings and Sacrifices of our lips, always praising and magnifying thy blessed Name through Jesus Christ our Lorde: to whom with thee & the holy Ghost, three persons and one God, bee all honour and glory from this time foorth for euermore.

O eternall and Gratious GOD, Father of peace and Protector of gouernment; who with a special eye of prouidence watchest ouer the heads of Princes, vpon whose safetie the liues of many thousands doe depend: We thy humble Seruants doe bowe downe the knees of our hearts, and powre foorth our soules in thankfulnesse before thee, for thy so gratious and mercifull deliuerance of our dread Soueraigne thy Handmayde, from the Traiterous intents and desperate Conspiracies of disloyall Subiects, who haue risen vp against thine Anoynted, and like vnnaturall Children haue rebelled against the Mother of their owne liues, that tooke them vp from their Cradles, and cherished them in her owne bosome, and laded them with Honours and preferments; to the great dishonour of thy Name, to the slander of thy Gospel, to the danger of confusion to their owne natiue Countrey. But thou, O Lord of Hostes, our deliuerer, diddest ouerthrowe them in their owne imaginations, and by thy iudgements hast declared them enemies to thine owne Maiestie; Thou diddest put thy obedience into the heartes of thy faithfull people, and without shedding of their innocent blood, diddest miraculously beate downe the Swords of all that rose vp against thine ordinance. For which thy vnspeakable goodnesse towards vs, vouchsafe, we beseech thee, to receiue the freewill offrings of our hearts, and calues of our lippes in prayses to thy glorious Name; Who notwithstanding our manifolde sinnes and transgressions, hast not yet forgotten to be Gracious, but heapest mercie vpon mercie, and causest blessing to followe and ouertake blessing, as the waues of the Sea. To thee therefore our Sauiour and Defender, our Watch-tower and our Rocke, we wil sing the Songs of thankefulnesse, and call upon thy blessed Name for euermore; Beseeching thee so to continue the fauour of thy countenance towards thine owne anoynted Magistrate, and vs her faithfull people; that our Light may neuer goe out, and our Song may neuer cease in this land: but that thy glorious acts may sound in euery Congregation, euer praise & honour and glory to thee, that sittest vpon the Throne for euer and euer. Amen.

Most mightie God, which art the authour of order, and the hater of confusion, to which purpose thou hast generally shewed thy wisedome in aduancing Princes to rule, whom it hath pleased thee to dignifie with thine owne name, and more particularly in thy exceeding loue to this our lande, hast placed ouer vs a most renowned Queene, religious to thee her God, kinde to her Subiectes, mercifull euen to her enemies: As wee magnifie thy glorious name, for that vnspeakable benefit, so at this time principally we yeeld thee in all humble duetie most heartie thankes for this thy late protection, both of her sacred Royall person, and of her faithful people from this mutinie thus rebelliously complotted, this rebellion so outragiously attempted, this outrage so dangerously continued, by defeating their popular hopes vpon which they trusted, by vniting true subiects hearts vnto their Prince annointed, by appeasing this suddaine vproare without much bloodshed, and in the ende by quelling the enraged spirits of the chiefe Conspirators: who, if either their Soueraignes countenance, and continuance of her gracious fauours, or her magnificence in their extraordinarie aduancements, or her clemencie in pardoning their manifold contempts, could haue moderated them: would neuer haue shewed themselues either causelessly discontented, or discontentedly disobedient. Lord, how often hath thy power and mercie beene manifested in reuealing Conspiracies deuised, in preuenting treasons intended, in terrifying hearts outraged, in scattering forces assembled? All which we ascribe not to any merit of ours, whose sinnes doe daily prouoke thy fauour to wrath, but onely to that loue which thou bearest vnto thy chosen Annoynted, and to thy Gospel professed. The prosperous continuance of them both we humbly craue of thee most gratious God, with assistance of thy grace to make vs more thankefull then heretofore we haue beene, that walking worthy of our vocation, and loyally to her Maiestie, we may performe that due obedience to them both, which in thy sight is better then sacrifice, and adorneth those which professe the name of thy sonne Christ Jesus, to whom with thee and the holy Spirite, wee acknowledge all praise and glory for this late & all other thy mercies extended now and for euermore. Amen.

The more thy prouidence (O Lorde) doeth euen visibly from heauen still manifest itselfe, by so many, so strange deliuerances of thine Annointed our Queene, & in Her, of vs al: the more & the more often are we bound to haue our hearts bent to the considering, & our mouthes opened to the magnifying of thine vncessant goodnes towards vs, to no people of the earth euer the like. The more are we bound, and as we are bound, (as is our duetie) so is it our desire thus to doe: and though we haue no thankefulnesse, wherewith to come neere it, yet it is our desire in some sort to seeke to expresse it: and the more our desires, the lesse our deserts haue bene, euer to see such and so many mercies, so often shewed vpon vs. For what are we Lord? or what is there in our vnworthy profession of thy holy Trueth, that thou shouldest respect vs at all? Yet how many, how marueilous haue bene those demonstrations, which heretofore thou hast vouchsafed vs? in preseruing thy chosen seruant our Souereigne from a number of plots and practises, some forreigne, some domesticall, some deepe and secret, some sudden and violent, all of them to the hazzard of her Sacred person and life: on whose life, dependeth the life and lifes-ioy of so many thousands. And this was yet a small thing in thy sight (O Lorde:) but euen now againe, euen at this very instant, thou hast renewed thy mercie, in discouering and disappointing this late dangerous and desperate resolution. And what can wee say more vnto thee? for thou Lorde knowest thy seruants. For thy trueths sake, and according to thine abundant louing kindnesse and compassion ouer vs hast thou done all these great things. O Lorde our God, as they should, and as wee would they should: so cause these, all these thy mercies, first and last, to enter into our hearts, and keepe them for euer in the mindes and memories of this people, and prepare our heartes to bee thankefull vnto thee: And O Lord (for it is thou that hast done this) let it please thee to confirme for euer thine owne worke: and as thou hast, by thus often deliuering thine Handmaid our Queene, brought her hitherto, that shee is nowe thy First-borne, the most renowmed and ancient Prince of all that professe thy Name: so let her bee blessed for euer with thy blessing, that she may long enioy this honour. And now and euer shew thou thy marueilous louing kindenesse, that shee may long enioy it, remaining euer happie, happie in the loue and loyaltie of her people, happy in the follie and fall of her enemies, and thrise happie in the continuall comfortable experience of thy fauour, power, and care, stil vpon euery occasion thus mightily, mercifully, miraculously preseruing her, to the continuance of thy trueth still among vs, of the comfort and contentment of thy people, and of the euerlasting remembrance of thy goodnesse, and praise of thy holy Name, through Christ our Lorde. Amen.

Most holy and euerliuing God, the inestimable riches of whose mercies toward vs, we are more willing to confesse then able to comprehend, dayly and hourely drawing from that infinite Treasurie which we neuer can consume, from the deepest acknowledgement of our owne wretchednesse and highest admiration and adoration of thy glorious goodnesse, we blesse thy sacred Maiesty, & from the ground of our hearts ascribe honor to thy praiseworthy Name: that it hath pleased thee from time to time with the early and late showres of all sufficient blessings to water thine inheritance this litle Kingdome, and by infallible arguments of continuall graces to make knowen to the whole world that thou louest the Gates of *England* more then all the Habitations of our neighbour Countreys about vs. Namely thou hast dwelt in the midst of vs with the presence and protection of thy good will to keepe vs from the danger of those fires, which both abroad and at home, men of vnquiet spirits haue kindled against vs. Many mischiefs haue the vngodly deuised, which they were not able to bring to passe. The bottomlesse deepe of thy Councell hath layed open their shallow and vngrounded pollicies. Thy faithfulnesse aboue the Clouds, hath preuented their trecherous, vnfaithfull earthly conspiracies, and thy iudgements as the great mountaines haue ouerwhelmed and dasht in pieces all the power of their malice.

Why did the vngodly of late so rage, and the children of this Land imagine a vaine thing? The Princes banded themselues, and assembled together against thee (O Lord) & against thine Anointed, saying amongst themselues, Let vs breake their bonds, and cast their cords from vs. But thou that sittest in heauen hast laughed them to scorne, thou hast had them all in derision, thou hast dissolued their knots, dissociated their bandings, defeated and frustrated their whole designments. They trauelled with winde, and brought forth a whirlwinde, which hath scattered their deuices and brought a wofull recompense vpon their owne heades.

We are not worthy to intreat mercy at thy hands (wormes of the earth) of thee who art the Former of our spirits, & Creator of all things, transgressers from our mothers bellies, and laden with sinne, of thee that hast pure eyes. The sacrifices we offer vp either of our praises or prayers, proceed but from hearts of ashes and polluted lips: but vnder the warrant and wings of thy deare Sonne, in whom thou art pleased, and we hid, hoping that the sacrifice of his most precious bloud shall answere all our defects, and couer our infirmities, we powre out our whole soules before thee, humbly beseeching thee for thy Christs sake, that the line of thy mercies and the line of her life may be lengthened and run forth together: that thou wilt always quiet her Realmes both from forreigne inuasions and intestine Rebellions, secure her person, keepe her people in allegiance to her Highnes, and amitie amongst themselues, and meet wth the purposes and practises of all ambitious *Absalons*, blasphemous *Shemeis*, seditious *Sheuas*, traiterous *Achitophels*, rebellious *Cores*, which striue against thine ordinance in her Heroicall hands.

Finally, O our strongest Redeemer, make vs mindfull of all thy forepassed benefits, thankfull for the present, fearefull of nothing but of thy plagues, carefull of nothing but of thy seruice and worship, that with hands & hearts euerlastingly lift vp to heauen, Prince and people knit together as it were in one soule, we may glorifie thy holy Name, and seeke the aduancement of thy kingdome through our blessed Redeemer and Intercessor, Jesus Christ.

1601–S   Fast days against general sinfulness

Sunday 21 June – Sunday 28 June 1601 (Scotland)

The general assembly of May 1601, which met with the king present, discussed several causes of 'defection' from religious purity, including the contempt of the gospel, the continued influence of catholics at court and in the country, conversions to catholicism, negligent ministers, vacant churches, decaying schools. Various remedies were proposed, including this fast, which was evidently presented as a response to general sinfulness rather than specific faults.

Order: by the general assembly, 14 May 1601, described in Calderwood, VI, 115–16.
Additional sources: *BUK*, III, 965–6; Spottiswoode, III, 96–7.

DESCRIPTION OF ORDER

Order by the general assembly: 14 May 1601
The Generall Assemblie having entered in consideratioun of the causes of the said great and fearefull defectioun of all estats of persons within this land, from the true and sincere professioun of the gospell presentlie sounding within the same; and having found the principall causes of this fearefull change to be, no doubt, the just wrathe of God kindled against the whole land, for the unreverent estimatioun of the gospell, and for the sinnes of all estats, and dishonouring of their professioun, and making the name of God to be blasphemed by the profane world without remorse: Which horrible judgements have fallin in everie estat, for the contemptuous hearing of the Word of God, in so farre as there is none that have worthilie esteemed the said pretious Word, according to the dignitie therof: Therefore, and for removing of the former evills and causes, and farther judgements, if they be not prevented by speedie repentance, this Assemblie has concluded and ordeanned a generall humiliatioun to be keeped solemnelie throughout the whole land, with fasting and prayer, two severall Sabboth dayes, in all congregatiouns, both in burgh and land, within this realme; and likewise in burrow touns, to be observed throughout the whole weeke, betuixt the said two Sabboths; and the causes of the said humiliatioun to be onlie the sinnes of the land, by the which the professioun of the gospell has beene dishonoured, and the wrathe of God provoked. Which generall humiliatioun is ordeanned to be upon the two last Sabboth dayes of Junie nixtocum.

1602–E   Thanksgiving prayers for victory at the battle of Kinsale

January 1602 (England and Wales)

On 24 December 1601, Charles Blount, Lord Mountjoy (Essex's replacement in Ireland) routed Tyrone's forces outside Kinsale as they attempted to join up with troops sent by Philip III to assist the Irish rebels, and now occupying the town. On 24 January 1602, Richard Bancroft, bishop of London, organized preachers to deliver a 'narration' and 'other points' from the London pulpits. The following day and under royal authority, Whitgift ordered an unidentified bishop to arrange public prayers for the victory and for further success, and sermons to 'notifie to their parishioners theise admirable workes of God and his p[ro]ceedinge great mercies multiplied vppon vs'. No form of prayer survives. Though Tyrone did not surrender until 1603, Mountjoy's victory effectually ended the Irish wars.

Order: Whitgift to [a bishop?], 25 Jan. 1601/1602 [i.e. 1602], LPL, Whitgift Register, III, fos. 138r–v [also in *Concilia*, IV, 367].
Form of prayer: none found.
Additional sources: Bishop Richard Bancroft to Cecil, 23 Jan. 1602, HH, CP 181/93, fo. 156r; *Records of the old archdeaconry of St Albans: a calendar of papers, AD 1575 to AD 1637*, ed. H. R. Wilton Hall (St Albans and Hertfordshire Architectural and Archaeological Society, St Albans, 1908), pp. 112–13.

ORDER

Archbishop of Canterbruy to [a bishop?]: 25 January 1602
Salutem in Ch[rist]o: your Lordshipp cannot bee ignorante of the great and manifolde blessinges and benefittes which wee haue receiued from God, since it pleased him to advance hir Maiesty to this Crowne. First by directinge hir Royall hart to establishe and meinteine true religion amongest vs; then by defendinge hir sacred person ageinst many and divers secrett plottes and cruell designementes: Thirdlie by protecting this whole Realme from intended inuasions of the kinge of Spaine, to the great admiration almost of all the world, and at this tyme by frustratinge this kinge of Spaine of his intended invasion and conquest of the Kingedome of Ierland, that thereby he might make his enterance the more easy for the subduinge of this Realme. To which intente likewise he combined with the Pope, and of late sente great forces into that Kingedome to the ayde and assistance of the Rebells there, which fortified them selves in three places besides Kijnsale with resolution never to haue departed that Kingedome, till they had subdued it to there Maister the Kinge of Spaine: Neverthelesse thoroughe Godes great goodnes and mercies they are subdued and forced to become intercessors that they might departe, and leave that enterprise, and haue surrendred and yeilded vpp all the places wherein before they had fortified them selues: Moreover the forces of both the Traytors Tyrone and Odonell are vanquished, Tyrone into the North parte of Ierland, and Odonell into Spaine; For which great goodnesse of the Almightie God in frustratinge of theise and divers other plottes and enterprises ageinst hir Maiestie and hir Kingedome, and speciallie ageinst the true religion, which wee professe, devised as well by the late Kinge of Spaine, as by this his sonne that nowe reigneth, who hath vowed to followe his fathers stepps, where in wee can never bee sufficiently thankefull: And therefore your Lordship shall doe well, and it is hir Maiesties pleasure to take order within your Dioces, that the preachers in there Sermons shall notifie to their parishioners theise admirable workes

of God and his exceedinge great mercies multiplied vppon vs, and moue them to render thankes vnto God for the same, and to praie for the continuance thereof …

1603–E   Services and weekly fast days during a plague epidemic

Wednesdays (fast days), Fridays and Sundays (services) [April onwards?] 1603 (England and Wales)

Queen Elizabeth died on 24 March 1603. In the following month, while the new sovereign, James VI of Scotland and now also James I of England, travelled south, plague broke out, and delayed his entry into London. Geographically, the epidemic varied in severity: cities such as London and Norwich as well as parts of Essex were particularly badly hit, whereas Exeter and parts of rural Devon were affected less, if at all. In the south-east, about a quarter of the population died and in London, attendance at the coronation on 25 July of James and his wife, Anna of Denmark, was diminished. Plague orders (first ordered in 1587) were enforced more widely than on earlier occasions, which may have contributed a pamphlet war during these months between those who believed that the plague was sent as a divine warning and those who stressed the importance of natural causes. No order for this occasion is extant. The form of prayer is based upon those for previous plague epidemics, especially that of 1563–E. In contrast to that for 1593–E, a much fuller text for the services was given. Various changes were made, chiefly the additions of four new prayers (replacing the collect of the days), a service for evening prayer, a 'short preface' and 'an exhortation for the time'. This exhortation was to be read in the place of the usual sermon or homily, and experienced preachers were expected to make their own exegeses of its main points. Non-preaching ministers were to read out the 'short preface' before reciting the exhortation. The 'order for the fast' largely followed the text as revised for 1593–E, with small verbal changes, the injunction that the one substantial meal of the day should be eaten after evening prayer, and significant additions to the closing 'admonition'. A second sermon was now specified, perhaps because a service for evening prayer was now provided. But a firmer stand was expressed against the puritan 'abuse of fasting': the arguments against excessive sermonizing were extended, and a warning was issued against those who 'factiously' arranged their own public fasts 'without consent of authority' – a precursor of canon 72 contained in the new church canons published in 1604.

Order: none found.
Form of prayer: *Certaine prayers collected out of a forme of godly meditations, set forth by his maiesties authoritie: and most necessary to be vsed at this time in the present visitation of Gods heauy hand for our manifold sinnes. Together with the order of a fast to be kept euery Wednesday during the said visitation* (32 pp.; STC 16532)*.
Additional sources: Stowe, *Abridgement of the English chronicle*, p. 445; James Balmford, *A short dialogue concerning the plagues infection* (1603; STC 1338); Thomas Lodge, *A treatise of the plague* (1603; STC 16676); Thomas Darling, *A potion for the heart-plague* (1603; STC 20132.5); Henoch Clapham, *An epistle discovrsing vpon the present pestilence* (1603; STC 5339); *Anglican canons*, ed. Bray, pp. 362–5.
Printed sermon: Nicholas Bownd, Norton (STC 3439).

FORM OF PRAYER

PREFACE

Wee be taught *[as 1563–E*: by many and sundry examples … prouoked by vs to*]* visit vs at this present with the plague and other grieuous diseases: It hath bene thought meete to excite and stirre vp all godly people within this Realm, to pray earnestly and heartily to God to forgiue vs our sinnes, and consequently to turne away his deserued wrath from vs, and to restore vs to his gracious fauour, and to our bodily health. And although it is euery Christian mans duety *[as 1563–E*: of his owne deuotion … his duetie.]* For the effectuall accomplishment whereof, it is thought meete that this order of prayer following should at this time be published, being such as may be vsed not only by the minister in the Church, but by euery man in his priuate family.

THE FORME OF PRAYERS PRESCRIBED FOR THE TIME

Let all Curats and Pastours exhort their Parishioners to endeauour themselues to come to the Church, with so many of their families as may be spared from their necessarie businesse (hauing yet a prouident respect in such assemblies to keepe the sicke from the whole in places where the Plague reigneth) and they to resort thither not only on the Sundayes and Holydayes: but also on Wednesdayes and Frydayes during the time of these present afflictions: exhorting them to behaue themselues there godly and reuerently, and with penitent hearts to pray vnto God to turne these Plagues from vs, which wee through our vnthankfulnesse and sinfull life haue deserued.[244]

MORNING PRAYER

Let the Minister beginning seruice, reade with a loude voyce one of these sentences of Scripture as they are set downe in the Communion booke. *[Joel 2; Dan. 9; Jer. 10]*

Then reade the Exhortation to Confession, and so the rest as in the Communion booke of Morning prayer vntill you come vnto the Psalme: *O come let vs sing vnto the Lord.* In place whereof reade this Psalme which hereafter followeth: *O come let vs humble our selues.*

After which Psalme, let two or three of these Psalmes bee read as they are already set downe in the Communion booke. *[9, 38, 39, 51, 86, 90, 91, 130]*

The Psalmes ended, reade one of these Chapters following for the first Lesson. *[Deut. 28; Deut. 30; 1 Kgs. 8; 2 Sam. 24; Joel 2; Jonah 3]*

Then reade, *We praise thee O God*, as in the Communion booke, is vsually after the first lesson.

For the second Lesson, reade one of these Chapters. *[Matt. 6; Matt. 8; Matt. 9; Luke 13; Luke 21]*

After the first Lesson, reade *Benedictus*, and so foorth as it followeth in the Communion booke, in the order of Seruice for Morning prayer vntill you come to the first Collect. In place whereof, reade the Prayer hereafter following which beginneth: *Almightie most iust and mercifull God.* Which ended, then reade these two Collects, that for *Peace*, and the other for *Grace*, as they follow in order in the Communion booke.

---

[244] I.e. as 1563–E, except that 'exhorting them to behaue themselues there godly and reuerently' replaces 'exhortyng them there reuerently and godly to behaue them selues'.

LITANY

Toward the end of the Letanie, and after these words: *As wee doe put our trust in thee*, Reade the prayer here newly Printed, which beginneth: *O eternall and euerliuing God, most mercifull Father, &c.* Which ended, then reade the Collects in order as they are set downe in the Communion booke. Viz. *We humbly beseech thee, &c.* The prayer for the King: the prayer for the Bishops and Curates, &c. The prayer of Chrysostome, and the blessing Viz. *The grace of our Lord Jesus Christ, &c.*

Here if the Minister bee no Preacher, let him sometimes reade the Exhortation hereunto annexed, and sometimes the Homilies, either of Prayer or of Fasting, or of repentance. And if he be a Preacher, it is very expedient that he should sometime insist vpon sundrie of the points in the said Exhortation.

EVENING PRAYER

Reade one of the sentences of Scripture before mentioned. Then reade the Confession and Absolution as at Morning prayer: Then follow the order of Euening prayer as in the Communion booke, vntill you come to the Psalmes, and then in place of the ordinarie Psalmes, Reade two or three of the Psalmes appointed for this time, which were not read in the forenoone.

For the first Lesson, reade one of the Chapters appointed before for Morning Prayer.

After the first Lesson for Magnificat, reade the Psalme which was read at Morning prayer in place of, *O come let vs sing vnto the Lord.* It beginneth: *O come let vs humble our selues, &c.*

For the second Lesson, reade one of these Chapters *[1 Cor. 10:1–15; 1 Cor. 13; 2 Cor. 9; or 1 Thess. 4]*.

Then reade the ordinarie Psalme after the second Lesson, Viz. *God be mercifull vnto vs, &c.*

Then proceede with the Beleefe, and so follow the order of the Communion booke, vntill you come to the place where the first Collect should be read. Instead whereof, reade any of the Prayers now set foorth, which were not read before at Morning prayer. Which prayer ended, reade the second ordinarie Collect at Euening prayer: Also the Prayer for the King at the end of the Letanie, Viz. *O Lord our heauenly Father, high and mightie, &c.* And lastly the ordinarie Collect at Euening prayers, Viz. *Lighten our darknesse, &c.*

A Psalme, whereof one verse its to be said of the Minister, and another by the people or Clerke.
O Come, let vs humble our selues, and fall downe before the Lord, with reuerence and feare. (Ps. 95) [95:6] *then as 1563–E, until]*
For we knowledge our faults: and our sins be euer before vs. (Ps. 51) [51:3]
Wee haue sore prouoked thine anger, O Lord, thy wrath is waxed hote, and thy heauie displeasure is sore kindled against vs. (Lam. 3) [Lam.3]
But there is mercie with thee, that thou mayest be feared: and thou art full of compassion. [?]
Thou hast in thine indignation striken vs with grieuous sickenesse, and by and by we haue fallen as leaues beaten downe with a vehement winde (Esay. 64) [Isa. 64]
[Then as 1563–E, to end of psalm]

Godly Prayers specified to be vsed at the Seruice in the Morning.

O almightie, most iust and mercifull God *[as 1563–E:* we here acknowledge ... chasten vs in thy mercie*]*. Regard not the horrour of our sinnes, but our vnfained repentance. Perfite that worke which thou hast begun in vs *[as 1563–E:* that the whole worlde ... according to*]* the seueral state of life wherunto thou Lord hast ordeined vs in godly feare and trembling before thee. And although we are vnworthy *[as 1563–E:* (O heauenlye father ... especially to*]* this our Realme, and to our most gracious King and gouernour King *Iames.* Queene *Anne,* Prince *Henrie,* and the rest of that Royall Progenie, increase the number of godly Ministers *[as 1563–E:* indue them ... Amen. (*with changes of gender*)*]*.

O Eternall and euerliuing God *[as 1563–E:* most mercifull father ... nowe partly vpon vs, by*]* plaguing vs so (with most dreadfull and deadly sicknes) whereby great multitudes of vs *[as 1563–E:* are dayly afflicted ... Amen*]*.

These Prayers following may be vsed at the choice of the Minister, in place of the other two alreadie prescribed.

It had beene the best for vs *[as 1563–E]*.

Another.

O Lord, we haue sinned, we haue sinned, and multiplied our abhominations in thy sight, the wanton prouocation of lust in our meates, the vncleane pollution of whoredome like that of Israel is on our Tables, and in our Tents: and wee haue magnified our selues in the multitude and mightinesse of our Nation as did Dauid, and thy wrath is incensed, and the plague is great amongst vs: iust art thou (O God) in thy iudgements, and it is thy mercy that wee are not vtterly consumed. And yet (O Lord) such is the hardnesse of our hearts, and so great is our security in the custome of sinne, as that we are not truely touched in our soules and consciences, either with that feeling apprehension of thine indignation against vs, or with that fearefull expectation of further calamities, as might direct and cast vs downe before thee with that consternation and confession as becommeth such miserable and wretched sinners as we are. Notwithstanding (O father of pity and of much mercie) deale not with vs according to our sinnes, neither reward vs according to our iniquities, but sanctifie vnto vs this thy visitation: wound our flesh with thy feare: possesse our soules with an awfull dread of thy power, thou which hast the hearts of all men in thy hands to preuent and prepare as it shall please thee. Conuert vs, and we shall be conuerted: turne vs, and wee shall be turned vnto thee, take on wickednesse from vs, and thou shalt finde none. But being pleased to be reconciled againe vnto vs in the name and mediation of our onely Aduocate and Sauiour Jesus Christ, burying those great and grieuous sinnes of our Nation in the graue of that thy Sonne: heale vs againe, O Lord, thou that hast wounded vs; let the voice of ioy and health be in our dwellings: So that we giue thankes vnto thee in the great Congregation, and record thy mercies for euer and euer.

Another.

Thou hast smitten vs (O Lord) thou hast plagued vs, and scattered the noysome pestilence in our chiefe Cities, and in our habitations round about, and we cry vnto thee (O Lord) but the sore runneth and ceaseth not. Yet is not thine eare heauie that thou canst not heare: neither is thine arme shortned, that thou canst not helpe: but our sinnes haue made a separation betweene thee and vs. Teach vs therefore (O Lord) truely to repent vs of all our wickednesse, that thou also maiest repent thee of the euill intended against vs. And as the stench and brimstone sent of our sinnes hath ascended vp into thy nosethrils to prouoke thy wrath and procure this plague against vs: So let our humble supplications testified with our teares and sighes powred foorth before thee, sanctified through faith in the intercession of our Sauiour, and thy Sonne Jesus Christ, come vp into thy sight (as did sometime *Aaron* with his golden Censer standing betweene the liuing and the dead) to turne away thy wrathfull indignation from vs. Oh, let vs liue, and we will praise thee, and thy iudgements shall teach vs, and informe vs in thy feare, that we may frame the rest of our life in all holy obedience according to thy will: and in the end of our dayes may be receiued through thy mercie and compassion into thy eternall glory without end. Amen.

Another.

O Lord our God most gracious and mercifull, we most miserable wretches humbly beseech thee in mercie and compassion to beholde our grieuous afflictions; for thine indignation lyeth hard vpon vs, thine arrowes sticke fast in vs, and the venime thereo[f] doeth drinke vp our spirits, and thy terrours doe fight against vs. We confesse (O Lord) that these thy iudgements are iust: for wee haue multiplyed our transgressions like the sand of the sea, and the cry of them hath bene so great, that it hath pierced the Heauens, and called for vengeance against vs. But yet wee beseech thee, O Lord, forget not thou to be gracious, and shut not vp thy louing kindnesse in displeasure: turne thee againe at the last, and be gracious vnto thy seruants. Helpe vs, O God of our saluation, for the glory of thy Name: O deliuer vs, & be mercifull vnto our sinnes for thy names sake: take thy plague away from vs, for wee are euen consumed by the means of thy heauie hand: cause thine Angel to sheath his sword againe, and preserue thou those which are appointed to die. O satisfie vs with thy mercie, and that soone; so shall wee reioyce and bee glad all the dayes of our life. Comfort vs againe now after the time that thou hast plagued vs: So shall we that be thy people and sheepe of thy pasture, giue thee thankes for euer; and wee will alwayes be shewing forth thy praise from generation to genera-tion. Graunt vs (O Lord) wee beseech thee, these graces, for Jesus Christ his sake thy onely Sonne and our onely Sauiour. Amen.

Another.

Almighty God and heauenly Father, whose iustice and iudgement is most seuere and fearefull against those that wittingly and willingly transgresse thy holy comman-dements, and stubbornly continue in their sinnes and wickednesse: whose mercie againe is infinite, and most ready to pardon and succour all such as in true repent-ance turne from their sinnes vnto righteousnesse, and come vnto thee in the faith and mediation of Jesus Christ: Wee thy humble seruaunts and miserable sinners, now visited and sore afflicted with this grieuous plague and pestilence, most worthily sent amongst vs for our iniquities and transgressions, in true acknowledgement of our manifold wickednesse, and thy iust iudgement vpon vs for the same, in vnfeigned repentance and hearty sorow for our sinnes, with a full purpose and promise by thy gracious assistance of a better life hereafter, doe now come vnto thy Throne of grace in the name and mediation of thy deare Sonne (in whome thou art well pleased our Lord and Sauiour Jesus Christ) in assured faith of atonement purchased for vs, by his blood, and full confidence of thy generall pardon proclaimed vnto vs in the Gospel: most humbly beseeching thee for his sake, to pardon and forgiue vs all our sinnes past, in thought, word, and deed, any wayes committed against thy diuine Maiestie, and holy Lawes: to giue vnto vs euery day more earnest and vnfeigned repentance for the same: to plant in our hearts by the grace of thy holy Spirit, a setled feare of thy Name, and full resolution to lead the rest of our life in the carefull obedience of thy holy will in our callings, and faithfull hope of a better life to come: and so to remooue from vs speedily this heauie plague and grieuous affliction (which now reigneth and rageth amongst vs) least wee be vtterly consumed. Graunt vs good Lorde (of thy grace and mercie) all meanes needfull hereunto: seasonable weather & good ayre, wholesome meats and medicines, and whatsoeuer else thou knowest profitable for vs: together, with a due care and conscience in our selues, to vse the same accordingly: that neither we tempt thy Maiestie by presumption, in contemning of the contagion; or neglecting the meanes of auoiding, remoouing, and repressing the same: neither despaire of thy goodnesse, or murmure against thy prouidence (if we be not so soone eased and deliuered as we desire:) but that wee may (submitting our selues in all things to thy good will and pleasure) seeke thy mercifull fauour for our release and succour by true faith and repentance: vse the meanes for ease which thou giuest vs, with care and diligence: helpe the afflicted, and preserue the whole with compassionate pitie and charitie: and finally depend vpon thy prouidence, and wait for thy gracious deliuerance, with constant hope and patience. Heare vs, and helpe vs, O Lord God of mercie, and Father of compassion, in the name and for the sake of thy deare Sonne our most gracious Mediatour and Redeemer, and most glorious Lord and Sauiour Jesus Christ. Amen.

A SHORT PREFACE TO BE VSED BEFORE THE EXHORTATION FOLLOWING, BY THE MINISTER WHO IS NOT A PREACHER.
When the Apostles wrote their seuerall Epistles to diuers Churches, they were to be read (by the Ministers especially) in the Publike Congregations. As it may appeare, in that S. Paul hauing written at large of many poynts of Religion to the Thessalonians, concludeth in this sort: *I charge you in the Lord, that this Epistle be read vnto all the brethren, the Saints.* And in the end of his Epistle to the Colossians: *When this Epistle* saith he, *is read of you: cause that it be read in the Church of the Laodiceans also: and that yee also reade the Epistle written from Laodicea.*

The name of Homilies by a misunderstanding conceit, is not acceptable with many: and yet they are nothing else in effect, but Epistles or Declarations grounded vpon the word of God, to teach Christian men and women their dueties to his Diuine Maiestie, howe to beleeue, and what to practise: carefully & soundly written vnto vs by Apostolicall men, with the approbation of the Church. There is here set downe, agreeable to the time, a godly Exhortation or Epistle, (as it may well be termed) written vnto you all here present, by such as are in authoritie, and do loue you with an vnfained loue in Christ Jesu, who intreat you by the mercies of God, That you wil be content and willing to heare, what for your good, vpon mature deliberation they do write vnto you: not as of themselues, but in the blessed Name of the most glorious Trinitie: to whom they cease not to commend you all in their dayly prayers.

AN EXHORTATION FIT FOR THE TIME.

In the due consideration of the mortalitie and plague, wherewith God at this time hath grieuously visited us, two principall things are to be looked into: First what may be the cause of this infectious disease: then what cure, or remedie may be prouided to remoue, stay, or mitigate the spreading and the increase thereof. The Philosopher and Phisition doe alledge such naturall causes as these: the infection of the ayre, the corruption of the blood, and humors in the body of man: the contagion which the sound partie may receiue from persons, or places alreadie infected: and all these are true in their kind. But ouer & aboue these causes alledged, the graue and weighty authoritie of the word of God must informe vs of an other cause, a cause not naturall, but supernaturall: namely the wrath of God prouoked and incensed by the sinnes of any Nation or people, hath often brought in the pestilence, as the sworde and scourge of God to destroy them, or chasten them for their sinnes. The people of Israel murmured against God in the wildernesse, and not regarding his louing care and prouidence ouer them (who fed them miraculously with water out of the Rocke, and with Manna from Heauen) waxed wanton in their desires, and required flesh also for their lust which though they obtained, yet notwithstanding while the meate was in their mouthes, the plague of God fell vpon, them and slew the wealthiest of them, and smote downe the chosen men that were in Israel, as you may read.[245] Againe the multitude of the people of Israel taking part with those factious and seditious conspirators, *Corah Darhan* and *Abiram*, murmured against *Moses* and *Aaron*, and grudged against that their authoritie of magistracie and priesthood wherein God himselfe had established them: wherefore a plague came vpon them and there dyed 14700.[246] Againe the same people of Israel committed whoredome with the daughters of *Moab* which called them also to the sacrifice of their gods; wherefore the wrath of the Lord was kindled against Israel, and there dyed in that plague 24000.[247] Againe in the dayes of King *Dauid* the wrath of the Lord was kindled against Israel,[248] and Sathan mooued *Dauid* to number Israel and Iuda: and the Lord sent a pestilence, and there died of the people from *Dan* to *Berseba* 70000. The Apostle Saint *Paul* also, signifieth in his Epistle to the Corinthians, that for their prophanation and abusing the holy Sacrament of the Lords supper,[249] many of them were sicke and weake, and many died. Lastly, of all sinne the same Apostle saith, that for such things commeth the wrath of God vpon the children of disobedience.[250] So that from these examples wee see that sinne mooueth the Lord to wrath, and the wrath of the Lord sendeth the plague, mortalitie, diseases, and death amongst men.

Which being so euident a trueth, confirmed by so many examples out of the holy Scriptures, it must be confessed & acknowledged that the same cause hath procured the same punishment with vs: and that in these daies, these euil daies of ours, our transgressions in number more & in degree more hainous then those of Israel, haue filled full the measure of iniquitie, & caused God to fil ful the cup of his wrath, and giuen vs this deadly wine to drinke, The people of Israel required meat for their

---

245 In margin: 'Numb. 11. Psal. 78.30.'
246 In margin: 'Numb. 25.'
247 In margin: '2. Sam. 24.'
248 In margin: '1 Chron. 21. 1[?]'.
249 In margin: '1. Cor. 11.'
250 In margin: 'Epe. 5.'

lust[251] & the people of England nourish their lust for their meat, giuing ouer themselues to surfeting & drunkennesse, and as those that make their belly their God, and
their glory their shame, are become a by-word vnto neighbor Nations for gluttony,
and belly-cheare.[252] The people of Israel murmured and rebelled against *Moses*, and
Aaron their leaders:[253] and there haue been also among vs in England not onely
such as haue despised gouernment, & spoken euil of those that are in authoritie :
but such also as S. *Paul* prophesied of, that there should come in the latter dayes
Traitours,[254] heady, high minded, murmurers, malecontents, fault-finders, as S. *Iude*
calleth them:[255] such as haue attempted reformation, aud alteration; with no lesse
disturbance to the Church of God amongst vs: no lesse danger and perill to the
state, and common wealth; and therefore with as much offence assuredly in the
sight of God, as was the contradiction of *Corah* and his complices.[256] The people
of Israel committed whoredom with the daughters of *Moab*: and there are many of
the daughters of England like those daughters of *Moab* and too many like vnto that
Zimri a prince in Israel, whose fornications are notorious in the sight of the world,
and who with a strumpets forehead, and a face of brasse, care not to conceale their
abhominations, and there wanteth greatly the zeale of *Phinehes* to punish them; and
therefore no marueile, if God himselfe stand forth to plague the land for them. Adde
vnto these that happely with *Dauid*,[257] wee haue lifted vp our hearts in the multitude
of our people, and magnified our selues, that we are a mightie and populous Nation,
ascribing vnto our selues, and our owne strength the honour, and victorie ouer our
enemies, which God with his owne right arme hath gotten vnto himselfe for his
glory. Adde moreouer, that swearing, outragious oathes, and cursed speakings are to
bee heard out of the mouthes of all estates, yea euen of very children in our streetes,
whereby the name of God is very grieuously prophaned. Adde also that our trades
and traffique is become the practise of deceite, and theft, while we make our gaine
by lying, forswearing, false measure, false weights, and false lights which are an
abhomination vnto the Lord. And therefore no maruell if that flying booke of the
curse of God against the swearer,[258] and the thiefe, haue entred into our houses, and
taken hould of the stone, and timber thereof. Besides all these, the Lords Sabboth is
not kept holy, but polluted: the word of God and the ministery thereof is not reuer-
enced, but despised: his holy Sacraments are either neglected, or abused: generally
the name of God is euill spoken of among the aduersaries of the trueth through vs,
and our dissolute and licentious conuersation: and therefore the cause is apparant
why the plague is broken in amongst vs: God hauing threatned vs in his word as the
people Israel, that because we wil not obey the voice of the Lord our God to do al
his commandements, and his ordinances which he commands vs, he will smite vs
with a consumption, and with a feuer, and with a burning ague, and shall cause the
pestilence to cleaue vnto vs vntill hee haue consumed vs from the land. And thus
much of the cause of the pestilence.

Now let vs examine & see what hope of helpe, what cure or remedie, remaineth

---

[251] In margin: 'Numb. 11. Psal. 78.'
[252] In margin: 'Numb. 16.'
[253] In margin: 'Iude 8.'
[254] In margin: '2. Tim. 3.4.'
[255] In margin: 'Nomb. 11. Psal. 78. 30.'
[256] In margin: 'Numb 25.'
[257] In margin: '2 Sam 2 4.'
[258] In margin: 'Zach. 4. 5.'

vnto vs in this visitation. The remedie is to be sorted out answerable to the cause of the disease: so y[t] if Gods anger against sinne hath caused this mortalitie amongst vs (as heretofore hath bin shewed amongst other people) if wee shall remooue our sinnes out of the sight of God, his wrath shal cease, and with his wrath our punishment. For the applying of this soueraigne balme vnto our present sore, there is by publike Order prescribed, that Fasting and Prayer, the true signes and tokens of our vnfeined repentance, and conuersion vnto God, should bee exercised in all Congregations: especially in and about London, that all degrees and Estates of people might thereby be admonished to humble themselues vnder the mightie hand of God, to acknowledge their sinnes and by their humiliation and detestation of their former wicked life, to testifie vnto the world, that they desire nothing more then to bee reconciled againe to their good and gracious God, that hee may cause his indignation to cease, and turne away this his fearefull chastisement from amongst vs. And as fasting and prayer are meanes spirituall, appointed in the word of God, and alwayes practised in the Church of God at such times as hee afflicteth his people with any contagious diseases or plagues for sinne: So are there also other naturall and ordinary meanes not to be neglected, but to be receiued and vsed against the naturall causes of this infection. For though it be true that all things are guided by Gods prouidence: and that he doeth what he will doe in heauen and in earth: yet hee effecteth and bringeth his will to passe by order and by meanes that himselfe hath determined. The eyes of all things looke vp vnto the Lorde, and trusting in him he giueth them their meate in due season: but yet the Lord will haue all men to labour, and eate the labors of their hands, for the maintenance of their life. It is the Lord that bringeth backe againe from the gates of death, and restoreth men that were sicke to their former health: and yet hath he ordained the Phisition, and created many medicinable and comfortable things to procure and preserue the health of man, & hath commaunded vs to vse them. Men must plant and water: though it be God onely that giueth the increase. If the husbandmen should giue ouer their tillage and pretend that they meant to depend vpon Gods prouidence, looking either to bee fedde from Heauen, or that the earth should of her owne accord bring foorth vnto them grayne and corne, and all necessarie fruits for their reliefe: were it not in respect of themselues extreame madnes, and towards God a most wicked temptation: It cannot bee denied but that this greeuous sickenes which now reigneth amongst vs, both is, and shall be gouerned by Gods prouidence, doe men what they list: But yet such as truely feare God, and are truly instructed out of his word, will submit themselues vnto his heauenly prouidence in such sort as hee hath appointed them. When good king *Ezechiah* was sicke of this disease of the plague as diuines doe deliuer, he prayed and wept and vsed those meanes meete to pacifie the anger of God. And when God had determined that he should not die of that sickenesse: though hee could no doubt haue healed him without meanes by his word only, yet he directeth his Prophet to signifie vnto him the medicinable meanes of his helpe, namely, that he should apply a plaster of figges to his sore to ripen and heale it. So that we see, first prayer to God, and then the vse of other necessary and profitable meanes must not be neglected.

Now if any man should obiect or say: this visitation commeth of God, and I know not whether I may pray against it, hee bewrayeth greatly his ignorance in the Scripturres of God. For in euery visitation of this, or any other plague there mentioned, you shall finde that the holy men of God still laboured by prayer and supplication vnto God to remoue the same from themselues and their people. *Moyses* is said to haue stood in y[e] gap to turne away ye wrath of God,[259] and *Aaron*, ran with his golden censer to stand betweene the liuing and the dead,[260] & *Phinees* the priest stood vp and praied, and the plague ceased. *Dauid* seeing the Angel ready to destroy Ierusalem.[261] built an Altar, offered sacrifice, and brake forth into that his most ardent, and earnest supplication for the people.

Againe, because in this great mortality of ours we find by experience, that not so much any general corruption of the aire, nor any distemperature in the blood, or humors of mens bodies haue bene the causes of the spreading & continuing of this infection, as the contagion that the disease it selfe hath bred, and which one man receiueth from another, the sound from those that are sicke: Therefore also men are to learne that one chiefe and ordinary meane of their preseruation in this dangerous time is, the auoyding of the contagion that commeth by mingling disorderly the sound, & the sicke together. And if there be any that being yet sound doe thinke they are not bound in conscience to shun and auoyd the persons & places that are infected, except it be in case of necessity: or if those that are diseased, or do keepe in houses where the disease is knowen to be, shall thinke much that they are shut vp, and restrained from comming abroad or frequenting the common and publique assemblies of those that are cleare, hauing in the meane time such things as are necessary for their sustenation: They must be content to heare out of the word of God their errour therein and ignorance. The disease of the leprosie was infectious as is the pestilence, and whensoeuer any were smitten with that disease, it was not surely without the will or prouidence of God: and yet we may safely learne euen of God himselfe without any preiudice to his good prouidence, how we ought in that and other kinde of infectious maladies to demeane our selues for the auoyding of the damage thereof. The Leper (saith the Lord in the 13. Chapter of Leuiticus,) in whom the plague is, shall haue his clothes rent, and his head bare, and shall put a couering vpon his lips, and shall cry: *I am vncleane, I am vncleane*. And as long as this disease shall bee vpon him he shall dwell alone, without the campe shall his habitation be. The renting of his clothes here mentioned was a signe of his mourning and lamentation for that affliction: hee dwelt alone for feare of infecting others. And if at any time hee went abroad to take the ayre, his lips were couered, that his breath might not infect such as came neere him. And besides he was to giue warning, that all men might the more carefully auoyde him by crying out vnto them: *I am vncleane, I am vncleane*.

Furthermore it was ordered by the Lorde, that the cloathes that were infected should be burnt, the houses purged, and in some cases of more danger of infection pulled downe and vtterly defaced. In which respect, there was a generall commandement giuen to the people, That they should take heede of the plague of the Leprosie. All these and diuers other rules and cautions prescribed by GOD himselfe, were chiefly grounded vpon this, That the disease of the leprosie was infectious. Whereby we are to learne, that forasmuch as the disease of the plague is farre more infectious, contagious, and dangerous, then that was of the leprosie; wee should be so much the more carefull to auoid it: and such as are infected, more charitably minded and religiously humbled vnder the hand of God, then disobeying all authority, to thrust themselues into the company of others, whereby the mortalitie dayly so increaseth.

---

[259] In margin: 'Nomb. 16.'
[260] In margin: 'Psal. 106.'
[261] In margin: '2 Sam. 24.'

And if any man should thinke, that the disease of the plague were not contagious and infectious, so grosse a conceit is rather to be pitied, then confuted, being contrary to the common & lamentable experience of these times, and contrary to the iudgement of all learned and wise men in all ages. If therefore wee desire that Almighty God should withdrawe his heauie hand from vs, and deliuer vs from this affliction, it is not sufficient for vs by fasting and prayer, to humble ourselues vnto his diuine Maiestie, except we ioyne therewith our best endeauours and diligence, by vsing such other meanes as God hath appointed for the staying of it. Otherwise, if wee despise all good meanes: if we neither regard to keepe our selues in good estate of our bodily health by the counsell of the learned Physician: if wee make a mocke of all preseruatiues of Art: if wee neglect all euill and infectious sauours, and refuse the benefit of the purer ayre: if wee run desperately and disorderly into all places and amongst all persons, and pretend our faith and trust in Gods prouidence, saying: *If he will saue me, he wil saue me: and if I die, I die.* This is not faith in God, but a grosse, ignorant, and foole-hardy presidence and presumption, little different from that subtill temptation of Sathan to our Sauiour Christ, to throw himselfe headlong from the toppe of the pinacle, in hope that God would send his Angels to hold him vp, which were a wanton & dangerous tempting of God: or else with Saint *Peter*, to leade himselfe into temptation, and by desiring to walke on the water, to bring his life into a needlesse and vnnecessary hazard and perill without any warrant of an ordinarie calling, or any comfort of a good conscience therein.

Moreouer, if men at any time will prepare themselues to death, then should they especially when they are in the greatest danger, as they are who are already infected, or doe without vrgent cause resort vnto them. Now in preparing our selues to leaue this world, what one thing almost is more necessary then a charitable heart towardes all men, which they cannot haue by any possible meanes, who either knowing themselues to be infected do keepe company with such as are cleare; or that being whole, do enter without any necessitie into places infected, and afterwards resort into all companies, as if they were sure that neither they themselues nor their clothes were tainted. When king *Azariah* became a leper, because he knew the danger of his disease, and found by the Law of God, the restraint of those that were so diseased, though a King, yet was hee content to dwell in an house apart all the dayes of his life, and *Iothan* his sonne gouerned in his stead. This his obedience must needs condemne their disordered licentiousnesse, who though the meanest among the people, yet being infected thinke scorne to keepe their houses though but for a short time; and breake abroad they will whatsoeuer come of it, no authoritie, orders, lawes, or proclamations can restraine them: and others there are as wilfull to associate and mingle themselues with them. Wherein howe cruell the one sort are against themselues in hazarding their owne liues and theirs that depend on them; how vncharitable the other sort are towards their brethren by deriuing their infection into them, and how iniurious both sorts are to the state and commonwealth wherein they liue, by prolonging and spreading the danger, which otherwise by their better gouernment might be sooner supprest, all wise men of sound iudgement are very sorie either to see, or heare it.

Wherefore, considering all that hath been spoken tendeth to this end, To shew that our sinnes haue caused this fearefull Visitation to breake foorth against vs; and that the remedy left vnto vs for our hope of helpe herein, is our speedy repentance, with prayer and fasting, together also with the good vse of ordinarie meanes, and the wary and carefull cariage of our selues out of the danger of contagion: let vs bee truely wise, and demeane our selues in this time of our triall, as those that make good vse of Gods corrections: let vs neither murmure nor grudge against the will of God, nor take impatiently what our sinnes haue deserued, and God in his fatherly care hath inflicted vpon vs for our amendment: let vs not nowe adde sinne vnto sinne, but forasmuch as the desperate securitie of those that seeme neither to feare, nor to flie from this infection, is but a tempting and prouoking of the iudgement of God: seeing it may be an hinderance vnto the fruit of the prayers, and fasting of the Church, which be they neuer so strict and zealous, shall hardly procure a release of this burden of God, if wilfull and intemperate spirits will not be kept in order: seeing such their vnruly licentiousnes extendeth it selfe to the breach of all charity, and bringing vpon their owne heads no lesse then the guilt of wilfull murder both of themselues, their children, their families, and neighbours, which hatefull crueltie against their owne kind, Turkes and infidels would abhorre: seeing it procureth also a publicke, and manifest detriment to the State, and places where they dwel, by hindering their trafficke, and impouerishing their neighbours in their trades and occupations: let men at the last be warned, and if there be any feare of God, any obedience to his word, any conscience of the magistrates authoritie, any fruits of our faith and Christian profession, whose badge and cognizance is mutuall loue and charitie, to further and procure the common good of all: let vs not go forward to tempt GOD, to continue so cruell to our selues and harmefull to others: let vs be more humble in the day of our affliction, submitting our selues to those good and wholsome orders, and decrees already published for preuenting the further infection of this our calamitie, and making account of all good meanes, and medicinable helpe made knowne vnto vs for our better preseruation: least wee may seeme to mocke God by prayer and fasting, to begge a mitigation of this his irefull chastisement, and yet we frame our actions contrary and opposite to the successe we pray for.

And among all other things yet spoken of, let this one aduise bee added without offence vnto any: That though it be a Christian and laudable custom to accompany the bodies of the dead vnto the graue, and commend them in decent manner vnto their rest: yet seeing the ende of such assemblies as are then gathered together is, by the vse of Prayer and the word preached rather to giue comfort vnto the liuing, then any benefit vnto the dead; let men be aduised, perswaded, and content, that their dead should be buried with no more company then is needful for the inter-ring and laying them vp in the earth, because the gathering together of friends and neighbours in so common a contagion, cannot be without present danger, and hazard of their health and liues: and it is verely thought that infection by this meanes of meeting hath ensued vnto many. And heere if time and place serued the Magistrates might be admonished of their ouersight, in that they haue taken no more care in the beginning for the stay of the ouerflowing of this euill. But now the contagion being growen so generall, there is no probable meanes, especially in the Citie of London, how they can by any circumspection doe that good which might at the first entrance haue beene effected. So that now the chiefe remedie to be expected from man is, that euery one would be a Magistrate vnto himselfe, and his whole familie, and endeuour by all good care both to preserue themselues being yet sound: or being diseased, not to scatter their infection vpon others. If men acquainted with the custome of other countreys, should compare the great seueritie there vsed in such times as these are, with the remisse indulgence which our Magistrates haue vsed, they shall find great difference of care & gouernment; which is not here remembred to vrge any sharper directions, then may well agree with the nature of our people.

The conclusion of all is this, that though there cannot be too much care taken for the preseruing of those that are yet sound, and for the secluding and sepa-rating of those that are sicke: yet must this warning be therewith giuen, That the infected housholds may not be so shut vp, as that they be also shut out from all succour, and reliefe of necessary maintenance, very many of those families which haue beene, and are yet visited, being of the poorer sort. To whose affliction, if you shall adde affliction, and suffer them to want meanes of ordinary sustenation, alas, what shalt become of them, seeing necessitie knoweth no law, and want and hunger breake stone walles? In which case of neede they must, and will breake forth for the succour of their liues, though with neuer so much danger to themselues, or others. Wherefore it shall well beseeme those that are rich, and able to shew their fellow feeling of their brethrens necessitie: it shall well become the misery of the time for men to be fruitfull in good workes, whereby their Christian duetie may be testified vnto God and men. And it shall well agree also with the exercise of Fasting and Prayer now in hand, that in euery assembly gathered together to that end, there be a collection made of the beneuolence of the people, to bee faithfully and truely distributed by those that are put in trust, vnto the poore shut vp, and visited with this affliction. So shall your Prayers, Fasting and Almesdeedes, as the incense, and odours of the faithfull, qualifie the stench and corruption of our sinnes, and as sacri-fices wherewith God is wel pleased, being made acceptable in that sweete smelling sauour of our sauiour Christ his intercession, shall mitigate the wrath of God, and turne away this his indignation from vs, restoring vs againe to his wonted fauour, and our former health and safetie: Which grace God the Father of all mercy and consolation graunt vnto vs euen for his dearely beloued Sonne Christ Jesus his sake, our onely Lord and Sauiour. Amen.

ORDER FOR THE FAST

The godly vse of Fasting, in time of common calamitie, as Warre, Famine, Pestilence, and also when any weightie matter was in hand, for the Church and Common-wealth, is euident in holy Scriptures. Wherefore it is necessarie in so contagious time of sicknesse (our sinnes procuring iustly the wrath of God) that following the godly examples of King *Iosaphat*, and the King of *Niniue* with others, Fasting with prayer bee commanded to the people by their Preachers.

1. Let this Fast bee helde euery weeke vpon the Wednesday.

2. All Persons (children, olde, weake, and sicke folks, and necessarie Haruest labourers, or the like excepted) are required to eate vpon that day, but one compe-tent and moderate Meale, and that towards night after Euening prayer: obseruing sobrietie of diet without superfluitie of ryotous fare, respecting necessitie and not voluptuousnesse.

3. The quantitie being but sufficient, it is not fit that any delicacie should be regarded. Let no publike order be contemned herein, nor dissimulation with God committed, pretending godly abstinence, but doing nothing lesse.

4. The welthier sort are earnestly to bee mooued to bestow the price of the meale forborne, vpon the poore, considering the miserie and distresse of a number of hungrie soules, either almost staruing for lacke of foode, or being sicke with eating vnseasonable meates.

5. The people are to be warned to forbeare this day their bodily working, and common buying and selling (necessarie occasions and labourers excepted) and to be exercised all the time in holy prayer, godly Meditations, and reuerend hearing of

the Scriptures, either read or preached. And especially they are to take heede that they spend it not in playes, pastimes, idlenesse, haunting of Tauernes, lasciuious wantonnesse, surfeiting and drunkennesse: for which sinnes (the proper sinnes of our Nation) the heauie displeasure and wrath of God is fallen vpon vs.

6. Admonition is here lastly to be giuen, that on the said Fasting day there be but one Sermon at Morning prayer, and the same not aboue an hower long, and but one at Euening prayer of the same length, to auoyde the inconuenience that may grow by the abuse of Fasting: Some esteeming it a meritorious worke: others a good worke, and of it selfe acceptable to God without due regard of the end: others presuming factiously to enter into publike Fasts without the consent of Authority, and others keeping the people together with ouermuch wearines and tediousnesse a whole day together: which in this time of contagion is very dangerous, in so thicke and close assemblies of the multitudes. God giue vs grace to repent, and in his mercie turne away his punishment from vs. *Amen.*

1604–E   Thanksgiving services for decline of the plague

Wednesdays, Fridays and Sundays, [late autumn/winter?] 1604 (England and Wales)

Among the revisions of the Book of Common Prayer in 1604 was the addition of 'occasional' thanksgiving prayers, as counterparts of the occasional (petitionary) prayers for exceptional circumstances published in the 1559 BCP. These thanksgiving prayers included two alternative prayers 'for deliverance from the plague'. Nevertheless, as the plague declined during 1604, the authorities decided to mark this with the issue a special service. It is possible that the thanksgiving prayers in the BCP were considered to be for local use, as the plague subsided in particular parishes or areas, but that a celebration throughout the kingdom required a service. The form of prayer followed the format of Elizabethan special services: it was based on the BCP with specially selected psalms, readings and prayers. There are no extant orders to indicate when the thanksgivings began and the wide geographical variation in the outbreak makes it impossible to establish this. However, it is likely that they began in late autumn because mortality declined sharply after mid-September in key cities such as Norwich, though it remained at epidemic proportions in cities such as Chester and Newcastle for some years. Though two of the prayers included in the form make reference to 'our chiefe Citie' and 'this Citie', this does not necessarily mean that special worship was limited to the capital.

Order: none found.
Form of prayer: *A short forme of thanksgiving to God, for staying the contagious sickenes of the plague: to be used in common prayer, on Sundayes, Wednesdayes and Fridayes. Set forth by authoritie* (15 pp.; STC 16533)*.

FORM OF PRAYER

Read the ordinary Seruice till you come to the Psalmes. And in stead of those which are appointed of course, read some of these: Viz. 34. 95. 103. 116. 107. 118. 145. 146. 147.

After the second Lesson, read this Psalme following.

Lord, thou art become gratious vnto thy Land, thou hast turned away the afflictions of thy seruants. (Ps. 85) [85:1]

Thou hast taken away all thy displeasure, and turned thy selfe from thy wrathfull indignation. [Ps. 85:3]

For if thou Lord hadst not helped vs, it had not failed, but our soules had bene put to silence. (Ps. 94) [94:17]

But when we said our feete haue slipped, thy mercie, O Lord, helped vs vp. [Ps. 94, 18]

In the multitude of the sorrowes that we had in our hearts, thy comforts haue refeshed our soules. [94:19]

Our soules waited still vpon the Lord, our soules hanged vpon his helpe, our hope was alwayes in him. (Ps. 62, 63) [62:5; 63:9]

In the Lords word did we reioyce, in Gods word did we comfort our selues. (Ps. 62 & 63) [?]

For the Lord said: Call vpon mee in the time of trouble, and I wil heare thee, and thou shalt praise me. (Ps. 50) [50:15]

So when wee were poore, needy, sickly, and in heauinesse, the Lord cared for vs: hee was our helpe and our Sauiour according to his word. (Ps. 40, 69) [40:20; 69:30]

In our aduersitie and distresse hee hath lift vp our heads, and saued vs from vtter destruction. (Ps. 27) [27:6?]

Hee hath deliuered our soules from death, hee hath fedde vs in the time of dearth, hee hath saued vs from the noysome Pestilence. (Ps. 33, 91) [33:18; 91:3]

Therefore will we offer in his holy Temple, the oblation of Thankesgiuing with great gladnesse: we will sing and speake praises vnto the Lord our Sauiour. (Ps. 27) [27:7]

We will giue thankes vnto the Lord, for hee is gratious, and his mercy endureth for euer. (Ps. 106) [106:1]

The Lord is full of compassion and mercie, long suffering, plenteous in goodnesse and pitie. (Ps. 86, 103) [86:15; 103:8]

His mercy is greater then the heauens, and his gratious goodnesse reacheth vnto the cloudes. (Ps. 57, 108) [57:11; 108:4]

Like as a father pitieth his owne children: euen so is the Lord mercifull vnto them that feare him. (Ps. 103) [103:13]

Therefore will we praise thee and thy mercies, O God, vnto thee will wee sing, O thou Holy one of Israel. (Ps. 71) [71:20]

Wee will sing a New song vnto thee, O God, we will praise the Lord with Psalmes of Thankesgiuing. (Ps. 98) [98: 1, 6]

O sing praises, sing praises vnto our God: O sing praises, sing praises vnto our King. (Ps. 47) [47:6]

For God is the King of the earth, sing praises with vnderstanding. (Ps. 47)

Wee will magnifie thee, O God our King, wee will praise thy Name for euer and euer. (Ps. 145) [145:1]

Euery day will we giue thankes vnto thee, and praise thy Name for euer and euer. [Ps. 145:2]

Our mouth shall speake the praises of the Lord, and let all flesh giue thanks to his holy Name for euer and euer. [Ps. 145:21]

Blessed be the Lord God of Israel for euer: and blessed bee the Name of his Maiestie world without end. AMEN. AMEN. (Ps. 21, 72) [21:?; 72:18–19]

In stead of the other Prayers vsed in the time of the Sicknesse, Read some of these following.

Wee will magnifie thee, O God our King, and we will praise thy name for euer and euer: because in the midst of thine anger, thinking vpon mercie, thou hast deliuered our soules from death, and preserued vs from that noysome pestilence, which not long since, raged in this Citie, sweeping away the rich with the poore, and aged with the young, leauing whole houses desolate, and filling all places with dead bodies: So that in mans iudgement there was no hope remayning, but that this yeere would haue thereby prooued yet more dreadful and infectious then the former. But because thou wilt haue it knowen, that thou onely woundest and canst heale againe, that thou killest and reuiuest, bringest euen to hell and backe againe: thou hast vouchsafed, contrarie to all humane expectation (such is thy power and goodnesse) to command thine Angell to stay his hande, and spare this Citie, and hast turned thine anger and the fiercenesse therof vpon many other Cities and Townes within this Realme. Wee therfore at this time offer vp vnto thee a double sacrifice, at once, *of hearty Thankesgiuing* for this our strange deliuerance, and *of humble and earnest Prayers*, for those dolefull places, thus grieuously afflicted: beseeching thee for thy Sonne Jesus Christ his sake, to be gracious vnto them also, that both they and we in ioynt affection, may acknowledge thy iustice in thy punishments, and recorde thine infinite mercies in sparing vs miserable sinners, through Jesus Christ thy Sonne, and our Sauiour, to whom, &c.

O most gracious God, seeing it hath pleased thee in the multitude of those sorrowes which we had in our hearts, by reason of that grieuous contagion which thou lately didst send amongst vs (besides the feare and expectation of the like, or a more violent infection this present yeere) to sende thy comfortes for the refreshing of our soules, and to remooue that fearefull pestilence from vs, not for any desert of ours, who are most wretched sinners; nor by any meanes of mans deuise, but onely of thine owne fauour, and for thy mercies sake: we yeeld vnto thy diuine Maiestie all thankes and praise, for this thine especiall goodnesse; trusting that we shal take warning, by this last dreadful iudgment, for euer prouoking thee to such a wrathfull indignation againe. And hauing felt the weight of thy heauie hand vpon our selues, tenderly compassionating the wofull case of those Cities and Townes in this Realme, which are nowe stricken with the same; we most humbly beseech thee, most mercifull Father, to extend the like mercie to them, that thou hast done to vs. Good Lord spare them, and heare their praiers, now crying vnto thee in the vexation of their spirits, and the anguish of their soules, and vs for them, that so this whole land may ioyfully prayse thy Name, and say; *Lord thou art become gracious vnto thy land, thou hast turned away all thy displeasure.* Graunt this O Lord, for thine onely Sonnes sake, Jesus Christ our Lord and onely Sauiour. Amen.

Almightie and eternall God, which strikest and healest, bringest downe to death and quicknest againe, who in thy iust iudgement for our sinnes diddest lately sore plague vs in our chiefe Citie and round about, with great sickenesse and mortalitie: yet remembring thy mercie hast turned thy selfe most graciously vnto vs, and comforted vs againe, by ceasing the plague therein, euen then when as by all likelihoode both of the time and place, and concourse of people, and our litle amendment of life, we could not but iustly feare & expect the continuance and encreasing of the same: wee most humbly acknowledge with all due thankefulnesse from the bottome of our hearts, this

thine exceeding gracious goodnesse and vndeserued mercie, euermore praysing thy
great & glorious name, for so wonderfull grace and clemencie towards vs most vile
and wretched sinners so freely and mercifully extended: most humbly beseeching
thee of thy fatherly goodnesse, not onely to continue this gracious course of thy
louing fauour, in mitigating and lessening more and more this noysome Pestilence,
till it be cleane remoued from vs: But also to powre thy heauenly Grace into our
hearts, that we neuer forgetting how grieuously and iustly wee haue bene chastened
for our sinnes, and yet in Mercy not consumed, but raised vp againe and comforted,
may learne thereby, both to feare thy dreadful iudgements against sinne, and so by
true Repentance to turne vnto thee from our wicked wayes, least a worse Plague fall
vpon vs; And also to put our whole trust in thy Mercy, and approch with confidence
vnto thy Throne of Grace, for help and succour in all our troubles and aduersities,
Euermore thanking & praysing thy glorious Maiestie for this thy most mercifull and
marueilous deliuerance, through Jesus Christ our Lord and Sauiour.

O God the Father of our Lord Jesus Christ, the God of all Mercie and Comfort, which
art Lord of life and death, and rulest all things in heauen and earth by the word of thy
Power: Looke downe mercifully from thy Holy place, vpon the people of this Land
yet grieuously afflicted in many places, with great sicknesse and mortalitie. And
as by thy great Mercy, the Plague which lately raged in our chiefe City, threatning
vtter consumption and desolation to the same, is now slaked and asswaged to our
great comfort, for which we praise and magnifie thy glorious Name: So likewise we
most humbly beseech thee, in the tender bowels of thy endlesse Compassion, to be
gratious and mercifull to the other parts of this land, now fearefully affrighted and
afflicted with this grieuous Plague & pestilence. Send them good Lord, speedy help
and succour from thy Holy habitation; And as thou diddest sometimes turne away
thy fierce wrath from the *Niniuites*, being iustly threatened out against them, and
euen hanging ouer their heads, by giuing them Repentance through thy Grace: So
now visite the hearts of thy people in this Land with thine heauenly Grace, and holy
Spirit, that they may speedily and soundly returne vnto thee from all their wicked
wayes, in true Repentance, and a liuing Faith in Jesus Christ: That so wee may bee
deliuered from this heauy wrath & Plague, which our sinnes haue pulled downe and
scattered amongst vs; And learne by thy fearefull Judgements to walke hereafter
before thee, in continuall reuerence and obedience, And for thy gratious mercie to
giue thee Euerlasting praise and glory, through Jesus Christ our Lord.

O Almightie God, which art the Resurrection of the dead, and the Life of them which
liue, who in thy displeasure cariest vs downe in a moment to the gates of death, and in
thy mercie recallest our Soules backe to dwell in the land of the liuing: Wee giue thee
humble thankes, that it hath pleased thee to restore vs when wee were almost past
hope, to strengthen vs in the extremitie of our weakenesse, to deliuer vs thy people
of this Citie from the Contagion, when in the eye of mans reason it was most likely
to haue encreased. This we acknowledge to be thy doing, O Lord, and it is wonderful
in our eyes, which haue seene these thy great mercies surpassing the strength of our
hope: and wee beseech thee to continue thy gracious goodnesse towards vs still,
whereby all the world may see and knowe, that thou art our mercifull Father, and
wonderfull Deliuerer, to the glory of thy holy Name, and to the comfort of vs thy
children, through Jesus Christ our Lord.

O heauenly Father, which art the Fountaine of Life, and the GOD of our health, in whome alone wee liue, and mooue, and haue our being: we beseech thee, that as thou hast beene gracious vnto this Citie, and the parts about it, in remoouing from hence that fearefull Plague, which for our sins thou haddest most iustly sent among vs. So it would please thee to heare these our intercessions for our brethren, which in other places of this Realme do yet grone vnder thy punishing hand. O Lord, be gracious also vnto them, and command thine Angel to sheath his Sword, that a remnant may be saued. So shall wee all ioyntly magnifie thy Mercies, and compasse about thine Altars with songs of deliuerance, to our vnspeakable comfort, and to thy euerlasting Glory, through Jesus Christ our Lord. Amen.

1605–E1   Prayers during the pregnancy of Queen Anna

[January–March?] 1605 (England and Wales?)

James's wife, Anna of Denmark, became pregnant in 1604; it was her first pregnancy since James acceded to the English throne. She already had two sons (Henry Frederick, b. 19 February 1594 – see 1594–S1 – d. 6 November 1612; and Charles, later Charles I, b. 19 November 1600) and a daughter (Elizabeth b. 19 August 1596, later queen of Bohemia). She had suffered a number of miscarriages and two children, Margaret (b. 24 December 1598) and Robert (b. 27 May 1602), died in infancy. Given Queen Elizabeth's failure to marry, this was the first time since 1554–E3 that prayers had been ordered in England for a queen's safety during pregnancy. The occasion is known only from the existence of a form of prayer. The form copied the practice of some Elizabethan texts (e.g. 1590–E2, 1597–E) in providing prayers to be incorporated into the BCP service (probably at the end of the litany), rather than a full liturgy.

Order: none found.
Form of prayer: *Prayers appointed to be vsed in the church at morning and euening prayer by euery minister, for the queenes safe deliuerance. Set foorth and inioyned by authoritie* (8 pp.; STC 16534)*.

FORM OF PRAYER

A prayer for the Queenes Maiesties safe deliuerance in her Childbirth.

O Mercifull Lord and heauenly Father, by whose gracious gift mankind is encreased, who hast promised that the seede of them that feare thee, shall be mightie vpon earth: wee beeech thee for our gracious Queene *ANNE*, that thou wilt preserue her in the great paines and perill of childbirth: grant her a safe and happie deliuerance, and send thy blessing vpon her and the fruite of her wombe, to the ioy and comfort of this land, and to the euerlasting praise and glory of thy Name, through Christ our Lord. Amen.

Or this.

Almightie God, from whose only blessing the fruitfulnesse of the wombe with safe and happy deliuerance from the paines and danger in childbirth doe proceed: giue this thy blessing wee humbly beseech thee vnto thy handmaid our gracious Queene, that she may be comforted with thy sauing health, and become a ioyfull mother of many children. So shall the King reioyce, and thy people be glad therof, and we all with thankefull hearts shall praise thy glorious Name for such an increase of the Kings royall issue, tending to the good of this thy Church, and vnto the comfort both of vs and of our posteritie, through Jesus Christ our Lord.

Or this.

Most gratious God which hast blessed vs with a Queene of a fruitfull wombe, and an happie offspring, and preserued her heretofore in the prosperous birth of that royall issue, which we with comfort and ioy daily behold : grant her we humbly beseech thee at this time also, a safe deliuerance of that noble babe which now she beareth, and prolong her dayes with the life of our most renowned King, that they may both together see their childrens children for many generations, vnto the honour and glorie of thy name, and the full establishment of our peace and happinesse, through Jesus Christ our Lord.

Or this.

O Lord our God, seeing it hath pleased thee of thy mercifull goodnesse to make our gracious Queene *ANNE* as a fruitfull Vine to multiply and encrease the royall Line of this Kingdome: wee beseech thee to blesse and preserue her, together with the happie fruite of her wombe formed and quickened by thine owne hand, that shee may in her fulnesse of time haue safe deliuerance, and we together with her may receiue thereby such ioy and comfort, as may tend to the good of this Kingdome, and to the eternall praise of thy holy Name, through Jesus Christ our Lorde. Amen.

Or this.

Most mercifull Father, seeing thou hast in thy wisedome appointed to all the sonnes of *Eue*, one and the same entrance into life, through the sorrowes and pangs of Child-birth: Wee most humbly beseech thee of thine infinite goodnesse, to protect and strengthen thy seruaunt *ANNE*, our most gracious Queene, against all danger and paines of Trauell, that through thy heauenly protection shee may be safely deliuered of the blessed fruit of her body, and become a ioyfull Mother of a happy issue, to the vnspeakable comfort of this thy Church, and to the praise and honor of thy glorious Name, through Jesus Christ our Lord. Amen.

Or this.

O almightie and most mercifull Father, heare the prayers of thy Church for thy hand-mayd our gratious Queene *ANNE*: looke downe from heauen vpon her with the eyes of thy tender compassion, and be euermore mercifull vnto her, assist her with thy comforts in her trauell of childbirth, mitigate the panges thereof for sinne inflicted, strengthen her, that without perill she may passe those daungers, and recei-uing ioy by an happie issue we thy people may haue comfort and consolation in her safe deliuerance, through Jesus Christ our Lord and onely Sauiour. Amen.

Or this.

O most mercifull God and louing Father, wee commend vnto thy Diuine proui-dence, the present estate of our most gracious Queene *ANNE*: Protect and defend her among all the changes and chances of this mortall life: preserue and keepe her amidst the paines and perils of Child-birth, and giue her the comfort, both safely to bring foorth, and ioyfully to bring vp the conceiued Issue of her fruitfull wombe.

So shall we ioyntly for such thy Fatherly mercie, giue thankes vnto thee in the great Congregation, and praise thy Name for euer and euer. Amen.

1605–E2   Thanksgiving prayers for the birth of Princess Mary

[after Monday 8 April] 1605 (England and Wales?)

Anna gave birth to her sixth child, Mary, on 8 April 1605 (erroneously dated 9 April in the form of prayer). This occasion appears to have been ordered immediately because, on 9 April, the bishop of London's chancellor, Edward Stanhope, informed the archdeacon of St Albans that the form of prayer was being printed and would be ready for collection and use the following morning. It was the first time since 1537–E2 that celebrations had been ordered in England for the birth of a royal child. The form contained a choice of six prayers, one of which was to be read, probably at the end of the litany. In contrast to other thanksgivings, the period for use of the prayers was not stated: Stanhope told the archdeacon that the prayers were to be used so long as was seen fit. Mary died in September 1607 after an illness and was buried in the Henry VII chapel, Westminster Abbey. Neither Anna nor James attended the funeral; they had not attended any funerals since the death of their third son, Robert, aged five months, in 1602.

Order: none found.
Form of prayer: *Thanksgiuing for the queenes maiesties safe deliuerance. 9. April 1605* (8 pp.; STC 16535)*.
Additional source: Edward Stanhope to Dr Bill, archdeacon of St Albans, 9 Apr. 1605, HALS, ASA 5/4/181, p. 803.

FORM OF PRAYER

Thanksgiuing for the Queenes Maiesties safe deliuerance.

Most gracious God and mercifull Father, of whose onely gift it doeth proceede, that mankinde is increased, and thy Kingdome vpon earth thereby enlarged: Wee giue thee most humble and hearty thanks, that it hath pleased thee, of thy especiall fauour towards vs and this Lande, to preserue our vertuous Queene *ANNE* in her late paines and perill of childbirth. Lord, thou hast made her a ioyful Mother of many Children: Send downe, wee beseech thee, thy continuall blessings vpon Her, and the hopefull Issue of her wombe, as may bee most to the perpetuall ioy and comfort of this Realme, and to the euerlasting prayse and glory of thy Name, through Jesus Christ our Lord. Amen.

Or this.

We humbly acknowledge O most gracious and louing Father, thy manifolde mercies extended vnto vs in our dread Soueraigne. Thou hast crowned him with great ioy and gladnesse, in that thou hast often, and at this present made his noble Queene to be as the fruitfull Vine, and the number of his Children like Oliue branches round about his table. Giue vs grace, O heauenly Father, duely to consider of thy great goodnesse declared vnto her and vs in this her happy deliuerance, and to yeeld thee acceptable thanks for the same, in the great Congregation, through Christ our Lord and onely Sauiour.

Or this.

O eternall and onely wise God, that hast ordained, that we should be fearefully and wonderfully made: Our bones are not hid from thee, though we bee made secretly, and fashioned beneath in the earth: thine eyes do see our substance being yet vnperfit, & in thy booke are all our members written. Wherefore we reioyce in feare and giue thee thankes in reuerence, that thy sauing health hath beene present day by day with our gracious Queene, both in the conception of her late borne Babe, and in her safe deliuerance. Thou hast multiplied our nation, and increased our ioy, wee reioyce before thee according to the ioy in haruest, and as men reioice when they diuide the spoile. Accept, we beseech thee, this our sacrifice of praise and thankesgiuing, and continue thy manifold blessings vpon our dread Soueraigne, his vertuous Queen and the Royall Issue, as long as the Sunne and Moone endureth. Grant this, O Lord, for Jesus Christs sake our onely Mediatour and aduocate.

Or this.

Almightie God, who makest thy prouidence to appeare most euidently in the greatest dangers, at this time more especially in granting to our gracious Queene a safe, speedie and happy deliuerance from her late great labour and perill in Childe-birth: We yeelde thee hearty thankes for this thy mercifull kindnesse, beseeching thee to continue her watchfull keeper both day and night, and to renew her former strength: that as she hath happily brought foorth, so shee may comfortably bring vp this newe borne Babe, and may liue to see her a faithfull member of thy Church, and a ioyfull mother of children, to the glory of thy Name, through Jesus Christ our Lord.

Or this.

Eternall God, whose power is perfected in weakenesse, we giue thee humble thanks for protecting our gracious Queene *ANNE*, in her late trauaile of Childe-birth, giuing her strength safely to bring foorth her blessed Infant, whereby the Line of the Kings royall Progenie may be lengthened, the number of thy elect children multiplied, the ioy and comfort of this land more and more secured and increased, to the prayse and honour of thy glorious Name, through Jesus Christ our Lord, and onely Sauiour.

Or this.

Most mighty God and gracious Father, wee acknowledge both thy power and mercie, in that it hath pleased thee to deliuer our most noble Queen *ANNE*, from the fearefull paines and dangers of Child-birth, and to blesse her with an happy issue: We further beseech thee of thy fatherly goodnesse, that thou wouldest giue thine Angels charge ouer her to strengthen her afresh, and prosper the workman-ship of thine owne hands, in blessing this new borne Babe, that she may growe vp as a fruitfull Vine to multiply and encrease the happy Offspring of the Kings royall Seede, to the comfort and quiet of this Realme, and to the euerlasting glory of thy Name, through Jesus Christ our Lord. Amen.

1605–E3 Daily thanksgiving services for the discovery of the gunpowder plot

Daily, after Friday 8 November 1605 (England and Wales?)

The gunpowder plot was conceived by Robert Catesby, Thomas Winter, John Wright, Thomas Percy and Guy Fawkes in response to the failure of widespread hopes of toleration for catholics after James VI's accession to the English throne. The plotters initially aimed to destroy parliament, but soon decided to replace James as king with his third child, the eight-year old Elizabeth (on the grounds that Prince Henry would be present with James in parliament and that it would be too difficult to secure Prince Charles, who was in London). One of the conspirators, probably Francis Tresham, warned the former catholic, William Parker, Lord Monteagle, that an attack on parliament was planned. James was informed and ordered a search of parliament. Though nothing was found apart from large quantities of firewood in a storeroom, the king remained convinced that a plot was brewing so ordered a second search on the night of 4 November led by Sir Thomas Knyvett, keeper of Whitehall Palace. This time, on moving away some of the firewood, the barrels of gunpowder were discovered and, later, fuses and matches were found in Fawkes' possession. The trials of eight conspirators, including Fawkes, were conducted at Westminster Hall on 27 January; all were found guilty and were executed in St Paul's Churchyard (30 January) or the Old Palace Yard, Westminster (31 January). Immediately after the discovery of the plot James VI and I, who argued that the plot had been discovered through divine intervention, considered ordering an annual thanksgiving for its failure, likening it to the failure of another plot against him while he was in Scotland, the Gowrie plot (see Anniversary commemorations, volume 3); this suggestion was implemented by parliamentary statute early in 1606 (see Anniversary commemorations, volume 3). There was also a more immediate response. On 8 November, Richard Bancroft, bishop of London, ordered the archdeacon of St Albans to ensure that prayers and thanksgivings were observed in all parish churches within his jurisdiction, an instruction that was evidently repeated throughout the diocese of London and the whole kingdom. A form of prayer appears to have been commissioned for this occasion, though its precise identity is unclear. In his letter, Bancroft referred to 'Certayne prayers by publicke aucthoritie nowe sett forthe to that end and Comaunded to be vsed in everie parishe Churche through owte the whole Realme at all tymes of Common prayer.' Bancroft may have been referring to a form which has not survived or to *Prayers and thankesgiuing to be vsed by all the kings maiesties louing subiects, for the happy deliuerance of his maiestie, the queene, prince, and states of parliament, from the most traiterous and bloody intended massacre by gunpowder, the 5 of Nouember 1605. Set foorth by authoritie.* The latter form (transcribed below) is undated but was described by the editors of STC as [1606?]. However, with no reference to the *annual* celebration of 5 November in this form, it is possible that it is the form described by Bancroft and should be dated to 1605. On 10 November, Bishop William Barlow of Rochester preached about the plot at Paul's Cross.

Order: Bancroft to the archdeacon of St Albans, 8 Nov. 1605, HALS, ASA 5/4/189, p. 825.
Form of prayer: Possibly *Prayers and thankesgiuing to be vsed by all the kings maiesties louing subiects, for the happy deliuerance of his maiestie, the queene, prince, and states of parliament, from*

the most traiterous and bloody intended massacre by gunpowder, the 5 of Nouember 1605. Set foorth by
authoritie. ([1606?]; [48] pp.; STC 16494)* (transcribed below).
Additional sources: Bancroft to the archdeacon of St Albans, 30 Nov. 1605, HALS, ASA 5/4/191, pp.
831–3; St Michael le Querne, London, churchwardens' accounts, LMA, 2895/1, fo. 278v; St Bartholomew Exchange, London, churchwardens' accounts, LMA, 4383/1, p. 90; St Mary Magdalene, Milk
Street, London, LMA, 2596/1, fo. 234v.
Printed sermon: Barlow, Paul's Cross, London (STC 1455; variant edn, STC 1455.5).

ORDER

Bishop of London to the archdeacon of St Albans: 8 November 1605
After my hartie Comendacons. It hathe pleased of to worke soe mercifully for our
moste gratious Soueraigne kinge and the whole State of Parliament in discoveringe
the moste barbarous and trecherous practize that ever was devised to have destroyed
both our kinge and the estates of this Realme assembled in parliament for the which
we can never shewe any sufficient dutifull thanckfulnes vnto our heavenly Father
but onely by prostratinge our selves in prayer & thanckes givinge for this his blessed
discoverie and preventinge of the same. There beinge Certayne prayers by publicke
aucthoritie nowe sett forthe to that end and Comaunded to be vsed in everie parishe
Churche through owte the whole Realme at all tymes of Common prayer. Theis are
to requiere you that forth with you Cawse with all the speede you Can the said booke
of prayer and thanckes givinge to be sent to everie particuler Churche to be vsed by
the minister thereat with in your Jurisdiction at all tymes of Common prayer.

FORM OF PRAYER

MORNING PRAYER

I exhort you therefore *[as 1 Tim. 2:1–3]*

First the Minister shall with a lowd voyce pronounce one of these three sentences
following.
[Ps. 51:9; Jer. 10:24; Luke 15:18–19]

[As BCP to the psalms]

[Ps. 35, 68, 69]
[First lesson: 2 Sam. 22]
[Te Deum]
[Second lesson: Acts 23]
[Benedictus or Jubilate Deo]

[Then as BCP to the Lord's prayer]

Minister: O Lord shew thy mercie vpon vs.
People: And grant vs thy saluation.
Minister: O Lord saue the King.
People: Who putteth his trust in thee.
Minister: Send him helpe from thy holy place.
People: And euermore mightily defend him.

Minister: Let his enemies haue no aduantage against him.
People: Let not the wicked approch neere to hurt him.
Minister: Indue thy Ministers with righteousnesse *[and as BCP]*.

Prayers and Thankesgiuing for the happy deliuerance of his Maiestie, the Queene, the Prince, and the States of Parliament, &c.

Almighty God, who hast in all ages shewed thy power and mercy, in the miraculous and gracious deliuerances of thy Church, and in the protection of righteous and religious Kings, and States professing thy Holy and Eternal trueth, against the wicked Conspiracies, and malicious practises of all the Enemies thereof: Wee yeeld vnto thee from the very ground of our hearts all possible praise and thankes for the woonderfull, and mightie deliuerance of our gracious Souereigne King *IAMES*, the Queene, the Prince, and all the Royall branches, with the Nobilitie, Clergie, and Commons of this Realme, assembled together at this present in Parliament, by Popish treacherie appointed as sheepe to the slaughter, and that in most Barbarous and Sauage maner, no age yeelding example of the like cruelty intended towards the Lords Anointed, and his people. Can this thy goodnesse, O Lord, bee forgotten, worthy to be written in a pillar of Marble, that wee may euer remember to praise thee for the same, as the fact is worthy a lasting monument, that all posteritie may learne to detest it? From this vnnaturall Conspiracie, not our merite, but thy mercie, not our foresight, but thy prouidence hath deliuered vs, not our loue to thee, but thy loue to thine Anoynted Seruant, and thy poore Church, with whome thou hast promised to bee present to the end of the world. And therefore not vnto vs, not vnto vs, Lord, but to thy Name be ascribed all honour, and glory in all Churches of the saints, throughout all generations: For thou Lord hast discouered the snares of Death, Thou hast broken them, and we are deliuered; Be thou still our mighty Protectour, and scatter our cruel enemies, which delight in blood: infatuate their counsels, and roote out that Babylonish and Antichristian Sect, which say of Jerusalem, Downe with it, downe with it, euen to the ground. And to that ende strengthen the handes of our gracious King, the Nobles and Magistrates of the Land with iudgement & iustice to cut off these workers of iniquitie, (whose Religion is Rebellion, whose Faith is Faction, whose practise is murthering of soules and bodies) and to root them out of the confines and limits of this Kingdome, that they may neuer preuaile against vs, and triumph in the ruine of thy Church, and to giue vs grace by true and serious repentance, to auert these & the like iudgements from vs. This Lord we earnestly craue at thy mercifull hands, together with the continuance of thy powerfull protection ouer our dread Soueraigne, the whole Church, & these Realmes, and the speedy confusion of our implacable enemies, and that for thy deare Sonnes sake, our onely Mediatour and Aduocate.

Almighty God and heauenly Father, which of thy euerlasting prouidence and tender mercy towards vs, hast preuented the extreme malice and mischieuous imagination of our enemies, reuealing and confounding their horrible and deuilish enterprise plotted against our Soueraigne Lord the King, his Royall house, and the whole State of this Realme, for the subuersion thereof, together with the trueth of thy Gospel and pure Religion amongst vs, and for the reducing into this Church and land of Popish superstition and tyrannie: We most humbly praise and magnifie thy glorious Name, for thine infinite gracious goodnesse in this our marueilous deliuerance; we confesse it was and is thy mercy, thy mercy alone, (most mercifull Father) that we are not consumed, that their snare is broken, and our soule is escaped. For our sinnes cried to heauen against vs, and our iniquities iustly called for iudgment vpon vs: but thy great Mercy towards vs hath exalted it selfe aboue Judgement, not to deale with vs after our sinnes, to giue vs ouer (as we deserued) to bee a pray to our enemies, but taking our correction into thine owne handes, to deliuer vs from their blood-thirstie malice, and preserue from death & destruction our King and State, with thy holy Gospel and true Religion amongst vs. Good Lord giue vs true repentance, and vnfained conuersion vnto thee, to preuent further iudgements: increase in vs more & more a liuely faith and fruitfull loue in all obedience, that thou maiest continue thy louing fauour with the light of thy Gospel, to vs and our posteritie for euermore. Make vs now and alwayes truely thankefull in heart, word and deed, for all thy gracious mercies, and this our speciall deliuerance. Protect and defend our Soueraigne Lord the King, with the Queene and Prince, and all the Royall progenie, from all treasons and conspiracies, preserue them in thy faith, feare and loue, vnder the shadow of thy wings against all euill and wickednes, prosper their raigne with long happines on earth, & euerlasting glory following in the kingdome of heauen. Blesse the whole State and Realme with grace and peace, that with one heart and mouth we may praise thee in thy Church, and alwayes sing ioyfully, That thy mercifull kindnesse is euer more and more towardes vs, and the trueth of the Lord endureth for euer, through Jesus Christ our onely Sauiour and Redeemer. Amen.

[Then as BCP to the end of morning prayer]

LITANY

[As BCP, inserting before the prayer 'We humbly beseech thee' the following]

Eternall God, and our most mighty protector, wee thy people of this Land, confesse our selues, aboue all the Nations of the earth, infinitely bound vnto thy heauenly Maiestie, for thy many vnspeakable benefits conferred and heaped vpon vs, especially for planting thy Gospel among vs, and placing ouer vs a most gracious King, a faithfull professor and defender of the same; both which exasperate the enemies of true Religion, and enrage their thoughts to the inuention of most dreadfull designes: All which notwithstanding it hath pleased thee hitherto either to preuent or ouerthrow, at this time principally thou hast most strangely discouered an horrible and cruell plot and deuice, for the massacring as well of thy deare Seruant and our dread Soueraigne, as of the chiefe States, assembled in thy feare, for the continuance of thy trueth and good of this Realme. Wee humbly present our selues at thy feete, admiring thy might and wisedome, and acknowledging thy grace and fauour, in preseruing them and the whole Realme, by their safetie, beseeching thee for thy Sonne Jesus Christ his sake, to continue still thy care ouer vs, and to shield our gracious King vnder the shadow of thy wings, that no mischieuous attempt may come neere, nor the sonnes of wickednes may hurt him, but that vnder him wee may still enioy this his peaceable gouernment, with the profession of the Gospel of thy Sonne Christ Jesus, to whom with thee and the holy Ghost, &c.

O God, Infinite in power and of endlesse mercie, wee giue thee all possible thankes, that it hath pleased thee so miraculously to discouer, and defeat the mischieuous plots of thine and our enemies: thou hast deliuered our dread Soueraigne from the snare of the fowler, and his Nobles from the fire and the fury of the wicked: hee shall reioyce in thy saluation, and we his people shall trinmph in this thy woonderfull deliuerance, thy Gospel shall prosper, and thine aduersaries shall bee confounded. And multiply (good Lord) wee beseech thee, thy great goodnesse towards our gracious King, and his kingdoms, from this time forth, through Jesus Christ our Lord, Amen.

[After the prayer 'we humbly beseech thee', the BCP prayer for the clergy and people]

[The prayer of St Chrysostom; the grace]

COMMUNION

If there be a Communion, then let the Epistle, Gospel, and Prayers of thankesgiuing newly appointed for the present occasion, be vsed in the places as they are here following set downe, to bee vsed when there is no Communion.

[As BCP to the end of the ten commandments]

Almighty God, whose kingdom is everlasting *[as BCP]*

[No prayer in place of the collect for the day was specified; probably one of the special collects at morning prayer was to be used]

[Epistle: Rom. 13:1–7]
[Gospel: Matt. 27:1–10]
[Nicene creed]
[Offertory sentence: Matt. 7:12]

[The prayer for the whole state of the church]

Assist vs mercifully, O Lord *[as BCP]*

Almightie God, which hast promised *[as BCP, followed by the blessing]*

1606–E   Prayers during the pregnancy of Queen Anna

[January–May?] 1606 (England and Wales?)

Soon after the death of Princess Mary (see 1605–E2), Queen Anna became pregnant again, and prayers were issued. No orders are extant; the text of the form of prayer followed that for 1605–E1. On 22 June 1606 the queen gave birth to another daughter, Sophia. The child died within twenty-four hours, evidently before any thanksgiving prayers could be issued.

Order: none found.
Form of prayer: *Prayers appointed to be vsed in the church at morning and euening prayer by euery minister, for the queenes safe deliuerance. Set forth and inioyned by authority* (8 pp.; STC 16537)*.

FORM OF PRAYER

[As 1605–E1]

1611–E   Services during a time of drought

1611 (England and Wales?)

There is no specific evidence about weather conditions in 1611, but the previous summer had been unusually dry. It was the first time since 1585–E2 that prayers had been ordered for bad weather. It is unclear why prayers had not been ordered in the interim, when the realm had been subject to harsh winters and both dry and wet summers; severe drought in 1607 had caused widespread rioting in the midlands. War and the products of bad weather – notably dearth – seem to have been regarded as more pressing reasons for special worship during this period. The form issued in 1611 provided a full liturgy but was printed in abbreviated form as instructions and two new prayers, one to be read after the third collect and the other at the end of the litany. Like some of the late Elizabethan prayers, the second of these was very long. For only the second time (see 1566–E), were specific instructions given on conducting evening prayer.

Order: none found.
Form of prayer: *A forme of praier to be vsed in London, and elsewhere in this time of drought. Set forth by authoritie* (16 pp.; STC 16538)*.

FORM OF PRAYER

MORNING PRAYER

At Morning Prayer after the 95. Psalme, O Come let vs Singe vnto the Lord, &c. *Reade the 105. Psalme, and the 107. Psalme.*
  For the first Lesson, the 26. of Leuiticus, or Deuteron. 28.
  For the second Lesson, the 24. of Matthew, or the 11. of the Acts of the Apostles.

After the Collect, O Lord our heauenly Father, Almighty and euerlasting God, &c, *say this Praier.*
  O almightie God, for as much as wee are taught by thy Word, that when thine anger is kindled against vs for our sinnes, among other punishments thou doest shut vp the Heauen, that there may bee no Raine, and causest that the earth may yeeld no fruite: Wee humbly confesse this immoderat Drought, to be inflicted vpon vs for our disobedience vnto thee, and thy holy Commandements, which we haue often violated with contempt of thy Sacred Maiestie, We are sorry for these our transgressions, Wee mourne that we haue straied from thy paths of Righteousnesse, and do beseech thee to haue mercy vpon vs, and not to punish vs with thy scorching and burning furie; Our fruitfull land is at this time like to become a barren place, and the labour of our handes is almost spoiled for want of thy good blessing, in sending downe moderate and seasonable showers. But, Father of all mercies, and God of consolation, bee mercifull vnto vs, and as thou hast bene prouoked by our manifold sinnes, so be pacified with our feeling and vnfained Repentance, mitigate thy iust iudgement by thine aboundant, (although vndeserued) Mercie: Vouchsafe so to mollifie our stony and hard hearts, that we may be truely humbled in thy sight, And thou remembring the riches of thy loue towards vs in thy Sonne Christ, mayest bee gracious vnto vs, and powre out of the Heauens such moderate and temperate Showers, that we may enioy the ordinary increase of the earth, and may loue and priase thy Name through the mediation of thy Sonne, and our Sauiour Jesus Christ.

Then reade the Letany, where after the Prayer, Almighty and euerlasting God, which onely workest great marueiles, &c, *say this Prayer.*

O eternall God, who hast created the world by thy mighty power, and by thy great prouidence doest rule and guide all things therein contained for the good of man; Ordayning thy creatures sometimes to bee instruments of thy Loue and Mercie vnto vs, to stirre vs vp vnto Thankefulnesse, and sometimes declarers of thine anger and fury against vs for our sinnes, to humble vs, mortifie vs, and to bring vs vnto true and serious Repentance: Wee wretched and sinfull creatures, humbly prostrated before thy glorious Maiestie, acknowledge thy blessings vpon our Land, in making it in great aboundance to bring foorth the bud of the hearbe, and of euery greene and liuing thing according to his kinde, to haue bene at sundry times exceedingly multiplied. For these thy Mercies our mouthes should haue bene filled with the voyce of vncessant Prayse and Thankesgiuing: wee should haue offered vp our selues, our soules, our bodies, and our whole man as a reasonable sacrifice vnto thy diuine Maiestie, all the dayes of our life: But such hath bene our blindnesse in beholding thine innumerable benefits, our dulnesse in meditating vpon them, and so horrible our ingratitude, that the more thou hast powred downe thy fauours vpon vs, the more haue wee multiplied our sinnes, abusing thy good gifts vnto riot, luxurie, wantonnesse, and vnto all kinde of intemperance. Most righteous God, so grieuous are our transgressions, that thou art iustly angrie with vs, and now doest manifest this thy displeasure, in shutting vp the windowes of Heauen, and in hardening them as iron, or brasse, in scattering the Cloudes, and commanding them that they drop not vpon the drie and thirstie earth, euen parched with the heate of thine indignation. We haue a liuely sense and feeling of this thy heauie displeasure kindled against vs, We groane vnder the burthen of our manifolde sinnes and transgressions, which terrifie vs from approching vnto thy Tribunall to begge any thing at thy hand; But yet because such is thy gracious goodnesse towards the sonnes of men, that by thy Prophet Zachary thou hast mercifully promised vs: Aske you of the Lord Raine in the time of the later Raine, so shall the Lord make white clouds, and giue you showers of Raine, and to euery one grasse in the fielde: Wee acknowledging our vnworthinesse, and onely relying vpon thine infinite Mercies, do presume to powre out our humble supplications before thee, and with lowly, contrite and broken hearts, doe beseech thee, That thou wouldest heare our Prayers, as thou diddest sometimes the earnest supplications of Helias: who prayed, and the Heauens gaue Raine, and the earth brought forth fruit. It hath pleased thee (most Gracious God) to promise by the mouth of thy seruant Moses vnto Israel, That if that people would hearken vnto thy Commandements, and loue thee, and serue thee with all their heart, and with all their soule, that thou wouldest giue raine vnto that Land in due time, the first Raine, and the later, that they might gather in thy Wheat and thine Oyle, and that thou wouldest send grasse in their fieldes for cattell, that they might eate ynough: And againe vnto the same people by thy Prophet Hosea, That vpon their true Repentance, and vnfained turning vnto thee, thou wouldest heare the Heauens, and they should heare the earth, and the earth should heare the grasse, the Corne and the Oyle, and wouldest haue Mercie vpon them that were not pitied.

Mercifull Father, with an humble confession of our former ingratitude and vnthankefulnesse, a loathing and hatred of our transgressions committed with a high hand against thy sacred Maiestie, with a serious purpose of walking in the wayes which thou hast commanded vs, with bitter mourning and heartie Repentance we turne vnto thee. Turne then vnto vs, most mercifull Father, extend thy great goodnes and compassion towards vs, and not onely sprinckle our consciences with the dew of thy grace, but also outwardly powre downe thy fruit-bringing Showres, that we may taste and see, how gracious thou art in the seasonable yeeld of the earth: to the honour of thy great Name, and the comfortable refreshing of thy seruants, for the merits of thy Sonne Jesus Christ our onely Lord and Sauiour.

EVENING PRAYER

At Euening Prayer, Reade the 78. Psalme, in steade of the Psalmes appointed for the day.
   For the first Lesson, reade 1. Kings 18. or Ioel the first Chapter.
   For the second Lesson, reade Iames 5. or Apocal. 6.
Before the Collect, Lighten our darkness, &c. *Reade the former prayer,* O eternall God, who has created, &c.

1613–E   Services during heavy rains and threats to the harvest

1613 (England and Wales?)

After the dry years of 1610, 1611 and 1612, heavy rain fell in 1613, once again threatening the harvest. The form of prayer copied the format of that issued for 1611–E. The prayer to be read at the end of the litany includes references to 'an vnusuall disease' that affected the country at the same time; this has not been identified. No orders are extant for this occasion.

Order: none found.
Form of prayer: *A forme of prayer to be publikely vsed in churches, during this vnseasonable weather, and aboundance of raine. Set forth by authoritie. Hosea 5.15. In their affliction they will seeke me early.* (14 pp.; STC 16539)* (with illegible text supplied from BL, C.133.f.13(2)).

FORM OF PRAYER

MORNING PRAYER

At Morning Prayer after the 95. Psalme, O Come let vs Singe vnto the Lord, &c. *Reade the 105. Psalme, and the 106. Psalme.*
        For the first Lesson, the 6. and 7. of Genesis.
        For the second Lesson, the 17. of Luke, or the 24. of Matthew.

After the Collect, O Lord our heauenly Father, Almighty and euerlasting God, &c. *Say this Prayer.*
   Most gracious God, and mercifull Father, forasmuch as wee are taught by thy holy Word,[262] that thou wilt breake the pride of our power, bring vpon vs burning Agues to consume vs, make our hearts heauie; And that thou wilt suffer vs to sow our Seed in vaine, and breake the staffe of our Bread, when we despise thy sacred Ordinances, and walke stubbornly against thee: in that thou hast partly visited, partly threatned vs with thy dreadfull punishments, thou doest thereby graciously admonish vs of our

---

262 In margin: 'Leuit.26.'

manifold sinnes, and wilfull transgressions against thy most scared Maiestie. Wee haue a long time securely slumbred in the senselessenes of our iniquities, and it hath pleased thy Gracious goodnesse by these thy chastisements mercifully to awaken vs. Wherefore we see the grieuousnes of our impietie, and beholding it, our hearts are filled with sorrow, and our eyes are watered with penitent teares. We do humbly acknowledge and confesse our great vnthankefulnesse for the continuall multiplying of thy blessings vpon vs. For the more thou hast heaped on vs thy Mercies, the more haue we, wretched sinners, by our transgressions prouoked thy Justice: and therefore most iustly hast thou laid thy heauie hand vpon vs, in smiting some of vs with a lingering sicknesse, & by vnseasonable wether menacing dearth, and further scarcity. These extraordinarie afflictions, are infallible signes of thy wrath & anger kindled against vs, yet because we know thee not onely to be a iust, and righteous, but likewise a mercifull God in thy deare Sonne Jesus Christ; through his media-tion, wee presume to prostrate our selues before thy Throne of grace, most humbly beseeching thy Fatherly goodnesse to wash away the vncleane pollutions of our sinnes with his precious blood, and to cast them into the bottome of the Sea, that their lowd crie may no longer pearce the Heauens, and thence pluck downe thine irefull indignation vpon vs: but wee being receiued into thy fauour, and henceforth walking in pietie, obedience, temperance, sobriety, and bringing forth fruits worthy of amendment of life, may to our comfort enioy thy temporall blessings in this life, and in that which is to come eternall glory, for Christ his sake our onely Aduocate and Mediatour. Amen.

LITANY

Then reade the Letanie, where, after the Prayer, Almighty and euerlasting God, which onely workest great marueiles, &c, *say this Prayer.*

O most Omnipotent Creator, who by thine infinite power hast framed the whole world, and all things therein contained, of nothing, and out of thine vnspeakable loue towards man hast placed glorious lights in the firmament to shine vpon the earth, and to be signes for Seasons, for Dayes, and for Yeeres, & hast appointed the Heauens to shed down fruitful showres, and the earth to bring foorth euery greene and liuing thing in due season: for this thine inestimable goodnesse we are inces-santly bound to dedicate our selues, our soules and bodies, yea, all our thoughts, and endeauors to be perpetuall sacrifices of thankefulnesse vnto thy holy Name, and euermore to praise and magnifie the riches of thy mercy towards vs. But wee, like a disobedient, and sinfull people, haue bin altogether vnmindfull of thy great clem-encie, and made thy gracious blessings instruments of horrible ingratitude against thy diuine Maiestie: abusing them to pride, wantonnesse, surfetting, drunkennesse, and all kind of riot and excesse; wherewith wee most iustly haue prouoked thy fearefull wrath, and indignation against vs. And as we by the multitude of our sinnes haue frequently violated thy diuine ordinances, and Statutes, so hast thou of late commanded the heauens, the earth, and the times and seasons depending on them, to breake and alter their course, so to punish vs for these sinnes, with an vnusuall disease, and with feare of future famine, if out of thy bottomlesse mercy thou stretchest not out thy sauing hand to stop the streame of thy fury, like to be powred downe vpon vs. We haue sinned, we haue sinned, O Lord, and in the immoderate showres, vnnaturall seasons of the yeere, and long lingring sicknesse continuing yet amongst vs, We haue felt the weight of thy heauie displeasure. But now from the ground of our hearts, We grieue and are sorry, We mourne, and lament for these our transgressions: Lord then let thy heauie displeasure cease, and be no longer angry with vs. We doe vnfainedly repent vs of all our iniquities, and through the gracious assistance of thy holy spirit doe most seriously purpose to turne vnto thee: Lord then turne vnto vs, and let the light of thy countenance shine vpon vs, in vouchsafing vnto vs moderate showres, healthfull seasons, and the fruitfull increase of the earth. Blesse vs O Lord, that we may blesse thee; giue vnto vs strength, and health, that we may praise thy sauing health: graunt vnto vs seasonable weather, and with it, thy plenty and aboundance, that so we may be taught to magnifie the abundance of thy mercies through all generations, to our euerlasting saluation, and thy endlesse honor and glory, through Jesus Christ our onely Lord and Sauiour. Amen.

EVENING PRAYER

At Euening Prayer, Reade the 78. Psalme, in steade of the Psalmes appointed for the day.

For the first Lesson, reade Deut. 28.

For the second Lesson, reade the Epistle of S. Iude, or 1. Cor. 10. vnto the end of the thirteenth verse.

Before the Collect, Lighten our darkness, &c. *reade this Prayer.*

Eternall God, whose perfect holinesse being euery where present, cannot suffer the wilfull encrease of wickednes and sinne: and therefore by thy manifest and visible iudgments thou declarest vnto grieuous sinners, both the greatnesse of thine indignation, and the weightinesse of their offences: we miserable & wretched sinners, being admonished by the apparent signes of thy displeasure now vpon vs, into what danger wee haue brought our selues by sinne, doe here humbly confesse our multiplied transgressions against thy diuine Maiestie, earnestly desiring thy singular goodnes, to respect vs with the eye of mercy, and to grant vnto vs vnfained repentance, that so the course of thy deserued anger may bee stayed against vs. O Lord, we behold and acknowledge thy hand powring vpon vs this chastisement of immoderate raine and waters: and the long continuance of this vnseasonable weather, hath wrought vpon our consciences (which are not so sensible as they should bee) at length to be affrighted, and to call vpon thee. Saue vs therfore, O God, that we perish not: deliuer vs out of the mire, that we sinke not: preserue vs, O Lord, for the waters are come in, euen vnto the soules of many of vs. Let not the water flood drowne vs, neither let the deepe swallow vs vp: and let not the pit shut her mouth vpon vs. We confesse, O God, that iniquitie doeth abound, that our sundry pollutions haue cried euen to the heauens for all thy stormes and tempests to fall vpon vs: but we beseech thee rather of thy infinite mercy to wash vs in the merits of thy Sonne Jesus Christ our Sauiour: for his sake accept our teares, our sighes, and hearty sorrow for our sinnes, and by the assistance of thy gracious spirit, make good our true purposes of amendment of life: Let thy blessed Name rather bee glorified in our saluation. Father of mercies, and God of al consolation, looke vpon the signe of thy Couenant in the clouds, and as thou sauedst thy people in the red sea; so we beseech thee to restraine thy showres, and to deliuer vs from this plague of waters. Furthermore, O heauenly Father, we doe feele that wrath is already gone out from thee, that thou doest threaten vs with scarcitie, and dearth: by these intemperate ouerflowings to make our fruitfull land barren, for the wickednesse of them that dwell therein: wee earnestly desire thee to forgiue the ignorances of the people, that the multitude of poore may not perish whome thou hast created. Our manifold sinnes, O Lord, do deserue, that thou shouldest visit vs with all thy roddes: As thou hast scourged vs heretofore with pestilence, & doest now weaken vs with a new disease: so thou maiest more deseruedly consume vs with scarcitie, and waste vs with death: but we flie vnto the Sanctuary of thy louing kindenesse, and the multitude of thy mercies towards vs, which exceede the variety of our sinnes. Remember thy wonted fauours to this land, how long thou hast giuen vs moderate raine from heauen, and fruitfull seasons, filling our hearts with ioy and gladnesse. Which blessings although we haue abused like prodigal sonnes, by riot, and intemperance, by forgetfulnes and vnthankfulnes, yet for thy goodnes receiue vs when we turne vnto thee by the intercession of thy only obedient Sonne, and grant vs the continuance of these temporall benefits, whereof we haue necessitie in this life, vntill wee haue passed to immortalitie, and things eternall in the life to come, by the grace and mercy of our Sauiour Jesus Christ, who liueth and reigneth, &c.

Or this.

Almightie, and most merciful Father, which vsest to be prouoked by offences, and yet pacified againe by repentance: which by thy punishments desirest the destruction of the sinnes, and not of the soules of thy seruants: We miserable and grieuous sinners doe beseech thee, to encline thine eares vnto our prayers, and to deliuer vs from the future calamities and afflictions, which (we haue iust cause to feare) doe now hang ouer our heades. Thou hast changed already the ordinary custome of the season, and by the ouerflowing of raine and waters doest threaten to wash away the strength and fatnes of the earth; to send scarcity and want amongst vs: We humbly beseech thee to turne away this thy deserued displeasure from vs, to consider our infirmities, and vpon our sorrow and repentance to alter the sentence of seueritie, if any be gone out against vs, and that for thy tender mercy in Christ Jesus, who liueth and reigneth, &c.

1621–S Fast days during anxieties over contempt of religion, safety of the royal family, the Ottoman threat and persecution of German and French protestants

Sunday 24 June – Sunday 1 July 1621 (Scotland)

This national fast, the first in Scotland for twenty years, seems to have been ordered in preparation for the parliament which met in Edinburgh on 25 July 1621 to levy taxation and ratify the five articles of Perth, controversial liturgical reforms that had excited considerable opposition within the Kirk. It is unclear who called the fast, though it is likely that the order came from the bishops or the government. The causes mentioned by Calderwood reflect the perennial themes of low religious standards and fears for the royal family, as well as the dangerous position of European protestantism following the outbreak of the Thirty Years War in 1618. For opponents of the crown's religious policies, who thought the imposition of episcopacy and the Perth articles were reasons for humiliation, these causes did not go far enough. According to Calderwood, the leading clergy among the opposition tried to organize their own fast for the Sunday before the meeting of parliament. Large numbers of these ministers were in Edinburgh, where they hoped to apply pressure on the parliament. The presbytery of Perth, which received the order on 20 June, appointed that the fast be observed across the first two Sundays in July, to avoid a fair in the final week of June.

Order: described in Calderwood, VII, 463.
Additional sources: Calderwood, VII, 463–4; Row, pp. 328–9; presbytery of Perth minutes, NRS, CH2/299/1, p. 62; Sir Patrick Hume to Sir Robert Ker, *c.* June 1621, NRS, GD40/2/13/14.

DESCRIPTION OF ORDER

Calderwood, *History*
Upon the Lord's day, the 17th of June, intimation was made efter sermon in Edinburgh, of a fast to be keeped through all the kingdome the nixt two Sabboth-days, for the generall contempt of the Word; the preservation of the king and his children; the preparation of the Turke, lying in wait to invade Europe, and seeking advantage of the division of Christians; and the persecution of the kirk in Germanie and France.

1622–S   Fast days during anxieties over sinfulness, dearth and threats to French, German and Bohemian protestants

Sunday 12 May – Sunday 19 May 1622 (Edinburgh)

This fast is known only from a description in Calderwood's *History*, which does not describe the ordering process. The fast may have been observed outwith Edinburgh. It was a response to the onset of dearth (see 1623–S1) and to the Thirty Years War. As in several of his other descriptions of fasts, Calderwood noted that the Church of Scotland's own failings – the result, he believed, of the imposition of episcopacy – were not specified as a reason for fasting.

Source: Calderwood, VII, 548.

DESCRIPTION

Calderwood, *History*
Upon the Lord's day, the 12th of May, there was a solemne fast keeped in the kirk of Edinburgh, and the weeke efter there were two sermons in two kirks everie day … The causes of the fast were, grouth of sin, appeirance of dearth and famine, the troubled estate of the Kirks of France, Germanie, and Bohemia; but noe mention was made of the rent that was in the kirk at home.

1623–S1   Fast days during famine and anxiety over idolatry and Prince Charles's proposed marriage

Sunday 29 June – Sunday 6 July 1623 (Scotland)

A severe famine, caused by two successive harvest failures, afflicted Scotland in 1622 and 1623. There was considerable mortality and internal migration, as parochial poor relief failed to meet the demand. At the same time, the projected marriage between Prince Charles and the Spanish Infanta (see 1623–S2) exacerbated fears concerning catholicism and idolatry. According to Row, contemporaries were surprised that a meeting of bishops, who were thought to be hostile to the practice of fasting, appointed this observance.

Order: by the meeting of bishops and ministers, 22 Apr. 1623 (described by Calderwood, VII, 571, 577). **Additional sources:** Calderwood, VII, 577; Row, pp. 332–3; presbytery of Perth minutes, NRS, CH2/299/1, pp. 87–8; presbytery of Ellon minutes, NRS, CH2/146/2, fo. 178r.

DESCRIPTION OF ORDER

Order by the meeting of bishops and ministers: 22 April 1623
Upon the 22d of Aprile, there was a meeting at St Androes, where the Bishops of St Androes, Brechine, Aberdeene, Murrey, Rosse, and Dumblane, and some ministers written for, conveened … They appointed a fast to be keeped universallie the last Sabboth of June, and the first Sabboth of Julie … The causes of the humiliation were, the present famine, the feare of idolatrie to creepe in againe, the danger the prince was in both for bodie and soule.

1623–S2   Thanksgiving service for Prince Charles's return from Spain

Monday 13 October 1623 (Edinburgh)

After concluding the negotiations for marriage between Charles and the Spanish Infanta (an alliance that was not solemnized), the prince and the duke of Buckingham returned to England, arriving at the royal hunting lodge at Royston, Hertfordshire, on 6 October 1623. Their return prompted spontaneous celebration in England and Scotland. This official thanksgiving was appointed at short notice for Edinburgh alone (compare 1594–S1 and 1600–S). Calderwood reported that the earl of Melrose, the president of the privy council, received a report of Charles's return on 13 October. Melrose then met the Edinburgh ministers, and engaged John Guthrie to preach at St Giles' that afternoon.

Order: privy council proclamation, 13 Oct. 1623, *RPC*, 1st ser., XIII, 374–5. **Additional source:** Calderwood, VII, 580.

ORDER

Privy council proclamation: 13 October 1623
Forsamekle as it hes bene the goode pleasour of God in his exceiding grite favour and mercye towardis this Iland to blisse the same with the most confortable, happie,

and saulff returne of the Prince his Heynes; for the whilk, as it becometh all goode
subjectis in most submissive and humble maner to acknoulege this so inestimable a
benefeit quhairwith it hes pleasit the Almightie God to conforte and blisse thame, so
thay aught to utter and expresse thair joy and thankfulnes by a solemne and publict
thankisgeving, and for this effect to conveene with thair pastouris in the House of
God and to concur and joyne togidder in a most solemne maner to gif all honnour,
praise, and thankis to his divyne Majestie for this his grite kyndnes; and whereas
this publict thankisgeving is appointit to be in the grite Kirk this present day at three
after noone: Thairfoir ordanis herauldis and purseuantis to pas to the mercatt croce
of Edinburgh and thair to mak publicatioun heirof, and to warne all the inhabitantis
of this burgh to repair to the kirk at the ringing of the bell, and with humble and
thankfull hartis to praise God for the premissis, and thairafter to manifest thair joy
and thankfulnes by setting oute of bonefyris and making all otheris taikynnis of joy,
according as the nature and circomestanceis of the caus and thair bundin dewtie
requiris.

1625–E   Weekly fast days during the plague epidemic, for Charles I, the realm and the naval and military forces

Wednesday 20 July 1625, and every Wednesday during the plague (England and Wales)

Plague had broken out in some towns and parishes in 1624 but the disease hit a
peak in 1625 and 1626. The new king, Charles I, was also committed to James I's
policy of supporting an Anglo-French force under Count Mansfeld to regain the
Palatinate for his (Charles's) brother-in-law, Frederick. Frederick had accepted the
crown of Bohemia from its citizens, but had lost both Bohemia and the Palatinate to
Maximilian of Bavaria, who had launched successful invasions in retaliation with the
help of his Habsburg in-laws. As a result, war with Habsburg Spain also threatened.
On 21 June 1625 in the House of Commons, Sir Miles Fleetwood proposed a public
fast for a blessing on the new king, in support of persecuted protestants abroad, a
blessing on the navy, and because of the plague, to be preceded by a private fast
within parliament. Sir William Strode seconded the motion, and suggested that
they should also petition the king for appointment of the public fast, to be observed
throughout the kingdom. After some debate on whether the Commons needed to
seek royal permission for a parliamentary fast, and on whether by petitioning for
a general fast they might lose the opportunity to hold a parliamentary fast, it was
agreed to petition the king for a general fast. A committee drew up a petition which,
in contrast to Fleetwood's original motion, placed much emphasis on the 'heavy
judgements' (such as plague) that God had laid on the realm. The implication was
that the Commons would not consider the king's business until the issue of the fast
had been considered. On 23 June the petition was presented to the House of Lords,
which concurred with the Commons and presented it to the king. On 24 June, Charles
expressed his agreement in principle, though stating that he needed time to consider
the form and manner of the fast. On 28 June, he informed the two houses that he
left the arrangements of the private parliamentary fast to them, and suggested that
the public fast should be held on Thursday, 7 July. On the proposal of the House of

Lords later that day, it was agreed that the parliamentary fast should be held on the following Saturday, 2 July; but it considered that 7 July was too soon for notices for the general fast to reach all parts of the kingdom, and suggested that the fast might be held in London on 2 July, in Westminster on Monday 4 July, and in the rest of the kingdom on Saturday 16 July. For reasons which are unknown, the king by proclamation instead appointed the general fast for Wednesday 20 July. The fast was to be repeated every Wednesday thereafter during the plague epidemic.

The form of prayer was composed by George Abbot (archbishop of Canterbury), George Mountain (bishop of London), Richard Neile (bishop of Durham), Samuel Harsnett (bishop of Norwich), Lancelot Andrewes (bishop of Winchester and dean of the chapel royal), William Laud (bishop of St David's) and John Buckeridge (bishop of Rochester). The form was largely derived from the previous form of prayer during the plague, 1603–E, including the 'short preface', the 'exhortation fit for the time', and the 'order for the fast', with its warnings against excessive sermons and against public fasts arranged without official authority. For the first time, it was stated that the psalms to be read at evening prayer, after the Lord's prayer and the versicles, were to be those which had not been read at morning prayer. This became a common practice during the 1620s and 1630s. Some editions of the form of prayer added a prayer for parliament at the start of the form. This prayer was reprinted in the special forms for 1628–E1, 1661–E and 1662–E, and was then (in slightly modified form) added to the 1662 BCP. One version of the form indicated the uncertainty about the prospects of war: it added that a prayer for the navy was not to be read out publicly until the navy had sailed.

The House of Lords resolved on 1 July that at their private fast in Westminster Abbey the next day, peers should contribute to collections for the poor, and on 10 August it agreed to fine those who had not been present to contribute: this was a common practice in the Lords. On 2 August, some MPs complained that the general fast was not being observed because of the failure of bishops to distribute copies of the form, or because parishes were being charged too much for them (between 10d and 3s) and sellers were making a profit. Certainly, some forms had been purchased by private individuals: the biblical scholar Joseph Mede obtained one in Cambridge for his friend, Sir Martin Stuteville. This is the earliest evidence of the private purchase of forms of prayer, which became a common practice by the mid-eighteenth century. There were also growing concerns that gatherings of people to hear the fast sermons on Wednesdays contributed to the spread of the contagion. The controversies of 1603–4 were revived, regarding why plague occurred, how it was spread and how best to combat it, and a number of pamphlets were reprinted.

This occasion was significant for two reasons. It was the first time that a general fast had been successfully initiated in parliament (a motion made by Sir Dudley Digges in 1624 had been ignored by James). This became characteristic not only of Charles's reign – when there was a motion for a general fast in every parliament until the outbreak of the civil war – but of the seventeenth century as a whole. Second, it was the first time that nationwide special worship was ordered in all three of the monarch's realms, though worship in Ireland was not ordered until October (see 1625–S and 1625–Ir).

Order: royal proclamation, 3 July 1625, STC 8787* [also in Larkin, II, 46–8].
Form of prayer: *A forme of common prayer, together with an order of fasting: for the auerting of Gods heauy visitation vpon many places of this kingdome, and for the drawing downe of his blessings vpon*

❧By the King.

¶ A Proclamation for a publike, generall,
and solemne Faft.

He Kings moft Excellent Maieftie, vpon the humble Petition of the Lords Spirituall and Temporall, and Commons in the prefent Parliament affembled, taking into his Princely confideration the many important caufes, and extraordinary occafions calling vpon him, and his people for a ioynt and generall humiliation of all Eftates of his Kingdome, before Almighty God in Prayer and Fafting, afwell for auerting this heauy Vifitation of Plague and Peftilence, already begun, and dangeroufly difperfed in many parts of this Kingdome, as alfo for drawing downe his Bleffing vpon his Maiefty and His people, and Armies both by Sea and Land, hath therefore (according to the Royall and laudable example of other godly Kings) by the aduice and affiftance of His Prelates and Bifhops, caufed an Order or Direction for publique Prayer and Fafting, to be conteined and publifhed in Print, in a Booke for this fpeciall purpofe, to be generally obferued and folemnized, in humble hope and confidence, that when both Prince and People together through the whole Land, that ioyne in one common & folemne Deuotion, of fending vp their faithfull and repentant Prayers to Almighty God at one inftant of time, the fame fhall bee more auaileable to obtaine that mercie, helpe and comfort from him, which in the prefent important occafions this Church and Common-wealth doe ftand in neede of.

His Maieftie doeth therefore by this prefent Proclamation ftraitly charge and command, That a generall, publike, and folemne Faft be kept and holden, as well by abftinence from food, as by publike Prayers, Preaching, and hearing of the Word of God, and other facred duties, according to the direction of the faid Booke, in all collegiate and parifh-Churches and Chappels within this Kingdome of England, and Dominion of Wales, vpon Wednefday, the twentieth day of this inftant moneth of Iuly, and from thenceforth continued vpon the Wednefday of euery weeke following, by the reuerend, religious, and deuout Affembly of the whole Congregation of fuch of the Inhabitants in each feuerall place, as are free and fafe from danger of Infection, and may in euery Family be conueniently fpared: willing and requiring, afwell all Archbifhops, and Bifhops, in their feuerall Prouinces, and Dioceffes, and all Parfons, Vicars and Curats, within their feuerall Parifhes and Charges, as alfo all Maiors, Sheriffes, Iuftices of Peace, and other Officers in their feuerall places, limits, and iurifdictions, refpectiuely to take efpeciall care, that this His Maiefties Royall commandement be duly executed and obferued: And that they themfelues be lights of good example to the reft; And that all others in manner aforefaid, doe diligently and deuoutly follow and performe the fame, as they tender their duties to Almighty God, and to their Prince and Countrey, and will anfwere for their prophane, or contemptuous neglect hereof at their vttermoft perils.

Giuen at the Court at White-Hall, the third day of Iuly, in the firft yeere of his Maiefties Reigne of Great Britaine, France and Ireland.

God faue the King.

¶ Printed at London by Bonham Norton and Iohn Bill,
Printers to the Kings moft Excellent Maieftie.
M. DC. XXV.

7 The first surviving printed royal proclamation issued to order an occasion of special worship, for the English services and fast days during the plague outbreak, 1625–E (1625; STC 8787); Huntington Library, San Marino, CA, Rare Books 53525, single sheet folio.

vs, and our armies by sea and land. The prayers are to be read euery Wednesday during this visitation. Set foorth by his maiesties authority (112 pp.; STC 16540)* with first page of the prayer for parliament supplied from BL, 3406.d.1(1).

Form of prayer (other edition): STC 16541.

Additional sources: *LJ*, III, 440–1, 443, 447–8, 451–2, 486; *CJ*, I, 799, 801–2, 810; HMC, *Thirteenth rep., app. IV*, p. 174; *APC*, XL, 125; *Memoirs of the life and works of the right honorable and right revd. father in God, Lancelot Andrewes*, ed. Arthur T. Russell (Cambridge, 1860), pp. 505–6; Mead to Stuteville, 4 Feb. 1626, W. B. Bidwell and M. Jansson (eds.), *Proceedings in parliament, 1626* (4 vols., New Haven, 1991–6), IV, 264.

Printed sermons: Hildersham, Ashby? (STC 13459, 13460); Preston, House of Commons (STC 20262, 20263, 20264, 20265, 20265.5).

ORDER

Royal proclamation: 3 July 1625

The Kings most Excellent Maiestie, vpon the humble Petition of the Lords Spirituall and Temporall, and Commons in the present Parliament assembled, taking into his Princely consideration the many important causes, and extraordinary occasions calling vpon him, and his people for a ioynt and generall humiliation of all Estates of His Kingdome, before Almighty God in Prayer and Fasting, aswell for auerting this heauy Visitation of Plague and Pestilence, already begun, and dangerously dispersed in many parts of this Kingdome, as also for drawing downe his Blessing vpon his Maiesty and His people, and Armies both by Sea and Land, hath therefore (according to the Royall and laudable example of other godly Kings) by the aduice and assistance of His Prelates and Bishops, caused an Order or Direction for publique Prayer and Fasting, to be conceiued and published in Print, in a Booke for this speciall purpose, to be generally obserued and solemnized, in humble hope and confidence, that when both Prince and People together through the whole Land, shal ioyne in one common, & solemne Deuotion, of sending vp their faithfull and repentant Prayers to Almighty God at one instant of time, the same shall bee more auaileable to obtaine that mercie, helpe and comfort from him, which in the present important occasions this Church and Common-wealth doe stand in neede of.

His Maiestie doeth therefore by this present Proclamation straitly charge and command, That a generall, publike, and solemne Fast be kept and holden, as well by abstinence from food, as by publike Prayers, Preaching, and hearing of the Word of God, and other sacred duties, according to the direction of the said Booke, in all collegiate and parish-Churches and Chappels within this Kingdome of *England*, and Dominion of *Wales*, vpon Wednesday, the twentieth day of this instant moneth of *Iuly*, and from thencefoorth continued vpon the Wednesday of every weeke following, by the reuerend, religious, and deuout Assembly of the whole Congregation of such of the Inhabitants in each seuerall place, as are free and safe from danger of Infection, and may in euery Family be conueniently spared; Willing and requiring, aswell all Archbishops, and Bishops, in their seuerall Prouinces, and Dioceses, and all Parsons, Vicars and Curats, within their seuerall Parishes and Charges, as also all Maiors, Sheriffes, Justices of Peace, and other Officers in their seuerall places, limits, and iurisdictions, respectiuely to take especiall care, that this His Maiesties Royall commandement be duly executed and obserued: And that they themselues be lights of good example to the rest; And that all others in manner aforesaid, doe diligently and deuoutly follow and performe the same, as they tender their duties to Almighty God, and to their Prince and Countrey, and will answere for their prophane, or contemptuous neglect hereof at their vttermost perils.

A
FORME OF
Common Prayer,

Together with

An Order of Fasting:

For

The auerting of Gods heauy Viſitation vpon
many places of this Kingdome, and for the drawing
downe of his Bleſſings vpon vs, and our Armies by Sea and Land.

---

*The Prayers are to be read euery Wedneſday during
this Viſitation.*

Set foorth by His Maieſties Authority.

¶ Imprinted at London by *Bonham Norton* and *Iohn Bill*,
Printers to the Kings moſt Excellent
Maieſtie. ANNO 1625.

---

8 The title-page of an early Stuart form of prayer, 1625–E. *A forme of common
prayer, together with an order of fasting: for the auerting of Gods heauy visitation
vpon many places of this kingdome, and for the drawing downe of his blessings vpon
vs, and our armies by sea and land. The prayers are to be read euery Wednesday
during this visitation. Set foorth by his maiesties authority* (4°, London, 1625; STC
16540), Folger Shakespeare Library, STC 16540 Bd.w. STC 14992.

FORM OF PRAYER

A Prayer For the High Court of Parliament, to be read during their Session in such place of these Prayers after the Letanie, as the Minister shall thinke fit.

Most Gracious GOD, wee humbly beseech thee, as for this kingdome in generall, so especially for the High Court of Parliament, vnder our most Religious and Gracious King, at this time assembled; That thou wouldest bee pleased to blesse and direct all their Consulations, to the preseruation of thy glory, the good of thy Church, the safety, honour, and welfare of our Souereigne & his Kingdoms. Lord look vpon the humility and deuotion with which they are come into thy Courts; And they are come into thy house in assured confidence vpon the merits and mercies of Christ (our blessed Sauiour) that thou wilt not deny them the Grace & Fauour which they begge of thee. Therefore O Lord, blesse them with all that wisdom, which thou knowest necessary to speed, & bring great Designes into Action, and to make the maturity of his Maiesties and their Counsels, the happinesse and the blessing of this Commonwealth. These and all other necessaries for them, for vs, and thy whole Church, we humbly begge in the Name and mediation of Iesus Christ our most blessed Lord and Sauior. Amen.

PREFACE
Wee be taught *[as 1603–E:* by many and sundry examples … in their*]* distresse of warres and forreine inuasions. So did the King and people of Nineue, and *Hester*, fall to humble prayers *[as 1603–E:* in lyke perils … by euery man in his priuate family.*]*

A FORME OF COMMON PRAYER, PRESCRIBED FOR THIS TIME OF VISITATION, AND OTHER NECESSITIES
Let all Pastours and Curates [as 1603–E]

MORNING PRAYER

Let the Minister beginning seruice reade with a lowd voice one of these sentences of Scripture [Joel 2:13, Dan. 9:9–10, Jer. 10:24].

[The exhortation, 'Dearely beloued brethren'; the general confession; the absolution, the Lord's prayer and versicles]

A Psalme, where of one verse is to be said of the Minister, and another by the people or Clarke.
    O Come, let vs humble our selues *[as 1603–E]*

[Ps. 6, 9, 32, 38, 39, 51, 86, 90, 91, 102, 130, 143]

The Psalmes ended, reade one of these Chapters following for the first Lesson. [Deut. 28; Deut. 30; 1 Kgs. 8; 2 Sam. 24; Joel 2; Jonah 3]
[Te Deum]

For the second Lesson, reade one of these Chapters, [Matt. 6; Matt. 8; Matt. 9; Luke 13; Luke 21]

[Benedictus or Jubilate]

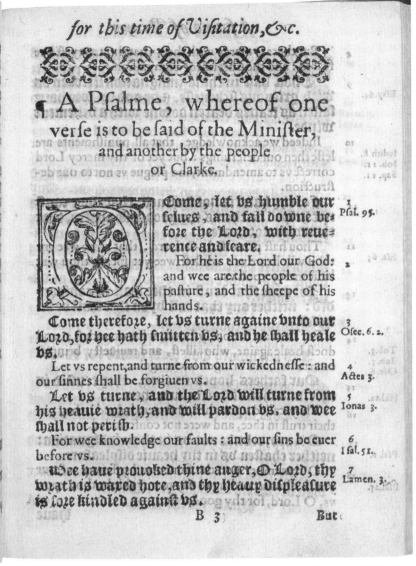

for this time of Uisitation, &c.

¶ A Psalme, whereof one
verse is to be said of the Minister,
and another by the people
or Clarke.

Come, let vs humble our
selues, and fall downe before the Lord, with reue-
rence and feare.
     For he is the Lord our God:
and wee are the people of his
pasture, and the sheepe of his
hands.
     Come therefore, let vs turne againe vnto our
Lord, for hee hath smitten vs, and he shall heale
vs.
     Let vs repent, and turne from our wickednesse : and
our sinnes shall be forgiuen vs.
     Let vs turne, and the Lord will turne from
his heauie wrath, and will pardon vs, and wee
shall not perish.
     For wee knowledge our faults : and our sins be euer
before vs.
     Wee haue prouoked thine anger, O Lord, thy
wrath is waxed hote, and thy heauie displeasure
is sore kindled against vs.

1
Psal. 95.

2

3
Osee. 6. 2.

4
Actes 3.

5
Ionas 3.

6
Isal. 51.

7
Lamen. 3.

B 3   But

9 An extract from a typical service in an early Stuart form of prayer, 1625–E. It shows a 'composite' psalm, created from verses taken from various parts of the Bible and recited as a call and response by the minister and congregation (or clerk). Such psalms were a common feature of Elizabethan and early Stuart special services. *A forme of common prayer, together with an order of fasting: for the auerting of Gods heauy visitation vpon many places of this kingdome, and for the drawing downe of his blessings vpon vs, and our armies by sea and land. The prayers are to be read euery Wednesday during this visitation. Set foorth by his maiesties authority* (4°, 1625; STC 16540), Folger Shakespeare Library, STC 16540 Bd.w. STC 14992, sig. B3r.

[Apostles' creed]

And after that, these prayers following, as well at Euening Prayer, as at morning prayer, all deuoutly kneeling the Minister first pronouncing with a loud voyce.
The Lorde be with you.
And with thy Spirit.
Let vs pray.

[Kyrie eleison]

[The Lord's prayer]

Then the Priest standing vp, shall say.
O Lord shew thy mercy vpon us.
And grant vs thy saluation.
O Lord saue the King.
And mercifully heare vs when we call vpon thee.
Indue thy Ministers with righteousnesse.
And make thy chosen people ioyfull.
O Lord saue thy people,
And blesse thine inheritance.
Giue peace in our time; O Lord.
Because there is none other that fighteth for vs, but onely thou, O God.
O God make cleane our hearts within vs.
And take not thy holy Spirit from vs.

The first Collect
    O almightie, most iust and mercifull God *[as 1603–E to end of collect, with monarch's and queen consort's names changed to Charles and Mary (sic) and omission of references to royal children]*

[The collects for peace and grace]

LITANY.

[The litany to the versicle before 'We humbly beseech thee']

O eternall and euerliuing God *[as 1603–E]*

[Prayers 'It had beene the best for vs', 'O Lord, we haue sinned', 'Thou hast smitten vs', 'O Lord our God most gracious', 'Almighty God and heauenly Father': all as 1603–E]

['We humbly beseech thee' to the end of the litany]

THE LATTER SERUICE[263]

The Priest standing at the North side of the Lords Table, shall say [The Lord's prayer, followed by the communion service from the BCP until and including the prayer for the king, 'Almighty God, whose kingdom is everlasting']

---

263   I.e. the communion service.

The prayer for the Nauie[264]

O eternall God, and our most gracious Father: Thou art the Lord of Hostes, and the strength of all Nations is from thee; if thou keepest not the Citie, and the king-dome, the watchman waketh but in vaine: And no Victorie can waite vpon the iustest designes, vpon the wisest Counsels, vpon the strongest Armies, if thou teachest not their hands to warre, and their fingers to fight. Thou art the steddy hope of all the ends of the Earth, and of them which goe and remaine in the broad Sea. Lord at this time we neede thy more speciall assistance both by Land, and Sea, and for the mercy of Christ denie vs neither. Be with our Armies, and the Armies of our Allyes and Associates by Land: Bee with Our Nauie at Sea. Bee not from the one, or from the other in power, and in great mercy, vntill thou hast brought them backe with honour, and a setled peace. Lord turne our enemies sword into their owne bosome; for wee sought peace, and ensued it, and while wee did so, they did more then make themselues ready to battaile. Wee are thy seruants, truly and heartily sorry for our sinnes; Lord forgiue them; and then we will trust vpon thee, that thou wilt power downe all thy blessings vpon this and all other Designes and Actions of this Sate, vndertaken for thy glory, the honour of our most gracious King CHARLES, and the Peace and welfare of his Church & Commonwealth. Grant this wee humbly beseech thee, for Jesus Christ his sake, our only Mediatour and Aduocate. Amen.

[The BCP prayer in time of war; in place of the collect for the day, the BCP collect for Ash Wednesday]

[Epistle: Joel 2:12–17]
[Gospel: Matt. 6:16–21]
[Nicene creed]
[Offertory sentence: Matt. 5:16]

[The prayer for the whole state of the church]

The Prayer for seasonable weather.

Most gracious Lord, we humbly beseech thee to pardon and forgiue vs all our many, great and grieuous transgressions. We may not hope thou wilt take off thy punishment, vntill thou hast forgiuen our sinne; Wee may not thinke thou wilt forgiue our sinne, vntill our Humiliation and Repentance come to aske forgiuenesse. Wee haue beene too slow to come, and now thou hast apparelled thy mercie in Justice to force vs to thee. Lord wee beleeue, but doe thou encrease our Faith, our Deuotion, our Repentance, and all Christian vertues in vs. At this time the vials of thy heauie displeasure drop downe vpon vs; and while we smart vnder one Judgement, thou threatnest the rest. The pestilence spreadeth in our streets, and goeth as if it sought whom to deuoure. No strength is able to stand against it, and it threatneth to make Families, nay Cities desolate. While the pestilence eateth vp the people, wee heare the sound of warre, and the sword calleth for such as it would deuoure. In the meane time the heauens are blacke ouer vs, and thy clouds droppe leannesse, and it will be famine, to swallow what the pestilence and the sword shall leaue aliue, vnlesse thou sendest seasonable weather to receiue the fruits of the earth in their season. Lord our sinnes haue deserued all this, and more, and we neither doe, nor can deny

---

264   STC 16541: 'This prayer is not to be read publikely till the Nauie be gone.'

it: wee haue no whither to goe but to mercy: wee haue no way to that, but by the all-sufficient merite of thy Son our blessed Sauiour. Lord for his merite and mercies sake looke downe vpon vs thy distressed seruants. Commaund thine Angell to stay his hand; and remember that in death wee cannot praise thee, nor giue thankes in the pit. Goe foorth with our Armies when they goe, and make vs remember that all our strength and deliuerance is in thee. Cleare vp the heauens ouer vs, and take not from vs the great plentie, with which thou hast crowned the earth; but remember vs, thou that sendest the Rauens when they call vpon thee. Lord wee need all thy mercies to fall vpon vs, and thy mercies are altogether in Christ, in whom, and for whose sake wee begge them of thee, who liuest and reignest with him in the vnitie of the Spirit, one God world without end. Amen.

[The prayers 'O most mighty God and mercifull Father' and 'Turn thou us, O good Lord' from the BCP commination service, followed by the collects 'Asssist us mercifully' and 'Almighty God, which hast promised' and the blessing from the BCP communion service]

EVENING PRAYER

[Opening sentence: Matt. 3:2]
Dearely beloued brethren, the Scripture mooueth vs, &c. *As in Morning Prayer.*

A generall confession to be said of the whole Congregation after the Minister kneeling [The general confession]

The absolution or remission of sinnes to bee pronounced by the Priest alone. [The absolution]
The people shall answer, Amen.

[The Lord's prayer]

[Versicles]

Reade the Psalmes that were left vnread at Morning prayer.

For the first Lesson, reade one of the Chapters appointed, and vnread at Morning prayer, as in the Rubricke before Te Deum.

[The Magnificat]

A Psalme, whereof one verse is to be said of the Minister, and another by the people or Clerke.
    O Come, let vs humble our selues *[as at morning prayer]*

For the second Lesson, read one of these Chapters, [1 Cor. 10:1–15; 1 Cor. 13; 2 Cor. 9; 1 Thess. 4].

[Deus misereatur]

[Apostles' creed]

[Kyrie eleison]

Then the Minister, Clerkes and people, shall say the Lords Prayer in English with a loud voyce. [The Lord's prayer]

Then the Priest standing vp, shall say.
    O Lord shew thy mercy vpon you *[as at morning prayer].*

Then one of those appointed prayers which were left vnread at Morning Seruice.

[The second collect from the BCP service for evening prayer; 'A prayer for the King's Majesty' and 'A prayer for the Queen, Prince Fredericke, the Lady Elizabeth, and their children' from the BCP litany; the third collect from the BCP service for evening prayer and the grace]

A SHORT PREFACE TO BE VSED BEFORE THE EXHORTATION FOLLOWING, BY THE MINISTER WHO IS NOT A PREACHER.
    When the Apostles *[as 1603–E]*

AN EXHORTATION FIT FOR THE TIME.
    In the due consideration *[as 1603–E]*

ORDER FOR THE FAST.
    The godly vse of Fasting *[as 1603–E]*

1625–S   Fast days during the plague epidemic in London, for the armed forces and for an abundant harvest

Wednesdays and Sundays, beginning July 1625 (Scotland)

This fast was ordered by the king, whose instructions were conveyed by the archbishop of St Andrews to the other Scottish bishops. The ordering process is less well documented than that of earlier fasts ordered by the general assembly. In his letter to Bishop Forbes, Spottiswoode wrote that Charles I had requested fasting in his three kingdoms to pray for the removal of the plague afflicting London, the success of the king's armies and a bountiful harvest (see 1625–E and 1625–Ir). In Spottiswoode's diocese, the fast was to begin on Wednesday 20 July, and to be observed on Wednesdays and Sundays in burghs, and Sundays in rural parishes, until further order. Presumably, the fast began somewhat later in other dioceses, with the same pattern of urban and rural observance. According to Row, godly congregations added other causes of fasting to those specified by the king.

Sources: Archbishop John Spottiswoode of St Andrews to Bishop Patrick Forbes of Aberdeen, 13 July 1625, NRS, GD188/20/9/5; Row, pp. 339–40.

1625–Ir   Weekly fast days during the plague epidemic in England

Wednesdays, beginning October 1625 (Ireland)

This occasion is only known through a unique copy of a proclamation, issued by Henry Carey, Viscount Falkland, the lord deputy of Ireland, in October 1625. It ordered a weekly fast on Wednesdays for the alleviation of the plague in England (see 1625–E and 1625–S) and to avert God's indignation against the Irish. There was no plague in Ireland at this time; it was free from the disease between 1608 and 1650. It is unclear why special worship was ordered three months after it was ordered in England and Scotland. This is the first occasion of a day of prayer or fasting in Ireland with an extant order (for the first documented case, see 1589–Ir). Unlike the English occasion, no form of prayer was issued. Instead, bishops were expected to draw up and distribute their own forms for the service, along with 'other prayers'. Ministers were also expected to preach a weekly sermon. Considering the general lack of able protestant ministers in Ireland, the strength of catholicism and the poverty of bishoprics and parish livings, these orders were probably not widely implemented or followed.

Order: proclamation by the lord deputy and council, 13 Oct. 1625, STC 14202; SoA, Proclamations Ireland, fo. 42r.
Form of prayer: none found.

ORDER

Proclamation by the lord deputy and council: 13 October 1625

Forasmuch as it hath pleased Almighty God to visit some parts of England, especially the Cities of London and Westminster, & thereabouts with a most grieuous sicknesse of Plague or pestilence, Whereof infinit numbers haue died & do daily die, signifying thereby that His Divine Maiestie is highly offended with vs for our manifold sinnes and transgressions. And because there is no better means to pacifie his wrath, then by hearty and vnfayned repentance, which is best expressed by Fasting and Prayer, alwaies practised vpon like occasions, aswell before, as since the Incarnation of our blessed Sauiour, in the Church of God, & is now vsed in England by the most pious & speciall commandement of the Kings most excellent Maiestie. We, who are to haue a sence of the miseries of others, and a feare of like punishment for our owne sinnes, haue no better meanes to pacifie and auerte the indignation & vengeance of Almighty God then by our humiliation, & imitation of the most godly & Christian course, which his Maiestie hath prescribed in England: In example whereof, hauing first taken a course (as farre as humane iudgement can) to preuent the infection like to be brought in by such as frequently come from infected parts in England: We doe now order, commaund and proclayme, publike Fasts and Prayers, to be obserued in all Parts, Parishes, and Congregations within this Kingdome once a weeke vpon every Wednesday, And therefore We will and require that the Minister, and parishioners of euery Parish within this Kingdome doe duely repayre to their parish-Church euery Wednesday, to heare diuine Seruice and Sermons (or to some conuenient place to be appointed for the purpose where there is no Church) upon which day the Minister is to call vpon the people, that they abstaine from labour, and from pleasure, and from the ordinarie workes of their calling, and dedicate themselues that day to Fasting, prayer, and meditation, bewayling aswell their owne sinnes, as the great and knowne sinnes of the kingdome, with vnfayned thankesgiuing for the manifold blessings ioyned with peace, plenty, and prosperitie, which this Kingdome hath long enioyed, whiles the neighbour Christian Kingdomes haue beene turmoyled with warrs and bloudie afflictions.

And in each Parish where there are Preachers, it is requisite, and they are hereby straightly charged that they preach duly euery Wednesday.

And Wee will and require euerie Archbishop, and Bishop, to call vpon his Cleargie for the diligent and due performance thereof: And because it may be, that some of the Cleargie cannot preach, nor make such forme of zealous prayer as the time requireth: We will and require that the Bishop of euery Diocesse doe prepare, and send to such Ministers, a Prayer or prayers, such as it shall please God to inspire them to frame, which prayer or prayers the said Ministers are to vse upon euerie Wednesday to their Congregations (amongst other prayers) in their diuine Seruice.

1626–E1   Thanksgivings days and services for decline of the plague epidemic

Sunday 29 January 1626 [and services on following days?] (London, Westminster and adjacent places); Sunday 19 February 1626 [and services on following days] (elsewhere in England and Wales)

In London, the plague epidemic of 1625–6 was the most severe of the century, apart from that in 1665. It claimed approximately 45,000 lives and was spread quickly to neighbouring Essex and more distant places by fleeing citizens (see 1625–E). In Exeter, approximately a fifth of the population died; in Plymouth, it was nearly a sixth. The order was issued by proclamation, which emphasized the king's own pious observance of the petitionary services during the outbreak of plague, as well as his 'acknowledging the gracious mercie of the Diuine Maiestie'. Such references to Charles's observance of special worship became common in proclamations. Joseph Mede wrote to Sir Martin Stuteville that he had been unable to obtain a copy of the proclamation in Cambridge because they had all sold out. The order was issued by proclamation, which now adopted the proposal made unsuccessfully by the House of Lords for 1625–E, that the special worship should be held on different days for London and Westminster, and for the rest of the kingdom: this accommodated the problem of delays in sending proclamations and forms of prayer to more distant areas. The proclamation also emphasized the king's own pious observance of the petitionary services during the outbreak of plague, as well as his 'acknowledging the gracious mercie of the Diuine Maiestie'. Such references to Charles's observance of special worship became common in proclamations. Joseph Mede reported to Sir Martin Stuteville that he had been unable to obtain a copy of the proclamation in Cambridge because they had all sold out. The form of prayer was based on that for 1604–E, which presumably explains a discrepancy between the proclamation and the form: the proclamation ordered the thanksgivings to be observed on Sunday 29 January or Sunday 19 February; the title of the form suggested that they were to be observed on Wednesdays, Fridays and Sundays, though it did not provide different liturgical forms for these days. It appears that those compiling the form in 1626 copied the title-page of the earlier form in 1604, unaware or forgetting that the thanksgiving was only to be observed on a Sunday. The plague continued: Norwich experienced a second peak of deaths in March, while in Plymouth, the disease was sustained well into 1627 by sailors returning from the Île de Ré campaign (see 1626–E2).

Order: royal proclamation, 22 Jan. 1626, STC 8821* [also in Larkin, II, 84–6].
Form of prayer: *A short forme of thankesgiuing to God for staying the contagious sickenesse of the plague: to be vsed in common prayer, on Sundayes, Wednesdayes, and Frydayes set forth by authority* (24 pp.; STC 16542)*.
Additional sources: Mead to Stuteville, 4 Feb. 1626, in Bidwell and Jansson (eds.), *Proceedings in parliament, 1626*, IV, 264; John Le Neve, *The lives and characters ... of all the protestant bishops* (1720), p. 124; MacLure, p. 130.
Sermons: Fuller, Paul's Cross, London (STC 11467)

ORDER

Royal proclamation: 22 January 1626

Whereas the Kings most Excellent Maiesty, vpon the fearefull increase, and spreading of the late Infection of the Plague, in the Imperial City of this Kingdome, and places adiacent, and from thence in the more remote places of the Land, out of his most Religious consideration of the immediate hand of God therein, did command, that all his people throughout this whole Realme, should by fasting & prayer humble themselues vnto Almighty God, and by their true repentance and humiliation seeke to diuert his wrath, and fearefull Visitation; And his Maiesty himselfe in His owne Person did giue a memorable example thereof to all his people, which Religious duety, being accordingly obserued, and for diuers monethes continued, it hath pleased God of his abundant mercie and goodnesse to stay his hand, and beyond the policie and hopes of man, to withdraw his Rod, and almost wholly to remoue the same.

Now the Kings Maiestie, with all possible Thankes, acknowledging the gracious mercie of the Diuine Maiestie, towards Himselfe and His people, and acknowledging also, that they are not worthy of future fauours, who are not truly thankful for benefits already receiued, Hath thought fit, that, by His Royal authority, there should be a generall and publike Thankesgiuing to God throughout this whole Kingdome, for so great & gracious a deliuerance. And therefore He doth hereby command, and publish His Royal pleasure to be, That vpon Sunday, the nine & twentieth of this present moneth of January, in, and throughout the Cities of *London* and *Westminster*, and places adiacent; And vpon the nineteenth day of February next, in all other places of this Realme, there shall be celebrated a publike Thankesgiuing to God for this so great mercie.

The manner and forme whereof, shall be directed by a small Booke, which shall to that purpose be composed by the Reverend Bishops, by His Maiesties expresse direction, and by them shal be sent and dispersed through their seuerall Diocesse; Whereof His Maiesties pleasure is, that all His louing Subiects shall take notice, and religiously, with that deuotion which appertaineth to so pious a Worke, shall solemnize the same.

FORM OF PRAYER

MORNING PRAYER

Reade the ordinary Seruice till you come to the Psalmes:

And in stead of those Psalmes which are appointed of course, reade some of these: Viz. 30, 34, 91, 103, 107, 116.

Then shal follow for the first Lesson, Isaiah *38. Or, 2* Samuel *24. beginning at the 16. Verse: and so to the end of the Chapter.*

For the second Lesson, the 5. of Luke, *beginning at the 13. Verse, to the end of the 26. Verse.*

After the second Lesson: reade this Psalme following.
Lord, thou art become gracious … (Ps. 85)
[Then as 1604–E until]
Hee hath deliuered our soules from death, hee hath fed vs in the time of dearth, hee hath saued vs from the noysome Pestilence. (Ps. 33, 91)
It is of the Lords mercies that we are not consumed, because his compassions fayle not. (Lam. 3, 22)
Therefore will wee offer in his holy Temple … (Ps. 27)
[Then as 1604–E to end]

[Apostles' creed]

And so forth, as in the booke of Common Prayer.

The first Collect.
Almightie LORD, the Father of mercies, and God of all consolation, wee doe with all humblenesse confesse, that, as our sinnes have surpassed the number and measure of the transgressions of our fathers; so thou hast most iustly and deseruedly laide vpon vs thy heauie hand, by sending a plague more dreadfull then hath beene felt in their dayes: Yea, in the very time of thy Visitation, whilest thy angry coun-tenance was bent against vs, wee haue not performed that degree of repentance and humiliation, which so sharpe a scourge did call for at our hands; but rather in the middes of that danger, did holde on the same our former course of carnall securitie, and neglect of thy Commandements. Yet now (O gracious Lord) to thy glory, and our comfort, wee acknowledge thy vnspeakeable mercy, in staying the hand of thy destroying Angel, and restoring suddenly, beyond expectation, the voice of Joy and Health in our habitations. It is thy goodnesse, and meere fauour to vs, that thou hast rather chosen to glorifie thy Mercy in sauing vs, then to magnifie thy Justice in our destruction. Goe on, mercifull Lord, we beseech thee, continue and perfect this thy blessed worke of preseruation throughout euery Congregation and Family of this Kingdome: enlarge thy fauours to thy Church, our King, and State; enrich them with all inward and outward blessings: and giue vs such effectuall grace, that wee looking euery of vs into the plague of his owne heart, may abhorre our owne corruptions, & turne from our euill wayes, euermore acknowledging, that thy long suffering calleth vs to repentance; that the prolonging of our dayes should be the breaking off of our sinnes; and that this restoring of health and safetie vnto thy people, is to worke in vs a perpetuall thankefulnesse both in word and obedience to thee, by the Merits and Intercession of thy blessed Sonne, by whose stripes wee are healed of the wounds and infection both of soule and body: To him our onely Sauiour, with thee, and the holy Ghost, be all praise and glory. Amen.

The second Collect.
O Lord God of all power and might, wee magnifie and laude thy great mercy, that it hath pleased thee in this late dreadfull sickenesse, to spare our soules from

death, whereby wee should have beene consumed and brought to nothing. For these, and all other thy gracious fauors, wee present vnto thee our selues, our soules and bodies, in all thankefulnesse and humilitie, beseeching thee to continue this thy goodnesse and preseruation ouer vs, that being hurt by no calamities, wee may liue to doe thee seruice, and euermore giue thankes in thy holy Church, to thy great and blessed Name, through our Lord Jesus Christ. Amen.

LITANY

[Epistle: 2 Cor. 7:8–13]
[Gospel: Luke 17:11–19]

Then reade some of the following.
   We will magnifie thee *[as 1604–E*: O God our King ... pestilence, which*]* not long since, raged in the Land, sweeping away *[as 1604–E*: the rich ... all places with*]* dead bodies: So that there may be feare that thine indignation may continue among vs, and breake foorth into a further punishment. But because thou wilt haue it knowen, that thou, O LORD, onely woundest *[as 1604–E*: and canst heale againe ... command thine Angell to*]* stay his hande, and spare vs: Wee therefore offer vp *[as 1604–E*: vnto thee ... and of*]* humble and earnest Prayers, for all those that are yet afflicted, beseeching thee for thy Sonne Jesus Christ his sake, to be gracious vnto them and vs, that both they and we *[as 1604–E*: in ioynt affection ... to whom, &c.]*

O most gracious GOD, seeing it hath pleased thee in the multitude of those sorrowes which we had in our hearts, by reason of that grieuous contagion, lately spread among vs, to send thy comforts *[as 1604–E*: for the refreshing ... for this*]* thine especiall goodnesse, beseeching thee to giue vs grace, that by our transgressions we doe not further kindle thine indignation against vs: Grant this, O Lord, for thine onely Sonnes sake, Jesus Christ our Lord and onely Sauiour. Amen.

Or this.
   Almightie and eternall God *[as 1604–E*: which strikest ... diddest lately*]* sore plague vs with great sickeness and mortalitie: yet remembring thy mercie hast turned thy selfe most graciously vnto vs, and comforted vs againe: we most humbly acknowledge *[as 1604–E*: with all due thankefulnesse ... through Jesus Christ our Lord and Sauiour]*.

O almightie GOD, which art the Resurrection *[as 1604–E*: of the dead ... our weakenesse, to*]* deliuer vs from the Contagion *[as 1604–E*: when in the eye of mans reason ... Jesus Christ our Lord]*.

[The blessing]

1626–E2   Fast days during war with Spain

**Wednesday 5 July 1626 (London, Westminster and adjacent places);
Wednesday 2 August 1626 (elsewhere in England and Wales)**

The war with Spain over Bohemia and the Palatinate that had threatened England
in 1625 had come to pass, and Charles's military campaign – which had ultimately
focused around an attack on the Spanish fleet – had proved disastrous. In 1626,
the king summoned parliament to vote further subsidies for the war effort. Plague
also continued to rage across England (see 1625–E and 1626–E1). Following the
precedent of 1625, the Commons proposed a general fast. The motion was made
by Sir James Perrott three weeks into the session, but he did not specify why a fast
was necessary, arguing that the reasons 'shall be set down in the conference with the
lords'. This was criticized by the vice-chamberlain, Sir Dudley Carleton, who argued
that it was usual, in other countries, to set down the reasons for a fast before one
was appointed. Sir Nathaniel Rich, who seconded Perrott's motion, cited a (probably
erroneous) precedent from Edward III's reign that fasts were ordered for the good
success of parliament and for good relations between parliament and the king, both
of which were relevant to 1626 because of deteriorating relations between the two
on the war, subsidies, the redress of grievances and controversy over the influence of
the king's favourite, the duke of Buckingham. The Commons appointed a committee
to draw up a petition to the king but it took over a month to complete its work and
report back to the house; the text of the petition does not survive and appears never
to have been presented either to the Lords or to Charles. Parliament was dissolved
on 15 June. A fortnight later, Charles, who had not been opposed to the Commons'
desire for a fast, issued a proclamation ordering a general fast, which, like that for
1626–E1, emphasized his own piety and religious observance. Although the title of
the form of prayer referred to pestilence, this was not a form for the plague, which
was described in the proclamation as having already passed. As for 1625–E, the fast
was ordered for different days for London and the rest of the realm to allow the form
to be distributed. This form was substantial and included a lengthy exhortation at the
end, probably intended to be read by the minister, as in 1603–E and 1625–E.

Order: royal proclamation, 30 June 1626, STC 8834* [also in Larkin, II, 97–9].
Form of prayer: *A forme of prayer, necessary to bee vsed in these dangerous times, of warre and
pestilence, for the safety and preseruation of his maiesty and his realme. Set forth by authoritie* (88 pp.;
STC 16543)*
Form of prayer (other edition): STC 16544.
Additional sources: Thomas Cruse to Lady Carnsew, [July?] 1626, SP16/32/114, fos. 170r–171r; *CJ*, I,
851, 853, 867, 869, 871; *Diary of Walter Yonge*, p. 94.
Printed sermon: Hampton, Paul's Cross, London (STC 12741).

ORDER

Royal proclamation: 30 June 1626
The fresh memory of the late fearefull visitation of the Plague, as in many other
places and parts of this Realme, so especially in and about the Cities of *London* and
Westminster, and places adiacent, and the spreading thereof in many parts of this
Kingdome at this time, ought to moue vs to consider, that it was, and is the immediate
hand of God for the sinnes of this Land, so to visite and correct his people; And

againe, the contemplation of the infinite goodnesse of God, so vnexpectedly to heale this great and populous Citie (the seate of this Empire) ought to draw vs to a due and thankefull acknowledgement of so great a deliuerance: The remembrance of the scarcitie and famine lately threatned vnto vs in all the borders of this Land, ought to humble vs, And the blessing of God vpon the fruits of the earth in the time of our greatest distresse, ought to stirre vp our thankfulnesse vnto that diuine Maiesty, who was the giuer of these blessings: The present estate of his Maiesties Dominions, and of His friends and Allies imbarked in a warre, with a potent and vigilant enemy, setting Us in an open Hostilitie abroad, and threatning vs with a powerfull inuasion at home, ought to perswade vs, not onely to a timely preparation for all things necessary for a defensive warre, but also to looke vp to Him, whose prouidence gouernes, and whose power ruleth all things vpon earth: And our former deliuerances in like distresses, ought to raise our thoughts, not to neglect the ordinary meanes, and yet to trust in him onely who is the Lord of hostes, and who alone can deliuer in times of danger: These Pious and Religious considerations haue so wrought in the Princely heart of the Kings most excellent Maiestie, That He hath not onely had recourse to that great and Diuine Maiestie, who is the King of kings, in His priuate deuotions, to implore his mercie and fauour to himselfe and His people; But according to the example of all good Kings in former ages in the times of common calamities, which equally concerne both Prince and people, to command a solemne, a generall, and a publike Fast throughout all this whole Land, wherein the whole Kingdome (as one man) may present to God their hearty and vnfained thankes for His benefits already receiued, and may powre out their supplications with strong cryes vnto Him, to send a blessing vpon our endeauours, and to diuert those punishments from vs, which the sinnes of this Land haue worthily deserued.

To this purpose, His most Excellent Maiestie, (moued therunto, the rather by the good inclination of the Commons House of Parliament, lately assembled, who being the representatiue Body of this Realme, and best knowing the necessities of them all, did intimate their desire thereof) hath consulted with His reuerend Bishops, and resolued vpon a graue and religious forme of solemnizing thereof, which His Royall Pleasure He doth hereby publish and declare to all His louing Subiects, And doth straitly charge and command, That on Wednesday next, being the fift day of July, this Fast be religiously and solemnly obserued and celebrated in the Cities of *London* and *Westminster*, and places adiacent, wherein His Maiestie in His Royall Person, and with His owne family and Royall houshold, will giue an example to the rest of His people. And that on that day moneth, being the second of August, the like be kept and duly obserued, thorowout the rest of this whole Realme of *England* and Dominion of *Wales*. And for the more orderly solemnizing thereof without confusion, His Maiestie, by the aduice of His Reuerend Bishops, hath directed to be Composed, Printed, and Published, the forme of such Prayers and publike Exhortations, as he thinketh fit to be vsed in all Churches and places at these publike meetings. And Hee hath giuen charge to His Bishops to disperse the same thorowout His whole Kingdome. All which, His Maiestie doth expresly charge and command, shall be reuerently and deuoutly performed by all His louing Subiects, as they tender the fauour of Almighty God, and would auoide his iust indignation against this Land; and vpon paine of such punishments, as His Maiestie can iustly inflict vpon all such, as shall contemne, or neglect so religious a Worke.

FORM OF PRAYER

MORNING PRAYER

First the Minister shall say. [Jer. 10:24]

[The exhortation, 'Dearly beloved brethren'; the general confession; the absolution; the Lord's prayer and versicles]

Then shall be said or sung this Psalme following, in stead of Venite exultemus.

I Will loue thee, O Lord, my strength: the Lord is my stonie rocke and my defence, my Sauiour, my God and my might in whom I will trust, my buckler, the horne also of my saluation, and my refuge. (Ps. 18) [18:1]
In my trouble I will call vpon the Lord, and complaine vnto my God: so shall I be safe from mine enemies. [18:5, 2]
So shall hee heare my voyce out of his holy Temple: and my complaint shall come before him, it shall enter euen into his eares. [18:6]
Heare my prayer, O Lord: and let my crying come vnto thee. (Ps. 102) [102:1]
Hide not thy face from mee in the time of my trouble: incline thine eare vnto me when I call, oh heare me, and that right soone. [102:2]
The enemie cryeth so, and the vngodly commeth on so fast: for they are minded to doe mee some mischiefe, so maliciously are they set against mee. (Ps. 55) [55:3]
Thou art my King, O God: send helpe vnto Jacob. (Ps. 44) [44:5]
Through thee will wee ouerthrow our enemies: and in thy Name will wee tread them vnder that rise vp against vs. [44:6]
For I will not trust in my bow: it is not my sword that shall helpe me. [44:7]
But it is thou that sauest vs from our enemies: and puttest them to confusion that hate vs. [44:8]
There is no King that can bee saued by the multitude of an hoste: neither is any mighty man deliuered by much strength. (Ps. 33) [33:15]
Therefore in thee, O Lord, haue I put my trust: let me neuer bee put to confusion, deliuer mee in thy righteousnesse. (Ps. 31) [31:1]
Bow downe thine eare to me, and saue mee: make haste to deliuer me. [31:2]
My time is in thy hand, deliuer mee from the hand of mine enemies: and from them that persecute me. [31:17]
Pleade thou my cause, O Lord, with them that striue with mee: and fight thou against them that fight against me. (Ps. 35) [35:1]
Lay hand vpon the shield and buckler: and stand vp to helpe mee. [35:2]
Bring foorth the speare, and stop the way against them that persecute mee: say vnto my soule, I am thy saluation. [35:3]
Let them bee confounded, and put to shame that seeke after my soule: let them bee turned backe, and brought to confusion that imagine mischiefe for mee. [35:4]
Let them be as the dust before the wind: and the Angel of the Lord scattering them. [35:5]
Let their way bee darke and slippery: and the Angel of the Lord persecute them. [35:6]
But let the eye of the Lord be vpon them that feare him: and put their trust in his mercie. (Ps. 33) [33:17]
To deliuer their soules from death: and to feed them in the time of dearth. [33:18]

O Lord, take heed vnto mee and heare mee: how I mourne in my prayer, and am vexed. (Ps. 55) [55:2]

For I will confesse my wickednesse: and be sorry for my sinne. (Ps. 38) [38:18]

I said, I will confesse my sins vnto the Lord: and so thou forgauest the wickednes of my sinne. (Ps. 32) [32:6]

For this shall euery one that is godly make his prayer vnto thee in a time when thou mayest bee found: but in the great water floods they shall not come nigh him. [32:7]

The sacrifice of God is a troubled spirit: a broken and contrite heart, O God, shalt thou not despise. (Ps. 51) [51:17]

O bee fauourable and gracious vnto Sion: build thou the walles of Ierusalem. [51:18]

And now, Lord, what is my hope? truly my hope is euen in thee. (Ps. 39) [39:8]

Let thy mercifull kindnesse be vpon vs: like as wee doe put our trust in thee. (Ps. 33) [33:21]

Glory be the Father, and to the Sonne, and to the holy Ghost:

As it was in the beginning, is now and euer shall be, world without end, Amen.

[Ps. 3, 27, 46, 83]

For the First Lesson *is appointed to be read* The Second Booke of the Kings, *from the seuenteenth Verse of the eighteenth* Chapter, *to the end of the nineteenth* Chapter. *Of* Hezekiah and Sennacherib.

Or

The Second Booke of the Chronicles, *the thirteenth* Chapter, *to the end of the twentieth Verse. Of* Abijahs *warre against* Ieroboam.

[Te Deum]

For the Second Lesson *is appointed to be read the foure and twentieth* Chapter *of Saint Matthew.*

[Benedictus]

[Apostles' creed]

The prayers, all deuoutly kneeling.
   The Lord be with you *[and as BCP].*

[The Lord's prayer]

The Priest standing vp, shall say:

O Lord shew thy mercy vpon vs *[as BCP until]*

Answer: And mercifully heare vs when we call vpon thee.

Priest: O Lord saue thy seruants.

Answer: Who doe put their trust in thee.

Priest: Send them helpe from thy Holy place.

Answer: And euermore mightily defend them.

Priest: Let our enemies haue no aduantage ouer vs.

Answer: Nor the wicked approach to hurt vs.

Priest: Be vnto vs O Lord a strong Tower.

Answer: From the face of our enemies.
Priest: O Lord heare our prayer.
Answer: And let our cry come vnto thee.
Priest: Indue thy Ministers with righteousnesse *[and as BCP]*

The first Collect for the day. [The BCP prayer in time of war]

Or this.

O Lord God of hostes, that giuest victory in the day of battell, and deliuerance
in the time of trouble, wee beseech thee to strengthen the hands, and to encourage
the hearts of thy seruants, in fighting thy battels, and defending thy Altars that are
among vs. Let thy Church be kept in safetie, and the state of thine Annoynted bee
free from all that shalbe attempted against it, either by Sea or Land. And although
for our manifold sinnes, wee deserue to bee now consumed by the sword, as of late
wee were wasted by the pestilence, Yet vpon our humble and vnfained contrition let
the multitude of thy mercies saue vs, and the merits of thy Sonne Christ our Lord
deliuer vs, that when we have escaped the furie of our enemies, and seene them sent
backe the same way they came, wee may blesse thy glorious Name, and serue thee
without feare in holinesse and righteousnesse all the dayes of our life, who liuest
and reigneth, &c.

Or this.

O eternall God and most mercifull Father, we humbly beseech thee to bee mercifull vnto vs, and be neere to helpe vs in all those extremities which our sinnes
threaten to bring vpon vs. Our enemies are strengthened against vs by our multiplied
rebellions against thee, and wee deserue to suffer what our enemies threaten, euen
suddaine surprisall and destruction to desolation. But there is mercy with thee that
thou mayest be feared; and there is mercy with thee, that they may not bee feared.
Shew vs therefore thy mercy O Lord, and let vs so feare thee, that wee may neuer
bee brought to feele or feare them, And when thou wilt correct vs for our sinnes, let
vs fall into thy hands, and not into the hands of men, euen for Christ Jesus sake our
onely Mediatour and Redeemer. *Amen*

[The second and third collects from the BCP service for morning prayer]

LITANY

[After 'We humbly beseech thee']
Then shall be said this prayer.

O eternall God and most gracious Father, wee confesse that by our manifold
transgressions, wee haue deserued whatsoeuer thy Law hath threatned against
sinners. Our contempt of thy diuine Seruice is great, and we heare thy word, but
obey it not. Our charitie to our neighbour is cold, and our deuotion to thee is frozen.
Religion is with vs, as in too many places besides, made but a pretence for other
ends then thy Seruice; and there hath beene little or no care among vs to keepe
Truth and Peace together, for the preseruing of our Church and State. Forgiue vs, O
Lord, forgiue vs these, and all other our grieuous sinnes. Send vs light in our vnderstanding, readinesse and obedience in our will, discretion in our words and actions,
true, serious, and loyall endeauours, for the peace and prosperity of Jerusalem, the

vnitie and glory of this Church and State; that so we may loue it, and prosper in it, full of grace in this life, and bee filled with glory in the life to come, through Iesus Christ our Lord. Amen.

Or this.

Looke downe, O gracious King of glory, looke downe from the habitation of thy holinesse, and behold vs with the eye of pitie, that lift vp our hearts and hands vnto thee for mercie. At the footstoole of thy Throne of grace, we prostrate our soules and bodies, with fasting, with teares, and supplications, beseeching thee, for the death and passion of our blessed Sauiour, to accept this our vnfained submission. To thy glory, O Lord, and to our owne shame, we confesse, that thy fauours and blessings haue made this Kingdome to be admired by our friends, and enuied by our enemies: but the sinnes thereof haue called for such punishments vpon vs, as may make vs to be pittied by all. Grieuous it is, and euen a part of this our humiliation, to remember the waste of late made in the principall parts of this kingdome by the deuouring Pestilence. And this thy Scourge, though ceasing now to smite where it strucke deepest before, yet making still further entrance into other parts of this Land, it reuiueth our sorrow, and redoubleth our humiliation before thee; that thou mayest heare the groanes of thy afflicted children, and binde vp the wounds of our deare brethren. Stop the course of thy destroying Angell, O Lord, and for the stinting of this dreadfull Infection of our bodies, cleanse, by thy purifying grace, the sinfull staines of our soules.

Let not the enemies of this Church and State triumph in our continued afflictions, and much lesse prosper in their designes for our fall and ruine. Though their power were greater then their malice against vs, yet is thy wonted fauour a safe protection against both. Shew vs therefore, O Lord, thy fauours and mercies, which haue beene euer of old, and be gracious vnto thy seruants. Watch ouer thy Sion, when it is most encompassed with danger, inspire her with wholsome counsailes, assist her with vndaunted courage, and crowne her with prosperitie and victorie ouer all her enemies. So shall our mourning be turned into ioy, and our drooping fasts, into feasts of spirituall comfort and grace, which shall leade vs to endlesse glory, by the merits of him, who hath purchased all these blessings for vs, thy onely Sonne, our euer blessed Sauiour. Amen.

[The prayer for the king, to the end of the litany]

THE SECOND SERUICE[265]

[The BCP communion service, with the collect for the king ('Almighty God, whose kingdome is everlasting') preceding the collect for the day following]

Shew forth the power of thy might, O Lord, and come among vs, and with great strength succour vs, that whereas by sin we are set in the midst of so many and great dangers, wee may by mercy be brought out againe, and the right hand of thy Maiestie may be our defence against all our enemies, through Iesus Christ our Lord. Amen.

---

[265] I.e. the communion service.

Or this.

God, our refuge and strength, whose power no creature is able to resist, who teachest our hands to warre and our fingers to fight, and without whom the horse and chariot is in vaine prepared against the day of battell, Defend vs, wee beseech thee, with thy mighty power, and saue vs with thine outstretched arme, that by the glory of thy strength our forces may bee preserued, and our Armies made victorious both at sea and land, euermore seruing vnder his banner who hath lead captiuity captiue, and as a mighty Conquerour hath by his Crosse triumphed ouer his enemies, euen Jesus Christ our Lord, To whom with thee and the Holy Ghost, &c.

[Epistle: Joel 2:12–17]
[Gospel: Matt. 5:1–12]
[Nicene creed]

[After the prayer for the whole state of the church]
Then some of these Prayers.

O most gracious and louing Father, wee haue felt thy manifold mercies & deliuerances, no Nation more; and we haue gone beyond many people in sinning against thee. Enter not into iudgement with thy seruants, O Lord, but for the all-satisfying passion of Christ deliuer vs from thy wrath, and saue vs from the malice and crueltie of our Enemies. They be our loud and crying sinnes, that haue called them vpon vs. Let it bee an addition to thy wonted mercy, to put thy bridle into their mouthes, and thy bit betweene their teeth, to restraine their fury, and to diuert their designes, that they may finde no way in our Seas, nor any path in our flouds, but may bee scattered with thy tempest, and followed with all thy stormes; and that wee being deliuered by thy hand, may blesse and honor thy Name, deuoutly seruing thee all our dayes, through Jesus Christ our Lord, Amen.

[The BCP collects for the third Sunday after Epiphany and the third Sunday before Lent]

[The first, second and sixth collects after the offertory from the communion service]

[The blessing]

EVENING PRAYER

[Opening sentence: Matt. 3:2]

[As the BCP service for evening prayer, with the Venite exultemus *replaced with the same psalm as at morning prayer]*

[Ps. 7, 86]

The first Lesson, 2. Chron. Chapter *20. to the end of the 30. verse. Of* Iehoshaphats *Prayer and Victory.*

[The Magnificat]

The second Lesson. Hebrewes *11. or,* Ephesians *6. Of the Armour of God.*

[As the BCP service for evening prayer with the suffrages after the Lord's prayer as at morning prayer]

[In place of the collect for the day, either the BCP collect in time of war]
Or this.

O Lord Creatour of all things, and gouernor of all the kingdomes of the world, looke downe, we beseech thee, in mercy vpon the estate of this Realme which is now in danger to bee assaulted by the enemies thereof. Thou seest, O Lord, how they make a murmuring, how they conspire daily and take counsell together against thee and against thine Anoynted. We therefore humbly pray thee to extend thine accustomed goodnesse to vs in the defence of our land, saue and deliuer vs from the hands of all such as threaten our destruction. Protect the person of our gracious Soueraigne, direct his Counsels, goe forth with his Armies, be vnto him, and to vs all a wall of brasse, and a strong tower of defence against the face of our enemies; that so we being safe through thy mercy, may liue to serue thee in thy Church, and euer to giue thee praise and glory, through Jesus Christ our Lord, Amen.

Or this against the Pestilence.

O most mercifull God, we give thee praise and thankes for the wonderfull ceasing of the late raging pestilence in the chiefe city of our kingdome. Thou didst most graciously accept our vndeserued Repentance before thee; we beseech thee to giue vs the grace of greater humiliation, and to shew vs yet further mercy. Lord looke vpon all parts of this kingdome with compassion, and keepe backe the destroying Angel, that hee enter not into the places that bee free, nor make further waste of those which bee already visited. Comfort them that are sicke, preserue them that are sound, receiue them that die, to mercy; that liuing and dying, they and we may continue thy faithfull seruants, through Jesus Christ our Lord, Amen.

[Then as the BCP service for evening prayer]

A GENERALL AND CHRISTIAN EXHORTATION, IN THE TIME OF DANGER, AND FEARE OF GODS IVDGEMENTS.
It is not long since (as you know) that Almighty God, who iustly scourged vs with his Chastizing rods, of Famine, and the latter by Pestilence, did after that his Fatherly correction, vpon our publique Humiliation, both satisfie our hungry soules with plentie, and likewise so miraculously deliuer vs from the iawes of death, in the principall part of this Kingdome, as if wee had heard him command his *Destroying Angell,* saying, *Stay thy hand, it is sufficient,* and immediatly the Plague ceased. As therefore the sense of his fiery indignation may terrifie vs from all further prouocation of his wrath, by custome of sinning; so ought the experience of his exceeding mercy challenge from vs an humble thankefulnesse, and constant obedience to his will. Notwithstanding, (O, the perfidiousnesse of the carnall heart of man!) who seeth not that God hath discouered our hypocrisies, by his Plague yet remaining in diuers parts of this Realme? seeing that we cannot but know that these coales of his fierce wrath, had not further burned, except they had been kindled by our rebellious affections, which are *set on fire of hell.* For what els are the visible Iudgements of God, but reall reproofes of our sinnes, and expressions of his wrathfull displeasure against

vs? Wherefore we may much suspect our selues, that wee by Gods late affliction were rather humbled, than truely humble; being as it were forced to that our outward humiliation, more by a slauish feare, than by any filiall sorrow for our transgressions of his will, and for abuse of his patience; much lesse by loue of that his mercy towards us, in our marueilous deliuerance.

Yet may you not understand this so spoken of vs, as thereby to condemne all outward Humiliation in *Feare*, whensoeuer we are vnder Gods hand of correction: No; for the holy Ghost noteth such Obstinates, who being [266]*Strucken of God grieued not at all,* [267]*nor trembled at his presence,* [268]*nor said in their hearts, Let vs serue the Lord*: and condemneth them, as *Foolish and ignorant of the wayes of the Lord, & the Iudgments of their God*; & accordingly denounceth Gods iust vengeance against them. For what greater affront and irreuerence can be done to the Maiestie of God, then not to quake and tremble, when they see Gods hand of vengeance present before them? or how can they conceiue that God will compassionate their miseries, whose hearts are so hard, that the furnace of Gods wrath cannot melt them? Know yee therefore, Beloued, and let it be printed in your soules, as a necessarie trueth, that the greatest cause of feare, is our not fearing of the visible Iudgements of God. This God himselfe sheweth, by binding himselfe with an oath, that they who gaue themselues [269]*To eating, drinking, and reioycing, in the daies of mourning and weeping*, should certainely *die and perish*.

Neuerthelesse, all they that would truely vnderstand themselues, that their conuersion vnto God, is sincere and vnfained, let them not bee contented to bee driuen to a religious walking before God, onely by feare of punishment; but contend especially by all holy meanes, to be animated with that loue of the goodnesse of God, whereof the Apostle speaketh, saying, [270]*The goodnesse of God leadeth to repentance*: The roote of the former is somewhat bitter, and the fruit sowre; the other of loue is as a spirituall wine, which may be said to [271]*glad the heart both of God and man*; men on earth, blessed Saints and Angels in heauen, and euen God himselfe being delighted at the true conuersion of a sinner.

All this while haue we spoken of Plague and Famine, the two instruments of death, and executioners of Gods vengeance; and wish that no other matter of horrour and dread, could be represented vnto you. But (alas the intollerable burthen of our sinnes!) the *Watchmen* that stand on the highest tower of this kingdome, *being asked what they see*, doe answere, and behold, a compleat, vast, and eminent preparation to warre against vs, by an Enemy, mighty in power, in malice implacable, in rage bent and incensed to the vtter destruction of our nation, as being that which chiefely maintaineth the Euangelicall trueth, and withstandeth his boundlesse and vnsatiable ambition.

This being our present doubtfull and dangerous condition, what can wee conceiue or pretend, that we should not thinke our selues lyable and subiect to this the greatest and most terrible vengeance euen *the deuouring sword*? Shal we now conceit, that wee are become more conformable to the Commandements of God, than heretofore? Let euery one open his eyes both of minde and body, looking as well inwardly into

266 In margin: 'Ier. 5. 3.'
267 In margin: '& cap. 22.'
268 In margin: '& cap. 24. 4.'
269 In margin: 'Isa. 22. 12.'
270 In margin: 'Rom. 2.'
271 In margin: 'Iudg. 9. 13.'

the closet of his owne heart, as outwardly vpon the actions of other men, and then let him tell; are not men, commonly, as sensually prophane as they haue been? their drunkennesse as generall and loathsome, their swearing as prodigious, their pride as Satanicall, their hatred as rankorous and inueterate, and, of all other reigning sinnes, some as vnprooued by Preachers, many as vnpunished by Magistrates, & almost all as vnrepented of by transgressours themselues? who after their afflictions are now growen so obstinate, as if they had made their hearts as anuells, to bee more and more hardened by the late strokes of Gods vengeance. Wherefore, as long as wee rebelliously oppose against God an army of our sinnes, let vs expect hee will bring vpon vs his hoste of reuengefull enemies, as hee once denounced against his people, saying, that hee would [272]*Hisse for the Flie that is in the vttermost part of the riuers of Egypt, and for the Bee that is in the land of Assyria; which* (sayth hee) *shall come with arrowes and bowes,* that is to say, in huge multitudes of armed enemies suddainely prest and prepared to execute Gods iudgements.

O, but some will say, Are not we the professours of Gods trueth, hauing the light of his Gospel among vs, together with the holy seales of his Couenant? True, our *Church of England,* by the singular mercie of God in Christ Iesus, may truely and confidently boast her selfe, in comparison with any other, that shee vnder a most gracious and religious King, is for trueth of doctrine and puritie of worship, as truely Catholike and Orthodox, as euer any Church of Christ hath been since the dayes of the Apostles; insomuch that in this our English and Spanish Warre, Trueth may seeme to fight against Falsehood, Innocence against Antichristian cruelty, and syncerity of worship against flat Idolatry, and therefore (say you) what can bee expected from God by vs in this battell, but victory and great triumph? Nay, deceiue not your owne selues, by claime of false priuiledges, as though, forsooth, *Israel* (euen the peculiar and onely people of God, carrying the signe of his Couenant in their flesh, acquainted with his Oracles, and possessed of the Arke and Temple of God) did not (notwithstanding) complaine that God, [273]*went not out with their Armies,* but forsooke them, so that they *turned their backe vpon their enemies*; that [274]*Gods Arke* (the glory of Israel, and Ensigne of the victorious God) *was taken* of the heathen; and that their whole nation was often enthralled in manifold *Captiuities* in *Egypt* and *Babylon*: a iustice against Gods people, which God himselfe did auow, when he spake of the sword saying, [275]*O Assyrian; The rod of mine anger, I will send thee against an hypocriticall nation, to destroy them.*

In which processe of Gods iudgement against his people, we are to contemplate and consider, the Holines, Iustice, and Power of our iealous God, together with the abomination of our owne sinnes. So holy a God is he, that he will not acknowledge any Professour of his Law, who is not also a practiser of Pietie and Holinesse; so Iust, that hee will at length afflict his owne children for their wilfull transgressions; so Powerfull, that hee can of beasts, elements, diseases, and (if these will not serue) of the very heathen and enemies of Gods Truth, and of their mortally malicious swords, make rods to correct them. Whereunto the Prophet giueth his acclamation, saying [276]*O mighty God, thou hast ordained them* (viz. the heathen) *for correc-*

---

[272] In margin: 'Isa. 7. 18.'
[273] In margin: 'Psal. 44.'
[274] In margin: '1. Sam. 4.'
[275] In margin: 'Isa. 10. 5.'
[276] In margin: 'Hab. 1. 12.'

tion. And how shall not the transgressour himselfe appeare to bee abominable, who prophaneth that Religion of God with his wicked life, which hee professeth with his breath; thereby causing, as much as in him is, the Name and Truth of God, to be blasphemed among the aduersaries thereof, as if God were a patronizer and protector of wickednesse. But say not with your selues, that the light of Gods glory shall be any whit eclipsed by punishing his owne people: No, but the contrary, as the Prophet sheweth, saying, [277]*The Lord of hostes will be exalted in iudgement, and God that is holy, will bee sanctified in righteousnesse*, that is, in his auenging Iustice. This may be sufficient for remoouing those fond pretences, which, like false Prophets, most commonly seduce the hearts of men.

In the next place, it will concerne you (deare Brethren), to seeke the meanes of pacifying Gods wrath, and of preuenting his fearefull Iudgements, and by a true reconciliation to God, your sins being put away by repentance, to obtaine, that you may become victorious in battel. To this end, you are to examine what is your greatest hinderance. Surely no greater danger can be imagined, then mans security & neglect of danger; nor can there be any greater security, then either not to be willing to know, or knowing, not to prepare against it. Vnderstand it we ought, because [278]*when God* (saith the Prophet) *giueth his alarme to warre, and bloweth his Trumpet*, that is, giueth you full assurance of battell, and you *will not hearken, surely the sword shall come*: And when God [279]*setteth vp his Ensigne*, that is, sheweth manifest euidences of the approach of the sword, and men are [280]*possessed with a spirit of slumber, and wil not see*: When they rather imbrace such false prophets, who cry [281]*Peace, peace*, vnto them; when they *make a couenant with death*,[282] as if they should say, Come what come will, wee will shift for our selues, all this *shall be disanulled*, say the Prophets; so that indeed, each one of these men are no better then *Salomons* [283] *Foole*, that would needs bee *sleeping vpon the top of the mast*, and therefore is in a desperate case.

Furthermore, what helpeth it vs to haue true and infallible intelligence of a malicious & puissant enemie, and yet not to prouide how to encounter him, as well with Spirituall, as Corporall weapons? Our Spirituall preparation is prescribed vnto vs, in the Word of God; [284]*Sanctifie a Fast vnto mee*, saith God by his Prophet; and certainely a *Sanctified Fast* it must bee, by holy abstinence in afflicting our selues by holy deuotion in Prayer, and worshipping of God, by holy Repentance, and abrenuntiation of our former sinnes, by holy vowes and promises of amendment of life & performance thereof. For wonderfull are the conquests which the Worthies of God haue atchieued and gotten in their true humiliation of Abstinence, Prayer, & Deuotion. *Moses* vanquished *Amalek*; King *Iehosaphat* sheathed the sword of the *Amorites* and *Moabites* in their owne bowels; King *Hezechias* frustrated the huge hoste of *Senacherib*, and turned them backe to their owne home: And our *Gracious Soueraigne* followeth the examples of those religious Kings, by his royall *command*

---

277   In margin: 'Isa. 5. 16.'
278   In margin: 'Ier. 6. 17.'
279   In margin: 'Is. 5. 26 & cap. 18.'
280   In margin: 'Isa. 29.'
281   In margin: 'Ezech. 9.'
282   In margin: 'Isa. 28.'
283   In margin: 'Prou. 23.'
284   In margin: 'Ioel. 1.'

of a Fast, and personall performance of Deuotion, and that (as wee pray, and hope, to obtaine) with like glorious successe.

Our next Spirituall preuention, to wit, our *Repentance*, is the subiect of most Sermons, and can neuer bee superfluously taught, because neuer sufficiently learned: Yet at this time it may suffice to take out this one Lesson, euen the obseruation of [285]*Achior*; that Gods people could neuer bee ouercome, so long as they were at peace with God; nor could they euer preuaile against their enemies, so long as their owne sinnes, as their deadliest enemies, fought against them, because of vnrepentance. Hence was that *Caueat*, which God gaue vnto the impenitents in Israel, [286]*Goe not vp against your enemies to war, lest ye die*. No maruaile then, if when man in his peruersenesse, turneth his necessitie of Repentance into a libertie and licencious-nesse of sinning, God in his Iustice turne his libertie of pardoning into a necessitie of punishing. Aboue all things therefore (Brethren) seeke after him in faith and repent-ance, in weeping, fasting, and praying, who is our reconciliation with the Father, Iesus Christ our Lord; so shall the voyce of his blood, shed for vs, crie downe the voyce of all our crying and bloody sinnes.

But are men spirits onely? Are they to fight their Battels onely with Spirituall Armour? No; for were not that to tempt God, in neglecting the good meanes ordained by him for that end? Merely politique preparations are Gods ordinance, and haue euer beene vsed by his good seruants, in their greatest confidence of his protection, euen when God himselfe hath commanded them to goe out to battell against his & their enemies. *Abraham, Moses, Ioshua, Dauid,* were all warriers, and famous in their generations, in fighting the Lords battels; yet read we not, that any of them euer went out to battell without due preparation of meanes. Wee reade of the great, mightie, and numerous armies of Gods owne people, and their strength and meanes imployed for their warres. Wee reade of *Lawes of Armes*[287] and *Counsels of warre*;[288] and we find also Gods incouragement to Captaines, and Warriers, as in raising [289]*Iudges* to *Israel*, to know and prouide against the dangers approching and to gather the people together, to conduct and direct them to fight their battels; such as were *Othniel* and *Shamgar*, of whom it is said, [290]*The spirit of the Lord came vpon them, and they fought*. And we read of [291]*The sword of the Lord, and of Gideon*, that is, Gods powerfull helpe by the hand of *Gideon*, and the people with him.

And it is the same Spirit of the Lord that informeth the hearts of good people in their duties to God, their King, and their Countrey; and inflameth the affections of all loyall Subiects with a ready and cheereful resolution, to imploy their bodies, strength, and meanes for the preseruation of *Gods Annoynted*, their *Gracious Souer-aigne*, and the safetie of the kingdome, especially in a Defensiue Warre, as this is, in which, Gods cause, and true Religion is also assaulted. And who is there, a subiect of this State, and member of this Church, of what degree and calling soeuer, that hath not his share & part herein, and is not imbarked in this ship of the care of the publike safety? So that the welfare of the whole is his welfare, and the ill speeding of this vessell, cannot but be the ship wrack and ruine of himselfe, & of all that are

---

[285]   In margin: 'Iudith 5.'
[286]   In margin: 'Deut. 1.'
[287]   In margin: 'Leu. & Num.'
[288]   In margin: 'Isa.'
[289]   In margin: 'Iudg. 3. &c.'
[290]   In margin: 'Iudg. 3.'
[291]   In margin: 'Iudg. 7.'

most deare vnto him. And therefore if through our backewardnes, and neglect of due preparation, to resist and oppose an inuading enemie, as well by the people and Souldiers, as by the Prince and the Leaders, wee shall become guilty of our owne ruine, and giue opportunitie and incouragement to the maleuolent mighty enemie, to exercise his rage and cruelty, with vnbounded and vnlimited fury, against all places and persons that come in his way: shall wee not iustly bee taxed of failing in our duety in respect both of publicke and priuate?

Yet in the height and best of our care, meanes and preparation, then doeth our hope become victorious, when in confidence of Gods helpe and protection, our Spirituall and Temporall forces are vnited together; but much more relying vpon our Spirituall munition, which hath an obligation of promise with God, then vpon our politique, temporall, and corporall.

Memorable and admirable is the story of *Moses*, who was praying while his Captaines and Souldiers were fighting with *Amalek*; and so it fell out, that while *Moses* held vp his hands in prayer, *Israel* had the better, but so soone as his hands failed and fell downe, *Amalek* the enemy preuailed. What else doeth this teach vs, but that whosoeuer they be that fight, Victory is absolutely in the will and power of God; and therefore when wee prepare for battell, not to put our trust in the arme of flesh, but to put and haue our confidence onely in our God, the Lord of Hostes; and hauing, as it behooueth vs, in the feare of God, made due preparation of all good meanes, to put on our Armour, and goe to the seruice with bended knees, and penitent hearts, strengthened with Faith, to call by feruent Prayer for His helpe and protection, that couereth our heads in the day of battell, giueth victory to Kings, protecteth His faithfull, and neuer faileth them that faithfully call vpon him in the time of necessitie?

The Prophet *Dauid* hath summed vp all that can be spoken hereof, in one verse, [292]*Our helpe is in the Name of the Lord, which hath made heauen and earth.* So then, whosoeuer shall distrust the arme of the Almightie, or doubt of the strength of the Lord of Hosts, hee thereby offendeth against both heauen and earth, because all kinde of creatures both in heauen and earth are the Armies and prest Souldiers of God, to fight his battels, euen from the hoast of his Angels aboue, to the flies, lice, and wormes that are ingendred in the dust: and hee can execute his iudgements by what meanes soeuer, whether they be ordinary or miraculous: For hee threw downe the walls of *Iericho* by the blast of [293]*Rams hornes*; hee gaue victory to *Israel*, by the holding vp of *Moses* his [294]*hands*: he discomfited the host of the *Madianites*, at the sound of [295]*Trumpets*, and noyse of *mens voyces*, and clashing of *pitchers* together: hee infused strength into the very haire of *Samsons* head, when *Samson* exulted, saying of his slaine, [296]*Heapes vpon heapes of a thousand, by the jaw-bone of an Asse.* But miracles now are for vnbeleeuers.

In the last place therefore, let vs examine the more ordinary prouidence of God, which may beget confidence in all extremities of warfare. What can man feare, being in reconciliation and confederacy with God, when our enemies are made the enemies of God? Is it the policy of their Counsells? But hee confoundeth the

---

292   In margin: 'Psal. 126.'
293   In margin: 'Ios. 6.'
294   In margin: 'Exod. 17.'
295   In margin: 'Iudg. 7.'
296   In margin: 'Iudg. 15.'

counsell of *Achitophel*. Is it that enemies combine together in the name of an *holy league*? But when they say, [297]*a Confederacy*, God maketh them like *a wheele* turned with the spirit of giddinesse. Is it the courage of their hearts? But he posses-seth the enemies hearts with [298]*feare*, and maketh the hearts of [299]*Canaanites to melt*. Is it their strength or hugenes of stature? But were they the children of *Anakims* and *Gyants*, and wee but as *Grashoppers* in comparison of them; yet [300]*Feare them not* (saith God) *I will goe before you*. Is it the multitude of their hoasts? But it is the glory of God to ouerthrow many [301]*thousands* by a few *hundreds*. Is it their ioynt and vnited forces? But hee [302]*setteth the Egyptians against the Egyptians*. Is it their importunitie, not to bee satisfied till they fight? But either, hee will draw *[303]Senacherib* backe from warring against *Israel*, by a *rumour of warres* begun in the bowels of his owne kingdome, or else, if they will needes battell, hee will hale them on thereunto [304]*to their owne destruction*. Is it because no man can tell, when there shall come deliuerance? But hee can doe this to our astonishment, before wee can thinke on it. [305]*When God turned the Captiuitie of Sion, wee were like vnto them that dreamed*, saith *Israel*: as not perswaded it was so, no not when they saw it. Againe, what greater matter of confidence can wee haue then our former experi-ence of Gods prouidence? *Dauids* remembrance of his deliuerance from the [306]*Lyon and the Beare*, did animate him in the encountering with that huge *Goliah*. And is there any Nation at this day vnder heauen that hath greater experience of Gods manifold deliuerances, then this our kingdome, especially from the fiery *Powder-plot,* and from the *Spanish Inuasion* by water?[307] in respect whereof we might here take vp a song answerable to that of *Deborah* of the riuer *Kishon*; so we, [308]*The maine Ocean swept them away, the ancient and maine Ocean*. To conclude, doe we cleaue fast to God? then their armes cannot touch vs; [309]*It is he that maketh Warre to cease, knappeth the Speare asunder, and burneth the Chariot with fire*. Nor can our enemies auoyd the sword, when it shall bee inforced vpon them; for then, as saith the Prophet, who can say to the sword of the Lord, *Put vp thy selfe into thy scabbard, rest and bee still?* It is answered, [310]*How can it be quiet, seeing the Lord hath giuen it a charge against Askalon*.

Finally (deare Brethren) bee you exhorted againe and againe, to serious and speedy repentance, the onely meanes whereby the wrath euen of the omnipotent God is made impotent: And (howsoeuer God shall be pleased to dispose of your bodily liues) aboue all things seeke to be furnished with the *compleate spirituall armour of God*, consisting of truth, hope, inward righteousnesse, and purity of a good conscience, whereby we may subdue all spirituall enemies that may assault our

---

297 In margin: 'Psal, 83.'
298 In margin: 'Deaut. 2.'
299 In margin: 'Ios. 5.'
300 In margin: 'Num. 13. & 14.'
301 In margin: 'Iudg. 7.'
302 In margin: 'Isa. 19.'
303 In margin: '2. Kings. 19.'
304 In margin: 'Iosh. 11.'
305 In margin: 'Psal. 126.'
306 In margin: '1. Sam. 16.'
307 In margin: 'In 1588.'
308 In margin: 'Iudg. 5. 21.'
309 In margin: 'Psal. 46.'
310 In margin: 'Ier. 47.'

soules, and in the end bee made possessours of that euerlasting kingdome of bless-
ednesse, which hath been so deerely purchased by Christ our Sauiour, and prepared
for all that with faith and patience expect the glorious appearance of his comming,
according vnto the euerlasting mercy of our most gracious and omnipotent God,
to whom bee rendred all praise, power, and thanksgiuing, both now and euermore.
AMEN.

1626–E3 Prayers during war and plague, and for Christian IV of Denmark

After 21 September (Canterbury)

In September, Charles ordered public prayers to be said in the province of Canterbury
because of the great dangers that hung over the realm – war and plague – and on
behalf of his uncle and ally, King Christian IV of Denmark. Christian was leading the
protestant defence against the catholics in central Europe, and had been defeated by
the Catholic League at Lutter the previous month. Charles argued that such prayers
were necessary because not only was Christian his kin, but also his defeat threatened
both the Palatinate and England. He also criticised the Commons for failing to grant
sufficient subsidies, which had contributed to Christian's defeat, and blamed them
for the deteriorating relationship between him and parliament. As no fast days or
services were intended, this special worship was ordered by letters missive from the
archbishop of Canterbury, rather than by royal proclamation.

Order: Letter missive from Abbot to [a bishop], 21 Sept. 1626, LPL, Abbot Register, Part II, fos.
218v–219v [printed *Concilia*, IV, 471–3].
Form of prayer: none found.

ORDER

Letter missive from archbishop of Canterbury, to [a bishop]: 21 September 1626

My very good Lorde I haue received from the Kinges Maiestie both pious and prudent
Instructions necessary for this tyme: the perticulers whereof doe heere follow /

Most reuerend father in God right trusty and right welbeloved Counsellor we
greete you well. wee have observed that the Church and the State are so neere vnited
and knit togeather, that though they may seeme two bodyes, yet indeede in some
relacon they may be anounted [*sic*] but as one, in as much as they both are made
vpp of the same men which are differenced only in relations to spirituall or Civill
endes. This neerenes makes the Church call in the helpe of the state to succour and
support her, whensoeuer she is pressed beyond her selfe And the same neerenes
makes the state call in for the service of the Church, both to teach that duty which
her members knowe not and to exhort them to, and encourage them in that duty
which they knowe. It is not longe since, wee ordered the State to serve the Church
and by a timely proclamation settled the place of it, And nowe the State lookes for
the like assistance from the Churche, that shee and all her ministers may serve God
and vs, by preaching peace and vnity at home that it may be the better able to resist
forraine forces, vniting and multiplying against it, And to the end, that they to

whome wee have Comitted the gouerment of the Church vnder vs may be the better able to dispose of the present occasions wee have with the advise of our Councell thought fitt to send to you theis instructions following to be sent by you to the Bishoppes of your Prouince and such others whom it may concearne and by them and their officers directed to all the ministers throughout the severall Diocesses that according to these punctually[?] the [illegible] instruct and exhort the people to serve God and vs, and labour by their prayers to divert the dangers which hang over vs. The danger in which wee are att this tyme is greate. It is increased by the late blowe given our good unkle the King of Denmarke who is the on chiefe person in those partes that opposed the spreading forces of Spaine. / If he cannot subsist, there is little or nothing left to hinder the house of Austria from being Lord and Master of Germany. And that is a large and mighty Territory as such as should it bee gotten, would make an open way for Spaine to doe what they pleased in all the west partes of Christendome for besides the great strength which Germany once possessed would bring to them, which are to strong already you are to consider first, howe it will enable them by land in that it will ioyne all or the most parte of the Spaniardes nowe distracted territories and be a meanes for him safely and spedily to drawe down forces against any other Kingdome that shall stand in his way; Nor can it be thought the Lowe Countreyes can hold out longer against him, if he once become Lord of the vpper partes. And Secondly, you are to weigh howe it will advantage him by Sea and make him strong vs [sic] in our particular, which is of easy apprehention to all men. And besides if he once gett Germany, he wilbe able though he had noe gold from India to supply the necessity of those wars and to hinder all trade and traficke of the greatest Staple Comodities of this Kingdome Cloath and wooll, and so make them of litle or noe value. You are to knowe therefore, that to prevent this, is the present Care of the King and the State and there is no probably way left, but by sending forces and other supplies to the saide Kinge of Denmarke our deare Vnkle to enable him to keepe the ffeilde that our enimies be not Masters of all on the Suddance, you are farther to take notice howe that wee and this whole State stand bound in honour and conscience to supply the present necessity of the Kinge of Denmarke, for this quarrell is more nearly ours the recovery of the auntient inheritance of our deare Sister and her Children. The King of Denmark stands not soe neere in bloud vnto her as wee doe. Yett for her and our sakes that brave and valiant King hath adventured into the feild, and in that engagement hath not only hazarded his person but as thinges goe nowe, it may turne to some dainger to his owne Kingdome and posterity, should he not receive ayde and succour from vs with out delay; which should it happen (as God forbidd) wilbe one of the greatest dishoners that ever this Kingdome was stayned withall, Nor is dainger and dishonour all the mischeife that is like to followe this disaster: ffor if he be not presently releived the cause of Religion is not only likely to suffer by it in some one parte (as it hath already in a fearefull manner in the Palatinate) but in all places where it hath gotten any ffooting, Soe that if wee supply not presently, our Allies and Confederats in this Case, it is likely to prove the extirpation of true Religion and the replanting of Romish superstition in all the neighbouring partes of Christendome, And the Coldnes of this State shall suffer in all places, as the betrayer of that Religion elsewhere, which it professeth and honoureth att home, which wilbe an imputation never to be washed of. And God forbid this States should suffer vnder it. Neither may you forgett rightly to enfourme the people Comitted to your Charge, that this warre which nowe growes full of dainger was not entred vpon rashly, and with out advise but you are to acquaint them, that all former treaties by a peaceably way, were in the later end of our deare father of Ever blessed memory, dissolved as fruitelesse and vnfitt longer to be helde on foote. And this by the Counsell of both houses of Parliament then sitting, so those two greate a[n]d honourable bodyes of the Peeres and people represented in Parliament led on this Counsell and Course to a warre with Spaine. To effect this they desired our ayde and assistance, and vsed vs to worke our saide deere Father to entertaine this Course. This vpon their perswations and promises of all assistance and supply wee redylie vnder tooke and effected, and cannot nowe be left in that busines but with the sinne and shame of all men, Sinne becayse ayde and supply for the defence of the Kingdome and the like affayres of the State, especially such as are advised and assumed by Parlementary Counsell are due to the Kinge from his people by all lawe both of God and men: And shame if they forsake the Kinge while he pursues their owne Counsell, iust and honourable, and which could not vnder God but have bene successfull if it had bene followed and supplied in tyme as wee desired and laboured for. One thing there is which proves a great hinderance of this State, and not continued amongst the people without great offence against God, detriment both to Church and state, and our great disservice in this and all other businesse. It is the breache of vnity which is growne too great and Common among all sortes of men. The danger of this goes farre: for in all States it hath made way for enemies to enter. Wee have by, all meanes, endeavoured vnion, and require of you to preach it and Charitye the mother of it, frequently in the eares of the people. Wee knowe their loyall hearts and therefore wonder the more what should cause distracted affections. If you call vpon them (which is your duty) wee doubt not butt that God will blesse them with that love to himselfe, to his Church and their owne preservation, which alone wilbe able to bynd vp the Scatteringes of devided affections into Strength. To this end you are to lay before them what miseries home divisions have brought vpon this and many other Kingdomes, and to exhort all men to embrace it in tyme. The danger it selfe, besides all other Christian and prudent motives is of force enough (where it is duly considered) to make men ioyne in all amity against a Com[m]on, a greate and a growing enemy. And to doe it in tyme before any secrett and cunninge working of his, maye vse one parte in a division to weaken the other. And in the last place, (but first and last and all times to be insited [sic] vpon) you are to call vpon God your selves, and to incite the people to ioyne with you in humble and hearty prayers vnto God, that he wilbe pleased nowe after long afflictions of his deare people: and Children to looke in mercy both vpon them and vs. And in particular, for the safetye of the Kinge of Denmarke, and that army which is left him, that God would blesse and prosper him against his and our enimies. Thus you are to Stating then the [illegible] and the hopes of our loyall subiectes and people in and vpon God. And whereas the greatest confidence men have in God, ariseth not only from his promises but from their experience likewise of his goodnesse, you must not fayle often to recall to the memory of the people with thankfulnesse, the late great experience wee have had of his goodnesse toward vs, ffor the three greate and vsuall Judgements which he darts downe vpon disobedient and vnthankfull people are pestilence famine and sworde. The pestilence did never rage more in this Kingdome then of late, And God was gratiously pleased in mercy to heare the prayers which were made vnto him, and the ceasing of the Judgement was litle lesse then a miracle. The famine threatned vs this present yeere, and it must have followed, had God rayned downe his anger, a litle longer vpon the fruites of the earth. But vpon our prayers he stayed that Judgement, and send vs a blessed season and a most plentifull harvest. The sworde is the thinge which wee nowe to looke to, and you must call the people to their prayers againe against the Enemy, that God wilbe pleased to send the like deliverance from this Judgement also, that in the same mercy, he will vouchsafe to strengthen the hand of his people, that he will sharpen their sworde, but dull and turne the edge of that which is in our enimies handes, that soe while some fight, others may pray, for the blessing And you are to be Carefull that you faile nott to direct and hearten our loving people in this and all other necessary services, both of God, his Church and vs that wee may have the comfort of our peoples service; the States safety; the Church Religion; and the People the enioying of all such blessinges as followe these. And wee end with doubling of this Care vpon you, and all vnder you in their severall places. Given att our Palace att Westminster in the second yeere of our raigne, the 21 of September 1626.

The Care which your Lordshipp is to vse in the behalfe is to see them made knowne to the worthy preachers and ministers in your diocesse, and soe farr a[s] your Lordship may, in your owne person to putt these thinges in execucion and to call vpon the Clergy, which is vnder you in their preaching and private conferences to stir vpp all sorte of people to expresse their zeale to God, their duty to the Kinge and their love vnto this Countrey and one to another, that all good and Christian Courses may bee taken for the preservation of the true Religion hath, in this Land, and throughout all Christendome which not doubting but your Lordshipp with all diligence and speede will see effected, I leave you to the Almighty and remaine: /

1627–E Prayers during English and allied military and naval campaigns against France

Daily [June?] 1627 (England and Wales)

This prayer cannot be dated precisely from internal evidence, and there is no extant order. Charles Cox argued that the prayer dated from 1625; it is dated to '?June 1627' in *CSPD*, while ESTC suggests '?1628'. The most likely date is 1627 because the form issued for 1625–E included prayers for war as well as plague; this prayer differs from those for documented days during 1628, and its references to the English army and navy and those of 'our Friends and Allies' are particularly relevant to the situation in 1627. Buckingham's diplomacy led England into war with France as well as Spain, and he launched an ultimately disastrous attack on the Île de Ré, in support of the Huguenots against the French crown. Christian IV continued to suffer defeats in Germany at the hands of Count Tilly and Albrecht von Wallenstein, commanders of the Catholic League.

Order: none found.
Form of prayer: *A prayer, to be vsed with the other prayers of the day, so long as his maiesties nauie and forces are abroade* (1 p.; STC 16545; SoA, Lemon 287)
Form of prayer (other edition): STC 16545.5.
Additional sources: *A prayer, to be vsed with the other prayers of the day* (1 p.; STC 16545; SP16/68/75, fo. 117r); Charles Cox 'Special forms of prayer: II, James I and Charles I', *Newbery House Magazine*, 7: 3 (1892), 260–1.

FORM OF PRAYER

O most gracious God, and mercifull Father; Thou art the Lord of Hosts, all victory over our Enemies, all safety against them is from thee: Wee humbly beseech thee to goe on, as thou hast in great mercy begun to go with our Armies, and blesse them: That thy selfe wouldest be with their Wind, and Anchor at Sea, and with their Sword and Shield at Land: That wisedome may attend all their counsels; and courage and successe all their enterprises: That so thou by them wilt be pleased to bring safety to this Kingdome; strength and comfort to Religion; victory and reputation to our Countrey: and accomplish and crowne that great blessing which thou hast begun to bring vpon vs. Blesse likewise, we beseech thee, the Armies of our Friends and Allies, giue them victory in thy cause, and preserve them from the might and the malice of their and our enemies. And when thou hast blessed both them and vs, and our most gracious King and State by their seruice, grant good Lord, that their Returne may be with safety and honour to heale our many afflictions; and that our thankfulnesse may then blesse thee, as we blesse thee this day, for shewing mercie to vs thy vnworthy, yet penitent and faithfull Servants. Grant this for thy deare Sonnes sake Jesus Christ our Lord. Amen.

1627–S   Fast days in response to increasing popery, persecution of continental protestants, war against France and fears of famine

Wednesday 8 August and Sunday 12 August 1627 (Scotland)

On 17 July 1627, a meeting of bishops and other commissioners of the Kirk chosen by the government was held at Edinburgh. It appointed commissioners to the crown, partly in response to pressure for a full meeting of the general assembly, and ordered this fast. Contrary to the account in the *Bannatyne miscellany*, Row alleged that no causes were agreed by the meeting; it is possible that they were not widely publicized. They responded to prevalent sins, the Thirty Years War, the crown's military expedition to the Île de Ré (see 1627–E), and heavy rains creating fears of famine.

Order: act of the commissioners of the Kirk, 18 July 1627, in *The Bannatyne miscellany* (Bannatyne Club, Edinburgh, 1855), III, 222.
Causes: agreed by the commissioners, 19 July 1627, *Bannatyne miscellany*, III, 223.
Additional sources: Row, p. 344; presbytery of Peebles minutes, NRS, CH2/295/2, fo. 28v; presbytery of Perth minutes, NRS, CH2/299/1, p. 178.

ORDER

Act of the commissioners of the Kirk: 18 July 1627
The whilk day, after reasoning, it was agreed upon be all the Brethren, in one voice, That there should be ane publick Humiliation with Fasting, to be upon the second Wednesday of August, and the Sabbath following, being the eight and twelt dayes of the said moneth, and intimation to be made upon the Sabbath day preceiding, being the fift day: And the Brethren of the Ministrie of Edinburgh, togidder with Dr

Theodore Hay and Dr Johne Michelsone, Mr Robert Scot, Mr Patrick Schaw, Mr Henry Blyth, and Mr William Erskin, should conveene, and condescend upon the particular Causes of the said Fast.

CAUSES

In everie Parish of this Kingdome the Pastors shall exhort their people to humble themselves before the Lord in true repentance, with tears and fasting, for these speciall causes:

1. Because of the great increase of Papistrie, and of all sorts of sinne in all degrees of persons within this land, both against Law and Gospell; which increase, being in the time of so cleare a light, cannot but provoke God's heavie wrath against us, which cannot be averted without true and sincere Repentance.

2. For the distres and cruell persecution of the Reformed kirks in Bohemia, and the adjoining Provinces in Upper and Lower Germanie, and the Palatinate, to intreate God that he wold be appeased towards his people, and pittie them, who are by the enemies designes destinat to death, and whose blood is shed as water in the streetes; that he wold cutt the coards of the wicked, and turn the rage of his enemies to his praise.

3. Because our King's Maiestie is imbarked in a most necessar and lawfull warre, and hes Armies both by sea and land for the maintenance of the true Religion and his royall Allyance, to pray to the Lord of Hosts that he wold lead these and all other Armies for the defense of the trueth, and powre shame upon his enemies, and smite them through the thigh, that they be not able to stand against him.

4. Because of the extraordinar raines, which now threaten rotting of the fruits of the ground before they be rype, and so a fearfull famine upon this land in so dangerous a time, when the seas are closed be the enemies, and no hope of help from other countreyes, if God shall send a famine, to intreat the Lord that He wold cause the Heaven answer the Earth, and the Earth to answer the Corne, and the cornes to answer our necessitie, and us to answer His will, in faith, repentance and obedience.

1628–E1 Fast days during war against France and persecution of protestants in Europe

Saturday 5 April 1628 (London, Westminster and adjacent places); Monday 21 April 1628 (elsewhere in England and Wales)

On 20 March, William Strode (second son of Sir William Strode) proposed that the Commons should petition the king for a general fast, following precedents set at the opening of the previous two parliaments. His motion was supported by Perrott and by Sir Robert Phelips, who argued that a fast was 'so necessary at this time' because 'this state [n]ever stood in more danger'. The war went from bad to worse; many MPs were concerned about the continuing influence of Buckingham, Charles's reluctance to redress grievances, the rise of Arminianism (the doctrines of Jacob Arminius which were contrary to Calvinism, especially on predestination) and of arbitrary government, the latter demonstrated by the Forced Loan of 1626–7. The Commons' petition was presented to the Lords on 21 March. It used Charles's own words – that the reformed churches were threatened with 'utter destruction' and that this would cause the 'subversion of this church and state' – to emphasize the plight of Calvinists at home and abroad; stressed the 'miseries' that lay on the protestant church (i.e. Arminianism and arbitrary government); argued that parliament played an important *rôle* in giving advice to resolve national problems, and sought divine blessing on their proceedings and the king. The petition was approved by the Lords and presented to Charles, who agreed to it on 24 March. Jeremiah Dyke (minister of Epping, Essex) and Walter Balcanquhall (dean of Rochester) were chosen to preach before the Commons; the bishops of Salisbury and Exeter, and the dean of Westminster before the Lords.

The royal proclamation was based on that for 1625–E, but with an explicit acknowledgment that the initiative for the fast had come from parliament, and that parliament had been assembled to consult and advise on weighty matters of state. More particularly, the proclamation included a lengthy eulogy on the king and his piety. The form of prayer was based on 1626–E2, but emphasized the plight of continental protestants rather than the plague. Like previous forms (see 1603–E, 1625–E and 1626–E2), it also contained a lengthy exhortation which was to be read aloud as part of the service. The form appears to have been reissued the following year for the fast for good relations between the king and parliament, the success of parliament and on behalf of the reformed churches abroad (1629–E). Identifying precisely which copies were printed for each occasion is difficult: the editors of the *STC* described STC 16547 as issued in 1629 and 16547.5 as issued in 1628. Though there is no evidence in the texts to support this, this identification is followed here and STC 16547.5 is transcribed below. Taken together, the proclamation and the form of prayer reveal the growing tensions between Charles and his more godly subjects. The proclamation stated that the form had been commissioned so that the fast could be 'performed with all decencie and vniformitie', indicating the authorities' concerns about 'godly' enthusiasts. The 'Prayer for all the reformed churches in Christendom' to be read during the litany emphasized the concerns of 'puritan' parliamentarians about the threats posed to protestantism from foreign and domestic enemies alike. In early April, a number of bishops expressed concern that the fast day coincided with parish fairs and markets. John Williams, bishop of Lincoln and dean of Westminster, had already appointed an alternative date for the fast in his jurisdiction, but others argued that such action required royal approval. Similar concerns were voiced by some MPs when they realized that the fast clashed with the meeting of Suffolk county court. Charles told the Lords that he was happy for bishops to authorize necessary changes in their dioceses. The mayor and alderman of Canterbury complained to the lord lieutenant of Kent that soldiers billeted in the town would refuse to observe the fast and would take the opportunity to protest about their food and lodging; they requested support to enable parishioners to observe the fast.

Order: royal proclamation, 29 Mar. 1628, STC 8889* [also in Larkin, II, 193–4].
Form of prayer: *A forme of prayer, necessary to bee vsed in these dangerous times of warre: wherein we are appointed to fast according to his maiesties proclamation, for the preseruation of his maiestie, and his realmes, and all reformed churches* (94 pp.; STC 16547.5)*.
Additional sources: *CJ*, I, 873–5; *LJ*, III, 693–9, 711, 734; *Commons debates, 1628*, ed. Robert C. Johnson (6 vols., New Haven, 1977–*c*.1983), II, 32–5, 46–7, 401, V, 189–90, 192, 197–8, 206, 208; the king's answer to the petition of the parliament, 24 Mar. 1628, SP16/98/38, fo. 89r; petition of both Houses of parliament to the king, 31 Mar. 1628, SP16/98/83, fos. 163r–168v; speech of the Lord Keeper

Coventry, 31 Mar. 1628, SP16/98/87, fos. 177r–177v; king's speech on receipt of the petition, 31 Mar. 1628, SP16/98/88, fo. 178r; mayor and aldermen of Canterbury to Philip, earl of Montgomery, 17 Apr. 1628, SP16/101/29, fo. 62r; John Millington to Gilbert Millington, [26 Mar.?] 1628, SP16/98/63, fo. 130r.

Printed sermons: Davenant, House of Lords (STC 6299); Dyke, House of Commons (STC 7424); Hall, House of Lords (STC 12692); Williams, House of Lords (STC 25729).

ORDER

Royal proclamation: 29 March 1628

The Kings most Excellent Maiestie, hauing by His Royall Authority assembled His high Court of Parliament, in that great Councell which is the representatiue body of His whole Kingdome, to Consult, Debate, and Conclude of those weighty, and most important matters, which concerne the glory of God, the honour of the King, the safetie of his Kingdomes, and support of His Friends and Allyes. Taking into His most pious and Princely consideration the present state of the true Religion, and of the affaires of Christendome, Himselfe, His people, His Friends and Allyes, being imbarked in an open warre, with potent and vigilant enemies, although Hee neither doth, nor will neglect any ordinary meanes, which may conduce to their iust defence, yet Hee neither doeth, nor will make His reliance vpon the arme of flesh, but in His priuate deuotions dayly lifteth vp His heart and hands to God, who is the King of kings, and Lord of hostes, from him to begge and obtaine a blessing vpon His Counsels and indeauours, and to take His owne cause into his owne hand. Yet to the end, that in a common calamitie, wherein Prince and people are inuolued, both Prince and people might humble themselves before Almighty God, and be reconciled vnto him, His Maiestie being mooued thereto by the ioynt petition of His Lords and Commons in Parliament, Himselfe in his owne pietie easily inclining to so religious and seasonable a motion, according to the examples of all good Kings in former ages, in like cases, hath resolued, and doeth hereby command a generall and publique Fast to be held and solemnized throughout this whole Land, in such manner as hereafter is directed and prescribed, that so both Prince and people, euen the whole kingdome as one man, may offer vnto Almighty God, their hearty & unfained thanks for his manifold mercies formerly vouchsafed vnto them, & may powre out their supplications with strong cries, vnto him, who is able to deliuer in times of greatest difficulty and danger, to send a blessing vpon the Counsels of this great assembly, to prosper their Actions and indeauors, and to diuert those iudgements, which the sinnes of this Land haue worthily deserued.

To this purpose His most excellent Maiestie hath consulted with His reuerend Bishops, and to the end so Religious an exercise may bee performed with all decencie and vniformitie, His Maiestie hath resolued vpon a graue and Religious forme of solemnizing thereof; which His royall pleasure Hee doeth hereby publish and declare to all his louing Subiects, and doeth straitly charge and commaund, That on Saturday next being the fift day of Aprill, this fast bee Religiously and solemnely obserued and celebrated in the Cities of London and Westminster, Borough of Southwarke, and other places adiacent, wherein His Maiestie in His Royall person, and with His owne Family and Royall household, will giue an example to the rest of His people: And that on Munday the one and Twentieth of the same Moneth of Aprill the like be kept and duely obserued, throughout the rest of this whole Realme of *England* and Dominion of *Wales*. And for the more orderly solemnizing thereof without confusion, His Maiestie, by the aduice of His Reuerend Bishops, hath directed to bee composed, printed, and published, the forme of such Prayers and publique Exhortations, as he thinketh fit to bee vsed in all Churches and places at these publique Meetings; And he hath giuen charge to His Bishops to disperse the same throughout His whole Kingdome. All which, His Maiestie doeth expressely charge and command [as 1626–E2: shall be reuerently … so religious a Worke].

FORM OF PRAYER

MORNING PRAYER

[As 1626–E2, adding Ps. 86 to the list of psalms for the day]

LITANY

[After 'We humbly beseech thee', the following prayer is to be said]
   O eternall God and most gracious Father [as 1626–E2]

A Prayer for all the reformed Churches in Christendome.
   Almighty God, and gracious Father, Wee confesse against our selues, that wee are most worthy of all the iudgements that thou hast threatned against vs, these Kingdomes, this Church, and other Reformed Churches much more, which are vnder the Crosse, and neere to vtter ruine and extirpation. And howsoeuer the clamour of their and our crying sinnes hath ascended into thine eares, and stirred vp destroyers to roote vs out, that we be no more a people, and that thy name bee no more called vpon, nor hallowed by them and vs; Yet wee most humbly beseech thee to heare the prayers and supplications, with strong cryes and teares, which once our blessed Sauiour offered for vs vpon the Crosse, & in the garden, and dayly represents vnto thee, and for his reuerence, piety, and all sufficient merits, which speake better things then the blood of *Abel*. Heare not the cry of our sinnes, but heare the cry of his blood, and therin wash away all our sinnes. Let their and our great miseries and dangers suffice for that which is past: and let that Oratour in thine owne bosome, that is, thine owne fatherly goodnesse perswade and preuaile for them and vs, and purchase their deliuery and our safety. Heare vs as fellow members of one and the same mysticall body, that haue a fellow feeling of one anothers calamities. Looke vpon vs both with the eyes of pitty and compassion, and looke vpon and consider our Enemies, how many and mighty they are, and they beare a tyrannous hate against vs. Our goods, our lands, our liues will not suffice their boundlesse Ambition: Our Religion, our Soules, and if it were possible, our God, is that they strike at. Curse thou their Anger, for it is fierce, and their wrath, for it is cruell. Diuide them in Jacob, and scatter them in Israel. As for vs, deliuer vs out of their hands, and vnite vs together in the bond of Peace, that beeing freed from our many and tyrannous enemies, we may euer blesse thy sacred and holy name, and euermore serue thee without feare, in holinesse and righteousnesse all the dayes of our liues, through Jesus Christ our Lord and onely Sauiour. Amen.

[Then as 1626–E2, adding the prayer for parliament (as in 1625–E1) after the prayer for the queen.]

THE SECOND SERUICE[311]

[As 1626–E2, adding the following prayer for the reformed churches after the gospel]
Another Prayer for all the reformed Churches in Christendome.

O God of all might and mercy, who by thine onely grace hast incorporated vs into that mysticall body of Christ, which is his Church; We, as liuely members therof, Mourning with them that mourne, and reioycing with them that reioyce, doe in a speciall sympathy and fellow-feeling as well of the Calamities, as of the Prosperities of our Brethren, now present our supplications and prayers before thy fatherly goodnesse, in the behalfe of all the reformed Churches in Christendome: Beseeching thee first to looke downe, with thy woonted eye of mercy and pittie vpon the now-mournfull and miserable estate of such of them, whom thou hast already deliuered ouer to bee chastened (as by thine owne rods and scourges) into the hands of superstitious and mercilesse men vnder their more then Egyptian bondage. For the Taskemasters of Egypt vexed thy people onely with bodily pressures, but neuer (as these) compelled them to defile their soules with their Idol-worships: Wherefore stretch out thine arme (O our iealous and iust God) and suffer not the Vilifiers of thy sacred Oracles, the Innouators and Forgers of new faiths, the Corrupters of thy Sacraments, the Polluters of thy holy worship, and the Abandoners of thy Catho-like Church to triumph ouer them, who desire nothing more, then that enioying the libertie of a good conscience, they may publikely professe thy Gospel of life, and celebrate thy Worship in Spirit and Truth.

Furthermore, in our humble and thankefull acknowledgement of thy gracious prouidence, in still protecting diuers other Churches of the same Catholique faith, in freedome from all Antichristian tyrannie; Continue, we beseech thee (O our heauenly Father) thy powerfull assistance vnto them, that their hearts (maugre the malice of whatsoeuer Enemie, whether ghostly or bodily) may bee all vnited together, both in the sinceritie of one Christian faith, and in an inuiolable and mutuall faithfulnesse one with another. And seeing that the insultations of our Aduersaries are come vp to thine eares, (O God) crying among themselues, and saying, A Confederacie, a confederacie, boasting that they can doe mischiefe, and threatning our vtter destruction: Arise, thou Lord of hosts, and aduance thine owne power. Make them like a wheele, that through the spirit of giddinesse, the Egyptians may fight against the Egyptians: & let thy word against the Enemies of Israel bee verified vpon ours, That they may flie away, crying one to another, Stand, Stand, and yet none daring to looke backe.[312]

Nor doe wee offer these our prayers and supplications vnto thee (O Lord our God) as presuming of our owne strength, wisdome, or worthinesse, but in that thy accustomed goodnesse, which vseth to manifest and magnifie thy mercie in mans miserie, thy wisedome in his folly, and thy power in his infirmitie: but in the experience of thy marueilous deliuerances vnto vs (who now in humiliation of body and soule, prostrate our selues before thee) when suddenly and immediatly thou didst banish thy Plague from vs, and vanquish that Nauie prepared for Inuasion, euen that huge Nauie; and in the boast of our Aduersaries, Inuincible; and didst curse and confound that matchlesse Treason hatched in the Vault, as it were in the forge of Hell. But especially our trust is in the Mediation of Christ Iesus our Lord and

---

[311] I.e. the communion service.
[312] In margin: 'Nahum 2.8'.

Sauiour, by whom wee are inuited to approach with boldnesse before the throne of Grace, in confidence to receiue aide in the time of need. Wherefore heare vs, O heauenly Father, for thy mercie sake, and for the Merit of thy deare Sonne; to whom, with thee, and the holy Ghost, wee ascribe all prayer, praise and thankesgiuing for euer and euer. Amen.

EVENING PRAYER

[As 1626–E2 to the collects for the day]

[Collects in place of the collect for the day as at morning prayer, followed by the prayer of St Chrysostom and the grace]

A GENERALL AND CHRISTIAN EXHORTATION, IN THE TIME OF DANGER, AND FEARE OF GODS IVDGMENTS
You may remember, beloued, how often Almighty God hath condemned our wickednesse, and discouered our hypocrisies by plague and famine; but now, (as if our sinnes were come to the full) he threatneth vs with a more mercilesse vengeance, euen the sword of the enemie, except by speedie humiliation, and vnfained repentance wee preuent his iudgements: For there can be no more infallible argument of Gods irreconcileable wrath against sinners, then is mans obstinacie in sinning, especially when his hand of correction is vpon them, as wee may reade concerning *[as 1626– E2:* those obstinates, who being … conuersion of a sinner*]*.

But alas the intolerable burthen of our sinnes! *[as 1626–E2:* The *Watchmen* … the Euangelicall trueth*]*.

And now what can wee pretend *[as 1626–E2:* wee should not be liable … to execute Gods iudgements*]*.

Yet, *[as 1626–E2:* some will say … to end of exhortation*]*.

1628–S   Fast days in support of persecuted protestants in continental Europe, during anxieties about general sinfulness, and for success in war against France

Sunday 18 May – Sunday 25 May 1628 (Scotland)

This fast seems to have been appointed by a synod meeting at Edinburgh; it was evidently approved by the crown. Yet, neither the proceedings of the synod nor the royal sanction can be documented. *Scotlands warning*, by the Edinburgh minister William Struther, was 'Written at the appointment of Superiors' (title-page) as an official announcement of the fast. Struther's pamphlet resembled the 1566 *Ordour and doctrine of the generall faste* (see 1566–S1), but provided no form of worship. It was instead a lengthy justification of the fast, explaining its causes under three heads, and discussing providential history, and the nature of repentance and abstinence. According to the 'History of the church and state', the fast was not universally observed throughout Scotland.

Order and causes: William Struther, *Scotlands warning* (Edinburgh, 1628; STC 23370)*.
Additional sources: presbytery of Perth minutes, NRS, CH2/299/1, p. 194; 'History of the church and state of Scotland', NLS, Wod. Qu. IX, fos. 251–2.

ORDER AND CAUSES

Jer. 36:5–7.[313]

And Ieremiah said vnto Baruch, I am shut vp, I cannot goe into the house of the Lord. Therefore goe thou, and read in the roule which thou hast written from my mouth, the words of the Lord, in the eares of the people, in the Lordes House vpon the Fasting day, and also thou shalt read them in the eares of all Iuda, that come out of their Cities.

It may bee they present their Supplications before the Lord, and will returne euerie one from his euill way: For great is the anger and wrath that the Lord hath pronounced against this Place.

2. Chr. 34:27–8.

Because thine heart was tender, and thou didst humble thy selfe before God, when thou heardest his wordes against this Place, and against the Inhabitants thereof, and humblest thy selfe before me, and diddest rent thy clothes and weepe before mee, I haue euen heard thee also, saith the Lord. Behold, I will gather thee to thy Fathers, and thou shalt bee put in thy graue in peace, neither shall thine eyes see all the euill that I will bring vpon this Place, and vpon the Inhabitants of the same.

It is the duetie of the LORDS Watch-men, whom hee hath sette on the Walls of *Ierusalem, Ezek. 3:33.* To consider diligentlie both the estate of it within, and the dangers imminent from without: And according as they see, to giue faithfull and tymous aduertisement to the people, *Hab. 2:1. Isa. 21:8.* That thereby they may both deliuer their owne Soules and direct the people by speedie Repentance, to preuent the approaching wrath.

This their Calling craueth; for they stand betwixt God and his people, as the *Interpreters* of his will to them. *Job. 33:23.* And as their *Remembrancers* to God, to present them and their necessities to him continuallie. *Isa. 62:6–7.* Hee calleth them vp to the Mountaine to see further than other, and (beside their giftes ând graces, as Christians) giueth them a Pastorall eye to see, and a pastorall heart to consider, and a pastorall mouth to declare what they see and consider.

This also he commandeth them vnder a most heauie paine. *Sonne of man, I haue sette thee a Watch-man vnto the House of Israel, therefore thou shalt heare the word from my mouth, & warne them from mee: When I say to the wicked, O wicked man, thou shalt surelie die, if thou doest not speake to warne the wicked from his way, that wicked man shall die in his sinne, but his blood will I require at thine hand.* Ezek. 3:17. 33:7–8.

And God commnendeth this as wisedome in Pastors according to his heart, *Who is the wise man to vnderstand this? and who is hee to whome the mouth of the Lord hath spoken, that hee may declare it? for what the Land perished.* Jer. 9:12.

Vpon these considerations, the Clergie of this land, taking to heart the Estate of the Church of God, both in this Kingdome and other reformed Countries, haue thought it necessar, *(Supreme authoritie commanding also the same)* That all the Congregations of this Land keepe a solemne and publicke Fast, the third and fourth Sundayes of this instant Moneth of *May*, and the weeke dayes betwixt these two Sabbaths: To intreat GOD, in all humilitie, and repentance for pardon of our sinnes,

---

[313] Biblical references have been standardized and modernized.

and for auerting of his just wrath, where it is alreadie begunne, and to hold it off these who are threatned with it.

And for the better informing of euery one in the equitie & necessitie of that religious work of *Fasting* and *Prayer*, and their better stirring vp therevnto: The just and weightie causes thereof are to bee considered, which may bee reduced to these heads.

1. First the most *lamentable estate of the reformed Churches of* Germanie, *and other Countries in* Europe: Where the Gospel did shine, and Gods worshippe was exercised fruitfullie to his glorie: But nowe by the crueltie of the preuailing *Papists*, fearefull desolation is wrought in these places, GODS Sainctes bereft of their liues, their blood spilt as water in the streetes, their women shamefullie abused, their goods taken from them: And the estate of them who haue escaped the rage of the sword, worse than the slaine. Their liberties lost and themselues either driuen from their dwellings or compelled to forsake their God & Religion, & take themselues to Romish Idolatrie, or to banishment. And vnder the name of an Imperiall reformation, there is nothing but a *Godlesse deformation*, setting vp the abomination of ignorance, and errour where the light hath beene.

How many Prouences sometimes pleasant, in a peaceable professing of the Trueth, as the Paradise of God, are now turned in a wildernesse: And the Houses of God prepared sometime on the top of the Mountaines, and exalted aboue the Hills, wherevnto people did flowe, are destroyed: And the Lords displayed banner, vnder which many did merch in comelie order, is cast down, & manie mothers in Israel, *famous Colledges and Universities* are scattered, and the abomination of desolation erected in them.

So wee may say with the Prophet, *Come, & behold the workes of the Lord, what desolations hee hath wrought in the Earth.* Ps. 16:8. *The Heathen are come in the inheritance of the Lord, his holie Temple haue they defiled, and made Ierusalem heapes of stones: The dead bodies of Gods Saincts haue they giuen to bee meate to the Fowles of heauen· and the flesh of thy Saincts to the beastes of the earth: Their blood haue they shed as water about Ierúsalem, and there was none to burie them: They haue deuoured Iacob, and made his dwelling place waste.* Ps. 79:1, 3–4.

God hath forsaken the Tabernacle of Shiloh, the tent which he placed among them: He deliuered his strength in captiuitie, and his glorie in the enemies hand. Ps. 78:61.

And wee may lament with *Ieremie. How doeth the Citie remaine solitarie, that was full of people? Shee is a widow: Shee that was great among the Nations, And Princesse among the Prouince is made tributarie.* And wee may wish with that same Prophet, *Oh, that mine head were waters, and mine eyes a Fountaine of teares, that I might weepe day and night, for the slaine of the Daughter of my people.* Jer. 9:1

This worke is a part of Antichrists persecution, for now hee is both breathing threatnings & slaughter, against the reformed Churches, and executeth his crueltie against them, because of their obedience to Gods voyce in comming out of Babell, and that according to the bloodie decrees of the Counsell of *Trent*. For after that Sathan had for a long space vented his *first propertie of lying* by Antichrist his first borne involuing and holding these Westerne places of *Europe* vnder the errours of a false Religion: And seeing that Mauger his malice, God in the appointed time brought in the Light of the Gospel, and discouered that darkenesse: Then hee tooke him to his other *propertie and practise of blood*, to maintaine by force his discouered

Heresies: And hee set Antichrist and his supposts to worke, to put out the Light of the Gospel, in destroying the professours of it.

So the indyting of the Counsell of Trent beares: *Ad reformandum Ecclesiam & exstirpandas Haeresies, To reforme the Kirke, and roote out Heresies;* That is to say in the Romane sense, *To confirme and establish the deformities and corruptions of their Church, and roote out the Trueth,* which God hath brought in againe by the Gospel. And from that tyme, hee hath sent out his *Emissaries, Iesuites* and other *Locusts* from the bottomlesse pit, to stirre vp the Kings of the Earth to fight against the Lambe: This is the quarrell now debated in *Europe*.

And albeit hee hath cast in the mixture of ciuill respects, in rights to Kingdomes and Dignities, and such like, to blind the eyes of the simple, as to make them belieue that all these warres are onelie for ciuill and not for Sacred things: Yet sure it is, that all this matter is directed and sweyed by the *Pope*: For his maine end is to roote out the Gospel, and reestablish his false Religion: His purpose serueth to the end of his associat Kings & Princes, and their power serueth his end. As they plotte and worke joyntlie in the worke, so they share in the end for their seuerall aduantage: For the Countreyes subdued, fall as a prey and a reward to the enlarging of Princes Dominions, and therein Idolatrie is established, as the *Popes* recompence.

Beside, what euer be the mixture of the cause, yet their maine intention is manifeste from themselues: For one of them in his alarme to this warre, stirreth vp the *Emperour to destroy the Protestants, as Moses did the Moabits: And if he did not so, his life should goe for their life, as Achabs* for the King of *Syria. Sciopp. Classicum belli Sacri. cap. 1. 2. 18.*[314]

Next, their *Cardinals* consulting, how to restore their Church to her auncient integritie aduised the *Pope, that there was no better way to doe it, than by prosecuting this warre, to the rooting out of Protestants. Aphorisml. Cardinal. Anno 1623.*[315] And for this end, a new order is instituted called the *sodalitie of the Christian defence,* that is to say, of Antichristian offence of the *Protestants, Cancell. Hispani. Consid. 1.*[316]

This course as others of the like stampe of the mysterie of iniquitie is drawne deepelie, for now Antichrist vnder the Name of Christs *Vicar* persueth Christ; vnder the Colours & banners of the *Crosse* of Christ hee destroyeth the doctrine of the *Crosse:* Vnder name of the *Church,* hee oppresseth the true Church: Vnder the name of the pretended *Verity,* he rooteth out the *Trueth* of God, to establish his owne *heresie:* And vnder the name of an old *Religion,* hee setteth vp *a new vp-start Religion.* This is *Iudas* his betraying of Christ with an Haile Master: When his pretended *Vicar* turneth all his usurped power to the destruction of his Kingdome: The Titles and Names that of old were the notes of the Apostolicke Church, are claimed now of the Antichristian Synagogue, and made signes for the persecution of the Church of Christ.

God doeth so afflict his Church, not for her Religion, but for the abuse of it: He hath called vs out of *Babell,* and wee haue obeyed his voyce in comming out,

---

[314] Kasper Schoppe, *Classicum belli sacri; sive Heldus redivivus* (1619).
[315] Michele Lonigo, *[Aphorismi] de statv ecclesiæ restavrando, ex decreto & adprobatione collegij Cardinalitij, collecti ex consilio Gregorio XV* (1623).
[316] [Ludwig Camerarius], *Cancelleria Hispanica. Adjecta sunt acta publica, hoc est: scripta et epistolae authenticae, e quibus partim infelicis belli in Germania partim proscriptionis in Electorem Palatinum scopus praecipuus apparet. Adjecti sunt sub finem Flores Scopiani, ex classico belli sacri* (Amsterdam, 1622). We are grateful to Dr Nicole Reinhardt for this reference.

and haue vndertaken to walke in the Light of God; but wee haue contemned that Light, and in the midst of it brought out the workes of darknesse: Sinne is grieuous in euery person, tyme, and place, but most grieuous in the Church, in the time of so cleare a Light: And where euer men sin, they are in Gods sight, but his eye in a more particular manner is ouer his Church.

A Father is angrie at faults in his seruant, but more angrie at them in his Sonne: The more liberall and bountifull God is to a people, the greater is their sinne, and heauier shall bee their judgement *Woe to thee Chorazin, woe to thee Bethsaida, for if the great works which were done in you, had beene done in Tyrus and Sydon, they had repented long agoe in sack-cloth and ashes: But I say to you it shall bee more easie for Tyrus and Sydon at the last day than for you.* Matt. 11:21–2. And it is a strange forme of reasoning with Israel, *You onely haue I knowne of all the Families of the Earth sayeth the Lord: Therefore will I punish you for all your iniquities.* Amos 3:2.

God may justlie compleane of vs, as hee did of the Iewes. *Hee planted a Vineyard in a fruitefull Hill, and fenced it, and gathered out the stones of it, and planted it with the choisest Vines, and built a Tower in the midst of it, and a Winepresse in it: And hee looked that it should bring foorth Grapes, but it brought foorth wylde grapes: And now, O Inhabitants of Ierusalem, and men of Iudah, iudge I pray you betweene mee and my Vine-yard: What could I doe more to my Vineyard, than I haue done? And now I will tell you what I will doe to my Vine-yard, I will take away the hedge thereof, and it shall bee eaten vp, and breake down the wall thereof, and it shall bee troden downe, and I will lay it waste.* Esa.[Isa.] 5:1–4.

As hee threatned them, so hee performed it. Hee brake downe her hedges, so that all that passed by plucked her *The wilde Boare out of the woode destroyed it, and the wilde beastes of the fielde did eate it vp.* Ps. 80:12–13. For after that hee had chastened his people by *Edomites, Moabites, Philistims,* and other bordering Nations, and they became incurable: In end hee chased them out of the Land: And that not at once, but by degrees, for hee powred out that wrath first vpon the tenne Tribes, reseruing to himselfe the Tribe of *Iudah*: And when *Iudah* was not made wise by the sinne and punishment of *Ephraim*, but *Ierusalem* did justifie *Samaria* by her greater sinnes, God sent *Iudah* also away in captiuitie to *Babylon*: And after hee had brought them againe, and settled them in the pleasant Land, they returned to their olde sinnes, till in end God cast them off altogether.

Thus God dealt with the *Iewes,* and after the like manner hee is now dealing with the Churches reformed, to bring them to amendement in time, that they may eschew a finall destruction: Their heauie calamities who are now vnder that bloodie persecution of Antichrist, are cleare documents to vs in this Land, commanding vs in time to turne to God, lest the like or a worse befall vs.

Wee can no wayes compare with these worthie Churches, neither in Grace nor in the fruites of the Gospel: And yet God hath begunne at them. If hee haue done so to the greene tree, what will hee doe to vs, who are a dry and a barren tree.

God in our sight and hearing these eight years, hath smitten seuerelie, thogh justlie these Churches, and that to teach vs Repentance: But wee are as *Iudah*, who mended not at the captiuitie of Israel *VVhen I had put away backslyding Israel for all her iniquities, and giuen her a bill of diuorcement, then trecherous Iudah feared not, nor turned not to mee with all her heart, but fainedlie.* Jer. 3:8–9.

Though euerie report of their calamitie bee Gods calling vs to sack-cloth and mourning, yet for all the newes of their trouble, wee are not turned to Repentance.

They were not the greatest sinners in *Ierusalem*, on whome the Tower of *Siloh* fell, neither were they the worst *Galileans* whose blood *Pilate* mingled with their sacrifices: They are not the worst *Protestants* whose blood is shed by this Romane Tyrannie and persecution, *but except we repent we shall all likwise perish.* Luke 13.

Their tryall is our lesson, and their chastisement is our document: VVee shall learne it, and tak it out wiselie, if their example turne vs to God: But if we doe not so, the heauier judgement abideth vs: *They haue drunken the brimme of the Cup of wrath, but the dregges of the bottome are reserued for vs.* except in time wee repent.

Neither let vs thinke, that their affliction doeth not concerne vs, because they are farre distant from vs: For the communion of Saincts knoweth no distance of place, and the Church of Christ which is his Bodie, as it hath him for the Head, so his Spirite for the life, and that Spirit quickning all the Bodie, indueth it with a fellow-feeling of others miseries: If wee haue fellowship with them in Christ, vve must feele their troubles, and mourne with them: If wee doe not so, wee proue wee haue no fellowshippe with them.

Let such hard-hearted and sensles Christians reade their Doome and dittay in the Prophet *Amos, Woe to them that are at ease in Sion, they put the euill day farre from them: They lye on their beddes of Yvorie, and stretch themselues on their beddes, and eate the Lambes of the Flocke, & the Calues out of the midst of the stall: They drink wine in bowles, but no man is sorie for the affliction of Ioseph: Therefore now shall they goe into Captiuitie with the first that goe captiue, & the sorrow of them that strech out themselues, is at hand.* Amos 6:1. 3–4, 6–7.

These are twinne branches of a senslesse and carelesse heart, in the day of the Churches affliction: First they put the euill day farre from themselues & mak a couenant with Death, as though it neuer should, nor would come neere to them: Next, they put the affliction of their Brethen far from their feeling and affection, as a thing that concerneth them not, The first is a fleshlie dreame of their owne immunitie: The other, a senslesse mis-regarde of their Brethren· and both of them a just cause, and certaine presage of a grieuous ruine to come vpon them, who are so graceleslie disposed.

But the godlie are otherwayes affected with the troubles of Syon: *For they take pleasure in the stones, and delight in the dust thereof.* Ps. 102[:14]. Though *Nehemiah* was in the fauour of his King and great prosperitie, yet when he heard that the *Iewes* were in great affliction and reproach, and the wall of *Ierusalem* broken downe, and the gates thereof burnt with fire, hee sate downe and weeped, and mourned certaine dayes, and fasted and prayed before the God of Heauen. Neither could all his courtlie happinesse smoother the griefe of his heart: But when the King perceiued the sadnes of his countenance, and asked the cause of it, he said, *VVhy should not my countenance bee sadde, when the Citie, and House of the Sepulchre of my Fathers lyeth waste.* Neh.1. If hee was so grieued for the violation of the Sepulchres of the dead: Shall not the cruell murther of the liuing Temples of the holie Ghost, moue vs more?

And *Ieremiah*, though hee was at libertie among the people, and well looked to by *Nebuzaradan*, yet when hee saw *Ierusalems* desolations: *For these thinges I weepe, mine eyes casteth out water, because the Comforter that should refresh my Soule is farre from mee, my Children are desolate, because the enemie preuaileth.* Lam. 1:16.

Beside, the respect of their persons, their cause should also moue vs to this holy griefe: The Gospel of Christ & true Religion in them, is persecuted and oppressed: And if wee haue found grace and comfort in that Gospel, should we not be grieued when so glorious a meanes of grace is obscured, and the cause of our good God borne downe by his enemies. God hath lighted that candle, to discouer the darknesse of Sathan, and destroy his worke: And when the prince of darknesse preuaileth so farre as to put out that Candle, and to cast downe the Candle-stickes on which it shined, if wee bee the Children of Light, wee must sorrow for that change: Therefore if vve feele not their sorrowes, wee declare wee haue no communion with them in the Bodie of Christ, and no part in the grace of the Gospel, which in their handes is persecute. No feeling, no Communion, and no Communion, no vnion with them, and Christ: If wee haue no griefe for the Light put out, vvee haue no part in the Life and Grace, that the Light carrieth.

We ought then a brotherlie compassion to them, vnder their trouble, because they are Brethren, and fellow members of Iesus Christ, and the more, because their affliction, is not for ciuill or common causes, but for Religion: As wee are commanded to mourne, with them that mourne, so much more, with them that suffer for the Gospel: *Bee partaker of the suffering of the Gospel, according to the power of God.* 2. Tim. 1:8.

Shall Sathan make errour and heresie, so forcible in his Suppostes, as to joyne their heartes and hands, to giue their power to the Beaste, to fight against the Lambe? And shall not Trueth and Charitie, in the Children of God, procure at least, a brotherlie compassion of the griefes of other? The first is a wonder, to see the Spirit of diuision make such an union among his adherents: But it is a greater wonder, not to see that compassion in them who are one Spirit in Christ Iesus.

But though wee would in the hardnesse of our heart cutte our selues off from all feeling of their miseries, that would not secure vs from punishment but rather double our sinne, and hasten a double punishment vpon vs: Wee stand in that same case with them: In a true Religion, in the abuse of it, and so vnder Gods processe for our sins: And it is a great mercie of God, that hee hath spared vs so long, and giuen vs so large a time of Repentance: When hee might haue begunne his Iudgement at vs, hee hath begunne at other, that by their example we might turne in time, & preuent his heauie strok: If forraine miseries beyond Sea, will not moue vs to sorrow, let our own home sins & dangers moue vs to repentance.

And for this ende, wee haue to consider, our owne state in this Land, *as the second cause of our Humiliation:* God hath blessed vs with his Law & Gospel, but we haue sinned against them both: There is no precept of the Law, whose breach is not shameleslie practised & avowed 1. Euerie one maketh himselfe *his owne god*, and seeketh themselues, their owne glorie, and gaine, directing all their wayes from their own heart, and turning all to themselues. 2. *Idolatrie* (once alluterlie banished) is cropen in, and setteth vp the head in this Land, and manie who professed the Trueth, are gone backe to Poperie: They close their eyes from the shining light, that is readie to resolue and reforme them: And are so possessed by errors and darkenes, that they abhorre the light, which wold pull them out of their fleshly delights. Their case is to be pitied. who so wilfullie losse themselues, refusing Saluation, and running head-long to Hell. 3. The abuse of the *glorious Name* of the Lord our God, is growen a popular disease, & reigneth in all Estats, & the better sort out-run the common people in so grieuous a sinne. And the rifenesse of it hath put it out of the respect of a sinne, and hath turned it in the flower of their language, as though all speech were but wersh,[317] and could neither fill the mouth of the speaker, nor the

---

[317] Unpalatable.

eare of the hearer, except the Name of GOD bee profaned, and God himselfe thereby thrust through. If the flying *Booke* of the curse of God, light vpon the house of euerie swearer, to destroy the Timber and stone. *Zach.* [Zech.] 5. How few houses shall escape the curse of God in this Land, which groaneth vnder the multitude of oathes. 4. The *profanation* of the Lords Day is vniuersall, and no difference made betwixt the obseruation of it, and other dayes: But rather more libertie is taken in vaging, in drinking, & chalmering, & wantonnesse, in idle and profane speaking in it, than in other days: As if God had set it apart, not for his owne honour, but for the workes of the flesh. Though wee bee not bound to judaize in the Sabbath, yet are wee bound Christianlie to spend the Lords day in abstaining from euill, and busying our selfe in the works of Pietie & Charitie, as the Sabbaths proper Exercise: as a memoriall of the Resurrection of Christ, & our Redemption perfected thereby: and a token of our eternall Sabbath, & rest in heauen.

5 *Disobedience to Superiours*, is a reigning sinne: Though God for their further honouring hath placed the Precept that commandeth their obedience, Next to the Precepts of Pietie, and calleth the dueties of it by the Name of Pietie, yet it is least respected. *Parents* naturall are misregarded: *Pastours* who beget and feede people in Christ, are contemned: And supreme *Authoritie* disobeyed of the most part. 6. Innocent blood is shedde in many places, as water, and the Earth groaneth vnder it, and the cry of it ascendeth to Heauen to bring down a judgement vpon vs all. 7. Filthinesse, hath layed off the former vaile of shame, and is now impudent: *Fornication, Adulteries & Incests*, out-face the Light and multiplie out of number: And the couenant of God in marriage is lesse respected and keeped then light prom- ises amongst men: Whereby thogh their were none other sinnes, a way is made to ouerthrow families, for God cannot blesse Inheritance in the hands of wrongous Heires. 8. Secret and open hurting of the lots of men, is a common practise, and no man standeth in awe, to make his Neighbours ruine a stepping stone to his owne exalting. The most part without regarde of God, Conscience, or humanitie lose their Soule, and quite the Heauen for the baggage of this life.

9. And Calumnies are now so frequent, that their is no godlie man who findeth not the scourge of the Tongue. And no man almost, who lendeth not to Sathan, his eare to heare and his heart to belieue lies, and his tongue to bee a scourge to his Neighbour.

10. As for the abominations of the heart, though they bee hidde from vs, yet they are manifest to God, and by these and the like fruites, the world may see, that the heartes of the most parte are voyde of God, and are vyle puddles to defile themse- lues, and ouerflow this Land with sinne: These filthie fountaines are not seasoned with the salt of Grace, but send out the deadlie waters of filthienes, to burden this Land, and make it spew vs out.

These and the like grieuous sinnes against the Law, doe swarme in this Land: But the sinnes against the Gospel, are more grieuous, both because of their kind, and because they are sinnes against the remeede of sinne.

Faith, a speciall part of our Euangelicall duetie, is rare to bee found: God daylie is offering Grace & Saluation in the Gospel, yet few do receiue it by Faith: And so his greatest mercie in offering Christ, is mett with greatest wickednesse on our parte, in not belieuing: Wee count Fornication or Thift, or Murther, to bee sinnes, but *Infidelitie* worse than anie of them, is counted no sinne, and yet it is among the greatest pardonable sinnes.

This Infidelitie bringeth out all sortes of *Disobedience:* When the heart by Faith is not purified, and ioyned to God, it is casten loose to all kinde of iniquitie, without any restraint of euill, or constraint to good: Our hearing, and reading, is not mixed with Faith, and so bringeth not out the obedience of faith, if wee neither belieue the promised reward, nor threatned punishment, wee cannot obey the directing Precept.

With these sins, is a fearefull *Apostasie* to Poperie in many partes of this Land: Many & these of the better sort, are seduced and drawen away to Romish superstition, and that because they were voyde of the Trueth of God, and beeing ledde with their owne lustes, they haue rendered themselues to that fleshlie Religion which giueth them libertie to sinne.

I speake of you, and to you, O *seduced Papists*, how long will it bee, ere yee open your eyes to see how your blinde Guides are leading you to damnation? If yee will not try this matter by Conscience try it at the least by common sense, & see what sort of Guides these are, who take you by the hand, with this condition, to close your eyes, that yee neither inquire, nor care whether they lead you: Tell mee if you would commit your selfe in a dark Night to such a Guide, as would close your eyes, put out the Lanterne in your hand & not suffer you to know how & what way hee leadeth you: Yee might think he were a Ruffian, to mislead you to a Bordell, or to rob you & yet ye hazard your Saluation vpon such cousening: Yee know your *Iesuites* and seducing *Seminaries,* strictlie discharge you the reading of Scriptures, and holde you hood-winked vnder the vaile of *implicite Faith*, or rather *explicite Ignorance*. They propone to you worse conditions, than *Nahash* the *Ammonite* did to the men of *Iabesh Gilead*: hee craued that one of their eyes should bee put out: But they craue, and yee agree, to haue both your eyes pulled out of you: It was *Israels* priuiledge to haue light in *Goshen,* in the midst of *Egypts* darknesse, but your delight is to haue darknesse in the midst of *Goshen*, and to winke in the cleare Noone-day of the Gospel, shining in this Land.

You know, they haue drawne your Houses within the compasse of Treason, and are a Moth and canker-worme to eate vp your State: And how euill they recompence your good intreating them in secrete, by defiling your Houses, in joyning bodilie whoredome with spirituall? For the married Women, they keepe their old direction, *Si non caste, tamen cautè, If not cleanelie, yet Cannalie.* But with Maides they cannot so conuoy it: The professed Chastitie of these Ghostlie Fathers, maketh Virginitie fruitefull: And their *Auricular confession is found to bee a carnall pollution.*

These thinges, and worse, you knowe of your seducers, yet you will not see them: But choose to couer your errours by a selfe-deceate, and least you should let men see, that yee know your abuse, yee remaine still vnder that your willing and wilfull Captiuitie.

This is none other, than that *strong delusion, making you beleiue lies, because you will not receiue the loue of the Trueth.*

They abuse you as their Slaues vnder blind Credulitie to belieue their lies, and base Obsequiousnesse to doe all their direction.

It is time for you to auenge your selues on these Philistines for your two eyes by pulling downe the house of their Dagon, and to vendicate your *Goods, Children, Wiues, and Conscience from their Tyrannie.* Though it bee a benefite to the Church, that you separate your selues from it, as the bodie is relieued, when noysome and excrementitious humours draw themselues to byles and Apostemes, yet your Apostacie bringeth guiltinesse on the Land.

Further more, vvho seeth not *Atheisme* an uniuersall disease in this Land: Many professe the true Religion, and some are fallen to Poperie. But *Atheists* are moe than true *Protestants,* and superstitious *Papists*. The most part doe liue, as though there were not a God, or an Heauen for the godlie, or an Hell for the wicked: Some more openlie expresse in wordes and actions, their grosse *Atheisme,* other more closelie couer it with a ciuill life, and a morall honestie: But all of them say in their heart, *That there is no God.* So the Lord may say to vs as by *Ieremiah, Run to and fro in the streetes of Ierusalem, and inquire in the open places of it, if there bee any that executeth iudgement, and seeketh the Trueth, and I will spare it* Jer. 5:1.

As *Impietie* hath spred it selfe ouer all, so God hath punished it with the *breach of Charitie*. All Estates of this Land, are rent from other, and euerie one of them diuided in it selfe. It was an vntimous strife betweene the seruants of *Abraham* and *Lot, when the Canaanites (enemies to them both) were in the Land:* Gen. 13:7. Peaceable *Abraham* reproued and amended it, saying, *Why doe wee striue, since we are Brethren.* And Moses tooke that lessoun of him, and reproued the two *Israelites* for their strife, *VVhy striue yee together, yee are Brethren,* Our renting is like the *diuisions of Reuben, strong thoughts of heart.* Judg. 5:15.

Weaknesse of judgement cannot discerne thinges, but breadeth scruples, and the scrupling weake minde is strong to hold fast the apprehension, and refuse better information and for to intertaine Schisme.

They are sinfull of themselues, & dangerous to vs all: VVhen the *Papist* taketh occasion of our diuisions, to strengthen himselfe, and waiteth opportunitie for our ruine. If wee can reconceale our selues to God, hee will soone bind vp our diuisions with brotherlie loue, in the bond of Peace. It is oftimes an ominous presage of ruine, *if ye byte & deuoure one another take heed ye be not deuoured one of another* Gal. 5:15.

And among all the sinnes against the Gospel, *the contempt of the Gospel, and the Ministrie of it,* is a great one, and so vniuersall, that few can cleanse themselues of it.

1. *Papists* abhorre them, because the light of their *doctrine* discouereth their abominable errours, as Theeues in their thift abhorre a Torch-bearer. 2. *Atheists* hate them deadlie, because their *Doctrine* suffereth them not to sleepe peaceablie in Sathans armes but suggesteth to them the thoughts of God, of the Soules immortalitie, of the last judgement, and eternall rewardes in heauen and hell: These, things make their Conscience checke them, and so troubleth their false peace. 3. *Deboshed and dissolute men* pursue them for their *Discipline,* because they suffer them not to run on in the workes of the flesh without censure.

4. And *Politickes* care not for their message, but serue themselues of them, for gaining a name of good professours, they cannot abide faithfull and free Pastours, but labour for a *Trencher Ministrie,* and to haue them as baselie obsequious, as their foote-boyes: If they with *Michah* can finde a *Leuite* for ten shickles of siluer, and a sute of apparell, they care not for the Gospel, nor the Ministerie of it.

5. And other who possiblie doe neither mislike their Doctrine, nor Discipline, nor sinceritie, doe grudge at them for *Church Patrimonie*. This is counted a great degree of *Iulians* persecution (though they bee not of his minde) by withdrawing the maintenance of the Professours, to vnderminde the Profession and Religion it selfe. This hath beene since the Reformation, and yet it is a great sinne in this Land: Men of the greatest sort pulling Gods portion from his Church, and turning it to the increase of their own estat. Whereby the Gospel is spoiled, & many thousand

Soules perish: *Where there is no vision, the people perish*. And where there is no maintenance, how can there bee prophecie or vision?

It is now a question greatlie debated, how it commeth to passe, that moe great Houses are decayed within these few yeares, than in some three Ages before? But it is easilie answered, 1. In the *generall*: Sinne is the ruine of all Estates. 2. In the particular the abuse of the Gospel: For as one hotte day rypneth the cornes more, than twentie colde dayes: So one yeare vnder the cleare Light of the Gospel, filleth more the cuppe of the sinnes of an House, than twentie yeares vnder idolatrie. 3. And Sacriledge is a consuming moth, to destroy a State, other wayes well acquired and guided.

It falleth to them as to the *Eagle*: Shee was not content of her free booting abroad, but pulled a collop from the Altar wherein was fastned an hotte firie coale, and when shee brought it to her nest, & filled her birds with that sacrilegious morsel, the coale fired her nest and burnt her birds in ashes: It is manifest to the worlde, that Houses moste ladened with Church Patrimonie, haue gone most to ruine. If one *Achan* stealing a part of things consecrate to God, and not as then conuerted to the use of the Tabernacle, brought wrath on all *Israel*: What shall wee looke for, where so many pull from God, these things, which beside their *devoting*, may pleade *prescription*, for many ages. And if in the beginning of the Gospel, God gaue an exempler punishment, on *Ananias* and *Saphira*, for interuerting a part of that which was once their owne, and was not sacred by that *primarie separation* of God, but by a *secondarie mortification* in their owne voluntarie offering, what shall bee their punishment, who draw that to themselues, which was neuer theirs but hath long stood both vnder a *sacred separation* and a *religious* use.

God compleaneth of the *Iewes*. *Will a man robbe God? Yet yee haue robbed mee. But yee say, Wherein haue wee robbed thee? In Tithes and offerings. Yee are cursed with a curse: For yee haue robbed mee, euen this whole Nation. Bring yee all the Tithes into the store-house, that there may bee meate in mine House, and proue mee now heerewith, sayeth the LORD of Hostes, if I will not open to you the windows of Heauen, and powre you out a blessing, that there shall not bee roome enough to receiue it.* Mal. 3:8–10.

Such is the state of the Gospel, concerning the *maintenance of it* in this Land, that had not God in mercie stirred vp the Heart of *King IAMES*, of happie memorie, and made now our gratious *King CHARLES* to succeede Him, in that Religious affection, as well as in the Thrones of these Kingdomes, to proue a *Nurse-Father* to the Church, and maintaine her maintenance. *Pouertie would banish the Gospel out of this Land.*

And with these sinnes is joyned *Impenitencie:* All men sinneth, but no man repenteth, or mourneth either for his owne sinnes, or the sin of his time. God hath giuen vs a time of Repentance, but we let it passe without turning, *And though hee hewed vs by his Prophets*, by denouncing judgements, yet wee feare not. *Hos. 6:5.* And though hee haue smitten vs with *Famine, Pest,* and *Mortalitie*, yet we haue not turned. *The Lord hath stricken, but wee haue not sorrowed, thou hast consumed vs, but wee haue not receiued Correction, wee haue made our face harder than a stone, and refused to returne.* Neither know wee the time of our mercifull visitation, and the thinges that concerne our peace, neither our just Correction to amend.

And with all, this wicked disposition, a worse is joyned, that the most parte will neither forsake sinne, nor repent, nor suffer it to be called sin, or themselues to be reproued and censured for it. It is not now sinne, to commit sinne, but to call sinne

sinne, and in an holy zeale, for the wakening of mens Conscience to reproue it, that is now called sinne, and an intolerable thing. And so to fill vp the cuppe of our sinnes, many are come to this degree of vncurablenesse, as to quarrell the reprouers of their sinne, as God noteth it in *Israel. Let no man reproue another, for my people are as they that striue with the Priest.* Hos. 4:4.

This is a great policie and preuailing of Sathan, hee desireth nothing more, than to holde men sleeping to death in sinne: And hee knoweth no meanes more able to waken them, than faithfull Pastours: Therefore hee laboureth to discredite them by contempt, that their warning may bee fruitlesse: And thus hee doeth by secrete and close degrees: Hee maketh not men at the first to contemne Pastours, and their Callings, but to mislike their reproofes and taxing of sinne, as vndisereet: From that hee leadeth them to hate their *Person*, and then their Calling: And so to contemne the Gospel, and make it fruitlesse to themselues. When he hath thus far preuailed, he can lead them further, as to mak them thinke that hating and abhorring of them, is a marke of true zeale: And to persecute them, is good seruice to GOD: As Christ foretelleth, *Whosoeuer killeth you, will thinke hee doeth God seruice.* John 16:2.

It is a forerunner of a grieuous judgement: *Amos* was euill handled of *Israel*, immediatelie before their Captiuitie: And *Ieremie* was foullie intreated, and *Uriah* slaine, immediatelie before the Captiuitie of *Iudah*: And *CHRIST* Himselfe, and his *Apostles* persecuted to death, before their last destruction. It cannot fall otherwayes to them, for contemning the meanes of Grace: They are left to themselues, and so fill vp the measure of their sinne to the hight.

There is some hope, so long as God holdeth Pastours in a land: But when the people contemne that his mercifull ordinance, it is iust with him, to send them harder Messengers of wrath.

So long as Gods Ambassadours are welcome, there is appearance that GOD is working Peace: But when they are contemned, and reproached for their fidelitie, GOD is no more to negotiate peace, but to proceed to destruction.

If *Dauid* reuenged so seuerely the indignitie done to his Ambassadours by the *Ammonites*, What shall GOD doe, when his Messengers of peace are so spitefullie intreated of men?

The signes of a desparate and incurable disease in man, are foure speciall which are all to bee found in this Land.

1. The first is, *senslesnesse of all paine*: Sicknesse after a long strife with nature, preuaileth so farre against her, that as it hath expelled health, so it taketh away the feeling of that losse. 2. *Next conceate of Health* vnder that state: That notwithstanding of the great disease, yet they conceate of strength and integritie the minde affected with the bodie, mistaketh the true estate of it. 3. A *carlesnesse* to bee cured: Conceated health expelleth all care of helpe against sicknesse. 4. *A neglect of the wholesome Counsell of the Physitian*, with a *reproaching and iniuring,* his person.

All these are spirituallie in this Land. 1. An uniuersall senslesnesse, of our spirituall State: All Doctrine of the *sicknesse of the Soule by sin: Of the nature of Conscience: The sense of God of his mercie and wrath, and such like,* are to the most part but as free discourses, without trueth or use: There is not so much of the life of God in them, as to know or feele that there is such a thing: All are closed vp in the fatnes of a hard and senslesse heart. *This is senslesse Atheisme.* 2. And notwithstanding of this, there is a strong conceate of perfection in some: They judge themselues in their owne light, & ponder them in their own ballance, and thinke all that is spoken in Scripture against sinners pertaineth not to them, but others, and all that is spoken of grace, and promises, is layed in their lappe alone: *This is proud Pharisaisme.* 3. Many smoothing themselues vnder this sweete sleepe, ly still in sinne, and neuer thinke of a Physitian: *This is fleshlie Securitie.* 4. And the last are worse, they tak not the information of Pastours, neither can they abide their Admonitions, when they are rebuked for sinne. Then they cry out as against *Ieremie. The Earth dow not beare this mans words and railings.* And take vpon them to prescriue to their Pastours, both mater and manner of Doctrine, *They say to the Seers, See not, & to the Prophets, Prophecie not vnto vs right things: But speak vnto vs pleasant wordes, prophecie deceites.* Isa. 30:10.

They will gladlie heare the sweete Doctrine of the Gospel, but not of the Law: Theorie but not practise; discoursing of Doctrine and Controuersies, but not vsefull application: And will heare the sinnes of other men, other callings, other Countreyes and Superiours, but not their owne sinnes reproued.

This is a desparate resolution, not to bee cured at all.

This is the pittifull state of this Land, in all Callings and Persons: *From the crowne of the Head, to the sole of the Foote, there is nothing whole therein, but wounds and swelling, and sores.* Isa. 1:4–6. &c. He may justlie pronounce against vs, as hee did against the *Iewes, Shall I not visite for these thinges, sayeth the Lord, and shall not my Soule bee auenged on such a Nation as this.* Jer. 5:9. *Therefore the Lord hath that same plea with vs, that hee had with rebellious Israel. Heare the Word of the LORD, ye Children of Israel: For the Lord hath a controuersie with the Inhabitants of the Land, because there is no Trueth, nor Mercie, nor Knowledge of GOD in the Land: By swearing, and lying, and killing, and steeling, and Whoring, they breake out and blood toucheth blood. Therefore shall the Land mourne, and euery one that dwelleth in it, shall languish.* Hos. 4:1–3.

Hee seeth vs lying in our sinnes, *and is going to his Place, to see if wee will seeke him. I will returne, and goe to my Place, till they acknowledge their offence, and seeke mee, in their affliction they will seeke mee earlie.* Hos. 5:15.

The third cause of our Humiliation, is for an happie *successe to our Kings Majesties weightie Affaires, at Home and abroad, both in Peace and Warre.* To pray to God, who hath the hearts of Kings in his hand, to multiplie more and more on his Ma[jesty] all Princelie Giftes and Graces, that Hee may walke before GOD in the *Vprightnesse* of *Dauid,* the *Sinceritie* of *Hezekiah,* and *Tendernesse* of heart, like *Iosiah.* That Hee would inlarge his heart more and more like *Solomon,* to goe out and in before his people.

And because His MAIESTIE is ingaged in a necessarie and dangerous Warre, for the defence of Trueth, and His Royall Allyance, whereby great Princes are become His Enemies, and His Kingdomes are threatned with a bloodie inuasion: It is the duetie of all, to intreate the LORD, for preseruation to his Ma[jesty] and His Dominions. When *Iehoshaphat* was beset by the *Moabites* and *Ammonites: He set himselfe to seeke the Lord, with Fasting and Prayer: And all his people gathered themselues together to aske helpe of God, and all Iudah with their Wiues, and little Ones, stood before him, who commanded them to stand still, and see the Saluation of the Lord, and gaue them a glorious deliuerie.* 2. Chr. 20.

And when *Hezekiah* receiued the blasphemous and boasting Letter of *Senacherib,* hee went vp to the Temple, and sprede it before the Lord, and prayed for saftie, and the Lord sent away his enemies, with slaughter and shame. Wee haue at these times, to pray to God, that hee would *bow downe his eare, and heare the blasphemie and boasting of the Enemies, and open his eye, and behold their bloodie decrees,* and the plotting of Princes to execute them, and their insulting for preuailing against vs.

And since God hath put it in our Kings Ma[jesty's] Heart, both to appoint to all His Subiects, and to keepe in His Royall Person, a solemne Fast. wee may the more confidentlie pray, that the Lord of Hostes, *to whom pertaineth the issues of Death, would merche before our Armies.* Ps. 68:20. *That hee would wound the head of our Kings Enemies, and thrust them through the thigh: And giue to Him their neckes and backes alwayes: That hee would cloath them with shame, and make his Crowne to flourish on His Head.* Ps. 132.

Two punishments are most to bee feared at this time, *the remouing of the Gospel, and the Sword of man*: The one to destroy the Soule, the other the Bodie. 1. God is threatning the *remouing of the Word*, because it hath beene long among vs without fruite: Wee haue not receiued it as the word of God, to belieue and obey it, and to delight and walke in the light of it: Though God haue his owne amongst vs, yet the most parte doe contemne it, and the Preachers of it: It is counted an intolerable burden, because it curbes their lustes, and reproueth their sinnes so plainelie: they would bee glad to want it, that they might sinne freelie.

God brought it wonderfullie amongst vs, few Martyrs sealing it with their blood, and yet great opposition made to it: But God by his owne good meanes, lighted that Candle amongst vs: At that time this Nation was as a new laboured ground, with little labour it rendered great increase: Light was then pleasant to men comming out of darknesse, and the taste of Grace was sweete at the first hearing of the Gospel: But now, after long hearing of it: Wee haue lost our first zeale, and are become as an out-worne & barren ground.

VVee are as the Earth, which drinketh in the raine that commeth oft vpon it, but bringeth out nothing, but thornes and briers, which is neere vnto cursing, & whose end is to be burnt. Heb. 6:7–8. The Lord hath patientlie waited on our fruits, and hath spared vs, like that figge tree, *not for three, but three score and seuen yeeres*, and yet neither is there fruite, nor Repentance, for want of fruite: *VVhat remaineth in his Iustice, but that hee cutte vs downe, and cast vs in the fire?*

Let vs not feede our selues with idle and groundlesse conceates, as that the Gospel is pure amongst vs, and wee haue a true Religion & a glorious Profession, &c. The lik conceat possessed the *Iewes* in their greatest guiltines & danger: They cryed, *The Temple of the Lord, the Temple of the Lord, this is the Temple of the Lord*, Jer. 7:4.

But ye trust, sayeth the Lord, in lying words, which cannot profite: VVill ye steale murther, and commit adulterie, and sweare falslie, and come and stand before mee in this House, which is called by my Name, and say, VVee are deliuered, though wee haue done all these abominations: But goe yee now into my Place, which was in Shiloh, where I set my Name at the first, & see what I did to it, for the wickednes of my people Israel. Jer. 7:8–10.

They thought they vvere secure vnder their profession, and God would not forsake them, but hee tolde them plainelie hee vvould cast them off, as hee did *Shiloh*.

The *Iewes* had his presence, and now they are casten off, The *Greeke* Church in *Asia*, *Africke*, and the Easterne partes of *Europpe*, had the Gospel, but abused it, and now are giuen ouer to *Mahumets* carnall, and absurde delusions. And the Westerne places of *Europ*, and *Rome* at the first did shine as a glorious Church, It vvas then an *hammer of Heretickes, and an harbour of distressed and persecuted Sainctes*, and yet falling from that Trueth, is novv for manie Ages, the nest of *Antichrist*.

And this Nation at the first inlightned with the Gospel, enjoyed Peace (when other Nations were ouer-runne with Warre, and had almost lost both learning and Religion.) Then this Church proued *a Mother Church* and sent out her Schollers as Apostles to conuert the most parte of *England*, and other Nations beyond Sea: But when shee was therafter first compelled, and then willingly yeelded to Romane superstition, God put out that candle of the Gospel, which had shined some seuen or eight Ages: And now since many Ignorants relapse to *Poperie,* and the most part fall in *Atheisme*, who are we after so many fearfull examples to thinke that God will still dwell amongst vs, not withstanding of all our rebellions, This fleshly conceat is an high degree of fleshly securitie, & as odious to God, as our other sins, for it would blemish him, *whose eyes are purer, than that they can behold iniquity*, as a fauourer of sin: As though he were tyed to dwell with obstinate and impenitent sinners, whom his Soule abhorreth: & to keepe his couenant with them who proudlie breake it, which is all one, *as to make GOD and Beliall dwell together.*

The *discouerie of the Newefound Land,* reserued till the laste times, offereth a remarkable consideration for this purpose: Some doe rest vpon naturall causes, as the perfection of sailing, & the inuention of the Sailers compasse, and other naturall reasons: But *Diuinitie* leadeth vs a steppe further, in the cause of this diuine prouidence: That as Light came out from *Sion* at the first, and spred it selfe through all parts: & *error* and *heresie* came after treacing the steps of trueth, to the out most-parts of the earth, yet many Nations either remaining in, or returning to *Paganisme,* other falling in *Mahumetisme*, & other were caried in that horrible *Apostasie* within the Church to *anti-christianisme*. The Kirk groning vnder these abuses, & heresies within it selfe, did lute for *Reformation*. In this mean time God discouered another world to tel this old one, that if they wold not reforme themselues, he had prouided him a soyle & dwelling place, & set vp a people that were not of our knowledge, to prouocke vs to I*ealousie.*

God hath indeede taken vs by the hand, but when nothing can moue vs to our duetie, what can hee but giue vs a *bill of deuorcement*, and put vs from him? God this day, and wee in his Name, are speaking as hee did to the Church of *Ephesus. I haue something against thee, that thou hast forgotten thy first Loue. Remember therefore, from whence thou art fallen, and repent, and doe the first workes, or else I will come against thee shortlie, and remoue the Candlesticke out of his place, except thou repent.* Rev. 2:4.

The Iewes promised continuance of all happinesse to themselues, because they were *Abrahams* seede: But Christ telleth them that God will not want a people, though they were destroyed; *For hee could raise vp Children vnto Abraham out of the stones of the fielde*: And hee letteth them see (if they would see it) to the griefe of their hearte, *that hee is better serued of the Gentiles, than euer hee was of them:* If we joyne to our other sins, this fleshlie conceat also, that hee will want a people, if hee cast vs off: He can make either *Barbarians* or *Iewes* (or those who now are the enemies of the Gospel, turning them to the Gospel) better seruants to him than wee are: And will teach vs to our by eternall sorrow, that hee can haue a people, though wee bee not his people: But where shall wee finde a God, if in his Iustice hee cast vs off for our sin: He will euer prouide himselfe a Church, *But woe to vs when hee departeth from vs.* Hos. 9:12.

The second plague to bee feared, is the *Sword of Man*: God hath shaken many roddes on vs, and smitten vs with them, but we mend not: *Hee hath broken the staffe of bread, and giuen vs cleannesse of teeth in our Cities, and multitudes in the streetes dying for famine*: Hee hath stricken vs with *Pestilence,* and made that flying arrow rage fearfullie: And great *Mortalitie* on men and beastes, hath almost latelie taken the *tith of this Land,* and yet wee haue not amended: The Sword onlie remaineth as the last and most fearfull plague, which God then useth, when all other chastisements haue not wrought his end to bring vs to repentance.

Wee are as *Israel,* whome God did smyte with plague after plague: *And yet for all this, they returned not to me, sayeth the Lord.* Amos 4. And therefore, *why should I smite them any more?* Isa. 1:4. *And thou hast forsaken mee, saith the LORD, thou art gone backeward: Therefore will I stretch out mine hand against thee, and destroy thee, I am wearie with repenting.* Jer. 15:6. When hee had taken paines on them, and they were not mended hee cast them a way. *The bellowes are burnt, the Leede is consumed in the fire, the Founder melteth in vaine, for the wicked are not plucked away: Reprobate siluer shall men call them, because the Lord hath reiected them.* Jer. 6:29–30.

It is now dangerous to sleepe in Securitie, as though our enemies were farre off, and wee compasseth with the walls of a great Sea: We haue our enemies within; so long as sin increaseth, & is not repented, we want not enemies to destroy vs: God wanteth neuer instruments, when he wil punish a Land, *He can hisse on the Flee at the Riuer of Egypt, and on the Bee in the Land of Ashur.* Isa. 7:18. *And though there were but men halfe wounded and halfe dead, they shall rise vp euery man in his tent, and burne Ierusalem with fire, when God is angrie with her.* Jer. 37[:10]. *Grashoppers* are but weake Creatures, yet when God sent them on *Israel,* they could not bee resisted, *because the Lord uttereth his voyce before his Armie, for his camp is very great, for he is strong that executeth his word.* Joel 2:10. As for our *walls of Water,* if our sinnes remaine, they will bee *Shippes and bridges* for our Enemies, to bring ouer the wrath of God, vpon vs: Though wee would build our nest into the toppe of Rockes, yet the hand of God can pull vs downe, where euer a man dwelleth, hee is a blacke marke for God to shoote at, and the arrowes of his wrath to light on, so long as guiltines abideth in him.

Wee should not indeede *neglect* or *contemne lawfull meanes* of our defence, for that were to tempt God. Though the *Apostle* had an expresse promise, that none of his companie should perish in the Storme, yet when the *Mariners* minded to conuoy themselues away, hee said, *Except these men abyde, wee can not bee saued.* Acts 27[:31]. Neither ought wee on the other part with *Asa,* to *put our trust in meanes,* as to rely on the *reede of Egypt, or the Arme of flesh,* for that is to prouocke God to *Iealousie.*

Both extremes, make God our Enemie, either in *tempting* him by neglect of meanes, or *prouocking* him, by trusting on them: The midst is his ordinance, which hee will euer blesse, to wit, the use of them, in holie wisedome and confidence in God. Our maine care should bee to bee at peace with him, that so the *Lord of Hostes may bee with vs, and the God of Iacob may bee our refuge.* Ps. 46[:11].

In this case wee are inclosed in Gods *pannall,* and he is set on his Throne to Iudgement, and the decreete will come foorth in the sentence, & bring forth the own execution, except in time wee agree with our God. Long hath hee spoken by his Prophets, in his *reforming, directing,* and *exhorting* Word: But wee haue neglected all that faire proceeding: He is gone to an *harder Word,* euen the worde of *Iudgement, and Processe*: And let vs assure our selues, hee will not leaue off, till hee bring it to some end: *When I beginne, I will also make an end*: 1. Sam. 3:12.

And there is none end, but one of two, either *our iust destruction,* or *mercifull preseruation*. If wee dispute with him, hee is righteous, *for we cannot answere to one of a thousand*: And wee cannot flee from him, *Whether shall wee goe from his Spirit*? Neither can we resist him, for he is Almightie. Since then we can neither *answere* to him, nor *flee* from him, nor resist him, our onelie best is to flee to him with the *forlorne Sonne* and cast our selues in the Armes of his fatherlie mercie.

Thus, God who knoweth best how to bee intreated, *commandeth vs. Come, let vs reason together.* Isa. 1:18. *Call a solemne Assemblie, sanctifie a Fast.* Joel 2[:15]. *Onelie acknowledge your iniquitie.* Jer. 3:13. And as hee commandeth, so he *promiseth a blessing. Though your sins were as the Skarlet, they shalbe as the Snow: Thogh they were as the Crimson, they shall be as wooll, If ye returne and repent.* Isa. 1:18. *And he will leaue a blessing behind him.* Joel 2[:14]. *Call vpon mee in the day of thy trouble, I will deliuer thee.* Ps. 50[:15]. *And I will bee with him in trouble, I will deliuer him, I will glorifie him.* Ps. 91:15.

And as he promised a blessing, so in all time hee hath *performed it*, for his people did neuer sincerelie humble themselues before him, but hee gaue them a visible blessing. The *Book* of *Iudges* is full of this practise. 1. *Israel sinned* against him, 2. And hee *gaue them ouer in the hand of some Enemie.* 3. And when they felt their miserie, they cryed vnto God, by *Prayer & Fasting.*

4. The Lord raised vp a *Iudge* or *Sauiour*, who deliuered them. When *Niniuie* was threatned with destruction, and humbled themselues in Fasting and praying, the Lord spared them, *Jonah 3:4.* And though *Ahab* was a wicked Hypocrite, yet when hee put on Sacke-cloath and fasted, the Lord said to *Eliah, Seest thou how Ahab is humbled before mee? Because hee hath submitted himselfe to mee, Therefore I will not bring this euill in his dayes.* 1. Kgs. 21[:29].

Prayers, and *Teares, are the kindlie weapons of Gods Church*, which they use in all their necessities and dangers: And that neuer without an euident blessing. They ouercome God, and bow him to mercie, because hee hath bound himselfe to accept the Sacrifice of a contrite heart: *A contrite and a broken Spirit, hee can not refuse.* Ps. 51:17. And vvhen hee is reconcealed to vs in *Christ,* and our sinnes pardoned, hee becommeth our Friende, and Protectour. So long as sinne remaineth, hee is our Aduersarie, and our sinnes bind his hand, *that hee cannot helpe, and stoppeth his eare, that hee cannot heare.* Isa. 59:1 But vvhen God is appeased, then he becommeth our deliuerer from all our dangers. And though they seeme but vveake vveapons to the Naturall man, vvho would haue his eyes filled with bodilie meanes, yet they are most forcible against our enemies.

And Sathan himselfe is affraied of nothing more, than solemne humiliation and Repentance. Hee knoweth so long as God is angrie with his people, hee will finde both great *permissions, & large commissions* against them, to their hurt: But when God and his people reason together, and his mercie pardoneth their sinne, then Sathans permissions are *restrained*, and his commissions *end,* and a certaine shame and disapointment is concluded against him.

There is neuer a solemne humiliation in the Church, but it bringeth a notable ruine to his kingdome: Our groanes and teares are as great *Ordinances* to batter and beate downe his building of iniquitie: All the Armories in the world haue not so terrible *Canouns* to Satan, as faithfull hearts grieued for sinne: Neither so fearefull *Bullets*, as feruent prayer and supplications sent vp with strong cryes and groanes to God: Though such hearts bee broken, in sending them vp, yet they batter Sathans Kingdome, and bringe health to themselues.

To these Prayers and Teares, wee haue now a cleare calling: As God in his word

commandeth, so he is by his worke applying that command to vs. 1. By the obseruation of all his *Seruants*, the Prophets who with a pastorall heart and eye, seeth the
present iniquities of this Land, and wrath hanging aboue our head.

This burden is layed on vs, who are Watch-men, *to stand on our Watch, and sitte
vpon our Tower, and see what God will say to vs, Sonne of man, if the Watch-man,
when hee seeth the Sword comming, blow the Trumpet, and warne the people: Then
whosoeuer heareth the sounde of the Trumpet, and taketh not warning, if the Sword
come, & take him away, his blood shall be vpon his owne head. Hee heard the sound
of the Trumpet, and tooke no warning, his blood shall bee vpon him. But hee that
taketh warning· shall deliuer his Soule.*

*So thou, O Sonne of man, I haue sette thee a Watch-man vnto the house of Israel:
Therefore, thou shalt heare the VVorde at my mouth, and warne them from mee.*
Ezek. 33:2–5, 7.

Vpon this heauie charge layed on vs, and the care to saue our selfe, and our
people, *we cry a loude, and spare not, wee lift vp our voyce as a Trumpet, to shew
to Israel his sinne, and to the house of Iaacob their transgression.* Isa. 58:1.

*Therefore, gather your selues, O Nation not worthie to bee loued, before the
decree come foorth, and yee bee as chaffe that passeth in a day, & before the fierce
wrath of the Lord come vpon you, & before the day of the Lords anger come vpon
you, Seeke ye the Lord all ye meek of the Earth: It may be ye shall be hid in the day
of the Lords anger.* Zeph. 2:1–3[.]   2. The obseruation of good people of euery sort,
falleth vpon this necessitie and cryeth for a publicke humiliation.

The causes are so manifest and vveightie, that anie who is not blinded may
perceiue them, & vvhat is this else, than a mutuall exhorting one of another. *Come,
let vs returne to the Lord: For he hath spoiled, and he will heale vs, Hee hath
wounded vs, and hee will bind vs vp* Hos. 6:1.[318]

Gods prouidence is a reall calling & a commanding of vs to this *Fast.* Hee hath
begun his Iudgements in other places, & we are vnder the same sinnes, and hee is
shaking that rod vpon vs. It vvas time for *Dauid* to pray for *Ierusalem*, vvhen hee
saw the Angell stretch his Sword ouer it: Hee prayed, and God made the Angell stay
his hand, *2. Sam. 24.*

Seeing then vvee are ladened with so many sinnes, and compassed vvith so
many troubles, and God by his vvord and vvorkes, and our *Conscience* calleth vs
to Repentance & Fasting, vve may not neglect this *Fast. For he who will not afflict
his Soule in the day of expiation, that Soule shall bee cut off from his people.* Lev.
23:29.

*And in that day, sayeth the Lord, I called to weeping & mourning & to baldnes,
& girding with sackcloth: And behold ioy & gladnesse, slaying Oxen, and killing
Sheepe, eating flesh, and drinking wine: Let vs eate and drinke, for tomorrow wee
shall die: And it was reuealed to mee, by the Lord of Hostes, Surelie this iniquitie
shall not bee purged from you, till you die, sayeth the Lord.* Isa. 22:12–14.

Neither let vs keepe the *Fast of Hypocrites who disfigure their faces, and looke
sowrlie, that they may bee knowne of men to fast.* Matt. 6:16. *They afflict their
Soules for a day, & hing their heads as a bulrush, and yet they finde pleasure, and
oppresse their Neighbour in the day of their Fast.* Isa. 58:5.

Neither let vs keepe the *Papists Fast*, who are *Hypocrites* in their externall shewe
and *Epicures* in the dyet of their Fasting: There can bee no afflicting of their bodie,

---

[318] The text reads 'Hos. 3.6.1.'

where for *qualitie*, they haue libertie to eate bread, Confections, Conserues, Fruits, & to drinke all sorts of Wine: & for *quantitie,* to tak their satietie, & fill of them, and yet in so doing, they breake not their Ecclesiasticall Fast. This is a mocking of the Christian Fast, a scorning of the VVorld, the feeding of the flesh, and a deceate of themselues in that wil-worship a Feasting for Fasting.

But let vs keep the *Christian Fast,* in a simple abstinence from all that may comfort the bodie, in true and vnfained Repentance, and forsaking of our euill wayes, turning *to the Lord our God with all our hearts that he may haue mercie on vs. If vvee seeke the Lord vvhen hee may bee found, then vvee shall cry, and hee will answere, wee shall call, & hee shall say, Behold, heere I am if thou take away from the midst of thee the yocke of sinne,* Isa. 58:9.

And for this ende, wee muste first *inquire* where these sinnes are, that so grieu-ouslie offend God, & that not by prying in our Neighbours, to lay all the blame on them, and *transferre* it from our selues, and so to foster a conceate of our owne innocencie in this common guiltinesse.

It is a deepe policie of Sathan, to cousen men in this case, to cleanse themselues, and blame their Neighbours. This is one olde lesson, wee haue of our first Parents. *Adam* layed the sinne vpon the Woman, and the woman on the Serpent: Wee are forward to commit sinne, but are ashamed of it, when it is committed, and would father it on another: Wee defile our selues reallie by the guiltinesse of it, and labour to cleanse vs by a conceate: But God will not bee so put off, and that shifting is a doubling of our guiltinesse.

So, after that *Core*, and his complices were punished, the people murmured against *Moses* and *Aaron*, saying, *Yee haue killed the people of the Lord.* Num. 16:41. The cause of *Corahs* punishment, was not in *Moses* and *Aaron*, but in *Corahs* sinnes, who inuying their credite, ambitiouslie affected the like, and seditiouslie made a faction, and drew the people after him, against them whom God had set ouer them: But the foolish people, not considering his sinne, nor their owne factious following of him, layed all the blame vpon *Moses* and *Aaron*.

This is to harden our selfe in our sinne & impenitencie, *and to freeze on our dregges.* Zeph. 1:12. But euerie one of vs ought to *examine first & most our selues*, and wee shall finde seuen abominations in our hearts: If we looke in the glasse of Gods Law, we shall see our leprosie, & bee forced with the Lepers to cry out, *I am vncleane, I am vncleane.*

So *Dauid* (albeit GOD beeing angrie at *Israel* suffered him to number the people) said to the Lord, *I haue sinned, and I haue done wickedlie, but these sheepe what haue they done?* 2. Sam. 24:1. And *Ieremie* putteth himselfe in with the rest, *vvee haue sinned, and thou hast not spared.* Lam. 3. And *Daniel, Wee and our Fathers haue sinned.* Dan. 9. It is a token of true Grace, in the censure of our selfe, with the *Apostle*, to count our selues *the first of all sinners*: and a token of true Repentance. 1. Tim. 1:5. In the appearance of sin with *Ionah*, to say, *I know, that for my sake, this storme is come vpon you.* Jonah 1:12. Euerie one of vs, hath broght his coale to this great fire of Gods wrath, so, let euery man come and take out the coale, hee hath cast in it, & draw waters out of his broken heart and powre out the teares of true Repentance to quench it withall: *Let vs search and try our vvayes, and turne againe to the LORD.* Lam. 3:40.

As on the one part wee ought not *Pharisaicallie* to lay all the fault on others, so neither should wee lazelie waite vpon the Repentance of other: Euerie one ought indeede to stirre vp another to this holie Exercise: But if other remaine in their hardnesse, and will not bee stirred vp to seeke the Lord, wee ought not to delay Repentance by their euill example.

Euerie one is bound to keepe his owne Soule: If yee vvill not repent, my Soule shall mourne in secrete for your pryde. Jer. 13:17. As the multitude of the godly cannot secure an euill man from Gods justice, hee found out *Achan* among the thousands of *Israel,* and punished him: So the multitude of impenitent Sinners, shall not hyde one mourning Sinner from his mercie: He sendeth not out his wrath, till *first hee marke them, that sigh and cry for the abomination of Ierusalem* Ezek. 9. And promiseth to *Baruch his life for a prey.* Hee had the *Arke* readie to saue *Noah,* and a *Zoar* to receiue *Lot.*

2. Next, for this holy Exercise, *let vs rent our hearts*, and that by a true and godlie sorrow for our bygone and present offences, *afflicting our Soules by a true contrition,* Joel 2. As wheate or corne, is brayed betweene the nether and vpper milstones, so is the penitent Soule, bruised betweene the *griefe for sinne*, and *feare of wrath*, with an holie indignation at our selues, for offending so good a God, and taking an holie reuenge or sythment, on our selues for that vylnesse. *2. Cor. 7.* That when wee remember our wayes, and all our doings, wherin wee haue beene defiled, wee may loath our selues in our owne sight, for all the euills that wee haue committed.

The reasons of this renting are, 1. Our heart is the fountaine, from which all proceedeth, that defileth the man, and ought to bee stopped. 2. It is the forge-house, wherein Sathan forgeth all iniquitie, and must bee ruined. 3. And the place of the conception of all our miseries, therefore by an *heart-breaking godlie sorrow,* it must be so disabled, as it losse the power of conceiuing, or bringing foorth of sinne as of before. 4 It is the bellie of the *Viper* for conceiuing, but it is not rent in the deliuerie of that venemous brood: Therefore it ought to bee rent in remorse for it, and with that renting, wee must bring out the birth of a sincer confession of our sinne, *Let vs lift vp our heartes and our hands to heauen, and say, VVee haue sinned and haue rebelled, and thou hast not spared.* Lam. 3:41–2.

3. Thirdlie, for the time to come, we must *purpose with our selfe, and vow to God amendement of our life,* & the studie and practise of new obedience: These holie vowes, will both bind our corruption, that it breake not out at all occasions, and stirre vp the grace of God to a life worthie of God.

True Repentance will so presse our corruption, that it may finde for the present a weight to bow it downe, and a knyfe to cutte the throate of it: And it will strengthen Gods grace by remouing sinne, which is the bane of it. It is a repeating of our first conuersion, and a notable promouing of Sanctification, by so solemne a worke, adding a sensible degree of killing the old *Man*, & the quickning the new.

This is the fruite of our wrestling with God, euen to halt with *Iacob:* Though wee haue preuailed, our corruption will bee so disjoynted, as it be not so strong therafter. So, God in mercie to his owne, by true Repentance, slayeth sin, which Sathan augmented by our falling & disappointing him of his end, turneth his work of sinne in vs, to a destruction of our sinne.

Fourthlie, wee must strengthen our hearts with *confidence on God*, that hee will haue mercie on vs: We can neuer goe to him with boldnesse, without this confidence in Iesus Christ, but wee runne from him as a *consuming fire.*

For this end, we ought first to fixe our mind vpon him, as hee hath discryued himselfe. 1. A *God full of goodnesse, for hee is gratious*, freelie to pittie vs not looking to our deseruing, *but beside, aboue, & contrare* to it, to helpe vs, bringing all the reasons of his goodnesse to vs from himselfe, and respecting none other thing in vs, than our miserie to cure it.

2. Hee is *Mercifull*, to pardon our sinnes, and remoue all euill from vs, whom gratiouslie hee accepteth, and giueth vs euerie good thing that wee neede.

3. And *slow to anger*, because the best men are often falling in sinne, and so giue matter of his prouocation, yet hee is not soone moued at their sinnes, but waiteth on their Repentance.

4. And of *great Kindnesse*, that euen in the time of his just anger, keepeth euer his Fatherlie loue and benignitie to them: His anger can stand well with his loue, though wee doe not well consider it: *Hee doeth not afflict vs willinglie*. Lam.3:33. *But in the midst of his wrath, hee remembreth mercie*, in the change of his work and action, from blessing to crossing, his heart and affection is not changed vpon vs Hee is not hastie to anger, and long in it, but slow to it, and soone from it.

Anger is in men according to their seuerall disposition: It is in the *Melancholian*, a vertue, that hee is *slow* to anger, but a vice, that hee *abydeth long* in it: And it is the *Cholerians* fault, that hee is *soone* angrie, but a vertue that hee is as *soone* from it. Our good God, speaking of himselfe according to man, expresseth his anger by the vertues of them both: With the first, hee is slow to anger, and with the second hee is soone appeased: And this is to our great comfort.

5. And he *repenteth him of euill*: Althogh our sinnes force strokes out of his hand, yet hee is grieued for vs vnder them, and by his sudden relieuing of vs, so soone as wee repent, doeth testifie, that hee hath neither pleasure in the death of sinners, nor in the troubles of his owne: *In all their afflictions hee is afflicted.* Isa. 63:9. And these diuine properties and their worke is not as his *strange vvorke, and strange Act,* but in those thinges, *hee delighted, because mercie pleaseth him.* Isa. 28:21. Jer. 9:24. Mic. 7.

And for our fuller confidence, wee haue not simplie to consider this his good-nesse in himselfe, but as it is presented and offered to vs in a *Couenant*, which is confirmed by Christ.

His goodnesse is in himselfe as a Fountaine superabounding, but the *Couenant* is as a *Chariot*, or *Conduit*, conuoying it to vs. His goodnesse assumed our Nature in Christ, to a personall vnioun with the Sonne; to assure vs both of the grounds of that communication of his goodnesse, and of our right to it; and of the way how it is: That beeing and belieuing in Christ our Brother, wee may haue *boldnesse and accesse by that way, which his blood hath consecrate toward the Throne of Grace.* Heb. 10. When in our mourning for sinne, our Faith looketh to Christ, whome our sinnes haue pierced, and intreate God, to looke on the Sonne of his loue, in whome hee is well pleased, *wee haue confidence to bee heard in that wee pray for:* Zach. [Zech.] 13. No man can tryst and meete with God in Christ the great *Peacemaker*, who is both the *Prince* and *pryce* of our peace, but hee shall finde reconciliation in him.

Thirdlie, our owne *Experience* may giue vs confidence: When this Yland was inuaded by that great Nauie, that was called, *Invincible*: God made the Seas to burie our Enemies, as it did the *Aegyptians: Anno* 1588.

Next, when Sathan saw, that our GOD vvas God of the Seas, hee tooke him to fire, and put it in the heartes of cruell Papists, to attempt the blowing vp by *Powder*, of the King, the *Parliament*, the Flower of all Estates of *England*: But God discouered that hellish plot, and brake their bow at the lowsing of their Arrow. *Anno* 1605. When *Mortalitie* passed through all this Land, and remoued many, God vvas intreated by our Prayers, and stayed it. *Anno.* 1623. When hee brak in with a fearefull *Pest* among vs, and we humbled our selues before him, he commanded the destroying Angel to depart from vs. *An.* 1625.

When hee threatened extreame *Famine*, in the rotting of all our Cornes, wee called on him by Fasting and Praying, & immediatelie thereafter for seuen weekes gaue such serenitie as scarcelie any man doeth remember the like. *Anno* 1626.

Hee is that same God, that hee was then: And if we will run to him in true Repentance, hee both can and will deliuer vs as of before.

In a word, we must *processe* our selues seuerelie before God. 1. In presenting our selues before his fearefull *Tribunall,* and standing there, compare our selfe to that righteousnesse of the Law, and our God, and wee shall finde that our sins are *moe, than the haires of our head.*

2. When wee haue found it so, wee must cry in the bitternesse of our heart, with the *Publican, knocking on our breast, The Lord bee mercifull to mee, a sinner.* Luke 18:3. This sight of our vilenesse, and sorow for it, must chase vs to God, to begge remission of sinne, and to be couered with the righteousnesse of Christ, *Wash mee throughlie from my sinne, and cleanse mee from mine iniquitie.* Ps. 51:4. We must striue to find remission sealed vp in the peace of conscience. All this processe before God, must be formed in our *conscience*, & led in a *spirituall* feeling: Many a time we doe the worke of God negligently, and content our selues with a light thoght & motion of these things: But we must labour to bring our conscience to a sight & our heartes to a feeling of them, without which God cannot bee pleased, nor we blessed in this worke.

And this processing is a great blessing of God, because it bringeth vs back to the first processe, that God formed in vs, at the time of our conuersion; and acquainteth vs with that Processe, which wee shall see at the last day; and shall secure vs from the terrour of it.

Wee shall then count our selues happie, for tymous processing our selues, when we shall see others condemned, who now neglect to doe it.

Further, wee must remember our *ordinarie measure of Deuotion* will not serue our turne in Fasting: But as the solemnitie is more than customable occasions: So our Deuotion in it must as far exceede our ordinarie, as it is aboue ordinarie occasions: The Sabbaths seruice had the own measure aboue the daylie Sacrifice: So our Griefe, Zeale, Faith, and softnesse of heart, must bee seuen fold more, than at other times: Therfore, is it compared to the greatest sorrow as the sorrow of a *woman mourning for her first borne*, and for the *Husband of her Youth,* and that as the mourning of *Iudah* in the *Vallay of Megiddo* for the slaughter of *Iosiah.* Zach: 12.

When our Soules by the Grace of GOD, are brought to this holie Disposition, we must also take order for our *Bodie*, that it may know in the owne kinde this Exercise; that defrauding it of the owne desires, wee may bring it to some feeling of that worke, that is within it euen of the *reasoning betweene God and our Soule*; that pinching of it, is both the chastining and amending of it.

Wee must abstaine from mirth and solace: When *Gods Sword is forbished, shall wee then make mirth, and contemne his rodde.* Ezek. 21:10.

Let the Bride-groome goe foorth of his chamber, and the Bride out of her Chamber. VVhen God is angry, it is not timous, nor comelie for vs to sport, or giue our selues to any delight.

If *Nehemiah* forbade the people to weepe at the reading of the Law, because that day was a *festiuitie to God*, Nehem. 8. Shall it not bee more vnseemelie to laugh, and rejoyce in the dayes, wherein God calleth vs to mourning and teares? It is not a day of *libertie or loosing* our minde and body to delights, but *inclosing and shooting vp our selfe in secrete.* That wee retrinch, and call in all our thoughtes, that at other times, may goe out to our businesse, and keepe them all, as a mourning widow, clothed vvith dule, in tokens of the affliction of our Soule.

The maine thing indeed, that God requireth in publicke humiliation is true *Repentance*, in godlie sorrow for our sinnes, and earnest imploring of his mercie in Iesus Christ. *Rent your hearts, and not your garments,* and yet with all, hee requireth also a bodilie *Fasting*, that our bodies bee defrauded, not onelie of their superfluous and vnlawfull desires, but also of their due and lawfull necessities in nourishment and rest, and that for these speciall reasons.

1. That the bodie by that abstinence, may bee afflicted and punished, as one *instrument of euill to the Soule:* Though strength and health of the bodie bee a blessing of God, yet ofttimes it affecteth the Soule, and either stirreth it vp to euill, or else is a readie weapon of vnrighteousnes, to execute the euill desires of it.

2. That it may bee taught by that defrauding and punishing, *what is the punishment of sinne.* 3. That since it is a great *impediment to our Soule in good*, when it is satisfied in all the desires: it may not hinder, but rather further the Soule in so holie an exercise, but the felt necessities of it, make it to spurre our Soule to bee earnest in the seruice of God, who is onlie able to saue both Soule and bodie.

4. Lastlie, for the *compleete Humiliation of the whole Man*: that as both Soule and bodie haue sinned, and euerie one of them haue had their owne parte in that wickednesse, they may now suffer conjunctlie, and bee humbled for it before God.

VVith prayer and Fasting other things must bee joyned: First *course and base Apparrell*, that none come before God in their best cloathing, but in their course and common garmentes: Costlie rayment doeth no more agree with Fasting and Repentance, than *laughing* and *surfette:* An heart *sopped with sorrow and bitternesse* for sinne, can neither desire, nor take paines vpon the *busking of the bodie.* Remorsfull thoughts can neither breed nor dwell vnder a *painted face*, and a *husked bodie*: Contrition in the heart commandeth a neglect of the flesh: As our flesh ought to bee taught by defrauding of nurishment, so also in basnesse and neglect of apparrell.

In most of our former Fastes, this hath beene a blotte, that people haue come to the Lords House in their best garments, vvhen hee hath cryed for sacke-cloth and ashes: They mak no difference betwixt *Fasting* and *Feasting*: Betwixt *Repentance* and other *ioyfull solemnities*, as *Communion* and *Thankesgiuing. Naomie* thought her name (vvhich signifieth beautifull) not fitting for her pittiefull estate, and the bitternesse of her heart, and desired not to bee called *Naomie,* but *Marah* or bitternesse.

VVhen our Parents sinned in *Paradise*, their nakednes made them ashamed, and that shame made them couer ther nakednesse vvith anie thing that come first to hand. Busking at Fasting is not of *shamefastnesse*, but a *shamelesse out-facing* of the vvorld, their own Conscience and the Iustice of God. That deuotion will neuer pierce heauen, vvhere the *ratling of silkes and Veluets out-cryeth the groanes of their Spirits.*

The sorrowfull *Iewes:* rent their garments, and cast dust on their heades: Dolour in the heart biddeth the bodie hing out sorrowfull ensignes, and these in blacke or base clothing: But in a busked bodie, there is not no such dulefull ensigne, and therefore, no sorrow in the heart. These painted *Puppies* seeme to bee sent of Sathan to Congregations to bee blots in them, and scoffers of God in his Face.

The *Primitiue Church* enjoyned their Penitents to come before the Congrega-tion in sackcloth, and cast themselues on the ground, so that ofttimes their teares moystening the dust, *defiled their faces with clay*: A face *so ouerlaide, is more beautifull* in the sight of God, than *Iezabells fairding*. They seeme to read *Silke* for *Sacke* in the Prophets exhortations to Fasting; at least they put on *Silke* instead of *Sacke*.

To heare Doctrine of Humiliation, and to bee richlie cled, doe not agree: To pretend griefe in heart, and bee sumptuouslie arrayed, is abomination in the sight of God, and a uisible *Solecisme*, in the eyes of Man.

2. The second thing to bee joyned with Fasting, *Is a large offering for the support of the Poore:* It is our tyme of supplication to God for his grace, whereof wee both desire and expect a large measure: VVhy should we not then bee liberall to the Poore? As vvee vvould haue him open handed to fill our hearts with grace, VVee should be free to helpe their necessities: Beside the measure of our daylie offering to them, wee are bound to conuert the charges of our house to their comfort, that vvhat wee spare on our selues in Fasting, may bee lent to God, and giuen to the Poore.

Vnlesse this way wee helpe them, vvee offer to God but a lame sacrifice, and turne his seruice to our owne worldlie gaine, because that vvhich we spare on our selues, remaineth vvith vs To be large in *Deuotion*, & *niggard* in our *contribution* to the poore, is to proue, that we count more of our *moneyes* than of *Deuotion:* And to moue God to respect it as little, as wee doe

This hath also beene a great fault in our former Fastings.

Wee ought therefore to giue our dinner to them that are hungrie, that Christ hungring in the poore, may receiue that which the fasting Christian doth abate: And so our Fastes may bee filled and fatted with Almous deedes, and wee may reioyce that our Fasting hath made another to eate.

3. Thirdlie wee must also joyne heerewith all *requisite godlie Exercises*, to bring our hearts to that holie Disposition, that God, requireth, as, 1. The *reading and hearing of the Law of GOD,* that vvee may see our *dittay* in the Commands that wee haue broken, and our *Doome* in the threatned wrath, vvherevnto vvee are lyable by these breaks: So *Iosiahs heart melted, when hee heard it read,* because hee saw great sinne in *Iudah*, and heauie wrath hinging ouer their heads.

2. The *hearing of Pastours,* apply that Law to vs, and lance our Conscience by their Doctrine: So *Peters* Sermon pierced the *Iewes* hearts vvhen their sins vvere layed to their charge, & they were forced to seeke ease to their wounded Consciences: *Acts 2.* And when the *Leuits* did expound the Law, the people mourned before the Lord. *Neh. 8.* That piercing sharpnesse of the worde, chaseth them that are wounded to God: The heart pierced with conscience of sinne, can find no rest, but in him.

3. The *reading of Bookes of deuotion*, which among other good ends, are vvritten by godlie men to stirre vp the heart to a tendernesse, and affectuousnesse in the worshippe of God.

4. *Conference with Pastours, and other well affected Christians,* For the mutuall stirring vp of our hearts to that holie Exercife: As coales joyned to coales, augment the heate, so godlie conference increaseth both zeale & affection.

5. Heerewith must be joyned holie *Meditation*: All worldlie thoughts must bee put out of our Soule, and the thoughts of God onelie keeped in it: Our heartes are hard; and not soone moued wee must labour on them painefullie, and hold them on

the bentsell[319] of spirituall disposition: *Hard stones are dissolued by strong waters and Vineger*, and the *hardest heart* will be softned by laying it in the strong water of *Contrition,* & that piercing *Vineger of bitter remorse*, all which things are furdered by constant meditation.

6. And aboue all, *feruent prayers to God, and singing Psalmes of Repentance*, that our desires be not a *sound and multitude of words*, but a *powring out of our verie heartes*, as water before him: We must wrestle with him as *Iacob* in power of his owne grace, and not suffer him to depart, till hee blisse vs with the remission of our sins.

It is not enough that one sort of people fast, but all of euery sort and state; For all haue sinned, and are impannelled at the barre of Gods Iustice: *Gather the people, sanctifie the Congregation, assemble the Elders, gather the Children, and these that sucke the brests*. Joel 2:16. And the King of *Niniuie* did fast, & made *all his seruants to fast also*. Jonah 3.

1. Pastours haue their part in this worke. To informe the people of their sin and danger of wrath, and waken vp their conscience by the terrours of the Law, that being priked in their hearts, they may cry out, *Men and Brethren, what shall wee doe*. Acts 2.

2. And not that onelie but also in example to goe before them: *Let the Priestes the Lordes Ministers weepe betweene the Porch & the Altar*. Joel 2. That thereby, they may shew to the people, that they themselues belieue the things which they speake of sinne and death, and that the worke of Humiliation is good when they practise it affectuouslie.

3. To interceede with God for their people, that hee would pardoun and spare them: *Spare thy people, O Lord, and giue not thine Inheritance to reproach*. Joel 2. *Moses* was so zealouslie carefull of the peoples safetie. that hee wished *his name to bee rased out of the Booke of Life, rather than they were destroyed:* And *Phineas* seeing the plague, breake into the Campe, made atonement for them. This is to *stand in the gappe, and make vp the breach from staying the proceeding of Gods anger.* Ezek. 22:30.

And the *bearing of the names* of the Tribes of *Israel,* on the *Breast-plate of our heart*, in a *Pastorall loue,* and on the two *Shoulders* of an *earnest care* and *assiduous labour*: Presenting them and their necessities daylie to God.

Our tyme is like the tyme of Ieremiah and Ezechiel. God hath now presented the *roule of his Booke vnto vs, and it is all written within and without, Lamentation, mourning, and woe.* Ezek. 2:10.

Our duetie is as *Noah,* to fore-warne the world of the Floode: As *Ionah* to denounce destruction against *Niniuie*: And as men that *stand in the counsell of God, to discouer the iniquitie of the people, to turne them from their sinne, and turne away their captiuitie.* Jer. 23.

Now the Shippe of Gods Church, is tossed and beaten with the stormie Seas of calamities, and the multitude, like *Ionah* in the sides of the Shippe, and are *fast asleepe in their sinne*: Wee ought to rouse them vp, and cry, *What meanest thou, O sleeper?* Arise, *and call vpon thy God: If so be, God will thinke vpon vs, that we perish not.* Jonah 1:6. *VVhy will yee die in your sinnes, O house of Israel.* Ezek. 18:31.

---

319 'bensel', meaning 'spring'.

The people also ought to consider their dueties heere[i]n. 1. To count it a blessing of God to haue Pastours that will waken them, for none of themselues, can awak out of the sleepe of sin: *Dauid* a Prophet, & tender hearted, had neede of a *Nathan* to waken his sleeping Conscience. 2. Therefore they should *heare and receiue information from their Pastours*, whom God hath set ouer them: As hee hath bound Pastours vnder heauiest paine to informe them, so are they bound in Conscience to heare them, and receiue their instruction. 3. To deale with their pastors, to interceed for them with the Lord: *Cease not to cry to the Lord for vs, that hee would deliuer vs from the Philist[in]es, said Israel to Samuel.* 1. Sam. 7:8. *And pray to the Lord, for thy seruants, that wee die not ibid.* 1. [1. Sam. 12:19]

4. To *ioyne their prayers* with the prayers of their Pastors: If they lye still in senslesnesse, the prayers sent vp to God for them will not auaile. *Pharaoh* desired *Moses* to pray for him, but prayed not for himselfe. Thogh *Moses* and *Samuel* stood before me, *yet my mind could not be toward this people.* Jer. 15:1. But when *Pastors* & people joyne their prayers together, then God suffereth himselfe to bee bound with the bonds of his owne making, euen his mercie and trueth in the promise layed vpon him by faith, in feruent prayers.

A cleare proofe of all these dueties, in Pastours and people, is in *Samuel* the Prophet, and the *Israelites*: When hee reproued them for their sinne *the people drew out water (not out of wells, but out of their broken hearts) and powred it out at their eyes, and fasted, and weeped that day,* and said, *Wee haue sinned against the Lord,* and besought the Prophet to pray to God for them. Then hee offered a sacrifice, and cryed to the Lord for them, and the Lord heard him, and deliuered in their handes the Hoast of the *Philistimes,* which was come vp against them. 1. Sam. 7.

If wee minde sincerelie to approue our selues to God in Fasting, it must bee both *publicke and priuate. Publicke humiliation* at such solemne times, is both first and most required, for sindrie reasons. 1. *To iustifie God,* who hath arrested vs, and threatned or begunne judgementes, by publicke confession of our sinnes, proclaiming that hee hath just cause of wrath against vs; and so by that publicke homage done to him, to acknowledge our obligement to him, for a newe holding of the life that hee spareth to vs.

2. Secondlie, to make a more *forcible onset on him,* by all our prayers joyned together. For he who hath promised to heare vs in secret apart, and to bee in the midst of two or three, that are met in his Name, will not he be in the midst of some hundreths, and thousands when they are come before him. Matt. 6:6. And he who said *Moses, Let me alone* (as thogh *Moses* prayers did bind him) shall hee not suffer himselfe to bee stayed from executing his wrath, when many thousands feruent and faithfull prayers lay holde vpon him at once.

3. For our *mutuall and greater incitation*: Many who in Congregations meete together, possiblie haue gone before other in euill example, and some haue offended and stumbled at the fall of other.

It is therfore moste expedient, that these see one another in that solemne Deuotion: That they who haue giuen euill example in sinne may giue good example by their Repentance: & they who haue conceiued just offence of other, may lay aside their offence, when they see them ryse from their sin. *Dauid* offended manie by his sinnes, but doubtlesse his Repentance satisfied them, and conuerted moe people to God.

4. For *Sathans greater conuiction,* hee intendeth no lesse in drawing vs to sinne, than to yock God and vs together, & so to set vs before him as guiltie persons to

bee destroyed, both in this life, and at the day of our last reckoning: But in these publicke Assemblies hee seeth the case altered, that God hath *preuented the terme*, and in place of a *wrathfull meeting*, to come to a *friendlie commoning*, & to end in a gratious reconciliation. *When God commeth downe in these meetings, and melteth the hearts of his people, and reconcealeth them to him, such a sight is an heart-breake to Sathan.*

VVe ought also to joyne *priuate Humiliation in our Houses, with that publicke Exercise. And they shall mourne euery Familie apart. The Familie of the house of Dauid apart, and their wiues apart: The Familie of the house of Nathan apart,* &c. Zech. 12. And that for sindrie causes. 1. We *pollute* our houses by sinne, and therefore ought to sanctifie them to God particularlie, in the time of a solemne Fast. *Dauid* sanctified his House after *Absoloms* sin, and shall not wee much more conse-crate our houses for our owne sinne?

2. For *Preparation* to the publicke worship: If wee come out of our owne houses to Gods House, without anie preparation, wee cannot looke for a great blessing in the Sanctuarie: Priuate worshippe before wee come out, is as a seede for the greater and publicke worke.

3. And when we haue beene in the Sanctuarie, and returned to our houses, wee ought to turne it in an *Haruest* in them in reaping the fruit that we haue found in publick: Our Houses then are both the *Barne* and the *Garner:* wherein wee prouide the seede that wee take out to the Sanctuarie, and to the which wee bring in the *Haruest,* and increase that we haue found in it.

4. Priuate worship is *a seale of the sinceritie of Grace*, for manie doe counter-feate Deuotion & Repentance in publicke, who haue none exercise of it in their houses, all their care is to be seene of men, and so they are *holie in the Church, and profane at home*: But to exercise Gods worshippe feruentlie in priuate, is a token of a true and vigorous grace of God.

5. For *greater libertie, to utter groaning, weeping, humbling, and prostrating of our bodie in priuate, than wee can in publicke,* there wee doe manie things which would finde an vncheritable censure, if they were seene of men: *Affections once loosed, will breake out in sindrie actions, which in publicke wee must suppresse; but in priuate wee giue them libertie.* Hannah vttered griefe of heart in the Temple, and was misconstrued by *Eli,* but her priuate deuotion at home, though with greater libertie was not offensiue, but a cause of her husbands more tender affection to her. 1. Sam. 1. *Dauid* in priuate, *watered his bedde with teares.* Ps. 6. *And filled his house with roaring, which in publicke hee did moderate.* Ps. 32. And by this priuate worship, is not onlie to be vnderstood, when the whole Family meeteth together in their Hall, or other conuenient roome, but beside that, when the Master of the house hauing discharged that duety with his Family, goeth a part to some reteered corner of the house, & there is yet more free in his deuotion than hee can bee in the sight of his Familie: And so other of the house, who are come to vnderstanding or any measure of Grace: *This is, the Familie aparte and their wiues aparte.*

In end, we haue three thinges to consider in all his work 1. First our *prepara-tion for it:* The worke is *transcendent* to the naturall man, and craueth preparation to lift him aboue Nature, in so heauenlie an exercise. Though sudden ejaculations waite not on preparation, because in them wee are set to worke vpon an instant, by some urging occasion, yet in the set dyet of his worshippe, we are bound to an holie preparation: And in this solemnitie we haue neede to double the measure of our deuotion, beeing called to the highest extent both of afflicting Nature, and stirring vp the grace of God in vs.

It is therefore needfull, to try if God prepare vs for the worke. This we shall know. 2. If he open our eyes, to see how needfull this humiliation is for vs, by seeing our sin & his just wrath, that wee may be driuen to that resolution that wee must either breake off our sinne by Repentance, or else be consumed in his anger 3. And by this sight, if he waken our sleeping conscience and make it to set vs to worke, *that we giue God no rest, till hee giue rest to his beloued.* 4. This is some proofe of that which God telleth *I haue beene sought of them that answered not, and found of them that sought mee not: And before they call I will answere.* Isa. 65:1. Where our miserable State hid from our selfe, is seene of him, so as hee pittieth it to helpe it, that our miserie vnwitting of vs, calleth for mercie: As the sores of a sleeping Childe moue the Father to compassion: And though wee neither seeke him, nor call on him, in anie knowne or sensible incalling, yet his Fatherlie pittie answereth the cry of that our necessitie, when wee know not: *This is a preuenting Grace in this point*: Whereby God finding vs in the pitte of miserie, setteth downe *Iacobs Ladder* to vs, afore wee know of our estate, or thinke of a deliuerie.

Next, wee should try *our disposition in the worke* it selfe, if Gods preuenting Grace in preparation bee seconded by an assisting Grace, which standeth in those points. 1. If hee *soften our heart,* to powre out it selfe as water before him, and bruse it, so as to bee an acceptable Sacrifice.

2. If hee powre vpon vs the *Spirit of Grace and Supplication*, his Spirite making intercession for vs, to helpe our infirmities, in teaching vs both what to aske, and how to pray, with groanes that cannot bee expressed.

3. If hee giue vs *Boldnesse* to draw neere to the Throne of Grace, and to finde accesse to him in the blood of Christ, and libertie of Spirit in all our deuotion.

4. If he giue vs the *desire* of our heart, in *disposing* it as we *desire*, to be both casten down for his offence, and raised vp in *hope and confidence* of his mercie: To feele our hearts melting in a godlie sorrow, is matter of vnspeakable joy; while that sorrow is melting the heart, the sense & conscience of that disposition, comforteth our heart when we find Gods Spirit hath giuen vs our will ouer our hard heart, to sacrifice it to God.

5. If wee see his beautie in the Sanctuarie, when hee *holdeth the golden Scepter of Peace, like Assuerus*, and commeth downe, and moueth people to teares and groanes. When the Angel of the Lord, or the Prophet charged the people of their sins, they did mourne, so that the place was called *Bochim or mourners.* And assisteth euery one according to their necessitie and place, making the Pastours *as Trumpets, to speak and not spare, his words in their mouth is as the Hammer, that breaketh the Rocke in pieces.* Jer. 23:23.

When hee casteth downe, and raiseth vp, woundeth, and healeth vs againe, and worketh so in the Congregation, that it may bee seene *hee hath appointed that meeting, and keepeth it to reconceale his people to himselfe.*

6. If as hee worketh a godlie sorrow in our heartes, *so hee putteth wordes in our mouth for his intreatie: Take to you wordes, and turne to the LORD, and say to him, Take away all our iniquitie, and receiue vs gratiouslie, so will we render the calues of our lippes.* Hos. 14:2.

And againe, *Let them say, Spare thy people, Lord, and saue thine Inheritance.* Joel 2:17.

It is a token, God will heare vs, when he giueth vs his Spirit to helpe our infirmities, and dytteth our bill: *Hee cannot refuse that supplication, which hee formeth himselfe.*

Hee heard *Daniel, and send him comfort while he prayed: While I was speaking, and praying, and confessing my sinne, the Man Gabriel beeing caused to flee to mee swiftlie touched mee, and said, At the beginning of the supplication, the Commandement came foorth.* Dan. 9:20. So sonne as wee are humbled on Earth, and send vp our supplications to God, hee is readie to answere vs to our heart.

Thirdlie, how vvee close that *Exercise:* If as it beginneth in sorrow for our felt miseries, so it *end in ioy,* because our sacrifice is turned in ashes. VVee haue sufficient grounds of good successe vpon his promises: But beside these promises in his vvord, his vvorke in preparing vs for it, and disposing vs in it, are a good inducement to our hope: When hee *powreth out the* Spirit *of Supplication* on *Ierusalem,* then assuredlie hee will *breake vp a Fountaine to the house of Dauid for sinne, and for vncleannesse,* Zech. 13:1.

VVee know not his purpose and thoughts concerning vs, but his Spirit vvho knoweth his minde, reuealeth them, and this is an sort of reuelation by his working: For as he knoweth the minde of God, so hee vvorketh the godly to that disposition vvhich he knoweth is most requisite, for obtaining the purposed blessing. Therefore that holie and heauenlie, libertie, is some sort of euidence to vs, that God hath both purposed for vs, and will giue vs the blessing, which wee craue after that manner. When he strengtheneth vs to wrestle with him, like *Iacob,* hee will not depart, till hee blesse vs, and of wrestling *Iacobs,* make vs his preuailing *Israel* on whom is his peace.

But, let none deceiue himselfe by a voluntar *apprehension of Peace,* or fainzie to himselfe *a ioy* where hee hath none: God hath giuen *vs the infalible mark of good successe of Fasting in new obedience: Who so after Fasting walketh not in a newnesse of life, is deceiued by his seduced heart.*

This is cleare, both by the Nature of Repentance, and remission: True *Repentance* is not onelie in a sorrowing for sinne, and refraining from it, for a day or two, but for all our lifetime thereafter. The purposes & vowes of obedience, which we make in our Repentance, must be practised and performed: Though the act of Repentance indure not euer in it selfe, yet the vertue of it remaineth constantlie in the godlie.

In Baptisme we are Sacramentallie changed, and at the time of our effectuall calling, wee feele that Sacramentall grace in justification, and sanctification, and all our following dayes vvee are bound to goe forward in them: Since Repentance then is nothing but Sanctification contracted: And sanctification all our life is nothing, but Repentance inlarged and continued, it will follow that if sanctification doe not kyth constant after our Fasting, there hath beene no true Repentance in it.

Remission of sinne proueth the same: For though Iustification, and Sanctification be two seuerall graces in themselues, and bring seuerall *respects* & *dispositions* in vs, yet they are inseparable, for God neuer pardoneth the guilt of sin, but iontlie therewith he slayeth sin originall: As he washeth away the blot of all sinne, so he woundeth deadlie the roote of sinning sin in vs: And the conscience of our washing in the blood of Christ, doeth euer beget in vs a care to keepe these garments cleane which God hath cleansed.

Therefore, if there be not after our Fastings a visible amendement of life, neither haue wee repented, nor God pardoned our sinne, but we haue added greater and worse sinnes to the former, and brought vpon vs a degree of *judiciall induration* and hardnesse of heart: When Christ had healed the sicke man at the *Poole* of *Bethesda*, hee commanded him, *Sinne no more, lest a worse thing befall thee.* John 5[:14]. So when we are washed in the house *of the Lords aboundantlie powred out mercie,* let vs keepe our selfe from sinne thereafter.

If God be with vs, & accept our Prayers, then we may be sure of these following fruits. 1. Of *Remission of sinnes*, in Iesus Christ: So when *Dauid* confessed his sinnes, and said, *I haue sinned against the Lord*: hee was answered by *Nathan: The Lord hath also put away thine iniquitie*: he had a warrand more speedilie to absolue him, than he had to accuse him. 2 Sam. 12. *And when the Publicane knocked on his breast*, & said, *The Lord haue mercy on me, a sinner, he went home iustified:* Luke 18. And when the forlorne Son came in Repentance to his Father, he receiued him in his fauour & house againe. Luke 15 He seeth no sin in *Iacob*, nor transgression in *Israel*: Our God pardoneth iniquitie, & passeth by the transgression of the remnant of his Inheritance; hee retaineth not his anger for euer, because hee delighteth in mercie.

Hee will turne againe, he will haue compassion on vs, hee will subdue our iniquities, and thou wilt cast all their sinnes in the bottome of the Sea. Mic. 7:18.

2. He will *accept of our persons*, vnder his shaddow, nothing holdeth vs out of that secrete refuge, but our sinne, because hee is of purer Eyes, than hee can beholde sine, and he pursueth sinne in all, and can no more protect an impenitent sinner, than hee can denie, his iustice. But when the heart is purged from euerie euill conscience, then his refuge is open to vs.

3. As for our *Enemies.* wee should consider their estate, better than themselues, they are in Gods *worke* for our punishment, but neither in his *fauour*, nor of his disposition.

They are more foolish than Sathan, hee durst not hurt *Iob*, without a *Commission* of God, but they think all possible & lawfull to them: And when he set on to execute that *Commission*, though malice blinded his desire, yet not his minde, for hee did fore see a disappointing, because hee knew Gods loue to *Iob,* by so manie pledges and testimonies of his sinceritie in Grace: But our enemies are not so wise as hee: They goe on without *Commission, sought & obtained* they expound their preuailing, as Gods sentence approuing their cause, and see not that all their businesse is a prouyding of a *Coffine,* and beare-trees, to carrie them out of this combate with shame & confusion. God will pleade his cause against them. Hee hath giuen them a hard, but a iust commission against vs for our sinnes. *Assur is the rodde of mine anger, I will send him against an hypocriticall Nation, against the people of mine anger will I giue him a charge to take the spoile*: But they passed the bounds of their commission, and satisfied their owne wicked heart vpon the people of God. *For Assur meaneth not as God doeth, but his heart is to destroy and cutte off Nations*, Isa. 10.

They say, *Let vs defile Sion, but they know not the thoughts of the Lord, neither vnderstand his Counsell.* Mic. 4:12. And when God suffereth them to preuaile, for the humiliation of his owne, they sacrifice to *their owne net*, and impute all this successe to their owne Idols. Hab. 2:11.

When God hath humbled vs, and pardoned our sinnes, then their *Commission expyreth*, and God will plague them in his furie for their own wickednesse in doing his work peruerslie. And therefore, he will turne him against them, & plead his cause saying, *I am verie sore displeased with the Heathen, that are at ease: For I was but a little displeased with my people, & the Enemies helped forward the affliction: I was angrie with my people, and polluted mine Inheritance, and giuen them in thine hand: But thou hast shewed them no mercie, thou hast layed vpon the Auncient a verie heauie yocke.* Zech. 2:16. Isa. 47:6.

And in his due time, hee will turne the *rage of the enemie to his praise, the remnant of their rage hee will restraine.* Ps. 76. *Hee will stretch out his hand against the wrath of our enemies,* and his right hand shall saue vs. Ps. 138:7.

So that wee may iustlie say to them, *Reioyce not against mee, O mine Enemie, when I fall, I shall rise, when I sitte in darknesse, the Lord shall bee a light vnto mee: I will beare the indignation of the Lord, because I haue sinned against him, vntill hee pleade my cause, and execute Iudgement for mee. Hee will bring mee foorth to the Light, and I shall behold his Righteousnesse: Then shee that is mine Enemies shall see, and shame shall couer her, which said vnto mee, Where is the Lord thy God? Mine eyes shall behold her, now shee shall bee troden downe as myre in the streete.* Mic. 7:8–10. They are nowe an instrument in his hand, to execute his anger on vs, but they shall be the *Bute and marke* of his greater anger.

4. As for the *Churches now desolate,* God will returne to them in mercie, in his own time: And this time is, when they are purged from sinne, and the sinnes and insolencie of the Enemie are come to an hight: *Then God will ryse, and haue mercie vpon Sion: For the time to saue her, euen the sette time is come.* Ps. 102:13.

It is time for the Lord to worke when they haue made voyde his Law. Ps. 119:126. So long as sinne remaineth in the Church, the commission giuen to our enemies, is in force.

If wee moue the question, *O thou Sword of the Lord, how long will it bee ere thou bee quiet? Put vp thy selfe in thy Scabbard and bee still:* It will be answered, *How can it bee quyete, seeing the Lord hath giuen it a charge.* And the charge will lest till sin bee repented. When sin is pardoned, the Lord will speake to his reconcealed people, *Feare not, thou worme, Iacob, I will helpe thee, saith the Lord, and thy Redeemer the holie One of Israel: Feare not, for I am with thee, I will vphold thee, with the right hand of my Righteousnesse. Behold, all they which were incensed against thee shall bee ashamed and confounded, and they that striue with thee, shall perish.* Isa. 41:10–11. *For I know the thoughts that I thinke towards thee, sayeth the Lord, euen thoughts of peace, and not of euill, to giue you the exspected end* Jer. 29:11.

He will build vp the Tabernacles of Dauid that are fallen downe, and make vp the breaches thereof, and repaire the ruines thereof, as of old: Amos. 9:11. *And will say, I am returned to Ierusalem with mercie, mine House shall bee built in it, sayeth the Lord of Hostes, and a line shall bee stretched out vpon it.* Zach. [Zech.] 1:5.

As *for vs,* whom as yet in mercie, hee hath spared from cruell persecution, hee is now crying to vs, *Come my people, enter into thy Chambers, and shute thy doores about thee, Hide thy selfe, as it were for a little moment, vntill the indignation be ouerpassed: The Lord will ordaine peace for vs, when hee hath wrought all our workes, euen the workes of true Repentance and Conuersion in vs.* Isa. 26:12, 20.

If wee repent truelie· the Riuer of his Grace will flow among vs, and the *Streames of it will make vs glad*: Hee will dwell in the midst of vs, and helpe vs tymouslie. Ps. 46. Hee will be a *fierie wall round about vs, and a glorie in the midst of vs.* Zach. [Zech.] 2:5.

This is the summe of all: That wee *returne* to the LORD our GOD, and seeke him vvhen hee may bee found, euen in this acceptable time vvhen hee is seeking vs: That wee *afflict our Soules* for sinne, and call for remission of them, vvithout which wee cannot be saued: That euery one of vs forsake our euill wayes, and renew our

Couenant with him: And among the rest, let vs mourne for this madnes that wee offended such a GOD, who as hee hath power to destroye vs, so also hee hath that Grace in his hand, vvithout the vvhich vvee cannot repent; our sinnes at once both pulling downe destruction, and closing the doore of his Grace vpon vs, except his vnspeakable mercie open it vnto vs againe.

The LORD our GOD, the Father of Lights, from whom euery good Gift and perfect Donation commeth downe: And who hath the hearts of all men in his hand, worke in vs all, in this and all other Humiliations, that which may bee acceptable to him: That by his Grace wee may bee enabled to offer the sacrifice of a contrite and a broken heart, and obtaine at his hand full pardon and remission of all our sinnes.

And the good LORD pardon all our sinnes, and the verie infirmities of that our Repentance for sinne: And bee mercifull to euerie one that prepareth his heart to seeke the LORD GOD of his Fathers, though hee bee not cleansed according to the purifications of the Sanctuarie: 2. Chr. 30:18–19. Through IESVS CHRIST our LORD, *AMEN*.

1628–Ir   Weekly fast days during war, cattle disease and fears of famine and plague

Weekly [May–July?] 1628 (Ireland?)

This occasion is known only from a letter from the lord deputy of Ireland, Henry Cary, Viscount Falkland, to Lord Conway, the secretary of state in London, which does not state the reason for the weekly fasts. It is likely that they were ordered in response to the war with France and Spain, mirroring similar events in England, Wales and Scotland (see 1628–E1 and 1628–S), as well as to dearth, famine, plague and cattle disease which affected Ireland alone. Charles's failure to secure sufficient money to pay for the war played into the hands of the (largely catholic) Irish nobility (the 'Old English'). For the promise of a modest financial contribution, they secured significant concessions on a range of longstanding grievances, including the oath of supremacy and office-holding. These were enshrined in the 'Graces' in May 1628.

Source: lord deputy to Lord Conway, 14 May 1628, SP63/246/58, fos. 141r–v.

DESCRIPTION OF ORDER

Lord deputy to secretary of state: 14 May 1628

For our partes in Ireland, we abound in Wantes and Calamityes of all sortes: Noe Fortificacions in state of defence: Noe Armes, Noe Munition, Noe monnye [illegible] a mortality of Catle dearth of Corne presently susteyned; famyne and Pestilence threatened to ensiew yf God of his greate mercy, doe not meruaylously diuerte them: or his Maiesty by his Gratious and Royall Prouidence, causeinge vs to be Tymely supplyed out of England, (which now happely aboundes,) they be not preuented. For the pacifiyng of the Wrathe deuyne and obteyneing mercy there we haue ordeyned a faste for one daye in a Weeke to be continued for two Monthes. For obteyneing his Maiestyes gracious consideracion and Releefe, we haue Quallifyed Sir Roger Jones our Agent to sollicite for vs, and beseech your Lordship that he may be fayrely heard and soe beleeued That we maye fynd the Effortes in his preuayling …

1628–E2 Prayers for the success of the naval expedition against France

[After Friday 22 August–September] 1628 (England and Wales)

Despite the failure of the Île de Ré expedition (see 1627–E) and a severe shortage of money, Charles and Buckingham remained committed to their aggressive policies towards France and Spain. After parliament reluctantly granted the king five subsidies (with conditions attached), Buckingham planned a second foray on La Rochelle, assembling troops at Portsmouth in early August. In July, Charles attended prayers at the Chapel Royal for the navy's success, but he did not order nationwide prayers until August. On 15 August, the privy council instructed Abbot as archbishop of Canterbury to compose a form of prayer for this occasion, even though Charles had entrusted his metropolitical authority to five bishops since October 1627 because of his refusal to license the printing of a sermon in favour of the Forced Loan by Richard Sibthorpe (Abbot's authority was not restored until December 1628). Abbot appears to have been slow in meeting this request because, on 22 August, Secretary Conway ordered Laud, newly appointed as bishop of London, to prepare the form instead. The reason for Abbot's dilatoriness is not known. He suffered from recurrent poor health in this period but he was also at odds with Charles over Arminianism, the Forced Loan and the duke of Buckingham. Laud was the obvious alternative because, as bishop of London, he was dean of the province of Canterbury and Abbot's deputy; he was also an increasingly powerful figure at court. His form comprised one prayer, as had been usual for special worship during naval and military expeditions. On 23 August Buckingham was assassinated, which threatened to halt the expedition, but on the 26th Conway reiterated his order to Laud and asked him to have the form printed and distributed. Laud reminded Conway that 'I cannot command the use of the prayer, further than in mine own diocese' and forwarded the secretary's letter to Abbot. Though this was characteristic of Laud's desire to do things 'by the book', it also represented the belief of many bishops and archbishops across the 400-year history of special worship that such worship could only be ordered on a nationwide basis by the archbishop of Canterbury acting under the authority of the crown.

Order: privy council to the archbishop of Canterbury, 15 Aug. 1628, *APC*, XLIV, 103.
Form of prayer: *A prayer to bee publiquely vsed at the going foorth of the fleete this present yeere, 1628* (1 p.; STC 16546; SoA, Lemon 286).
Form of prayer (other edition): STC 16546.5.
Additional sources: MS copy of the prayer, [1628], LPL, MS 933/47; Secretary Conway to Bishop William Laud of London, 22 and 24 Aug. 1628, SP16/113, fo. 93r, SP16/114/3, fo. 3r; Laud to Conway, 26 Aug. 1628, SP16/114/14, fo. 19r; William Fairfax to Sir Thomas Fairfax, [27 July] 1628, *The Fairfax correspondence*, ed. George W. Johnson (2 vols., 1848), I, 141–2.

ORDER

Privy council to the archbishop of Canterbury: 15 August 1628

Wheras ther is a greate Fleete prepareing, and is in shorte tyme to put to Sea. His Majestie thinks it fitt, that your Grace cause a forme of prayer to be conceaved, to be used in all Churches throughout the Kingdome for the good successe therof: and that your Grace will by your letters signifie his Majesties pleasure to the Lord Arch Bishopp of Yorke, that he will see the said prayer used in his Province. Soe recommending to your speciall Care this Religeous and zealous consideracion of his Majestie, we bid etc.

FORM OF PRAYER

O eternall God, and mercifull Father, vouchsafe, wee beseech thee, to hearken to vs thy most unworthy seruants, who, in hope of thy louing kindnesse, are bold to come vnto thee. And whereas now, for the reliefe of some of our distressed brethren, our Gracious Soueraigne thy beloued seruant, is mooued, out of zeale to thy House, and compassion of the Members of thy Mysticall Bodie, to send foorth a Fleete to Sea for their reliefe; wee are humble and earnest suiters to thy Diuine Maiestie, that thou wilt mercifully bee pleased to accept of this endeauour, as a Sacrifice offered to thy selfe. And to blesse this Nauie, and all that serue in it, that they may effect that, about which they are sent, and then returne with safetie, to the honour of thy Name, the comfort of our gracious King CHARLES, the refreshing and encouragement of all those that wish well to the happinesse and prosperitie of the Reformed Churches. This wee humbly desire, and with it the flourishing of these Kingdomes in true Religion, Justice, and vnion of hearts, euen for thy blessed Sonnes sake, IESVS CHRIST, our onely Sauiour and Redeemer. AMEN.

1628–E3 Prayers during the pregnancy of Queen Henrietta Maria

[Autumn] 1628–[spring] 1629 (England and Wales)

No order is extant for this occasion. It was issued after Henrietta Maria became pregnant, for the first time, in the autumn of 1628. However, a letter from Thomas Vicars, vicar of Cuckfield, Sussex, suggests that he did not receive the form until the following spring. He wrote to his cousin on 22 April, 'We have a prayer, or rather praise, for the Queen's being with child. Do you believe it?' Vicars attributed the form to a 'Thomas', but he cannot be identified. Henrietta Maria gave birth prematurely to a son in May 1629 but he died within two hours. His death explains why no thanksgiving prayers were issued as they were in 1605 (see 1605–E2).

Order: none found.
Form of prayer: *A thankesgiuing and prayer for the safe child-bearing of the queenes maiestie* (1 p.; STC 16548)*.
Additional sources: Thomas Vicars to John Vicars, 22 Apr. 1629, SP16/141/27, fo. 34r; Clergy of the Church of England Database, www.theclergydatabase.org.uk, person ID 15889; 'Provisions to be made against the queen's majesty's delivery', [Apr.?] 1629, SP16/141/84, fos. 125r–126r.

FORM OF PRAYER

O eternall GOD and mercifull Father, All peace and strength of Kingdomes is from thee, and lineall Succession is thy great blessing both vpon Princes & States, the great meanes to preserue Unitie, and confirme Strength: Wee therefore giue thee humble and hearty thankes, as for all thy blessings, so especially at this time for thy great mercie and louing kindnesses to our dread Souereigne, his Royall Queene, and this whole State, in giuing her Maiestie hope of a long desired Issue, and so for filling our hearts with gladnesse. Lord goe along with thine owne blessings, to perfect them.

Bee with her in soule and in body. Preserue her from all dangers. Keepe her safe to & in the houre of Trauell, that there may be strength to bring foorth her ioy and our hope; And make her a ioyful mother of many Children, to the Glory of thy great Name, the happinesse of his Maiestie, the securitie of this State, and the flourishing of the Church and true Religion amongst vs. Grant this euen for Jesus Christ his sake, our onely Lord and Sauiour. Amen.

1629–E   Fast days for the preservation of Charles I, his realm and his allies and continental protestants

Wednesday 18 February 1629 (London, Westminster, Southwark and adjacent places); Friday 20 March 1629 (elsewhere in England and Wales)

On 26 January 1629, at the end of a short speech on the dangers of catholicism and Arminianism, Phelips made the now customary motion in the House of Commons for a general fast. The petition, presented the following day, justified the need for a fast to effect a 'perfect and a most happy Union and Agreement' between parliament and Charles, for the 'happy Success' of the session and on behalf of the 'continued and increasing Miseries of the Reformed Churches abroad'. Conflict had escalated between king and parliament over foreign policy, finance, religion and the duke of Buckingham, culminating in 1628 with the Petition of Right and the Remonstrance against Buckingham's conduct of the war. Yet, according to Robert Barrington, MP for Newtown, Isle of Wight, members were confident that Charles would agree. In his reply on 29 January, the king ignored the references to reconciliation and pointed out that 'Fighting will do them [the reformed churches] more Good than Fasting.' He also stated he did not expect to be constantly petitioned for fasts, other than on 'great Occasions'. Nonetheless, he agreed to the fast. The form of prayer appears to have the same text as 1628–E1, which was, in turn, based primarily on that for 1626–E2. This makes it difficult to identify which copies were printed for which occasion. The editors of the STC ascribe STC 16547 to 1629 (and STC 16547.5 to 1628) and, though there is no evidence for this, that attribution is followed here. In mid-February, the Commons asked the royal printer to ensure that there were sufficient copies of the form for MPs to have copies. This was a sign of the growing demand for personal copies of forms (see 1625–E).

Order: royal proclamation, 14 Feb. 1629, STC 8915* [also in Larkin, II, 220–2].
Form of prayer: *A forme of prayer, necessary to bee vsed in these dangerous times of warre vvherein we are appointed to fast, according to his maiesties proclamation; for the preseruation of his maiestie, and his realmes, and all reformed churches* (94 pp.; STC 16547)*.
Additional sources: *CJ*, I, 922–31; *LJ*, IV, 13–34; *Barrington family letters, 1628–1632*, ed. Arthur Searle (Camden Society, 4th ser., 28, 1983), pp. 51, 53, 55–6; Sir Francis Nethersole to Elizabeth, queen of Bohemia, 28 Jan. 1629, SP16/133/24, fos. 35r–37v.

ORDER

Royal proclamation: 14 February 1629
The Kings most Excellent MAIESTIE, taking into His most pious and Princely consideration, the present estate of the affaires of Christendome, and the deplorable

condition of those who professe the true Reformed Religion, together with Us, and the great and vnspeakable mercie and blessing of Almighty God vnto, and vpon His Maiestie and this Kingdome, that amidst the many miseries, which the true professors of the Religion haue of late yeeres suffered in forreine parts, Wee of this Kingdome haue enioyed a happy peace at home, & that peace, which aboue all other is of most esteeme, the peace of conscience. And His Maiestie, hauing at this time assembled His High Court of Parliament, in that great Counsell (which is the representatiue body of the whole Kingdome) to consult, debate, and conclude of those weighty and important matters which concerne the glory of God, the honour of the King, the safety of His Kingdomes, and the comfort and support of His Friends and Allies, Hee being thereto mooued at this time, by the ioynt Petition of His Lords and Commons in Parliament, whereto, out of His owne Religious disposition, Hee was easily inclined, hath resolued according to the examples of all good Kings in former ages, to command a generall and publique Fast to bee solemnized throughout this whole Kingdome; That so, although Hee is resolued to neglect no ordinary meanes, which may conduce to the iust defence of Himselfe, His people, and His Friends and Allies, yet not making His Reliance thereon, His Maiestie, both in His priuate deuotions, doth dayly lift vp His heart and hands to God Almighty, the King of Kings, and doth direct, that now in publique, both Hee and His whole people, as one man, may humble themselues by fasting and prayer before His Footestoole, who is able and ready to deliuer those (in his owne good time) who faithfully call vpon him; And therefore His Maiestie, to prayse God for his mercies vpon this Land, and other His Maiesties Dominions, and to implore his gracious fauour vnto, and vpon the distressed estate of those of the Religion in forreine parts, and his blessing vpon the counsels of this present Parliament, doth hereby commaund a generall and publique Fast to bee held, and solemnized throughout this whole Land, in such manner as hereafter is prescribed.

To this purpose His most Excellent Maiestie hath consulted with His Reuerend Bishops, and to the end so religious an exercise may bee performed with all decency and vniformitie, His Maiestie hath resolued vpon a graue and religious forme *[as 1626–E2*: of solemnizing thereof ... (*with change of date to 18 February*) ... celebrated in the*]* Cities of *London* and *Westminster*, Borough of *South-warke*, and other places adiacent *[as 1626-E2*: wherein ... (*with change of date to 20 March*) ... Dominion of *Wales]*. And for the better solemnizing thereof, without confusion, His Maiestie, by the aduice of His Reuerend Bishops, hath directed to bee composed, *[as 1626-E2*: Printed, and Published ... publike meetings*]*. And Hee hath giuen charge to His Bishops, to procure so many Bookes, and disperse the same throughout His whole Kingdome, in such manner, that the Minister and Clerke of euery Parish may in conuenient time be furnished with those Bookes. And His Maiestie, for the more deuout performance of so religious an exercise, doth command, that on that day the publike Markets be forborne in the Cities of *London* and *Westminster*, and the Suburbes thereof, and the Borough of *South-warke*. All which His Maiestie doth expresly charge *[as 1626-E2*: and command ... so religious a Worke*]*.

FORM OF PRAYER

[As 1628–E1]

¶ A Thankesgiuing for the safe deliuery
of the Queene, and happy birth of the
yong PRINCE.

Most mercifull God and gracious Father, thou hast giuen vs the ioy of our hearts, the contentment of our soules for this life, in blessing our deare and dread Souereigne, and His vertuous Royall Queene with a hopefull Sonne, and vs with a Prince, in thy iust time and his, to rule ouer vs. Wee giue thy glorious Name most humble and hearty thankes for this : Lord make vs so thankefull, so obedient to thee for this great mercie, that thy goodnesse may delight to increase it to vs. Increase it good Lord to moe children : the prop one of another against single hope. Increase it to moe Sons: the great strengthening of his Maiesty & his Throne. Increase it in the life and well fare of this Prince already giuen. Increase it in the ioy of the Royall Parents, & all true hearted Subiects. Increase it with his Christian and most happy education, both in faith and goodnes : That this kingdome and people may be happy: First in the long life and prosperity of our most gracious Souereigne, and his Royall Consort : And when fulnesse of dayes must gather him, Lord double his graces (if it be possible) and make them apparent in this his Heire, and his Heires after him for all generations to come, euen for Iesus Christ his sake our Lord and onely Sauiour. Amen.

¶ Imprinted at London by ROBERT BARKER, Printer
to the Kings most Excellent Maiestie. 1630.

10 A later example of a single prayer, printed as a half sheet folio, for the thanksgiving after the birth of the future Charles II, 1630–E2. *A thankesgiuing for the safe deliuery of the queene, and happy birth of the young prince* (1630; STC 16549), Houghton Library, Harvard University, P EB65 A100 B657b v. 1.

1630–E1 Prayers during the pregnancy of Queen Henrietta Maria

[After Saturday 2 January–June] 1630 (England and Wales)

Henrietta Maria became pregnant again in autumn 1629. No order is extant for this occasion but it was probably not ordered until January 1630. On 2 January, Laud wrote to Dudley Carleton, Viscount Dorchester and one of Charles's principal secretaries, that 'the busynes of thanksgiving & prayer cannot be done to morrowe for this great blessinge', because 'there must be a prayer made'. There is no other recorded thanksgiving between 1628 and June 1630, and it was usual in Charles's reign for thanks to be offered for the queen becoming pregnant, simultaneously with prayers for her safe delivery. This suggests that Laud might have been involved in writing the form and that the date printed on the *Thankesgiuing* (1629) must be Old Style (i.e. the new year beginning on 25 March).

Order: none found.
Form of prayer: *A thanksgiuing and prayer for the safe child-bearing of the queenes maiestie* (1 p.; STC 16548.3)*
Form of prayer (other edition): STC 16548.7.
Additional source: Laud to Dorchester, 2 Jan. 1630, SP16/158/5, fo. 7r.

FORM OF PRAYER

O eternall God and mercifull Father, since lineall Succession is vnder thee the great security of Kingdomes, and the very life of peace: Wee therefore giue thee most humble and hearty thankes, for the great blessing which thou hast begun to worke for our Royall King *Charles*, and this whole State, in giuing the Queenes Maiestie second hopes of a long desired Issue. And as we giue thee hearty and bounden thankes for this; so wee humbly pray thee to perfect this great blessing thus begunne, to preserue her from all dangers, and to be with her by speciall assistance in the houre of Trauell. Lord make her a happy Mother of successefull Children, to the increase of thy Glory, the comfort of his Maiestie, the ioy of her owne heart, the safety of the State, and the preseruation of the Church and true Religion amongst us. Grant this euen for Jesus Christ his sake, our onely Sauiour and Redeemer, Amen.

1630–E2 Thanksgiving prayer for the birth of Prince Charles

[June] 1630 (England and Wales)

Henrietta Maria gave birth to a son, the future Charles II, on 29 May 1630 at St James's Palace. The following day, the king with the privy council attended the sermon at Paul's Cross. No order is extant for this thanksgiving occasion, but news of the prince's birth travelled relatively quickly and celebrations were swiftly organized. In Hinton St George, Somerset, for instance, John, Lord Poulett reported that the news of the queen's delivery arrived on 3 June and was immediately celebrated with bell-ringing, bonfires and public thanksgivings. According to ESTC, the form was written by Laud.

Order: none found.

Form of prayer: *A thankesgiuing for the safe deliuery of the queene, and happy birth of the young prince* (1 p.; STC 16549)*.
Additional sources: Arthur Hopton, *Hoptons concordancy enlarged* (1635; STC 13781), sig. Q3r; MacClure, p. 135; John Lord Poulett to Dorchester, 6 June 1630, SP16/158/24, fo. 32r.

FORM OF PRAYER

O most mercifull God and gracious Father, thou hast giuen vs the ioy of our hearts, the contentment of our soules for this life, in blessing our deare and dread Souereigne, and his vertuous Royall Queene with a hopefull Sonne, and vs with a Prince, in thy iust time and his, to rule ouer vs. Wee giue thy glorious Name most humble and hearty thankes for this: Lord make vs so thankefull, so obedient to thee for this great mercie, that thy goodnesse may delight to increase it to vs. Increase it good Lord to more children: the prop one of another against single hope. Increase it to more Sons: the great strengthening of his Maiesty & his Throne. Increase it in the life and well fare of this Prince already giuen. Increase it in the ioy of the Royall Parents, & all true hearted Subiects. Increase it with his Christian and most happy education, both in faith and goodnes: That this kingdome and people may be happy: First in the long life and prosperity of our most gracious Souereigne, and his Royall Consort: And when fulnesse of dayes must gather him, Lord double his graces (if it be possible) and make them apparent in this his Heire, and his Heires after him for all generations to come, euen for Jesus Christ his sake our Lord and onely Sauiour. Amen.

1630–S   Thanksgiving prayer for the birth of Prince Charles

June 1630 (Scotland)

On 2 June 1630, Viscount Dupplin, the chancellor of Scotland, read to the privy council a royal letter announcing the birth on 29 May of Prince Charles (later Charles II). The council resolved that letters be written to Scotland's chief burghs, conveying the news and ordering acts of thanksgiving. The council did not prescribe the nature of this thanksgiving, which may not have involved special worship in all places. In Edinburgh, however, the news was celebrated with worship in the churches and bonfires in the streets.

Order: privy council order, 2 June 1630 (described in *RPC*, 2nd ser., III, 551–2).
Additional sources: *Edin. recs., 1626 to 1641*, pp. 76–7; 'History of the church and state of Scotland', NLS, Wod. Qu. IX, fos. 275v–276r.
Printed sermon: Struther, Edinburgh (STC 23369).

DESCRIPTION OF ORDER

Order of the privy council: 2 June 1630

[The king's] letter being read, heard and considderit be the saids Lords, and they with most humble and thankfull hearts to God, acknowledging the great and inestimable blessing showin by his Divine Majestie to this whole yland by blessing his Majestie with a sonne, they ordained notice to be givin thairof to the burgh of Edinburgh, and ordains missives to be writtin to the burrowes of Perth, Dundie, Aberdein, Linlithgow, Stirline, Glasgow, Air, advertising thame of thir most joyfull and happie tydings and desyring thame to expresse thair joy and thankefulnesse after the most solemne maner they can.

1630–Ir   Thanksgiving day for the birth of Prince Charles

Thursday 15 July 1630 (Dublin; and possibly elsewhere in Ireland)

The observance of a day of thanksgiving in Ireland for the birth of Prince Charles was mentioned in a letter from the lord justices to the king. No further information regarding the occasion has been found; it is not clear whether there was thanksgiving beyond Dublin.

Source: lords justices to King Charles, 18 July 1630, SP63/251/22, fo. 40r.

DESCRIPTION

Lords justices to King Charles: 18 July 1630
The xxix^th of the last moneth wee did with vnexpressable ioy and contentment receaue by the handes of this speciall bearer one of your Maiesties officers of armes and honor, your Maiesties most princely lettres, which brought vnto vs the blessed and happy tideings of the birth of our most illustrious Prince, which for the matter and gratious manner of expression thereof vnto vs your humblest seruants, wee in all humility confesse doth merrit more ample acknowledgment from vs then is with in the compasse of our capacities to expresse.

Wee did with vndelayed care communicate the same to your Maiesties Councell here and with vnanimous aduise and consent concluded and made dispatches to apointe the Fifteenth of this moneth to be kept as a Festiuall through out this whole Kingdome, to the end that vpon that day all the hartes and handes of your Maiesties Subiectes might be eleuated in giueing God thankes for this inestimable blessing of his infinite grace and goodnes vouchsafed to your Maiesty and to all your Subiectes in euery your Kingdomes. Thursday last was that day of celebrity with vs here at Dublin where there was (for soe short a time of notice) an vnexpected assembly of the Nobility Clergy Gentry and Communalty and all possible expressions of generall ioy and ioyfull exultacion in such sorte as in our memories wee haue not seene or heard the like vpon any occasion and wee assure our selues it was the same in all partes of this Realme, which wee hold it our bounden duties to make knowne to your Maiesty, to whose incomparable goodnes wee known it will be acceptable to vnderstand the dutifull and louing acclamacion and applaus of your people here for Gods infinite blessing bestowed vpon your Maiesty and through you vpon them all …

1631–E1   Prayers during the pregnancy of Queen Henrietta Maria

1631 (England and Wales)

Henrietta Maria became pregnant again early in 1631. No order is extant for this occasion. The prayer is similar to 1630–E1.

Order: none found.
Form of prayer: *A thankesgiuing, and prayer for the safe child-bearing of the queenes maiestie* (1 p.; STC 16549.5)*.

FORM OF PRAYER

O Eternall God *[as 1630–E1*: and mercifull Father … for the*]* great blessing which thou art working for our Royal King *CHARLES* and this whole State, in giuing the Queenes Maiestie further hopes of a desired and happy Issue. *[As 1630–E1*: And as we giue thee … Amen*]*

1631–E2   Thanksgiving prayer for the birth of Princess Mary

[November] 1631 (England and Wales)

Henrietta Maria gave birth to her first daughter, Mary, on 4 November 1631 at St James's Palace. The birth was celebrated immediately by bonfires and bell-ringing: Lady Judith Barrington reported to her mother-in-law, 'We had great bon fyers and ringing last night for the queen's deliverance of a daughter the night before about 2 of the clocke being at 11 at a playe'. It was thought that the child might not survive so she was christened by Laud the same day. But Mary did survive and married; her only child, William (later William III), was born in November 1650. There is no evidence that Mary's birth was celebrated in Scotland or Ireland. However, as thanksgivings were ordered in Scotland for the birth of another princess, Anne, in 1637 it is likely that royal births were regularly celebrated in Scotland without prayers being ordered by a central authority.

Order: none extant.
Form of prayer: *A thankesgiuing for the safe deliuery of the Queene, and happy birth of the yong princesse* (1 p.; STC 16550)*.
Additional source: *Barrington family letters*, ed. Searle, pp. 213, 215–16.

FORM OF PRAYER

O most gracious God, and louing Father, Wee giue thee, as wee are bound, most humble and hearty thanks for thy great mercy extended to vs, and this whole State, in blessing the Queenes Maiestie with a happy deliuerance, in, and from the great paines, and perils of Childbirth. We humbly beseech thee to continue and increase this blessing; To giue her strength that Shee may happily ouercome this, and all dangers else. That his most gracious Maiestie may long haue ioy in her happy life. That Shee may haue like ioy in His Maiesties prosperity. That both of them may haue comfort in the Royall Prince *CHARLES*, the new-borne Princesse the Lady *MARY*, and with them in a hopefull, healthfull, and a successefull Posterity. That the whole Kingdome may haue fulnesse of ioy in them. And that both they and we may all haue ioy, in the true honour and seruice of God. That both Church and Kingdome may bee blessed, and their Royall persons filled with honour in this life, and with eternall happinesse in the life to come. Euen for Jesus Christ his sake, our onely Lord and Sauiour. Amen.

1632–E   Thanksgiving prayer for the recovery of Charles I from smallpox

[December] 1632 (England and Wales)

In early December 1632, Charles fell ill with a mild case of smallpox. He was not seriously ill and recovered quickly. There is no order extant for this occasion.

Order: none found.
Form of prayer: *A thanksgiuing for the happy recouery of his maiesties health* (1 p.; STC 16550.3)*.
Additional sources: Edward Nicholas to Capt. John Pennington, 6 Dec. 1632, SP16/226/17, fos. 29r–v (*CSPD, 1625–32*, p. 454); same to same, 7 Dec. 1632, SP16/226/19, fo. 33r (*CSPD, 1625–32*, pp. 454–5).

FORM OF PRAYER

O eternall GOD, and mercifull Father, Wee giue thee all humble and hearty thankes for our most Gracious Souereigne Lord King CHARLES; Both for the Gentleness of thy hand, in a Disease otherwise so troublesome, and fearefull: And for the Mercifulnesse of thy hand, in taking it off so soone, and so happily. Wee know and acknowledge before Thee our sinnes, and what grievous punishment they haue deserued. But Lord Wee beseech thee still to remember vs in mercie, and long to blesse our Gracious King, with Life, and Health, and Strength, and Happinesse; and aboue all with the feare of thy Holy Name: That so Hee may continue vnder Thee, and ouer Us, a Father of the State, a Patron of the Church, a Comfort to His Royall Queene; till hee see His Childrens Children, and Peace upon Israel. Grant this good Lord, euen for Jesus Christ his sake. Amen.

1633–E1   Prayers during the pregnancy of Queen Henrietta Maria

After 31 May to October 1633 (England and Wales)

Henrietta Maria became pregnant again early in 1633 and, in May, the privy council ordered Archbishops Abbot of Canterbury and Neile of York to organize public prayers and thanksgivings in their provinces. The form was identical to 1631–E1.

Order: privy council to George Abbot, archbishop of Canterbury, 31 May 1633, PC2/43, p. 87.
Form of prayer: *A thanksgiving, and prayer for the safe child-bearing of the queens maiestie* (1 p.; STC 16550.5; Keble College, Oxford, Brooke 219a (10)).

ORDER

Privy council to George Abbot, archbishop of Canterbury: 31 May 1633

[W]hereas her maiestie at our attendance this day upon her at Greenewich was graciousely pleased to giue us knowledge, of her being quick with Child. We takeing it into Consideracon as a duty requisite, and agreeable to former President, that publique Thanksgiueing and Prayre for her maiesties happie deliuerie, should be made and vsed in all Churches throughout the Realme haue thought good hereby, to recomend the Care therof to your Grace, Praying you to giue direccon for publique Prayer to be made on that behalfe in all places wthin your Jurisdiccon, as was formerly vsed upon the lyke occacon. And this aduise and direccon, we haue alsoe thought fitt to giue unto our verie good Lord the Lord Arch Bishopp of York his Grace, for that which concerns his Province And see[.]

FORM OF PRAYER

[As 1631–E1]

1633–E2   Thanksgiving prayer for the birth of Prince James

[October] 1633 (England and Wales)

Henrietta Maria gave birth to James, duke of York (later James VII and II) on 14 October 1633 at St James's Palace. No order is extant; the form was based on 1631–E2.

Order: none found.
Form of prayer: *A thankesgiuing for the safe deliuerie of the queenes maiestie, and happy birth of the duke of Yorke* (1 p.; STC 16550.7)*.

FORM OF PRAYER

Most gracious God, and louing Father, we giue thee all humble and hearty thankes, for thy great Mercy, in blessing *[as 1631–E2*: the Queenes Maiestie … continue and*]* increase this Blessing, that shee may happily ouercome this, and all other Dangers. That his most gracious Maiestie may long haue ioy in her most happy life, and both of them comfort in the Royall Prince *Charles* and the rest of their Princely Issue, particularly in the new-borne Prince the Duke of *Yorke*. That they all may prooue a healthfull, hopefull, and a successefull Posterity; That both Church and Kingdome may haue fulnesse of Ioy in them. That so their Maiesties Royall Persons may be filled with Honours in this life, and with eternall happinesse in the life to come. And this euen for Jesus Christ his sake our onely Sauiour and Redeemer. Amen.

1635–E   Prayers during the pregnancy of Queen Henrietta Maria

1635 (England and Wales)

Henrietta Maria became pregnant again in the spring of 1635. No order exists to date precisely when this prayer was issued. The form is almost identical to 1631–E1.

Order: none found.
Form of prayer: *A thankesgiuing, and prayer for the safe child-bearing of the queenes maiestie* (1 p.; STC 16552*).

FORM OF PRAYER

O Eternall God *[as 1630–E1*: and mercifull Father … which thou hast*]* again *[as 1630–E1*: begun to work … the Queenes Maiestie*]* further hopes of a desired and happy Issue *[as 1630–E1*: And as we … Amen*]*.

1636–E1   Thanksgiving prayer for the birth of Princess Elizabeth

[January] 1636 (England and Wales)

Princess Elizabeth was born on 28 December 1635 at St James's Palace and was baptized there by Laud on 2 January. This prayer was issued soon afterwards to ministers in England and Wales. It was based on 1633–E2. Elizabeth remained in England as a ward of parliament throughout the civil war and died on the Isle of Wight on 8 September 1650 from a cold; she was buried in St Thomas's Church, Newport.

Order: none found.
Form of prayer: *A thanksgiving for the safe delivery of the queenes maiestie, and happy birth of the new-borne princesse* (1 p.; STC 16555.5; Keble College, Oxford, Brooke 219a (14)).

FORM OF PRAYER

[As 1633–E2 with 'new-borne Prince the Duke of *Yorke*' replaced by 'new-borne Princesse'*]*

1636–E2   Prayers during the pregnancy of Queen Henrietta Maria

1636 (England and Wales)

Henrietta Maria became pregnant again soon after the birth of Princess Elizabeth (see 1636–E1). No order survives to date this occasion precisely; the form was identical to 1635–E. However, there is no evidence that a thanksgiving was ordered after the birth of the child, Anne, on 17 March 1637. As the birth of all of Henrietta Maria's children had been celebrated in England and Wales, and the birth of Anne was marked in Scotland (1637–S), it is likely that thanksgivings were ordered, but no orders or forms survive.

Order: none found.
Form of prayer: *A thanksgiving, and prayer for the safe child-bearing of the queenes maiestie* (1 p.; STC 16555)*.

FORM OF PRAYER

[As 1635–E]

1636–E3   Weekly fast days during the plague epidemic

Wednesdays, beginning October 1636, during plague (England and Wales)

A new strain of plague entered England through Hull and Yarmouth in 1635 and spread to neighbouring areas along major travel routes, into Kent, London, the Thames valley, the midlands, Wales and, possibly via coastal shipping, to the north (mainly

Yorkshire, Durham and Northumberland). However, orders for days of prayer and weekly fasts were not issued until October. This was probably because the relatively cold spring and early summer had meant that mortality did not rise significantly until August and September. It was also a less severe outbreak than previous ones in 1603 and 1625. As was ordered by the privy council on 9 October, the form of prayer was based on the form issued for the previous fast days for plague, 1625–E. However, a number of changes were made, presumably under the supervision of Laud, who had succeeded Abbot as archbishop of Canterbury in 1633. A collect was revised, using text from the form for the first plague fasts (1563–E). Most notably, the 'admonition' added at the end of the 'order of the fast' for 1593–E and extended for 1603–E was altered. Most of the anti-puritan injunctions were removed: the comments on the abuse of fasting and the warnings against fasts arranged without authority. Yet the limitations on the number of sermons (only one during the morning and evening services) and on their length (no more than an hour) were retained, and injunctions on the conduct of services were now added to the terms of the proclamation: this too declared that sermons should not exceed an hour, and added that the services were to be conducted only in accordance with the official form of prayer. These changes, and especially the effort to limit sermons, aroused protests from puritan controversialists, particularly Henry Burton and William Prynne. In his pamphlet *Newes from Ipswich,* Prynne criticised the 'new Faste-book' in detail as the work of 'Romish Prelates' who aimed to 'suppresse the preaching and Preachers of his Word when it was most necessary and usefull', and to 'countenance, justifie and set up Popery, *superstition, idolatry*, error and disorder'. In consequence, Burton and Prynne were convicted of sedition before Star chamber in 1637, and suffered punishment by cropping of their ears and facial mutilation.

London recorded over 10,000 deaths, Hull nearly 3,000 and Newcastle-upon-Tyne over 5,000. The outbreak did not subside until December, and cases remained relatively common in 1637 (3,000 in London alone). In contrast to earlier outbreaks, no thanksgivings appear to have been ordered after the plague declined. This seems unusual and it is more likely that evidence simply does not survive.

Order: royal proclamation, 18 Oct. 1636, STC 9075* [also in Larkin, II, 538–40].
Form of prayer: *A forme of common prayer, together with an order of fasting: for the auerting of Gods heauie visitation vpon many places of this kingdome, and for the obtaining of his blessings vpon vs. The prayers are to be read euery Wednesday during this visitation. Set forth by his maiesties authority* (100 pp.; STC 16553)*
Form of prayer (other edition): STC 16553a.
Additional source: privy council order to reprint the 1625–E form of prayer, and to prepare a proclamation, 9 Oct. 1636, PC2/46, pp. 432–3; William Prynne, *Newes from Ipswich discovering certaine detestable practises of some domineering lordly prelates* (8pp.; STC 20470).
Printed sermon: Swadlin, St Paul's, London (STC 23509).

ORDER

Royal proclamation: 18 October 1636
The heauie Iudgement of God in His present Visitation of the Cities of *London, Westminster,* and diuers other parts of the Kingdome at this time with the Pestilence, ought to moue vs to acknowledge the immediate hand of God therein, for the sinnes of this Land, so to afflict and correct His people: And His Maiestie hauing taken into His Religious care, that in common Calamities the speciall meanes to remoue the Euill, is by serious humiliation to implore the grace and fauour of that

Supreme offended Maiestie, who hath smitten the Land, and can onely heale it; Hath resolued, according to the example of pious Kings in former ages, and in like cases, to command Generall and Publike Fasts to be held through the whole Realme, in such manner as is herein directed. And to the end so Religious an Exercise may be performed with all Decencie and Uniformitie; His most Excellent Maiestie hath, with the aduice of His Reuerend Bishops, resolued vpon a graue and Religious Forme of Solemnizing thereof.

And this His Royall Pleasure He doth hereby Publish and Declare to all His louing Subiects, and doth straitely Charge and Command, that this Fast be Religiously and Solemnely obserued and Celebrated Weekely, from the time of the Publishing of this Proclamation, vpon euery Wednesday, thorowout the whole Kingdome, during the Continuance of the present Infection: With this limitation neuerthelesse, that in the Citie of *London* and Suburbs thereof, and in all other Cities, Townes, and places, where the Infection now is, or hereafter shall happen to be, and during the continuance of the Contagion in any of those places, the said Fasts shall be no otherwise Celebrated in publike in such seuerall Parish Churches, then by a Deuout and Religious vse of the Prayers in the Printed Booke, now appointed to be set forth. And that no Minister shall in *London*, or any other place infected, detaine their assemblies any longer time together to heare either Sermons or other Diuine Seruice, because such detaining of the people so long together, may proue dangerous to the further increase of the Sicknesse. And further, that all other Duties of Prayer and Humiliation requisite, to the keeping of such a Fast, be obserued by euery person in their priuate Families, at home: But in all Cities, Towns, and other places not infected, His Maiestie requireth that the said Fast be publikely solem-nized, not onely by reading the said Booke, but by the vse of Sermons or Homi-lies, also as upon like Occasions hath beene commanded and obserued; the same Sermons not exceeding the space of an houre. And for the more orderly solemnizing thereof, without confusion, His Maiestie, by the aduice of His Reuerend Bishops, hath directed that the Booke of Prayers formerly set forth by Authority, shall be reprinted and published, which, with the publike Exhortation therein, His Maiestie thinketh fit, and commands to be vsed in all Churches and places at these publike meetings: And he hath giuen charge to His Bishops to disperse the same thorowout this whole Kingdome, so farre as in these sickly times they may be able. All which His Maiestie doth expresly charge and command *[as 1626–E2*: shall be reuerently … so religious a Worke*]*.

FORM OF PRAYER

PREFACE
 Wee be taught *[as 1625–E]*

A FORME OF COMMON PRAYER, PRESCRIBED FOR THIS TIME OF VISITATION, AND OTHER NECESSITIES
 Let all Pastours and Curates [as 1625–E]

MORNING PRAYER

Let the Minister beginning Seruice, reade with a lowd voyce one of these sentences of Scripture. [Joel 2:13; Dan. 9:9–10; Jer. 10:24]

[As 1625–E until]

[Ps. 6, 32, 38, 39, 51, 90, 91, 102, 130]

The Psalmes ended, reade one of these Chapters following for the first Lesson, [Deut. 28; Deut. 30; 1 Kgs. 8; 2 Sam. 24; Joel 2; Jonah 3]

[Te Deum]

For the second Lesson, reade one of these Chapters, [Matt. 6; Matt. 8; Matt. 9; or Luke 13]

[As 1625–E until]

The first Collect.
    O almightie, most iust and mercifull God *[as 1563–E 'A prayer, conteynyng also a confession of sinnes'*: we here acknowledge … worthyly to expresse*]*. Thou hast released vs from the hard seruitude of Sathan. But wee most vnmindfull in times of prosperitie, of these thy great benefits, haue neglected thy Commandements, haue abused the knowledge of thy Gospel *[as 1563–E*: and have folowed … although thou shouldest*]* punish vs more grieuously then thou hast done, and for one plague send vs many, if thou shouldest powre vpon vs *[as 1563–E*: all those testimonies … chasten vs in thy mercie*]*. Regard not the horrour of our sinnes, but our vnfained repentance. Perfite that worke which thou hast begun in vs *[as 1563–E*: that the whole worlde … and especially to*]* this our Realme, and to our most gracious King and Gouernour King *Charles* and Queene *Mary* increase the number of godly Ministers *[as 1563–E (with changes of gender)*: indue them … continue thyne, and*]* euer praise thy holy Name, and by thy great mercy be partakers of grace in this life, and eternall glory in the life to come. Grant vs these and all other our humble petitions (O mercifull Father) for thy deare Sonnes sake Iesus Christ our Lord. Amen.

[The collect for peace; the collect for grace.]

LITANY

[After the versicle]
    O eternall and euerliuing God *[as 1563–E*: most mercifull father … nowe partly vpon vs, by*]* plagueing vs so (with most dreadfull and deadly sicknesse) whereby great multitudes of vs *[as 1563–E*: are dayly afflicted … Amen*]*.

[The prayers 'O Lord, we have sinned', 'Thou hast smitten us (O Lord)', 'O Lord our God most gracious and merciful' and 'Almighty God and heavenly Father' from 1603–E, followed by 'We humbly beseech thee' and the rest of the litany]

THE LATTER SERUICE[320]

[As 1625–E to the collect for the day, which is the BCP collect for Ash Wednesday]

---

[320] I.e. the communion.

[Epistle: Joel 2:12–17]
[Gospel: Matt. 6:16–21]
[Nicene creed]
[Offertory sentence: Matt. 5:16]

[After the prayer for the whole state of the church, the prayers 'O most mighty God and merciful Father' and 'Turn thou us, O good Lord' from the BCP commination service, 'Assist us mercifully', 'Almighty God, which hast promised', and the peace]

EVENING PRAYER

[As 1625–E]

A SHORT PREFACE TO BE VSED BEFORE THE EXHORTATION FOLLOWING, BY THE MINISTER WHO IS NOT A PREACHER.
When the Apostles *[as 1603–E]*

AN EXHORTATION FIT FOR THE TIME.
In the due consideration *[as 1603–E]*

ORDER FOR THE FAST
[As 1603–E, until]
6. Admonition is here lastly to be given, that on the said Fasting day in places where Sermons are allowed to be by the Proclamation, there bee but one Sermon at Morning prayer, and the same not above an houre long, and not above one at Evening Prayer of the same length. God give us grace to repent, and in his mercie turne away his punishment from us. Amen.

1637–S   Thanksgiving prayer for the birth of Princess Anne

March 1637 (Edinburgh; possibly elsewhere in Scotland)

News of the birth of Henrietta Maria's fifth child, Anne, on 17 March 1637, reached Edinburgh on 22 March. The privy council met and ordered national thanksgiving; cannons were later fired from Edinburgh Castle. The order resulted in preaching in Edinburgh on 23 March, but as with the thanksgiving for the birth of Prince Charles (1630–S), it is not clear whether prayers were said nationally. It seems that the other royal births of the 1630s were celebrated without prayers being ordered by central authority in Scotland. Moreover, local responses to royal births may have had an essentially secular character, as in Edinburgh after the birth of the future James VII and II in 1633. No evidence survives that Anne's birth was celebrated in England and Wales, though this is probably because no orders or forms survive rather than because no thanksgiving was ordered (see 1636–E2).

Order: privy council order, 22 Mar. 1637, *RPC*, 2nd ser., VI, 418.
Additional sources: 'History of the church and state of Scotland', NLS, Wod. Qu. IX, fo. 407r; Craighall, p. 57; *Edin. recs., 1626 to 1641*, p. 133.

ORDER

Privy council order: 22 March 1637

Forsamekle as it hes pleased God to grant unto the Queen's Majestie ane happie and confortable deliverie of a daughter, for the quhilk inestimable blessing it becometh all good subjects to expresse thair joy and thankfulnes in als solemne a forme and maner as formerlie hes beene accustomed in the like caises, thairfoir the Lords of Secreit Counsell ordains all his Majesteis subjects to expresse thair joy and thankfulnes in ane usuall and accustomed maner, and that the ministrie of this burgh [Edinburgh] at the first preaching day acquaint the people with the said happie deliverie and to stirre up the people to be thankfull to God for this so great a benefite.

1638–S1   Fast day for the success of the general assembly and an end to divisions

Wednesday 7 November 1638 (Scotland)

The imposition of a prayer book on the Church of Scotland in 1637 provoked riots in Edinburgh, and gave rise to a campaign of petitioning by opponents of the crown's religious policies, which culminated in the signing of the National Covenant on 28 February 1638. In the following months, pressure mounted on Charles to make concessions to his critics. By the summer, Charles and the covenanters were both preparing for war (see 1639–E), but in September, the king was persuaded to call a general assembly to address the grievances. Charles ordered this fast at the same time as he appointed the assembly to meet at Glasgow on 21 November. In some places, including Edinburgh, Paisley and Perth, the fast was observed on Sunday 4 November, in addition to, or instead of, Wednesday 7 November. In Aberdeen, a centre of opposition to the covenanting movement, the fast may not have been observed, at least by the burgh council.

Order: royal declaration, 19 Sept. 1638, approved by the privy council, 22 Sept. 1638, *RPC*, 2nd ser., VII, 66.
Additional sources: *RPC*, 2nd ser., VII, 64–7; 'History of the church and state of Scotland', NLS, Wod. Qu. IX, fo. 446v; presbytery of Perth minutes, NRS, CH2/299/1, pp. 374–5; presbytery of Paisley minutes, NRS, CH2/294/2, p. 115; *Letters and journals of Robert Baillie*, ed. David Laing (3 vols., Bannatyne Club, Edinburgh, 1841–2), I, 111; *Diary of Sir Archibald Johnston of Wariston, 1632–1639*, ed. George Morison Paul (Scottish History Society, 1st ser., 61, 1911), p. 397; *Aber. recs., 1625–1642*, p. 143.

ORDER

Royal declaration: 19 September 1638

… And that this Assemblie may have the better successe and more happie conclusion our will is that there be a solemne fast proclamed and keeped be all our good subjects of this our kingdome a fourteene dayes before the begining of the said Assemblie, the causes thairof to be a begging a blessing frome God upon that Assemblie and a peaceable end to the distractions of this church and kingdome, with the aversion of Gods heavie judgement frome both; and our pleasure is that this fast be keeped in the most solemne maner hes beene in this church at anie time heertofore upon the most extraordinar occasion.

1638–S2   Thanksgiving day for the achievements of the general assembly

Sunday, December 1638 – January 1639 (Scotland)

This thanksgiving was appointed in the closing session of the 1638 general assembly, on 20 December. By this date, the assembly had sat for a month, had defied the royal commissioner's attempt to dissolve it and had abjured episcopacy, all to the satisfaction of the presbyterian clergy who had taken control. No day was specified for the thanksgiving; ministers were to announce it to their parishioners on the first Sunday after their return from the assembly, and the thanksgiving itself was to be observed on the Sunday following. It was observed in Edinburgh on 30 December, and in Dalkeith and Perth on 6 January; presumably, many other lowland parishes observed it around this date. The act was unprinted, and the assembly's minutes do not give the text of the act itself.

Order: act of the general assembly, 20 Dec. 1638 (described in the register of the general assembly, 1638–9, NRS, CH1/1/4, p. 181).
Additional sources: 'History of the Church and state of Scotland', NLS, Wod. Qu. IX, fo. 451v; presbytery of Dalkeith minutes, NRS, CH2/424/2, p. 119; presbytery of Perth minutes, NRS, CH2/299/1, p. 376; 'An index of the principall unprinted acts of the assembly at Glasgow, 1638', in *The principall acts of foure generall assemblies* (Edinburgh, 1642; Wing C4233A), facing title-page.

DESCRIPTION OF ORDER

Act of the general assembly: 20 December 1638

The Moderator said There is a motion made concerning thanksgiving to be keeped when ye go home to your particular congregations. And truly considering our evill deservings, and what the Lord hath done to us of mere favour, we have no less nor great reason to acknowledge it, both publikly in our Congregations, and privatly in our families, and to delight in the honour of God, and make frequent commemoration of it at the first convenient occasion, after ye return to yoʳ Presbytries and Paroches. And I trust it shall be acceptable unto God, and give no just occasion of offence to any.

The assembly alloweth this article, and ordaineth ministers to make intimation in their pulpets of the Conclusion of this assembly, the first Sabbath after their return home; and desire their people to prepare themselves against the next sabbath thereafter, not for a carnall festivitie, but for a humble thanksgiving.

1639–E   Prayers during Charles I's military campaign to Scotland

[April] 1639 (England and Wales)

Despite his concessions to the covenanters in Scotland (see 1638–S1), Charles made preparations to crush the movement by force. He slowly gathered a military force of 15,000, and on 13 March 1639 ordered a prayer for a successful campaign. This was written under the direction of Laud, who was also ordered to have the prayer printed and distributed to the bishops. Charles decided not to order a fast because these were appointed 'only upon occasion of publicke and great calamityes'; this may have been a deliberate attempt to underplay the seriousness of the situation. Nevertheless, Henrietta Maria ordered the usual Saturday fasts (preparatory to taking the mass) to be kept and sermons to be read every Saturday at Somerset House during the king's absence. Charles's campaign was a failure: it antagonized the Scots, while the slowness with which the king assembled his troops enabled the Scots to mobilize. It also divided his English subjects. Although some, such as John Pocklington (a Laudian sympathizer), welcomed the expedition calling it 'the King's happy journey and joyful return out of Scotland', there was widespread sympathy in the English army for the covenanters and some clergy, such as Edward Bright, vicar of Goudhurst, Kent, refused to read the prayer. This occasion is significant because parliament appeared to question the king's authority to order nationwide prayers. In December, parliament's committee for religion investigated Wiliam Kingsley, archdeacon of Canterbury, who had suspended Bright for failing to read the prayer. They demanded 'what authority enjoyned him to enjoyne others to reade and publish that prayer, and by what authority he suspended Mr Bright for not reading what as not commanded'. Kingsley responded that 'he received no such commandes' (this appears to refer to Bright's suspension) but referred to a letter from an officer in the vicar-general's office to the registrar of Canterbury 'to some such effect as the publishing or dispersing of the said prayer'.

Order: privy council order, 13 Mar. 1639, *Privy council registers preserved in the Public Record Office reproduced in facsimile* (12 vols., 1967–8), V, 152.
Form of prayer: *A prayer for the kings majestie, in his northern expedition, to be said in all churches, in the time of divine service, next after the prayer for the queen, and the royall progenie* (1 p.; STC 16556)*.
Additional sources: 'His graces lettres to the commissaryes of Lincoln dioces', 26 Mar. 1639, LPL, VB.2/1, fo. 42; George Garrard to Edward, Viscount Conway and Killultagh, 28 Mar. 1639, SP16/415/65, fos. 182r–183r; [Edmund Rossingham to the same], 1 Apr. 1639, SP16/417/3, fos. 6r–7r; Dr John Pocklington to [Sir John Lambe], 4 Mar. 1639, SP16/414/25, fos. 44r–v; *Proceedings principally in the county of Kent in connection with the parliaments called in 1640* , ed. Lambert B. Larking (Camden Society, original ser., Westminster, 1862), p. 91.

DESCRIPTION OF ORDER

Order of the privy council: 13 March 1639
It was this day ordered by his Matie wth the Advise of the Boord, that the Lord Arch Bishopp of Canterbury his Grace calling to his Assistance such other Bishops as he thinkes fitt, and are now in Towne, should compose a prayer to bee publiquely read in all Churches att all tymes of prayer for the happie success of his Ma^ts expedition to the Northren parts But some mention beeing then made of a Fast it was not thought fitt that any should bee proclaymed att this tyme, being not agreeable to the practise of the Catholique Church, where Fasts were appointed, only upon occasion of publicke and great calamityes

FORM OF PRAYER

[After the prayer for the queen and the royal family]
O eternall God, and mercifull Father, by whom alone Kings reign, thou Lord of Hosts, and Giver of all Victory, We humbly beseech thee, to guard our most gracious Soveraign Lord King CHARLES: To blesse Him in His Person with Health and Safetie, in His Councels with Wisdom and Prudence, and in all His Actions with Honour and good Successe: Grant, blessed Lord, that Victory may attend His

Designes; And that His liege people may rejoyce in thee, but that shame may cover the faces of Thine and His treacherous Enemies. Give Him, blessed Father, so to settle His Subjects in Peace, and the true fear of thy Divine Majestie, that He may return with Joy and Honour, and proceed long to govern His Kingdoms in Peace, and Plenty, and in the happinesse of true Religion and Piety all His dayes. These Blessings, and whatsoever else shall be necessary for Him, or for our selves, we humbly beg of thee, O mercifull Father, for Jesus Christ his sake, our onely Mediator and Redeemer. Amen.

1639–S   Fast day for general evils and for the general assembly and parliament

Sunday 10 November 1639 (Scotland)

When the covenanters confronted the king's army in Berwickshire in June 1639, Charles quickly decided to negotiate for peace. In the treaty of Berwick, the king agreed to allow the general assembly and the Scottish parliament to meet in August. The assembly confirmed the abolition of episcopacy, and was dissolved on 30 August with a promise from the royal commissioner, the earl of Traquair, that its acts would be ratified in the ensuing parliament. Thus, the assembly appointed this 'fast and thanksgiving' in anticipation of a considerable triumph for the covenanting cause. When in early November the presbytery of Edinburgh, acting on the assembly's instructions, announced the date of the observance, the covenanters' success was still incomplete: despite weeks of discussion by the lords of the articles, no acts had been presented to parliament. The causes of the fast, communicated by the presbytery of Edinburgh, reflected the pessimism inspired by parliament's proceedings. The Edinburgh presbytery's records are not extant, but the causes were recorded in the register of the presbytery of Dalkeith on 7 November.

Order: act of the general assembly, 30 Aug. 1639 (described in the register of the general assembly, NRS, CH1/1/4, p. 266).
Causes: presbytery of Dalkeith minutes, NRS, CH2/424/3, pp. 18–19.
Additional sources: address of the commissioners of the general assembly to the king, 1639, SP16/445/74, fo. 139r (*CSPD, Oct. 1639–Mar. 1640*, p. 472); Craighall, p. 111.

DESCRIPTION OF ORDER

Act of the general assembly: 30 August 1639

The assembly considering that if it should please God to conclude all matters in the assembly and parliament, it were necessary there should be a solemne fast and thanksgiving through all the Land, for this great favour from God and the kings majestie. And because they could not well appoint the dyet now, did therefore ordaine the Presbytrie of Edinburgh to advertise all the rest.

CAUSES

Evills of punishment
    1. The long sitting of this parliament, yet no good done neither to the Kirk, nor cuntrey

2. Our hopes suspended, and just feares, lest they be frustrat be the malice craft and power of enemies at Court or elsewhere

3. The barbarous oppressions, and roberies in the north, yea even in tyme of parliament sitting, no redress, bot appearance of greater dissolution

4. The great scaircitie of faithfull Labourers in the Lords harvest, and small hope of help, because no course taken for seminaries

5. Manie congregations destitute of Pastours quhilk can not be helped without ane happie conclusion to this parliament

6. Multitud of strong beggers, inordinat livers, and no care hade of those, whoe are poore indeed

Evills off sin, the causes theroff

1. Unthankfulnes after recept of so great favours, and Wonderfull delyverance

2. A deepe securitie, When never more need of watching and prayer, by reason of the malice of our adversaries both at home and abroade, being so farre disappointed, because of this Work of reformation begun in Religion

3. No cair to reforme our Lyvs according to our Covenant

4. Neglect and slighting of Gods word in publick, neglect of it in privat and in families

5. Grosse ignorance

6. Manie mor reigning sinnes, as blasphemie &c

The Lord to be supplicated

To remeed and remove all those forsaid Evills.

To grant ane happie conclusion to this parliament.

To grant good information to our King.

To bles the commissionars sent up to that effect.

1640–S1   Fast days in response to general evils, shortage of ministers and the failure of parliament and the peace negotiations

Friday 10 April and Sunday 12 April 1640 (Scotland)

This fast was appointed in March 1640 by the presbytery of Edinburgh, which had been commissioned by the 1639 assembly to act for the Kirk as a whole. Politically, the covenanters' position had changed little since the observance of 1639–S. Parliament had not been allowed to vote on any religious and constitutional reforms, and had been prorogued until June. Since July 1639, royal forces had been rebuilding and rearming Edinburgh Castle, apparently in preparation for renewed conflict. In March, tensions were inflamed when the covenanters ordered a guard to observe activities at the castle. The presbytery's order for the fasts also reflected concerns about the sins of the people, the parochial effectiveness of the church and constraints on religious reform. It appears that this fast may also have been observed privately in England (and Germany): Robert Woodford, a godly provincial lawyer who became steward of Northampton in 1635, recorded in his diary 'a general fast was held this day [10 April] amongst xxians [i.e. Christians] privately in England Scot[land] Germany ut dicitur pro successe of the parliament'.

Order: by the presbytery of Edinburgh, *c*. 20 Mar. 1640 (described in presbytery of Dalkeith minutes, NRS, CH2/424/3, pp. 36–8).
Additional sources: presbytery of Perth minutes, NRS, CH2/299/1, p. 385; presbytery of Paisley minutes, NRS, CH2/294/2, p. 137; *Woodford*, p. 349.

DESCRIPTION OF ORDER

Order by the presbytery of Edinburgh: *c.* 20 March 1640

Quhilk day the Ministrie of Edenburgh standing at this tyme in the chiefest watche tour of this kirk wairned the brether that it was concluded to be most necessar that all who tak the cause of God to hart renew thair humiliation and repentance w^t earnest prayers to God for mercie help and delyv^{r}ance in this day of trouble: And for this end a publick and solemne fast be sanctified in all the kirks the 10 and 12 of Apryle instant: quhilk the brether appoints to be intimat this nixt sabbath

Causes ordinarie

Grosse ignorance, strong inclination to superstition, charming, inchantment, sorcerie, common blasphemie w^{t}out anie kynd of reverence to the blessed name of God prophanation of the lords day, the sanctification y^{r}of in manie places altogither neglected, and in other places abridged to ane houre of customarie service w^{t}out ather familie or personall worship in privat, and without inward worship in publik; whiche is the caus of muche uncleennes, intemperancie, fraudulent and violent dealing The cry whairof is now greater by reason of our Late obligation w^t god of our covenant and of the notable mercies of God towards us

Causes extraordinarie

1 The perfidious dealing of some, the perfunctorious dealing of others, and the indifferencie and lookwarmnes of manie in the cause of God, Notw^{t}standing of theire solemne oath and subscription to the contrare

2 The desolate condition of manie congregations at this tyme of commun calamitie most deplorable when people have so great need to be directed strengthned aind incouraged for the just defence of thaire religion, liberties, lyves, and estats

3 Act of parliament is denyed for ratifeing what was concluded in the Assemblie The ratification of the acts off Assemblie refused except with limitatione and declaratione. Ane act rescinding particular acts standing in vigor to the contrare (altho no thing more necessare, reasonable, and usuale) was also denyed. Manie particulars proponit by the ministrie for the good of the kirk was reiected The Praelats still keep theire former titills, subscription, state, and respect, and the service book in als highe esteem, and als manie pleading for it by word and writ, as ever before. Thus the table hath beene covered and the meat presented, and we go hungrie away.

4 The act of pacification was refused, except it sould import the acknowledgement of our rebellion against the king: and thus for all the peace that was mad w^t us we are still reput rebells. The meanes for releiving the great charges bestowed on this work since the beginning thairof are denyed. The kingdome hath nether counsell nor Session, nor anie common judicatorie sitting for ministration of justice

5 All dewties in all treuth and loyaltie have been cairfullie and punctualie performed on our syd The Articles of Pacification keeped to the outmost, all forces dismissed, all moderation in our proceedings in Parliament, Humble and readie obedience givin to the prorogation theirof, Commissioners sent to render reasons of our just desyres, and no thing whiche beseemed good subiects or might ather pacifie

or satisfie left unassayed: And yit, by the prevalent malice of oᵣ enemies, no thing can be accepted; all favour denyed, fortifications are made, and great garrisons are keeped at Bervik and Carlile, The castell of Edenburᵗ furnished wᵗ men and munition to destroy the toun, Armies by sea and land prepairing, a terrible Commission givin to Northumberland, all acts and wayis used for working division among oᵣselves

All thease call for humiliation of heart & reformation of lyf

---

1640–E1   Fast day for averting plague and war

Wednesday 8 July 1640 (England and Wales)

The plague that broke out in 1635–6 lingered until 1642. Laud complained to Viscount Conway in August that Hampton Court was infected and that he had had to leave 'all my stuff' there and go to the palace at Oatlands where he had no accommodation. Within three days of parliament (the 'Short Parliament') being assembled (for the first time in eleven years), the Commons drew up a petition for a general fast, which was presented to the Lords. Charles quickly agreed to the petition but left the choice of dates to be decided by the Lords. Contrary to procedure, the Commons then proposed that parliament should observe the fast on 2 May, but the Lords refused to meet its delegation to assent to this choice 'by reason of the very great and weighty Businesses they are now in, the King being there present'. The Lords were also unimpressed by the Commons' breach of its privilege. As a result, the Commons did not observe the fast because it did not have the authority to decide the date alone, and parliament was dissolved shortly afterwards. The proclamation for the general fast was not drawn up until 31 May, probably because Charles was busy trying to raise money for his campaign against the covenanters. The fast was ordered to be observed on 1 July. When the proclamation was issued on 16 June, however, the date had been changed to 8 July. It is unclear why this change was made; it may have been simply because issuing the order had been delayed, and more time was required to print and distribute forms of prayer. Although the forms largely followed the format and content of those for previous fasts, changes were made to the preface and to the psalm which took the place of the *Venite exultemus*. As the title of the form emphasizes, the intention was to 'avert' a renewed visitation of the plague, as well as other 'judgements'; accordingly, the style of forms of prayer used earlier during actual epidemics (1563–E, 1593–E, 1603–E, 1625–E, and 1636–E3) was not considered appropriate for this occasion. For the first time, the rubrics specified which psalms were to be read after the first lesson in evening prayer, instead of directing the minister to read the psalms which had not been read at morning prayer. The fast coincided with military preparations against Scotland, and some soldiers, such as those at Cirencester, forced recusants into church to participate in the services.

Order: royal proclamation, 7 June 1640, STC 9159* [printed in Larkin, II, 714–15].
Form of prayer: *A forme of common prayer; to be used upon the eighth of July: on which day a fast is appointed by his majesties proclamation, for the averting of the plague, and other judgements of God from this kingdom. Set forth by his majesties authority* (85 pp.; STC 16557)*.
Additional sources: *CJ*, II, 4–11; *LJ*, IV, 61–5; *Proceedings of the Short parliament of 1640.* ed. Esther S. Cope and Wilson Coates (Camden Society, 4th ser., 19, 1977), pp. 241–2; parliamentary proceedings,

BL, Harleian MS 4931, fo. 48v; order of council, 31 May 1640, SP16/455/96, fo. 233r; [Edmund Ross-ington to Conway], 21 July 1640, SP16/460/56, fos. 137r–138v.

ORDER

Royal proclamation: 7 June 1640

The Kings most Excellent Majestie acknowledging the great goodnesse and mercy of the Almighty in preserving of His Kingdoms and dominions in plenty and tranquillity during all the time of His Majesties most blessed Reign (to the admiration and astonishment of all neighbouring Nations) and in delivering this His Majesties Kingdom of *England* in particular from severall heavy visitations of the Plague and Pestilence: And His Majestie taking into His Princely consideration the many important causes, and extraordinary occasions calling upon him, and His people for a joynt and generall humiliation of all estates of this Kingdom, before Almighty God in prayer and fasting, aswell for averting the heavy calamities of Sicknesse and War, justly deserved by unthankfulnesse to him for his blessings upon this Nation above all others, and the other crying sins of the people, as also for drawing down His blessing upon His Majestie and His people: His Majestie therefore doth by His Royall Proclamation straightly charge and command, that a generall, publike, and solemn Fast be kept and holden, aswell by abstinence from food, as by publike prayers and hearing of the word of God, and other Sacred duties, in all Cathedrall, Collegiate, and parish churches, and chappels within this Kingdom of *England*, and Dominion of *Wales*, upon Wednesday the eighth day of July, next ensuing the date hereof: And for the more orderly solemnizing *[as 1626–E2*: thereof ... such Prayers and*]* publike exhortations, as are fit to be used in all churches and chappells, on that day and occasion. And he hath given in charge to His said Arch-bishops, and Bishops, to disperse *[as 1626–E2*: the same throwout His whole Kingdome ... so religious a Worke*]*.

FORM OF PRAYER

PREFACE

We are taught by many and sundry examples of holy Scriptures, that upon occasion of particular Punishments, Afflictions, and Perils, which God of his most just judgement hath sometimes sent amongst his people, to shew his anger against sin, and to call them to repentance, and to the amendment of their lives, all men ought to be provoked *[as 1563–E*: and styred vp ... in that transgression*]*. This was done by the vertuous Kings, *David*, *Iosaphat*, and *Ezekias*,[321] in their distresses of Pestilence, War, & forraign Invasions. So did the King and people of *Nineve*, and *Hester*[322] fall to humble Prayers in like perils of their people. So did *Daniel* in his Captivity,[323] & many other moe in their severall troubles and afflictions. Now therefore calling to minde that God hath been provoked by us to threaten, and begin to visit us at this present both with the Plague, and other grievous Judgements; It hath been thought meet to excite and stir up all godly people within this Realm, to pray earnestly and heartily to God to forgive us our sins, and consequently to turn away his deserved wrath from us, and to restore us to his gracious favour, and to our bodily health. And

---

[321] In margin: '2 Sam 24.14 2 Chro. 20.5 2 Kings 19.1 Jonah 3'.
[322] In margin: 'Esth.r 14 13.'
[323] In margin: 'Dan 9.4'.

although it is every Christian mans duty, of his own devotion to pray at all times; yet for that the corrupt nature of man is so slothfull and negligent herein, he hath need by often and sundry means to be stirred up, and put in minde of his duty, according as is now commanded by His most Pious and Sacred Majestie.

MORNING PRAYER

Let the Minister beginning Seruice reade with a loud voice one of these sentences of Scripture *[Jer. 10:24, Joel 2:13]*

[The exhortation, 'Dearely beloued brethren'; the general confession; the absolution, the Lord's prayer and versicles].

A Psalme. Then shall be said this Psalme following, in stead of *Venite exultemus*, one Verse by the Priest, and another by the People or the Clerk.
O come, let us humble our selves, and fall down before the Lord with reverence and fear. (Ps. 95) [95:6]
For he is the Lord our God, and we are his people, and the sheep of his pasture. (Ps. 100) [100:2]
If a man will not turn, God will whet his sword, he hath bent his bowe, and made it ready. (Ps. 7) [7:13]
Let us repent … [as 1563–E until]
We have provoked thine anger, O Lord, and thy heavy displeasure is kindled against us. (Lam. 3) [Lam. 3:?]
But there is mercy with thee, that thou mayest be feared, and thou art full of compassion. (Ps. 130) [130:4]
Thy hand is not shortned … *[as 1563–E until]*
Help us, O God of our salvation, for the glory of thy Name: O deliver us, and be mercifull unto our sins, for thy Names sake. [Ps. 79:9]
The sacrifice of God is a troubled spirit: a broken and contrite heart, O God, shalt thou not despise. [Ps. 51:17]
O be favourable and gracious unto Sion: build thou the walls of Jerusalem. [51:18]
So we that be thy people … *[as 1563–E to end of psalm]*

The Psalmes appointed, are the 6. 32. 38. 39. 51. 90. 91. 102. 130. 143. whereof the five first are to be read at Morning, and the five last at Evening prayer.

The Psalmes ended, reade one of these Chapters following for the first Lesson. [1 Kgs. 8; 2 Sam. 24; Joel 2; or Jonah 3]

[Te Deum]

For the second Lesson, reade one of these Chapters,
[Matt. 6; Matt. 8; Matt. 9; or Luke 13]

[Benedictus or Jubilate]
[Apostles' creed]
[The creed]

And after that, these prayers following, as well at Euening Prayer, as at Morning prayer, all deuoutly kneeling, the Minister first pronouncing with a loud voice.
  The Lorde be with you.
  And with thy Spirit.

Let vs pray.

[The Lord's prayer]
[Kyrie eleison]

Then the Priest standing vp, shall say.
  O Lord shew thy mercy vpon you *[as 1625–E]*

The first Collect.
  O most mercifull and gracious Lord, we wretched and miserable sinners humbly beseech thee in mercy and compassion to behold our great afflictions: for thy wrath is gone out, and thine indignation is kindled against us. We confesse, O Lord, that thy judgements are just, for we have multiplied our transgressions like the sand of the sea, and the cry of them hath been so great, that it hath pierced the heavens, and called for vengeance against us: But we beseech thee, O Lord, forget not thou to be gracious, and shut not up thy loving kindnesse in displeasure; turn thee again, and be mercifull unto thy servants. Help us, O God of our salvation, for the glory of thy Name; O deliver us, and be mercifull unto our sins for thy Names sake: Take thy Plague, and all other Judgements from us, that we be not consumed by the means of thy heavy hand upon our sins. O satisfie us with thy mercy, and that soon; so shall we that be thy people, and sheep of thy pasture, give thee thanks for ever, and will always be shewing forth thy praise from generation to generation. Grant this, O mercifull Father, we beseech thee, for Jesus Christ his sake our onely Saviour and Redeemer. Amen.

[The collects for peace and for grace]

Litany

[The litany to the versicle before 'We humbly beseech thee' at the end of the litany, the three prayers following (the second was based on the BCP collect for the fourth Sunday in Lent)]
  O eternall God, and most gracious Father *[as 1626–E2]*

Grant we beseech thee, Almighty God, that we which for our evill deeds, and our great unthankfulnesse are worthily punished, by the comfort of thy Grace may mercifully be relieved through our Lord Jesus Christ. Amen.

Almighty and most mercifull Father, who for our many and grievous sinnes (those especially which we have committed since our last solemn humiliation before thee) might most justly have cut us off, but in the multitude of thy mercies hast hitherto spared us: Accept, we most heartily beseech thee, our unfeigned sorrow for all our former transgressions, and grant that we may never so presume of thy mercy, as to despise the riches of thy goodnesse, but that thy forbearance, and long suffering may lead us to repentance, and amendment of our sinfull lives, to thy honour and glory, and our eternall salvation at the last day through Jesus Christ our Lord. Amen.

['We humbly beseech thee' to the end of the litany]

THE LATTER SERUICE[324]

The Priest standing at the North side of the Lords Table, shall say
[The Lord's prayer, followed by the communion service from the BCP to the end of the prayer for the king, 'Almighty God, whose kingdom is everlasting']

[In place of the collect for the day, the BCP collect for Ash Wednesday and the following (based on the BCP collect for the fifth Sunday after Trinity)]
Grant Lord, we beseech thee, that the course of this world may be so ordered by thy governance, that thy Church may joyfully serve thee in all godly quietnesse, through Jesus Christ. Amen.

[Epistle: Joel 2:12–17]
[Gospel: Matt. 6:16–21]
[Nicene creed]
[Offertory sentence: Matt. 5:16]

[After the prayer for the whole state of the church, the prayer 'O Most mighty God and merciful Father' from the BCP commination service; the BCP collect for the third Sunday after Epiphany; the BCP collect for Septuagesima; the collects 'Assist us mercifully, O Lord' and 'O almighty Lord and everliving God' from the BCP communion service; the BCP collect for the twlfth Sunday after Trinity; the collect 'Almighty God, which hast promised to hear' from the BCP communion service]

[The blessing]

EVENING PRAYER

[Opening sentences: Jer. 10:24, Joel 2:13]
[The general confession; the absolution; the Lord's prayer and versicles].

Read the Psalmes that were left unread at Morning Prayer.[325]

For the first Lesson, reade one of the Chapters appointed, and unread at Morning prayer.

Then the Magnificat, or the Psalme, O come let us humble our selves, *&c, as before in Morning Prayer.*

[The Magnificat]

---

[324] I.e. the communion service.
[325] I.e. Ps. 90, 91, 102, 130, 143.

For the second Lesson, read one of these Chapters, [Rom. 6; 1 Cor. 10:1–15; 2 Cor. 9; or 1 Thess. 4]

[Apostles' creed]
[Kyrie eleison]
[The Lord's prayer]

Then the Priest standing up, shall say.
   O Lord shew thy mercy vpon you *[as at morning prayer]*

[In place of the first collect, the prayer 'Turn thou us, O good Lord' from the BCP commination service; after the second collect, the prayer 'We humbly beseech thee' from the end of the BCP litany, the BCP prayers for the king, for the royal family, and for the bishops and curates]

AN HOMILY OF REPENTANCE, AND OF TRUE RECONCILIATION UNTO GOD.[326]

1640–S2   Fast days during preparations for war with England

Sunday 23 August and Thursday 27 August 1640 (Scotland)

This fast was appointed by the general assembly which met at Aberdeen from 28 July to 5 August. The assembly's act was not printed, instructions regarding the fast being conveyed to presbyteries by their commissioners to the assembly. The sources differ about the dates of the fast; it may have been observed on 28 August in some places. The fast coincided with preparations for war. Sir John Conyers reported that the causes made particular reference to the safety of Edinburgh, to the king's commission to the earl of Northumberland to raise forces against Scotland and to the continuing lack of courts of justice (see 1640–S1), in spite of which there were no serious dissensions.

Order: act of the general assembly, *c.* 1 Aug. 1640 (not found).
Sources: presbytery of Dalkeith minutes, NRS, CH2/424/3, p. 56; presbytery of Peebles minutes, NRS, CH2/295/2, fo. 103v; presbytery of Perth minutes, NRS, CH2/299/1, p. 389; *Letters and journals of Robert Baillie*, I, 258; Sir John Conyers to Sir Henry Vane, 21 Aug. 1640, SP16/464/59, fo. 131r (*CSPD, Apr.–Aug. 1640*, pp. 614–15).

1640–E2   Prayers during Charles I's military campaign against the Scottish covenanters

[After Wednesday 8 July?–August] 1640 (England and Wales)

Although the 'Short Parliament' had refused to vote Charles any subsidies to pay for the war with Scotland, the king continued to plan his military campaign. In

---

[326] *Two books of homilies*, pp. 525–49

England, there was growing support for the Scots, especially after the convocation of the Church of England, instructed by Charles to remain sitting after parliament was dissolved, passed a new set of canons, drawn up by Laud. These enforced many of the changes to ceremony and practice introduced by Laud and opposed by puritans. They stated that taxes were due 'by the law of God, nature and nations' and introduced a new oath not to consent to alter the state of the church in the future. The former was interpreted as supporting arbitrary government; the latter potentially bound those who took the oath to oppose any act of parliament that lawfully altered the church settlement. No order is extant to indicate when this prayer was issued, but it was presumably after the fast day for plague on 8 July (see 1640–E1). There were a number of cases of non-observance, including in the puritan strongholds of Northampton and Bedford; the regime also investigated reports about those loyal to Charles who did not conform exactly to the orders. Matthew Hazard (or Hassard) of St Andrew's, Bristol, was reported for replacing the words 'especially against those his traitorous subjects, who, having cast off all obedience to their anointed Sovereign, do at this time, in rebellios manner, seek to invade this realm' with 'and now and evermore detect and reveal unto him [the King] all those traitorous enemies in this kingdome that disturb the peace of the realms, and that vex and molest the hearts of Thy Church and faithful people'. Some parishioners also reported their ministers for failing to observe the day properly. Those of Tenterden in Kent complained to parliament's committee for religion that 'to their great greife' their minister, Dr Humphrey Peake, had 'very slightly performed' 'so holy and religious a work' (i.e. the prayer). He and his curate being absent, the newly ordained schoolmaster was forced to conduct the service but had preached for 'little more than halfe an houre'; a fast (it is unclear if this was organized by the parish or was ordered by the crown) 'not being continued a competent and convenient time, as hath beene heretofore used, a good part of the day was, by the ruder sorte, spent in the alehouses, to the great dishonour of Almighty God'.

Order: none found.
Form of prayer: *A prayer for the kings majestie in his expedition against the rebels of Scotland; to be said in all churches in time of divine service, next after the prayer for the queen and royall progenie* (1 p.; STC 16558)*
Form of prayer (other edition): STC 16558.5.
Additional sources: examination of Thomas Pidgeon, joiner, 28 Sept. 1640, SP16/468/76, fos. 127r–127v; answer of John Bradshaw, clerk, 7 Oct. 1640, SP16/469/52, fo. 107r; note of the words interposed by Mr Hazard of Bristol, 23 Sept. 1640, SP16/467/147, fo. 286r; *Proceedings principally in the county of Kent*, ed. Larking, pp. 229–33.

FORM OF PRAYER

O eternall God, *[as 1639–E*: and mercifull Father … Honour and*]* good Successe; especially against those His Trayterous Subjects, who having cast off all obedience to their Anointed Soveraign, do at this time in Rebellious manner seek to invade this Realm. Grant, blessed Lord *[as 1639–E*: that Victory … Thine and His]* treacherous Enemies. Inable Him (blessed Father) so to vanquish and subdue them all, that His Loyall Subjects being setled in Peace, and the true fear of thy holy Name, He may return with Joy and Honour, and continue to govern His Kingdoms in Peace, and Plenty, and in the happinesse of true Religion and Piety all His dayes. These blessings, and whatsoever else shall be necessary for Him, or for our selves, we humbly beg of thee, O mercifull Father, for Jesus Christ his sake, our onely Mediatour and Redeemer. Amen.

1640–E3 Fast days during plague, war and momentous public affairs

Tuesday 17 November 1640 (London, suburbs and specified adjoining parishes); Tuesday 8 December 1640 (elsewhere in England and Wales)

On 20 August 1640, an 18,000-strong Scottish covenanter army led by Alexander Leslie invaded England. It defeated the king's forces, commanded by Conway, at the battle of Newburn on 28 August, and occupied much of Northumberland and the town of Newcastle. Although the king travelled north with reinforcements, he gradually accepted the weakness of his military and political position, and sought to conciliate his critics by summoning a Great Council of Peers at York on 24 September and then agreeing to call a new parliament and negotiating a truce with the Scots, by the treaty of Ripon on 26 October. Three days after what became known as the 'Long Parliament' had been convened on 3 November, Sir Miles Fleetwood proposed that the House of Commons should petition the king for a general fast. He himself did not specify a reason for this, but the petition subsequently submitted by the Commons declared that a fast would prepare parliament to address the problems of the condition of religion and the safety and welfare of the king and realm, and would help the two houses to obtain divine assistance in their deliberations. Joined by the House of Lords, royal approval was easily secured. But in contrast to earlier fasts that had been initiated by parliament, the royal proclamation ordering the fast days made little reference to its contribution – presumably an indication of the king's strained relationship with parliament. The form of prayer very largely re-used the text for 1640–E1, with the addition at the end of the litany of the prayer for parliament from 1625–E (though, as in a number of forms in the 1620s, this prayer was printed at the beginning of the form). The occasion is the first for which we have descriptions of how the service was conducted in parish churches. The Northampton lawyer Robert Woodford noted in his diary on 17 November that 'This day was held a publiq fast here in London & some adiacent parishes by his Majesty's proclamacon ... god did wonderfully enlarge the harts of his ministers & people, I was at Aldermanbury Church [i.e. St Mary Aldermanbury, London] about 14 houres together where 3 ministers prayed & preached one after another, Mr [Edmund] Calamy & 2 strangers.' He also reported that Stephen Marshall and Cornelius Burges preached before the Commons at St Margaret's, Westminster: 'they delivered glorious things with extraordinary zeale & fervor'. '[T]his hath bene a heavenly day Lord heare the prayers of thy people worked a holy reformacon & make this nacon a pray ... the whole earth for the Lords sake', he concluded. Woodford observed the fast again on 8 December in his home parish of St Peter's, Northampton. Here, William Holmes, the curate, preached in the morning, and the minister, Thomas Ball, 'stood about 4 houres & dimi in the afternoon & prayed and preached very well'. In a comment that reveals the rapid shift in puritan attitudes, Woodford remarked: 'blessed be god Lord remove Bishops & Idolatry & superstition & pestering Ceremonyes & thy plagues out of the Land, & send forth thy light & thy truth for the Lords sake'.

Order: royal proclamation, 11 Nov. 1640, STC 9170* [printed in Larkin, II, 734–6].
Form of prayer: *A forme of common prayer: to be used upon the 17th of November, and the 8th of December: on which dayes a fast is appointed by his majesties proclamation, for the removing of the plague, and other judgements of God, from this kingdome. Set forth by authority* (88 pp.; STC 16559)*.
Additional sources: *CJ*, II, 20–3; *LJ*, IV, 84–6, 92–3, 116; *Woodford*, pp. 375, 380.

ORDER

Royal proclamation: 11 November 1640

The Kings most Excellent Majestie, observing the correcting hand of God upon the Kingdom in many yeers Pestilence, the present interruptions of that long continued blessing of Peace, and other signes of his anger for the sins of the Land; and seriously considering the weighty affairs of State now in agitation in the high Court of Parliament, out of His truly Religious heart to God, and His tender care of His Kingdom and peoples welfare (according to the practise of pious Kings and Princes in former ages, in times of common calamities, which concern both Prince and people) hath resolved (with the humble advice of the Lords and Commons now assembled in Parliament) by a solemn and publike Fast, in the first place to have recourse to the Divine Majestie, to implore his mercy and favour to Him and His people, as well for removing the present Judgements, as for a blessing upon the great Affairs and businesses in hand concerning His Majestie and the Publike. And therefore His Majestie doth hereby straitly charge and command that a generall and publike Fast be kept and holden, as well by abstinence from Food, as by publike Prayers and hearing the Word of God, and other sacred Duties, in all Cathedrall, Collegiate, and Parish Churches and Chappels within the City of *London*, the Suburbs thereof, and the adjoyning Parishes of Saint *Clement Danes*, Saint *Giles in the fields*, Saint *James* at *Clarkenwell*, Saint *Katharine Tower*, Saint *Leonard Shoreditch*, Saint *Martins in the fields*, Saint *Mary Whitechappell*, Saint *Magdalene Bermond*, and *Savoy* Parish, upon Tuesday the seventeenth day of this instant November: And in all other Cathedrall, Collegiate, and Parish Churches and Chappels within the Kingdom of *England*, and Dominion of *Wales*, upon Tuesday the eighth day of December next ensuing the date hereof: All which His Majestie *[as 1626–E2*: doth expresly charge and command … so religious a Worke*]*.

FORM OF PRAYER

PREFACE
We are taught *[as 1640–E1*: by many and sundry examples … to turn away his deserved wrath from us, and*]* to restore us to his gracious favour. And although it is every Christian mans duty *[as 1640–E1*: of his own devotion … His most Pious and Sacred Majestie*]*.

[As 1640–E1 until]

LITANY

[At the end of the litany, the following prayer for parliament was to be read in place of the other appointed prayers at the minister's discretion]

Most gracious God, wee humbly beseech thee *[and as 1625–E, 'A prayer for the High Court of Parlament']*.

[As 1640–E1 to end]

1641–ES Thanksgiving day for the peace treaty of London

Tuesday 7 September 1641 (England and Wales, Scotland)

Following the truce agreed at Ripon in October 1640, negotiations between Scottish commissioners and the crown continued, leading to the treaty of London, which the king ratified on 25 August during a visit to Scotland. Under its terms, Charles recognized the abolition of episcopacy in Scotland and consequently the full establishment of presbyterian church government there, together with various constitutional reforms which had been proposed by the Scottish parliament in June 1640. The treaty also provided for a public thanksgiving in both kingdoms, the first time special worship was held on the same day and for the same purpose in the two realms. In England and Wales, this was ordered by parliamentary ordinance, possibly because Charles was absent in Scotland; even so, the ordinance was a notable constitutional innovation. The ordinance was printed in two versions. It is not clear why, as both were printed by the same printers, the royal printers, Robert Barker and the assignees of John Bill. Printed below is the longer of the two; the variant omitted the final two paragraphs. No Scottish order has been traced. As was normal, no form of prayer was commissioned for use in Scotland. Nor was an official form of prayer ordered or published for England and Wales. This was very much in contrast to normal practice since the 1550s, given the provisions and assumptions of the act of uniformity. Instead, the only text that was ordered to be read in every parish church was the text of the ordinance itself, with its requirement that all the king's subjects should manifest their 'loyalty and faithfulnes' at the time of the thanksgiving. This requirement, agreed by the king, had been requested by the Scottish treaty commissioners, presumably as a form of covenant and commitment to the terms of the treaty. Otherwise, the ordinance 'ordained' that the thanksgivings on the appointed day, Tuesday 7 September, should be expressed through unspecified 'Prayers, Reading, and Preaching of the Word'. The absence of any text for services or prayers resulted from the hostility of many godly MPs and peers towards set forms of prayer, including, increasingly, the BCP itself. This was also demonstrated by the reaction of the House of Commons to the publication by John Williams, bishop of Lincoln and dean of Westminster, of a form of prayer for use in his own diocese and at Westminster: the text of this form is printed below. Bishops and other senior clergy had been entitled since 1559 to order and commission prayers and services in their own jurisdictions, and Williams's form did not infringe the act of uniformity nor the terms of the parliamentary ordinance. Nevertheless, on 6 September the House of Commons declared that Williams had no right to issue a form of prayer, and ordered that it should not be used. Despite the growing religious and political tensions between the king and his critics, the thanksgiving services were reported to be well attended. Stephen Marshall and Jeremiah Burroughes were appointed to preach before the Commons at St Margaret's; both their sermons were printed.

Order: ENGLAND AND WALES: parliamentary ordinance, 27 Aug. 1641, Wing E1797* (shorter variant, Wing E1796); SCOTLAND: not found.
Form of prayer: none ordered.
Form of prayer (other edition): *A form of thanksgiving, to be used the seventh of September thorovvout the diocese of Lincoln, and in the jurisdiction of Westminster* (s.n.; 7 pp.; Wing C4181A)* [attributed to John Williams on BL, Thomason E.171[12]].
Additional sources: *RPS*, 1641/8/21, 1641/8/23, 1641/8/24; order of the Lords and Commons, 30 Aug.

1640, SP16/483/100, fo. 196r; *CJ*, II, 253, 273–82, 286; *LJ*, IV, 158, 343–4, 359–62, 375, 377–84, 395; *FSP*, I, 5–6; presbytery of Dalkeith minutes, NRS, CH2/424/3, p. 77; presbytery of Elgin minutes, NRS, CH2/144/1, p. 51.
Printed sermons: Marshall, House of Commons (Wing M766; *FSP*, I, 205–60); Burroughes, House of Commons (Wing B6119; *FSP*, I, 261–332).

ORDER

England and Wales: parliamentary ordinance, 27 August 1641

Whereas it hath pleased Almighty God to give a happy close to the Treaty of Peace between the two Nations of ENGLAND and SCOTLAND, by his wise providence, defeating the evill hopes of the subtill Adversaries of both Kingdoms; For which great Mercy it was by the Kings most Excellent Majestie, the Lords and Commons in this present Parliament Enacted, That there should be a publike Thanksgiving in all the Parish Churches of his Majesties Dominions;

It is now ordained and declared by the Lords and Commons in Parliament, That the time for the Celebration of that publike Thanks to Almighty God for so great and publike a Blessing shall be on Tuesday the seventh of September next, by Prayers, Reading, and Preaching of the Word in all Churches and Chappels of this Realm, whereof We require a carefull and due observance: That we may joyn in giving Thanks, as we partake of the Blessing, with our Brethren in SCOTLAND, who have designed the same day for that duty.

According to the Act of this present Parliament *For confirmation of the Treatie of Pacification between the two Kingdoms of* ENGLAND *and* SCOTLAND, where it was desired by the Commissioners of *Scotland*, that the loyalty and faithfulnes of His Majesties Subjects might be made known at the time of the publike Thanksgiving in all places, and particularly in all Parish Churches of His Majesties Dominions; which Request was graciously condescended unto by His Majestie, and confirmed by the said Act:

It is now ordered and commanded by both Houses of Parliament, that the same be effectually done in all Parish Churches thorowout this Kingdom upon Tuesday the seventh day of September next coming at the time of the publike Thanksgiving by the severall and respective Ministers of each Parish Church, or by their Curats, who are hereby required to read this present Order in the Church.

FORM OF PRAYER

[For diocese of Lincoln and Westminster Abbey]

Read after, O Lord open thou our lips, *&c, these Psalmes: Psal. 95. Psal. 96. Psal. 122. 126. 133. 136. Being all short Psalmes.*

Then   1. Lesson. *Jerem.* 31
        2. Lesson. *Matth.* 24.

Adde to the Collects this Prayer.

We humbly acknowledge before thee, O most mercifull Father, that all the punishments which are threatned in thy Law, might justly have fallen upon us, by reason of our great transgressions, and hardnesse of heart. It was most just, O Lord, that thou didst lately threaten us with a pulling back and withdrawing of all those Spirituall Graces and Temporall Blessings, wherewith this Island did flow and abound above all the nations of the earth: It was most just (and our sins did well deserve it) that thou, by withdrawing the Cooperation of thy holy Spirit, shouldest suffer our Faith to grow weak and feeble, our Charity cold, our Hope wavering and without foundation, our hearing of thy holy word, our partaking of thy blessed Sacraments, our Praying and Invocating of thy sacred Name, to become in both Priest and People, for want of true Devotion and the inward guidance of thy Spirit, but as it were so many outward Fashions, Forms, and Complements. And especially most agreeable it was unto all the Rules of thy Divine Justice, that from those in whom these Spirituall could not be found, thy Temporall blessings should be withdrawn: That our Plentie should be turned into Want and Famine, our Health into Sicknesses, Plagues, and Pestilences, and our long Peace (the Crown of all these blessings, and the Envie of all the Nations round about us) into the worst and most miserable of all Wars, a Civil War, a War of Christian against Christian, Neighbours against Neighbours, Brethren against Brethren, a War of *Ephraim* against *Manasseh*, of *Manasseh* against *Ephraim*, and of both these against thy *Judah*.

But the more justly, O Lord, thou mightest have visited us in this thy fury and anger, the more are we, dust and ashes, worms & no men, most wretched and miserable sinners, bound to praise and blesse thy holy Name for thy unspeakable goodnesse and mercies shewed unto us at this time: That it hath pleased thee, upon our weak and unworthy humiliation, to begin some small measure and degree of Reformation in us, to plant in our hearts some more sense and feeling of thy spirituall Graces, some more steadinesse of Faith, fervencie of Love, assurance of Hope, Zeal in Prayer, Devotion in the Hearing of thy holy Word, and in the receiving and administring of those heavenly Seals and Pledges of the same. And by and by after, as delighted with these green and raw fruits, which thine own hand had planted, to reward and crown them, unripned as they be, with great abundance of temporall blessings, with Corn, and Wine, and Oyl, with good times and seasons, with a shew rather then any showre of Diseases, which serve only to keep us awake, that we fall not into that former drowsinesse and forgetfulnes of our selves and thee.

But especially, as a strong fence and hedge to compasse in and preserve all these outward Blessings, thou hast given us a speedy and a happy Union and Peace with all our Neighbours and Brethren of this Island, making us a multitude of one Heart and of one Soul, as thou hadst before made us a multitude of one Lord, one Faith, and one Baptisme. The which thy great work of Union thou hast thus atchieved and effected, not (as thou mightest have done) by putting a sword into the hand of the stronger to devour the weaker, but by sending down thy holy Spirit, the Spirit of Wisdom and Understanding, the Spirit of Counsell and Providence, into the Hearts of our Gracious King, and the Peers and Commons now assembled in Parliament, thus by a wise and timely disposing of a few drops of our trash and worldly pelf, to prevent the unnaturall spilling of whole Channels and Rivers of Christian blood, to the great danger and hazard of so many bodies and souls.

For these thy great and unspeakable mercies, O Lord, we praise thee, we blesse thee, we worship thee, we glorifie thee, we give thanks unto thee for thy great glory, O Lord God heavenly King, God the Father Almighty, the onely begotten Son Jesus Christ; to whom with the Holy Ghost be all praise, honour and glory this day particularly, and withall for evermore.

Lastly, that we may be the better disposed to take thy Prayses into our mouths, plant in our hearts a true desire to be reformed. Convert us, O Lord, that we may be converted. Perfect this work of sanctification which thou hast begun in us. Encrease our Faith, enflame our Charity, strengthen our Hope, kindle our Devotion in the hearing, & our care in the practising of thy holy Word. Seal up all these graces in our Souls by the reverent and awfull receiving of thy holy Sacraments, make us to run the wayes of thy Commandments, now that thou hast set our hearts at liberty. And let these spirituall, O heavenly Father; be unto thee a further occasion to pour upon us more and more of thy temporall Blessings; by preserving our King, Queen and the Royall Issue, in all health and prosperity, by increasing more and more the Spirit of Wisdom and Understanding upon the Lords and Commons assembled in Parliament, by a stronger knitting and uniting of the Hearts of all these Nations one with another, which thou hast thus united under one Crown and Scepter, and by increasing our thankfulnesse and acknowledgement unto thee, in some measure and proportion of this increase of thy favours and mercies towards us: That so we may (as much as flesh and blood is permitted to do) begin the Church Triumphant in this Church Militant, and practice those Praises here on earth, which we shall more perfectly sing out in the kingdom of Heaven, by the Grace and Merits of our Lord and Saviour Jesus Christ. To whom with the Father, and the Holy Ghost, three Persons, and one Eternall, Everliving God, be all honour, glory, praise and dominion this day especially, and withall for evermore. Amen.

1641–S   Fast days in response to domestic divisions, the Irish rebellion and distress of continental protestants, for the success of the Scottish and English parliaments and for the security of the church

Sunday 14 November 1641 (Edinburgh and where possible); Sunday 28 November 1641 (elsewhere in Scotland)

In August 1641, Charles I arrived in Edinburgh to attend parliament, which then approved the treaty of London, ratifying the covenanters' reforms (see 1641–ES). However, tensions between the king and the covenanters were inflamed by a rumoured royalist plot to seize three leading nobles (the 'Incident' of 12 October) and, in late October, by news of the rising of Irish catholics. Parliament appointed this fast on the request of the commission of the general assembly. The causes reflected the importance of events in Ireland and England, but also showed an awareness of the circumstances of continental protestants.

Order: parliamentary ordinance, 4 Nov. 1641, *RPS*, 1641/8/138.
Causes: *RPS*, A1641/8/103 [from *The acts of the parliaments of Scotland*, ed. Thomas Thomson and Cosmo Innes (12 vols., Edinburgh, 1814–75), V, 692].
Additional sources: minutes of the commission of the general assembly, 1641, NLS, Wod. Fol. LXV, fos. 14v, 15r; Balfour, III, 136, 153; presbytery of Perth minutes, NRS, CH2/299/1, p. 407; Sir Henry Vane to Edward Nicholas, 9 Nov. 1641, SP16/485/67, fos. 167r–v (*CSPD, June 1641–Dec. 1643*, pp. 160–1).

ORDER

Parliamentary ordinance: 4 November 1641

The quhilk day the paper produceit be the commissioneres of the kirke, conteyneing the causs of the publict fast to be indicted, being publictlie red in audience of the parliament, his majestie and estates of parliament appoyntes the same to be givine to the ministeres that they may cause intimat the same to all the kingdome; and appoynt the fast to be upoun Sonday cum eight dayes for this sherefdome and all places adjacent that may be adverteised in due tyme, and for the rest of Scotland upoun the last Sonday of this moneth. For whilke end, the paper was instantlie givine to Maister James Bonar to be delyvered to the ministeres.

CAUSES

1. The divisiounes and distractiones in this kingdome, the rebellioun in Ireland, the distresses of the Palatinat and of the reformed kirkis of Germanie, quhich tend to the incres of poperie, the ruyne of the reformed religioun and to the disturbance of the peace of the kingis majestie and his kingdomes.

2. In place of thankfulnes and zeale, our ingratitude for so great mercies as we have laitlie receaved, our many sinnes of all sorts witnessing our want of the love of God and our nichtbour, contrair to our late solemne oath and Nationall Covenant, and our deepe securitie and indispositioun in the most pairt to the exerceiss of pietie.

3. To pray the more earnestlie to God for a speedie and happie cloise of the parliamentis of both kingdomes, for the preservatioun of this kirk in the treuthe and the kingdomes in unitie under his majesties happie governement, to disapoynt all secreit conspiracies and oppin rebelliounes, and to blisse all the reformed kirkis with puritie of religioun and peace.

1641–Ir   Weekly fast days during the rebellion

Fridays weekly [starting December] 1641 (Ireland)

This occasion is only known through Steele. ESTC lists no extant copies of the proclamation, and no form of prayer. Without either, it is difficult to establish the precise reasons for the occasion but it should be noted that, in October, the Irish rebellion, led by Rory O'More, Lord Conor Maguire, Hugh MacMahon and Sir Phelim O'Neill, broke out in response to English plantations, the harsh governance of Lord-Lieutenant Wentworth and his successors, religious grievances and poor harvests. Approximately 3,000 people were massacred and many others fled to England. As rumours circulated about the growing number of dead, suspicions rose that the king was involved; these were reinforced when O'Neill claimed they had risen in response to Charles's order.

Order: proclamation by the lords justices and council, 27 Nov. 1641, Wing I613 [no copy found; formerly Dublin PRO (destroyed); see Steele, II, no. 356].
Form of prayer: none found.

1641–E Fast days and monthly fast days during the Irish rebellion [and continued after until 1649]

Wednesday 22 December 1641 (parliament and London); Thursday 23 December 1641 (Westminster); Thursday 20 January 1642 (elsewhere in England and Wales); Wednesday 23 February 1642 and last Wednesday of every month during the Irish rebellion [and continued until 1649] (England and Wales)

Rumours of large-scale massacres in Ulster – of as many as 20,000 people – circulated in London throughout November and December, making tensions run high. On 13 December, the Commons ordered the Committee for Irish Affairs to consider the ordering of a general fast together with a special collection on behalf of those protestants fleeing the Irish rebellion (see 1641–Ir); a delegation from the lower house met with the Lords on the same day. On 14 December, the Commons' proposal was read in the Lords, but there was no further action because a dispute over parliamentary privileges developed immediately afterwards when Charles came to parliament to criticize its delay in passing the bill for the pressing of soldiers to go to Ireland. There was no further discussion of the fast until 17 December, when the proposal was approved by the Commons. Following a conference, both Lords and Commons agreed that the fast be held on Wednesday 22 December for parliament and the City of London, on Thursday 23 December for Westminster and on Thursday 20 January for the rest of the kingdom. On 18 December, the Commons received news from the Lords that Charles had assented to the fast and the proposed dates for it. It then ordered that City MPs should 'take the best and speediest Course they can, for publishing through the City the Directions for the Fast to be observed on *Wednesday* next'. Edmund Calamy and Stephen Marshall were appointed to preach before the Commons; John Williams, formerly bishop of Lincoln and recently elevated to York, and James Ussher, archbishop of Armagh, were appointed to preach before the Lords. As had been common in the 1620s, parliament and Westminster observed the fast on different days because MPs and Lords needed to use St Margaret's, Westminster and the Abbey for their own services. The fast had been proposed in the midst of conflict between parliament and the crown over the Grand Remonstrance, which attacked some of Charles's advisors as 'Jesuited Papists' and called for a general synod of the godly to be assembled to reform the church. By the time the parliamentary fast took place tensions had risen further: the City elections had put allies of the Commons' leader John Pym in control of the common council, and the king had responded by appointing Colonel Thomas Lunsford as lieutenant of the Tower. On 23 December, doubtless responding to the delay in the issuing of a royal proclamation for the fast, the Commons, having thanked its preachers, resolved that its order, 'reciting his Majesty's Royal Assent thereunto', be printed and sent to sheriffs, for distribution to constables and other local officers in their counties and boroughs. This was the first time that the Commons had been directly and publicly involved in ordering the distribution of orders or forms. The incident also revealed the growing tension between the parliamentary majority and the king, both specifically over the ordering of nationwide prayers, fasts and thanksgivings, and more generally over the condition of the church and the nature of royal government.

    Later on 23 December, the rift between king and parliament became wider, when the Commons received Charles's letter rejecting the Grand Remonstrance. As part of its response, on the next day the Commons passed a resolution, which was agreed to by the Lords on 28 December, petitioning the king to issue a proclamation not only for the public fast on 20 January, but also for a monthly fast, to be observed by parliament and the whole kingdom 'during the Troubles of *Ireland*'. On 30 December, the Commons impeached twelve bishops for petitioning the king to declare parliament's proceedings null and void because they had been excluded from the House of Lords; the Lords consented to this motion. On 2 January, Charles issued articles of high treason against five MPs; on the 4th, he unsuccessfully stormed parliament with an armed force to arrest them. On 5 January, Charles was mobbed by Londoners after failing to force the City council to surrender the five members and, five days later, he and his family left London. The royal proclamation, requested by parliament, was finally issued on 8 January, and significantly, like that for 1640–E3, it made no mention of parliament at all. Nor, however, did it order the composition of a form of prayer, the issue which had caused controversy in September. This proclamation inaugurated the series of monthly fasts which were to be continued after the suppression of the Irish rebellion, and which provided the occasion for a stream of parliamentary propaganda in the form of the fast sermons preached before the Commons and Lords. In October 1643, Charles responded to this hostile use of the fast days by ordering the end of the observance of the Wednesday fast and its replacement by a fast on the second Friday of every month (see 1643–E11(R)). But parliament continued to observe the Wednesday fast right through the first and second civil wars, until its abolition by the Rump on 23 April 1649 (see 1649–E2). In December 1644, the Westminster assembly of divines (see 1643–E7(P)) published directions for the observance of fast days, establishing a presbyterian model to replace the Church of England's order of fasting first issued in 1563. Observance of the fasts apparently became lax (see 1649–E2), but some historians have seen the days as a platform for radical preaching which encouraged the polarization of the parliament and country.

Orders: resolution of the House of Commons, 17 Dec. 1641; *CJ*, II, 348; agreement of the House of Lords, 17 Dec. 1641, *LJ*, IV, 480; royal proclamation, 8 Jan. 1642, Wing C2582* [printed in Larkin, II, 758–60].

Form of prayer: none ordered.

Additional sources: Sidney Bere to Sir John Pennington, 23 Dec. 1641, SP16/486/87, fos. 165r–166r; *CJ*, II, 341, 348–9, 353, 355–6; *LJ*, IV, 473–4, 480–1, 485, 488, 493; *CJ*, II, 341, 348–9, 353, 355–6; *LJ*, IV, 473–4, 480–1, 485, 488, 493; *Die Jovis 23. Decem. 1641* (1641; Wing E2778); *FSP*, II, 1, 4–5; warrant to the attorney general to prepare a proclamation, 3 Jan. 1642, SP16/488/3, fo. 11r; *Westminster assembly*, V, 154–8.

Printed sermons: Calamy, House of Commons (Wing C235; other editions C236, C237, C238, C239; *FSP*, II, 12–80); Marshall, House of Commons (Wing M770; *FSP*, II, 81–136).

ORDERS

Resolution of the House of Commons: 17 December 1641

Resolved, upon the Question, That this House doth assent unto *Wednesday* next to be the Day for the Fast for both Houses and the City of *London*; and *Thursday* for *Westminster*; [and] *Thursday* come Month for the whole Kingdom.

Agreement of the House of Lords: 17 December 1641

To let there Lordships know, that the House of Commons do fully agree to the Three Days appointed for the Fast; to which this House likewise agreed, and appointed the Lord Steward and the Lord Chamberlain to present the humble Desires of both Houses to the King, for keeping the Fast those Three Dayes accordingly.

Royal proclamation: 8 January 1642

His Majestie taking into His Princely and Pious consideration the lamentable and distressed estate of His good Subjects in His Majesties Kingdom of *Ireland*, and conceiving it to be a just and great occasion calling upon Him, and His people of this His Kingdom of *England* for a generall humiliation of all estates of this Kingdom before Almighty God, in Prayer and Fasting, for drawing down His Mercy and Blessing upon that Kingdom: His Majestie doth therefore by this His Proclamation straitly charge and command, that a Generall, Publike, and Solemn Fast be kept, and holden, as well by abstinence from Food, as by publike Prayers, Preaching, and Hearing of the Word of God, and other Sacred duties, in all Cathedrall, Collegiate, and Parish Churches and Chappels within this His Majesties Kingdom of *England*, and Dominion of *Wales* (His Majesties Cities of *London* and *Westminster* onely excepted, where it hath already been observed) on the twentieth day of this present moneth of Januarie.

And His Majestie doth further by this His Proclamation straitly charge and command, that a Generall, Publike, and Solemn Fast be kept and holden, as well by abstinence from Food, as by publike Prayers, Preaching, and Hearing of the Word of God, and other sacred Duties, in all Cathedrall, Collegiate, and Parish Churches and Chappels within this Kingdom of *England* and Dominion of *Wales* (without any exception) on the last Wednesday of the moneth of February next following the date hereof, and from thenceforth to continue on the last Wednesday of every moneth during the Troubles in the said Kingdom of *Ireland*. All which His Majestie doth expresly charge and command shall be reverently and devoutly performed by all His loving Subjects, as they tender the favour of Almighty God, and would avoid His just indignation against this Land, and upon pain of such punishments as His Majestie can justly inflict upon all such as shall contemn or neglect so religious a Work.

1642–Ir1 Monthly fast days during the Irish rebellion

Fridays monthly, beginning May 1642 (Dublin and surrounding area)

This occasion is known only through the proclamation of 30 April 1642. The context for the prayers was the continuation of the Irish rebellion (see 1641–Ir and 1641–E). The precedent for monthly fasts had been set by the proclamation for England in January (1641–E).

Order: proclamation by the lords justices and council, 30 Apr. 1642, Wing I395, National Library of Ireland, Dublin, MS 2541, fo. 26 [summarized in HMC, *Ormonde*, II, 7–8].
Form of prayer: none ordered.

ORDER

Proclamation by the lords justices and council: 30 April 1642

Forasmuch as Almighty God hath been pleased to shew his infinite goodnesse and mercie to His most Excellent Majestie, and all his liege people in this Kingdome, in the wonderfull discoverie of an horrible Treason and Conspiracie, intended by divers malignant and ill-affected Irish, and Papists, and their Adherents, against His Majesties Crown and Dignitie, the Professors of the Protestant Religion, and all the Brittish, and the descendents and Branches of the Brittish Nation, planted throughout this Kingdome, and other His Majesties loyall Subjects here, whom these Traytors threaten to extirpate and utterly roote out of this Land. And although the horrid and bloudie effecting and execution of the said intended Treason and Conspiracie, is hitherto by Gods Providence and mercie (to the unspeakable joy of His Majestie, and all His loyall and true-hearted people) prevented in His Maiesties Castle of Dublin, & in the Citty of Dublin, and in some other places of this Realme, Yet neverthelesse the said trayterous Conspiracie hath taken effect in many parts of this Kingdome, and the Conspirators and Actors therein, have with rage, and fury committed, and doe commit daily great outrages, spoiles, and inhumane cruelties upon great numbers of Protestants and persons of the Brittish Nation, and other His Majesties loyall Subjects in this Realm, and have made great destruction and depopulation of them, to the displeasure of Almighty God, the scandall of Christian Religion, and the dishonour of His Majestie. And now all the miseries of Warre and Famine doe imminently threaten this Cittie and Kingdome, and a further execution of Gods indignation may justly be expected to be powred down upon this City and Kingdome, for the sinnes and abominations thereof. Wherefore that laud and thanksgiving may be rendered to Almightie God, for this wonderfull discoverie and deliverance, and for those happy and prosperous successes, which God in mercie hath given unto Us against those Rebells, that Prayer and Supplication may be made unto God, to avert his severe wrath and indignation from this Kingdome, that his divine aid and assistance (who is the Lord of Hoasts) may be implored, still to strengthen and conserve His Majesties Armies for the utter subduing of the said ungracious and disloyall Rebells and Traytors, and that some relief in these calamitous times may the better be afforded for the poore of this Citty and suburbs thereof, and for such indigent persons as these Traytors by their rapine and crueltie have deprived of their fortunes, and left naked and miserable; We the Lords Justices and Councell doe in His Majesties name straitly charge and command, that once every moneth a Publique and Religious Fast be devoutly and piously observed and solemnized, in and throughout this whole City of Dublin and suburbs thereof, by all His Majesties people therein, and that Divine Service and Sermons be celebrated and heard upon the Fast day, in every Cathedrall and other Church and Chappell in this Citty and Suburbs thereof, and that on the Fast day, all Shops be kept shut, and no buying or selling admitted that day, so that neverthelesse the ordinarie defence of the said Citty and Suburbs be not thereby neglected. And We doe hereby command that the said Fast be observed monthly upon each Friday before the Sacrament, and shall continue so monethly untill Declaration be made to the contrarie. All which premises We command all His Majesties good Subjects within the places and precincts aforesaid, reverently and Christianly to performe, as they tender the Favour of Almighty God, and would avoid his just indignation, and upon paine of such punishment and censures as may be inflicted upon all such as shall neglect or contemne so Religious a work. And We doe hereby exhort and declare that We hold it a fitting and charitable thing, that every Housholder and Master of Familie, should designe and contribute in Almes upon every Sunday following the Fasting day, the value of so much as was the former week spared and saved by this commanded Abstinence, towards the relief and succour of the poore afore mentioned.

1642–S   Fast days in response to ignorance, wickedness, the Irish rebellion, English divisions and for religious unity and a good harvest

Sunday 11 September and Wednesday 14 September 1642 (Scotland)

The general assembly, which met in St Andrews from 27 July to 6 August 1642, received a declaration from the English parliament, affirming its desire to reform the Church of England in a manner 'agreeable to Gods Word' and conducive to 'a most firme and stable Union between the two Kingdomes' (*The principall acts of the foure generall assemblies*, second part, pp. 11–12). The assembly responded enthusiastically, urging the English to abolish episcopacy. Addressing Charles I in more measured terms, it stressed the importance of religious uniformity as a basis for peace between Scotland and England. The assembly's fast act reflected this agenda, and expressed pessimism about the situation across Charles's kingdoms. The terms of the act were communicated to presbyteries by letters or verbally, with the causes then being 'sent in write by the clerk of the assemblie' (presbytery of Peebles minutes, NRS, CH2/295/2, fo. 144v). The act was later included in the assembly's printed acts, which may have been published after the fast itself, probably because it appointed continuing prayers for the king and parliament.

Order: act of the general assembly, 6 Aug. 1642, Wing C4233A*, second part, pp. 34–5 [also in *Acts of the general assembly of the Church of Scotland, M.DC.XXXVIII.–M.DCCC.XLII* (Edinburgh, 1843), p. 72].
Additional sources: *The principall acts of the foure generall assemblies* (Edinburgh, 1642; Wing C4233A); *CJ*, II, 683–4; *LJ*, V, 227; presbytery of Dalkeith minutes, NRS, CH2/424/3, p. 92; presbytery of Peebles minutes, NRS, CH2/295/2, fo. 144; presbytery of Elgin minutes, NRS, CH2/144/1, p. 70; *Letters and journals of Robert Baillie*, II, 53.

ORDER

Act of the general assembly: 6 August 1642
The Generall Assembly being desirous to promove the great work of Unity in Religion, and Uniformity in Church-government, in all thir three Dominions, for which the Assembly hath humbly supplicat the Kings Majestie, and remonstrate their desires to the Parliament of *England*, lest they should be wanting in any meane that may further so glorious and so good a Work: Doe ordaine, that not only the said Declaration to the Parliament, and supplication to the Kings Majestie, shall be accompanied with the earnest Petitions and prayers of the whole Brethren in private and publick, for the Lords blessing thereunto, according to the laudable custome of our predecessors, who in the year of God 1589. ordaines that the Brethren in their private and publick prayers, recommend unto God the estate of the afflicted Church of *England*: But having just cause of fear, that the iniquities of the Land, which so much abound, may marre this so great a Work, doe also ordain a solemne Fast to be kept on the second Lords day of *September*, and the Wednesday following throughout the whole Kingdome for the causes after specified.

I. Grosse ignorance and all sort of wickednesse among the greater part, security, meer formalitie and unfruitfulnesse among the best, and unthankfulnesse in all.

II. The sword raging throughout all Christendome, but most barbarously in *Ireland*, and dayly more and more threatned in *England*, through the lamentable division betwixt the King and the Parliament there, tending to the subversion of Religion and Peace in all the three Kingdomes.

III. That God may gratiously blesse the supplication of the Assembly to the Kings Majesty, and their motion to the Parliament of *England*, for Unity in Religion, and Uniformity of Kirk-government, and all other means which may serve for the promoving of so great a Worke, and advancement of the Kingdome of Christ every where.

IV. That God may powerfully overturne all wicked plots and designes of Antichrist and his followers, and all divisive motions against the course of Reformation, and the so much longed for Union of the King and Parliament.

V. That God may blesse the harvest.

1642–E1(R)   Thanksgiving prayer for the royalist victory at the battle of Edgehill

[November] 1642 (England and Wales)

The first battle of the civil war occurred at Edgehill on 23 October after the king's army, while moving south towards London, encountered parliamentarian forces under their captain-general, the third earl of Essex. A fierce conflict ensued, characterized by bickering over tactics and poor decision-making on both sides. It was resolved, not by victory, but by mutual exhaustion and both sides withdrew having suffered approximately the same number of casualties (*c.* 750 each). Royalist claims of a 'victory', therefore, were slightly disingenuous: Charles lost more officers during the battle, though he had, at least, opened up a path to London. The form of prayer appears to have been reissued in October 1643 after the equally indecisive battle of Newbury (see 1643–E10(R)). It was reprinted in *His maiesties declaration and manifestation to all his souldiers* (1642) and in a collection of royalist prayers, compiled by Brian Duppa in 1643. Duppa's collection itself was reprinted in 1644 as *The cavaliers new common-prayer booke unclasp't*, 'with some briefe and necessary observations, to refute the lyes and scandalls that are contained in it'.

Order: none found.
Form of prayer: *A prayer of thanks giving for his majesties late victory over the rebells* ([Oxford], s.n.; 1 p.; Wing P3193)*
Form of prayer (other editions): Wing P3194; Wing P3195.
Additional sources: *His maiesties declaration and manifestation to all his souldiers, by himselfe declared in the head of his army at Southam, 10 miles on this side Coventry, Octob. 21 for direction in their marching, that the goods of no inhabitants be despoiled or unjustly pillaged, but that due satisfaction be given for meat or drink or whatsoever shal be convenient and necessary for them* (1642; Wing C2178 and variants Wing C2178A and Wing C2179, printed in Oxford); *A collection of prayers and thanksgivings, vsed in his maiesties chappell and his armies. Vpon occasion of the late victories againat the rebells, and for the future successe of the forces* (Oxford, 1643; Wing C4094A and variant editions C4094B, C4094C); *The Cavaliers new common-prayer booke unclasp't. It being a collection of prayers and thanksgivings used in his majesties chapel, and in his armes. Upon occasion of the late (supposed) Victorians against the parliaments forces, and for the future successe of the cavalier forces* (1644; Wing C1578).

FORM OF PRAYER

O thou God of Hosts, who goest forth with our Armies, and pleadest the cause of thine Anoynted against them that strive with Him, we acknowledge with all lowlinesse of mind, that it is not our sword, nor the multitude of our Host that hath saved us, but it is thy Hand alone that hath dispos'd of Victory to thy Servant the King, that hath covered his Head in the day of Battaile, and hath kept His Crown from being thrown down to the ground. Not unto us therefore, not unto us, but unto thee, O God, do we give the praise, beseeching thee to accomplish the great worke thou hast begun for us, to continue the blessings of Good successe on the head of our Soveraigne, and on His Army, that the happinesse thereof may flow from thence to the very skirts of His People, to continue the fear, and consternation which thou hast already cast upon the Hearts of those who have rebelliously risen up against Him, to enfeeble their strengths, to infatuate their Counsels, undeceive and disabuse the seduced part of them, that they may know, and feele, that to take up Arms against thy Vice-gerent, is to fight against Heaven, that so by a timely and conscientious submission to the just Authority of him whom thou hast set over them, the effusion of more bloud may be prevented, the peace of this distracted Kingdom setled, Faction may be cast out of the State, and Schisme out of the Church, to the advancement of thy Glory, the Kings Honour, and the Peoples good. Grant this, O God, for thy old mercies sake, which thou wert wont to show unto this Nation, that both Prince and People may joyne in giving praise to thee, who livest and raignest world without end, AMEN.

1642–Ir2   Thanksgiving day for the anniversary of the failure of the Irish rebellion

[After Friday 28 October–November] 1642 (Ireland)

This occasion is known only through a letter from the lord justices and the privy council of Ireland to William Lenthall, speaker of the English House of Commons. They had ordered a thanksgiving to celebrate the first anniversary of the failure of the plot to seize Dublin Castle and the arrest on 23 October 1641 of two of the leaders of the Irish rebellion, Lord Conor Maguire and Hugh MacMahon. There is no form extant and the council's letter does not allude to one, suggesting that none was issued.

Order: lords justices and the council to William Lenthall, 28 October 1642, HMC, *Ormonde*, II, 216–19. **Form of prayer:** none extant

DESCRIPTION OF ORDER

Lords justices and the council to William Lenthall: 28 October 1642
… The [Irish] rebels have lately published a proclamation, a copy whereof coming to our hands, we have adjudged it fit to transmit here inclosed a copy of it. We have also thought fit to send here inclosed a copy of an Act of Council lately made at this Board, for celebrating the 23rd of October in a public thanksgiving to God for that miraculous deliverance which by the abundant mercy of God was granted to his Majesty and his good subjects in this kingdom on that day, and for the miraculous preservation of us hitherto far above our own and our enemies expectation …

1642–E2(P)   Thanksgiving prayers for the parliamentarian victory at Winchester

Sunday 18 December 1642 (City and liberties of London, Westminster, Middlesex and Southwark)

The recovery of Winchester on 12–13 December by Sir William Waller came after a series of military defeats and growing divisions within the parliamentary leadership over whether to make peace with the king. Waller allowed his troops to sack the town. Ironically, this included his own house, and he saw this disaster as divine punishment for agreeing to his men's demands for plunder. The thanksgiving was initiated by the earl of Essex, who on 16 December requested that the House of Lords issue orders to the mayor of London, and justices of Westminster, Middlesex and Southwark for celebrations on Sunday 18 December. Parishes were also authorized to ring their bells and make the 'usual Expressions of Joy' in the meantime. The Commons agreed to the order on the same day. No form was issued because the Commons opposed set prayers and the use of the BCP (see 1641–ES). However, in lieu of any alternative, ministers may have continued to use the BCP if they were uneasy or unable to provide extemporary prayers. The Commons did commission Sir Henry Vane the younger to prepare a 'Narrative' of the victory (no longer extant) to be read out during the service. This publication of a 'narrative' explanation quickly became common for special worship ordered by parliament, and was the only text which was required to be read out in churches on these occasions. These lengthy accounts, usually of military campaigns, sieges and battles, were normally printed separately from the parliamentary orders, and in these cases they are not printed in this edition. The narratives are printed only when they were integral parts of the text of the orders.

Orders: order of the House of Lords, 16 Dec. 1642, *LJ*, V, 494; order of the House of Commons, 16 Dec. 1642, *CJ*, II, 892.

ORDERS

Order of the House of Lords: 16 December 1642
Hereupon this House ORDERED, That the Lord Mayor of the City of *London* be hereby desired, to cause Public Thanks to be given, within the said City and Liberties thereof, on *Sunday* next, for the great Victory lately obtained at the City of *Winchester*, by the Parliament Forces; and that usual Expressions of Joy, by ringing of Bells, may be in the mean Time.
The like Order to be directed to the Justices of *Westm[inster]* and *Midd[lesex]* and *Southwarke*.

Order of the House of Commons: 16 December 1642
Resolved, That, in the several Churches of *London* and *Westminster*, and the Suburbs and Liberties thereof, and the Borough of *Southwarke*; publick Thanks shall be given unto God, on the next Lord's Day, for the good Success it pleased God to give the Parliament Forces against the Cavaliers and Forces under the Command of the Lord *Grandesan* at *Winchester*.

1643–E1(P) Thanksgiving prayers for the parliamentarian victory at Chichester

Sunday 8 January 1643 (City and liberties of London and Westminster)

Waller's success at Winchester (1642–E2(P)) was quickly followed by victory at Chichester: he arrived at the city on 21 December and it surrendered six days later. One of Waller's detachments also successfully besieged Arundel Castle at the same time. A thanksgiving was ordered by the House of Lords on 4 January; there is no corresponding entry in the Commons' journal. Bell-ringing and 'Expressions of Joy' were ordered for 4 January. Waller's military successes earned him the sobriquet 'William the Conqueror'.

Order: order of the House of Lords, 4 Jan. 1643, *LJ*, V, 526.

ORDER

Order of the House of Lords: 4 January 1643
ORDERED, That the Lord Mayor of the City of *London* shall be sent to, to give Order, That Public Thanks shall be given to Almighty GOD, in all the Parish Churches of *London*, and the Liberties thereof, on the next Lord's-day, for the late Victory at *Chichester*, obtained by the Parliament Forces; and Bells and Expressions of Joy this Night to be done, as is usual.
And the like Order for *Westm[inster]* and the Liberties thereof.

1643–E2(P) Thanksgiving prayers for the parliamentarian victory at Leeds

Sunday 5 February 1643 (England and Wales)

Waller's victories in the south were followed by the military success of Ferdinando Fairfax, second Lord Fairfax, and his son, Sir Thomas (or 'Black Tom') at Leeds on 23 January. On 30 January, the Commons ordered a public thanksgiving for the victory the following Sunday in all churches in England and Wales; the Lords approved the order on the same day. Lord Fairfax's account of his victory and those of others in the north, the duke of Newcastle's use of catholics in the royalist army and the persecution of protestants in the north (as well as how parliament starved Fairfax of resources) was printed, and ministers were expected to read it out during the service.

Order: order of the House of Commons, 30 Jan. 1643, *CJ*, II, 947.
Additional sources: *CJ*, II, 948; *LJ*, V, 578–80; *The good and prosperous successe of the parliaments forces in Yorkshire against the earle of New-Castle and his popish adherents* (1643; Wing F114).

ORDERS

Order of the House of Commons: 30 January 1643
Ordered, That the next Lord's Day, publick Thanks shall be given unto God, in the Churches through *England*, by the Ministers, for the great and good Success it has

pleased him to give the Forces raised by the Parliament in *Yorkeshire*: And that the Letters that give the Information be read at the same time.

1643–S1 Fast days in response to declining zeal, catholic threats and persecution of continental protestants and for union between Scotland and England

Sunday 26 February and Thursday 2 March 1643 (Scotland)

Appointed by the commission of the general assembly in early January 1643, this fast was an intervention in the controversy about how Scotland ought to respond to the English civil war. On 20 December, the privy council had voted to publish a letter from the king critical of a declaration by the English parliament requesting Scottish assistance. With the support of the commission, a meeting of covenanters drew up a petition against the council's decision, arguing that by publishing the letter the council would be seen to be taking the king's side against the English parliament. A group of nobles and lairds more sympathetic to the king then produced a rival address, known as the Cross Petition. The commission in turn issued a *Declaration against the Crosse Petition*, accusing its authors of undermining the pursuit of religious uniformity, and of threatening the peace between Scotland and England. The commission's fast act was printed together with a more general *Warning to the ministerie* against papists, sectaries and malignants. As well as the immediate political situation, the fast act referred to sinfulness in Scotland and threats to European protestantism.

Order: act of the commission of the general assembly, *c.* 4 Jan. 1643, Wing N369*, 11–13 [also printed in Wing T2606, 5–6; and in ESTC 006349816, 6–8].
Additional sources: *A declaration against the Crosse Petition* (Edinburgh, 1643; Wing C4203AB); *A necessary warning to the ministerie* (Edinburgh, 1643; Wing N369); presbytery of Dalkeith minutes, NRS, CH2/424/3, p. 97; presbytery of Peebles minutes, NRS, CH2/295/2, fo. 152v; presbytery of Elgin minutes, NRS, CH2/144/1, p. 77; presbytery of Ellon minutes, NRS, CH2/146/3, p. 168; presbytery of Paisley minutes, NRS, CH2/294/2, p. 184; *Letters and journals of Robert Baillie*, II, 60; Craighall, p. 186.

ORDER

Act of the commission of the general assembly: *c.* 4 January 1643

Whereas by the late Generall Assembly, power is committed to us to consider and perform what wee finde necessary by all lawfull and Ecclesiastick wayes, for furtherance of the Union in Religion, and Unity in Kirk-government, for continuance of our own Peace at home, and of the common Peace betwixt the Kingdomes: We finde it necessary, that there shall be a Solemne Fast and Humiliation kept in all the Kirks of this Kingdome, on the last Sabbath of *February*, and the Thursday next thereafter, for the causes and motives following.

I. Although within these few years we renewed the Covenant, and vowed solemnly to stand to the former Reformation of Religion, and to reforme our selves and Families, we have not withstanding fallen from the zeal and fervencie of our Profession at that time; Persons of all ranks and callings are grown luke-warme, and are content with a meere formalitie, and shew of Godlinesse, without the inward power; yea, the most part are profane; so that Blasphemie, Profanation of the Sabbath, Fornication,

Adultery, Drunkennesse, and other vices abound as much as before in the time of corruption, Family worship, mutuall edification, and stirring up one of another by information, admonition, consolation, rebuke much neglected, and Ministers negligent in urging the same. All which are so much the more hainous, because of our unthankfulnesse after so great mercies, and breach of Covenant.

II. The danger of this Kirk and Kingdome, arising partly from within, by the insolencie of Papists in these troublesome times, the divisive motions of the malignant party, and creeping in of the errours of separation; and partly from without, from the Popish Armies and Prelaticall party in England and Ireland, which aime undoubtedly at the disturbance of our Peace, and over-throw of the Work of Reformation. The consideration whereof should move us to pray to God to direct us in all lawfull meanes which may serve for unitie among our selves, that we may be the more strengthened against the common enemies.

III. In respect of the fellow-feeling which we ought to have with the members of Christs body far and near, we have cause to lament the long lasting troubles of the Kirks of God abroad in Germany, and elsewhere, and specially the present combustions in England, and almost utter desolation in Ireland.

IV. That the Lord may blesse all lawfull meanes to be used for preserving the Union and Peace betwixt the two Kingdomes, and procuring the unity of Religion, and uniformity of worship and Kirk-government within His Majesties Dominions; especially that God would grant a good successe to the treaty and travels of the Commissioners for the conservation of Peace, and a gracious acceptance to the Supplications unto His Majesty from the Lords of Councell, and the Commissioners both of Parliament, and of the Generall Assembly.

V. Because the unhappy division betwixt the King and the Parliament of England is a great impediment to the work of Reformation, and to the setling of a firme Peace in His Majesties Dominions, it is our dutie to recommend earnestly to the Lord, that the differences may be composed in such a way as may most conduce to advance the so much wished for Unity of Religion, and uniformitie of worship and Kirk-government.

VI. Finally, that the Lord would discover and disappoint all the conspiracies, counsells, and machinations, which tend to the execution of the bloudie decrees of Trent, the fountain whence hath issued all the troubles and persecutions to the Reformed Kirks, and quickly destroy the man of Sinne.

1643–E3(P)   Thanksgiving prayers for failure of a royalist plot in Bristol

Sunday 19 March 1643 (City and liberties of London and Westminster)

In early March, Prince Rupert, the king's nephew and commander of the royalist cavalry forces, failed to take the parliamentarian stronghold of Bristol, the second most important town in the kingdom and a key port. This may have been because of the failure of an alleged plot to open the city's gates for him. On 13 March, the Commons received letters informing them of a 'cruel Plot and Design of Divers Malignants of that Town'. That day and the next, it met the Lords to discuss the plot. As a result, the two houses ordered a thankgiving to be held on 19 March for parliament's delivery from the conspiracy. They also agreed to publish the letters narrating the plot (as *An extraordinary deliverance*), to seize the estates of the conspirators and to urge parliamentarian forces across the country to disarm all royalists as a matter of priority.

Orders: parliamentary orders: House of Lords, 14 Mar. 1643, *LJ*, V, 648; House of Commons, 16 Mar. 1643, *CJ*, III, 4.

Additional source: *CJ*, II, 1001–3; *An extraordinary deliverance, from a cruell plot, and bloudy massacre contrived by the malignants in Bristoll* (164[3]; Wing F873).

ORDERS

Order of the House of Lords: 14 March 1643

ORDERED, That an Order be sent to the Lord Mayor of the City of *London*, to desire him to give Order, That Public Thanks be given to Almighty GOD on *Sunday* next, in all Parishes, Churches and Chapels, within the said City and the Liberties thereof, for the great Deliverance from the Conspiracy at *Bristoll*.

The like Order to be directed to the Justices of *Westm[inster]* for the City of *Westm[inster]* and the Liberties thereof.

Order of the House of Commons: 16 March 1643

Ordered, That Mr. *Vassall* and Mr. *Ashe* do move the Lord *Mayor*, that Publick Thanksgiving may be given in all the Churches within his Liberties and Jurisdiction, on *Sunday* next, for the Delivery from the Conspiracy at *Bristoll*; and that the Letters concerning that Business, printed by Order of both Houses, may be likewise read.

1643–E4(P) Thanksgiving prayers for the parliamentarian capture of Reading

Sunday 30 April 1643 (City and suburbs of London and Westminster)

In mid-April, Essex besieged the strategically important town of Reading and soon forced its surrender. Though Charles and Prince Rupert arrived soon afterwards with an army of *c*.10,000 men, the king was forced to agree to the surrender. Charles demanded that his troops be allowed to leave the town with their arms and equipment. Parliament agreed to this, but the royalist troops nevertheless were attacked by parliamentarian soldiers as they left. On 29 April, the Commons requested a day of thanksgiving to be held on the following day, a request approved by the Lords. Both houses also agreed to the publication of a letter narrating the siege (probably Sir Philip Stapleton's *An exact relation*), one of many that were printed.

Order: parliamentary order, 29 Apr. 1643, *LJ*, VI, 22.

Additional sources: *CJ*, III, 63–4; *By the King. His majesties proclamation and declaration concerning a clause in one of the late articles at Reading* (1643; Wing C2547); Sir Philip Stapleton, *An exact relation of the delivering up of Reading to his excellencie the earl of Essex* ... (1643; Wing S5256).

ORDER

Parliamentary order: 29 April 1643

A Message was brought from the House of Commons by Sir *Rob't Harley* Knight; which consisted of divers Particulars:

1. Whereas it hath pleased GOD to give the Lord General good Success, in the taking of *Reading* with so little Blood, the House of Commons hath voted to have Public Thanks to be given in all Churches and Chapels, in the Cities of *London* and *Westm.* and the Suburbs there, To-morrow, for so great a Mercy GOD hath vouchsafed to us; wherein they desire their Lordships Concurrence.

Agreed to; and Ordered to be sent to the Lord Mayor of *London*, and the Justices of the Peace for the City of *Westm.*

1643–E5(P)   Thanksgiving prayers for the parliamentarian capture of Wakefield

Sunday 28 May 1643 (London, Westminster, Southwark and suburbs)

In May, Sir Thomas Fairfax led a raid by parliamentarian forces on Wakefield, and captured the city after two hours of fierce fighting and a cavalry charge, despite facing numerically superior royalist forces. Receiving news of the victory, the Commons requested the Lords to order a thanksgiving for the following day (as it had for their earlier victory at Reading: see 1643–E4(P)). As for earlier thanksgivings, an account of the battle, derived from Fairfax's letters, was printed (probably *An exact relation*); other accounts were also produced.

Order: order of the House of Commons, 27 May 1643, *CJ*, III, 106; order of the House of Lords, 27 May 1643, *LJ*, VI, 65.

Additional sources: *LJ*, VI, 65; Anon., *An exact relation of an honovrable victory obtained by the parliaments forces in Yorkshire as it was sent in a letter, and read in both houses of parliament, on Saturday, Maii 27, 1643* (1643; Wing E3675A); *A miraculous victory obtained by the right honorable, Ferdinando Lord Fairfax, against the army under the command of the earl of Newcastle at Wakefield* (1643; Wing F121AB); *A fuller relation of that miraculous victory which it pleased God to give unto the parliaments forces under the command of the right honourable the Lord Fairefax* (1643; Wing F2491A).

ORDER

Order of the House of Commons: 27 May 1643

Resolved, &c. That a publick Thanksgiving shall be given, in all the Churches and Chapels of *London, Westminster*, Borough of *Southwark*, and Suburbs, for the great and good Success it has pleased God to give the Forces under the Command of the Lord *Fairfax*, at the taking in of *Wakefield*.

Order of the House of Lords: 27 May 1643

That a Public Thanksgiving shall be given, in all the Churches and Chapels of *London, Westm[inster]* and Suburbs, for the great and good Success it hath pleased GOD to give the Forces under the Command of the Lord *Fairfax*, at the Taking of *Wakefeild*; and that both Houses do send to the City the Letters, the better to quicken them therein.

Agreed to.

1643–S2 Fast days in response to declining zeal, catholic threats and persecution of continental protestants, and for union between Scotland and England

Sunday 11 June and Wednesday 14 June 1643 (Scotland)

In May 1643, the divisions among Scots created by the English civil war, and exacerbated by the Cross Petition (see 1643–S1), remained unresolved. On 12 May, a proclamation was issued summoning a convention of estates, which went on to negotiate an alliance with the English parliament. This fast was observed in the week before the convention met, but may have been ordered before the meeting was summoned. The causes issued for 1643–S1 were to be used.

Order: act of the commission of the general assembly, *c.* 15 May 1643 (described in presbytery of Elgin minutes, NRS, CH2/144/1, pp. 82–3).
Causes: 1643–S1 (Wing N369) was to be used.
Additional sources: presbytery of Peebles minutes, NRS, CH2/295/2, fo. 159r; presbytery of Dalkeith minutes, NRS, CH2/424/3, p. 104; presbytery of Paisley minutes, NRS, CH2/294/2, p. 193; Craighall, p. 189.

DESCRIPTION OF ORDER

[Act of the commission of the general assembly, *c.* 15 May 1643]
The said day the moderator presented to ye rest of the presbyterie a Letter directed from the Commissioners of the generall assemblie the purpose qrof was to signifie y^t in respect ther is a conventione of the Estates of this Kingdome to meit in Edinburgh the twentie tuo day of June Instant about effaires of verie great Importance, and the saids commissioners conceiving that the conclusions of that great meeting may be of great concernment to this kirk, Have thairfor appoynted a solemne fast & Humilia^{o}ne to be keeped through all this kingdome upon the [Sun]day & wednesday the allevint and fourtenth dayes of this Instant for the same causs for qlk the Late fast in Feb[ruary] Last was indicted, excepting onlie the Last part of the fourth cau[se] anent o^r commissioners who ar now returned, the remanent causs as yet remaining as great motives to bring us againe in all humilitie befor the Lord Bot especiallie for this caus that the Lord wold blesse that meeting of estates with such counsells consulta^{o}ns and Conclusions as may tend to the securing of the Religione and peace of this kirk and kingdome.

1643–E6(P) Thanksgiving days for discovery of a plot against parliament

Thursday 15 June 1643 (London, Westminster and suburbs); Tuesday 11 July 1643 (elsewhere in England and Wales)

On 31 May, Edmund Waller, a royalist and MP for St Ives whose speeches circulated widely in print, was arrested by parliamentarian officers for plotting a campaign of passive resistance, and possibly an uprising, against parliament. John Pym, revealing the plot to the Commons on 6 June, requested, among other things, that a day of thanksgiving be ordered for the whole realm and that 'a Vow' be administered 'to distinguish the good Party from the bad; and to unite faster together the good Party'. Pym's proposals were accepted by the Commons and then by the House of Lords, which on 8 June ordered the day of thanksgiving for Tuesday 13 June in London and Westminster, and for a month later throughout England and Wales. The order is notable as the first to name the ministers who had been appointed to preach before the House of Lords: Edmund Calamy and Charles Herle. (The preachers for the House of Commons, Stephen Marshall and Obadiah Sedgwick were not named in the order, but it was separately ordered that the sermons for both houses were to be published.) For reasons which are unknown, on 9 June, the day after the order had been agreed, the House of Lords postponed the date of the observance in the London and Westminster areas by two days, to Thursday 15 June, and the Commons instructed the lord mayor of London to notify ministers in the city of this change of date. On 14 June, the day before this first thanksgiving day, the House of Commons ordered that a printed account of the plot, *A brief narrative of the late treacherous and horrid designe*, should be distributed to all churches in the London and Westminster areas, to be read out by ministers during the thanksgiving services. The date originally appointed for the second thanksgiving day, throughout England and Wales, was Tuesday 11 July. This date was also changed. Again, the reason is unclear, but it may have been connected with the arrangements for Pym's second proposal, the administration of a 'vow' or oath, because this was now included with this thanksgiving. On the day that the first thanksgiving day was celebrated in Westminster, the House of Commons asked the Lords to appoint – in practice, to re-appoint – the thanksgiving day for the whole kingdom. Two days later, the Lords and Commons jointly ordered that both this thanksgiving and the administration of the oath should take place together on Thursday 13 July. This combination of an order for special worship and a requirement of an expression of loyalty was unusual but not quite new, as a similar arrangement had been ordered for 1641–ES. The oath was to be administered either at the end of the sermon, or at the end of the evening service. Edmund Waller escaped trial, either because he was willing to implicate others whom parliament felt unable to punish (including the earls of Portland and Northumberland), or because he bribed other MPs. He was imprisoned for eighteen months, and eventually fined £10,000 and allowed to go into exile.

Order: order of House of Lords on a motion from the House of Commons, 8 June 1643, *LJ*, VI, 85; order to hold the thanksgiving on Thursday 15 June 1643, House of Lords, 9 June 1643, *LJ*, VI, 87, House of Commons, 9 June, *CJ*, III, 122; order for the distribution of the narrative, House of Commons, 14 June 1563, *CJ*, III, 130; order of the House of Commons for a nationwide thanksgiving, 15 June 1643, *CJ*, III, 130; order of parliament, 17 June 1643, *A collection of the publicke orders ordinances and declarations in both houses of parliament from the ninth of March 1642. until December 1646* (by T.W. for Edward Husband; 1646; Wing E878), 218*.
Additional sources: *CJ*, III, 117, 121–2, 130, 132; *LJ*, VI, 85, 87–8, 99; *A collection of all the publicke orders, ordinances, and declaration of both houses of parliament from the ninth of March, 1642 untill December, 1646* (1646; Wing E878), p. 218; *The vow and covenant, appointed by the Lords and Commons assembled in parliament, to be taken by every man, in the cities of London, Westminister, the suburbs and liberties thereof; and throughout the whole kingdom* (1643; Wing E2459); Lambert, *Printing*, p. 61; Francis Rous, *A brief narrative of the late treacherous and horrid designe, which by the great blessing and especiall providence of God hath been lately discovered* (1643; Wing B4614); *Mercurius Aulicus ... the sixe and twentieth weeke* (1643; Thomason E.59 [24]); *FSP*, VI, 5–7.
Printed sermons: Calamy, House of Lords (Wing C261; *FSP*, VI, 246–311); Herle, House of Lords (Wing H1556; ESTC 006478134; *FSP*, VI, 313–43); Marshall, House of Commons (Wing M789; *FSP*, VI, 345–96); Sedgwick, House of Commons (Wing S2374; *FSP*, VI, 397–434).

ORDERS

Parliamentary order: 8 June 1643

ORDERED, That *Tuesday* next, being the 13th of this Instant *June*,[327] is appointed for the Celebration of Public Thanksgiving to GOD, for this Discovery, and great Deliverance, by the Lords and Commons, the Cities of *London* and *Westm[inster]* and the Suburbs; the Lords to keep it in the Abbey Church at *Westm[inster]* and Mr. *Calamy* to preach in the Morning, and Mr. *Herle* to preach in the Afternoon: And further it is ORDERED, That *Tuesday* come Month is appointed for the keeping the Thanksgiving throughout the whole Kingdom.

Order for the Thursday: House of Lords: 9 June 1643

ORDERED, That the Day of Thanksgiving shall be on *Thursday* next.

Order for the Thursday: House of Commons: 9 June 1643

Ordered, That Mr *Spurstoe* desire the Lord Mayor to give Notice to the Ministers of the several Parishes within his Jurisdiction, that the Lords and Commons have appointed the Day of publick Thanksgiving, for the Discovery and great Deliverance from the late horrid Design, to be kept on *Thursday* next.

Order for the distribution of the narrative: House of Commons, 14 June 1643

Ordered, That the Narration and Commission be read in all Churches and Chapels in and about *London* and *Westminster*, on *Thursday*, being the Day of Thanksgiving for the Deliverance of the Parliament and City from the late horrid Plot: And Sir *Rob. Pye* and Mr. *Wheeler* are to take care to send printed Copies thereof to the Churches in *Westminster*, to be read there: And the Lord Mayor to see them read in *London*; and Sir *John Francklyn* to take care they be read in the adjacent parishes in *Middlesex*; and Mr. *White*, for *Southwark*.

Order for a thanksgiving for the whole kingdom: House of Commons, 15 June 1643

Ordered, That a Message by sent to the Lords to desire them to appoint a Day for a publick Thanksgiving to be given unto God, by the whole Kingdom, for his great Mercy in the Discovery and Deliverance from the late horrid and treacherous Design.

Parliamentary order: 17 June 1643

It is this day Ordered by the Lords and Commons Assembled in Parliament, That publike thanksgiving through the whole Kingdome for the discovery of the late Plott, shall be on Thursday come three weekes, being the thirteenth day of *Iuly* next ensuing, at which time the Covenent and Oath shall be tendred to every man in the severall parish Churches and Chappells through the Kingdome, after the Sermon or Evening prayers shall be finished.

---

[327] This was changed to Thursday, 15 June, by the Lords on 9 June, for reasons which were not stated (*LJ*, VI, 87).

1643–E7(P)   Day of humiliation for parliamentarian defeats in the north and west

Friday 21 July 1643 (London, Westminster, suburbs and adjacent places within the bills of mortality)[328]

After Fairfax's success at Wakefield in May (see 1643–E5(P)), the parliamentarians suffered a series of serious setbacks in the midlands, Oxfordshire, Devon and Cornwall. Parliament's control of the north and south west was eradicated, the army was virtually destroyed, key commanders (including Lord Brooke and John Hampden) were killed, morale collapsed and there were bitter recriminations at Westminster. The proposal for a 'day of humiliation' was made by members of the 'Westminster Assembly of Divines' during its first meeting on 19 July. The Westminster assembly was a gathering of clergy, MPs, peers and Scottish presbyterian ministers which had been commissioned by parliament to revise the doctrine, liturgy and government of the Church of England. On being informed by two MPs, John Selden and William Pierrepont, that it had no authority to order public occasions of special worship independently of parliament, the assembly asked the Lords and Commons to order 'a Publike and extraordinary day of Humiliation ... that every one may bitterly bewaile his owne sinnes, and cry mightily unto GOD for Christ his sake, to remove his wrath, and to heale the Land'. They also requested that parliament should take action to implement a programme for the reformation of manners. Each house agreed to the request for a day of humiliation; a joint order was issued and printed the same day. This was the first time that the term a 'day of humiliation' was used in an official order for special worship, although the significance of the change is not obvious: the day was to be observed with fasting as well as prayer. It was also the first time that an order by parliament for a day of special worship had been printed. A printed notice of the Lords' order was sent to the lord mayor, one of only two extant examples of such a printed notice (see also 1645–E3(P)). The following day, the Commons, or more likely a committee meeting at Grocers' Hall, issued an order to ministers to exhort their parishioners to make financial contributions to support Sir William Waller's parliamentarian army; there is no reference to this order in the Commons' journal. Thomas Hill, William Spurstowe and a Mr Burgess (probably Anthony Burgess) were appointed to preach before parliament, but Burgess was later replaced by Richard Vines. All three clerics were subsequently invited to print their sermons, though Vines appears not to have done so.

This occasion brought further innovations. First, the fast was to be observed 'within the bills of mortality'. It is unclear whether this represented a wider definition of the London and Westminster areas, or whether parliament was just being more specific about which parishes constituted 'adjacent places'. Second, the House of Lords attended the same special service as the House of Commons, in St Margaret's Westminster, the Commons' traditional place of worship since 1614, rather than having a separate service in Westminster Abbey, as had been its own tradition.

---

[328] I.e. the weekly printed broadsides listing the numbers of baptisms and deaths in the City of London, the City and Liberty of Westminster and parishes in Middlesex (including Spitalfields, St Giles in the Fields, Hackney, Islington, Shoreditch, Whitechapel and Bethnal Green) and Surrey (including the borough of Southwark and parishes in Lambeth, Rotherhithe and Bermondsey).

This is perhaps an indication of the changing relationship between the two houses of parliament.

Order: *Die Mercurii, 19 July, 1643. The Lords and Commons assembled in parliament, out of the deep sense of Gods heavy wrath now upon this kingdome,* 19 July 1643, (s.n., s.p., n.d.; Wing E1640B)* [also in *LJ*, VI, 139].
Additional sources: *LJ*, VI, 136–9, 143; *CJ*, III, 173–4, 177; *Iuly 20, 1643. The House of Commons taking into their serious consideration how much it imports the safety of this city, and the whole kingdome, that the forces under the command of Sir William Waller* ... ([London: s.n., 1643]; Wing E2579); Lambert, *Printing*, p. 64; *FSP*, VII, 5–6; *Westminster assembly*, V, 9–11.
Printed sermons: Hill, parliament, St Margaret's, Westminster (Wing H2024; *FSP*, VI, 229–65); Spurstowe, parliament, St Margaret's, Westminster (Wing S5094; *FSP*, VI, 267–302).

ORDER

Parliamentary order: 19 July 1643

The Lords and Commons assembled in Parliament, out of the deep sense of Gods heavy wrath now upon this Kingdome, and more particularly manifested by the late discomfeiture of the Forces, both in the North and in the West; Have for themselves resolved to set apart and keepe, and do ordaine, and command, That *Friday* the 21. of this present *July*, 1643. be set apart and kept as a day of publique and extraordinary humiliation by Prayer and Fasting, throughout the Cities of *London* and *Westminster*, and the Suburbs, and places adjacent, within the Bils of Mortality; That every soule may bitterly bewaile his owne sinnes, and the sinnes of the whole Nation, And cry mightily to God for Christ his sake, that he will be pleased to turne from the fiercenesse of his wrath, and heale the Land. And the Lord Mayor of the City of *London*, is hereby required to give present Order for the due performance of this Order.

1643–E8(P)   Thanksgiving prayers for the parliamentarian relief of Gloucester

Sunday 17 September 1643 (London, Westminster and parishes within the bills of mortality)

The royalists were prevented from exploiting recent victories by marching on London because their armies in Yorkshire and the south-west were unwilling to leave their own counties. Instead, Charles laid siege to Gloucester, intending to disrupt parliament's communications between Oxford and the south-west. Though poorly fortified and having only a small military force, the city refused to surrender. Charles withdrew his army on 5 September on hearing that a substantial parliamentarian force under Essex was on its way to relieve the city. The 'victory' was reported to parliament within three days, and a public thanksgiving was ordered for 17 September following the usual procedure: the Commons proposed the fast and sought the consent of the Lords.

Order: order of House of Commons, 15 Sept. 1643, *CJ*, III, 242; order of House of Lords, 16 Sept. 1643, *LJ*, VI, 218.
Additional source: *CJ*, III, 241–2.

ORDER

Order of the House of Commons: 15 September 1643
Ordered, That publick Thanksgiving be given on the next Lord's Day, in all the
Churches of *London* and *Westminster*, and the Parishes within the Bills of Mortality,
in Acknowledgment of God's great Mercy and Goodness, shewn in the Relief of
Gloucester.

Order of the House of Lords: 16 September 1643
That a Public Thanksgiving be given, on the next Lords-day, in all the Churches of
London and *Westminster* and the Parishes within the Bills of Mortality.
ORDERED, To send to the Lord Mayor of *London*, and the Justices of the Peace
of *Westm[inster]* to give Directions and Command that the same may be done
accordingly.

**1643–E9(P)   Thanksgiving prayers for the parliamentarian successes
at Gloucester and the first battle of Newbury**

Sunday 24 September 1643 (London, Westminster and their liberties)

After his success at Gloucester, Essex attempted to hurry back to London but he and
his army were cut off by Charles at Newbury. In a fierce but indecisive battle on 20
September, approximately 3,500 men were killed, including senior royalists such
as the secretary of state, Viscount Falkland, Lord Caernarvon and Lord Sutherland.
However, the parliamentarians were unable to secure a clear victory, though Charles's
withdrawal allowed Essex to return to London as a conquering hero. Charles's
reception at Oxford was similar, at least publicly. In another change to the ordering
process, the Lords asked the Commons to join it in a request to the common council
of London to order a public thanksgiving for Essex's 'victories' at Gloucester and
Newbury. The council comprised the lord mayor, aldermen and representatives from
each of the wards. This was the first time that special worship had been ordered by
the council or the lord mayor and, though it reflected parliament's wish to wrest
control of fasts and thanksgivings from the church, it also represented a surprising
delegation of authority by parliament itself. Parliament ordered two official accounts
of the battle to be printed: one in English by Ralph Routhwaite and the other its Latin
translation. The purpose of the latter was 'so it may be dispersed into Foreign Parts;
to give them a true Relation of that Battle'.

Order: resolution of the House of Commons, 23 Sept. 1643, *CJ*, III, 253–4.
Additional sources: *LJ*, VI, 231, 287; Ralph Rounthwaite, *A true relation of the late expedition of his
excellency, Robert Earle of Essex, for the relief of Gloucester with the description of the fight at Newbury*
(1643; Wing T2979); *Descriptio rerum gestarum in expeditione, quam suscepit illustrissimus heros,
Robertus comes Essexiae* (1643; Wing D1138).

ORDER

Resolution of the House of Commons: 23 September 1643
The Lords ... have appointed Six of their Lords to be a Committee, to join with
a Committee of a proportionable Number of this House, to go to the Common

Council: And desire, that the Committee may have Power to desire the Lord Mayor, that Notice may be given to all Ministers, that publick Thanksgiving be given, To-morrow, in all Churches, for the great Success it has pleased God to give the Army, under the Command of the Earl of *Essex* ...

That this House has considered their Lordships Message; and have appointed a Committee, to go with a Committee of a proportionable Number, to his Excellency my Lord General; and have appointed a Committee to go with a Committee of a proportionable Number, to the Common Council, this Afternoon at Three of Clock, upon the Votes and Propositions of both Houses; and do agree to the additional Instructions and Propositions for the Committee appointed to go to the Common Council.

1643–E10(R) Thanksgiving prayer for the royalist success at the first battle of Newbury

After Monday 9 October 1643 (England and Wales?)

This occasion is known only because of marginal comments made by the book collector, George Thomason, in his copy of the printed prayer. The prayer was a reprint of that issued in November 1642 (1642–E1(R)) and Thomason wrote 'at Newbery' against the title. The prayer appears to date from 9 October: this was the date Thomason noted at the bottom of the sheet, which is filed with other items from this week. However, the ornaments show that it was printed in London, not Oxford. The battle of Newbury, fought on 20 September, had been inconclusive and both sides claimed victory (see 1643–E9(P)).

Order: none found.
Form of prayer: *A prayer of thanksgiving for his majesties late victory over the rebels* (s.n., [1643]; Wing D2664; 1 p.)*.
Additional source: Falconer Madan, *Oxford books* (3 vols., Oxford, 1895–1931), II, nos. 1048, 1465.

FORM OF PRAYER

[As 1642–E1(R)]

1643–S3 Fast day [unspecified dangers to the church and kingdom]

Sunday 8 October 1643 (Scotland)

In August 1643, the convention of estates negotiated the Solemn League and Covenant with commissioners from the English parliament, and then voted to send troops to assist parliament against the king. This was a triumph for the many covenanters who wanted to use a military alliance with England to advance the cause of presbyterianism there. It is unclear precisely what motivated the commission of the general assembly to appoint this fast. By 5 October, the presbyteries of Dalkeith and Peebles had received letters from the commission notifying them of the fast.

Order: act of the commission of the general assembly, *c.* 15 Sept. 1643 (described in presbytery of Dalkeith minutes, NRS, CH2/424/3, p. 108).
Additional source: presbytery of Peebles minutes, NRS, CH2/295/2, fo. 163r.

DESCRIPTION OF ORDER

[Act of the commission of the general assembly, *c.* 15 September 1643]
The Commissioners of the Generall Assemblie Ordained a fast to be keiped the following Sabbath because of the dangers Imminent to the churche & kingdome

---

1643–E11(R) Monthly fast days for success of the royalist cause

Second Friday of each month, beginning 10 November 1643 (England and Wales)

In November 1643, the king ordered that observance of the monthly fast, first ordered by royal proclamation on the prompting of parliament during the Irish rebellion (see 1641–E), should cease, and that it should be replaced by a new monthly fast, observed on a different day and in a different week – on the second Friday of each month. The purpose of the new fasts was 'for the diverting of his heavy judgements from Us, for the continuing of his Gracious *Protection* over Us and this Nation, for the avoyding of all Malicious practices against Us, and the Setling and Establishing of a happy Peace amongst Us'. The king argued that, while the original monthly fasts had been ordered 'for the support and preservation of that Kingdome', they were now being used by parliament for its own purposes, for 'the destruction of Us and of this Kingdome of *England*'. This occasion was significant for further reasons. The king publicly asserted that only fasts ordered by the crown were legal, thereby denying the authority of parliament or its associated bodies to order special worship. The new fasts were more traditional than those ordered in 1641. They were to be observed on the conventional (and catholic) day for fasting, Friday. A form of prayer was issued; none had been commissioned in 1641. In the rubrics, the minister was referred to as the 'priest', not a term now acceptable to the parliamentarians. The form pointedly included the Elizabethan homily against disobedience, and the 'Prayer against rebellion', which had both first been published in 1570–E: this prayer was to be read after the homily or after a sermon. Three prayers from the new form – 'A thanksgiving for the Queenes safe returne' (Queen Henrietta Maria had rejoined the king after a long period in Holland and the nother of England), 'A Hymne or generall Thanksgiving' and 'O Most Glorious and Powerfull Lord God' (said after the prayer for the bishops and the clergy) – were republished, in some cases lightly edited, in a collection of royalist prayers which was compiled by Brian Duppa in 1643, and reprinted in 1644 as *The cavaliers new common-prayer booke unclasp't* : see 1642–E1(R). The fast days were to be observed and the form of prayer used throughout England and Wales, but in practice they were adopted only in areas of royalist control. The monthly fasts ordered in 1641 for the last Wednesday of each month continued to be observed in areas under parliamentarian control, so in effect two rival series of fast days were available in the kingdom. On 13 October, the sheriffs of London brought to the House of Commons several bundles of the royal proclamation and the writs for printing them, which had been delivered to the lord mayor and the under sheriff of Middlesex. The Commons banned continued publication of the proclamation, and ordered that the messenger who had brought the copies from Oxford should be apprehended and tried under martial law as a spy.

Order: royal proclamation, 5 Oct. 1643 (Leonard Litchfield, Oxford, 1643; Wing C2583)* [also Wing C2584; also in Larkin, II, 954–5].

Form of prayer: *A forme of common-prayer, to be used upon the solemne fast appointed by his majesties proclamation upon the second Friday in every moneth. Beginning on the tenth day of November next, being Friday. For the averting of Gods iudgement now upon us; For the ceasing of this present rebellion; and restoring a happy peace in this kingdome. Set forth by his majesties authority, & commanded to be duely read in all churches and chappels within this kingdome, and the dominion of Wales* (Oxford, Leonard Lichfield; Wing C4111*; 76 pp.).

Forms of prayer (other editions): 76 pp., York, Stephen Bulkley, 1643, Wing C4109; Bristol, Robert Barker and John Bill, 1643; Wing C4110; 70+ pp.; Oxford [i.e. York or Bristol], Leonard Lichfield, Wing C4111A; 76 pp. [for the last version, see Madan, *Oxford books*, II, no. 1470].

Additional sources: *CJ*, III, 296–7; *A collection of prayers and thanksgivings, vsed in his maiesties chappell and his armies. Vpon occasion of the late victories againat the rebells, and for the future successe of the forces* (Oxford, 1643; Wing C4094A and variant editions C4094B, C4094C); *The cavaliers new common-prayer booke unclasp't* (1644; Wing C1578).

ORDER

Royal proclamation: 5 October 1643

When a generall Fast was first propounded unto Us, in contemplation of the miseries of Our Kingdome of *Ireland*, We readily gave Our Consent unto it, and in Our Court, and in Our Person have duely observed it, as a Religious duty, fit to be exercised in a time of common Calamity. But when we have seen what ill use hath been made of those publique meetings under the pretence of Religion, in the Pulpits, and Prayers and Sermons of many seditious Lecturers to stirre up and continue the Rebellion raised against Us within this Kingdome; And that those, who first moved and seemed to affect the relief of Our distressed Subjects of *Ireland*, have deserted the care thereof, and diverted the Means ordained for the support and preservation of that Kingdome, to the destruction of Us and of this Kingdome of *England*; We have thought it fit to Command, That such an Hypocriticall Fast, to the dishonour of God, and the slander of true Religion, be no longer continued and countenanced by Our Authority, which hath been too long continued already, to such false and Trayterous ends. And yet we being desirous (as by Our duty to Almighty God We are bound) by all possible means to expresse Our own Humiliation, and the Humiliation of Our People, for Our own sinnes and the sinnes of this Nation, (as We have great cause) are resolved to continue a Monthly Fast, but not on the day formerly appoynted and so much abused by those who are in Rebellion against Us, they using it as a Principall Engine to work their own designes. We doe therefore hereby Command, That from henceforth no Fasts, or publike Meetings under that name be held on the last Wednesday of the Moneth in any part of this Our Kingdome of *England*, as for many Moneths it hath been, nor upon any other day, then as hereby is appoynted by Us, which we are well assured, none of Our Subjects may or ought to doe without, much lesse against Our Command: but instead thereof We do expresly Charge and Command, That in all Churches and Chappels in all the parts of this Our Kingdome of *England* and Dominion of *Wales*, there be a solemne Fast held, and Religiously observed on the second Friday in every Moneth, with publike Prayers to God, and Preaching in all places where it may be had, when and where we may all both Prince and People, as one man, earnestly powre out our Prayers to God, for the diverting of his heavy judgements from Us, for the continuing of his gracious *Protection* over Us and this Nation, for the avoyding of all Malicious practices against Us, and the Setling and Establishing of a happy Peace amongst Us. And to the end that with one Heart and one Voyce We may performe so Religious an Exercise, We have caused devout formes of Prayers to be Composed and Printed, and intend to disperse them into all the parts of this Our Kingdome, and doe Command that they be used in all Churches and Chappels at these solemne and publique Meetings. And if thus We shall heartily and unfainedly apply Our selves to Our good God and gratious Father, whom We have offended, and prayse him for his many and even Miraculous deliverances past, we may with Comfort and Confidence hope that he will in mercy look upon Us, and be reconciled unto Us.

FORM OF PRAYER

[Opening sentence: Jer. 10:24]

[The exhortation; general confession; absolution; the Lord's prayer and versicles]

Then shall be said or sung this Psalme following, in stead of *Venite exultemus [as 1626–E2].*

Psalmes for Morning and Evening Prayer. [27, 35, 37, 59, 74, 83, 94, 144]
For the First lesson is appoynted to be read 2. *Sam.* 15. & 16. *Chap.* of the Rebellion of *Absolon.* OR, *Numb.* 16. The Conspiracy of *Corah, Dathan*, and *Abiram.*

[Te Deum]

For the *Second Lesson* is appointed to be read *Rom.* 13.

[Benedictus]
[Apostles' creed]

The prayers, all devoutly kneeling.
    Lord be with you *[as BCP to the end of these prayers].*

[The Lord's prayer]

The Priest standing up, shall say: O Lord shew thy mercy upon us.
Answer: And grant us thy salvation.
Priest: O Lord guard the Person of thy Servant the King.
Answer: Which putteth His trust in thee.
Priest: Send to Him & to His Armies help from thy holy Place.
Answer: And evermore mightily defend them.
Priest: Confound the designes of all those that are risen up against Him.
Answer: And let not their Rebellious wickednesse approach neare to hurt Him.
Priest: O Lord heare our prayer.
Answer: And let our cry come unto thee.
Priest: Indue thy Ministers with righteousnesse.
[As BCP to end of these suffrages]

The first Collect for the day.
[The BCP collect in time of war]

A Prayer.

O eternall God and most mercifull Father, Wee humbly beseech thee to be merci-full unto us, and in the Riches of thy unspeakable mercies, be neare to help and succour us, in all those extremities which our sinnes threaten to bring upon us. The Rebellious are strengthned against us, by our multiplied Rebellions against thee: and wee deserve to suffer what our enemies threaten, even suddaine surprisall & destruction to desolation. But there is mercy with thee, that thou maist be feared: and there is mercy with thee that they may not be feared. Shew us therefore thy mercy O Lord; and let us so feare thee, that we may never be forced to feel or feare them. And when thou wilt correct us for our Sinnes, O Lord in judgement remember mercy, and let us fall into thy hands, and not into the hands of men, let us fall into thy hands, and not into the hands of ungratious and ungodly men: into thy hands, and not into the hands of Sacrilegious and seditious men: into thy mercifull hands, and not into the cruell hands of thine and our enemies. Even for Iesus Christs sake, our only mediator and Redeemer. Amen.

The second Collect.
[The second collect, for peace, from the BCP service for morning prayer]

The third Collect.
[The third collect, for grace, from the BCP service for morning prayer]

LITANY

[After the prayer for the bishops and clergy]

O Lord of heaven and earth, God of the spirits of all flesh, we a most sinfull, and therefore now a most miserable People, doe in the bitternesse of our afflicted Soules humbly fall downe at the footstoole of thy grace, most sadly bewailing our many and most haynous sinnes. We have multiplied our iniquities into a violation of thy whole Law, having neither performed to thee our God, nor to man the duties thou requirest of us, so that by our wicked workes we have denied that most holy faith, whereof our mouthes have for so long a time made profession. These things O Lord, have we done, and because in goodnesse thou wert pleased to keep silence, how many of us have thought wickedly, that thou wert altogether such an one as our selves; which either did'st approve or at least would'st not punish the Crimes that we doted on. And now in thy just Iudgements thou hast set our sinnes in order before our eyes; In the continued scourge of this wasting Rebellion, we may well perceive, that the sinnes we have done have not been barely infirmities, but Rebellions against thee. In the Rapines acted upon the substance thou hast given us, we cannot but consider that by Oathes and Blasphemies we have robbed thee of thine Honour, and have oftimes stolen much of that pretious time which should have been spent in thy service. Nay we have added sinne unto sinne, so that one Crime hath brought forth another Transgression, and thou hast shewed us even this in thy Iudgements we now feele, in that this present warre hath brought forth an infectious disease, and doth now threaten famine to us. We confesse O Lord with all thankfulnesse of heart, that thou hast been pleased to sweeten the bitternesse of this Cup by many strange successes, by frequent and unexpected Victories, and yet thou hast so allayed each favour of thine hand with the mixture of some sudden crosse, that herein thou hast set our Repentance too before the sight of our eyes, and let's us see 'tis mixt with so much coldnesse and Hypocrisy, that there may be as much guilt in such a kind of Repentance as before there was in our sinnes. Yet returne O God, in great mercy returne unto the many thousands of thy people: doe thou accept, and increase in our hearts our detestation of all wickednesse, that our sorrowes for sinne may be as compleatly perfect as we desire thou shouldst make our Victories, and that for times hereafter, our hearty observance of thy whole Law may still runne along with such sorrowes. O let not thy scourge end in a desolation, nor thine anger goe on unto the height of an everlasting ruine: But heare us mercifull Father, hasten the aresion [*sic*] of these thy sharp judgements from us, and let not the noyse of this accursed Rebellion be any longer heard in our streets. Scatter thou the People that delight in Warre, and let the blessing of Peace be upon the Heads of all those who strive and pray for this blessing; and that for his sake by whose hand thou givest every blessing Iesus Christ our Lord. Amen.

[The BCP prayer in time of war, or the prayer, 'O God, whose nature and property is ever to have mercy and to forgive', to the end of the litany]

THE SECOND SERVICE.[329]

[The communion service from the BCP until the collect for the day]
Shew forth the power of thy might *[as 1626–E2]*

[Epistle: 2 Tim. 3:1–9]
[Gospel: Matt. 23:13–39 or Rev. 7–13 [sic] or Matt. 5:1–12]
[Nicene creed]

After the Creed, if there be no Sermon, shall follow, a Homily*, set forth in the end of this Book.*

[Offertory sentence: Matt. 5:16]

[After the prayer for the whole state of the church]
A Hymne or generall Thanksgiving
   Glory be to God on high, and in Earth Peace, good will towards men. We praise thee, we blesse thee, we worship thee, we glorifie thee; and at this time, in a more especiall manner, with the highest expressions of our devoutest Hearts, we most humbly give thankes unto thee, for that thou hast been pleased out of thine infinite goodnes, mercifully to look down upon the late low estate of our gratious Soveraigne; That thou hast brought him from so much scornfull neglect, to appeare so terrible unto those desperate Rebells, who dare yet stand in Armes against him; That thou hast blest him with many, and those eminent Victories. O Lord God, heavenly King, God the Father Almighty, O Lord the only begotten Sonne Iesus Christ, continue these thy favours to us, and perfect, we beseech thee, that glorious worke,

---

[329] I.e. the communion.

the happy Peace of this Land, which none but thine owne strength can finish. And to that end, thou that takest away the sinnes of the world, take this foule sinne of Rebellion from us; thou that sittest at the right hand of God the Father, smite through the loynes of those Sacrilegious men, who have not spared at all to prophane thy house, and thy service; so shall we still blesse and magnifie thy Name in the midst of the great Congregation; so shall we thy servants never cease to be still praysing thee and saying; Thou only, art holy, thou only art the Lord, thou only O Christ, with the holy Ghost, art most high in the glory of God the Father. To thee be all Praise and Honour, and Glory ascribed, world without end. AMEN.

A thanksgiving for the Queenes safe Returne

O most mercifull Lord God, we farther render thee all Praise and thankes, for that thou hast been pleased to extend thy hand of deliverance unto the Person of our gratious QUEENE; that thou hast made Her an Instrument of so much good to this Kingdome, & brought her safely hither, through so many dangers both by Sea and Land. Lord make the KING and His People daily more and more happy in her, that as by thine especiall favour She is already become the Mother of so many hopefull Princes, so Shee may be daily fruitfull in the addition of more blessings to vs, through Iesus Christ our Lord, to whom with thee, and the holy Ghost, be all Honour and Glory, world without end. AMEN.

Almighty and everlasting God, mercifully looke upon our infirmities and miseries, and in all our dangers and necessities, stretch forth thy right hand to helpe and defend us, through Jesus Christ our Lord. AMEN. *[This is the collect for the third Sunday after Epiphany, with the addition of 'and miseries']*

[The BCP collect for the third Sunday before Lent]

[The first, second and sixth collects after the offertory from the communion service in the BCP]

[The blessing]

EVENING PRAYER

[Opening sentence: Matt. 3:2]

[The exhortation, the confession; the absolution; the Lord's prayer and versicles]

Then shall be said or sung this Psalme following, in stead of Venite exultemus.
I will love thee *[as at morning prayer]*

The Psalmes appointed to be read for the Evening Prayer, are the 74. 83. 94. 144. *as they are joyn'd to the Psalmes for the Morning prayer, beginning at pag. 17.*

The first Lesson. 2. Sam. 17 and 18. the Residue of Absolon's Conspiracies. OR, 2. Sam. 20. Shebah's Rebellion.

[The Magnificat]

[Second lesson: 1 Pet. 2]
[Nunc dimittis or Deus misereatur]
[Apostles' creed]
[The Lord's prayer]

Then the Priest standing up shall say.
    O Lord shew thy mercy upon us *[as at morning prayer]*

The first Collect of the day
[The BCP collect in time of war]

O Lord God of Hosts who givest victory unto Kings, and didst deliver *David* thy
Servant from the perill of the Sword, heare us, we beseech thee, most miserable
sinners, who doe here powre out our Soules before thee, entirely desiring the protection
of thine hand upon thy servant the King: let Him find safety under the shadow of thy
wings, and preserve His Person as the apple of thine own eye. Suffer not that sword
which thou hast put into his hands to be wrested out by the hand of man: but blesse
his Counsells with successe, and His enterprises with victory, that He may goe on to
be a terror to all those that oppose Him, and to be as the dew of the latter raine upon
the hearts of all those who doe still remain Loyall to Him. And ô thou who takest no
delight in the misery of one single sinner, spare mercifull Lord, spare a great, though
most sinfull Nation, pitty a despised Church, and a distracted State, heale up those
wounds which our sinnes have made so wide, that none but thine own hands can
close them. And in the tendernesse of thine unspeakable compassion hasten to put so
happy an end unto these wasting divisions, that thy service may be the more duely
celebrated, thine Annoynted more conscientiously obeyed, that the Church may be
restored to a true Christian unity, and the Kingdome to our former Peace, and that
for his sake who is the Prince of Peace, and that shed his pretious blood to purchase
our Peace, even Iesus Christ our Lord, to whom with thee, ô Father, and thy blessed
Spirit be &c.

The second Collect.
[The second collect, for peace, from the BCP service for morning prayer]

The third Collect.
[The third collect, for grace, from the BCP service for morning prayer]

*[The prayer for the king; a prayer for the queen; the prayer for the bishops and
clergy]*

O most Glorious and Powerfull Lord God, without whose aid and influence all
our strength is weaknesse, and our Counsell folly: we thy unworthy Servants in a
gratefull commemoration of thy frequent and often repeated blessings, with humble
and unfained hearts offer up to thee the sacrifice of prayse, calling Heaven and Earth
to witnesse with us, that it is thy Power alone by which we stand, thy Strength by
which we prosper. We humbly begge of thee, O Lord, to continue in all our dangers
thy speciall assistance to us, to break the speare of the Disobedient, and melt the
hearts of the Rebellious into water, to strike the mindes of the perverse, with a true
touch of Conscience, which they goe about to stifle, and a true sense of that duty to

thine Annoynted, which they labour to forget; that we thy miserable and distressed People, may no longer groane under those heavy Iudgements, which our sinnes have pulled downe upon us, but may at last be reunited and knit in the happinesse of a long wisht for Peace, and with one mind, in the same true Religion, worship thee the only true God, and obey our King whom thou hast set over us: grant this, O mercifull Father, for thy dear Sonnes sake who raigneth with thee, and thy holy Spirit world without end. *Amen.*

[The 'thanksgiving for the queenes safe returne' from the communion service, followed by the residue of evening prayer]

AN HOMILY AGAINST DISOBEDIENCE AND WILFULL REBELLION, TAKEN OUT OF THE BOOK OF HOMILIES, PUBLISHED IN THE TIMES OF QUEENE ELIZABETH.[330]

A PRAYER AGAINST REBELLION, PUBLISHED BY THE AUTHORITY OF QUEEN ELIZABETH IN A REBELLIOUS TIME, AND PRINTED IN THE BOOK OF HOMILIES.

1644–S1 Fast days for ungodliness, dangers to church and kingdom and for success of the army and commissioners in England

Sunday 7 January and Wednesday 10 January 1644 (Scotland)

The appointment of this fast coincided with the raising of an army to intervene in the English civil war, as agreed by the convention of estates in August (see 1643–S3). The fast act also referred to the Scottish commissioners to the Westminster assembly of divines, who had recently travelled to London. The commission's act is not extant; the description given below was recorded in the register of the presbytery of Dalkeith for 8 December.

Order: act of the commission of the general assembly, *c.* 15 Nov. 1643 (described in presbytery of Dalkeith minutes, NRS, CH2/424/3, p. 111).
Additional sources: presbytery of Peebles minutes, NRS, CH2/295/2, fo. 166v; Craighall, p. 201.

DESCRIPTION OF ORDER

[Act of the commission of the general assembly, *c.* 15 November 1643]
This day a Letter was presented by M[r] Ol[iver] Colt from the Commissioners ordaineing a fast to be keiped upon the 7 & 10 dayes of Januarie throughout this whole churche & kingdome The cheife causes of the fast wer 1. o[r] not valueing the Inestimable benefits of the Gosp. nor walking worthie of the same 2 The dangers threatned to this churche & kingdome & distressed estate of the nighbour kingdomes 3 That the Lord would blesse the Labours of o[r] commissioners in England 4 That in the expedition we trust not in the arme of fleshe but in the Lord of hoastes.

---

[330] *Two books of homilies*, pp. 550–600.

1644–E1(P)   Thanksgiving day for the discovery of a plot against parliament and London

Sunday 21 January 1644 (England and Wales)

In January 1644, a second plot to effect a peace between the king and the City of London was discovered (see 1643–E6(P)); it was led by Sir Basil Brooke (an iron-founder and prominent catholic), Theophilus Riley (scoutmaster-general of London), Colonel Riley and Thomas Violet. On 13 January, the Commons accepted an invitation from the lord mayor and the City's aldermen and common council to attend a thanksgiving feast at the Merchant Taylor's Hall on 18 January, and suggested that the banquet be prefaced, at eight o'clock in the morning, with a sermon by a preacher of their choice. Stephen Marshall was chosen to preach at Christ Church, and members of the Westminster assembly were invited to attend. On 13 January, the Commons also proposed a day of thanksgiving to be organized on the 21st, a proposal agreed by the Lords on the 20th. For the first time, parliament's resolution was printed, on the title-page of an account of the plot, *The vote of both houses of parliament*. This account, which also implicated Lord Digby, Queen Henrietta Maria and the duchess of Buckingham and was full of invective, was ordered to be read during the thanksgiving service. However, parliament had left little time for *The vote* to be printed and distributed – in fact, it was not printed until 22 January – and there can have been little expectation that it would be used. It is possible that *The vote* was designed to be read in the following months and thus had a propaganda purpose entirely separate from the thanksgiving itself.

Order: *The vote of both houses of parliament; upon the discovering of the late designe. Or, A narrative of a seditious and Iesuiticall practice upon the parliament, and city of London, lately discovered; and some observations upon it by Mr. Soliciter. Die Sabbathi, 20 Ian. 1643. It is this day ordered...* (Peter Cole; 12 pp., 1643; Wing E2433, title-page)* [a similar text is in *LJ*, VI, 385].
Additional sources: *CJ*, III, 365–6, 371; *LJ*, VI, 385; *FSP*, IX, 6–8; *The vote of both houses of parliament; vpon the discovering of the late designe* (1643; Wing E2433); *A cunning plot to divide and destroy, the parliament and the City of London. Made knowne (at a common hall) by the earle of Northumberland, master solliciter, and Sir Henry Vane* (1644; Wing C7586); Marshall, Christ Church, London (Wing M772; *FSP*, IX, 228–66).

ORDER

Parliamentary order: 20 January 1644

It is this day Ordered, by the Lords and Commons, That the 21. day of this instant, January, being the Lords day, be kept as a Day of Publique Thanksgiving, for the great Deliverances which God hath given to the Parliament and City, from the severall Plots and Designes against them; and more particularly, in discovering the late Designe: And that the Vote of both Houses upon the late Designe be printed, and read in the Churches.

1644–E2(P) Thanksgiving prayers for Scottish military assistance, the parliamentarian victory at Nantwich and the relief of Nottingham

Sunday 4 February 1644 (City of London and suburbs)

On 25 January 1644, parliamentarian forces led by Sir William Brereton and Sir Thomas Fairfax defeated John, Lord Byron who had laid siege to Nantwich, parliament's last stronghold in Cheshire, earlier in the month. On receipt of the news on 2 February, the House of Commons ordered thanksgiving in churches on the following Sunday, 4 February. For the first time, the Lords were not involved in the ordering process, as it was not sitting on 2 February. When the final order was drawn up later that day, the Commons decided to add thanksgivings for the successes of the parliamentary forces at Nottingham, which had withstood the marquess of Newcastle's siege, and the covenanter army, led by the earl of Leven, which had taken Newcastle-upon-Tyne. The support of the Scots had been sealed when parliament had signed the Solemn League and Covenant on 25 September 1643 in order to increase its military forces and to unite the English and Scottish churches and establish presbyterianism. The order for the thanksgiving was to be distributed by the lord mayor and the 'Committees for the Suburbs', probably the Committee of the Militia in the City (established in March 1642) or, more likely, one of its subcommittees. An account of the siege of Nantwich was to be printed exclusively by parliament's printer, Bernard Alsop. Presumably, the account was to be read out during the church service as previous accounts had been, though the order did not specify this. For the first time, the names of ministers who refused to publish the order had to be submitted to the Commons.

Order: *Die Veneris 2 Feb, 1643. It is this day ordered that publike thankes be given unto God in all the churches of London, Westminster, suburbs, and within the bills of mortality, upon the next Lords day* (Robert Bostock; 1 p., 1644; Thomason 669.f.7(62))* [also in *CJ*, III, 386].
Additional sources: *CJ*, III, 386; *A famous victory obtained by Sir William Brewerton, Sir Thomas Fairfax, Sir William Fairfax* (1644; Wing I1062).

ORDER

Parliamentary order: 2 February 1644

It is this day Ordered, that publike thankes be given unto God in all the Churches of London, Westminster, Suburbs, and within the bills of mortality, upon the next Lords day, for his great goodnesse in sending so seasonably to our aid, our brethren of Scotland, and in giving so great and absolute a victory unto the Forces for the Parliament neer Namptwich in Cheshire, and for the great deliverance of the Garison at Nottingham. And that copies of this Order be sent forthwith to the Lord Major of the City of London, and to the Committees for the Suburbs who are to see that this Order for the publike thanksgiving be dispersed accordingly, and that the names of such Ministers as shall refuse to observe the same, be returned to this house …

Taken neer Namptwich Ianuary 25, when the siege was raised.
5 Collonels.
2 Lieutenant Collonels.
1 Major.

14 Captains.	Slain about the Town at the
20 Lievtenants.	Siege 500.
26 Ensignes.	

14 Captains.   Slain about the Town at the
20 Lievtenants.   Siege 500.
26 Ensignes.
2 Quartermasters.   One Lieutenant
2 Cornets.   Collonel.
40 Drums.   Whereof,
41 Serjants.   4 or 5 Captains.
63 Corporalls.   And many other
22 Cullers   Officers.
The Chaplain to the Regiment.
Common souldiers above 1500.
Ordnance 6 Peeces 5 of Brasse.
Slain Lieutenant Collonel *Vain*, and many others on the enemies party,
All without the losse of one Officer, and not 20 Souldiers.
At Nottingham slain of the Earl of Newcastles Forces 200, taken 80, all with the losse
of one boy of the Garrison.

1644–S2   Fast day because of the poor condition of the Scottish army in England

Wednesday, February–March 1644 (Scotland)

The Scottish army, which crossed into England on 19 January 1644, was reportedly short of troops and supplies. The committee of estates in Edinburgh took steps to remedy the situation, and the commission of the general assembly appointed this fast. The order instructed presbyteries to appoint a fast on the next possible Wednesday. The fast was observed in Dalkeith presbytery on 21 February, and in Perth presbytery on 13 March.

Order: act of the commission of the general assembly, *c.* 15 Feb. 1644 (not found).
Sources: presbytery of Dalkeith minutes, NRS, CH2/424/3, p. 115; presbytery of Perth minutes, NRS, CH2/299/1, pp. 465–6; presbytery of Elgin minutes, NRS, CH2/144/1, p. 92.

1644–E3(R)   Thanksgiving service for the royalist victory at Newark and for the pregnancy of Queen Henrietta Maria

[March] 1644 (England and Wales)

On 21 March, Prince Rupert relieved Newark, an important royalist stronghold controlling communications between Oxford and York, which had been under siege by Sir John Meldrum for a fortnight. The prince's victory also led to parliament withdrawing from the nearby towns of Lincoln, Gainsborough and Sleaford. A form of thanksgiving was issued shortly afterwards (no order survives) which also included a prayer for Queen Henrietta Maria's safety during pregnancy. The form differed from previous royalist forms. Rather than providing a full liturgy, it comprised a single sheet to be used alongside the BCP service, listing the psalms and readings to be used and printing a collect for the military victory and a prayer for the queen (closely based on that for 1630–E1). Such economy may have been because the royalists had found it more difficult to print large quantities of long works since they left London, where the vast majority of printers had their presses. This form was printed by the University Press in Oxford. It is unclear where in the service the collect and prayer would have been read: the former may have replaced the collect of the day, the latter may have been read at the end of the litany. Henrietta Maria gave birth to her ninth and last child, Henrietta Anne, on 16 June.

Order: not extant
Form of prayer: *A forme of thanksgiving for the late defeat given unto the rebells at Newarke* (Oxford, Leonard Lichfield; Wing C4179B; 1 p.)*.

FORM OF PRAYER

[Ps. 103, 107, 115]
[First lesson: 2 Sam. 22]
[Second lesson: Rev. 19]

The Collect

O most just, most mercifull Lord God, who hast been pleased that the crying sins of this Land, should be scourg'd by a devouring Rebellion; and yet hast allayed the sharpnesse of these stripes, by acts of Mercy and Loving kindnesse to us: We doe here approach to thy Throne of Grace, with hearts full of praise and thanks, magnifying thy Name, for that thou hast been pleased to blesse thine Annoynted the King with many eminent Victories in diverse parts of this Kingdom: Particularly, for that late Notable Defeat given to the Rebells at *Newarke*, by besieging the besiegers, and for delivering those things for a prey unto us, which they intended for our destruction. Let the King still rejoyce in thy strength, O Lord, that all Loyall hearts may be exceeding glad to behold thy Salvation on Him. Goe thou still out with His Armies, and let the Sword of Thine hand fight His battailes; let Him and His evermore returne with Honour and Victory, and doe Thou hasten to reestablish Him in His Fathers Throne, with the blessing of a well setled Peace, through Iesus Christ our Lord and only Saviour. Amen.

A Prayer for the Queenes safe Delivery:

O eternall God and mercifull Father, since Lineall succession is under Thee, the great security of Kingdoms, and the very staffe of our Publique hopes: We therefore give thee most humble thanks for that especiall favour which thou art now working for our Gratious King, and this whole Realme, in giving the QUEEN more confirmed hopes of an addition to those Royall Branches which already thou hast blest us with. And as we heartily render thee all due thankes for this, so we humbly beseech thee to perfect this great blessing thus begunne *[and as 1630–E1, with 'the king' instead of 'his Maiestie'].*

[Epistle: Rom. 13:1–8]
[Gospel: John 18:1–10]

1644–E4(P)   Thanksgiving days for the parliamentarian victory at the battle of Cheriton

Tuesday 9 April 1644 (London, Westminster, parishes within bills of mortality and lines of communication); Sunday 14 April 1644 (elsewhere in England and Wales south of the Trent); Sunday 28 April 1644 (elsewhere in England and Wales north of the Trent)

Parliamentary forces, led by Waller, secured an important victory at Cheriton Wood on 28 March, having initially been routed by the royalist army. It was parliament's first offensive victory, which halted the royalist advance on the south-east and made a royalist invasion of London unlikely. It strengthened the 'War party' who were opposed to negotiating a peace with Charles. Once again (see 1643–E9(P)), the Lords initiated the ordering process and the Commons agreed to its ordinance[331] for a day of public thanksgiving to be held on 14 April on the south side of the Trent and on the 28th on the north side. However, during the following day, both houses agreed that the thanksgiving should take place on 9 April in London and surrounding parishes. The ordinance stated that Waller's victory was a result of the 'Prayers and Humiliation upon the late Solemn Fast' on Wednesday 27 March (i.e. the monthly fast: see 1641–E and 1643–E11(R)). Unlike previous thanksgivings, no account of the victory appears to have been printed. Obadiah Sedgwick and Thomas Case were appointed to preach the thanksgiving sermons to the Commons. On 8 April, the Commons ordered that a collection be made at the thanksgiving to aid maimed soldiers.

This occasion was marked by several innovations in parliament's ordering of special worship. It was the first time that the order was printed as a separate pamphlet; that MPs were requested to distribute the printed order to the counties; that special worship was specifically ordered to be observed at different times outside London and the first time that special worship was ordered to be observed along 'the lines of communication'. These 'lines' were a series of twenty-three fortifications which parliament ordered to be built to protect the City and its liberties from attack. They stretched from the Tower northwards to the Whitechapel Road, across to Hackney Road and Kingsland Road near Shoreditch, turning south-westwards to St John Street, Gray's Inn Lane and Oxford Road and then to Hyde Park Corner, Chelsea Turnpike, and Tothill Fields. South of the river, the lines ran north-east from Vauxhall to St George's Fields, Borough Street, Kent Street, Deptford Street and to a point on the Thames opposite the Tower.

Orders: *An ordinance of the Lords and Commons assembled in parliament for appointing a solemne day of thanksgiving for the happy success of the forces under Sir William Waller and Sir William Balfore: against the forces under the command of Sir Ralph Hopton, who were totally routed on the 29 of March last, 1644. Together with an ordinance of the Lords and Commons assembled in parliament to enable the merchants of Levant company, to import in English bottomes any currans and to land them within any port within the power of the parliament*, 1 Apr. 1644, Wing E1858* [also in *LJ*, VI, 495].
Additional sources: *CJ*, III, 444–5, 453–5; *LJ*, VI, 495, 497, 509; *FSP*, X, 5.

---

331   Though parliament increasingly used the term 'ordinance' to describe their orders, this was technically incorrect because ordinances were statutes that had been passed by parliament but did not have royal approval (see 1641–ES).

Printed sermons: Case, House of Commons (Wing C839; *FSP*, X, 263–302); ?Herle, mayor of London (Wing H1550); Sedgwick, House of Commons (Wing S2381; *FSP*, X, 227–62).

ORDERS

Parliamentary order: 1 April 1644

The Lords and Commons in Parliament assembled, having certain Information of the great mercy of our good God, in the happy successe of the Forces of the Parliament, under the command of Sir *William Waller* and Sir *William Balfore*, on Friday last the 29 of March, 1644. Do in their acknowledgement of Gods mercy herein Order, That upon the Lords day, which will be on the 14. of this instant April, publique Thanksgiving be given in all churches and chappels on the South side of Trent, within the power of the Parliament, unto the Lord of hosts that giveth all Victory, for the seasonable and extraordinary blessing, whereby the Army under the Command of Sir *Ralph Hopton* was totally routed, with the losse of very few of the Parliaments Forces; And all Ministers in their respective churches and chappels, are hereby directed and commanded to give notice therof, and to exhort and excite their people to acknowledge and improve this great blessing in a spirituall way, that as this mercy was bestowed in return of our prayers and humiliation, upon the late and solemn Fast the VVednesday before this Victory, so God may have the sole honour and glory of it in our praises and Thanksgivings, and that the like Thanksgiving shall be made on the North side of Trent fourteen dayes after, which will be on the 28. of this instant April.

1644–E5(P) Thanksgiving day for the parliamentarian victories at Selby, York and in Pembrokeshire

Tuesday 23 April 1644 (London, the lines of communication and the bills of mortality)

On 11 April, parliamentarian forces led by Lord Fairfax, his son, Sir Thomas, and Colonel John Lambert captured the royalist town of Selby. This was a significant victory, destroying the royalist army in Yorkshire, breaking its dominance of the north and allowing the Scots to move southwards and join with parliament's forces. On 17 April, the Commons proposed a day of thanksgiving for the victory to be held in all parishes within the lines of communication and the bills of mortality. There is no reference to the thanksgiving in the Lords even though it was sitting on this and subsequent days. Though it is possible that this is an error in record-keeping, it is more likely that the Commons had ordered the thanksgiving itself and not consulted with the Lords. Fairfax's account of the battle and a list of officers and gentlemen taken prisoner were ordered to be published and read out during the service. A collection was also ordered to be taken during the thanksgiving services on behalf of parliamentary soldiers imprisoned in Oxford; the money collected was to be paid to John Pocock, William Greening, John Randall and Richard Hutchinson, treasurers of the Maimed and Sick Soldiers, at Chandlers' Hall by 26 April. Andrew Perne and Joseph Caryl preached the sermons at St Margaret's, Westminster, but, if Perne's was printed, it is no longer extant.

Order: *A letter sent from the right honorable the Lord Fairfax, to the committee of both kingdoms: concerning the great victory, lately obtained (by Gods blessing) at Selby in York-shire. Wherein is more exactly set forth the manner of performing that gallant service, then hath been published in former relations. Together with a list of the commanders that were there taken prisoners*, 17 Apr. 1644, Wing F121,* 8 [also in *CJ*, III, 462].

Additional sources: *CJ*, III, 462–3, 468; *LJ*, VI, 522; *A collection of all the publicke orders, ordinances, and declaration of both houses of parliament* (Wing E878), p. 484; *A letter sent from the right honourable the Lord Fairfax, to the committee of both kingdoms* ([London], 1644; Wing F121); *FSP*, X, 6.

Printed sermons: Caryl, House of Commons (Wing C787; *FSP*, X, 303–58).

ORDER

Fairfax to the committee of both kingdoms: 17 April 1644

It is this day Ordered by the Commons assembled in Parliament, That the Ministers in the severall Churches and Chappels within the Line of *Communication*, and Parishes vvithin the Bills of Mortallity, do give notice to their Parishioners, of the great Success it hath pleased God to give the Parliaments Forces in Yorkshire and Pembrokeshire; And to acquaint them that the Houses have appointed, and set apart Tuesday next, for a Publique Thanksgiving, to be given to Almighty GOD for his great Blessings and Successes.

1644–E6(P)   Thanksgiving prayers for the parliamentarian relief of Lyme

Sunday 23 June 1644 (London and within the bills of mortality)

Prince Maurice, nephew of Charles I and younger brother of Prince Rupert, unsuccessfully besieged Lyme for six weeks before abandoning it (on 15 June) just before the earl of Essex arrived with reinforcements. The port had been able to hold out by receiving supplies and reinforcements by sea. On 17 June, the Commons ordered thanksgiving prayers in parishes in London and within the bills of mortality. Once again, there is no record that it consulted with the Lords or sought the House's agreement, making it more likely that the previous thanksgiving had also been ordered solely by the Commons. For the first time, the lieutenant of the Tower was ordered to distribute orders to the lord mayor, who was then to distribute them to parishes. On 19 June, the Commons also ordered that ministers should 'stirre up' their congregations 'to relieve their [the inhabitants of Lyme] hunger and nakednesse, with a charitable contribution'. The lifting of the siege and the order for the thanksgiving were both reported in *Mercurius Britannicus*.

Order: *Die Lunae 17. Junii. 1644. It is this day ordered ...* (s.n., 1644; Wing E2605C)*.

Additional sources: *CJ*, III, 524, 532–3; *LJ*, VI, 588; *A letter from the Right Honourable Robert Earle of VVarwicke, lord high-admirall of England: to the speaker of the house of peeres. VVith an exact diurnall of all the most speciall and remarkable passages which have hapned during the siege of Lyme in Dorsetshire by Pr. Maurice his forces, from the 21 of February to this present* (1644; Wing W1000); *Mercurius Britannicus*, 40 (17–24 June 1644), Thomason E.52 [8].

ORDER

Order of the House of Commons: 17 June 1644

It is day this Ordered by the Commons in Parliament, Assembled, That the severall and respective Ministers in and about the Cities of *London* and *Westminster*, and the

Parishes within the Bills of Mortality, doe on the next Lords Day, take notice of the great blessing of God in preserving the Towne of *Lyme*, and raising the Siege, and returne him humble and hearty Thankes for the manifestation of his great goodnesse and blessing herein.

1644–S3   Fast days during anxieties for the Scottish army in England

Sunday 7 July and Thursday 11 July 1644 (Scotland)

The general assembly appointed this fast on 3 June 1644, amid continuing concerns about the likely fortunes of the Scottish army in England (see also 1644–S2). The assembly expected its commission, which was to meet soon after the assembly's dissolution, to specify full causes for the fast, but details of these have not been traced.

Order: act of the general assembly, 3 June 1644, NRS, CH1/1/9, p. 250 [listed in Wing C4236, 29].
Additional sources: presbytery of Dalkeith minutes, NRS, CH2/424/3, p. 121; presbytery of Elgin minutes, NRS, CH2/144/1, p. 96; presbytery of Paisley minutes, NRS, CH2/294/2, pp. 206–7; Balfour, III, 214; Craighall, p. 207.

ORDER

Act of the general assembly: 3 June 1644
The Generall Assembly Thinks it very expedient that a solemn Fast and Humiliation be kept throughout this Kingdome upon [the] first Sabboth of July next, and the next Thursday following [espe]ciallie for commending the condition of our Army to God, And appoints that other reasons and causes necessar to be set down by the Comm^{rs} of this Assembly and sent to severall Presbyteries[.]

1644–E7(P)   Thanksgiving days for the parliamentarian and Scottish victory at the battle of Marston Moor

Thursday 18 July 1644 (London, Westminister and the lines of communication); Thursday 25 July 1644 (elsewhere in England and Wales)

The battle of Marston Moor is reputedly the biggest battle ever fought in England and involved five armies (Prince Rupert's and Newcastle's for the royalists; Lord Leven's covenanters and the armies of Fairfax and Manchester for parliament); it lasted just two hours. A surprise offensive secured victory over Prince Rupert, who was forced to hide in a beanfield to avoid capture, and Newcastle's spirited stand against the Scots was insufficient once Oliver Cromwell arrived with reinforcements. The battle ended the royalist stranglehold on the north, crushed its army and led to key officers either abandoning the royalist cause (Newcastle and Lord Eythin) or defecting to parliament (Lord Inchiquin). The Commons proposed that a day of thanksgiving should be organized in all parishes in the lines of communication on 18 July. The order for the thanksgiving was finalized on 10 July and commanded to be printed. It was presumably at this point that it was decided that the thanksgiving would also be observed across England and Wales. As for 1644–E4(P), the order was printed by Edward Husbands and distributed by MPs. Although accounts of the battle were printed, there was no explicit order for these to be read during the service as had been the case for earlier occasions. Matthew Newcomen and Richard Vines were appointed to preach the sermons at St Margaret's, Westminster, but, on 10 July, Newcomen, who was ill, was replaced by Alexander Henderson.

Orders: *Die Lune, 8 Iulii, 1644. It is this day ordered by the Lords and Commons assembled in parliament* ... 8 July 1644 (s.n., s.p., n.d.; Wing E1620A)* [also in *CJ*, III, 554]; *Die Mercurii, 10. Julii, 1644*, 10 July 1644, Wing E1638*.
Additional sources: *CJ*, III, 554–6, 561, 564; *LJ*, VI, 621, 625, 629, 631, 634–6; *A letter from Generall Leven, the Lord Fairfax, and the earl of Manchester; to the committee of both kingdoms* (1644; Wing L1816); the committee of both kingdoms to the three generals (Lords Fairfax, Manchester and Leven), 9 July 1644, SP21/18, pp. 203–4; *FSP*, XI, 5–6.
Printed sermons: Henderson, House of Commons (Wing H1441, H1442; *FSP*, XI, 333–68); Vines, parliament (Wing V559, V560, V560A; *FSP*, XI, 306–31).

ORDERS

Parliamentary order: 8 July 1644
It is this day Ordered by the LORDS and COMMONS assembled in Parliament, That *Thursday* come sevennight shall be set apart and appointed for a day of Publike Thanksgiving to be rendred unto Almighty God, for his great Blessing and full Uictory over Prince RVPERTS Army in *York*-shire, to be kept in *London* and *Westminster*, and all other parts of the Kingdome.

Parliamentary order: 10 July 1644
The *Lords* and *Commons* in Parliament assembled having certain Information of the great Mercy of our Lord God, in the happy successe of the Forces of both Kingdoms, against our Enemies near *York*, the second of this Instant Iuly, Do in their acknowledgement of Gods mercy herein Order, That upon Thursday next, which will be the eighteenth of this Moneth instant, Publique Thanks be given in all churches and chappels within the cities of *London* and *Westminster*, and the Lines of communication, unto the Lord of Hoasts that giveth all Victory, for this seasonable and extraordinary Blessing; whereby the Armies under the command of Prince *Rupert* and the Earl of *Newcastle*, were totally Routed and overthrown. And all Ministers in their respective churches and chappels, are hereby directed and commanded to give notice thereof, and to excite and exhort their people to acknowledge and improve this great Blessing in a spirituall way; That as this mercy was bestowed upon us of his meer grace and goodnesse, so God may have the sole Honour and Glory of it, in praises of Thanksgiving: And that the like Thanksgiving shall be made in all other the churches and chappels throughout the whole Kingdom, on Thursday the Five and twentieth of this instant Iuly.

1644–S4   Thanksgiving days for the Scottish and parliamentarian victory at the battle of Marston Moor

July 1644 (Scotland)

On 2 July 1644, Scottish and parliamentary forces defeated Prince Rupert's royalist army at the battle of Marston Moor, allowing parliament to take York. News of the victory reached Edinburgh by 7 July, and on 12 July a letter from the earl of Lindsay, who was with the army, was read in the Scottish parliament. An ordinance for a thanksgiving was passed, and the commission of the general assembly presumably responded by ordering presbyteries to observe the occasion. It is not clear whether a specific date was appointed by the commission.

Orders: parliamentary ordinance, 12 July 1644, *RPS*, 1644/6/141; act of the commission of the general assembly, *c.* 12 July 1644 (not found).
Additional sources: Balfour, III, 214–15; Craighall, p. 207; *RPS*, A1644/6/3; presbytery of Dalkeith minutes, NRS, CH2/424/3, p. 122; presbytery of Elgin minutes, NRS, CH2/144/1, p. 98; presbytery of Paisley minutes, NRS, CH2/294/2, pp. 207–8; *Life of Blair*, p. 172.

ORDER

Parliamentary ordinance: 12 July 1644
The esteates of parliament recommendis to the moderator and remanent commissioneres of the generall assembly the maner and way for ane speedie and solemne thankesgiveing throw the whole kirkes of this kingdome for the glorious victorie of our army at Yorke aganes our enemyes.

1644–E8(P)   Fast day for the safety of the parliamentarian army in Cornwall

Tuesday 13 August 1644 (St Margaret's, Westminster; St Olave's, Southwark and four other churches in the lines of communication)

During the summer of 1644, the earl of Essex campaigned in the royalist south-west, taking Weymouth, Taunton, Tavistock, Plymouth and Exeter before arriving at Lostwithiel in early August. Here, he found his supply lines overstretched, and he was surrounded by royalist forces and a hostile local populace. At the meeting of the Westminster assembly on 9 August, the Baptist minister, Hanserd Knollys, moved for a fast to be held in six churches in and around London, led by members of the assembly, in order to seek divine protection for Essex and his army. The assembly quickly agreed to Knollys's motion and appointed 'Dr Burgis' (probably Cornelius Burges), Stephen Marshall, Obadiah Sedgwick, William Spurstow and Humphrey Hardwick to put the proposal before parliament. Whether by coincidence or because prompted by the motion, the assembly proceeded to discuss directories for fasts and thanksgivings, that is to say the proposed sub-directories of the Directory of Public Worship, intended to replace the BCP: the main cause of disagreement was whether a whole day could or should be laid aside for either activity. It was only at the end of the session that the assembly returned to the issues of which six churches should observe the fasts, and who should lead the services. Those recommended were St Margaret's, Westminster (Herbert Palmer and Thomas Hill), St Olave's, Southwark (Charles Herle, John Conant, (Thomas?) Carter of Dinton), St Paul's Cathedral (Burgis, Marshall and Spurstow), St Michael Cornhill (Thomas Coleman, Hardwick and John Maynard), St Botolph Aldgate (Thomas Valentine, Gasper Hickes and John Bond), and St Andrew, Holborn (Sedgwick, Joseph Caryl and Daniel Cawdry). Both houses of parliament agreed to the appointment of a fast day, and to the churches and preachers. It is possible that the fasts were observed at churches other than those selected, because the assembly ordered its members to 'give notice of the[d] fast in their severall churches', and the parliamentary order also allowed the fast to be observed elsewhere.This was the second time during the civil war that a day of special worship had been initiated by the clergy (see 1643–E7(P)), and the first to be held officially in a limited number of churches. Thomas Hill and Herbert Palmer were appointed to preach before parliament.

Order: order of the House of Commons, 9 Aug. 1644, *CJ*, III, 584; approved by the House of Lords, 9 Aug. 1644, *LJ*, VI, 665.
Additional sources: *CJ*, III, 585; *FSP*, XII, 4–5; *Westminster assembly*, III, 222–7.
Printed sermons: Hill, parliament (Wing H2027; *FSP*, XII, 119–63); Palmer, parliament (Wing P235; *FSP*, XII, 48–118).

ORDER

Order of the House of Commons: 9 August 1644
Resolved, &c. That there shall be a publick solemn Fast kept on *Tuesday* next, in Six Churches within the Line of Communication (Two whereof are to be *Saint Margaret's, Westminster*, and one in *Southwarke*) to desire a Blessing from God upon my Lord General, and the Forces under his Command in the West: And that it be referred to the Assembly of Divines, to provide the Ministers that shall perform this Duty in those Six Churches; and to make Choice of the Churches: And that this Fast may be kept in such other Churches as shall desire it.

Order of the House of Lords: 9 August 1644
That there shall be a public solemn Fast kept on *Tuesday* next, in Six Churches within the Line of Communication, whereof One to be at *St Margarett's Westminster*, and One in *Southwarke*, to desire a Blessing from GOD upon my Lord General, and the Forces under his Command in the West, and that it be referred to the Assembly of Divines, to provide the Ministers that shall perform this Duty in those Six Churches, and to make Choice of the Churches; and that this Fast may be kept in such other Churches as shall desire it.
    Agreed to.

1644–E9(P)   Fast and day of humiliation for the parliamentarian defeat at Lostwithiel

Thursday 12 September 1644 (Westminster and parishes in the lines of communication and bills of mortality)

Defeated at Lostwithiel, Essex was forced to flee to Plymouth by fishing boat; many of his troops deserted or were attacked by local people as they retreated. On

9 September, the Commons proposed a solemn fast and a 'Day of Humiliation' to be held on 12 September in St Margaret's, Westminster, and other churches in the lines of communication and bills of mortality. It was agreed by the Lords and, for the first time, the Westminster assembly. It is unclear why the assembly's approval of the motion was necessary, or sought, but news of Essex's defeat distracted the assembly from its business of considering synodical church government, prompting instead a discussion of the causes of God's displeasure, made evident by the earl's defeat, including the extent to which the Solemn League and Covenant had not be observed. This debate continued for two more days. Thomas Coleman and Matthew Newcomen were appointed preachers by the Commons, a choice approved by the Lords and the assembly.

Order: parliamentary orders: House of Commons, 9 Sept. 1644, *CJ*, III, 622; House of Lords, 9 Sept. 1644, *LJ*, VI, 700.
Additional source: *FSP*, XII, 5–6; *Westminster assembly*, III, 279–99.
Printed sermons: Coleman, parliament (Wing C5051; *FSP*, XII, 318–54); Newcomen, parliament (Wing N913; *FSP*, XII, 271–317).

ORDER

Order of the House of Commons: 9 September 1644
Resolved, &c. That *Thursday* next shall be set apart for a publick Fast, and Day of Humiliation, to be kept by both Houses, the Assembly of Divines, and in the Parishes and Chapels within the Lines of Communication, and Bills of Mortality: And that the Lords Concurrence be desired herein: And that *Saint Margarett's* Church shall be the Place for this House to keep and observe it in[.]

Order of the House of Lords: 9 September 1644
That their Lordships agree to set *Thursday* next apart for the Fast; and approve of the Preachers[.]

1644–E10(P) Fast and day of humiliation in support of the parliamentarian armies

Tuesday 22 October 1644 (Lines of communication)

The royalists inflicted further defeats on parliamentarian forces after their victory at Lostwithiel, despite a shrinking in the size of the royalist army as many soldiers deserted to bring in the harvest, and despite divisions among its leaders over the favour shown to Prince Rupert. On 17 October, the Commons proposed and the Lords agreed to the appointment of another public fast and 'day of humiliation'. Advice was sought from the Westminster assembly about the day for the fast, though the assembly's minutes indicate that members were concerned more with where the fast should be observed (in six churches, or more widely), and with trying to ensure that the fast would be more strictly observed than previous ones. Either the assembly or the Commons appointed the fast to be observed within the lines of communication on 22 October. Ministers were ordered to 'specially remember this Occasion in their prayers', and there were specific injunctions against working or opening shops on the day. The orders were disseminated by the lord mayor. Benjamin Calamy, Richard Vines and Obadiah Sedgwick were appointed to preach before the Commons at St Margaret's, Westminster; Thomas Temple, Herbert Palmer and Humphry Chambers were appointed to preach before the Lords. Only those who preached before the Commons subsequently had their sermons printed. An entry in the Commons' journal suggests that this occasion may have been observed by the Westminster assembly on 23 October. On that day, two MPs were instructed to ask the assembly to 'employ this Day in Prayers unto Almighty God, for his Blessing upon the Parliament Forces'.

Order: order of the House of Commons, 18 Oct. 1644; *CJ*, III, 669; order of the House of Lords, 19 Oct. 1644, *LJ*, VII, 29.
Additional sources: *CJ*, III, 669–70, 673; *FSP*, XIII, 4–5; *Westminster assembly*, III, 413–14.
Printed sermons: Calamy, House of Commons (Wing C233, C234; *FSP*, XIII, 120–71); Sedgwick, House of Commons (Wing S2364; *FSP*, XIII, 205–39); Vines, House of Commons (Wing V563, V564, V564A; *FSP*, XIII, 173–202).

ORDER

Order of the House of Commons: 18 October 1644
Resolved, &c. That *Tuesday* next be set apart for a Publike Fast, and Day of Humiliation, to be observed within the Lines of Communication, to desire a Blessing from God upon the Armies: And that none do presume to use their Trade, or ordinary Labour, or to open their Shops, within the Places afore-mentioned, upon that Day; and that speedy Notice hereof be given to the Lord Mayor, and he desired to send Notice hereof to the particular Ministers of the several Places: And the Ministers are further desired, to recommend unto God the Condition of the Armies the next Lord's Day.

Order of the House of Lords: 19 October 1644
That this House agrees to the Ordinance concerning the Fast.

1644–E11(P) Thanksgiving service for the Scottish capture of Newcastle

Sunday 27 October 1644 (London, Westminster and the lines of communication)

While things looked bleak for the parliamentarians in the south of England during October, the covenanter army, led by the earls of Callendar and Leven, scored an important success when Newcastle fell on 19 October after a two-month siege. This sealed parliament's control of the north of England, ensured a supply of fuel to London and boosted Scottish morale. On 25 October, the Commons proposed thanksgivings for the following Sunday, and on 27 October; the Lords agreed immediately. Unlike on previous occasions (1644–E9(P), 1644–E10(P), 1644–E11(P)), neither the advice nor the approval of the Westminster assembly appears to have been sought. As was now usual, the orders were to be disseminated by the lord mayor of London. No account of the victory was printed and there is no record that ministers were appointed to preach before parliament.

Order: order of the House of Commons, 25 Oct. 1644, *CJ*, III, 677; approved by the Lords, 25 Oct. 1644, *LJ*, VII, 35.

ORDER

Order of the House of Commons: 25 October 1644

The Lords and Commons, in Parliament assembled, having received certain Intelligence of God's gracious Providence, in delivering the Town of *Newcastle* into the Hands of our Brethren of *Scotland*, come in to our Assistance; do *Order*, That publick Thanks be given to God on our and their Behalf, by all the Ministers within the Cities of *London* and *Westminster*, and the Lines of Communication, on the Lord's Day next, for this great Blessing from the Lord of Hosts: And the Lord Mayor of *London* is desired to take care, that timely Notice be given to the several Ministers of the several Parishes and Places aforesaid.

Approval of the House of Lords: 25 October 1644

That this House doth affectionately concur, for a Thanksgiving on the next Lords-day, for the taking of *Newcastle*.

1644–S5 Fast days during anxieties about the church, civil discord and military defeats

Sunday 27 October and Wednesday 30 October 1644 (Scotland)

In the summer of 1644, the marquis of Montrose joined a force of Irish and highland troops to lead the first major royalist campaign against the covenanters within Scotland. This fast seems to have been appointed soon after Montrose's victories at Tippermuir (near Perth) on 1 September, and at Aberdeen on 13 September. The printed causes for the fast (which do not include the commission's fast act itself) were undated; they had been received by the presbytery of Dalkeith by 17 October.
Order: act of the commission of the general assembly, *c.* 25 Sept. 1644 (not found).
Causes: *Causes of a solemne fast and humiliation* (Wing C4201CB)* [EEBO copy compared with EUL, Df.1.32(3); also printed in Wing T2964, 15–17].
Additional source: presbytery of Dalkeith minutes, NRS, CH2/424/3, p. 126.

CAUSES

We have great cause to be humbled in solemne manner by Fasting and Prayer, because we see the anger of God is kindled against us, in an unwonted and extraordinary way, as is evidently seen and felt. 1. By the slow progresse of the much-wished and desired Work of Reformation and intended Uniformitie in Publike Worship and Church government in all his Majesties Dominions. 2. By the long continuance of these bloody and unnaturall Warres within these Kingdomes. 3. By this unhappy Division betwixt the King and his Subjects, fomented by the Popish and Praelaticall Faction, with their adherents, Malignants and Delinquents. And 4. By the breach already made by a contemptible crew, naked and unarmed, upon our dear Brethren in Stratherne, Fyfe, Aberdeen, and other parts in the North, with effusion of much Christian blood, forcing of women, and spoiling of goods, whereby many honest women are made desolate Widows, many children Fatherlesse, and whole Families brought to extreame povertie.

I. It is to be lamented, that notwithstanding these judgements while the Lord is thus sharply chastising us, yet we look more to the immediate and second Causes of these evils than to the Supreme, Gods Providence and Permission in his justice correcting us.

II. There is no Reformation of our lives, notwithstanding of our solemne Vowes made by our Covenants, and promises of amendment in our frequent Humiliations by Fasting and Prayer; Family Exercises being neglected, and by many mocked; The Lords Sabbaths profaned, and Fornications, Adulteries, Incests, Drunkennesse, and other hainous sins still abounding.

III. The great and fearfull sinnes of our Armies abroad (as we are informed) meeting with our sinnes at home, as uncleannesse, blasphemy, spoyle and rapine indifferently, of our friends, as well as of these who are disaffected, whereas before their piety and devotion was admired, and so they were the more formidable to their enemies, now little difference twixt ours and the Malignant Armies, save in the formality of Worship.

IIII. No exact tryall of the Members of Ecclesiasticall and Civill Judicatories, which the Lord principally requires, both for a paterne of Reformation to others, and a powerfull meane to redresse enormities and abuses in others; for there is no such exact tryall of corruptions at the entrie of Ministers, nor of their carriage afterward, nor of Judges, and other Members of Civill Courts and Judicatories, as this present Reformation requires.

V. Impunitie, or slight censure, or punishment, of known Incendiaries and Malignants, wherein both Ecclesiasticall and Civill Judicatories are faultie, and thereby themselves made guilty likewise of the cruelty, villany, and other mischiefs committed by these un-naturall Countrey-men, and their Followers.

VI. Perjurie, in not discovering and delating Incendiaries and Malignants, conforme to our vow and promise in our late solemne League and Covenant; for Malignant Ministers are not delated for wresting the good intentions of the chief Instruments of this Work of Reformation; for carping at the equitie and lawful-nesse of our Covenants, and of our defensive Warres, or for their silence in not informing and confirming from time to time the people therein: Neither are Profes-sors, whereof there are a great number, delated for their Malignancie in taxing our Covenants, and the proceedings of Persons and Judicatories in the publick Cause.

VII. Perjurie, for not assisting our Brethren joyned with us in Covenant, in person, or by our meanes and moyen in this present Cause, according to our promise in our Covenants.

VIII. Confidence in our Armies at home and abroad, and their Commanders, and an arrogant conceit of our own valour and zeale to the puritie of Religion; for at first when we were naked men without Arms, without experience of the Discipline of Warre, without the mutuall help of our Neighbour Nation, we did depend on God who fought for us, and made us see his salvation: But now presuming upon our power, number of Men and Arms, skill in Warre, and of our confederacy with England, and puft up with our former successe and Victories, we have fallen off from God, leaned to the Arme of Flesh, pleasing our selves in the name of courage, to which our late punishment by Gods just judgement is made suteable; for being left to our selves, albeit armed and carrying Bows, with *Ephraim* we turned back in the Day of Battel, and fled as the *Israelites* before *Ai*, so we fled before a base un-armed, and inconsiderable Enemy.

IX. Thanksgivings for any victories the Lord hath given us, either coldly performed, or soon forgotten.

X. The great and deep security we are into, not being wakened by the noise of Gods judgements on the Churches of Germany, England, and Ireland, neither yet being sensible of the judgements hanging over this Land, yea, begun to fall already, the bloody Sword which heretofore threatned us at our Borders, being come even to the heart of our Kingdome; Nor have we that fellow-feeling of the pitifull estate of our afflicted Brethren, farre from *Uriah* and *Nehemiahs* zeale, who sympathized in their Brethrens crosses, yet who is moved amongst us, or layes to heart.

1644–E12(P) Thanksgiving days for the Scottish victory at Newcastle and parliamentarian victories at the second battle of Newbury, at Liverpool, in Lincolnshire and at Tynemouth

Wednesday 30 October and Tuesday 5 November (Lines of communication)

On 19 October, the covenanter army successfully stormed Newcastle (see 1644–E11(P)). On 27 October, the royalist and parliamentarian armies met (in the second battle of Newbury) between Newbury and Donnington Castle, a strategically important point that connected London to the west and Plymouth and Oxford to the north. Though the parliamentarian army was numerically stronger, it was unable to secure an outright victory because of low morale among soldiers, squabbling among the leaders, a reluctance to launch a frontal assault on the royalist army and the spirited defence mounted by Charles's troops. Nevertheless, as the king temporarily withdrew his troops to Oxford, parliament claimed victory. On 29 October, the House of Commons ordered that a thanksgiving for these two victories should be observed within the lines of communication on 30 October (the date of the monthly fast) and 5 November (commemoration of the failure of the gunpowder plot). On 4 November, the Commons ordered that thanks should also be offered for the recovery of Liverpool and victories in Lincolnshire. On 5 November, before the house adjourned to observe the thanksgiving at St Margaret's, it was ordered that one of the two appointed preachers (Anthony Burgess and Charles Herle) were to 'take Notice' of the surrender of Tynemouth Castle (27 October). Although the Lords observed the anniversary of 5 November – appointing John Strickland and William Spurstowe to preach before them at Westminster Abbey – and their concurrence was sought by the Commons to recognize the victories at Liverpool and in Lincolnshire, there is no record in its journals that it was involved in ordering parliamentary victories to be observed on either 30 October or 5 November.

Order: order of the Commons, 29 Oct. 1644, *CJ*, III, 680–1; resolution of the House of Commons, 4 Nov. 1644, *CJ*, III, 686; order of the House of Commons, 5 Nov. 1644, *CJ*, III, 687.
Additional sources: *CJ*, III, 680–1, 686, 687; *LJ*, VII,42, 48; *FSP*, XIV, 3–5.
Printed sermons: Burgess (Wing B5655; *FSP*, XIV, 89–116); Herle, House of Commons (Wing H1554; *FSP*, XIV, 118–40); Spurstowe, House of Lords (Wing S5093; *FSP*, XIV, 7–42); Strickland, House of Lords (Wing S5971; *FSP*, XIV, 44–88).

ORDER

Order of the House of Commons: 29 October 1644

Ordered, That To-morrow, being the Day of Publick Humiliation, a Commemoration be observed of God's great Mercy in the great and good Success it pleased God to give the Parliament's Forces, over the Enemies Forces near *Newbury* and *Donnington Castle*; and for the great Success it pleased God to give the Forces of our Brethren the *Scotts*, come in to our Aid, at *Newcastle*: And that, on *Tuesday* next, being the Fifth of *November*, the Day of Commemoration of our Deliverance from the Gunpowder Treason, a Commemoration be likewise had of these great Blessings of God; and publick Thanks given to God for his great Mercies: And that Mr. *Ashherst* do desire Mr. *Herle* to preach before the Commons on that Day: And that Mr. Recorder do desire my Lord Mayor to give Intimation of these Orders, both for To-morrow and Gunpowder Treason Day, to all the Ministers of all the Parishes and Places within the Lines of Communication.

Order of the House of Commons: 4 November 1644

Resolved, &c. That in the Publick Thanksgiving appointed to be had To-morrow, Notice to be taken of the great Success it has pleased God to give the Parliament Forces, in the Recovery and Retaking of *Liverpoole*: And likewise that Notice be taken of the great Success the Parliament Forces have lately had over the Enemies Forces in *Lincolneshire*.

The Lords Concurrence was desired herein by Mr. *Ashherst*: And

It is *Ordered*, That Notice hereof be given to the Lord Mayor, to send particular Intimations thereof to the particular Ministers.

Order of the House of Commons: 5 November 1644

Ordered, That Sir *Thomas Widdrington* do give Notice to the Preacher to take Notice of the Surrender of *Tynmouth* Castle: And that he give Thanks therefore in *St. Margarett's* Church.

1644–S6   Thanksgiving days for the capture of Newcastle

November–December 1644 (Scotland)

The thanksgiving for the Scottish army's capture of Newcastle on 19 October is not well documented, but (as with the other thanksgivings in this period) it seems that the commission of the general assembly instructed each presbytery to select a day for its own area. It was kept on 17 November in Dalkeith, and before 5 December in Peebles.

Order: act of the commission of the general assembly, *c.* 31 Oct. 1644 (not found).
Sources: presbytery of Dalkeith minutes, NRS, CH2/424/3, p. 127; presbytery of Peebles minutes, NRS, CH2/295/3, fo. 9v ; presbytery of Elgin minutes, NRS, CH2/144/1, pp. 102–3.

1645–S1 Fast day for the meetings of parliament and the general assembly

Sunday 5 January 1645 (Scotland)

This fast was appointed in anticipation of forthcoming meetings of parliament (on 7 January 1645) and of the general assembly, which had been summoned for 22 January to consider the Directory of worship and propositions concerning church government issued by the Westminster assembly. As the description of the fast (from the minutes of Dalkeith presbytery for 12 December) suggests, the causes printed for 1644–S5 were to be used, with additional prayers for the success of parliament and the assembly.

Order: act of the commission of the general assembly, *c.* 1 Dec. 1644 (described in presbytery of Dalkeith minutes, NRS, CH2/424/3, p. 128).
Additional sources: presbytery of Peebles minutes, NRS, CH2/295/3, fo. 11v; presbytery of Elgin minutes, NRS, CH2/144/1, p. 103; presbytery of Paisley minutes, NRS, CH2/294/2, p. 216.

DESCRIPTION OF ORDER

[Act of the commission of the general assembly: *c.* 1 December 1644]
Quhilk day The brethren resaved a letter from ye Commissioners of ye generall assemblie for a Fast to be keeped ye fyft of Januare Causs one w^t ye former, and to crave a blissing to this ensuing parliament, and generall assemblie.

1645–E1(R) Fast day during the peace negotiations at Uxbridge

Wednesday 5 February 1645 (England and Wales)

In November 1644, the House of Lords initiated peace negotiations with the king, which were conducted over the following weeks at Uxbridge. The three main areas of discussion were religion – particularly the alternatives of episcopacy or presbyterianism, and the BCP or the Directory of worship – control of the militia and the navy, and the political and religious position of Ireland. The two sides differed markedly on these issues, but ultimately the negotiations failed for other reasons: neither side was committed to peace, they deeply distrusted each other, and both were busy strengthening their armies for a new campaign in the spring. On 27 January 1645, the king issued a proclamation for a solemn fast, to be held on 5 February. The ostensible reason was to support the cause of peace, but evidently the main purpose was to claim divine favour for the renewed royalist campaign. As the royal court had returned to Oxford, the form of prayer was printed by Leonard Lichfield, at the University Press, and it is presented in a very odd format. The opening pages print the beginning of the BCP service for morning prayer, giving the full text of standard elements such as the confession and absolution, followed by a 'Psalme composed out of severall passages in the Booke of Psalmes' to be said in place in the *Venite*. But then, on pp. 9–10, the form simply lists the psalms and lessons to be used at morning prayer and evening prayer, followed by the instruction that the rest is 'to go on as it is in the former Fast-Book [that is, 1643–E11(R)], with the addition of some

Prayers'. Then the details of the epistle and gospel for the communion service are given, after which the text of three new prayers is printed, including one composed by the king's 'speciall Direction and Dictates'. It almost appears as if the printer abandoned setting the full text of the form after the first few pages. If this were the case, it might be explained by a realization of the difficulty of printing a full form in the relatively short space of time between the king's proclamation on 27 January and the fast on 5 February, especially given the limited number of presses available in Oxford. Although the fast was supposed to be observed 'in all places within our Dominions', the king himself recognized that it was unlikely that his proclamation could be widely distributed in time.

Order: royal proclamation, 27 Jan. 1645 (Leonard Litchfield, Oxford, 1645; Wing C2585)* [also in Larkin, II, 1055–6].
Form of prayer: *A forme of common-prayer, to be used upon the solemne fast appoynted by his majesties proclamation upon the fifth of February, being Wednesday. For a blessing on the treaty now begunne, that the end of it may be a happy peace to the king and to all his people. Set forth by his majesties speciall command to be used in all churches and chappels.* (Oxford, Leonard Lichfield; Wing C4112; 16 pp.) [annotated on BL, Thomason E.27(4): 'Feb: 3ᵈ'].
Form of prayer (other edition): Oxford [i.e. London], Leonard Lichfield; Wing C4112; 8 pp. [see Madan, *Oxford books*, II, no. 1704].
Additional sources: *CJ*, IV, 67.

ORDER

Royal proclamation: 27 January 1645

Whereas Almighty God in his Iustice to punish the Common and Crying sinnes of the Land, hath sent a Civill Sword throughout all Our Dominions, which hath miserably wasted and threatens a speedy and utter desolation to the same. And now in the height of these Calamities, a Treaty is assented to, to beginne at *Vxbridge* on *Thursday* the Thirtieth day of this Instant *January*, touching the Composing and ending of those unhappy differences and distractions, about which so much blood hath been already spilt, which Treatie, may by the blessing of God (who is the disposer of all mens hearts and of all events) be a meanes to produce a Peace. And whereas it is the duty, and hath been the practice of Christians under affliction, to set apart some time for publique and solemne Humiliation and Prayer, for removing of Gods judgements, and particularly for a blessing and good successe to the meanes conducing to their deliverance. We doe therefore by this Our Proclamation appoynt and straitly Charge and Command, that on Wednesday being the Fifth of *February* next ensuing, a solemne Fast be kept in all places within Our Dominions, whether the notice of this Our Proclamation shall or may come before that time, that both Prince and People may then joyne together in a true Humiliation and Devout and earnest Prayers to God, that he would be pleased so to blesse and prosper this intended Treaty, that it may produce a happy Peace in all Our Dominions, such as may be for his honour and the good of his Church, and of Us and all Our Subjects. And We doe hereby charge and require all Our Subjects, of what degree or condition soever they be, which shall have notice of this Our Proclamation, That they doe religiously prepare and apply themselves to a due observation of the same, by Fasting, Humiliation, and Prayer on that day, and in hearing of Gods word, as they will answer to God their neglect of this Christian duty, and as they will answer to Us the neglect of this Our Just and necessary Command. And for the better and more orderly observation of this Fast, We doe hereby appoint, that the Forme of Prayer and Service of God set forth in the

Booke heretofore published for the Monthly Fast, with such alterations and additions as shall be prepared and fitted for this present purpose, and published in Print before the said day, shall be used in all Churches and Chappels where this Fast shall be kept.

FORM OF PRAYER

MORNING PRAYER

First the Minister shall say. [Opening sentence: Jer. 10:24]

[The exhortation, the confession, the absolution, the Lord's prayer and versicles]

In stead of the Venite Exultemus, *shall be us'd this Psalme composed out of the severall passages in the Booke of Psalmes.*

Unto thee will I cry, O Lord my strength: thinke no scorne of me, least if thou make as though thou hearest not, I become like them that goe downe into the Pit. (Ps. 28:1)
Heare the voyce of my humble Petitions, when I cry unto thee: when I hold up my hands towards the Mercy seat of thy holy Temple. (2) [Ps. 28:2]
O God, wherefore art thou absent from us so long: why is thy wrath so hot against the sheep of thy pasture? (Ps. 74.v.1) [74:1]
Lord, how long wilt thou be angry: shall thy jealousy burn like fire for ever? (Ps. 79:5)
Hath God forgotten to be gratious: or will he shut up his loving kindnesse in displeasure? (Ps. 77:9)
Lord, where are thy old loving kindenesses: which thou swarest unto David in thy truth? (Ps. 89:48) [89:49]
O think upon thy Congregation: whom thou hast purchased, and redeemed of old. (Ps. 74:2)
Thinke upon the tribe of thine Inheritance: and mount Sion wherein thou hast dwelt. (3) [Ps. 74:2]
Thou shalt arise and have mercy upon Sion: for it is time that thou have mercy upon her, yea, the time is come. (Ps. 102:13)
And why? thy servants thinke upon her stones: and it pittieth them to see her in the Dust. (14) [Ps. 102:14]
Be thou my Judge, O Lord, for I have walked innocently: my trust hath been also in the Lord, therefore shall I not fall. (Ps. 26:1)
Examine me, O Lord, and prove me: try out my reines, and my Heart. (2) [Ps. 26:12]
Let my sentence come forth from thy presence: and let thine eyes look upon the thing that is equall. (Ps. 17:2)
Shew thy marvailous loving kindnesse, thou that art the Saviour of them which put their trust in thee: from such as resist thy right hand. (7) [Ps. 17:7]
Call to remembrance, O Lord, thy tender mercies: and thy loving kindnesse which hath been ever of old. (Ps. 25:5)
For thy Names sake, O Lord, be mercifull unto my sinne: for it is great. (15) [Ps. 25:15]
The sorrowes of my Heart are enlarged: O bring thou me out of my troubles. (16) [Ps. 25:16]
Look upon mine adversity and misery: and forgive me all my sinne. (17) [Ps. 25:17]

Thou shalt shew us wonderfull things in thy Righteousnesse, O God of our salvation: thou that art the Hope of all the ends of the Earth, and of them that remaine in the broad Sea. (Ps. 63:5)
Which stilleth the raging of the Sea: and the noise of his waves, and the madneße of his People. (7) [Ps. 63:7]
Remember me, O Lord, according to the favour that thou bearest unto thy people: O visit me with thy salvation. (Ps. 106:4)
That I may see the felicity of thy chosen: and rejoyce in the gladnes of thy People, & give thanks with thine Inheritance. (5) [Ps. 106:5]
O let the sorrowfull sighing of the Prisoners come before thee: according to the greatnesse of thy power preserve thou those that are appointed to dye. (Ps. 79:12)
Comfort us again now after the time that thou hast plagued us: and for the yeares wherein we have suffered adversity. (Ps. 90:15)
The fiercenesse of man shall turne to thy Praise: and the fiercenesse of them shalt thou refraine. (Ps. 76:10)
For God will save Sion, and build the Cities of Juda: that men may dwell there, and have it in poßeßion. (Ps. 69:36)
O tarry thou the Lords leisure: be strong and he shall comfort thine heart, and put thou thy trust in the Lord. (Ps. 27:16)
And the glorious Majestie of the Lord our God be upon us: Prosper thou the worke of our Hands upon us, O prosper thou our handy worke. (Ps. 90:17)
Glory be to the Father ...

Psalmes for Morning and Evening Prayer.

[Morning prayer: Ps. 42, 46, 61, 80, 122]
[Evening prayer: Ps. 77, 80, 85, 126, 132, 133]

[Morning prayer: first lesson: Isa. 51:9–23]

[Te Deum]

[Morning prayer: second lesson: Rom. 12:9–21]

[Benedictus]

[Evening prayer: first lesson: Isa. 54]

[The Magnificat]

[Evening prayer: second lesson: 1 John 4]

[Nunc dimittis]

The rest to go on as it is in the former Fast Book [i.e. 1643–E11(R)] *with an addition of some Prayers.*

[COMMUNION]

[Epistle: Heb. 12:1–15]

[Gospel: Matt. 5:1–12]

A Prayer drawne by His MAJESTIES *speciall Direction and Dictates.*

O Most mercifull Father, Lord God of Peace and Truth, we a People sorely afflicted by the Scourge of an unnaturall Warre, doe here earnestly beseech Thee, to command a Blessing from Heaven upon this present Treaty, begunne for the establishment of an happy Peace. Soften the most obdurate Hearts with a true Christian desire of saving those mens blood, for whom Christ himselfe hath shed His. Or if the guilt of our great sinnes cause this Treaty to breake off in vaine, Lord let the Truth clearly appeare, who those men are, which under pretence of the Publick good doe pursue their own private ends; that this People may be no longer so blindely miserable, as not to see, at least in this their Day, the things that belong unto their Peace. Grant this gracious God, for his sake who is our Peace it selfe, even Jesus Christ our Lord. AMEN.

A Prayer for Peace

Almighty God, terrible in thy *Judgements*, but more wonderfull in thy *Mercies*, who turnest man to *Destruction*, and againe, thou saist, *Come* againe ye children of Men; we miserable sinners prostrate this day before thee, humbly confesse with *Horror* in our *Hearts*, and *Confusion* in our *Faces*, that every one of us hath, more or lesse, contributed to that vast heap of crying sins which hath now in so high a measure drawne down thy vengeance on us, that we have abused thy *Patience* so long, till we have at last turn'd it into *Fury*, compelling thee, by our often provocations to visit us in blood, to make us teare out our owne bowels, and by a strange unnaturall Warre, raised we know not why, (thy *Justice* and our *Sinnes* excepted) to become executioners of our selves, and so to sinne afresh in the very punishments of sinne. But alas! what profit is there in our *Blood*? or what *Glory* can come to thee by our *Ruine*? Let it suffice, O God, that thou hast thus farr rebuked us in thine *Anger*, but *consume* us not utterly, for we are all thy People. Say to the destroying *Sword*, *It is enough*, and let it be no longer *drunk* with the blood of thine *Inheritance*: But look down upon our unfained *Humiliation*, heare the *Prayer* which in the bitternesse of our Soules we powr out this day before thee, accept of our *Repentance*, and where it is defective, let thy *Holy Spirit* make it up with *Groanes* that cannot be expressed. Look upon thy *Moses* who standeth in the gap, beseeching thee to turn thine anger from thy People; remember what he hath *suffer'd*, and the *heavy things* that thou hast shewn him; and in the day, when thou makest *Inquisition for Bloud*, forget not his *desires of Peace*, the *endeavours* which he hath used, and the *Prayers* which he hath made to Thee for it. Return all this, O Lord, with *comfort* into his *Bosome*. And since thou hast already wrought so much for him, as to bring these unhappy entangled differences to a *Treaty*, take not off thine *Hand*, till thou hast *untyed* every *knot*, and *cleared* every *difficulty*. Send *thy Spirit* into their Hearts who are entrusted with this *great worke*, give them *Bowells of Compassion* toward their *bleeding, and expiring Country*, strike a *Sense* into them of the Bloud *already* shed, and the *Desolation* to come, which threatneth all if they prevent it not. But above all, let *thy Feare* run through all their *consultations*, that remembring the *sad account*, which in the last *great day* will be required of them, they may lay aside *every Sin*, and *every Interest* that may divert them from *the wayes of Peace*; and by the guidance of *thy Wisedome* (for in this all humane wisedome failes) find out those *blessed Expedients* as may restore the voyce of Joy and Peace into our Dwellings, in such a way, as may be most to the *Glory* of thy *Great Name*, the Settlement of the *true Religion* so long professed among us, the *Honour*, and *Safety* of the *King's Sacred Person*, and the *Good* of *all His People*. Heare these our Prayers, and perfect this great work, through the mediation of thine owne dear Son Jesus Christ our Lord. *Amen*.

A Prayer

O most just and powerfull Lord God, to whom vengeance belongeth, we cannot but acknowledge that the manifold miseries which have befallen us are the due reward of our deeds, and that we have deserved that the things which belong to our peace should still be hid from our eyes. For when of thy owne free mercy thou wert pleased to grant us a long time of plenty and prosperity, more then thou gavest to any of the Nations that are about us, we became weary of our happinesse, and by our ingratitude pulled upon us those judgments which now threaten desolation to this late flourishing Kingdome. And since the time of our affliction thou hast given us space to repent, and we repented not; Iniquity hath still more and more abounded. As heretofore thy mercies did not allure us, so now thy judgments have not humbled us to a serious consideration of our misdeservings. Now, O Lord, we finde our selves intangled and wearied by our owne counsels; The troubles of our heart are inlarged; Our iniquities and the punishments which attend upon them, are a burden too heavy for us to bear. And therefore in the anguish and bitternesse of our soules we returne unto thee, humbly beseeching thee, in whom alone is our helpe, to have respect unto the prayers of thy servants. O shut not up thy loving kindnesse in displeasure, let not thine anger burne against the sheepe of thy pasture: But binde up the breach of this people. Let the sighing of the prisoners come before thee; Behold the teares of the distressed Orphans and widowes, and of all such as are oppressed and have no comforter. How long, O Lord, holy and true, doest thou forbeare to command deliverances? Remember thy tender mercies which have beene ever of old, and save us as thou hast done heretofore. Remember thy promise of deliverance to those who call upon thee in the day of trouble. And when the bloud that hath beene shed by oppression calls aloud for vengeance, O then hearken unto the voice of thy Sonnes bloud which speakes better things; behold the Lambe of God, who was wounded for our transgressions, and bruised for our iniquities. And to this end regard the sincerity of thine Anointed, maintaine thy owne cause, and preserve unto him that power which thou hast given him: binde his soule in the bundle of life, let mercy and truth preserve him, and let his Throne be established for ever before thee. Blesse them that are peaceable and faithfull in the land: And as for those that have risen up against him, we beseech thee melt & mollify their hearts to the entertainment of compassion and love; reclaime them to obedience, lay not their sinne to their charge, but guide their feet into the way of peace. Give to those that have done wrong the grace to repent, and to those that have suffered wrong, minds ready to forgive. And if any shall be averse from peace, O thou that art the wonderfull Counsellour, turne their wisedome into foolishnesse, confound their practices, and let their mischeife returne upon their owne heads. And when thou hast vouchsafed to give us that tranquillity which we begge at thy hands, give us grace to embrace it with all thankfulnesse, to obey our Governours, to live at unity among our selves, evermore blessing thy glorious name which is exalted above all blessing and praise, through Jesus Christ our Lord. *Amen*.

1645–E2(P)   Thanksgiving day for the parliamentarian victories at Weymouth, Shrewsbury, Scarborough, Plymouth and Lancaut

Wednesday 12 March 1645 (Lines of communication)

During and after the treaty negotiations at Uxbridge, parliament scored a number of victories, including those at Plymouth (January), Scarborough and Shrewsbury (both 22 February), and Weymouth (28 February). Sir Edward Massey, the parliamentarian governor of Gloucester, defeated the royalist forces of Sir John Winter (or Wintour) at Lancaut on 25 February, forcing Winter into a desperate escape by swimming across the River Wye. On 4 March, the Commons proposed a general thanksgiving for these events to be held on 12 March. Although this received the Lords' approval, the printed version of the order stated that the day was ordered by the Commons alone. On 10 March, the Lords and Commons jointly ordered a collection be made during the services for the relief of widows, injured soldiers and others of Plymouth, Melcombe Regis and Weymouth. The Commons also commissioned an account of the victories, *God appearing for the parliament*, which was ordered to be read during the thanksgiving services; it included the text of the order at the end of the pamphlet. This was part of parliament's increasing use of print to disseminate orders, acts, protestatations, rates, speeches and other information across the country. John Arrowsmith and a Mr Harris were appointed preachers for the occasion, though Harris was later replaced by Richard Vines on account of his old age and 'the Lowness of his Voice'. At the Lords' suggestion, the service for parliament was held in Christ Church, not at the usual places, St Margaret's and the Abbey. The lord mayor was ordered to distribute the order to all ministers within the lines of communication; he was also expected to attend parliament's service.

Orders: parliamentary orders, 4 Mar. 1645, Wing G906*, p. 20 [also in *CJ*, IV, 67]; 10 Mar. 1645 (s.n., s.p., n.d.; Wing E2603K)* [also in *CJ*, IV, 72–3].
Additional sources: *LJ*, VII, 262, 264, 267; *CJ*, IV, 69, 72–3; *Die Lunae, 10. Martii, 1644. The Lords and Commons in parliament assembled, taking into their consideration the great distresse and calamity of the town of Plymouth, Melcomb Regis, and Weymouth* (1645; Wing E1643); *God appearing for the parliament, in sundry late victories bestowed upon their forces* (1645; Wing G906); *FSP*, XVI, 3–4.
Printed sermons: Arrowsmith, parliament (Wing A3775; *FSP*, XVI, 9–48); Vines, parliament (Wing V551, V552, V552A; *FSP*, XVI, 50–80).

ORDERS

Parliamentary order: 4 March 1645

Resolved upon the Question by the Commons Assembled in Parliament; That Publique Thankes shall be given unto God for his great Mercy and bleßing upon the Parliament Forces, in the regaining of *Weymouth*, the gaining of *Shrewsbury*, and *Scarborough*, the late deliverance at *Plymouth*, and the great Victory over the Forces under Sir *Iohn Winter*.
Resolved upon the Question,
That Wednesday come seven-night (being the 12. of this present *March*, be appointed for this day of publique Thanksgiving.
Ordered that the Lord Major of the Citie of *London* be desired to give notice of this day of publique Thanksgiving, to all the Ministers within the Lines of Communication,

that they may give notice of it to their Parishioners in their Pulpits on the next *Lords Day*.

Parliamentary order: 10 March 1645

It is this day Ordered by the Commons assembled in Parliament; That the day of publique Thanksgiving, appointed by both Houses to bee kept on Wednesday next the 12th. of this instant *March*, bee observed on the same day, in all the Churches and Chappels within the Lines of Communication. And the Assembly of Divines are desired to take notice hereof, and to employ their best endeavours and care herein. And my Lord Major is further desired to give notice hereof to all the severall and respective Ministers.

1645–S2   Fast day after defeats by Montrose's royalist forces

Wednesday 26 March 1645 (Scotland)

The marquis of Montrose wintered his troops in the highlands, where they plundered Campbell lands in Argyll, before defeating an army of covenanters at Inverlochy (now Fort William) on 2 February 1645. These setbacks moved the general assembly to appoint a fast, and to call on parliament and the church courts to act vigorously against supporters of Montrose. On the other hand, the printed causes of the fast, and the assembly's *Solemne and seasonable warning* (with which the causes were distributed), acknowledged that progress had been made towards religious uniformity with England.

Order: act of the general assembly, 7 Feb. 1645 (unprinted; not found) [listed in Wing C4239, 46].
Causes: *The causes of the fast: appointed by the generall assembly to be kept the last Wednesday of March. 1645* (Wing C42011; EUL, Df.1.32(5)) [also Wing C4267].
Additional sources: *A solemne and seasonable warning to the noble-men, barons, gentlemen, burrows, ministers, and commons of Scotland* (Edinburgh, 1645; Wing C4259G); *RPS*, 1645/1/74; presbytery of Dalkeith minutes, NRS, CH2/424/3, pp. 131, 133; presbytery of Peebles minutes, NRS, CH2/295/3, fo. 18v ; presbytery of Paisley minutes, NRS, CH2/294/2, p. 218.

CAUSES

The wrath of GOD incumbent on us, waxing more and more hote, and threatning day by day greater destruction, calleth and crieth aloud to prepare our selves To meet our God, To acknowledge our offences, and Seek his face: Though one of the causes of our last solemne Humiliation (to wit, the slow progresse of the much wished and desired Work of Reformation, and intended Uniformitie in Publike Worship, and Kirk-Government) be in a fair way and good measure removed by our gracious LORD, who is a GOD that heareth Prayer, and who in the midst of Wrath remembreth Mercy; yet all the rest of the Causes, both of the evil of Sin and of Punishment, are rather increased than abated.

For, 1. The unnaturall bloody War between King and Subjects still continueth, and though this War be fomented by the Popish and Prelaticall Faction, by Malignants, Delinquents, and their Complices; By the Queen, her compassing Sea and Land to that purpose; Yet for any thing we can see or learn, Our King, led by ill counsell, is guilty of shedding much innocent blood, both by Sea and Land; whereof we have presently dolefull experience, in sending against us cruell Irishes, *Skilfull to destroy.*

2. These bloody Butchers, led by one excommunicate, perfidious in the Covenant, do range and run from place to place, Plundering, Spoiling, Burning, Slaying, without any respect to Sex or Age, they practise all mischief, and prosper; a pregnant evidence, as of the LORD his feeding and fitting of them to the day of slaughter; so of his anger and indignation against us, for our Rock hath for a time sold us, he goeth not forth with our Armies as before, he giveth not the wonted blessing to our Resolutions, nor the former successe to our Expeditions: And not onely is the Sword of a Barbarous Enemy, eating Flesh and drinking Blood; but we are threatned also with the Plagues of Famine and Pestilence, which is breaking out into divers corners of our Countrey.

No wonder: For 1. *The whole head is sick, and the whole heart faint: from the sole of the foot unto the head there is no soundnesse in it, but wounds and bruises, and putrifying sores, there is no Truth, no Mercie, nor knowledge of God in the Land: By Swearing, Lying, Killing, Stealing, and committing Adultery, they break out, and Blood toucheth Blood.* None have taken to heart nor repented that foule Defection and Back-sliding of our Kirk, in time of Prelacie; Princes, Rulers, Pastors, People, all have sinned hainously and done foolishly: These in whose hands the Sword of Justice is put, have been slow to execute Justice unpartially: The Watchmen also in many places are often asleep, keep silence, or speak amisse, prove not faithfull, labour not upon the souls committed to them, for instructing and informing of their judgements, for quickning and rectifying of their affections towards the Way and VVork of the LORD; but rather temporise, doing all things for the Time, and nothing for the Trueth; they do rather weaken then strengthen heart and hand in the Work of the LORD, notwithstanding of their Oath to the contrary. No marvell therefore that the Multitude be over-grown with Prophanity, Security, Neutrality, and fall on murmurings against publike Ordinances for the common safety of the Kingdom.

2. Our Covenant doth binde us to Reformation of Judicatories, as well as to a Reformation of Persons and Families, and doth obliege those who have Servants and Followers to endeavour their Reformation: But where is there any Reformation to be seen? Our LORD is working wonders for advancing Religion in the Power, Puritie, and Spiritualitie of it: But where is any Power or Life of Godlinesse to be found? It is rather hated and mocked, Christ and his Gospel dis-esteemed: Many of all ranks do rest upon meer formality, and content themselves with the bare name of a Covenant, and of a Profession; Yea, Sin did never more abound then now, though amidst many Mercies on the one hand, and many sad Judgements on the other. And among these who are Covenanters, and stand in Arms for the Covenant, nothing almost to be heard or seen, but fearfull Oaths, Sabbath-breakings, Oppressions of very friends, Quarrellings, VVhorings, Carousings, and such fearfull abominations, which make the Land to mourn.

3. Never a Nation hath tasted of higher Favours, of rarer Mercies: Yet where is there any Nation lesse deserving? more regardlesse of the Works and Wonders of the LORD, or more unthankfull? Not any more ready to forget unparalleld Blessings; not any more prone to Murmure, to Quarrell, to Distrust; None more ready to kisse their own right hand, when any thing is done; None more ready to trust in man, when any thing is to be done; None more ready to quarrell with God, and to speak evil of his Way and Covenant, when any thing is mis-done: No looking up to the Hand that smites us, nor to the Hand that bindes up and heales us.

For these and such like causes, *Jacob is given for a spoile, and Israel to the robbers*. The worst of the heathen are brought among us: Yet if we will bestirre our selves to call on GOD, To lay hold on him, To wrestle with him for the Blessing, To Repent all our Sins; our hardnesse of heart, our slight and superficiall performance of our former Fasts and Humiliations, we may be confident that there is yet hope in Israel: And though this be the time of Jacobs trouble, he shall assuredly be saved out of it: and that the rather, because of the glorious and stately Steps whereby the LORD hath been pleased to manifest himself, in all the Passages of this great Work, and now in this Assembly: whereby we may easily perceive, That he keepeth still a purpose of Love towards us, and doth but *Hide himself for a time*, till we *Seek him early*, and Return to him heartily.

1645–E3(P)   Thanksgiving prayers for Montrose's retreat from Dundee

Sunday 20 April 1645 (Lines of communication)

This thanksgiving reflects the decline in the morale of the parliamentary leadership in the spring of 1645 as Montrose's actions at Dundee can hardly be called a 'great defeat'. His troops quickly overran the town but, hearing that Sir John Urry (or Hurry), major-general of foot and horse in Scotland, was coming to the town's defence, Montrose voluntarily withdrew and successfully eluded capture. Nevertheless, on 15 April, the Lords proposed that thanksgivings be held on 20 April in all churches and chapels within the lines of communication, and that extracts of the letters they had received describing events should be printed and read during the service (*An extract of severall letters*). The Commons agreed to this, and to the proposal that delegates from both houses should personally congratulate the Scottish commissioners on this 'great Victory'. The printed order from the Lords (Wing E1734) is one of only two extant printed slips which conveyed the Lords' order to the lord mayor (see also 1643–E7(P)).

Orders: parliamentary order, 15 Apr. 1645, Wing E3910* [same text in *Die Mercurij 16. Aprill, 1645* (s.n., s.p., n.d.; Wing E1734)].
Additional sources: *CJ*, IV, 111; *LJ*, VII, 319; *An extract of severall letters from Scotland* (1645; Wing E3910; another edition Wing E3911); *Die Mercurij 16. Aprill, 1645. Ordered by the Lords and Commons in parliament assembled, that the lord major of the city of London is hereby desired and required to give direction that publike thanksgiving be made on the next Lords day* (1645; Wing E1734); Lambert, *Printing*, p. 96.

ORDER

Parliamentary order: 15 April 1645
Ordered by the Lords and Commons Assembled in Parliament, that publike Thanksgiving be made on Sunday next in all Churches and Chappels within the Lines of Communication for the great blessing God hath given to our Brethren of *Scotland*, in the late Victory obtained against the Forces under the Command of the Earle of *Montrosse*: And it is further Ordered, That this Relation and Order be forthwith Printed and published.

1645–E4(P)   Thanksgiving prayers for parliamentarian success at Taunton

Sunday 18 May 1645 (Lines of communication and bills of mortality)

Parliamentarian forces under Colonel Robert Blake had regained control of Taunton during the summer of 1644, but were then faced by a prolonged royalist siege. A relief force commanded by Colonel Welden reached the garrison on 11 May 1645, and three days later, the Commons ordered thanksgivings to be observed on 18 May. The Lords' *rôle* in the process is unclear: though they received news of Welden's victory, there is no record in its journal of assent to the thanksgivings. As usual, the orders were distributed by the lord mayor. An account of the siege, in the form of two letters from Fairfax and Welden, was ordered to be printed and was entered in the Stationers' Register on 14 May. A collection for the inhabitants of Taunton was not ordered until 24 May, after the thanksgivings had been held. In the event, the thanksgivings and the belief that the town had been relieved were premature, as royalist forces under Lord Goring were able to renew the siege, which continued for another two months (see 1645-E6(P) and 1645-E7(P)).

Order: parliamentary order, 14 May 1645, *CJ*, IV, 142.
Additional sources: *LJ*, VII, 372, 374; *Two letters the one from the Right Honourable, Sir Thomas Fairfax. The other from Colonell Ralph Weldon. Being an exact relation of the raising of the siege, and releeving of the town of Taunton* (1645; Wing F251); *Die Sabbathi, 24 Maii, 1645. It is this day ordered by the Lords and Commons assembled in parliament, that a collection be made of all well-affected persons ... to be imployed for the relief of the poor distressed inhabitants of the town of Taunton* (1645; Wing E1621).

ORDER

Parliamentary order: 14 May 1645
Ordered, That Publick Thanks be given unto Almighty God, on the next Lord's Day, in all the Churches and Chapels within the Lines of Communication, and Bills of Mortality, for the good Success it has pleased God to give the Parliament Forces in the Relief of *Taunton*: And my Lord Mayor is desired ... , that timely Notice hereof may be given to the several Ministers respectively.

1645–S3   Fast day during Montrose's military advances

Sunday 1 June 1645 (Scotland)

This fast was appointed due to Montrose's continuing royalist military campaign in northern Scotland. The presbytery of Dalkeith recorded the commission's letter on 12 May 1645, suggesting that the fast was ordered shortly before Montrose's victory at Auldearn (see 1645–S4).

Order: act of the commission of the general assembly, *c.* 1 May 1645 (described in presbytery of Dalkeith minutes, NRS, CH2/424/3, p. 135).

DESCRIPTION OF ORDER

[Act of the commission of the general assembly: *c.* 1 May 1645]
Ane Letter wes sent from the Commissioun of the Assembly ordaineing ane Solemne
Fast to be keipit on the first of Juny. Becaus of the sines and Judgementis so heavie
on the Land.

1645–E5(P)   Thanksgiving days for the parliamentarian victory at the battle of Naseby

**Thursday 19 June 1645 (London, Westminster and parishes within the lines
of communication and bills of mortality); Friday 27 June 1645 (counties
under the power of parliament)**

Although the battle of Naseby on 14 June initially went in the royalists' favour,
the size of the New Model Army (*c.* 15,000–17,000) and the tactics employed by
Fairfax and by Cromwell, newly made lieutenant-general of the cavalry, ultimately
secured a parliamentary victory. The victors lost only about 150 men compared to
1,000 men, 2,000 horses and all the artillery on the royalist side. On 16 June, the
Commons proposed a day of thanksgiving to be held in and around the capital on
Thursday 19 June and 'in the several Counties under the Power of Parliament' – the
first time such a designation was used – on Friday 27 June. On the following day, 17
June, the Westminster assembly debated the order, more particularly whether it was
appropriate that the thanksgiving day should be observed in the same week as the
monthly fast day. It concluded that the fast might not be observed that week. Despite
the assembly's decision, the fast went ahead. On 16 June the letters of Fairfax,
Cromwell and the army committee were ordered to be printed, but the account of
the battle (*An ordinance*) was not printed until the 20th. This suggests that it was
only to be read during services in the counties; indeed, the account includes the text
of the order for this later thanksgiving. Stephen Marshall and Richard Vines were
appointed to preach the parliamentary sermons at Christ Church. Contrary to usual
practice, the sermons were both preached in the morning in order to accommodate
the dinner to which the lord mayor, aldermen and common council of London were
invited by both houses at the Grocers' Hall, which was some distance from Christ
Church. Vines's sermon was either not published or is no longer extant; Marshall's
printed the date of the thanksgiving as 19 June. At Clare Hall, Cambridge (now Clare
College), the Fellows were allowed 'exceedings at Dinner and a Supper, provided
neyther consist of theire ordinary fish commons in part'. They were also ordered to
have a bonfire. At Hesket-in-the-Forest, the parliamentary commissioners informed
David Leslie, lieutenant-general of the horse, that they would not be able to meet
with him on 27 June because it was the thanksgiving day. Whether Leslie observed
the thanksgiving is unclear: he was laying siege to Carlisle which only surrendered
on the 28th.

A month after Naseby, parliament was able to make capital from the publication
of Charles's secret correspondence captured during the battle. *The kings cabinet
opened* (Wing C2358) revealed Charles's attempts to obtain foreign support, his
distrust of parliament and his subjects, and his willingness to abandon all penal

laws against English and Irish catholics if they would join the royalists. It damaged Charles's ability to recruit soldiers in some areas and fortified less moderate members of parliament to fight for the king's unconditional surrender.

Order: parliamentary ordinance, 16 June 1645, Wing E2072*, 6 [also in *CJ*, IV, 175].
Additional sources: *CJ*, IV, 175–6, 179; *LJ*, VII, 432–3, 436–7, 439–40; *Westminster* assembly, III, 620–1; *An ordinance of the Lords and Commons assembled in parliament* (1645; Wing E2072); *Three letters, from the Right Honourable Sir Thomas Fairfax, Lieut. Gen. Crumwell and the committee residing in the army. Wherein all the particulars of the great victory obtained by our forces against his majesties, is fully related, fought the 14 of Iune, 1645* (1645; Wing F240); *A more exact and perfect relation of the great victory (by Gods providence) obtained by the parliaments forces under command of Sir Tho. Fairfax in Naisby field, on Saturday 14. June 1645* (1645; Wing M2699); HMC, *Second rep.*, p. 116; HMC, *Seventh rep., appendix*, p. 454; Sir William Armyne and other commissioners to Lieutenant-General David Leslie, 26 June 1645, SP16/507/145, fo. 216r; *FSP*, XVII, 4–5.
Printed sermon: Marshall, parliament (Wing M773; *FSP*, XVII, 159–98).

ORDER

Parliamentary ordinance: 16 June 1645
Ordered by the Lords and Commons in Parliament, That Thursday next shall be set apart for a day of Publique Thanksgiving to Almighty God, in all the Churches and Chappells within the Cities of *London* and *Westminster*, and Lines of Communication, and weekly bills of Mortallity, For the Great & Glorious Victory obtained by the Parliaments Army under the Command of Sir THOMAS FAIRFAX, against the Forces of the KING. And M. *Marshall* and M. *Vines* be desired to preach at *Christ-Church*, before the Parliament. And that the Lord Mayor, Aldermen, and Common-Councell doe meete the Parliament there. And it is further Ordered, That Friday being the twenty seventh day of this instant *Iune*, be set apart for a publique day of Thanksgiving for this Victory, in all the Churches and Chappells in the severall Counties of the Kingdome under the power of the Parliament.

1645–E6(P)   Prayers for a blessing on parliament's army in the south-west

Tuesday 1 July (parliament; Westminster Abbey and eight churches within the lines of communication)

After the parliamentarian victory at the battle of Naseby, the only part of the royalist army that could mount an effective challenge to the New Model Army was that led by Lord Goring in south-west England, which had declined to join the king at Naseby because he was engaged in the siege of Taunton. In London, there was considerable support for Blake, the parliamentarian commander at Taunton, who had defended the town for nearly twelve months, and much expectation that the parliamentary army should now assist him. Following the battle of Naseby, Fairfax had focused on capturing Leicester, but in late June he led his army on a swift march to the south-west. On 30 June, the House of Commons instructed three MPs, Francis Rous, Denis Bond and Edmond Prideaux, to ask the Westminster assembly to arrange for special prayers on the following day in support of Blake and of Fairfax's army. The House of Lords appears not to have been consulted. As for 1644–E8(P) the prayers were only to be observed in specified churches, although this time these were to be chosen by the Westminster assembly, which was also directed to nominate one of its members to pray in the House of Commons for an hour during the morning of the appointed day. The assembly selected Westminster Abbey and eight churches in the City of London and in Southwark, and also decided to appoint ministers from among its own members to say the prayers and to preach in these places of worship. By this time, the royalist siege of Taunton was already being ended (see 1645–E7(P)).

Order: order of the House of Commons, 30 June 1645, *CJ*, IV, 189; order of the Westminster assembly, 30 June 1645, Wing A168*.
Additional source: *Westminster assembly*, V, 203.

ORDER

Order of the House of Commons: 30 June 1645
Ordered, That Mr. *Rous*, Mr. *Bond*, and [Mr.] *Prideaux*, do desire the Assembly of Divines to set To-morrow apart, and to appoint several Churches, to meet to seek God for a Blessing upon our Armies and Forces now in the West; and that one of them do pray an Hour at the House Tomorrow Morning.

Order of the Westminster Assembly: 30 June 1645
According to an Order from the Honourable House of Commons to the Assembly of Divines, Desiring them to set *Tuesday* the first of *Iuly* apart, and to appoint severall Churches to meet in, to seek God for a Blessing on our Armies and Forces now in the West; It is Ordered by the Assembly, That these Churches following be designed for that purpose; *Viz.*

Abbey VVestminster.
Dunstanes VVest.
Christs Church.
Black-Fryers.
Aldermanbury.
Michael Cornhill.
Aldgate.
Dunstanes East.
Olaves Southwark.

Severall Members of the Assembly of Divines, are appointed to Pray and Preach in the Churches above mentioned.

1645–S4   Fast day after defeat at Auldearn and during plague epidemic

Thursday 3 July 1645 (Scotland)

The decision of the commission of the general assembly to appoint another fast, soon after 1645–S3, reflects the severity of conflict and disease in Scotland at this time. Montrose's royalist forces won a surprise victory over Sir John Urry's (or Hurry's) covenanters at Auldearn (near Nairn) on 9 May 1645, killing nearly 2,000. At the same time, Edinburgh was suffering a serious outbreak of plague, brought from the north of England by returning soldiers.

Order: act of the commission of the general assembly, *c.* 15 May 1645 (described in presbytery of Dalkeith minutes, NRS, CH2/424/3, p. 136).
Additional sources: presbytery of Peebles minutes, NRS, CH2/295/3, fo. 25v; presbytery of Paisley minutes, NRS, CH2/294/2, p. 226.
Printed sermon: ?Skeldie, Edinburgh (ESTC 006469117).

DESCRIPTION OF ORDER

[Act of the commission of the general assembly: *c.* 15 May 1645]
Ane Letter wes presentit from the Commissioun Ordaining ane solemne fast to be keipit on the first thursday of July becaus of the sines of the Land and Sword & pestilence

---

1645–E7(P) Thanksgiving day for the parliamentarian victory at the battle of Langport, and for London remaining free of the plague

Tuesday 22 July 1645 (England and Wales under the power of parliament)

The parliamentarians followed up their victory at Naseby with the recapture of Leicester (18 June), Taunton (29 June) and Langport (10 July). The last victory destroyed the royalist cavalry, as Naseby had done to the infantry, and, from a position of relative strength at the start of the year, Charles suddenly faced defeat. At the same time, a serious epidemic of plague had broken out, affecting towns such as Oxford and Exeter. On 14 July, the Commons proposed a day of thanksgiving to be held on 22 July for the victory at Langport and to thank God for his mercy in preserving London from plague. Collections were proposed to be taken at the services to relieve those who had fled from the south-west. The Lords agreed to the motion. Dissemination of the orders appears to have been delegated to both the 'Committee of the Several Counties'[332] and to MPs. The Commons proposed Gasper Hickes and Mr Meddop to preach the sermons before them at St Margaret's Church; Meddop was later replaced by Humphrey Chambers, for reasons unknown. As was usual, the Lords observed the service at Westminster Abbey; the sermons were preached by John Ward and Obadiah Sedgwick. On 21 July, the Lords ordered, and the Commons assented, that all sermons were to be preached in the morning, beginning at 8 am; no reason for this was stated. Neither Chambers nor Hickes was invited by the Commons to print their sermons. Though both Ward and Sedgwick were invited by the Lords to print theirs, only Ward did so.

Order: parliamentary order, 14 July 1645, *CJ*, IV, 207.
Additional sources: *CJ*, IV, 208, 212, 214; *LJ*, VII, 496–7, 503; *FSP*, XVII, 6–7.
Printed sermon: Ward, House of Lords (Wing W774; *FSP*, XVII, 315–58).

---

[332] Probably not a committee but a reference to the county committees, established in the summer of 1643.

ORDER

Parliamentary order: 14 July 1645

Ordered, &c. That *Tuesday*, being the Two-and-twentieth of this Instant *July*, shall be set apart for a publick Day of Thanksgiving to Almighty God, in all Churches and Chapels through the whole Kingdom, under the Power of the Parliament, for the great and glorious Victory obtained by the Parliament's Forces, under the Command of Sir *Thomas Fairefax*, over the Enemies Forces in the West: And that on the same Day the Ministers do likewise take Notice of the great Mercy of God in preserving this City, during the Sitting of this Parliament, from the Infection of the Plague: And this Order be printed and published.

1645–S5   Fast days for the gathering of troops at Perth, and for the success of parliament

Saturday 26 July and Sunday 27 July 1645 (Scotland)

Following another defeat of the covenanters by Montrose (at Alford on 2 July 1645), parliament met at Stirling from 9 to 11 July. Reflecting concerns that defence against the royalists had hitherto been insufficiently resourced, parliament ordered a general rendezvous of troops at Perth on 19 and 24 July. Parliament then concurred with a suggestion from the commission of the general assembly that a national fast appointed for the weekend after the rendezvous be observed with special ceremony at Perth. According to the register of Peebles presbytery, the commission instructed that ministers should refer to the causes of humiliation detailed in the *Solemne and seasonable warning* issued by the previous assembly (see 1645–S2).

Orders: act of the commission of the general assembly, *c.* 10 July 1645 (described in presbytery of Dalkeith minutes, NRS, CH2/424/3, p. 137); parliamentary ordinance, 10 July 1645, *RPS*, 1645/7/8/23 [also in *The acts of the parliaments of Scotland*, ed. Thomson and Innes, VI: 1, 437].
Additional sources: *RPS*, 1645/7/8/7, 1645/7/24/5; Balfour, III, 298; presbytery of Peebles minutes, NRS, CH2/295/3, fo. 28v; presbytery of Paisley minutes, NRS, CH2/294/2, p. 227; *A solemne and seasonable warning to the noble-men, barons, gentlemen, burrows, ministers, and commons of Scotland* (Edinburgh, 1645; Wing C4259G); *Life of Blair*, pp. 174–5.

DESCRIPTION OF ORDER

[Act of the commission of the general assembly: *c.* 10 July 1645]

Ane Letter sent from ye Commissioun Ordaineing ane solemne humiliation to be keipt on saturday the 26. of July and ye Sabboth following: because of sines and judgements prevailing And for ane blissing to ye present Parliament

ORDER

Parliamentary ordinance: 10 July 1645

Mr Robert Blair, accompanyed with diverse of the ministrie appeiring in face of parliament, desyred the estates to take into thair consideratione if it were not fitting thair should be ane fast appoynted before the generall randevous at Pearth, and quhat nomber of the ministrie they thought fitt to attend thair, and if the commissioners of the generall assembly should attend that meitting. The estates of parliament thinkes it fitting that Satirday eftir the generall randevous (being the 26 of this instant) should be appoynted to be ane fast day, and that thair come ane minister out of ilke presbetrie to attend at Pearth with the commissioners for the generall assembly at the dyet appoynted for the parliamentes meiting. And the estates of parliament declaires that they are verie sensible of the cairfullnes of the ministrie, quhilke they accept with thankefullnes, and ordeanes the same to be recordit.

1645–E8(P) Thanksgiving prayers for the parliamentarian victories at Bridgwater and Pontefract

Sunday 27 July 1645 (lines of communication and bills of mortality)

On 21 July, Colonel-General Sydenham Poyntz took Pontefract from the royalists, ending a siege that had begun in January. Two days later, Fairfax captured Bridgwater in Somerset, cutting off royalist communication between the south-west and Bristol (Charles's main port and magazine). On 24 July, the Commons ordered that 27 July would be observed by thanksgivings in all churches and chapels within the lines of communication and the weekly bills of mortality. The Commons may have acted unilaterally in ordering this thanksgiving as there is no record of any consultation with, or assent by, the Lords in their journal. The order was printed and, as usual, copies were distributed to the clergy by the lord mayor.

Order: parliamentary order, 24 July 1645, SP16/510/19, fo. 30r.
Additional sources: *CJ*, IV, 216, 218, 220; *LJ*, VII, 511; *A brief relation of the taking of Bridgwater by the parliaments forces under the command of Sir Tho: Fairfax* (1645; Wing B1666); William Fuller, *A fuller relation from Bridgwater since the last fight* (1645; Wing F2489); *Sir Thomas Fairfax's letter to the Honorable William Lenthall Esq. speaker of the House of Commons of all the particulars concerning the taking of Bridgwater* (1645; Wing F193).

ORDER

Parliamentary order: 24 July 1645
Ordered by the Commons assembled in Parliament, That, on the next Lords day, being the seven and twentieth of this present *July*, notice be taken of Gods Mercies and Blessings upon the Parliaments Forces in the West and in the North, particularly in the taking in of *Bridgewater*, and *Pontefract* Castle: And that in all the Churches and Chappels within the Lines of Communication, and Weekly Bills of Mortality, the Ministers doe return Thanks unto Almighty God, for these great mercies. And that the Lord Major be desired to give timely notice of this Order to the Ministers of the severall Churches and Chappels.

1645–E9(P) Thanksgiving day for parliamentarian victories, especially at Bath, Bridgwater, Scarborough, Sherborne and in Pembrokeshire, and for the Scottish victory at Canon Frome

Friday 22 August 1645 (London, Westminster, the lines of communication and bills of mortality)

The parliamentarians consolidated their control of the north and the south-west by victories at Scarborough (25 July), Bath (31 July), Colby Moor, Pembrokeshire (1 August), Haverfordwest (5 August) and Sherbourne Castle (17 August). For this occasion, the earlier victory at Bridgwater was again celebrated, following the thanksgiving prayers for 1645–E8(P). Thanks were also ordered to be made for the 'Dispersing of the Clubmen' in Somerset and Dorset. 'Clubmen' were local defence forces formed to resist both parliamentarians and royalists. The groups in the south-west caused particular difficulties for parliamentarian forces, until they were defeated and disbanded by Cromwell's forces on 4 August. The thanksgiving was proposed by the Commons on 18 August and ordered by the Lords on the 19th; the Lords amended the order to include thanks for the taking of Canon Frome in Herefordshire by the covenanters (23 July). John Bond and Thomas Case were appointed to preach before the Commons at St Margaret's, Westminster because Andrew Perne and John Ward were not in London. The order was distributed by the lord mayor as usual.

Orders: order of the House of Commons, 18 [or 19?] Aug. 1645, *CJ*, IV, 245; order of the House of Lords, 19 Aug. 1645, *LJ*, VII, 543.
Additional sources: *CJ*, IV, 245–7; *LJ*, VII, 543; *FSP*, XVIII, 5; *Two letters: the one, sent to the Right Honorable, the Lord Fairfax, from Sir Tho: Fairfax his son, commander in chief of the parliaments forces; concerning his besieging Sherborn. The other sent to Sir Tho: Fairfax, from Lieutenant Generall Cromwell; concerning the late fight at Shaftesbury* (1645; Wing F252); *A true relation of the taking of Sherborn-castle* (1645; Wing T3054); *Sir Thomas Fairfax's letter to the Honorable William Lenthall Esq: speaker of the House of Commons; concerning the taking of Sherborn Castle* (1645; Wing F194).
Printed sermons: Bond, House of Commons (Wing B3572A, B3573; *FSP*, XVIII, 135–86); Case, House of Commons (Wing C842; *FSP*, XVIII, 187–224).

ORDERS

Order of the House of Commons: 18 [or 19?] August 1645
Ordered, That *Friday* next be set apart for a Day of Publick Thanksgiving to Almighty God, to be observed and kept within all the Parishes in *London* and *Westminster*, the weekly Bills of Mortality, and Lines of Communication, in all the Churches and Chapels thereof, for his several Mercies to the Forces of the Parliament in divers Parts of the Kingdom, in the Gaining of the Towns of *Bath* and *Bridgewater*, and of *Scarborough-Castle*, and *Sherborne-Castle*, and for the Dispersing of the Clubmen, and the good Success in *Pembrokeshire*: And

It is further *Ordered*, That the Lord Mayor of *London* be desired to give speedy Notice of this Order to the Ministers of the several Places aforesaid.

Order of the House of Lords: 19 August 1645
Ordered, That *Friday* next be set apart for a Day of Public Thanksgiving to ALMIGHTY GOD, to be observed and kept within all the Parishes in *London* and *Westm[inster]* the Weekly Bills of Mortality and Lines of Communication, in all

the Churches and Chapels thereof, for His several Mercies to the Forces of the Parliament, in divers Parts of the Kingdom, in the gaining of the Towns of *Bath*, *Bridgwater*, *Scarborough Castle*, and *Sherburne Castle*; and for the dispersing of the Clubmen, and the good Success of *Pembrookshire*.

And it is further ORDERED, That the Lord Mayor of *London* be desired to give speedy Notice of this Order to the Ministers of the several Places aforesaid.

Agreed to, with this Addition, ['and for the good Success of the *Scottch* Army, as the Taking of Cannon Frome, &c.']

1645–E10(R) Thanksgiving prayers for the royalist relief of Hereford

Sunday 7 September 1645 (Hereford and possibly elsewhere)

On 30 August, Charles's army marched from Oxford to raise the siege of Hereford. Hearing of the army's arrival at Worcester on 1 September, Lord Leven abandoned Hereford and Charles entered the city on 4 September. As contemporaries noted, it was an important victory because it appeared to secure royalist dominance of Wales and the Welsh Marches. This occasion is only known from a reference in a letter of George, Lord Digby, to Charles, prince of Wales. It is unclear how widely the thanksgiving was celebrated, because the king faced growing difficulties in printing forms of prayers and distributing prayers and orders across the country after his departure from London, the centre of printing and of the country's communications network. However, it is possible that, if parishes received word of the victory, they could have adapted one of the prayers in *A collection of prayers and thanksgivings*, a compilation of prayers from previous occasions (see 1642–E1(R) and 1643–E11(R)) and new prayers compiled by Brian Duppa in 1643. This raises the question of whether other royalist victories were ordered to be celebrated, what form of prayer was ordered to be used (if any) and how widely any such thanksgivings were observed. The appendix in volume 3 of this edition lists other possible royalist occasions in the 1640s.

Order: none found.
Form of prayer: none found but parishes could have used *A collection of prayers and thanksgivings, vsed in his maiesties chappell and his armies. Vpon occasion of the late victories againat the rebells, and for the future successe of the forces* (Oxford, 1643; Wing C4094A and variant editions C4094B, C4094C).
Additional source: George, Lord Digby, to Charles, prince of Wales, 7 Sept. 1645, SP16/510/99, fos. 167r–168v.

DESCRIPTION OF OCCASION

George, Lord Digby, to Charles, prince of Wales: 7 September 1645

… his Maiestie is now in this place at a solemne thankesgiving for the successe, and incouraging all others by his favour to this Citty to follow their example in such eminent expressions of Loyalty, then which there was never any thing more happy or seasonable, for had this seidge continued but a weeke longer, the generallity of all Wales had certainly revolted to the Parliament, whereas now this Country is likely to be most entirely settled in their obedience, and to be a magazine of men for his Maiestie against the next spring.

1645–E11(P) Days of humiliation for Scottish defeats and Fairfax's army and during the plague

Friday 5 September 1645 (lines of communication); Friday, 19 September 1645 (parliament's quarters)

After taking Sherborne Castle (1645–E9(P)), Fairfax's parliamentarian army marched to Bristol and laid siege to the city. In Scotland, the covenanter army under William Baillie suffered a major defeat against the marquis of Montrose at Kilsyth (between Glasgow and Stirling) on 15 August. Losses on the battlefield, as well as the ruthless slaughter of fleeing soldiers, left the whole of Scotland in Montrose's hands. Plague continued, particularly in Edinburgh, Leeds and the west country. On 30 August, and in contrast to other recent occasions, the Commons resolved (rather than ordered) that a day of humiliation would be observed on 5 September within the lines of communication, and on 21 September in 'parliament's quarters'. (This is the only time this phrase was used for occasions of special worship. Its meaning is unclear; it probably denoted additional areas in parliament's control, beyond the lines of communication.) On 2 September, the Lords agreed to the Commons' resolutions. Only the parliamentary order for 19 September was printed; orders could be disseminated verbally within the lines of communication by MPs and the lord mayor, and this was common practice by this point. John Ward, Daniel Cawdrey and George Gillespie were ordered to preach before the Commons, and Alexander Henderson and Lazarus Seaman to preach before the Lords. None of the preachers were invited to print their sermons. Parliament received news of Fairfax's taking of Bristol before the second day of humiliation was observed (1645–E12(P)) but there is no evidence to suggest that it sought to cancel this observation.

Orders: resolutions by the Commons, 30 Aug. 1645, *CJ*, IV, 258; agreement by the Lords, 2 Sept. 1645, *LJ*, VII, 563; parliamentary order, 2 Sept. 1645, Wing E1733D*.
Additional sources: *CJ*, IV, 258; *LJ*, VII, 563; *FSP*, XIX, 3–4.

ORDERS

Resolution by the House of Commons: 30 August 1645
Resolved, &c. That *Friday* next be set apart, and appointed, for a Day of Humiliation, within the Lines of Communication, to be humbled for the Miseries of *Scotland*; and to desire God's Blessing upon the Army under Sir *Thomas Fairfax*, and for the Ceasing of the Plague in the Kingdoms of *England* and *Scotland*: And that Mr. Recorder do acquaint the Lord Mayor with this Order; and desire him, that this Order may be published, in all the Churches and Chapels within the Lines of Communication, by the several and respective Ministers, To-morrow, being the Lord's Day …

Resolved, &c. That *Friday* next come Fortnight shall be a Day appointed for publick Humiliation, through all the Parliament-Quarters, to be humbled for the Miseries of *Scotland*, and to desire God's Blessing upon the Army under Sir *Thomas Fairfax*, and for the Ceasing of the Plague in the Kingdoms of *England* and *Scotland*.

Agreement of the House of Lords: 2 September 1645
A Message was brought from the House of Commons, by Mr. *Knightly*, &c.
To desire their Lordships Concurrence in these Particulars:

1. An Order, That *Friday* next be appointed for a Day of Humiliation, within the Lines of Communication, to be humbled for the Miseries of *Scotland*; and to desire GOD'S Blessing upon the Army under Sir *Tho. Fairefax*; and for ceasing of the Plague in the Kingdoms of *England* and *Scotland*.
Agreed to …

2. An Order, That *Friday* next come Fortnight shall be a Day appointed for Public Humiliation, through all the Parliament Quarters, to be humbled for the Miseries of *Scotland*; and to desire God's Blessing upon the Army under *Sir Tho. Fairefax*; and for ceasing of the Plague in the Kingdoms of *England* and *Scotland*.
Agreed to.

Parliamentary order: 2 September 1645
Ordered by the Lords and Commons assembled in Parliament, That *Friday* next come fortnight, shall be a day appointed for publique Humiliation through all the Parliaments Quarters; to be humbled for the Miseries of *Scotland*; and to desire Gods Blessing upon the Army under Sir *Thomas Fairfax*: And for ceasing of the Plague in the Kingdoms of *England* and *Scotland*.

1645–E12(P) **Thanksgiving prayers for the parliamentarian victory at Bristol, and the Scottish victory at the battle of Philiphaugh**

Sunday 21 September 1645 (London and surrounding area); Sunday 5 October 1645 (elsewhere in England and Wales)

On 11 September, Fairfax stormed Bristol after a six-day bombardment. Prince Rupert, who had been unable to defend the city, was later dismissed from royal service. On 17 September, the Commons proposed thanksgiving prayers for the taking of Bristol and a collection for maimed soldiers. Two days later, the Commons ordered that the successes of parliament's Scottish allies should be included in the thanksgivings. Montrose's royalist forces had obtained a series of victories, notably at Kilsyth (1645–E11(P)), but then suffered a decisive defeat by the convenanters' army led by General David Leslie at Philiphaugh, near Selkirk, on 13 September. Once again, the House of Lords appear not to have been involved in ordering the thanksgiving. The house did not sit on 17 September, and, although it was sitting on 19 September and received news of Fairfax's and Leslie's victories, its journal records neither a consultation with the Commons about the thanksgiving nor assent to its order. An account of the taking of Bristol (*Lieut: Generall Cromwells letter*) was ordered to be read out during the service. The order was distributed in London and the surrounding area by the lord mayor and by MPs elsewhere. It appears that no preachers were appointed to preach before the Commons.

Orders: parliamentary order, 17 Sept. 1645, Wing C7114, 8* [also in *CJ*, IV, 277]; 19 Sept. 1645, *CJ*, IV, 279.
Additional sources: *CJ*, IV, 273, 277; *Lieut: Generall Cromwells letter to the House of Commons* (1645; Wing C7114, C7114A); *A true relation of the storming Bristoll, and the taking the town, castle, forts,*

ordnance, ammunition and arms, by Sir Thomas Fairfax's army, on Thursday the 11. of this instant Septemb. 1645 (1645; Wing R2336A).
Printed sermon: Beech, Basing (Wing B1680).

ORDERS

Parliamentary order: 17 September 1645

Ordered by the Commons assembled in Parliament, That on the next Lords-Day thanks be given unto God for the great Successe he hath given unto the Parliaments Forces under Sir *Tho: Fairfax* their Generall, in taking in the City of Bristoll, with the Castle and Forts, in all the Churches and Chappels within the Lines of Communication, and Bills of Mortality; and that on the next Lords-Day come Fortnight, being the fift day of October, in all the parts of the Kingdom, within the power of the Parliament; And that the Lord Major of the City of London, do give timely notice hereof, to all the Ministers within the Lines of Communication, and Bills of Mortality; And that the Knights and Burgesses of the severall Counties, Cities, and Burroughs, do give notice hereof, and send Copies of this Order, to the severall Counties, Cities, and Burroughs: It is further Ordered, That the Relation sent up from Lieutenant Generall *Cromwell*, by the command of the Generall, of Septemb. 14. be Printed, and Read upon the dayes on which publique thanks are to be given unto God, for his great blessing in this Successe given at Bristoll.

Parliamentary order: 19 September 1645

Ordered, That, the next Lord's Day, Thanks be given to Almighty God in all Churches and Chapels within the Lines of Communication, for his great Blessing upon the Forces of our Brethren of *Scotland* against the Enemy's Forces under the Command of the Earl of *Montrosse*, in *Scotland*: And that the like be done, on *Sunday* come Fortnight, in all Parts of this Kingdom under the Power of the Parliament: And that the Lord Mayor be desired to give timely Notice hereof to the Ministers within the Lines of Communication, and Bills of Mortality: And that the Members do give notice hereof to the several Counties.

1645–S6   Thanksgiving day for victory at the battle of Philiphaugh

September–October 1645 (Scotland)

After Leslie's victory at the battle of Philiphaugh on 13 September (see 1645–E12(P)), the commission of the general assembly ordered a general thanksgiving. As with other Scottish thanksgivings in this period, it appears that the commission did not itself appoint a particular date, but instructed presbyteries to select a convenient day for their own parishes. Dalkeith presbytery recorded its receipt of the commission's order on 25 September, and appointed the thanksgiving to be kept on Sunday 28 September.

Order: act of the commission of the general assembly, *c.* 20 Sept. 1645 (not found).
Source: presbytery of Dalkeith minutes, NRS, CH2/424/3, p. 140.

1645–E13(P)   Thanksgiving days for parliamentarian victories, especially at Chester, Devizes and in Pembrokeshire, and for the Scottish victory at the battle of Philiphaugh

Thursday 2 October 1645 (London, Westminster and within the lines of communication); Thursday 16 October 1645 (elsewhere in England and Wales)

As in August (1645–E9(P)), victories which had already been celebrated (Bristol and Philiphaugh: 1645–E12(P)) were the subject of further thanksgiving. In addition, thanks were given for the victories at Picton Castle, Wales (20 September), Devizes (21–2 September) and Rowton Heath, near Chester (24 September). The thanksgiving was proposed by the Commons on 27 September and ordered by the Lords the same day. John Ley and [Thomas?] Coleman were appointed to preach before the Commons at St Margaret's, Westminster, though neither was subsequently thanked for his sermon or invited to have it printed. Simeon Ash and Gaspar Hickes were appointed to preach before the Lords; only Ash was thanked for his sermon and, though he was invited to have it printed, he appears not to have done so. The lord mayor continued to be responsible for distributing orders in London and the surrounding area; MPs were ordered to distribute the order to the county committees for further dissemination. In addition, the Commons proposed that, notwithstanding the official thanksgiving, ministers in parishes within the lines of communication should offer thanks for Poyntz's victory at Chester on 28 September.

Order: parliamentary order, 27 Sept. 1645, *LJ*, VII, 606.
Additional sources: *CJ*, IV, 290–2; *LJ*, VII, 604–7; *FSP*, XIX, 6–7 (which erroneously identified the second preacher to the Commons as Thomas Temple, not Coleman); *A letter concerning the storming and delivering up of the castle of the Devises unto Lieutenant Generall Cromwell* (1645; Wing N1326); *The kings forces totally routed by the parliaments army, under the command of Major Generall Poyntz and Cheshire-Forces, on Routon-Heath* (1645; Wing K595); *A fuller narrative of the late victory obtained by Col: Generall Poyntz against his majesties forces neer Chester* (1645; Wing F2488); *A letter from Colonell Generall Poynts, to the Honourable William Lenthall speaker of the House of Commons: concerning Sir Tho. Glenham, Colonell Gerard, [brace] and [brace] Sir Marmaduke Langdale, in the last fight neere Chester* (1645; Wing P3135).

ORDER

Parliamentary order: 27 September 1645

ORDERED, by the Lords and Commons in Parliament assembled, That *Thursday* next shall be set apart, for a Day of Public Thanksgiving unto ALMIGHTY GOD, for His great Mercies and Blessings upon the Parliament's Forces under Colonel General *Poynts*, against the King's Forces, near *Chester*, on *Wednesday* last, *September* 24th, 1645, and likewise for GOD'S great Mercy upon the Parliament's Forces, in the taking of *Bristoll, Devizes*, the Success in *Pembrookesheir* given to the Forces under Major General *Langherne*, and for GOD'S great Mercy in *Scotland*, in all Churches and Chapels of *London* and *Westm[inster]* and within the Lines of Communication, and on *Thursday* next come Fortnight in all other Parts of the Kingdom; and Alderman *Penington* is appointed to desire the Lord Mayor to give timely Notice hereof to the Ministers of the Churches and Chapels within the Lines of Communication: And it is further ORDERED, That the Members of the House of Commons, of the several and respective Counties, do send Copies of this Order to the several respective

Committees of the several Counties, to the End that they may be so dispersed, that the Counties may take timely Notice hereof, that the Day may be kept with that Observation as is due to so great Blessings.

1645–E14(P) Thanksgiving prayers for parliamentarian victories at Winchester, Basing House and Chepstow

Sunday 19 October 1645 (London, Westminster and parishes within the lines of communication and bills of mortality)

Immediately after the taking of Devizes, Cromwell's forces moved to Winchester, which surrendered 5 October, and to Basing House, which surrendered on 14 October. Meanwhile, Sir Thomas Morgan forced Chepstow to surrender on 10 October. The Commons proposed a thanksgiving for the victories at Basing House and Winchester on 15 October, adding Chepstow on 17 October when they received the news. Though the house was sitting during this time, the Lords do not appear to have been involved in ordering this occasion. Indeed, its journal records that it received news only of the taking of Basing House, and did so two days later than the Commons. No preachers were appointed to preach before either house. Two accounts of the taking of Basing House (*Lieut: Generall Cromwells letter* and *The full and last relation of all things concerning Basing-House*) were 'Commanded to be Printed, and published according to Order', though there is no explicit reference in the Commons' journal that they had to be read during the services as had been the case on previous occasions. The lord mayor was again ordered to disseminate the orders.

Orders: parliamentary orders, 15 Oct. 1645, Wing C7108C, 8* [also in Wing P1702, facing title-page; similar text in *CJ*, IV, 309]; 17 Oct. 1645, *CJ*, IV, 312.
Additional sources: *Lieut: Generall Cromwells letter to the Honorable William Lenthall Esq., speaker of the House of Commons* (1645; Wing C7108C); *The full and last relation of all things concerning Basing-House* (1645; Wing P1702).

ORDERS

Parliamentary order: 15 October 1645
Ordered by the Commons in Parliament assembled, That the next Lords day publique thanks be given unto Almighty God for his great mercies and blessings upon the Parliaments Forces under Lieutenant Generall *Cromwell*, and Col. *Dalbier*, for taking in *Winchester* Castle and *Basing house*, in all Churches and Chappels in the Cities of *London* and *Westminster*, and within the Lines of Communication; And Alderman *Pennington* and Colonell *Venn* are appointed by this House to desire the Lord Major to give timely notice hereof to the Ministers of the Churches and Chappels within the Lines of Communication.

Parliamentary order: 17 October 1645
Ordered, &c. That Thanks be given to God, for delivering into the Parliament's Hands the Town and Castle of *Chepstowe* in *Wales*, upon *Sunday* next, in like manner as it is ordered to be given for *Winchester* and *Basing-House*: And the Lord Mayor

is desired to give notice hereof to all the Parish-Churches of *London*, and within the Lines of Communication, and Bills of Mortality.

1645–E15(P) Thanksgiving days for parliamentarian victories at Sherburn and Tiverton, and in Wales

Sunday 26 October 1645 (parishes within the lines of communication); Sunday 9 November 1645 (elsewhere in England and Wales)

On 15 October, Colonel Copley routed the royalist forces at Sherburn-in-Elmet, near Leeds. Elsewhere, the royalists surrendered Cardigan, Rowland Laugharne occupied Carmarthen (12 October) and Fairfax took Tiverton in Devon (17–19 October). On 20 October, the Commons proposed a day of thanksgiving, which was approved and ordered by the Lords on the 22nd. On the 25th, the Commons added Laugharne's victories to the roster of events requiring thanks. As usual, the lord mayor communicated the orders to local ministers, but no preachers were appointed to preach before parliament and no accounts of the victories were explicitly ordered to be read during the services. Both the Commons' proposal and the final order laid new stress on the need 'to stir up the People, and to make them sensible of these great Blessings and Mercies; and to stir up their Hearts to an hearty Thankfulness', suggesting that the Commons believed that people were not observing these occasions as enthusiastically as they should.

Orders: order of the House of Lords, 21 Oct. 1645, *LJ*, VII, 654; order of the House of Commons, 25 Oct., *CJ*, IV, 321.
Additional sources: *CJ*, IV, 315, 317; *LJ*, VII, 653; *A letter sent to the Honorable William Lenthall Esquire, speaker of the honorable House of Commons, concerning the miraculous taking of Tiverton-Castle with the church* (1645; Wing R2323); *Generall Fairfax's letter to the Honorable William Lenthall Esquire, speaker of the honorable House of Commons. Concerning the storming and taking of Tiverton Castle and Church* (1645; Wing F197); *Major Generall Laughorn's letter to the Honourable William Lenthall Esq; speaker of the honorable House of Commons. VVherein is truly related the taking of Carmarthen town and castle* (1645; Wing L402).

ORDERS

Order of the House of Lords: 21 October 1645
Resolved, by the Lords and Commons in Parliament, That, on the next Lord's-day, Public Thanks be given unto ALMIGHTY GOD in all the Churches and Chapels within the Lines of Communication, and on the next Lord's-day come Fortnight in all other Parts of the Kingdom, for the great Blessings and Success it hath pleased God to give the Parliament's Forces in the North, near *Sherborne* in *Yorkesheir*, and in other Parts of the Kingdom; and that the Ministers be required to stir up their Hearts to an hearty Thankfulness; and that the Lord Mayor be desired to give timely Notice hereof to the Ministers of the several Churches and Chapels within the Lines of Communication.

Order of the House of Commons: 25 October 1645
Ordered, That To-morrow, being appointed for a Day of Publick Thanksgiving for several Mercies and Victories obtained by the Parliament's Forces against the Enemy,

the Ministers do likewise, in their Thanksgivings, make Mention of the great Blessing upon the Forces under Major-General *Langherne*, in Reducing of the Counties of *Pembroke, Caermarthen*, and *Cardigan*, to the Obedience of the Parliament.

1645–S7   Fast days because of general sinfulness

[November?] 1645 (Scotland)

Despite the covenanters' victory over Montrose at Philiphaugh (see 1645–S6), the commission continued to perceive much evidence of divine anger at Scotland's sins, most notably in the plague outbreak around Edinburgh. Like the presbytery of Dalkeith, the presbytery of Paisley met on 6 November, ordering the fast to be intimated on the following Sunday, to be observed on 16 November.

Order: act of the commission of the general assembly, *c*. 20 Oct. 1645 (described in presbytery of Dalkeith minutes, NRS, CH2/424/3, p. 142).
Additional source: presbytery of Paisley minutes, NRS, CH2/294/2, pp. 229–30.

DESCRIPTION OF ORDER

[Act of the commission of the general assembly: *c*. 20 October 1645]
The said day ane letter came from the moderato^r of ye commission of ye generall assembly ordainet ane solemne humilia^{o}n to be keepe because of the sinnes of the land etc. The brether ordainet ye same to be intimat the first sabboth day and keipet ye nixt sabboth day following

1645–E16(P)   Thanksgiving prayers for parliamentarian victories at Camarthen and Monmouth

Sunday 2 November 1645 (London and surrounding area)

Though Laugharne's victories in South Wales were included, at the last minute, in the thanksgiving on 26 October for parishes within the lines of communication (1645–E15(P)), on 27 October the Commons proposed a separate date for these to be celebrated. The Lords agreed and ordered the thanksgiving the same day. This additional celebration of parliament's Welsh victories enabled Sir Thomas Morgan's capture of Monmouth on 25 October to be included. Again, the lord mayor distributed the orders to the parishes.

Order: parliamentary order, 27 Oct. 1645, *LJ*, VII, 662.
Additional source: *CJ*, IV, 323
Printed sermon: Ashe, St Pauls, London (Wing A3964).

ORDER

Parliamentary order: 27 October 1645

ORDERED, That, on the next Lord's-day, Public Thanks shall be given to ALMIGHTY GOD, in all Churches and Chapels within the Lines of Communication and Weekly Bills of Mortality, for the great Blessing and Success it hath pleased GOD to give the Parliament Forces in *Wales*, in the taking in, and reducing to the Obedience of the Parliament, the Town and Castle of *Caermarthen*; and for the taking in and reducing of the Town and Castle of *Monmouth*; and that Mr. Alderman *Pennington* and Colonel *Venn* do acquaint the Lord Mayor with this Order, and desire him, that timely Notice may be given hereof to the respective Ministers within the Limits aforesaid.

1645–E17(P)   Thanksgiving prayers for the fifth anniversary of the Long parliament, and parliamentarian victories at Carlisle and Denbigh

Wednesday 5 November 1645 (London, Westminster, lines of communication and bills of mortality)

On 1 November, the Commons ordered that, during the annual commemoration of the failure of the gunpowder plot on 5 November, thanks be offered also for the fifth anniversary of the opening of the Long parliament (3 November 1640) and for the defeat of the northern royalist force on the Solway Firth, near Carlisle, on 21 October. It was the second time that the house had chosen to co-opt this anniversary to celebrate key events or its own military victories (see 1644–E12(P)). On 4 November, the Commons ordered that the victory of Thomas Mytton and Michael Jones over Sir William Vaughan at Denbigh (1 November) should also be remembered. Richard Vines and Edmund Calamy were appointed to preach on the day, but Vines was replaced by Matthew Newcomen on 1 November because the former would not be in London on the day specified. Neither preacher was formally thanked for his sermon or invited to print it. Although the Lords observed the annual commemoration of the gunpowder plot, there is no record in its journals that it was involved in ordering the thanksgiving for the anniversary of the Long parliament or for the recent military victories.

Order: orders of the House of Commons, 1 Nov. 1645, *CJ*, IV, 330; 4 Nov. 1645, *CJ*, IV, 333.
Additional sources: *CJ*, IV, 326, 328; *FSP*, XX, 3–4; Nathaniel Lancaster, *A true relation of a great victory obtained (through Gods providence) by the parliaments forces in Cheshire, under the command of Sir William Brereton, against the kings forces under the command of Sir William Vaughan, neer Denbigh, November 1. 1645* (1645; Wing L312).

ORDER

Order of the House of Commons: 1 November 1645

Ordered, &c. That, on *Wednesday* next, the several Ministers of the respective Churches and Chapels within the Cities of *London* and *Westminster*, and within the Lines of Communication, and weekly Bills of Mortality, do take notice of the great Mercy of God in preserving and keeping together this Parliament now Five Years complete, notwithstanding all the Practices and Endeavours of the Enemy to dissolve and destroy it; and likewise the Mercy of God upon the Forces under Colonel Sir *John Browne*, in defeating the Forces under the Lord *Digby* and Sir *Marmaduke Langdale* in *Scotland*; and to render Thanks to Almighty God for it: And the Lord Mayor is desired to give the Ministers Notice: And Colonel *Venn* is to acquaint the Lord Mayor with this Order.

Order of the House of Commons: 4 November 1645
Ordered, &c. That To-morrow, being the Fifth of *November*, and set apart to praise God for his great Mercies to this Kingdom, in the Deliverance from the Powder-Treason; and the respective Ministers of the several Churches and Chapels within the Cities of *London* and *Westminster*, Lines of Communication, and weekly Bills of Mortality, being, by former Order, appointed to take notice of the great Mercy of God in Preserving and Keeping together of this Parliament, now Five Years complete, notwithstanding the Practices of the Enemy to dissolve and destroy it; and of God's Mercy in defeating the Enemies Forces under the Lord *Digby*, in *Scotland*; It is this Day further *Ordered*, That they do likewise give Thanks to Almighty God for his further Mercies to the Forces of the Parliament under the Command of Colonel *Mitton*, in defeating the Enemies Forces under Sir *Wm. Vaughan*, in *Wales*: And that the Letter from Mr. *Lancaster*, relating this Success, be likewise read: And that they do earnestly stir up the People to a serious and hearty Thankfulness to Almighty God for all these several Mercies: And my Lord Mayor is desired to give them notice of this Order: And Mr. *Vassall* is to acquaint my Lord Mayor herewith accordingly.

1645–E18(P) Thanksgiving prayers for the parliamentarian victory at Lathom House

Sunday 14 December 1645 (London, Westminister and lines of communication)

The parliamentarians gained a number of victories in November, including Shelford Manor and Wiverton Hall near Newark and Beeston Castle near Chester. However, it was the taking and destruction of Lathom House in Lancashire (home of the earls of Derby) on 2 December that prompted the next thanksgivings. The Commons ordered these on 9 December; the Lords appear not to have been involved in the ordering process because there are no references to the thanksgiving in their journal. The lord mayor, as usual, distributed the orders.

Order: parliamentary order, 9 Dec. 1645, *CJ*, IV, 370.
Additional source: *CJ*, IV, 373.

ORDER

Parliamentary order: 9 December 1645
Ordered, That the Ministers within the Cities of *London, Westminster*, and Lines of Communication, do, on *Sunday* next, remember and give Thanks unto Almighty God, for his great Blessing, in Reducing of *Latham-House*.

1645–E19(P) Thanksgiving prayers for the parliamentarian capture of Hereford

Sunday 28 December 1645 (lines of communication)

On 18 December, Colonel Sir Thomas Morgan and Colonel John Birch captured Hereford in a surprise attack. On 22 December, the Commons proposed thanksgivings; this was agreed by the Lords on the same day, but no explicit order is recorded in its journal. No preachers were appointed. The lord mayor was again responsible for communicating the orders to ministers.

Order: parliamentary order, 22 Dec. 1645, *CJ*, IV, 381–2.
Additional sources: *LJ*, VIII, 53, 59–60; *Two letters sent to the Honorable W. Lenthall Esq; speaker to the honorable House of Commons; concerning the taking of Hereford on the 18. of this instant Decem. 1645* (1645; Wing M2753); *Severall letters from Colonell Morgan governour of Gloucester, and Colonell Birch. Fully relating the maner of the taking of the city and garrison of Hereford* (1645; Wing M2749).

ORDER

Parliamentary order: 22 December 1645
Resolved, &c. That, on the next Lord's Day, publick Thanks be given unto Almighty God, in all the Churches and Chapels within the Lines of Communication, for his great Blessing upon the Parliament's Forces under the Command of Colonel *Morgan*, Governor of *Gloucester*, and of Colonel *John Birch*, now Governor of *Hereford*: And that the Lord Mayor be desired to give timely Notice hereof to all the Ministers of the said Churches and Chapels; to the end that their Hearts may be enlarged to render Thanks and Acknowledgment unto Almighty God, in some sort answerable to the Greatness of this Blessing.

1646–E1(P) Thanksgiving days for parliamentarian victory at Dartmouth

Thursday 5 February 1646 (London, Westminster, lines of communication and ten miles around); Thursday 12 February 1645 (elsewhere in England and Wales)

Fairfax took Dartmouth on 18 January 1646, completing a series of parliamentary victories in the south-west that included Bovey Tracey (9 January) and Plymouth (12 January). On 22 January, the Commons proposed thanksgivings for all of these victories, as well as that at Hereford celebrated in December (see 1645–E19(P)). However, the Lords narrowed the purpose of the thanksgiving to the taking of Dartmouth only. On 31 January, the Commons ordered that a collection should be made during the thanksgiving services to support Fairfax's troops. John Bond and Anthony Harford were appointed to preach before the Commons at St Margaret's, Westminster, and William Strong and John Ley before the Lords at St Martin's-in-the-Fields (which had been unsuccessfully proposed as the location for both houses to observe the thanksgiving for the victory at Langport, 1645–E7(P)). None of the sermons appear to have been printed. In a change to their usual practice, the

Commons included parishes within ten miles of London, Westminster and the lines of communication in the first day of thanksgiving, suggesting that its ability to disseminate orders quickly (through the lord mayor) was increasingly effective.

Order: *Die Iovis 22 Ianuarii 1645*, 22 Jan. 1646 (s.n., s.p., n.d.; Wing E2815)* [another issue: Wing E1663A]
Additional sources: *CJ*, IV, 410, 414, 416, 424; *LJ*, VIII, 116, 121; *FSP*, XXI, 5–6; *A true relation of the fight at Bovy-Tracy* (1646; Wing R2336); *The parliaments severall late victories in the west, obtained by Sir Thomas Fairfax army* (1646; Wing P524); *A full and exact relation of the storming and taking of Dartmouth* (1646; Wing E2279); *Sir Thomas Fairfax letter to both houses of parliament; more exactly and fully relating the storming and taking of Dartmouth* (1646; Wing F121).

ORDER

Parliamentary order: 22 January 1646
The Lords and Commons in Parliament assembled do Order and appoint this day fortnight for a day of Thanksgiving, for taking in of DARTMOUTH, to be kept within the Cities of *London and Westminster*, Lines of Communication, and ten miles about; And this day three weeks for all other places in the Countrey.

1646–S1   Fast day for measures against Montrose's supporters

Thursday 5 February 1646 (Scotland)

This fast was ordered during a session of parliament, which punished supporters of Montrose and took steps to reorganize the army for another campaign against him. The presbytery of Paisley recorded that the commission's letter ordering observance of the fast also requested that malignants be censured by the church courts. Dalkeith presbytery did not record this detail, instead acting on an instruction from the commission for the use of the Directory of Public Worship produced by the Westminster assembly of divines. The Directory had been approved by the general assembly for use in Scottish churches in February 1645, but ministers were slow to adopt it.

Order: act of the commission of the general assembly, *c.* 10 Jan. 1646 (described in presbytery of Dalkeith minutes, NRS, CH2/424/3, p. 143).
Additional sources: presbytery of Dalkeith minutes, NRS, CH2/424/3, pp. 143–4; presbytery of Paisley minutes, NRS, CH2/294/2, p. 231; *Life of Blair*, p. 180.

DESCRIPTION OF ORDER

[Act of the commission of the general assembly: *c.* 10 January 1646]
The said day an Letter cam from the moderato^r of ye commission of generall assembly for the keeping of a fast the first Thursday of Februar, and practising of the directorie.

1646–E2(P) Thanksgiving days for parliamentarian victories at Chester and thanksgiving prayers for the battle of Torrington

Thursday 19 February 1646 (London, Westminster, the lines of communication and parishes up to ten miles about); Thursday 5 March 1646 (parishes in England and Wales more than ten miles from London and Westminster)

Chester, a royalist stronghold since the start of the civil war and Charles's only remaining major port, had been under parliamentarian attack since February 1645. Royalist reinforcements were routed at Rowton Heath in September 1645 (see 1645–E13(P)) and the city finally surrendered on 3 February 1646. On 6 February, the Commons proposed a day of thanksgiving and the order was made jointly by the Commons and Lords in a statement from the Lords on 7 February. In designating when parishes would observe the day, parliament maintained the new distinction between those within ten miles of London and Westminster and those further away (see 1646–E1(P)). On 23 February, the Commons ordered that these more distant parishes should also give thanks for Fairfax's victory at Torrington on 17 February: see 1646–E3(P). The lord mayor was deputed to disseminate orders to parishes within ten miles of the lines of communication and MPs to those outside. Francis Woodcock and Thomas Case were appointed to preach before the Commons; Daniel Cawdrey and Joseph Caryl preached before the Lords.

Orders: order of the House of Lords, 7 Feb. 1646, *LJ*, VIII, 146–7 [similar text in *CJ*, IV, 429]; order of the House of Commons, 23 Feb. 1646, *CJ*, IV, 449.
Additional sources: *CJ*, IV, 429, 431; *LJ*, VIII, 146–7; *Sir William Breretons letter concerning the surrender of the city of Chester for the parliament* (1646; Wing B4368); *FSP*, XXI, 6–7.
Printed sermons: Caryl, House of Lords (Wing C780; *FSP*, XXI, 181–216); Case, House of Commons (Wing C833; *FSP*, XXI, 217–60); Woodcock, House of Commons (Wing W3430; *FSP*, XXI, 261–95).

ORDERS

Order of the House of Lords: 7 February 1646

ORDERED, by the Lords and Commons assembled in Parliament, That *Thursday* next come Sevennight shall be set apart for a Day of Public Thanksgiving to ALMIGHTY GOD, for His great Mercy, in giving up that strong City of *Chester* into the Hands of the Parliament; to be observed and kept in all Churches and Chapels in the Cities of *London* and *Westm[inster]* and within the Lines of Communication, and Ten Miles of the said Cities; and that the Lord Mayor be desired to give the several Ministers within the Limits aforesaid timely Notice hereof, to the End they may stir up the People to a due Thankfulness, in regard both of the Seasonableness and Greatness of the Mercy.

Agreed to.

ORDERED, by the Lords and Commons in Parliament assembled, That *Thursday* next come Three Weeks shall be set apart for a Day of Public Thanksgiving to ALMIGHTY GOD, for His great Mercy, in giving up that strong City of *Chester* into the Hands of the Parliament; to be observed and kept in all Churches and Chapels in the several Counties above Ten Miles distant from the Cities of *London* and *Westm[inster]*; and that the Gentlemen that serve for the said several Counties and Places do take Care that timely Notice may be given to the several Ministers within the said respective Counties, to the End they may stir up the People to due Thankfulness, in regard both of the Seasonableness and Greatness of the Mercy.

Agreed to.

Order of the House of Commons: 23 February 1646

Whereas *Thursday* Sevennight is, by former Order, appointed to be set apart for a Day of Publick Thanksgiving, for the great Mercy of God, in giving up the City of *Chester* in .. [*sic*] the Hands of the Parliament: And whereas it hath pleased God to add a further Mercy, in the happy Success of the Forces of the Parliament, against the Forces of the Enemy, at *Torrington* in *Devonshire*: It is thereupon *Ordered*, That, on the same Day, the respective Ministers, in the several Counties under the Power of the Parliament, where the said Day of Thanksgiving is appointed to be observed, do praise God for this other Mercy at *Torrington*: And that they do stir up the People to a due Thankfulness for the same. And the Knights and Burgesses of the several Counties are to take care, that this Order be sent to the several Counties and Places they serve for; to the end that the Ministers may have timely Notice hereof.

1646–E3(P)   Thanksgiving day for parliamentarian victories at the battle of Torrington and at Cardiff

Thursday 12 March 1646 (London, Westminster, the lines of communication and parishes up to ten miles about)

After taking Dartmouth, Fairfax secured victory against royalist forces led by Lord Hopton in a moonlit pitched battle at Torrington on 17 February. Fairfax was nearly killed when an explosion of gunpowder caused a thick web of lead from a church window to fall near him. On 23 February, the House of Commons proposed that, in addition to the thanksgiving prayers added to 1646–E2(P) for use across England and Wales, this victory should be marked by a thanksgiving day on Tuesday 10 March in London, Westminster, the lines of communication and parishes within ten miles. On the same day as the Commons' order, the House of Lords independently proposed thanksgiving days for the victory on 1 March (London, Westminster, the lines of communication and parishes up to ten miles about) and 8 March (elsewhere). The Lords subsequently acceded to the Commons' proposals to the extent of abandoning the thanksgiving outside the London area, but appointed Thursday 12 March. The reason for the Lords' preference is not stated in the journal; thanksgivings were usually observed on Thursdays but some (such as 1645–E7(P)) had been observed on Tuesdays. On 28 February, parishes were also ordered to give thanks for Laugharne's victory at Cardiff (20–2 February). On 7 March, the Commons ordered an account of recent victories to be drawn up and ministers informed, presumably so that they might include this information in their sermons. This is probably the narrative that was appended to the printed parliamentary order (Wing E2785B). John Bond and either Obadiah or William Sedgwick were appointed to preach before the Commons; William Strong and Gaspar Hickes were appointed to preach before the Lords. None of the preachers chose to print their sermons, even though they were all invited to do so.

Orders: order of the House of Lords, 26 Feb. 1646, *LJ*, VIII, 187; order of the House of Commons, 28

Feb. 1646, *CJ*, IV, 458; *Die Sabbathi, 7. Martii, 1645*, 7 Mar. 1646 (Richard Cotes; 1 p., 1646; Wing E2785B)* [also Wing E2787 and in *CJ*, IV, 467].

Additional sources: *CJ*, IV, 448–9, 452–4, 458; *LJ*, VIII, 181, 184–5; *FSP*, XXII, 3–4; *Die Sabbathi, 7. Martii, 1645. Whereas Thursday next is by former order appointed for a day of publique thanksgiving for the great mercy of God in giving successe to the parliaments forces against the enemy at Torrington in Devonshire* (1646; Wing E2785B); *A true relation concerning the late fight at Torrington* (London,1646; Wing R2334A); *Sir Thomas Fairfax letter to the Honoble William Lenthal Esq; speaker of the honorable House of Commons. Concerning all the passages of his army since his advance from Exeter* (1646; Wing F195).

ORDERS

Order of the House of Lords: 26 February 1646

It is this Day ORDERED, by the Lords and Commons assembled in Parliament, That *Thursday* Fortnight be set apart for a Day of Public Thanksgiving to ALMIGHTY GOD, for His great Mercy, in giving Success to the Parliament Forces, against the Forces of the Enemy under the Command of Sir *Ralph Hopton*, at *Torrington*, in *Devonsheir*; to be observed and kept in all Churches and Chapels within the Cities of *London* and *Westm[inster]* Lines of Communication, and Ten Miles about; and that the Lord Mayor be desired to take Care that the respective Ministers within the Limits aforesaid may have timely Notice hereof, to the End they may excite and stir up the People to a due Thankfulness for the same.

Order of the House of Commons: 28 February 1646

Ordered, &c. That the Ministers of the several Churches and Chapels within the Limits, where the Day of Publick Thanksgiving for the Victory over the Enemies Forces at *Torrington* in *Devonshire* is appointed to be kept, do, on the same Day, take special Notice of the great Mercy in the Success of Major-General *Langherne*, over the revolted Forces of the Enemy at *Cardiffe*, in the County of *Glamorgan*: And that the Lord Mayor be desired to take care, that the respective Ministers may have notice hereof.

Parliamentary order: 7 March 1646

Whereas *Thursday* next is by former Order appointed for a day of Publique Thanksgiving for the great mercy of God in giving successe to the Parliaments forces against the Enemy at *Torrington* in *Devonshire*: And whereas since the appointment of the said day of Thanksgiving the Parliaments Forces in severall Parts of the Kingdome have given the Enemie divers defeats, and gained severall strengths which are now in the posseßion of the Parliament: It is thereupon Ordered, That the respective Ministers within the Limits where the said day of Thanksgiving is appointed to be observed, and kept; do make mention of these severall mercies and successes, and stirre up the People to a due thankfulnesse for the same; And to the end the said mercies and successes may bee the better taken notice of, *Mr. Rouse, Sir Peter Wentworth, Mr. Gourdon*, and *Mr.* Alderman *Pennington* are to collect the same; to the end the Ministers may bee acquainted with the particulars thereof. And the Lord Major of *London* is desired to take care that the Ministers may have timely notice of this Order.

1646–E4(P)   Thanksgiving days for Fairfax's victories in the south-west, and the parliamentarian victory at Stow

Thursday 2 April 1646 (the cities and liberties of London and Westminister, the lines of communication and ten miles around); Thursday 16 April 1646 (parishes more than ten miles from London within the power of parliament)

Fairfax sought to consolidate parliament's hold on Devon and Cornwall, still widely perceived as a royalist stronghold. He took Launceston (25 February) and Bodmin (2 March), and negotiated the surrender of Hopton's army (10–14 March). On 21 March, the House of Commons proposed a thanksgiving for these events to be observed on Tuesday 31 March in and around London, and on Thursday 16 April in areas elsewhere under parliament's control. A change and an addition were made to these proposals during 23 March, apparently as a result of discussions with representatives of the House of Lords. First, it was agreed to change the first date to Thursday 2 April. The journals of the two houses give no explanation of this change, though it may have resulted from the Lords' preference for thanksgivings to be held on Thursdays, as shown earlier in the month for 1646–E3(P). Second, apparently on the proposal of the Commons, following receipt of new reports, it was agreed to add further thanks for a parliamentarian victory at Stow-in-the-Wold, and the capture of the royalist commander, Sir Jacob Ashley. The order for the London area was printed at the end of an account of Fairfax's actions, *Sir Thomas Fairfax's letter from Cornwall*, which was published by an order of the Lords on 24 March. Although there were no explicit instructions, the account was presumably meant to be read out during the services. The order for the thanksgiving day for the rest of the kingdom on 16 April was printed separately, bearing (incongruously) the date of the Commons' original proposal on 21 March. Joseph Caryll and Hugh Peters were appointed to preach before both houses at Christ Church, which had last been used by parliament for special worship in June 1645 (see 1645–E5(P)). Peters's sermon lasted three hours. As in June 1645, the lord mayor and aldermen of London were invited to the service; in return, they invited members of both houses to a dinner afterwards at the Grocers' Hall 'to preserve Love and Unity between the Parliament and City, which some did endeavour to divide'. The orders were disseminated by the lord mayor and MPs.

Orders: parliamentary orders, *LJ*, VIII, 230, 231.
Additional sources: *CJ*, IV, 483–5, 491, 495–6; *LJ*, VIII, 227, 230–1, 237, 240–1, 243, 248–9; *Sir Thomas Fairfax's letter from Cornwall, relating the whole businesse in the West. With the articles at large, concluded upon by His Excellencies commissioners and Sir Ralph Hoptons. And an order of both Houses for a day of thanksgiving for the same. Die Lunae, 23 March. 1645. Ordered by the Lords assembled in Parliament, that this letter with the articles shall be forthwith printed and published* (1646; Wing F171); parliamentary orders, 21 [i.e. 23] Mar. 1646, Wing E1751*; *FSP*, XXIII, 2–4.
Printed sermons: Caryl, parliament (Wing C751, C752; *FSP*, XXIII, 9–56); Peters, parliament (Wing P1704; *FSP*, XXIII, 57–116).

ORDERS

Parliamentary orders: 23 March 1646
Ordered, by the Lords and Commons assembled in Parliament, That *Thursday* Sevennight be set apart for a day of Public Thanksgiving to Almighty God, for the great Success of the Army under the Command of *Sir Thomas Fairfax,* General

against the enemy in the West, in breaking and destroying their Armies, and giving them up into the hands of the Parliament; to be observed and kept in all the Churches and Chapels within the Cities of *London* and *Westm[inster]* and Liberties thereof, and Lines of Communication, and Ten Miles about; and that the Lord Mayor be desired to take care, that the respective Ministers within the Limits aforesaid may have timely notice hereof.

...

Ordered, by the Lords and Commons in Parliament assembled, That on *Thursday* Sevennight, and on *Thursday* Three Weeks, being the Days appointed to be set apart for Days of Public Thanksgiving in the Cities of *London* and *Westm[inster]* and in the other Parts of the Kingdom, for the Success of the Army in the West, under the Command of *Sir Thomas Fairefax* General, the several Ministers do, on the said Days respectively, take Notice of the great Blessing of God upon the Forces of the Parliament, in taking of *Sir Jacob Ashley* Prisoner, and total Routing and Defeating the Forces under his Command, near *Stow*, in the County of *Gloucester*.

1646–S2   Fast day during fears of continued rebellion

Thursday 30 April 1646 (Scotland)

After his defeat at Philiphaugh, Montrose had returned to the highlands, where he struggled to raise troops for a renewed attack on the covenanters. Despite the royalists' weaknesses, the commission of the general assembly thought that they continued to pose a threat. On 31 March 1646, the commission issued a *Declaration* against the 'Humble Remonstrance' of the earl of Seaforth, which had proposed a compromise between royalists and covenanters, but was interpreted by the commission as a new anti-covenanter band. At around the same time, the commission appointed a fast, reflecting this political situation, the country's sinfulness and the welcome retreat of the plague.

Order: act of the commission of the general assembly, *c*. 1 Apr. 1646 (not found).
Causes: *Causes of a solemne fast* (Wing C2401D)*.
Additional sources: *A declaration against a late dangerous and seditious band* (Edinburgh, 1646; Wing C4203AE); presbytery of Dalkeith minutes, NRS, CH2/424/3, p. 147.

CAUSES

I. Besides the diverse causes of our former solemne Humiliations, both for the evill of Sin and of Punishment, lying still in a great measure upon the whole Land, wee should lay to heart the late shamefull backsliding and compliance of many with the Enemies, in the houre of temptation.

II. It is to be lamented, though the Lord our God hath taken pains to purge us by his Judgments of Sword and Pestilence, yet there is no reformation of our lives, our scumme remains in us, many returning with the dog to their former profanenesse, neglect of Gods worship in Families, uncleannesse, drunkennesse, and other great provocations, as if they had been delivered to do all these abominations: Have we not just cause to mourn and be afraid that the Lord kindle the fire again, heap on more wood, and cause his fury to rest upon us?

III. It is high time when the whole Land is threatned with a new breach from the North, to acknowledge our great and senselesse ingratitude, who have no wayes rendred to the Lord according to the benefits received, though the Lord hath begun to draw back his hand in a sensible and unexpected delivery from the raging Pesti-lence, and hath given us a little breathing from the cruell insulting Enemie, yet all our promises and vows uttered in the day of our trouble, have proven to be as the early dew and morning cloud; neither have we brought forth the fruits of right-eousnesse, and amendment of our wayes, while the Lord looked for them, after so gracious a Delivery: so that it is just with our God to disappoint us of our expecta-tion, when we look for healing to send new troubles, and to raise up in his wrath some, who have banded themselves together in the North, contrary to our solemne Covenants.

IV. Seeing our God hears Prayer, it is our duty to run to him in this day of trouble, and to wrestle with tears and supplications, that our God in the might of his power would crush this Cockatrice Egge, that it break not forth into a fierie flying Serpent; that the insolent pride of the contrivers of this divisive and seditious Bond, may be rebuked by the Lord; that the simple who have been mis-led, may be convinced and drawn out of the snare, that these who stand, may be stablished by grace in their stedfastnes, and strengthened with the spirit of Unity and Courage to oppose that divisive motion: Lastly, that the Work of Uniformity in Church-government may be finished, our Armies blessed and compassed with Gods favour, and a firme and well-grounded Peace settled betwixt the Kings Majesty and Parliaments of both Kingdomes.

1646–E5(P)   Thanksgiving days for parliamentarian victories in the south-west and in Wales

Tuesday 12 May 1646 (London, Westminster, the lines of communication and parishes within twenty miles); Tuesday 19 May 1646 (elsewhere in England and Wales within the power of parliament)

Parliament enjoyed a string of successes in the spring of 1646, including Portland Castle (6 April), Ruthin (12 April), Exeter (13 April), Aberystwyth (14 April), Barnstaple (20 April), Dunster Castle (20 April) and St Michael's Mount (23 April). On 28 April, the Commons proposed days of thanksgiving on 12 and 19 May, extending the reach of the former to parishes within twenty miles of London and Westminster, rather than the usual ten. The Lords ordered the occasions on 12 May. Samuel Torshell and Charles Herle were appointed to preach before the lower house; both men were invited to print their sermons but only Torshell appears to have done so. The Lords' journal does not record any formal invitations to preach sermons but in the list of sermons printed at the end of William Goode's sermon, *Jacob raised*, Daniel Cawdrey and Richard Lee were named as preachers for this thanksgiving. On 9 May, the Commons added an order that the surrender of Newark (6 May) and Banbury (9 May) after long sieges should also be marked on these days; the Lords' reponse is not known because there is no reference to it in its journal.

Orders: order of the House of Lords, 2 May 1646, *LJ*, VIII, 293; order of the House of Commons, 9 May 1646, *CJ*, IV, 540.

Additional sources: *CJ*, IV, 526, 529–30; *LJ*, VIII, 291–2; *FSP*, XXIII, 5–6; William Goode, *Jacob raised: or, The means of making a nation happy both in spiritual and temporal priviledges. Presented in a sermon preached before the Right Honorable House of Peeres in the Abby Church at Westminster, at the late solemne monthly fast, Decemb. 30. 1646* (1647; Wing G1094), 31.
Printed sermons: Ford, St Botolph's Aldersgate, London (Wing F1487, F1487A); Torshell, House of Commons (Wing T1940; *FSP*, XXIII, 254–83).

ORDERS

Order of the House of Lords: 2 May 1646

ORDERED, by the Lords and Commons assembled in Parliament, That this Day Fortnight, being the 12th Day of *May* next, shall be set apart for a Day of Public Thanksgiving, within the Cities of *London* and *Westm[inste]r*, and Lines of Communication, and Twenty Miles of the said City, for the several Mercies of GOD upon the Forces of the Parliament, in reducing and taking-in the several Castles and Garrisons of *Portland, Ruthin, Execeter, Barnstable, The Mount in Cornwall, Dunster Castle, Tutbury Castle, Aberistwith Castle, Woodstock Mannor*, and the Castle of *Bridgnorth*; and that the Lord Mayor of the City of *London* be desired to take Care that the several Ministers within the Limits aforesaid may have timely Notice of this Order.

Ordered, by the Lords and Commons assembled in Parliament, That this Day Three Weeks, being the 19th of *May* next, shall be set apart, and observed and kept, for a Day of Public Thanksgiving, within the several Counties, Cities, and Places, within the Power of the Parliament, for the several Mercies of GOD upon the Forces of the Parliament, in reducing and taking in the several Castles and Garrisons of *Portland, Ruthyn, Exeter, Barnestable, The Mount in Cornwall, Dunster Castle, Tutbury, and Aberristwith Castle, Woodstock Mannor*, and the Castle of *Bridgnorth*; and that the Knights and Burgesses that serve for the said Counties and Places do take Care that the respective Ministers may have timely Notice hereof.

Order of the House of Commons: 9 May 1646

Ordered, That, on *Tuesday* next, being the Twelfth of this instant *May*, and, by former Order, set apart for a Day of Publick Thanksgiving for several Mercies on the Forces of the Parliament in divers Parts of the Kingdom, Thanks be likewise given to Almighty God, for his great Blessing in the Surrender of the Garisons of *Newarke* and *Banbury-Castle*: And that the Lord Mayor of the City of *London* is desired to give notice hereof to the several Ministers within the respective Limits and Parishes where the said Day is appointed to be observed and kept. And

It is further *Ordered*, That this great Blessing of the Surrender of *Newarke* and *Banbury-Castle* be likewise commemorated, on *Tuesday* the Nineteenth of this instant *May*, in the several Counties and Places where the said Day is appointed to be observed and kept as a Day of Thanksgiving for several other Mercies to the Forces of the Parliament in divers Parts of the Kingdom: And that the Knights and Burgesses of the said several Counties and Places do take care, that timely Notice hereof may be given to the respective Ministers within the said several Counties and Places accordingly.

1646–E6(P)   Thanksgiving prayers for parliamentarian victories in the west

Sunday 14 June 1646 (London, Westminster, the lines of communication and bills of mortality)

Following the king's flight from Oxford on 27 April 1646 and surrender to the Scots at Newark on 13 May, his forces surrendered more castles and towns, including Tutbury in Staffordshire (20 April), Dudley Castle (13 May), Hartlebury Castle (16 May), Ludlow (before 23 May) and Borstall House on the Oxfordshire–Buckinghamshire border (early June). On 8 June, the Commons proposed thanksgivings for 14 June in all parishes in London, Westminster and within the bills of mortality and lines of communication, reverting to a more limited geographical area for observance than on previous occasions. The Lords appear not to have been involved in the ordering process: there is no record of the Commons' proposal in the Lords' journal, even though the upper house received news of Fairfax's victories and the terms of the treaties he had made. There was no thanksgiving proposed for the rest of the country under parliament's authority and no preachers were appointed to preach before either house. The orders were disseminated by the lord mayor.

Order: parliamentary order, 8 June 1646 (s.n., s.p., n.d.; Wing E2603E)* [also in *CJ*, IV, 568].
Additional sources: *CJ*, IV, 568; *LJ*, VIII, 363, 365.

ORDER

Parliamentary order: 8 June 1646
It is this day Ordered by the Commons now Assembled in Parliament, That on the next Lords Day the respective Ministers of the severall Churches, and Chappels within the Cities of *London* and *Westminster*, and Lines of Communication and Weekely Bills of Mortality, doe take notice of the late severall Mercies of Almighty God to the Forces of the Parliament in the regaining and reducing of the severall Garrisons of *Tudbury* Castle, *Dudley* Castle, *Hartlebury* Castle, *Ludlow* Towne and Castle, and of *Bostoll* House; And to acknowledge and returne hearty thanks for the same. And that the Lord Major of the City of *London* be desired to take care that timely notice may be given hereof to the Ministers. And Mr. Alderman *Atkin*, is to acquaint the Lord Major with this Order.

1646–S3   Fast day after the Scottish defeat at the battle of Benburb, Ireland

Thursday 9 July 1646 (Scotland)

This fast was a response to the victory of a confederate army (formed of Irish catholics loyal to Charles) over the Scottish army in Ireland at Benburb on 5 June 1646. This defeat, together with the arrival of a body of confederate soldiers in Argyll, represented a new blow to the covenanters, although the threat from Montrose had now dissipated. The general assembly's act was not printed, but at least two copies of the printed causes exist, unrecorded by ESTC.

Order: act of the general assembly, 17 June 1646 (unprinted; not found) [listed in Wing C4239, 26].
Causes: *Causes of a solemn fast and humiliation* ([Edinburgh?], 1646; EUL, Df.1.32(8)) [another copy in NRS, GD16/50/29; not in ESTC].
Additional sources: presbytery of Dalkeith minutes, NRS, CH2/424/3, p. 155; presbytery of Elgin minutes, NRS, CH2/144/1, p. 111.

CAUSES

Besides the divers Causes of our former solemne Humiliations, both for the evil of Sin and of Punishment, lying still in a great measure upon the whole Land; Great Prophanenesse, neglect of Gods Worship in Families, Uncleannesse, Drunkennesse, and other great provocations; we should at this time, in a speciall manner, acknowledge our great unthankfulnesse, and unanswerable walking to the Lords gracious Work of Reformation within this Kingdom: for which cause it is just with God hitherto to disappoint our expectation in a great measure of the intended Uniformity in Church-Government.

II. The late overthrow given to our Armie in *Ireland*; with *Ephraim* we have turned back in the day of Battell, we have not kept the Covenant of God, and have refused to walk in his Law: we lifted up our selves in the pride of our heart, and the Lord in his righteous Judgement hath humbled us by a contemptible Enemy; the Lord threatens to vex us with Strangers come into the west Sea, and lets us see he will not want one Rod after another to correct a stubborn and impenitent nation.

III. Notwithstanding our great and many Sins, and the heavy Judgements inflicted, Who layes to heart the evil of their wayes? No man repents him of his wickednesse, saying, What have I done? The people are senceless of their provocations against God, and our King layes not to heart the violence committed, and blood shed within this Kingdome, by wicked men cloathed with his Commission.

IIII. Seeing our God hears Prayer, it is our duty by teares and supplications to wrestle with him, that our hearts who fainted shamefully in the hour of temptation, and complyed in any sort with the Enemy, may be established in his Truth and our holy Profession, for the time coming: That the Lord would heal all division both in Kirk and State, that by his grace in the sense and conscience of our Covenant we may endeavour to keepe the Unity of the Spirit in the bond of Peace: That it may please the Lord who put it in the hearts of his people to joyne in that Solemne League and Covenant, to preserve the Kingdomes in Union: That the Lord who turnes the hearts of Kings where he will, as the rivers of waters, would incline our Kings heart to the Counsells of Trueth and Peace. And it is our duty to pray to the God of Armies to compasse our Armies with his favour, that by their endeavours a well grounded Peace may be settled within these United Kingdomes.

1646–E7(P)   Thanksgiving day for parliamentarian victories at Oxford, Faringdon, Anglesey and Lichfield

Tuesday 21 July 1646 (London, Westminister and the lines of communication,)

During the latter part of June news reached parliament of the surrender of further royalist strongholds including Anglesey (14 June), Oxford and Faringdon Castle (both 24 June). On 3 July, the Commons proposed a thanksgiving for these successes to be held on 14 July in London, Westminster and parishes within ten miles, and on 21 July for those beyond. The Lords, however, did not reply to the Commons until 9 July, when it refused to assent to the proposal. The reasons for this were not stated but could reflect the growing tension between the Lords and the Commons, particularly over the New Model Army, whose victories were being celebrated. Though the Commons seems previously to have ordered thanksgivings independently, the Lords' explicit refusal to give assent on this occasion seems to have led them, on 11 July, to postpone the thanksgiving in London and the surrounding area until 21 July. On 17 July, having received news of the taking of the royalist garrison at Lichfield Cathedral (10 July), the Commons ordered that the thanksgiving on the 21st should mark this success as well. It appears that the thanksgiving was limited to London, Westminster and the lines of communication, possibly because there was insufficient time to disseminate the order to more distant parishes. The Commons observed the day at its usual church of St Margaret's, Westminster. Sermons were preached, in the morning, by Henry Wilkinson and, in the afternoon, by Walter Cradock (replacing William Bridge, who was ill); both were printed. It is unclear if the Lords observed the day: it did not sit on 21 July and its appointment, on 9 July, of Edmund Calamy and Simeon Ashe to preach 'at the next Fast-day' referred to the monthly fast on 29 July.

Orders: orders of the House of Commons, 3 July 1646, *CJ*, IV, 600; 11 July 1646, *CJ*, IV, 616; 17 July 1646, *CJ*, IV, 621.
Additional sources: *CJ*, IV, 603, 611; *LJ*, VIII, 424; *FSP*, XXIV, 3–4.
Printed sermons: Cradock, House of Commons (Wing C6764, C6764A, C6765; *FSP*, XXIV, 54–95); Wilkinson, House of Commons (Wing W2224; *FSP*, XXIV, 9–53).

ORDERS

Order of the House of Commons: 3 July 1646

Ordered, That *Tuesday* Sevennight, being the Fourteenth Day of this instant *July*, be set apart for a Day of Publick Thanksgiving within the Cities of *London* and *Westminster*, Lines of Communication, weekly Bills of Mortality, and Ten Miles about, for the great Mercy of God, in delivering up into the Hands of the Parliament the strong Garison of *Oxford*, and the Garison of *Farringdon*, and for reducing the Island of *Anglesey*: And that the said Day be duly observed and kept within the several Churches and Chapels within the Limits aforesaid: And that the Lord Mayor of the City of *London* be desired to give Notice hereof to the several Ministers aforesaid.

The Lords Concurrence to be desired herein.

Ordered, That *Tuesday* Fortnight, being the One-and-twentieth Day of this instant *July*, be set apart for a Day of Publick Thanksgiving within the several Counties, Cities, and Places within this Kingdom, in the Power of the Parliament, above Ten Miles distant from *London*, for the great Mercy of God, in delivering up into the Hands of the Parliament the strong Garison of *Oxford*, and the Garison of *Faringdon*, and for reducing the Island of *Anglesey*: And that the Members of this House that serve for the said several Counties, Cities, and Places, do take care that timely Notice hereof be given to the several Ministers within the Limits aforesaid.

The Lords Concurrence to be desired herein.

Order of the House of Commons: 11 July 1646

Resolved, &c. That the Day of Thanksgiving for the Taking in and Reducing of *Oxford* be put off and deferred until *Tuesday* come Sevennight: And that Colonel *Venne* and Mr. *Vassall* do acquaint the Lord Mayor with this Order; and to desire him, that Notice hereof may be given in the several Churches within the Cities of *London* and *Westminster*, and Lines of Communication.

Order of the House of Commons: 17 July 1646

Ordered, That the Ministers within the Cities of *London* and *Westminster*, and Lines of Communication, do, on *Tuesday* next (being appointed for a Day of Publick Thanksgiving for the Gaining of *Oxford*), take notice of the great Mercy of God in reducing the strong Garison of *Lichfield*: And that the Lord Mayor of *London* be desired to give the Ministers Notice of this Order.

1646–E8(P)   Thanksgiving days for parliamentarian victories at Worcester, Wallingford, Ruthin, Raglan and Pendennis

Tuesday 8 September 1646 (London and surrounding area: London, Westminster, parishes within the lines of communication and bills of mortality and up to ten miles beyond); Tuesday 22 September 1646 (counties beyond ten miles from London and Westminster and in parliament's power)

Worcester surrendered to Colonel Rainsborough on 22 July, after a long siege which had begun in May. Similarly, Wallingford, besieged by Fairfax from 4 May, surrendered on 25 July. In Wales, Pendennis Castle surrendered on 17 August, followed by Raglan Castle (19 August) and Flint (24 August). On 21 August, the Commons requested that the speaker of the house inform MPs of these recent successes, although a thanksgiving was not proposed until the house met again on the 25th. A collection was ordered to be made in the London area for the relief of the poor and sick in Devon. The Lords agreed to this proposal on the 28th. As usual, the lord mayor and MPs were responsible for distributing these orders. Obadiah Sedgwick and Thomas Goodwin were appointed to preach before the Commons at St Margaret's; neither had their sermons printed, though both were invited to do so.

Orders: parliamentary orders, 28 Aug. 1646 (John Wright; 1 p., 1646; Wing E1735)* [also in *LJ*, VIII, 475]; 28 Aug. 1646 (John Wright; 1 p., 1646; Wing E1704)* [partially illegible; missing text supplied by Wing E878*, 916; also in *LJ*, VIII, 475].
Additional sources: *CJ*, IV, 651–3, 656–7; *LJ*, VIII, 474–5; Lambert, *Printing*, p. 121; *FSP*, XXIV, 6–7.

ORDERS

Parliamentary order: 28 August 1646

Ordered by the Lords and Commons Assembled in Parliament, That Tuesday, being the eight day of *September*, now next coming, be set a part for a day of Publike thanksgiving within the Cities of *London* and *Westminster*, Lines of Communication, and weekly Bils of Mortality and ten miles about, For the great blessing of God upon the Forces of the Parliament, in the reducing of the severall Castles and Garrisons of *Worcester*, *Wallingford*; *Ruthen*, *Ragland*, and *Pendennis*; And that the Lord Mayor of the City of *London* doe take care, that the Ministers of the severall Churches and Chappels, within the City of *London*, and Liberties thereof, may have timely notice hereof.

Parliamentary order: 28 August 1646

Ordered by the Lords and Commons Assembled in Parliament, That Tuesday, being the two and twentieth day of *September* now next coming, be set apart for a day of Publike Thanksgiving to be observed and kept in all Churches and Chappels, in the severall Counties, Cities and Places, in the Kingdome of *England*, above tenne miles distant from the Citie of *London*, For the great mercy of God to the Forces of the Parliament, in the reducing of the severall Garrisons and C[astles of] *Worcester*, *Wallingford*, *Ruthen*, *Ragland*, and *Pendennis*; [and that] the Members of this House that serve for the said severa[l Count]ies, Cities and Places, do take care that timely notice here[of may] be given to the respective Ministers within the places afo[resaid].

1646–S4 Fast day for sinfulness, peace talks, rebellion, defeat in Ireland and a good harvest

Sunday 20 September 1646 or the first Sunday after receipt (Scotland)

When this fast was appointed, Charles I was a prisoner of the Scottish army in Newcastle, where he was encouraged to agree peace terms. Listing the causes of the fast, the commission of the general assembly requested prayers for the success of these negotiations, and also expressed the need for further repentance in response to Montrose's rising and the defeat of the army in Ireland (see 1646–S3). Because the commission's register is extant, this is the first observance appointed by that court that can be fully documented. After appointing the fast on 26 August, the commission arranged for the causes to be printed, dispatching them to presbyteries with a circular letter the following day.

Order: act of the commission of the general assembly, 26 Aug. 1646, *RCGA*, I, 48.
Causes: *Causes of a publike fast and humiliation* (Wing C4201A)* [also in *RCGA*, I, 48–9].
Letter: commission of the general assembly to presbyteries, 27 Aug. 1646, *RCGA*, I, 55.

ORDER

Act of the commission of the general assembly: 26 August 1646

The Commission of Assemblie appoints a solemne fast and humiliatione to be keeped in all the congregationes of this Kirk vpon the 3d Sabbath of September nixt for the reasones and causes following

CAUSES

I. Notwithstanding of our profession in the last Article of our Solemne League and Covenant, yet to this day the Son of God is not honoured amongst us in the excellencie of his Person, nor imployed in the vertue of his Offices; But the unsearchable riches of Christ and the inestimable treasure of the Gospell are neglected and despised as things of no value.

II. We doe not tremble under the threatnings of the Law, verified upon us in many sad and sore judgements, Nor doe we follow the direction thereof as a rule of our obedience, but the whole Land almost and many in our Armies still lie in a deep security, and live under grosse prophanity and hardnesse of heart.

III. We have reason to mourn for the issue of that horrid Rebellion, as a testimony of the continued indignation of the most High against our backslidings and provocations.

IIII. The lamentable condition of our Brethren in *Ireland*, almost brought unto fainting, and neere to be swallowed up by the power and cruelty of the Rebells there, Together with the danger that we are threatned with from them, and the afflicted estate of those parts of this Kingdome which yet lie under the feet of the Enemies.

V. Seeing the Lord hath been pleased to stain the pride of all our glory, by blasting all our carnall confidence and making the emptinesse of means to appear, we would seriously intreat him that he would make himself glorious in the midst of us, by the manifestation of his free grace and wonted favour, in pardoning our sins, reclaiming us from our backslidings, and healing our Land for his own Name sake.

VI. That the Lord would soften the Kings heart, and give unto him the spirit of Humiliation that he may mourn for his iniquity, and that the spirit of wisdom and understanding may be given to him, and all these that are imployed in the publike affairs in both Kingdoms, that all their councells and actions may be means for the advancement of the Kingdom of the Son of God, promoving the work of Uniformity, holding fast the League betwixt the Nations, and for procuring a firm and well-grounded Peace in all the three Kingdomes.

VII. That the spirit of Faithfulnesse, Unity, and Zeal, may be poured upon all the Ministers of the land, that in integrity and love they may bear burden one with another, for seeking the honour of Jesus Christ and the edifying of his Body the Church.

VIII. That the Lord would crowne the year with his goodnesse in granting a fair and fruitfull Harvest.

LETTER

Commission of the general assembly to presbyteries: 27 August 1646

We haue found it necessar at this time to enjoyne a publict fast for the reasones which we haue sent to yow in print. Ye will be carefull that the same be religiouslie observed, and if this come not to your hand in time so that ye cannot keep it vpon the day appointed, that ye keep it the nixt convenient Sabbath therafter ...

1646–S5   Fast day in support of parliament

Friday 13 November 1646 (Edinburgh)

The Scottish parliament reassembled on 3 November 1646. Charles was now a prisoner of the Scottish army at Newcastle, and the estates faced the question of what to do with him if he refused to accept peace terms. The nature of parliament's 'conference with the ministrie' before the appointment of this fast is unclear, but on

Die Veneris, 4. *Decemb.* 1646.

ORdered by the Lords and Commons affembled in Parliament, That *Wednefday* next be appointed for a Day of Publique Humiliation, to be obferved in all the Parifhes and places
within the Cities of *London* and *Weftminfter,* Lines of Communication, and weekly Bills of Mortality. And *VVednefday* next
come fortnight to be obferved by the whole Kingdom, For the
removing of the great Judgment of Rain and Waters now upon
the Kingdom, and for preventing the fad Confequences that may
infue thereupon.

H: Elfynge, Cler. Parl. D. Com.

Die Jovis, 3. *Decemb.* 1646.

*ORdered by the Commons affembled in Parliament, That the Order for
appointing* Wednefday *next come fortnight a Day of publique Humiliation, to be obferved throughout the Kingdom, For removing this heavy
Iudgement of Rain and Waters, and for preventing the fad confequences that
may infue thereupon, be forthwith printed ; And that the feveral and refpe-
Ctive Knights and Burgeffes of the feveral and refpeCtive Counties, Cities
and Boroughs, do fend Copies thereof to the feveral and refpeCtive Committees; The faid Committees are to give timely notice thereof to the feveral
and refpeCtive Minifters, and to take care that the faid day may be more ftriCt-
ly obferved then many of the former have been.*

H: Elfynge, Cler. Parl. D. Com.

LONDON:

Printed for *Edward Husband,* Printer to the
Honorable Houfe of Commons.

11 After the outbreak of civil war, parliament ordered its own occasions of
special worship. These orders were often printed, either as single sheets or
at the ends of narratives which were to be read out in church. This order,
for 1646–E9(P), was issued during a period of bad weather: it survives in a
unique copy. Parliamentary order, 4 Dec. 1646, Wing E1735D (Alexander
Turnbull Library, Wellington, NZ; R Fletcher 18); half sheet folio.

11 November the commission of the general assembly nominated ministers to preach to parliament on the fast day.

Order: parliamentary ordinance, 7 Nov. 1646, *RPS*, 1646/11/14.
Additional source: *RCGA*, I, 99.

ORDER

Parliamentary ordinance: 7 November 1646

The estates of parliament, eftir conference with the ministrie, appointis Fryday nixt for keiping of ane solemne fast all that day in Edinburgh for ane blessing from God to this parliament in ther proceidingis therin.

1646–E9(P)   Days of humiliation during heavy rain and floods

Wednesday 9 December 1646 (London, Westminster, lines of communication and bills of mortality); Wednesday 23 December 1646 (elsewhere in England and Wales)

This day was initiated by the Westminster assembly for 'Removing of this great Judgement of immoderate Rain and Waters upon this Kingdom and for the preventing the sad Consequence that may ensue upon it'. It was the first time that the assembly had initiated a day of special worship since 1644–E8(P) and the first time that special worship had been ordered for anything other than civil war since the outbreak of plague in 1640 (1640–E3). It is unclear why the assembly chose to initiate this occasion. No reason is given in its records, and there were few perceived signs of divine disapproval of parliament's actions, especially as royalist castles continued to surrender (Denbigh, 26 October; Conway, 18 December). Other significant changes were also afoot: episcopacy had been abolished on 9 October; parliament asserted its authority to take charge of Charles's person (28 November); it was in negotiation with the earl of Ormond, the royalist leader in Ireland; and the assembly itself formulated the Confession of Faith (4 December). The Commons heard and assented to the assembly's request on 3 December, and the Lords on the following day. For the first time, the orders were disseminated not only by the lord mayor and MPs, but also by the JPs of Middlesex, Westminster and Surrey. John Ward and Jeremiah Whitaker were appointed to preach before the Commons; neither subsequently printed their sermons. Francis Roberts and a Mr Martyn were appointed to preach before the Lords in the Henry VII Chapel, Westminster Abbey. On 5 December Roberts was ill and was replaced by Charles Herle. Though Roberts printed his sermon, Herle did not.

Order: parliamentary order, 4 Dec. 1646, Wing E1735D (Alexander Turnbull Library, Wellington, NZ; R Fletcher 18) [similar text in *LJ*, VIII, 590].
Additional sources: *CJ*, IV, 737–8; *LJ*, VIII, 590–92, 601; *FSP*, XXV, 6–7; *Westminster assembly*, III, 669, IV, 98, 354–5.
Printed sermons: Roberts, House of Lords (Wing R1580; *FSP*, XXV, 309–56); Bryan, Coventry (Wing B5242).

ORDER

Parliamentary order: 4 December 1646
Ordered, by the Lords and Commons assembled in Parliament, That *Wednesday* next be appointed for a Day of Publique Humiliation, to be observed in all the Parishes and places within the Cities of *London* and *Westminster*, Lines of Communication, and weekly Bills of Mortality. And *Wednesday* next come fortnight be observed by the whole Kingdom, For the removing of the great Judgement of Rain and Waters now upon the Kingdom, and for preventing the sad Consequences that may insue thereupon.

1647–E1(P)   Day of humiliation for religious errors, heresies and blasphemies

Wednesday 10 March 1647 (England, Wales and Berwick-upon-Tweed)

This day of humiliation was proposed by the Commons on 27 January. It was agreed by the Lords on 4 February; on 13 February the Commons ordered that the ordinance be printed and then distributed by MPs. Ministers were expressly ordered to publish the ordinance on 7 March, the Sunday preceding the day of humiliation, though this seems to have revived or formalized an earlier practice whereby ministers were fined by their bishop for failing to advertise days of special worship a week in advance. It was the first usage of the designation 'England, Wales and Berwick-upon-Tweed', which was to be common from 1650 to 1801, and used periodically thereafter. This probably reflected the hegemony of parliament and ending of the (first) civil war. The purpose of the day was 'to set forth this our deep sence of the great dishonor of God, and perillous condition that this Kingdom is in, through the abominable Blasphemies, and damnable Heresies' which threatened the care and protection that God had offered England since the drawing up of the Solemn League and Covenant in August 1643. It is unclear what, if any, specific events triggered the Commons' action. Parliament had taken custody of the king from the Scottish army, which had now withdrawn from Newcastle, and the Westminster assembly continued to develop the confession of faith as well as draw up the long and short catechisms. However, there were conflicts between presbyterians and independents in the Commons, and between the Commons and Lords, over religious sectarianism and the New Model Army (seen by many as a harbour for religious sectarianism), so this occasion may have been an attempt by the presbyterians to seize the initiative from more radical groups. On 4 February, the Lords appointed Richard Vines and a Mr Martyn to preach before them at Westminster Abbey. However, Vines had already been appointed to preach before the Commons, with Calamy; if the Lords appointed a substitute, it is not known who this was. The Commons also had problems appointing preachers. On 1 February, Calamy was replaced by Burgess (it is unclear whether this was Anthony Burgess or Cornelius Burges) but he immediately asked to be excused and Thomas Hodges was appointed in his place. Both Hodges and Vines printed their sermons.

Order: parliamentary ordinance, 4 Feb. 1647, Wing E1823* [also Wing E1824; also in *LJ*, VIII, 706–7; *Acts and ordinances of the interregnum 1642–60*, ed. C. H. Firth and R. S. Rait (3 vols., 1911), I, 913–14].

Additional sources: *CJ*, V, 66, 69–70, 86; *LJ*, VIII, 705–7, IX, 18; *FSP*, XXVII, 4–5.
Printed sermons: Hodges, House of Commons (Wing H2315; *FSP*, XXVII, 273–340); Vines, House of Commons (Wing V545, V545A; *FSP*, XXVII, 197–272).

ORDER

Parliamentary ordinance: 4 February 1647

We the Lords and Commons assembled in the Parliament of *England*, having entred into a Solemn Covenant, to endeavor sincerely, really and constantly, the Reformation of Religion, in Doctrine, Discipline and Worship, and the extirpation of Popery, Superstition, Heresy, Schism, Prophanenesse, and whatsoever shall be found contrary to sound Doctrine and the power of godlinesse; and having found the presence of God wonderfully assisting us in this Cause, especially since our said ingagement in pursuance of the said Covenant, Have thought fit (lest we partake in other mens sins, and thereby be in danger to receive of their plagues) to set forth this our deep sence of the great dishonor of God, and perillous condition that this Kingdom is in, through the abominable Blasphemies, and damnable Heresies vented and spread abroad therein, tending to the subversion of the Faith, contempt of the Ministery, and Ordinance of Iesus Christ: And as we are resolved to imploy and improve the utmost of our power, that nothing be said or done against the Truth, but for the Truth; so we desire that both our selves and the whole Kingdom may be deeply humbled before the Lord for that great reproach and contempt which hath been cast upon his Name and saving Truths, and for that swift destruction which we may justly fear will fall upon the immortal souls of such who are or may be drawn away, by giving heed to seducing Spirits. In the hearty and tender compassion whereof, We the said Lords and Commons do Order and Ordain, That Wednesday being the tenth day of *March* next, be set apart for a day of publique Humiliation for the growth and spreading of Errors, Heresies and Blasphemies, to be observed in all places within the Kingdom of *England* and Dominion of *Wales*, and Town of *Berwick*, and to seek God for his direction and assistance for the suppression and preventing the sam. And all Ministers are hereby enjoyned to publish this present Ordinance upon the Lords day preceding the said Tenth day of *March*.

1647–S1 Fast day for the army's campaign against royalists in northern Scotland

Sunday 4 April 1647 or the first Sunday after receipt (Scotland)

After handing over Charles I to English custody and receiving payment from the English parliament, the Scottish army withdrew from Newcastle in early February 1647. Having remodelled the army on a much smaller scale, parliament then sent troops to fight the remaining royalist leaders in the north of Scotland. The commission of the general assembly, which had called for action against the royalists, ordered this fast to pray for the success of the covenanting forces.

Order: act of the commission of the general assembly, 24 Feb. 1647, *RCGA*, I, 216.
Letter: commission of the general assembly to presbyteries, 24 Feb. 1647, *RCGA*, I, 216–17.

Additional sources: *RPS*, 1646/11/243; *The humble remonstrance of the commissioners of the general assembly* (Edinburgh, 1647; Wing C4229AB); *Strathbogie presbytery*, pp. 74–5.

ORDER

Act of the commission of the general assembly: 24 February 1647

The Commission appoynts a solemne Fast and humiliation to be keeped upon the first Lords Day in Appryle, and that letters be written to that purpose; …

LETTER

Commission of the general assembly to presbyteries: 24 February 1647

Hearing that our forces ar to marche northward against these bloody rebells that have infested this poor kingdome, we conceive it our dutie to put up our prayers for the Lords speciall assistance unto them in their undertakings; and for that effect have appoynted that the first Sabboth of Appryle be keeped for a day of publik fasting and humiliation before the Lord, that he may be intreated for his blessing and assistance to them in their persute of these rebells; wherin ye will remember also the common sins of the land, and the causes and reasones of our former humiliations yet remaining; And if these presents shall not come in due tyme to your hands, that yow set apart the first Sabboth which conveniently yow can observe after the receipt heirof for a day of fasting for the reasones and causes aforesaid …

1647–S2   Fast day for the general assembly, against threats from English religious independents, for the king and for parliament

Sunday 25 July 1647 (Scotland)

This fast had been appointed by the general assembly of 1646 to precede its next meeting. Though the order was made more than a year in advance of the fast, the causes written by the commission of the general assembly reflected more immediate concerns, notably developments in England. The growth in influence of the independents, particularly in the army (which seized Charles I on 4 June 1647), weakened the cause of English presbyterianism and undermined religious uniformity between the kingdoms. According to the commission, English proponents of religious toleration threatened the subversion of true doctrine and renewed civil conflict. The causes of the fast also referred to the plague, which revived this summer in several parts of Scotland.

Order: act of the general assembly, 18 June 1646, Wing C4240*, 22 [also in *Acts of the general assembly of the Church of Scotland, M.DC.XXXVIII.–M.DCCC.XLII*, p. 147].
Causes: *Causes of a publike fast, and solemne humiliation* (Wing C4201B)* [also in *RCGA*, I, 286–7].
Letter: commission of the general assembly to presbyteries, 14 July 1646, *RCGA*, I, 287–8.
Additional source: *RCGA*, I, 285, 289–96.

ORDER

Act of the general assembly: 18 June 1646

The Assembly having considered an Act of the Assembly 1644 *Sess. Ult.* enioyning a publike Fast to be keeped in all the Kirks of the City where the General Assembly holds upon the first day of the meeting of the Assembly; And finding some inconveniencies therein, Therefore at this time untill the matter be further considered, Appoints a publike Fast and Humiliation for the Lords blessing to the meeting of the next Assembly, to be universally observed in all the congregations of this Kirk upon the Sabbath next except one preceding the said next Assembly; The exercises for the members of the Assembly at their first meeting, Being still observed according to the ancient and laudable practise of this Kirk, This appointment notwithstanding.

CAUSES

That notwithstanding of our solemne ingagement, in the Covenant, our Obligations from great and singular mercies, and our many warnings from judgments of all sorts; Yet not only doe we come farre short of that sobriety, righteousnesse and holinesse that becometh the Gospell of *Jesus Christ,* but ungodlinesse and worldly lusts abound every where throughout the Land, unto the grieving of the Lords Spirit, and provoking the eyes of his glory to make him increase his plagues upon us, and to punish us seaven times more, because we continue to walke contrary unto him.

Secondly, That the Lords hand is still stretch'd out against us, in the judgment of the Pestilence, which spreadeth not only in severall places of the Country, but continueth and increaseth in many of the most eminent Cities in the Kingdome.

Thirdly, The great dangers that threaten Religion, and the worke of Reformation, In these Kingdomes from the number, Policy and power of the Sectaries in *England,* which are like not only to interrupt the progresse of uniformity, and the establishing of the Ordinances of God in their bewty and perfection, but to overturne the foundation already layd, and all that hath beene built thereupon, with the expences of much bloud and paines.

First, And therefore we are earnestly to pray the Lord that the solemne League and Covenant may bee kept fast and inviolable, notwithstanding of all the purposes and endeavours of open enemies and secret underminers to the contrary.

Secondly, We are to entreate the Lord on the behalfe of the Kings Majesty, that he may be reconciled to God, and that he may be now furnished with Wisdom and Councell from above, that hee bee not involved in new snares, to the endangering of himselfe and these Kingdomes, but that his heart may encline to such resolution, as will contribute for setling of Religion and Righteousnesse.

Thirdly, We are also to entreat the Lord on the behalfe of the Parliament of *England* of the Synod of Divines, and of all such in that Land as doe unfainedly minde the work of God, that they may not be discouraged or swarve in the day of temptation, but that each of them in their stations, and according to their places and callings may bee furnished with light and strength from heaven for doing of their duty with faithfulnesse and zeale.

Fourthly, We are to supplicate for direction to our Committee of Estates, that they may discerne the times, and know what is fitting to be done, for securing our selves and incouraging our Brethren.

Fifthly, We are to pray for a spirit of light and of law unto our Assembly, that they may be instrumentall in preserving the truth, and advancing holinesse amongst our selves, and for carrying on the work of God amongst our Neighbours.

Finally, *That the Lord would power out upon all sorts of persons in these King-domes a spirit of grace and supplication, that it may repent us of all our iniquities, and that we may be reconciled to the Lord; that so all the threatens of his wrath may bee removed from amongst us, and he may blesse us with the sweet fruits of truth and peace.*

LETTER

Commission of the general assembly to presbyteries: 14 July 1646

… In the mean while we have sent yow the Causes of a publik fast which we conceive necessary to be kept the 25 of this moneth, not only in reference to the approaching Assembly according to the Act of the preceeding Assembly, but also in reference to the present condition of affairs. In the first cause wee have kept upon a generall, leaving it to your own knowledge and discretion to discend unto the particular sins that abound in the land and in your bounds …

1647–E2(P)   Thanksgiving days for the parliamentarian victory at the battle of Dungan's Hill, Ireland

Tuesday 31 August 1647 (London, Westminster, lines of communication and parishes within the bills of mortality); Tuesday 7 September 1647 (elsewhere in England and Wales)

Though the civil war had ended in England and Wales, fighting continued in Ireland. In August, Thomas Preston, younger son of the fourth Viscount Gormanstown, attempted to seize Dublin for the royalists; the capital had earlier been surrendered to parliament by the earl of Ormond to prevent it falling into catholic hands. However, on 8 August, Preston was intercepted at Dungan's Hill by parliamentarian forces under Colonel Michael Jones and his army destroyed. On 18 August, the Commons proposed days of thanksgiving to be held on 31 August and 7 September. The Lords agreed to its request on 20 August. This occasion thus reverted to the usual practice of ordering two observances – one for the London area and another for the rest of England and Wales – after the innovation of one nationwide observance for 1647–E1(P). Thomas Temple and Sidrach Simpson were appointed to preach before the Commons, though neither man availed themself of the Commons' invitation to have their sermons printed.

Order: *Die Veneris 20 August, 1647*, 20 Aug. 1647, Wing E1735A (Guildhall Library, London, Bside 25.113) [also in *LJ*, IX, 390].
Additional sources: *CJ*, V, 276, 280, 287; *LJ*, IX, 388; *An exact and full relation of the great victory obtained against the rebels at Dungons-Hill in Ireland, August 8. 1647* (1647; Wing R2068); *FSP*, XXIX, 7–8.

ORDER

Parliamentary order: 20 August 1647

Ordered by the Lords and Commons in Parliament assembled, That Tuesday next come seven-night be observed as a day of publike Thansgiving [*sic*] unto Almighty God within the Cities of *London* and *Westminster*, Lines of Communication, and Parishes within the weekly Bills of Mortalitie, for the great Victory obtained against the Rebels in *Ireland* on Sunday the eighth of this present August, by the great blessing of God upon the Forces under the command of Colonell *Michael Jones*, and Tuesday next come fortnight in all the Parishes and places in all the Kingdome of *England* and dominion of *Wales*.

1647–S3 Thanksgiving day for victory in Argyll, resistance to English sectaries and relief from plague

Sunday 26 September 1647 (Scotland)

In the summer of 1647, the covenanting army moved against the royalists in Argyll, causing the flight to Ireland of Alasdair MacColla, a leading MacDonald clansman who had led troops alongside Montrose. The campaign against other royalist figures was continuing when the assembly appointed this thanksgiving, but the army's success seemed assured. On 20 August, the assembly adopted a *Declaration and brotherly exhortation*, addressed to English presbyterians, denouncing the attitudes and influence of independents and sectaries, and calling for presbyterian government to be settled. Compared to previous years, the plague of 1647 affected fewer parts of Scotland. Members of the presbytery of Strathbogie complained that the thanksgiving day was abused by soldiers in the area.

Order: act of the general assembly, 1 Sept. 1647 (unprinted; not found) [listed in Wing C4241, 42].
Causes: *Causes of a publike thanksgiving* (Wing C4201CA; Beinecke Rare Book and Manuscript Library, Yale University, New Haven, CT, BrSides By6 1647).
Additional sources: *A declaration and brotherly exhortation of the general assembly* (Edinburgh, 1647; Wing C4205); *Strathbogie presbytery*, p. 80.

CAUSES

That the Lord hath been pleased to grant so happy and glorious a successe to our Army imployed against the Rebels, which mercy as it is considerable in it self, so is it much more eminent, in regard of these and other circumstances which do accompany it.

1. That after so many essayes wherein we were put to the worse before the Enemie, the work was apprehended, not only to be difficult, but almost impossible in the judgements of men.

2. That notwithstanding of all the difficultie thereof, The Lord hath brought it to passe in a very short time, and with the expence of very little blood.

3. That he carried our Army as on Eagles wings over Sea and Land, and in his gracious providence so disposed of all events and difficulties as they did contribute for furthering of the Work.

4. That in the midst of the greatest straits he kept the Army from murmuring, and not only furnished them with patience and courage in the wants of things necessary, but subdued their Enemies before them, and gave into their hands many Garisons and strong holds, in an unexpected and more then ordinary way.

5. That hee hath been pleased to dispence so great a mercy in such a point of time, wherein the pride and insolencie of the adversaries of the Work of Reformation in our Neighbour Land is come to so great a height, And not only threatneth the interruption thereof, But the overturning of all that is already done.

I. That the Lord hath been pleased in this point of time, wherein the confusions of our Neighbour Land and our feares from thence are so great, To give us a Generall Assembly, which hath with much Unanimity of judgement issued a publike Declaration against the errours in *England*, And done those things that may contribute for preserving of Truth, and advancing of Holinesse amongst our selves.

II. That the Lord hath been graciously pleased, to keep the Pestilence from spreading over the face of the Land, and to deliver the most eminent City of the Kingdome therefra, in a short time, after many thousands had fallen in her streets.

1647–S4   Fast day during the plague epidemic, and against English independents and other troubles

Sunday 31 October 1647 (Scotland)

The political and epidemiological circumstances that led the assembly to appoint the previous thanksgiving (1647–S3) were mixed, as were the reasons for ordering this fast. As well as the challenges posed by the independents and sectaries in England (see 1647–S3), and the continuing, if declining, outbreak of plague, the position of the king, who was still a prisoner, was unclear.

Order: act of the general assembly, 1 Sept. 1647 (unprinted; not found) [listed in Wing C4241, 42].
Causes: *Causes of a publike fast* (Wing C4201BA; EUL, Df.1.32(11)).
Additional source: presbytery of Paisley minutes, NRS, CH2/294/3, p. 9.

CAUSES

1. That notwithstanding of the Lords dispensation unto us in his Word and his Works both of Mercy and Justice; Yet we continue to provoke the eyes of his Glory by our impenitencie, security, unthankfulnesse, and a multitude of hainous sins which abound every where throughout the Land.

2. That many tokens of the Lords displeasure lie heavy and sad upon the Land, such as the want of the power of the Gospel, the continuing of the Pestilence in places where it hath been of a long time, and the spreading of it in these parts where the Sword did formerly waste and destroy.

3. That the Lord hath been graciously pleased, to keep the Pestilence from spreading over the face of all the Land, and to deliver the most eminent City of the Kingdome therefra, in a short time, after many thousands had fallen in her streets.

4. That fearfull Apostacy and Defection from the Truth and Solemne League and

Covenant that is in our Neighbour Land, which threatens most eminent danger both to Religion and Policie, and to all Government both Civill and Ecclesiastick.

5. The distressed condition of such as are straight for the Work of God in that Land, under the tyranny and oppression of those, who under a pretext of liberty seek to bring all in thraldome to themselves.

6. Lastly, We are earnestly to intreat the Lord that he would give repentance and remission of sins to his People, and wisdome and courage to those that are intrusted with publike affaires; And that he would so dispose of all these confusions and difficulties, that the Excellencie of his Power may appear in the weaknes of his People, when all opposition shall evanish, and the Head-Stone of his Work brought forth unto his praise and their consolation.

We are to pray that the Lord would be pleased to save our King from farther snares, and to bow his heart unto the obedience of his Will in all those things that concern Religion and Righteousnesse.

1647–E3(P)   Thanksgiving prayers for the parliamentarian victory in Munster

Sunday 5 December 1647 (London, Westminster, their liberties and the late lines of communication); Sunday 19 December 1647 (elsewhere in England and Wales)

In the summer of 1647, the president of Munster, Lord Inchiquin (who had defected to parliament in 1644) consolidated his control of the province through a harsh military campaign, which culminated in a clash with the catholic confederate army, under Viscount Taaffe, at Knocknanuss, near Cork, on 13 November. Though Inchiquin was outnumbered, he managed to rout the confederates. This victory put the whole of southern Ireland in parliamentarian hands. The occasion seems to have been ordered solely by the Commons; there are no references in the journals of either house to consultation with the Lords. The lord mayor and MPs were responsible for disseminating the orders. The Commons also ordered that a collection be made on 5 December for the relief of protestant refugees from Ireland. This is the first occasion for which there is evidence of how many orders were produced and distributed: ten quires for the City of London and more than 9,500 copies for the rest of England and Wales. Counties such as Lincolnshire (630), Norfolk (625) and Yorkshire (563) received large quantities, whereas Rutland (47), Northumberland (40) and most Welsh counties received very few.

Order: parliamentary order, 29 Nov. 1647, Wing E2669E* [also in *CJ*, V, 371].
Additional sources: *CJ*, V, 371; Note of the particulars of the several printed orders delivered by Mr Husband to the several members of the House of Commons for a thanksgiving for the Lord Inchiquin's victory, 3 Dec. 1647, SP16/515(pt 2)/125, fos. 98r–99v; *A true relation of a great victory obtained by the forces under the command of the Lord Inchiquine in Munster in Ireland, against the rebels under the command of Lord Taaff, Novemb. 13, 1647* (1647; Wing I136).

ORDER

Parliamentary order: 29 November 1647

Ordered by the Commons assembled in Parliament, That on the next Lords day being the Fifth day of December, publique Thanks be given to Almighty God by the respective Ministers within the Cities of *London* and *Westminster*, and liberties and parts adjacent within the late Lines of communication, for his great Blessing upon the Parliament Forces in *Munster* in *Ireland*, under the Command of the Lord *Inchiquine*, against a force of the Rebels under the Command of the Lord *Taaff*, obtained the Thirteenth of this present November, 1647. And that on the next Lords day come fortnight the Nineteenth day of December, publique Thanks be likewise given in all the Churches and chappels of *England* and Dominion of *Wales*, by the respective Ministers thereof, for the same Blessing upon the said Forces: It is further Ordered, That upon the said respective Lords days of the Fifth and Nineteenth of December, there be a Collection in the said Churches and chappels, for Relief of the poor English Protestants driven out of *Ireland*; and that the Moneys that shall now be collected, be added to the sum formerly collected upon a late Ordinance of Parliament which directs a collection for relief of such poor English Protestants; and that the said Moneys now to be collected, be paid in the same maner to the same Treasurers appointed in that Ordinance, and be disposed by Order of the same Committee. It is further Ordered, That the Lord Major do give timely notice of this Order for a Thanksgiving on the next Lords day, to all the Ministers within the cities of *London* and *Westminster*, and late Lines of communication: And the respective Knights of the Shires, and Burgesses of the several cities and places, are required to send copies of this Order to the several counties, cities and places; and the Ministers in the several places are required to move and stir up the people to a chearful contribution in acknowledgement of their thankfulness for this great and seasonable Blessing.

1648–S1 Fast day during negotiations on the Engagement with Charles I

Sunday 21 February 1648 (Edinburgh?)

On 26 December 1647 at Carisbrooke Castle on the Isle of Wight, where he was confined, Charles I and the earls of Lanark, Lauderdale and Loudoun signed the Engagement. This treaty offered the king military assistance in pursuit of a peace settlement with the English parliament. The Engagement was subject to approval in Edinburgh, and there the committee of estates began negotiations with the commission of the general assembly about the religious dimensions of the treaty. Responding to a proposal from the commission, the committee agreed to participate in this fast. Because it was appointed at short notice, the fast may not have been observed much beyond Edinburgh. It may have been for members of the commission and committee only.

Order: act of the commission of the general assembly, 17 Feb. 1648, *RCGA*, I, 358–9.
Additional source: *RCGA*, I, 352–3, 356–7.

ORDER

Act of the commission of the general assembly: 17 February 1648

The answer from the Comittee of Estates being reported that their Lordships are heartily content to joyne in the fast, remitting the day to the Comission, Therfor the nixt Sabboth is appointed as the fittest day for it, and desire Messrs. Andrew Cant and David Dickson to intimat it to their Lordships.

1648–S2 Fast day during parliament's consideration of the Engagement with Charles I

Sunday 12 March 1648 (Edinburgh and surrounding area)

When parliament met on 2 March 1648, a majority of members seemed ready to approve the Engagement with the king (see 1648–S1). However, on 1 March, the commission of the general assembly had adopted a *Declaration* expressing its opposition to the Engagement, which it claimed served the interest of malignants, undermined the Solemn League and Covenant and threatened peace and uniformity between the kingdoms. Despite having had the *Declaration* printed, the commission reluctantly agreed to parliament's request not to distribute copies until after the observance of this fast, ordered by the commission at the request of parliament.

Order: act of the commission of the general assembly, 10 Mar. 1648, *RCGA*, I, 386–7.
Additional sources: *A declaration of the commissioners of the generall assembly* (Edinburgh, 1648; Wing C4217); *RPS*, 1648/3/30, 1648/3/31; *RCGA*, I, 387–90.

ORDER

Act of the commission of the general assembly: 10 March 1648

This day Arthur Erskin of Scotscraige having represented the Parliaments desire that ther might be a fast vpon the nixt Lords day for them selves in the Parliament house, which they wished also might be keiped in all the kirks of this town, and in the Cannogait, Leith, and St. Culberts, the Comission according heartily to their Lordships desire, Doe appoint that the nixt Lords day be keiped for a solemne fast and humiliation for the Lords blessing to the Parliament, and to pray for his directione and counsell to their Lordships in maters now in hand; and appoints intimation heirof to be sent to the ministers of this citie, and of Leith, Cannogait, and St. Culberts, and doe againe appoint their brethren, Messrs. Androw Cant and John Livistoun to preach in the Parliament house the nixt Lords day, and that Messrs. Robert Birnie and Alexander Livistoun preach that day in the Colledge Kirk.

1648–E1(P)   Thanksgiving prayers for the end of riots in London

Sunday 16 April 1648 (Lines of communication)

Opposition to the existence and costs of a standing army, as well as to the suppression of festivals, especially Christmas, erupted in the spring of 1648. Charles I's accession day (27 March) was celebrated in London and Norwich; royalist supporters in the capital made occupants of passing carriages drink to the king's health, and an effigy of his gaoler, Colonel Hammond, was dragged through the streets before it was hanged, drawn, quartered and burned. On 9 and 10 April, between 3,000 and 4,000 apprentices rioted in the city in favour of Charles. On 13 April, the lord mayor and common council of London petitioned the Lords to order thanksgiving for the capital's deliverance. The Lords agreed, as did the Commons on the same day; the Lords issued the order on the 14th. The printed order comprised the common council's account of the disorder, their request to parliament for the thanksgiving and for powers of oyer and terminer to try offenders, as well as parliament's assent to this account and their order for the thanksgiving. The council's account and request were to be read by ministers during their services.

Order: parliamentary order, 13 Apr. 1648, Wing L2852, 3* [also in *CJ*, V, 529; *LJ*, X, 195].
Additional sources: *CJ*, V, 528–9; *LJ*, X, 188, 192; *An act and declaration of the Common Council of the city of London, touching the late insurrection* (1648; Wing L2852); *A full narration of the late riotous tumult within the City of London* (1648; Wing F2349).

ORDER

Parliamentary order: 13 April 1648
Ordered by the Lords and Commons in Parliament assembled, That a publique Thanksgiving be made by the several Ministers within the late Lines of Communication, on the next Lords Day, for the great mercy of God, in delivering the City of *London* from the late horrid Outrage and Tumult; And that the Lord Major of the said City do give Notice thereof to the several Ministers within the said Lines of Communication.

1648–E2(P)   Thanksgiving days for the parliamentarian victory at the battle of St Fagans

Wednesday 17 May 1648 (the City and liberties of London, the late lines of communication and bills of mortality)

Popular disaffection towards parliament and sympathy for Charles, along with divisions in the governing elite in England, Scotland and Ireland about whether to allow Charles to return to the throne, ignited the second civil war. South Wales was one of the first battlegrounds, after Colonel John Poyer and Major-General Laugharne defected to the royalists and attempted to gain an early victory against parliament's forces led by Colonel Thomas Horton at St Fagan's, near Cardiff, on 8 May. Though Poyer's infantry vastly outnumbered Horton's, they were ultimately defeated through lack of cavalry, and royalist morale suddenly plummeted. On 11 May, the Commons proposed days of thanksgiving to be observed in and around London on 17 May, and in the rest of the country on 7 June. However, when the Lords agreed to the proposal the following day, they ordered observance only in London and the surrounding area. As usual, the order was distributed by the lord mayor; sermons were preached in the Commons by William Bridge and Stephen Marshall and at St Paul's by William Strong. How well the day was observed is unclear. An anonymous letter (perhaps to the earl of Lanark) reported that it was 'so much neglected as in most of the Churches of London 5 or 6 were a great Congregation'. The author, however, had strong royalist sympathies, remarking that 'if they can appease gods wrath with a few hipocriticall prayers and 3 sermons, they will endeauor it'.

Orders: parliamentary order, 12 May, 1648, Wing E2244, Cambridge University Library, Broadsides.B.64.45 [also in *LJ*, X, 254].
Additional sources: *CJ*, V, 556–7; *LJ*, X, 251, 253–4; *A fuller relation of a great victory obtained against the Welsh forces by Col: Tho: Horton* (1648; Wing F2490); *FSP*, XXX, 8–9; letter to Q.V.E.R, 23 May 1648, NRS, GD406/1/2466.
Printed sermons: Bridge, House of Commons (Wing B4451; *FSP*, XXX, 270–99); Marshall, House of Commons (Wing M753; *FSP*, XXX, 229–68); Strong, St Paul's, London (Wing S6011).

ORDER

Parliamentary order: 12 May 1648

Resolved by the LORDS and COMMONS in Parliament Assembled, that *Wednesday* next be appointed for a day of publique Thanksgiving to Almighty God for his great mercy and blessing, in giving so great and seasonable a Victory to the Parliament Forces under the Command of Colonell *HORTON*, over all the Forces of the Enemy in South-Wales, on Monday the eight of this instant *May*, 1648. to be observed within the City of *London* and Liberties thereof, late Lines of Communication, and weekly Bils of Mortality.

And that the Lord Mayor be desired to give timely notice hereof to all the Ministers within the places aforesaid.

1648–S3   Fast day during divisions over the Engagement with Charles I

Sunday 28 May 1648 (Scotland)

In its letter to presbyteries of 28 April 1648, the commission of the general assembly expressed its frustration at the Scottish parliament's approval of the Engagement and the attempts of the promoters of that agreement to create a pretext to invade England on Charles I's behalf. The commission, which had repeatedly voiced reservations about the Engagement (see 1648–S2), now believed that parliament had usurped the church's right to make judgments about the religious relations between Scotland and England. On the same day that it appointed this fast, the commission sent a 'Humble representation' to parliament dissenting from the planned invasion.

Order: act of the commission of the general assembly, 28 Apr. 1648, *RCGA*, I, 485.
Letter: postscript to the commission of the general assembly's letter to presbyteries, 28 Apr. 1648, *RCGA*, I, 488.

Additional sources: *RCGA*, I, 485–512; presbytery of Paisley minutes, NRS, CH2/294/3, p. 20; *Strathbogie presbytery*, p. 88.

ORDER

Act of the commission of the general assembly: 28 April 1648
The Comission thinks fitt that there be a fast through all the kirks of this Kingdome vpon the last Sabboth of May nixt.

LETTER

Postscript to the commission of the general assembly's letter to presbyteries: 28 April 1648
It is evident from the premises how great and many difficulties the Kirk of God in this land is brought vnder by reasone of the sinnes and provocationes of his people, and how deip revolting from the Cause of God many are come to, and what cause we have to fear the overturning of all that God hes done for ws: Therfor we have resolved that ther should be a fast keiped in all the congregations of this land the last Sabboth of Maij, for intreating the Lord for help and mercie in this day of our great need, which we desire yow to keip in all your severall congregationes …

1648–E3(P)   Thanksgiving prayers for the parliamentarian victory at Maidstone

Sunday 4 June 1648 (London, Westminster and the late lines of communication)

A royalist rebellion broke out in Kent when the county committee attempted to suppress a petition calling for Charles's return and the disbanding of the New Model Army. The royalists took Canterbury, Rochester, Sittingbourne, Faversham, Sandwich, Dartford and Deptford; some of parliament's ships went over to the royalist cause; the forts of Deal, Sandown and Walmer surrendered and Dover Castle was besieged. Fairfax, who was preparing to go north, rallied the New Model Army and on 1 June attacked Maidstone, securing it after fierce fighting. Around 1,000 royalists were captured and 300 killed; one of the leaders, the earl of Norwich, fled. Two days later, the Commons ordered a thanksgiving to be held on 4 June in London, Westminster and the lines of communication. Though the Lords received several accounts of Fairfax's success, they appear to have taken no *rôle* in ordering this thanksgiving. The orders, as usual, were distributed by the lord mayor.

Order: parliamentary order, 3 June 1648, *CJ*, V, 583.
Additional source: *A letter sent to the honorable William Lenthal Esq; speaker of the honorable House of Commons, of the fight between his excellency's the Lord Fairfax forces at Maidstone, and the Kentish forces, June 1. 1648* (1648; Wing R2324).

ORDER

Parliamentary order: 3 June 1648

Ordered, That, on the next Lord's Day, the Fourth of this instant *June*, Thanks be given unto Almighty God, by the several Ministers, in the Churches and Chapels within the Cities of *London* and *Westminster*, and late Lines of Communication, for his great Blessing upon the Parliament Forces, under the Command of his Excellency the Lord *Fairefax*, against the *Kentish* Forces, at the Fight near and at *Maidstone*, and in the Taking in of *Maidstone*: And the Lord Mayor is desired to give timely Notice hereof to the several and respective Ministers within the several Places aforesaid. Colonel *Venne* is desired to acquaint the Lord Mayor herewith.

1648–E4(P)   **Thanksgiving prayers for parliamentarian suppression of a rebellion in Kent**

Sunday 18 June 1648 (London and the late lines of communication)

Fairfax continued to quash the rebellion in Kent. Dover Castle surrendered on 6 June and Canterbury on 8 June. A second thanksgiving was therefore ordered by the Commons on 13 June. Again, the Lords appears not to have been involved in ordering the occasion, even though it received news of Fairfax's actions and the articles of surrender. Insurrections continued elsewhere, notably in Essex, Suffolk and the city of Norwich. The order was distributed by the lord mayor of London and the appropriate county committees.

Order: parliamentary order, 13 June 1648, *CJ*, V, 597.
Additional sources: *The lord general's letter to to [sic] the honorable William Lenthal Esq; speaker of the honorable House of Commons, wherein is fully related, the particulars of the fight at Maidstone* (1648; Wing F198); *A narrative and declaration of the dangerous design against the parliament & kingdom, carried on in the county of Kent and elswhere* (1648; Wing N166).

ORDER

Parliamentary order: 13 June 1648

Ordered, That, on the next Lord's Day, Thanks be given unto Almighty God, for His great Blessing upon the General, and his Forces, in reducing the County of *Kent*, and quieting the Insurrections and Distempers there: And the several Ministers in the Churches and Chapels within the City of *London*, and late Lines of Communication, are enjoined to take Notice of this great Deliverance, and declare it to their Congregations; and render Thanks unto Almighty God for the same: And the Lord Mayor of the City of *London* is desired to give timely Notice hereof to the Ministers within the City of *London*, and the Liberties; and the respective Committees to the several Ministers within the late Lines of Communication.

1648–S4   Fast days in protest against the Engagement and military campaign against the English parliament

Thursday 29 June and Sunday 2 July 1648 (Scotland)

Having decided to invade England under the terms of the Engagement, the Scottish parliament ordered military levies to take place in May 1648. Numerous civil and church courts petitioned against the policy, and the commission of the general assembly continued to advise parliament to reconsider the invasion. On 7 June, the commission moved for a fast, but although a paper containing causes was read in the meeting on 10 June, the commission did not then approve the causes, instead awaiting the outcome of a new address to parliament. Parliament failed to respond, and the commission sent the causes of the fast to presbyteries on 12 June. In the presbytery of Strathbogie, the fast seems to have been kept on 9 July, apparently because the order arrived late.

Order: act of the commission of the general assembly, 7 June 1648, *RCGA*, I, 559.
Causes: *RCGA*, I, 567–8 [also in Wing S2018, 5–8].
Letter: commission of the general assembly to presbyteries, 12 June 1648, *RCGA*, I, 569.
Additional source: presbytery of Paisley minutes, NRS, CH2/294/3, p. 22; *Strathbogie presbytery*, p. 91.

ORDER

Act of the commission of the general assembly: 7 June 1648
The Comission findes a necessity at this tyme of great difficulties and dangers, That their be a Fast vpon the last Thursday of Junij and the first Sabboth of Julij, and that the reasons be drawen vp be Messrs. James Gutterie, James Nasmith, and George Lesly.

CAUSES

1. We are to mourne for all the sins and provocations mentioned in the Causes of our former Humiliations which doe continue and abound, notwithstanding of all our obligations to reform our wayes, and many former solemn professions of repentance, and of all the sharpe rods wherewith God hes corrected ws, and heavy judgments wherwith he now threatens ws.

   2. We are in a speciall way to be humbled for the countenance that hath been given, and complyance that hath been made, by too many with Malignants and persons disaffected to the work of Reformation, which in the just judgment of God hes at last put such power and strength in their hands as is terrible to the people of God and threatens his work with ruine.

   3. We are to bewaile the small proficiency vnder the preaching of the Gospell in many, the great contempt thereof in others, and the great obstinacy and hardnesse of heart in some, not onely vnto the dispysing and reproaching of the ministry, but vnto the rejecting of the most powerfull word of exhortation in the mouths of his servants.

   4. We are to be humbled for the grievous backsliding that is amongst ws, which hath prevailed vnto the vndertaking of an unlawfull Ingagement in war, notwithstanding of the many Petitions from Burghs and Shires, Presbyteries and Synods to the contrary; Which vndertaking, beside many sad effects amongst ourselves, is

like to rend in sunder the Vnion betuixt the Kingdomes, and not only obstruct the progress of the work of Vniformity, but overturn the foundation already laid.

5. We are to lament before the Lord for the oppression of his people in many places of this Kingdom, vnto the spoiling of their goods, offering violence vnto their persons, and forcing of their consciences, and by causing them either to indure great affliction, or to sin against God by being accessory to a sinfull course.

6. We are deeply to be humbled that the Parliament being now risen, they have been so far from satisfying any of the just and necessary Desires of the Kirk, or hearkening to the Petitions presented vnto them, that they have enjoyned obedience to all their orders vpon the grounds of their Declaration published in April.

7. We are to entreate the Lord in the behalf our King that he may be convinced and repent of the evill of his former wayes, and be inclined vnto the love and appro-bation of the work of God; and in the behalf of these who have the power of the Kingdom in their hands that they may desist from every sinfull course and satisfie the just and necessary Desires of the Kirk, and the consciences of the well-affected in the land, by securing of Religion and preserving Vnion between the Kingdoms and Monarchicall Government in the person of the King and of his posterity.

8. As we are to beg of God that all the purposes, both of Sectaries and of the Popish, Prelaticall, and Malignant Party in all the three Kingdoms, against the truth and work of God may be disappointed and their power crushed, so also that the Lord would strengthen his people in all these dominions to adhere without shrinking or fainting vnto the Cause of God, and to bear a faithfull testimony thereto in the day of Tentation.

Lastly, we are to pray for a blessing vpon the ensuing Generall Assembly that they may meet in peace and love, and being furnished with the spirit of vnity, faithfullnesse, wisdom, and zeale, they may so carry them selves in every thing, as that the hopes and designes of disaffected men may be disappoynted, truth may be preserved, holiness promoved amongst our selves, and the work of Vniformity advanced amongst our neighbours.

LETTER

Commission of the general assembly to presbyteries: 12 June 1648
… We have sent yow herewith the causes of a Solemne Fast and Humiliation to be keept on the last Thursday of this instant Junij and the first Sabboth of Julij …

1648–E5(P)   Thanksgiving prayers for parliamentarian victories at Cartington and Willoughby Field

Sunday 9 July 1648 (London and the late lines of communication)

On 5 July, the Commons proposed thanksgivings for Robert Lilburne's victory over the royalist forces under Sir Richard Tempest at Cartington, Northumberland, four days earlier. On 8 July, they ordered that Colonel Rossiter's victory against the royalists at Willoughby Field, near Nottingham, should also be celebrated. It appears that this addition was made after their original proposal was sent to the Lords (also on

8 July), to which the Lords assented. This may explain why the Commons proposed a second thanksgiving to mark Rossiter's victory a few days later (see 1648–E6(P)).

Order: parliamentary order, 8 July 1648 (John Wright; 1 p., 1648; Wing E1733F)*.
Additional sources: *CJ*, V, 625, 628–9; *LJ*, X, 369–70.

ORDER

Parliamentary order: 8 July 1648
Ordered by the Lords and Commons assembled in Parliament, That on the next Lords day publique thanks be given to Almighty God, in all Churches within the City of *London,* and late Lines of Communication, for his great mercy in giving the Parliaments Forces a great Victory in the North. And the Lord Maior is desired to give notice hereof, to the Ministers in the severall Parishes within the City.

1648–E6(P)   Thanksgiving day for recent parliamentarian victories

Wednesday 19 July 1648 (parishes within the late lines of communication and bills of mortality)

On 12 July, the Commons proposed a thanksgiving to mark Rossiter's victory at Willoughby Field, which suggests that its attempt to incorporate this into the thanksgiving ordered on 8 July had failed because the Lords had already given its assent to the original request to mark the victory at Cartington (see 1648-E5(P)). The Lords assented to the request and ordered the thanksgiving on 13 July. An account of Rossiter's actions, *An impartiall and true relation*, was printed by command of the Commons, although the order for the thanksgiving did not specify that it had to be read out during the service, as had been the case on earlier occasions. John Bond and Obadiah Sedgwick were appointed to preach before the Commons, but only Bond took up the house's subsequent invitation to print his sermon.

Order: order of the House of Lords, 13 July 1648, *LJ*, X, 381.
Additional sources: *CJ*, V, 633, 635; *An impartiall and true relations of the great victory obtained through the blessing of God* (1648; Wing I80, I80A); *FSP*, XXXI, 5.
Printed sermon: Bond, House of Commons (Wing B3570; *FSP*, XXXI, 55–106).

ORDER

Order of the House of Lords: 13 July 1648
ORDERED, by the Lords and Commons assembled in Parliament, That *Wednesday* next be set apart for a Day of Public Thanksgiving unto ALMIGHTY GOD, for His great Blessings and Mercies bestowed upon the Parliament's Forces, in giving them lately many great and signal Victories; to be observed in all the Churches and Chapels within the late Lines of Communication, and Parishes within the Bills of Mortality: And the Lord Mayor of the City of *London* is desired to take Care, that timely Notice may be given of this Order to the several Ministers.

1648–E7(P)   Thanksgiving day for further parliamentarian victories

Wednesday 9 August 1648 (England and Wales)

Before the previous thanksgiving had taken place, the Commons proposed another, probably to mark Lord Monson's successful defence of Reigate Castle (6 July), the surrender of Pembroke Castle (11 July) and the taking of Walmer Castle (12 July). The process for ordering appears different from previous occasions. On 17 July, a 'Declaration' was introduced to the Commons, read twice and ordered to be read a third time the following day. Although it is unclear whether this third reading took place, the order was passed on 18 July and commanded to be printed for distribution on 27 July. This change in the ordering process might be regarded as an attempt by the Commons to avoid the problems of 1648–E5(P), for which the Lords appear to have prevented it from adding Rossiter's victory to the order. However, the Commons had regularly ordered thanksgivings without the Lords' explicit assent during the first civil war; the Lords, now reduced to a rump, did not sit on 18 July and do not appear to have received news of that month's successes.

Order: parliamentary order, 18 July 1648, *CJ*, V, 639.
Additional source: *CJ*, V, 638, 649.

ORDER

Parliamentary order: 18 July 1648
Ordered, That, To-morrow Three Weeks, 9° *Augusti*, be appointed for a Publick Thanksgiving to Almighty God, in the several Parish Churches in the several Counties within the Kingdom of *England*, and Dominion of *Wales*, for the several great Victories lately given to the Parliament Forces.

1648–E8(P)   Day of humiliation for heavy rain and threatened harvest

Thursday 10 August 1648 (London, Westminster and the late lines of communication and bills of mortality)

The summer of 1648 was unusually cold and wet, endangering the harvest; it was described as worse than many recent winters. On 5 August, the Commons proposed a 'day of solemn humiliation', to include a public fast on 10 August. Though the Lords agreed to this proposal, the order itself may have issued from the Commons, as there is no record of it in the Lords' journal.

Order: parliamentary order, 5 Aug. 1648, *CJ*, V, 662.
Additional source: *LJ*, X, 420–1.

ORDER

Parliamentary order: 5 August 1648

Whereas it hath pleased Almighty God, among other his heavy Judgments upon this Nation, to manifest his sore Displeasure against the Kingdom, by Abundance of Rain, and such unseasonable Weather, the like whereof hath scarce been known at this Season of the Year; by reason whereof the Corn, and other Fruits of the Earth are in Danger to be utterly spoiled, or rendered so unwholsome, as may produce a general Dearth and Mortality: In Consideration whereof, the Lords and Commons have thought fit to set apart a Day for Solemn Humiliation, and Seeking of the Lord, for averting this and other his most heavy Judgments; and do thereupon *Order*, That *Thursday* next, being the Tenth of *August*, be appointed for this Purpose; and be observed within the Cities of *London, Westminster*, and late Lines of Communication, and Bills of Mortality: And the Lord Mayor of the City of *London* is desired to give present Notice to all the Ministers accordingly.

1648–E9(P) **Thanksgiving day for parliamentarian victories at the battle of Preston and at Colchester**

Thursday 7 September 1648 (England and Wales)

On 23 August, the House of Commons proposed a thanksgiving for recent successes, later identified as including Winwick Pass (19 August), Deale Castle (14 August) and the defeat of the royalist force between Radnor and Montgomeryshire (17 August). It argued that it was particularly important to offer thanks because these victories proved God's favour at a time when parliament faced a host of rebellions in Essex, Kent, Suffolk, Wales and elsewhere. By the time that the proposal was considered by the House of Lords, celebrations focused on fuller news of the battle of Preston. Over three days from 17 to 19 August the parliamentarian army under Cromwell defeated the combined forces of the invading Scots of the Engagement and various English royalists. The parliamentary order of 23 August accordingly specified only the battle of Preston, which was to be marked by a day of thanksgiving. On 26 August, the House of Commons ordered a collection to be made on behalf of those in Lancashire who had suffered from war, plundering by the Scots and plague; it also ordered that 10,000 copies of the order and two accounts of the recent victories, *A particular of the several victories* and *A full relation of the great victory*, were to be printed and circulated to parishes. Though there is earlier evidence of how many orders were ordered to be printed (see 1648–E3(P)), this is the earliest evidence of how many copies of accounts of victories were printed. Ten thousand copies were sufficient for each parish to have one copy, as there were a little over 9,000 parishes in England and Wales. On 31 August, the Commons ordered that the surrender to Fairfax of Colchester, one of the leading centres of royalist insurrection, should also be celebrated on 7 September. Stephen Marshall and Obadiah Sedgwick were appointed to preach before the Lords in Westminster Abbey, though on 4 September the Lords ordered that the venue of its thanksgiving was to be changed to St Martin's-in-the-Fields. Only Sedgwick was thanked by the house for his sermon (and invited to have it printed, which he declined); it is possible that Marshall was excused but, if so, there is no record of his replacement. The Commons initially appointed Joseph Caryl and Richard Heyricke to preach before them but, at some point, Heyricke was replaced by John Bond. Neither Caryl or Bond chose to have their sermons printed, though they were both invited to do so. John Clopton, a parliamentarian gentleman from Little Wratton in Essex, observed the thanksgiving as prescribed on 7 September, listening to a sermon by a Mr Fayreclot on Psalm 115:1. However, he also recorded in his diary for 29 September that 'Mr Fayrecloth preacht at Romford a thanksgiving sermon for the comittee men's deliverance out of Colchester: the thanksgiving was the day before.' This is the only reference to a second thanksgiving for the delivery of Colchester, and its status as an official or unofficial and local event is unclear.

Orders: parliamentary order, 23 Aug. 1648, Wing E2153, 8* [also Wing E1734F; Wing F2362, 8; also in *LJ*, X, 452]; order of the House of Commons, 31 Aug. 1648, *CJ*, V, 695.
Additional sources: *CJ*, V, 680–1, 683, 685–6; *LJ*, X, 452, 485, 493; *A particular of the several victories and the occasions of the solemn day of thanksgiving* (1648; Wing E2153); *A full relation of the great victory obtained by parliaments forces* (1648; Wing F2362); *FSP*, XXXI, 7–8; Clopton diary, 7, 29 Sept. 1648.

ORDERS

Parliamentary order: 23 August 1648
Ordered by the Lords and Commons in Parliament assembled, That Thursday come fortnight, the seventh of *September* next, be appointed a Day of Solemn Thanksgiving through the whole Kingdom unto Almighty God, for his wonderful great mercy and success bestowed upon the Parliament Forces, under the Command of Lieut. General *Cromwel*, against the whole Scots Army, under the Conduct and Command of Duke *Hamilton*, on the Seventeenth, Eighteenth and Nineteenth of this present *August* in *Lancashire*.

Order of the House of Commons: 31 August 1648
Ordered, That this great Mercy of God in reducing the Town and Garison of *Colchester* into the Hands and to the Obedience of Parliament, be in an especial manner remembered on the next solemn Day of Thanksgiving; and hearty Thanks given unto Almighty God for his great Mercy herein: And that this be forthwith printed.

1648–S5   Fast day for general assembly's protest against invasion of England

Sunday 10 September 1648 (Scotland)

By the time the general assembly met on 12 July, the army of the Engagement had crossed into England. The assembly refused to accept the committee of estates' justifications of the invasion, and issued a declaration against the 'unlawfull engagement in war' (*Principall acts*, 11–26). The assembly appointed this fast; the act and causes were unprinted and have not been traced.

Order: act of the general assembly, 11 Aug. 1648, described in Wing C4242*, 67.
Additional sources: *The principall acts of the generall assembly* (Edinburgh, 1648; Wing C4242), pp.

11–26; presbytery of Paisley minutes, NRS, CH2/294/3, p. 24; *Life of Blair*, p. 205; *Strathbogie pres-bytery*, p. 92.

DESCRIPTION OF ORDER

Act of the general assembly: 11 August 1648
Indiction of a Fast on the second Sabbath of *September*, with the causes thereof.

1648–E10(P) Day of humiliation during negotiations between parliament and Charles I at Newport

Tuesday 12 September 1648 (late lines of communication and bills of mortality)

Despite its recent successes, parliament was acutely conscious of how divided it was in itself, how unpopular its regime was and how strong (relatively) support was for the king. Consequently, on 18 September they opened peace negotiations with Charles, imprisoned at Newport on the Isle of Wight. On 1 September, the House of Commons proposed a day of public humiliation for the 12th, to seek God's blessing on the negotiations. This was agreed by the Lords the following day and ordered. Gasper Hickes and Edmund Calamy were appointed to preach before the Commons; Thomas Horton replaced Hickes, who was ill and, on 11 September, Marshall was also appointed to preach. None of the preachers were formally thanked by the Commons nor invited to print their sermons. Thomas Valentine and Stanley Gower were initially appointed to preach before the Lords at Westminster Abbey but were replaced by William Gouge and Cornelius Burgess respectively on 5 and 6 September. On 11 September, the Lords ordered that the house observe the thanksgiving at St Martin's-in-the-Fields, as it had for the previous thanksgiving (see 1648–E9(P)). Gouge printed his sermon, though it is not clear whether this was at the Lords' invitation. The king responded by observing his own day of fasting and humiliation on 15 September. It is unlikely that this fast day was observed beyond his immediate circle at Newport, but the occasion was used for royalist propaganda. *A forme of prayer used at Newport* was published, reprinting the text of the form published during the earlier negotiations at Uxbridge, 1645–E1(R). This was again important in demonstrating the king's continued loyalty to worship based on the now proscribed BCP; printing (and using) the form was for royalists an act of defiance. The bookseller and pamphlet collector, George Thomason, wrote 'Sept ye 22' on his copy of the form, which perhaps gives the date of publication. A prayer asking for a blessing on the new negotiations, said to have been composed at the king's direction, was also published as part of a royalist broadsheet, *The commencement of the treaty*.

Order: parliamentary order, 2 Sept. 1648, Wing E1735B (BL, Cup.21.g.42/26) [also ESTC 006127980; also in *LJ*, X, 485].
Additional sources: *CJ*, V, 697, VI, 1–2, 6, 17; *LJ*, X, 482–3, 485, 490, 492, 498; *FSP*, XXXI, 8–9; *A forme of prayer used at Newport in the Isle of Wight upon the 15 of September, 1648. Being the day of fasting and humiliation for the obtaining a blessing upon the personall treatie betweene the king and his two houses of parliament* (1648; Wing C4165; annotated on BL, Thomason E.1146(2)); *The commencement of the treaty between the king's majesty, and the commissioners of parliament at Newport* (1648; Wing C5546).

Printed sermons: d'Espagne, Durham House, London (Wing E3254); Gouge, House of Lords (Wing G1394; *FSP*, XXXI, 187–230).

ORDER

Parliamentary order: 2 September 1648

Ordered, by the Lords and Commons assembled in Parliament, That Tuesday-come-Seven-night, the twelfth of this instant September, be appointed and observed as a day of publique Humiliation, by the Members of both Houses, and in all the Churches and Chappels within the late Lines of Communication and weekly Bills of Mortalitie, to seeke God earnestly for a Blessing upon the Treaty.

1648–E11(P) Thanksgiving prayers for parliamentarian successes at Carrickfergus, Belfast and Coleraine

Sunday 1 October 1648 (London, Westminster, the late lines of communication and bills of mortality)

General Monck and Colonel Michael Jones were able to exploit divisions among the confederates in Ireland to consolidate parliament's hold of Leinster, Dublin and the Pale. Monck took Belfast, Carrickfergus and Coleraine in September. On 28 September, the Commons ordered thanksgivings to be held on 1 October in the London and Westminster areas. The lines of communication were described in the order as 'late', recognizing the end of the civil war. As for many previous occasions, the Lords do not appear to have been consulted. As usual, the order was distributed by the lord mayor. An account of Monck's victories sent to the MP, John Moor, was ordered to be printed by the Commons. It may have been designed to be read out during thanksgiving services, though there are no explicit instructions to this effect.

Order: parliamentary order, 28 Sept. 1648, *CJ*, VI, 37.
Additional source: *A letter concerning Colonel Monks surprizing the town and castle of Carrickfergus and Belfast, in Ireland and his taking General Major Monro prisoner. For the honorable, Col: Iohn Moor, a member of the House of Commons* (1648; Wing C4487).

ORDER

Parliamentary order: 28 September 1648

Ordered, That Thanks be given to Almighty God, on the next Lord's Day, by all the Ministers in all the Churches and Chapels within the Cities of *London* and *Westminster*, late Lines of Communication, and weekly Bills of Mortality, for the great Blessing of God upon the Conduct of the Parliament's Forces in the North of *Ireland*, under the Command of Colonel *George Moncke*, in the regaining into the Hands of the Parliament the strong Towns and Castles of *Carickfergus* and *Belfast*, in the North of *Ireland*: And the Lord Mayor of the City of *London* is desired to give timely Notice hereof to the several and respective Ministers.

1648–E12(P) Thanksgiving prayers for parliamentarian victories in Anglesey

Sunday 8 October (London, Westminster, the late lines of communication and bills of mortality)

In the summer and autumn of 1648, Colonel Mytton campaigned to secure North Wales for parliament. Having gained the surrender of Caernarfon in June, on 2 October he took Beaumaris after a short skirmish at Red Hill. Two days later, the Commons ordered thanksgivings for 8 October. With no references to the thanksgiving in the Lords' journal, it was likely that the lower house acted independently as usual. No account of Mytton's success was printed and no preachers appear to have been appointed to preach before parliament.

Order: parliamentary order, 4 Oct. 1648, *CJ*, VI, 43.

ORDER

Parliamentary order: 4 October 1648

Ordered, That Thanks be given to Almighty God, by all the Ministers in all the Churches and Chapels within the Cities of *London* and *Westminster*, late Lines of Communication, and Weekly Bills of Mortality, on the next Lord's Day, for his great Mercy in blessing the Parliament Forces, under the Command of Colonel *Mitton*, with Success against the Enemy in the Isle of *Anglesey*, and in reducing that Island into the Hands, and to the Obedience, of the Parliament: And the Lord Mayor of the City of *London* is desired to give timely Notice hereof to the Ministers of the several and respective Places aforesaid.

1648–S6 Fast days on the renewal of the Solemn League and Covenant

Thursday 14 December and Sunday 17 December 1648 (Scotland)

After the defeat of the army of the Engagement at the battle of Preston (17–19 August 1648), a radical party of anti-engagers seized power in Scotland. Most clergy had seen the Engagement as an unlawful breach of the Solemn League and Covenant (see 1648–S5), and in October the commission of the general assembly called for the covenant to be sworn afresh on a national basis, excluding those who had been involved in the Engagement. This ceremony was to take place on the second of two fast days, which were intended to stimulate national repentance. The commission produced a *Solemn acknowledgment of publick sins and breaches of the covenant*, which was to be read publicly to prepare congregations for the covenant renewal. On 14 October, the committee of estates, from which engagers had been removed, passed an act approving the commission's order for fasting and covenant renewal.

Order: act of the commission of the general assembly, 6 Oct. 1648, Wing C4259E*, 14–16 [also in *RCGA*, II, 78–9].
Additional sources: *RCGA*, II, 78–96, 136–9; *A solemn acknowledgment of publick sins and breaches of the covenant* (Edinburgh, 1648; Wing C4259E); *An information of the present condition of affairs*

(Edinburgh, 1648; Wing I170); *The explanation of a former act of the sixth of October* (Edinburgh, 1648; Wing C4224B); *Strathbogie presbytery*, p. 95; *Life of Blair*, p. 212.

ORDER

Act of the commission of the general assembly: 6 October 1648

The Commission of the General Assembly considering that a great part of this Land have involved themselves in many and grosse breaches of the solemn League and Covenant; And that the hands of many are grown slack in following and pursuing the duties contained therein, And that many who not being come to sufficient age, when it was first sworn and subscribed, have not hithertills been received into the same, Do upon these and other grave and important considerations Appoint and Ordain the Solemn League and Covenant to be renewed throughout all the Congregations of this Kingdom; And because it is a duty of great weight and consequence, Ministers after the sight hereof would be carefull to take pains in their Doctrine and otherwise, that their people may be made sensible of these things wherein they have broken the Covenant, and be prepared for the renewing thereof with sutable affections and dispositions: And that these things may be the better performed, we have thought it necessary to condescend upon a solemn acknowledgement of publick sinnes and breaches of the Covenant; and a solemn Engagement to all the duties contained therein, Namely, those which doe in a more speciall way relate unto the dangers of these times: And this solemn Acknowledgement and Engagement sent herewith shall bee made use of, And the League and Covenant shall be renewed in such manner as followes. First, There shall be intimation of a solemn publick humiliation and Fast the second Sabbath of *December* To bee kept upon the next Thursday and Lords Day thereafter, At which intimation the League and Covenant, and the publick acknowledgement of sinnes and Engagement unto duties are to be publickly read by the Minister in the audience of all the people, And they are to be exhorted to get copies thereof that they may be made acquainted therewith; And the Humiliation and Fast is to be keeped the next Thursday thereafter in reference to the breaches of the Covenant contained in the solemn publick Acknowledgement as the causes thereof, And the next Lords Day thereafter which is also to bee spent in publick Humiliation and Fasting, immediately after the Sermon, which is to be applied to the businesse of that day, The publick acknowledgment and Engagement is again to be publickly read, And thereafter prayer is to be made containing the confession of the breaches mentioned therein and begging mercy for these sinnes, and strength of God for renewing the Covenant in sincerity and Truth; After which Prayer the solemn League and Covenant is to bee read by the Minister, And then to be sworn by him and all the people, who are to ingage themselves for performance of all the duties contained therein, Namely these which are mentioned in the publick acknowledgement & Engagement and are opposit unto the sinnes therein confessed: And the action is to be closed with Prayer to God that his people may be enabled in the power of his strength to doe their duty according to their Oath now renewed in so solemn a way. It is also hereby provided, that all those who renew the League and Covenant shall again subscribe the same, And that none be admitted to the renewing or subscribing thereof who are excluded by the other act and direction sent herewith.

1649–S1   Fast day after the execution of Charles I and to mark the accession of Charles II

Thursday 22 February 1649 (Scotland)

In January 1649, the Scottish parliament sat, annulling the legislation that facilitated the Engagement and, with the act of classes of 23 January, purging from office the engagers. On 3 February, the news of Charles I's execution on 30 January arrived in Edinburgh. Parliament adjourned itself, before assembling to proclaim Charles II on 5 February. As parliament's proclamation made clear, the new king was required to guarantee that he would accept Scottish presbyterianism and the covenants 'before he be admitted to the exercise of his royall dignitie' (*RPS*, 1649/1/71). On 2 February, parliament had proposed a fast for its own members; the news of the regicide prompted it to ask the commission to appoint a national fast.

Order: act of the commission of the general assembly, 6 Feb. 1649, *RCGA*, II, 194.
Letter: commission of the general assembly to presbyteries, 6 Feb. 1649, *RCGA*, II, 194–5.
Additional sources: *RCGA*, II, 193–4; *RPS*, 1649/1/64, 1649/1/71; presbytery of Paisley minutes, NRS, CH2/294/3, p. 30.

ORDER

Act of the commission of the general assembly: 6 February 1649
The Commission, having considered the desires of the Parliament, Doe appoint the 22 day of this moneth to be set apart for fasting and humiliation, and that the letter following be sent to Presbyteries for that effect, and appoints the Clerk to cause print the samyne for the more speedy dispatch.

LETTER

Commission of the general assembly to presbyteries: 6 February 1649
… we have thought fit that a solemn publick humiliation be kept on Thursday the 22 of this instant, as for all the sines and provocatiouns of the land, so to pray the Lord in a speciall maner for these things following: 1. That He would deliver the King from the snares of evill counsell, in which he is now involved, and teach him in his youth in the knowledge of His way, that he may fear His name, and imploy his power for establishing and advancing the Kingdom of Jesus Christ, and the Worke of Reformatioun. 2. That the Lord would be pleased to blesse those addresses, that are now to be made to his Majestie for the securitie of Religion, the vnion betuixt the Kingdoms, and the peace and safety of this Kingdome. 3. That He would strengthen and deliver our afflicted brethren in England, who suffer by the violence and strange practises of the Sectaries. 4. That He would in His mercy prevent all those calamities and confusions, that the present great revolution of affaires doth threaten these Kingdoms with. So hoping that yow will be carefull to stirre vp yourselves and others to wrastle with God in such an exigent, and to intimate the Fast timeouslie, and to keepe the same in your severall Congregatiouns the foirsaid day

1649–E1 Fast day for the establishment of the Commonwealth government

Thursday 19 April 1649 (England and Wales)

This fast day was probably ordered to set the godly tone for the newly established Commonwealth after the execution of Charles I (30 January) and the abolition of both the house of lords and the monarchy (6–7 February). Its origins are obscure: it was first ordered before 28 February but there are no records in the Commons' journal to identify when. It was postponed twice for unknown reasons (on 28 February until 24 March, and on 8 March until 5 April), and the 'Grounds' or justification for the fast day was not drawn up until after 8 March. These contrasted 'our unthankfulness and unfruitfulness' with the 'wonderful goodness and assistance of God', who had helped 'The Commons of England assembled in Parliament' to restore to the nation 'their just Liberties and laid Foundations for the well Government thereof'. It was eventually observed on 19 April across England and Wales, the first time that parliament had ordered one nationwide fast since the end of the first civil war (1647–E1(P)). John Owen, John Warren and Joseph Caryl were appointed to preach before parliament, though Caryl chose not to have his sermon printed subsequently. John Clopton recorded in his diary that the fast 'was not kept' in and around his parish. This occasion is significant because it brought an important change in the ordering process. It was the first time that special worship had been ordered by an act of parliament and read three times before being put to the vote (17 March); a 'Declaration' for the thanksgiving had been read twice, or possibly three times in July 1648, but it was still issued as a parliamentary order and not an act of parliament (1648-E7(P)). Thus, the occasion seems to have produced a development of parliament's use of ordinances (technically acts of parliament which did not have the royal assent) which had begun with 1644–E4(P). The printed act was much longer than previous orders and was comparable to a royal proclamation, containing an extended justification for the fast day.

Order: *An act of the Commons of England assembled in parliament, for the keeping of a day of humiliation upon Thursday the 19 day of April, 1649*, 17 Mar. 1649, Wing E2505*.
Additional sources: *CJ*, VI, 152, 158, 166; *FSP*, XXXII, 8–9 (with incorrect Wing number for Owen's sermon); Clopton diary, 19 Apr. 1649.
Printed sermons: Owen, House of Commons (Wing O789; *FSP*, XXXII, 313–60); Warren, House of Commons (Wing W976; *FSP*, XXXII, 282–311).

ORDER

Act of parliament: 17 March 1649

Whereas this Nation hath long laboured under many Miseries and Judgements, as a just fruit of our multiplyed transgressions, and amongst other sins, more especially for our unthankfulness and unfruitfulness under unparalleld mercies and deliverances, and for our unbelief, to the dishonor of our mighty, wise, and good God, who hath through a Wilderness of Temptations brought us even to the entrance of a *Canaan*, and to the hope of a blessed Reformation; as also for our uncharitablenes and want of a good affection to the publique, and of love one to another, the very fountain of our late Civil Wars and Desolations: And whereas we have learn'd from the word of God, and the example of his people in all ages, and our own experience, That the humbling of our souls for sin, and the seeking the favor of God in the mediation of our Lord and Savior Jesus Christ by prayer and fasting, hath been, through his grace and acceptance, effectual both for the preventing & removal of the greatest Judgements, and also for procuring the choycest Mercies: The Commons of *England* assembled in Parliament, having through the wonderful goodness and assistance of God, restored this Nation (as far as in them lieth, and the present interruptions will yet admit) to their just Liberties, and laid Foundations for the well Government thereof in the way of a Commonwealth, Do Enact and Ordain, and be it Enacted and Ordained by this present Parliament, and by Authority thereof, That *Thursday* the *19* day of *April, 1649.* shall be observed and kept in all Parishes and other places in *England* and *Wales*, a solemn day of Fasting, Prayer, and Humiliation, for the aforementioned sins, and all other the abominations whereof this Nation is guilty; and for the imploring of the Lord our God, (who is Holiness, Love, and Wisdom, and the Father of Spirits) to give unto this people the Spirit of Reformation, Faith, Understanding, and Union, That so our sins, the cause of our sufferings, may be forgiven, and this Commonwealth may be setled in a lasting Peace and Happiness: And be it further Enacted and Ordained, That all Ministers, and other people within *England* and *Wales*, do with all possible care & pious diligence, solemnly observe the same accordingly, under the penalties contained in any Order or Ordinance of Parliament heretofore made, concerning the due observation of the Lords-day, or days of publique Humiliation.

1649–E2 Fast days marking the end of monthly fasts, for ending divisions and in support of the Commonwealth campaign in Ireland

Thursday 3 May 1649 (London, Westminster, the late lines of communication and bills of mortality); Thursday 17 May 1649 (elsewhere in England, Wales and Berwick-upon-Tweed)

On 17 April, troops were chosen by lots to go to Ireland under the overall command of Oliver Cromwell to prevent Charles II using the country as a base for an invasion of England. On 20 April, the Commons ordered a day of public and solemn humiliation in support of Cromwell's troops and to repeat the admonitions against sinfulness made on the previous fast day (1649–E1). On 23 April, the order was read twice before being passed after the question. The act also repealed Charles's proclamation for a monthly fast in response to the Irish rebellion (1641–E) and it allowed secular duties, including the sitting of law courts, to be conducted on these days once again. By 1649, parliament argued that these monthly fasts had become neglected, 'prophaned' or mere formalities. As on the previous occasion, the printed act of parliament looked like a royal proclamation and contained an extensive justification for the fast, drawn up by Sir James Harrington and Miles Corbett. However, in a return to older practices, the fast was held on different days in and around London and elsewhere in England and Wales. Thomas Goodwin, Isaac Knight and Ralph Venning were all appointed to preach but none subsequently printed their sermons.

Order: *An act for setting apart a day of solemn fasting and humiliation, and repealing the former*

monethly-fast, 23 Apr. 1649, Wing E1075* [also in *Acts and ordinances of the interregnum*, ed. Firth and Rait, II, 79–81].
Additional sources: *CJ*, VI, 190, 193; *FSP*, XXXIII, 3.

ORDER

Act of parliament: 23 April 1649

Whereas by a Proclamation the eighth of *January*, in the Seventeenth year of the Reign of the late King, a general Publique and Solemn Fast was appointed to be kept and holden, as well by abstinence from Food, as by publique Prayers, hearing of the Word of God, and other sacred Duties in *England* and *Wales*, on the last Wednesday of the Moneth of *February* then next following, and from thenceforth to continue during the Troubles in the Kingdom of *Ireland*; which was strictly commanded to be observed, upon pain of punishments to be inflicted upon all such as should contemn or neglect so religious a work: And whereas several Ordinances or Orders of Parliament have since been made for the holding and observing of the said Fast on the same day;

The Parliament of *England* finding by sad experience, how much the observation of the said Monethly Fast hath been for divers years last past, in most places of this Commonwealth wholly neglected, and in other places where the same hath been retained, it hath declined by degrees from that Solemnity and due Reverence wherewith the same was at the first Institution thereof entertained, and as is suitable unto such an Ordinance of Christ, whereby the same hath been much prophaned, the Spirits of those that truly fear God, and desire to Worship him in sincerity and truth, been grieved, the Lord highly dishonored and provoked, and much guilt contracted, by the taking of Gods Name in vain: And seriously considering how apt such set times for extraordinary duties of Worship are to degenerate into meer Formality and Customary observances; and that it is more agreeable to the nature of such extraordinary Worship, and to the approved and successful Examples of the people of God in Scripture, to set apart special times for such solemn Duties, according to the particular occasions, to the end the same might be observed with greater care and intention: For the better reforming of which abuses, and prevention thereof for the future, Be it Enacted and Ordained, and it is Enacted and Ordained by this present Parliament, and by authority thereof, That the said Proclamation be declared *Null* and void; and that all Orders and Ordinances of Parliament, touching the observation of the said Fast on the day or days afore mentioned, be and are hereby Repealed and made void: And that it shall and may be lawful for all and every the Courts of *Westminster*, and all other Courts to sit; and all other person and persons whatsoever, to follow the works of his or their lawful Calling upon those days, without incurring any penalty thereby.

And forasmuch as the multiplyed sins of this Nation, the contempt of God and his Ordinances, that general prophaneness, opposition to Reformation, murmuring at the various and gracious Providences of God and the general unthankfulness for the mercies and preservations this Nation hath received, together with a proneness and endeavor to relapse into that former condition of Tyranny and Superstition, out of which God hath in much mercy lately brought us, do minister just cause of Humiliation, together with the present miseries and straights of our poor Brethren in *Ireland*, through the Apostacy and perfidiousness of some, and the united Malice and power of others; and the Parliament being resolved, by Gods assistance, to send some Forces for the speedy Relief of the Parliament Forces there, and the reduction of the enemy unto the Obedience of the Parliament and Commonwealth of *England*; Be it therefore further Enacted and Ordained by this present Parliament, and the authority of the same, That Thursday the third day of *May, Anno Dom. 1649.* be set apart and appointed for a publique and solemn day of Fasting and Humiliation, to be observed in all Churches and Chappels within the cities of *London* and *Westminster*, and all places within the late Lines of Communication, and Bills of Mortality, earnestly to seek unto Almighty God, through our Lord Jesus Christ, that he will be graciously pleased to pardon the Sins of this Nation, and in a special maner the Sins beforementioned, and the Iniquities of the former Monethly Fast-days; and that he will be pleased to heal the Divisions and Breaches of this Land, and give a blessing and success to the Forces of the Parliament now in *Ireland*, and such as are shortly to be sent thither, and at the last to establish his pure Worship, and Righteousness and Peace in this Nation. And be it further Enacted and Ordained by the Authority aforesaid, That *Thursday* the Seventeenth day of the same Moneth of *May, 1649.* be set apart and appointed for the like publique and solemn day of Fasting and Humiliation, upon the grounds and to the ends aforesaid, to be observed and kept in all other Churches and Chappels, in all other Cities, Boroughs, Towns, Parishes and places within *England* and *Wales*, and the Town of *Berwick*: And all Pastors and Ministers, of and in all and every the Cities, Boroughs, Towns and places aforesaid, be enjoyned and required to publish this present Act, in the several Churches and Chappels in and under their several and respective charges, on the Lords-day next before the day by this present Act appointed for the observation of the said Fast, and to take care that the same be Solemnly and Religiously observed: And that all Majors, Justices of the Peace, Bayliffs, Constables, and all other Officers within their several and respective Liberties and Precincts, be hereby authorized and required to restrain all persons from the publique doing of any work, or using any exercise of a wordly nature, either contemptuously or unnecessarily, to the prophaning or neglect of the said Fast on the days aforesaid respectively by such penalties, or as were heretofore by any Ordinance of Parliament to be inflicted for prophaning the said Monethly Fast.

And be it further Enacted and Ordained by the Authority aforesaid, That this present Act be forthwith printed and published; and that the Sheriffs of the several Counties and Cities in *England* and *Wales*, do cause the same to be proclaimed and set up in the usual and publique places within the said several Counties. And all the People of this Nation are hereby required and enjoyned, with all due Reverence and Devotion to observe the said Fast at the days aforesaid respectively, as they tender the glory of God, and the good and peace of this Commonwealth.

1649–S2   Thanksgiving day for victory against royalist forces at Balvenie

Friday 25 May 1649 or the first convenient day after receipt (Scotland)

On 11 May 1649, the commission of the general assembly approved a *Declaration and warning* against the rising in the north of royalist opponents of the Scottish parliamentary regime. On the following day, news arrived of the defeat of these rebels at Balvenie, near Dufftown, on 8 May. The commission appointed this thanksgiving for the victory, also expressing thanks for the quick suppression of a mutiny in the garrison at Stirling. The causes of the thanksgiving, attached as a postscript to the *Declaration*, reflected the wider satisfaction of the commission, after the overturning of the Engagement (see 1649–S1) and the passage of various acts of parliament for moral reform and in favour of the church. The thanksgiving was observed on Sunday 3 June in Elgin presbytery, the order having arrived too late for the specified date.

Order: act of the commission of the general assembly, 12 May 1649, *RCGA*, II, 264.
Causes: *A declaration and warning to all the members of this Kirk* (Wing C4207)*, 7–9 [also in Wing C4208, pp. 7–9; *RCGA*, II, 264–6].
Letter: commission of the general assembly to presbyteries, 12 May 1649, *RCGA*, II, 266.
Additional sources: *RCGA*, II, 252–8; *A declaration and warning to all the members of this Kirk* (Edinburgh, 1649; Wing C4207); presbytery of Elgin minutes, NRS, CH2/144/1, p. 222; presbytery of Paisley minutes, NRS, CH2/294/3, p. 39; Lamont, p. 5; *Life of Blair*, p. 219.

ORDER

Act of the commission of the general assembly: 12 May 1649
The Commission of Assembly haveing seriously considered the Lords mercifull defeat of the enemies of the peace of this land, Thinke it necessarie that there be a solemne day of thanksgiving, vpon the 25th of this instant, for so great a mercie, and that the same be added as a postscript to the Declaratioun and Warning, and the letters concluded yesterday

CAUSES

Within a short time after that we had resolved and concluded thus to Declare and give warning concerning the Insurrection in the North, We received certain Intelligence by an Expresse sent of purpose from thence, that upon *Tuesday* last at *Balvenie* upon *Spey* side, by a party of an hundred and twenty horse, commanded by Lieutenant Generall *Leslie* to attend these fields under the conduct of Colonell *Ker*, Lieutenant Colonell *Hacket*, Lieutenant Colonel *Strachen*, the Lord hath defeat the most considerable part, if not all the strength of the Rebels in the North, to the number of twelve hundred, of whom betwixt sixty and eighty are killed, near eight hundred taken prisoners, and amongst those, the now L. *Rae* with his most considerable officers, and many considerable gentlemen and officers of the name of *Mac-kenzie*: Which as it is a great and most seasonable mercy that carries upon it a lively impression of the power and goodnesse of the Lord, so doth it engage his people to acknowledge and bear Testimony to the same before the sons of men.

    And therefore having now for a long time past, had thoughts of a publick thanksgiving for the many mercies bestowed upon, and deliverances wrought for the Land; Wee conceive this day of salvation to be a fitting opportunity, wherein the Lords people should make mention of his loving kindnesse and exalt his Name by publick thanksgiving and praise, for all the great things which he hath done for them, especially for these which follow.

    1. That as the Lord since the beginning of the work of Reformation hath alwayes gone before his people, and visited them with most seasonable deliverances in the day of their difficulties and distresses; so also that of late, when all the power of the Kingdom both in Judicatories and Armies was come into the hands of Malignant and dis-affected men, the Lord was pleased to preserve in this* Land (having

been over them in a piller of direction and protection) a remnant in the Parliament to dissent from, and protest against the proceedings of the greater part tending so much to the prejudice of Religion and the work of God, and that he directed and enabled his servants of the ministry to bear so free and faithfull Testimony in their Sermons, Warnings and Declarations against that unlawful Engagement, and put it in the hearts of many of his people to petition against it, and to refuse to concur therein notwithstanding of their great sufferings.

2. That whilst the Malignant and dis-affected party in the Land were in the height of their strength, and pride of their power, God was pleased to break their horn, and to scatter them and bring them down, and to put it in the hearts of his people to come forth for their own defence against the remnant of their Forces, and so to dispose, that after that Malignant party at *Stirling* had shed blood, yet things were concluded in a peaceable way, and both their Armes and the Civill power gotten out of their hands, and put into the hands of those that have been honest and faithfull in the Cause from the beginning.

3. That the Lord was pleased to give unto us in such a period of time, a Parliament consisting of so many able and faithfull men, who did walk so straightly in all things concerning Religion and his Majesties Government, and make so many pious and laudable Acts for the suppressing of profanitie and iniquity, and advancing Piety, and Righteousness in the Land.

4. That the Lord hath disappointed and defeated so many secret Plots and devises, tending to the undermining of his Cause, especially that at the Isle of *VVight* so prejudiciall to the Covenant and the Union betwixt the Kingdoms.

5. That the Lord hath been pleased at such a time when all the Malignants of the Kingdom were hatching new devices, and strengthening themselves at home, and expecting Forces from abroad, by so small a number, and in so unexpected a way, to defeat so many of them, and give such victory and salvation to his People, without so much as one being killed on our side.

6. That the LORD was pleased to direct and assist both State and Kirk, in giving so seasonable, full, and harmonious Testimony against the proceedings of the Sectaries in *England*.

LETTER

Commission of the general assembly to presbyteries: 12 May 1649
The Postscript of the Declaratioun will shew that, vpon a new emergent of the Lords goodness, Wee have resolved vpon a publick Thanksgiving to be kept throw all the Kirks of the Kingdom, vpon Fryday the 25 of this instant; And therefore, after yow read from your pulpits the Declaratioun, yow will also read the Postscript, togither with the causes of the Thanksgiving, the Lords day before the foresaid dyet, and make intimatioun of the same, to be kept at the time appointed; And if these shall not come tymously, yow shall keep the Thanksgiving vpon the first convenient day after these shall come to your hands.

1649–E3 Thanksgiving days for suppression of the Levellers, and for naval successes

Thursday 7 June 1649 (London, Westminster, the late lines of communication and bills of mortality); Thursday 28 June 1649 (elsewhere in England and Wales)

During May 1649, inspired by the radical agitation of the Levellers, some of the regiments ordered to go to Ireland (see 1649–E2) rebelled against arrears of pay and the Rump parliament's refusal to call new elections. Fairfax and Cromwell, whose regiments were free from trouble, led a surprise attack on the rebellious soldiers and shot three of the leaders by firing squad. Cromwell reported his success to the Commons on 25 May; the following day, it ordered a public thanksgiving, the order for which was passed on 1 June after three readings. The act was printed with a lengthy justification for the thanksgiving. On 5 June, parliament ordered that thanks should also be offered on 7 June for recent naval successes. This probably refers to Robert Blake's capture of ten English merchant ships chartered to Portugal which he tried to use to secure control over Prince Rupert's fleet. Reviving earlier practice, the lord mayor, aldermen and common council of London invited the Commons to dine with them at the Grocers' Hall after the sermons at Christ Church. There, the City presented Fairfax with a large basin and a gold ewer; Cromwell received a plate worth £300 and 200 pieces of gold. The sermons were preached by John Owen and Thomas Goodwin; neither preacher chose to have their sermons printed. For the first time, the speeches made at the dinner at the Grocers' Hall – by Hugh Peter and the aldermen, Thomas Atkins and Isaac Pennington – were printed. Clopton reported that the thanksgiving was 'kept of very few', though he claimed that he and his wife did not attend church only because their 'house lay open in many places where the carpenters had pulled it down to set up the brewhouse'. However, he remarked that a local minister preached on Judges 5 on this day, using the same text again three days later.

Orders: *An act for setting apart a day of publique thanksgiving, and declaring the reasons and grounds thereof*, 1 June 1649, Thomason E.1060[34]*; parliamentary order, 5 June 1649, *CJ*, VI, 224–5.
Additional sources: *CJ*, VI, 218, 220–1; *FSP*, XXXIII, 4; *Whitelocke diary*, pp. 241–2; Thomas Atkins, *Hosanna: or, A song of thanks-giving, sung by the children of Zion, and set forth in three notable speeches at Grocers Hall, on the late solemn day of thanksgiving, Thursday June 7. 1649* (1649; Wing A4124A and other editions A4124B and H2887bA); Clopton diary, 28 June, 1 July 1649.

ORDERS

Act of parliament: 1 June 1649

How often and eminently Almighty God hath been graciously pleased to appear in the Cause of the Parliament and People of *England*, against the Common Enemy both of the true Religion and the Liberties of the Nation, since the beginning of the late Wars, the world is not ignorant: And when through his providence and especial blessing on the Councels and Endeavors of the Parliament and their Forces, the Power of the Enemy was broken, their Garisons taken or surrendered, and all of them subdued, there arising another cloud, that threatned not onely a storm, but an inundation of Misery, by the revolt of divers Castles at once, the defection of a great part of the Navy, Insurrections in many several counties, open Rebellions in *Wales,*

Surrey, Kent; when many of those at home, who had formerly shewed themselves on the part of the Parliament and Nation, were become uncertain friends, if not certain Enemies; and at the same instant, a numerous Army from the Neighbor Nation, poured in like a flood, and uniting with a Malignant party in the North, endeavored a conjunction with the rest, that so they might swallow up all the honest party, and restore the former Tyranny, against which both Nations had not long before engaged; and all this at such a time, when the Army (which was, under God, the most visible means of preserving both Parliament and Nation from utter ruine) was dispersed so far asunder, as did render them less able to oppose so potent an enemy, & to defend themselves; The Lord did then gloriously make bare his arm, in the seasonable reduction of *Wales*, the total defeat of that great Army, by less then half their number of men, wearied with Service and long Marches, giving in divers victories (whereof we could not have wanted any one, without danger of ruine; and our miscarrying in any one, had been enough for the Enemies advantage) the dissipating of the several parties, the Rendition of *Colchester*, and all others the Towns and Castles, which by force or treachery they had surprized; and thereby was pleased to give, not onely a wonderful deliverance to this Nation, from being ruined in a second War, but a second compleat conquest over the Enemy at home, and to bear witness against the Hypocrisie & Injustice of those Invaders from abroad, as well by an utter overthrow here, as by breaking in their own Countrey, the whole power of that party, who had promoted that perfideous Engagement by such an Authority as might denominate the Breach National: All which considered, the Mercy appears so eminent and admirable, that the Parliament cannot but recount it with all humble thankfulness unto God, and transmit the memory of it to Posterity, that the Generations to come may praise him: And after all these great Deliverances and strange Providences of the almighty, carrying on the Parliament in the execution of Justice upon the chief Author, and some of the most eminent Instruments of both these Wars, and that some hopeful progress hath been made in setling the Government of this Commonwealth, in such a way as (by Gods blessing) may secure it against the like Tyranny for the future, and be a foundation of Happiness and Freedom; And that the Parliament (having by these troubles in *England*, been interrupted from sending relief to *Ireland*) did now resolve (by Gods assistance) to speed a considerable Force thither, for reducing that Land to the obedience of the Parliament of *England*: It could hardly have been suspected that any, especially such as have professed a zeal for God, his Truth, and People, should have retarded so good a work, but rather should have unanimously given assistance thereunto, the security of *England*, and Religion it self being so much concerned in it: Yet at this time a new distemper discovered it self, kindled and fomented by some turbulent Spirits, acted Jesuitical Councels and Principles, destructive to Government; who, disliking every thing whereof themselves might not have the honor, did design to pluck up all that hath been planted, to bring the Nation into confusion, destroy all property, eradicate Law and true Liberty at once, and obstruct the relief of *Ireland* (which otherwise might by this time have been sent thither) And to that end, by traducing the actions of the Parliament in the things, which before they were done, themselves petitioned for, and since seemed to rejoyce in; and by unjust scandals upon some chief Officers in the Army (the General himself not being exempted) whom God had made Instrumental in so many Victories and Preservations of the whole Nation; and by holding forth specious pretences of Liberty and benefit to the People, had seduced some few of the inferior Officers of the Army, and a considerable number of the Soldiery to decline the Service of *Ireland*,

and wrought a disaffection thereunto in many of those who were designed to that work: How dangerous the Design was in it self, and how deeply laid to the apparent hazard of *Ireland*, and the embroiling this Nation in a further and more desperate War, The Parliament of *England* being very sensible, and considering the especial providence of God in the timely discovery of it, and the seasonableness of the mercy, in crushing the Serpent in the egge; and by his good hand upon the Forces under the General, suppressing that Rebellion and Insurrection, and so preventing the sad and fearful consequences which it might have produced, Held themselves in duty bound, publiquely to acknowledge Gods goodness therein, and to look upon it as a pledge of future mercies to this poor and unworthy Nation, and of his willingness to heal it, if yet it will be healed. And therefore the Parliament do Enact and Ordain, and be it Enacted and Ordained, That a day of publique Rejoycing and Thanksgiving to our gracious God, for this wonderful and signal mercy, be observed and kept on Thursday the seventh of *June, 1649.* in all Churches and Chappels within the Cities of *London* and *Westminster*, the late Lines of Communication, and weekly Bills of Mortality, and in all other Churches and Chappels within *England* and *Wales*, on Thursday the *28* day of the same moneth of *June, 1649.* And the Parliament do earnestly exhort and require all that truly fear God in this Commonwealth, to lay aside all bitterness and opposition against the present dispensations of God towards this Nation, and to consider how much it concerns the Interest of Christ, his Truth and *People*, to unite themselves, and to serve the Lord and his providences with one shoulder; And to take notice of the hand of God in this mercy, appearing visibly to all that do not wilfully shut their eyes, and to rejoyce in it, and earnestly to beseech God to rebuke that Spirit of Division, and to knit the hearts of his own *People* in Love and Unity; and likewise to beg from God a special blessing upon the Forces intended for *Ireland*, and a perfecting of his own work to his own glory. And the *Parliament* do enjoyn all the Ministers of the Gospel throughout the Nation, to use their utmost endeavor, That the said day of Thanksgiving be Solemnly and Religiously observed, that God be not dishonored and provoked thereby; And to that end, that they and every of them do give publique notice thereof, by publishing this Act in their several Churches and Chappels, as well on the Lords day next before the day of Thanksgiving, as also on the day so to be observed; And that all Majors, Sheriffs, Justices of the peace, and other Officers, do take care for the due observation of the said day of Thanksgiving, that God may be pleased to accept the praises of his people in this particular, and delight in, and rejoyce over them to do them good, and to make this Nation a praise in the Earth.

Parliamentary order: 5 June 1649

Resolved, &c. That Notice be taken, on the next *Thursday*, being a Day appointed for Publick Thanksgiving, for the great Mercy of God in the Success given to the Fleet at Sea, and the State of our Affairs there; and to give hearty Thanks to God for the same; and beg a further Blessing on their Undertakings: And that Sir *James Harrington*, Mr. *Gurdon*, and Mr. *Strickland*, do withdraw; and pen an Order to be sent to the Ministers for that Purpose.

1649–E4 Fast days for the Commonwealth campaign in Ireland

Wednesday 11 July 1649 (London, Westminster, the late lines of communication and bills of mortality); Wednesday 1 August 1649 (elsewhere in England and Wales)

On 6 July, the Rump parliament ordered another day of solemn fasting and humiliation in support of Cromwell's troops going to Ireland, where they faced resurgent royalist forces under Ormond, Inchiquin and Sir George Munro in Leinster and Derry. The ordering process reverted to older practices: the day was authorized by parliamentary order, not by act of parliament; the fast was observed on different days in the London area and elsewhere in the country; the printed order was brief, and copies of it were distributed in and around London by the lord mayor, and elsewhere by the sheriffs. Ministers were expected to publish the order in their churches a week before the fast day and JPs were required to ensure that the fast was observed. This was the first time since 1647–E1(P) that ministers had been explicitly instructed to publish the order in advance. It was also the first time that JPs were ordered to enforce attendance, though punishments for non-observance had been regularly alluded to in sixteenth-century orders for special worship, and measures to identify clerical and lay wrong-doers had been periodically devised (e.g. 1644–E2(P)). Both of these measures may reflect the Commonwealth's anxieties about its unpopularity. William Strong and Samson Bond were appointed to preach before the Rump at St Margaret's, Westminster, marking a return to the traditional Commons' place for special worship. If their sermons were printed they are no longer extant. Bulstrode Whitelocke, MP and member of the council of state, recorded in his diary how he and Cromwell had observed the occasion at Windsor. After Cromwell arrived 'in great & stately equipage', 'they had a meeting to seek God by prayer, for his blessing upon their intended journey for Ireland, three Ministers & Cromwell prayed, C[ollonells] Goffe & Harrison expounded some scriptures pertinent to the purpose' (*Whitelocke diary*, 241). Clopton remarked in his diary that many called this fast day 'Cromwell's fast'. It was not widely observed around Clopton's parish of Little Wratton, Essex: 'Few hereabouts preacht but Mr Burrell, his text "Soe let thine enemies perish oh God" – a text he first made use of at the previous thanksgiving for the army's victory against the Levellers' (1649–E3). Clopton attended morning service, but his workmen were not given the day off.

Orders: order of the House of Commons, 6 July 1649, *CJ*, VI, 251; parliamentary order, 6 July 1649 (1p., 1649; Wing E2671C)*.
Additional source: *CJ*, VI, 251, 253–4; *Whitelocke diary*, p. 241; Clopton diary, 1 Aug. 1649.

ORDERS

Order of the House of Commons, 6 July 1649
ORDERED, That *Wednesday* next, being the Eleventh Day of *July* instant, be set apart, and appointed, for a Day of Publick and Solemn Fasting and Humiliation, to be observed in all Churches and Chapels within the Cities of *London* and *Westminster*, and the late Lines of Communication, and weekly Bills of Mortality, for the Seeking of Almighty God, for his especial Blessing upon the Forces now designed and going for the Relief of *Ireland*; And that the Lord Mayor of the City of *London* be required to cause timely Notice hereof to be given to the Ministers of the several

Parish Churches within the City of *London*, and Liberties thereof; and to take care the same be duly observed accordingly: And that every of the Ministers of the Churches aforesaid be required to publish this Order, in the several Churches, on the next Lord's Day.

Parliamentary order: 6 July 1649

Ordered by the Commons assembled in Parliament, That Wednesday next come three weeks be set apart and appointed for a day of publique Fasting and Humiliation, for seeking unto Almighty God in an especial maner, for his blessing upon the Forces designed, and now going for the relief of *Ireland*, to be observed in all Cities, Towns and places in *England* and *Wales*, besides the Cities of *London* and *Westminster*: And that the Sheriffs of the several Counties in *England* and *Wales*, do take care to disperse this Order unto the Ministers of the several Churches aforesaid: And the Iustices of peace in the several counties, are required to take care for the due observation thereof; And that the Ministers do publish this Order in their several Churches, on the Lords day next before the day appointed for the due observation of the said Fast.

1649–S3 Fast day during anxieties over witchcraft, threats in England and Ireland, Charles II's policies and the harvest

Sunday 26 August 1649 (Scotland)

This fast was appointed by the general assembly shortly before it dissolved on 6 August 1649. The causes reflect Scotland's many problems: the huge surge in prosecutions for witchcraft, the threat of invasion by the English or by royalists and shortages of food. Scottish commissioners had met Charles II at The Hague in the spring, but he had failed to accept parliament's terms for his travelling to Scotland, and he continued to take advice from opponents of the regime, notably the marquis of Montrose. On 20 July, the assembly passed an act requiring supporters of the Engagement publicly to testify their repentance, or face excommunication. Lamont's diary suggests that the announcement of this act in the parishes coincided with the observance of the fast. The fast seems to have been kept a week late in Strathbogie.

Causes: *Edinburgh, August 6. 1649. Cavses of a solemn publick humiliation and fast* (Wing C4201G)* [listed in Wing C4243, p. 38].
Additional sources: *The principall acts of the generall assembly* (Edinburgh, 1649; Wing C4243), pp. 2–5; presbytery of Elgin minutes, NRS, CH2/144/1, p. 227; presbytery of Paisley minutes, NRS, CH2/294/3, p. 41; Lamont, pp. 8–9; *Strathbogie presbytery*, pp. 113–14; *Inverness and Dingwall records*, pp. 152–3.

CAUSES

I. Wee are to mourn for the continuance and increase of sinne and profanity; Especially of the abominable sin of Witchcraft, which abounds in the Land, as appeares from the many and frequent discoveries thereof, in all the corners and quarters of the Countrey.

II. We are to afflict our soules before the Lord, for the sad Interruption of the

Lords Work in *England* and *Ireland*, and for the sore oppression of his people, and such as are stedfast in his Cause in these Kingdomes, by a prevailing party of Sectaries in the one, and of Malignants in the other.

III. It is matter of Humiliation unto us, that our King hath not as yet granted the just and necessary desires of this Kirk and Kingdome, for securing of Religion, and that he hath made Peace with the *Irish Rebels*, who have shed so much of the blood of the Lords people, and hath granted unto them the full Liberty of Poperie.

IV. Wee are to entreat the Lord to deliver the King from the snare of Malignant Counsels, and to incline his heart to give satisfaction in these things that concern Religion, that he may be established upon his Throne.

V. We are to pray for stedfastnes to this Land, especially to those who have the charge of publick Affairs, that in the midst of so many Snares and Tentations, they may keep their Integrity, and not decline neither to the right hand, or to the left.

VI. Wee are to entreat the Lord that he would strenthen those who suffer for his Cause in *England* and *Ireland*, and that he would break the yoke of their oppressours from off their neck, and carry on his Work amongst them, unto the praise of his own Name, the comfort of his people, and shame of his Enemies.

VII. Wee are to beg of God that he would regard the necessities of the Poor, who cry for want of bread, by a faire and seasonable Harvest, and Crowning the yeer with his goodnesse, in bestowing upon his people a plentifull measure of the fruits of the earth, that so the famine which hath been long threatned, and is much feared, may be prevented, and the Kingdome enabled to beare necessary burthens, without repining.

1649–E5   Thanksgiving day for the Commonwealth victory at the battle of Rathmines, in Ireland

Wednesday 29 August 1649 (England, Wales and Berwick-upon-Tweed)

On 2 August, the royalist forces of the earl of Ormond took Baggotrath Castle, between Rathmines and Dublin, but failed to secure its defences before the castle was attacked by Commonwealth forces under Colonel Michael Jones. Jones routed the royalist cavalry and overran their infantry. Hearing of Jones's victory on 14 August, the Rump parliament proposed a day of thanksgiving to be held on 29 August. Though this culminated in an act of parliament, there are no records of the three readings in the Commons' journal. The act was to 'requir[e] the due Observation' of the thanksgiving, though (like the royal proclamations before it) it specified no penalties for non-attendance. This might suggest that the recent change in the ordering process was about enforcing observance and punishing non-attendance as well as the authority to order; acts of parliament defined actions as legal or illegal. It certainly demonstrates the blurred distinctions between orders, ordinances and acts of parliament during this period. A 'declaration' of the grounds for the thanksgiving was drawn up and printed as part of the act. Extracts from Jones's letters and the report given to parliament were also printed. There was a new system for broadcasting the order: the Commons' serjeant-at-arms was ordered to distribute copies to the sheriffs, his servants being paid four pence a mile to do so. William Greenhill and William Cooper were appointed to preach before the house at St Margaret's on 29 August.

Though both men were requested to print their sermons, only Cooper appears to have done so. In Essex, Clopton attended two sermons on this day – by Burrell in the morning and, in the afternoon, by the prominent godly preacher and writer, Daniel Rogers, at Wethersfield (on Ephesians 2) – before dining with Sir Nathaniel Bardnardiston, his wife and others at Kitton Hall.

Order: *An act for setting apart a day of publique thanksgiving, to be kept on Wednesday the 29th of August, 1649. Together with a declaration & a narrative of the grounds and reasons thereof*, 16 Aug. 1649, Thomason, E.1060[55]*.
Additional sources: *CJ*, VI, 278–9; *An act for setting apart a day of publique thanksgiving* (1649; Thomason E.1060[55]), pp. 451–6; *Lieut: General Jones's letter to the Councel of State, of a great victory which it hath pleased God to give the forces in the city of Dublin under his command, on the second of this instant August* (1649; Wing J983); *FSP*, XXXIII, 5–6; Clopton diary, 29 Aug. 1649.
Printed sermon: Cooper, House of Commons (Wing C6064; *FSP*, XXXIII, 12–54).

ORDER

Act of parliament: 16 August 1649
Since the time that the *Lord* brought up his *People* from the *house of Bondage*, by the Outgoings of his Almighty Power, in Signs and Wonders, it can hardly be observed, That ever His Almighty Arm was made more visibly bare in promoting, or that He hath by more evident demonstrations declared to the world, His approbation and owning of any *Cause*, then he hath done *that*, in which *this Parliament* hath been engaged, for asserting and recovery of their just *Rights* and *Liberties*, with the establishment of *Truth* and *Righteousnes*, and suppression and removal of *Tyranny*, and all the effects of it. And this hath been seen the more evidently and absolutely, since the time that the *Parliament* hath engaged most *expresly* and *impartially* against the greatest and highest Enemies of *Religion* and *Liberty*.

With what a *Series* of Mercies, and Miracles of *Victory* and *Deliverances* we have been followed from the hand of our Merciful God, since the Battel of *Naseby* till this present, cannot, we hope, be so far out of either the sense or memory of any good *Patriot*, as to need a Recapitulation or Rehearsal. *He* hath made us to *Triumph* over our Enemies, and *wherein they dealt proudly, He was above them*; giving them leave oft-times to *swell* their *Waves*, that *He* might set them limits, and say unto them, *Hitherto shall you come, and no further. He* hath made them *feel* the liftings up of his hand, which they would not *see*; and by His own Almighty *wonder-working Power*, defeated their Strengths, and confounded them in their Confidences: *When* heightened to *Assurances* of undoubted *Success*, they have *promised* themselves nothing but *Victory, Spoil*, and the full harvest of their Hopes, *then* sudden destruction hath befaln them from the *Lord*, and that so *signally*, and beyond ordinary Providences, as if *the Stars in their courses had fought against them: When* they have gone from Mountain to Hill to seek for *Divinations against Israel*, and called in *Moab*, and *Ammon*, and *Amaleck, and the inhabitants of Mount Seir*, against the *worm Jacob, through* the Power, and Presence of our *God*, no *Sorcery* hath prevailed, no *weapon found against* us hath *prospered*: The Lord hath declared to the world, That he is a *God of Mountains and of Valleys*, and every where a *strong Rock*, a mighty *Defence* for those that serve and *trust* in Him. Against all *persons*, and in all *places*, He hath appeared for *Us*, as against the old professed *Malignants* and *Royalists* all along in *England*; against the pretended *Covenanters* the last year from and in *Scotland*; so now of late most *seasonably*, and even *miraculously* in

Ireland, against both *Scots*, Renegado *English*,[333] and *Irish* formerly Commanded by *Taaff, Preston, Clanrickard, Inchiquin*, and now united and grown into a numerous Army under the *Apostate Ormond*,[334] amounting in the whole, at their own account, to Nineteen thousand men. Now when by the Revolt of *Inchiquin*, all *Munster* was theirs; and by the force of *Clanrickard*, all *Connaught*, by the defection of the *Scots*, and treachery of the *English* deserting their Trust, all *Ulster* was lost, except *Derry*; and *Lempster*, even to *Dublin*. When all the *English* Interest in *Ireland* was reduced, and shut up in those two Towns, and the latter straightly besieged by so *potent* a force, whereby the Enemy was arrived to such a *Confidence*, as that the Lord *Ormond* began to be solicitous, and full of trouble to himself, what to do with our Men, when they should be in his power (*whereof he made no doubt*) inclining (as he said) to send them to the *Barbadoes*, and our other Plantations, if sufficient shipping could be gained; and the Lord *Taaff*, to ease him of that care, suggested (as an easier expedient) the throwing them into the *Sea* (such are the Mercies of the Wicked;) *Then*, when they onely staid but for the coming up of their additional forces, to effect all this the more securely, *then* the Lord look'd down from *Heaven, the habitation of his Holiness*, and His Glory, and *defeated* them; *Then* He sent forth *his wrath, and consumed them as stubble*, or *as chaff before the wind*. And thus hath *He* begun to avenge his *Israel* there, and visit for the *Blood* of his people *shed* in that Kingdom, *with a rage reaching up to Heaven*, and therein given his Servants *here* cause with triumphant *joy* to say, *Who is like unto thee, O Lord, among the gods? Who is like thee, glorious in Holiness, fearful in Praises, doing wonders?*

The particulars of which *wonderful* Mercy now given, are more fully and clearly certified in several *Expresses* from Lieutenant General *Jones*, the principal and most honorable Instrument in the Hand of *God* for this great Deliverance and Success, summ'd up into the ensuing *Narrative*.

Since *Ormonds* first setting himself before *Dublin*, (where he continued from the twentieth of June, to the second instant) little was done against this City; He aiming first at the gaining the principal Out-Garrisons, as *Droghedah, Dundalk* and *Trym*, the last being taken the one and twentieth past.

On the two and twentieth, Col: *Venables* landed with his Foot; the five and twentieth, Colonel *Reynolds* with his Horse; the six and twentieth, Colonel *Moor*, and Colonel *Hunks* with their Foot, and Captain *Norwood*, and Major *Eliot* with their Troops, whereby this Party became in some sort considerable. Wherewithal, and by the report of the Lord *Lieutenant's* following soon after with the whole Army, the Enemy being awakened, thereupon resolved to set themselves wholly to this work; And in the first place, they did cut off that *Water*, whereby our Mills were driven, and thereby was our condition something straightned; but principally upon

---

333 Royalists who fought under the earl of Inchiquin, the marquis of Clanricard, Viscount Taaffe and Thomas Preston. This was a more diverse group than the declaration implies. Inchiquin had defected to parliament in July 1644 and defeated Taaffe at Knocknanuss in 1647, before returning to the royalist cause in April 1648. Taaffe went over to the confederates after Ormond surrendered Dublin to Colonel Jones in 1647. Preston rejected the First Ormond Peace, negotiated by the earl, in 1646 and fought against Jones in 1647. Clanricard was unable to persuade him to return to Ormond's service until 1648.

334 This may refer to Ormond's surrender of Dublin to parliament in June 1647. Though the earl was loyal to the king, he did not want the Irish capital to fall into Catholic hands. However, he immediately left Ireland, returning in September 1648 with French troops to press the royalist cause again.

the second instant, they cast up a Work at *Baggarath*, within a quarter of a mile of this City, whither having drawn about fifteen hundred Foot, besides Horse, they thence purposed to work themselves forward in their approaches, and to take from us our forrage for our Horse, and grass for our Cattle, without which this place could not long have subsisted; and they built Forts towards the Sea, to deprive us of the landing place, for our coming Supplies, and this was the onely safe landing left for our Forces in the Dominion of *Ireland*.

The *Enemies* Horse and Foot appearing at *Baggarath*, the second of this instant, about nine in the morning, Lieutenant General *Iones* drew out twelve hundred Horse, and four thousand Foot; intending then onely to beat up the Enemies quarters, and not to engage with so small a party, their Camp being at *Rathmines*, within less then a mile of *Baggarath*; but *God* blessing our men with success, and by the coming on of parties on all sides, it came at length to a general engagement, and after more then two hours hot dispute, the Enemy was *totally* routed: *Ormond* hardly escaped with eight horse, and few had escaped of their whole numbers, but that these was cause to provide against a body of a thousand fresh Horse of the Enemies, commanded by Sʳ *Thomas Armstrong*, which coming up fresh, and in our mens disorder, might have endangered all; but they in stead of advancing (which our men expected) fled toward *Drogheda*.

Our loss of men was *little*, there not being *twenty* missing, but many wounded.

Of the Enemy were slain about four thousand, some of considerable quality, and two thousand five hundred and seventeen taken prisoners, amongst whom Colonel *Christopher Plunket*, the Earl of *Fingale*, and Colonel *Richard Butler*, the Earl of *Ormonds* brother, were Principals, and with them sixteen Colonels and Field Officers, forty one Captains, Lieutenants fifty eight, Ensigns forty two, of Cornets, Quatermasters, and other persons of inferior Offices and quality, great numbers; most of them of *Inchiquins* English, and our run aways. To which is to be added Mʳ· *Iohn Herbert* (servant to the pretended King) who about six days before landed his Masters houshold-stuff in *Galloway*. Our men took in the place three *Demi canons*, one large square Gun, carrying a Ball of twelve pound, one Sacre-Drake, and one Morter-piece, all these Brass. And our men also gained about two hundred *Oxen* for the *Trayn*, besides carriages. The next day our men seized a *Brass Canon*, within five miles of the Camp, which Camp was richly furnished with great store of Velvets, Silks, Scarlets and other clothing of value, Wines, Grocery, with some convenient quality of *Money*: all which they left behinde them, and the neighbouring villages plentifully stored with *cattle* of all sorts, fit for food.

They are also taken of *Train carriages* and *waggons*, belonging to the Enemies Army, at the least three hundred, Tents five hundred, Cows three hundred, and Irish Nags, termed by them Garroones, eight hundred.

It was for our advantage that *Inchiquin* had some days before gone towards *Munster*, yet intending to return shortly. As also that our men so engaged before *Clanrickards* coming up with his three thousand men out of *Connaught*, and seven thousand *Vlster Scots* also upon advancing.

All this was done but by a *handful* of men, and not the *third* part of our Foot coming in to the principal part of the Work; yet by *them* the *Lord* defeated an Enemy, by themselves now acknowledged Nineteen thousand, and they having a fresh *reserve* of Horse, little short of our numbers.

The same night *Rathfurnans* (Sʳ *Adam Loftus* his house) lately taken by the Enemy, was regained, and the Soldiers in number about Seven score, entertained into the Parliaments service, professing their *abhorrence* to accompany any longer with those *bloody* Irish *Rebels*, and that they were *forced* to do what they did, and that hereafter they would *live* and *dye* with us. Nor did their fear leave them till they had also quitted *Mannoroth*, (the Earl of *Kildares* house, and one of the strongest pieces in *Ireland*) the *Naas, Donahedy*, and *Richardstown*, each twelve miles at the least distant from *Dublin*.

Never was any duty in *Ireland* like *this*, to the *confusion* of the Irish, and to the raising up the spirits of the poor English, and to the restoring of the English Interest; Which, from their *first* footing in *Ireland*, was never in so *low* a condition, as at that very instant: there not being any one considerable *landing* place left *us*, but *this* alone, and *this* also almost *gone*.

Upon consideration of all which, the Parliament for manifestation of their high and extraordinay sence of so signal and seasonable a Mercy, Have thought it fit, and their duty to set apart a time for Publique and Solemn Thanksgiving, to be rendred to the Lord the Author of that Mercy: And they do therefore Enact and Ordain, That *Wednesday* the Twenty ninth of this instant *August*, be observed and kept as a day of publique and holy Rejoycing and Thanksgiving to the Lord, in all the Churches and Chappels, and places of Divine Worship within this Commonwealth of *England*, Dominion of *Wales*, and Town of *Berwick* upon *Tweed*; and that the Ministers of the respective parishes and places aforesaid, be and hereby they are required and enjoyned to give notice on the Lords day next preceding the said Twenty ninth of *August*, of the day so to be observed, to the end the people of their several Congregations may the more generally and diligently attend the publique Exercises of Gods Worship and Service there to be dispensed upon this occasion; at which time, that the people may be more particularly and fully informed of this great Deliverance and Success, the said Ministers are hereby required to publish and read this present Act and Declaration: And for the better observation of the day, The Parliament doth hereby inhibit and forbid the holding or use of all Fairs, Markets, and servile works of mens ordinary Callings upon that day: And all Majors, Sheriffs, Justices of Peace, Constables, and other Officers, be and are hereby enjoyned to take especial care of the due observance of the said day of Thanksgiving accordingly.

1649–E6 Thanksgiving day for Commonwealth victories in Ireland

Thursday 1 November 1649 (England, Wales and Berwick-upon-Tweed)

On 11 September, Cromwell and General Henry Ireton successfully took Drogheda after five hours of bombardment and very fierce fighting. The royalist forces were brutally killed (including Sir Arthur Aston, the governor, who was bludgeoned to death with his own wooden leg) and many civilians were massacred on Cromwell's order, including a hundred people burned to death in St Peter's church. Though such a massacre could be justified in contemporary terms because the city had failed to surrender, it was widely seen as revenge for the massacre of protestants during the uprising in 1641, and it made Cromwell a hated figure. After the fall of Drogheda, the royalists abandoned Trim and Dundalk. On 2 October, parliament ordered a thanksgiving day to be observed on 1 November; the act was read twice and passed on 11 October. A 'Declaration' explaining the reasons for the thanksgiving was commissioned and 12,000 copies of this and the act were ordered to be printed (an increase of 2,000 since the previous occasion for which there is evidence of how many copies were printed: see 1648–E9(P)). They were distributed across the country by the sheriffs. *Letters from Ireland*, a further account of the military campaign with a list of commanders and numbers of those killed, was also ordered to be printed; it is not clear if it was to be read during the service. Stephen Marshall and Peter Sterry were appointed to preach before parliament at St Margaret's, Westminster; only Streey chose to have his sermon printed. On 30 October, the lord mayor was ordered to distribute copies of *A letter from the lord lieutenant of Ireland*, an account of the taking of Wexford by Cromwell (11 October), to ministers in London and its liberties; it was to be read out on the thanksgiving day. Clopton reported that the thanksgiving was not widely observed in Essex.

Order: *An act for a day of publique thanksgiving to be observed throught England and Wales on Thursday the first of November, 1649. Together with a declaration of the grounds thereof,* 11 Oct. 1649, Wing E993*.
Additional sources: *CJ*, VI, 300, 301, 305, 315; *Letters from Ireland, relating the several great successes it hath pleased God to give unto the parliaments forces there* (1649; Wing L1778); *A letter from the lord lieutenant of Ireland, to the honorable William Lenthall Esq; speaker of the parliament of England: giving an account of the proceedings of the army there under his Lordships command* (1649; Wing C7101A); *FSP*, XXXIII, 6; Clopton diary, 1 Nov. 1649.
Printed sermon: Sterry, parliament (Wing S5476; *FSP*, XXXIII, 56–130).

ORDER

Act of parliament: 11 October 1649
The great and wonderful Providences, wherein the Lord hath eminently gone forth in mercy towards this Nation, have been such, that howsoever many do shut their eyes, or murmure against them, or at least refuse to joyn in Publique Acknowledgements, and Thanksgiving to Almighty God for the same; Nevertheless, the Lord hath been pleased to publish to all the world, That it is the work of his own hand: Nor hath his infinite goodness and favor been restrained to *England* onely, but extended to *Ireland*, which he hath been pleased to remember in its low estate; and when his People there were as dry bones, He hath not onely revived them in a way almost as miraculous as a Resurrection from the Dead, but been pleased to raise both them and us to a high pitch of hope, That the Lord will go on to perfect his work in that Land, and make it likewise at last a quiet Habitation for his People, and establish the power and purity of the Gospel there. The consideration whereof, and of the Goodness and Power of God in the late wonderful Victory, which he hath been pleased to give unto the Parliaments Forces there before *Dublin* (never to be forgotten) And the further progress God hath made in giving in *Drogheda*, a place of great Strength and Consequence, defended by a considerable number of their prime Officers and Soldiers, the particulars whereof are expressed in the Lord Lieutenants and other Letters, lately Printed; and since that, by striking Terror into the hearts of the Enemy, so as they have yielded up or deserted many other considerable Castles and Garisons, as *Trym*, *Dundalk*, *Carlingford*, the *Newry*, and other Places, and some other additional Victories which God hath cast in since, cannot but make a deep impression on the hearts of all that fear the Lord, and provoke them to exceeding Thankfulness and Rejoycing.

Upon consideration of all which, the Parliament out of their deep sense of so great and continued Mercies, Have thought fit, as in duty to God, to set apart a day for publique and solemn Thanksgiving to the Lord, the Author of these Mercies: And they do therefore Enact and Ordain, That *Thursday* the First of *November* next, be kept as a day of publique Thanksgiving to the Lord, in all the Churches and Chappels, and places of Divine Worship within this Commonwealth of *England*, Dominion of *Wales*, and Town of *Berwick* upon *Tweed*: And that the Ministers of the respective Parishes and places aforesaid, be and hereby they are required and enjoyned to give publique notice of the Lords-day next preceding the said First of *November*, of the day so to be observed, to the end the People of their several Congregations may the more generally and diligently attend the publique Exercise of Gods Worship and Service, there to be dispensed upon this occasion; At which time, that the People may be more particularly and fully informed of this great Victory and Successes, the said Ministers are hereby required to publish and read this present Act. And for the better observation of the day, the Parliament doth hereby inhibit and forbid the holding or use of all Fairs, Markets, and servile works of mens ordinary Callings upon that day: And all Majors, Sheriffs, Justices of the Peace, Constables and other Officers, be and are hereby enjoyned to take especial care of the due observance of the said day of Thanksgiving accordingly.

1649–Ir   Thanksgiving day for Commonwealth victories in Munster

Saturday 24 November 1649 (Ireland)

This occasion is only known through a letter from Cromwell to William Lenthall, speaker of the Rump parliament, dated 19 December, in which he refers to a day of public thanksgiving throughout Ireland for successes in Munster: the taking of Carrick (19 November) and the securing of lines towards Waterford. This appears to have been ordered around 18 November and was held on the 24th, when the Commonwealth secured another Irish victory at Passage Fort near Waterford. Though Cromwell failed to take Waterford itself, his campaign had been so successful that Charles II abandoned his plan to use Ireland as the springboard for an invasion of England.

Source: Oliver Cromwell to William Lenthall, 19 Dec. 1649, HMC, *Seventh rep., appendix*, p. 74.

DESCRIPTION OF ORDER

Oliver Cromwell to William Lenthall: 19 December 1649

… It is not unworthy taking notice that, having appointed a public day of thanksgiving throughout your territories in Ireland (as well as a week's warning would permit) for the recovery of Munster, which proves a sweet refreshment to us, even prepared by God for us after our weary and hard labour, that that very day and that very time that men were praising God, was this deliverance [the taking of Passage Fort] wrought …

1649–E7 Thanksgiving prayers for Commonwealth victories in Munster

Sunday 16 December 1649 (London, the late lines of communication and bills of mortality)

On 12 December, parliament issued an order for thanksgivings in and around London for the recent victories in Munster; it is unclear why they did not use an act of parliament. Unlike the Irish occasion (1649–1r), it appears that only prayers were ordered, not a day of thanksgiving. Indeed, parliament may not have been aware that a similar thanksgiving had already been held in Ireland, as Cromwell's letter to Lenthall describing it was not read to parliament until early January. Extracts of Cromwell's letters were ordered to be printed and read during the service (*A letter from the right honorable, the lord lieutenant of Ireland*). This account discussed the taking of Ennistery, Passage Fort, Carrick, Bandonbridge and Kinsale.

Order: parliamentary order, 12 Dec. 1649, Wing C7101*, p. 2 [also in *CJ*, VI, 331].
Additional source: *A letter from the right honorable, the lord lieutenant of Ireland, to the honorable William Lenthall esq* (1649; Wing C7101).

ORDER

Parliamentary order: 12 December 1649
Ordered, That publique Thanks be given to Almighty God on the next Lords Day, in all the several Churches in and about the City of *London,* and within the late lines of Communication, and Bills of Mortality, for his great Mercies, in giving us these seasonable and great Victories in *Ireland;* And that this Letter of the Lord Lieutenant General be then publiquely read in all the said several Churches in and about the said City, and within the lines of Communication and Bills of Mortality.

1650–E1 Day of humiliation during anxieties for the Commonwealth government

Thursday 28 February 1650 (England and Wales)

On 29 January, the Rump parliament ordered a group of its members to draw up a declaration for a day of public humiliation. They proposed this special worship for the 'Solemn Seeking of God for his Direction in, and Blessing upon, the Councils and Endeavours of the Parliament, and their Forces raised by them'. This probably referred to the extension of the Oath of Engagement to all adult males (2 January), proposals for new regulations for future elections, and Cromwell's preparations to consolidate his hold of Munster. The English parliament was also well aware that the Scots had proclaimed Charles II king of Scotland, England and Ireland, and were ready to fight on his behalf. The act was read for the first time on 2 February and passed after two readings on the 4th. John Owen and Vavasor Powell were appointed to preach before the Rump at St Margaret's, Westminster. Clopton did not observe the fast, busying himself buying and swapping horses, but he may have attended church: he recorded that a Mr Burrell preached two sermons, both on the same text ('Thou hast torne us thou canst heale us').

Order: parliamentary act, 4 Feb. 1650, Wing E981*.
Additional source: *CJ*, VI, 352, 356–7; *FSP*, XXXIII, 7–8.
Printed sermon: Owen, parliament (Wing O808; *FSP*, XXXIII, 237–96); Powell, parliament (Wing P3081; *FSP*, XXXIII, 131–236); Clopton diary, 28 Feb. 1650.

ORDER

Act of parliament: 4 February 1650
The Lord who Ruleth over the Nations, who disposeth and ordereth all things, according to the good pleasure of his own Will, hath in our Age (as in former Generations) exceedingly glorified his Wisdom, Power and Mercy, That he might warn and awaken the Inhabitants of the Earth unto a diligent enquiry after him, a faithful and fruitful living before him; His Voyce and his Hand hath been heard, and seen in this Land most eminently, in rescuing Us out of the destroying hands of Tyranny, Popery and Superstition: Which experience of the Lords wonderful Goodness and Mercy towards this Nation, might have wrought an answerable return of Duty and Obedience; and the sense of the want hereof ought to fill us with shame, astonishment and confusion of face, especially when (in stead thereof) we finde in the midst of it, such crying Sins, hideous Blasphemies, and unheard of Abominations (and that by some under pretence of Liberty, and greater measure of Light) as after all our wondrous Deliverances, do manifest themselves to the exceeding dishonor of God, and reproach of our Christian Profession: To the end therefore that this Nation in general, and every one in particular may have an opportunity to know and acknowledge their Sins in the sight of God, and be truly humbled for them; and that earnest Prayer and Supplication may be put up on behalf of this Commonwealth, for the advancement of the Kingdom of Christ, and propagation of his Gospel throughout the same, and all the Dominions thereof; That the good hand of God may be continued with us in perfecting his great works, which have been carryed on to so good a degree in *England* and *Ireland*; That all Differences among Brethren might be reconciled in love; That the Designs, Combinations and Conspiracies of all wicked men (whether within or without us) to imbroil this Nation in a New War, may be discovered and prevented; and that whilest ungodly men do make the Arm of Flesh their Confidence, We may testifie (from an abundant experience of the Lords Goodness) That our Strength is onely in the Living God: Be it therefore Enacted and Declared, That *Thursday* the last day of *February, 1649.* be appointed and kept as a Solemn day of Fasting, Prayer and Humiliation, for the ends aforesaid.

1650–S1   Fast day during negotiations with Charles II

[Sunday 7 April or another convenient day] 1650 (Scotland)

In January 1650, on request of the Scottish commissioner George Winram, Lord Liberton, Charles II invited the committee of estates and the commission of the general assembly to send commissioners to treat with him at Breda in the Low Countries. On 21 February, both bodies responded, nominating some of their members to travel to the king. Presumably because the commission was not due to meet again until May, the date of this fast was to be agreed and publicized by the presbytery of Edinburgh. That presbytery's minutes are not extant, but other presbytery registers show that Sunday 7 April was recommended (though Strathbogie observed 14 April instead).

Order: act of the commission of the general assembly, 22 Feb. 1650, *RCGA*, II, 379.
Additional sources: *RCGA*, II, 354–5, 367–73; HMC, *Leybourne-Popham*, pp. 59–61; presbytery of Paisley minutes, NRS, CH2/294/3, p. 69; presbytery of Elgin minutes, CH2/144/1, p. 276; *Strathbogie presbytery*, p. 136.

ORDER

Act of the commission of the general assembly: 22 February 1650
The Commission thinks fitt that there be a solemn Fast for a blessing to the travells of the Comissioners with his Majestie, beside the vther causes of our former humiliation, and refers the day to be given notice of by the Moderator and the brethren of Edinburgh, after conference with our Comissioners thereanent.

1650–S2   Thanksgiving day for victory over Montrose's forces at Carbisdale

Wednesday 15 May 1650 or the first convenient day after receipt (Scotland)

The marquis of Montrose raised forces in Scandinavia in the summer of 1649; they landed in Orkney in September, wintering there until the arrival of Montrose in March 1650. Encouraged by a letter from the king, Montrose ordered an invasion of mainland Scotland; his forces were defeated by David Leslie's army at Carbisdale on 27 April. In Edinburgh, this thanksgiving was observed on 15 May, on which day parliament reconvened to discuss the continuing negotiations with the king, and to try the captured Montrose. In the presbytery of St Andrews, the thanksgiving was kept on 23 May; in Strathbogie, the commission's act was not received until 5 June.

Order: act of the commission of the general assembly, 9 May 1650, *RCGA*, II, 380.
Letter: commission of the general assembly to presbyteries, 9 May 1650, *RCGA*, II, 380–1.
Additional sources: *A true relation of the happy victory* (Edinburgh, 1650; Wing T2996); *RPS*, M1650/5/1; HMC, *Leybourne-Popham*, pp. 73–4; presbytery of Paisley minutes, NRS, CH2/294/3, p. 73; presbytery of Elgin minutes, NRS, CH2/144/1, pp. 284–6; *Strathbogie presbytery*, p. 146; Nicoll, p. 11; Lamont, p. 18; *Inverness and Dingwall records*, pp. 188–9.

ORDER

Act of the commission of the general assembly: 9 May 1650
The Commission of Assembly appoynts Wednesday nixt, the 15th of this moneth, to be a solemne day of Thanksgiving for the late victorie in the North, in the defeating of James Grahame, and that the letter following, with the printed relation of the victorie, be sent to Presbyteries for that effect.

Commission of the general assembly to presbyteries: 9 May 1650
By the inclosed relation of the Lords great and mercifull deliverance of this Kirk
from the intended violence and oppression of that excomunicat traitor, James
Grahame, who, with the assistance of strangers and some vnnaturall contriemen,
had invaded the North parts of this Kingdome, yow will perceive how farre we are
ingaged to acknowledge and beare testimony to the goodnes and power of our God
for so wonderfull and seasonable a mercie. Therefore, that for this day of salvatioun,
amongst many vther former mercies, the Lord may have the praise and glory, to
whom it only belongeth, We have appoynted the fyftene day of this moneth to be
a day of publick and solemne thanksgiving in all your Congregations; and if this
advertisment come not tymely to your hands, yow shall take the nixt convenient day
thereafter …

1650–E2   Fast day following royalist successes

Thursday 13 June 1650 (England, Wales and Berwick-upon-Tweed)

On 16 May, the Rump parliament proposed a day of public fasting and humiliation
to be held on 13 June in respect of the nation's sins and 'the pernicious Deigns of
the Enemies of this Commonwealth'. The latter probably referred to Prince Rupert's
attack on the parliamentary fleet at Lisbon (13 April) and Charles II's alliance with
the Scottish presbyterians (treaty of Breda, 1 May). As with other recent days of
humiliation, the Rump appointed a committee to draw up a declaration. This was
read twice on 17 May and passed, after amendments, on the 21st. The declaration
was ordered to be read during the services and 10,000 copies of it were ordered to be
printed. John Owen, Joseph Caryl and William Strong preached before parliament;
none chose to have their sermons printed. According to Clopton, Mr Burrell, a local
minister, preached twice on the same text he had used for the previous fast (1650–
E1).

Order: parliamentary act, 21 May 1650, Wing E982*.
Additional sources: *CJ*, VI, 412, 414; *FSP*, XXXIII, 8–9; Clopton diary, 13 June 1650.

Act of parliament: 21 May 1650
Although this Nation hath enjoyed many Blessings, and great Deliverances from
the hands of God; yet have the People thereof multiplied their Sins, as God hath
multiplyed his Blessings upon them, especially the Sins of Unthankfulness and
Unfruitfulness, under such Gospel means and Mercies, which may most justly
provoke the Lord to multiply his Judgements upon this Nation. The Parliament
taking the same into serious consideration, as also the pernicious Designs of the
Enemies of this Commonwealth, to engage the same in a New and Bloody War; and
being truly sensible of their own inability to prevent or disappoint the same; and to
testifie, That their whole dependance is upon the Lord alone, and upon the Freeness
of his Grace in Christ, Do Enact and Ordain, and be it Enacted and Ordained, That

Thursday the Thirteenth of *June* next ensuing, be observed and kept in all Churches and Chappels in *England* and *Wales*, and the Town of *Berwick* upon *Tweed*, a solemn Day of Fasting and Humiliation for the fore-mentioned Sins, and for all other the Transgressions whereof this Nation is guilty; and for imploring the Favor of God, for a Blessing upon the Counsels and Endeavors of the Parliament, and upon their Forces by Land and by Sea; and that our gracious God would be pleased to give the People of this Nation a heart to serve him in sincerity; and to unite them against all Combinations and Practices of Forreign or Domestique Enemies to this Cause of God (which the Parliament hath, and shall by his Blessing and Assistance, maintain to the end) That so at last, through the Goodness and Mercy of God, this Commonwealth may be Established in all Truth and Peace, to the Glory of God, and Happiness of this Nation. And the Ministers of the respective Churches and Chappels aforesaid, are hereby required to give notice hereof on the Lords-day next preceding the said Thirteenth of *June*; at which time also the said Ministers are required to publish this present Act.

1650–S3 Fast day during fears of invasion by English Commonwealth forces and revival of Scottish royalists

Sunday 30 June 1650 or the first Sunday after receipt (Scotland)

This fast was appointed amid fears of an imminent invasion by Cromwell's English army. The causes also expressed a concern that the royalist insurgency would revive, despite the execution of Montrose on 21 May. On 29 April, the Scottish commissioners at Breda had invited Charles II to Scotland, although the king had failed to agree to all of the committee of estate's terms, and he was reluctant to swear the covenants. The fast was observed on Sunday 7 July at Largo, Fife, and later in Elgin.

Order: act of the commission of the general assembly, 21 June 1650, *RCGA*, II, 420.
Causes: *Causes of a publick and solemn humiliation* (Wing C4201bA; EUL, Df. 1.32(17)) [also in *RCGA*, II, 420–1].
Letter: commission of the general assembly to presbyteries, 21 June 1650, NRS, GD112/2/141/28/5 [not in *RCGA*].
Additional sources: *A seasonable and necessary warning concerning present dangers and duties* (Edinburgh, 1650; Wing C4258dA); presbytery of Elgin minutes, NRS, CH2/144/1, pp. 296–7; Lamont, pp. 20–1.

ORDER

Act of the commission of the general assembly: 21 June 1650
The Commission appoints a Fast to be keeped vpon the Sabboth cum eight dayes, the last of this instant, where advertisement cumes timeously, vther wayes the first Sabboth after advertisement, for the causes following:

CAUSES

The Lords dispensations hath often called this Land to Humiliation and Fasting, sometimes by fear of snares, sometimes by threatned violence; But the grounds of this holds forth an eminent degree of both these, as a fruit of many mis-spent and abused solemn occasions. And although we have no cause to faint, or cast away our confidence in any difficulty, yet we conceive it becomes all the Lords people throughout this Kingdom seriously to be humbled for these causes following,

I. First the great danger the land and work of reformation are into, by the sudden and unexpected approaching of the Sectarian Forces in our neighbour Kingdom of England; Which as it is without all cause or provocation from us, and inconsistent with the Oath of God, in the Solemn League and Covenant, and the large Treaty betwixt the Nations, So except the Lord prevent it, it threatnes no lesse then the ruine of this Kingdom and obstructing of the work of God within the same.

II. The present distressed Estate of the people of God in *England* and *Ireland* now groaning under the Tyrany of that partie, which should the more affect us, seeing if providence do not otherwayes dispose, ere long we our selves may be brought to the like or worse extremitie.

III. Beside the danger we are in from that party in *England*, we are not without the reach of hazard from the Malignant party; whose inveterate malice against the work of God holds them on to pursue the same designs hitherto by the blessing of God disappointed.

IV. Notwithstanding all these imminent dangers, the Land lies in security, ignorance, profanity and formality; little conscience[335] is made of the Oath of God in our solemn vowes, the guiltinesse of short-coming wherein, and the breaches wherof before the Lord pleads against Rulers, Ministers, Souldiers, and people of all sorts, beside the great unthankfulnesse for mercies old and late, and the great abounding of sorcery so common in many parts of this Kingdom.

Wee are therefore to pray,

I. That God would keep us from the danger of that proud party now in arms drawing towards our border, That wee may neither be infected by their errours, nor harmed by their violence, and that he would dis-appoint all their designs against this Land and the work of God, and break their yokes from off the necks of his people in our neighbour Kingdoms.

II. That he would purge the Land from profanitie, malignancy and all other our sins, stir up all sorts to their duty, direct and blesse them in it for the furtherance of his work and defence of his people, and that he may keep us straight therein, that enemies get no advantage by our declining from the Covenant either to the right hand or to the left.

III. That he would shew mercy to our King, and cause his wrath to cease from his Fathers house, and blesse the labours of our Commissioners with him, in bringing that Treaty to such a solid close, as we may be keeped from sin and snares, and he so brought to his Throne, as may be for the good of Religion and comfort of his people.

IV. That as hitherto the Lord has ever been for a defence to the Assemblies of his Kirk, so he would be pleased graciously to countenance this ensuing General Assembly both in the gathering and procedour thereof.

---

[335] 'conscience' in *RCGA*, II, 421; variously 'conscience' and 'constancy' on copies of Wing C4201bA.

LETTER

Commission of the general assembly to presbyteries: 21 June 1650

We have found a necessitie to appoynt a solemne fast & humiliation to be keeped upon the last day of this moneth of Junij Therfore you will make Intimation of it this next sabbath and if these come not to you tymouslie you will keepe some convenient day thereafter. Lett not this fast be any hind[r]ance or delay of your Comissioners coming to the assemblie but be carefull to sent them tymouslie ...

1650–E3 Thanksgiving day for Commonwealth victories in Ireland

Friday 26 July 1650 (England, Wales and Berwick-upon-Tweed)

Sir Charles Coote and General Venables, who had already secured much of Ulster for the Rump, launched a joint attack on the Ulster confederate army at Scarriffhollis on 21 June. After fierce hand-to-hand fighting, Coote ordered an attack on the Irish flank which made his enemies flee; they were chased and cut down for ten miles. The battle ended the confederate army in Ulster – most of its leaders and *c.* 3,000 men were killed – and opened up the whole of Ulster to the rule of parliament. On 9 July, the Rump received news of the victory and proposed a day of thanksgiving; a declaration and act were ordered to be drawn up by a committee of named individuals. The act was passed after two readings on 11 July; it and the lengthy declaration (*An act for the setting apart a day of publique thanksgiving*) were ordered to be printed. There was a notable innovation in the method of distribution: for the first time, the orders were sent across the country by post. William Bridge and John Bond were appointed to preach at St Margaret's, Westminster; neither chose to have their sermons printed.

Order: parliamentary act, 11 July 1650, Thomason E.1061[7]*, pp. 917–24 (partially extant also in Wing E1123aA).

Additional sources: *CJ*, VI, 438, 440, 442; *An act for the setting apart a day of publique thanksgiving, to be kept on Friday the twenty sixth of this instant July together with a declaration and narrative, expressing the grounds and reasons thereof* (1650; Wing E1123aA); *A declaration of the Irish armie in Ulster sent to the parlament in a letter from William Basill, esquire, atturney [sic] general of Ireland* (1650; Wing B1025); Lambert, *Printing*, p. 175; *FSP*, XXXIII, 9.

ORDER

Act of parliament: 11 July 1650

The mighty Wonders that God hath wrought in and for *England*, and the multitude of Mercies with which he hath followed the PARLIAMENT throughout, in this great Cause which they have undertaken, for Asserting and Recovery of their Just Rights and Liberties, with the Establishment of Truth and Righteousness, are always to be had in thankful Remembrance by us and our Posterities, and ought to endear this Commonwealth, after a most peculiar maner to seek the Lord, and become a People in whom his Soul may take delight. For he it is that hath removed our shoulders from the Burthen, and hath delivered us from Tyranny and Bondage; He hath gone forth with our Armies, and the Weapons that have been formed against us, He hath not suffered to prosper. A most eminent Example of this His Grace and Goodness to us, we have occasion at this time to Celebrate in respect of *Ireland*, where God hath

not onely begun his saving and delivering Work, to our Admiration, and the Astonishment of all our Enemies, but hath almost made an end, and that in a most glorious
and remarkable maner; so as we may truly say, The Lord hath soon subdued our
Enemies in that Nation, and turned his hand against our Adversaries; *The haters of
the Lord have been found lyars, and have not been able to stand in the day of Battel*;
but those Cruel and Blood-thirsty men have had his just Vengeance so seasonably
poured out upon them, that the Innocent Blood of the many Thousands Protestants
there slain since this Rebellion, hath been Revenged and Punished upon the prime
and eminent Actors of it. God (that *is unsearchable in his Councels, and in his ways
past finding out*) having called them to a strict Accompt, and *given them blood to
drink*, of which they were worthy, *that all Nations may fear before him*, and take
heed how they set themselves against him and his People. It is as yet very little more
then Twelve Moneths, when *Dublin* and *London-derry* were the onely considerable
places in all *Ireland*, that remained under the Power of the Parliament; and those
were so straightly block'd up and besieged by powerful Armies of the Enemies,
that there was nothing left, but marvellous & extraordinary appearances of God,
whereby to set them free, and make passage, & give footing unto the Army sent last
year from hence for the reduction of that Dominion; whose progress, by the Blessing
of God, hath been such, as that neither in Field nor Garison the Enemy is much
considerable. The particulars of this last great Mercy given unto the Parliaments
Forces under Sir *Charls Coot*, Lord President of *Connaught*, against the whole
Army of Irish Rebels in *Vlster*, commanded by the Popish Bishop of *Clogher*, have
been by an Express from the said Lord President, certified to the Parliament, and
are summ'd up in the Narrative following, and the Letters and Papers themselves
herewith, and heretofore printed and made publique.

   It having pleased God so to bless our Armies in *Lemster* & *Munster*, that the
enemy durst no longer keep the Field in those parts, The Irish Rebels (having
reduced themselves into a Body meerly Popish, putting all Protestants, of what
quality soever, from amongst them, and till when, they thought themselves less
capable of Success or any Blessing) look'd upon the Province of *Vlster* as the fittest
Refuge for their preservation and subsistence, where the Parliaments Forces lay
scattered in smallest proportion, and (as the nature of that large Countrey required)
at greatest distances, and where the Countrey was well-near wholly at their Devotion, the Papists (which in those parts are the most zealous, and therefore the first in
the Rebellion, and most bloody in the Execution) upon their own account entirely,
and the Scots upon their Kings, by whose Authority, and for whose Service this
Army was raised; and therefore as by the last years experience they were sure of
the Scots upon that Common Interest, so for their encouragement now, they did by
many Declarations disperst amongst the Scots, assure them of Security and Protection, if they continued to own the said Kings Authority. These Forces, which upon
the death of *Owen Roe O Neal*, were destitute of a Commander, were supplied with
Ever mac Mahon Bishop of *Clogher*, by Commission from *Ormond*, Authorized
thereunto by *Charls Stuart*, Eldest Son to the late King, into whose Service and
Protection they were taken, by a Treaty mentioned in the said Commission it self of
the said *Ormonds*, herewith Printed.

   This is that Army, which while it was under the Conduct of *Owen Roe* the last
year, did occasion some jealousies and reproaches upon the Proceedings of this
present Parliament, as if they had been taken into their Service, and that such bloody
Rebels should have been made use of against the Protestant Party of English and

Scots, then under the Command of *Ormond* and *Monroe*, that had declared them-selves against the Parliament of *England*, as Sectaries, and Murtherers of the late King: And great use was made thereof by Ministers and others, not affected to this present Government, to alienate the mindes of men from their duty to this Parlia-ment, and foment new Distractions and Divisions amongst us. But as we did then in the sight of God and sincerity of our hearts, vindicate our innocency in reference to any such Designs, as by the Votes we then passed doth appear; so the vigorous and constant opposition all along maintained against them, and the thorow execution now done by our Forces upon them, gives an undenyable evidence of our clearness therein, and leaves to future Ages, the marks of our just Indignation against them. This Army provided of this General about the end of *May* last, fell down into Sir *Charls Coot*'s Quarters, and presently took by storm a place upon the Frontier of *Vlster*, called *Dungeven*, where they put all to the Sword, except the Governor, whom they sent dangerously wounded to *Charlemont*; from thence they marched to *Bally* Castle, which was presently surrendred to them without opposition, by the treachery of some therein. These successes exceedingly puft up the Rebels, and made them considerable, not in their own eyes onely, but to the judgement of *Ormond, Clanrikard,* and the rest of their Party, who therefore advise their General, by all means to keep off from putting things to the hazard of a Battel, having hopes upon this foundation, and by the well managing of this so well begun Success, to recover again, not onely their late Interest in, but the whole Dominion of *Ireland*: For though the Army in effective force did not consist of above Six hundred Horse and Four thousand Foot, yet they were reckoned Fourteen Regiments of Foot, and had Officers of all degrees proportionable to that number, which by their Interest in the Countrey as aforesaid, and by the countenance of these successful begin-nings, they might reasonably promise themselves; & by them upon the place it is belived, that within a very few days they would have gathered in a force of Soldiers, answerable to those Officers: In the mean time, all the force that the Lord President of *Connaught* could draw into the Field to resist this powerful inroad (leaving the Garisons tollerably provided for) was but Eighteen hundred Foot, and Six hundred Horse, whereof One thousand Foot came up to him under Colonel *Fenwick*, but three days before he engaged the Enemy: But *England* may say as well as Israel, *It is as easie with the Lord to save with few as with many*; who was pleased to put such zeal and courage into the Soldiers of the Parliament, that on the One and twentieth of June last, they marched up towards this Army (so exceeding them in number, and heightned Resolution by late successes) as it lay Encamped near *Letterkenny* upon the side of a Mountain, inaccessible either for Horse or Foot; upon sight of which, the Enemy drew forth upon a piece of ground (being indeed inticed thereunto by the giving back of some of our Forlorn-Hopes (ordered for that purpose so to do) and though that ground were extreamly bad, yet it pleased God to put it into the hearts of our Forces, with that small Body to advance towards them, where they presently engaged them, and by the wonderful blessing of God, after an hours hot dispute, even to push of Pike, with great resolution on both sides, the Enemy was totally Routed, many of them killed upon the place, and the Execution pursued ten or eleven Miles every way that night; so as the number computed to be slain that day in the pursuit, and the next day, was Three thousand at the least, in which Action were slain and taken Prisoners most of their Officers, from the highest to the lowest, few escaping; and many of the Heads of the principal Septs or Families in that Countrey of the old Irish Rebels, some of whom are since Executed, and their

Heads set upon the Walls of *London-Derry*, for the terror of others, and as Monuments of Gods goodness in their overthrow; the most considerable of all which, so far as they were then discovered and known, are set forth in the List herewith printed. There were also taken in that glorious Day, all their Arms, Ammunition, Colours, Bag and Baggage, and most of their Horse; and though their General the Bishop got off with a Party, yet he was met with (so sure doth Divine Justice pursue, and overtake the men of Blood) and taken by Major *King* and his Troops near *Eniskellen*, whose Head was also sent for by Sir *Charls*, to accompany the rest of his wicked Accomplices at *Derry*. In this day of *Vlsters* Danger and Distress, it might reasonably have been expected, That the Scots (who notwithstanding their general defection from the Parliament to the contrary Party the last year, had yet enjoyed Peace and Protection from us) would have come out against this perfectly-Popish Army, and *help the* LORD *against the mighty*; but such was their ingratitude, and so great their hatred to them whom they term Sectaries, above what they bear to the worst of Papists, and the most bloody Rebels, as that they sate Neutral all the while, as reserving themselves to declare, and fal in with the Conqueror, which they also did accordingly.

In all this Business, the loss on our side was very small, so mercifully *did the* LORD *cover the heads of his servants in the day of Battel*; so as onely Captain *Sloper* of Colonel *Venables* Regiment, with eleven or twelve private Soldiers, were slain, and Colonel *Fenwick*, Major *Gore*, Captain *Gore*, and an Ensign, with some few others, wounded: And it is a thing most worthy Observation, That those who first began the Rebellion in that very Countrey of *Vlster*, and where they executed most Cruelty and Inhumanity, should be reserved for Gods Vengeance to be poured out upon them in that place; so that we may justly say, *Who is a* GOD *like our* GOD, *our enemies themselves being Iudges!* To him alone therefore be the Praise and the Glory.

Nor was this great Mercy more Wonderful then Seasonable, in regard of the terms wherein we stand to *Scotland*, and the Necessity of our Armies marching thither, amongst other things, for pursuing the Head of this Army of Popish and Irish Rebels, CHARLS STUART, Eldest Son of the late King, who being beaten out from his Confidences and Intimacies with the Popish Army in *Ireland*, by the wonderful Success which God hath been pleased to give our Army this year and the last, hath now no other Refuge left him but *Scotland*, where his hopes are (*Montross* also having run out his course, upon whose Assistance 'tis known he most affectionately depended) to do that by Stratagem and Deceit, with the Reformed Party, which he could not carry on by Force and Power, by means of the Popish Rebels, and purely Malignant Party; And thinks now, under the fair Vizard of Reformation and the Covenant (which he hath swallowed, like ill-pleasing Physick, for a desperate Cure) to raise up a Party for himself in this Nation also, for the Rooting up this present Government, and with it the English Liberty, Purchased at so high a Rate, and whatever else is near and dear to honest and good men: But the same God, who is mighty in Strength, and also wise in heart, and having shewn himself in Power to subdue open Enemies, will not suffer his Arm to be shortned, in his going forth against Hypocrites and false Friends, that he in all may be glorified, and his Praise spread abroad throughout the whole Earth.

Upon consideration of all which, together with the taking of *Trecroghan* about the same time, and other prosperous proceedings of our Forces in *Ireland*, The Parliament, for manifestation of their high and extraordinary Sense of so signal and seasonable Mercies, have thought it fit, and their duty, to set apart a time for publique and solemn Thanksgiving, to be rendred to the Lord, the Author of these Mercies: And they do therefore Enact and Ordain, That *Friday* the Twenty sixth of July, be observed and kept as a Day of publique and holy Rejoycing and Thanksgiving to the Lord, in all the Churches and Chappels, and places of Divine Worship within this Commonwealth of *England*, Dominion of *Wales*, and Town of *Berwick* upon *Tweed*; And that the Ministers of the respective Parishes and places aforesaid, be, and hereby they are Required and Enjoyned to give notice on the Lords-Day next preceding the said Twenty sixth of *July*, of the day so to be observed; to the end the People of their several Congregations may the more generally and diligently attend the publique Exercises of Gods Worship and Service there to be dispensed upon that occasion; At which time, that the People may be the more particularly and fully informed of this great Deliverance and Success, the said Ministers are hereby Required, and (under the Penalty set down in the *Resolves of Parliament* of the Ninth day of *July*, One thousand six hundred forty nine) Enjoyned to publish and reade this present Act and Declaration. And for the better observation of the day, the Parliament doth hereby inhibit and forbid the holding or use of all Fairs, Markets, and servile workes of mens ordinary Callings upon that day: And all Majors, Sheriffs, Justices of the Peace, Constables, and other Officers, be, and are hereby Enjoyned to take especial care of the due observance of the said day of Thanksgiving accordingly.

1650–S4   Fast days following the Commonwealth invasion of Scotland

[July–August] 1650 (Scotland)

On 22 July 1650, Cromwell's army entered Scotland. The general assembly, which sat until 24 July, appointed this observance, probably in response to the invasion. The presbytery of Strathbogie's minutes suggest that the assembly ordered its members to intimate the fast on 'the first day after ther return' to their presbyteries (*Strathbogie presbytery*, p. 150), with the consequence that different days were kept across the country. Paisley presbytery noted that the assembly had called for 'frequent fasting & humiliation in families, & in congregations' (NRS, CH2/294/3, p. 77), and appointed several days of humiliation for its area.

Order: act of the general assembly, *c.* 24 July 1650 (not printed; described in presbytery of Elgin minutes, NRS, CH2/144/1, p. 301).
Additional sources: presbytery of Paisley minutes, NRS, CH2/294/3, p. 77; *Strathbogie presbytery*, p. 150; *Life of Blair*, p. 232; *Inverness and Dingwall records*, p. 192.

DESCRIPTION OF ORDER

[Act of the general assembly, *c.* 24 July 1650]
The brethren … reported that they hade Intimate and keeped the fast appointed by the Generall Assemblie for the present great dangers wherin this kingdome is by the being of a strong and numerouse armie of Secta[ries] within the bosome of this kingdome, and for the causes of the pr[eced]ing fasts not removed, wherof the[y] hade gotten no advertisement till [after] the last meiting dissolved

1650–Ir1 Fast days during plague epidemic

Tuesday 6 August 1650 (army camp, garrisons at Clonmel, Youghal and Cork, and other places that receive the order in time); Tuesday 13 August 1650 and Tuesday 20 August 1650 (whole of Ireland)

On 30 July, the lord deputy of Ireland, Henry Ireton, ordered three days of fasting and humiliation in response to an outbreak of plague in Dublin, Wexford, Ross, Kilkenny, Carrick, Clonmel, Youghal and among the English armies in Leinster and Munster. The first day, 6 August, was to be observed in the army and in garrisons and other places that had received the order by that date; the further two days were to be observed both in these places (which accordingly had three fast days in total) and in the rest of Ireland (in practice, the additional areas that accepted the authority of the lord deputy, which thus observed two fast days). Despite the vicissitudes in the ordering process in England since 1642, the process in Ireland remained the same and special worship continued to be ordered by the Lord Deputy. The order included a lengthy account justifying the fast day. This stated that God had afflicted Ireland with plague in order to stir up the English to greater piety and better behaviour and to persuade 'the poor deluded Popish people' of Ireland of their 'malice and cruelty … [and] their continued abominable Treachery towards all that concur not with them in their own Superstitions, Idolatry and affected Ignorance, or indeed that worship not the Beast as they do'. Although there were no specific instructions about the format of religious services, the order stated that everyone must be involved in prayers and religious exercises and must abstain from food, worldly labour, sports and recreations. It was permissible to punish, by imprisonment or other means, those who neglected or actively flouted the fasts. The order also exhorted people not to be distracted by 'the Troubles and Temptations of their Brethren' in England and Scotland, probably an illusion to the continuing conflict between royalists and the Commonwealth in Scotland. The order was printed in Ireland and in London; the latter may have been so that it could be disseminated for propaganda purposes.

This occasion is significant for two reasons. It was the first occasion of special worship known to have been ordered in Ireland since 1642–Ir2 and only the eighth occasion since the break with Rome. Yet, it represented the start of a short, but intense, period of special worship in Ireland which probably owed much to Ireton's own religious beliefs and commitments: he ordered twice as many occasions in his two years as lord deputy as had been ordered in the previous twenty-five years. Second, it was the first time that any Irish order had been accompanied by an extensive account justifying the event, though this was common practice in England.

Order: order of the deputy general, 30 July 1650 (s.n., Cork, 1650; Wing I1030)*.
Additional source: Steele, II, no. 462.

ORDER

Order of the deputy general: 30 July 1650
It hath pleased the Lord our God, now a long while to stretch forth his heavy hand over this Nation in general, and the Inhabitants thereof, in those capital Judgements of the Sword and Pestilence (with somewhat of Famine also in many places;) and especially by that Plague of Pestilence (as with his *own* more *immediate hand*)

to sweep away, in a maner, whole Towns and Cities, and lay waste almost whole Countreys, and to spread the contagion throughout into all parts (as sadly is to be seen at this day) And that eminent hand of his (which *of late* was so heavy onely, or *chiefly,* upon *the Enemies* of his and his Peoples Cause, and upon others the Natives of the Land, with *distinguishing Mercy,* and forbearance towards those his poor creatures that serve him in that Cause) hath of late been extended to the taking away of many of them also, and not Soldiers onely, but many Officers (and more of them, in proportion, then of the other) as also many other *English Protestant people,* both of the ancient Inhabitants, and such as have more lately come over to us; and of all these, not onely the common sort, but many even of those that have more eminently professed his fear, and divers such as we have cause to esteem his own people, dear and precious in his sight, so as that former discriminating Mercy of his, seems now to be turned into *a general displeasure,* and universal Indignation: And his destroying Angel (striking here and there round about us) seems to come near to us, to the Doors, and even into the Houses or Tents of us that yet survive, even of those that are esteemed *best* amongst us. And thus those, whom he hath so wonderfully preserved and provided for in times and places of greatest hazard and scarcity, and owned both here and in *England,* in doing great things for them and by them, as yet he ceaseth not to do (*which I desire we and all his people may ever acknowledge to his praise,* and that his and our Enemies might to their conviction) Though he yet delivers them not over into the hands of men, but rather makes them still more and more Masters over their Enemies, and those that hate them, yet (as in some other kindes both of Diseases and Hardships, wherewith he hath formerly afflicted us, so in this now) he is pleased *to chastise* with his own hand, and taking away many (whether in Judgement for their own and our sins or unworthiness, or in Mercy, as from the evil to come) doth every way threaten and warn those of us that remain, and *calls upon all men every where to repent,* and not to think that those he hath thought fittest to take away, *were greater sinners then our selves,* but all of us to *search our hearts, and try our ways, and turn unto himself, that he may heal us, and have mercy upon us.* Now though none of the *works* of our God are without their grounds or ends, or without *their speakings and teachings* intended to the Sons of men, and especially to those whom he hath given eyes to see: And though in these cases of Judgements, no men (no not the most sanctified amongst us) need to seek far for causes more then sufficient of his just displeasure against them (further then Mercy through our Mediator Christ Jesus, and Faith in given him, turns it into Free-grace and favor) yet such *extraordinary dispensations, being not without their extraordinary grounds and ends,* It is the duty of all, and must needs be the desire and practice of the Faithful (through the grace and wisdom given them) to search in themselves, and humbly to seek from the Lord, that they may understand what those are, that in such dealings of his *he would have them especially take notice of.* And though such as have interest in the sure and everlasting Covenant of Mercy, need not, and so (so far as it is sealed unto them) they do not or ought not fear that God hath, or ever will break that Covenant, or take away those everlasting Mercies of his in Christ Jesus towards them, yet even such (considering how they through the flesh do unworthily abuse that Mercy, and all the gracious fruits thereof, and do many other ways provoke him) ought more then others (as *kindely children* toward *such a Father*) to be jealous of his just displeasure, and tenderly sensible of, and affected with any significations thereof, and most sollicitously to search and seek out (that they may be *kindely humbled for,* and *in future avoid*) *the occasions* thereof in themselves: And considering that in those things which concern our Temporary being, and the comfort or discomfort thereof (wherein he hath foretold he would correct even the seed of *David* (his chosen and anointed one) when they offend, *notwithstanding his sure Covenant for everlasting mercies,* which he would not break or take away) *He doth not vainly afflict nor grieve the children of men;* and then especially not those he hath adopted for his own, but does it *for some ends* of good towards them (as for *reproving, or restraining, for awakening, or quickning, for humbling, teaching or instructing, for purging or purifying, for trying or perfecting of them, &c.* as he findes *they need*) and of glory to himself in and from them, they ought not to be regardless and unsensible of, but carefully to observe each motion of his hand, and *pointing* of his finger, and to watch, study, and humbly to seek, that they may finde out his minde and meaning in all, and especially in such *signal dispensations* of his towards them, as these are, and may obtain the fruit to themselves, and render to him the glory he intends them for.

Having therefore (upon the aforesaid *eminent occasion,* given to my self and others in this Nation) some sense and consideration (through Grace) in my own heart concerning these things, and much more then I have the time or faculty to bring forth in suitable expressions, I thought good to commend the same to others, and provoke them to a further sense and consideration of them, and to a *diligent practice suitable thereunto,* leaving and recommending them to be further improved and *heightned,* both in my self and others, through the working of the same Spirit of Grace in Christ Jesus, by which alone, any such sense is wrought in me: And considering, that as the people of God ought to be sensible of, and duly affected with all the Judgements of God in the world (even against wicked men, and their enemies, so as to give glory to God in them *(which worldly men themselves will not)* to pray and intercede for Mercy and forbearance towards them (so far as may stand with his honor and good pleasure) and to be humbled under the consideration of their own equal unworthiness and ill-deserving (further then as infinite Mercy passeth by, or Grace makes a difference) and to take warning, and be bettered in themselves by such examples) so much more ought they, many other ways, to be affected, when they see God smite their fellows (those that are dear to him as themselves) and so, or otherwise, striking at or near themselves (which should, amongst other effects, awaken and stir us up to consider what, and how great those evils must be, that so provoke or engage God to seem (as it were, for the time) to act against the glory of his Mercy and Truth, to those that profess and trust his Name, for the *necessary vindication* of his Justice, and greater glory of his Mercy at the last) And that when his mighty hand is so eminently lifted up, as he expects and requires all the children of men should be humbled under it, and his own especially; so it becomes those that are so indeed, to express and declare it, both before Him, and his Angels, and Men, in all the ways he hath required or declared his acceptance of, and to take shame to themselves, and witness to his Righteous Judgements, and implore his mercy and forbearance; I do therefore commend unto all that have any thing of *true Christianity* in them, within this Dominion, the frequent exercise of Prayer with Fasting *(such as is without Super-stition)* and (suitable to the Faith, Simplicity, Truth and Purity of the Gospel) during the time of this our Calamity, with humble Acknowledgements and Confessions before God (to our shame and his glory) and fervent Intercessions (as the Spirit of Christ shall enable) in behalf of the many places and people of this Land, now so sadly visited and afflicted therewith; especially of *Dublin, Wexford, Ross, Kilkenny, Carrick, Clonmel* and *Youghall,* and the several parts of the Army throughout our

Quarters, in Garison or Field, especially in *Leinster* and *Munster,* That God would stay that his afflicting hand, and spare his poor people (*especially those that serve and truly seek him* in this Countrey and Cause) that he would shew us wherein we have especially offended, or do displease him; what his minde and meaning is towards us; what he would have us learn by these his loud and dreadful speakings, and (especially) what our carriage and dealings *should have been,* and what he would have it be, towards the *generality* of the people, and our Enemies here, whether in respect of *Justice (for innonocent Blood)* or of more *moderation* and mercy towards any; and that he would guide us in his way, to do according to his own minde therein; bow and bend our hearts to conform unto, and faithfully to follow and pursue what he shall teach us to be *his minde and will in all things;* and *give out a true Spirit* of Humiliation for, and universal Reformation of those many evils that abound amongst us, and a faithful zeal for it (especially in us the Officers towards those under our charge) and this as in respect of all evils, so especially of those that are most crying and prevailing (as Swearing, Blaspheming, Drunkenness, Plundring, Exaction and Cruelty towards people in protection (where any opportunity with hope of privacy is found) cursed Covetousness, and *Self-seeking* in general (the root of many other Evils) and neglect of God, his ways and worship) that he would every way *enlarge his Spirit* upon his poor Servants here, and advance the truth and *power of Godliness more* amongst us, make us a people fit for him to own, use and bless yet further in his Work, for good in the world, and not onely to destroy, and be destroyed; and would so take off his afflicting hand from us, and restore health and safety to us, and soundness within our Tents and Dwellings, and turn our *now required Mourning* into Praises; and also in behalf of the *poor deluded Popish people of this Nation* (captivated and kept in miserable darkness and bondage by their *seducing Priests and Leaders*) and, amongst them, even for our very Enemies, that all of them (so far as may stand with the good pleasure of God, and with the glory and *Righteousness of his Works and Judgements in the world*) may at length be made sensible of the *great weight* of so much crying innocent Blood, whereof (as principals or participants) they generally stand guilty; of their malice and cruelty (so far as they finde power and opportunity) and of their continued abominable Treachery towards all that concur not with them in their own Superstitions, Idolatry and affected Ignorance, or indeed that *worship not the Beast* as they do: And also of the eminent and glorious hand of God, exalted *so conspicuously and constantly* every where against them, for these and the many other Iniquities and Abominations abounding amongst them; so as from Conviction thereof, they may take shame and confusion to themselves and *their Idols,* and give glory to the living God; and (if possible) the wrath of God may be appeased towards them, and *not utterly destroy them and their Nation;* and that those of them who are capable of his eternal Mercies, may be truly and *spiritually humbled* under his mighty hand, taken off from the foundations of any Self-or-Creature-confidence, and brought to see, and finde the pure and free mercies of God in Jesus Christ; and, for that purpose, may have their eyes opened, and hearts enlarged to discern and embrace the *true light* and freedom of the *Gospel,* and be converted from their carnal conceptions to a spiritual reception thereof, *and from their vain Idols to the living God;* and in order thereunto (if the Lord have any purpose of a Church or People to himself to be called out amongst them) we may, through his Grace, be made instruments thereof, as well as of subduing their outward man; and (however) may so walk towards them and amongst them, both in word and life, as not to give them occasion of further offence, or stumbling at the Gospel we profess, or cause it to be the worse thought or spoken of amongst them.

And the same exercise of Fasting and Prayer, which I thus recommend for frequent use to those within this Nation (now more immediately concerned in the occasion of it) I do earnestly desire may be used for the same purposes and in the same behalfs (as God shall give freedom and opportunity) by other Christians of the Reformed Religion in other places (who shall take notice hereof, and whose hearts God shall touch with a fellow-feeling of our condition; to whom I desire our Judgments and our Shame may be as notorious, to the glory of God, as our Mercies and Successes) and particularly *by the Saints and Churches of Jesus Christ,* and those especially of the Army in our native Land *(our Brethren by double and treble relation;)* And, for those within this Dominion (that all, who have interest at the Throne of Grace, may at once meet there with their joynt cryes) I have thought fit (in the Place I stand in here) to Appoint, and do hereby Appoint accordingly, the first, second and third Tuesdays in the ensuing Moneth of *August,* to be kept and observed as times especially set apart for *Publique Humiliation* with Fasting and Prayer, upon the occasions, and for the ends and purposes before expressed: On the first whereof to begin the same at the Head-quarters or Camp, and at *Clonmel, Youghal, Cork,* and other Garisons and places to which notice hereof shall come before; and the second and third to be observed both at the same, and all other places (as notice hereof shall be further spread:) On which days at the several places as aforesaid respectively, I require all Officers (both Military and Civil, for those under their respective Charges) carefully to see to it, that there be a general abstinence, so far as comeliness and necessity will permit, from all worldly labors, bodily food, and other the outward comforts of this life (whereof our unprofitableness and iniquities, and particularly our usual excess in them, and over-valuing, or other abuse of them, render us most unworthy) as also from all sports and recreations; And likewise to take notice of, and punish (by Imprisonment, or other fitting Penalties proportionably to the Offences) not onely such as shall contemptuously do to the contrary hereof, but also any such as shall be found (from Idleness, or from contempt or slighting of Religion, or *of the hand of God* in his present dispensations) to neglect the joyning with others in Prayer and Religious Exercise, to the purposes aforesaid, in one place & Society or other (not according to the Popish way:) And I exhort all *true* Professors of the Reformed Religion, in the fear and dread of God, for the love of Jesus Christ, and from the bowels of Charity, and fellow-feeling of each others Miseries, to be *seriously affectionate in this Exercise;* and that in their Addresses to the Throne of Grace for the aforesaid concernments of their own, they be mindeful also of the *Troubles and Temptations of their Brethren,* wherewith they are conflicting (though in differing kindes) in other Nations, and especially in *England* and *Scotland;* where (besides many other both Iniquities and Judgements) that most sad and abhorred evil is now more then ever to be found, and further to be feared, That *Brethren,* professing, and in each party some (as there's reason to believe) really having the same Faith, and hope of the Gospel, and the same Cause of Common Concernment (against the world of enemies to Christ, his Spirit and Kingdom, that thirst and watch to destroy both parties) yet (either from offence and weakness, or peevishness, or from worldly interest) not onely have been and are loaded and wounded (the one part by the other) with foul and hateful reproaches (to the dishonor and scandal of the Gospel, and the rejoycing and advantage of those their Enemies) and provoked one at the other, and one of them *to take the interest and assistance of the said Enemies,* against the other, and to execute (the one upon the other) that destruction, by those Enemies designed against both; which *sad spectacle (most grievous to every true Christian heart)* as it calls for *deepest* Humiliation on *both* parts (*especially* on that whence the cause hath been most given, or the offence with least cause and most impatience taken) so it requires most earnest Prayer and Intercession to our God and Father of those that are faithful on either part (which I desire accordingly in these our Exercises may be used) that, for the Merits and Mediation, and by the Power and Spirit of his Son Christ Jesus (our Lord, Head, and eldest Brother, *the great Reconciler* and Peacemaker *betwixt God and Man,* and amongst men, his Members, each with other) and from his Fatherly bowels and pity towards his weak and froward children, he would now in the extremity of time appear, and mercifully interpose and *bring forth some expedient (when men can or will finde none)* to avoid and hinder (if it be his will) *this hateful and dreadful evil* and mischief; and for that purpose would put forth and enlarge, in all that are his children *in both Nations,* that sweet Spirit of Peace and Love (as well as Righteousness and Judgement) which is his Sons; to convince and reprove every one of them for their several offences and evils, that any way occasion this or lead to it; and to overpower and work them unto *a disposition of giving and receiving* satisfaction, and of bearing and forbearing towards each other (and that especially in the stronger towards the weak) and every one (as far as they have been faulty givers, or impatiently and unjustly takers of the offence) to take shame to themselves, and give glory to God; and that so he would pardon the sin, take away the offences, and *heal the breaches betwixt his people,* and discover the hypocrisie, and defeat the designs of those his enemies (that watch the advantage for the ruine of them all, and to raise thereupon their own corrupt interests against Godliness and Honesty) that none that have interest in Jesus Christ, may further be drawn into, or proceed in any Engagements to the destruction of their Brethren, the opposing of his *Spiritual Kingdom* and work in the world, or the partaking with those parties and powers that are enemies thereunto: But (if it be his good pleasure, and he see it conducing to the glory of his work at last, That there should be any such Engagement, even to Blood and further War) That then (pardoning the weaknesses and failings) he would still witness to the integrity and simplicity of those his poor Servants in this same *old Cause of His,* who have (through his Grace) followed him therein, *according to their light,* with faithfulness, to the *original Grounds,* substance, and principal ends thereof, with least mixture of their own, or other worldly corrupt interests, in the prosecution of it, and with truest desires and endeavors for the suppressing or restraining of the Common Enemies thereof, for the Deliverance, Protection and Advancement of those that love and fear the Lord, and wait for his appearance; and in the mean time, for preserving amongst all such the unity of faith in the bond of peace and love: And that if he shall yet see it good to compleat, or prosecute any further the outward Victories of his people, against their outward Enemies and Oppressors in the world, he would glorifie the Power and Vertue of the Spirit of his Son in them, now at last, in giving them (through it) to overcome spiritually the Temptations of prosperity, and of the good things of the world, as hitherto it hath been, by their overcoming all Tryals and Sufferings in the evils thereof.

Now lastly, for the better and speedier communication of what is herein required or desired, I do hereby further Appoint the same to be Printed and Published.

1650–E4 Thanksgiving prayers for Commonwealth victories at Carlow, Waterford and Duncannon

Sunday 1 September 1650 (London, Westminster, the late lines of communication and weekly bills of mortality); Sunday 15 September 1650 (elsewhere in England, Wales and Berwick-upon-Tweed)

The remaining Irish forts in southern Ireland surrendered to the Commonwealth's forces: Carlow on 24 July, Waterford on 6 August after a week-long siege and nearby Duncannon fort on the 12th. This destroyed both the confederate army in the south and Irish loyalty to its leader, Ormond. The Rump parliament received news of these victories on 27 August, proposed a thanksgiving and commissioned Thomas Scott to prepare a declaration outlining the grounds for the day. This was presented on 30 August when, after two readings, it was passed and 12,000 copies of the declaration were ordered to be printed.

Order: parliamentary order, 30 Aug. 1650, Wing E1691*.
Additional sources: *CJ*, VI, 459–60; order in parliament, 30 Aug. 1650, SP25/88, p. 39.

ORDER

Parliamentary order: 30 August 1650

Ever since that Wonderful and unexpected Victory, which the Lord was pleased the last Summer to give unto a small Party of the Parliaments Forces then in *Dublin*, against that numerous and potent Army under *Ormond*, which was a Door of Hope to the Parliament, and their Army then on their way for *Ireland*, That the Lord, who had made so open a way for them, would vouchsafe his Presence with them, to carry on and perfect that Work which himself had so eminently begun in that admirable Providence, wherein he had, as it were, by a Worm threshed the Mountains: The same gracious Hand hath gone along from time to time with his Servants there, vouchsafing them many Victories, giving in many strong Cities, Towns, Castles and Garisons into their hands, raising up their Spirits, overcoming great Difficulties, furnishing seasonable Supplies, and dismaying the hearts of the Enemies, and that in such a Series of continued Successes, as is just matter of high Admiration, and perpetual Thankfulness in all that truly fear the Lord, and love his Cause and People. And seeing every Addition of Mercy, is a further Obligation to Thankfulness and Duty; and that the Lord hath been pleased, as a further Manifestation of his Goodness, to give up into the hands of the Parliament Forces there, *Carlo*, a Garison of much Strength and Importance; *Waterford*, a great and populous Town, and the most considerable Harbor in all *Ireland*, upon Saturday the Tenth of *August* instant; together with the strong Castle of *Duncannon*, since likewise Surrendred upon Articles: The Parliament of *England* have thought fit not to let such great Mercies pass, without an especial return of Thankfulness, but to publish the Narrative thereof, as it comes to us in a Letter from the Deputy General of *Ireland*; (*viz.*) The effect whereof is as followeth: The Deputy having received at the late Leaguer before *Catherlagh*, several Alarms of great Forces of the Enemies rising and appearing within the Counties of *Cork, Kerry, Limrick* and *Tipperary*, to the distressing and endangering of our Parties and Garisons in those parts; where the Enemy threatned to destroy our Quarters, and probably designed a conjunction of their most considerable

Forces, in order to the Relief of *Waterford*, and an Attempt upon that small party that was left to Block it up; after he had disposed divers of his Forces to secure *Carrick*, to repel and oppose the Enemy in *Carbery*, and the Western parts, and to march to the Relief of our Forces in *Kerry* and *Limrick*, leaving Sir *Hardress Waller* with the Body of the Army, to carry on the business about *Catherlagh*, did himself draw down with a small party of Foot towards *Waterford*, to Beleaguer it more straitly: Coming before *Waterford* with those Foot, and some small parties left there before, to Block it up at a distance, applied himself to a closer Siege of it, making two Quarters within shot of their Walls, which with our Foot at the Abbey on the other side of the Water, kept them close within the Town on every side; and then trying them with a Summons, the Enemy within so despised our small Numbers, as that they made an offer, as if they durst set open one of their Gates, and let in all our Foot to make the best of it: And to that being answered, It was but a vain Brag, and they durst not make it good; they in Reply, for their Honors sake, seemed to adhere to their former Vanity, but with such conditions and cautions, as they might be sure would not be accepted: But that the Power of God might appear in our despised Weakness against this Pride of Man, These Sons of Honor, as they would be thought, did even in both the same Letters, unequally subjoyn to these high Vapors, an offer of Treaty for Surrender: During which time, News came from *Catherlagh*, That it had pleased God, beyond, or much before Expectation, upon our Mens Battering, and then taking by Storm (without Loss on our part) a small Tower on their Bridge over the *Barrow*, to bring down the Enemies hearts to a Treaty, and Surrender of that strong and important Place. Hereupon the Deputy conceiving *Waterford* to be attemptible by force in one or two places, though otherwise exceedingly fortified: while preparations were made for that Attempt, the Lord wrought upon the hearts of the Enemy to desire a Treaty, without their terms of Honor, which formerly they insisted on; by which, after high Demands, rejected on our part with Indignation, they were on Tuesday the Sixth of this instant *August*, brought to Surrender upon Articles, which was performed on Saturday following; At which time there marched out about Seven hundred men well armed, the Townsmen more numerous then before was believed, and the Town better Fortified in all parts, and more difficult to be attempted then our Forces conceived, there being many private Stores, sufficient to have maintained them a long time: whereby we may see the Hand of God, in over-powering the hearts of the Enemy, which was the onely cause of their present Surrender. By this of *Waterford* and *Catherlagh*, God was pleased to extend his Hand toward *Duncannon*, the Enemy there (though a Priest were Governor) having on the same Saturday, with Colonel *Cooks* leave, sent one to *Waterford*, to see whether it were Surrendred, did on the Eleventh of this Moneth desire a Treaty, which produced, through the same Divine Mercy, a Surrender of the same Castle of *Duncannon*, upon Articles, on Saturday the seventeenth of this Moneth; since which time, the strong Garison and Castle of *Charlemount* is likewise Surrendred, whereby the whole Province of *Ulster* is now intirely in the Power of the Parliament.

For all which great Mercies, the Parliament doth Order and Appoint, That all Ministers of the several Congregations within the Cities of *London* and *Westminster*, and the late Lines of Communication, and Weekly Bills of Mortality, do in their respective Churches and Chappels return humble Thanks unto Almighty God, on the next Lords-Day, being the First day of *September* next: And all Ministers of all other Churches and Chappels within *England*, *Wales*, and Town of *Berwick* upon *Tweed*, do upon that day Fortnight, being the Fifteenth day of the said Moneth of

September, render Thanks to God for the same. And that upon the said respective days, all and every the said Ministers do Reade this Order and Narrative in their said Congregations, immediately after the Psalm before the Sermon, for the better stirring up of the hearts of the People to praise God for the same.

1650–S5   Fast days after Scottish defeat at the battle of Dunbar

September 1650, at the appointment of presbyteries (Scotland)

On 3 September 1650, the Scottish army was defeated by Cromwell's English forces at Dunbar in East Lothian. The English victory provoked panic in Edinburgh, prompting an evacuation of civil and ecclesiastical officials. Before a quorum of the commission of the general assembly could be assembled, a few of its members, together with other ministers who had been with the army, sent the causes of a fast to presbyteries. Although the commission, meeting at Stirling, approved this action on 11 September, some ministers, notably in the synod of Fife, objected to the causes, seeing them as the work of a small faction. Most controversially, the causes reflected hard-line ministers' dissatisfaction with the agreement with Charles II (see 1650–S3), and their distrust of the king, who had reluctantly sworn the covenants and landed in Scotland on 24 June. James Wood of St Andrews, who had been one of the Kirk's commissioners to Charles at Breda (see 1650–S1), successfully requested that article two of the causes be changed. According to Balfour, the original text had read: 'Togider with the crooked and precipitant wayes that wer takin by our commissioners for carinng one the trettey with the King' (Balfour, IV, 108). The dates on which the fast was to be observed were to be determined by presbyteries.

Order: act of the commission of the general assembly, 11 Sept. 1650, *RCGA*, III, 48–9.
Causes: *The causes of a publick fast and humiliation* (Aberdeen, James Brown; Wing C4201C)*, pp. 3–6 [also in *RCGA*, III, 49–52].
Letter: commission of the general assembly to presbyteries, 12 Sept. 1650, Wing C4201C*, pp. 7–9 [also in *RCGA*, III, 54–6].
Additional sources: *RCGA*, III, 43–8, 56–8; *RPS*, A1661/1/69; presbytery of Elgin minutes, NRS, CH2/144/1, p. 304; Balfour, IV, 98–108; *Life of Blair*, pp. 245–6; Lamont, p. 23; Nicoll, p. 34.

ORDER

Act of the commission of the general assembly: 11 September 1650
The Commission of Assembly, vnderstanding that the brethren, mett here before the meeting of the Commission, found it verie necessarie that at this tyme the whole land should be humbled before the Lord in respect of the great wrath appearing against the same, and that they did draw some grounds and causes for a Fast and humiliation, and did send them to Presbyteries, recommending to them to observe a day of humiliation for the same; The Commission, having considered those reasones and Causes, doe approve thereof, and appoint the same to be sent to Presbyteries that did not receave them before; tenour of which Causes follow.

CAUSES

Albeit the Solemn Publick Humiliations, hath bene much slighted, and gone about in a formall way, by many in this LAND: So that it is not one of the least of our provocations, that wee haue drawn near to GOD with out[336] mouthes, and kept our hearts far away from Him. For which the LORD hath turned the Wisdom of the Wyse, into Follie; and the Strength of the Strong, into Weakness. Yet, seeing it is a duetie, that hath often proven comfortable vnto vs; Unto which GOD now calleth vs in a speciall way, by a singular dispensation, and knowing that all that are acquainted with GOD in the LAND, will make conscience of it; Wee conceaue it expedient, the whole LAND bee humbled, FOR THE CAUSES following:

The continued ignorance and profanitie of the Bodie of the Land; And the obstinacie and incorrigibleness of many; not-with-standing all the payns that GOD hath taken vpon vs, by His WORD, and by His Works, of Mercie and Iudgement, to teach vs, in the knowledge of His Name and Way, and to reform vs, from the evill of our wayes.

II The manyfold Provocations of the Kings Houss; Which we fear are not yet throughly repented of; nor forsaken of him, to this day: Together with the crooked and praecipitant wayes, that were taken by sundry of our States-men, for carrying on the Treatie with the King.

III The bringing home with the King a great many Malignants; and endeavouring to keep some of them about him, and many of them in the Kingdom yet; not-with-standing of Publick Resolutions, to the contrarie.

IV The not purging of the Kings Familie, from Malignant and Profayn men; and constituting the same of Well-affected and Godly persons; Al-be-it it hath bene often pressed vpon the Parliament and Commissioners of Estates; and vndertaken, and promised, to bee performed by them.

V The levying of a most Profane and Malignant Gaurd of Horses, to bee about the King: Who being sent for, to bee purged some two dayes, before the Defeat, were suffered to bee, and fight in our Armie.

VI The exceeding great slackness of many, and aversness, & vntowardness of some, in the chieff judicatories of the Kingdom; And in the Armie, in good Motions, and Publick Dueties: Especially, in these things that concern the Purging of judicatories & the Armie, from Malignant, and Scandalous persons: And not filling all Places of Power and Trust, with men of known integritie, and of Blameless and Christian Conversation: Together with greater inclinations, and endevours, to bring & keep in Malignants, to the judicatories, and the Armie; As though the Land could not bee guyded, nor defended, without these; And great repyning, and crying out agaynst all that is done, in the contrarie; And studying to make the same vneffectuall.

VII The exceeding great Diffidence of some of the chieff Leaders of our Armie; And others amongst vs: Who thought, That wee could not bee saved, but by a numerous Armie: And who when wee had gotten many thousands together; Would not hazard to act any thing; Not-with-standing that GOD offered sundry fayr opportunies, and fitted the Spirits of the Souldiours, and for the carnall confidence, that was in many of the Armie, vnto the despysing of the Enemie; and promised Victorie to themselues, without eying GOD.

---

[336] 'our' in *RCGA*, III, 49.

VIII The Loosness, Insolencie, and Oppression, of many, in the Armie; And the little, or no care, that was taken by any to preserue the Corns: By which it hath come to pass, that very much of the Food of the Poor people of the Land, hath bene needlessly destroyed: And whylst wee remember this, wee wish, that the Profanitie and Oppression of sundry of our Officers, and Souldiours, in ENGLAND; Whylst wee were fighting, for the Assistance of the Parliament of that Kingdom, may not bee forgotten, Because as it was matter of great Stumbling to many in the Land: So is it lyke, That it is one of the CAUSES of the LORDS Indignation, now manifested agaynst vs, by the hands of these men.

IX Our great Unthankfulness, for former Mercies, & Delyverances: And, even for many Tokens of the LORDS Favour, and Goodness, towards our present Armie; whylest they were together; and the great Impatience of Spirit, that was to be seen in many these weeks past; which made them to limit the LORD, and complayn; and weary of His Delay, to giue Delyverance.

X The owning and eying of the Kings Quarrell, and Interest, by many, without Subordination to Religion, and the Liberties, and Safties, of these Kingdoms.

XI Next, the Carnal Selfe-seeking, and crooked-wayes, of sundry of our judicatories, and Armie; Who make their places and imployments, rather a matter of Interest, Gayn, and Praeferment to themselues, than of advancing Religion, & Righteousness, in the Land.

XII The not putting difference, betwixt those that serue GOD, and those that serue Him not, in our Services, our Company, and Imployments; But accounting all men alyke, many tymes praeferring those, who haue nothing of GOD in them.

XIII And lastly: The Exceeding Great Neglect, That is in Great Ones, & others; in performing of Dueties, in thier Families: Not-with-standing of our former acknowledgement of this Sinne: As also, The Neglect of Dueties, of Mutuall Edification, & great Fruitlessness, and Barrenness, that is to be seen in al sorts of persons; together with the folowing of Dueties, with a great deall of mixture, of Carnall Affections, and Fleshly Wisdom; Which grieveth the Spirit of GOD; And taketh away much of the LORDS Image, from our judicatories; As wee would bee humbled for these things: So would wee also intreat the LORD; That Hee would sanctifie this sad Affliction, to His People, That they neither despyse His Chastisments; nor faynt, when they are rebuked of Him: But that they may bear His Indignation patiently; And cleaue steadfastly, to the TRUETH, & the COVENANT, & the CAUSE of GOD: Without yeelding to the Furie of the Enemie; Or receaving their Errours; or complying either with them on the one Hand; or Malignants on the other Hand: And, That the LORD would powr out His Spirit, vpon His People; That their Spirit may bee raysed vnto their Duetie: And that they may bee fitted, and furnished of GOD, with Wisdom, and Resolution, to act agaynst their Enemies; For the Honour of GOD, and their own Praeservation: And, That the LORD will not suffer them to bee tempted, aboue that they are able to bear: But that Hee would break the Yoak of their Oppressours from off their Necks; And giue them Salvation, and Delyverance: AMEN.

LETTER

Commission of the general assembly to presbyteries: 12 September 1650

Wee perswade our selves, that ere this come to your hands, you are deeply affected with the sadde report of the Lords displeasure, declared against the Land by the

Defeat of our Armie, instant September 3. And by the woeful consequences & desolation which is lyke to ensue therevpon, if the tender Mercies of the Lord do not speedily prevent vs, and move Him, for His Names sake, to lift up a Standart agaynst that Enemy, which is now come in as a flood vpon vs, and is prevayling and rageing in our bosoms. And wee doubt not, but you are seriouslie bethinking your selves about your duety, and what the Lord is calling you to as the watchmen of His people in so dark a tyme. Wee beleeve you haue gotten the Letters sent to you from such Members of the Commission, and other Ministers who had beene with the Armie bearing their advyce for keeping of a Solemn publique Humilation with your severall flocks, according to the CAUSES which were sent you. The Commission being now mett, thought good to wryte vnto you, and requyre you in the Lord, as wee do also confidently expect of you, that you will be carefull and diligent, to make your people sensible of the Lords Hand, that they do not dispyse & slight so great a wrath; so to stir up, & encowrage them to the dueties, which this tyme and the Lords dispensation calleth for at their hand; that men bee not found now with their hands vpon their loyns, as women in travail, fainting under the chastising and rebukes of the Lord: for though it bee the day of Iacobs trouble, hee shall bee saved out of it, for we are not to doubt, but if wee shall return and seeke the Lord with all our heart, after all this that is come vpon us, that there is hope in Israel, concerning His work and people which are in the dust for the tyme. In a speciall way, wee do recommend to you, that you do carefully and instantly warne your people, agaynst the snares, which they for their tryall may meete with, to draw them to complyance with the present Enemy, their errors and way: and that they patiently wayte on the Lord, vntill the indignation passover, and not feare their feare, neyther be dismayed, but would sanctifie the Lord God in their hearts, that He may be their feare and their dread, so that they do not for their safety & preservation choyse the courses of flesh and blood, tending eyther to complyance with Sectaries on the one hand, or Malignants on the other. But that the work of God may be carryed on, and His people may, follow & adhere vnto it in their stations & places according to the Covenants & former grounds, & principles. We conceive, that these who feare the Lord and make conscience of duety, & desyr to be faithful, wil be so far from slacking their hands in their duety, & in a straight way of persueance therof for any thing that hath befallen now, that they wil rather look vpon themselves, as called & obliedged to their duetyes, in a more speciall way of strictnes and watchfullness than formerly, and that the present difficulties and dangers of the tyme, be not abused for flattering of men in any way, that may tend to turning aside to crooked courses. And because the Lord is trying vs, how far we wil follow our duety, in the fayth of His strength, in a weak & low condition; & there being som endevors at this tyme for making vp the Army, We expect that you will not be wanting in your stations, according to your power, for furthering of the levies appoynted by the Committy of Estates, & for the speedie returning of such Officers & Souldiers, who are come home, since the Armie was broken, also such of your own number, who were appoynted to wayte vpon Regiments of horses, & are now at home, your selves would appoint to repair with all diligence to Sterling, where the Randivouss is appointed: for there is of every Regiment a considerable number remaineing, and are together here, and about, without Ministers, though this be a time wherein they have most neede of them. Thus praying the Lord to powre out upon His people and servants through-out the land, such a measure of the lyf and consolation of His Spirit, as may furnish them, for their duetyes & tryalls, at such a time as this.

1650–E5 Thanksgiving prayers for Commonwealth victory at the battle of Dunbar

Sunday 8 September 1650 (within the lines of communication)

Cromwell, appointed to lead the Commonwealth's army in Scotland after Fairfax had resigned his commission, initially enjoyed little success and was unable to draw the Scottish army out of Edinburgh. However, in early September the main Scottish forces, under David Leslie, positioned themselves near his army at Dunbar, and on the morning of 3 September Cromwell executed a surprise attack on the Scots which, after two hours of fighting, gave him victory. He probably exaggerated in claiming that his army had killed 3,000 men and captured 10,000 others, but his ability to gain victory against overwhelming odds contributed to Dunbar being regarded as his finest victory. On receiving the news on Saturday 7 September, while parliament was not sitting, the council of state immediately ordered that the account of the battle should be printed and distributed by the lord mayor to all parish churches within easy reach, and that it should be read out and thanksgivings expressed during the next day's Sunday services. Later during its meeting, the council appears to have received fuller news of the scale of the victory and a printed copy of the *Brief narrative of the great victorie*, and so expanded its order and resolved to ask parliament to appoint a general thanksgiving day, for which see 1650–E5.

Order: orders of the council of state, 7 Sept. 1650, SP25/9/77 (*CSPD 1650*, p. 330).
Additional sources: *A brief narrative of the great victorie, which it hath pleased God to give to the armie of this common-wealth against the Scots armie, near Dunbar, in Scotland, on Tuesdaie morning, the third of this instant September, related to the council of state by an express messenger of the lord general, sent from the armie; which messenger was present at the action* (1650; Wing B4613).

ORDER

Orders of the council of state: 7 September 1650
The relation of the success of the army against the Scots to be printed and sent to the lord mayor, and he desired to order the publication thereof to-morrow, in all the parish churches within the lines of the communication, and thanks to be returned to God for his great mercy shown to this nation, in that happy success.
…
It having pleased God to give the army of the commonwealth now in Scotland a great victory against the Scots, and the Parliament not now sitting, it is ordered that the following brief narrative be published in all churches and chapels within the late lines of communication to-morrow, that thanks may be given for so great and wonderful a mercy, until Parliament shall give order for a more general and solemn thanksgiving; and that the lord mayor and sheriffs of London cause this narrative to be distributed in all the said churches and chapels, and all the ministers thereof are required to publish the same.

1650–E6 Thanksgiving day for Commonwealth victory at the battle of Dunbar

Tuesday 8 October 1650 (England and Wales)

When the Rump Parliament reconvened on 10 September, it accepted the proposal of the council of state for a general day of thanksgiving (see 1650–E5). As usual, MPs ordered a committee to draw up a narrative; this was completed and the bill passed, after two readings, on 17 September. The council of state was ordered to ensure that the act and narrative were distributed to the sheriffs outside London and to report back to parliament. Joseph Caryl and John Owen were appointed to preach before parliament at St Margaret's, but were replaced, at some point, by William Strong and Thomas Brooks (St Thomas Apostle, London). Isaac Knight was appointed to preach at St Martin's-in-the-Fields, and the lord mayor and the commissioners for the local militias were ordered to ensure that all parishes in and around London were supplied with sufficient preachers to preach on the day. It appears that observance of the thanksgiving was patchy. Clopton noted in his diary that it was 'observed by very few' in Essex; he himself 'stayd at home all day'. In October, Thomas, Lord Grey informed the council of state that the thanksgiving had not been widely observed in Leicestershire and that 'the best affected' in the county wanted the council to address 'such Contempt' otherwise 'it may produce many Inconveniences'. Two weeks later, the council ordered the lord mayor and the commissioners of the local militias to report to them the names of ministers who had refused to observe the day.

Order: parliamentary act, 17 Sept. 1650, Thomason E.1061[17] [also in *The acts of the parliaments of Scotland*, ed. Thomson and Innes, VI: 2, 806–9].
Additional sources: *CJ*, VI, 464–5, 468, 484; *Fast sermons*, XXXIII, 10; *An act for setting apart Tuesday the eighth of October next, for a day of publique thanksgiving* (1650; Thomason E.1061[17]); *Die martis, 17 Septembr. 1650. ordered by the parliament, that the sheriffs ... send to the ministers ... the act for setting apart Tuesday the eighth day of October* (1650; Wing E1749bA); Clopton diary, 8 Oct. 1650; Lord Grey to the lord president of the council of state, 13 Oct. 1650, Zachary Grey, *An impartial examination of the fourth volume of Mr Daniel Neale's history of the puritans* (1739), p. 450; council of state, 8 Nov. 1650, SP25/12/65 (*CSPD 1650*, p. 421).
Printed sermons: Brooks, parliament (Wing B4949; *FSP*, XXXIII, 298–327); Fenwicke, Sherburn (Wing F721); Homes, Christ Church, London (Wing H2576).

ORDER

Act of parliament: 17 September 1650

If any Nation in the World hath at this day upon them mighty and strong Obligations unto the Lord, for his peculiar Manifestations of Mercy and goodness unto them; wherein he hath filled with Admiration and Astonishment, all that have been Spectators and Observers of the out-goings of his Power, in Deliverances and Preservations; It is the Parliament and People of *England*, in the midst of whom the Lord hath walked most eminently for these Ten years last past, and constantly exercised them, by various and wonderful Providences; being pleased to make use of a few weak and unworthy Instruments, contemptible in the eyes of men, to bring great things to pass, and carry on his own Work, that the Power might appear to be of God, and not of Man; and this in the weakest and lowest conditions of his Servants, when we have been reduced to the greatest Straights, and had, as it were, *the sentence of death in our selves*; and our Enemies heightned and hardned by their Power and

Multitudes, in their Confidences, even to Pride and Arrogance, ready to swallow us up and destroy us: So that upon most of the Victories vouchsafed unto us, there hath been written in broad and visible Characters, *This hath God wrought, Thus far hath God helped us.*

And as it is the duty of all persons in this Commonwealth, especially those that fear the Lord, to observe these his marvellous and gracious Dispensations, and be taught by them not onely to submit unto, and close with the Actings and Appearances of the Lord (*who worketh all things according to the Councel of his own Will*) but to be enlarged in Rejoycings and thankful Acknowledgements, and to trust him in like straights for time to come; So the memorial of such Mercies and glorious Deliverances of the Almighty, deserve to be transmitted to Posterity, and for ever recorded unto his Praise.

In the Number of these, and as that which may have the first place, The Parliament is most exceedingly affected with the late Wonderful and gracious dealing of the Lord, towards their Army under the Command of their present General, General CROMWEL in *Scotland*, and with the glorious Victory which he hath there wrought for them in an unexpected season against the *Scots*: For which inestimable Blessing of God unto the Parliament and People of *England*, enriched with so many remarkable circumstances, that all along evidence his Divine Presence, this Commonwealth can never be sufficiently thankful; especially if it be considered, That in this is given in a Seal and Confirmation from Heaven, of the Justice of our Cause, and of the Sincerity of his Servants, that are his unworthy Instruments in the carrying of it on, after that most Solemn Appeals were made on both sides to God himself, the Righteous Judge, in this necessitated War between *England* and *Scotland*; And that all means of Christian love and tenderness towards those that bear the Name of Godly in the *Scotish* Nation, have been used to inform, and perswade them, and prevent (if it had been the will of God) a decision by the Sword, and the same rejected.

And indeed, such is the riches and fulness of this high and unexpressible Mercy, that the value and consequence thereof, is not in a short time to be apprehended, but is of that nature, as succeeding Generations will be tasting the sweet and good of it, as often as they look back upon it, and penetrate into it. For in the bosom of it is comprehended the safety of all that hath been fought for these many years late past: And together with this Victory, God hath renewed Being and Life it self to this Commonwealth, and the Government thereof; whose total Ruine and Subversion was not onely contrived and designed, but almost ripened unto an Accomplishment, by all the Enemies of it, under the fairest Vizards and Disguises they could clothe themselves with; that is to say, of *The Cause of God, The Covenant*, and *Priviledges of Parliament*, the more easily to seduce and deceive a Party within this Nation, who lay waiting for it, and to concentre in one all the Strength that could be heap'd up together, of various destructive Interests unto the Power of Godliness, and true Liberty and Freedom of the People, the maintenance whereof is so much in the desires and endeavors of this Commonwealth.

In this Combination the Popish, Prelatical, Prophane and Malignant Parties stood behinde the Curtain, and seemed for a season to be quite laid aside, that the Cause of God, the Covenant, and Work of Reformation might bear the Name, and the Promoters thereof the onely Power and Sway, through whose seeming Credit and Authority our hands might be weakned, our Cause blemished, and general Insurrections from all parts of *England* procured, and so obtain that through Deceit and Hypocrisie joyned with Power, which by Force alone they durst not attempt, as having found by frequent and dear Experiences, the mighty hand of God drawn out against them, as often-soever as they appeared in a way of meer and open Force; And now when the Design was thus subtilly and dangerously laid, and the Enemy in his own thoughts was in so fair a way of accomplishing thereof, that they doubted nothing less, then of having our Army at their mercy, and of marching up unto *London* without opposition, with their new King at the Head of theirs: The following *Narrative* will declare how suddenly the Lord turned himself against them, and arose *like a Gyant refreshed with Wine*, bestowing upon *England* the most seasonable and wonderful Victory over his Enemies, that it hath ever known, or been made partaker of.

The Narrative.

After the march of our Army into *Scotland*, upon the grounds of Justice and Necessity, and in the prosecution of those ends heretofore declared by us; And that all means had been used by the General, and his Councel of War, for to prevent the effusion of Blood, and bringing the guilt of it upon their own heads, which might incur upon their obstinacy, especially of such as we beleeved might fear God in the *Scotish* Nation: Our Army did often press upon them, and several times tempt them to engage with us; which they did as often avoid, waiting for their advantage over us by our weaknings and sickness, and their own strengthning, by the continual access of forces to them. And when it was found, notwithstanding all ways used by us, it would work no effect to fight us; It was at length by the General and his Councel concluded to march with the Army back as far as *Dunbar*, for the more convenient supplying it with victuals, and providing for our sick and weak men, who fell so fast down of the Flix, that we were compelled to Ship away at *Muscleborough* Five hundred of them.

The Enemy mistaking the Grounds of our March took Courage on a sudden, perswading themselves we now durst not Engage with them, as verily imagining we had with our sick men shipp'd away our Ordnance already (which was indeed onely sent with a Party before towards *Haddington*) and having been informed that we intended after we were come to *Dunbar*, to send away all our Infantry by Sea, and with our Horse to return back into *England*; Between which and our Quarters then, they knew there were many Passes, where they might have an advantage easily to annoy us.

Upon our rising therefore from *Muscleborough* the last of *August*, our Army having with them but four days Provision, The Enemy, who by the coming of their Kings Guard of *English*, and several other Recruits from the North to them, were made effectively Twenty two thousand men, ours being weakned to Eleven thousand, rise also and marched close after us, attempting the disordering of our Rear, especially upon the lodging our Army at *Haddington*; wither coming neer night, and having passed most of our men over the River, the Enemy fell on so hot, that though we brought up our Rear-Brigade of Horse to succor our Rear-Forlorn, which the Enemy had faln and broke in upon, yet we could not have come off without a considerable loss, the Enemies whole Army being neer at hand, had not the goodness of God seasonably interposed by his Providence, and so ordered it, that a dark Cloud passing over the Moon, we had the opportunity given us of drawing off our Horse again, undiscerned by the Enemy, and of sheltring it with our Foot, and the rest of the Army by *Haddington* Town-side, the Enemy having got nothing by the scuffle.

The whole Body of the Enemies Army lying within two Miles of the Town, about midnight they sent up a Party of Horse and Foot to try what success they should have upon our Quarters. The General having notice of their approach, commanded out Captain *White* with his Troop to charge them, which he accordingly did; but meeting with greater numbers, both Horse and Foot then was expected, was put to a Retreat, the Enemy pursuing to the Town-Wall: But the General drawing out another Party, they retired to their Army, leaving without any loss of ours, some few of their men slain.

The next morning (the Enemy lying upon a very good Ground for Battel) our Army put themselves into order, as thinking it had been the Enemies intention to fight: And moving towards them there, where the Enemy had drawn some of his men over a Pass, the Enemy thinking not then his best time, commanded his men back again, and the River interposing, our Army in this order faced them four or five hours, when a motion was made by some of the Officers to send to them to offer them Battel; but this Proposal took no effect, as not judging it fit to anticipate the time and design of Providence, which they had ever found best patiently to wait upon.

Perceiving therefore they would come to no resolution to fight, our Army proceeded in their march again to *Dunbar;* and the Enemy having received a fresh Recruit of Three new Regiments, sent some of our men that they had taken Prisoners in to inform us of their supply, and that they were now bent to fight us. Their Confidence upon this supply, and their former mistakes of us, being greatned to a very high degree, so that they followed our Army with that eagerness, that before we got within a mile of *Dunbar* (where we came that night) their whole Bodies of Horse and Foot were in our Rear, within Canon shot, where our Army being to pass over a small River that had pretty high Banks, made a Halt, and drew up in Battalia: The Enemy again declined to joyn, and espying an advantage he had, drew off to the Right Hand, marching in great haste to possess himself of some Hills that did intercept between us and *England*; which he accordingly did (we being not able to prevent it, without leaving our Train and Provisions behind us) his Camp overlooking our Army, and sending afterward a considerable number of Horse, did possess himself likewise of the Pass at *Copperspeth*; we placing our Tents in the mean time close by the Sea, and leaving *Dunbar* behind us.

Here begun the pride of the *Scots* Army so to swell, as they quite forgot an overruling Providence, their Scouts upbraiding us, They now had us safe enough, and that though they had afforded us a Summers Quarters, they hoped to have it quickly repaid them, when they come to take up their Winter Quarters, intending, as they said, to convoy up our Rear for us to *London*; yea, so far had their Passion blinded them, and their Presumption prevailed upon them, That as we were informed by some of their own, they sate in Consultation what Conditions it was fit they should offer us, whether or no Quarter was to be allowed to any for their lives, and to whom onely, and upon what terms.

And indeed, many were the difficulties that it pleased the Lord at that time to set before our Army, the ground the Enemy had gotten being inaccessible, and not possible for us to engage him upon, without apparant hazard; on either hand, and on the Rear of our Army was the Sea, and before them onely a narrow Pass, and the Hills where the Enemy lay; nor were we without straights in our selves, our Army being so sickly, as a hundred of them fell down of a day, and our Provisions growing scanty for those that were well.

But in this began the Wisdom, Power and Goodness of God, the more to break forth in upholding, notwithstanding the hearts both of the Officers and Soldiers, quietly and patiently to expect the glorious Appearance of his Divine Presence in this their Distress, of which they had oft times humbly boasted, and by which they had no time hitherto been deserted.

All the next day we lay still; toward the Evening, on Monday, the Enemy drew out nigh three parts of four of their Horse, South of *Dunbar*, intending to interpose and shut up quite the way of our Army to *Berwick*; which the General observing, declared to Major General *Lambert*, That now in his apprehensions there was an opportunity given of attempting something upon the Enemy; which the Major General having at the same time upon his spirit also, was about to prevent him in; and after advice taken with the Councel of Officers (who were all consenting) it was resolved to be ordered in this maner, That Six Regiments of Horse, and Three Regiments and half of Foot, under the command of the Major General should first fall on, and that Four Regiments and half of Foot, and Two Regiments of Horse should bring up the Canon and Rear; the time of the Onset to be break of day.

The night proved blustering and wet, so that our Army fell not upon the Enemy at the hour appointed, till it was somewhat later in the Morning; their Motions being soon descryed by the Enemy, who before any of ours came up, had put himself in so good a posture to receive them, as he had the advantage of his Canon and Foot against our Horse onely, which according to order first charged the Enemy, while that our Foot was coming up, opposition was made by the Enemy with very great Resolution; a very hot dispute at Swords point being between our Horse and theirs. Five Companies of our Foot that were first commanded out, after they had discharged their dutie, being over-powred by the Enemy, received some repulse, which they soon recovered; the Generals Regiment timeously coming in, who (God eminently assisting them with Courage) at the push of Pike, did break the stoutest Regiment the Enemy had, and totally routing them, did full execution upon them; which proved as great an advantage to us, as it was a terror & amazement to the residue of their Foot; nor was the issue in the mean time less successful in our Horse, who being carried on by the same Divine Power and Presence) did with a great deal of spirit and valour daunt the Resolution of the Enemy, charging through and through the Bodies both of the Enemies Horse and Foot, who after the first Repulse were as Stubble before them. And now the best of the Enemies Horse and Foot, being in less then an hours dispute broken, and their whole Army put into confusion, it became a total Rout, our men having the chase and execution of them near eight miles; in all which Fight, notwithstanding it is credibly affirmed, our Army lost not thirty men, so great was the mercy and protection of God over them.

And thus in the thing wherein they dealt proudly, the Lord shewed himself to be above them, causing their foot to slide in the duest time, even when he had reduced our Army into such straights, that room was onely left for Believing.

While our Army having rested themselves, and given thanks to God for this great Victory, were preparing their march to *Edenburgh*, news was brought to the General, That *Edenburgh* and *Leith* were both quitted: The Provost of *Edenburgh* having acquainted the people of the overthrow of their whole Army, unsafety of their present condition, and that visibly there was nothing appeared that could protect them: Whither our Army sooner after marching, did quietly take up their Quarters, not meeting with the least resistance; The Enemy being retired to the other side of *Sterling*.

In this Battel were kill'd upon the place and near about it, above Four thousand men.

Of private Soldiers taken Prisoners, above Ten thousand.

Of their Horse taken, killed, and made unserviceable, about Two thousand.

Commission Officers taken Prisoners, as Colonels, Lieutenant Colonels, &c. about Two hundred and ninety.

Two of their Committee of Estates taken Prisoners, the Lord *Lybberton* and Sir *Iames Lunsden,* who was also Lieutenant General of their Foot, and some of their Ministers.

The Foot Arms taken, were about Fifteen thousand.

About Two hundred Colours taken.

Two and Thirty peeces of Ordnance, with the rest of their Artillery, Bag and Baggage, and all their Ammunition taken.

There was not above Five thousand Horse and Foot of ours ingaged in this Battel.

The Enemies word was *The Covenant,* ours *The Lord of Hosts,* who manifested himself to be with us.

Their King, as some of their Prisoners said, was within a day or two expected to come into their Army.

The serious consideration of all which, as it doth give the Parliament cause of great Thankfulness unto God, for this his unspeakable Goodness: So they do most earnestly desire, That the whole Nation, together with themselves, may be deeply sensible of the same; And therefore they do Enact and Ordain, and be it Enacted and Ordained by this present Parliament, and the Authority thereof, That *Tuesday* the Eighth day of *October,* One thousand six hundred and fifty, be set apart, and appointed for a day of Publique Thanksgiving and Holy Rejoycing in all the Churches and Chappels within *England,* *Wales,* and Town of *Berwick* upon *Tweed,* for this great Mercy; And that the Ministers of the respective Parishes and places aforesaid, be, and hereby they are Required and Enjoyned to give notice on the Lords day next preceding the said Eighth day of *October,* of the day so to be observed; to the end the people of their several Congregations may the more generally and diligently attend the publique Exercises of Gods Worship and Service there to be dispensed upon that occasion: At which time, that the people may be the more particularly and fully informed of this great Deliverance and Success, the said Ministers are hereby Required and Enjoyned to publish and reade this present Act and Narrative. And for the better Observation of the Day, the Parliament doth hereby inhibit and forbid the holding or use of all Fairs, Markets, and servile works of mens ordinary Callings upon that day; And all Majors, Sheriffs, Justices of Peace, Constables, and other Officers, be and are hereby Enjoyned to take especial care of the due observance of the said day of Thanksgiving accordingly.

1650–Ir2 Thanksgiving day for the Commonwealth victory at the battle of Dunbar

Thursday 7 November 1650 (Ireland)

Lord Deputy Ireton ordered a public thanksgiving in Ireland for 7 November to celebrate Cromwell's victory at Dunbar (1650–E5). Unlike the previous Irish occasion (1650–Ir1), however, the instruction was issued by proclamation not order, the first time since 1625–Ir. This may have been to enforce the closure of fairs and markets, which had not been explicitly required in August 1650. Once again, the proclamation included a lengthy narrative of events as well as calls to offer thanks for God's protection more generally. Though Ireton had received copies of the act for the thanksgiving in England and an account of the battle, the narrative appears to owe little or nothing to either. The rallying nature of the account, as well as the importance of special worship to British national identity, may explain why army officers were expected to take particular care that the day was observed in garrisons.

Order: proclamation by the deputy general, 12 Oct. 1650 (s.n., Cork, 1650; Wing C7104, sigs. C1ᵛ– C4ʳ)*.

Additional source: *A letter from the lord general Cromwell to the parliament of England* (Cork, 1650; Wing C7104); council of state: day's proceedings, 21 Sept. 1650, SP25/10, fo. 37v (*CSPD, 1650*, p. 350).

ORDER

Proclamation by the deputy general: 12 October 1650

Although God hath not been pleased to grant that, which in our late Publique Addresses to him was (I hope with sincerity) desired by us, for the preventing of Engagement unto blood betwixt our Army in *Scotland*, and those of that Nation that professe his feare; But hath seene it good (for the further discovering of the hipocrisy of them, that for the promoting of their owne worldly Interests, doe abuse his Name, and make use of the most specious Pretences of Religion, and Godlynesse, for their corrupt ends) to suffer their proceedings there, unto such an issue of warre as we heartily wished might have been avoyded, Yet, on the other part, he hath been pleased to answer the Prayers, And indeed to exceed the weake faith, and expectations of us and others his poore people who have sought him in that behalfe, By witnessing many wayes to that which is indeed his owne and his peoples Cause, and to that measure of Integrity he hath given to his poore servants that have followed him therein, and against both the Persons, and pretences of all that oppose the same, and especially (when it came to a grand ingagement in the Field) By giving to our Army there, not onely a deliverance from the streights and extremities, as well as from the Enemyes wherewith they were surrounded, And ready to have been destroyed, But also a totall and easy victory over the Enemyes Army (though double to them in number, And haveing all outward advantages on their part) as is at large set forth in the Lord Generalls Letter to the Parliament, and the Parliaments Act for a publique Thanksgiving thereupon, both which for more generall notice throughout this Dominion, I have caused herewith to be reprinted.

Now these are therefore further added to excite all persons within this Dominion, who have hearts in any measure capable of it unto a due sence, and consideration of the glorious workings of God in these things, And that they may more fully appeare to be such I desire that these (amongst other things tending to set forth the same) may be especially taken notice of, and considered.

1. That as the marching of our Army into *Scotland* was not from any desires of obtaining Dominion, or other worldly advantages over that Nation, but meerely to prevent their Invading us againe (which they had done so lately before upon the very same score and under the same pretexts, as they were againe (but with greater advantage and more heightened pretentions of the same kinde then before) formeing and preparing all things unto, so as by their Transactions with their King, and many other wayes; All men not onely in *England, Scotland* and *Ireland*, but even throughout Europe, did take notice and understand it so and to have obtayned securitie, or assurance to *England* against the like invasions from that Nation (though to the declining or remitting of our just demands, of satisfaction for the former dammages and violations (to the Truth of all which in the Intentions of the Parliament of *England* & their Army God hath now most graciously testified) so it pleased God both to carry forth the Army thither with a Spirit of Prayer for Peace, and Agreement (if it might be) with all that appeared godly in *Scotland*, and for the reall good of them as for their owne, and (when they were there) to carry themselves on with bowells of Love towards all such in that Nation, and all Tendernesse towards the generallity of that people nowithstanding the so much contrary Practise of their former, and last Army in *England*, and great Provocations of our men to the contrary from the People of *Scotland* wherever they came) and to incline and guide them both in their Declarations, Letters and other intercourses and also by their whole carriage, and deportment to seeke Peace, and Agreement with the satisfieing and undeceiving of any such who (meaning well to our first Common Cause) had really stumbled; and taken offence at any carriages of things in *England*, and so to make all faire Tenders and try all meanes possible (without subjecting or exposeing *England* to a forreigne power, or deserting the worke of God, and Interest of his People) to have obtained that Agreement and security they came for (if it had beene the will of God) without engagement unto blood betwixt them and the Parties professing Godlinesse in *Scotland*, yet all this would availe nothing with them who (it seemed) had nothing but War in theire hearts, and the worldly advantages expectable thereby in their eyes, although they had the Confidence to dissemble it before the allseeing God, and the discerning world.

2. That before this great ingagement that Party in *Scotland* resolving with themselves to carry on their whole businesse with a faire forme of Godlinesse and an appearance of holding true to their former professions, that way thereby to gaine the better Party both in *England*, and elsewhere to favour and further their proceedings (and indeed resting too much in (if not minding onely) that bare forme, and appearance, and conceiveing it necessary (in conformity thereunto) that before their avowed owneing of their young Kings Interests against the Commonwealth of *England*, he should not only subscribe the severall Covenants in which they formerly were engaged, but appeare as a man really, and from inward divine Conviction brought over thereunto; and for that purpose should both disclaime his former evill Councells, and wayes in opposition thereunto, and professe (as a man Divinely converted) a deepe sence of and repentance for the great guilt and sinns both of himselfe, his Father, Mother, and his Fathers house in that kinde, wherewith those of *Scotland* had so often, and so deeply charged them before the world as could not be retracted) they therefore formed a Declaration to that purpose, for him to owne and signe, which indeed as it holds forth the fairest semblance that may be of such

a thing so (in the whole Tenor of it) it carryes such an exact and formall counterfeite of a Divine conversation and repentance, as one would thinke none but such as had a reall taste thereof in themselves, could devise, Which Declaration, against his Nature and heart (as by his severall refusalls thereof, and many other wayes is too evident) they haveing him in their Power did by threats, and otherwise necessitate him at last to signe, and publish as his owne, and haveing therein fulfilled their intended forme and brought him to this verball conformitie thereunto (Though they could not but see how farr it was from his heart) they now owned him, and held him forth to the People as a man really converted and brought over to the Cause of God, and under such a Notion began Publickly to owne him and that which was the Interest of him, and his Father in other things; which bold Hypocrisy, and shame-less abuse of Gods holy Name did indeed ripen them for Gods Righteous Iudgments and (when with appeales to him thereupon Haveing thus prepared all things, as they conceived sutable to their designed forme, they came forth with Confidence, to fight our Army) It is good that all men take notice, how God met with it, and severely witnessed against the Same.

3. That when by such their specious carriage of their whole businesse in order to the stateing of their intended Warr against us, added to the strange representa-tions which they and other of their Temper, and Interest, had made of the late great Transactions in *England* (in putting the Late King to death, and changeing (in part) the forme of Government (there) most men were apt to conceive (as it has beene the great endeavor both of them and all the Royallists and Discontented parties every where to make it beleived) that there was now a totall change of the Cause and Interest on our Parts, as well as of the persons or Parties now engaged against us, and that we were become breakers of the Covenant, Backsliders from God, and his Cause, and Apostates from the principles, and ends of our first common engage-ment, and thereupon to expect an Answerable change of Successe therein, to our ruine; (So as many good men were much at a stand, and their hearts apt to faint through doubtfull apprehensions thereof) It pleased God thus seasonably to come in, and give a cleare Testimony that (as through his grace, we had acted in Truth of heart for the same first ends of Publique good to men, with safety and wellfare to the People of God and glory to his Name therein so,) he was still the same God unto us, vouchsafeing the same presence still amongst us, and Carryeing us on in the same spirit, and with the same successe, as formerly, and giveing a Change, both to the spirit in acting, and also to the successe of those engaged against us, in Comparison to what they had in former engagements against that Party, and Cause, with which (though they endeavoured to Dissemble it) They were now really united.

4. That while our Army was in it's full strength & Vigour God would not suffer it to come to any such Engagement, but saw it good first, both to exercise their Faith and Patience in following, and Trusting him throuh manifold hardships, & Diffi-culties, and to bring them to great streights, and dangers of utter ruine, and when they were reduced to the greatest weaknesse, and the Enemy swollen to their full expected strength and accompanied with all visible Advantages, (in both which they appeared to be exalted with Pride, and fleshly Confidence, So as even to Triumph before the Victory) then to give that great successe against them, so as it might appeare a deliverance as well as Victory, and that men might more clearly see it to be the worke of his hand, and not wrought by Prevalence in fleshly power.

5. That after all provocations from that People, and the Advantages now gained over them, God is pleased to keepe yet his poore Servants in our Army, as from

being exalted in themselves before him so from Insulting or Domineering over that People, or useing those Advantages to their oppression or ruine & to preserve in his Servants the same Bowells of Love towards those that may yet be found truly Godly in *Scotland*, and of Compassion, and Tendernesse towards their Deluded Enemy there, as is expressed (amongst other things) by the Care of their Wounded, Weake, or Aged Prisoners; and the free Release of Thousands of them being found in such a condition; Now from these and other such Considerations of this glorious working of God, I desire that all men within this Dominion (as it Concernes all every where, (so farr as the Notice of it shall extende) may be awakned, (at last) to see and acknowledg his hand, that is so eminently lifted up, and may discerne him as he is pleased to come forth more visibly then in former Ages to execute Righteous Iudgments in the world, and may learne to Tremble, and feare before his Dreadfull Presence (when he appeares so neere at hande to take notice of the wayes, and pretentions of men when they appeale to him) and may take warning henceforth not to Dare so to take his Name in vaine, or to abuse it in Hypocrisy, or to cover any crooked, or Corrupt Designes with false pretences of Religion, that all those who professe Godlinesse may take heed of resting in the forme thereof, or goeing about to set that up against the power of it, or of closeing and taking parte (for worldly Interests sake) with wicked men or any Corrupt Powers of the World in their wayes of opposition against God, and the True Spirituall Kingdome of Christ his Sonne, in, and over the hearts of his People least they also be pertakers of their Plagues in the Day of his sore Visitation; And that all that Truly love and feare the Lord, may be stirred up, and be enlarged in their hearts to rejoyce and blesse and prayse his Name for ever for his Righteous Iudgments in their behalfe, and for his goodnesse, and faithfullnesse towards those, whose hearts he hath Drawne forth to seeke and serve him, may be established in their faith, and Patience to follow and Trust him, and waite for his more full appearance, and may be provoked to more Zeale of his glory, and to a Godly Ielousie over their hearts, and wayes that they may not be, (or walke) unworthy of his glorious presence amongst them, and Dispensations of Mercy and goodnesse towards them, but may obtaine grace to bring forth fruits in some Measure answerable therunto.

For the furtherance of these ends, & Considering the greatnesse of this Mercy, & of what Vast importance it is, and further consequence it may be, to the security and great good not only of the Commonwealth of *England*, and all that have Interest in it (both there and here) but also of all the People of God every where; (the Parliament by the Act herewith Printed haveing appointed a Day of Publique Thanksgiving which is already past before there could be a generall notice of it in this Nation) I have thought it my duty to appoint a further day for the same purpose to be observed within this Dominion, And doe hereby accordingly appoint Thursday the seauenth day of November next ensueing to be set a part, and observed as a day of Publique Thanksgiveing upon the foresaid occasion in the said Act and Letter of the Lord Lieutenants recited and for the ends, and purposes in that Act contained, at which tyme more especially (Though I wish it may at no time be neglected or forgotten) I Desire all Officers and Souldiers, and others under the obedience of the Parliament in the severall Garrisons and Quarters throughout this Dominion, and especially those who are acquainted with the Lord to endeavour (as God by his spirit shall enable them) to render hearty Thankes, and prayse unto his holy Name for those great Mercies and glorious workings of his, to acknowledg and Testifie to each other, and before him, his sole Power, Wisdome, Goodnesse, Righteousnesse, and Faithfulnesse appearing therein, to provoke, and stirr up one another to a due sence, and consideration thereof that it may have impression upon all our hearts and never be forgotten.

And upon this occasion I desire also that wee may call to remembrance his many other glorious and gratious workings with and for us, & other his poore Servants upon our manifold engagements in his Cause both in this and our Native Country, and that wee may implore, and importune him (by the sure argument of his free Covenant of grace with his People in Iesus Christ) that he who doth these great and glorious things, for his owne name sake in behalfe of his People and against their Enemies would also in his due time worke all suteable effects, and impressions, and bring forth all answerable fruites of them in all sorts of men: and (as all others so) those especially which I have herebefore desired they may (according to theire severall Conditions and Capacities) be awakened, and stirred up unto from the Considerations aforegoeing, And that he would still pitty the weaknesses, and frailties of his poore Servants, and Pardon the many Provocations by which wee have, and doe still requite him evill (especially in our aptnesse so soone to forget him and his Mercies, and to repine, and Distrust in straights or Difficulties) That wee may henceforth abstaine from murmuring against so good a God, who hath never left those that have patiently waited upon him in distresses That he would vouchsafe still to abide with us, and Continue his blessing and presence unto us, and all others, who labour in his Cause, to the compleating of his worke with Peace (if it be his will) in these Nations; That he would purge out wickednesse, and iniquity from amongst us, more, and more, quicken and strengthen us to every good way, and worke, and make us, more fit for him yet further to use and owne, and Communicate himselfe unto: And (for our Brethren of the Army in *Scotland*) that he would still carry them on and enlarge them in the same spirit of faith, and prayer of humility selfe-denyall and liveing above all the Advantages and Temptations of the world, in continued Love, and tendernesse of heart and way towards such as professe (and may yet be truely possessed with, his feare in that Nation, that if it be his will none such may continue engaged in crooked corrupte or deceitfull wayes, or united in councells and interest with ungodly and wicked men, That Envyings, heart-burnings, strife and debate betwixt his People may be laid aside, and Cause, and that in Mercy they may be called and gathered together in one, from amongst the men of this world by the spirit, and good hand of the Lord, to rejoyce and praise his Name together, and hold fast the unity of the faith in the Bond of Peace, and Love: And (for our selves perticularly in this Nation) that he would be pleased to let us understand more of his minde, and will, concerning his worke, and our proceedings therein here, and give us hearts to doe his Worke, and fulfil his will with faithfulnesse and diligence, and to endure all hardships, and encounter streights, and difficulties for his sake without repineinges, yea with rejoyceing so to suffer for him; That he would shew, and teach us in all things what he would have us doe, and how he would have us deale with the People of this Nation that if it be his will, we may be instrumentall for their good; rather then Distruction; And hee would be pleased at last to open their eyes to see their owne Darknesse and Bondage with the Corruption of their wayes, and enlarge their hearts to the imbraceing of the Gospell in the Truth, and spirit, and Power of it, and that (with removeall of their, and our sinns that provoke him to Iudgement, he would be pleased to take off, and cease his sore Visitation in the plague from all places amongst us, and especially to spare his poore People that serve him in this Cause; And for his gratious beginnings of abatement thereof in many places, and totall Ceaseing of it in some (as at *Clonmell, Kilkenny, VVaterford,* &c) as we have cause to owne the same, as a fruite and answer to our poore prayers, in our late dayes of humiliation: So I desire it may be parte of the Matter of that dayes Thanksgiveing.

And lastly let us especially begg of him that our thankfulnesse may not rest or terminate in the words, or services of a day, but that we may (Through his grace) live to his praise all our dayes, and our Conversations may be as a continuall Song of praise for his great goodnesse to his People, and for his Righteous Iudgments, and wondrous workings, in our dayes amongst the Children of men.

Now for the better observation of the said day, as appointed, I doe hereby inhibit, and forbid, the holding or useing of any Faires, Marketts, or servile workes of mens ordinary callings upon that day. And all Officers both Military and Civill in their severall places within this Dominion, are hereby required to take especiall care of the due observation of the said day of Thanksgiveing accordingly, for more generall and speedy notice thereof, I doe further appoint that this Proclamation be forthwith Printed, and Published.

1650–E7   Thanksgiving prayers for Commonwealth victory at Meelick Island, Ireland

Sunday 1 December 1650 (London, its liberties and the late lines of communication)

Following a succession of setbacks, in late 1650 Ormond relinquished command of the Irish royalist and confederate forces to the marquis of Clanricade, a catholic. Under cover of darkness on 25 October, parliamentarian forces led by Colonel Axtell launched a surprise attack on Clanricarde's troops at Meelick Island on the River Shannon; they had withdrawn there in the face of Commonwealth reinforcements after a summer of defending Connaught. After fierce hand-to-hand fighting, Axtell overcame Clanricarde's forces. Soldiers fled, some drowning in the river; the marquis also escaped. On 26 November, the Rump parliament ordered a day of thanksgiving in celebration of the victory and instructed the lord mayor and, for the first time since 1646–E9(P), JPs to distribute the order. A narrative, *A letter from William Basill*, was ordered to be printed.

Order: parliamentary order, 26 Nov. 1650, Wing B1027, 8* [also in *CJ,* VI, 501].
Additional source: *CJ,* VI, 501; *A letter from William Basill esq* (1650; Wing B1027).

ORDER

Parliamentary order: 26 November 1650
Resolved by the Parliament,

That publique Thanks be given by the respective Ministers in the several Parish Churches, Chappels and Places of Publique Worship within the City of *London,* and Liberties thereof, and within the late Lines of Communication, on the next Lords day, being the first day of *December, 1650.* for Gods great mercy in giving a Signal and Seasonable Victory to the Parliaments Forces in *Ireland,* against the bloody

Rebels there, on the Five and twentieth of *October* last, and mentioned in this Letter: And it is Ordered, That the Lord Major of *London* do take care that timely notice hereof be given to the Ministers of the several Parishes within the said City of *London* and Liberties thereof; And that the respective Justices of Peace within the late Lines of Communication, do take care that timely notice hereof be given to the Ministers of their several and respective Parishes within the said late Lines of Communication.

1650–S6   Fast days before Charles II's Scottish coronation, for general sinfulness

Sunday 22 December and Thursday 26 December 1650 (Scotland)

These fasts were ordered in preparation for Charles II's coronation, which was held at Scone on 1 January 1651. The appointment of the fasts should be seen in the context of divisions in the commission of the general assembly exposed by the Western Remonstrance, an outspoken criticism of the Scottish government's relations with Charles, whom the document's authors considered insincere, unrepentant and untrustworthy. Supported by a minority of the clergy and laity, the Remonstrance was condemned by the committee of estates meeting in Perth on 25 November, and (in milder terms) by the commission on 28 November. On 23 November, the commission had instructed James Wood and James Durham to compile causes for two fasts, incorporating causes agreed with the king in August for a fast postponed due to the defeat at Dunbar. When the causes were approved on 29 November, supporters of the Remonstrance had withdrawn from the commission, and it is possible that this division may have disrupted the observance of the fasts in some places. In Strathbogie presbytery, the fasts were kept in January due to the late arrival of the commission's instructions.

Order: act of the commission of the general assembly, 29 Nov. 1650, *RCGA*, III, 143.
Causes: *Reasons of a fast* ([Aberdeen], [James Brown]; Wing C4251B)* [also in *RCGA*, III, 143–52]; *RCGA*, III, 152–4 [also NRS, GD157/1347].
Letter: commission of the general assembly to presbyteries, 29 Nov. 1650, *RCGA*, III, 154–5.
Additional sources: *RCGA*, III, 43–8, 57–8, 115–18, 124–5, 131–2; *RPS*, A1650/11/2, A1650/11/26, M1650/11/2, M1650/11/5, A1661/1/69; presbytery of Elgin minutes, NRS, CH2/144/1, p. 310; presbytery of Paisley minutes, NRS, CH2/294/3, p. 84; *Strathbogie presbytery*, p. 169; *Life of Blair*, pp. 254–5; Lamont, p. 25; Nicoll, p. 40; *Inverness and Dingwall records*, p. 204.

ORDER

Act of the commission of the general assembly: 29 November 1650

The Commission of Assembly, being very sensible of the great wrath gone out from the Lord against this land, Therefore think fitt that the whole land, King and people, be humbled before the Lord, and that two dayes of solemne fasting and humiliation be kept through all the congregations of this Kirk, the first to be upon the 22 of the moneth of December nixt, being the Sabboth for the contempt of the Gospell, which is one of the great contraversies which the Lord hes against this land, the particulars whereof are to be branched out in a severall paper, and sent to Presbyteries in print. The other day of fasting and humiliation is to be upon Thursday, the 26 of the said moneth of December, for the King, his familie and court.

Causes

[For 22 December]
The Commission of the Generall Assemblie, seriously considering, That howso-ever this Land lyeth under the Guiltiness of many-fold Provocations of al sorts, against the Commandements of the Law of GOD, abounding, in all Rancks & Conditions of People: Yet, that the despysing and refusing of the Gospell, and of the Rich Free Grace of GOD in CHRIST held foorth therein, is the Great National Sinne of this Kirk and Kingdom, against which the LORD is most evidently and remarkeably, pleading a Contraversie in His present judgements vpon the Land: And, that this is the very Fountayn and Cause of so great abounding of all other sinnes. Considering, also, that this Sinne having been often mentioned and held foorth amongst the Causes of former Fasts, hath been little, or no wayes at all, layd to heart. Yea, not well understood what it meaneth by the most part of People. And, therefore, having appoynted a Fast and Humiliation to bee kept especially for this Sinne, on the LORDS Day, December xxij. 1650, throughout all the Congregations of this Kirk, it is thought fit, to the effect, That all may haue the more clear and distinct apprehension of the foresayd Sinne, and bee helped the better, to discern their guiltiness therein; To hold foorth unto People, the Mayn Branches thereof, in this Paper which is desyred to bee read in all Congregations.

Sinnes relating to the Gospell-Ordinances.
First: To the WORD. Neglecting to come and attend on the Preaching of the Word, both on the LORDS Day, and on week dayes, in these places where such Exercises, are on these dayes.

2. Not comming to the Preaching of the Word, for the right end, viz to fynd communion with Christ, and a taste of His goodnes and excellencie, & to be built vp in the most holy fayth: but eyther out of custome or to eschew censures, or to satisfy & hold off the challenges of a naturall conscience; or some other by-respect. And not preparing the heart befor hand in secret, to come with Godly fear and reverence, humility, spiritual hungring and thirsting after the Kingdom of God, and the Righteousnes thereof, and desyring as new born babes the sincere milk of the Word, to grow thereby,

3. That when People are at the preaching of the word, besyds great carelesnes, overlines sleeping, wandring of the heart, & in advertencie to what is preached; the Word is not heard as an Ordinance and meane appoynted of God to work vpon, and carry in grace and comfort vnto the heart, but is only reguarded as other discourses proceeding from mens ability and parts, and is accordingly esteemed by the most part, or at most is only made vse of, as a mean of informing the judgement.

4. That in the preaching of the Word, neyther doeth Ministers speak the same as the Oracles of God, not remembring themselves to be the ambassadours of Christ, speaking in Gods stead: nor doeth people present themselves in so immediat a way befor God Himself as to receive the Word not as the Word of man, but as the true Word of God; whence it commeth to pass that there is litle trembling at the Word, and so litle rejoycing in it.

5. That people in the hearing of the Word, contents themselves with mans teaching, and doeth not in the conviction of their own blindnes & vtter inability of themselves to perceive the things of the Spirit, and of the insufficiencie of the outward means without Gods immediat work therewith vpon the heart; imploy

Him self to teach them inwardly by His Spirit, joyning with the outward means, according to the promise of the Covenant. They shal be al taught of God: whence it commeth to pass that there is so much Preaching, and so little profiting, so much Learning, and so little speed comming in the knowledge of GOD.

6. The not mixing of the Word preached with Fayth, whyle as in the hearing thereof; even these who seem to giue most heed thereunto do for the most part, rather imploy the judgement, to consider and judge of the pertinencie, coherence, the way of uttering of the doctrine delivered; or in a meer speculatiue way to apprehend the matter & trueth of what is spoken than they do labour, with the heart to close with, embrace and apply to themselues the Trueth preached.

7. No care to lay up, & hyde the words of CHRIST in the heart, to remember the same for usemaking: But letting them slip and run thorow; which the Apostle accounteth a neglecting of the Great Salvation of GOD, (HEB. 2.1.3) Nor imploying the Spirit to bring the Word that hath been heard; but forgotten, to remembrance: Not making conscience to conferre on the Word Preached, and to whet it on, upon an other. Not taking payns, nor delight in it, in private, to reade, and meditate on it.

2. In relation to the Sacraments. And first in general & common: Not making vse of them as Seals of the Covenant of Grace, and promises thereof made to us in Christ; but laying al the weyght of confidence vpon themselves & being content with the deed done, which was the ordinary sin of the Iews in the vse of Circumcision, & other Rits and ceremonies of the Law, so often charged vpon them in Scripture. Then particularly.

In Baptisme. 1 In Parents bringing their Children therevnto, eyther out of meer fashion and custome, as meerly to have a difference put between them, and vnchristned people, or in effect as vnto a meer ceremonie: and not from any sense that they are vnclean from vnclean, born dead in sins, and children of wrath of themselves, defyled with original guilt and corruption, nor from a desyre that they may be spiritually regenerated, incorporated vnto Christ, to be made partakers of the vertue of His Death & Resurrection, to be washed from their filthines in the blood of Christ, and to get interest in the Covenant of grace, and promises thereof, sealed vp vnto them.

2 Not setting themselves in the administration of this Sacrament to consider & pryze the free love and grace of God, which hath prevented vs, & our seed in provyding such a fountain for sin & vncleanes in Christ, making such a Covenant with vs, so well ordered in al things, & sure preventing vs and our seed with the seall thereof; nor to apply the Covenant and the promises thereof for our selves and our seed, and this Sacrament as the seall of the same.

3. The great & evident slighting of the administration of this Sacrament, while as few in the Congregation joyneth therin eyther for their own edification, or to hold vp the baptized to God, that He might bless His own ordinance to them, and receive them in amongst His Children in Christ: and many with-draweth themselves from the administration thereof, as if it did not concern them and only the Minister and Presenter were to be actors in it.

4 Parents not making conscience, to make known vnto their Children when they come to years of Capacity their Baptism, the ends and vse thereof, and the obligation therby layeth vpon them as consecrated to Christ.

5 The not making vse of this Sacrament all a-long the course of our, lyf for renewing & strengthening our comfort in the Fayth and assurance of our Regenera-

tion & Adoption; and of our interest in God, as our GOD and Father in CHRIST: and for strenthening through Christ our resolutions & endeavours of Mortification, and newness of lyf. Which is a great despysing of this Ordinance.

In the Lords Supper. 1. The great profanation ther of, by the comming and admitting there vnto: of many gross Ignorants, who cannot discern the Lords Body, nor knoweth how to examine themselves, many profane Ones, Godless Livers, without the Worship of GOD, in private, and into many places al sorts of persons promiscuously without making a difference between the precious & the Vyle: whereby the Blood of Christ, is much profaned (altho the constitutions of our Kirk were they well observed doth sufficiently guard against these evills) Which no doubt is one of the mayn sins, for which GOD hath beene provoked to suffer so much of our blood to be shed. See 1, Cor. 11. 30.

2. The little or no care or payns that is taken for preparation to so high and holy an Ordinance, wherein we are called to the nearest and most familiar Communion with Christ, that is heere vpon earth: most part contenting themselves giving their presence at a Preparation Sermon, many not making conscience of so much as this. Very few separating themselves, as is needfull to examine themselves; that being sensible of their Guiltyness, Spirituall inlacks &c. They might come with humble, broken, and contrite Spirits, with Spirituall hunger and thirst, for Christ Crucified. And sincere purposes of heart, to forsake their former sinfull courses, and to renew their Covenant with GOD, in the strength of CHRISTS Grace.

3 The great and lamentable Blockishness of the most part, in the participation of this Ordinance, who may be, have some kynd of amazement at the Solemnityes thereof, but doth no wyse therein exercyse themselves in remembring the Lords Death, till He come agayn to apply the same to themselves: for peace with GOD, and mortifying the Body of Sin, for working deep Repentance, and Gospell sorrow for Sin, and getting the Love of Christ, more kindled in them, and their hearts enlarged with greater thankfulness towards Him, Who loved vs, and gave Himselff for vs. And on the other hand the great heartless sinfull Dejection of many sensible Souls, who at no tyme are readyer to be plunged in legall heavyness; & feeding as it were on gall, and Worm-wood: then at this Ordinance, wherein they ought to be most rejoycing through Fayth, on the propitiation in the Death of Christ, so familiarly set foorth therein to them.

4 That the tyme and occasion of this Sacrament, is vsed by the most part, only for some outward restraint of grosser sins, for a day or two before and after; but all such goodnes being as a morning clowd, no constancie nor reall reformation: but presently turning to wonted, naturall, worldly, and carnall courses; Not-withstanding renewed remembring of the Death of CHRIST, and Profession of renewing Covnants with GOD.

3. In Relation, To the Ordinance of Discipline: 1. Which partiality in the administration of thereof, with respect of persons, and according to affection; which appeareth in that, whyle as Offences and Scandalles, in meaner persons, are taken notice of, challenged and censured: There is not the lyke Christian-Freedom, Faythfulness and Zeall used, towards such as are more eminent for Wealth, Place, or Dignitie, in the World.

2 Want of a Spirit of Meekness, sometymes in the administration thereof; whereby men, if GOD peradventure would give them Repentance, might bee recovered out

of the Snare of Satan. And, on the other hand, want of Zeall often tymes, to saue others with fear, plucking them out of the Fyre.

3 Much Vilifying, Contemning of the Censures & Exercise of Discipline: Yea, hateing thereof, and the Officers of the Kirk for it.

4 Not making use of it, as a Spirituall Medicine, and Means of Salvation: but as a meer Punishment, which as it is in itselff a miss-apprehension and abuse of this Ordinance: So is (no doubt,) the cause of so much impatience and indignation agaynst it in people; and of so much inaequality, and mixture of selfish affection, in the administration thereof.

5 The great Formality, that is every where, in the vse thereof, whyle as, so bee it, that persons under censure continue out their set tyme and dayes of censure, little care or respect is had of the effects for which it was instituted: To wit, Humilia-tion of heart, and Godly sorrow, bringing foorth Repentance, not to bee repented of, which maketh the administration thereof, to look too lyke the way of Popish Pennance.

4. In Relation to Prayer: 1. Great neglect thereof by most part of persons and fami-lies throughout the Land in private and secret.

2 Many more imminent[337] persons in the World, accounting the performance thereof in their families, (altho this bee incumbent to them, by their Place and Station,) a disparidgement; and therefore turning it over vpon others, as a Service bee low them.

3 In the publick Prayers of the Kirk, Peoples lying by, from joyning therein, al along with their Spirits, which should bee stryving together with the Minister; either mutering words of their own; or taking liberty to themselues, to bee ydle in the work, and raving in their thoughts: As if the Minister only were to bee an Actor in that Service.

4 Not using this Ordinance, as a mean of communion with GOD, and of obtay-ning blessings from Him: But using it meerly as a Duety; and many as a matter of meer task. Whereof many may bee convinced by this; That they do not make conscience, nor setteth themselues to obserue what commeth of their Prayers; how they are taken off their hand, what speed they haue come, and what answer they get.

5 The little care that is had either by Ministers, or others, to pray in the Spirit; or to inploy the Spirit of Grace, and Supplication for this Service: The most part in their performances thereof, too evidently acting meerly their own memory, inven-tion, wit, &c. And that often tymes with apparent affectation.

5. Relating more immediatelye to CHRIST Himself, and the Free Grace of GOD in Him, which is the Matter and Object of the Gospell, as:

1 Gross ignorance in the most part, and great short comeing of the best in the knowledge of Iesus Christ His Person, offices, His blessings and benefits, of the Covenant of grace; established in Him and the way of making vse of Christ and the covenant of grace.

2 Undervaluing and misprysing of Christ, communion with Him, & His spiritual graces and blessings. Which appears most evidently, by the great neglect of the vse of these means and exercyses, publick, privat & secret wherein He offereth Himself to be sought & found: the great wearying of them: great willingnes and readines to

---

[337] 'eminent' in *RCGA*, III, 148.

bestow tyme and payns vpon things worldly even vanityes & trifls than on these; preferring the interests of creatures to the interests of Christ; and not giving Him the preheminence above al: by the readines which appears in people in tymes of tryall to comply with sinful courses; to the prejudice of Christs causs and the hazarding of their own peace with God, for maintayning their case; temporary safety and worldly commodities rather then to deny themselves: take vp their cross and follow Him.

3 Not receiving of Christ, nor making vse of Him as He is held foorth in the Gospell, in His fulnes of grace, nor living in fayth by Him, more especially in Not receiving and making vse of His free gifted and imputed Righteousnes for Iustification, acceptation befor God, and for peace of conscience while as most part securely rest on meer outward church priviledges: many confyde in their own Morall Honesty, performances; and Duetyes So going about to establish their own Rigteousness, and following Duetyes this way to make their Peace, and Reconciliation there-by with GOD: AND even the Best Professours no not so purely & inteirly rest on his righteousnes as the Gospell requyreth: as well[338] appear by these things amongst many others: heartless fears, miss-be-lieff, scarring to apply Christ, and to make vse of the promises, not rejoicing in Christ, and His propitiation with humility, when there is a discovery, challenges and apprehensions of want, short comming & failing of duetyes, which in effect is in a degree, and in part an establishing our own righteousness and not submitting to the Righteousness of GOD. Not making vse of Christ, for Sanctification, according to the promises of the Covenant, and not acting in a way of dependence on Him, in al the performances of our common Christian calling, and of particular lawful vocations, for direction, quickning, strength to mortify corruptions, to every duety and to carry vs through agaynst discowragements, & tentations: but acting only or most part by the strength of our own wits, abilityes, and payns.

In not making vse of the Mediation and intercession of Christ, in approaching to the Throne of Grace, in prayers, supplications, and thanksgivings: while as many doeth neglect prayer altogether albeit they have some course of performance of this duety, yet knoweth not what it is to put their prayers vp to GOD thorow the Mediator, tho they may perhaps name His Name, but doth as that Uzziah who would offer incense himself, neglecting the high priest: and even believers themselves doth not directly, distinctly, and steadfastly in their approaches to God, eye Christ, to offer in al their service through Him, nor do come with that humble boldness and full assurance of fayth in God as a Father, where with the intercession of Christ warrandeth them to come, Heb 10. 19, 20, 21, 22

4 Not walking as becometh the Gospell of Christ, in Righteousnes, godlines, and sobriety: many not-with-standing their profession of the gospell, and claming interest in Christ, and His grace, yet living loose, profane, godless, carnall, and earthly in their way, in effect turning the grace of God, vnto wantoness & securety, and taking liberty to sin, because grace doth abound. And even best not so constrayned with the love of Christ, to live to Him, who dyed for them, not stryving to keep the thoughts of the love of Christ, and the free grace of God, in Him, vpon their hear[t]s, so fresh & constant, as they should be, to keep them watchfull, tender zealous, & enlarged for God, and His Honour.

---

338 'will' in *RCGA*, III, 149.

6 In relation to the operations of the Spirit wherein the Gospel is the Ministration, & maketh it effectuall, as:

1 Profane mocking, miscalling, & mis-interpreting the tender & acurat w[a]lking of the Godly in the wayes of God; as vnnecessary and prowd precyseness: And their Spirituall exercyses, as fantastickness, melancholy, or madness. Which is a horrible sin, sib to that which is vnpardonable: yet, very frequent amongst carnall and natu-rall people.

2 The meer naturall and morall way of living, in a civill honesty, and sitting down contented therewith, of the most part of people not labouring in their conver-sation, to walk after the Spirit: i.e. upon Spirituall Principles, according to the Spir-ituall Rule, (of Gods revealed Will in His Word,) nor for Spiritual ends the Honour of God, Glory, and immortality.

3 Not observing and yeelding vnto the knockings of the Spirit, whereby Christ maketh tender to come in to hearts, that He may sup with them, and they with Him: resisting and quenching His motions, whereby He stirreth vp to Duetyes stiffling or putting by His challenges, whether in publick or secret, which tendeth to repent-ance, humiliation, or with-draw-ing from sin; not being tender of His presence and consolations, to entertayn the same; but grieving Him, by mispryzing them, refusing them, careless walking, in not attending on His direction and guiding, in giving way to known sinfull thoughts, and lustings in a continued tract, altho not growing vp to a full accomplishing of them; and sometymes in giving way even to grosser out-breakings, and in not watching agaynst predominant corruptions, whereof even the best are much guilty.

4 Not delighting in, nor improving Spiritual company and spirituall exercises.

7 Of Ministers, in relation to their preaching of the Gospell, as:

1 Many not labouring to sett foorth the Excellency of Christ in His Person, Offices, and the vnsearchable Riches of His Grace, the new Covenant, and the way of living by Fayth in Him: nor making this the mayn and chief Theme, and matter of their preaching, as did the Apostle, 1. Cor. 3.2. 2. Cor. 4.5. Coloss. 1.28. Nor preaching other things with a relation to Christ; To wit, Not preaching convictions, reproofs, discoveries of sin, and of short commings in Duetyes, and threatnings, to leade to Christ, to pryze Him the more highly, and to embrace Him the more earnestlie; especially for justification; and pressing Duetyes, in a meer legall way; not urging them, as by the authority of Gods Commandements; so from the love of Christ, & the grace of the Gospell, nor poynting and directing people to their furniture for them in Christ: often tymes craving hard, but giving nothing wherwith to pay.

2 What they preach of Christ, and the matters of the Gospell, not preaching the same in a Gospell way whereof. See 1 Cor. 3. from the beginning at length.

3 Not commending as they ought, neither their own work, whether of meditation, or delyverie, nor their hearts to Christ, that He might give the increass: but going about the work, either altogether in their own strength, or much that way.

4 Often tymes not speaking, because they believe, and many not seeking for communion with Christ, in their own personall estate; and to feele the power of the Word, vpon their own hearts: that they might speak so.

These branches of contemning and abusing of the Gospell, are thought fitt for the better Information of all to bee held foorth at this tyme, as beeing most obvious, recommending with all to Ministers, to apply themselues, to make a more full and particular discovery thereof; as is not doubted, but they will do, according to their wisdom and vnderstanding, in the Gospell; and the experience they have by observation of their own hearts, and of the wayes and consciences of people.

It is also found needfull and appoynted, that in reguard it is not one or two, but many provocations of the people of God in this Land, which have drawn on the present sad calamities and judgements: and that the servants of God, tho they have condescended vpon many sinnes of the King and his Family of Iudicatories and of the people as vndoubted Causes thereof: yet are perswaded, that there is need of a fur[t]her discovery. Therfore vpon the foresayd day of Humiliation, & at other tymes both in publick and private earnest supplications to be made to God, for light and unanimity to His servants in this matter; that the causes of Gods wrath being more fully and throughly seen; and the hearts of al humbled accordingly befor God, wee may bee yet sett in a Way to fynd the Lords Mercy in due tyme.

[For 26 December]
1. The long opposition hes beine made by the Royall familie to the worke of God and progresse of the Gospell, and persecution that hes beene by their authoritie of many godlie and faithfull men since the Reformation began in this land.

2. That King James, after his swearing and subscriving the Covenant, should so foullie have fallen from the same, and, contrare thereto, have altered the governement of this Church, brought in bishopps, and many other ceremonies.

3. The persecution that was followed by him against many faithfull ministers, for their adhering to the Covenant and liberties of the Church, and testifieing against the corrupt cours of the tyme.

4. His laying of a foundation for bringing in all the ceremonies of the Church of England on this Church, whence hes flowed so many sad inconveniences as these yeires past have produced.

5. King Charles his entering upon that same course and prosecuting that same designe, whereby, after many particular offences, it came at last to ane arbitrarie and violent obtruding of the Booke of Common Prayer and Cannons upon this Church.

6. His allying and marying with one of the Popish Religion, and his tollerating the Masse and exercise of these abominations in view of the Lords people, to the great prejudice of the Reformed Religion, and the putting himself and his Kingdomes under snaires and wrath.

7. The great profanitie of his Court for many yeares, too much tollerated and countenanced by him, in maskes and Sabboth breakings, at last publictlie allowed by him in many things by the *Booke of Sports*, etc.

8. His arbitrarie governement, whereby many of all sorts hes beene brought to suffering, without proceeding according to the laws of the Kingdome.

9. His establishing the Court of High Commission, and authorising them in many things destructive to the liberties of this Church and Kingdome.

10. His prosecuting by armes, being misled by evill counsell, a warre against those who adhered to the Covenant and necessarlie and lawfullie withstood the inbringing of these corruptions unto this Church, whereby he made himself guiltie of much innocent blood of the Lords people in these Kingdomes.

11. The present King his entering to tred these same stepps: – (1) by closeing a treatie with the Popishe Irishe rebells, who had shedd so much blood, and granting them not onlie their personall libertie, but also the full exercise of the Popish religion, so that he might make use of them against his Protestant subjects; (2) by his

commissionating of excommunicatt rebells, James Grahame, to invaid againe this Kingdome, who were stryving to be faithfull to the Cause and to him, and to give Commissions to sundrie by sea for that end; (3) by his refuising for a tyme the just satisfaction was desyred by this Church and Kingdome; (4) His intertaining privat correspondencies with Malignants and enemies of the Cause, contrarie to the Covenant, whereby he was at last drawen to ane publict and scandalous deserting of the publict judicatories of this Kingdome, so contrarie to his oath, treattie, declaration and professions (whereupon followed many offences and inconveniences), and to joyne with Malignants and perverse men, who wer by his warrand incouraged to take armes at such a tyme, to the hazarding of the Cause, and fostering of jealousies, and disturbing of the peace of the Kingdome.

These sinnes being sensiblie layd out before the Lord, He is with ardent prayers to be intreated to doe away the contraversie he hes against the King and his house for these transgressions, and that he may be graciouslie pleased to blesse the Kings persone and governement.

LETTER

Commission of the general assembly to presbyteries: 29 November 1650

This sadd time of the Lords dispensation towards this Kingdome calles for mourning and searching of the causes of his great wrath; and, after serious tryell and enquyrie, we find the great contempt of the Gospell, so plentifullie given to this land, to be one of the great reasones of the provocation, for which we have appoynted a solemne fast and humiliation to be kept in all the congregations of this Kirk upon the 22 of December, being the Lords day, and have branched out in severall partes the same, which will be sent unto you in print in due tyme. And becaus the Lord is certainlie highly provocked by the sinnes of the King, his familie and court, we have also appointed Thursday, the 26 of December, to be kept as a solemne fast and humiliation for these sinnes ...

1651–E1 Thanksgiving day for victories by Commonwealth armies and navy

Thursday 30 January 1651 (England and Wales)

Cromwell's victory at Dunbar in September 1650 was followed by Major-General Lambert's against the Scottish Western Association under Ker at Hamilton (1 December) and Cromwell's own success at Edinburgh (24 December). A rising in Norfolk in December was quickly and easily suppressed. In addition, the royalist fleet was wrecked in a storm near Cartagena when fleeing from General-at-sea, Robert Blake, on 6 November. On 31 December, the Rump parliament proposed that a day of thanksgiving be held for these events on 30 January 1651. This was the anniversary of Charles I's execution and, though this was not explicitly mentioned in the journal, it is possible that the date was chosen deliberately so the Rump could compete with, or challenge, the observance of this day which had developed quickly and clandestinely among royalist sympathizers. The significance of the date would not have been lost on MPs and, though some thanksgivings had been organized with a month's notice (e.g. 1650–E2), they were usually organized more promptly by the 1650s. The act was read twice and passed on 3 January and an account of the victories complied by a committee was ordered to be printed along with various letters, the articles of surrender and a list of ordnance taken from Edinburgh. Joseph Caryll and Ralph Venning were appointed to preach before the house at St Margaret's, Westminster.

Order: parliamentary act, 3 Jan. 1651, Thomason E.1061[33].
Additional sources: *CJ*, VI, 516–17, 519; *An act for setting apart Thursday the thirtieth day of January, 1650. for a day of publique thanksgiving: together with a declaration of the grounds and reasons thereof* (1650; Thomason E.1061[33]).

ORDER

Act of parliament: 3 January 1651
If it be considered what the Lord hath done for this Commonwealth of *England* within the space of a year last past, when threatened on every side at home and abroad, by Sea and by Land, insomuch as it became incompassed with the strongest Combinations, and most mischievous Designs that were remaining within the power of Enemies to set on foot for the Unsetling and Subverting this present Government, and bringing back this Nation into Thraldom and Confusion. And if it be also observed (as God hath made it most signally appear) That in all the Deliverances and Salvations out of these Difficulties and Dangers, the Lord hath magnified his Power and Wisdom in the weakness of the Instruments by such a concurrence of Providences, so seasonable and unexpected, as the Wit of Man could not have contrived, nor Humane Strength have effected. Who is there but must acknowledge, to the Glory and Praise of the Divine Majesty, That *it hath not been by Might, nor by Power, but by the Spirit of the Lord*, that *Englands* Safety and Deliverances have been obtained? So that the People of God throughout this Nation have abundant cause not onely of Admiration, but of Exaltation in the Lord their God: For it is He that hath displayed his Mercy, Faithfulness and Power, in preserving and prospering the Endeavors of his unworthy Servants (though but a Remnant) that have been kept through his Grace, and made in any measure Faithful to the Cause and Interest of Him and His People. It is the Lord of Hosts that hath gone forth in Justice and in Fury against his and their Enemies, and hath *arisen against the house of evil doers, and against the help of them that work iniquity.*

And besides the continued Series of Glorious Salvations afforded by the good hand of God to this Nation for the year past, some fresh and memorable Instances of his Divine Power and Goodness manifested to this Commonwealth, the Parliament hath inserted in the ensuing Narrative, the better to stir up and provoke the Good People of this Nation, not onely to render Praise unto his most Holy Name on the Solemn Day of Thanksgiving set apart by them for that end, but in all Humility and Thankful Acknowledgement, desire through the Assistance of his Divine Grace, to fear and walk before him the remainder of their days, as becomes a People so immediately and wonderfully saved by the Lord.

And in the first place it is not to be passed over in silence, how timely it pleased the Lord to Discover and Disappoint the late desperate Design that was by the Enemies of this Commonwealth closely contrived and laid in several Counties, to raise a New War, or at least such Commotions and Insurrections as might make way for the coming in of a Foraign Enemy. This Design actually brake forth in *Norfolk*, which (being before the adjacent Counties of *Suffolk, Cambridge, Lincolnshire* and others (where it was also laid) were in a readiness) was seasonably disappointed. And that very Party in *Scotland* under the Command of Colonel *Ker*, which was expected to have come into *England* at the same time, and to have joyned with them, as by several Examinations taken appear, was by Divine Providence dissipated and broken, being taken also in the very Net and Snare they had laid for others: For it pleased God that they having knowledge of our Forces under the Conduct of Major General *Lambert* at *Hamilton* in *Scotland*, after that the General had parted from him, and was marched on the other side of the River with the greatest Body of his Forces, there attempting to fall into our Quarters (with the greatest Confidence to have utterly destroyed our Forces there, by surprizing them in the midst of the Night, so as not one should have been able to escape) proved through Divine Grace to their own Destruction and Ruine; so that their whole Party was scattered and broken, their Commander in Chief, Colonel *Ker*, taken Prisoner, and sore wounded, together with many other Prisoners, and a considerable number of Horse taken: And hereby a way became opened very seasonably for Major General *Lambert* to possess himself of the West part of Scotland, and of the Town of *Ayre*, a considerable Port and Garison there.

Since which also the Lord hath given in the strong Castle of Edinburgh, with Fifty three pieces of Ordnance, and Fifteen of Iron, about Eight thousand Arms, and store of Ammunition and Provisions; A more particular Accompt of all which hath been sent by the General unto the Parliament, and by their Order made publique: whereby it will abundantly appear, That it was the hand of the Lord alone that wrought out, and extended such great Salvations to us.

And together with these Mercies vouchsafed, the late Successes are not to be forgotten that the Lord hath been pleased to give unto a small part of the Parliaments Fleet at Sea, when the Season and Expectation of Service (in the apprehension of man) was at an end: It being lately certified from *Cathagena* from a Commander in the Parliaments Fleet, by his Letter dated the 22 of November, That the Squadron of Ships left under the Command of General *Blake*, having first surprized a considerable part of the *Portugal Brasil* Fleet fraughted with Sugars, and since sent home into England, did set sail and went in pursuit of *Rupert*, and the Revolted Ships with him, whom they followed into the Streights beyond *Allegant*, where they have also taken and destroyed Seven of *Ruperts* Fleet; and the said General *Blake* is in pursuit of the rest to the places whether he had Intelligence *Rupert* was then sailed: All which, as it is of great Importance to the Traffique and Commerce of the Merchants of this Nation, So thereby also the Mercies of the Lord towards this Commonwealth are sounded forth into the Ears of Foraign Princes and States, who now begin to see and acknowledge, That God hath been with the Parliament of the Commonwealth of ENGLAND, and is their Strength and Establishment.

For all which wonderful Mercies and signal Salvations, The Parliament desire by themselves, and all the Good People of this Nation, to publish their humble and thankful Acknowledgements unto the Lord; And therefore do Enact, and by the Authority of this present Parliament be it Enacted and Ordained, That *Thursday* the Thirtieth day of *January*, One thousand six hundred and fifty, be set apart and observed as a Day of Publique Thanksgiving and Holy Rejoycing for the forementioned Mercies, in all Churches and Chappels within *England* and *Wales*, and Town of *Berwick*. And all Ministers and Pastors, and all the People of this Commonwealth, are Enjoyned duly and diligently to observe the same, by attending upon the Publique Worship of God solemnly to be performed upon that Day. And be it Enacted, That the said Ministers do upon the Lords-day next before the said Thirtieth day of *January* publish this Act, by Reading the same in their respective Churches and Chappels, to the end notice may be given, and observation had thereof accordingly.

1651–E2   Fast days during political, military and diplomatic anxieties for the Commonwealth

Thursday 13 March 1651 (London, Westminster, the late lines of communication and weekly bills of mortality); Wednesday 2 April 1651 (elsewhere in England, Wales and Berwick-upon-Tweed)

On 4 March, the Rump parliament proposed a day of solemn fasting and humiliation; the act was read twice, received a negative vote to be engrossed and was passed and ordered on 7 March. The negative vote for the engrossment was probably a short cut to enable the bill to pass more quickly: it stopped the bill from going to committee and allowed it to move immediately to a final vote. It was the first time this had happened for bills of special worship, but occurred again later in 1651 and in 1652 (see 1651–1 and 1652–EIr). Though a declaration was compiled to explain the reasons for the fast day, it identified these only very broadly and focused instead on previous signs of divine providence. The likely reasons for the fast day were the coronation of Charles II by the Scots (1 January); the recruitment of royalists into parts of the Scottish army; Cromwell's ill-health and Ireton's failure to take both Limerick and Athlone. In addition, in mid-February the Commonwealth had sent a delegation to negotiate an alliance with the Dutch states-general. Owen, Leigh and John Simpson were appointed to preach before parliament. Owen's and Leigh's sermons were well received (Owen was immediately made dean of Christ Church, Oxford), but Simpson's caused furore and the Rump debated it for more than two hours, criticizing John Harrison, who had nominated Simpson, and rebuking the preacher himself. Reflecting growing divisions within the Rump, parliament rarely offered formal thanks to preachers or ordered sermons to be printed after this episode.

Order: parliamentary act, 7 Mar. 1651, Thomason E.1061[42], pp. 1317–19*.
Additional sources: *CJ*, VI, 544, 546; *FSP*, XXXIV, 3–4; Bernard Alsop, *A perfect account of the daily intelligence from the armies*, 12–19 Mar. 1651, Thomason E.626[9], p. 77; Blair Worden, *The Rump parliament, 1648–1653* (Cambridge, 1974), p. 242.

ORDER

Act of parliament: 7 March 1651
The wonderful Dispensations of the Providence of God in the Salvations which he hath wrought for this Nation, and the Alterations he hath made within a few years for our good; as they call for continual Acknowledgements and Praises from his people, so they are strong Encouragements to them to depend upon him, till he hath made his Work perfect: In these the Lord hath exceedingly magnified his own Mercy, and his Infinite Power and Wisdom hath been greatly exalted, not onely in carrying on the Work to a higher pitch then what either the wisest men could foresee, or the

best of men had their hopes elevated unto, but also in drawing forth the Spirits of some of his Servants beyond their first intentions, to follow him in untrodden paths of danger and difficulty, which he by his eminent Providences did trace out to them; and to which he did as it were guide them with his Eye, that it might appear to be not by Humane Wisdom or Power, but by his Spirit. In all which, and many other special Manifestations of himself, the people of God in this Nation have grounds of hope, That these are but the First-fruits of an Harvest of Mercy; and that the Lord, who hath gloriously exceeded their Expectations in what is past, will shew forth his Faithfulness in guiding them safe through the remaining Dangers and Difficulties they are to pass, and in the speedy effecting of the great things yet behinde, which he hath promised to do for his Church in the latter days; for which so many Prayers have been put up to Heaven in the Ages past, and are renewed with more fervency and longings, to which the Lord hath raised up the Spirits of his people in this present Age. And as the Lord by setting out the Rage of the Enemy, and permitting them to continue their mischievous Designs against those that are his in this Nation, doth thereby awaken those who fear him, from Security, and call upon them to improve their Counsels and Power for the carrying on his Work to his Glory (wherein he is alway pleased to provide for their good and safety) so it should put them in minde, That their Salvation being onely in him, they ought to have recourse to him at all times, both for his Direction and Blessing.[339]

The Parliament out of a sense of their Duty herein, and the many Experiences they have had, though very unworthy, of the gracious Returns of Prayer which God hath vouchsafed them (in which respect they have cause to say, They never sought him in vain) and to manifest, That their whole Dependance both for Wisdom and Strength is in the Lord alone: (whose Ends they desire to serve) and perfectly to trust in him for the consummating the Work of his own Glory, and their Peace in the Ruine of his and their implacable Enemies, the Vindication of his own Cause, and the Sincerity of his Servants, the Uniting the Hearts of all that love the Lord Jesus Christ in Sincerity, and Establishing this Nation in Truth and Peace, Do Enact and Ordain, and be it Enacted and Ordained by this present Parliament, and the Authority thereof, That *Thursday* the Thirteenth day of *March*, One thousand six hundred fifty, be set apart for a Day of Publique Fasting and Humiliation, to be observed in all Churches and Chappels within the Cities of *London* and *Westminster*, the late Lines of Communication, and Weekly Bills of Mortality, to seek the Lord earnestly for the pardon of the Great and Crying Sins of this Nation; and to vouchsafe his especial Presence with, and Blessing upon the Counsels of this Nation, and their Forces both by Land and Sea, for perfecting his work in *Scotland* and *Ireland*; as also to vouchsafe his Direction and Blessing upon their Treaties with Forraign Nations now in Agitation, and so to carry on his own great Design, as that the Enemies of the Lord may be found Lyars, and that all those who fear the Lord in this Nation, may say, This is our God, we have waited for him, and he hath saved us.

And be it Enacted by the Authority aforesaid, That *Wednesday* the Second day of *April*, One thousand six hundred fifty one, be set apart as a Day of Publique Humiliation for the ends aforesaid, in all other Churches and Chappels within *England* and *Wales*, and Town of *Berwick*. And all Ministers and People of this Commonwealth are enjoyned duly and diligently to observe the same, by attending upon the publique Worship of God solemnly to be performed upon those days respectively.

---

[339] At this point the type changes from roman to black letter.

And the said Ministers are hereby Required to publish this Act the Sabbath day next before the said several days respectively, to the end notice may be given, and observation had thereof accordingly.

1651–S1   Fast days during English occupation and domestic divisions

Sunday 13 April 1651 or the first Sunday after receipt (Scotland)

At the time of the appointment of this fast, Scotland south of the Forth was occupied by English troops, and serious divisions had emerged within the Kirk between supporters and critics of the commission of the general assembly. In its public resolutions of 14 December 1650, the commission meeting in Perth had given its approval for a military levy of all fencible men other than excommunicates, opponents of the covenants and the notoriously scandalous. This decision, which allowed former engagers and royalists to join the army, prompted a series of dissenting protests from presbyteries, and led some ministers to preach against the commission. The day after it ordered this fast, the commission issued a *Short exhortation*, to be read to congregations, lamenting the English occupation, and forbidding ministers from speaking or writing against the resolutions. It is likely that the fast and the reading of the *Short exhortation* were boycotted by the commission's critics, who became known as Protesters.

Order: act of the commission of the general assembly, 19 Mar. 1651, *RCGA*, III, 340.
Causes: *RCGA*, III, 340–3.
Letter: commission of the general assembly to presbyteries, 20 Mar. 1651, *RCGA*, III, 353.
Additional sources: *Perth, 20 March, 1651. A short exhortation and warning* ([Aberdeen], [1651]; Wing C4259A); *RPS*, M1651/3/11; Lamont, p. 30; *Inverness and Dingwall records*, pp. 210–13.

ORDER

Act of the commission of the general assembly: 19 March 1651
The Commission of Assembly think it necessar that there be a Solemne Fast and Humiliation keept upon the second Sabboth of the moneth of Aprile, it being the 13 day thereof.

CAUSES

We need not to search farre in the causes of a humiliation. There is none who lookes upon the present posture of the Kingdome, the sadd judgements that are incumbent and imminent, and the sinfulnesse thereof notwithstanding of all that is comed upon us, but will find them palpable, as:

1. First. Our continueing in the guiltinesse of sinnes formerlie mourned for, tho the Lords hand hes been streatched out against us, the same seeds of evills springing afresh even while the Lord is pleading against them.

2. Our generall security and universall unprofitablenesse under and unanswerablenesse unto the Lords way with us, whither of goodnesse or severity, so that we are neither bettered by the one nor the other; whereby, if mercie prevent not, our wound may become uncureable.

3. The profanitie of many in the land, even of these who are imployed in armes, which makes unfaithfulnes in levies, oppression and violence in quarterings, etc., to the hazard of the worke and scandall of the Gospell.

4. The slownesse and negligence in acting against the enemie of trueth and of the peace and government of these Kingdomes – notwithstanding of the pressure of the troubles themselves, cryes and groanes of the people, and frequent exhortations and remonstrances of the Kirk – which, as it cannot be looked upon but as a great token of wrath from the Lord, so must we acknowledge it to be a great part of our guiltinesse that now, after so many moneths wherein God hes wonderfullie given us a breathing in this part of the land, that yet litle or nothing is done against the enemie.

5. The selfinesse of the time, tho that many in the thrie Kingdomes, and even members of this same Kingdome, and particularlie these of the cheefe citie, be suffering, yet the most parte of the land is secure and tenacious of, and selfie in pursueing particular interests, as if the publict were not concerned.

6. The rysing and great differences of judgement upon the unclearnesse of some anent the Publict Resolutions, whereby the worke of God and delyverance of this Kirk and Kingdome is obstructed.

7. The extreme distress of our brethren and desolation of the land be south Forth, and especiallie of our cheefe citie, the cruell and barbarous usage of our brethren that are prisoners, the feare of famine, the many scattered congregations whose pastors are driven away and necessarlie detained from them, the hazard of their soules that are under the feet of the enemie, the falling away of some to their pernitious wayes, and the sadd distresses of our brethren and fellow Covenanters in England and Ireland.

8. That the Lord in his just displeasure against our great and manifold sinnes goes not foorth with our armies, but gives up the most considerable part of the land and our strongholds therein into the hands of the enemie.

We are therefore in all humility and earnestnes to pray:

1. First, That God would poure out of his Spirit of repentance upon all sorts, that we may not fast to stryfe and debate, but that there may be an impartiall searching of the sinnes which have provocked God, and a sincear turning from them to the Lord, and that he would forgive the iniquity of all ranks in the land, and turne from his fearce wrath which is burning against the same.

2. That God would stirre up the spirits of people for their dueties to doe in their places as he calles them; that Magistrats may be faithfull in their place, studieing the publict good, and be furnished with counsell for that end; that officers and souldiers may be sanctified and fitted with faithfulnes, abilitie, and courage for their places; and that all who have professed repentance in returning from former Malignant wayes may be established by grace to walk so as the Gospell may not suffer by any of their miscariages.

3. That God would delyver these Kingdomes from the present enemie, and would againe restoir the whole land to the former bewtie of the enjoying of the libertie and purity of ordinances, and that he would guard his people from their snares, and reclame any that are intangled therein.

4. That God would make his people willing and stirre them up for the defence of their brethren, and blesse and gather our armies together, and may sanctifie them to be holie unto him and instrumentall for the delyverie of this distressed land; and

that the Lord would judge these who have unjustly invaded and spoyled us, trampled on authority, tred downe Gods sacred ordinances, and murdered so many of Gods dear people.

5. That the Lord, who is One, may give his people and servants one heart and one way to serve him in his worke with one consent against all the enemies thereof, and that he would remove and prevent the growing offences of these times.

6. That God would looke upon the afflictions of the Royall familie and blesse the King, that he may be keeped free both from the snaires and dangers of these times, and in due time be restoired to his just right, sett on the throne of all his thrie Kingdomes, made a comfortable instrument for the good of the work and people of God, and terrible to all the enemies within the same.

7. That the Lord would mercifully remember our distressed brethren in our cheefe citie and other desolate partes of the land under the feet of the enemie, releeve our prisoners, prevent the feared famine, gather together his scattered congregations unto the publict and free use of his ordinances, recall them who have fallen unto the wayes or errours of the enemies, and lift up the standart of the Gospell in all the thrie Kingdomes.

8. That till the delyverance come all the Lords people may glorifie him in their patient bearing of the crosse, without grudging or murmuring, untill he plead their cause, and bring them foorth unto the light.

LETTER

Commission of the general assembly to presbyteries: 20 March 1651

… Yow shall also receave the Causes of the Fast and be carefull to observe it diligentlie, and report your diligence therein; and if this letter shall not come tymeously to your hands, yow shall keepe it upon the first Sabboth after this shall come unto yow …

1651–S2 Fast days for the army, Charles II and the reformed church

Thursday 19 June and Sunday 22 June 1651 (Scotland)

In the early months of 1651, the Scottish army was remodelled and concentrated in Stirling, where it awaited a major confrontation with the English troops occupying the south-east of the country. The uncertainty of the standoff was reflected in the commission's fast act, which ordered that the fast was to be kept earlier in the army if it marched before 19 June. The day before appointing the fast, the commission had further alienated the Protesters (see 1651–S1) by signalling that it was prepared for parliament to repeal the acts of classes, statutes of 1646 and 1649 that had excluded royalists and engagers from public office. Thus, the fast was not kept by the Protesters, although those in the presbytery of Paisley boycotted the observance less out of opposition to the commission than from a desire to comply with the rest of the synod of Glasgow and Ayr. In the presbytery of Strathbogie, the commission's act arrived late and the fast was kept on 29 June and 3 July.

Order: act of the commission of the general assembly, 25 May 1651, *RCGA*, III, 447.
Causes: *RCGA*, III, 447–9.
Additional sources: *RPS*, M1651/5/8; presbytery of Paisley minutes, NRS, CH2/294/3, pp. 100–1;

Lamont, p. 30; *RCGA*, III, 489; *Strathbogie presbytery*, pp. 199–200; *Inverness and Dingwall records*, pp. 221–3.

ORDER

Act of the commission of the general assembly: 25 May 1651

The Commission approves the causes of the Fast, and appoints a Solemne Fast and Humiliation to be kept through the Kingdome upon the 3ᵈ Thursday of Junij and the Sabboth following; and if the Armie march before that time, this Fast it to be keeped in the Armie upon any weeke day that shall be found convenient before the Armies march, and upon the Sabboth following. The tenor of the causes follow:

CAUSES

Beside the causes formerlie emitted for fasting and humiliation by the Commission:

1. We are to bewayle the great stupidity and profanity which everie where abound in all the land, so as there are verie few who are sensible of their sin or sorrowfull for the chastisement wherewith God hath chastised us, or who stand on the gape to make up the hedge that the fierce wrath of God doe not overturne the remnant of the land, neither doe they profite by the rod as to turne to him that smites them.

2. Though many in the Army and generallie throughout all the land have profest their repentance for their Malignant courses, and have been receaved into Ecclesiastical society, yet these who were in that course ought constantly to remember their evill wayes, and be ashamed, and mourne after the Lord for the same.

3. We are to wrastle earnestly with the Lord, that, laying aside his fierce wrath, he will be graciously pleased to bless our King, restore him to the possession of his just rights, and sanctifie him to be the instrument of God for promoving the worke of Reformatioun in England and Ireland, and preserving it in Scotland; that the Lord would be pleased to assist him in the managing of the weightie affaires of the Kingdome, particularly in the conduct of the Armie, and to blesse all that have charge under him with faithfulnes, courage, and authority, and sanctifie and strengthen the souldiers to doe their duty effectually and obediently.

4. That seing this blasphemous enemy now infesting the land is a most violent adversar to the work of Reformation and union of the Kirks in the 3 Kingdomes in Religion, Worship, and Government, according to the Solemne League and Covenant, and that the truly godly in all the 3 Kingdomes are under the violence of his persecution, the Lord would poure abundance of the Spirit of grace and supplication, and stirre up the spirits of all the godly in the 3 Kingdomes to wrastle with God for a delyverance at this time from this our common and treacherous enemy.

5. That God would graciously unite the hearts of all these who are concerned and in hazard by the present enemy to act joyntly in their stations for the cause of God and against the enemy with ane heart and mynd, and remove all jealousies and heart-burnings from among them.

6. That as God hath gotten honour in making many of all ranks who were opposed to the worke of Reformation to acknowledge their guiltines, and to submitt to discipline, so he wald be graciously pleased to make them manifest the reality of their repentance by their sincere and effectuall actings against the enemy and constant good cariage in all tyme coming.

7. That the Lord would provide for the necessarie preservation of the lyves of his people from the sword and feared famine.

8. That the Lord would mercifully lead out our armie, and enable everie one therein to keep them selves from everie wicked thing, cover their heads in the day of battell, teach their hands to warre and their fingers to fight, and make them have good successe, that the enemy may fall and flie before them; and that the Lord would graciously please by their means to deliver our brethren that are under the foot of that enemy, and preserve the remnant of this oppressed Kirk and Kingdome from unjust violence of the cursed and cruell adversary.

1651–E3   Thanksgiving prayers for Commonwealth victory at Inverkeithing

Sunday 27 July 1651 (London, the late lines of communication and weekly bills of mortality)

In July, Lambert attempted to disrupt Scottish supply lines from Fife to Stirling, where Leslie's army was stationed. Although Leslie's commanders, Holbourne and Brown, scored some initial successes, Lambert routed their troops at Inverkeithing on 20 July while sustaining very few losses. The victory opened up the Firth of Forth and Fife to the English forces. The Rump parliament ordered a thanksgiving to be observed on 30 July. The order was distributed by the lord mayor and the sheriffs of London, Middlesex and Surrey; Cromwell's letter describing the victory was ordered to be printed.

Order: parliamentary order, 25 July 1651, *CJ*, VI, 609.
Additional source: *A letter from the lord general, dated the one and twentieth day of July, to the right honorable William Lenthal esq* (1651; Wing C7095).
Printed sermon: Masterton, St Clement Danes, London (M1072).

ORDER

Parliamentary order: 25 July 1651
Ordered, by the Parliament, That upon the next Lord's Day, the Ministers in all the Congregations within the City of *London*, and late Lines of Communication, and weekly Bills of Mortality, do render Thanks to Almighty God for his great Mercy in the great Success given to the Parliament's Forces in *Scotland* against the Enemy there, upon the last Lord's Day, being the Twentieth Day of *July* instant; and implore the Continuance of God's Blessing upon the Proceedings of the Forces of this Commonwealth there, and the Perfecting of his own Work to his Praise.

Ordered, That this Order be forthwith printed and published: And that the Lord Mayor of the City of *London*, and the Sheriffs of *London, Middlesex*, and *Surrey*, respectively, do take care that timely Notice hereof be given to the several Ministers, accordingly.

1651–Ir1 Fast day during plague, Scottish invasion of England and English divisions

Thursday 28 August 1651 (Dublin?)

This occasion is only known from Steele's handlist of proclamations, which recorded the existence of this order in manuscript before it was destroyed by fire at the former Dublin Record Office in 1922; Steele saw the order only in manuscript. The disease continued to grip Dublin (see 1650-Ir1): in August, between fifty and sixty people died a week. There were also outbreaks in Limerick and Kilkenny. The fast was also concerned with events in England. Charles II began to march south from Stirling at the head of a 14,000-strong Scottish army, entering Carlisle on 6 August where he was proclaimed king of England. The Rump parliament continued to be divided over religion. The mayor of Dublin was responsible for giving notice of the fast day.

Order: order by commissioners, 25 Aug. 1651, not extant [formerly Dublin PRO, Order Book 42, p. 3; described in Steele, II, no. 481].

DESCRIPTION OF ORDER

Order by commissioners, 25 August 1651
On account of plague in Dubline, invasion of England, and the spirit of division among the Parliamentary party, a solemn fast is ordered on Thursday next, 28 August. Mayor to give notice.

1651–E4 Thanksgiving prayers for Commonwealth victories at Wigan and in Scotland

Sunday 31 August 1651 (London, the late lines of communication and weekly bills of mortality)

The earl of Derby landed in Lancashire, from the royalist stronghold of the Isle of Man, with a small force (*c.* 750–1,500 men) to support Charles II, but was routed at Wigan on 25 August by Harrison and Lambert. Meanwhile, in Scotland, Lieutenant-General Monck took Inchgarvie (24 July) and Burntisland (29 July), and Perth surrendered to Cromwell (1 August). On 29 August, the Rump parliament ordered thanksgivings to be observed for these victories in two days time. When it received news of the surrender of Stirling to Monck (the town on 6 August, the castle on 14 August), it amended the order. Narratives of the victories were commissioned and printed, though these cannot now be traced. It is unclear why these thanksgivings were only ordered to be observed in and around London.

Order: parliamentary orders, 29 Aug. 1651, *CJ*, VII, 8; 30 Aug. 1651, Wing E2124* [also in *CJ*, VII, 9].

ORDERS

Parliamentary order: 29 August 1651
Resolved, That, on the next Lord's Day, Thanks be given to Almighty God, by the Ministers in all Churches and Congregations within the City of *London*, and all

Places within the late Lines of Communication, and weekly Bills of Mortality, for the great Mercies of God to this Nation, in the great and seasonable Defeat of the Earl of *Derbie's* Forces in the County of *Lancaster*: And likewise for the great Successes it hath pleased the Lord to give the Parliament Forces in *Scotland*: And that the Lord Mayor of the City of *London* do take Care, that timely Notice be given to the said Ministers, accordingly.

    Resolved, That it be referred to the Council of State, to prepare a Narrative upon these Two Subjects, to be published, as the Ground of this Thanksgiving; and to report it to the House To-morrow Morning.

Parliamentary order: 30 August 1651

    The Parliament having received Intelligence of the taking of the Castle of *Sterling* in Scotland (wherein were the Records of Scotland, Forty Pieces of Ordnance, Five thousand Arms, with several Provisions and Ammunition) As also of the Dispersing of the new Levies of the Enemy in Scotland; and likewise of the total Rout and Overthrow of the Earl of *Derby,* and all the Forces under his Command in Lancashire, by the Parliaments Forces under Colonel *Robert Lilborne* (the Particulars whereof, together with the Number and Names of divers of the Colonels slain or taken Prisoners, is contained in a Letter sent to the Parliament from the said Colonel *Robert Lilborne*) Do Order, that on the next Lords day, Thanks be given to Almighty God by the Ministers in all Churches and Congregations within the late Lines of Communication, and weekly Bills of Mortality, for these Great and Seasonable Mercies; and that they do then also beg of Almighty God, a Blessing upon the Parliaments Army now ready to Ingage with the Enemy. And that the Lord Mayor of the City of *London* do take care, That timely notice be given to the said Ministers accordingly.

1651–S3   Fast day during domestic anxieties and divisions

Sunday 31 August 1651 (Scotland)

The general assembly met at St Andrews from 16 to 21 July, when it was adjourned to Dundee on news of the English victory at Inverkeithing (see 1651–E3). The Protesters, who had been excluded from the assembly, denounced the meeting as unfree. The reconvened assembly approved the commission's decisions over the previous six months with respect to the public resolutions, and deprived some of the Protester ministers, confirming the schism in the Kirk. The reconvened assembly also appointed a fast, which was presumably boycotted by the Protesters.

Order: act of the general assembly, *c.* 31 July 1651 (not found).
Causes: described in *Inverness and Dingwall records*, pp. 227–8.
Additional sources: *The protestation of diverse ministers* (Edinburgh, 1651; Wing P3861); *A warning and declaration from the generall assembly* (Aberdeen, 1651; Wing C4272A); Lamont, p. 34; *Strathbogie presbytery*, p. 211.

DESCRIPTION OF THE CAUSES

Strathbogie presbytery
Inverness and Dingwall records

1. Albeit the lord be evidentlie p'seving his controversie for the abounding of sinne in the land, yet no man sayth what have I done, bot everie man following his ovne way as the horse rusheth into the battell.

2. Tho in the midst of wrath the lord doth remember mercie towards ws, and stretcheth forth his arme still with the offer of reconciliation throgh Christ in the preaching of the gospell, yet the offer of his grace is not seriouslie imbraced.

3. The holie ordinance of God nov in so long a tyme continued with ws in puritie and plentie are neglected and dishaunted by many, sleigtlie and p'functoriouslie made wse of by others.

4. The wniversall evill of preferring ovr ovne things of ch[rist's].

5. Ovr obstinate continuing in those evills qlk we must have palpablie read in the rod, qrby the lord hath beine scourging ws, such as covetousnes, etc.

6. As if continuance in sinne wnder judgment were too little we grov worse wnder afliction, fighting with God in the furnace, blasphemie, etc.

7. As for these thingis, and many things els which the prudence and faithfullnes of Ministers will easily lead them to observe, we ought to be humblie before the lord and poure spirits before him; So we are particularlie to pray and request y[t] the lord wald be pleasit to give pardon to ovr king, states, airmie, ministerie, and people of all rankes, y[t] the lord wald looke wpon the lov condition of the land, how justlie soever smitten by him yet most wnjustlie invaded by a blasphemous and p'fidious enemie.

8. That as he hes made judgment begin att his ovne house, he wald make the enemies drink of the dregs of the cup, heale ovr backslydings, make wp our begun rentings, save us from the spirit of separation, prosper ovr wndertakings, and yet be pleasit to goe ovt with ovr airmie and relieve his borne dovne truth and oppressed people in the 3 kingdomes, y[t] truth may triumph over errour, Gods people may after there sad dayes injoy peace and truth, and our king, now in covenant with God and ws, may be restored wnto and settled in his due right, for the good of religion in the thre kingdomes, in Scotland, England, and Ireland, according to the covenant.

1651–E5 Thanksgiving prayers for Commonwealth victory at the battle of Worcester

Sunday 7 September 1651 (the late lines of communication and weekly bills of mortality)

Charles II occupied the loyal but weakly fortified town of Worcester on 22 August with a much depleted, weak and tired army. On 3 September, Cromwell, who had hurried south after his victory at Perth, organized a two-pronged attack on the town from the east and south. Having breached the city's walls, he launched an outright attack on the city in the evening and, after bitter fighting, was victorious. Charles was persuaded to flee. The Rump parliament intended to organize a nationwide thanksgiving for this victory, which saw an unexpected, though shortlived, rise in the regime's popularity due to hostility towards Charles's Scottish soldiers. In the meantime, it took 'into Consideration how to improve this extraordinary Blessing for the publick Service of the Commonwealth, and the Advantage thereof' and ordered thanksgivings on 7 September in and around London. The Rump does not seem to have observed these prayers as a body, but delayed its observance until the nationwide thanksgiving was ordered. Bulstrode Whitelocke, who was appointed to offer Cromwell formal congratulations for the victory on the 10th, spent at least part of the day meditating on Nahum 2.13, 'Behold, I am against thee, saith the lord of hosts, and I will burn her chariots in the smoke, and the sword shall devour thy young lions [i.e. Charles II]: and I will cut off thy prey from the earth, and the voice of thy messengers shall no more be heard.'

Order: parliamentary order, 5 Sept. 1651, Wing C7105*, pp. 6–7 [also in *CJ*, VII, 12 and Wing C7096, pp. 7–8].
Additional sources: *CJ*, VII, 12; *A letter from the Lord General Cromvvel, touching the great victory obtained neer Worcester* (1651; Wing C7105); *A letter from the Lord General Cromvvel, dated September the fourth, 1651. To the Right Honorable William Lenthal Esq; speaker of the parliament of the Commonwealth of England* (1651; Wing C7096); *Whitelocke diary*, p. 279.

ORDER

Parliamentary order: 5 September 1651
The Parliament being very sensible of the wonderful and seasonable Mercies God hath been pleased to vouchsafe unto this Nation, by his great Blessing upon their Army near *Worcester*, in Routing the Army of the *Scots* on Wednesday last, As is expressed in a Letter from the Lord General to the Speaker of the Parliament, herewith Printed, and intending to set apart a day of Solemn Thanksgiving unto God, to be observed through this Commonwealth; Do in the mean time Order, That the Ministers in all Churches and Congregations within the late Lines of Communication and weekly Bills of Mortality, on the next Lords day, give Publique Thanks to Almighty God for this great Mercy; And that the Lord Major of the City of *London*, Do take care that timely notice be given to the said Ministers for that purpose; and that the said Ministers do then read the said Letter.

1651–1   Thanksgiving day throughout the British Isles for Commonwealth victory at the battle of Worcester

Friday 24 October 1651 (England and Wales; Scotland and Ireland)

Following the thanksgiving prayers for 1651–E5, on 6 September, the Rump parliament proposed a thanksgiving day to be observed on 2 October in England and Wales, Scotland and Ireland for Cromwell's victory at Worcester. The act for the thanksgiving was read on 16 September and, again on 18 September, at which point the day of observance was changed to 24 October for reasons that were not stated. On 26 September, the house rejected engrossing the bill – as it had done for 1651–E2 – probably in order to enable the bill to move immediately to its final reading, whereupon it was passed. An account of the battle was commissioned (*A letter from the Lord General Cromwell*) to be read out during the service. The Rump attended the thanksgiving service at St Margaret's, Westminster. It was supposed to dine at the Banqueting House at Whitehall after the service, but this order was cancelled on 30 September; the reason for this is not clear. Thomas Goodwin and John Owen preached the sermons; if Goodwin's was printed, it is no longer extant.

The Rump and its supporters sought to capitalize on the victory. On 6 September, an annual thanksgiving for the victory was proposed and a bill for it was read for the first time on 18 September. However, it appears to have garnered little support because there are no further references to it in the journal, though parliament did observe the anniversary in 1652. In 1654, however, although the new parliament met (under the terms of the Instrument of Government) on Sunday 3 September and attended divine service in Westminster Abbey, there is no evidence that the day was observed specifically as a thanksgiving for Worcester.

Cromwell made a triumphal entry into London on 10 September; prisoners were paraded through the streets (11 September) and some of the royalist leaders were executed, including the earl of Derby (15 October). The Rump parliament exploited news that royalists in Scotland and France had held 'Thanksgivings and Triumphs' in preparation for Charles's march southward, only to be 'ashamed' when the king was roundly defeated. It also tarnished the royalists with accusations of popery: one report stated that 'The late Queen of England [Henrietta Maria] seemeth to mourn too, yet not so much as others' because 'by general report' she often criticized Charles 'for not adhering to the Pope (though she had taught him Popery.) It is likely the titular Duke of York [the future James II] will try his fortunes that way.' Nevertheless, although Charles had not gained much support in England, there was opposition to the thanksgiving. William Clewer, minister of Blisworth, was ejected from his living for refusing to observe the day; John Fisher, minister of Weston, was ejected for reading the forty-first psalm during the service at his college (probably Queen's College, Oxford). Peter Ince, rector of Donhead St Mary, Wiltshire, preached that 'the parliament men did deserve to have their heads some of them cut off'.

This occasion was significant because it was the first time that special worship had been ordered simultaneously in all four nations by one uniform order; in 1625, fast days during the plague had been ordered separately in England and Wales, Scotland and Ireland. Indeed, the council of state even ordered that 100 copies of the act and narrative be sent to New England. How far the occasion was observed in Scotland and Ireland, to which 2,000 copies were sent, is unclear. The Rump had no authority to order special worship in Scotland: not only had Scotland not been fully conquered, but worship was normally ordered by the Kirk. No evidence survives to show whether the thanksgiving was observed in Ireland.

Order: parliamentary act, 26 Sept. 1651, Thomason E.1061[57].
Additional sources: *CJ*, VII, 12–13, 18–22, 173, 365; *FSP*, XXXIV, 5–7, 9; *An act for setting apart Friday the four and twentieth day of October* (1651; Thomason E.1061[57]); *A letter from the Lord General Cromwell, dated September the fourth* (1651; Wing C7096); John Goodwin, *Two hyms, or spirituall songs; sung in Mr. Goodwins congregation on Friday last being the 24. of Octob. 1651* (1651; Wing G1212); *Weekly Intelligencer of the Common Wealth*, 40 (30 Sept. –7 Oct. 1651), pp. 308–9; *Several proceedings in Parliament*, p. 106 (2–9 Oct. 1651; Thomason E.787[30]), p. 1643; *Perfect account of the daily intelligence from the armies*, 38 (24 Sept.–1 Oct. 1651; Thomason E.643[1]), p. 303; petition of William Clewer, MA, 30 May, 1660, SP29/1/9I, fo. 19r; John Fisher to Sir Joseph Williamson, 14 Dec. 1677, SP29/398/90, fo. 124r; *CSPD, 1677–8*, pp. 506–7; *SP Thurloe*, III, 648; *CSPD, 1660–1*, pp. 2, 142; *Walker revised: being a revision of John Walker's Sufferings of the clergy during the Grand Rebellion, 1642–60*, ed. H. G. Matthews (Oxford, 1948), p. 32; *CSPC 1574–1660*, p. 362; SP25/23, fo. 3.

Printed sermons: Coler, Broughton (Wing C5062A); Owen, parliament (Wing O711, O711A, O712; *FSP*, XXXIV, 13–50); Speed, Bristol (Wing S4907).

ORDER

Act of parliament: 26 September 1651

The Works of Providence, by which the Lord hath pleaded the Cause of this Parliament and Commonwealth in the sight of the Nations round about, are Glorious, and will be sought out by all those that have pleasure in them; and therefore must not pass under the common Title of *Events and Chances of War*: The Lord having so done this marvellous Work for Time and Place, with a Concurrence of all other remarkable Circumstances, That it ought to be had in Everlasting Remembrance, both by our Selves, and by the Generations which shall be born; as will eminently and convincingly appear by this brief ensuing *Narrative*.

After the Lord (the Great and Righteous Judge of Heaven and Earth) was pleased so Signally to bear Witness to the Justice and Necessity of our Armies marching into *Scotland*, by giving Sentence (when Solemn Appeals were made unto him by both Parties) on our side, in that glorious Victory vouchsafed unto our Army the Third day of *September*, One thousand six hundred and fifty, against the *Scots* near *Dunbar*: The same Divine Providence led on our Forces there to the gaining of many Towns and Garisons; and in particular, *Leith, Edinburgh*, and not long after, the Castle there, though in the Esteem of the Enemy impregnable. But the Enemy not resting in that decision, did reinforce themselves, and relying on the advantage of the Town and Pass at *Sterling*, and other Intrenchments, would by no Provocation or Endeavors on our part used, be drawn forth to an Engagement, though our Forces faced them up to their Works, when the *Scots* (as some of themselves have since confessed) were Twenty seven thousand, and ours nothing near that number, suffering a strong Garison of theirs to be stormed and taken within the view of their Camp, without once offering to relieve it. The Consideration hereof, and of the Charge and Difficulties of a Winters War (which the Enemy seemed chiefly to Design, and might the better effect whiles they had *Sterling*, and thereby the Command of the rich Country of *Fife* at hand to Quarter their Forces in, and by means of St. *Johnstons* (a second Pass) the whole North of *Scotland* to furnish them with Recruits of Men and Supplies of all Provisions; and likewise many Sea Ports to let in Forreign Assistance) produced a Resolution to put over a Force into *Fife* (notwithstanding all Hazards) to straiten their Quarters and hinder their Supplies; Which Attempt the Lord was pleased to Crown, not onely by giving us speedy and happy Footing, but a notable Victory to that part of our Army commanded by the Major General, over the Forces of the Enemy, whereof the greatest number were a commanded Party of their choice Men out of their whole Army: In which Defeat near One thousand five hundred were taken Prisoners, together with Sir *John Brown* their Commander in Chief, and the greatest part of the residue slain, Forty two Colours taken, and all this (which made the Mercy the more remarkable) with the loss onely of Four of our Men slain on the place, and some wounded. About this very time the General marched up near *Sterling* to engage the Enemy, who having quitted their Camp at *Torwood*, were march'd through *Sterling*, Sixteen Miles toward our Forces in *Fife*; And finding the Enemy would not Engage (having disposed on this side of the River such Force as could well be spared to hinder the Enemies Levies and Provisions; of if they should Advance for *England*, to be upon our Borders, and to joyn with other Parties there in Readiness to retard their March) The General Remarch'd to *South-Ferry*, and Landed the Residue of his Army in *Fife*; upon which, the strong Castle of *Enisgarvy*, in the Middle of the River, with Sixteen Pieces of Canon, and *Brunt-Island*, were Surrendred, and the Army marcht forthwith towards St. *Johnstons*. The Enemy being thereby awakened, sent a Party of about One thousand Foot, with a Governor, into St. *Johnstons*, who arrived there Two hours before the General sate down with the Army: And finding by this Interposition his Northern Supplies cut off, marcht directly for *England* with an Army of Sixteen thousand Horse and Foot, and a Light Train of Artillery; being come near *Carlile*, their King caused himself to be Proclaimed King of *England*, and sending out his Declarations full of fair Promises to all that should come in to him or not oppose him, marched forward, being attended in his Motions by some of our Horse. The General (St. *Johnstons* being Surrendred, leaving a Garison there, and about Seven thousand Horse and Foot under the Command of the Lieutenant General of the Ordinance, for reducing the Castle of *Sterling* and other Garisons, and preventing any Levies by the Enemy) with the rest of the Army came back for *Lieth*, and the same day sent away Five Regiments of Horse and Dragoons to fall into the Rear of the Enemy, whiles himself with the rest of his Horse, his Body of Foot, and Train of Artillery, Advanced after with all possible speed towards *England*. The Enemy being come to *Warrington*, and attempting the Pass there, our Forces (who a day or two before were joyned and got into his Van) thought not fit long to Dispute it, in respect the River was in many places Fordable, the Lands and Inclosures inconvenient for the Horse; and the Foot, whom they found at the Bridge, though full of Courage, and desirous to Engage, no way proportionable to the Enemies great numbers, the General also being at that time about Four days March off them, but marched off to *Knotsford* Heath; where in the way the Enemy twice Charging our Rear-gard, was beaten back with the loss of about Thirty of theirs (slain and taken Prisoners) we not losing above Three or four in the March, and at the Pass: On that Heath our Forces drew up in a Posture to receive and fight the Enemy, but he declined it, and marcht to *Nantwich*.

In their passage through *Lancashire*, the Enemy had left the Earl of *Derby* with Three hundred Foot and a Troop of Horse, which he brought from the *Isle of Man*, together with Sir *William Widderington*, Sir *William Throckmorton*, Sir *Timothy Fetherstonhaugh*, Major General Sir *Thomas Tildsey*, Colonel *Boynton*, with many Commanders and other Gentlemen of quality, to raise Six thousand Foot and One thousand five hundred Horse in that County, as an Additional Strength to their Army; Major General *Massey* being also left with him to assist that Work, whiles the Enemy himself marcht on in a direct course to *Worcester*, in his way summoning *Shrewsbury*, and attempting by Letters and Declarations to gain more assistance, but without success.

The Two and twentieth of *August*, with five hundred Horse and Dragoons, about Noon, he entred *Worcester*, then which no Place seemed more to answer all his Ends, it being a City seated on the *Severn*, within twelve Miles of five Counties, near unto *Glocester*, the Forest of *Dean* and *Southwales*, where *Massey* (who was a little before called off from the Earl of *Derby* to serve this Design) pretended his greatest Interest to be; and by gaining that Place, the Enemy well knew he should be Master of all the Passes upon *Severn*, from *Shrewsbury* to *Glocester*, and (there not being One hundred of the Parliaments Forces within twenty Miles of him) he might lie the more secure for refreshing his wearied men, imploy his Interest to get what Additional Strength he could from those Parts, or at least make it a winter War; and thereby gain time for Forreign Assistance, and better opportunity for his Agents to stir up Tumults in *England*, and for the Raising of a new Army in *Scotland* under the Earl of *Leven* (whom he had left General there for that purpose) to come also into *England*: Our Forces in *Worcester* being few, and finding the Place untenable (though threescore onely of them beat the Enemy twice out of the Town, and killed and wounded some of them) withdrew in safety to *Glocester*.

The General with his Forces (which on the Third of *August* were at *St. John-stons* in *Scotland*) upon the Twenty eighth of the same moneth with a continued March, except one days Rest, took up his Head-quarters within two Miles of the East side of *Worcester*, being from *St. Johnstons* about three hundred Miles, the rest of the Forces which had hitherto attended the Enemy being joyned with him; the Lieutenant General, with the Forces under him, quartered the same day about seven Miles from *Worcester* near *Upton* Bridge, of which Pass the Enemy was possessed, and in *Upton* Town on the other side the River, was Major General *Massey* with Sixty Dragoons and Two hundred Horse to secure it. Whiles a small Party of ours went to view the Bridge, without Design or expectation at that time to gain the Pass, and finding the Bridge broken down by the Enemy (one piece of Timber onely left, which reached from one Arch to another) twenty Dragoons and dismounted Troopers with Carbines being commanded over to possess the Church near the Bridge, crept over the piece of Timber, and got to the Church, whereupon the Enemy took the Alarm, and advanced towards them and offered them quarter, and were attempting to fire the door; mean while a hundred Dragoons more came up, and in like maner got over and beat off the Enemy, whose whole Party was now come down upon them; in which Action Major General *Massey* had his horse killed under him, himself received several Shots and was wounded, and forced to retreat with his Party in disorder towards *Worcester*. The Lord having been pleased thus unexpectedly and happily to give us this Pass, the Lieutenant General marched over, and lodged part of his Forces that night in *Upton*.

Whiles the General was on his March from *Scotland*, he sent off Colonel *Lilborn* with his Regiment of Horse to wait upon the Enemies Rear; who finding the Earl of *Derby* raising Forces in *Lancashire*, in his endeavoring to prevent him was forced to engage, where the Lord was graciously pleased by that Regiment of Horse (though harrazed by a tedious March from *Scotland*) and three Companies of Foot, to defeat the Earl of *Derby*'s whole Forces, being One thousand five hundred Horse and Foot near *Wiggon* in *Lancashire*, where were slain Sir *William Widderington* Major General, Sir *Thomas Tildsey*, Colonel *Boynton* (sometimes Governor of *Scarborough* for the Parliament, which Place he betrayed to the Enemy) and Colonel *Trollop*, and taken, Four hundred Prisoners, together with Sir *William Throckmorton*, Sir *Timothy Fetherston-haugh*, and several Colonels and Commanders of quality: The Earl of *Derby* with about thirty Horse escaping, carried the News of his own Defeat to *Worcester*. In which Mercy the Lord was graciously pleased to appear for our small Forces (who were engaged upon great Disadvantages of place and number beyond their intentions) and that most seasonably, in destroying that growing Army, and giving in the same as a Pledge of what he would yet do for his People.

These glad Tidings were followed by the News from *Scotland* of the Surrender of *Sterling* Castle, in which were many thousand Arms, Forty Pieces of Ordnance, Six and twenty Barrels of Powder, the Publique Records of *Scotland*, the Sword, Cloth and Chair of State. Not long after this followed the Routing of the New Levies of the Enemy in the West of *Scotland*, taking the Lord *Osbarston* and others prisoners; The gaining *Anstruther* by Storm with Fifteen Ships in the Harbor, the Surprizing the Earl of *Leven* General of their Forces in *Scotland*, the Earl *Craford-Lindsey* Lieutenant General, the Earl *Marshal*, with four Lords more, and divers Knights, Ministers and Gentlemen of quality; with the scattering and dispersing of Four thousand, which at that time were Rendezvouzed at *Ellit* in *Perth*, to relieve *Dundee* then besieged by our Forces; the taking many Prisoners at *Dumfreeze* and Dissipating them, attempting again new Levies there, and the gaining *Dundee* it self by Storm, in which were Forty Pieces of Ordnance, Six hundred of the Enemy slain, with Major General *Lumsden* the Governor, Colonel *Coningham* late Governor of *Sterling*, and many others of quality, four hundred taken Prisoners, great store of Ships and other Vessels found in the Harbor; to which was since added, the giving up of *St. Andrews*, *Montross* and *Aberdeen*.

On Saturday the Three and twentieth of *August*, the Scotch-King with his whole Army marched into *Worcester*, and applied himself to the Fortifying thereof, and had soon made up some Works, and repaired the Royal Fort on the East side of the City, and planted Canon upon it, the General being encamped before the Town: On the Third of *September* (being the self same Day of the moneth upon which a year before we obtained that Memorable Victory at *Dunbar*) our Forces at *Upton*, under the Command of the Lieutenant General, in pursuance of former Councels (the Execution whereof Providence had delayed till this day, without any such Prede-termination on our part) advanced towards the Enemy at *Worcester*, but by reason of some hinderances reached not to *Teame* River (which lying on the West side of *Severn*, empties it self thereinto about a Mile beneath *Worcester*) till between two and three of the Clock in the Afternoon, Boats also being brought up at the same time, two Bridges were made over the Rivers. The Enemy taking no Alarm till the Van of our Forces were marcht within the sight of the Town, did now draw down his Horse & Foot from his Leaguer at *St. Jones's* lyning all the Hedges from their Pass at *Poyick* to the River *Severn* with Musqueteers to oppose our Advance: The General commanded some Forces over *Severn* towards the Enemy, whiles others were sent over *Teame* to the same ground; the Enemies Foot with some difficulty were beaten from the Hedges, which they for some time disputed, and were at length driven back to the Body of their Horse and Foot, which was then drawn up in *Wickfield* near *Poyick* Bridge, being the same Field where the late king first engaged the Forces of the Parliament, in the same moneth of *September*, One thousand six hundred forty two: Our horse and Foot marched up with great resolution to the Enemies Body, and came to push of Pike with them, and through the Goodness of God drove back and wholly routed them, killing many upon the place, and pursuing the rest to the Draw-bridge and Gate of the City. Whiles this was in action, some Horse and Dragoons sent to a Pass over *Teame* about two Miles above *Poyck* Bridge (which the Enemy had broken down) gained that Ford, where our Horse passed over, and pursued such of the Enemies Horse as could not get into the Town, and secured that Bridge at the West-gate, that none might escape that way.

The greatest part of our Army was now drawn over to the west of *Severn*, where it was conceived the Stress of the Battel would be, which the Enemy perceiving, and supposing them too far engaged to get back over the Bridge of Boats that night, he poured forth at the several Gates of the City all his Horse and Foot upon that part of our Forces left on the East side of the River, which being seasonably discovered, our General himself hastened back to that part of the Army, which the Enemy presently charged with good Resolution; yet through the good hand of our God upon that part of the Army, after about two hours sharp Dispute, they were beaten back into the Town, and our men passing by their great Fort and Canon, entred the Town with the Enemy, whiles others of our Forces ran up and stormed the Royal Fort it self, possessed themselves of it, turning the Canon upon the Enemy.

The Scotch King (having in vain used all Endeavors to make the Horse and Foot in the Town face about for Defence thereof) fled away, and about Three thousand Horse and some High-land Foot, leaving the rest in the Town, fled towards *Bewdley*, whether the General sent the day before One thousand Horse and Dragoons to secure that Pass, who took more Prisoners then themselves were in number, and many of those who escaped them and the Horse sent in their Pursuit, were met with by other of the Army and Countrey Forces (Expresses being the same night the Battel was fought sent into all the Northern Counties and *Scotland*, giving notice of the Successes) so as they were gathered up by Hundreds and Fifties, that very few of those who fled from *Worcester* escaped.

Thus was our gracious God pleased to appear as *The Lord of Hosts* (which was our Word in this and the Battel at *Dunbar*) with and for his People, in destroying this desperate and insolent Enemy, and working a glorious salvation for us.

Of the Enemy, which were about Sixteen thousand Horse and Foot, there were slain in and about *Worcester* and in the Pursuit, about Three thousand; The Prisoners taken in the Town and in their Flight, about Twelve thousand; amongst whom were Duke *Hamilton*, the Earls of *Derby, Cleveland, Rothes, Lauderdale, Kinmore*; the Lords, *Montgomery, Peasly, Cranston, Grandison*, with many other persons of quality; as also *David Lesley* Lieutenant General of their Army, Lieutenant General *Middleton*, Major General *Massey*, and divers other General Officers, besides Seven hundred other Officers, above an hundred Colours, with all their Arms, Artillery, Bag and Baggage; and all this with the loss of about Two hundred of our men, whereof but Three Commission Officers, and about Three hundred of our Soldiers wounded.[340]

The Parliament taking the Premises into their serious consideration, and being exceedingly affected with the glorious Appearances of God for them, and for all the good People throughout *England*, *Ireland* and *Scotland*, in vouchsafing these wonderful and unparalled Successes and Victories to their Armies and Forces (wherein the forwardness of the Counties to send out their respective *Militia's*, and the Courage and Resolution of their Soldiers expressed in this Service, by owning this Cause and present Government against the Common Enemy, is a Mercy greatly to be acknowledged by us, and receive a lasting Memorial) Have thought fit to Enact and Ordain, and be it Enacted and Ordained, That *Friday* the Four and twentieth day of *October*, One thousand six hundred fifty one, be observed and kept as a day of Publique and Holy Rejoycing and Thanksgiving unto the Lord, in all the Churches and Chappels, and Places of Divine Worship within *England*; and also in *Ireland* and *Scotland*: And that the Ministers of the respective Parishes and Places within this Commonwealth, be and are hereby required and enjoyned to give notice on the Lords-day next preceding the said Four and twentieth day of *October*, of the day so to be observed, to the end the People may more Generally and Diligently attend the Publique Exercises of Gods Worship to be Dispensed upon that occasion; at which

---

[340] At this point the font changes from roman to black letter.

time, that the People may be the more particularly and fully informed of this great Mercy, The said Ministers are hereby required and enjoyned to publish and reade this present Act and Declaration; and for the better Observation of the day, The Parliament doth hereby inhibit and forbid the holding and use of all Fairs, Markets, and servile works of mens ordinary Callings upon that day; and all Majors, Sheriffs, Justices of the Peace, Constables and other Officers, be and are hereby enioyned to take special care of the due Observation of the said day of Thanksgiving accordingly.

1651–E6 Thanksgiving day for Commonwealth victories in Jersey

Wednesday 5 November 1651 (London, Westminster, the late lines of communication and the weekly bills of mortality)

Robert Blake and James Heane began to attack Jersey on 20 October; the island was a royalist stronghold and a regular base for attacks on parliament's ships. Though they took St Helier and St Orgueil easily (22 October), Elizabeth Castle was virtually impregnable. Consequently, when, on 30 October, the Rump ordered a thanksgiving in celebration of the victory, fighting was far from over and the castle did not surrender until 12 December when its supplies were nearly exhausted. Obadiah Sedgwick and Peter Sterry preached before parliament at St Margaret's, Westminster, and William Ames preached before the lord mayor and aldermen of London at St Paul's, the first time the cathedral is known to have been used for the City elite to observe special worship since the sixteenth century. Sedgwick was not thanked for his sermon nor invited to have it printed. It is unclear whether 5 November – the annual thanksgiving for delivery from the gunpowder plot – was chosen deliberately to make a connection between divine providence in 1605 and the righteousness of the Commonwealth's cause in 1651. The date had been used previously to mark parliamentary military victories (see 1644–E12(P) and 1645–E17(P)). Opponents of the Commonwealth, such as William Jenkyn, chose to mark the gunpowder plot in their sermons, not the victory at Jersey.

Order: parliamentary order, 30 Oct. 1651, *CJ*, VII, 31.
Additional source: *FSP*, XXXIV, 7–8.
Printed sermons: Ames, St Paul's, London (Wing A3009), Jenkyn, St Mary, Aldermanbury, London (J651, J652), Sterry, parliament (Wing S5478, S5479; *FSP*, XXXIV, 52–106), T.W., St Michael's Cornhill, London (Wing W130).

ORDER

Parliamentary order: 30 October 1651
Ordered, That the Ministers in the several Congregations in the Cities of *London* and *Westminster,* and the late Lines of Communication, and weekly Bills of Mortality, do, on the Fifth of *November* next, render humble Thanks to Almighty God, for his great Mercy vouchsafed to this Commonwealth, in the gaining of the Isle of *Jersey*; and that the Lord Mayor of *London* do take Care to give Notice to the Ministers of the several Congregations, accordingly.

1651–Ir2 Thanksgiving day for Commonwealth victories at Limerick and in the Isle of Man, Guernsey and Jersey

Wednesday 26 November 1651 (Ireland)

This occasion is only known from Steele. It was ordered for the capture of Jersey (see 1651–E6) and Guernsey. Limerick, one of only three towns remaining in Irish hands, surrendered on 27 October after a long siege. The Isle of Man surrendered on 31 October. Work was suspended on the thanksgiving day.

Order: order by commissioners, 18 Nov. 1651, not extant [formerly Dublin PRO, Order Book 42, p. 69; described in Steele, II, no. 484].

DESCRIPTION OF ORDER

Order by commissioners: 18 November 1651
Wednesday, 26 Nov., declared a day of thanksgiving for the taking of Limerick, and the reduction of Man, Guernsey, and Jersey. Ordinary vocations not to be followed. This to be proclaimed and published.

1651–E7 Thanksgiving prayers for Commonwealth victories at Limerick and in Jersey and the Isle of Man

Sunday 7 December 1651 (London, Westminster, the late lines of communication and the weekly bills of mortality)

News of the surrender of Limerick (see 1651–Ir2) reached parliament on 28 November and thanksgivings were immediately ordered. Thankgivings for the victories on Jersey (already marked in and around London on 5 November: see 1651–E6) and the Isle of Man were also ordered to be observed.

Order: parliamentary order, 28 Nov. 1651 (John Field, 1651; Wing I1032, 24)* [also in *CJ*, VII, 45].
Additional sources: *CJ*, VII, 45; *A letter from the lord deputy-general of Ireland, unto the honorable William Lenthal Esq; speaker of the parliament of England; concerning the rendition of the city of Limerick* (1651; Wing I1032).

ORDER

Parliamentary order: 28 November 1651
Ordered by the Parliament.
That the Ministers in the several Congregations within the Cities of *London* and *Westminster*, and the late Lines of Communication, and weekly Bills of Mortality, Do, on the next Lords-day come Seven-night, render solemn Thanks to Almighty God for his great and seasonable Mercy to this Commonwealth, in the delivering up into the hands of the Parliament Forces in *Ireland*, under the Command of the Deputy-General, the strong and Populous City of *Limerick*, with all the Artillery, Arms and Ammunition therein, upon the Thirtieth of *October*, One thousand six hundred fifty one; and in the taking of the Isle of *Jersey* and the Isle of *Man*; with all the Castles and Forts, Ordnance and Ammunition, therein.

Ordered, That the Lord Mayor, and Committees of the Militia's, be required to take order for notice of this Order to be given.

1651–Ir3 Days of humiliation for the lord deputy's death, plague epidemic and storms

Thursday 11 December 1651 and Thursday 18 December 1651 (Ireland)

As with most other Irish occasions during this period, this day of humiliation is only known through Steele. Lord Deputy Ireton died from a fever on 26 November at Limerick. Limerick, Dublin and other towns in Ireland continued to suffer from plague. Storms persisted around the coast of the British Isles, hampering parliament's fleet and general shipping.

Order: order by commissioners, 6 Dec. 1651, not extant [formerly Dublin PRO, Order Book 42, p. 84; described in Steele, II, no. 485].

DESCRIPTION OF ORDER

Order by commissioners: 6 December 1651
Thursday, 11 and 18 December, to be days of public humiliation for the death of the Lord Deputy, plague in Limerick and elsewhere, and storms at sea. This to be proclaimed and observed according to the Act.

1652–EIr Fast days during threat of conflict with the Dutch Republic

Wednesday 9 June 1652 (London, Westminster, Middlesex, late lines of communication and the weekly bills of mortality); Wednesday 30 June 1652 (elsewhere in England, Wales and Berwick-upon-Tweed); Wednesday 30 June 1652 (Ireland)

During the first half of 1652, parliamentary forces secured the surrender of remaining royalist and Irish strongholds in the British Isles, America and the West Indies: Tipperary and Waterford (23 March); Roscommon; Galway (May); Barbados (11 January); Virginia, Maryland and the Bermudas (March) and Jamestown (April). Strangely, none of these victories were celebrated with official thanksgivings, though they were probably the 'abundant mercies' referred to in the English parliamentary act which ordered this occasion. In May, relations with the Dutch Republic deteriorated as English ships harried their Dutch counterparts in the Channel and a full-scale battle ensued on the 19th. On 1 June, the Rump proposed days of fasting in response to these 'new Dangers'. The act was passed after two readings on 4 June; as in previous occasions (1651–E2 and 1651–1), the House rejected engrossing the bill, probably in order to speed its passage through parliament. A declaration outlining the reasons for the fast was commissioned and printed by parliament's printers in England and Scotland (though the fast days were not explicitly ordered to be observed in Scotland). A parliamentary order was also issued stating that the declaration was not to be printed by anyone else. Joseph Caryll and William Strong were appointed to preach before the house at St Margaret's, Westminster; neither chose to have their sermons printed. On 21 June, the Irish parliament meeting at Cork ordered a day of humiliation to be observed across the country on 30 June. The order only survived in manuscript and is known only through Steele.

Order: ENGLAND AND WALES: parliamentary act, 4 June 1652, Wing E1118* (and variant E1118A); IRELAND: order by commissioners, 21 June 1652, not extant [formerly Dublin PRO, Order Book 42, p. 255; described in Steele, II, no. 496].
Additional sources: *CJ*, VII, 137, 139; *A declaration of the parliament of the Commonwealth of England, relating to the affairs and proceedings between this Commonwealth and the states general of the United Provinces* (1652; Wing E1511); *A declaration of the parliament of the Commonwealth of England, relating to the affairs and proceedings between this Commonwealth and the states general of the United Provinces* (Leith, 1652; Wing E1511A); *FSP*, XXXIV, 8.

ORDER AND DESCRIPTION OF ORDER

England and Wales: Act of Parliament, 4 June 1652
The Parliament acknowledging from the bottom of their Hearts the abundant Mercies of their good God continually heaped upon this Nation, Notwithstanding their great Unworthiness and unproportionable Returns of Thanks in their Lives and Actions; And being sensible withal of those new Dangers which this Nation seems to be threatned with, and hath most justly Deserved, Have thought fit to have recourse to the same God by publique Humiliation and Prayer, for averting his Judgements, and removing those Sins which otherwise may call for those Judgements, and for obtaining a Blessing upon the Councels and Forces of this Commonwealth both by Sea and Land: Be it therefore Enacted by this present Parliament, and by Authority thereof, That a day of solemn Fasting and Humiliation be set apart to be observed on Wednesday the Ninth of *June*, One thousand six hundred fifty two, in the Cities of *London* and *Westminster*, and within the late Lines of Communication and weekly Bills of Mortality; and upon Wednesday the Thirtieth of *June* following, in all other Cities, Towns and places within *England*, *Wales*, and the Town of *Berwick* upon *Tweed*: And that the Ministers of the respective Parishes and places aforesaid, be and hereby are required and enjoyned to give notice hereof on the Lords-Day next preceding the day so to be observed: To the end the people may more diligently attend the publique Exercises of Gods Worship and Service on that Day; And for the better observation thereof, The Parliament doth inhibit and forbid the holding or use of all Fairs, Markets, and servile Works of mens ordinary Callings on the respective Days aforesaid: And all Majors, Sheriffs, Justices of Peace, Constables, and other Officers, be and are hereby enjoyned to take special care of the due Observation of the said Day accordingly.

Ireland: order by commissioners, 21 June 1652
Wed., 30 June, has been ordered by Parliament, No. 2970, Eng., q.v., to be kept as a day of humiliation. This is to be published.

1652–S   Fast days during anxieties about religion, the church and Charles II's policies

Sunday 12 September and Sunday 19 September 1652 (Scotland)

The assembly met at Edinburgh in late July and early August. Its fast act does not seem to be extant, and little can be reconstructed about its appointment. The fast was boycotted by the Protesters. Several gentlemen of Renfrewshire requested that the Paisley presbytery observe the fast, but it refused to recognize the legitimacy of the general assembly, and appointed its own fast day.

Order: act of the general assembly, *c.* 5 Aug. 1651 (not found).
Causes: described in *Inverness and Dingwall records*, pp. 242–4.
Additional sources: *RCGA*, III, 519–22; presbytery of Paisley minutes, NRS, CH2/294/3, p. 120; Lamont, pp. 45–7; *The diary of Alexander Brodie of Brodie, MDCLII.–MDCLXXX. and of his son, James Brodie of Brodie, MDCLXXX.–MDCLXXXV.*, ed. David Laing (Aberdeen, 1863), 24; *Strathbogie presbytery*, p. 224; *Inverness and Dingwall records*, p. 245.

DESCRIPTION OF THE CAUSES

Inverness and Dingwall records

Albeit our sadd conditione of itself cry aloud to mourneing, it being our deutie to stir wp the lords people to tak on him in this day of his displeasour, we find it incumbent to all the land, and charges in it uppon them as they wold have the lord to turne away from his fearce wrath so hoate perscheweing and burneing ws wp, that they wold search and try y^r wayis and murnefullie befoire ye lord, and at this tyme ly in ye dust, for all these provoca^{one}s w^h ar ye chiefe causes of all the evills that ar come wpon ws.

1. Besydes manie sinnes heirtofoire mentioned in former causes of fasts, we ar to mourne for the land destroying sinne, The contempt of the gospell, qlk the comprehensone of so manie oy^r sinnes set doune be ye commissione of the assemblie 1650, a sinne so odious in y^e sight of God, that neglecting so gryte a salua^{o}ne and slichting the bloode of y^e covenant, we cannot escape y^e vengeance of y^e gospell.

2. Becaus the sadd dispensatione we haue mett w^t and the wonderfull work wrought amongst us ar $neiy^r$ exed nor improwen be ws, our wound is greivous that we hawe not greived, the lord hes smitten ws, bot we refused to retarie, zea none taking y^e lord for thair partie nor accepting y^e punishment of y^e iniquitie, we revolt more and more, this is a lamentatione and salbe for a lamentatione.

3. Becaus of Covenant bracking, especiallie in this our day of our calamitie and tryall, committed oppinly in ye midds of all the land, and ye schameless dispyseing of ye oathe of God so often and so solemly sworne be ws, nor thinking to escape by iniquitie lyes y^{re} refuge, thus ye lord is mocked and his name prophaned, for which he will not hold ws guiltless.

4. Becaus of Zions breach which seemes wnreparable, shee is brocken breach uppon breach, hir vaile is torne, hir headge brocken downe, hir pretious thing defyled, blasted, exposed to foxes and beares, and q^{ll} it is thus with hir, hir louers forget hir, hir children still contending in y^e fornace, notwithstanding of y^e gryte contraversie y^e lord hath w^t the wholl land.

5. Becaus of y^e fowle dep'tor from y^e true doctrine of C[hrist] receawed in yis kirk, and separa^{o}ne from y^e communion and government $y^r$of, y^t some ministers and some wy^r wnsteable soules hes turned asyde wnto, contrarie to y^e solemne covenant and wowes, to y^e hiest contempt of y^e name of God and gryt scandell of y^e gospell.

6. Becaus of gryte oppositione made to y^e work of God be y^e royall familie, and manie eminent families of ye blood, oppressione, ignorance of God, wnbeleiffe, wncleanenesse, covetousnes, falshood, decept, hypocrisie, and wy^r grosse iniquities that hes abounded among all rankes of ye land, both in ye preceiding and present genera^ones.

7. Becaus of ye manie sinnes of ye ministers, the work hes not bene strenthned, nor those quho hes bene driven away soucht for, for we have not worked for soules, bot done dueties by commissione, nor the thingis of God, for theise we aught to mourne and requeist ye Lord through Jesus C. that he would pardone all these abominationes, subdue ws by his spirit, that we may fall in love w^t Chryst, be obedient to ye gospell, y^t seeing many things we may observe them and regard the works of ye lord and opera^one of his hands, yat he wald heale our backslydings, repaire our breaches, reclame ye seduced, and tak away all our iniquities, furnishe ye contrarie w^t ye king, nobles, ministers and ye people, comfort our prisoners, and y^t he wald be pleased to stay amongst ws and preserve vnwiolable ye liberties of his house, and help ws for his names sack, becaus we are brought werie low, and y^t remediing ye distressed esteate of Gods people in these lands, wald carie on ye work of reforma^one to the w^c we ar ingadged by covenant, and wald build his Zion, and appeire in his glorie.

1652–E   Fast day during the first Dutch war

Wednesday 13 October 1652 (England, Wales and Berwick-upon-Tweed)

After further assaults on Dutch shipping in June, the Commonwealth formally declared war against the United Provinces on 8 July (the first Anglo-Dutch war, 1652–4). On 10 August, a day of fasting and humiliation to be observed on 8 September was proposed in parliament; the proposal was read twice on 19 August and was committed for review to the Committee for Propagating the Gospel, established in February 1650 to eject ungodly ministers and to fund puritan missionaries in Wales. This change in procedure was probably caused by growing concern about religious radicalism, especially the fifth monarchists, a dissenting group which believed that Christ would return in 1666. On 1 September, the act was passed with amendments, though moving the day of observance to 13 October. This may have been to allow more time for the order and declaration, outlining the reasons for the fast day, to be printed and distributed. The Rump observed the day at St Margaret's, Westminster. John Owen, Thomas Goodwin and, perhaps surprisingly because he was a prominent fifth monarchist himself, Christopher Feake were ordered to preach. Feake was nominated by another fifth monarchist, Thomas Harrison, after parliament sought a third person 'to assist in the carrying on the Exercises of the Day'. Only Owen's sermon is extant. Together with that by Goodwin, it was well received, but Feake's was not and he was not officially thanked by parliament for his efforts.

Order: parliamentary act, 1 Sept. 1652, Wing E1077*.
Additional source: *CJ*, VII, 162, 165–6, 173; *FSP*, XXXIV, 9–10; *Perfect account*, p. 94, 13–20 Oct. 1652 (1652; Thomason E.678[16]), p. 745.
Printed sermon: Owen, parliament (Wing O806; *FSP*, XXXIV, 107–62).

ORDER

Act of parliament: 1 September 1652

Whereas the most wise God, whose Judgements are unsearchable and ways past finding out, hath by his over-ruling Providence made a breach upon that Amity (which the Parliament hath in all sincerity endeavored to conserve) between this Commonwealth & the United Provinces; The Parliament of *England* well knowing it to be their duty, in all the turns of Providence to acknowledge God, and to seek unto him to direct their Paths; and also considering the Word of Truth doth teach, That Sin onely doth separate between God and a People, Have thought fit to admonish and stir up the People of this Nation to confess their sins unto the Lord, and to seek his Face, That he would be pleased to grant unto us Repentance and Pardon through the Blood of his dear Son Jesus Christ who is our Peace, and by the Blood of his Cross reconciles all things in Heaven and Earth: And humbly to beseech him to direct and bless the Councels and Actions of the Parliament, to the spiritual and temporal welfare of the people of this *Commonwealth*; and more particularly, That he will be pleased to shew them the way how the saving truth of the Gospel may be best advanced and propagated, and whatsoever is contrary to sound Doctrine & the power of Godliness suppressed: And likewise, That he would vouchsafe his Presence with, and Blessing upon the Forces and Navy of this Commonwealth, and out of all the Troubles wherewith he is pleased to exercise us, to bring forth a righteous and lasting peace to his People to his own Glory: And to the end the People of this Nation may have an opportunity for this purpose, Be it Enacted by this present Parliament, and the Authority thereof, That Wednesday the Thirteenth day of *October, 1652.* be set apart to be observed as a day of solemn Fasting and Humiliation in all Cities, Towns and places within *England*, *Wales*, and the Town of *Berwick* upon *Tweed*; and that the Ministers of the respective Parishes & places aforesaid, upon the Lords day next preceding the day so to be observed, do give notice hereof, that the people may the better attend the Exercises of that day. And for the more full observation thereof, The Parliament doth forbid the holding or using of any Fairs, Markets, and servile Works of mens ordinary Callings on the Day thus set apart: And all Majors, Sheriffs, Justices of Peace, Constables and other Officers, are hereby enjoyned to take special care for the observation of the said Day accordingly.

1653–E1   Thanksgiving prayers for naval victory at the battle of Portland

Sunday 27 February 1653 (London, Westminster, the late lines of communication and the weekly bills of mortality)

The Commonwealth's fleet was reorganized and refitted in the winter of 1652–3 and defeated the Dutch at the battle of Portland (18–20 February), securing control of the Channel. On 24 February, parliament ordered thanksgivings to be observed in three days' time; it thus occurred earlier than the fast day ordered earlier, on 9 February (1653–E2). It is not clear if observance of this thanksgiving was deliberately limited to an area in and around London to ensure that it could be organized before the nationwide fast day and therefore allow the nation to focus on petitioning God for assistance against the Dutch. The victory at Portland was considered sufficiently important to warrant a thanksgiving day at a later date: see 1653–E3.

Order: parliamentary order, 24 Feb. 1653, Wing E1747*.
Additional source: *CJ*, VII, 262.

ORDER

Parliamentary order: 24 February 1653
Ordered by the Parliament,
    That the Ministers in the several Congregations within the Cities of *London* and *Westminster,* and the late Lines of Communication and weekly Bills of Mortality, Do on the next Lords-day render Thanks to Almighty God for his great Mercy vouchsafed to this Commonwealth, in the great Success he hath been pleased to give unto the Navy of this Commonwealth against the Dutch Fleet, on the Eighteenth, nineteenth and twentieth days of this instant *February;* wherein many of their Men of War and other Ships were sunk and taken, and the rest put to flight and scattered.
    Ordered by the Parliament, That it be referred to the Lord Major of the City of *London,* to give timely notice of this Order to the Ministers within the places afore-said.

1653–E2   Fast day for the Commonwealth government and forces during the first Anglo-Dutch war

Thursday 3 March 1653 (England and Wales)

In early January 1653, the council of officers (established in 1647 to govern the New Model Army) met for a week of prayers to discuss the future of the Commonwealth, including the proposed dissolution of the Rump parliament. There were also ominous developments abroad because Denmark allied with the United Provinces on 29 January and banned English shipping from the Baltic. On 27 January, the Rump 'resolved' to hold a public fast on 3 March; it is not clear if this represented a change in procedure or just of language. The order was agreed on 9 February and ordered to be printed and distributed across the country by the sheriffs. Stephen Marshall, William Ames and Ralph Venning were appointed to preach before the Rump at St Margaret's, Westminster. On 2 March, Nicholas Lockyer was asked to '[assist] in carrying on the Work of a Day of Fasting and Humiliation', though it is unclear what this meant. None of the preachers was thanked for his sermon or invited to print it.

Order: parliamentary resolution, 9 Feb. 1653, Wing E2451* [similar text in *CJ*, VII, 257].
Additional sources: *CJ*, VII, 251, 257–8, 263; *FSP*, XXXIV, 11.

ORDER

Parliamentary resolution: 9 February 1653
Resolved upon the Question by the Parliament,
    That Thursday the third day of *March* next, be set apart for a Day of Publique Fasting and Humiliation, to be observed throughout this whole Nation, to seek unto

Almighty God for a Blessing upon the Councels of this Commonwealth, and upon their Forces by Sea and Land.

Resolved upon the Question by the Parliament,

That this Vote be Printed and Published, and Copies thereof sent to the Sheriffs of every County; and that they be required to send the same unto the Ministers of the several Parishes, that Notice thereof may be given in convenient time.

1653–S   Fast days during anxieties over domestic divisions and sinfulness

Sunday 27 March and Sunday 3 April 1653 (Scotland)

The commission of the general assembly's discussions at its meetings on 23–5 February 1653 principally concerned relations with the Protesters. The commission considered a paper from the party lamenting the failure to heal the schism in the Kirk, and wrote to presbyteries condemning the Protester James Guthrie's *Nullity of the pretended-assembly*, an account of the 1651 general assembly. This fast was boycotted by protesters; according to Nicoll, they kept their own day in response.

Order: act of the commission of the general assembly, 24 Feb. 1653, *RCGA*, III, 540.
Causes: *Causes of an humiliation* ([Edinburgh?]; Wing C4201H)* [also in *RCGA*, III, 544–5].
Letter: commission of the general assembly to presbyteries, 25 Feb. 1653, *RCGA*, III, 543.
Additional sources: *RCGA*, III, 538–43; James Guthrie, *The nullity of the pretended-assembly at Saint Andrews and Dundee* ([Leith], 1652; Wing G2263); *Strathbogie presbytery*, p. 235; Lamont, p. 53; Nicoll, pp. 106–8; *The diary of Alexander Brodie of Brodie*, p. 26; *Inverness and Dingwall records*, p. 252.

ORDER

Act of the commission of the general assembly: 24 February 1653

The Commission of the Generall Assembly, having taken to their serious consideration the great sins and distempers of the Kirk and countrey, appoynt a Fast and Humiliation to be keeped the last Lords day of March and first Lords day of Aprile, Mr Robert Ker and the Clerk appoynted to draw the Causes.

CAUSES

As we conceive, that the many crying evils, for which the Lord hath been and is smiting us, which hath been held forth formerly as causes of Solemn Humiliations, should be seriously laid to heart and mourned for, and especially that maine and Fundamentall evill, the woefull source and root of all our other Provocations, the contempt of the Glorious Gospel of Jesus Christ, the ignorance of him amongst the generality of the Land, and the great negligence even amongst the best of seeking to him for Reconciliation with God, and entertaining Communion with God through him, and obtaining grace from him for walking acceptably in our Persons and Callings; So particularly we judge the Lord in his Providence is calling us to mourn before him;

I. For the growing evidences of his displeasure against the Land, in the continuance of his sad afflictions upon all ranks of Persons, notwithstanding our former

Humiliations before him, the Lord testifying his anger even against the prayers of his People: and no wonder, considering the great abuse of that holy Ordinance by our formalities and Fasting unto our selves and not unto God.

II. The grouth of sin of all sorts; particularly, Pride, Uncleannesse, Contempt of Ordinances, Oppression, Violence, Fraudulent dealing, and that under the Rod, the most part of the People are growing worse and worse, and revolting more and more, few or none accepting of the punishment of their iniquity, and labouring to get their uncircumcised hearts humbled.

III. The encrease and heightning of all our woefull differences and divisions, to the great scandall of the Reformed Christian Religion, and apparant ruine of the Work of Reformation established amongst us, if the Lord in mercy do not prevent.

IV. The many sad encroachments from diverse hands made and like to be made upon the precious Liberties of the Kingdom of our Lord Jesus, a precious trust committed to us from him, and transmitted to us from our zealous and faithfull Predecessors, who, in the obtaining and preservation of them, loved not their lives, even unto the death.

V. The generall distemper on the spirits of all sorts of People, all or the most part of all ranks in this time, while the Lord is casting down what he builded and plucking up what he planted, seeking their own things and few or none seeking the things of Jesus Christ.

For these, amongst many things, we desire the People of God throughout the Land may mourn, every man searching his way, and saying, *What have I done*, rather then to lay all the weight on the sins of others; And withall, humbly to pray, That the Lord would powre on the Land the spirit of mourning and repentance, that, in the depth of his own wisdome and goodnesse, he would finde out wayes of healing of our woefull differences, and in the mean while possesse our hearts with the spirit of love, stedfastnesse, and a sound mind, and with resolution and courage for enduring whatsoever the Lord in his wise Providence shall call us to suffer in the maintainance of his truth.

LETTER

Commission of the general assembly to presbyteries: 25 February 1653
… We shall add no more but that we have herewith sent the Causes of a Fast to be keeped on the last Lords day of March and first Lords day of Aprill nixtocome …

1653–E3 Thanksgiving day for naval victory at the battle of Portland

Tuesday 12 April 1653 (England and Wales)

A month after the Rump parliament had ordered thanksgiving prayers in and around London to celebrate victory at the battle of Portland (1653–E1), it ordered a thanksgiving day throughout the Commonwealth, to be observed on 12 April. Once again, the language of 'resolution' was used in the journals (see 1653–E2) though no changes in the ordering process can be discerned. Thomas Scott and Nicholas Love were commissioned to compose a declaration outlining the reasons for the thanksgiving; on 29 March, it was ordered to be printed and distributed. For the first time, distribution of the order was delegated to the council of state. In the absence of other evidence, it is reasonable to assume that the sheriffs continued to be used in forwarding orders to parishes. Oliver Bowles and Isaac Knight were appointed to preach before the house. However, on 24 March, Bowles was excused and replaced by Walter Cradock; Cradock himself was excused on 1 April in favour of Obadiah Sedgwick; and, on 5 April, Sedgwick was excused and Philip Nye was appointed in his stead. Neither Knight nor Nye were formally thanked for their sermons or asked to print them. This is the first day of prayer or thanksgiving attended (in Tavistock) by Thomas Larkham, parliamentary chaplain, preacher, author, independent minister and diarist; he gave sixpence to the parish collection.

Order: parliamentary resolution, [Mar.] 1653, Wing E1693* [also in *CJ*, VII, 266].
Additional sources: *CJ*, VII, 265–6, 271, 273, 274; *FSP*, XXXIV, 11–12; *Larkham diary*, p. 62.

ORDER

Parliamentary resolution: [March] 1653
Resolved by the Parliament,
    That Tuesday the Twelfth of *April,* One thousand six hundred fifty three, be set apart for a day of Publique Thanksgiving to the Lord throughout the whole Commonwealth, for the great and seasonable Victory vouchsafed to the Navy of this Commonwealth, upon the late Engagement with the Dutch Fleet, on the Eighteenth, Nineteenth and Twentieth days of *February* last.

Tuesday the Nine and twentieth of March, 1653.
    Ordered by the Parliament, *That the Order appointing the Twelfth of* April*, One thousand and six hundred fifty three, a Day of Publique Thanksgiving, be forthwith Printed and Published; And that it be referred to the Councel of State to cause the same to be forthwith sent into the respective counties within this Commonwealth, to be observed accordingly.*

1653–Ir   Fast days after change in the Commonwealth government

Wednesday 4 May 1653; Wednesday 11 May 1653 (Ireland)

There had been discussions throughout the first half of 1653 about the future of the Rump parliament and the need for new elections, but little agreement. On 20 April, Cromwell forcibly dissolved the Rump and a few days later *A declaration of the lord-general* was printed to explain his reasons. On 29 April, Charles Fleetwood, commander-in-chief of Ireland, and his council ordered two fast days to be observed throughout Ireland in order to petition God to give 'wisdom and strength unto those his servants, on whom the burthen and care of preserving the Commonwealth in peace, and setling the same in Righteousnesse, doth principally lie'. No evidence survives to indicate how well these fasts were observed, though the dissolution of the Rump was not welcomed by religious radicals in Ireland. The same day that Fleetwood ordered the fast days, a new council of state was established in England to rule in the Rump's stead, comprising ten members including Cromwell (and hence referred to as the Decemvirate).

Order: order by commissioners, 29 Apr. 1653, (Edward Griffin, n.p., n.d.; Thomason E.213[13])*.
Additional source: Steele, II, no. 514 [describing Dublin PRO, Order Book 44, p. 108].

DESCRIPTION OF ORDER

Order by commissioners: 29 April 1653
The Declaration of his Excellency the Lord Generall, and his Councell of Officers comming to our knowledge; we hold it our duty to publish the same unto all who are intrusted with the mannaging of publique Affairs in this Countrey, and to mind them that it is now their duty (more then ordinary) notwithstanding the present Alteration, to Act carefully and industriously in their severall charges, and diligently to discharge their respective Trusts, that the common Enemy may not have advantage from hence to worke new disturbance against the publique peace and welfare: And that such as are in the service of the Commonwealth in this Land, must expect to be called to a strict account for their neglect therein.

And in regard the present posture of affaires is such, as extraordinarily concernes the interest and welfare of all good people; we hold it our duty earnestly to exhort them unto a specially fervent wrestling with the Lord by humble prayer and supplication, for wisdome and strength unto those his servants, on whom the burthen and care of preserving the Commonwealth in peace, and setling the same in Righteousnesse, doth principally lie. For which end we doe appoint Wednesday the fourth of *May* next, and that day sevennight being the eleventh of *May*, to be set apart for solemne seeking the face of the Lord by all his people in Ireland on that behalfe.

1653–E4   Thanksgiving day for naval victory at the battle of the Gabbard

Thursday 23 June 1653 (England and Wales)

Though both Cromwell and his Dutch counterpart, Johan de Witt, were keen to bring the first Anglo-Dutch war to a conclusion, the Commonwealth's victory at Portland (see 1653–E1 and 1653–E3) encouraged the council of state to pursue the war further. The council was rewarded with an English victory at the Gabbard, between Harwich and Yarmouth, on 2–3 June. On 12 June, the council ordered the publication of an order and declaration for a thanksgiving to be observed across the nations. This was a change in the usual ordering process, brought about by the dissolution of the Rump parliament (see 1653–EIr). The declaration differed from previous ones, by listing the key points about the victory rather than giving a prose account. It also included several biblical passages, though it is unclear whether these were to be used during the services.

Order: declaration by the general and council of state, 12 June 1653 (Giles Calvert, Henry Hills and Thomas Brewster; 1 p., 1653; Wing E775aA)* [also Wing E775].

ORDER

Declaration by the general and council of state: 12 June 1653
It hath been a Custom much exercised to enjoin Days and Duties of Thanksgiving for Mercies received from the Lord: The suitablenesse of which practise with Gospel

Times, and that Gospel Spirit, which is only to bear Rule in the Churches of God (where the Worship is to be in Spirit and Truth, exercised by a Free and willing People) is besides the intent of this Paper to dispute.

But considering how welcom to the Lords People every occasion of praise, ministred by the Lord himself, and minded by those that manage the Publique Affairs, is, to such as wait for his Salvation, we have thought fit to commend this high and Heavenly Exercise and Privilege, to all those, who are faithful in these Lands, in the words of the Prophet *Isaiah*.

Isa. 12. 4. *In that day ye shall say, Praise the Lord, call upon his name, declare his doings among the People, make mention that his name is exalted.*

Ver. 5. *Sing unto the Lord, for he hath done excellent things; this is known in all the Earth.*

Ver. 6. *Cry out and shout, thou inhabitant of* Zion; *for great is the Holy One of* Israel *in the midst of thee.*

Truly this is such a Day, if not that Day, it may be the dawning of it.

Isa. 10. *A day of wo to unrighteous Judges, to Tyrants, to all the proud of the Earth.*

Isa. 11. *The day of him who is the rod, the branch, and the root of* Iesse.

Ver. 5. *The day of his Righteousness and Faithfulness.*

Ver. 6. *Of his beginning to heal the Creation.*

Ver. 12, 13. *The day of gathering his People, and taking away their envyings of one another, and making up their breaches.*

This great Success against the Dutch (who, a few daies before, were lifted up with their Success in getting out their Fleets for Trade, and bringing their Ships loaden with Merchandise home in safety, and in their braving it upon our Coasts, shooting against our Towns and Castles in the absence of our Fleet) was a most Signal, and every way, a most seasonable mercy.

The Victory was a compleat one.

The Enemy flying with great Terrour and Astonishment, having received great loss of Men and Ships, and this in the view and hearing of the Subjects of *France*, and *Spain*, and their own Countrymen.

It was without the loss of one Ship on our part.

It was also seasonable, in abasing Pride, Haughtiness and fleshly Confidence, and in discovering Hypocrisie.

It was an Answer to the Faith and Prayers of Gods People, and to their great hopes and expectations from the Lord.

It is a Mercy minding us of, and sealing to us, all our former Mercies.

A mercy at such a time as this, to say no more; what Mercies it hath in the Bowels of it, time will declare: who knows?

One of which we desire from our Hearts, and Hope may be, as of Establishment and Union to all those that fear the Lord amongst us: So of conviction to that Nation (at least to all those that fear the Lord there) of their Opposition to the Work of the Lord in the midst of us: And of their Duty to be serviceable to *Christ* (with their Brethren) in that which He is doing in the World, preferring their usefulness therein, before all their Worldly advantage.

We shall conclude our Exhortation with that of *David*.

Psal. 107. ver. 1. *O give thanks unto the Lord, for he is good, for his mercy endureth for ever.*

Ver. 2. *Let the redeemed of the Lord say so, whom he hath redeemed from the hand of the Enemy.*

Psal. 118. ver. 1. *O give thanks unto the Lord, for he is good, for his mercy endureth for ever.*

Ver. 2. *Let* Israel *now say, that his mercy endureth for ever.*

Ver. 3. *Let the house of* Aaron *now say, that his Mercy endureth for ever.*

Ver. 4. *Let them now that fear the Lord say, that his Mercy endureth for ever.*

Ver. last. *O give Thanks unto the Lord, for he is good, for his mercy endureth for ever.*

The General and Council of State have appointed the 23. of this instant *Iune* to meet (if the Lord permit) with the Council of Officers, to praise him.

1653–E5   Thanksgiving day for naval victory at the battle of Scheveingen

Thursday 25 August 1653 (England and Wales)

Peace negotiations between the Dutch and the English failed because the Dutch refused to accept liability for reparations and because the terms threatened their independent sovereignty. The English and Dutch navies clashed again at the battle of Scheveingen on 29–31 July, from which the English emerged victorious. A week later, a thanksgiving was proposed in the nominated assembly (or Barebone's parliament), a body which had been formed in June to replace the Rump (dissolved by Cromwell in April). The assembly commissioned a declaration 'to invite the People of God in this Nation, to join in the Observation thereof'. On 12 August, this declaration was read twice, amended, passed, and ordered by the council of state to be printed and to be distributed. Though this process was broadly similar to that in the past, there were two modifications. People were 'invited', rather than ordered, to observe the thanksgiving; this probably expressed Cromwell's reluctance to order or compel people to worship. Second, the instruction for the thanksgiving was issued by parliamentary declaration, not by a parliamentary act, order or ordinance. How well this occasion was observed is difficult to gauge because of shortage of evidence, but the Venetian ambassador remarked to his counterpart in France that 'it may be freely stated that the greater part of the population does so out of fear rather than from any love for the present'.

Order: parliamentary declaration, 12 Aug. 1653, Wing E1510*.
Additional sources: *CJ*, VII, 297, 299; *SP Thurloe*, I, 416; Lorenzo Paulucci to Giovanni Sagredo, 6 Sept. 1653, *CSPV, 1653–4*, p. 121.

ORDER

Parliamentary declaration: 12 August 1653

It having pleased the Lord, after those many signal Tokens of his presence with his People in this Nation, in the several Straights and Changes, through which he hath by a mighty Hand and an out-stretched Arm led them hitherto, Yet again to manifest his wonted power and goodness to them in that late and great Success of our Fleet at Sea, when it pleased the Lord at the end of *July* last, so to bless the Forces of this

Commonwealth engaged by the Dutch (who by Advantages not a few, to humane Appearances, were likely to have prevailed) as that after a most sharp and doubtful encounter, he Crowned us with Victory, and made our Enemies to feel the Stroak of his Righteous Hand against them, who have abundantly manifested it to be in their Intentions to have made us (wearied by a long Intesttine War) a spoil to their Avarice and Ambition, by their first unjust Invasion of us, and their earnest prosecuting since of a War against us, notwithstanding all the endeavors used on our part to compose so sad, and to us so unwelcome a Breach between the two Nations: We being desirous to be deeply sensible hereof before the Lord, and bearing also in minde what cause we have at all times to make mention of his Name in this Nation, with all humble and thankful Acknowledgements, but especially when he hath thus seasonably made bare his Holy Arm in this late Mercy, before the eyes of all the Nations round about us, Have thought it requisite at a particular time, and in an especial maner to acknowledge the Hand and Goodness of our God to us in this great Work which he hath wrought for us; And we have therefore set apart Thursday the Five and twentieth of this present *August*, for the end aforesaid. And in regard the Mercy is general, and we hope will be of great advantage to this whole Commonwealth, and to all that fear God in it; We do earnestly desire them to contribute their help in this great Work of Thankfulness to the Lord, and to suffer us to call upon them, to sing together with us unto the Lord a new Song, *He hath dealt bountifully with us, for his mercy endureth for ever*; and that as the Lord shall move and direct them, they would seriously set themselves in his presence and praise him, together with us, that so we may all with one Heart and Voice, offer up a free Sacrifice of Prayer and of Praise, and all of us endeavor in our several Stations, to improve so great a Deliverance to the alone Glory of our great God, and the good of his People throughout the World.

1654–E Fast days during a severe drought

Friday 24 March 1654 (London, Westminster and outlying parishes); Friday 7 April 1654 (elsewhere in England and Wales)

Cromwell was made Lord Protector on 15 December 1653. On 20 March, he and his council ordered fast days in response to a fourth successive year of hot, dry weather which threatened the country's crops. Though Cromwell has often been called 'king in all but name', his power and authority was less straightforward and this, along with his reluctance to compel worship, may account for the continued use of declarations to 'order' special worship during this period. The drought was blamed on the sins of the realms, particularly the lack of godliness and prevalance of drinking, revelling and 'all manner of licentiousness', and on the failure of the magistracy to curb such behaviour. Cromwell heard three sermons on the thanksgiving day, preached by his chaplains Nicholas Lockyer, William Strong and [Walter?] Cradock.

Order: declaration by the lord protector, 20 Mar. 1654, Wing C7068A*[341] [also Wing C7077; printed in

---

[341] Wing catalogues two separate declarations with the same number, C7068A – one for this occasion, the other for 1654–1. The declaration for this occasion is represented in EEBO by the copy in the BL.

The writings and speeches of Oliver Cromwell, ed. W. C. Abbott (4 vols., Cambridge, MA, 1937–47), III, 225–8].

ORDER

Declaration by the lord protector: 20 March 1654

The common and notorious sins so boldly and impenitently practised amongst us, notwithstanding all our Deliverances and Mercies, together with the present Rod of an Exceeding and an Unusual Drought, which hath layen upon us for some years, and still continues and increaseth upon us, threatning Famine and Mortality, are no less than the Voice of God, calling aloud in our ears to Fasting, and Mourning, and great Abasement of Soul before him.

And although the General End and Intendment of inviting to a Day of Fast, be, that all of every Condition and Quality whatever, do try and examine their heart and way more especially, according to their own Light, and in the use of such Helps and Means as the Lord in His Providence shall afford to each one, before and upon the said day of Meeting; yet finding some thoughts set seriously upon our Heart, We judged it not amiss to recommend the same to Christian Consideration, not to impose them upon any, or to confine any within the compass thereof; but leaving every man free to the Grace of God, and to the work of his Spirit, who worketh all things in the Hearts of the Sons of Men, according to the Counsel and Good Pleasure of His own Will.

It cannot be denied but that God hath vouchsafed to appear very much in working the Deliverance of the Nation from their bondage and thraldome, both Spiritual and Civil, and procuring for them a just Liberty by His own People.

Do we now walk worthy of our high Calling in humbleness and lowliness of mind, holding forth the Virtues of Christ in time of Peace, which was our strength, by the efficacy of which all our great things were accomplished in time of War?

Have we a heart prepared as willingly to communicate the said Just Freedom and Liberty to one another, as we were industrious to get it?

Do we thankfully acknowledge our mercy in the Liberty of Worshipping God in Holiness and Righteousness without fear, being delivered out of the hands of our Enemies?

Is Brotherly Love, and a Healing Spirit of that force and value amongst us that it ought?

Do we own one another more for the grace of God, and for the Spiritual Regeneration, and for the Image of Christ in each other, or for our agreement with each other in this or that form, or opinion?

Do we first search for the Kingdom of Christ within us, before we seek one without us? Or do we listen to them that say concerning the comming of Christ, Lo here, and lo there?

Do we not more contend for Saints having rule in the world, than over their own hearts?

Are there not too many amongst us that cry up the Spirit, with a neglect of Love, Joy, Peace, Meekness, Patience, Goodness, Temperance, Long-suffering, Forbearance, Brotherly kindness, Charity, which are the fruits of the Spirit?

How do we carry our Selves, not only to the Churches of God, and the Saints, but towards them that are without?

Do not some of us affirm our selves to be the only true Ministry, and true Churches of Christ, and only to have the Ordinances in purity, excluding our Brethren, though of equal gifts, and having as large a Seal of their Ministry, and desiring with as much fervor and zeal to enjoy the Ordinances in their utmost purity?

Do we remember old Puritan, or rather Primitive simplicity, Self-denyal, Mercy to the Poor, Uprightness, and Justice? or are we not herein put to shame by those we easily call Anti-Christian or Carnal?

Hath one that we judge to be without equal justice with one we will call a Brother?

Do we contend for the *Faith once delivered unto the Saints*, as the things of Faith ought to be contended for, with Love, Patience, Tenderness, Zeal, by perswasion? Or rather imposingly, proudly, carnally, provokingly, sensually, thereby prejudicing the Truth, and, whilst we are calling aloud for the propagating of the Gospel, do we not put stumbling-blocks in the way of the same, and too much endanger to make good the slander of the world in charging Profession with *Faction*?

For want of Circumspection and care herein, and a due regard to sincerity and uprightness, have not many apostatized, running after *Fancies* and *Notions*, listning to filthy *Dreams, worshipping of Angels*, and been carried by their Impulsions; and instead of contending for the Faith, and holding the form of sound words, contended against *Magistracy*, against *Ministery*, against *scriptures*, and against *Ordinances*, too much verifying the Prophesies of *Peter* and *Jude*, in these following words.

2. Pet. 2. 1. *But there were false Prophets also among the people, even as there shall be false Teachers among you, who privily shall bring in damnable heresies, even denying the Lord that bought them, and bring upon themselves swift destruction.*

2. *And many shall follow their pernicious waies, by reason of whom the way of truth shall be evil spoken of.*

3. *And through covetousness shall they with feigned words make merchandize of you; whose judgement now of a long time lingreth not, and their damnation slumbreth not.*

10. *But chiefly them that walk after the flesh in the lust of uncleanness, and despise Government, presumptuous are they, self-willed, they are not afraid to speak evill of dignities.*

11. *Whereas Angels which are greater in power and might bring not railing accusations against them before the Lord.*

12. *But these as natural Brute Beasts made to be taken and destroyed, speak evil of the things they understand not, and shall utterly perish in their own corruption.*

13. *And shall receive the reward of unrighteousness, as they that count it pleasure to riot in the day time: spots they are and blemishes, sporting themselves with their own deceivings while they feast with you.*

15. *Having eyes full of adultery, and that cannot cease from sin, beguiling unstable souls; an heart they have exercised with covetous practices, cursed children;*

Jude ver.4. *For there are certain men crept in unwares, who were before of old ordained to this condemnation, ungodly men, turning the grace of our God into lasciviousness, and denying the only Lord God, and our Lord Jesus Christ.*

8. *Likewise also these filthy Dreamers defile the flesh, despise Dominion, and speak evil of dignities.*

10. *But these speak evil of those things which they know not, but what they know naturally, as brute beasts, in those things they corrupt themselves.*

11. *Wo unto them, for they have gone in the way of* Cain, *and ran greedily after the errour of* Balaam *for reward, and perished in the gain-saying of* Core.

12. *These are spots in your feasts of Charity when they feast with you, feeding themselves without fear: clouds they are without water, carried about with winds; trees whose fruit withereth, without fruit, twice dead, plucked up by the roots.*

13. *Raging waves of the Sea, foaming out their own shame; wandering stars, to whom is reserved the blackness of darkness for ever.*

16. *These are Murmurers, complainers, walking after their own lusts, and their mouth speaketh great swelling words, having mens persons in admiration because of advantage.*

19. *These be they who separate themselves, sensual having, not the Spirit.*

And notwithstanding all these evils, and worse, are upon, and in the midst of us, like gray hairs, here and there, and we *know it not, our pride testifying to our face Hos.* 7.9,10. and we not return to the Lord our God, nor seek him for all this, but these things are contended for, and justified under the notion of Liberty, it being too commonly said that the Magistrate hath nothing to do either in repressing, or remedying these things. We do hereby appeal to the hearts and consciences of all fearing the Lord, whether there be not as great cause as ever to lay our *Mouthes in the dust*, and to *abhor our selves* before the Lord, *for these abominations*, whereby the eyes of his jealousie are provoked, and to seek pardon and remedy from himself of these things.

Add we to these, The resistance, hatred, and neglect of the Gospel by the generality of men, the contempt and despite done to the sincere professors of it, even for the image of Christ in them (although they have been instruments of many mercies, and of the obtaining a just freedom for the nation) The wickednesses, oaths, drunkennesses, revellings, and all manner of licentiousness, for which things sake, the Scriptures have said, that the wrath of God shall undoubtedly overtake the children of disobedience.

And lastly, the impunity of these things, through the neglect of the Magistracy, throughout the Nation, and then judge whether there be not cause, that we be called upon, and do call upon each other seriously, to lay all these things to heart, being greatly abased before the Lord for them.

Upon the serious consideration of these things, We judge it not only warrantable, but a duty, to call upon you, and ourselves, to set apart time to humble our souls before the Lord, to cry unto him for broken & penitent hearts, and that he would turn away his wrath, & be reconciled to us; for the Lord he is merciful, gracious, long-suffering, and abundant in goodness and truth, forgiving iniquity, transgression and sin, and will by no means clear the guilty, who are only such as go on in their hardened and impenitent hearts, refusing the grace offered by Jesus Christ.

It is therefore hereby declared, That We, and our Council, do purpose (by the grace of God) to set apart *Fryday* next, being the 24. of this present *March*, for a day of *Humiliation.*

And it is hereby Ordered that timely notice be given to the Cities of *London* and *Westminster*, who (together with the out-Parishes) we doubt not, will willingly keep the same day, And that like notice be given throughout *England* and *Wales*, to have their several meetings upon the same day Fortnight; And that Copies hereof be Printed and published, to be sent to the several Parts of the Nation, to invite them unto the performance of this duty.

1654–1   Thanksgiving day for peace treaty with the Dutch Republic, and the end of drought

Tuesday 23 May 1654 (England and Wales, Scotland, Ireland)

Peace between the protectorate and the United Provinces was concluded on 5 April in the treaty of Westminster. On 9 May, Cromwell declared a day of thanksgiving for 23 May. Although his declaration did not specify which parts of the Commonwealth were to observe the occasion, his references to 'we the Nations' and, more importantly, the terms of the ordinance of 12 April 1654 uniting England and Scotland, would imply that it was to be observed across all kingdoms. There was a corresponding thanksgiving in the United Provinces. Cromwell exhorted people, in addition to giving thanks for the peace, to remember God's mercy in sending rain after four years of drought (see 1654–E). As for previous occasions, the declaration included a number of biblical passages which, though used to justify and set the tone for the thanksgiving, could have been used during the service. The thanksgiving was marked among English communities in the United Provinces but, according to an English newsletter, the English preachers (Mayden and Price) used the occasion to preach against the protectorate, and to call for the restoration of Charles II and the assassination of Cromwell.

Order: declaration by the lord protector, 9 May 1654, Wing C7080* [also Wing C7080A; printed in *Writings and Speeches*, ed. Abbott, III, 289–91].

Additional sources: A letter of intelligence from Holland, 5 June 1654 [New Style], *SP Thurloe*, II, 319; *Larkham diary*, p. 91.

ORDER

Declaration by the lord protector: 9 May 1654

That this hath been a Nation of blessings in the midst whereof so many wonders have been brought forth by the out-stretched arm of the Almighty, even to astonishment, and wonder, Who can deny? Ask we the Nations of this matter and they will testify, and indeed the dispensations of the Lord have been as if he had said, *England* thou art my first-born, my delight amongst the Nations, under the whole Heavens the Lord hath not dealt so with any of the people round about us.

The Lord having added another Link to this golden Chain of his loving kindness by giving us a Peace with Our Neighbours the United Provinces, (whereby he hath not only stopped a great issue of blood, but We trust also given us hearts to unite Our bloud and strength for the mutual defence of each other) cals for great return of Thanks for the same.

It is therefore thought fit to set apart *Tuesday*, being the 23. of this present *May*, as a day for Praise, and for the Thankful Acknowledgement of this blessing of Peace, which we hope hath in the womb of it many other blessings.

And let us not forget our other Mercies, was not the Earth lately so unusually parcht up, that it threatned Famin, and did cause the Beast of the field to mourn for want of food, and water to sustain it? And hath not the Lord so watered the Earth that he hath turned those fears into the expectation of the greatest plenty that ever was seen by any now living in this Nation? Consider we also the way whereby the Lord imparted this mercy to us, did any amongst us, foreknow it was coming, was it not by stirring up our hearts to seek the same by prayer, and that immediately before the Lord vouchsafed us this mercy? And doth not this bespeak? 1. That the manner of conveying this mercy is the best part of the mercy.

2. That the Lord has not cast us off, that his Spirit yet strives with us, that he hath a people of his love amongst us, and loves the Nation so far as to provoke it to be in love with calling upon the Name of the Lord for better things than Corn and Wine.

3. That he knows best how and when to answer the expectation of the Husbandman, and when to hear, even the mourning of the brute Beast, who will yet much more hear the desires of them that fear him, and that in the fittest season.

4. That the Heavens having thus declared the glory of God, and the Earth answering thereunto in its fruitfulness, Why should not we be melted and softned, humbling our selves under these marvellous kindnesses, and abounding unto all fruitfulness in every good word and work of love; And if every place hath been made partaker of his showres, Why should not we (laying aside our differences) be inlarged also each to other?

5. That seeing the Lord hath been thus universal in this Mercy, why should we not universally turn from the National Evils and vain Practices which yet are too superstitiously and customarily exercised amongst us, which we need not repeat here, because they are too well known, and We trust will be remembred by those godly Ministers who shall be called to preach unto the People upon this occasion? Conclude we with the words of *David*, *Psalm* 107. v.

30. *Then they are glad, because they be quiet, so he bringeth them unto their desired Haven.*

31. *O that Men would praise the Lord for his goodness, and for his wonderfull works to the Children of Men.*

32. *Let them exalt him also in the Congregation of the People, and praise him in the Assembly of the Elders.*

33. *He turneth Rivers into a Wilderness, and the water-springs into dry ground.*

34. *A fruitfull Land into barrenness, for the wickedness of them that dwell in it.*

35. *He turneth the Wilderness into a standing water, and dry ground into Water-springs.*

36. *And there he maketh the hungry to dwell, that they may prepare a City for Habitation.*

37. *And sow the Fields, and plant Vineyards, which may yield fruits of increase.*

38. *He blesseth them also, so that they are multiplied greatly, and suffereth not their Cattel to decrease.*

O that Men would praise the Lord for his goodness, and for his wonderfull works to the Children of Men.

1654–Ir   Fast day for support of the new lord deputy of Ireland

Thursday 21 September 1654 (Ireland)

This occasion is only known through Steele who saw the proclamation in manuscript. On 22 August, Charles Fleetwood was appointed lord deputy of Ireland, having previously only been commander-in-chief because parliament had been reluctant to use the title of lord deputy after the death of Ireton. The exact reason for this fast day is unclear, but Ireland was wracked with divisions at this time over the nature of government, the perceived conservatism of the protectorate, land allocation and the power of the army.

Order: order by the lord deputy and council, 14 Sept. 1654, not extant [formerly Dublin PRO, Order Book 5, p. 2; see Steele, II, no. 536].

DESCRIPTION OF ORDER

Order by the lord deputy and council: 14 September 1654
21 September to be a fast day for aid to the Lord Deputy in the discharge of his magistracy.

1654–2   Day of humiliation in the three nations for general repentance of sins

Wednesday 11 October 1654 (England and Wales, Scotland); Wednesday 1 November 1654 (Ireland)

The proposal for a day of fasting and humiliation in England, Wales, Scotland and Ireland was one of the first actions of the new protectorate parliament, which opened on 3 September. Cromwell faced opposition, particularly over his position as lord protector and, as the declaration for the fast made clear, there was continuing concern that the realms were not godly enough and that further religious and moral reform was required. Initially, it was proposed that there would be separate fast days for London (13 September), for the rest of England, Wales and Scotland (4 October) and for Ireland (1 November). But, on 14 September, the house resolved that the fasts for London, England, Wales and Scotland be postponed until 11 October; it is unclear why. A declaration prepared by a group of MPs, including Sir William Masham, Sir James Harington and Sir Arthur Hesilrigge was brought before the house on 15 September. It was passed after several amendments and then sent to Cromwell for his approval, which was given on 19 September. On 9 October, the burgh council of Edinburgh ordered that the day was to be observed. In Ireland, Lord Deputy Fleetwood and the council received the order and copies of the printed declaration for distribution. However, support for the fasts was not universal. George Fox, one of the founders of the Quakers, had printed a critique of the declaration, *A warning from the Lord*. John Nicoll, clerk of the Society of Writers to the Signet in Edinburgh, noted in his journal that 'the Church of Scotland did not agrey thairunto, bot exprest thameselffis aganes the present governament'.

Order: declaration by the lord protector and parliament, 19 Sept. 1654, Thomason E.1064[46] (see also Wing C7068A, Bodleian Library and 1654–E above).
Additional sources: *CJ*, VII, 366–8; council to the sheriffs of the counties, and same to General Monck, 20 Sept. 1654, SP25/75, 571; draft of the president and council to the lord deputy and council of Ireland, 20 Sept. 1654, *CSPI, Charles [and Commonwealth]*, III, 807; *Writings and speeches*, ed. Abbott, III, 479; *Edin. recs., 1642 to 1655*, pp. 350–1; George Fox, *A warning from the Lord* (Wing F1980); Nicoll, p. 138; *Larkham diary*, p. 99.

ORDER

Declaration by the lord protector and parliament: 19 September 1654

Who is such a stranger in our *Israel* that hath not taken notice of the great things God hath brought to pass amongst us by his out-stretched arm? What nation is there who hath had God more nigh unto them, than the Lord our God hath been to us, in all things we have called unto him for? Ask of the daies that are past, which have been before us, in these later ages, whether, there have been any such things as those many blessings and signal deliverances vouchsafed to us from his own hand, in answer to the voice of tears and blood that have been powred forth.

But in the mean while this is matter of great lamentation, whilst God, by a continual series of his loving kindnesses and providences, hath multiplied mercies and forgivenesses to us, we of these Nations, instead of an answerable return of thankfulness and obedience, have, as the highest aggravation of our sin, multiplyed our provocations against him;

In that general ignorance, unthankfulnes, and unfruitfulness, under all those dews of grace and Gospel-mercies.

In not acknowledging fully to this very day our calamities to have come upon us from the hands of God alone, provoked by us, who useth what instruments he pleaseth to execute his indignation.

In not bemoaning our selvs, as sons, and smiting upon our thighs with *Ephraim*, in the sense of our own iniquities, and of the patience & forbearing mercies of our heavenly Father.

In that prophane, sensual, worldly, formal and *Laodicean* spirit generally amongst us, some hating the power of godliness, and despising the true professors thereof, for having the image of God upon them; and others, by being loose in their opinions and practices, *have turned the grace of God into wantonness*.

In that great neglect and want of zeal and courage in Magistrates, and other officers & persons therein concerned, to suppress enormities, in conscience to perform the duty incumbent upon them to God and man.

All which, with other the crying sins of these three Nations, call aloud upon us, that as we are now united to be one Commonwealth under one Government, so, having been sinful and sufferers together, we would with one heart and lip be perswaded to unite in our humble and serious addresses and supplications to Almighty God.

That the fruit of all our mercies might not be with *Jesurun*, to kick, or to be found fighters against him, nor opposers of his will, as if we were preserved to commit yet more abominations.

That we may wrestle and prevail with him for pardon and removal of our darkness, vanities, blasphemies & prophaness, with all that worldly mindedness, formality, and other abominations which are yet found amongst us under the glorious light of the Gospel.

That as God hath been pleased to make choice of these Islands wherin to manifest many great and glorious things, so he would answerably make us a chosen generation, and a peculiar people, that in thankfulness to him, and example to others, we might shew forth his praises, who hath separated us from other nations, and called us out of darkness into his light.

That God would now speak with a strong hand to quiet the spirits of men that are apt to murmure, by causing them clearly to see where the true and spiritual interest of Christians lieth, and that in keeping close thereunto is wrapt up their safety, that so *When he uttereth his voice, All flesh may be silent before him, and know that he is raised out of his holy habitation.*

That though he hath had just cause to be angry with us for our murmurings, back-slidings, and other iniquities, and hath therefore smitten us, yet that he would now heal us, and restore comfort to us and our Mourners.

And especially that God would inable the Rulers of these Nations now in consultation about their peace, settlement & welfare, to proceed with faithfulness, zeal, wisdom and union, to fulfill the end of their being called together, and to be such, and do such things for the interest of Christ and his members, and for the good of all the People, as they ought, and as he hath promised Governours should be and do in subserviency to those glorious ends.

That so at last, through the goodness and mercy of our God, these three Nations, after so great and various revolutions, may be establisht together upon the sure foundations of Truth, Righteousness and Peace.

It is therefore declared by His Highness the Lord Protector and the Parlament of the Common-wealth of *England, Scotland* and *Ireland*, that for the ends and purposes aforesaid they doe appoint *Wednesday*, being the eleventh day of *October* next, for a day of solemn humiliation and seeking the face of God, through the mediation of Christ, in all places within *England* and *Scotland*; and *Wednesday* the first day of *November* next, in all places in *Ireland*. And doe therefore hereby incite and encourage all such whose hearts God shall perswade and make sensible of their duty, and of the Commonwealths present condition, that the respective daies aforesaid be set apart by them for the purposes aforesaid; whereof the Ministers and Preachers of the respective Parishes and Congregations are to take notice. For which end, It is Ordered that Copies of this Declaration be printed and sent into the severall parts of the three Nations, that the same may be Published accordingly.

1655–Ir1 Fast day during plague epidemic

Thursday 3 May 1655 (Ireland)

On 28 April, the lord deputy and council ordered a day of public fasting to be observed on 3 May in response to the plague which continued to dog the country (see also 1651–Ir1, 1651–Ir3). The order, which included a reference to Isaiah 58:3 ('Wherefore have we fasted, say they, and thou seest not?'), was seen by Steele only in manuscript; it is unclear if it was printed. The mayor of Dublin was ordered to give notice of the fast day.

Order: order by the lord deputy and council, 28 Apr. 1655, not extant [formerly Dublin PRO, Order Book 5, p. 142; see Steele, II, no. 554].

DESCRIPTION OF ORDER

Order by the lord deputy and council: 28 April 1655
Whereas the hand of the Lord was stretched ... Orders a fast on Thursday, 3 May, in view of the pestilence; quotes Isaiah lviii. 3. Mayor of Dublin to give notice.

1655–EIr   Fast days in support of the persecuted protestants of Savoy

Thursday 14 June 1655 (England and Wales); Thursday 5 July 1665 (Ireland)

On 25 May, Cromwell ordered a day of solemn fasting to be observed and a collection taken on 14 June on behalf of the Vaudois (or Waldensian) protestants who had been evicted from their homes and some massacred in Savoy between January and April. Though the ordinance for the union of England and Scotland (12 April 1654) enabled the protector to order special worship jointly for England, Wales, Ireland and Scotland, this occasion reverted to being ordered only for England and Wales, and a separate order was issued by the lord deputy and Irish council in June. This occasion was also the first time that special worship had been ordered on behalf of foreign protestants since 1629–E and it was a personal decision by the protector who had 'soe taken to hart' their fate. Cromwell also wrote to other European rulers seeking to build a protestant alliance against Charles Emmanuel II, duke of Savoy, and broke off treaty negotiations with Louis XIV until the French king agreed to intercede with the duke for the Vaudois. Thomas Larkham's diary shows that he contributed five shillings to his parish collection 'To the distressed protestents in Savoy', rather than the usual sixpence on other fast days or thanksgivings. On 12 July, Cromwell issued a proclamation exhorting those parishes which had not observed the fast – which he blamed on officers failing to distribute his declaration – to organize a financial collection; he also required those who had not delivered their collections to the state's officers to do so immediately. On 15 June, Lord Deputy Fleetwood and the council in Ireland ordered a day of humiliation to be observed on 5 July in Ireland. As with the English and Welsh occasion, a collection was also ordered: the money was to be collected by ministers and sent, within four days, to the local town council or JP and they, in turn, passed it to the mayor or aldermen of Dublin within twenty days. Over £1,000 was raised. The Irish order also contained Cromwell's invitation to the English and Welsh to participate in a fast day and instructions on collecting the financial contribution.

Orders: ENGLAND AND WALES: declaration by the protector, 25 May 1655, Thomason E,1064[54]*; proclamation by the protector, 12 July 1655, Thomason 669.f.20[5]*; IRELAND: order by the lord deputy and council, 15 June 1655, Wing C7077A*.
Additional sources: Lord Protector to the sheriffs, 12 July 1655, SP25/76, pp. 177–8; *SP Thurloe*, III, 549; Evelyn, III, 152 n. 1; *Larkham diary*, p. 113; Steele, II, no. 560.
Printed sermon: ? Crofton, London (Wing C6994).

ORDERS

England and Wales: declaration by the protector, 25 May 1655

The poor Inhabitants of the valleys of *Lucern*, *Angrona*, and others within the Dominions of the Duke of *Savoy*, professing the Reformed Religion, and refusing to abandon the same, which hath been transmitted unto them from their Ancestors (the Old *Waldenses*, those famous Martyrs, who with their Lives and Fortunes have born their frequent Testimonies to the Truth) were by an Edict from the said Duke enjoyned in the hardest season of the Winter, to quit their Habitations, upon penalty of Loss of Life and Confiscation of their Estates, unless they should within twenty days after Publication of the said Edict make it appear, that they had embraced the

Roman Religion; which hard and rigorous Command was soon after most severely put in execution by an Army sent amongst them, which by continual Slaughters, Massacres and other intolerable Violences daily exercised upon them, inforced them to retreat to the Mountainous Parts of their Countrey, the better to secure themselves from the Fury of their Adversaries, who putting many of them to the Sword, and continuing daily to prosecute them with barbarous and inhumane Cruelties and Tortures, forced the rest to flie for their Lives, who are now wandering with their wives and little ones, destitute and afflicted by Hunger, Cold and Nakedness, in such desolate places of the Mountains where they may best hide and shelter themselves from the remainder of their most implacable Enemies Rage and Violence: This being the sad condition of Our poor Brethren and Fellow-Members in the Body of Christ, should those of the same Faith and Hope with them (who through the Stretcht-out hand of God, enjoy Deliverance and Protection from the like Fury and Violence) neglect or disregard them in this Day of their Distress for the Testimony of Jesus, Assistance and Relief would arise to them some other way; But we should be little able to give an Accompt with Chearfulness of this Call of God that is now upon Us, for the exercise of Mercy and Compassion towards them: God who hath given them to suffer for Christs sake, hath given Us the Liberty of the Gospel in that measure, with those Attendances of Peace and Plenty, as we must needs look upon it as a great Contempt of his Distinguishing Mercy, should not we improve our utmost Interest in him, and lay out what he hath intrusted Us withal as we have opportunity, for their Relief. Out of Our deep sence therefore of the sad calamitous Estate of Our poor Brethren, as also of the future Danger upon all the Protestant Churches in general, that We may enjoy the gracious presence of Our good God in Christ to guide Us in what he shall call Us to do or suffer for, or with Our Brethren, We do hereby Appoint *Thursday* the Fourteenth day of *June*, One thousand six hundred fifty five, to be set apart for a Day of Humiliation and Seeking the Face of God, in the behalf of the Oppressed Witnesses of Christ; and earnestly desire, That all the People of God in this Nation would joyn with one heart and lip in this so great and necessary a Duty. And We do also further desire, That on the same day the Ministers of the several Congregations will stir up the People to a free and a liberal Collection and Contribution for their Relief, to be made on such day and in such maner, as shall be expressed in certain Instructions hereunto annexed; And the respective Ministers are hereby Required to cause this Declaration to be Read and Published in their several Congregations on the said Day of Humiliation.

England and Wales: proclamation by the protector, 12 July 1655

Whereas His Highness from a deep Sence of the sad Calamities of the poor Inhabitants of the Valleys of *Lucern, Angrona,* and others within the Dominions of the Duke of *Savoy* (occasioned by their faithful Adherence to their profession of the Reformed Religion) and from a Confidence that the Good People of this Nation would (in this day of their Brethrens Trouble) manifest a serious Sense of the Sufferings of their Fellow-Members, professing the same Faith and Hope, did in *May* last (by and with the Advice of the Council) publish a Declaration, thereby inviting the People of *England* and *Wales,* to set apart the Fourteenth of *June* last for a Day of Solemn Fasting and Humiliation, and seeking the Face of God on behalf of those oppressed Witnesses of Jesus Christ, expressing withal His desire, that the People might then be stirred up to a free and liberal Contribution for their Relief, to be made in such way and maner as was set forth in certain Instructions thereunto annexed:

And whereas His Highness hath received Information, That (although the People of many Parishes and Congregations have with a liberal hand extended their Bounty, in contributing largely to their Relief, yet) through the negligence of some, to whom the dispersing of the said Declarations and Instructions to the respective Parishes, was intrusted, the said Fast and Collection hath been in many places wholly omitted; To the intent therefore that those whose Hearts God shall stir up, may not be deprived of so precious an Opportunity of Refreshing the Bowels of the afflicted Members of Christ, His Highness (upon Advice with His Council) doth hereby recommend it to all the several Parishes and Congregations in *England* and *Wales,* where the said Collection hath not been made, that they would improve this present Season of drawing out their Compassion on behalf of their said distressed Brethren; As also to the Ministers of the said several Congregations, to stir up the People thereof to a Free and Liberal Contribution as aforesaid, and to pursue the way for Collecting and Paying in the said Moneys prescribed in the said Instructions. And whereas several Sums of Money already collected are not yet returned nor certified, according to the said Instructions, His Highness doth hereby Will and Require the several Ministers, Churchwardens, and other persons imployed about the said Collections, and the several Justices of Peace, to whose hands any of the Moneys so collected have been paid, speedily to return as well the Certificates as the said Moneys, according to the purport of the said Instructions, that so those Ends which have been propounded, and shall be faithfully prosecuted for imploying the said Moneys for the said Protestants Relief, may with more speed and advantage be accomplished; On which Accompt His Highness doubts not, but all persons who bear the Name of Christ, will (according to their several Concernments herein) lay out their Interests and faithful Endeavors in this so pious, necessary and honorable a work, with Chearfulness and Expedition.

Ireland: order by the lord deputy and council, 15 June 1655

Ordered, That Thursday (being the fifth of *July* next ensuing) be set apart for a day of *Humiliation* and seeking the face of the Lord for the ends and purposes in his Highness the Lord Protectors said Declaration set forth; and all the people of God in this Nation are earnestly desired to join with one heart and lip in this so great and necessary a Duty.

And it is farther desired, That upon the same day the Ministers of the several Congregations within this Nation do stirr up the people to a free and liberal Collection and Contribution for their relief; who are hereby required to cause the said Declaration of his Highness to be read and published in their several Congregations on the said day of *Humiliation*. And it is farther Ordered, That all moneys so collected (together with the said Schedule and Declaration so endorsed) be returned and payd by the said Ministers respectively, within four days then next ensuing, unto the respective Governers of such City or Town, or to the next Iustice of Peace to the Parish where such Collection shall be made, or such other fit and responsible person, as the said respective Governers of that Precinct shall appoint to receive the same, who is hereby impowered and required to receive the same, and to give his acquittance to such person so paying the same; and within 20 days after, or sooner (if it may be) to return the sum or sums so received unto *Thomas Hooke* Esq; Mayor of the City of *Dublin*, Alderman *Daniel Hutchinson* and Alderman *John Preston*, or any one of them, who are hereby appointed Treasurers for receiving the whole sum which shall be gathered upon this Collection, whose acquittance shall be a sufficient discharge for such sum so payd in; and that the said Ministers do within ten days after such Collection certifie unto *Thomas Herbert* Esq; Clerk of the Council, the sum so collected in such City, Town or Parish, to the end an exact Accompt may be taken thereof. Which moneys so collected and payd are to be returned to the Committee in the said Instructions named, to be disposed of for relief of the said poor Protestants, according to the intent of the Givers, and not otherwise.

1655–Ir2   Fast day in support of the persecuted protestants of Savoy and of the lord protector's policies

Thursday 8 November 1655 (Ireland)

On 3 November, the lord deputy and council ordered a fast to be observed on 8 November in support of the Savoy protestants and the lord protector; it was the second fast to be ordered in Ireland in response to events in Savoy (see 1655-EIr). Elsewhere, tension grew between England and Spain; Cromwell was asked to negotiate between Sweden and the United Provinces over control of the Baltic Sea; the legitimacy of the protectorate had been challenged by the Leveller, John Lilburne, in the summer, and, on 31 October, the major-generals were authorized to enforce the law, collect taxation and instil more godly behaviour in England and Wales.

Order: order by the lord deputy and council, 3 Nov. 1655, not extant [formerly Dublin PRO, Order Book 5, p. 275; see Steele, II, no. 574].

DESCRIPTION OF ORDER

Order by the lord deputy and council: 3 November 1655
When Wee reflect upon the great … Cites Deut. xxxiii. Last verse and Ps. cvii., and the sufferings of the Protestants of Savoy. A fast to be kept on Thursday, 8 November, for direction to the Lord Protector in foreign affairs, and a blessing on home undertakings.

1655–1   Day of humiliation for general repentance of sins

Thursday 6 December 1655 (England and Wales, Scotland, Ireland)

By late 1655, Cromwell was increasingly troubled by his own ungodliness and that of the rest of the country. He interpreted the royalist uprisings in the spring (including Penruddock's uprising, 11 March) and the failure of the Western Design (to attack Spanish shipping in the Caribbean in order to damage trade and weaken catholic influence in the New World) as divine warnings prompted by such ungodliness. As a result, he ordered a day of humiliation to be observed on 6 December. His declaration did not specify whether the day was to be observed throughout the Commonwealth but this is implied by the terms of the ordinance of 12 April 1654 in which England, Wales, Ireland and Scotland had been united under one government. References to the 'People in these Nations' in the order may also suggest that the day was to be observed across the Commonwealth. This day of humiliation was the first of a series over the next two years. More practically, Cromwell instituted the rule of the major-generals across England (31 October): direct military rule aimed at enforcing godliness and order more effectively than previously. Cromwell appears to have planned this occasion well in advance of his declaration. For instance, he and the council wrote to the mayor of Chester authorizing the printing and distribution of the order and declaration in the city a week before it was officially issued.

Order: declaration by the protector, 21 Nov. 1655, Wing C7078*.
Additional sources: HMC, *Eighth rep., Appendix*, p. 387; *SP Thurloe*, IV, 207.

ORDER

Declaration by the protector: 21 November 1655

When We call to mind, together with the repeated loving kindnesses of God to his People in these Nations, the late rebukes We have received, the Tares of Division that have been sown by the envious one, and the growth they have had, through his Subtilty, amongst Us, the abhominable blasphemies vented, & spreading of late, through the Apostacy of, and the abuse of liberty by, many professing Religion, the continued Series of Difficulties We have been, and are exercised under, by the secret and open practises of those, that, bearing evil will unto *Sion*, have *Balaam*-like attempted all waies to frustrate Our hopes and endeavours of such a Settlement and Reformation as hath been so long contended for; as also the weight of the work of this Generation.

We have thought it a duty becoming Us, not only Our Selves to lie low before the Lord, and to have recourse to him by Prayer and Humiliation, but also to call upon, and invite, all the People of God in these Nations to joyn with Us in Solemn and Earnest Supplications to the Throne of Grace (a way wherein We have often experimented the good presence of God) That the Lord will be pleased truly to humble Us and the Nation under his righteous hand, that We may be every one searching out the plague of his own heart, and turn unfeignedly from the evil of Our waies, that notwithstanding all Our provocations, the Lord may be pleased to return & smile upon Us.

That he will disappoint the Designs of those that labour to lift themselves up against the interest of Christ and his People.

That he will rebuke the aforesaid evils, and give his people to know the things that belong to their Peace, that so We may with one heart and shoulder serve the Lord both Theirs and Ours.

That his presence may be with those that are more especially engaged in, and entrusted with the great Affairs of the Nation, by a Spirit of Counsel and Wisdom to enable them faithfully to discharge their weighty Trust, and that they may bear some proportion of serviceableness to the great Works, Designs and Promises of God concerning the Kingdom of his Son, our blessed Lord, in these later times, and may be used as Instruments in his hand for the continuance and increase of the Reformation, and the Security and Settlement of these Nations.

Upon these and such like grounds, We have appointed *Thursday* the sixth day of *December* next, to be set apart for a day of Publick Humiliation. And the Ministers of the several Congregations are to give notice hereof on the Lords day next before the said sixth day of *December*.

1656–1 Days of humiliation for general repentance of sins

Friday 28 March 1656 (England and Wales, Scotland, Ireland); Thursday 3 April and Thursday 17 April 1656 (Ireland)

This was the second in a series of days of humiliation prompted by Cromwell's increasing sense that his own sins, as well as those of the commonwealth, had provoked God's wrath. Spain attacked English ships in response to continued attempts to secure control of the West Indies; Sweden and the United Provinces fought for control of the Baltic; the duke of Savoy's persecution of his protestant subjects in Piedmont resulted in a massacre in April; Cromwell's attempts to form an anti-catholic protestant alliance failed; royalists and sectaries (especially the fifth monarchists) destabilized domestic order. As in 1655–1, this occasion was probably ordered to be observed in England, Wales, Ireland and Scotland under the terms of the ordinance of 1654, with Cromwell referring in his declaration to 'We all in these Nations'. But, on 28 March, Lord Deputy Fleetwood and the council issued a separate order for days of humiliation to be observed in Ireland on 3 and 17 April. Whether their actions mean that the ordinance of 1651 did not automatically enable special worship to be ordered across the Commonwealth by declaration of the protector is unclear. The mayor of Dublin and the sheriffs were appointed to distribute the Irish order; no markets and fairs were to be held and no servile work could be done.

Order: ENGLAND AND WALES [SCOTLAND, IRELAND?] declaration by the protector, 13 Mar. 1656, Wing C7078B* [also Wing C7079 dated 14 Mar.]; IRELAND: order by the council, 28 Mar. 1656, not extant [formerly Dublin PRO, Order Book 10, p. 47; see Steele, II, no. 576].

ORDER AND DESCRIPTION OF ORDER

England and Wales, Scotland, Ireland: declaration by the protector, 13 March 1656

That We all in these Nations have more than ordinary cause to humble Our selves, and to lay Our mouthes in the dust in Fasting and Prayer before the Lord at this time will undoubtedly be agreed by all.

Amongst many others let these following motives induce Us to be very solemn and serious in this Duty.

I. We having made Peace with all Our Neighbour Nations, and upon righteous grounds deeply engaged in a War with the *Spaniard*, with whom We had no peace, but where he pleased, and from whom we could obtain none for the future, without subjecting the Lives, Liberties and Estates of the People of these Nations trading thither, to the bloody Inquisition and other Papall determinations, nor unless we would quit Our claims of satisfaction for multiplied injuries done Us in shedding the innocent blood of this people, and expulsing them out of divers Islands, of which they were justly possessed, as is more at large expressed in the late Declaration, holding forth the grounds and reasons of Our undertaking against them. The Lord hath been pleased in a wonderful manner to humble and rebuke Us, in that expedition to the *West Indies,* which although we apprehend was not in favour of the Enemy, yet gives Us just reason to fear, that We may have either failed in the spirit and manner wherewith this business hath been undertaken, or that the Lord sees some abomination, or accursed thing by which he is provoked thus to appear against Us.

II. That whilest the Lord has thus abased Us (instead of humbling Our selves under the mighty hand of God, and each man searching and repenting of the plague and evil of his own heart, and mourning for so great an affliction upon the whole Land, and more principally on the interest and profession of the Gospel in all the world) some most unnaturally rejoice, others are apt hastily to apply according to their fancies; being too forward to give a reason of the Judgements of God, which are so great a deep, and particularly to assign the reason of this sharp dispensation, not considering that the Lord may for tryal as well as in judgement, exercise the faith of his people. Others imputing the cause onely to the evil of the Majestrate, who profess (if there were no other provocation) even for their own sins justly to have incurred all this, and much more, and hope they can in some measure desire to redeem the losse sustained by this heavy stroke, with their lives, desiring nothing more than a conviction from the Lord. And have appointed this day of Humiliation, that the Majestrate, together with all such as fear the Lord, may deal impartially with their own souls, before the Lord, in a matter of so great concernment.

III. That the People of God continue still in their animosities, and improve not such strokes unto Love and Union, whilest by the advantage thereof, the common Enemy, both at home and abroad, take encouragement to hope, that the time hast-neth wherein they shall swallow Us up; but instead thereof, some of the same faith in all things necessary to salvation, upon private thoughts of their own, hold up still a quarrel with, and opposition to their Brethren, about Christs Kingdome, or rather their own understanding of the time, and manner of it, We mean those of them, who will not give way that others wait upon the Spirit of God for light in this matter. Others still differing about forms, even to the breach of the Royal Law. Others repining at the present begun Reformation, though having much tendency to good, both as to the comfort and security of the Godly, and discountenance of wicked men, and wickedness; wherein through God it hath had some small effect, and also, which (which is most sad) even because it hath had the success to unite more good men upon the old principles of Love and truth then any expedient the providence of God hath brought forth since these troubles.

IV. That still We murmur and are unquiet, unthankful to the Lord, weary of our Peace, making it a light thing to run again into blood; We despise Magistracy, and are become weary of the preaching of the Gospel, and other Ordinances of Christ.

V. Oathes, prophanness, unmercifullness, oppression, covetousness, and seeking great things in such shaking times, not mourning when the Lord calls to it, nor being sensible of our condition.

These and many more are just causes and provocations to us to mourn, especially taking in this aggravation that the Lord hath done for us, yea even for his people here, above what he hath done for any people.

VI. Adde to these the condition of the Protestant Churches abroad, the members whereof have very lately been massacred in *Piedmont* without sparing age or sex, are bleeding in *Switzerland*, divers there having been put to death for no fault, but being Protestants; the designes upon the whole Interest by the Popish party almost in all places of *Europe*, and the grounds of their quarrel and persecution for Religion, more clear and avowed then in many years before.

VII. And lastly, That the Lord would pardon the iniquities both of Magistrate and people in these Lands, wherein the Magistrate desires first to take shame to himself and find out his provocation, as well as lay it upon others, and that the Lord would pardon our iniquities and convert us unto himself, and bless our poor friends in the *Indies*, and go out with our Fleets, and prosper our undertakings as formerly by his own blessed presence, and unite us in love, causing mercy and truth to meet together, and righteousness and peace to kiss each other, and thereby exalt his own great name, make our Land glorious and bless his cause and people in all the world, and hasten the time of the pulling down of Antichrist, and expelling out of these Lands the unclean Spirit, Is this day of solemn humiliation and prayer appointed to be upon *Friday* the 28. of *March* 1656.

Ireland: Order by the Council, 28 March 1656

Whereas His Highness for the reasons expressed … Cites Declaration No. 3069, Eng., q.v. A fast to be held on Thursday, 3 April and 17 April. Mayor and sheriffs to give notice. No fairs, markets, &c., to be held or servile work to be done.

1656–2   Thanksgiving days for naval victory at the battle of Cadiz

Wednesday 8 October 1656 (London, Westminster and the late lines of communication); Wednesday 5 November 1656 (elsewhere in England and Wales, Scotland, Ireland)

Conflict between England and Spain increased, especially after Philip IV of Spain signed the treaty of Brussels with Charles II to provide military support for a proposed royalist invasion of England (2 April; ratified 5 June). During the summer, Spanish shipping at Vigo and Malaga was attacked and Cadiz was blockaded by English ships. On 9 September, Captain Stayner attacked the Spanish plate fleet from Cuba off Cadiz, capturing two richly ladened ships and sinking three others. News of his success was received at the second protectorate parliament on 2 October, just as members began to discuss the Anglo-Spanish war. Parliament proposed a thanksgiving and sought Cromwell's approval. The lord protector assented to the order and approved the narrative (*A true narrative*) on 17 September. The ordering process for this occasion, therefore, returned to the procedure common in the 1620s, when parliament proposed special worship and then sought the consent of the head of state. It is unclear why parliament reverted to this procedure. It is not clear if the date for observance of the thanksgiving outside London (5 November) was chosen deliberately to draw a parallel between God's favour shown at Cadiz and in the discovery of the Gunpowder plot in 1605. As in 1656–1, the Irish privy council also issued its own proclamation. The order and declaration were distributed in and around London by the lord mayor and JPs. Joseph Caryll and John Row were appointed to preach before the house at St Margaret's, Westminster. In Ireland, the Irish privy council ordered *A true narrative* to be reprinted in Dublin. John Nicoll, the Scottish chronicler, reported that 'This solempnitie of thankisgeving was not obeyit by our Scoottis ministrie.'

Orders: ENGLAND AND WALES, SCOTLAND, IRELAND: parliamentary order, 2 Oct. 1656, *CJ*, VII, 432; IRELAND: a proclamation by the Irish council, 21 Oct. 1656, not extant [formerly Dublin PRO, Order Book 10, p. 198; Minute Book 48; see Steele, II, no. 582].
Additional sources: *CJ*, VII, 432–4, 438, 440; *SP Thurloe*, V, 472; *A true narrative of the late success which it hath pleased God to give to some part of the fleet of this common-wealth* (1656; Wing T2800A;

ESTC 006470907 (Dublin reprint)); draft of the privy council to the lord deputy and council of Ireland, 21 Oct. 1650, *CSPI*, XVIII, 832; Nicoll, p. 186.
Printed sermons: Carpenter, ? (Wing C622); Caryl, parliament (Wing C788); Rowe, parliament (Wing R2065).

ORDER AND DESCRIPTION OF ORDER

England and Wales, Scotland, Ireland: parliamentary order, 2 October 1656

Resolved, That, a Day of Thanksgiving be appointed to bless the Lord for the great Mercies by him vouchsafed to this Commonwealth, in the Success given to some of their Ships, against the Fleet of the King of *Spaine*, coming from the *West Indies*, on the 8th of *September* last.

Ordered, That Wednesday next be the Day set apart for a Day of Thanksgiving for this House; to be observed also within the Cities of *London* and *Westminster*, and all Places within the late Lines of Communication …

… *Ordered*, That the Fifth of *November* be appointed as a Day of Publick Thanksgiving throughout *England, Scotland*, and *Ireland*, for the great Mercies which the Lord hath vouchsafed to this Commonwealth in the Success of Part of their Fleet against the *Spanish West India Fleet*.

Ireland: order by the Irish council, 21 October 1656

5 Nov. to be a day of thanksgiving. The narrative of the defeat of the Spanish fleet to be printed with this order.

1656–3   Day of humiliation for general repentance of sins

Thursday 30 October 1656 (England and Wales, Scotland, Ireland)

Though this day of humiliation, like the thanksgiving that preceded it (1656–2), was proposed by parliament, it seems to have been another in the series of days of humiliation prompted by the fears of Cromwell and others that the nations' sins had provoked God's wrath. In addition to continued hostilities with Spain, the protectorate faced growing opposition at home, and Cromwell issued special instructions to the major-generals to maintain order. On 18 September, the day after parliament assembled, this day of humiliation was proposed and a declaration outlining the reasons for it was commissioned. The order and declaration were read for the first time on 20 September and for a second time on the 22nd, when a number of amendments were made, including the banning of recreations and bodily labour on the day. The proposal having passed the house, a committee was appointed to seek Cromwell's approval. This was given on 22 September, though he amended the date of observance from 24 October to the 30th because the earlier date was when the lord mayor of London would be formally presented to his office. In Ireland, Lord Deputy Fleetwood was informed of the fast immediately and appears to have been supplied with copies of the declaration to distribute to parishes. Though the order was distributed in and around Edinburgh, it does not appear to have been widely observed beyond the burgh council because of opposition to it by the Scottish Kirk.

Order: declaration by the lord protector and parliament, 23 Sept. 1656, Wing C7069* [also Wing C7071, C7071A (Edinburgh reprints)].

Additional sources: *CJ*, VII, 423–4, 426–7; *Burton diary*, I, 181–2; *Larkham diary*, p. 148; further orders of the [council of state], 26 Sept. 1656, *CSPI*, XVIII, 831; *Edin. recs., 1655 to 1665*, p. 39; Nicoll, p. 186; John Nicoll to the laird of Glenorchy, younger, 11 Oct. 1656, NRS, GD112/39/101/13.
Printed sermon: Owen, parliament (Wing O757).

ORDER

Declaration by the lord protector and parliament: 23 September 1656

Such have been the out-goings of our God for his people in this our generation, that none as men, but must say, *It is Marvellous in our eyes*: And none as Christians, but must cry out; *It is the Lords doing*, he hath alwaies been a ready help in time of need, and never did his poor servants seek his face in vain, neither did he ever lend a deaf ear to the voice of their weepings. *Who can utter the mighty Acts of the Lord? who can shew forth all his praises? But Israel doth not know, my people doth not consider*, for in the midst of such unequalled and signal mercies, how great hath been, and is our ingratitude and unfruitfulness? Verily such, that nothing can be greater, but that inexhausted mercy, which hitherto hath not consumed us. Should the Lord say unto us, as once he did unto *Ephraim, Ephraim is joined unto Idols, let him alone*. That heavy sentence would be but our desert. As insensibility is our crime, so it might be too justly made our punishment; for who has been melted by mercies, who has been broken by judgement? *Ah sinful Nation! a people laden with iniquity, a seed of evill doers, children that are corrupters, they have forsaken the Lord, they have provoked the holy one of Israel to anger, they are gone away backward: why should ye be stricken any more? ye will revolt more and more.* As these sad words do Characterize us as fully as they did those of *Juda* to whom they were first spoken; so if that sad Denunciation should also be our Doom, we could not yet but acknowledge; *the Lord is righteous in all his wayes, and holy in all his works*. How deeply have we grieved our good God, in not mourning as we ought, even as one that mourneth for his first-born, for that ignorance, profaneness and barrenness that is so ripe amongst us, even under such rich means of knowledge, reformation and grace, in not being sensible under, nor making a sanctified use of, those Rebukes we have of late received; But rather charging such miscarriages upon Instruments, chiefly, if not only, when every Individual hath helped to fill up the measure of those sins after which such Judgements were to follow.

In not improving mercies so fully as might have been, to his glory, from whom alone they were received.

In the sad neglect and want of Activity, Resolution and Integrity, in Magistrates and others impowred therein, for the punishment and suppression of vice and crying Enormities.

In the abominable Blasphemies vented and spread of late through the apostasie of, and the abuse of liberty by, many professing Religion.

In that little love and tenderness which is even amongst professors themselves towards one another, who whilst they contend for things disputable, lose that which is certain, even *Charity, which is the bond of perfectness*, and without which they become as *sounding Brass, or a tinckling Cimball*: To love one another is Christs new Commandement, nay, the very Badge of his Disciples. *By this shall all men know that you are my Disciples, if you have love one to another*, in allowing difference in forms, more power to divide Christians, then Agreements in fundamentals has to unite them, one of the dangerousest and fruitfullest seed that hath been sown by the envious one.

In not being truly sensible, that though the Lord in the depths of his wisedome and righteous Judgement, hath for some years last past been overturning several Authorities in these Nations, and hath as it were been pouring them out from vessel to vessel: He hath yet been pleased ever since his people publickly contended for his Truths, still to set up Rulers, who have allowed them the free exercise & profession of them.

In that Atheistical and Luke-warm Spirit, too commonly amongst us, whereby not only the form but power of godliness is reproached, and accounted as a vile thing, but also too many have fallen from their first love, and others *Laodicean* like, esteem themselves *rich and to have need of nothing*, whilest indeed they are *wretched, and miserable, and poor, and blind, and naked*, sins which are the highlier aggravated, by being committed in Countreys where the Glorious light of the Gospel shines clearest.

In being more dissatisfied that we have not obtained all we aymed at, then thankfull that we have obtained so much, as through mercy we now enjoy.

All which, with other the grievous sins of these three Nations, call aloud upon all the good people in them, to lye Low in the sight of our offended God, and by prayer and humiliation; (a way which in our deepest distresses, we have found both our duty and comfort to tread in) to seek to appease his wrath; And that he will for his own Names sake be pleased, to remove whatever accursed thing there is amongst us, and that as he is our God, so we may be his people.

That he will infatuate the Counsels, and defeat the Designs, of all those that labour to exalt themselves, against the interest of his Son and his People.

That he will be pleased in a most especiall manner to vouchsafe his presence to those who are intrusted with the mannagement of the affaires of these Nations:

That as he is the *mighty Councellor* in himself, so also that he would appear such experimentally unto them.

That he would in all things spirit them to the work unto which they are called, And give them unitie amongst themselves, even the best *Unitie*, That *of the Spirit, In the* best *Bond*, That *of Peace*; That as they are a people abounding in Mercies, so they may abound in Returns.

And that at last through the unwearied goodness of our God, these three Nations, after such memorable revolutions, may be setled upon the sure foundations of Truth, Mercy & Peace, and his people henceforth, *being delivered from* their *Enemies, may serve him without fear, in Holiness, and Righteousness, before him all the dayes of their lives.*

It is therefore declared by his Highness the Lord Protector, and the Parliament of the Commonwealth of *England*, *Scotland* and *Ireland*, That for the end and purposes aforesaid, They do appoint *Thursday* being the thirtieth day of *October* next, for a day of solemn humiliation and seeking the face of God, through the Mediation of Christ, in all places within *England*, *Scotland* and *Ireland*, And do therefore hereby incite, and encourage all such whose hearts God shall perswade and make sensible of their duty, and of the Commonwealths present condition; that the day aforesaid be set apart by them for the purposes aforesaid. And all persons whatsoever, are hereby enjoyned and required, to abstain from the works of their ordinary calling, and from any recreations, or other things against the fitting and due observation of that day. And all Faires and Markets are hereby prohibited to be kept upon that day, but may be proclaimed to be kept upon the day next ensuing. And all Officers of Justice are hereby required to cause due observation to be had hereof, And the Ministers and

Preachers of the respective Parishes and Congregations, are to take notice hereof: For which end, *It is Ordered*, That Copies of this Declaration be Printed, and sent into the several parts of the three Nations, that the same may be published accordingly.

1657–1   Thanksgiving days for discovery of an assassination plot against Cromwell

Friday 20 February 1657 (England and Wales, Scotland, Dublin); Friday 27 February 1657 (elsewhere in Ireland).

In January 1657, Miles Sindercombe, John Toope, John Cecil and others, under the influence of the Leveller, Edward Sexby, tried several times to assassinate Cromwell. On a number of occasions, their resolve faltered; once, when they planned to shoot the lord protector in Hyde Park, Cromwell himself unconsciously foiled the plot by inviting Cecil over to enquire about his horse. They were finally captured when Toope betrayed their plot to blow up parliament. Toope and Cecil became informers and Sindercombe was tried for treason in February, found guilty and sentenced to be hanged but committed suicide before his sentence was carried out. On 19 January, reports of these plots were read out in parliament and it was proposed to hold a thanksgiving for Cromwell's deliverance. A declaration setting out the reasons for the day was commissioned and, on 31 January, read and passed. The proposal and declaration were approved by the lord protector on 2 February. Patrick Gillespie and John Warren were appointed to preach at St Margaret's, Westminster, on 20 February; all MPs were invited to dine with Cromwell at the Banqueting House, Whitehall. Parish ministers were instructed to read out the declaration during the service and congregations were exhorted to prayer for the protector. Although the declaration ordered thanksgivings to be held in Ireland, another declaration was issued in the lord deputy's name (Fleetwood had been recalled to England in September 1655 though he retained his position until September 1657) which ordered the thanksgivings to be held in Dublin on the 20th but elsewhere in Ireland on the 27th. The reason for this may simply have been to give more time to distribute the order across Ireland: the Irish declaration was not issued until the 16th. The thanksgiving may not have been widely observed in Scotland. General Monck told Secretary Thurloe that 'truly I doubt there are a few Scotch ministers who will observe it', but he agreed to convey orders to them as well as to English regiments.

Orders: ENGLAND AND WALES, SCOTLAND, IRELAND: declaration by the lord protector and parliament, 2 Feb. 1657, Wing C7066*; IRELAND: declaration by the lord deputy and council, 16 Feb. 1657, not extant [formerly Dublin PRO, Order Book 10, p. 268; see Steele, II, no. 586].
Additional sources: *CJ*, VII, 481, 483–4, 493; declaration of the protector and parliament for a day of thanksgiving on Friday 20 Feb., 2 Feb. 1657, *CSPD, Interregnum*, X, 258–9; *Burton diary*, I, 356–63; *A true narrative of the late trayterous plot against the person of his highness the lord protector* (1657; Wing T2801); *A true account of the late bloody and inhumane conspiracy against his highness the lord protector, and this Commonwealth* (1657; Wing T2381); Major John Rawdon to [Lord Conway], 9 Dec. 1657, SP63/287/88, fos. 130r–131v; draft letter from the protector and council to the lord deputy and council of Ireland, 3 Feb. 1657, *CSPI: Charles and the Interregnum*, XVIII, 837; W. Nieuport to the Dutch ambassador in Enghland, 9 Mar. 1657 [New Style] and resolutions about some design of an

A DECLARATION

OF

His Highnefs the Lord PROTECTOR

AND THE

PARLIAMENT,

For a Day of

Publique Thankfgiving

On *Friday* the Twentieth of *February* 1656.

Monday, the fecond of February, 1656.

ORdered by the Parliament, That the Declaration for a day of Thankf-giving on the Twentieth of February inftant, be forthwith Printed and Publifhed, and that the fame be fent to the Sheriffs of the refpective Counties and Shires, who are required to take care that the fame be deli-vered to the Minifters of the refpective Parifhes and Congregations.

Henry Scobell, Clerk of the Parliament.

London, Printed by *Henry Hills* and *John Field*, Printers to His Highnefs the Lord Protector. 1656.

12 The title-page of a lengthy declaration issued by the protectorate government, dated in old style as 1656 but for 1657–1, ordering a thanksgiving day after the failure of assassination attempts against Oliver Cromwell, the lord protector. *A declaration by his highness the lord protector and parliament*, 2 Feb. 1657, Wing C7066, Folger Shakespeare Library, Washington, DC, 156–316f, 2º.

insurrection, 2 Feb. 1657, in *SP Thurloe*, VI, 84–5, 163–4; *Edin. recs., 1655 to 1665*, pp. 48–50; Nicoll, p. 192; Lamont, p. 97.
Printed sermon: Warren, parliament (Wing W974).

ORDER AND DESCRIPTION OF ORDER

England and Wales, Scotland, Ireland: declaration by the lord protector and parliament, 2 February 1657

The good People of this Commonwealth after a long and sharp Contention, with the greatest of Hazards and Difficulties, for the preservation of their Native Rights, being at length, by the Goodness and Power of God, restored to the blessings of Peace and Freedom, and their Enemies given into their power, Did nevertheless by all tenderness and milde proceedings, endeavor the regaining of their Countreymen, and not their destruction:

Yet such was the rancor of many of them, that they ceased not to design and labor to raise new Troubles amongst us, and open fresh veins of English blood; for which end, they lately were in actual Arms in several places, endeavoring again to kindle the flames of Civil Dissension in these Nations, had not the same by the good Hand of the Lord been quenched and prevented.

Besides these, have risen up a sort of discontented Spirits, called *Levellers*, plotting to disturb Our Peace, divide Our Strength, and to bring new Miseries upon Us; but by the same good Hand of Providence, these were likewise seasonably discovered, and at that time suppressed.

The latest of these wicked Practices, was chiefly by some of that Party, together with the former Adversary; and these have so far degenerated, as to associate themselves with the inveterate Enemies of the English Nation and Protestant Religion, those of *Spain*; and for malice and hire, to submit themselves to be executioners of their barbarous Designs, and against their Native Countrey; and finding themselves disabled to prosecute the same by open Violence, and well knowing that in all precedent Passages and Deliverances from the beginning of our Troubles to this present, it pleased God to make use of, and to own the Lord Protector, as a most Eminent and Principal Instrument, and the Leader of his People:

These Conspirators fell to that which is detested even by the People who know not God, yet after the practice of our Foreign Enemy (whereof our publique Ministers imployed in Foreign parts have had sad experience) they fell to secret and unworthy Plots against the life of the Lord Protector, to commit base and horrid Murther upon His person, bloodily and inhumanely to Assasinate Him, whom they durst not by open Force attempt.

The particulars whereof in the ensuing Narrative appear, by Examination upon Oath, and Confession of some of the parties themselves who were engaged in this Design of Blood and Confusion.

That about four Moneths since one *Miles Sundercomb* acquainted *John Cecill*, that there was a Design in hand among some very considerable persons, for killing the Lord Protector, perswading him to engage therein; and that it would be a very acceptable Service to take off the Protector, whereby things would come to Confusion, and the People rise.

That there was no attempting him in the Field, nor any other way, but by falling upon his person at an advantage, and that money should be provided.

Upon these and such like discourses, *Cecill* engaged to joyn in this work (*viz.*) to attempt and kill the Lord Protector.

First they provided good horses, and agreed to attempt him as he went upon the Road, and the intention was to make a Party of Horse, of about forty to have assaulted him, but that proving a difficult business to get so many men together, it was resolved to be done by a lesser party, and these two agreed to take the first opportunity to Assacinate the Protector when he went abroad, and one *Toop* of the life-Guard, whom *Sundercomb* had engaged to serve them in this attempt, was to give them notice when the Protector went abroad; and *Sundercomb* and *Cecill* were upon the Road five or six times, on purpose to have made this attempt, and had notice of the Protectors going abroad by *Toop*, but had no opportunity to effect the design.

That *Sundercomb* went once into *Hide Park* with intention to have attempted the Protector there, having a Sword and Pistol to that purpose, being confident that if he could have come neer him, he could have done it and escaped.

That this way proving not effectuall, they took a house at *Hammer-smith*, where there is a garden-wall, and upon the wall a Banquetting-house which is upon the street, out of which the intention was to shoot as he came by, with Guns made on purpose for that business, which should carry twelve or more Bullets at a time.

That at the same time they had a design to fire *Whitehall*, and a fire-work was prepared for that purpose, and made up in a hand-basket with two matches hanging out of each side.

That *Sundercomb* and *Toop* viewed several places where they might put the fire-work, and *Toop* undertook to place it.

That they & *Cecill* on *Thursday* the 8. of *January* instant, between five and six of the clock in the Evening, came to the Chappel at *White-hall*, and brought thither and placed their fire-work with the matches lighted, that they conceived it would have fired between twelve and one of the clock at night.

That one *Boyes* (a principal actor in these designes) did assure them, that when the Protector was dispatched, Forces were to come from *Flanders*, in ships to be hired with the King of *Spaines* money.

That a Port Town was to be seized upon, where Forces were to be landed, and that a very great sum of money would be given for such a place.

That their design is going on for taking away the life of the Protector, and that there are thirty or forty men engaged therein.

That there was a design to take away the Protectors life the first day of the Parliament, the intention being to shoot the Protector as he went by in his Coach, but there being no possible way of escaping, they were discouraged from that enterprise.

Then they hired a house neer the *Abby* in *Westminster*, thinking to shoot him as he went from the Sermon to the Parliament, but they not having time to make conveniences, and finding so many people standing on both sides the way before the Protector came by, and as he passed, they durst not do any thing for fear of being discovered before they shot.

That *Sundercombs* discourse was such, that another of his companions believed that he was hired, and set on work by the King of *Spain*.

That he assured him that within half a year, he himself should be a Colonel of Horse, and that the other should have a Troop of Horse and fifteen hundred pounds in money, when the Protector should be killed; and said, that it was better that *Charles Stuart* should raign here then the Protector.

That there were five of them besides *Toop* who knew of this design and were ingaged to effect it.

This Bloody and barbarous design thus carried on, though by so few persons, yet it pleased the just God (who detesteth wickedness) so to work upon the heart of one of that small number, that he voluntarily came and discovered it to his Highness.

Thus did they imagin a Mischievous device, which (through the goodness of God) they were not able to perform; but the Lord hath brought their Counsel to nought, and made their Devices of none effect.

It is God who delivered us, and doth deliver, and in whom we trust, that he will yet deliver us.

For this eminent Mercy and great deliverance which the Lord hath wrought for our Chief Magistrate, and for all the good People of this Commonwealth; whose peace and comforts were designed to be taken away with the life of the Protector, and thereby new Calamities, Blood and Confusion upon all the Inhabitants of the three Nations.

For this and many other Mercies, His Highness the Lord Protector, and this present Parliament, hold themselves obliged, with all humble and thankfull acknowledgement, to praise his Name, who is the Author of all our Mercies; And for this purpose have thought fit, and do hereby appoint, That *Friday* the Twentieth day of *February* One thousand six hundred fifty six, shall be set apart for a day of Publique thanksgiving to the Lord, in all the three Nations of *England*, *Scotland* and *Ireland*; And do hereby incite and encourage all persons, who are sensible of the Mercy of God to them, to come together in their several Congregations for the performance of this Duty, to praise the Lord for his goodness, humbly to intreat the continuance of his loving kindness to us, (though we have departed from him) that our God may be exalted in his own strength; and that Peace and Righteousness may flourish in these Nations.

And all persons whatsoever, are hereby Required and Enjoyned to abstain from bodily labour, and from the ordinary workes of their calling upon that day, under the penalties which by Law are to be inflicted for such offences.

And that all Ministers in their respective Congregations, be Required to publish this Declaration and Narrative on the Lords day, next before the said day of Publique Thanksgiving: And that they be Exhorted on all occasions in their prayers in the Publique Congregation, to pray for the Lord Protector and all that are in Authority in this Commonwealth.[342]

Ireland: Declaration by the Lord Deputy and Council, 16 February 1657

Whereas his Highness ... and the Parliament ... Cites Declaration 2 Feb. Friday, 27 February, to be a day of thanksgiving in 'this nation (20th in Dublin) for the preservation of the Lord protector. Sheriffs to distribute this declaration to all ministers.

---

[342] The first and last sections of this text are in black letter type; the middle section is in roman.

1657–E1   Thanksgiving day for naval success at Santa Cruz

Wednesday 3 June 1657 (London, Westminster, the late lines of communication and the weekly bills of mortality)

On 20 April, Blake mounted a successful attack on the Spanish plate fleet that had docked at Santa Cruz on Tenerife; all seventeen ships were destroyed. As a result, Philip IV was unable to pay his troops in the Netherlands and Portugal. On 28 May, Secretary Thurloe read reports of Blake's victory to parliament and a thanksgiving was proposed for 3 June; a declaration was also commissioned. Cromwell assented to the proposal for the thanksgiving on 29 May. Thomas Manton and William Carter were appointed to preach before the house at St Margaret's, Westminster. Blake was rewarded with a jewel worth £500, commensurate with the reward that Fairfax had received after Naseby. It is unclear why this occasion was ordered to be observed only in and around London, though such circumscribed special worship – limited to the capital or to England and Wales – became common for the rest of the decade.

Order: parliamentary order, 28 May 1657, Thomason E.1065 [14]* [also in Wing E1694; Wing E1694A, p. 1; *CJ*, VII, 541].
Additional source: *CJ*, VII, 541; *An order of parliament, with the consent of his highness the lord protector* (1657; Thomason E.1065 [14 and also Wing E1694), pp. 2–5; *Whitelocke diary*, p. 468.

ORDER

Parliamentary order: 28 May 1657
Ordered by the Parliament, That Wednesday next be set apart for a Day of Publique Thanksgiving, within the Cities of *London* and *Westminster*, and the late Lnies of Communication, and Weekly Bills of Mortality, for the marvellous Goodness of God to this Nation, in Preserving the Fleet of this Commonwealth in their late Action at *Sancta Cruz*, in the Island of *Teneriff*, under General *Blake*; and giving them great Success against the Ships of the King of *Spain*.

1657–E2   Fast day during severe sicknesses

Friday 21 August 1657 (London, Westminster, the late lines of communication, the weekly bills of mortality and, where possible, elsewhere in England and Wales)

Plague broke out in England and Ireland in 1657. Parts of England also suffered from viral infections, only some of which were fatal, and which may have included influenza. In England, the death rate is estimated to have been over 40 per cent above the average. This occasion is only known through the printed order issued by Cromwell and the privy council on 13 August. There is no evidence that special worship was ordered in Scotland or Ireland.

Order: order by the lord protector and privy council, 13 Aug. 1657, Wing E2926D*.

ORDER

Order by the lord protector and privy council: 13 August 1657

His Highness the Lord Protector and His Privy Council, taking notice of the Hand of God, which at this time is gone out against this Nation, in the present Visitation by Sickness that is much spread over the Land, which calls upon the People of this Nation to humble themselves in a solemn maner before the Lord, and to seek his Face in reference thereunto; His Highness and the Council have thought fit to set apart to Morrow Seven-night being *Friday*, the One and twentieth day of this Moneth, for a Day of Solemn Fasting and Humiliation for the ends aforesaid, to be observed within the Cities of *London* and *Westminster*, and the late Lines of Communication, and Weekly Bills of Mortality, and all other places in this Nation to which notice hereof shall come; not doubting but the People of God in other parts of the Nation also will be forward in their particular Congregations to a Duty so necessary at this time.

1657–E3   Thanksgiving day for the anniversaries of the battles of Dunbar and Worcester

Thursday 3 September 1657 (London, Westminster, the late lines of communication, weekly bills of mortality and elsewhere in England and Wales where notice shall come)

On 25 August, Cromwell and the privy council ordered a thanksgiving in celebration of the anniversaries of victories at the battles of Dunbar and Worcester (3 September 1650 and 1651). Both had been the subject of thanksgivings (see 1650–E5 and 1651–1) but an earlier attempt to establish an annual commemoration for the victory at Worcester had been unsuccessful (though parliament itself had observed the anniversary in 1652; see 1651–1). There is no evidence to indicate why it was decided to order an annual thanksgiving at this juncture. The battle of Dunbar was regarded as Cromwell's finest hour; Worcester was a decisive victory which had ended the political independence of Scotland. There had also been attempts to establish annual anniversaries of other major victories in the civil war (e.g. 1642–Ir2). In the absence of other evidence, it seems plausible that the thanksgiving was ordered because of Cromwell's continuing concerns that the nation's ungodliness continued to provoke God's wrath.

Order: order by the lord protector and privy council, 25 Aug. 1657, Wing E2926B*.

ORDER

Order by the lord protector and privy council: 25 August 1657

His Highness and the Council, calling to minde the memorable Mercies which the Lord was pleased to vouchsafe to this Nation of *England*, in the admirable successes and Victories given to their Forces, on the third day of *September*, in the year 1650. at *Dunbar*, and on the same day in the year 1651. at *Worcester*, and being desirous that such eminent salvations wrought by the Lord, should not be forgotten, but continued in thankfull remembrance, Have thought fit to appoint and set apart *Thursday* the third day of *September* next, to be a day of Publique and Solemn Thanksgiving to the Lord, in the remembrance of the Mercies aforesaid, to be kept and observed in the Cities of *London* and *Westminster*, and all places within the late Lines of Communication, and Weekly Bills of Mortality, and all other places where the notice hereof shall come, not doubting but the Ministers and such as fear the Lord in this Nation, will with all readiness joyn in a Duty to which God hath engaged them by such signal and redoubled providences.

1657–E4   Fast day during severe sicknesses

Wednesday 30 September 1657 (England and Wales and Berwick-upon-Tweed)

On 10 September, less than three weeks after the previous fast day for plague, Cromwell and the privy council ordered a second day of solemn fasting and humiliation in response to the plague and other viral infections which continued to afflict the Commonwealth (see 1657–E2). This was another in the series of humiliation or fast days prompted by Cromwell's fears that God's wrath had been provoked by ungodliness: the order described the plague as 'the Hand of the Lord … which calls upon all men to Repent and turn from their evil Ways'.

Order: order by the lord protector and privy council, 10 Sept. 1657, Wing E2926C*.

ORDER

Order by the lord protector and privy council: 10 September 1657
His Highness the Lord Protector and his Privy Council, being very sensible of the Hand of the Lord, which for some Moneths past hath layen sore upon this Land, in the present Visitation by Sickness throughout the Nation, which calls upon all men to Repent and turn from their evil Ways, and in a Solemn maner to Humble themselves before the Lord, and to seek his Face and Favor, His Highness and the Council have though fit to Invite and Stir up all that fear the Lord in this Nation, to the said Duty of Solemn Fasting and Humiliation; and for that end have appointed Wednesday the Thirtieth day of this instant *September*, to be observed in all places within *England*, *Wales*, and the Town of *Berwick* upon *Tweed*; not doubting but all who have a due sence of the Tokens of Gods Displeasure, will be excited to the performance of this necessary Duty, in such a maner as is suitable to the present Dispensation, and may not become a further Provocation.

1658–E   Fast days during plague epidemic

Wednesday 5 May 1658 (London, Westminster, the late lines of communication and weekly bills of mortality); Wednesday 19 May 1658 (London, Westminster, late lines of communication, bills of mortality and elsewhere in England and Wales and Berwick-upon-Tweed)

Though the plague and other viral infections continued to trouble the Commonwealth, there was no further nationwide fast day for seven months. A proposal for a national fast day in January was unsuccessful, though a day of humiliation was observed by parliament itself on 27 January 1658. However, the purpose of this occasion is not known and may not relate to plague. On 29 April, Cromwell declared fast days on 5 and 19 May; once again, the order emphasized that the plague was a providential sign of God's wrath at the nation's sins. For the first time, London and the surrounding area were ordered to observe the fast twice: once on their own and again simultaneously with the rest of the country.

Order: declaration by the lord protector, 29 Apr. 1658, Wing C7072*.
Additional sources: *CJ*, VII, 581; *Burton diary*, II, 372–3; *Larkham diary*, p. 177.

ORDER

Declaration by the lord protector: 29 April 1658

His Highness the Lord *PROTECTOR* and the Council, being (as becomes them) very sensible of, and deeply affected with the hand of the Lord, in the present general Visitation, with which not onely these populous Cities, but mo[s]t parts of the Nation are sorely afflicted, and many have been taken away; Do hold it their duty to invite the People of this Nation to humble themselves greatly before the Lord, whose displeasure We have highly provoked by Our unthankfulnes for and abuse of Gospel Mercies, and that Peace, Health, and Plenty, which for diverse years last past We have (through his goodness) enjoyed, and by that spirit of Division, murmuring, prophaneness and enmity against the power of Godliness, which is so prevalent amongst Us, besides many other abominations: His *HIGHNESS* therefore, with the advice of His Council, hath thought fit to declare and appoint, that *Wednesday* the Fifth of *May* next, be observed as a Day of solemn *Fasting* and *Humiliation* within the Cities of *London* and *Westminster*, the late lines of Communication, and Weekly Bils of Mortality, And *Wednesday* the Nineteenth day of the same Moneth within the places aforesaid, and all other places within *England* and *Wales*, and Town of *Berwick* upon *Tweed*; Exhorting all, especially those that fear the Lord, to humble themselves before him, and turn from their evil wayes, and seek the Lord, that he will be pleased to forgive our sins, and heal Our Land: And that there may not onely be a lengthning out of our Tranquillity, but such returns of special Mercy, as may evidence to his people, and convince all that have evill will unto their Peace, that the Lord hath not forsaken Us, but doth yet for his own Great Names sake take delight in Us, to make Us (though most unworthy) a People of his Praise. And His Highness doth earnestly recommend it unto all such as are touched with the sense of Gods hand and displeasure, to set themselves to the performance of this Duty, in such a Solemn and Spiritual manner as becomes such an extraordinary Duty, and as so sad an Occasion as this calls for. His Highness pleasure also is, that notice hereof be given in the several Churches and Congregations by the respective Ministers, on the Lords Day before the respective days aforesaid, for the better publication hereof.

1658–ES Thanksgiving days for the failure of invasion attempts and plots, for the end of plague and for a good harvest

Wednesday 21 July 1658 (England, Wales and Berwick-upon-Tweed); Thursday 29 July 1658 (Edinburgh and county); Thursday 19 August 1658 (elsewhere in Scotland)

Between May and July, a plot to organize an invasion of England by Charles II was discovered and the conspirators (including John Mordaunt, Dr John Hewitt and Sir Henry Slingsby) were arrested and tried. On 4 June, an Anglo-French army won a decisive victory over the Spanish at the battle of the Dunes. Ten days later, Dunkirk surrendered after a month-long siege; control of the town passed to England under the terms of the Anglo-French military treaty. After raging for more than a year, the plague epidemic subsided. On 3 July, Cromwell ordered a thanksgiving for these successes to be held across England and Wales on 21 July and a lengthy declaration was printed for distribution. The council of state sent copies of the declaration to the Scottish council, instructing it to call a thanksgiving. Ministers were told to read both the English declaration and the Scottish council's declaration from their pulpits. On 23 July, Edinburgh's burgh council summoned ministers to receive the printed declaration, and issued an order closing shops in Edinburgh, Leith and Canongate on the day of the thanksgiving. There is no evidence that the thanksgiving was ordered for Ireland.

Order: ENGLAND AND WALES: declaration by the lord protector, 3 July 1658, Wing C7067* [also Wing C7068, 1–6 (Edinburgh reprint)]; SCOTLAND: declaration by the council in Scotland, 21 July 1658 (Christopher Higgins, Edinburgh, 1658; Wing C7068, 7–9)*.
Additional sources: council of state, day's proceedings, 6 July 1658, *CSPD Interregnum*, XII, 87–8; *Whitelocke diary*, p. 494; General George Monck to Gideon Scott, 21 July 1658, NRS, GD157/2070/1; *Edin. recs., 1655 to 1665*, p. 108; Nicoll, pp. 215–16.

ORDER

England and Wales: declaration by the lord protector, 3 July 1658
We being conscious of the Mercy of those dispensations, which have come very thick upon Us within the space of Five moneths last past, cannot but think Our Self obliged to call for a Day of Thanksgiving in these Nations; which that it might be the more seriously and spiritually performed, We have thought it meet to make a brief Remembrance, and as it were in a Glass, to represent the state of Our Affairs, as they stood much about the beginning of the time before mentioned, and summarily to rehearse those things, which God hath wrought for Us within that time; that so all such as fear God, and are wise to observe these things, and thereby understanding the loving kindness of the Lord, may have their hearts and mouths filled with his praise.

It is well known that the last Parliament did, by Adjournment, meet the Twentieth day of *January* last past, and that these Nations had very good hopes, by those preparations made in their former Sitting, that We should have gone on upon those Foundations, to an happy Settlement: But those hopes were soon dashed, through the intemperance of some mens Spirits; Notwithstanding it was throughly represented, that the old Enemy had a design of an immediate Invasion, with an Army consisting of Papists and Atheists, upon the accompt of *Charles Stuart*, in conjunction with the King of *Spain*, in whose Counsels it was agreed more adviseable to give Us work in *England*, rather then that We should assist the *French*, to engage them in their own Countrey. It being also at the same time most visible, that diverse of the inferiour sort of people (set on by men of the same Spirit with them before hinted at) and naturally fluctuating, were enclined to dangerous commotions, seeing the disputes were more readily taken up and improved, then the putting in execution, and prosecuting the agreements before made; and that the Army seemed to have some unsettlement in it self, partly arising from the before mentioned disappointment; partly from the great wants which were upon them, and fears of being necessitated to take free Quarter upon the People (then which, nothing could be more abhorrent to them) the Trade of the Nation, and Our Honour at Sea ready to be hazarded and lost for want of due Supplies, We being forced to keep Our men of War out at Sea, not having money to pay Our Mariners when they came in. In the mean time Our Neighbours every where preparing greater Fleets then usual, and even they in *Flanders* themselves, having made ready a Fleet of above twenty men of War at *Ostend*, for the transporting of *Charles Stuart*, and his *Spanish* Forces to invade Us. In order whereunto, divers of Our Garrisons were by Bribes endeavoured to be gained, for receiving the said invading Army, and Insurrections designed and laid in several Counties by the Malignant Party, to rise in assistance of the said Invasion, accompanied also with that desperate design of firing the City of *London*, and seising upon the Treasure that could be found there; which wicked Plot was managed by many Colonels, and other chief Officers, who were to head this Tragical Action: All which hath been made evident, as well by clear proofs against, as by the confessions of divers of the persons engaged therein; some of which have already suffered the paines of Death; and further Examinations touching others are still going on, that all the world may see that these things have not been matters of invention or surmise, but real and demonstrable truths, and things, that as they heighten greatly the danger, so also the recital of them tends to Our end in making this Narrative, which is the magnifying of the good hand of God towards Us in Our deliverance.

And lastly, (which did not the least afflict Us) We had cause deeply to apprehend, that the Lords hand was upon Us in that Epidemical sickness, which was so long continued upon the Nation, and lay sore upon the City of *London*, and in the marvellous unseasonableness of the Spring, threatning Us even with a deprivation of the fruits of the earth, and consequently with a sore famine.

That this hath been the danger hanging over the head of these Nations, no honest or ingenuous man can deny. And therefore let us now consider in what State and Condition We are, and what the Lord by his own Arm and for his own Names sake, hath wrought for Us.

It is very true, We are not yet setled, but it hath fared with Us as with the burning Bush, though We have for these five Moneths last past, and longer too, been in a burning condition, yet We are not consumed. We yet live in the enjoyment of a sweet peace, to praise the Lord in hope of better things: We are not yet weltring in bloud. It appears, that as God was in the midst of the Bush, so he hath been in the midst of Us, and therefore We are not consumed. He disappointed the Invasion, by giving Us timely notice of the Enemies preparations, and of the place thereof; by means of which Our Ships were layed to break their designe. He discovered to Us their attempts to gain Our Sea-garisons into their hands, and disappointed them. He revealed the conspiracies in the Counties in order to Insurrections, and prevented them. He brought to light also the bloudy and hellish design for the destruction of the City of *London* by fire and sword, and hath brought the guilty persons under judgement for the same.

He hath given Our Souldiery a spirit of union, of honesty and integrity, so that, notwithstanding the great temptations of want upon them, and the contrivements to divide them, to the praise of God We speak it, they retain that good old spirit that hath carried them through all their difficulties. Those that have had too much distemper upon them, through murmuring and discontents, are We hope (at least some of them) sensible of the evil thereof, and instead thereof both Counties and Cities have testified a very contrary spirit, a spirit owning mercies, blessing the Lord for them, and thirsting after the continuance of them, and for a just settlement. As for that sore Visitation, how hath the Lord, upon the prayers of his poor People, ceased that? and tis not without remark, that the two weeks Bills of Mortality, immediately after the Fast upon that occasion, were brought to the half of what they were the week before, and did amount not to more discernably then in the healthiest times. And as to the evils threatned by the unseasonableness of the spring, the Lord hath so contradicted our fears, that We are all of Us to be convinced by sence, that the hopes of greater plenty hath been seldom seen upon the face of the Earth.

And lastly in that place where the Enemy layd all his designs from whence to invade Us, and to give Us trouble, and had brought it to that pass for the heightning of their confidence both there and here, that they were ready even to triumph, as having as good as obtained their wishes, even there hath the great God abased them, and brought them low in a signal victory gained by the *French* and Us over them: In which success the *French* themselves have owned much to the honour of the *English* Nation, not without admiration, observing that the *English* on Our part should behave themselves with so much valour and undaunted resolution, and the *English* on *Charls Stuarts* part more cowardly then any in the *Spanish* Army. The Lord also hath in the same place given Us a Port Town, not the worst in *Flanders*, which We beg we may make use of to the glory of God, and the good of the Christian cause. These things being thus, how could We forbear, for the honour of God, to give you a remembrance of them? And how can you and We forbear the returning of our humblest and heartiest thanks to the Lord? How can We refraine any longer from breaking forth into the high praises of Our God, for he is good, for his mercy endureth for ever? Let the redeemed of the Lord say so; Let Israel now say so, Let them now that fear the Lord say, that his mercy endureth for ever. And when We have with our mouthes and with our hearts thus blessed God, let Us like a People blessed by him, keep in our hearts a thankfull remembrance of these, and all other Our mercies, giving glory to God and Christ through the spirit, seeking the Peace and the truth for evermore.

We have therefore though fit to appoint *Wednesday* the one & twentieth day of *July* instant to be a day of Publique Thanksgiving unto the Lord for these great and eminent mercies, to be observed in all places within *England*, *Wales* and Town of *Berwick* upon *Tweed*, and do Command and require all Ministers and Pastors to give notice thereof in their Congregations on the Lords-day next before the said day of Thanksgiving, and that upon the said day of Thanksgiving they do read this Declaration in their respective Congregations; And We do hereby prohibite the keeping of all Fairs and Markets upon the day aforesaid.

Scotland: declaration by the council in Scotland, 21 July 1658

His Highnesse Council here having received the fore-going Declaration of His Highnesse the Lord Protector, for a Day of Publick Thanksgiving, with a Letter from his Highnesse and the Council, recommending it to his Highnesse Council here to do the like in *Scotland*, upon such a convenient day as they should think fit; And his Highnesse Councill here being very sensible of the Lord's Mercies towards these Nations, divers of which are expressed in the said Declaration; and considering that the whole Commonwealth being concerned in the Mercies the LORD hath vouchsafed, are therefore obliged to joyn in the return of Praises.

They have therefore thought fit to appoint Thursday the Twenty ninth of *July* instant, to be observed in the Burgh of *Edinburgh*, and Shire thereof, as a Day of Publique Thanksgiving; And that throughout all the other Shires and Burghs in *Scotland*, Thursday the Nineteenth day of *August* next, be observed as a Day of Thanksgiving unto the Lord, for these great and eminent Mercies: And the said Council do hereby recommend it to the Presbyteries, and Ministers and Pastors within the Burgh of *Edinburgh*, and Shire thereof, to give notice of the said Day of Thanksgiving appointed for those Places, in their Congregations, on the next Lord's-day: And, in like manner, do recommend it to the other Presbyteries, Ministers and Pastors, to give notice of the said Day of Thanksgiving appointed for those places, in their respective Congregations, on the Lord's-day next before the said Nineteenth of *August*; And that all the said Ministers and Pastors do on those Dayes of their respective Publick Thanksgivings, reade the said Declaration of His Highnesse, together with this Order, in their respective Congregations. And the said Council do hereby prohibit the keeping of all Fairs and Markets within the Burgh of *Edinburgh* and Shire thereof, As likewise all Traders and Work-men from trading or labouring on the said Day of Thanksgiving for those places; And also they do hereby prohibit the keeping of all Fairs and Markets in the other Shires and Burghs, and all trading and bodily labour there on the said Nineteenth of *August* next; And do require the Sheriffes and Justices of his Highnesse Peace in the respective Shires, and the Magistrates of the Burghs respectively to cause this Prohibition of Fairs and Markets, Trade and bodily Labour on the Publick Thanksgiving Day to be duely observed.

1658–EIr   Fast days on the death of Cromwell, and during plague epidemic

Wednesday 13 October 1658 (England, Wales and Berwick-upon-Tweed); Thursday 14 October (Ireland)

The thanksgiving in July for the ending of the plague (1658–ES) proved premature and, in October, a further fast day was ordered. The occasion also marked the death of Cromwell at Whitehall on 3 September, the anniversaries of the battles of Dunbar and Worcester. His eldest surviving son, Richard, succeeded him as lord protector though there was – and is – debate as to whether he was nominated by his father or not. Richard had been inconspicuous in parliament and had not held any major office until the final months of his father's life, when he was appointed to the council of state. According to Bulstrode Whitelocke, Richard Cromwell and the privy council observed their own day of humiliation for the lord protector's death on 10 September and 'the keeping of it att another time in London'. No official order for observance in London is extant and it is unclear whether such an occasion was ordered. Rather, on 24 September, Richard and the council ordered a day of fasting and humiliation for 13 October in England and Wales. On the same day, Richard's younger brother, Henry, lord deputy of Ireland, ordered a day of solemn fasting and humiliation to be observed in Ireland on 14 October; it is unclear why the two occasions were not co-ordinated. Declarations were issued in England and Wales and in Ireland, and ordered to be read out during the services. Although both declarations emphasized that Oliver Cromwell's death was a providential sign of God's wrath at the nations' sins, the lengthy Irish declaration was more explicit in its condemnation of ungodliness and instructed parishioners to pray for their new lord protector, his council, the army and their foreign alliances. All fairs, markets and bodily labour were to be suspended on the fast days. In Ireland, mayors, governors of garrisons, JPs, constables and other officers were 'to take care that the said day be solemnly kept and observed'. There is no evidence that any fast day was ordered in Scotland.

Order: ENGLAND AND WALES: declaration by the lord protector, 24 Sept. 1658, Wing C7181*; IRELAND: declaration by the lord deputy and council, 24 Sept. 1658, Wing I382B*.
Additional source: *SP Thurloe*, VI, 369; *Whitelocke diary*, p. 497.
Printed sermons: Lawrence, Cross's Hospital, ? (Wing L659); Slater, St Edmundsbury (Wing S3968).

ORDER

England and Wales: declaration by the Lord Protector, 24 September 1658
As it is the Duty, so it hath been the constant practise of the People of God in all ages, not onely to take special notice of the Providential dispensations of God towards them, whether they concerned them as a Nation, or as particular persons, but also to meet the Lord in the way, both of his Judgements, and of his Mercies, in a solemn maner, suitable to such Dispensations, to which the Lord hath been pleased to give such visible testimonies of his gracious acceptance, as hath been and still is a great encouragement to his people to make their addresses to him under the like providences. And as no Nation under heaven hath been exercised with more various and wonderful Providences then these Nations of *England*, *Scotland* and *Ireland*, so none have had more eminent experiences of the goodness of the Lord in the speedy and merciful returns he hath made to the prayers of his people; And therefore of all others, it becomes them to let no Providence of God go unobserved or unregarded, especially such as seem to carry upon them Characters of the displeasure of that God, from whom alone We have professed to all the world, We have received all Our mercies past, and that We depend on him alone for greater things, which are yet in his peoples expectation. Upon these grounds, His Highness the Lord Protector and the Council, sadly reflecting on the late dispensation of Divine Providence, in removing from Us His Highness the late Lord Protector, whom the Lord hath used as a choice Instrument for carrying on his Work, and under him to be both a Sun and a Shield unto those that fear the Lord abroad and at home (which they cannot but be deeply sensible of as a sore stroak of his mighty hand) as also in the general visitation of Sickness and great Mortality, which is now upon many parts of this Nation, hold it their duty to invite the people of these Nations to humble themselves greatly under the mighty hand of God, in the sence of the many great and crying sins of this Nation, which have deserved his sore displeasure, and to accept the punishment of their sins.

And likewise to seek the Lord for a blessing upon His Highness and his Government and Counsels for the good of these Nations, that thereby the breach which he hath made upon Us may be healed, and the present tokens of his displeasure removed, and that he will be pleased yet to continue his gracious presence among Us, and delight in Us as his people, that his own Work may by his assistance be carried on, and peace and truth may be established in the midst of Us. For which purpose His Highness the Lord Protector, with the advice of his Privy Council, hath thought fit to set apart *Wednesday* the Thirteenth day of *October* One thousand six hundred fifty and eight, to be observed as a day of Solemn Fasting and Humiliation in all places within *England* and *Wales*, and the Town of *Berwick* upon *Tweed*, earnestly exhorting all the people of God in this Nation to cry mightily unto the Lord, and to wrestle with him by prayer and supplication for the ends aforesaid. And that the Ministers of the several Churches and Congregations, do diligently and conscientiously attend their duties on that day, as is suitable unto so solemn a work, and that they give notice hereof on the Lords day next before the said Thirteenth day of *October* in their Publique Meeting-place, and read this Declaration on the said day. And His Highness doth hereby prohibit all Fairs, Markets, and all bodily labour in the works of mens callings, which may interrupt or hinder the Religious observation of the day aforesaid.

Ireland: declaration by the lord deputy and council, 24 September 1658

God blessed for evermore, who *worketh all things after the Counsel of his own will*, and giveth no account of any of his matters, having lately taken from our heads our Chief Ruler, under whose shadow we said we shall live, (the Instrument of his Hand, whereby he hath wrought great things in and for these Nations) calls out aloud upon us to consider it, and to lay it to heart, (otherwise we may be sure there is *evil to come*) and to *prepare to meet our God*, even because he hath done this unto us. We judg it our duty also to call upon all that fear the Lord in this Land, to labour that they may be found of him with us, in ways of unfeined Humiliation and Reformation, *if it may be a lengthening of our tranquillity*: For, when *the people turneth not to him that smiteth them*, neither *do seek the Lord of Hoasts*, what can be expected but that he should set up Adversaries, and joyn their enemies together, who shall *devour them with open mouth*? And in order to an universal Abasement and Amendment of our selves, we think it most seasonable and needfull to stir up our selves and all under our care and charge seriously to consider, That *when Gods judgments* of a publick and general concernment *are abroad* in a nation or among a people, such a people ought to take special notice of Gods judgments: Those that *will not see when his hand is lifted up*, he will make them both see and feel too, before he hath done with them. It was EPHRAIM'S folly, not to know when *gray hairs*, (signs of a decaying and declining condition) *were here and there upon him*; And it is one of the highest points of wisdom in the world *to hear* the audible and awful *voice of the Rod*, and him *who hath appointed it*. They ought also then to *search* out *why the Lord contendeth with them*, to counsels, lay to heart, and *humble themselves* solemnly for their sins, procuring such judgments; To *pray and seek Gods face* earnestly; To reform themselves and their ways thoroughly and sincerely; This is *the work* whereunto the Lord at this day calleth us. And oh that our LORD, when he cometh to take a view of us, might (through the help of his blessed Spirit) *find us so doing*!

Consider we also that God hath taken away, & threatned to take away *Chief Rulers* and *Governours*, and him that holdeth the Scepter; both, for the Sins of the

Cheif Rulers themselves: as, for *not believing* fully in God, for *not Sanctifying God before the People*, and other miscarriages: and for the Sins of the people under their Rule and Government; as, their relying and *trusting to their own wisdom*, way, and Arme of flesh, rather then on the Lord; their *forgetting* and *forsaking God*; their *despising his word* and warnings; their *mocking and misusing his messengers*; their persisting and *proceeding on still to do wickedly*, even in despight of all Gods mercyes, and judgements; their grieving the Spirits of their Rulers, by their discontents, murmurings and strivings, and the like: And for the sins of the Prophets and Ministers, their unfaithfulness, not *discovering the peoples iniquities for preventing their captivity* and calamity; but *seeing vain and foolish things for them*, and for the sins of former Rulers, their *Idolatry, Bloodguiltiness, Profaneness*, these may bring judgements and ruin, notwithstanding the zeale and sincere endeavours of their Successors for a reformation. How should the thoughts of these things pierce our hearts, together with the sence of this severe stroak, wherewith the Lord hath at once smitten, not onely these three Nations, but all the professors of the Protestant Religion.

Let us also consider further, that God having honoured a people with great Privilidges, Deliverances and Salvations, doth sometimes *after all the good* that he hath done them, *again do them hurt*, judge aud destroy them; and that especially, for their *ingratitude* towards God, notwithstanding all his great goodness, when they *render not again according to the benefit done unto them*; for their *turning away their faces from the habitation of the Lord*, and turning their back upon him, his Worship and Ordinances; for their *Vnbelief, Idolatry, Vncleanness*, height of Impiety, and profaneness; for their *Sorcery, Blood, Oppression*, and violence, *dishonest gain*, and theft, *profanation of the Sabboth*, pollution of Gods Ordinances, violation of his *Covenant, Cursing, Swearing*, and forswearing; for their *Murmuring* against God and his Vice-gerents when afflictions press them; for their *Barrenness* under the means of grace, and contempt of the messengers thereof; for their hatred to *Reformation*, and *Enmity against Christ* and his Kingdom; and for their incorrigibleness and impenitency in all these, notwithstanding all his smitings; Now *shall not the Lord visit for these things*? and *shall not his Soul be avenged on* those that wallow in the guilt and filth of them? And are there not with us, even with us, such Sins as these to be found against the Lord our God? Are there not gross *Heresies* and horrid *Blasphemies* in the midst of us? much *Superstition* and *Idolatry, Ignorance*, and *Blindness*, not onely of the Papists, but of the generality of Protestants also? deadness and unprofitableness under the most lively and powerful means; neglect, contempt, reproach and prophanation of all the Ordinances of the Gospel, and instituted worship of the Lord Iesus. *What* abuse of *the glorious and dreadful name of the Lord our God*, not onely by customary and rash *Oaths* and imprecations (which are usually interwoven with the language of the Natives,) but also by formal giving and taking of oaths even in Courts and places of judicature, and by sleight and heartless discourses of Divine things; most men vain-gloriously aiming more therein to express their own guifts, then to attain or exercize grace, or to minister and communicate it unto others? *What* despising, undermining, and opposing the work, call, office, and persons of *Gospel-Ministers? What* profaning the *Lords-day*, not onely like beasts in wayes of pleasure, but like Devils spending that day in sin against the Lord, which should be spent in nigher communion with him? *What* unthankfulness for mercies enjoyed? *What* fighting against God after mercies, under mercies, yea with our very mercies? *What* loathing and making light of all that which we have and do receive, because of the absence of some particulars which we desire? And hath not *Blood* here *reached blood*? under the guilt whereof these Lands may yet justly be made to mourn; the blood of the Innocent shed by Enemies, and even the blood of the nocent shed by our selves, in an undue manner, without that grief and tenderness of Spirit which became the *followers of the Lamb* the Lord Iesus. *What* panting hath there been amongst us after the dust of the earth, as if all would not suffice for every man to take an handful? *What* labouring to *load our selves with thick clay? What* covetous and greedy *heaping up* worldly *Riches*? without regard to be *rich in good works, rich in faith, poor in spirit. what* seeking rather after a seeming then a real greatness; rather to be great in the sight of men, then in the sight of the Lord? *what* resolving to get earth, though with the loss of Heaven? what oppressing the poor Inhabitant, to ease and gratify the rich, in the apportioning and applotting the publique burthens and taxes? *what* depriving the poorer sort of the price and purchase of his blood and labour, by hard and circumventing bargains & insnaring agreements? and yet that daughter of the horse Leach still crying, give, give.

What divisions and breaches have there been amongst Brethren? and how many sinfull consequencies of those divisions? whispering, slandering, backbiting, reviling, and *an anger which teares perpetually*, (whereof God complaineth by the Prophet AMOS.) *What* sinful compliances even of subordinate Magistrates, Justices of the Peace, Officers of the Army, Ministers of the Gospel, and others, *with the unfruitful works of darkness*? not onely omitting the due Execution of the good Laws concerning Reformation: but too much patronizing wicked men in their evil ways for carnal ends; by which means also that great work of our Generation, in subduing the *Irish* Papists to the scepter of JESUS CHRIST, and removing from them the occasions of sin, in their usage of many barbarous and brutish customs, hath been in all places obstructed; and in most, totally neglected. *How little* have godliness and honesty been regarded by many *Magistrates*, as if to see to these were not included in their Commission? *How little* have many *Ministers* attended the *catechizing* the ignorant, *visiting* the sick, *rebuking* the profane, *instructing* from house to house, the due exercize of discipline, and right administration of Sacraments? whereby not onely the popish and profane have been more alienated than ever, from the truths and ways of God: but ignorance, heresie, heathenism and atheism increased; and through long fasting from the Institutions of *Christ*, many have lost their stomachs; and some, that very life which appeared formerly to act in them; and others unworthily partaking thereof, have been hardened and nuzled up in their evil ways, and sealed up under wrath and condemnation? *How* have *Family duties* in most places been neglected, even to provoke the LORD *to pour out his wrath* upon them, as upon *the heathens that call not on his name? What* infidelity and distrustfulness have prevailed in many spirits, in relation to our late Supream Magistrate, as if the Author of our mercies did not continue, & his cause the same, if that eminent instrument were removed? Though we have so many precious promises, so many strengthening experiences, as stays & props to our hope, even under the greatest shakings, and many soverain Cordials to prevent fainting; God not having left himself without many witnesses to his mercie, even to this *day of trouble and treading down*, which otherwise would have been indeed a day of grief, and of desperate sorrow. *And how* great hath been the *Ingratitude* and murmuring peevishness of others, as if our mercies were not mercies, because themselves were not the pipes of conveyance; or because those *waters* came not so plentifully into their *Cisterns* as unto others?

These and such like sins as these, seem stampt (as it were) on the face of this judgment, and are to be especially eyed in the frown thereof. And are they *Christians*, are they *men*, who are without the sense of these things? Have we like sheep, wandered from our Shepheard, and from one another in this our sun-shine? It is just for our God to send such a storm to drive us together, and into his fold. Have we played with the candle that burned so brightly among us, consuming himself to guide and refresh these Nations, or have we puffed at it? it is just for God to put it out.

And doth not the LORD now call from heaven unto us, as sometimes he did to backsliding ISRAEL, *Gather your selves together, yea gather your selves, search and sift your selves, O Nation not desired, before the decree bring forth*, (which seems now to hasten to the birth) *before the day pass as the chaf*, before all your light, and joy, and peace and plenty be blown away by the blast of the Lords displeasure; *before the fierce anger of the Lord come upon you*, before the day of the Lords anger come upon you? And we can not forbear, but call upon all the Lords people in this Land, as MOSES sometimes did to the *Israelites, Who is on the Lords side among you? Consecrate your selves to day unto the Lord, even every man* by punishing and witnessing against sin in his son, and in his brother; and especially by doing execution upon it in himself; That he may bestow a blessing upon us this day. Let us with one heart and mouth say, *To us belongeth confusion of face, to our Princes, to our fathers, and to our children; because we have sinned against the Lord*; Let us bewail and repent of our former *doings, which were not good*: not onely by sorrowing for them, (for there is sorrow enough even in hell;) nor onely by wishing them undone, (for so far even *Iudas* went;) but by true *repentance from dead works*, turning again to the Lord *to serve the living God*. Let all the Magistrates of the Land, let all the *Gospel-Ministers*, let all the Officers and Souldiers, let both great and small renew their *Covenant*, and engage their souls, and give the hand unto the Lord, and unto Vs, who do stretch forth ours unto you, saying, *Come and let us return unto the Lord, for he hath torn and he will heal us, he hath smitten and he will bind us up.*

And for our further help both in returning to him, and gaining some comfortable evidence that he doth accept us, and will heal us, It is ordered, That *Thursday* the fourteenth day of *October* next, be kept as an Holy day of Fasting and Prayer unto the Lord, *That* thereon we may *afflict our souls* before him, and lament, not so much the *fall of our Crown* and chief ornament, as our sins that caused it: *That* the eyes of all our Tribes, as of one man, may be toward the Lord, to beg mercy for his poor Church here on earth, scattered over the face of the whole world: *That* the Rightousness thereof may go forth as brightness, and the Salvation thereof as a lamp that burneth: and particularly, for that part thereof which his *own Right-hand hath planted* in these Nations, *That* he would *extend peace unto it, like a River, and glory like a flowing stream*; and to that end, *That* he would *make his face to shine* upon his Servant, whom the good hand of his providence hath now set over us; that as he hath called him to this great and weighty work, so he would carry him through it all his dayes in *the everlasting Armes* of his power and goodness, to the glory of his own name, and the joy of these Nations; that so, he may prove *the Minister of God* indeed *to us for good*, for all manner of good, natural, moral, civil, Spiritual; *That* he would bless his HIGHNESS Councils in these three Nations, and cloath them with a spirit sutable to their stations: and all other inferior Magistrates;

That the *mountains may drop down new wine,* and the hills flow with milk; that the *mountains may bring forth peace unto the people, and the little hills by rightousness; That* he would bless his HIGHNESS Forces both at home and abroad, by land and sea; with the continuance of a spirit of love and faithfulness, and with good success in all their lawful undertakings; *That* he would establish and strengthen his confederacies with other Nations, so far as may tend to the propagating the Gospel, and to the preservation and prosperity of the poor Protestants in other Countreys; *That* he would set up *burning and shining lights* in all the dark corners of this land, and bless the labours of those whom he hath already set and made faithful to the bringing in and building up of many souls, through the fellowship of the gospel, in an everlasting fellowship with the Father, & the Son, by the communion of the holy Ghost.

And it is further Ordered, That the Sherifs of the several Counties in this Nation, do forthwith (after receipt hereof) distribute the said Declarations to all and every the Ministers within their respective Balywicks, to the intent that seasonable and publick notice may be given unto the People by the Ministers in every their respective Parishes and Congregations, upon the Lords-day preceding the said fourteenth day of *October*. And the said Ministers are also to read this Declaration unto the People, at their being assembled upon the said Fast-day, appointed to be celebrated. For the better observation whereof, the servile works of mens ordinary Callings are to be forborn upon that day.

And all Sherifs, Mayors, Governors of Garrisons, Iustices of the Peace, Constables, and other Officers Civil and Military, are to take care that the said day be solemnly kept and observed.

1658–1 Fast days for the success of parliament and public affairs

Wednesday 29 December 1658 (England, Wales and Berwick-upon-Tweed); Wednesday 5 January 1658 (Scotland, Ireland)

The order for the fast day in Ireland on 14 October (1658–EIr) had directed parishioners to pray for the successful governance of all three nations; this was reiterated in a second set of fast days ordered for the three nations on 29 December and 5 January. The declaration by the lord protector, which was to be read out during the services, emphasized the benefits and warnings God had sent the realms over the previous year. It also drew attention to the new parliament to be convened on 27 January, and the effect it 'may have, not onely upon the Civil Peace and outward Prosperity of these Three Nations, yea of all the Protestants abroad, but also in reference to the Spiritual Liberties which the Lord hath in an especial maner reserved as a Blessing to be given in to this Generation'. In contrast to declarations issued under Oliver Cromwell, this one stated that the fast day was ordered by Richard Cromwell 'by Advice of His Privy Council'. The declaration was printed in England and Scotland; there is no surviving evidence that a version was also printed in Dublin.

Order: declaration of the lord protector, 16 Dec. 1658, Wing C7182* [also ESTC 006477084 (Edinburgh reprint)].

ORDER

Declaration of the lord protector: 16 December 1658

The Successes of all the Consultations and Actions of the Sons of Men have their Dependence on the Pleasure of that God, who is Wonderful in Counsel, and Mighty in Working: And therefore, as in all other Affairs, so especially in those which are of greatest concernment, it is our Duty to seek the Lord, with whom alone is Wisdom and Strength, that we may testifie our Hope to be in him, and our Dependence on him alone. It is the Priviledge of those who are in Covenant with the Lord, that they have a God nigh unto them in all that they call upon him for. The People of God in this Nation (if they had observed them, or have not forgotten them) may produce so large a Catalogue of Mercies given in answer to Prayers, as no Nation under the Heavens can parallel: in not a few of which the Lord hath as it were exemplified that Promise, *Before they call I will answer, and while they are yet speaking I will hear*; and in others, given a proof of his Faithfulness in what he had said, *Ask of me concerning my Sons, and concerning the Works of my Hands command ye me*: All of them so many real Demonstrations, that he hath not said unto the seed of *Jacob, Seek ye me in vain*: So that above all the People in the World, those who fear the Lord in these Nations have cause to say of him, *Because he hath heard my voice, therefore will I call upon him so long as I live*: And as if the Lord would try us whether we will do so or not, he is pleased to administer variety of occasions to prove the Faith of his People. This present season exhibits matter of deep Humiliation, and earnest Supplication. Who can look back on the Providences wherewith the Lord hath exercised us the Year passed, but hath cause to say, *My flesh trembleth for fear of thee, and I am afraid of thy Judgements*? And if we do but with an eye of common Prudence, take a Prospect of those great Actions which are like to be the Product of the ensuing Year, and weigh the Consequences of them, may we not say, *Lord, we know not what to do, but our eyes are unto thee*? His Highness the Lord Protector seriously considering these things, and having by the Advice of His Privy Council called a Parliament to meet in *January* next, and being not a little sensible how great an influence the Deliberations and Determinations of that His great Council may have, not onely upon the Civil Peace and outward Prosperity of these Three Nations, yea of all the Protestants abroad, but also in reference to the Spiritual Liberties which the Lord hath in an especial maner reserved as a Blessing to be given in to this Generation, and likewise to the concernments of the Gospel through the World: Therefore His Highness, by Advice of His Privy Council, holds it a seasonable and necessary Duty as in His own Person, so to call upon, and invite others who are concerned herein, in a Solemn maner to humble themselves before the Lord, and earnestly to seek his Favor and Blessing on the Counsels and Affairs of these Nations, and especially on that Great Council, that he who is the Counsellor and Prince of Peace, will sit among them, guide their Spirits, and lead them to such Counsels of Peace and Good for these Nations, and the Interest of the Lord Jesus in them, that the Generations to come may rise up and call them Blessed, and the Nations round about us may be filled with Admiration at the Lords gracious dealings with us, and we may have further cause to say, *The Lord is in the midst of us, therefore we shall be established.* For which purpose His Highness doth appoint, That in all Places within *England* and *Wales*, and Town of *Berwick* upon *Tweed*, Wednesday the Nine and twentieth day of *December* instant, and in *Scotland* and *Ireland*, Wednesday the Fifth of *January* next, be observed as a day of Solemn Fasting and Humiliation in all Churches, Chappels and Congregations within the same; earnestly exhorting all those whose hearts the Lord hath touched with a due sense of these things, to be instant with the Lord in this behalf, in such a Serious and Solemn maner, as the nature of so Spiritual and Extraordinary a Duty doth require, and that every one in their Places will study how they may second their Prayers with sutable endeavors, tending to Unity and Peace: And His Highness doth Will and Require all Ministers and Pastors of Congregations, to Read this Declaration in their Meetings for Publique Worship on the Lords Day next before the said Day of Publique Fasting, to the end the same may be the better taken notice of: And the holding of all Markets and Fairs are hereby Prohibited on that day.

1659–1   Fast day during general anxieties, and for the success of parliament

Wednesday 18 May 1659 (England and Wales, Scotland, Ireland)

A fast day was proposed in the Commons on 30 March; the declaration, drawn up by a committee of members including Sir Henry Vane and Sir Anthony Ashley Cooper, was read and amended on 2 and 4 April. The Commons' journal, Thomas Burton's diary and Sir Bulstrode Whitelocke's diary provide much insight into the lengthy process by which the day was finally ordered. There were debates about the date of the fast, whether a specific date should be named, the extent to which the upper house would delay the order and whether it should be ordered in parliament's or the protector's name, as well as extensive amendments to the declaration over two days. These reflected many of the concerns that had been aired in earlier debates, particularly over the Act of Recognition (recognizing Richard Cromwell as lord protector), the powers of the protector and whether there should be a second chamber in parliament and, if so, what its powers would be. The Commonwealth also seemed under threat in April from a number of royalist uprisings. The order was eventually passed on 14 April. Though the order included Scotland, there is no evidence that this fast was observed there and the Edinburgh council met on the day. This was not unexpected. MPs had recognized the potential for opposition from the Scottish Kirk during the debates on the fast, specifically that the Kirk would not administer any fast day ordered by a secular magistrate and that ministers would refuse to read out declarations because this was seen as a civil intrusion.

Order: declaration by the lord protector and parliament, ?14 Apr. 1659 (I.S., 1659; Wing C7183)*.
Additional sources: *CJ*, VII, 622–6, 639; *Burton diary*, IV, 300–1, 328–41; *Whitelocke diary*, p. 510; *Edin. recs., 1655 to 1665*, p. 147.

ORDER

Declaration by the lord protector and parliament: ?14 April 1659

We look upon it as a duty Incumbent upon us, who are set upon the Watch Tower to declare what we see, and seriously weighing the condition of these three Nations by Gods waies towards us, & our waies towards him, and the present posture of Affairs among us: We cannot but have sad thoughts and apprehensions of the tokens of Gods just displeasure against us; as for the waies of the Lord wherein he hath walked towards us, they have been waies of multitudes of mercies in vicissitudes of dangers; For, in the saddest dispensations of his providence towards us, he hath in the middest of Iudgment remembred mercy, and hath seemed to say as of old to *Ephraim*, and *Israell*; how shall I give thee up *England*? how shall I deliver you *Scotland* and *Ireland*? how shall I make you as *Admah*? how shall I set you a *Zeboim*? my heart is turned within me, my repentings are kindled together, yet we cannot say, that his wrath is turned away, but his hand is stretched out still, for though we have been emptied from vessell to vessell, yet we can finde no rest or settlement; we see not our signes, nor any that can tell us how long: This is a Lamentation, and if our wayes towards God in all this be considered, it must be for a Lamentation; for instead of humbling our selves under the mighty hand of God, and meeting him in the wayes of his Iudgements, we turn our backs upon him, cast him out of mind, vex his holy Majestie with our murmurings and complainings of Events, repining at the Miscarriages of Instruments; envying, censuring and fretting against one another, no man in the mean time laying his hand upon his own heart saying what have I done: how highly is God provoked by our great Apostacie and backsliding, arising Chiefly from want of receiving the truth in the love thereof, whereby these Nations are overspread with many blasphemies, and damnable heresies against God himself and his glorious attributes, against the Lord Iesus Christ his Person, his Offices, and his merits; against the holy spirit, against the word of God the onely rule of faith and life, by denying the authority thereof, and crying up the light in the hearts of sinfull men as the rule and guide of all their actions, besides many other abominable errours, which have opened a wide door for the letting in of the most horrible contempt of the Ordinances and Institutions of *Iesus Christ*, of the Ministers and Ministry of the glorious Gospell, together with the growth of grosse Ignorance, Atheisme and prophanesse of all sorts, such as are vaine, swearing and cursing, prophanation of the Lords-day, Drukennesse, Vncleanesse, and other ungodly courses for which the Land mourns: And besides all this, (that which should be cause of deepest humiliation to us, and is of high provocation to God) is the great scandall given by professors, and the sad divisions amongst them, whereby Religion hath been so wounded in the House of their Friends; And that which makes these abominations the more nationall (and gives us the more cause to be humbled for them) is the too much remissnesse and connivance of the civill Magistrates (to whom belongs the care of maintaining Gods publique worship, honour and purity of doctrine aswell as of punishing all sins against the second Table) in permitting the growth of these Abominations, by suffering persons under the abuse of Liberty of Conscience to disturbe the publick Ordinances, and to publish their corrupt principles and practises, to the seducing and infecting of others: And that which makes all those sinnes to be out of measure sinfull, is, That they are against so many signall deliverances and mercies under such a glorious sun shine of the Gospel, and contrary to so many Covenants, Vowes and Protestations personal and National. Nor are we in this day of our humiliation to forget the Iudgements of God, whereby he gives these Nations tokens of his displeasure; That in the mid'st of all our Changes and Unsettlements, he hath still left us in the dark, and hid Counsell from the wise, so that hitherto we have not attained unto that happy settlement in Church and State, which hath layn so much upon the spirits, and hath bin so much in the prayers and desires of all that fear him, That there hath bin so great a mortality upon man and beast in many places of this Nation, besides the decay of trade, & the great dearth which is amongst us, which if the Lord be not so mercifull as to send seasonable weather, may threaten a famine.

These things seriously considered; Is there not a cause to sanctifie a Fast, to call a solemn Assembly, to gather the Elders, and all the Inhabitants of the Land into the house of the Lord our God, to cry mightily unto the Lord: For which purpose, as also to implore a blessing from God upon the Counsels and proceedings of this present *Parliament*; his Highnesse the Lord *Protector* and the *Parliament* do appoint, That in all places within *England, Scotland* and *Ireland*, and the Dominions thereto belonging, the Eighteenth day of *May* next be set apart and observed as a day of solemn fasting and humiliation in all Churches, Chappels & Congregations within the same; and we do will and require all Ministers, and Pastors of Congregations, to read or cause to be read this *Declaration* in their severall Churches, Chappels and Congregations on the Lords day next before the said day of publick fasting to the end the same may be the better taken notice of; And we doe also hereby will and require all Iustices of the Peace, and other Officers to see that the said day be duly observed; And we do prohibit all Fairs, Markets, opening of Shops, and other ordinary Labours and employments, and all recreations upon the said day.

1659–2   Fast day during general anxieties, and for success in public affairs

Wednesday 31 August 1659 (England [and Wales?], Scotland, Ireland)

On 26 July, the Commons proposed another fast day, to be observed in all three nations on 31 August for all subjects 'to humble themselves for the great Provocations and Sins that are committed against God, and to seek the Blessing of God upon the Counsels and Affairs of this Commonwealth'. Government had slid quickly into chaos after Oliver Cromwell's death. The army, the republicans and, after its recall on 7 May, the Rump parliament distrusted Richard Cromwell and refused to recognize him as lord protector. Richard resigned on 25 May; his brother Henry resigned as lord deputy of Ireland on 15 June. The annual deficit and army arrears rose; there were growing fears of royalist conspiracies (see 1659–3) and fierce conflicts between parliament and military officers over control of both the army and the country. As with recent fast days, this occasion does not seem to have been observed in Scotland. It is unclear whether the declaration's failure to order observance in Wales was deliberate or an assumption that this was included in instructions concerning England.

Order: parliamentary order, 26 July 1659, Wing E1753* [also in *CJ*, VII, 732].
Additional sources: *CJ*, VII, 732; *Whitelocke diary*, p. 523.

ORDER

Parliamentary order: 26 July 1659
Ordered by the Parliament,
    That *Wednesday* the *31* of *August 1659.* be set apart for a day of Solemn Fasting and Humiliation throughout *England, Scotland* and *Ireland.* And the good People of this Nation are hereby invited to joyn in this Duty, and to humble themselves fo[r the] great Provocations and Sins that are committed against God, and to seek the Blessing of God upon the Counsels and Affairs of this Commonwealth.

1659–3   Thanksgiving days for the failure of royalist conspiracies and Booth's uprising

Thursday 6 October 1659 (London, Westminster and the late lines of communication); Thursday 3 November 1659 (elsewhere in England and Wales, Scotland and Ireland)

After Richard Cromwell's resignation as lord protector, Charles II authorized the establishment of the Great Trust and Commission, a plan to organize simultaneous royalist uprisings across the country. Though it garnered much support, the conspiracy was discovered and only one uprising took place, that of Sir George Booth in Cheshire and North Wales on 1 August. The rising was quickly put down by force, but though Booth was arrested and imprisoned in the Tower, he was never tried. On 24 September, the Commons resolved to order thanksgiving days on 6 October and 3 November. A declaration was composed and approved, with amendments, on 1 October. Joseph Caryll was appointed to preach before the house at St Margaret's, Westminster. As on previous occasions, members of the council of state, parliament and officers of the army were invited to dine with the lord mayor, aldermen and common council of London at Grocer's Hall after the service. According to Whitelocke, 'the Citty highly feasted them, & there were many mutuall expressions of respect and love among them'. This occasion does not seem to have been observed in Scotland, though a version of the declaration was printed in Edinburgh.

Order: parliamentary declaration, 1 Oct. 1659, Wing E1493* [also Wing E1493A (Edinburgh reprint)].
Additional sources: *CJ*, VII, 786, 790; *Whitelocke diary*, pp. 532–4.
Printed sermon: Homes, Christchurch, London (Wing H2577).

ORDER

Parliamentary declaration: 1 October 1659
The signal Mercies wherewith God hath blessed this Commonwealth for some years past, are so evident and convincing, that such onely who are offended at the hand from whence they come, can refuse to make acknowledgement. And had not the Concerns been more then humane, which were Imbarkt with the late Adventures in these Nations, their miscarriage might have been according to the expectance of the Adversary: But though not for our sakes, yet for his great Name sake, who sits in Heaven and laughs to scorn all the Plots and Devices of the ungodly, hitherto we have been delivered; *The snare is broken, and we are escaped.* 'Tis not unknown with what an outstretched Arm it hath pleased God, as well to prevent, as repel those dangers which seemed of late to threaten this Nations Peace, by the Apostasie of some from their former Engagements in conjunction with old Enemies, together with a neutral Generation, in so much as few Counties of *England* but have been in some measure infested, though not with open acts of Hostility, yet with secret Complottings and Attempts, to debauch the people to an Insurrection, but more especially the North-Western parts, where Sir *George Booth*, Sir *Thomas Middleton*, Colonel *Egerton*, Colonel *Werden*, and several others their Accomplices, upon pretence of adding to this Nations Freedom, would have by force of Arms, brought it into Bondage, by re-admitting a Kingly Interest and Family, against which God hath so long by a Successive and uninterrupted Series of Providences very fully witnessed; That when

in many other places of this Nation, even at once the Enemy hath attempted to break in upon our peace like a flood, 'tis wonderful to behold, how the Spirit of the Lord hath lifted up a Standard against him. All which the Parliament considering, hath reckoned it a duty incumbent on them to set apart *Thursday* next, being the sixth day of *October*, one thousand six hundred fifty nine, for a Day of solemn Praises and Thanksgivings, to be returned unto the Lord; And to the end, that all who are truly free to such a Duty, within the Cities of *London* and *Westminster*, and late lines of Communication, may have an opportunity to offer a Sacrifice of Praise on this behalf, the Parliament doth hereby Declare they are invited thereunto; and as for all other parts of this Commonwealth, upon the third day of *November* next: That as the true performance of this Duty is by such a people as are made free in the Sons freedom (for *Praise waiteth for God in Sion*) so an occasion is hereby given to render it to the Lord, even in the Great Congregation.

And although this Combination was so general, its appearance suddain, and there was not wanting a readiness of willing people to offer themselves in such a day of tryal; yet that it hath pleased God, with the loss of so little Blood, to still the raging enemy and avenger, yea, after his defeat and disappointment, that both Persons and Things are brought to light in this matter beyond expectation, are none of the least motives to quicken and excite even all that fear God, and work righteousness in these Nations, unto such a Duty at this Season, not doubting but as it hath pleased God to cause *the wrath of man to praise him*, so that the *remainder of wrath will he restrain*.

1660–Ir   Thanksgiving days for Irish repudiation of the Commonwealth government

Thursday 3 January 1660 (City and liberties of Dublin); Thursday 17 January 1660 (Ireland)

Sir Hardress Waller, major-general of the army in Ireland, had been personally allied to Oliver Cromwell, but after Richard and Henry Cromwell's resignations, he supported the republicans in parliament, and arrested Henry at Phoenix Park. However, in December 1659, he suddenly switched sides, supporting an uprising of Irish protestants and, on 13 December, seized Dublin Castle and called for the restoration of the Long parliament. Lacking real authority to order nationwide prayers, Waller 'seriously recommended and desired' all Irish subjects to join in thanksgivings for his success and to petition God for the success of a revitalized Long parliament.

Order: declaration by the major-general and the council of officers, 28 Dec. 1659, Wing W536*.

ORDER

Declaration by the major-general and the council of officers: 28 December 1659

The Signal Turns of Gods hand challenge of right our signal observation and improvement, that we may express in our heart and life, the due counterpane of his various dealings. Providence hath of late wrought wonders of mercy, as in these Nations, so particularly in this City and throughout this Land. The Lord hath remembred us in our low estate, because his mercy endures for ever. Who is so great a stranger in our Israel, that observed not the dreadfull symptoms of threatned ruine to our Religion, and all our Liberties Sacred and Civil? Hath not God saved us with a *notwithstanding*, by the late dispensations of his gracious appearances in our greatest straights and perplexities? Were not the mountains of sinfull provocations and strong oppositions raised up to their height, to obstruct the great work of Reformation, so happily begun, and so solemnly engaged for among us? Had not the Romish Emissaries and Ingeneers of darkness prevailed far, to divide and distract, to delude and destroy us? Were not the hopes of our Common Enemy exceedingly raised up, gaping for the confusion and dissolution of Christs interest and People in these Nations? Had not the powers and policies of Hell prevailed far, and laid the very necks of Magistracy and Ministry upon the block of direfull Anarchy and Arbitrary rule? Were not all foundations religious and politick so put out of course, in all Relations, as to threaten eminent ruine both to Church and State? Which Ordinance of God was not slighted, opposed, maligned and scorned by specious pretences and strong delusions? Were not Gods own people very deeply guilty of apostacie and hypocrisie, of unfaithfulness and breach of Covenant in all Relations? Were we not all ready to devour one another by sinfull mistakes and wofull miscarriages, whilst our ill neighbours were laughing at us, and combining against us? Did not unclean spirits range and rage among us, possessing many, foaming out their shame, torturing souls and all societies with deadly convulsions? Were not our distempers, personal and publick, grown so inveterate, so complicate, & so multiplicious, that our best Physicians could do little else then pity & bewail our expiring Liberties? Was not the name of Christ, and whatsoever is dear unto his people, ready to be made the scorn and prey of our ill neighbours? Were we not hastning to the sad Catastrophe of the German Tragedy, and *Munsters* desolations, procured by the like fanatick spirits, which then obstructed Reformation work? What cause then have we to admire the miraculous patience and bounty of our God, that have made us now the living monuments of undeserved Mercy? Should not we adore and celebrate that good-will of his, who dwelling in this Bush, hath thus prevented the consumption thereof? He that is our God, now appears indeed to be the God of all salvations, to whom belong all issues from death. He hath delivered, he doth deliver, in him we hope that he will still deliver. Thankfulness to him, verbal & actual, cordial and constant, will be the best preserver of mercy, and improver thereof. The choice circumstantials of this Salvation, are so many, and so remarkable, that the sense thereof cannot but engage and inflame our hearts to the highest expressions of gratitude and praise. That such a God, so highly provoked, should shew such favor, to such an unworthy people, in such a season, and by such means, in such a manner, and to such an end, this indeed is the wonder of Mercies, the complex and complement of Free-grace. That so great a change should be brought about with so little noise, so little bloud, so little opposition, and so hopefully; Is not this a miracle of Mercy? This day of small things should not then be despised, being the Lords doing, so marvellous in our eies. Though our Redemption be not yet perfected, yet do we see cause abundantly to provoke all Christs friends to solemn Acknowledgments. Should not they praise him, that have been seeking him? Do not the Signal returns of his mercy challenge proportionable returns of our Duty? Is not this the best way to assure and increase, to improve and hasten the blessings promised and begun? Doth he not command and commend such a course? hath it not been his own and his peoples method in all former ages? Have not we received notable experiences ever since the begining of our famous Parliament, to direct and strengthen us thereto? Doth not the posture of Gods reforming people, so signally foretold *Rev.* 15. challenge this from us? Those very persons who have been unhappily seduced into snares and illegal Engagements against the supreme Authority, may in this great *Turn*, find sufficient ground of blessing the Lord, that they have been stopt in such a career, posting to confusion. To be thus kept from sin and ruine will be then known and acknowledged for a singular mercy; when the Lord shall please to remove prejudice and pre-ingagements.

That all Gods people in this City and throughout Ireland *may orderly concurr in all humble return of praise to our good God, on this account; it is therefore seriously recommended and desired, That* Tuesday *next, being the 3. of* January 1659, *be set apart and solemnly observed as a day of publick Thanks-giving within the City and Liberties of* Dublin; *and the* Tuesday *fortnight, next after it, being the 17. of* January, *to be likewise observed for a solemn Thanks-giving throughout all the parts of this Nation; and the several Ministers of the Gospel in their respective places are desired to give publick notice thereof, on the first Lords day after the receipt hereof.*

1660–1   Fast day for the new parliament and restoration of stable government

Friday 6 April 1660 (England and Wales, Scotland, Ireland)

In December 1659, General Monck, commander-in-chief of the armed forces in England, Scotland and Ireland, marched south from Coldstream to demand the reinstatement of the Rump parliament, which had been dissolved by the army in October. He was hostile to English army officers and feared that the army would allow religious radicalism to increase further. As he marched south, there were riots and strikes in London and, in the face of these, the ruling Committee of Safety collapsed. The Rump was reinstated before Monck reached London, but popular pressure grew for new elections and a 'full and free' parliament'. After tense negotiations and stand-offs between Monck and the Rump, those MPs who had been purged in 1648 were reinstated and the Long parliament was restored (21 February). On 8 March, a bill was introduced in parliament for new elections for a new parliament to convene on 25 April. On 14 April, the Commons resolved to order a day of fasting to seek God's blessing on this endeavour. Two days later, the Long parliament dissolved itself. Despite the reinstatement of both the Rump and the Long parliament, the ordinance of April 1654 uniting England and Scotland remained in force; this day of fasting was technically ordered for the whole Commonwealth.

Order: parliamentary order, 16 Mar. 1660, Wing E2237A* [also Wing E2237B; also in *CJ*, VII, 880].
Additional sources: *CJ*, VII, 880; *Larkham diary*, p. 221; *Whitelocke diary*, p. 577; *Minutes of the Manchester presbyterian classis, 1646–1660 (Part 3)*, ed. William A. Shaw (Chetham Society, new ser., 24; Manchester, 1891), pp. 338–9.

ORDER

Parliamentary order: 16 March 1660
Resolved, &c.

   That *Friday*, the sixth Day of *April*, One Thousand, six hundred and Sixty, be set apart for a Day of Publick Fasting and Humiliation, to be solemnized throughout the Nation, under the sence of the great and manifold Sins and Provocations thereof: And to seek the Lord for his Blessing upon the Parliament now shortly to be Assembled, That the Lord will make them Healers of our Breaches, and Instruments to restore and settle Peace and Government in the Nations, upon Foundations of Truth and Righteousness.

1660–E1   Thanksgiving days for the dissolution of the Long parliament and restoration of the monarchy

Thursday 10 May 1660 (London, Westminster and the lines of communication); Thursday 24 May 1660 (elsewhere in England and Wales)

The convention parliament met on 25 April 1660, amid widespread expectation of the imminent restoration of Charles II. On 26 April, parliament resolved to appoint days of thanksgiving for the *rôle* of General Monck in bringing about the dissolution of the Long parliament and fresh elections (see 1660–1). On 1 May, parliament agreed that 'the Government is, and ought to be, by King, Lords, and Commons' (*CJ*, VIII, 8). Charles was proclaimed king on 8 May; on the following day, parliament passed a second resolution about the thanksgiving, to take account of this. The resolution required ministers to give thanks for Charles's various public letters and declarations, giving reassurances about the terms of a restored monarchy, and during services they were to read out in particular his letters to the houses of parliament. This resolution of 9 May was printed together with a separate order for ministers to pray for Charles and the royal family in their daily prayers. A long unofficial prayer was published 'by T. Mabb, for William Shears' (Wing F1572A). This was a response to the proclamation of Charles, and made no explicit reference to the thanksgiving days.

Orders: parliamentary resolutions, 26 Apr. 1660, Wing E2243C*; 9 May 1660, Wing E2265B*.
Additional sources: *CJ*, VIII, 2, 8, 15–16, 19; *LJ*, XI, 5, 21; *The diaries and papers of Sir Edward Dering, second baronet, 1644 to 1684*, ed. M. F. Bond (1976), 41; *A form of thanksgiving* (1660; Wing F1572A); *Minutes of the Manchester presbyterian classis, 1646–1660*, III, 342; HMC, *Fifth rep.*, p. 204; *CSPD, 1665–6*, p. 163.
Printed sermons: Baxter, St Paul's, London (Wing B1377); Buck, House of Lords (Wing B5308); Cole, Preston (Wing C5040A); Godman, Cambridge (Wing G941); Gregory, Oxford (Wing G1888); Newcombe, Manchester (Wing N900, N900A); Price, House of Commons (Wing P3336); Roberts, Wandsworth (Wing R1597AB); Walsall, ?Sandy (Wing W624); Walwyn, East Coker (Wing W696B); White, Wadhurst (Wing W1785B).

ORDERS

Parliamentary resolution: 26 April 1660
Resolved by the Lords and Commons in Parliament Assembled,
   That this Day fortnight be set apart for a Day of Thanksgiving to the Lord for Raising up His Excellency the Lord General, and other Eminent Persons who have been Instrumental in Delivery of this Nation from Thraldome and Misery.

Resolved by the Lords and Commons in Parliament Assembled,
   That this Day fortnight be the Day set apart for a Day of Thanksgiving for both

Houses of Parliament, and within the Cities of *London* and *Westminster*, and late Lines of Communication; And this Day Moneth for the whole Nation.

Parliamentary resolution: 9 May 1660

Resolved upon the Question by the Lords and Commons Assembled in Parliament,

That the Ministers who are appointed to officiate before both Houses upon *Thursday* next, being the day appointed for a Publick Thanksgiving, and all other Ministers within the Cities of *London* and *Westminster*, and the late lines of Communication, who in their several Churches, and Chappels, are to carry on the Duties of that day. And also all other Ministers who are on that day fortnight to perform the like duty throughout the Kingdome of *England*, and Dominion of *Wales*, and Town of *Berwick* upon *Twede*, shall be, and are hereby enjoyned to return Thanks to Almighty God for his Majesties several Gracious Letters to both Houses of Parliament, and to the Commanders in Chief of the Forces both by Land and Sea, and to the *Lord Mayor*, and *Common-Council* of the City of *London*, together with the Declarations enclosed, and the Just and Honourable Concessions therein contained, and for the hearty, loyal, and dutiful conjunction of the Lords and Commons now Assembled in Parliament, and the Universal Concurrence of all the Commanders and Forces both by Land and Sea, to receive his Majesty into his Dominions and Government, according to their bounden duty, and the Laws of the Land; And that the Ministers upon *Thursday* fortnight be enjoyned to read his Majesties Letters and Declarations to both Houses in their several Churches and Chappels at the same time.

1660–S   Thanksgiving day for the restoration of Charles II

Tuesday 19 June 1660 (Scotland)

This thanksgiving was appointed before the reconstruction of monarchical government in Scotland, and at a time when no national ecclesiastical courts were meeting. The initiative probably came from the presbytery of Edinburgh (whose register for this period is not extant). Its ministers first planned to appoint a thanksgiving day to follow Charles II's English coronation, expected to be held soon after his return to London in May 1660. When it became clear that the coronation would be delayed, the clergy in Edinburgh recommended that presbyteries elsewhere in Scotland follow their example by observing a thanksgiving in June. This suggestion was widely followed: printed sermons show that 19 June was kept as a thanksgiving day in Edinburgh, Aberdeen, Stirling and probably Linlithgow. In these and other towns, burgh authorities helped to organize celebrations. A sermon published by John Jameson suggests that the thanksgiving was kept on 27 June in Jedburgh. The diarist John Lamont recorded that in the presbyteries of St Andrews and Cupar the thanksgiving was delayed until 5 July.

Order: none found.

Sources: Robert Douglas to James Sharp, 19 June 1660, Glasgow University Library, MS Gen. 210, p. 136; Wodrow, *History*, I, 40–1; Nicoll, pp. 292–4; Lamont, p. 124; *Aber. recs., 1643–1747*, pp. 186–8, 191; *Extracts from the records of the burgh of Glasgow* (4 vols., Scottish Burgh Record Society, Glasgow, 1876–1908), *1630–1662*, p. 447; *Edin. recs., 1655 to 1665*, p. 203.

Printed sermons: Jameson, Jedburgh (Wing J442); Laurie, Edinburgh (Wing L694); Menzies, Aberdeen (Wing M1724); Paterson, Aberdeen (Wing P687); Ramsay, Linlithgow (Wing R222); Symson, Stirling (Wing S6373).

1660–E2   Thanksgiving day for the restoration of Charles II

Thursday 28 June 1660 (England and Wales)

On 29 May 1660, the day of his arrival in London, members of parliament attended Charles II at Whitehall to express their satisfaction with his restoration. On the following day, a bill was moved in the Commons for an anniversary celebration of the restoration of the monarchy (see AC–29 May), and members proposed an address to the king, requesting that he appoint a thanksgiving day. The Lords agreed to the address on 31 May. Charles responded by issuing a proclamation, dated 5 June, appointing a thanksgiving day on 28 June. The proclamation contained an explicit instruction that it was to be read in churches on a Sunday preceding the thanksgiving. It did not order a form of prayer. The future of worship in the Church of England was yet to be settled, though the parliamentary ordinance of 1645 prohibiting use of the BCP, like all legislation passed without royal assent between 1641 and 1660, no longer had the force of law. The king's printers, John Bill and Christopher Barker, published a form of prayer shortly before the thanksgiving (Thomason's copy is dated 'June 27'). On 30 June, a complaint was made in the Commons that the production of this form and other publications was a 'great Abuse to his Majesty' (*CJ*, VIII, 78). It should not be assumed, however, that the form was unauthorized. Nothing came of the Commons' enquiry, and there is little reason to doubt that a form of prayer published 'by Authority', under the imprint of the king's printers, with an elaborate royal coat of arms on the verso of the half-title, had the approval of the court, though no evidence survives to indicate who was responsible for composing the form. It also seems likely that the form was used at the chapel royal, where liturgical worship according to the BCP had already resumed. The late publication date would suggest that the form was unlikely to have been used widely across the country, though the fact that surviving copies include at least two variants indicates that it was printed in substantial numbers.

Order: royal proclamation, 5 June 1660, Wing C3426*.
Form of prayer: *A form of prayer, with thanksgiving, to be used of all the kings majesties loving subjects. The 28th. of June, 1660. For his majesties happy return to his kingdoms. Set forth by authority* (41 pp.; Wing C4170)*.
Additional sources: *CJ*, VIII, 49–51, 78; *LJ*, XI, 46, 49–50; *CSPD, 1660–1*, p. 3; Wodrow, *History*, I, 32, 40; HMC, *Fifth rep.*, p. 154; Pepys, I, 186.
Printed sermons: Creed, St Mary Woolchurch, London (Wing C6874); Ford, Northampton (Wing F1492, F1492A); Hodges, House of Lords (Wing H2317); Martin [not preached] (Wing M842); Nelme, Gloucester (Wing N415); Reynolds, House of Commons (Wing R1246); Sheldon, court (Wing S3068); Spencer, Cambridge (Wing S4952); Swetnam, Derby (Wing S6254); Towers, Exeter Chapel, near the Savoy (Wing T1960); Whynnell, ?Askerswell (Wing W2073).

ORDER

Royal proclamation: 5 June 1660

Whereas it hath pleased Almighty God to manifest his own immediate Goodness, Wisdom, and Power, in his late Providence towards Us, and Our Kingdoms, wherein, beyond all Humane Means and Contrivances, as well of Our Friends for Us, as of Our Adversaries against Us, he hath by the interposition of his own Power and Wisdom, after a long and tedious Exile, returned Us home to Our People, and, after a long, and seemingly invincible, Interruption, restored Our People and Kingdoms to their ancient Rights, Liberties, and Government; and all this brought about, by his most wise and over-ruling Hand, without any effusion of Blood: But, instead thereof, filling the Hearts of Us, and Our People, as full of mutual Love, Confidence, and Joy, as became such a Restitution of King and People, whereby the Mercy is not onely advanced, but the hopes of most happy consequences, thereupon, are increased: We cannot upon the due consideration hereof, but with all humility admire and adore the Mercy and Goodness of God, in these his signal manifestations thereof; and We looked, and still look upon them as invitations from Heaven to Us, and all Our People, unto most entire Thankfulness for the same unto Almighty God, and publick and chearful Expressions thereof.

And whereas in the midst of those Our considerations, both Our Houses of Parliament by their Address of the One and twentieth of *May* last, have humbly shewed unto Us, That such is the inestimable blessing of Our Restitution to Our Royal Throne, which at once hath put a period to the Calamities of Three Kingdoms, and to all the Sorrows and Sufferings of Our Royal Person and Family, that they cannot but account it as an entrance into the state of Joy and Happiness, which obligeth all Our Subjects to render an Everlasting Tribute of Praise and Thanksgiving to Almighty God, for these glorious Mercies to his afflicted People.

And to the end, some solemn Time may be set apart for the publick performance of this Duty; and that all Our Subjects in *England* and *Wales*, and the Town of *Berwick* upon *Twede*, do equally share in the joys of this Deliverance, may be united in these Devotions, which are offered for it, They therefore humbly beseeched Us, that We would be pleased by Our Royal Proclamation to set apart some Day, for a publick Thanksgiving throughout all these Our Dominions. We willing that the just Tribute of Praise and Thanksgiving to Our Great Soveraign the King of Heaven and Earth be returned by Us, and all Our People for these his Deliverances and Mercies; and that as his Mercy is of Universal concernment to Us and all Our Subjects, so, to the end, that the publick Returns of Our Praise to God, for the same, though it cannot equalize, yet it may in some measure answer the amplitude of the Benefit.

We do hereby Publish and Declare, That the Twenty eight day of this instant *June*, be set apart and observed as a day of Publick Thanksgiving to Almighty God, throughout Our Kingdom of *England*, Dominion of *Wales*, and Town of *Berwick*, for this his great Mercy; and We do direct and appoint, that this Our Proclamation be publickly read in all Churches and Chappels, on some Lords day, precedent thereunto, to the end that notice be taken thereof, and due Thanks and Praise may, upon the said Twenty eighth day of *June*, be offered up unto Almighty God by Us and all Our People, with one Heart, and that humble Supplications be poured out before him, for his continual Assistance and Improvement of this and all his Mercies, to the honor of his great Name, and the Safety, Peace and Benefit of all Our Kingdoms and Dominions. We willing and strictly commanding all Persons within these Our

Dominions, with all Sobriety, Reverence, and Thankfulness, to set apart that Day to this Duty, and to observe the same as becomes so solemn an occasion.

FORM OF PRAYER

MORNING PRAYER

[1 Tim. 2:1]

I exhort you therefore, that first of all, prayers, supplications, intercessions, and giving of thanks be made for all men: for Princes, and for all that are in authority, that we may live a quiet and peaceable life, in all godlinesse and honesty, for that is good and acceptable in the sight of God our Saviour.

First, the Minister shall with a loud voyce pronounce some one of these three Sentences, as in the Book of Common Prayer.
    [Ezek. 18:27; Joel 2:13; 1 John 1:8]

[Then as 1559 BCP to the end of the Venite*]*

[Ps. 20, 21, 85, 118]
[First lesson: 2 Chron. 1]
[Te Deum]
[Second lesson: Rom. 13]
[Benedictus]

[Then as 1559 BCP to the end of the Lord's prayer]

Then the Priest standing up, shall say,
    O Lord shew thy mercy upon us.
People: And grant us thy salvation.
Priest.: O Lord save the King.
People: Who putteth his trust in thee.
Priest: Send him help from thy holy place.
People: And evermore mightily defend him.
Priest: Let the enemies have none advantage over him.
People: Let not the wicked approach to hurt him.
[As 1559 BCP, to the end of the suffrages]

A Prayer for the Kings Majestie.
    O Lord our heavenly Father, high and mighty, King of kings, Lord of lords, the onely ruler of Princes, which doest from thy throne behold all the dwellers upon the earth, most heartily we beseech thee with thy favour to behold our most gracious Soveraign Lord King CHARLES, and so replenish him with the grace of thy holy Spirit, that he may alway incline to thy will, and walk in thy way, indue him plentifully with heavenly gifts, grant him in health and wealth long to live, strengthen him that he may vanquish and overcome all his Enemies, and finally after this life, he may attain everlasting joy and felicity, through Jesus Christ our Lord. Amen.

O Lord God, thou hast dealt exceeding graciously with this our sinful land, who by a manner, which passeth all humane understanding and skil, hast been pleased to grant us so suddain and miraculous a producing of Light out of Darknesse. We therefore thy most unworthy Creatures, finding our selves so undeservedlie, and yet so infinitely blessed, in the safe return of our dread Soveraign Lord thy Servant King *Charles* are at this time here most humbly gathered together, before Heaven and before Thee, disclaiming all Interest of us sinful men therein, and with joyful and faithful hearts, through the Spirit of thy Grace, blessing thy holy name alone, for this thy unspeakable Goodnesse, and with all Sinceritie, and prostration of our Spirits, offering up these our Vows, and Sacrifices of true Thanksgiving unto thy Divine Majestie. We fall down before the Throne of grace, and most humbly beseech the Lord of Heaven and Earth, in the infinite merits of our Redeemer Jesus Christ, the Eternal Son of the Father, God and man, to accept now from us, this most unworthy Oblation of our selves; who here now do vow, without all dissimulation or any disloyal affections, all holy, and free obedience, in thought, word, and deed; First unto thee O Lord, our Creator and Redeemer, and next, under thee, in thee, and for thee, through thy blessed assistance, unto our Soveraign Lord the King, whom thou hast so graciously restored unto us.

We therefore, O Lord, unfeignedly now promise for ever hereafter all Loialtie, and unsteined Allegiance unto him, his Heirs and Successors; And we beseech the Majestie of Heaven, that thou wouldest daily, O Lord; more and more endue his Royal Heart with Holinesse, and thy Heavenly grace, and begirt his Sacred Person with the increase of all Honour, Health, and Happinesse in this World, and at last, crown him with immortality and glory in the World to come; and that, for Jesus Christ his sake, our onely blessed Lord and Saviour. *Amen.*

[Then as 1559 BCP to the end of morning prayer]

Litany

[As 1559 BCP, except that the 'Prayer for the queen's majesty' is replaced by the following]

O Lord God most mercifull Father, who of thine especial grace and favour, hast placed thy servant King Charles our Soveraign, in the royall Throne of this Kingdome, thereby assuring us of the continuance of thy Gospel and sacred truth amongst us, to the great joy and comfort of our hearts: We thine unworthy servants, here assembled together in memorie of this thy mercy, most humbly beseech thy Fatherly goodness, to grant us grace, that we may in word, deed, and heart shew our selves alwayes thankfull unto thee for the same; and that his Majestie through thy grace may in all honour, vertue and godliness continue his glorious reign over us many and many years yet to come, and we dutifully obey him as faithfull and loyall Subjects: that so we may long enjoy him with the continuance of thy great blessings which by him thou hast powred upon us, through Jesus Christ our Lord.

Almighty God, the fountain of all goodness, We humbly beseech thee to bless *Mary* the Queen Mother, *James* Duke of *York*, and the rest of the Royall Progeny: Endue them with thy holy Spirit, enrich them with thy heavenly grace, prosper them with all happiness, and bring them to thine everlasting Kingdome, through Jesus Christ our Lord. Amen.

COMMUNION[343]

[As 1559 BCP to the collect of the day]

Here must follow the Collect for the day, the Priest standing up and saying,
God the strength of all them that trust in thee, mercifully accept our praiers: and because the weakness of our mortal nature can do no good thing without thee, grant us the help of thy grace, that in keeping of thy Commandements, we may please thee both in will and deed, through Jesus Christ our Lord.

O most gracious God, and merciful Father, we thine unworthy servants acknowledge it thy special care and fatherly providence over us, that it hath pleased thee, for the good of thy Church, and glory of this land, to place thy servant King *Charles* our Soveraign Lord, in the Royal seat of this Kingdome, giving us by him and with him, a happy restoring of thy sacred truth and Gospel, and of our former peace and prosperitie, together with a great increase of honour, power, and dignity: we beseech thee to grant unto him the defence of thy salvation, and to shew forth thy holy kindness and mercy, both to his Majestie thine Anointed, and to thy servants *Mary* the Queen mother, the illustrious *James* Duke of *Yorke*, with the rest of the Royal seed for evermore: and to stirre up in our hearts a dutiful and Loyal obedience unto this thy ordinance, and a religious and holy thankfulnesse unto thee for these thy great mercies, through Jesus Christ our Lord. Amen.

Stirre up, we beseech thee, O Lord, the wills of thy faithful people, that they plenteouslie bringing forth the fruits of good works, may of thee be plenteouslie rewarded, and particularlie with the long life and prosperous reign of our most gracious Soveraign, through Jesus Christ our Lord.

[Epistle: 1 Peter 2:11–17]
[Gospel: Matt. 22:16–22][344]
[Nicene creed]
[Offertory sentence: Matt. 5:16]

[Prayer for the whole state of the church]

O Lord our God, which upholdest and governest all things in heaven and earth, receive our humble praiers, with thanksgiving for our Soveraign Lord King *Charles*, set over us by thy grace and providence to be our King and Governour, and so together with his Majestie, blesse the rest of his Royal alliance with the dew of thy heavenly Spirit, that they ever trusting in thy goodness, protected by thy power, and crowned with thy gracious and endlesse favour, may continue before thee in health, peace, joy and honour, a long and happy life upon earth, and after death obtain everlasting life and glory in the kingdome of heaven, by the merits and mediation of Christ Jesus our Saviour, who with the Father and the holy spirit liveth and reigneth ever one God, world without end. Amen.

---

[343] In the original: 'The Second Service'.
[344] In original: Mat.2.16.

Almighty God, which hast promised to hear *[as 1559 BCP]*

[The blessing]

1661–Ir1 Fast day on the anniversary of the regicide of Charles I

Wednesday 30 January 1661 (Ireland)

No thanksgiving day was called in Ireland in response to Charles II's return to England, probably because the reconstitution of the Irish government was delayed until autumn 1660. Consequently, this fast was the first special observance appointed in Ireland after the restoration. Although the proclamation made no reference to a form of prayer, it nevertheless indicated the government's desire to impose religious uniformity and to restore the royal prerogative in religious matters. The proclamation gave unusually explicit instructions to ministers, requiring them to assemble their congregations at ten o'clock in the morning on the fast day, at which time they were to read out the proclamation. On 22 January, the lords justices issued another proclamation prohibiting meetings of catholic clergy and protestant nonconformists, which, it was alleged, had often assumed the function of appointing fasts and thanksgivings. The day appointed for the Irish fast was observed in England and Wales as the anniversary of Charles I's execution, 30 January having been appointed by act of parliament in 1660 as an annual fast day. Not until 1666 was there statutory authority for keeping the anniversary fast in Ireland (see AC–30 Jan.).

Order: proclamation of the lords justices and council, 21 Jan. 1661, Wing I610, SP63/306/19 [partially printed in *CSPI, 1660–2*, pp. 190–1].
Additional sources: *By the lords iustices and council* (Dublin, 1661; Wing I955); earl of Orrery to Lord Hyde, 23 Jan. 1661, Bod., MS Clarendon 74, fo. 98v.

ORDER

Proclamation of the lords justices and council: 21 January 1661
We cannot doubt of the happy condition of Our late dread Soveraign of ever blessed memory *CHARLES* the first, being assured by the voice of truth it self, that whosoever looseth his life for Christs sake shall find it; In which respect Martyrdom (wherewith he was undoubtedly crowned) hath been justly stiled the baptism of blood, and the anniversary days of the death of the Martyrs have been ever observed by the Church of God, as the birth days of their glory, so as it might seem half a crime to shed a tear for him whose Soul the Lord hath delivered from death, his eyes from tears, and his feet from falling, whom his bloody enemies did advantage more by their malice and cruelty, then they could have done by the pretension of Allegiance and Loyalty, snatching him from the sweet society of his dearest consort, and most hopeful and Royal Issue, and from the Government of all his Kingdoms and People, to place him in the bosom of the blessed Angels and Saints triumphant.

Yet when We consider our own loss to be deprived by a company of traiterous paracides of such a Prince, of so eminent and exemplary virtue and piety, with whom our Liberty, our Laws, our Religion had expired, if God in his great mercy had not miraculously restored them by the happy restitution of his Majesty; when

We consider the manner of his death, to be murdered by his own Subjects, who had sworn Allegiance to him, in his chief City, before the gates of his own Pallace, in the face of the Sun, in the sight of his good People, who durst not mutter whatsoever they thought, and that under a formality and fained pretence of Justice, after all the indignities and affronts imaginable, had been put upon him; And especially considering the guilt of innocent bloud, how it defileth the Land and lyeth heavy upon a whole Nation, being not to be washed away but by the bloud of them who shed it, God in his National Judgments oftentimes involving those who are innocent in the eye of man with the nocent, which he may still justly do considering that Our National sins deserved that he should permit that detestable paracide to be committed.

All these things being duly pondered, We the Lords Justices and Council have thought fit to set a part, and do hereby set a part the thirtieth day of this present month of *Ianuary* for a day of solemn Fasting and Humiliation of Our Selves before the Lord, at which time all his Majesties Subjects of this Kingdom of *Ireland* are required by Us to meet and assemble themselves at their several Parish Churches, to joyn with their respective Ministers in publick prayers that God will be graciously pleased to avert his Judgments from this Nation due unto so horrid and bloody a crime, and to discover more and more those who have been the principal Contrivers and Actors in that unparraleld murder, and to establish and radicate his Majesty in the just possession of his Hereditary Crowns and Kingdoms; And lastly to forbear all bodily labour, and all trading, and to shut up their Shops for that day; And We do further require all Ministers and Curates throughout this Kingdom of *Ireland* either dignitaries, or beneficiaries, or stipendaries, upon that day, at ten of the clock in the forenoon to assemble their Parishioners, and to read this Proclamation to them, to press [u]nto them the detestableness of this barbarous murder, which was so much the more abominable by how much it was endeavoured to be covered under the cloak of Religious piety and Justice; And to exhort their several Congregations to Loyal[t]y and Obedience, and a perfect detestation of those seditious principles from which so much Treason and Rebellion hath flowed, and doth and will daily flow for the future, unless such dangerous tenets destructive not onely to Piety but to all humane society be purged out of the minds of men, And We hope and do expect that all his Majesties good Subjects as they desire to appear innocent of the guilt of that bloud will seriously perform this Our injunction.

1661–Ir2 Fast day for the success of the parliaments

Thursday 2 May 1661 (Ireland)

ESTC lists no extant copies of the proclamation of this fast, and no form of prayer. According to Steele, the proclamation called for prayers for God's blessing on the forthcoming meetings of the Irish, English and Scottish parliaments, which assembled on 8 May.

Order: proclamation by the lords justices and council, 15 Apr. 1661, Wing I843, not found [formerly Dublin PRO (destroyed); see Steele, II, no. 642].

1661–E   Fast days during heavy rains and fears of a bad harvest and sicknesses

Wednesday 12 June 1661 (London, Westminster, Southwark and surrounding area); Wednesday 19 June 1661 (elsewhere in England and Wales)

The spring of 1661 was unusually wet. In late April, Ralph Josselin recorded that the heavy rains made ploughing the fields and sowing seeds difficult, and there were fears that food shortages would result. Acting on the precedent set in the 1620s (see 1625–E, 1626–E2, 1628–E1, 1629–E), parliament proposed the calling of a fast day. The Commons and Lords agreed on 31 May to ask the king to appoint a fast; Charles's proclamation was issued on 7 June. Convocation was sitting, and this seems to have been the reason for the unusual manner of the form of prayer's composition, which involved a committee of four bishops and eight members of convocation's lower house. By the time the form was completed, the weather had improved, and several collects of thanksgiving for the end of the rains were included. Noting this, Pepys described the observance as 'between a fast and a feast' (Pepys, II, 119). The form of prayer followed the services in the BCP of 1559 (as revised in 1604), which was widely used in the interval between the restoration and the introduction of the revised BCP in 1662.

Orders: royal proclamation, 7 June 1661, Wing C3298*; order of the king in council, 10 June 1661, in the form of prayer.
Form of prayer: *A form of prayer, to be used upon the twelfth of June, in all churches and chappels within the cities of London and Westminster; the suburbs of each, and the burrough of Southwark. And upon the nineteenth of the said moneth, in all other churches and chappels within the rest of his majesties dominions of England and Wales, and the town of Berwick upon Twede. Being the several days appointed for a general fast, to be kept in the respective places; for the averting those sicknesses and diseases, that dearth and scarcity, which justly may be feared from the late immoderate rain and waters: for a thanksgiving also for the blessed change of weather, and the begging the continuance of it to us for our comfort: and likewise for beseeching a blessing upon the high court of parliament now assembled* ([60] pp., Wing C4143)*.
Additional sources: *CJ*, VIII, 262, 266; *LJ*, XI, 269, 272–3, 278; *CSPD, 1661–2*, pp. 5, 426; *The diary of Ralph Josselin, 1616–1683*, ed. Alan Macfarlane (Oxford, 1976), pp. 479–80; Pepys, II, 119–20; Thomas Lathbury, *A history of the convocation of the Church of England* (1853), p. 284.
Printed sermon: Grenfield, House of Commons (Wing G1937, G1937A; ESTC 006109124).

ORDERS

Royal proclamation: 7 June 1661

The Kings most Excellent Majesty taking into His Pious and Princely consideration, that great and immoderate Rains and Waters have lately fallen in the Land, whereupon it may be feared, scarcity, and famine, and sickness, and diseases will ensue, if Almighty God of his great Clemency be not mercifully pleased to avert those Judgements and Punishments, which our many and manifold sins and provocations have justly deserved: And His Majesty having assembled His high Court of Parliament (the Representative Body of this Kingdom) which is now sitting, and being thereto moved by the Petition of both the Houses of Lords and Commons in Parliament, and out of His own Religious disposition readily inclined, hath resolved, and hereby doth Command a general and publick Fast to be kept throughout this whole Kingdom, in such manner as hereafter is directed and prescribed, that so both Prince and People, even the whole Kingdom, as one man, may send up their Prayers and Supplications to

Almighty God, to divert those Judgements which the sins of this Land have worthily deserved, and to continue the blessed change of weather now begun, and to offer up to him their hearty and unfained thanks for this, and other abundant mercies formerly vouchsafed unto them, and to beseech his blessing upon that great Assembly of this Nation, and to prosper their actions and endeavours.

And to the end so Religious an Exercise may be performed with all Decency and Uniformity, His Majesty hath resolved upon a Grave and Religious Form of Solemnizing thereof, which His Royal Pleasure He doth hereby Publish and Declare to all His loving Subjects, And doth Streightly Charge and Command, That on *Wednesday* next being the Twelfth day of this instant *June*, this Fast be Religiously and Solemnly observed and celebrated in the Cities of *London* and *Westminster*, Burrough of *Southwarke*, and other Places adjacent, wherein His Majesty in His Royal Person and with His Royal Family and Houshold, will give Example to the rest of His People; And that on *Wednesday* the Nineteenth day of the same Month of *June*, the like be kept and duly observed throughout the rest of This whole Realm of *England* and Dominion of *Wales*; And for the more Orderly Solemnizing thereof without confusion, His Majesty by the Advice of His Reverend Bishops hath Directed to be Composed, Printed and Published, the Form of such Prayers and Publique Exhortations as He thinketh fit to be used in all Churches and places at these Publique Meetings, and He hath given Charge to His Bishops to Disperse the same throughout the whole Kingdom. All which His Majesty doth expresly Charge and Command shall be Reverendly and Decently performed, by all His loving Subjects, as they tender the favor of Almighty God, and would avoid His just Indignation against this Land, and upon pain of such punishments as His Majesty can justly inflict upon all such as shall contemn or neglect so Religious a Work.

Order of the king in council: 10 June 1661

Our Will and Pleasure is, and We do hereby straightly charge and command, That *This Form of Divine Service* Printed by Our Authority, be read and used upon the twelfth day of this instant *June*, in all the Churches and Chappels within Our Cities of *London* and *Westminster*, and the Suburbs of each, and the Borough of *Southwark*; and upon the Nineteenth day of the same moneth in all Cathedral and Collegiate Churches and Chappels, in all Chappels of Colledges and Halls in both Our Universities, and of Our Colledges of *Eaton* and *Winchester*, and in all Parish Churches and Chappels within Our Kingdom of *England*, Dominion of *Wales*, and Town of *Berwick* upon *Twede*.

FORM OF PRAYER

[Order of the king in council, as above]

PREFACE

[As 1563–E: ... to shew his wrath agaynst sinne, and*]* to call them to repentance, and to the redress of their lives, all men ought to be provoked *[as 1563–E: and styred vp* ... in their distresse of*]* wars and forreign invasions. So did the king and people of *Nineve*, and *Hester [as 1563–*E: fall to humble prayers ... at this present with the*]* plague of rain and waters, whence we cannot but fear scarcity and famine, sicknesses and diseases, unless prevented by his infinite mercy and goodness: It is thought meet to excite and stirr up all godly people within this Realm, to pray earnestly and heartily

to God to forgive us our sins, and consequently to turn away his deserved wrath from us, and to restore us to his gracious favour, by continuing a blessed change of weather, for which also we are now to give thanks unto his holy Name. And likewise we are to beg a blessing upon the high Court of Parliament now assembled, that he would direct all their counsels and endeavours to his own glory, and the honour and prosperity both of King and People. And although it is every Christian mans duty, of his own devotion to pray at all times: yet for that the corrupt nature of man is so slothful and negligent herein, he hath need by often and sundry means to be stirred up and put in remembrance of his duty: For the effectual accomplishment whereof, it is thought meet that this order of Prayer following should at this time be published, being such as shall be used by the Minister in the Church, and may by every man in his private family.

MORNING PRAYER

Let the Minister beginning service, reade with a loud voice one of these sentences of Scripture.
[Joel 2:13; Dan. 9:9–10; Jer. 10:24]

[As 1559 BCP to the Venite*]*

Then shall be said or sung this Hymn following, instead of Venite Exultemus*; whereof one Verse is to be said of the Minister, and another by the People or Clerk.*
O Come, let us humble our selves, and fall down before the Lord, with reverence and fear. (Ps. 95) [95:6–7]
For he is the Lord our God: and we are the people of his Pasture, and the sheep of his Hands.
Let us repent, and turn from our wickedness: and our sins shall be forgiven us. (Acts 3) [3:19]
For we knowledge our faults: and our sins be ever before us. (Ps. 51) [51:3]
We have provoked thine anger, O Lord, thy wrath is waxed hot, and thy heavy displeasure is sore kindled against us. (Lam. 3)
But there is mercy with thee, that thou mayest be feared: and thou art full of compassion
For thy hand is not shortned, that thou canst not help: neither is thy goodness abated, that thou wilt not hear. [Isa. 59:1]
Thou hast promised, O Lord, that afore we cry thou wilt hear us: whilest we yet speak thou wilt have mercy upon us. (Isa. 65) [65:24]
For none that trust in thee shall be confounded: neither any that call upon thee shall be despised.
Our Fathers hoped in thee, they trusted in thee, and thou didst deliver them. (Ps. 22) [22:4–5]
They called upon thee, and were helped: they put their trust in thee, and were not confounded.
O Lord, rebuke not us in thine indignation: neither chasten us in thy heavy displeasure. (Ps. 6) [6:1]
O remember not the sins and offences of our youth: but according to thy mercy think thou upon us, O Lord, for thy goodness. (Ps. 25) [25:6]
For thine own sake, and for thy holy Names sake, incline thine ear, and hear, O merciful Lord. (Dan. 9)

For we do not pour out our prayers before thy face, trusting in our own righteousness: but in thy great and manifold mercies.

Wash us throughly from our wickedness: and cleanse us from our sins. (Ps. 51) [51:2, 9–10]

Turn thy face from our sins, and put out all our misdeeds.

Make us clean hearts, O God: and renue a right spirit within us.

Help us, O God of our salvation, for the glory of thy Name: O deliver us, and be merciful unto our sins for thy Names sake. [Ps. 79:9]

So we that be thy People, and sheep of thy Pasture, shall give thee thanks for ever, and will always be shewing forth thy praise, from generation to generation. (Ps. 79) [79:14]

Glory be to the Father, &c.

[Ps. 32, 90, 107]
[First lesson: Gen. 8]
[Te Deum]
[Second lesson: Luke 21]
[Benedictus]

[Then as 1559 BCP to the end of morning prayer, replacing the collect for the day with]

O eternal God, and most gracious Father, who by the late immoderate Rain and Weather, hast caused us to fear that scarcity and famine, sicknesses and diseases may ensue, and justly fall upon us for our iniquities. We humbly here confess, there can fall nothing so heavy upon us, but we have deserved, even whatsoever thy Law hath threatned against perverse and obstinate sinners. Our contempt of thy Divine Service is great, and we hear thy Word, but obey it not: Our charity to our neighbor is cold, and our devotion to thee is frozen: Religion is by many of us made but a pretence for other ends then thy Service; and there hath been little or no care among us to keep Truth and Peace together, for the preserving of our Church and State. Forgive us, O Lord, forgive us these and all other our grievous and heinous sins, and grant us a true and hearty sorrow and repentance for them all. Send us henceforward light in our understandings, readiness and obedience in our wills, discretion in our words and actions, true, serious and loyal endeavors for the Peace and Prosperity of *Jerusalem*, the Unity and Glory of this Church and State; that so we may love it, and prosper in it, enjoy the blessings both of Heaven and Earth upon it, live in thy grace and favor here, and be filled with thy glory in the life to come, through Jesus Christ our Lord. *Amen.*

O most gracious God, who in the multitude of those fears which were upon us by reason of the late immoderate Rain and Showers, wast pleased at last to clear up the Heavens, and give us hopes of plenty yet to crown the Earth, we bless and praise thy glorious Name, Humbly acknowledging, that as our sins most justly deserved thy wrath and indignation to be poured out upon us, and for our sakes upon the Earth, not onely in dearth and scarcity, but all other calamities; so it is thy mercy onely, and not our deservings, that thou hast thus again comforted and refreshed us. For which we humbly yeeld thee all thanks and glory; beseeching thee, that by our transgressions we may not anew enkindle thy displeasure, to dash our hopes in pieces, and recal thy mercies from us. Grant this, O merciful Father, for Jesus Christ his sake, our onely Lord and Saviour. *Amen.*

LITANY

[As 1559 BCP to the end of the prayer 'We humbly beseech thee']

Almighty and most mercifull Father, who for our many and grievous sins mightest most justly have continued those immoderate raines with which thou didst afflict us, and thereby bring upon us both plagues and sickness, dearth and famine, but in the multitude of thy mercies hast given us better hopes. Accept we most humbly beseech thee our unfeigned sorrow for all our former transgressions, and grant that we may never hereafter so presume of thy mercy, as to despise thy Judgments, but that thy forbearance and long-suffering may lead us to repentance, and amendment of our sinful lives to thy honor and glory, and our eternal Salvation at the last day, through Jesus Christ our Lord. *Amen.*

[The prayers for the king's majesty, for the royal family, for the clergy and people, and for the high court of parliament, all as in 1604 BCP]
O Lord God, who hast justly humbled us by thy late plague of immoderate rain and waters, and in thy mercie hast relieved and comforted our souls by this seasonable and blessed change of weather, we praise and glorifie thy holy name for this thy mercy, and will alwayes declare thy loving kindness from generation to generation, through Jesus Christ our Lord. *Amen.*

[The thanksgiving for peace and deliverance from our enemies, as in 1604 BCP]

[The prayer of St Chrysostom; the grace]

COMMUNION

The Priest standing at the North-side of the Lords Table shall say [as 1559 BCP to the end of the ten commandments]

Almighty God, whose Kingdom is everlasting *[as 1559 BCP]*

[The 1559 BCP collect for Ash Wednesday]

O most mighty God, and merciful Father, who makest thy Sun to rise upon the evil, and upon the good; and sendest Rain on the just, and on the unjust; who sometimes dost punish thy servants also by them both: Grant we beseech thee, that both the immoderate Rain and Waters which have lately faln, and the fair seasonable weather which thou hast since that time given us, may make both of them to our good; that notwithstanding our fears and sins, we may enjoy the fulness of thy mercies, and learn both truly to repent us of our iniquities, and be continually thankful for thy mercies, through Jesus Christ our Lord. *Amen.*

[Epistle: Joel 2:12–26]
[Gospel: Luke 13:1–9]
[Nicene creed]

[Offertory sentence: Matt. 5:16]

[The prayer for the whole state of the church]

O Lord we beseech thee favourably to heare the prayers of thy people, that we which have been justly punished for our offences by the late immoderate raine and waters, being now mercifully delivered by thy goodness, may give thee thanks and praise, through Jesus Christ our Lord. *Amen.*

[The 1559 BCP collect for the twenty-second Sunday after Trinity]

[The collects, 'Assist us mercifully' and 'Almighty God, who hast promised' from 'Collects to be said after the offertory' in 1559 BCP]

[The blessing]

EVENING PRAYER

[Opening sentence: Matt. 3:2]

[Then as 1559 BCP to the psalms]

[Ps. 65, 147, 148]
[First lesson: Gen. 9]
[Magnificat]
[Second lesson: James 5]
[Deus misereatur]

[Then as 1559 BCP, with, in place of the collect for the day, the prayers 'Almighty and most mercifull Father' from the end of the litany and 'O most gracious God, who in the multitude', as at morning prayer]

[The BCP second and third collects at evening prayer]

[The collect 'We humbly beseech thee', from the 1559 BCP litany]

[Then follows the litany above, from the prayer for the king's majesty to the end of the service, omitting the prayer 'O Lord God, who hast justly']

1662–E   Fast days during unseasonable weather and fears of scarcity and sicknesses

Wednesday 15 January 1662 (London, Westminster, Southwark and surrounding area); Wednesday 22 January 1662 (elsewhere in England and Wales)

This fast was prompted by a period of unusually warm winter weather, which it was feared would disrupt farming and bring an outbreak of plague. The king issued his proclamation without having received any formal representations from parliament, which returned from a Christmas adjournment on 7 January. Unlike 1661–E, the proclamation made no reference to the production and distribution of a form of prayer. Nevertheless, a form was produced; as with 1661–E, it followed the 1559 BCP. According to Evelyn, the observance of the fast was immediately followed by a change in the weather.

Orders: royal proclamation, 8 Jan. 1662, Wing C3299*; order of the king in council, 9 Jan. 1662, in the form of prayer.
Form of prayer: *A form of prayer, to be used upon the fifteenth of January, in all churches and chappels within the cities of London and Westminster; the suburbs of each, and the burrough of Southwark, and upon the two and twentieth of the said moneth, in all other churches and chappels within the rest of his majesties dominions of England and Wales, and the town of Berwick upon Twede. Being the several days appointed for a general fast, to be kept in the respective places; for the averting those sicknesses and diseases, that dearth and scarcity, which justly may be feared from the unseasonableness of the weather. Set forth by His Majestie's command* ([56] pp., Wing C4142)*.
Additional sources: *CSPD, 1661–2*, p. 238; *CJ*, VIII, 343; *LJ*, XI, 363; *The diary of Ralph Josselin*, ed. Macfarlane, pp. 484–5; Pepys, III, 10; Evelyn, III, 311–12.

ORDERS

Royal proclamation: 8 January 1662
The Kings most Excellent Majesty, taking into His Pious and Princely Consideration, the present unseasonableness of the Weather, whereupon it may be justly feared, Scarcity and Famine, Sicknesses and Diseases will ensue, if Almighty God of his great Clemency be not mercifully pleased to avert those Judgements and Punishments, which our many and manifold sins and provocations have most justly deserved, hath, out of His own Religious Disposition, resolved, and hereby doth Command *[as 1661–E*: a general and publick Fast ... those Judgements which the*]* sins of this Land have worthily deserved, and to send us such seasonable weather, whereby the Fruits of the Earth may be duely received, and Sicknesses and Contagious Diseases (so justly feared) be prevented.

And to the end so Religious an Exercise may be performed with all decency and uniformity, His Majesty doth hereby (by and with the Advice of His Privy Council) publish and declare to all His loving Subjects, and doth straitly Charge and Command *[as 1661–E*: That on ... (*with changes of date) England and*]* Dominion of *Wales*; And that the same be reverently and decently performed by all His loving Subjects *[as 1626–E*: as they tender ... so religious a Worke*]*.

Order of the king in council: 9 January 1662
[As 1661–E, with change of dates]

FORM OF PRAYER

[Order of the king in council, as above]

PREFACE
[As 1661–E]

MORNING PRAYER

[As 1661–E to the end of the hymn 'O Come, let us humble our selves', then]

[Ps. 32, 36, 90]
[First lesson: Amos 4]
[Te Deum]
[Second lesson: Acts 17:22–34]
[Benedictus]

[Then as 1661–E to the end of the service, replacing the collect for the day with]
O eternal God, and most gracious Father, who by this strange and unseasonable Weather, causest us to fear *[as 1661–E: that Scarcity and Famine … is cold, and our]* devotion to thee is frozen: Our unthankfulness to thee is very great; and we have not been throughly sensible, either of thy mercies, or thy judgments. Religion is by many of us *[as 1661–E: made but a pretence … repentance for them all]*. Send us henceforward light in our Understandings, that we may rightly apprehend thy dealings towards us; readiness and obedience in our Wills, that we may express in our lives, a due sence of thy goodness and special providence over us, True, serious and loyal endeavors *[as 1661–E: for the Peace and Prosperity … Amen]*.

O Lord God, in whom we live, and move, and have our being; thou hast preserved us hitherto, and held our souls in life: Yet givest us cause to fear, by this unseasonable weather, that Sickness and Mortality may ere long take us away: We therefore humbly beseech thee, that thou wouldst send us such wholsome Seasons, that we may continue in health, and strength, and safety, and use them all to thy honor and glory, through Jesus Christ our Lord. *Amen.*

LITANY

[As 1559 BCP to the end of the prayer 'We humbly beseech thee']

Almighty and most mercifull Father, we confess that for our many and grievous sins, thou mightest most justly punish us with the continuance of unseasonable and unwholsom weather, and thereby bring upon us noisom diseases, dearth and famine; But we most humbly beseech thee to accept our unfeigned sorrow *[as 1661–E: for all our former transgressions … Amen]*.

[The 1604 BCP prayer for parliament; the 1604 BCP prayer for peace and deliverance from enemies]

[The prayer of St Chrysostom; the grace]

COMMUNION

[As 1661–E to end of the collect for Ash Wednesday (1559 text)]

[The prayer 'O Lord God, in whom we live, and move', as at morning prayer]

[As 1661–E from the epistle to the end of the prayer for the whole state of the church]

[The BCP collect for the fourth Sunday in Lent (1559 text); the BCP collect for the twenty-second Sunday after Trinity (1559 text)]

[Then as 1661–E from 'Assist us mercifully' to the end of the service]

EVENING PRAYER

[As 1661–E to the psalms]

[Ps. 65, 107, 147]
[First lesson: Ezek. 14]
[Magnificat]
[Second lesson: James 4]

[Then as 1661–E to the collect of the day, in place of which are the special collects prescribed in place of the collect for the day at morning prayer]

[Then as 1661–E to the end of the service]

1665–E   Fast day after the outbreak of the second Anglo-Dutch war

Wednesday 5 April 1665 (England and Wales)

The commercial rivalry between England and the Netherlands resulted in growing calls for war during 1664. Preparations gathered pace over the winter, and on 22 February 1665, Charles II issued a declaration condemning various hostile actions of the Dutch and allowing English ships to attack Dutch vessels in retaliation. On 28 February, the Commons resolved to ask the king to appoint a fast day for a divine blessing on the fleet. The Lords concurred with this resolution on 1 March, and members of both houses waited on the king that evening, gaining his assent to the fast.

This was the first form of prayer to be composed following the passage of the Act of Uniformity in May 1662, requiring the use of the revised Book of Common Prayer of 1662. Accordingly, this and all subsequent forms of prayer in England and Wales are based on the 1662 BCP.

Order: royal proclamation, 6 Mar. 1665, Wing C3300*.
Form of prayer: *A form of common prayer to be used on Wednesday the 5th of April, being the day of the general fast appointed by his majesties proclamation, for imploring Gods blessing on his majesties naval forces. Set forth by his majesties authority* ([68] pp., Wing C4115; BL, 3407.c.37(1)).
Additional sources: *His majesties declaration* (1664[/5]; Wing C2950); *CJ*, VIII, 611–12; *LJ*, XI, 672–4; *CSPD, 1664–5*, pp. 242–3; Pepys, VI, 50, 73; Evelyn, III, 404–5; Robert Wigam to ?, postmarked 11 Apr. 1665, Tanner 45, fo. 3r.

ORDER

Royal proclamation: 6 March 1665

The Kings most Excellent Majesty having not had any the least satisfaction (although often demanded) from the States of the *United Provinces*, for several Injuries done to Himself and His people; but on the contrary is advertised of their great Preparations for War, and that they are resolved what they have done by Wrong, to maintain by Arms. And His Majesty being thereby forced for the just Defence and Vindication of the Rights of Himself and His Subjects, to prepare and set out Naval Forces; and being moved by the humble desire of both Houses of Lords and Commons lately Assembled in Parliament, and out of His Religious Disposition readily inclined, Hath Resolved, and doth hereby Command a General and Publick Fast to be kept through this whole Kingdom, in such manner as is hereafter directed and prescribed; that so both Prince and People may send up their Prayers and Supplications to Almighty God, for imploring His Blessing on His Majesties Forces imployed in this present Expedition. And for the more decent and uniform performance thereof, His Majesty doth hereby publish and declare to all His loving Subjects, and doth straightly charge and command, That on Wednesday the Fifth of *April* next, this Fast be Religiously and solemnly observed and kept throughout this whole Realm of *England*, Dominion of *Wales*, and Town of *Berwick* upon *Twede*.

And for the more orderly solemnizing thereof, His Majesty hath directed to be Composed, Printed and Published (by and with the advice of His Reverend Bishops) a Form of Prayers to be used in all Churches and Places at these Publick Meetings; and hath given charge to the Bishops for the dispersing thereof throughout their several Dioceses in the whole Kingdom. And His Majesty doth expresly charge and command, That the said Fasting and Prayers be Soberly, Reverently, and Decently performed by all His loving Subjects, as they tender the Favour of Almighty God, and upon pain of such punishments as His Majesty can justly inflict upon all such as shall contemn, or neglect so Religious a Work.

FORM OF PRAYER

MORNING PRAYER

Let him that ministreth read with a loud voice, one or more of these sentences of Scripture, and then say the Exhortation that followeth
[Joel 2:13; Dan. 9:9–10; Jer. 10:24].

[As 1662 BCP to the Venite*]*

Instead of the Venite exultemus, *shall be sung or said this Hymn following; one Verse by the Priest, and another by the Clerk and people.*
O Come let us humble our selves before the Lord: and fall down before him with reverence and fear. (Ps. 95:6)
For he is the Lord our God: and we are the people of his pasture, and the sheep of his hands. (Ps. 95:7)
Let us repent, and turn from our wickedness: and our sins shall be forgiven us. (Acts 3:19)
For this shall every one that is godly, make his prayer unto thee, O Lord: in a time when thou mayest be found. (Ps. 32:7.)
In my trouble I will call upon the Lord, and complain unto my God: so shall I be safe from mine enemies. (Ps. 18:2)
So shall he hear my voice out of his holy temple: and my complaint shall come before him, it shall enter even into his ears. (Ps. 18:6)
Hear my prayer, O God: and let my crying come unto thee. (Ps. 102:1)
Thou art my King, O God: send help unto Jacob. (Ps. 44:5)

Through thee will we overthrow our enemies: and in thy Name will we tread them under, that rise up against us. (Ps. 44:6)

For I will not trust in my bow: it is not my sword that shall help me. (Ps. 44:7)

But it is thou that savest us from our enemies: and puttest them to confusion, that hate us. (Ps. 44:8)

There is no King that can be saved by the multitude of an Host: neither is any mighty man delivered by much strength. (Ps. 33:15)

Therefore in thee, O Lord, have I put my trust: let me never be put to confusion; deliver me in thy righteousness. (Ps. 31:1)

Bow down thine ear to me, and save me: make haste to deliver me. (Ps. 31:2)

I will love thee, O Lord my strength; the Lord is my stony rock, and my defence: my Saviour, my God, and my might, in whom I will trust, my buckler, the horn also of my salvation, and my refuge. (Ps. 18:1)

Behold the eye of the Lord is upon them that fear him: and upon them that put their trust in his mercy. (Ps. 33:17)

O be favourable and gracious unto Sion: build thou the walls of Jerusalem. (Ps. 51:18)

Let thy merciful kindness, O Lord, be upon us: like as we do put our trust in thee. (Ps. 33:25)

Glory be to the Father, and to the Son: and to the holy Ghost.

As it was in the beginning, is now, and ever shall be: world without end. Amen.

[Ps. 3, 27, 28, 46]
[First lesson: Isa. 58]
[Te Deum]
[Second lesson: Luke 21]
[Benedictus]

[Then as 1662 BCP to the Lord's prayer]

Priest: O Lord shew thy mercy upon us.
Answer: And grant us thy salvation.
Priest: O Lord save the King.
Answer: And mercifully hear us when we call upon thee.
Priest: O Lord save thy servants,
Answer: Who do put their trust in thee.
Priest: Send us help from thy holy place;
Answer: And evermore mightily defend us.
Priest: Let the enemy have no advantage over us:
Answer: Nor the wicked approach to hurt us.
Priest: Be unto us, O Lord, a strong Tower,
Answer: From the face of our enemies.
Priest: O Lord hear our prayer,
Answer: And let our cry come unto thee.
Priest: Indue thy Ministers with righteousness.
[As 1662 BCP to the end of the suffrages]

Instead of the first Collect at Morning Prayer shall these two be used.
    O most glorious, and powerful Lord God, who alone hast spread out the heavens,

and compassed the waters with bounds, until night and day come to an end; at whose command the winds blow, and who rulest the raging of the sea; Thou art terrible in all thy works of wonder, the great God to be feared above all. We therefore adore thy divine Majesty, acknowledging thy power, and imploring thy goodness. Be pleased to receive into thine Almighty and most gracious protection the persons of thy servants that fight for us, and the Ships and Navies in which they serve: preserve them all from the dangers of the sea, and from the violence of the enemy, and from every sad accident: that they may be a safe-guard to our most gracious Soveraign, and his Kingdoms, and a security for such as pass on the seas upon their lawful occasions. Help, Lord, and save them for thy mercies sake; that they may return in safety, with honour and victory, and good success, to enjoy the blessings of the land, and the fruit of their labours; and that all the inhabitants of these Islands, being blest with plenty and prosperity, peace and quietness, may serve thee our God in righteousness, and true holiness, and with a thankful remembrance of all thy mercies may ever praise and glorifie thy holy Name, through Jesus Christ our Lord. *Amen.*

[The 1662 BCP prayer in time of war]

[Then as 1662 BCP to the end of morning prayer]

LITANY

[As 1662 BCP to the end of the prayer 'We humbly beseech thee'; then the BCP collect for Ash Wednesday, and then, from the BCP commination service, the prayers 'O Lord, we beseech thee mercifully hear our prayers', 'O most mighty God and merciful Father' and 'Turn thou us, O good Lord'. Then]

O almighty God, and our most gracious Father, the Soveraign Commander of all the world, in whose hand is power, and might, which none is able to withstand: Thou art the Lord of hosts, the God of battels, and the strength of all Nations. If thou keepest not the City, and the Kingdom, the watchman waketh but in vain: Nor can victory wait upon the justest Designs, upon the wisest Counsels, upon the strongest Armies, unless thou teachest their hands to war, and their fingers to fight. Thou art the steddy Hope of all the ends of the earth; and of them which remain in the broad Sea. Go forth, we humbly beseech thee, at this time by thy more especial assistance with His Majesties Fleet, and Naval Forces, and bless them all. Let thy mercies fill their Sails with prosperous gales, and thine Almighty power be their sure Anchor-hold, thy good Providence their Shield, and their impregnable Defence. In all their Counsels let Wisdom lead them; in all their Enterprises Courage assist them; and thy blessing every where crown them with victory, and good success: That so they may at last bring back Honour to our Soveraign; safety and strength to these His Kingdoms; and to all his Subjects plenty and prosperity and a lasting peace: and finally that by these, and all thy mercies we may be still more engaged to a true and real thankfulness to thee our God, such as may appear in our lives by an humble, holy, and obedient walking before thee all our days. Grant this, O merciful Father, for thy Son Jesus Christ his sake. *Amen.*

[The prayer of St Chrysostom; the grace]

COMMUNION

[As 1662 BCP to the end of the ten commandments]

Almighty God, whose kingdom is everlasting *[as 1662 BCP]*

[Then, in place of the collect for the day, the special collects prescribed for morning prayer]

[Epistle: Eph. 6:10–18]
[Gospel: Matt. 5:1–12]
[Nicene creed; the sermon]
[Offertory sentences: Matt. 5:16; Matt. 6:19–20]

[The prayer for the whole state of the church]

We humbly acknowledge before thee, O merciful Father, that all the punishments threatened in thy Law against sinners might justly fall upon us by reason of our manifold transgressions; and especially our great unthankfulness for thy late unspeakable mercies towards us. But though our crying sins call aloud for thy wrath, and vengeance to be poured down upon us; yet there is mercy with thee, O Lord, that thou mayest be feared; and with thee our God there is plenteous Redemption. Oh enter not into Judgement with thy servants: For if thou shouldst be extreme to mark what we have done amiss; O Lord, who would be able to abide it? At the Footstool of the Throne of thy Grace we prostrate our souls, and bodies with fasting, tears and supplications. Look down graciously upon us, we humbly beseech thee, from the habitation of thy Holiness, and of thy Glory; and for the all-satisfying Death, and Passion of thy blessed Son accept this our unfeigned Submission, and Humiliation. O deliver us from all our sins; and then our enemies cannot hurt us. Let us ever remember, what thou hast so strictly enjoyn'd,[345] That when the Host goeth forth against our enemies, we should then especially keep our selves from every wicked thing. Unite our hearts, that we may fear thy Name; and then we need not fear, what Man can do unto us. O let our ways be such, as may please Thee, that Thou mayest make even our enemies to be at Peace with us here; and when we have accomplish'd our Warfare upon earth, maist admit us to the blessed Vision of everlasting Peace in thine own glorious presence, through his Merit, and Mediation, who is both the Lord of Hosts, and the Prince of Peace, Jesus Christ our Lord and blessed Saviour. *Amen.*

O God the Protector of all, that trust in Thee, without whom nothing is strong, nothing is holy; who knowest us to be set in the midst of so many, and so great dangers, and seest, that we have no power of our selves to help our selves: Mercifully look upon our infirmities; Raise up thy power, and come among us, and with great might succour us: and in all our dangers and necessities stretch forth the right hand of thy Majesty to help, and defend us against all our enemies. Look, we pray thee, upon the hearty desires of thy humble servants; Encrease, and multiply upon us thy mercies; that we, who for our evil deeds do worthily deserve to be punished, by the comfort of thy Grace may mercifully be relieved: and that Thou being our Saviour and Deliverer,

---

[345]   In margin: 'Deut. 23.9.'

our Ruler, and our Guide, we may so pass the waves of this troublesom World, that finally we may come to the land of everlasting life, there to reign with Thee world without end, through Jesus Christ our Lord. *Amen.*

Almighty God, who has promised *[as BCP, followed by the blessing]*

EVENING PRAYER

[The rubric as in morning prayer, followed by the opening sentences: Joel 2:13; Dan. 9:9–10; Jer. 10:24]

[Then as 1662 BCP to the psalms, before which is inserted the prayer to be used in place of the Venite *at morning prayer]*

[Ps. 90, 91, 144]
[First lesson: Exod. 17:8–16]
[Magnificat]
[Second lesson: Heb. 11]
[Deus misereatur]

[Then as 1662 BCP from the Apostles' creed to the suffrages after the Lord's prayer, which are those used at morning prayer]

[The special collects prescribed in place of the collect for the day at morning prayer; the 1662 BCP second and third collects for evening prayer; the 1662 BCP collect for Ash Wednesday; then, from the BCP commination service, the prayers 'O Lord, we beseech thee mercifully hear our prayers', 'O Most mighty God and merciful Father' and 'Turn thou us, O good Lord']

[As 1662 BCP from the prayer for the king to the prayer for the clergy and people]

[The special prayer at the end of the litany, 'O Almighty God', followed by the special prayer 'O God' the Protector of all in the communion service]

[The prayer of St Chrysostom; the grace]

1665–S1   Fast day after the outbreak of the second Anglo-Dutch war

Wednesday 7 June 1665 (Scotland)

The outbreak of war against the Dutch occasioned the first Scottish fast appointed by the crown after the restoration (for the war, see 1665–E). James Sharp, archbishop of St Andrews, who had evidently seen the proclamation for 1665–E, proposed that the king's Scottish secretary, the earl of Lauderdale, ask Charles II to order a fast in Scotland. The resulting proclamation, which referred to Lauderdale's 'humble motion' to the king, was written at court in London and sent to the privy council in Edinburgh with instructions for its publication. The bishops, reintroduced to the church in 1661 and 1662, were to inform parish ministers of the fast. The bishop of Galloway distributed copies of the proclamation to his clergy at a synod meeting on 17 May, requiring them to preach twice on the day. The presbytery of Dingwall recorded an instruction from the bishop of Ross to announce the fast to their congregations. According to the historian Robert Wodrow, the few presbyterian clergy who continued to possess parish churches observed the day, expanding at length in their sermons on Scotland's sinfulness. It is unclear to what extent the fast was kept by lay presbyterians who did not conform to the established church, though the occasion seems to have been observed by some dissenters in Edinburgh. When proposing the fast to Lauderdale, Sharp wanted to issue a form of prayer for the occasion, but, he wrote, 'the condition of the tym, and temper of the people will not admitt of it' (NLS, MS 2512, fo. 72r.).

Orders: royal proclamation, 3 May 1665, Wing C3310A* [also in *RPC*, 3rd ser., II, 42–3; Wodrow, *History*, I, 420]; privy council order, 3 May 1665, *RPC*, 3rd ser., II, 43.
Additional sources: Archbishop James Sharp of St Andrews to earl of Lauderdale, 29 Mar., 15 May 1665, NLS, MS 2512, fos. 72r, 74r; *The register of the synod of Galloway, from October 1664 to April 1671* (Kirkcudbright, 1856), p. 24; *Edin. recs., 1655 to 1665*, p. 369; Robert Mein to Henry Muddiman, 10 June 1665, *CSPD, 1664–5*, p. 418; Wodrow, *History*, I, 420–1; *Alford exercise*, p. 65; *Inverness and Dingwall records*, p. 310; Nicoll, p. 434; Lamont, p. 179.

ORDERS

Royal proclamation: 3 May 1665
Forasmuch as We, by the great injuries and provocations from the States of the *United Provinces*, have been forced, for the just defence and vindication of Our Own and Our Subjects Rights, to prepare and set out Naval Forces, and to engage into a War upon most important reasons of Honour and Justice: And We, out of Our religious disposition, being readily inclined to approve of an humble motion made to Us, for commanding a general Fast to be kept throughout this Our whole Kingdom, for imploring the blessing of Almighty GOD upon Our Councils and Forces imployed in this expedition; Have thought fit, by this Our Proclamation, to indict a general and publick Fast and day of Humiliation, for the end foresaid. Our Will is herefore, and We straitly Command and Charge, that the said Fast be religiously and solemnly kept throughout this Our whole Kingdom, by all Our Subjects and People within the same, upon the first Wednesday of *June*, being the seventh day thereof: Requiring hereby the Reverend Archbishops and Bishops, to give notice hereof to the Ministers in their respective Dioceses, that upon the Lords-day immediatly preceeding the said seventh day of *June*, they cause read this Our Proclamation from the Pulpit in every Paroch Church; and that they exhort all Our loving Subjects to a sober and devout performance of the said Fasting and Humiliation, as they tender the favour of Almighty GOD, the duty they owe to Us, and the peace and preservation of their Country; Certifying all those who shall contemn or neglect such a religious and necessary work, they shall be proceeded against, and punished as contemners of Our Authority, and persons disaffected to the Honour and Safety of their Countrey.

Privy council order: 3 May 1665
The above-wrytten proclamation, with his Majesties letter to his Commissioner authorising his Grace to publish the same in his Majesties name, being this day read in presence of the Lords of Privy Councill, they ordaine the same to be printed and published at the mercat croce of Edinburgh and other places neidfull that none pretend ignorance.

1665–EIr1   Thanksgiving days for naval victory at the battle of Lowestoft

Tuesday 20 June 1665 (London, Westminster, Southwark and surrounding area); Tuesday 4 July 1665 (elsewhere in England and Wales; Ireland)

The English and Dutch navies engaged in battle off Lowestoft on 1–4 June 1665. Samuel Pepys hailed this a 'great victory, never known in the world' (Pepys, VI, 123). A royal proclamation appointing this thanksgiving was issued on 14 June. Yet the confrontation was highly damaging to the English fleet and, although the Dutch navy withdrew on the arrival of English reinforcements, the battle was not decisive. Gilbert Burnet claimed that celebrating a thanksgiving after the encounter was 'a horrid mocking of God, and a lying to the world' (*History*, I, 420). Like the thanksgiving 1660–E2, but unlike the recent fast days, there was an explicit instruction that the proclamation for this thanksgiving was to be read in churches on a Sunday preceding the thanksgiving day. The privy council ordered that charitable collections made on the thanksgiving day be donated to victims of the plague, which had appeared in London (see 1665–EIr2). News of the battle prompted celebrations in Dublin: on 16 June, the lord deputy attended a crowded service in Christ Church Cathedral. On 22 June, the lord deputy and council issued a proclamation for a national thanksgiving. Because this proclamation was based closely on the English order, it seems that the lord deputy acted on instructions from England. In common with the other surviving orders for Irish observances before 1679, however, the proclamation made no reference to a form of prayer. Presumably no special form was used.

Orders: ENGLAND AND WALES: royal proclamation, 14 June 1665, Wing C3312*; IRELAND: proclamation by the lord deputy and council, 22 June 1665, Wing I616*.
Form of prayer: ENGLAND AND WALES: *A form of common prayer, with thanksgiving, for the late victory by his majesties naval forces: appointed to be used in and about London, on Tuesday the twentieth of June; and through all England, on Tuesday the fourth of July. Set forth by his majesties authority* ([64] pp., Wing C4120)*; IRELAND: none ordered.
Additional sources: privy council register, PRO, PC2/58, fo. 89v; *CSPD, 1664–5*, p. 426; J. Knight to Williamson, 16 July 1665, Sir Robert Bradshaigh to Williamson, 21 July 1665, *CSPD, 1664–5*, pp. 478, 484–5; Pepys, VI, 117–19, 121–3, 129–30, 132; Burnet, *History*, I, 419–20; Bishop John Hacket of Coventry and Lichfield to Archbishop Gilbert Sheldon of Canterbury, 17 June 1665, Tanner 45, fo. 13r; *CSPI, 1663–5*, p. 592; ? to Joseph Williamson, 17 June 1665, *CSPI, 1663–5*, p. 592; Sir George Rawdon to Viscount Conway and Killultagh, 1 July, 4 July 1665, *CSPI, 1663–5*, pp. 602–3.
Printed sermons: Dolben, court (Wing D1832); Ford, Northampton (Wing F1504).

ORDERS

England and Wales: royal proclamation, 14 June 1665
Whereas it hath pleased Almighty God in his late Providence towards Us and Our People, to manifest at once the glory both of his Power and Mercy, in giving Us a happy Victory over Our Adversaries at Sea, filling the hearts of Us and Our People as full of joy and thankfulness, as becomes so transcendent a Mercy; We cannot upon the due consideration hereof, but with all humility admire and adore the mercy and goodness of God in this his signal manifestation thereof; and We look upon it as an invitation from Heaven to Us and all Our People unto most entire thankfulness for the same. And to the end some Solemn time may be set apart for the publick performance

of this Duty; and that We and all Our Subjects in *England* and *Wales*, and the Town of *Berwick* upon *Tweed*, may pay Our just tribute of Praise and Thanksgiving to Almighty God, We do hereby Publish and Declare, and also strictly Charge and Command, That *Tuesday* the Twentieth day of this instant *June* be set apart and observed as a day of Publick Thanksgiving in the Cities of *London* and *Westminster*, Borough of *Southwark*, and other places adjacent. And that *Tuesday* the Fourth of *July* next, the like be kept and duely observed through the rest of this whole Realm of *England*, and Dominion of *Wales*. And for the more orderly performance thereof, We by the advice of Our Reverend Bishops, have directed to be Composed, Printed and Published, the Forms of such Prayers and publick Thanksgivings, as We have thought fit to be used in all Churches and places at these publick Meetings; and have given charge to Our Bishops to disperse the same throughout the whole Kingdom. And We do also direct and appoint, That this Our Proclamation be publickly read in all Churches and Chappels, on some Lords-day precedent to the said days of Thanksgiving hereby appointed, to the end that notice may be taken thereof, and due thanks and praise may upon the said days be offered up unto Almighty God; And that humble supplications be poured out before him for his continual assistance, and improvement of this and all his mercies to the honour of his great Name, and the peace and benefit of Us and Our People; Willing and strictly Commanding all persons within Our said Realm and Dominions, with all sobriety, reverence, and thankfulness to observe this day, as becomes so solemn an occasion.

Ireland: proclamation by the lord deputy and council, 22 June 1665

Whereas it hath pleased Almighty God in his late Providence towards His Majestie and His people, to manifest at once the glory both of his power and mercy, in giving His Majestie a happy Victory over His Adversaries at Sea, filling the hearts of His Majestie and His people as full of joy and thankfulness, as becomes so transcendent a Mercy: We cannot upon due consideration thereof, but with all humility admire and adore the Mercy and Goodness of God in this His Signal manifestation thereof. And We look upon it as an invitation from Heaven to His Majestie and all His people unto most intire thankfulness for the same. And to the end some solemn time may be set apart for the publick performance of this Duty; and that We and all His Majesties Subjects throughout this Kingdom, may pay our just tribute of praise and thanksgiving to Almighty God; We do hereby publish and declare, and also strictly charge and command, That *Tuesday* the Fourth day of *July* next, be set apart and observed as a day of publick Thanksgiving, in and throughout this His Majesties Kingdom of *Ireland*. And We do also direct and appoint, That this Our Proclamation be publickly read in all Churches and Chappels on the Lords Day precedent to the said day of Thanksgiving hereby appointed; to the end that notice may be taken thereof, and due thanks and praise may upon the said day be offered unto Almighty God. And that humble supplications be poured out before him, for his continual assistance and improvement of this, and all his mercies to the honour of his great Name, and the peace and benefit of His Majestie and His people, willing and strictly commanding all persons within this His Majesties Kingdom of *Ireland*, with all sobriety, reverence and thankfulness to observe that day, as becomes so solemn an occasion.

FORM OF PRAYER

England and Wales

MORNING PRAYER

Let him that ministreth read with a loud voice these sentences of Scripture; and then say the Exhortation that followeth.
[1 Tim. 2:1–3]

[As BCP to the Venite*]*

In stead of Venite exultemus *shall be sung or said this Hymn following; one Verse by the Priest, and another by the Clerk and people.*

Not unto us, O Lord, not unto us: but unto thy Name be the praise. (Ps. 115:1)
Unto thee, O God, do we give thanks: yea unto thee do we give thanks. (Ps. 75:1)
For great things are they, that thou hast done: O God, who is like unto thee? (Ps. 71:17)
Thou art the God, that doth wonders: Who is so great a God as our God? (Ps. 77:14, 13)
The Lord hath done great things for us: yea the Lord hath done great things for us, for which we rejoyce. (Ps. 126:3–4)
Thou art our King, O God: the Help that is done upon earth, thou do'st it thy self. (Ps. 44:5, 74.13)
Through thee have we overthrown our enemies: and in thy Name have we trod them under, that rise up against us. (Ps. 44:6)
For I will not trust in my bow: it is not my sword that shall help me. (Ps. 44:7)
But it is thou, that savest us from our enemies: and puttest them to confusion, that hate us. (Ps. 44:8)
We gat not the Victory through our own sword: neither was it our own arm, that helped us; (Ps. 44:3)
But thy right hand, and thy arm, and the light of thy countenance: because thou hadst a favour unto us. (Ps. 44:4)
If the Lord had not been on our side (now may we say:) if the Lord himself had not been on our side, when men rose up against us; (Ps. 124:1)
They had swallowed us up quick: when they were so wrathfully displeased at us. (Ps. 124:2)
Yea, the waters had drowned us: the deep waters of the proud had gone even over our souls. (Ps. 124:3–4)
But praised be the Lord: who hath not given us over as a prey unto their teeth. (Ps. 124:5)
Our help standeth in the Name of the Lord: who hath made heaven and earth. (Ps. 124:7)
God hath shewed us his goodness plenteously: and God hath let us see our desire upon our enemies. (Ps. 59:10)
Therefore will we offer in his dwelling an oblation with great gladness: we will sing praises unto the Lord. (Ps. 27:7)
Let Heaven and Earth praise him: the Sea, and All that moveth therein. (Ps. 69:35)

Sing unto God, O ye Kingdoms of the earth: O sing praises unto the Lord. (Ps. 68:32)
Ascribe unto the Lord, O ye kindreds of the people: ascribe unto the Lord worship and power. (Ps. 96:7)
Ascribe unto the Lord the honour due unto his Name: bring presents, and come into his courts. (Ps. 96:8)
O love the Lord, all ye his saints: for the Lord preserveth them that are faithful, and plenteously rewardeth the proud doer. (Ps. 31:26)
Blessed be the Lord our God from everlasting, and world without end: and let all the people say Amen. (Ps. 106:46)
Glory be to the Father, and to the Son: and to the holy Ghost;
As it was in the beginning, is now, and ever shall be: world without end. Amen.

[Ps. 29, 33, 46]
[First lesson: Exod. 15:1–20]
[Te Deum]
[Second lesson: 1 Pet. 2]
[Benedictus]

[Then as BCP to the end of the suffrages after the Lord's prayer]

In stead of the first Collect at Morning Prayer shall these two be used.

O almighty God, the soveraign Commander of all the world, in whose hand is power and might which none is able to withstand; We bless and magnifie thy great and glorious Name for this happy victory, the whole glory whereof we do ascribe to thee, who art the only giver of victory. And, we beseech thee, give us grace to improve this great mercy to thy glory, the advancement of thy Gospel, the honour of our Soveraign, and, as much as in us lieth, to the good of all mankind. And, we beseech thee, give us such a sense of this great mercy, as may engage us to a true thankfulness, such as may appear in our lives by an humble, holy, and obedient walking before thee all our days, through Jesus Christ our Lord: To whom with thee and the holy Spirit, as for all thy mercies, so in particular for this victory and deliverance, be all glory and honour world without end. *Amen.*

[The BCP thanksgiving for peace and deliverance from our enemies]

[Then as BCP to the end of morning prayer]

LITANY

[As BCP to the end of the prayer 'We humbly beseech thee']

O most gracious and glorious Lord God, who by thy great power hast made, and by thine infinite wisdom dost dispose and order all things, the Protectour of those that trust in thee, and their Deliverer in time of their distress: Our Enemies compassed us about on every side, but thou hast also compassed us about with deliverance; They were many, and did rage horribly, but thou, O Lord, who dwellest on high art mightier; They intended that mischief, which through thy goodness to us they were not able to perform; And when they had marked us out for ruine, thou didst then bring upon them swift destruction. Out of the deep of the Sea we cried unto thee, O Lord, and thou didst hear us out of the depth of thy mercy, which hath more prevailed with thee to save us, than our many great sins to destroy us. We acknowledge and confess, O our God, that it is not our own strength that hath helped us, nor the number of our Ships, nor the courage of our Souldiers, nor yet the conduct of our Commanders, but thy alone wisdom and power that hath defeated the counsels and broken the strength of our Adversaries in pieces. It is thine own right hand that purchased us this Victory, a Victory beyond all example great and glorious, compleat and cheap, in the preservation of our Ships, and sparing of our persons. We want words to express our thankfulness, and thoughts to conceive the greatness of these thy manifold Deliverances which thou hast wrought for us; yet be thou pleased to accept the best praises that we can give, which we desire now to render unto thee from the bottom of our souls; and grant, O Lord, that we may never forget this thy wonderful blessing, which thou hast vouchsafed not onely to us, but to all our succeeding generations, that it may still prove an incitement unto us to obey and serve thee in holiness of life; and that improving this Victory to thy glory and our own good, we may obtain the like happy success in all our future Enterprizes, to the glory of thy Name, through Jesus Christ our onely Saviour and Deliverer. *Amen.*

Then shall follow this Prayer, which shall be used continually so long as the Navy is abroad.
    O most glorious, and powerful Lord God *[as 1665–E]*

[The prayer of St Chrysostom; the grace]

COMMUNION

[As BCP to the end of the ten commandments]

Almighty God, whose kingdom is everlasting *[as BCP]*

[Then, in place of the collect for the day, the special collects prescribed for morning prayer]

[Epistle: Phil. 4:4–9]
[Gospel: Matt. 5:43–8]
[Nicene creed; the sermon]
[Offertory sentences: Matt. 5:16; Matt. 7:12]

[The prayer for the whole state of the church]

O Lord God of our salvation, without whose Aids and Influence all our Strength is Weakness, our Courage Rashness, and our Counsel Folly; We thy unworthy Servants, the sinful People of these three Nations, (whom by thy miraculous Providence thou didst lately rescue from the Miseries of a Civil War at home, & hast now crowned with Victory against a potent Enemy abroad) in grateful acknowledgement of thy so great, and often-repeated Mercies, are here now before thee with humble, yet inflamed hearts, desirous to offer up unto thee our Sacrifice of praise and thanks; calling Heaven and Earth to witness with us, that as it was the Miracle of thy meer Mercy, which raised us out of the depth of those miserable Confusions, in which we lay; So it is thy Power alone, O our God, by which we stand; thy good Providence, by which we prosper. More particularly, with the highest expressions of our devoutest hearts we magnifie thy great and glorious Name, O Lord our God, for that eminent, and most remarkable Victory, wherewith thou hast lately so wonderfully blest the Arms and Naval Forces of our gracious Soveraign. O continue forth thy loving kindness towards him: Let thy tender Mercies prevent, and follow him all the days of his life: Let his Reign be prosperous, and his Arms victorious; & let the blessings of safety and happy success attend all those that fight his Battels. Subdue more and more unto him the People that is under him, and the Nations under his feet. Preserve him from the gathering together of the froward, and from the Insurrection of the evil doers. Let no weapon that is form'd against him prosper; but make Him and His always to return with Honour, and Victory, and Joy, and Triumph. O let all the Blessings of Heaven and Earth be poured out upon the sacred Head of thine Anointed, and from thence flow down even to the skirts of the meanest of his People, in Peace, and Plenty, and Prosperity: That so both Prince and People may with one mind, and with one mouth glorifie thee, O God most gracious, for this thy unspeakable goodness; not onely presenting thee (as this day) the fruit of the lips, giving thanks unto thy Name, but also through the entire course of a holy life ever offering up unto thee Souls and Bodies, which thou hast created, redeemed and preserved, to be a living and holy Sacrifice acceptable unto thee through Jesus Christ: To whom with thee, O Father Almighty, in the unity of the holy Ghost, be glory in the Church throughout all Ages world without end. *Amen.*

Almighty God, who hast promised *[as BCP, followed by the blessing]*

EVENING PRAYER

[The rubric as in morning prayer, followed by the opening sentence: 1 Tim. 2:1–3]

[Then as BCP to the psalms, before which is inserted the prayer to be used in place of the Venite *at morning prayer]*

[Ps. 66, 92, 147]
[First lesson: 1 Sam. 2:1–10]
[Magnificat]
[Second lesson: 1 Thess. 5]
[Cantate Domino]

[Then as BCP from the Apostles' creed to the suffrages after the Lord's prayer]

[The special collects prescribed in place of the collect for the day at morning prayer; the BCP second and third collects for evening prayer]

[As BCP from the prayer for the king to the prayer for the clergy and people]

[The special prayer at the end of the communion service 'O Lord God of our salvation', followed by the prayer 'O most glorious and powerful Lord God' to 'be used continually so long as the Navy is abroad']

[The prayer of St Chrysostom; the grace]

1665–EIr2   Monthly fast days and weekly prayers during the plague epidemic

Wednesday 12 July 1665 (London, Westminster and bills of mortality);
Wednesday 2 August 1665 and the first Wednesday of each month following
(England and Wales; Ireland); prayers every Wednesday [until November
1666 (1666–E)]

After some years of low infection rates, a plague epidemic afflicted London and other parts of southern England during 1665. A few deaths were reported in December 1664; during the spring, the disease spread, initially in London's western out-parishes. On 5 July, the privy council ordered the bishop of London to give notice to parishes within the bills of mortality of the first fast day; an order by the bishop to this effect was inserted in some copies of the form of prayer. The form of prayer drew heavily on those used for earlier fasts during epidemics of the plague (see 1603–E and 1625–E), going back ultimately to 1563–E. But some significant changes were made. Most notably, in 1665 the fast was ordered to be observed monthly; during all previous major outbreaks there had been weekly fasts. Perhaps as a consequence of this, the 'order of the fast' was moved from the end of the form of prayer to the beginning and was amended to include an announcement, to be read by ministers in church on the Sunday before each fast day, giving notice to the congregation. Otherwise, the text of the 'order of the fast' had one notable amendment – the omission of the anti-puritan 'admonition' introduced for 1593–E and expanded for 1603–E. The 'exhortation' was also amended to include a lengthy passage, which, with clear references back to the troubles of the 1640s and 1650s, condemned those who continued to 'strive both with their Princes and their Priests' and warned of the dangers of 'our proneness … to Sedition in the State, and Schisme in the Church'. Similar motives doubtless informed the inclusion of Numbers 16, telling the story of the Jews' revolt against Moses and Aaron, as the first lesson at morning prayer. The special collects and the adjustments to the litany were to be used weekly on Wednesdays. To reinforce the proclamation's request for charitable donations for plague victims, on 31 July the archbishop of Canterbury ordered regular collections in his diocese. The form of prayer was reprinted in York and Oxford, presumably because it was feared that the distribution of copies printed in London would spread the plague. Moreover, the court withdrew from London to Oxford in July. A proclamation of 26 September 1665 changed the observance in November from the 1st to the 8th, to avoid All Saints Day. Rules for JPs and others concerning the plague, issued by royal command on 11 May 1666, indicated that monthly fasts, as well as Wednesday and – not indicated on the form of prayer – Friday prayers, were still to be observed. Nevertheless, many Anglican clergy fled London during the outbreak, and dissenting ministers preached in some of the city churches. The monthly fast was discontinued after the thanksgiving for the retreat of the plague (1666–E). As this was the last occasion on which England was afflicted by an outbreak of plague, it was also the last time on which the 'order of the fast' was printed in a form of prayer. The Dublin PRO formerly had copies of four orders relating to this occasion in Ireland: orders dated 19 July and 20 July, the fast proclamation of 24 July listed by Steele and a proclamation of 19 October altering the date of the observance to avoid All Saints' Day. No copies of any of these orders have been traced. A letter from Sir George Rawdon at Lisburn mentioning arrangements for the September observance proves that the fasts were kept beyond Dublin. The 'severe hand of God in the pestilence raging' in England was also one of the causes for the fast ordered to be observed in Massachusetts on 22 November 1665.

Orders: ENGLAND AND WALES: order of the king in council, 5 July 1665, PC2/58, fo. 100r; order by the bishop of London, undated, Emmanuel College Library, Cambridge, S1.4.24; royal proclamation, 6 July 1665, Wing C3301* [also Wing C3301A, C3306A (misdated 1674)]; royal proclamation, 26 Sept. 1665, Wing C3232*; IRELAND: proclamation by the lord deputy and council, 24 July 1665, Wing I624 [no copy found; formerly Dublin PRO (destroyed); see Steele, II, no. 741]; proclamation by the lord lieutenant and council, 19 Oct. 1665, Wing I909 [no copy found; formerly Dublin PRO (destroyed); see Steele, II, no. 750].

Form of prayer: ENGLAND AND WALES: *A form of common prayer, together with an order of fasting, for the averting of God's heavy visitation upon many places of this realm. The fast to be observ'd within the cities of London and Westminster, and places adjacent, on Wednesday the twelfth of this instant July; and both there, and in all parts of this realm, on the first Wednesday in every moneth: and the prayers to be read on Wednesday in every week, during this visitation. Set forth by his majesties authority* ([84] pp.; Wing C4119)* [other impression, ESTC 006155408]; IRELAND: none ordered?

Form of prayer (other editions): Oxford, Ric. Davis, Wing C4119A; York, Stephen Bulkley, Wing C4119AB.

Additional sources: privy council register, PC2/58, fos. 100r, 101r, 102r; *CSPD, 1664–5*, pp. 466, 497, 573; the king to the bailiffs of Yarmouth, 21 Aug. 1665, Sir William Coventry to Lord Arlington, *CSPD, 1664–5*, pp. 527, 552–3; *Rules and orders to be observed by all justices of peace* (1666; Wing E819); Wilkins, *Concilia*, IV, 583–4; Bishop Seth Ward of Exeter to Archbishop Sheldon, 16 Sept. 1665, Bod., MS Add. c. 305, fo. 158r; Pepys, VI, 93, 120, 155; Evelyn, III, 415–16; Wood, II, 86; *The diary of John Milward, esq., member of parliament for Derbyshire, September, 1666 to May, 1668*, ed. Caroline Robbins (Cambridge, 1938), pp. 12, 37; Daniel Defoe, *A journal of the plague year*, ed. Louis Landa (Oxford, 1990), pp. 28–9, 104; *Report of the deputy keeper*, XXIII, app., p. 30; Sir George Rawdon to Viscount Conway and Killultagh, 5 Sept. 1665, *CSPI, 1663–5*, pp. 638–9; *Massachusetts records*, IV, pt. ii, 281.

Printed sermons: Hall, House of Lords, 3 Oct. 1666 (Wing H335); Perrinchief, House of Commons, 7 Nov. 1666 (Wing P1606); Reynolds, House of Lords, 7 Nov. 1666 (Wing R1281).

ORDERS

Order of the king in council: London, Westminster and bills of mortality, 5 July 1665

It was this day Ordered by his Ma[jes]tie in Councill, That the Right Reverend Father in God Humphrey Lord B[isho]p of London do cause Notice to be given to the seuerall Parishes within London, & the Weekely Bills of mortality of his Ma[jes]ties Proclamation for a Fast to be obserued on Wednesday next for imploring Gods mercy in putting a Stop to the present Plague & Contagion. And that his Lo[rdshi]p giue directions, that each of the said Parishes haue Copies of the Forme of Prayer prepared & imprinted by his Maties Command to be used on that day; Signifying unto them, that it's his Maties Pleasure that they make Collections in their seuerall Parish Churches on that day for the Releife of such poore People as are visited with ye Sicknes.

Order by the bishop of London: London, Westminster and bills of mortality [n.d.]

By an Order of His Majesty, present in Council, on Wednesday the Fifth of this instant *July*, I am commanded to require all Ministers of Parishes in the Cities of *London* and *Westminster*, as also those which are in the Bills of Mortality, to publish in their respective Churches, That His Majesty in His Religious and Princely care for the Spiritual and Temporal welfare of His people, hath appointed and commanded,

That Wednesday the Twelfth day of this instant *July* be set apart and observed for a Solemn Fasting, in all the foresaid Parishes; and that the said day be spent in the publick Worship of God, according to that Form of Prayer, both for the Morning and Evening, which is by His Majesties Authority, upon this occasion, now published, and in hearing of the Word of God; that so by Prayer, Repentance, and Works of Charity the People of this Kingdom may be prepared to seek and obtain of God the averting of his judgement of Plague and Pestilence from the land. I therefore require you, That upon the next Lords day, being the Ninth day of *July*, in the time of the Morning Service, immediately after the reading of the *Nicene* Creed, and before the Sermon, you read my Order, that so the Congregation may take notice of His Majesties pleasure and commands herein.

England and Wales: royal proclamation, 6 July 1665

Whereas it hath pleased Almighty God, after many years of Health, and many great and miraculous Mercies afforded to this Kingdom, to visit the Cities of *London* and *Westminster*, and places adjacent with the Plague and Pestilence, which by the spreading thereof into several Parishes, & other the more remote parts of this Kingdom, seems to threaten a general and most dreadful Visitation: To the end therefore that Prayers and Supplications may every where be offered up unto Almighty God for the removal of this heavy Judgement, and that some Solemn Days and Times may be set apart for the performance of these and other Religious Duties;

His Majesty is pleased, by the Advice of His Privy Council, to Declare, and doth hereby publish and declare his Royal Will and Pleasure, That Wednesday next being the Twelfth day of this instant *July*, shall be observed and kept within the Cities of *London* and *Westminster*, and places adjacent, as a Day of Fasting and Humiliation; And Wednesday three Weeks after being the Second day of *August*, shall be observed and kept in like manner in all parts of this Realm; and so from thence forward every First Wednesday of every Moneth successively, until it shall please God to withdraw this Plague and grievous Sickness.

And that the solemnization of these days may be with such Order and Decency as is requisite, His Majesty by the Advice of His Reverend Bishops hath directed to be Composed, Printed and Published the Form of such Prayers as His Majesty thinks fit to be used in all Churches and Chappels at these publick Meetings, and also upon Wednesdays in every Week; And hath given charge to His Bishops to disperse the same through the whole Kingdom. All which his Majesty doth expresly charge and command shall be reverently and devoutly performed by all His loving Subjects, as they will answer to God for the neglect of so great a Duty and Service, and upon pain of being proceeded against as wilful Breakers and Contemners of this His Royal Will and Command.

And His Majesty doth further declare, That upon all and every the said Days of Fasting and Humiliation, there shall be a Collection made of the Alms and Charitable Benevolence of the several persons in the respective Churches and Chappels then Assembled: Which Collections shall be paid in to the Bishops of the several Dioceses wherein such Collection shall be made, or to such Persons as the Bishops shall appoint to receive the same.

And the Bishops shall take care, That the Moneys so collected and paid in, be in the first place applyed to the Relief of such places as shall be visited with the Plague within the Diocese wherein such Collections shall be made. And the Overplus, if any be, shall be paid in to the Bishop of *London*, or such as he shall appoint to receive the same, and be applyed to the Poor who are sick and visited with the Plague in *London* or *Westminster*, or the parts adjacent.

And lastly, His Majesty doth Command, That the respective Preachers on the said Fast-days do earnestly exhort the people in the several Parishes to a Free and Chearful Contribution towards the Relief of their Christian Brethren, whom it hath pleased God to visit with Sickness.

England and Wales: royal proclamation, 26 September 1665

Whereas the Kings most Excellent Majesty did by His Royal Proclamation, bearing Date the Sixth day of *July* last, appoint that from the time therein mentioned, the First Wednesday of every Moneth successively should be observed and kept in all parts of this Realm, as a day of Fasting and Humiliation, until it shall please God to withdraw this Plague and grievous Sickness. And to the end that Prayers and Supplication may every where be offered up unto Almighty God for the Removal of this heavy Judgment: And whereas the First Wednesday in *November* (which according to that Order ought to be kept) falls out to be *All-Saints* day, which is a great Festival in the Church, and so not fit to be kept as a day of Fasting and Humiliation, His Majesties Pleasure is, and He doth hereby Declare, That the Next Wednesday following in the said Moneth, that is to say, Wednesday the eighth of *November*, shall be kept in all parts of this Realm as a day of Fasting and Humiliation, instead of the First Wednesday of that Moneth. And for the time to come, the First Wednesday in every Moneth shall be so kept as was appointed by the said former Proclamation; Except the same falls out to be on some day appointed to be kept Holy, and in that case it shall be kept the Wednesday following, as is hereby directed. And His Majesty doth hereby again call upon the Respective Preachers on the said Fast-days, that they do Earnestly Exhort the People, in the several Churches, to a Free and Chearful Contribution, towards the Relief of their Christian Brethren, whom it hath pleased God to visit with Sickness; And that the Moneys so gathered be disposed according as His Majesty hath directed by His said Former Proclamation.

FORM OF PRAYER

England and Wales

THE ORDER OF THE FAST; AND THE WARNING TO BE GIVEN OF THE SAME.

Upon the Sunday before the Monethly Fast, immediately after the Nicene Creed, the Minister shall in the Pulpit, or Reading-Pew, thus give the people warning of it.

Brethren, I am to give you notice, That *Wednesday* next is a day of Publick and Solemn Prayer and Fasting, set apart by His Majesties Authority to be observed by us and the whole Nation, for the averting of Gods heavy Visitation now upon us in many places of this Kingdom.

Upon which day (as also upon *Wednesday* in every Week, during the time of these present Afflictions) all Parishioners, with so many of their Families as may be spared from their necessary business, are to resort hither to the Church, and here to behave themselves godly, and reverently; and with penitent hearts to pray unto God to turn these Plagues from us, which we through our unthankfulness, and sinful lives have deserved.

All persons (children, old, weak and sick folk, and necessary Harvest-labourers, or the like, excepted) are required to eat upon the Fast-day, but one competent and moderate Meal; and that towards night, after Evening Prayer: observing sobriety of Diet, without superfluity of riotous fare, respecting necessity, and not voluptuousness.

The quantity being but sufficient, it is not fit that any delicacy should be regarded. Let no publick Order be herein contemned, nor dissimulation with God committed, by pretending godly abstinence, but doing nothing less.

The wealthier sort are earnestly moved to bestow the price of the Meal forborn, upon the poor; considering the misery and distress of a number of hungry souls in many places, either almost starving for lack of food, or being sick with eating unwholsom meats.

The people are to forbear that day their bodily working, and common buying and selling (necessary occasions, and labourers excepted;) and to be exercised all the time in holy Prayer, godly Meditations, and reverent hearing of the Scriptures, either read or preached: And especially they are to take heed, that they spend it not in Plaies, Pastimes, Idleness, haunting of Taverns and Ale-houses, lascivious Wantonness, Surfeiting or Drunkenness; for which, and other sins of our Nation, the heavy Displeasure and Wrath of God is fallen upon us.

God give us all grace to repent; and in his mercy turn away his punishment from us. Amen.

MORNING PRAYER

Let him that ministreth read with a loud voice these Sentences of Scripture; and then say the Exhortation that followeth.
[Dan. 9:9–10; Jer. 10:24]

[As BCP to the Venite*]*

Instead of Venite exultemus, *shall be sung or said this Hymn following; one Verse by the Priest, and another by the Clerk and people.*

O Come, Let us humble our selves, and fall down before the Lord: with reverence, and fear. (Ps. 95:6)
For he is the Lord our God: and we are the people of his pasture, and the sheep of his hand. (Ps. 95:7)
Come therefore, let us turn again unto our Lord: for he hath smitten us, and he will heal us. (Hos. 6:1)
Let us repent, and turn from our wickedness: and our sins shall be forgiven us. (Acts 3.19)
Let us turn, and the Lord will turn from his heavy wrath: and will pardon us, and we shall not perish. (Jonah 3:8–9)
We acknowledge indeed, that our punishments are less then our deservings: but yet of thy mercy, O Lord, correct us to amendment, and plague us not to our destruction. (Job 11:6; Wisd. 11:23)
We have provoked thine Anger, thy wrath is waxed hot: and thy heavy displeasure is sore kindled against us. (Lam. 3:42)
But thy hand is not shortned, that thou canst not help: neither is thy goodness abated, that thou wilt not hear. (Isa. 59:1)

Thou hast promised, O Lord, that before we cry thou wilt hear us: whil'st we are yet speaking, thou wilt have mercy upon us. (Isa. 65:24)

For thou art the only Lord, who woundest, and do'st heal again: thou killest, and revivest; bringest even to hell, and bringest back again. (Job 5:18; Hos. 6:2)

Thou forgivest all our sins: and healest all our infirmities. (Ps. 103:3)

Thou savest our life from destruction: and crownest us with mercy and loving kindness. (Ps. 103:4)

Our fathers hoped in thee: they trusted in thee, and thou didst deliver them. (Ps. 22:4)

They called upon thee, and were holpen: they put their trust in thee, and were not confounded. (Ps. 22:5)

And now in the vexation of our spirits, and the anguish of our souls we cry unto thee: hear Lord, and have mercy. (Bar. 3:1–2)

For many troubles are come about us: our sins have taken such hold upon us, that we are not able to look up. (Ps. 40:15)

O remember not our sins, and our offences: but according to thy mercy think thou upon us, O Lord, for thy goodness. (Ps. 25:6)

Hide not thy face from us in the time of our trouble: encline thine ears unto us, when we call; O hear us, and that right soon. (Ps. 102:2)

For thine own sake, and for thy holy Names sake, encline thine ear: and hear, O merciful Lord. (Dan. 9:18–19)

For we do not present our supplications before thee, trusting in our own righteousness: but in thy manifold and great mercies. (Dan. 9:18)

Help us, O God of our salvation, for the glory of thy Name: O deliver us, and be merciful unto our sins for thy Name's sake. (Ps. 79:9)

So we that are thy people, and sheep of thy pasture, shall give thee thanks for ever: and will always be shewing forth thy praise from generation to generation. (Ps. 79:14)

Glory be to the Father, and to the Son: and to the holy Ghost.

As it was in the beginning, is now, and ever shall be: world without end. Amen.

[Ps. 6, 32, 38, 39]
[First lesson: Num. 16; or Deut. 28:1–30]
[Te Deum]
[Second lesson: Luke 13; or Luke 21]
[Benedictus]

[Then as BCP to the end of morning prayer, replacing the collect for the day with the BCP collect for Ash Wednesday and the BCP special prayer in time of common plague or sickness]

LITANY

Here followeth the Litany; which, as it is here Printed, together with the other proper Collects in this Book, shall be used publickly in Churches, not onely upon the Monethly Fast-day, but on Wednesday in every Week (and may by every man be used daily in private Families) during the time of this Visitation.

[As BCP to the end of the prayer 'We humbly beseech thee']

The Priest and Clerk, or he that ministers (still kneeling in the place where they are accustom'd to say or sing the Litany) shall here repeat this Psalm.
[Ps. 51]

[Then, from the BCP commination service, the prayers beginning 'Minister: O Lord, save thy servants', 'O Lord, we beseech thee mercifully hear our prayers', 'O most mighty God and merciful Father' and 'Turn thou us, O good Lord'. Then]

O most gracious God, Father of Mercies, and of our Lord Jesus Christ; look down upon us, we beseech thee, in much pity, and compassion, and behold our great misery, and trouble. For there is wrath gone out against us, and the Plague is begun. That dreadful Arrow of thine sticks fast in our flesh; and the Venime thereof fires our bloud, and drinks up our spirits; And shouldest thou suffer it to bring us all to the dust of Death, yet must we still acknowledge, that Righteous art thou, O Lord, and just are thy judgements. For our Transgressions multiplied against thee, as the sand on the sea-shore, might justly bring over us a Deluge of thy Wrath. The cry of our sins, that hath pierc't the very Heavens, might well return with showers of Vengeance upon our Heads. While our Earth is defiled under the Inhabitants thereof, what wonder, if thou commandest an evil Angel to pour out his Vial into our Air, to fill it with Infection, and the noisom Pestilence, and so to turn the very breath of our Life into the savour of Death unto us all! But yet we beseech thee, O our God, forget not thou to be gracious: neither shut thou up thy loving kindness in Displeasure. For his sake, who himself took our Infirmities, and bare our Sicknesses, have mercy upon us; and say to the destroying Angel, *It is enough.* O let that bloud of sprinkling, which speaks better things than that of *Abel*, be upon the Lintel, and the two side-posts in all our Dwellings, that the Destroyer may pass by. Let the sweet Odour of thy Blessed Son's all-sufficient Sacrifice, and Intercession (infinitely more prevalent than the typical Incense of *Aaron*) interpose between the Living and the Dead, and be our full, and perfect Atonement, ever acceptable with thee, that the Plague may be stayed. O let us live, and we will praise thy Name; and these thy Judgements shall teach us to look every Man into the plague of his own Heart: that being cleansed from all our sins, we may serve thee with pure hearts all our days, perfecting holiness in thy Fear, till we come at last, where there is no more Sickness, nor Death, through thy tender Mercies in him alone, who is our Life, and our Health, and our Salvation, Jesus Christ, our ever blessed Saviour, and Redeemer. *Amen.*

Then shall follow this Prayer; which shall be used continually as long as the Navy is abroad.
    O most glorious, and powerful Lord God *[as 1665–E]*

[The prayer of St Chrysostom; the grace]

COMMUNION

[As BCP to the end of the ten commandments]

Almighty God, whose kingdom is everlasting *[as BCP]*

[Then, in place of the collect for the day, the special collects prescribed for morning prayer]

[Epistle: Joel 2:11–18]
[Gospel: Matt. 6:16–21]
[Nicene creed; the sermon]
[Offertory sentences: Matt. 5:16; Ps. 41:1]

[The prayer for the whole state of the church]

Then shall be added the prayer following.
Almighty God, our Heavenly Father, whose Judgements are most severe, and terrible against obstinate offenders; but thy Mercies infinite to all, that with hearty Repentance, and true Faith turn unto thee: We, the sinful people of this land, whom for our iniquities, and manifold transgressions thou hast in many places most justly visited with the noisom Plague, and Pestilence, come now before the Throne of thy Grace in the Name of thy dear Son, in whom thou art well pleased; and in confidence of that Atonement which he hath made for us, most humbly beseech thee to pardon, and forgive us all our sins in thought, word, or deed committed against thy Divine Majesty; to work in us daily more and more a true, hearty, and unfeigned Sorrow, and repentance for the same; so plant in our hearts a sincere and setled Resolution, by the assistance of thy Grace, to lead the rest of our lives in careful Obedience to thy holy Will in all things; and so to remove from us this Plague, and grievous Sickness, that we be not utterly consumed by means of thy heavy hand. To this end, grant us, good Lord, of thy grace and mercy, all things conducing hereunto; Seasonable Weather, and good Air, and wholsom Food, and powerful Medicines, and whatever else thou seest to be good, and profitable for us; together with a due Care, and Conscience in using of the same; that we neither presume, nor tempt thy Majesty by neglecting the Means, which thou hast appointed, nor yet despair of thy Blessing in the diligent use of them, nor in any event repine, or murmure at thy providence, what portion soever it allots us: But that submitting our selves to thy good pleasure in all things, we may commit the keeping of our Souls to thee in well-doing, as unto a faithful Creatour; with compassionate pity, and charity (as we are able) succouring the sick, and preserving the whole, and praying fervently for All: and finally, that depending entirely upon thy Goodness, we may wait the hour of thy gracious Deliverance in Faith, and Hope, and constant Patience, with perfect Resignation to thy wise, and just Appointment in all things; To the which we betake our selves, and the whole Nation, and whatever concerns us. Be merciful unto us, O God, be merciful unto us, for our souls trust onely in thee, and under the shadow of thy Wings shall be our refuge, till this Calamity be overpast; Which we beseech thee speedily to remove, if it be thy Will, O Lord God of Mercies, and Father of Compassions, and to restore the voice of Joy, and Health once more into our Dwellings, for the alone Merits sake of thy dear Son Jesus Christ, our onely Mediatour, and Advocate. *Amen.*

Here may be added one, or both these Collects following.
[The BCP collects for the fourth and second Sundays in Lent]

Almighty God, who hast promised *[as BCP, followed by the blessing]*

EVENING PRAYER

[The rubric as at morning prayer, followed by the opening sentences: Dan. 9:9–10; Jer. 10:24]

[Then as BCP to the psalms, before which is inserted the prayer to be used in place of the Venite *at morning prayer]*

[Ps. 90, 91, 130]
[First lesson: 2 Sam. 24; or Jonah 3]
[Magnificat]
[Second lesson: 1 Cor. 10:1–14]
[Deus misereatur]

[Then as BCP from the Apostles' creed to the suffrages after the Lord's prayer]

[The special collects prescribed in place of the collect for the day at morning prayer; the BCP second and third collect at evening prayer; and then, from the BCP commination service, the prayers 'O Lord, we beseech thee mercifully hear our prayers', 'O most mighty God and merciful Father' and 'Turn thou us, O good Lord'; and 'Almighty God, our Heavenly Father, whose Judgements are most severe']

[As BCP from the prayer for the king to the end of evening prayer]

AN EXHORTATION FIT FOR THE TIME
[As 1603–E to the paragraph beginning 'Which being so evident a truth'*]*
Which being so evident a truth, confirmed by so many examples out of the holy Scriptures, it must be confessed and acknowledged, that the same cause hath procured the same punishment with us: and that in these days, these evil days of ours, our transgressions in number more, and in degree more hainous than those of Israel, have filled full the measure of iniquity, and caused God to fill full the cup of his wrath, and given us this deadly wine to drink. The people of Israel required meat for their lust,[346] and the people of England nourish their lust for their meat, giving over themselves to surfeiting and drunkenness, and as those that make their belly their God, and their glory their shame, are become a by-word unto neighbour-Nations for gluttony & belly-chear. And what wonder, if we die with the very meats we lust after in our mouths, or if the heavy wrath of God come upon us, as sometime upon them, and smite us down with a very great Plague. The people of Israel murmured,[347] and rebelled against *Moses* and *Aaron* their Leaders: and there hath been also, and is yet amongst us here in *England*, a people that strive both with their Princes and their Priests, that obey not those that have the Rule over them, that submit not themselves to such as by Gods appointment watch over their souls: Such as not only despise Governments in their hearts, but speak evil of Dignities; Nor only curse in their Bed-chamber, but openly revile the Rulers of their people; Malecontents, and Murmurers, and Fault-finders (as S. *Jude* calls them) rashly mis-judging, and boldly censuring the Actions of their Governours, upon groundless jealousies and suspitions; Nay such,

---

[346] Num.11; Ps. 78.
[347] Num. 16.

as S. *Paul* prophesied should come in these last and perillous days, Traytors, Heady, High-minded, who have dared to lift up their hands also against the Anointed of the Lord; and what wonder that there is wrath gone out from the Lord, and the Plague is begun? The people of *Israel* committed whoredom with the daughters of *Moab*;[348] and are there not many of the daughters of *England* too like to those of *Moab*? and too many *Zimries* amongst us, whose Fornications are notorious, and scandalous in the sight of the World; who care not to conceal their abominations, blush not at their crimes, but impudently boast and glory in their shame? And therefore no marvail if God himself stand forth to plague the land for them. Add to these, that we have perhaps, with *David*,[349] lifted up our hearts because of the multitude of our people, magnified our selves that we are a mighty and a populous Nation, placing our confidence in the arm of flesh, and ascribing to our selves, and our own strength, or skill, our valour, or our conduct, that honour, and victory over our enemies, which God with his own right hand, and with his holy arm hath purchased unto himself for his own glory. And further, that by outragious swearing, vain and rash oaths, and blasphemies, and cursed speakings, to be heard out of the mouths of all estates, yea, even of very children in our streets, the holy Name of God is very grievously profaned amongst us; And not only by voluntary unlawful oaths (for which the Land mourns) but yet worse, by abominable perjuries, and careless, and profane violation of oaths lawfully imposed upon us, as in Courts of Justice: and those especially so solemnly made, and so often repeated to our Soveraign Lord, while we wilfully forget that such are the Oaths of God, and that he himself is a strict and most severe Avenger of them: And also, that our Trading and Traffick is become the practise of Deceit and Theft, while we make our gain by lying and false swearing, by false Measures, Weights and Lights, which are all abomination unto the Lord: And then it cannot appear strange, if God who still reserves great plagues for the ungodly, and in especial manner resists the proud, hath set himself in battel-array against us; or if that flying Roll of the curse of God against the Swearer and the Thief, hath entred already into our Houses, and taken hold of the Stones, and of the Timber thereof. In sum, the holy Word of God and the Ministery thereof is not justly reverenced, but despised; his holy Sacraments either totally neglected or abused, in many places neither rightly administred, nor received; the Lords day not kept holy, as commanded, but profaned; and other holy seasons, whether of Festivity or Fasting (appointed by just Authority, according to the example of Gods people in all Ages, for the procuring of his blessings, and for the averting these his heavy Judgements) not duly, nay, in too many places not at all observed; the awful presence of God, the honour due to his divine Majesty in his own house not at all regarded, but turned into meer scorn and mockery; the holy Service, and publick worship of God in the beauty of Holiness not frequented as it ought, but slighted and undervalued, and snuffed at, and opposed by a disobedient and gainsaying people; the Portion of God invaded, his Altars robbed of Tithes and Offerings, and holy things of all sorts profanely and sacrilegiously devoured; For which crying sins, and finally for our great Disobedience and Irreverence to all our Superiours, our untractable and ungovernable humour, our proneness upon no occasion to Sedition in the State, and Schisme in the Church (by raising, leading, and keeping up Parties and Factions, and fomenting uncharitable contentions, and animosities to the disturbance of publick peace) our Hypocrisie and Superstition,

---

348 Num. 25.
349 2 Sam. 24.

open profaness, and irreligion against God himself, and generally for our dissolute, and licentious, and most unchristian conversation of all sorts (most directly contrary to the righteous laws, and great example of the most holy Jesus our Lord) the name of God is polluted, and his blessed Gospel evil spoken of amongst the Adversaries of the truth *thorough us*: So that we need seek no further; the cause is apparent, why the Plague is broken out amongst us: God having threatned us in his Word, as the people of Israel, that because we will not obey the voice of the Lord our God to do all his commandments, and his ordinances which he commands us, he will smite us with a consumption, and with a fever, and with a burning ague, and cause the pestilence to cleave unto us, until he hath consumed us from the land. And thus much of the cause of the pestilence.

Now let us examine and see what hope *[as 1603–E: of helpe … to the paragraph beginning* 'And among all other things yet spoken of … ', *except that, in the paragraph beginning* 'Now let us examine and see what hope': *(a)* 'especially in and about London' *is deleted after* 'should be exercised in all Congregations'; *(b)* 'And as fasting & prayer are means' *begins a new paragraph; and (c)* 'doe men what they list' *is deleted after* 'shall be governed by Gods providence'*]*.

And among all other things yet spoken of *[as 1603–E*: let this one aduise bee added … this means of meeting hath ensued unto many*]*.

The conclusion of all is this *[as 1603–E, to the end of the exhortation]*.

1665–S2   Thanksgiving day for naval victory at the battle of Lowestoft

Thursday 13 July 1665 (Scotland)

News of the battle of Lowestoft on 1–4 June 1665 (see 1665–EIr1) arrived in Edinburgh on 11 June; cannons were fired and, on the following day, bonfires lit. On 10 June, the king had approved the text of a proclamation appointing a thanksgiving in Scotland. Like the order for 1665–S1, the proclamation was written in London and sent to Edinburgh to be issued by the Scottish privy council. It was recorded in the council register on 22 June, on which date the council ordered it to be printed and published. Unlike the orders for 1665–S1 and later Scottish fasts and thanksgivings, however, the printed proclamation was dated at Whitehall. The reason for this is not clear. The thanksgiving was observed with preaching, and there were bonfires in many places.

Orders: royal proclamation, 10 June 1665, Wing C3311A* [also in *RPC*, 3rd ser., II, 56–7; Wodrow, *History*, I, 423]; privy council order, 22 June 1665, *RPC*, 3rd ser., II, 57.
Additional sources: *CSPD, 1664–5*, p. 418; *Edin. recs., 1655 to 1665*, pp. 369, 371; *Aber. recs., 1643–1747*, p. 220; *Inverness and Dingwall records*, p. 311; Nicoll, pp. 435–6; Lamont, pp. 179–80.

ORDERS

Royal proclamation: 10 June 1665
Forasmuch as Our Navy Royal, under the command of Our dearest Brother the Duke of *York*, hath, upon the third day of *June* last, obtained a glorious Victory over the Fleet set out by the States of the *United Provinces*: And We finding it suteable, that

a solemn return of Praise be paid to Almighty GOD, by whose special Hand, and signal Appearance for Us and the justice of Our Cause, this great Salvation hath been wrought; Have judged fit, by this Our Proclamation, to indict a general and publick Thanksgiving for the cause aforesaid. Our Will is herefore, and We straitly command and charge, that the said Thanksgiving and solemn Commemoration of the goodness of GOD, manifested by the conduct and management of this late Action, be religiously and solemnly observed through this Our whole Kingdom, upon the second Thursday of *July* next, being the thirteenth day thereof; Requiring hereby Our Reverend Archbishops and Bishops, to give notice of this Our Royal Pleasure to the Ministers in their respective Diocesses; and that upon the Lords-day immediatly preceeding the said thirteenth day of *July*, they cause read this Our Proclamation from the Pulpit in every Paroch Kirk: And that they exhort all Our loving Subjects to a chearfull and devout performance of this so becoming a duty they owe to the Name of the LORD Our GOD, who has done these great and auspicious things for Us, and for the Honour and Interest of Our Kingdoms.

Privy council order: 22 June 1665
The Lords of his Majesties Privy Councill ordaines the above-wrytten proclamation to be printed and published.

1665–S3 Fast day during plague epidemic in England

Wednesday 13 September 1665 (Scotland)

On 12 July 1665, acting on reports of the epidemic in London (see 1665–EIr2), the Scottish privy council issued a proclamation prohibiting trade between Scotland and London and other English towns infected with the plague. On 8 August, the council appointed this fast day, apparently at the urging of the bishops. Unusually, the council seems to have ordered the fast on its own initiative, perhaps because the restriction on trade, or the flight of the court from London, limited the flow of official correspondence to and from the king. The proclamation is clearly by the council, rather than in the name of the king.

Order: proclamation by the privy council, 8 Aug. 1665, Wing S1784A* [not in *RPC*].
Additional sources: *RPC*, 3rd ser., II, 71–4; *Inverness and Dingwall records*, pp. 312–13; Lamont, p. 182.

ORDER

Proclamation by the privy council: 8 August 1665
Forasmuch as it has pleased Almighty GOD to visit the City of *London*, places adjacent, and several other Towns and Villages of the Kingdom of *England*, with the sore Plague of Pestilence; So that all Commerce and Trade with that Kingdom has been prohibited and forbidden, lest that by importing of Commodities, the Plague might be brought into this Kingdom, to the great prejudice and danger of the Lieges: And seing it has been moved to the Council, from the Right Reverend Fathers the Archbishops and Bishops, that a general Fast may be appointed and kept throughout the whole Kingdom, for imploring the goodness and protection of Almighty GOD,

that in His infinite mercy, He may preserve this Kingdom from that contagion, and compassionat the sufferings of those that are visited therewith in *England*, and hinder the spreading thereof in all places, which by His mercy are yet preserved there-from: As likewise, that the LORD may bless this Kingdom with a fair and seasonable Harvest, that the Fruits of the ground may be reaped for the comfort and maintenance of the people. Therefore, the Lords of His *Majesties* Privy Council, by these presents, command and charge, That a Fast be religiously and solemnly kept throughout the whole Kingdom, by all Subjects and People within the same, upon the second *Wednesday* of *September* next to come, in this instant year of GOD, being the thirteenth day of the said Moneth; requiring hereby, the Reverend Archbishops and Bishops to give notice hereof to the Ministers in their respective Dioceses, that upon the LORDS-day immediatly preceeding the said thirteenth of *September*, they make publick intimation thereof in every Parish Church; and that they exhort all their Parishioners to a sober and devout performance of the said Fast and Humiliation, as they tender the favour of Almighty GOD, the preservation of their native Country, and the suffering condition of their Neighbours and fellow Subjects in *England*: Certifying all who shall contemn or neglect such a religious and necessary duty, they shall be proceeded against as contemners of Authority, neglecters of religious Services, and unnatural and profane Persons. And Ordains these presents to be printed and published, that none pretend ignorance.

1666–EIr1   Fast days in support of the naval campaign against the Dutch (and in Ireland, of the government's direction of the war)

Thursday 31 May 1666 (London, Westminster, Southwark and surrounding area); Thursday 14 June 1666 (elsewhere in England and Wales); Wednesday 20 June 1666 (Dublin and suburbs); Wednesday 27 June 1666 (elsewhere in Ireland)

This fast in England was ordered at unusually short notice, on news that the Dutch navy had sailed. There was insufficient time to write a new form of prayer, and the proclamation ordered that the form issued for 1665–E be used. Before the fast day on 14 June, reports had arrived of English victory in the Four Days battle (1–4 June; see 1666–EIr2). Bishop Hall of Chester cancelled the fast (whether in the city or diocese is unclear). In anticipation of an order for a thanksgiving, he requested the use in the meantime of a thanksgiving collect from the BCP (presumably that 'for peace and deliverance from our enemies'). In Ireland, the fast day seems to have been ordered before news arrived of the Four Days battle. As with 1661–Ir1, the proclamation specifically instructed the people to refrain from labour on the fast days. It is possible that some Irish clergy chose not to observe the days after hearing reports of an English victory. Alternatively, the fasts may have been reclassified as thanksgiving days (see 1666–Ir1).

Orders: ENGLAND AND WALES: royal proclamation, 28 May 1666, Wing C3302*; IRELAND: proclamation by the lord lieutenant and council, 8 June 1666, Wing I678*.
Form of prayer: ENGLAND AND WALES: 1665–E (Wing C4115) to be used; IRELAND: none ordered.

Additional sources: privy council register, PC2/59, fo. 25v; *CSPD, 1665–6*, p. 415; Pepys, VII, 138; Bishop George Hall of Chester to Archbishop Sheldon, 13 June 1666, Bod., MS Add. c. 305, fo. 54r.

ORDERS

England and Wales: royal proclamation, 28 May 1666

The Kings most Excellent Majesty being necessitated for the just Defence and Vindication of His own and Subjects Rights, to continue His Forces at Sea, now in readiness upon a present Expedition; hath resolved, and doth hereby Command a General and Publique Fast to be kept throughout this whole Kingdom, in such manner as is hereafter directed and prescribed; That so both Prince and People may send up their prayers and supplications to Almighty God for imploring His blessing on His Majesties Naval Forces. And for the more decent and uniform performance thereof, His Majesty doth hereby Publish and Declare to all His loving Subjects, and doth straitly Charge and Command, That *Thursday* next, the last of this instant *May*, this Fast be Religiously and Solemnly kept and observed in the Cities of *London* and *Westminster*, Burrough of *Southwark*, and other places adjacent: And *Thursday* the Fourteenth of *June* next, the like be kept and duely observed through the rest of this whole Kingdom of *England*, Dominion of *Wales*, and Town of *Berwick* upon *Tweed*. And for the more orderly solemnizing thereof, His Majesty hath directed, That the Form of Prayers Composed and Published the last year upon the like occasion, be used in all Churches and places at these publique Meetings, and hath given Charge to the Bishops for the dispersing thereof through their several Diocesses in the whole Kingdom. And His Majesty doth expresly Charge and Command, That the said Fasting and Prayers be soberly, reverently, and decently performed by all His loving Subjects, as they tender the favour of Almighty God, and upon pain of such punishments as His Majesty can justly inflict upon all such as contemn or neglect so religious a work.

Ireland: proclamation by the lord lieutenant and council, 8 June 1666

We the Lord Lieutenant and Council, do Order, Command and Proclaim, publick Humiliation, Fasting and Prayers to be observed in all the parts and Parishes within this Kingdom; that is to say, in the City of *Dublin* and Suburbs thereof on *Wednesday* the Twentieth day of this Moneth of *June*, and on *Wednesday* the Seven and twentieth day of the said Moneth, in and throughout the whole Kingdom: And therefore We will and require, That the Ministers and Parishioners of every Parish within this Kingdom, do duly repair to the Cathedral or Parish Church on every of the said days as aforesaid, to Divine Service and Sermons: Upon which days the Minister is to call upon the people, that they abstain from labour, and from pleasure, and from the ordinary works of their callings, and dedicate themselves on those days to Humiliation, Fasting, Prayer, works of Charity and Devotion, bewailing as well their own sins, as the great and known sins of the Kingdom, and supplicating Almighty God of his Mercy and Goodness, to bless and prosper all His Majesties Councils, and all His Armies and Fleets by Land and by Sea, and particularly His present expedition: And We will and require every Archbishop and Bishop to call upon his Clergy for the diligent and due performance thereof.

1666–Ir1 Thanksgiving day for naval victory in the Four Days battle

[After 20 June] 1666 (Ireland)

According to the *Report of the deputy keeper*, there was formerly in the Dublin PRO an order dated 20 June 1666 for thanksgiving for the naval victory (of 1–4 June: see 1666–EIr2). The order was not listed by Steele. Possibly the fast appointed for 27 June was cancelled (see 1666–EIr1).

Order: 20 June 1666 [listed in *Report of the deputy keeper*, XXIII, app., 31; not in Steele].
Form of prayer: none ordered?

1666–S1 Fast days in support of the naval campaign against the Dutch

Wednesday 11 July 1666 (Scotland south of the River North Esk); Wednesday 18 July 1666 (Scotland north of the River North Esk)

As the proclamation shows, these fasts for a blessing on the naval campaign were appointed after news reached Edinburgh of the Four Days battle, in which royal forces were broadly successful (see 1666–S2 and, for the battle, 1666–EIr2). The proclamation was issued by the privy council in Edinburgh, although unlike 1665–S3, it was in the king's name. The council's register does not record a royal letter ordering a fast. Uniquely in the case of special worship, the River North Esk (the border of Forfarshire and Kincardineshire) was specified as the boundary between southern and northern Scotland.

Order: royal proclamation, 28 June 1666, Wing C3311, SP29/160/59 [also in *RPC*, 3rd ser., II, 173].
Additional sources: *CSPD, 1665–6*, p. 470; *RPC*, 3rd ser., II, 170; Wodrow, *History*, II, 14; *Edin. recs., 1665 to 1680*, p. 17; *Alford exercise*, p. 83; *Inverness and Dingwall records*, p. 316; Nicoll, p. 449; Lamont, p. 190.

ORDER

Royal proclamation: 28 June 1666

Forasmuch as We are necessitated, for Our just defence, and vindication of Our Own and Our Subjects Rights, to continue the War against the *United Provinces*, as likewise against the *French* King and King of *Denmark*, who are now joyned with them in their unjust quarrel; And for carrying on of the same, (after several Expeditions and Engagements of our Naval Forces heretofore, which it hath pleased Almighty GOD to blesse with great success and victory) of new again to make ready Our Royal Fleet, for encountering Our enemies, and maintaining Our just Rights, and securing the Trade and Commerce of Our Subjects: And We, having so great and eminent experience of the assistance of Almighty GOD, whose protection and favour, after keeping a solemn day of Fast and Humiliation, We have hitherto implored. And upon this great occasion finding, that the renewing the same may move Almighty GOD, in His infinite mercy, to continue His favour and protection, and to bless Our Naval Forces at this time with success and victory. Our Will is herefore, and We straitly command and charge, that the said Fast be religiously and solemnly kept throughout this Our whole Kingdom, by all Our Subjects and People within the same, upon the second Wednesday of *July* next, being the eleventh day thereof; and the third Wednesday of the same Moneth, being the eighteenth, in manner *respectivè* following, *viz.* By all these upon the south side of the north water of *Esk*, upon the said eleventh day; and these upon the north side thereof, upon the said eighteenth day: Requiring hereby the Reverend Archbishops and Bishops, to give notice hereof to the Ministers in their respective Dioceses, That upon the Lords dayes *respective*, immediately preceeding the said eleventh and eighteenth dayes of *July*, That they cause read this Our Proclamation, from the Pulpit, in every Paroch Church; and that they exhort all Our loving Subjects to a sober and devout performance of the said Fast and Humiliation, as they tender the favour of Almighty GOD, the duty they owe to Us, and the peace and preservation of their Country: Certifying all these who shall contemn or neglect such a religious and necessar a work, they shall be proceeded against, and punished as contemners of Our Authority, and persons disaffected to the honour and safety of their Country.

1666–Ir2 Thanksgiving day for naval victory in the Four Days battle

[August] 1666 (Ireland)

The *Report of the deputy keeper* listed an order for thanksgiving, formerly in the Dublin PRO, dated 25 July 1666 (see also 1666–Ir1). The occasion is otherwise unknown, and might not have been distinct from 1666–EIr2.

Order: 25 July 1666 [listed in *Report of the deputy keeper*, XXIII, app., 31; not in Steele].
Form of prayer: none ordered?

1666–EIr2   Thanksgiving days for naval victory in the battle of St James's day

Tuesday 14 August 1666 (London, Westminster, Southwark and surrounding area); Thursday 23 August 1666 (elsewhere in England and Wales); Thursday 6 September 1666 (Ireland)

Like the battle of Lowestoft of the previous year, the Four Days naval battle of 1–4 June 1666 was hailed as an English victory over the Dutch, despite significant losses of men and ships. Both sides claimed success; it was reported that the Dutch also appointed thanksgiving worship. In the battle of St James's Day (25 July), the English had greater success, quickly breaking through the enemy's lines, and pursuing its navy back to Holland. Despite continuing plague, the thanksgiving days were observed with preaching, bells, bonfires and volleys of gunfire in various parts of England and Wales. At court, as Pepys recorded, there was 'a special good Anthemne' (Pepys, VII, 245): Matthew Locke's 'Be thou exalted'. On 6 August 1666, the Irish lord lieutenant (the duke of Ormond) wrote to Secretary Arlington in

London reporting that the victory had been celebrated in Dublin, and that he would appoint a thanksgiving if one were ordered for England. An Irish thanksgiving was duly appointed, but it is not clear whether this was on the instruction of the government in Whitehall. Ormond, who was on progress, attended the thanksgiving day service in state at Cork Cathedral.

Orders: ENGLAND AND WALES: royal proclamation, 6 Aug. 1666, Wing C3313*; IRELAND: proclamation by the lord lieutenant and council, 15 Aug. 1666, Wing I617 [no copy found: formerly Dublin PRO (destroyed); see Steele, II, no. 768].
Form of prayer: ENGLAND AND WALES: *A form of common prayer, vvith thanksgiving, for the late victory by his majesties naval forces: appointed to be used in and about London, on Tuesday the 14th of August; and through all England, on Thursday the 23d of August. Set forth by his majesties authority* ([64] pp.; Wing C4121)* [other impression, Wing C4121aA]; IRELAND: none ordered?
Additional sources: *CSPD, 1666–7*, pp. 16, 17; Lord Arlington to Williamson, 6 June 1666, John Carlisle to Williamson, 7 June 1666, ? to Henry Smith, 15 June 1666, *CSPD, 1665–6*, pp. 430–2, 432–3, 442; John Carlisle to Williamson, 24 Aug. 1666, Anthony Thorold to Williamson, 25 Aug. 1666, M. Anderton to Williamson, 25 Aug. 1666, Hugh Acland to Williamson, 27 Aug. 1666, Jo. Man to Williamson, 27 Aug. 1666, H. Muddiman to George Powell, 30 Aug. 1666, *CSPD, 1666–7*, pp. 62–3, 65, 66, 69, 70, 79; Pepys, VII, 245–6; Robert Thompson, 'Locke, Matthew (*c*. 1622–1677)', *Oxford dictionary of national biography*; lord lieutenant to Secretary Arlington, 6 Aug., 26 Aug. 1666, *CSPI, 1666–9*, pp. 176, 197–8; *CSPI, 1666–9*, p. 208.
Printed sermon: Dolben, court (Wing D1833).

ORDER

England and Wales: royal proclamation, 6 August 1666

Whereas it hath pleased Almighty God in his late Providence towards Us and Our People, to manifest at once the glory both of his Power and Mercy, in giving Us a happy Victory over Our Adversaries at Sea, filling the hearts of Us and Our People as full of joy and thankfulness, as becomes so transcendent a Mercy; We cannot upon the due consideration hereof, but with all humility admire and adore the mercy and goodness of God in this his signal manifestation thereof; and we look upon it as an invitation from Heaven to Us and all Our People unto the most entire Thankfulness for the same. And to the end some Solemn time may be set apart for the Publick performance of this Duty, and that We and all Our Subjects in *England* and *Wales*, and the Town of *Berwick* upon *Tweed*, may pay Our just tribute of Praise and Thanksgiving to Almighty God, We do hereby Publish and Declare, and also strictly Charge and Command, That *Tuesday* the Fourteenth day of this instant *August* be set apart and observed as a day of Publick Thanksgiving in the Cities of *London* and *Westminster*, Borough of *Southwark*, and other places adjacent. And that *Thursday* the Three and twentieth of this instant *August*, the like be kept and duely observed through the rest of this whole Realm of *England*, and Dominion of *Wales*. And for the more orderly performance thereof *[as 1665–EIr1*: We by the advice of Our Reverend Bishops … so solemn an occasion*]*.

FORM OF PRAYER

England and Wales

MORNING PRAYER

[As 1665–EIr1, until]

[Ps. 29, 33, 46]
[First lesson: 1 Chron. 16:7–36]
[Te Deum]
[Second lesson: 1 Pet. 2]
[Benedictus]

[Then as BCP to the end of the suffrages after the Lord's prayer]

In stead of the first Collect at Morning Prayer shall these two be used.
    O almighty God, the soveraign Commander *[as 1665–EIr1]*

[The BCP prayer for peace and deliverance from enemies]

[Then as BCP to the end of morning prayer]

LITANY

[As BCP to the end of the prayer 'We humbly beseech thee']

O most gracious and glorious Lord God, *[as 1665–EIr1:* who … in time of their distress:*]* Our Enemies compassed us about on every side, but thou hast delivered us by thy mercy. They were many, and did rage horribly *[as 1665–EIr1:* but thou, O Lord … swift destruction*]*. Out of the deep of the Sea we cried unto thee, O Lord, and thou didst hear us. We acknowledge and confess *[as 1665–EIr1:* O our God … defeated the counsels and*]* broken the strength of our Adversaries. It is thine own right hand that purchased us this Victory. We want words to express our thankfulness, and thoughts to conceive the greatness of thy manifold Deliverances; yet be thou pleased *[as 1665–EIr1:* to accept the best praises … *Amen]*.

Then shall follow this Prayer; which shall be used continually as long as the Navy is abroad.
    O most glorious, and powerful Lord God *[as 1665–E]*

[The prayer of St Chrysostom; the grace]

COMMUNION

[As BCP to the end of the ten commandments]

Almighty God, whose kingdom is everlasting *[as BCP]*

[Then, in place of the collect for the day, the special collects prescribed for morning prayer]

[Epistle: Phil. 4:4–9]
[Gospel: Matt. 5:43–8]
[Nicene creed; the sermon]
[Offertory sentences: Matt. 5:16; Matt. 7:12]

[The prayer for the whole state of the church]

Then shall be added this Prayer following.

O Lord God our strength and our salvation; We thy unworthy Servants, the sinful People *[as 1665–EIr1:* of these three Nations, … of our devoutest hearts*]* we magnifie thy great and glorious Name, O Lord our God, for that remarkable Victory, wherewith thou hast lately blest the Naval Forces of our gracious Soveraign. O continue forth thy loving kindness *[as 1665–EIr1:* towards him … *Amen].*

Almighty God, who hast promised *[as BCP, followed by the blessing]*

EVENING PRAYER

[The rubric as in morning prayer, followed by the opening sentences: 1 Tim. 2:1–3]

[Then as BCP to the psalms, before which is inserted the prayer to be used in place of the Venite *at morning prayer]*

[Ps. 66, 92, 147]
[First lesson: 1 Sam. 2:1–10]
[Magnificat]
[Second lesson: 1 Thess. 5]
[Cantate Domino]

[Then as BCP from the Apostles' creed to the suffrages after the Lord's prayer]

[Then, in place of the collect for the day, the special collects prescribed for morning prayer]

[Then as BCP to the end of the prayer for the clergy and people, and then the prayer 'O Lord God our strength and our salvation' from the end of the communion service, and the prayer to 'be used continually so long as the Navy is abroad']

[The prayer of St Chrysostom; the grace]

1666–S2   Thanksgiving days for naval victory in the battle of St James's day

Thursday 23 August 1666 (Edinburgh and Lothian); Thursday 30 August 1666 (elsewhere in Scotland)

On 11 June 1666, the Scottish privy council heard reports of the navy's success against the Dutch in the Four Days battle, and ordered bonfires, bells and cannon fire in Edinburgh. On 14 August, the council received a letter from the king reporting that a thanksgiving had been appointed in England after the victory in the St James's Day fight (1666–EIr2), and ordering that an equivalent thanksgiving be observed in Scotland. Charles requested that 23 August be kept in Edinburgh and the surrounding area, and left the date for the rest of Scotland to the privy council's decision. The thanksgiving was observed on 5 September in the presbytery of Dingwall. During

June 1667 a Dutch naval attack on the British fleet anchored in the Medway, together with the cost of the war, persuaded the king to conclude a peace treaty.

Order: royal proclamation, 14 Aug. 1666, *RPC*, 3rd ser., II, 187–8 [no broadside listed in ESTC].
Additional sources: *RPC*, 3rd ser., II, 170, 187; Lord Bellenden to the earl of Lauderdale, 14 Aug. 1666, BL, Add. 23135, fo. 45r; *Edin. recs., 1665 to 1680*, p. 17; *Aber. recs., 1643–1747*, pp. 231–2; *Alford exercise*, p. 84; *Inverness and Dingwall records*, pp. 317–18; Nicoll, p. 450; Lamont, p. 191.

ORDER

Royal proclamation: 14 August 1666

Forasmuch as it hath pleased Almighty God to give to our royall fleit upon the 25 and 26 of July last a glorious and happy victory against the fleet of our enemies, the States Generall of the United Provinces, for which wee are resolved to acknowledge our thankfulnes for so signall and seasonable a mercy by a day of publick thanksgiveing to be solemnly keipt throughout our kingdomes of Scotland and England, and for imploreing the continuance of Gods blissing upon our fleet now remaining on our enemies coast, our will is herfore and we straitly command and charge all our subjects duelling and reseiding within our burgh of Edinburgh and the shyres of Eist, West and Mid Lotheans to observe and keip the 23 of this instant August as a day of publick thanksgiveing; and all others reseiding within any other burgh or shyre to keip and observe the threttieth day of the said moneth, requyring hereby our reverend archbishopes and bishops within their severall diocesses to give notice hereof to all ministers within the same that they intimat these presents upon the Sonday before out of their severall pulpitts, and exhort their parochiners to be present at sermon and to perform the deuties of that day as becomes good christians and loyall subjects, with certification that, if any neglect, they shall be esteemed as persons disaffected to our royall government and service.

1666–EIr3   Fast day after the great fire of London

Wednesday 10 October 1666 (England and Wales; Ireland)

The great fire of London started in the early hours of 2 September 1666, and burned destructively until at least 5 September, affecting around four-fifths of the area of the City of London. On 10 September, the privy council resolved to appoint a fast day, issuing a proclamation that gave detailed reports of the fire. The proclamation also made a special appeal to the whole of England and Wales for charity for the fire's victims; collections were to be sent to the lord mayor of London. The form of prayer opened with a paragraph which repeated the appeal for funds, to be made either in churches or by house-to-house collections. The form was based on that for the monthly fast for the plague (1665–EIr2), which continued to be observed, explaining the reference to the 'Visitation' in the instructions concerning the litany. Pepys recorded that St Margaret's, Westminster, was crowded on the fast day. On hearing of the fire, the lord lieutenant of Ireland, who was at Kilkenny, travelled to Dublin, arriving on 20 September. The council met and issued a proclamation for this fast day. It is likely that the date was chosen deliberately to match that observed in England. The lord lieutenant also wrote to the mayor of Dublin and other Irish magistrates, requesting donations for the victims of the fire.

Orders: ENGLAND AND WALES: royal proclamation, 13 Sept. 1666, Wing C3303*; IRELAND: proclamation by the lord lieutenant and council, 22 Sept. 1666, Wing I854 [no copy found; Dublin PRO (destroyed); see Steele, II, no. 773].

Form of prayer: ENGLAND AND WALES: *A form of common prayer. To be used on Wednesday the tenth day of October next, throughout the whole kingdom of England, and dominion of Wales, being appointed by his majesty, a day of fasting and humiliation, in consideration of the late dreadful fire, which wasted the greater part of the city of London. Set forth by his majesties special command* ([52] pp.; Wing C4116)*; IRELAND: none ordered?

Additional sources: privy council register, PC2/59, fos. 81r, 82r; *CSPD, 1666–7*, p. 122; Anthony Thorold to James Hickes, *CSPD, 1666–7*, p. 195; *Concilia*, IV, 586; Pepys, VII, 316–17; Evelyn, III, 464; *The diary of John Milward*, ed. Robbins, p. 19; George Warburton to Joseph Williamson, 22 Sept., 1 Oct., 13 Oct. 1666, *CSPI, 1666–9*, pp. 213, 219, 223–4.

Printed sermons: Sancroft, court (Wing S553, S554, S554A); Stillingfleet, House of Commons (Wing S5637, S5638, S5639, S5640); Stokes, Eton (Wing S5720).

ORDER

England and Wales: royal proclamation, 13 September 1666

Whereas it hath pleased Almighty God by a most lamentable and devouring Fire (which broke out upon Sunday the Second of *September*, about two of the Clock in the morning neer *Thames-Street*, and continued raging till Thursday night, or Friday following) to lay waste the greatest part of the City of *London* within the Walls, and some part of the Suburbs, whereof more then Fourscore Parishes, and all the Houses, Churches, Chappels, Hospitals, and other the great and Magnificent Buildings of pious or publique use which were within that Circuit, are now brought into Ashes, and become one ruinous Heap: A Visitation so dreadful, that scarce any Age or Nation hath ever seen or felt the like; wherein although the afflicting Hand of God fell more immediately upon the Inhabitants of this City, and the parts Adjacent, yet all men ought to look upon it as a Judgment upon the whole Nation, and to humble themselves accordingly. His Majesty therefore out of a deep and pious sence of what Himself and all his People now suffer, and with a Religious care to prevent what may yet be feared, unless it shall please Almighty God to turn away his Anger from Us, doth hereby publish and Declare His Royal Will and Pleasure, That Wednesday, being the Tenth of *October* next ensuing, shall be set apart and kept and observed by all His Majesties Subjects of *England* and *Wales*, and the Town of *Barwick* upon *Tweed*, as a Day of Solemn Fasting and Humiliation, to implore the mercies of God, That it would please him to pardon the crying sins of this Nation, those especially which have drawn down this last and heavy Judgment upon Us, and to remove from Us all other His Judgments which Our sins have deserved, and which We now either feel or fear: And to the end that His Majesties Subjects may be assisted in the performance of the duties of that Day, and that all His good People may be united in such common Devotions and Supplications as may be fit and proper for the occasion, His Majesty will take care, by and with the Advice of His Reverend Bishops, That a Form of Prayer fit for that purpose shall be timely and seasonably published; And His Majesty doth strictly charge and command all His Subjects of what Estate or Degree soever, That they duely observe this Day of Fasting and Humiliation in such decent and devout manner as becomes so sad and solemn an Occasion, as they will answer the neglect thereof unto Almighty God, and upon pain of incurring the utmost severities which can be inflicted upon the wilful breakers and contemners of this His Majesties Royal Command: And because many Persons and Families, who were formerly able to give great relief to others, are now become great objects of Charity themselves, having not only lost all they had by Fire, but being destitute of all Habitation; His Majesty doth therefore require and command all Ministers, Parsons, Vicars, or Curates who shall Preach on that Day, That they earnestly recommend the distressed estate and condition of those who have been undone by this Fire, unto the charity of all good and well disposed Christians. And that they cause Collections for this purpose to be made in all Churches and Chappels whatsoever, and the Monies so collected to be faithfully and entirely returned up to *London*, and there paid in to the Lord Mayor of the City of *London*, or such as he shall appoint, to the end the same may be duly and orderly distributed by the advice and directions of the Lord Mayor, and Lord Bishop of *London*, unto and amongst such poor Sufferers by this Fire, as shall be found to have most need thereof; And that all good people may be the better prepared for their Devotions, and provided for their charitable benevolence that Day, It is His Majesties further Pleasure, that this His Royal Proclamation be read in all Churches and Chappels on some Lords Day precedent to the said Day of Fasting and Humiliation.

FORM OF PRAYER

England and Wales
His Majesty hath Commanded all Ministers, with all possible earnestness to stir up the people of their several Congregations that Day to a Charitable and bountiful Contribution for the relief of those many poor distressed persons, who suffer by reason of this Fire: Which money so collected is speedily to be sent up to the Lord Mayor of the City of *London*, to be disposed of, as by His Majesties Proclamation is Graciously provided and declared. And this Collection is to be made, either in the publick Congregation, or by going from house to house, as shall be most conducing to this Charitable and Pious work.

MORNING PRAYER

Let him that ministreth read with a loud voice these Sentences of Scripture; and then say the Exhortation that followeth.
[Dan. 9:9–10; Jer. 10:24]

[As BCP to the Venite*]*

Instead of Venite exultemus, *shall be sung or said this Hymn following; one Verse by the Priest, and another by the Clerk and people.*
O Come, Let us humble our selves, and fall down before the Lord: with reverence and fear. (Ps. 95:6)
For he is the Lord our God: and we are the people of his pasture, and the sheep of his hand. (Ps. 95:7)
Come therfor, Let us turn again unto our Lord: for he hath smitten us, and he will heal us. (Hos. 6:1)
Let us Repent and turn from our wickedness: and our sins shall be forgiven us. (Acts 3:19)
Let us turn, and the Lord will turn from his heavy wrath: and will pardon us, and we shall not perish. (Jonah 3:8–9)

We acknowledge indeed, that our punishments are less than our deservings: but yet of thy mercy, O Lord, Correct us to amendment, and plague us not to our destruction. (Job 11:6; Wisd. 11:23)

We have provoked thine anger, thy wrath is waxed hot: and thy heavy displeasure is sore kindled against us. (Lam. 3:42)

How doth the City sit solitary, that was full of people: how is she become as a widow, she that was great among the Nations, and Princess among the Provinces? (Lam. 1:1)

How hath the Lord covered the Daughter of Sion with a cloud in his Anger: and cast down from Heaven unto the Earth the beauty of Israel, and remembred not his footstool in the day of his anger! (Lam. 2:1)

He hath cut off in his fierce anger the Horne of Israel, and consumed all that was pleasant to the eye: in the Tabernacle of the Daughter of Sion he poured out his fury like fire. (Lam. 2:4)

The Lord was an enemy; he hath swallowed up Israel, he hath swallowed up all her Palaces: he hath destroyed his strong holds, and hath increased in the Daughter of Judah mourning and lamentations. (Lam. 2:5)

But thy hand is not shortned that thou canst not help: neither is thy goodness abated, that thou wilt not hear. (Isa. 59:1)

Thou hast promised, O Lord, that before we cry, thou wilt hear us: whilst we are yet speaking thou wilt have mercy upon us. (Isa. 65:24)

For thou art the only Lord, who woundest and dost heal again: thou killest, and revivest; bringest even to Hell, and bringest back again. (Job 5:18; Hos. 6:2)

Thou forgivest all our sins: and healest all our infirmities. (Ps. 103:3)

Thou savest our life from destruction: and crownest us with mercy and loving kindness. (Ps. 103:4)

Our Fathers hoped in thee: they trusted in thee, and thou didst deliver them. (Ps. 22:4)

They called upon thee, and were holpen: they put their trust in thee, and were not confounded. (Ps. 22:5)

And now in the vexation of our spirits, and the anguish of our souls we cry unto thee: hear, Lord, and have mercy. (Bar. 3:1–2)

For many troubles are come about us: our sins have taken such hold upon us, that we are not able to look up. (Ps. 50:15)

O remember not our sins, and our offences: but according to thy mercy think thou upon us, O Lord, for thy goodness. (Ps. 25:6)

Hide not thy face from us in the time of our trouble: encline thine ears unto us when we call; O hear us, and that right soon. (Ps. 102:2)

For thine own sake, and for thy holy Names sake, encline thine eare: and hear, O merciful Lord. (Dan. 9:18–19)

For we do not present our Supplications before thee, trusting in our own righteousnesse: but in thy manifold and great mercies. (Dan. 9:18)

Help us, O God of our Salvation, for the glory of thy Name: O deliver us, and be merciful unto our sins, for thy Names sake. (Ps. 79:9)

So we that are thy people, and sheep of thy Pasture, shall give thee thanks for ever: and will alwaies be shewing forth thy praise from generation to generation. (Ps. 79:14)

Glory be to the Father, &c.

As it was in the beginning, &c.

[Ps. 25, 77, 86]
[First lesson: Isa. 1]
[Te Deum]
[Second lesson: Luke 21]
[Benedictus]

[Then as BCP to the end of morning prayer, replacing the collect for the day with the BCP collect for Ash Wednesday]

LITANY

Here followeth the Litany; which, as it is here Printed, together with the other proper Collects in this Book, shall be used publickly in Churches, not onely upon the Monethly Fast-day, but on Wednesday *in every Week (and may by every man be used daily in private Families) during the time of this Visitation.*

[As BCP to the end of the prayer 'We humbly beseech thee']

The Priest and Clerk, or he that ministers (still kneeling in the place where they are accustomed to say or sing the Litany) shall here repeat this Psalm.
[Ps. 51]

[Then, from the BCP commination service, the prayers beginning 'Minister: O Lord, save thy servants', 'O Lord, we beseech thee mercifully hear our prayers', 'O Most mighty God and merciful Father' and 'Turn thou us, O good Lord'. Then]

Look down, O Lord, in the bowels of thy mercy, upon the sorrows and distresses of thy servants, who in the deepest sense of thy amazing Judgements, and our own manifold provocations, lie prostrate in the dust before thee.

To thee O God holy and true, belong mercy and forgiveness, But unto us confusion of face as it is this day: For we are that incorrigible Nation who have resisted thy Judgements, and abused thy Mercies; we have despised the chastisements of the Lord, and turn'd his grace into wantonness.

What shall we then say unto thee, O thou Preserver of men? thou hast found out the iniquity of thy servants, and discovered our nakedness and pollution, in a vengeance suited and answerable to our grievous crying sins. Our pride, oppression, and fulness of bread, had made us like to Sodom, and thou hast afflicted us as Gomorrha. We would not be reclaimed by thy exemplary punishments upon others, or our selves, and thou hast made us a terrour and astonishment to all that are round about us.

And now, O Lord, thou art most just in all that is come upon us; for thou hast done right, but we have done very wickedly; yet behold we are all thy people, though an unthankful and rebellious people: Suffer us therefore to implore thy pity, and the sounding of thy bowels, and for thy Names sake; for thy mercies sake, for Christ Jesus sake encline thine ear to us and save us.

Above all, we beseech thee, abandon us not to our selves; but by what method soever it shall please thee to reduce us, though to this bitter cup of trembling thou shalt add more and more grievous afflictions, by any the severest course, subdue us unto thy self, and make us see the things belonging to our peace, before they be hid from our eyes, that being duely humbled under thy mighty hand, we may be capable of being relieved and exalted in thy due time, through Christ our Lord. *Amen.*

Then shall follow this Prayer; which shall be used continually so long as the Navy is abroad.
   O most glorious, and powerful Lord God *[as 1665–E]*

[The prayer of St Chrysostom; the grace]

COMMUNION

[As BCP to the end of the ten commandments]

Almighty God, whose kingdom is everlasting *[as BCP]*

[Then, in place of the collect for the day, the BCP collect for Ash Wednesday]

[Epistle: 1 Cor. 10:1–14]
[Gospel: Luke 17:26–37]
[Nicene creed; the sermon]
[Offertory sentences: Matt. 5:16; Ps. 41:1]

[The prayer for the whole state of the church]

We bless and magnifie thy Name, O Lord, for that wonderful mercy thou hast vouchsafed us in the midst of thy just and dreadful Judgements. It is of thy goodness that we are not consumed; That when we had provoked thee to give us all up to utter ruine and desolation, and thy hand was stretched out to execute thy whole displeasure upon us; yet thou hast preserved a remnant, and plucked us as a brand out of the fire, that we should not utterly perish in our sins. Add, we beseech thee this one mercy to all that thou hast hitherto so unsuccessfully cast away upon us: By thy mighty convincing Spirit awaken our sleepy consciences, soften and melt our hard hearts, that being humbled by thy chastisements, we may by thy goodness be led to repentance, and sin no more, lest a worse thing happen unto us; But contrariwise may faithfully improve this respite and relief, with all its precious advantages and opportunities, to a thankful, humble, profitable walking before thee, that so thy Name may be glorified, the gospel credited, and our souls saved in the day of the Lord; Grant this, O Father, for Jesus Christs sake our onely Mediatour and Redeemer. *Amen.*

Here may be added one, or both the Collects following.
[The BCP collects for the fourth and second Sundays in Lent]

Almighty God, who hast promised *[as BCP, followed by the blessing]*

EVENING PRAYER

[The rubric as in morning prayer, followed by the opening sentences: Dan 9:9–10; Jer. 10:24]

[Then as BCP to the psalms, before which is inserted the prayer to be used in place of the Venite *at morning prayer]*

[Ps. 90, 102, 130, 143]
[First lesson: Amos 4]
[Magnificat]
[Second lesson: 2 Pet. 3]
[Deus misereatur]

[Then as BCP with, in place of the collect for the day, the BCP collect for Ash Wednesday; the BCP second and third collects for evening prayer; then, from the BCP commination service, the prayers beginning 'O Lord, we beseech thee mercifully hear our prayers', 'O most mighty God and merciful Father' and 'Turn thou us, O good Lord'; the prayer beginning 'Look down, O Lord' from the end of the litany]

[Then as BCP from the prayer for the king to the end of evening prayer]

1666–E   Thanksgiving day for decline of the plague in London

Tuesday 20 November 1666 (London, Westminster and bills of mortality)

By November 1666, London's major plague outbreak had subsided, though a few plague deaths continued to be reported. This thanksgiving was appointed by privy council order, rather than the usual printed royal proclamation. It is unclear why this procedure was followed, though it may have been because the observance was limited to London and its environs. The use of a council order probably explains why the form was prefaced by an instruction to ministers to announce the thanksgiving in church on the Sunday preceding, a practice which was very uncommon for fast and thanksgiving days in England. According to Pepys, it was widely remarked that the observance was ordered precipitately, so as to allow the theatres to reopen. Perhaps the speed with which the occasion was planned explains the apparently incomplete rubric before the collect in morning prayer beginning 'Almighty Lord, the Father of mercies'. Unusually, the form of prayer included the BCP's rubric calling for the anthem in morning prayer. The selection of a Tuesday for the thanksgiving day explains why the litany, not normally read on Tuesday, was omitted from the form of prayer.

Order: privy council order, 9 Nov. 1666, PC2/59, fo. 108v.
Form of prayer: *A form of common prayer with thanksgiving to God, for asswaging the late contagion and pestilence, to be used on Tuesday the 20th of this instant November, in the cities of London and Westminster, and the several parishes within the weekly bills of mortality. Published by his majesties authority* ([28] pp.; Wing C4121A)*.
Additional sources: Pepys, VII, 376–7; *The diary of John Milward*, ed. Robbins, p. 44.

ORDER

Privy council order: 9 November 1666
It was this day Ordered by his Matie in Councill, That the Right Reverend Father in God the Lord Bishop of London do giue speedy notice to the Ministers of the seuerall

Parish Churches within the Citties of London and Westminster, and the Suburbs thereof, That it is his Maties expresse Will & Pleasure, That Tuesday the 20th of this instant November be set apart, and obserued as a day of Publique Thanksgiving in the Citties of London and Westminster and the seuerall Parishes within the Weekely Bills of Mortality humbly to acknowledge the great Mercy and Goodnes of Almighty God in abating and withdrawing the late heavy Visitation of the Plague of Pestilence in the Places aforesaid, And for the more orderly performance hereof, His Lo^p is desired to cause Coppys of the Forme of Prayer & Thanksgiving that shalbe prepared for that purpose to be distributed to the said Ministers.

FORM OF PRAYER

Upon the Sunday before the day of Thanksgiving, immediately after the Nicene Creed, the Minister shall give the people warning of it: And earnestly exhort them to express their thankfulness to Almighty God, and due sence of his great mercy and deliverance vouchsafed unto them.

MORNING PRAYER

Let him that Ministreth read with a loud voice these Sentences of Scripture, and then say the Exhortation that followeth.
[Ezek. 18:27; Dan. 9:9–10]

[As BCP to the psalms]

[Ps. 30, 103, 116]
[First lesson: Isa. 38]
[Te Deum]
[Second lesson: John 5:1–15]
[Jubilate Deo]

[Then as BCP to the third collect, replacing the collect for the day with both the BCP thanksgivings for deliverance from the plague or other common sickness]

[The anthem, and as BCP to the prayer for the clergy and people]

[The BCP prayer for parliament; the BCP prayer in time of war]

This Prayer is to be read every day until ---
   Almighty Lord, the Father of mercies, and God of all consolation; We thy bounden, but most unthankful people, who above all nations of the world, have seen the greatness of thy hand; have been from time to time the care of thy Providence, and Example of thy Goodness: with all humility and shame confess, that as our sins have surpassed the number and measure of the transgressions of our fathers, so thou hast most justly brought upon us the fruit of our own ways, by sending to us a Plague more dreadful far then any inflicted upon them: Yea in the time of thy visitation, whilst thy anger waxed hot against us, we have not returned unto our God that smote us, nor brought forth those meet fruits of repentance and humiliation, which so sharp a scourge did call for from us: but rather in the midst of that danger, did

hold on the same course of carnal security, and neglect of thy Commandments. Yet thou hast not cut us off in the midst of our sins and provocations, but hast stay'd the hand of the destroying Angel, and restored to us the voice of joy and health within our dwellings. It is thy goodness and meer favour to us, that, thou hast rather chosen to glorifie thy Mercy in saving us, then to magnifie thy Justice in our destruction. For this we praise thy great and holy Name, beseeching thee to continue and perfect this thy blessed work of Preservation and Deliverance. Inlarge thy favors to thy Church, our King and State, enrich them with all inward and outward Blessings, and give us such effectual Grace, that we looking every one of us unto the Plague of his own heart, may abhor our own corruptions, and turn from our evil ways, that thy long-suffering and forbearance may lead us to Repentance; and the prolonging of our days, may be the breaking off our sins, and the amendment of our lives. Grant this, O Father, for Jesus Christ his sake, our Lord and onely Saviour. *Amen.*

Then shall follow this Prayer; which shall be used continually so long as the Navy is abroad.

 O most glorious, and powerful Lord God *[as 1665–E]*

[The BCP general thanksgiving; the prayer of St Chrysostom; the grace]

COMMUNION

[As BCP to the end of the ten commandments]

Almighty God, whose kingdom is everlasting *[as BCP]*

[Then, in place of the collect for the day, the special collects prescribed at morning prayer]

[Epistle: Isa. 1:9–21]
[Gospel: Luke 17:11–19]
[Nicene creed; the sermon]
[Offertory sentences: Matt. 5:16; Heb. 13:16]

[The prayer for the whole state of the church]

Then shall be added the prayer following.
We will magnifie thee, O God our king, and will praise thy Name for ever and ever; because in the midst of wrath, remembring mercy thou hast delivered our souls from death, and preserv'd us from the noisom Pestilence. It is not for our righteousness, O Lord, nor for the cleanness of our hands in thy sight, that when thousands better then our selves have faln besides us, and ten thousand at our right hand, destruction has not come nigh us, but we yet remain alive, as it is this day. Tis thou, O Lord, who dost wound and heal again, killest and makest alive, bringest to Hell and back from thence. Thou hast vouchsafed above all humane aids and means, such is thy power and goodness, to command thy Angel to stay his hand, and spare us. We therefore offer up unto thee at once, the oblation of hearty thanksgiving for this our great deliverance, and of humble and earnest prayer for all those that are yet afflicted; beseeching thee for thy Son Jesus Christ his sake, to be gracious unto them and us; that both they and we in joint affection, may acknowledge the justice of thy

Punishment, and record thine infinite mercy in sparing us miserable sinners: and this we do in the Name of thy Son and our Saviour, to whom with thee and the holy Ghost, be all praise & glory now and ever. *Amen.*

Almighty God, who in thy late dreadful visitation, hast covered with thy hand, thine anointed servant our gracious sovereign Lord King *Charles*, so that no evil has happened unto him: And also hast compassed with thy merciful protection, the Queen and the whole Royal Family, so that no Plague has come nigh their dwelling: We acknowledge with all thankfulness this thy distinguishing, conspicuous mercy, vouchsafed at once unto his Majesty and his Dominions: beseeching thee to continue still thy gracious goodness towards them; to the glory of thy Name, and the welfare and prosperity of thy Church; and this we beg for Jesus Christ his sake. *Amen.*

Assist us mercifully, O Lord *[as BCP]*

Almighty God, who hast promised *[as BCP, followed by the blessing]*

1672–EIr   Fast days after outbreak of the third Anglo-Dutch war

Wednesday 27 March 1672 (London, Westminster, Southwark and bills of mortality); Wednesday 17 April 1672 (elsewhere in England and Wales; Ireland)

In the secret treaty of Dover (1670), Charles II had promised to join Louis XIV of France in war against the United Provinces. Although the crown's policy remained publicly anti-French, its preparations for the war became increasingly obvious from the summer of 1671. On 17 March 1672, a declaration of war was made; at the same time, the attorney general was ordered to produce a proclamation for this fast. Perhaps to save time, allowing the fast days to be observed at short notice, the form of prayer was identical to 1665–E, apart from two minor changes, which could have been introduced by the copyist or printer. In Ireland, the fast was appointed ten days after the crown's declaration of war; 17 April may have been chosen deliberately to co-ordinate with the equivalent English observance. Yet no instruction from Whitehall to the Irish authorities has been traced, and it is possible that the lord lieutenant acted on his own initiative. Unlike in the case of 1665–EIr1, where the equivalent English proclamation was the model for the Irish proclamation, there is no resemblance here.

Orders: ENGLAND AND WALES: royal proclamation, 22 Mar. 1672, Wing C3305*; IRELAND: proclamation of the lord lieutenant and council, 27 Mar. 1672, Wing I675*.
Form of prayer: ENGLAND AND WALES: *A form of common prayer to be used on Wednesday the 27th of March, 1672, within the cities of London and Westminster, &c. And on Wednesday the 17 of April next through the rest of the whole kingdom of England, dominion of Wales, and town of Berwick upon Tweed; being the days of the general fast appointed by his majesties proclamation, for imploring Gods blessing on his majesties naval forces. Set forth by his majesties authority* ([68] pp.; Wing C4117)* [other impression, ESTC R223748]; IRELAND: none ordered.
Additional sources: privy council register, PC2/63, fos. 104r, 106r; *CSPD, 1671–2*, p. 225; the king to the bishop of London, 29 Mar. 1672, Edward Bodham to Williamson, 17 Apr. 1672, *CSPD, 1671–2*, pp. 253, 334; Bishop Edward Rainbow of Carlisle to Archbishop Sheldon, 7 May 1672, Bod., MS Add. c. 305, fo. 48r; *CSPD, 1671–2*, p. 244.

ORDERS

England and Wales: royal proclamation, 22 March 1672

The Kings most Excellent Majesty, being necessitated, for the just Defence and Vindication of His own and Subjects Rights, to Declare War against the *States of the United Provinces*; And having His Forces now in readiness upon a present Expedition, Hath Resolved and doth hereby Command a General and Publick Fast to be kept throughout His whole Kingdom: That so both Prince and People may send up their Prayers and Supplications to Almighty God, for imploring His Blessing on His Majesties Naval Forces: And for the more decent and Uniform performance thereof, His Majesty doth hereby Publish and Declare to all His loving Subjects, and doth straitly Charge and Command that *Wednesday* next being the 27th day of this instant *March*, This Fast be Religiously and Solemnly kept and observed, within the Cities of *London* and *Westminster* and the Borough of *Southwark* and other Places adjacent within the Bills of Mortality: And that upon *Wednesday* the 17th of *April* next, the like Fast be kept and duly observed through the rest of this whole Kingdom of *England*, Dominion of *Wales*, and Town of *Berwick* upon *Tweed*.

And for the more orderly Solemnizing thereof, His Majesty hath directed that the Form of Prayers Compos'd and Published in the late War, upon the like occasion, be used in all Churches and Chappels, and hath given Charge to the Bishops for the dispersing thereof through their several Dioceses in the whole Kingdom.

And His Majesty doth expresly Charge and Command, that the said Fasting and Prayers be Soberly, Reverently, and Decently Performed by all His Loving Subjects, as they tender the Favour of Almighty God, and upon pain of such Punishments as His Majesty can justly inflict upon all such, as Contemn or Neglect so Religious a Work.

Ireland: proclamation of the lord lieutenant and council, 27 March 1672

We the *LORD LIEUTENANT* and *COUNCIL*, do Command and Proclaim Publick Humiliation, Fasting and Prayers to be observed in all the Parts and Parishes within this Kingdom, on *Wednesday* the 17th of *April* next. And therefore We Will and Require, That the Ministers and Parishioners of every Parish within this Kingdom, do duely repair to the Cathedral or Parish-Church on the said Day, as aforesaid, to Divine Service and Sermons: Upon which Day, the Minister is to call upon the People, That they abstain from Labour, and from Pleasure, and from the Ordinary works of their Callings, and dedicate themselves on that Day to Humiliation, Fasting, Prayer, Works of Charity and Devotion, Bewailing as well their own Sins, as the great and known Sins of the Kingdom; And supplicating Almighty God of his mercy and goodness, to bless and prosper all His Majesties Councils, and all His Armies and Fleets by Land and by Sea, and particularly His present Expedition. And We Will and Require every Archbishop and Bishop to call upon his Clergy for the diligent and due performance thereof.

FORM OF PRAYER

England and Wales

[As 1665–E, except]

[In the communion service, after the prayer for the whole state of the church]

We humbly acknowledge before thee, O merciful Father, that all the punishments threatned in thy Law against sinners might justly fall upon us by reason of our manifold transgressions; and especially our great unthankfulness for thy unspeakable mercies *[as 1665–E*: towards us ... what we have*]* done amiss; O Lord, who will be able to abide it? *[as 1665–E*: At the Footstool of the Throne of thy Grace ... *Amen]*

1674–E   Fast days during divisions over catholic influences, and during the third Anglo-Dutch war

Wednesday 4 February 1674 (London, Westminster, Southwark and ten miles around); Wednesday 11 February 1674 (elsewhere in England and Wales)

Amid growing opposition to the Dutch war and fears of catholic influence at court, parliament met on 20 October 1673. This followed a prorogation of seven months. The House of Commons twice addressed the king against the marriage of the duke of York to the catholic princess of Modena, proposed a test to exclude catholics from office and resolved not to grant supply to the crown until its grievances were resolved. The Commons addressed the king for a fast on 3 November, but on the following day Charles adjourned the session until 7 January. With the Lords' concurrence, the matter was resumed in the new year, and an address for a fast was presented to the king on 14 January. The king, now eager to conciliate the parliamentary opposition, agreed to order a fast. He also resolved to conclude peace with the Dutch. The proclamation's first sentence followed parliament's address almost verbatim. The form of prayer was based closely on 1665–E.

Order: royal proclamation, 16 Jan. 1674, Wing C3306*.
Form of prayer: *A form of common prayer, to be used on Wednesday the 4th of February, 1673/4, within the cities of London and Westminster, burrough of Southwark, and other places within ten miles distance. And on Wednesday the 11th of Febr. next through the rest of the whole kingdom of England, dominion of Wales, and town of Berwick upon Tweed; being the days of the general fast appointed by his majesties proclamation, for imploring Gods blessing on his majesty, and the present parliament. Set forth by his majesties authority* ([68] pp.; Wing C4118)*.
Additional sources: *CJ*, IX, 281–6, 291–3; *LJ*, XII, 603–5, 608; privy council register, PC2/64, fos. 163, 165; *CSPD, 1673–5*, pp. 4, 73, 109; Mostyn newsletters, 13 Jan., 22 Jan. 1674, University of Wales, Bangor, MS 9088, fos. 63v, 67.
Printed sermon: Croft, House of Lords (Wing C6974).

ORDER

Royal proclamation: 16 January 1674
Whereas Our most Loyal and Obedient Subjects, the Lords Spiritual and Temporal, and Commons in Parliament Assembled, being passionately Sensible of the Calamitous Condition of this Kingdom, not onely by reason of the War wherein it is at present involved, but many other Intestine Differences and Divisions amongst Us, which are chiefly occasioned by the undermining Contrivances of Popish Recusants, whose Numbers and Insolencies are greatly of late Encreased, and whose restless Practices threaten a Subversion both of Church and State; all which our sins have

justly deserved: And being now Assembled in Parliament, as the great Councel of this Our Kingdom, to Consult of such means as they conceive fittest to redress the present Evils wherewith this Nation is surrounded; Have in the first place humbly besought Us, That by Our special Command, One or more Days may be forthwith Solemnly set apart, wherein, both themselves and this Kingdom may by Fasting and Prayer seek a Reconciliation at the hands of Almighty God, and with humble and penitent hearts beseech him to heal the Breaches of this Nation, and remove the Evils it doth lie under, and to avert those Miseries wherewith it is threatned, and continue the Mercies it doth yet enjoy, and that he will be graciously pleased to bestow his abundant Blessing upon Us, and the present Parliament; That all their Councels and Consultations may tend to the Glory of God, and the Honour, Safety, and Prosperity of Us, and all Our People. Wherefore, and out of Our own Religious Disposition being thereto readily inclined, We have Resolved, and hereby do Command a General and Publick Fast to be kept throughout this whole Kingdom, in such manner as is hereafter Directed and Prescribed. And to the end so Religious an Exercise may be performed with all Decency and Uniformity, We have Resolved upon a Grave and Religious Form of Solemnizing thereof: And do hereby strictly Charge and Command, That on *Wednesday*, being the Fourth day of *February* next, this Fast be Religiously and Solemnly Observed and Celebrated, in the Cities of *London* and *Westminster*, Burrough of *Southwark*, and other Places within Ten Miles distance, wherein We in Our Royal Person, and with Our Royal Family and Houshold, will give Example to the rest of Our People. And that on *Wednesday* the Eleventh day of *February* next, the like be Kept, and duly Observed throughout the rest of this whole Kingdom of *England*, and Dominion of *Wales*, and Town of *Berwick* upon *Tweed*. And for the more orderly Solemnizing thereof without Confusion, We, by the Advice of Our Reverend Bishops, have Directed to be Composed, Printed, and Published, the Form of such Prayers, and Publick Exhortations, as We think fit to be Used in all Churches and Places at the Times aforesaid, and have given Charge to Our Bishops to Disperse the same throughout the whole Kingdom; And We Require and Command all Preachers, to Exhort their Congregations on the said respective Days, to Mercy and Liberality to the Poor, in this time of Dearth and Scarcity; All which We do Expresly Charge and Command shall be Reverently and Decently Performed by all Our Loving Subjects, upon Pain of Our High Displeasure, and such Punishments as We can Inflict upon all such as shall Contemn, or Neglect so Religious a Work.

FORM OF PRAYER

MORNING PRAYER

[As 1665–E, until]

[In place of the collect for the day, the following prayer]
    O most glorious, and powerful Lord God, who alone hast spread out the heavens, and compassed the waters with bounds, until night and day come to an end; We adore thy divine Majesty *[as 1665–E*: acknowledging thy power … *Amen]*.

[The BCP prayer in time of war, and the collect for peace, and then]

Most gracious and merciful Lord God, we thy most unworthy servants being deeply sensible of the calamitous condition of this Kingdom, involved in a War with Enemies abroad, and by the contrivances of the Adversaries of True Religion, distracted with intestine differences and divisions at home, do with all humility and sincerity acknowledge and confess, That by our unthankfulness for thy wonderful mercies and deliverances, insensibleness and stupidity under thy manifold judgments, impiety, and other daily provocations of thy vengeance, we have justly deserved thy wrath and indignation against us. Wherefore we are here met together this day, desiring with broken and penitent hearts to present our selves before the Throne of Grace, beseeching thee in mercy to pardon the great offences of us thy servants, and the crying sins of this Nation, to remove the evils which we now lie under, to avert those judgments which we justly deserve, to reconcile our differences, and heal our breaches, to unite our hearts in the profession of the True Religion, which thine own right hand hath planted and established in this Kingdom, and in an holy conversation answerable thereunto. To which end we humbly beseech thee abundantly to bestow the choicest of thy blessings temporal and spiritual, upon the Kings most Excellent Majesty, and the High Court of Parliament, that all their consultations may tend to the glory of thy great Name, the safety and honour of the King, the advancement of Piety, and preservation of the Church, and the security, peace and prosperity of all estates and conditions of men in this Kingdom. All which we humbly beg in the Name, and through the Mediation of thy Son and our blessed Saviour Jesus Christ. *Amen.*

[The BCP collect for grace]

LITANY

[As BCP to the end of the prayer 'We humbly beseech thee'; then the BCP collect for Ash Wednesday; and, from the BCP commination service, the prayers 'O Lord, we beseech thee mercifully hear our prayers', 'O most mighty God and merciful Father' and 'Turn thou us, O good Lord'. Then]

O Almighty God, and our most gracious Father, the *Soveraign* Commander *[as 1665–E: of all the world … His Majesties Fleet, and]* Naval Forces, and bless them all. In all their Counsels let Wisdom lead them; *[as 1665*–E: in all their Enterprises … *Amen]*.

[The prayer of St Chrysostom; the grace]

COMMUNION

[As 1665–E, until]

[After the prayer for the whole state of the church]

We humbly acknowledge before thee, O merciful Father, that all the punishments threatned in thy Law against sinners, might justly fall upon us, by reason of our manifold transgressions; and especially our great unthankfulness for thy unspeakable mercies *[as 1665*–E: towards us … what we have*]* done amiss; O Lord, who will be able to abide it? *[as 1665–E:* At the Footstool of the Throne of thy Grace … *Amen]*.

O God the Protector of all *[as 1665–E]*.

Almighty God, who hast promised [as BCP, followed by the blessing].

EVENING PRAYER

[As 1665–E, until]

[The special collects prescribed in place of the collect for the day at morning prayer; the BCP second and third collects at evening prayer; the BCP collect for Ash Wednesday; and then, from the BCP commination service, the prayers 'O Lord, we beseech thee mercifully hear our prayers', 'O Most mighty God and merciful Father' and 'Turn thou us, O good Lord']

[As BCP from the prayer for the king to the prayer for the clergy and people]

[The prayer 'O Almighty God, and our most gracious Father' from the end of the litany; the prayer 'O God the Protector of all' from after the prayer for the whole state of the church; the prayer of St Chrysostom; the grace]

1675–S   Fast days during dearth and drought

Wednesday 28 July 1675 (archdioceses of St Andrews and Glasgow, dioceses of Edinburgh, Dunkeld, Brechin and Dunblane); Wednesday 4 August 1675 or the first convenient Wednesday (elsewhere in Scotland)

This fast was called after a period of food shortages, the result of harvest failure in 1674. In June and July 1675, the privy council took steps to increase the supply of food; on 15 July, it fixed the prices of several staple crops, and forbade Leith merchants from hoarding grain. Unlike the proclamations for 1665–S1 and 1665–S2, but like that for 1665–S3, the order for the fast was probably written in Scotland. It was in the usual form of a royal proclamation, though it was described as an 'act' on the printed broadside and, unusually, was given under the signet. By the standards of this period, it was very detailed in its list of sins.

Order: royal proclamation, 15 July 1675, Wing S1398A* [also in *RPC*, 3rd ser., IV, 429–30; Wodrow, *History*, II, 280–1].
Additional sources: *RPC*, 3rd ser., IV, 406, 418, 430; *Alford exercise*, p. 248; *Inverness and Dingwall records*, p. 59.

ORDER

Royal proclamation: 15 July 1675
Forasmuch, as the Almighty God, in His most Wise and Righteous Providence, after the sinfull abuse of His most signal mercies of the blessed Gospel, of Our Own and Our Subjects wonderfull Deliverance from the Yoke of Usurpation and Bondage, by the almost Miraculous Restauration of Us to the exercise of Our Government, and of the long and mercifull Continuance of Our despised Peace and Plenty; Doth, by His Warnings and Judgements incumbent and impendent, manifestly discover His Anger and Displeasure against the grievous Sins of this Kingdom; and particularly by the sad and pinching dearth, whereby many indigent persons and families are

reduced to a starving condition, and by the long and threatning Drought, the Lord, in His Righteous Judgement, having so long bound up the Clouds, making the Heavens Brass, and the Earth Iron, thereby threatning Our Subjects of this Kingdom with the breaking of the Staff of their Bread, and with the dreadful plague of Famine: Which Dispensation doth with a loud voice call upon all ranks of people for speedy and true Repentance, and the National expression hereof by deep Mourning and solemn Fasting and Humiliation.

Therefore We, with Advice and Consent of the Lords of Our Privy Council, do Ordain a day of Publick and Solemn Fasting and Humiliation to be keeped and observed by all the people of this Kingdom in the several Paroches thereof; Strictly Commanding and Requiring them upon that day, to cease from all the Works of their ordinary Callings, and to repair to their respective Paroch Churches, and there make solemn Confession of their Sins, and implore the Divine Mercy for the Land, by Praying, Mourning, Fasting, and such other Devotions, as are requisite and usual upon such dayes of Publick Humiliation: And more particularly, Humbly to Confess and Mourn for the great Neglect and Contempt of, and Disobedience to the Blessed Gospel, and the Ordinances thereof, and the great and lamentable increase and prevalency of *Atheism*, Profaneness, and Irreligion which is thereby occasioned, and for the sinfull undervaluing of the great Blessing of Peace so long enjoyed by Our Subjects under Our Government. By all which, and many other crying Sins, the Lords Jealousie and Anger are kindled, and His hand is stretched out against this Kingdom, threatning the Destruction of the Fruits of the Ground, the necessarie Provision for the Life of Man and Beast, that by serious Mourning for, and sincere and hearty turning from these provoking Sins, the Lord may graciously pardon them and repent Him of the evil seemingly determined by Him, and most righteously deserved by us, and may open the Clouds and grant the latter Rain in its due season and measure, reserving for us the appointed weeks of the Harvest. And for this end and purpose, We, with Advice foresaid, do seriously recommend to, and require the Arch-Bishops and Bishops, to be carefull that this Fast be duely observed by the Ministers in their respective Diocesses, as followes; To the Arch-Bishops of St. *Andrews* and *Glasgow*, the Bishops of *Edinburgh*, *Dunkell*, *Brechin* and *Dumblane*, to cause it to be intimated in the several Paroch Kirks of their Diocies upon Sunday, the twenty fifth, and observed on Wednesday, the twenty eighth of *July* instant; and the remanent Bishops, whose Diocies are more remote, to cause it to be intimated on Sunday, the first of *August*, and to be observed the fourth of *August* next. And as to such Ministers, who, by reason of their distance from *Edinburgh*, cannot be so soon advertised, that they celebrate this Fast upon the next convenient Wednesday thereafter.

1678–E1 Fast days during political tensions between Charles II and the House of Commons

Wednesday 10 April 1678 (London, Westminster and bills of mortality);
Wednesday 24 April 1678 (elsewhere in England and Wales)

After years of domestic criticism of his pro-French policy, in late 1677 Charles II shifted the balance of his diplomacy, entering into an alliance with the Dutch states-general. Many in England remained suspicious of Charles's motives, particularly as he was unwilling to declare war on France. On 15 March 1678, the House of Commons approved an address calling for an immediate declaration of war. The Lords debated the address on 16 and 17 March, diluting its force with an amendment that was to prove unacceptable to the Commons. Perhaps to distract from the calls for war, on 16 March the Lords sent a message to the king desiring him to order a fast day. Charles accepted this proposal. Unlike 1674–E and 1678–E2, the proclamation made no reference to the parliamentary request for a fast. The proclamation's unspecific reference to divine judgments reflected the uncertain drift of events. The account of the distribution of forms of prayer in the Tanner papers reveals the number of copies ordered for each diocese.

Order: royal proclamation, 30 Mar. 1678, Wing C3307*.
Form of prayer: *A form of common prayer, for Gods blessing upon his majesty, and his dominions, and for the averting of Gods judgments: to be used upon Wednesday April the tenth next ensuing, in all churches and chappels within the cities of London and Westminster, the suburbs and liberties of the same. And upon Wednesday the four and twentieth of the same moneth in all the rest of this his majesties kingdom of England, the dominion of Wales, and town of Berwick upon Tweed. Set forth by his majesties authority* ([56] pp.; Wing C4108)*.
Additional sources: *CJ*, IX, 454–5, 458; *LJ*, XIII, 185, 186, 194; privy council register, PC2/66, pp. 268, 271; *CSPD, 1678*, pp. 82, 97; Thomas Holden to Williamson, 25 Apr. 1678, *CSPD, 1678*, p. 134; HMC, *Ormonde*, new ser., IV, 415–16; royal order, 6 Apr. 1678, Tanner 39, fo. 17r; account of the distribution of forms of prayer, Tanner 39*, fo. 21r; Samuel Crossman to Bishop Guy Carleton of Bristol, 22 Apr. 1678, Tanner 129, fo. 143r; Wood, II, 403.
Printed sermon: Thomas, House of Lords (Wing T982).

ORDER

Royal proclamation: 30 March 1678

For the imploring a Blessing from Almighty God upon His Majesty and all His Dominions, and for the averting of those Judgments which our manifold sins and provocations have most justly deserved; The Kings most Excellent Majesty hath thought fit, and doth hereby Command, That a General Fast, and day of solemn Humiliation be kept and observed throughout this His Majesties Kingdom of *England*, Dominion of *Wales*, and Town of *Berwick* upon *Tweed*. And to the intent the same may be performed with all Decency and Order, His Majesty doth hereby Publish and Declare to all his loving Subjects, and doth strictly Charge and Command, That on *Wednesday* being the Tenth day of *April* next, this Fast shall be religiously observed and kept within the Cities of *London* and *Westminster*, and other Places within the weekly Bills of Mortality; wherein His Majesty in His Royal Person, and with His Royal Family and Houshold will give Example to the rest of His People; and that on *Wednesday* the Four and twentieth day of the said Month of *April*, the like be observed and kept throughout the rest of this His Majesties Kingdom of *England*, the Dominion of *Wales*, and Town of *Berwick* upon *Tweed*. And His Majesty doth most strictly Charge and Command all His loving Subjects, That they do with all Christian Reverence observe and perform the same, according to the Directions that shall be given in a Form of Prayer to be by Our Order and Command Published and dispersed for that purpose, as they tender the Honour of Almighty God, and would avoid his just Wrath and Indignation against this Land, and upon Pain of receiving such punishment as His Majesty may justly inflict upon such as shall contemn or neglect so Religious and necessary a Duty.

FORM OF PRAYER

MORNING PRAYER

Let him that ministreth read with a loud voice these Sentences of Scripture, and after them the Exhortation following.
[Joel 2:13; Dan. 9:9–10; Jer. 10:24]

[As BCP to the Venite*]*

Instead of Venite, exultemus, *shall be said this Hymn following; one Verse by the Priest, and another by the Clerk and people.*
O Come, let us humble our selves, and fall down before the Lord: with reverence, and fear. (Ps. 95:6)
For he is the Lord our God: and we are the people of his pasture, and the sheep of his hand. (Ps. 95:7)
Come therefore, let us turn again unto our Lord: for he hath smitten us, and he will heal us. (Hos. 6:1)
Let us search, and try our wayes: let us lift up our hearts with our hands unto God in the heavens. (Lam. 3.40–1)
Let us repent *[and as 1665–EIr2, to ' ...that thou wilt have mercy upon us.' (Isa. 65:24). Then]*
For none that trust in thee shall be confounded: neither shall any that call upon thee be despised.
Our fathers hoped in thee: they trusted in thee, and thou didst deliver them. (Ps. 22:4)
They called upon thee, and were holpen: they put their trust in thee, and were not confounded. (Ps. 22:5)
And now in the vexation of our spirits, and the anguish of our souls we cry unto thee: hear, Lord, and have mercy. (Bar. 3:1–2)
For many troubles are come about us: our sins have taken such hold upon us, that we are not able to look up. (Ps. 40:15)
For thine own sake [as 1665–EIr2 to end].

[Ps. 6, 25, 51]
[First lesson: Isa. 50; or Isa. 58]
[Te Deum]
[Second lesson: Luke 13; or Luke 21]
[Benedictus]

[Then as BCP to the end of the Lord's prayer]

Priest: O Lord, shew thy mercy upon us *[as BCP until]*
Answer: Because there is none other that fighteth for us, but onely thou, O God.
Priest: O Lord save thy servants,
Answer: Who do put their trust in thee.
Priest: Send us help from thy holy place;
Answer: And evermore mightily defend us.
Priest: Let the enemy have no advantage against us:
Answer: Nor the wicked approch to hurt us.

Priest: Be unto us, O Lord, a strong towre,
Answer: From the face of our enemies.
Priest: O Lord hear our prayer,
Answer: And let our cry come unto thee.

[In place of the collect for the day, the BCP collects for Ash Wednesday and for the fourth Sunday in Lent]

[Then as BCP to the end of morning prayer]

LITANY

[As BCP to the end of the prayer 'We humbly beseech thee'; then, from the BCP commination service, the prayers beginning 'O Lord, we beseech thee mercifully hear our prayers'; 'O most mighty God and merciful Father' and 'Turn thou us, O good Lord'; then the BCP collect for the twenty-first Sunday after Trinity; the prayer of St Chrysostom; the grace]

COMMUNION

[As BCP to the end of the ten commandments]

Almighty God, whose kingdom is everlasting *[as BCP]*.

[Then, in place of the collect for the day, the special collects prescribed for morning prayer]

[Epistle: Joel 2:11–18]
[Gospel: Matt. 6:16–21]
[Nicene creed; the sermon]
[Offertory sentences: Ps. 41:1; Prov. 19:17]

[The prayer for the whole state of the church]

Glorious, and gracious God, whose Judgments against obstinate Offenders are most severe, and terrible; but thy Mercies infinite to All, that with hearty Repentance, and true Faith turn unto thee: We, sinful people of this Land, do acknowledge before thee, to thy Glory, and our own Shame, and Confusion, that never any Nation under Heaven had more Experience of all the Instances of thy Goodness, and the Methods of our Amendment; nor yet did ever any more shamefully abuse them. When thou gavest us great, and long Prosperities; we fed our selves to the full, waxed fat, and wanton, and kicked against thee. When thou threwest us into horrid Confusions, from which we saw then little Hope of arising; even in the time of that Distress did we trespass yet more against thee. When by Miracles of Mercy thou hadst turned our Captivities; we soon return'd to Folly, to our Vomit, and to our wallowing in our former, or greater Filthiness. Though thy Plagues have been since upon us to high, and dreadful Degrees; we did not then (as we ought) look every Man into the Plague of our own Hearts, nor return to him that smote us. We went through Fire, and Water; but were not by that severe Discipline purified from our Dross, or purg'd from our Pollutions. Even while thou wert fighting for us against our

Enemies abroad; we were by our Sins at home fighting against Heaven, & against thee. And now we are no more worthy to be called either thy Sons, or thy Servants; whom neither thy Fear hath driven, nor thy Goodness led to Repentance. It is of thy meer Mercies, O Lord, that we are not consumed; thy unwearied unconquerable Patience, that thou hast not long since given us over as incorrigible. We adore the unsearchable Depths of thy infinite Goodness, that we are still under thy Discipline: We are ready here before thee meekly to kiss all the smarting Rods, which we may justly fear thou now holdest over us; beseeching thee by the Aids, and Influence of thy Grace to make them effectual to our Correction, and not to our Destruction. In Mercy awaken our drowsy Consciences; Soften and subdue our hard hearts into deep Contrition, and Repentance; Pardon the many great Offences of us thy Servants, and the crying sins of the whole Nation; Remove the Evils we now lie under; Avert those Judgments which we justly fear, because we most justly deserve; Unite all our hearts in the Profession of the true Religion, which thine own right hand hath planted and established amongst us, and in a holy Conversation answerable thereunto. To this end Pour out the richest of thy Blessings spiritual, and temporal, upon our gracious Sovereign; that all his Counsels, Resolutions, and Endeavours may tend to, and end in the Glory of thy great Name, the Advancement of Piety, and Justice, the Preservation of thy Church, and the Security, Peace, and Prosperity of all Estates, and Conditions of Men in these, and all other his Dominions: All which we humbly beg in the Name, and through the Mediation of Jesus Christ, thy Son, our Saviour. *Amen.*

Almighty God, who hast promised *[as BCP, followed by the blessing]*

EVENING PRAYER

[The rubric as in morning prayer, followed by the opening sentences: Joel 2:13; Dan. 9:9–10; Jer. 10:24]

[Then as BCP to the psalms, before which is inserted the prayer to be used in place of the Venite *at morning prayer]*

[Ps. 32, 130, 143]
[First lesson: Amos 6; or Jonah 3]
[Magnificat]
[Second lesson: 1 Cor. 10:1–13; or 2 Pet. 3]
[Deus misereatur]

[Then as BCP from the Apostles' creed to the suffrages after the Lord's prayer, which are those used as at morning prayer]

[The special collects prescribed in place of the collect for the day at morning prayer; the BCP second and third collects for evening prayer; then, from the BCP commination service, the prayers beginning 'O Lord, we beseech thee mercifully hear our prayers', 'O most mighty God and merciful Father' and 'Turn thou us, O good Lord'; then the BCP collect for the twenty-first Sunday after Trinity]

[As BCP from the prayer for the king to the prayer for the clergy and people]

[The prayer beginning 'Glorious, and gracious God' from the communion service]

[The prayer of St Chrysostom; the grace]

1678–E2   Fast day on reports of a popish plot

Wednesday 13 November 1678 (England and Wales)

In August 1678, Titus Oates alleged that there was a popish plot to assassinate the king and foment civil war in the three kingdoms. Oates was a convert to catholicism and a former student at the English College in Valladolid; he claimed to have an insider's knowledge of Jesuit affairs. His reports of the plot were widely publicized and believed, creating much panic. Meeting on 21 October, the two houses of parliament addressed the king for a fast day to seek God's assistance in 'the further Discovery of the horrid Design' (*LJ*, XIII, 296). Parliament initiated its own investigations of the plot and the apparently connected murder of the magistrate Sir Edmund Berry Godfrey. Although the royal proclamation for the fast mentioned the plot, and the form of prayer composed for the day included a prayer derived from the 5 November service (beginning 'Almighty God, who hast in all ages shewed thy Power'), MPs including Colonel John Birch, Sir Thomas Meres and Sir Thomas Clarges complained that the form made no specific reference to the popish threat. On 8 November, the House of Commons addressed the king for the production of an additional, more explicit prayer to be read on the fast day in London and Westminster; on 9 November, a further Commons address to this effect was presented to Charles. An additional prayer, to be read after the prayer for parliament, was duly produced in three editions, and was inserted in many copies of the first form. The instructions on the additional prayer did not limit its use to the London area, but the short notice suggests that it was not read far beyond the capital. In Barbados the governor ordered a day of fasting and humiliation on the address of the assembly, although there is no evidence of any instruction from London to the colonies.

Order: royal proclamation, 25 Oct. 1678, Wing C3308*.
Forms of prayer: *A form of prayer, to be used on Wednesday November the thirteenth; being the fast-day appointed by the king, to implore the mercies of almighty God in the protection of his majesties sacred person, and in him of all his loyal subjects, and the bringing to light more and more all secret machinations against his majesty, and the whole kingdom. By his majesties special command* ([48] pp.; Wing C4145)*; *A prayer to be used on Wednesday November 13. In the office appointed for that day, immediately after the prayer for the high court of parliament (which is to be read during their session:) and next before the prayer of Saint Chrysostom, both in the morning, and evening service* ([London], [?John Bill, Christopher Barker, Thomas Newcomb and Henry Hills]; [1] p.; Wing C4145A)* [other impressions, ESTC 006147911, 006112726].
Additional sources: *LJ*, XIII, 296–8, 300; *CJ*, IX, 518, 535–9; *Debates of the House of Commons, from the year 1667 to the year 1694*, ed. Anchitell Grey (10 vols., 1763), VI, 170–2, 182–4; privy council register, PC2/66, pp. 426, 429; *CSPD, 1678*, p. 519; Bishop John Fell of Oxford to Archbishop Sancroft of Canterbury, 11 Nov. 1678, Bishop William Thomas of St David's to Archbishop Sancroft, 11 Nov. 1678, Tanner 39, fos. 134r, 135r; Thomas Horne to Bishop Carleton, 13 Nov. 1678, Tanner 129, fo. 49r; Morrice, II, 78; Evelyn, IV, 157; Wood, II, 423; *CSPC*, X, 317–18..
Printed sermons: Camfield, ?Aylston (Wing C385); Patrick, St Paul Covent Garden, London (Wing P840); Sancroft, House of Lords (Wing S568); Stillingfleet, House of Commons (Wing S5649, S5650, S5651, S5651A, S5652, S5653).

ORDER

Royal proclamation: 25 October 1678

Whereas the Lords Spiritual and Temporal, and Commons in Parliament Assembled, having been made acquainted by His Majesty, That there is Information given of an Horrible Design against His Sacred Life; And being very sensible of the fatal Consequence of such an Attempt, and of the dangers of the Subversion of the Protestant Religion, and Government of this Realm (which God in his infinite Mercy hath hitherto prevented, and it is to be hoped will prevent for the future) have most humbly besought His Majesty, That a Solemn Day of Fasting and Humiliation may be appointed, to Implore the Mercy and Protection of Almighty God to His Majesties Royal Person, and in Him to all His Loyal Subjects; and to pray that God will bring to light more and more all secret Machinations against His Majesty and the whole Kingdom: The Kings most Excellent Majesty, out of his own Religious Disposition, hath readily inclined thereunto; And doth therefore by this His Royal Proclamation, Command a General and Publick Fast to be kept throughout this whole Kingdom, in such manner as is hereafter Directed and Prescribed, that so both Prince and People may send up their Prayers and Supplications to Almighty God, to and for the purposes aforesaid. And to the end that so Religious an Exercise may be performed at one and the same time, His Majesty doth hereby Publish and Declare to all His Loving Subjects, and doth straitly Charge and Command, That on *Wednesday* being the Thirteenth day of *November* next, this Fast shall be Religiously kept and celebrated throughout His Kingdom of *England*, Dominion of *Wales*, and Town of *Berwick* upon *Tweed*. And that the same may be performed with all Decency and Uniformity, His Majesty, by the Advice of His Reverend Bishops, hath Directed to be Composed, Printed and Published, such a Form of Divine Service as he thinketh fit to be used in all Churches and Places at the time aforesaid, and hath given Charge to His Bishops to Disperse the same accordingly. All which His Majesty doth expresly Charge and Command shall be Reverently and Decently observed by all His Loving Subjects, as they tender the Favour of Almighty God, and would avoid his Wrath and Indignation against this Land, and upon pain of undergoing such Punishments as His Majesty may justly inflict upon all such as shall contemn or neglect so Religious a Duty.

FORMS OF PRAYER

MORNING PRAYER

Let him that ministreth read with a loud voice these Sentences of Scripture, and after them the Exhortation following.
[Joel 2:13; Dan. 9:9–10; Jer. 10:24]

[As BCP to the Venite*]*

Instead of Venite, exultemus, *shall be said this Hymn following; one Verse by the Priest, and another by the Clerk and people.*
Hear my prayer, O God: and hide not thy self from my petition. (Ps. 55:1)
Take heed unto me, and hear me: how I mourn in my prayer, and am vexed. (Ps. 55:2)
The enemy crieth so, and the ungodly cometh on so fast: for they are minded to do me some mischief, so maliciously are they set against me. (Ps. 55:3)

O deliver me from the wicked doers: and save me from the bloud-thirsty men. (Ps. 59:2)

Hide me from the gathering together of the froward: and from the insurrection of wicked doers. (Ps. 64:2)

For lo, they lie waiting for my soul: the mighty men are gathered against me without any offence or fault of me, O Lord. (Ps. 59:3)

They encourage themselves in mischief: and commune among themselves, how they may lay snares, and say, that no man shall see them. (Ps. 64:5)

Let God arise, and let his enemies be scattered: let them also that hate him, flee before him. (Ps. 68:1)

Like as the smoke vanisheth, so shalt thou drive them away: and like as wax melteth at the fire, so let the ungodly perish at the presence of God. (Ps. 68:2)

Let them be ashamed and confounded, that seek after my soul: let them be turned backward and put to confusion, that wish me evil. (Ps. 70:2)

Consume them in thy wrath, consume them, that they may perish: and know that it is God that ruleth in Jacob, and unto the ends of the world. (Ps. 59:13)

Help us, O God of our salvation, for the glory of thy Name: O deliver us, and be merciful unto our sins for thy Names sake. (Ps. 79:9)

For thou, Lord, art good and gracious: and of great mercy unto all them that call upon thee. (Ps. 86:5)

Behold, God is my helper: the Lord is with them that uphold my soul. (Ps. 54:4)

Shew some token upon me for good, that they who hate me may see it and be ashamed: because thou, Lord, hast holpen me and comforted me. (Ps. 86:17)

Thou shalt grant the King a long life: that his years may endure throughout all generations. (Ps. 61:6)

He shall dwell before God for ever: O prepare thy loving mercy and faithfulness, that they may preserve him. (Ps. 61:7)

So we that are thy people and sheep of thy pasture, shall give thee thanks for ever: and will alway be shewing forth thy praise from generation to generation. (Ps. 79:14)

Glory be to the Father, and to the Son: and to the holy Ghost;

As it was in the beginning, is now, and ever shall be: world without end. Amen.

[Ps. 20, 21, 46, 83]
[First lesson: Neh. 4; or Jer. 41]
[Te Deum]
[Second lesson: Acts 23]
[Jubilate Deo]

[Then as BCP to the end of the Lord's prayer]

Priest: O Lord, shew thy mercy upon us.
[As 1678–E1]

In stead of the first Collect at Morning Prayer shall these two be used.

Almighty God, who hast in all ages shewed thy Power and Mercy in the miraculous and gracious deliverances of thy Church, and in the Protection of righteous and religious Kings and States, professing thy holy and eternal Truth, from the wicked Conspiracies, and malicious practices of all the enemies thereof; Be thou still our mighty Protector, and scatter our enemies that delight in Bloud: Infatuate and defeat their Counsels, abate their Pride, asswage their Malice, and confound their Devices: Strengthen the hands of our gracious King CHARLES, and all that are put in Authority under him, with Judgment and Justice, to cut off all such workers of Iniquity, as turn Religion into Rebellion, and Faith into Faction; that they may never prevail against us, or triumph in the ruine of thy Church among us: But that our gracious Sovereign and his Realms being preserved in thy true Religion, & by thy merciful goodness protected in the same, we may all duly serve thee, and give thee thanks in thy holy Congregation, through Jesus Christ our Lord. *Amen.*

O God the Protector of all that trust in thee, without whom nothing is strong, nothing is holy, who knowest us to be set in the midst of many, and great dangers, and that we have no power of our selves to help our selves; Raise up, we pray thee, thy Power, and come among us, and with great might succour us; and in all our dangers & necessities stretch forth the right hand of thy Majesty to help and defend us against all our enemies: And grant that we who for our evil deeds do worthily deserve to be punished, by the comfort of thy Grace may mercifully be relieved, through the merits and mediation of Jesus Christ our Lord and only Saviour. *Amen.*

[Then as BCP to the end of morning prayer]

LITANY

[As BCP to the end of the prayer 'We humbly beseech thee'; then the BCP collect for Ash Wednesday; and then, from the BCP commination service, the prayers 'O Lord, we beseech thee mercifully hear our prayers', 'O most mighty God and merciful Father' and 'Turn thou us, O good Lord'; the BCP collects for the twenty-fourth Sunday after Trinity and for the twenty-first Sunday after Trinity]

In the office appointed for that Day, immediately after the Prayer for the High Court of Parliament (which is to be read during their Session:) and next before the Prayer of St Chrysostom, both in the Morning, and Evening Service. By the Kings Special Command.

Almighty God, who hast in part discovered the designs, and disappointed the attempts of those Popish Conspirators, who under the pretence of Religion, and thy Sacred Name, have conspired our destruction; labouring by the most unjustifiable methods of Murders, Treasons, and the Assassination of His Majesties Sacred Person, to introduce the tyranny of a foreign power, and the abomination of superstitious worship; and thereby to enslave the souls and bodies of thy servants, and to extinguish the light of thy Gospel amongst us and our posterity: We yield thee praise and thanksgiving for this thy mercy to us; imploring thy grace and favour in the farther discovery of these depths of Satan, this mystery of iniquity. Send forth thy light and thy truth, and let them preserve us. Give protection and defence to our Sovereign Lord the King, bind up his soul in the bundle of life, and let no weapon form'd against him prosper; Clothe all his enemies with shame; but upon Himself and His Posterity let His Crown ever flourish. To this end, knit together the hearts of all this People, as the heart of one man, in the defence of their King, their Laws, and their Religion. Teach them to see in this their day, the things belonging to their peace, before they are hid from their Eyes; Remove from among them the Accursed thing, those personal, and those publick guilts, whose cry is gone up to heaven, and calls aloud for thy vengeance; And being by true repentance reconcil'd to thee our God, let us by Christian Love and Charity be united to one another: That walking in the paths of thy holy Law which thou hast given us, its Blessing may be continued to us; and we thy people and sheep of thy pasture may give thee thanks for ever, and shew forth thy praise from generation to generation. Hear us, O God, for thy mercies sake, through Jesus Christ our Lord. *Amen.*

[The prayer of St Chrysostom; the grace]

COMMUNION

[As BCP to the end of the ten commandments]

Almighty God, whose kingdom is everlasting *[as BCP]*

[Then, in place of the collect for the day, the special collects prescribed for morning prayer]

[Epistle: 1 Pet. 2:13–23]
[Gospel: Matt. 21:33–41]
[Nicene creed; the sermon]
[Offertory sentences: Matt. 5:16; Gal. 6:10]

[The prayer for the whole state of the church]

O Most Glorious Lord God, whose Mercies are to be admired, and thy Judgments to be trembled at; We miserable sinners, with prostration of our bodies, with anguish of our souls acknowledge, that righteousness appertains to thee, and to us, and all the people of the Land confusion of faces; having disobeyed all thy precepts, having aggravated the profaneness of our lives by our unthankfulness for all our deliverances. Thou hast vouchsafed to us beauty for ashes; thou hast miraculously restored, and graciously preserved hitherto the breath of our nostrils, thine anointed Servant, and under his protection the Solemnities of thy Sacred Ordinances, the establishment of our Laws, the enjoyment of our Interests, to eat the fruit of our own Vines; our Swords being changed to Plowshares, our Spears to Pruning-hooks: But we have turned thy Grace to wantonness, having surfeted with Plenty and Security, like *Jeshurun* waxed fat, and kicked, having multiplied our provocations like *Sodom*; we have not relented nor been ashamed to be wicked, having pursued the works of darkness in the face of the Sun, to excite, and to dare thy fiercest displeasure.

Yet to thee, O Lord, belongeth mercy and forgiveness, though we have rebelled against thee. Let not the returns of our iniquities call back thy Judgments: Deprive us not of the light of thy Gospel, of the Purity, the Regularity of thy Worship, because we have not walked uprightly, and suitably to it; whilst strict, and Reformed in our Doctrines, having been Lewd and Licentious in our Conversation. Take into thy special tuition our dread Sovereign; hide him under the shadow of thy wings, give thy holy Angels charge over him, counsel his Counsellors, fortify his Guards, turn the wisdom of *Achitophel* to folly, defeat the Devices, and blast the Enterprizes of all his enemies. And that for the merits of thy blessed Son, and our alone Saviour Jesus Christ.

Almighty God, who hast promised *[as BCP, followed by the blessing]*.

EVENING PRAYER

[The rubric as in morning prayer, followed by the opening sentences: Joel 2:13; Dan. 9:9–10; Jer. 10:24]

[Then as BCP to the psalms]

[Ps. 57, 62, 140, 144]
[First lesson: Job 5]
[Magnificat]
[Second lesson: Rom. 13]
[Deus misereatur]

[Then as BCP from the Apostles' creed to the suffrages after the Lord's prayer, which are those used as at morning prayer]

[The special collects prescribed in place of the collect for the day at morning prayer; the BCP second and third collects for evening prayer; the BCP collect for Ash Wednesday; and then, from the BCP commination service, the prayers 'O Lord, we beseech thee mercifully hear our prayers', 'O most mighty God and merciful Father' and 'Turn thou us, O good Lord'. The BCP collects for the twenty-fourth Sunday after Trinity and for the twenty-first Sunday after Trinity]

[As BCP from the prayer for the king to the prayer for the clergy and people]

[The prayer beginning 'O most glorious Lord God' from the communion service]

[The BCP prayer for parliament]

[The additional form of prayer (Wing C4145A) as above]

[The prayer of St Chrysostom; the grace]

1678–S   Fast day on reports of a popish plot

Wednesday 18 December 1678 (Scotland)

After receiving reports of the popish plot, the Scottish government followed the lead of the English authorities, ordering this fast in imitation of 1678–E2. Archbishop Sharp proposed the fast in the privy council on 14 November 1678, and the council decided to appoint the occasion without waiting for the king's approval, to allow it to be observed before Christmas. A committee comprising the archbishops of St Andrews and Glasgow and the bishop of Galloway was instructed to prepare a proclamation. It seems that they had a copy of the proclamation for 1678–E2, which supplied some phrases for their own text. The proclamation, approved by the council on 15 November, was, like 1675–S, given under the signet.

Order: royal proclamation, 15 Nov. 1678, Wing S1785* [also in *RPC*, 3rd ser., VI, 62–3].
Additional sources: James Sharp to Lauderdale, 16 Nov. 1678, NLS, MS 2512, fo. 213r; *RPC*, 3rd ser., VI, 59, 63; Wodrow, *History*, II, 502; *Edin. recs., 1665 to 1680*, p. 361; Lauder, *Historical observes*, p. 104; *Alford exercise*, p. 300; *Inverness and Dingwall records*, p. 89.

ORDER

Royal proclamation: 15 November 1678

Forasmuch, as We considering the eminent Danger Our Royal Person and Government, and the Protestant Religion have been of late, and are still exposed unto, through an Damnable and Hellish Plot, contrived and carried on by the Papists, for taking away Our Sacred Life, and for the subversion of the Protestant Religion, and of the Government of these Kingdoms (which GOD of His Infinite Mercy hath hitherto prevented and disappointed, and We hope will prevent and disappoint for the future) And being very sensible of the Fatal Consequences of such an Horrible and Sanguinary Conspiracy and Designe; We, out of Our Religious Disposition, have readily approven of an Humble motion made to Us for commanding a General Fast, to be Religiously kept throughout this whole Kingdom, to Implore the Mercy of Almighty GOD for the preservation of the Protestant Religion, as it is by Law established, and for the protection of Our Royal Person and Government; As also, to pray that GOD will more and more bring to Light, and confound all Secret Contrivances and Machinations against Us, and in Us, against all Our Loyal Subjects; We, with advice of Our Privy Council, have therefore thought fit by this Our Proclamation, to Indict a General and Publick Fast and day of Humiliation, that all Our loving Subjects may send up their fervent Prayers and Supplications to Almighty GOD, to, and for, the purposes aforesaids. Our Will is herefore, and We strictly Command and Charge, that the said Fast be Religiously and Solemnly kept throughout this Our whole Kingdom, by all Subjects and People within the same, upon the third *Wednesday* of *December* next, being the eighteenth day thereof, to the end that so necessary and Religious an Exercise may be performed by all at one and the same time. Requiring hereby the Reverend *Arch-Bishops*, and *Bishops*, to give notice hereof to the Ministers in their respective Dyocesses, that upon the LORDS-Day immediately preceeding the said eighteenth day of *December*, they cause Read and Intimate this Our Proclamation from the Pulpit in every Parish Church, and that they Exhort all Our Subjects to a Serious and Devout performance of the said Prayers, Fasting and Humiliation, as they tender the Favour of Almighty GOD, and the Safety and Preservation of the Protestant Religion, and of Our Sacred Life and Government, and as they would avoid the Wrath and Indignation of GOD against this Kingdom: Certifying all those who shall contemn or neglect such a Religious and necessary Duty, they shall be proceeded against, and punished as Contemners of Our Authority, and Persons Disaffected to the Protestant Religion, as well as to Our Royal Person and Government.

1679–EIr   Fast days during fears of catholic conspiracies

Friday 11 April 1679 (England and Wales); Wednesday 28 May 1679 (Ireland)

In late 1678, anti-catholic fears encouraged by the popish plot intersected with revelations of Charles II's secret negotiations with Louis XIV to create a political crisis. Parliament sought to impeach the earl of Danby, the king's chief minister, prompting Charles to order the first dissolution since the restoration. Nevertheless, when the new parliament assembled in March 1679, investigation of the plot and the campaign against Danby continued. An address for a fast day was moved in the House of Commons, agreed to by the Lords and presented to the king on 25 March. Much of the text of this address was incorporated in the royal proclamation which was published three days later. According to figures especially sympathetic to the crown, such as Anthony Wood, disloyal parliamentarians deliberately fomented opposition to the king, and intended the fast to provide a platform for Charles's critics. Certainly, the febrile political atmosphere and the way in which the popish plot was being exploited by the parliamentary opposition to attack not only Danby but also the catholic duke of York and the catholic faction at court helps to explain some of the unusual aspects of this occasion. At least one MP had questioned the veracity of the plot, and the two houses agreed on a formal resolution asserting their belief in the allegations. This resolution was printed in the form of prayer for England and Wales, though apparently not in that for Ireland. It was the only occasion after the restoration for which a form of prayer included a parliamentary resolution. Unusually little time was allowed to prepare, print and distribute the form of prayer; the fast was ordered to take place just two weeks after proclamation. It is hardly surprising that Bishop Croft of Hereford reported the late delivery of forms of prayer to his diocese, which he feared would disrupt the observance of the fast.

After hearing of the appointment of the English observance, the lord lieutenant and council of Ireland sought permission from Whitehall to proclaim a fast in Ireland for the same reasons. This was approved, and it seems likely that the Irish proclamation (which has not been traced) repeated much of the text of that issued in England, since the purpose of the fast was described on the title-page of the form of prayer in words taken from the English proclamation. After its title-page, the Irish form of prayer was identical to the form for England and Wales. This was the first occasion on which it is known that a special form was issued for use in Ireland.

Orders: ENGLAND AND WALES: royal proclamation, 28 Mar. 1679, Wing C3309*; IRELAND: proclamation by the lord lieutenant and council, 14 May 1679, Wing I668 [National Library of Ireland, Dublin, copy not found; see also *Report of the deputy keeper*, XXIII, app., 34–5].
Forms of prayer: ENGLAND AND WALES: *A form of prayer, to be used on Friday the eleventh of April; being the fast-day appointed by the kings proclamation, to seek reconciliation with almighty God, and to implore him, that he would infatuate, and defeat the councels of the papists our enemies; continue his mercies, and the light of his gospel to us, and our posterity; and bestow his abundant blessings upon his sacred majesty, and this present parliament. By his majesties special command* ([8] pp.; Wing C4146)*; IRELAND: *A form of prayer to be used on Wednesday the 28th of May; being the fast-day appointed by proclamation of the lord lieutenant and council. To seek reconciliation with almighty God, and to implore him, that he would infatuate, and defeat the counsels of the papists our enemies; continue his mercies and the light of his gospel to us, and our posterity; and bestow his abundant blessings upon his sacred majesty, and this present parliament. By his majesties command* ([8] pp.; Wing C4194U)*.
Additional sources: *CJ*, IX, 571–2, 574; *LJ*, XIII, 472, 476, 479; privy council register, PC2/67, fos. 140, 144; *CSPD, 1679–80*, p. 110; HMC, *Ormonde*, new ser., IV, 368–71; Bishop Herbert Croft of

Hereford to Sancroft, 13 [i.e. 3?] Apr. 1679, Tanner 38, fo. 14r; Luttrell, I, 11; Morrice, II, 116; Wood, II, 448; Evelyn, IV, 166–7; HMC, *Ormonde*, new ser., V, 83; Sir George Rawdon to Viscount Conway, 17 May 1679, *CSPD, 1679–80*, pp. 149–50.

Printed sermons: Jane, House of Commons (Wing J456); Sharp, House of Commons (Wing S2984); Topham, ?Boston (Wing T1906).

ORDER

England and Wales: royal proclamation, 28 March 1679

Whereas the Lords Spiritual and Temporal, and Commons in this present Parliament Assembled, being deeply sensible of the sad and calamitous Condition of this Our Kingdom, occasioned chiefly by the impious and malicious Conspiracies of a Popish Party, who have not only Plotted and intended the Destruction of Our Royal Person, but the total Subversion of Our Government, and of the true Protestant Religion within this Realm by Law established (All which the many and grievous Sins of this Nation have most justly deserved) Have most humbly besought Us, That by Our Royal Proclamation, a Day may be Solemnly set apart; wherein all Our Loyal Subjects may by Fasting and Prayer, seek a Reconciliation with Almighty God, and with humble and penitent hearts implore him by his power and goodness, to Infatuate and Defeat the wicked Counsels and Imaginations of Our Enemies, and to continue his Mercies, and the Light of his Gospel to this Kingdom, and particularly to bestow his abundant Blessings upon Our Self, and this present Parliament, that their Consultations and Endeavours may produce Honour, Safety and Prosperity to Us, and to Our People: We have to this their humble Request most readily inclined; And do by this Our Royal Proclamation Command a General and Publick Fast *[as 1678–E2, with change of date, substituting 'we' and 'our' for 'his Majesty', 'he' and 'his'*: to be kept throughout this whole Kingdom … so Religious a Duty*]*.

FORMS OF PRAYER

[Included in the form for England and Wales only]
Die Martis, 25° Martii. 1679
Resolved, *nemine contradicente*, by the Lords Spiritual, and Temporal, and Commons in Parliament assembled; That they do declare, that they are fully satisfied by the proofs they have heard, that there now is, and for divers years last past hath been a Horrid, and Treasonable Plot, and Conspiracy, contrived, and carried on by those of the Popish Religion, for the Murdering of his Majesties sacred Person, and for subverting the Protestant Religion,and the ancient, and established Government of this Kingdom.
    Jo. Browne Cleric Parliamentor

England and Wales; Ireland

The Service shall be the same in all things with the Office appointed to be used upon Friday *in every Week, if it be Holiday; Except, where it is after herein otherwise directed.*

He that Ministreth, shall begin with these Sentences,
[Joel 2:13; Dan 9:9–10; Jer. 10:24]

(6.)   A   *Liturgies Ireland Ch. of. Particular serve*

FORMᵏ

OF

PRAYER.

To be used on

Wednesday the 28th of *May*;

BEING

The Fast-day

Appointed by Proclamation of the

Lord Lieutenant and Council.

To seek Reconciliation with Almighty *God*, and to implore him, that he would Infatuate, and Defeat the Counsels of the Papists our Enemies; Continue his Mercies and the Light of his Gospel to us, and our posterity; and bestow his abundant Blessings upon His Sacred Majesty, and this present Parliament.

By His Majesties Command

DUBLIN.

Printed by *Benjamin Took* and *John Crook* Printers to the Kings most Excellent Majesty, and are to be sold by *Mary Crok* at his Majesties Printing-house in *Skinner-Row*. 1679.

13 The title-page of the earliest known form of prayer issued for use in Ireland, published after the 'popish plots' against the crown for 1679–EIr. The description of the purpose of the fast copies the text of the proclamation that ordered the equivalent occasion in England and Wales. *A form of prayer to be used on Wednesday the 28th of May* (Dublin, 1679; Wing C4194U), British Library, 3407.b.46; quarto.

MORNING PRAYER

Instead of Venite, Exultemus, *shall this Psalm following be used; one Verse by the Minister, and another by the Clerk and People.*
 Hear my prayer, O God *[as 1678–E2].*

[Ps. 51, 32, 83, 20]
[First lesson: Isa. 1]
[Second lesson: Luke 13; or Acts 23]

Instead of the Collect for the Day, shall be used this, which followeth, both in Morning, and Evening Prayer, and in the Communion-Service.
 Almighty God, who of thy great Mercy toward us hast discovered the Designs, and disappointed the Attempts of those Popish Conspirators, who under the pretence of Religion, and thy most Holy Name, had contriv'd our Destruction, and labour'd by the most unjustifiable Methods of Treason, and Murther, and the Assassination of His Majesties Sacred Person, to introduce the Tyranny of a foreign power, and the Abomination of Superstitious Worship, and thereby to enslave both the bodies and souls of thy servants, and to extinguish the blessed light of thy holy Gospel amongst us: We yield thee praise, and thanks for this thine infinite goodness to us; imploring thy Grace and Favour in the farther Discovery of these depths of Satan, this mystery of iniquity. Send forth thy Light, and thy Truth, and let them preserve us. Protect, and defend our Sovereign Lord the King. Bind up his soul in the bundle of life, and let no Weapon form'd against him prosper. Cloth all his enemies with shame; but upon Himself, and His Posterity let the Crown ever flourish. To this end Bless the present Parliament now Assembled, and knit together the Hearts of this whole Nation, as the heart of one man, in the defence of our King, our Laws, and our Religion. Teach us to know, at least in this our Day, the things which belong to our peace, and let them not be hid from our Eyes. Remove from among us the Accursed Thing; those personal, and those publick Guilts, the cry whereof is gone up to Heaven, and calls aloud for Vengeance. And grant, that being by true repentance reconcil'd to thee our God, we may also be united by Christian Love, and Charity to one another: So that we walking in the paths of thy holy Law, thou maist continue the Blessing thereof to us, and our posterity, and we All may continue to give thee Thanks for ever, and shew forth thy praise from Generation to Generation; through Jesus Christ our Lord. *Amen.*

LITANY

*In the end of the Litany, after the Collect [*We humbly beseech thee, O Father, &c.*] shall be read in this Order, The Collect for* Ash-Wednesday, *The Three Collects in the Commination, The Collect for the XXI. Sunday after Trinity, The Prayer for the High Court of Parliament, and this which followeth,*

For Deliverance from the Papists our Enemies;
Taken out of the Office for the Fifth of November.
 Almighty God, who hast in all ages shewed thy Power and Mercy *[as 1678–E2].*

Then the Prayer of S. Chrysostom.

COMMUNION

[Epistle: 1 Cor. 10:1–16; or Joel 2:11–19]
[Gospel: Matt. 21:33–42; or Matt. 6:16–22]

Immediately after the Prayer For the whole state of Christs Church, *shall this be used.*

Glorious, and gracious God, who's Judgments *[as 1678–E1*: against obstinate Offenders ... to thy Glory, and*]* our own shame, that never any Nation had more Experience of thy Goodness; nor yet did ever any more unthankfully abuse it. When thou gavest us great, and long prosperity, we fed our selves to the full, waxed fat, and kicked against thee. *[As 1678–E1*: When thou threwest us ... and to our*]* wallowing in our former, or greater Filthiness. Even while thou hast of late appear'd for us, by discovering the Plots and Contrivances of our implacable Enemies of the Romish Faction, we have been in the mean time by our sins fighting against Heaven, and against thee. And now we are no more worthy to be called either thy sons, or thy servants; whom neither thy Fear hath driven, nor thy Goodness led to Repentance. In Mercy awaken our drowsie Consciences. Soften, and subdue our hard hearts into deep contrition. Pardon the many *[as 1678–E1*: great Offences ... which we justly fear*]*, because we most justly deserve. Discover more and more the snares of Death, and Popish Treachery: and let us never fall into the hands of those men, who's mercies are cruel. Unite all our hearts in the profession of the true Religion, which thine own right hand hath planted among us, and in a holy Conversation answerable thereunto. Pour out thy abundant Blessings upon our Gracious King, and his great Council, the present Parliament: Keep him as the Apple of thine Eye; hide him under the shadow of thy wings. Inform his Princes after thy will, and teach his Senators Wisdom: And grant that all their Counsels, Resolutions, and Endeavours may tend to, and end in the Glory of thy great Name, the preservation of thy Church, and true Religion among us, and the security, peace, and prosperity of these Kingdoms: All which we humbly beg in the Name, and through the Mediation of Jesus Christ thy Son, our Saviour. *Amen.*

EVENING PRAYER

[Ps. 21, 46, 57, 143]
[First lesson: Isa. 58]
[Second lesson: Rom. 13]

*Immediately after the Collect [*Lighten our darkness*] shall be read, in this Order, The Collect for Ash-wednesday, The three Collects in the Commination, and the Collect for XXI. Sunday after Trinity.*

*And after the Prayer for the High Court of Parliament, shall be added that for Deliverance from the Papists our Enemies, and the Prayer [*Glorious and gracious God, &c.*] as they are set down before in the Morning-Service.*

1680–E   Fast day during the exclusion crisis

Wednesday 22 December 1680 (England and Wales)

In May 1679, parliament's anti-popish campaign culminated in the introduction of a bill in the House of Commons to exclude the catholic duke of York from the succession to the throne. As the campaign for exclusion gained momentum, Charles first prorogued and then dissolved parliament in attempts to prevent discussion of the succession. A new parliament finally met in October 1680, and MPs revived the exclusion bill, this time securing its passage through the Commons. The measure faced opposition in the Lords, however, where the bill was defeated on 15 November. On 19 November, the Commons resolved to address for a fast. The text of an address was agreed with the Lords on 23 November and presented to Charles II two days later. As with 1678–E2, the proclamation's narrative was based on parliament's address. Bishops William Lloyd of St Asaph, John Dolben of Rochester and Henry Compton of London composed the form of prayer, re-using and revising some prayers from the forms for 1678–E1 and 1679–EIr. The tensions between the Commons and the court were evident on the fast day, when Gilbert Burnet preached a strongly anti-Catholic sermon to MPs. The Commons thanked Burnet, and his sermon was printed in three impressions. Thomas Sprat's sermon to the Commons offended MPs by suggesting that they were acting disobediently. Sprat received no thanks from the House (and his sermon was not printed), but his popularity at court increased.

Order: royal proclamation, 2 Dec. 1680, Wing C3310*.
Form of prayer: *A form of prayer, to be used on Wednesday the 22d of December; being the fast-day appointed by the kings proclamation: to seek reconciliation with almighty God, and to beseech him, that he would avert his judgments, defeat the counsels of our enemies, unite the hearts of all loyal protestants, continue his mercies, and the light of his gospel to us, and our posterity, and bestow his abundant blessings upon his sacred majesty, and this present parliament, and all their consultations, and endeavours. By his majesties special command* ([48] pp.; Wing C4148)*.
Additional sources: *CJ*, IX, 656, 660–2; *LJ*, XIII, 684, 688, 690; privy council register, PC2/69, fos. 158–9; *CSPD, 1680–1*, p. 97; Bishop William Lloyd of St Asaph to Sancroft, 29 Nov. 1680, Tanner 37, fo. 207r; Luttrell, I, 60; Morrice, II, 258; Evelyn, IV, 236; Burnet, *History*, II, 252.
Printed sermons: Burnet, House of Commons (Wing B5874, B5770, B5770aA); Dixon, Rochester (Wing D1748aA); Fell, House of Lords (Wing F621, ESTC 006407249); Fuller, Little Wakering (Wing F2393); Jekyll, Newland (Wing J534); Palmer, ? (Wing P252).

ORDER

Royal proclamation: 2 December 1680
Whereas the Lords Spiritual and Temporal, and Commons in this present Parliament Assembled, have by their Address to Us, made known unto Us, That they are deeply sensible of the sad and calamitous Condition of this Our Kingdom, occasioned by the Impious and Horrid Conspiracies of a Popish Party, who have not only plotted and intended the Destruction of Our Royal Person, but the total Subversion of the Government and true Religion established amongst us, and that the same detestable Machinations are still obstinately prosecuted by them, as well by fomenting Divisions amongst Our Loyal Protestant Subjects, as all other the most wicked Contrivances, notwithstanding the many Discoveries thereof by Gods great Mercy and wonderful Providence lately brought to light. All which dreadful Judgments are now impending over us most deservedly for our many and grievous Sins, and cannot otherwise in humane reason be prevented, but by the particular Blessing of

God upon the Consultations and Endeavours of Our great Council now Assembled in Parliament; Have most humbly besought Us that a day may be most Solemnly set apart, wherein Our Self and all Our Loyal Subjects may by Fasting and Prayer endeavour a reconciliation with Almighty God, and with humble and penitent hearts implore him by his Power and Goodness, to divert those Judgments, and defeat the wicked Counsels and Devices of Our Enemies, to Unite the hearts of Our Loyal Protestant Subjects, and to continue his Mercy and the Light of the Gospel to Us and our Posterities, and more especially to bestow his abundant Blessings on our Self and this present Parliament, that our Consultations and Endeavours may produce Honour, Safety and Prosperity to Our Self and Our People: We have to this their humble Request most readily inclined, and do by this Our Royal Proclamation Command a General and Publick Fast to be kept throughout this whole Kingdom, in such manner as is hereafter directed and prescribed, that so both We and Our People may send up Our Prayers and Supplications to Almighty God, to, and for the purposes aforesaid. *[As 1678–E2, with change of date, substituting 'we' and 'our' for 'his Majesty', 'he' and 'his':* And to the end that … so Religious a Duty.*]*

FORM OF PRAYER

MORNING PRAYER

Let him that ministreth read with a loud voice these Sentences of Scripture, and after them the Exhortation following.
[Joel 2:13; Dan. 9:9; Jer. 10:24]

[As BCP to the Venite*]*

Instead of Venite, exultemus, *shall be said this Hymn following; one Verse by the Priest, and another by the Clerk and People.*
O Come, let us humble our selves, and fall down before the Lord: with Reverence, and Fear. (Ps. 95:6)
Let us search and try our ways: Let us lift up our hearts with our hands unto God in the Heavens. (Lam. 3:40–1)
Let us repent, and turn from our wickedness: and our sins shall be forgiven us. (Acts 3:19)
Let us turn, and the Lord will turn from his heavy wrath: he will pardon us, and we shall not perish. (Jonah 3:8–9)
Our fathers hoped in thee, O Lord: they trusted in thee; and thou didst deliver them. (Ps. 22:4)
They called upon thee, and were holpen: they put their trust in thee, and were not confounded. (Ps. 22:5)
For thine own sake, and for thy holy Name's sake incline thine ear: and hear us, O merciful Lord. (Dan. 9:18–19)
Help us, O God of our salvation, for the glory of thy Name: O deliver us, and be merciful unto our sins for thy Name's sake. (Ps. 79:9)
For innumerable Troubles are come about us: our sins have taken such hold upon us, that we are not able to look up. (Ps. 40:15)
The Enemy crieth so, and the ungodly cometh on so fast: for they are minded to do us some Mischief, so maliciously are they set against us. (Ps. 55:3)

They encourage themselves in mischief, and commune among themselves how they may lay snares: and say, that no man shall see them. (Ps. 64:5)

O deliver us from the wicked Doers: and save us from the blood-thirsty Men. (Ps. 59:2)

Let God arise, and let his Enemies be scattered: Let them also that hate him, flee before him. (Ps. 68:1)

Like as the smoke vanisheth, so shalt thou drive them away: like as wax melteth at the fire, so let the ungodly perish at the presence of God. (Ps. 68:2)

Let them be ashamed and confounded that seek after our souls: Let them be turned backward, and put to confusion, that wish us evil. (Ps. 70:2)

Let them consume away like a snail, and be like the untimely fruit of a Woman: and let them not see the sun. (Ps. 58:7)

Shew some token upon us for good, that they who hate us may see it and be ashamed: because thou, Lord, hast holpen us and comforted us. (Ps. 86:17)

Thou shalt grant the King a long life: that his years may endure throughout all generations. (Ps. 61:6)

He shall dwell before God for ever: O prepare thy loving mercy and faithfulness, that they may preserve him. (Ps. 61:7)

So we that are thy people and sheep of thy pasture, shall give thee thanks for ever: and will alway be shewing forth thy praise from generation to generation. (Ps. 79:14)

Glory be to the Father, and to the Son: and to the holy Ghost;

As it was in the beginning, is now, and ever shall be: world without end. Amen.

[Ps. 51, 32, 80, 83]
[First lesson: Isa. 1]
[Te Deum]
[Second lesson: Luke 13]
[Jubilate Deo]

[Then as BCP to the Lord's prayer]

Priest: O Lord, shew thy mercy upon us.
[As 1678–E1]

In stead of the Collect for the Day, shall be used this which followeth, both in Morning, and Evening Prayer, and in the Communion-Service.

Almighty God, who of thy great Mercy *[as 1679–EIr*: toward us … a foreign power, and*]* the Abomination of Superstitious and Idolatrous Worship, and thereby to enslave *[as 1679–EIr*: both the bodies and souls … *Amen]*.

[Then as BCP to the end of morning prayer]

LITANY

[As BCP to the end of the prayer 'We humbly beseech thee'; then the BCP collect for Ash Wednesday; then, from the BCP commination service, the prayers 'O Lord, we beseech thee mercifully hear our prayers'; 'O most mighty God and merciful Father' and 'Turn thou us, O good Lord'; the BCP prayer for parliament. Then]

Blessed Jesu, our Saviour, and our Peace; who didst shed thy precious Blood upon the Cross, that thou mightest abolish, and destroy all Enmity among Men, and reconcile them in one Body unto God: Look down in much pity, and compassion upon this distressed Church, and Nation; who's bleeding wounds, occasion'd by the lamentable Divisions that are among us, cry aloud for thy speedy Help, and saving Relief. Stir up, we beseech thee, every soul of us, carefully (as becomes sincere Christians) to root out of our Hearts all Pride, and Vain-glory, all Wrath, and Bitterness, all unjust Prejudice, and causeless Jealousie, all Hatred, and Malice, and Desire of Revenge, and whatsoever it is, that may any way exasperate our Minds, or hinder us from discerning the things that belong unto our peace: And by the power of thy Holy Spirit of peace, dispose all our Hearts to such Meekness of Wisdom, and lowliness of Mind, such calm, and deliberate Long-suffering, and Forbearance of one another in love, with such due Esteem of those, whom thou hast set over us to watch for our souls, as may turn the Hearts of the Fathers to the Children, and the Hearts of the Children to the Fathers; that so we may become a ready people prepar'd to live in peace, and the God of peace may be with us. To this End, give us all Grace, O Lord, seriously to lay to heart, not only the great Dangers we are in at present by these our unhappy Divisions; but also the great Obligations to this godly Union, and Concord, which lie upon us: That as there is but one Body, and one Spirit, and one Hope of our Calling; one Lord, one Faith, one Baptism, one God, and Father of all; so we may henceforth be all of one Heart, and of one Soul, closely united in one holy bond of Truth, and peace, of Faith, and Charity; and may with one Mind, and one Mouth glorifie thee, O Lord, the Prince of peace, who with thy blessed Father, in the unity of the Holy Spirit, livest, and reignest ever one God world without end. *Amen.*

[The prayer of St Chrysostom; the grace]

COMMUNION

[As BCP to the end of the ten commandments]

Almighty God, whose kingdom is everlasting *[as BCP]*

[Then, in place of the collect for the day, the special collect prescribed for morning prayer]

[Epistle: 1 Pet. 3:8–16]
[Gospel: Matt. 10:24–39]
[Nicene creed; the sermon]
[Offertory sentences: Matt. 5:16; Gal. 6:10]

[The prayer for the whole state of the church]

Glorious, and gracious God, who's Judgements *[as 1678–E1*: against obstinate Offenders … to thy Glory, and*]* our own shame, that never any Nation had more Experience of thy Goodness; nor yet did ever any more unthankfully abuse it. Even while thou hast of late appear'd for us, by discovering the Plots and Contrivances of our implacable Enemies of the Romish Faction, we have been in the mean time by our sins fighting against Heaven, and against thee. And now we are no more worthy to be called either thy sons, or thy servants; whom neither thy Fear hath driven, nor thy Goodness led to Repentance. In Mercy awaken our drowsie Consciences, Soften, and subdue our hard hearts into deep contrition. Pardon the many great offences of us thy servants, and the crying sins of the whole Nation. Remove the Evils we now lie under. Avert the Judgments, which we justly fear, because we most justly deserve. Discover more and more *[as 1679–EIr*: the snares of Death, … *Amen]*.

Almighty God, who hast promised *[as BCP, followed by the blessing]*.

EVENING PRAYER

[The rubric as in morning prayer, followed by the opening sentences: Joel 2:13; Dan. 9:9–10; Jer. 10:24]

[Then as BCP to the psalms]

[Ps. 46, 124, 129, 144]
[First lesson: Isa. 58]
[Magnificat]
[Second lesson: 1 Pet. 4]
[Deus misereatur]

[Then as BCP from the Apostles' creed to the suffrages after the Lord's prayer, which are those used as at morning prayer]

[The special collect prescribed in place of the collect for the day at morning prayer; the BCP second and third collects for evening prayer; the BCP collect for Ash Wednesday; and then, from the BCP commination service, the prayers 'O Lord, we beseech thee mercifully hear our prayers', 'O most mighty God and merciful Father' and 'Turn thou us, O good Lord']

[As BCP from the prayer for the king to the prayer for the clergy and people]

[The BCP prayer for parliament]

Against the Papists our Enemies.
    Almighty God, who hast in all ages shewed thy Power *[as 1678–E2]*.

For Union amongst our selves.
    Blessed Jesu, our Saviour *[as in the litany above]*.

[The prayer of St Chrysostom; the grace]

1681–S   Fast days during drought, and in support of parliament against catholic conspiracies

Wednesday 29 June 1681 (archdioceses of St Andrews and Glasgow, dioceses of Edinburgh, Dunkeld, Dunblane and Brechin); Wednesday 6 July 1681 (elsewhere in Scotland)

Scotland received unusually light rainfall in the spring and early summer of 1681, raising fears of crop failure. The drought, together with the forthcoming meeting of the Scottish parliament in Edinburgh, appointed for 28 July, prompted the appointment of this fast. The duke of York had been serving as Charles II's commissioner in Scotland since October 1679, and parliament had been called in part to ratify the duke's succession to the throne, in the wake of the exclusion crisis in England. The fast proclamation attributed a large part of the blame for God's judgments on Scotland to the ideas and actions of the Cameronians, presbyterian extremists who had excommunicated the king and declared war on his government. Donald Cargill, field preacher to the group, remained at large, having evaded capture in May. According to Lauder, rain showers began on 24 June but the fast days were observed nonetheless.

Order: royal proclamation, 16 June 1681, Wing S1789* [also in *RPC*, 3rd ser., VII, 132–3; Wodrow, *History*, III, 246–7].
Additional sources: *Edin. recs., 1681 to 1689*, p. 21; Lauder, *Historical observes*, pp. 42–3; *Alford exercise*, p. 328; *Inverness and Dingwall records*, p. 102.

ORDER

Royal proclamation: 16 June 1681
Forasmuch, as Almighty God, who since His wonderful Restoring of Us to Our Royal Rights and Government, and Deliverance of this Our Ancient Kingdom from the Tyrannical Usurpation, under which, the late Fatal Rebellion enslaved it, hath been mercifully pleased to preserve its Peace, and bless it with Plenty; Doth now, by his Warnings and Judgements Incumbent and Impendent, manifestly discover his anger and displeasure against the grievous sins thereof, committed by the abuse of both; in permitting many, who have departed from the Communion of this National Church, to give themselves over to imbrace and believe sad, Blasphemous, Sanguinary and Treasonable Delusions, to the great Scandal and Reproach of the Protestant Name and Religion; And inflicting a long Scorching and threatning Drought, whereby the Fruits of the Ground, the necessary Provision for the Life of Man and Beast, are in danger to be burnt up and consumed; The Lord, for the luxurious abuse of our Plenty, having so long in his Righteous Judgements, bound up the Clouds, *making the Heavens Brass, and the Earth Iron*, thereby threatning Us *with pale Famine*: And now having called a Parliament, to Assemble at *Edinburgh*, on the twenty eight of *July* next, for Consulting and Establishing the Civil and Religious Interests of this Kingdom, and for suppressing, by Good and Wholsome Laws, such wicked Principles and Disorders, which tend to the Subversion of both. Therefore We, out of Our Religious Disposition, have thought fit, with advice of Our Privy Council, by this Our Proclamation, to Indict a General and Publick Day of Fast and Humiliation; that all Our Loving Subjects may be moved heartily, to turn speedily to God by a true Repentance, and to send up their Fervent Prayers and Supplications, for Wise

and Pious Direction unto, and a Blessing upon the ensuing Parliament; for healing the Breaches, and pardoning the sins of the Kingdom; especially, the contempt and disobedience of the Holy Gospel, the great prevalency of Atheism, Error, Schism, Profaneness and Irreligion; together, with the unthankful abuse of Peace, with which God hath so long time Blessed Our Government; that by serious Mourning for, and sincere turning from them, the Lord may Graciously Pardon them, and open the Clouds, for preserving the Fruits of the Ground, for the Comfort of Man and Beast. Our Will is herefore, and We straitly Command and Charge, that the said Fast be Religiously and solemnly kept throughout this Kingdom, by all Subjects and People within the same: Requiring hereby the Arch-Bishops and Bishops to be careful, that this Fast be duely observed in their respective Dioceses; as follows, *viz.* the Arch-Bishops of *St. Andrews* and *Glasgow*, the Bishops of *Edinburgh, Dunkel, Dumblain* and *Brechin*, to cause it to be intimated in the several Paroch Churches within their Diocesses, upon *Sunday* the twenty sixt day of *June* instant, to be observed on *Wednesday* thereafter, the twenty ninth day of the said Moneth; and the remnant Bishops, whose Diocesses are more remote, to cause it be Intimated on *Sunday* the third day of *July* next, and observed on *Wednesday* thereafter, the sixt day of the said Moneth; which Intimation is to be made by the Ministers Reading this Our Royal Proclamation from the Pulpit, and in Exhorting a Serious and Devout Performance of the Duties and Devotions becoming Fasting and Humiliation; as they tender the Favour of Almighty God, the Safety and Honour of the Protestant Religion, and Established Government, and as they would avoid the Wrath and Indignation of God against this Kingdom: Certifying all such as shall contemn such a Religious and necessary Duty, they shall be proceeded against as Contemners of Our Authority, as well as neglecters of so Religious a Duty.

1683–EIr Thanksgiving day after discovery of the Rye House plot

Sunday 9 September 1683 (England and Wales; Ireland)

After dissolving what would be the final parliament of his reign in March 1681, Charles II ruled in alliance with the tory nobility and gentry, purging supporters of exclusion from central and local office. In this context, the discovery in June 1683 of the Rye House plot, a conspiracy to assassinate both Charles and the duke of York, proved useful to the court, since it supplied evidence with which to prosecute leading whigs and to rally public loyalty to the king. The crown's version of events was published in a royal declaration issued soon after the trials of the conspirators were over. The declaration, far longer than most proclamations for special worship, was to be read in churches on the Sunday before the thanksgiving day and on the day itself. It seems that a Sunday was chosen for the thanksgiving in order to ensure as full an observance as possible during the harvest. The form of prayer reused sections from earlier forms: the second prayer in place of the collect for the day was based on a collect from the 5 November service, here directed against dissenting 'fanatics' rather than catholics. Likewise, the collect after the prayer for the whole state of the church drew phrases from an anti-catholic prayer in the 1679–EIr form. These borrowings were consonant with a broader propaganda campaign to turn accusations of popery against the whigs, which was manifested most clearly in claims that the whig theories of resistance were drawn directly from catholic writings. Following the appointment of the day in England, Charles II instructed the Irish lord deputy, the earl of Arran, to appoint a thanksgiving in Ireland. The king's declaration and the form of prayer were sent to Dublin, where they were reprinted and distributed to parish clergy. As with the English observance, the declaration was to be read in churches when the thanksgiving day was announced, as well as on 9 September itself. The declaration was also reprinted to be read on a thanksgiving day in Scotland (1683–S). In England, the thanksgiving was observed with public entertainments, bonfires and the ringing of bells in many places. Some of the celebrations were highly partisan: figures representing presbyterians were paraded and burned; preachers attacked dissenters and glorified monarchy. An unusually large number of sermons preached on the day were later printed. There were sporadic reports of non-observance by the disaffected, and criticism of what some regarded as the judicial murders of the convicted plotters. Thanksgivings were also held in some of the American colonies – Antigua, Barbados, Massachusetts, New Hampshire and New Plymouth – although it seems likely that these were ordered in imitation of events in England. Edward Cranfield, governor of New Hampshire, complained about the neglect of the occasion, claiming that it revealed the colonists' disaffection.

Orders: ENGLAND AND WALES; IRELAND: royal declaration, 28 July 1683, Wing C2998* [also Wing C2998C, Wing C2999: Dublin reprints; see 1683–S for Scottish reprints]; IRELAND: proclamation by the lord deputy and council, 13 Aug. 1683, Wing I420*.

Forms of prayer: ENGLAND AND WALES: *A form of prayer with thanksgiving, to be used on Sunday September the 9th; being the day of thanksgiving, appointed by the kings declaration: to be solemnly observ'd in all churches, and chappels within this kingdom, in due acknowledgment of God's wonderful providence, and mercy, in discovering, and defeating the late treasonable conspiracy against his sacred majesties person, and government. By his majesties special command* ([48] pp.; Wing C4172; Durham University Library, Routh 63T.18(7)); IRELAND: *A form of prayer vvith thanksgiving, to be used on Sunday September the 9th; being the day of thanksgiving, appointed by the kings declaration: to be solemnly observ'd in all churches and chappels within this kingdom, in due acknowledgment of God's wonderful providence and mercy in discovering and defeating the late treasonable conspiracy against his sacred majesties person and government. By his majesties special command* ([48] pp.; Wing C4172A)*.

Additional sources: the king to the lord deputy, 30 July 1683, Secretary Jenkins to the lord deputy, 31 July 1683, lord deputy to Jenkins, 8 Aug. 1683, John Gelson to ?, 12 Sept. 1683, examination of James Barham, 12 Sept. 1683, newsletter, 13 Sept. 1683, James Harris to Jenkins, 18 Sept. 1683, Jenkins to the archbishop of York, 25 Sept. 1683, *CSPD, July–September 1683*, pp. 225, 229, 267–8, 390–1, 392, 394–5, 405, 423; *CSPD, 1683–4*, pp. 283–4; HMC, *Ormonde*, new ser., VII, 66, 79, 83; HMC, *Fifth rep.*, p. 589; HMC, *Duke of Leeds etc.*, p. 198; Mostyn newsletter, 4 Aug. 1683, University of Wales, Bangor, MS 9091, fo. 128; Jenkins to the earl of Arran, 31 July 1683, Bod., MS Carte 216, fo. 317r; Arran to Jenkins, 8 Aug. 1683, Bod., MS Carte 168, p. 159; Morrice, II, 396; Luttrell, I, 273, 279; Wood, III, 72; *CSPC*, XI, 504, 510, 522, 540, 545–6; Thomas Hutchinson, *The history of Massachusettes* (3rd edn., 2 vols., Boston, 1795), I, 309.

Printed sermons: Anon., ? (Wing A439A); Barne, Cambridge (Wing B861, B862, B863, ESTC 006278679, 006420939); Bolton, Christchurch, London (Wing B3535); Calamy, St Lawrence Jury, London (Wing C217); Chapman, ?Barnard Castle (Wing C1954); Clapham, ?Wramplingham (Wing C4409); Fitzwilliam, Cotenham (Wing F1106); Foreness, Manchester (Wing F1554); Harrison, ?Pulborow (Wing H895); Hesketh, St Mary-le-Bow, London (Wing H1619); Long, Exeter (Wing L2972); E. M., Thomastown (Wing M20A); Milbourne, Great Yarmouth (Wing M2037); Payne, ?St Mary Whitechapel, London (Wing P912); Pearson, ?St Michael Crooked-lane, London (Wing P1014); Pelling, ? (Wing P1094); Pomfret, Ampthill (Wing P2800); Powell, South Marston (Wing P3046); Price, Petworth (Wing P3337); Scattergood, Blockley (Wing S844); Smith, Norwich (Wing S4281); Turner, court (Wing T3282); Turner, Epsom (Wing T3317); Wagstaffe, Stow (Wing W212).

ORDERS

England and Wales; Ireland: royal declaration, 28 July 1683

HIS MAJESTIES DECLARATION To all His Loving Subjects, concerning the Treasonable Conspiracy against His Sacred Person and Government, lately Discovered: Appointed to be Read in all Churches and Chappels within this Kingdom. Charles R.

It hath been Our Observation, That for several Years last past, a Malevolent Party hath made it their Business to Promote Sedition by False News, Libellous Pamphlets, and other wicked Arts; whereby they Endeavoured not only to Render Our Government Odious, and Our most Faithful Subjects Suspected to the People, but even to Incite them to a Dislike and Hatred of Our Royal Person: Whereupon it was evident to Us, That the Heads of this Party could have no other Aim, but the Ruine of Us and Our Government.

And whilst by Our utmost Care, We Manifested to all Our Subjects Our Zeal for the Maintenance of the Protestant Religion, and Our Resolutions to Govern according to Law; It was a great Trouble to Us to find, That Evil Persons by Misrepresenting Our Actions to the People, should so far Insinuate themselves into the Affections of the weaker Sort, as that they looked upon Them as the only Patriots and Assertors of their Religion and Liberties, and gave themselves up entirely to their Conduct.

As their Numbers increased, so did their Boldness, to that height, That by often shewing themselves in Tumults and Riots, and Unlawful and Seditious Conventicles, They not only Engaged, but Proclaimed an Impunity to their own Party, who thought themselves already too strong for the Laws; and they seemed to believe, That in a short time they should gain upon the People, so as to perswade them to a total Defection from the Government.

But it pleased God, by these their Violent Ways, to Open the Eyes of Our good Subjects, who easily Foresaw what Troubles these Methods would Produce; And thereupon with great Courage as well as Duty and Affection towards Us, upon all Occasions did Manifest their Resolution and Readiness in Defence of Our Person, and Support of Our Government, and the Religion Established: And did likewise Convince the Common People of the Villanous Designs of their Factious Leaders, and the Miseries that would befall them in pursuing such Courses.

By these means the Factious Party lost Ground daily, and finding that it was impossible to keep up the Spirits of their Followers, against the Religion Established, and the Laws; whilst we were Steady in the Maintenance and Execution of them, became Desperate, and Resolved not to Trust any longer to the slow Methods of Sedition, but to betake themselves to Arms; not doubting, but that they remained still strong enough by Force to Overturn the Government which they could not Undermine.

It is hard to imagine how men of so many different Interests and Opinions, could joyn in any Enterprize; but it is certain, They readily Concurred in the Resolution of taking Arms to Destroy the Government, even before they had Agreed what to set up in the place of it.

To which purpose, they took several Ways; For, whilst some were Contriving a General Insurrection in this Kingdom, and likewise in *Scotland*; Others were Conspiring to Assassinate Our Royal Person, and Our Dearest Brother, and to Massacre the Magistrates of Our City of *London*, and Our Officers of State, That there might be no Appearance of Government, nor any Means for Our Subjects to Unite for their Defence.

In case it had pleased God to permit these wicked Designs to have taken Effect, There could have been nothing in Prospect but Confusion: For, instead of the Reformation they pretended, their Success would have produced Divisions, and Wars among themselves, until the Predominant Party could have Enslaved the rest, and the whole Kingdom.

But the Divine Providence, which hath preserved Us through the whole Course of Our life, hath at this time in an Extraordinary manner, shewed it self in the Wonderful and Gracious Deliverance of Us and Our Dearest Brother, and all Our Loyal Subjects from this Horrid and Damnable Conspiracy.

As it is therefore Our desire that all Our Loving Subjects should joyn with Us in giving Thanks to Almighty God for this Mercy, so We thought it necessary they should be now in some measure Informed of the Fact as it hath been Discovered to Us by undoubted Proof, and the Confession of divers of the Accomplices in this Conspiracy; whereof, though We have not as yet perfectly Traced all the Particulars, the Principal and main Designs of it nevertheless, have appeared to be as followeth.

About the beginning of *October* last, when the Heads of the Faction saw the Magistracy of Our City of *London* Settled in Persons of Loyal Principles, they became impatient, and fell immediately to Consult of Rising in Arms; for which some thought their Party so well prepared, that they could not fail of attaining their ends whenever they should break out into open force.

Whereupon there was a Meeting of some of the Principal Conspirators, to Agree about the best means to Master Our Guards, and to Seize Our Person; but upon Consideration, they found it necessary to prepare their Friends in the several Counties, as also the Disaffected Party in *Scotland* to joyn with them, without which, any Attempt in Our said City, or upon Our Guards, appeared too rash to be undertaken; so that they laid aside the thoughts of a present Rising, and disposed themselves to find, by a Correspondence with *Scotland*, and with several parts of this Our Kingdom, how far they might be Assisted by a General Insurrection, so that they might not in Human probability fail of Success.

Whilst this first Design was Forming, some Villains were likewise carrying on that Horrid and Execrable Plot of Assassinating Our Royal Person, and Our Dearest Brother, in Our coming from *Newmarket*, and Mony was deposited for that purpose: But by the shortness of the time (We being then immediately upon Our Return) and for want of necessary Preparations, they were forced to defer the Execution of it till further Opportunity.

It was then proposed among them, Whether they should Attempt the same at Our next going to *Newmarket*, in *March* last? But some objected, That Our Guards which usually remain here some time after Our Departure, would be capable of making a great Opposition upon the Arrival of the News. For which Reason, and because they were not then in a sufficient Readiness; It was Agreed to be done at Our Return from *Newmarket*.

The Place Appointed was the House of one *Richard Rumbold* a Maltster, called the *Rye*, near *Hoddesdon* in the County of *Hertford*: And it was Resolved, That Forty Persons in number, who were to be Actors in this Assassination, under the Command of the said *Richard Rumbold*, should hide themselves in or near the said House; And when Our Coach should come over against them, then Three or Four were to Shoot with Blunderbusses at the Postilion and Horses, and if they should fail of killing the Horses, some were to be ready in the way, who in the Habit of Labourers should Turn a Cart cross the Passage, and so stop Our Coach. Others were appointed to Shoot into the Coach, where Our Royal Person, and Our Dearest Brother were to be: Others to Fire upon the Guards that should be then Attending Us. And it was further Resolved, That upon the same Day, Many Lords, and other Persons of Quality, whom they supposed favourable to their Design, should be Invited to Dine in Our City of *London*, That they might be the more ready to Appear among the Citizens upon Arrival of the News. The Actors in the said Assassination having Contrived the manner of their Escape, by a nearer Passage than the usual Road; By which means they hoped to get to *London* as soon as the News could be brought thither.

They thought it would be Easie upon their Perpetrating this Horrid Fact, to possess themselves of the Government, presuming upon the Numbers of the Disaffected.

But lest the Blackness of such an Action might Deter any from joyning with them, They Prepared to Palliate it, as far as they could, by some Remonstrance, or Declaration, which was ready to be Printed and Dispersed in that Confusion, to Amuse the People. And lest Our Officers of State, and the Magistrates of Our said City, with the *Militia* thereof, and other Our Loyal Subjects, should be able to put some Stop to their Carreir, They Resolved to follow this Blow with a Massacre; wherein they particularly Designed for immediate Slaughter, Our Officers of State, the Present Lord Mayor, and Sheriffs, and the Magistracy of Our City, and other Our Subjects that had been most Eminent for their Loyalty.

But it pleased Almighty God, by His wonderful Providence, To Defeat these Councels by the sudden Fire at *Newmarket*, which necessitated Our Return from thence before the time We had Appointed.

Yet these Villains were not thereby discouraged from Pursuing the same Bloudy Design, but Resolved to take the first Opportunity for Effecting the same, and proposed to themselves, That it might be done, either in Our Passage from *Windsor* to *Hampton Court*, or in Our Journey to *Winchester*, or when We should go by Water in Our Barge, or under *Bedford* Garden Wall, as We should pass that way, or at the Bull Feast, which was to be in Red-Lyon-Fields; they being informed, That We and Our Dearest Brother had Intentions of coming thither.

And that they might be the better prepared, when there should be occasion, by having a certain Number of Arms lying always ready for that Purpose; Arms for Forty Men were bespoke in all haste, (*vizt.*) Thirty Carbines with Belts and Swivels, Thirty Cases of Pistols, and Ten Blunderbusses, which were accordingly Made and Paid for.

And for the more easie Drawing their Party together against the time of Execution, they Contrived to Divide Our Cities of *London* and *Westminster*, and the Suburbs, into Twenty Parts; from each of which they expected Five hundred men to be ready at the first Onset; And some Agitators were to give an Account of the men to be furnished in each Division, and to give out Orders to them, as there should be occasion.

And to the end the Forces they should Raise might be the sooner Modelled into the Form of an Army, there were One hundred Old Officers, who had been Engaged in the late Rebellion, ready in Town to take the Command of them; In the pursuit of which Project they continued, till they knew that a Discovery had been made unto Us.

During all this time, the Principal Conspirators were Managing their other Design for a General Insurrection in both Kingdoms.

The late Earl of *Shaftsbury*, who had at first Pressed them to sudden Rising, which he would have had before the Seventeenth of *November* last, or upon that day at the farthest, sent to the Conspirators, at a Meeting appointed by them, to know their Resolution; and finding they would not adventure without farther Preparation, Conveyed himself secretly into *Holland*, to avoid the Danger he might be in by a Discovery.

His withdrawing himself from their Councels did not Discourage them from Pursuing their Design, onely made them more Cautious; Whereupon a new Councel was appointed of Six Persons that were to have the Chief Management of Affairs, in Order to a General Insurrection, by a Correspondency with their Party in *Scotland*, and several Counties of this Our Kingdom. And because a Correspondency by Letters was thought dangerous, it was held necessary that some Person should be sent into *Scotland*, to Invite the Heads of the Disaffected Party in that Our Kingdom, to come hither, under pretence of Purchasing Lands in *Carolina*; But, in truth, to Concert with them the best Means for carrying on the Design Joyntly in both Kingdoms: And a Treaty was thereupon had with *Archibald Campbell* late Earl of *Argile*, already Attainted of Treason, who demanded Thirty thousand Pounds at first; But afterward Agreed to accept of Ten thousand pounds, for Buying of Arms in *Holland*, and making other Provisions necessary for a Rebellion within Our Kingdom of *Scotland*.

In the said Councel of Six it was Debated, Whether the Rising in this Kingdom, should be first in Our City of *London*, where, by reason of the vast Numbers that might readily Unite, they thought they might easily Master the Guards, or rather in some remote parts, whereby We should be under a necessity of sending Our Guards to Suppress them, and thereby the Rising in Our said City would become more Secure and Effectual: But at last it was Resolved, as most convenient, That it should be in all parts at the same time, lest Our City might be Defended by the *Militia* thereof, without the help of Our Guards, which We might send for the Suppressing any Insurrection in the Countrey; And they did all dispose themselves accordingly, for the Compassing their Design, which was very near taking effect.

But such was the abundant Mercy of Almighty God, while they were yet meditating their Execrable Mischiefs against Our Royal Person, Our Dearest Brother, and the Government, a Discovery was made unto Us by one of the Accomplices, on the Twelfth of *June* last; since which time We have used the best Means We could for the Detecting, and Prevention of so Hellish a Conspiracy.

But so it has hapned, that divers of the Conspirators, having notice of Warrants Issued out for their Apprehension, are fled from Justice: *Viz. James* Duke of *Monmouth*, the Lord *Melvin*, Sir *John Cochrane*, Sir *Thomas Armestrong*, *Robert Ferguson*, who was the Common Agitator Entrusted by all Parties in the several Conspiracies, *Richard Goodenough, Francis Goodenough, Richard Rumbold* the Maltster, *William Rumbold* his Brother, *Richard Nelthorp, Nathaniel Wade, William Thompson, James Burton, Joseph Elby, Samuel Gibbs, Francis Charleton, Joseph Tyley*, [*blank in original*] *Casteers*, [*blank in original*] *Lobb*, both Non-Conformist Preachers, *Edward Norton, John Row, John Ayloff*, and *John Atherton*.

Ford Lord *Gray* being Apprehended, made his Escape out of the hands of a Serjeant at Arms, and *Arthur* late Earl of *Essex*, being Committed to the *Tower* for High Treason, Killed himself.

Others have been Taken and Committed to Custody, some of whom, *Viz.* the Lord *William Russel, Thomas Walcot, William Hone,* and *John Rowse,* have upon their Trials been Convicted, Attainted, and Executed according to Law.

This We thought fit to make known to Our Loving Subjects, that they being sensible (as We are) of the Mercy of God in this great Deliverance, may Chearfully and Devoutly joyn with Us in Returning Solemn Thanks to Almighty God for the same.

For which end We do hereby Appoint the Ninth day of *September* next, to be observed as a day of Thanksgiving in all Churches and Chappels within this Our Kingdom of *England,* Dominion of *Wales,* and Town of *Berwick* upon *Tweed,* in such manner as shall be by Us Directed, in a Form of Prayer with Thanksgiving, which We have Commanded to be prepared by Our Bishops, and Published for that purpose.

And it is Our Pleasure, That this Declaration be Publickly Read in all the said Churches and Chappels, as well on Sunday the Second of *September* next, as upon the Day of Thanksgiving aforesaid.

Ireland: proclamation by the lord deputy and council, 13 August 1683

It having pleased Almighty God by his wonderful Providence, and out of his unspeakable Mercy, in a most extraordinary manner to deliver His Majesty from a late horrid and damnable Conspiracy of bloody men; and His Majesty out of a deep sense thereof, having been pleased by his Declaration dated the *28th.* of *July 1683.* to appoint a day of Publick Thanksgiving to be observed & solemnly kept throughout the Kingdom of *England,* and Principality of *Wales,* upon the ninth of *September* next; and by His Letters to Us, the Lord Deputy, hath signified his pleasure, that the like be done in his Kingdom of *Ireland,* either upon the said ninth of *September,* or some other convenient day, as We should direct. Now We, the Lord Deputy and Council, in Obedience to His Majesties said Command, and to the end a particular time may be set a-part for a publick performance of this Duty, and that there may be an entire Uniformity of both Churches and Kingdoms in their Publick Thanksgiving to God for so great a Deliverance, do hereby Publish and Declare, and also strictly Charge and Command that the said ninth day of *September* next be set a part, and observed as a day of Publick Thanksgiving in and throughout His Majesties Kingdom of *Ireland.* And We do direct and appoint that His Majesties said Declaration, together with this Our Proclamation, be publickly read in all Churches and Chappels, as well on Sunday the second of *September* next, as upon the day of Thanksgiving aforesaid; and that the same form of P[r]ayer, with Thanksgiving, prepared in *England* for that occasion (which We have ordered to be printed here) be also on the said ninth day of *September* made use of in the publick Service and Worship of God.

FORMS OF PRAYER

England and Wales; Ireland

MORNING PRAYER

Let him that ministreth read with a loud voice these Sentences of Scripture, and after them the Exhortation following.
[1 Tim. 2:1–3; Dan. 9:9–10]

[As BCP to the Venite*]*

Instead of Venite, exultemus, *shall be said or sung this Hymn following; one Verse by the Priest, and another by the Clerk and People.*
O Come, let us sing unto the Lord: let us heartily rejoyce in the strength of our salvation. (Ps. 95:1)
Let us come before his presence with thanksgiving: and shew our selves glad in him with psalms. (Ps. 95:2)
Let Israel rejoyce in him, that made him: let the children of Sion be joyful in their King. (Ps. 149:2)
For the Lord hath pleasure in his people: and helpeth the Meek-hearted. (Ps. 149:4)
The Lord setteth up the Meek: and bringeth the Ungodly down to the Ground. (Ps. 147:6)
Great is our Lord, and great is his power: yea, and his Wisdom is infinite. (Ps. 147:5)
The merciful and gracious Lord hath so done his marvellous works: that they ought to be had in Remembrance. (Ps. 111:4)
O that Men would therefore praise the Lord for his Goodness: and declare the Wonders, that he doeth for the children of Men. (Ps. 107:21)
That they would offer unto him the sacrifice of Thanksgiving: and tell out his Works with Gladness. (Ps. 107:22)
That our posterity also may know them: and the children that are yet unborn. (Ps. 78:6)
And not be as their Fathers, a faithless, and stubborn Generation: a Generation that set not their heart aright, and whose spirit cleaved not stedfastly unto God. (Ps. 78:9)
As for us, *Our Song shall be ever of the loving kindness of the Lord: with our Mouth will we be shewing forth his Truth from one Generation to another.* (Ps. 89:1)
Praised be the Lord daily: even the God, who helpeth us, and poureth his Benefits upon us. (Ps. 68:19)
He is our God, even the God, of whom cometh Salvation: God is the Lord, by whom we escape Death. (Ps. 68:20)
God shall wound the Head of his Enemies: and the Hairy Scalp of such an One, as goeth on still in his Wickedness. (Ps. 68:21)
Give thanks O Israel, unto God in the Congregations: from the Ground of the Heart. (Ps. 68:26)
Thy God hath sent forth strength for thee: stablish the thing, O God, that thou hast wrought for us. (Ps. 68:28)
God hath shewed us his Goodness plenteously: and God hath let us see our Desire upon our Enemies. (Ps. 59:10)
Great prosperity giveth he unto his King: and sheweth loving kindness unto *David* his Anointed, and to his seed for evermore. (Ps. 18:51)
The Lord hath been mindful of us, and he shall bless us: even he shall bless the House of Israel, he shall bless the House of Aaron. (Ps. 115:12)
He shall bless them, that fear the Lord: both small, and great. (Ps. 115:13)
So that a Man shall say, Verily there is a Reward for the Righteous: doubtless there is a God that judgeth the Earth. (Ps. 58:10)
Glory be the Father, &c.
As it was in the beginning, &c.

[Ps. 9, 21, 118]

[First lesson: 2 Sam. 22]
[Te Deum]
[Second lesson: Acts 23]
[Jubilate Deo]

[Then as BCP to the end of the Lord's prayer]

Priest: O Lord, shew thy mercy upon us *[as 1678–E1].*

Instead of the Collect for the Day, shall be used these two which follow, both in
Morning and Evening Prayer, and in the Communion-Service.
[The BCP collect for peace and deliverance from our enemies]

Almighty God, who hast in all Ages shewed forth thy Power, and Mercy in the miraculous, and gracious Deliverances of thy Church, and in the protection of Righteous, and Religious Kings, and States, professing thy Holy, and Eternal Truth, from the malicious Conspiracies, and wicked practices of all their Enemies; We yield unto thee from the very Bottom of our Hearts unfeigned Thanks, and Praise for the late signal, and wonderful Deliverance of our most Gracious Soveraign, his Royal Brother, and loyal Subjects of all Orders, and Degrees, by the fanatick Rage, and Treachery of wicked and ungodly Men, appointed as sheep to the slaughter in a most barbarous, and savage Manner. From this unnatural, and hellish Conspiracy not our Merit, but thy Mercy; not our Foresight, but thy Providence; not our own Arm, but thy right hand, and thine Arm, and the light of thy countenance hath rescu'd and deliver'd us, even because thou hadst a favour unto us: And therefore not unto us, O Lord, not unto us; but unto thy Name be ascribed all Honour, Glory, and Praise, with most humble, and hearty Thanks in all Churches of the Saints: Even so, Blessed be the Lord our God, who onely doeth wondrous things; and Blessed be the Name of his Majesty for ever, through Jesus Christ our Lord, and onely Saviour. *Amen.*

[Then the BCP collects for peace and for grace]

LITANY

[As BCP to the end of the prayer 'We humbly beseech thee']

O God, whose providence neglects not the meanest of thy Creatures; but is most illustriously visible in watching over the persons of Kings, the great Instruments of thy Goodness to Mankind: We give Thee most hearty Thanks, and Praise, as for thy many wonderful Deliverances, formerly vouchsafed to thy Servant, our dread Soveraign, through the whole Course of his Life; so especially for the late Miracle of thy Mercy, whereby thou didst rescue Him, and Us all from those bloudy Designs, which nothing, but thine infinite Wisdom, and Power could have discovered and defeated. For this thy great Goodness (notwithstanding our great unworthiness, & many provocations) so graciously continued to us, we praise thee, we bless thee, we worship thee, we glorifie thee, we give Thanks to thee for thy great Glory: Humbly beseeching thee, that our present Sense of this thy Favour, and the fervent Affections now kindled in our Hearts thereby may never cool, or sink down into Forgetfulness, or Ingratitude; but may produce in every one of us firm Resolutions of future Thankfulness, and Obedience, with a suitable constant perseverance in the same. Let us never forget, how often, and how wonderfully Thou hast preserved thine Anointed, and his people; that being All duely sensible of our absolute Dependence upon thee, we may endeavour to answer the blessed Ends of this thy good providence over us. Continue Him a nursing Father to this thy Church, and thy Minister for Good to all his people: And let us, and all his Subjects look upon him henceforth, not onely as the Ordinance, but also as the Gift of God; promising and performing in thee, and for thee all faithful Duty, and Loyalty to Him, and his Heirs after him; with a religious Obedience, and Thankfulness unto thee for these, and all other thy mercies, through Jesus Christ thy Son our Lord; To whom with thee, O Father, and God the Holy Ghost be all Honour, and Glory world without end. *Amen.*

[The BCP prayer 'O God, whose nature and property is ever to have mercy']

[The prayer of St Chrysostom; the grace]

COMMUNION

[As BCP to the end of the ten commandments]

Almighty God, whose kingdom is everlasting *[as BCP]*

[Then, in place of the collect for the day, the special collects prescribed for morning prayer]

[Epistle: Rom. 13:1–7]
[Gospel: Matt. 21:33–46]
[Nicene creed]

After the Creed shall be publickly read the Kings Declaration to all his loving Subjects, concerning the treasonable Conspiracy against His Sacred Person, and Goverment, lately discovered.

Then shall follow the Sermon, or some part of the Homily formerly set forth by Royal Authority, against Disobedience, and wilful Rebellion: and after that shall be said,

[Offertory sentences: Matt. 5:16; Ps. 41:1]

[The prayer for the whole state of the church]

Almighty God, and Heavenly Father, who of thine unspeakable Goodness towards us hast in a most extraordinary Manner discovered the Designs, and disappointed the Attempts of those traiterous, heady, and highminded Men, who under the pretence of Religion, and thy most holy Name had contriv'd, and resolv'd our Destruction; As we do this Day most heartily, and devoutly adore and magnifie thy glorious Name for this thine infinite gracious Goodness already vouchsaf'd to us; So we most humbly implore the continuance of thy Grace and Favour for the farther and clearer Discovery of these Depths of Satan, this Mystery of Iniquity. Send forth thy Light and thy Truth, and make known the hidden things of Darkness: Infatuate, and defeat all the secret Counsels of the Ungodly; Abate their Pride, asswage their Malice, and confound their Devices; Strengthen the Hands of our gracious King *Charles*, and All that are put in Authority under him, with Judgment, and Justice, to cut off all such Workers of Iniquity, as turn Religion into Rebellion, and Faith into Faction; that they may never prevail against Us, or triumph in the Ruine of thy Church among us. To this End protect, and defend our Sovereign Lord the King, with the whole Royal Family, from all Treasons, and Conspiracies. Bind up his Soul in the Bundle of Life; and let no Weapon form'd against him prosper. Be unto him a Helmet of Salvation, and a strong Tower of Defence against the Face of his Enemies. Let his Reign be prosperous, and his Days many. Make him glad now according to the Time wherein thou hast afflicted him; and for the years wherein he hath suffered Adversity. As thou hast given him the Necks of his Enemies, so give him also every day more and more the Hearts of his Subjects. As for those that are implacable, clothe them with shame; but upon himself, and his Posterity let the Crown for ever flourish. So we that are thy people, and the sheep of thy pasture, shall give thee Thanks for ever, and will always be shewing forth thy praise from Generation to Generation, through Jesus Christ our only Saviour and Redeemer. *Amen.*

[The BCP collect for the fifth Sunday after Trinity]

Almighty God, who hast promised *[as BCP, followed by the blessing]*.

EVENING PRAYER

[The rubric as in morning prayer, followed by the opening sentences: 1 Tim. 2:1–3; Dan. 9:9–10]

[Then as BCP to the psalms]

[Ps. 92, 124, 144]
[First lesson: Num. 16]
[Cantate Domino]
[Second lesson: Jude or 1 Pet. 2]
[Deus misereatur]

[Then as BCP from the Apostles' creed to the suffrages after the Lord's prayer, which are those used as at morning prayer]

[The special collects prescribed in place of the collect for the day at morning prayer; the BCP second and third collects for evening prayer; the prayer 'O God, whose providence neglects not the meanest' from the end of the litany]

[Then as BCP from the prayer for the king to the prayer for the clergy and people]

A Prayer for our Enemies.
Father of Mercies, and lover of Souls, who art kind unto the Unthankful, and to the Evil, and hast commanded us also to extend our charity even to those that hate us, and despitefully use us: We beseech thee, as to accept our Prayers, and Praises, which we have this Day offered up unto thee in behalf of all that are Faithful and Loyal in

the Land; so also to enlarge thy Mercy, and Pity, even to those that are our Enemies. O most wise, and powerful Lord God, in whose Hands are the Hearts of all men, as the Rivers of Water, to turn them whithersoever thou wilt; Work mightily upon the Minds of all Parties amongst us. Turn the Hearts of the Children to the Fathers, and the Disobedient to the Wisdom of the Just; and so make them a ready people prepared for the Lord. Thou that sittest between the Cherubim, be the Earth never so unquiet; thou that stillest the Raging of the Sea, and the Noise of his Waves, and the Madness of the People: Stir up thy Strength, and come, and help us. Let the Wickedness of the Wicked come to an end: Take away his Ungodliness, and thou shalt find none. Let the Fierceness of Man turn to thy Praise; and the Remainder of Wrath do thou restrain. To this end take from them all their Prejudices, and all their Passions; their confident Mistakes, their carnal Ends, and their secular Interests. Open the blind Eyes, that they may see (at least in this their Day) the Things which belong to their Peace, and wisely considering thy Work, may say, This hath God done; and so hear, and fear, and do no more wickedly. Soften the most obdurate Hearts into a meek, and humble, and docible Temper, that they may no longer resist the Truth. Bow down the stiff Neck, and the iron Sinew, to the gentle and easie Yoke of thy most holy Law. Take away the Brow of Brass, and the Whores Forehead; and make their Faces ashamed, that they may seek thy Name. Sweeten (if it may be) the Gall of Bitterness; and loose the Bands of Iniquity; and guide their Feet into the Ways of Peace: And thus redouble, O Lord, upon us the Joys of this Day, that we may not onely triumph in the Disappointment of their wicked Imaginations, but with thy holy Angels in Heaven rejoyce for their Conversion: Which great Blessing with the most ardent Affections of our Souls we beg of thee, for thy tender Mercies sake, through the Merits, and Mediation of Jesus Christ, thy blessed Son, our onely Saviour. *Amen.*

[The BCP collect for the fifth Sunday after Trinity]

[The prayer of St Chrysostom; the grace]

1683–S   Thanksgiving day after discovery of the Rye House plot

Sunday 9 September 1683 (Scotland)

On 2 July 1683, a letter from Charles II was read to the Scottish privy council reporting the discovery of the Rye House plot (see 1683–EIr). Intending to call a thanksgiving day in response, the council instructed the bishops to prepare a proclamation, and mentioned its plan in a letter to Charles of 4 July. Presumably after further instructions from court, the council delayed for a month, and then appointed a thanksgiving for the same day as the equivalent English celebration. By this time, Charles's declaration concerning the plot had been issued; the council ordered that it be read in churches together with the proclamation. Bonfires and wine were provided at the crown's expense around Holyroodhouse on the thanksgiving day, but in many places observance was less enthusiastic. One reason for this was the lukewarm response of presbyterian ministers. The council later prosecuted several indulged presbyterians (those who had been licensed to preach in churches) for not reading the king's declaration or observing the thanksgiving.

Order: royal proclamation, 7 Aug. 1683, Wing S1948* [another version with an account of its proclamation at Edinburgh, 8 Aug. 1683 (Wing S1949); also in *RPC*, 3rd ser., VIII, 209–10; Wodrow, *History*, III, 503–4].

Declaration: *His majesties declaration to all his loving subjects, concerning the treasonable conspiracy against his sacred person and government, lately discovered. Appointed to be read in all churches and chappels within this kingdom. By his majesties special command* (Edinburgh, 1683; Wing C2998A) [also Wing C2998B: reprints of the order for 1683–EIr].

Additional sources: *RPC*, 3rd ser., VIII, 183–4, 186–7, 319–20, X, 36–8; *CSPD, July–September 1683*, pp. 24–5; Wodrow, *History*, III, 499–504, IV, 37, 40; Luttrell, I, 274; Lauder, *Historical observes*, p. 104; receipt for entertainments at Holyroodhouse, GD90/2/120; *Alford exercise*, p. 347; *Inverness and Dingwall records*, p. 115; Lauder, *Historical notices*, I, 456, 478; *Journal of the Hon. John Erskine of Carnock, 1683–1687*, ed. Walter MacLeod (Scottish History Society, XIV, Edinburgh, 1893), p. s28.

ORDER

Royal proclamation: 7 August 1683

Forasmuch as Almighty God in His great Mercy, and by His wonderful Providence, hath brought to Light, Defeated and Confounded a most Un-natural, Traitorous and Diabolical Conspiracy, contrived and carried on by Persons of Phanatical, Atheistical and Republican Principles, for taking away Our Sacred Life, and the Life of Our Dearest Brother *James* Duke of *Albany*, Subverting of Our Government, and Involving these Kingdoms in Bloud, Confusion and Miseries; Concerning which Treasonable Conspiracy, We have Emitted Our Royal Declaration to all Our loving Subjects, at Our Court at *Whitehall*, the 28th. of *July* last, in this 35th. year of Our Reign, which We have Ordered to be Re-printed here. And We being deeply sensible of the humble and grateful Praises and Adoration, We owe to the Divine Majesty, for this great and signal Instance of His watchful Care over Us, whom He hath so long Preserved, and so often Delivered by Miracles, Have out of Our Religious Disposition, readily approven of an humble Motion made to Us for commanding an Solemn and General Thanksgiving, to be religiously Observed throughout this whole Kingdom, to Offer up devout Praises and Thanksgiving to Almighty God, for this eminent and miraculous Deliverance granted to Us, and in Us, to all Our loyal and dutiful Subjects; as also, fervently to pray that God may continue His gracious Care over Us, and His Mercies to these Kingdoms, and more and more bring to Light, Defeat and Confound all Traitorous Conspiracies, *Associations* and Machinations against Us, Our Dearest Brother and Government; We with Advice of Our Privy Council, have therefore thought fit by this Our Royal Proclamation, to Indict a General and Solemn Thanksgiving, to be Observed throughout this Kingdom, that all Our loving Subjects may offer their devout Praises and Gratulations, and their fervent Prayers and Supplications to Almighty God for the Purposes foresaid; And We strictly Command and Charge, that the said Solemn Thanksgiving be religiously and devoutly Performed by all Our Subjects and People within this Our Kingdom, upon the ninth of *September* next; And to the end this part of Divine Worship, so pious and necessary, may be uniformly and at the same time offered by all Our loving and loyal Subjects; We hereby Require the Reverend Arch-Bishops and Bishops to give notice hereof to the Ministers in their respective Dioceses, that upon the Lords Day immediatly preceeding the said 9th. day of *September* next, as also upon the said 9th. of *September* they cause Read and Intimat this Our Royal Proclamation from the Pulpit in every Paroch Church, together with Our foresaid Declaration, Dated at Our Court at *Whitehall* as said is, and that they exhort all Our Subjects to a serious and devout Performance of the saids Prayers, Praises and Thanksgiving, as they tender the Favour of Almighty God, and the Safety and Preservation of Our Sacred Life and Government; Certifying all such as shall contemn or neglect this so religious and important a Duty, they shall be proceeded against, and punished as Contemners of Our Authority, and as Persons highly Disaffected to Our Person and Government. And ordains these Presents to be Printed.

DECLARATION

[As 1683–EIr]

1684–S   Fast days during bad weather and fears of famine

Wednesday 7 May 1684 (archdioceses of St Andrews and Glasgow, dioceses of Edinburgh, Galloway, Dunkeld, Aberdeen, Brechin and Dunblane); Wednesday 28 May 1684 (elsewhere in Scotland)

Following a severe winter and a late onset of spring, the diocesan synod of Edinburgh, meeting on 9 April 1684, resolved that two diocesan fast days should be appointed annually to beseech good weather in spring and at harvest time. Some clergy apparently doubted whether calling fast days was within the bishop's power, so the proposal was submitted for the privy council's approval. Perhaps as a consequence, the council soon after issued the proclamation for this national fast. According to the diarist John Erskine, churches were better attended on the fast day than on a typical Sunday.

Order: royal proclamation, 17 Apr. 1684, Wing S1949A* [also in *RPC*, 3rd ser., VIII, 452–4].
Additional sources: Wodrow, *History*, IV, 177–8; *Inverness and Dingwall records*, p. 119; Lauder, *Historical observes*, p. 123; Lauder, *Historical notices*, II, 530–1, 536, 539; *Journal of the Hon. John Erskine of Carnock*, ed. MacLeod, pp. 58, 60; *The diary of Alexander Brodie of Brodie, MDCLII.–MDCLXXX. and of his son, James Brodie of Brodie, MDCLXXX.–MDCLXXXV.* [1740], ed. David Laing (Spalding Club, Aberdeen, 1863), p. 489.

ORDER

Royal proclamation: 17 April 1684
Forasmuch as Almighty God, after a sinful abuse of the holy Gospel, and of the never to be forgotten Deliverance of this Our ancient Kingdom, from the Yoke of Bondage and Usurpation, and of Our Royal Person and Government, from the open Rebellions, and secret Plots and Conspiracies of Traiterous and Phanatical Enemies; and after a long and impious despising of Peace and Plenty, doth by his righteous Judgements, manifestly discover his Anger and Displeasure against the grievous sins of this Kingdom; and particularly, by the long continuance of the Rigor and Storms of the last Winter, and the severity and unnatural Coldnesse of the present Spring, whereby not only a great part of the Cattel and Bestial are already destroyed, and the remanent in apparent danger; but even the ordinary Season of Plowing and Sowing of the Ground, was in danger almost to be lost, thereby threatning the breaking of *The*

Staff of Bread, and the dreadful *Plague of Famine:* Which Dispensation, doth invite persons of all Ranks, to speedy and true Repentance, and the National Expression thereof, by deep Mourning, and solemn Fasting and Humiliation. Therefore We, with Advice and Consent of the Lords of Our Privy Council, Do appoint and ordain a Day of Humiliation to be observed by all Our Subjects of this Kingdom; strictly Commanding and Requiring them, upon that Day, to cease from all the Works of their ordinary Callings, and to repair to their respective Paroch Churches, and there, make solemn Confession of their Sins, and Implore the Divine Mercy to Us, and Our Subjects, by Praying, Mourning, Fasting, and such other Devotions, as are usual upon such Dayes of publict Humiliation, more particularly, contritely to Confess and Mourn for the great neglect and contempt of, and disobedience to the holy Gospel, for the sinful Separation from the Ordinances thereof, and for the great and lamentable prevalency of Atheism, Error, Prophaness, and Irreligion occasioned thereby; and for the sinful undervaluing of the great Blessings of Peace and Plenty, so long continued under Our Government: By all which, and many other crying Sins, the Lords Anger and Jealousie are kindled, and his Hand is stretched out to the Destruction of the Cattel, and threatning the Fruits of the Ground, the necessary Provision for the Life of Man and Beast, that by serious Mourning, and sincere turning from these provocking Sins, the Lord may graciously pardon them, and repent him of the evil threatned, and most righteously deserved. And for this end, We do require the Arch-Bishops of *St. Andrews* and *Glasgow,* the Bishops of *Edinburgh, Galloway, Dunkel, Aberdeen, Brichen,* and *Dumblane,* To cause it to be Intimated in the several Paroch Churches of their Dioceses, upon *Sunday* the fourth day of *May,* and to be Celebrated and observed, on *Wednesday* thereafter; and the remanent Bishops, whose Diocesses are more remote, to cause it to be Intimated on *Sunday* the twenty fifth of *May,* to be observed the *Wednesday* thereafter, by Reading the same from the Pulpit, after Divine Service, the Sabbath before the saids respective Dayes of Fasting and Humiliation.

1685–E   Prayers during the illness of Charles II

Daily from 5 February 1685 (England and Wales)

Charles II fell ill on 2 February 1685. News of the king's condition led ministers in various parts of the kingdom to read the BCP order for visitation of the sick: in London, prayers were said for Charles 'from the time he began to be in danger, til he expir'd' (Evelyn, IV, 407), and on 4 February John Lloyd, the vice-chancellor of Oxford, authorised use of the BCP order in college chapels. The special form of prayer, based closely on the BCP's prayers for the sick, was dated 4 February on the colophon, and was available in London on the following day. But the new form could not have been widely distributed before the king's death. After a report of Charles's partial recovery, the archbishop of York ordered a thanksgiving prayer to be said in the minster and York's parish churches on 6 February. Responding to the same news, Lloyd issued instructions for a thanksgiving form on 5 February, which was used until 7 February. The king, however, died on the morning of 6 February.

Order: none found.
Form of prayer: *Prayers for the king; to be used in all churches, and chapels immediately before the prayer of S Chrysostom, both in the morning and evening-service* (4 pp.; Wing C4188IBA)*.

Additional sources: *CSPD, 1684–5*, pp. 311–12; Evelyn, IV, 405–8; Wood, III, 125; HMC, *Buccleuch, Drumlanrig*, II, 204; Bishop Francis Turner of Ely to Sancroft, 5 Feb. 1685, Archbishop John Dolben of York to Sancroft, 7 Feb. 1685, Tanner 32, fos. 212r, 213r.

FORM OF PRAYER

[Before the prayer of St Chrysostom, at morning and evening prayer]
The Minister standing up, shall say,
    Brethren; Although it hath pleas'd Almighty God to be very gracious to these Three Kingdoms, in giving us so good Hopes of His Majestie's Recovery from His late dangerous sickness; Nevertheless it is thought fit, that, so long as his weakness shall continue upon him, Prayers be made without ceasing of the Church unto God for him. Wherefore I beseech you, to joyn with me in offering up Supplications at the Throne of the heavenly Grace for the restoring of him to his perfect Health.

Then, all kneeling down, the Minister shall say,
Minister: Remember not, Lord, our iniquities *[then as BCP order for the visitation of the sick until the end of the Lord's prayer]*

Minister: O Lord, save thy servant the King.
Answer: Who putteth his trust in thee *[as BCP]*

O Lord, look down from heaven, behold, visit and relieve thy servant, the King. Look upon him with the eyes of thy mercy *[as BCP]*

Hear us, Almighty and most merciful God and Saviour; Extend thy accustomed goodness to thy servant who is grieved with sickness. Sanctifie, we beseech thee *[as BCP]*

Almighty everliving God, maker of mankind, who dost correct those whom thou dost love, and chastise every one whom thou dost receive; We beseech thee to have mercy upon thy servant visited with thine hand, and to grant that he may take his sickness patiently, and recover his bodily health (if it be thy gracious will) and whensoever his soul shall depart from the body, it may be without spot presented unto thee, through Jesus Christ our Lord. *Amen.*

O Saviour of the world *[as BCP]*

The Almighty Lord, who is a most strong tower to all them that put their trust in him, to whom all things in heaven, in earth, and under the earth do bowe and obey, be now, and evermore his defence, and make him know and feel, that there is none other name under heaven given to man, in whom, and through whom he may receive health and salvation, but onely the Name of our Lord Jesus Christ. *Amen.*

Unto Gods gracious mercy and protection we commit him. The Lord bless him, and keep him. The Lord make his face to shine upon him, and be gracious unto him. The Lord lift up his countenance upon him, and give him peace, both now and evermore. *Amen.*

1685–S   Thanksgiving days for the defeat of the Monmouth and Argyll risings

Thursday 23 July 1685 (Edinburgh diocese); Thursday 13 August 1685 (elsewhere in Scotland)

The accession of James VII and II gave new impetus to Scottish and English whig exiles in the Netherlands, who began to plan co-ordinated risings against the king. The earl of Argyll, who had been forfeited for refusing the Test oath in 1681, intended to raise an army from among his tenants and kinsmen in the western highlands; at the same time, the duke of Monmouth would gather followers in the south-west of England. On 2 May 1685, Argyll sailed from Amsterdam, stopping in Orkney before landing in Kintyre. At Campbeltown on 20 May he issued a declaration justifying his rising and began to gather forces. But the rising lacked a clear strategy and quickly lost momentum. When Argyll was captured on 18 June, the delayed Monmouth had been in England for only a week. He recruited some supporters in the west country, but was defeated at the battle of Sedgemoor on 6 July and executed on 15 July. Argyll had suffered the same punishment on 30 June. This thanksgiving day was appointed on 16 July, five days after the proclamation for the equivalent English observance (1685–EIr). Probably as a deliberate show of loyalty, however, the thanksgiving was to be observed in Edinburgh diocese before it was kept in England. The occasion was celebrated with bells, cannon-fire and bonfires in Edinburgh.

Order: royal proclamation, 16 July 1685, Wing S1806* [also in *RPC*, 3rd ser., XI, 100–1].
Additional sources: Lauder, *Historical observes*, p. 207; Lauder, *Historical notices*, II, 656; *Journal of the Hon. John Erskine of Carnock*, ed. MacLeod, p. 152; *Alford exercise*, p. 365; *Inverness and Dingwall records*, pp. 122, 357–8.

ORDER

Royal proclamation: 16 July 1685
Forasmuch as *James Scot* late Duke of *Monmouth,* and *Archibald Campbel* late Earl of *Argile*, with their Traiterous Confederates and Accomplices, Having most presumptiously Invaded both Our Kingdoms of *Scotland* and *England* by Armed Force, of purpose to have destroyed Us, and all Our good and Loyal Subjects, and subverted Our Government in Church and State; but it having pleased Almighty God, (by whom Kings Reign, and Princes decree Justice) by his Miraculous Providence and Omnipotent hand, to confound and blast the Hellish Devices and Projects of these our Enemies, and utterly to discomfite and subdue them. We have therfore from a Due and Religious sense of Gods so great Mercy and Deliverance towards us, and Our People in these Realms, Thought fit, with Advice of Our Privy Council, Hereby to set apart solemn days of Thanksgiving, for offering solemn Praise to Almighty God, for so great and miraculous a Deliverance, and making humble Prayers and Supplications, that his Divine Majesty may continue his undeserved Goodness towards Us, and these Our Kingdoms: And to the end this Solemn and Religious a Thanks giving may be gone about in a devout manner, We do hereby Recommend to the Most Reverend the Arch-Bishops, and the Right Reverend the Bishops, that they cause the Ministers in their Diocesses respectively from their Pulpits, Read and Intimate this our Royal Pleasure on the Lords Day immediately preceeding the Dyets appointed for the said Thanksgiving, which are after-mentioned, *viz.* These

for the Diocess of *Edinburgh*, upon Thursday the Twenty Third Instant; and these of all the other Dioceses of this our Kingdom, upon Thursday being the Thirteenth Day of *August* next. And We hereby Require and Command all Our good Subjects Peremptorly and Religiously to Observe these Solemn Days of Thanksgiving, as they would tender the Glory of Almighty God for so Signal a Deliverance and not incur Our high Displeasure; yet We are not hereby to lessen the Resentments of our good Subjects on this Occasion, but allow them, after Divine Service performed, to use all lawful demonstrations of Joy and Gladness. And that Our Pleasure in the Premisses may be known, Our Will is, and We Charge you strictly, and Command, that in continent, these Our Letters seen, ye pass to the Mercat Cross of *Edinburgh*, and all the other Mercat Crosses of the Head Burghs of the Shires of this Kingdom, and there by open Proclamation, in Our Royal Name and Authority, make Publication of Our Pleasure in the Premisses, that all Our Subjects may have Notice thereof, and give Obedience accordingly.

1685–EIr   Thanksgiving days for the defeat of the Monmouth and Argyll risings

Sunday 26 July 1685 (England and Wales); Sunday 23 August 1685 (Ireland)

Two days after his defeat at Sedgemoor on 6 July 1685, the duke of Monmouth was captured and taken to London for execution (for an account of his and Argyll's risings, see 1685–S). The king ordered this thanksgiving at the privy council meeting of 10 July, and the proclamation was issued on the following day, by which time the form of prayer was being prepared. Nevertheless, the occasion was appointed at too short notice: on the day before the thanksgiving was to be intimated in churches, the archbishop of York complained that his clergy had not received copies of the proclamation. On 30 July, after the observance in England, the earl of Sunderland sent copies of the English proclamation and form of prayer to the lords justices in Dublin, instructing them to appoint a thanksgiving day in Ireland. The lords complied, basing their proclamation closely on the English text. It is unclear why no attempt was made to co-ordinate the dates of the Irish and English observances (cf. 1683–EIr). Unusually, the council of Waterford ordered a full civic observance of the occasion; the mayor's expenses were nearly twice those incurred on the previous 29 May, Restoration Day. As for 1683–EIr, while no evidence survives of any instructions from London, thanksgivings were held in some of the American colonies, and certainly in Barbados, Jamaica and Virginia.

Orders: ENGLAND AND WALES: royal proclamation, 11 July 1685, Wing J327*; IRELAND: proclamation of the lords justices and council, 10 Aug. 1685, Wing I615*.

Forms of prayer: ENGLAND AND WALES: *A form of prayer, and solemn thanksgiving to almighty God for his majesties late victories over the rebels; to be observed in all churches and chapels throughout the kingdom, upon Sunday the twenty sixth of this instant July. By his majesties special command* ([12] pp.; Wing C4122; Durham University Library, Routh 63T.18(9)); IRELAND: *A form of prayer, and solemn thanksgiving* ([12] pp.; Wing C4194N; Cashel Cathedral Library, M.9.17(12)).

Additional sources: *London Gazette*, 2049 (6–9 July 1685); privy council register, PC2/71, fo. 61r; Mostyn newsletter, 11 July 1685, University of Wales, Bangor, MS 9092, fo. 153; Bishop Peter Mews of Winchester to Sancroft, 11 July 1685, Dolben to Sancroft, 18 July 1685, Tanner 31, fos. 158r, 167; Luttrell, I, 353; Evelyn, IV, 460; earl of Sunderland to the lords justices, 30 July 1685, *CSPD, February–*

December 1685, p. 288; HMC, *Ormonde*, new ser., VII, 352; *Council books of the corporation of Waterford, 1662–1700*, ed. Seamus Pender (Dublin 1964), pp. 258, 260; *CSPC*, XII, 95–6, 99–100, 105; *Executive journals of the council of colonial Virginia* (6 vols., Richmond, 1925–66), I, 73–4.

Printed sermons: ENGLAND AND WALES: Allestree, Oxford (Wing A1081, A1081A); Cooke, Islington (Wing C6038); Frezer, Dordrecht, Dutch Republic (Wing F2204); Goodrick, Lincolns Inn (Wing G1144); Gostwyke, Cambridge (Wing G1323); Hesketh, court (Wing H1620); Heyrick, Market Harborough (Wing H1752); Hinton, Newbury (Wing H2068); Hutton, Uplyme (Wing H3840); Lee, Wakefield (Wing L885B); Long, Exeter (Wing L2983); Pelling, Westminster (Wing P1098); Scott, St Mary-le-Bow, London (Wing S2069); Wagstaffe, St Margaret Pattons and St Gabriel Fenchurch, London (Wing W214); Williams, St Mildred's Poultrey and St Anne's Aldersgate, London (Wing W2726); IRELAND: Anon., Co. Kilkenny (ESTC 006148268).

ORDERS

England and Wales: royal proclamation, 11 July 1685

Whereas it hath pleased Almighty God in the beginning of Our Reign, to manifest his great goodness towards Us and Our Kingdoms, in giving Us so absolute and signal Victories over the late Rebels, who in contempt of the Laws of God, and of these Kingdoms, rose up against Us in Open Rebellion, threatning the Subversion of the Peace and Tranquility of Our Kingdoms, whereby it hath pleased him in his infinite mercy not onely to Restore to Us and Our Kingdoms a perfect Peace, by an utter Dissipation of all those Rebels, but likewise to deliver into Our hands the Chief Heads of that Horrid Traiterous Conspiracy, in order to their Condign Punishment, that thereby nothing might remain to interrupt Our Peaceable Government for the future. Upon the due Consideration whereof, We do with all humility Admire and Adore the late Mercy and Goodness of God, in giving Victory to Our Arms, and Delivering Us and Our Kingdoms from the Miseries and Calamities that might and constantly do ensue an Intestine and Unnatural Rebellion. And considering that such signal and publick Mercies are Invitations from Heaven to Us and all Our Subjects, to render the most publick and cheerful Expressions of Thankfulness to the Divine Goodness: We are willing that the just tribute of Praise and Thanksgiving to Our Great Soveraign the King of Heaven and Earth, be Solemnly returned by Us and all Our People for this his late Mercy. And to the end some Solemn time may be appointed for the Publick performance of this Duty, that all Our Subjects in *England* and *Wales*, and Town of *Berwick* upon *Tweed*, who equally share in the Blessing and Joys of this Deliverance, may be United in the Devotions which are offered for it. We do hereby Publish and Declare, That *Sunday* the Twenty sixth day of this instant *July* be Observed as a Day of Publick Thanksgiving to Almighty God throughout Our Kingdom of *England*, Dominion of *Wales*, and Town of *Berwick* upon *Tweed*, for this his great Mercy; And We do Direct and Appoint, That this Our Proclamation be Publickly Read in all Churches and Chappels on *Sunday* precedent thereto, to the end that Notice be taken thereof, and due Thanks and Praise may upon the said Twenty sixth day of *July* be offered up unto Almighty God by Us and all Our People with one Heart, and that humble Supplications be made before him for his continual Assistance and Improvement of this and all his Mercies to the Honour of his great Name, and the Safety, Peace and Benefit of all Our Kingdoms and Dominions: We Willing and strictly Commanding all Persons within these Our Dominions with all Sobriety, Reverence and Thankfulness to perform this Duty on that day, and to observe the same as becomes so solemn an Occasion.

Ireland: proclamation of the lords justices and council, 10 August 1685

Whereas it hath pleased Almighty God *[as England and Wales above, substituting 'His Majesty', 'His' and 'His Majesties' for 'Us' and 'Our'*: in the beginning … such signal and]* publick Mercies are invitations from Heaven to us, and all His *MAJESTIES* Subjects to render the most publick and cheerful expressions of Thankfulness to the Divine Goodness; We are desirous that the just Tribute of Praise and Thanksgiving to our great Sovereign the King of Heaven and Earth be solemnly returned by Us and all his Majesties people, for this his late Mercy; and to the end some solemn time may be appointed for the publick performance of this Duty, that all His Majesties Subjects in this Kingdom, who equally share in the Blessing and Joys of this Deliverance, may be united in the Devotions which are offered for it: We do hereby publish and declare, That *Sunday* the three and twentieth day of this instant *August* be observed as a day of publick Thanksgiving to Almighty God throughout this Kingdom, for this his great Mercy. And We do direct and appoint *[as England and Wales above, with change of date and changes as before*: That this Our Proclamation … and Dominions:]* We willing and strictly commanding all persons within this Kingdom, with all Sobriety Reverence and Thankfulness, to perform this Duty on that day; and to observe the same, as becomes so solemn an occasion; And that the same Forme of Prayer with Thanksgiving prepared in *England*, for that occasion (which we have ordered to be printed here) be also on the said three and twentieth day of *August*, made use of in the publick Service and Worship of God.

FORMS OF PRAYER

England and Wales; Ireland

The Service shall be the same with the usual Office of the Day in all things; except where it is in this Office otherwise appointed.

Both the Morning and Evening Prayer shall begin with these Sentences.
[1 Tim. 2:1–3; 1 John 1:8–9]

MORNING PRAYER

In stead of Venite exultemus, *the Hymn following shall be said or sung; One Verse by the Priest, and another by the Clerk and People.*
Not unto us, O Lord, not unto us: but unto thy Name be the praise, for thy loving Mercy, and for thy truths sake. (Ps. 115:1)
O my God, I will give thanks unto thee for ever: yea, as long as I have any Being, I will sing praises unto my God. (Ps. 30:13; 146:1)
For great things are they, that thou hast done: O God, who is like unto thee? (Ps. 71:17)
The Lord hath done great things for us: yea, the Lord hath done great things for us, whereof we rejoyce. (Ps. 126:3–4)
For lo, thine enemies made a murmuring: and they that hate thee did lift up their heads. (Ps. 83:2)
They cast their heads together with one consent: and were confederate against thee. (Ps. 83:5)

The People stood up, and their Rulers took counsel together; against the Lord, and against his Anointed. (Ps. 2:2)

They said, Let us break their bonds asunder: and cast away their cords from us. (Ps. 2:3)

Their device was to put him out, whom God hath exalted: yea, they said in their hearts, let us make havock of them altogether. (Ps. 62:4; 74:9)

They said, Come, and let us root them out, that they be no more a people: and that their name may be no more in remembrance. (Ps. 73:4)

But salvation belongeth unto thee, O Lord: the help that is done upon earth, thou doest it thy self. (Ps. 3:8; 74:13)

Through thee have we overthrown our enemies: and in thy Name have we trod them under that rose up against us. (Ps. 44:6)

There is no King that can be saved by the multitude of an host: neither is any mighty man delivered by much strength. (Ps. 33:15)

A horse is counted but a vain thing to save a man: neither shall he deliver any by his great strength. (Ps. 33:16)

I will not trust in my bow: it is not my sword that shall help me. (Ps. 44:7)

But it is thou that savest us from our enemies: and puttest them to confusion that hate us. (Ps. 44:8)

If the Lord himself had not been on our side, (now may we say:) if the Lord himself had not been on our side, when men rose up against us. (Ps. 124:1)

They had swallowed us up quick: when they were so wrathfully displeased at us. (Ps. 124:2)

But God hath shewed us his goodness plenteously: and God hath let us see our desire upon our enemies. (Ps. 59:10)

Praised be the Lord: who hath not given us over, as a prey unto their teeth. (Ps. 124:5)

They are brought down, and fallen: but we are risen, and stand upright. (Ps. 20:8)

There are they fallen, all that work wickedness: they are cast down, and shall not be able to stand. (Ps. 36:12)

Give thanks, O Israel, unto God the Lord in the congregations: from the ground of the heart. (Ps. 68:26)

Thy God hath sent forth strength for thee: stablish the thing, O God, which thou hast wrought for us. (Ps. 68:28)

Let thy hand be upon the man of thy right hand: and upon the son of man, whom thou madest so strong for thy self. (Ps. 80:17)

He shall dwell before God for ever: O prepare thy loving mercy, and faithfulness, that they may preserve him. (Ps. 61:7)

Shew thy marvellous loving kindness: thou that art the Saviour of them, that put their trust in thee from such as resist thy right hand. (Ps. 17:7)

O let the wickedness of the wicked come to an end: but establish the just. (Ps. 7:9)

Let them that seek thee be joyful and glad in thee: and let all such as love thy salvation, say always, The Lord be praised. (Ps. 40:19)

Not unto us, O Lord, not unto us: but unto thy Name give praise, for thy loving mercy, and for thy truths sake. (Ps. 115:1)

Glory be to the Father, &c.

As it was in the beginning, &c.

[Ps. 9, 21]
[First lesson: Num. 16]
[Te Deum]
[Second lesson: Jude]
[Benedictus]

In stead of the Collect for the Day, shall this Thanksgiving which follows be used, For peace and deliverance from our Enemies.
[The BCP thanksgiving for peace and deliverance from our enemies]

LITANY

*In the end of the Litany after the Collect (*We humbly beseech thee, &c.*) shall this Thanksgiving,* For restoring publick peace at home, *be used.*
[The BCP thanksgiving for restoring public peace at home]

COMMUNION

In the Communion-Service in stead of the Collect for the day, shall be read, O Almighty God, who art a strong tower, &c. *as before in Morning Prayer.*
   [The BCP thanksgiving for peace and deliverance from our enemies]

[Epistle: 1 Pet. 2:11–17]
[Gospel: Matt. 22:15–22]
[Offertory sentence: Matt. 7:12]

After the Prayer, For the whole state of Christs Church, &c. *shall these following Prayers be used.*

O Lord, our God, who by thine Infinite Power and Wisdom dost govern all things, we adore and magnifie thy great and glorious Name, confessing, that to thy good Providence over us we entirely owe both our Being and our Preservation. We are here before thee this day to make this humble Acknowledgment, as every one of us for himself in particular, so all of us together in the name of this whole Nation; to which both now of late, and heretofore thou hast vouchsafed so many great and publick Deliverances. Thou art our God, who hast so often, and so wonderfully defeated the Designs of ambitious, restless, and bloodthirsty men: to whom hadst thou given us up for a prey (as our sins most justly deserved) our Blood would have been spilt like Water upon the ground; we must have lost all that is dear to us in this World, and we should have been overwhelmed in a Deluge of Sects and Heresies, of Wars and Confusions, of which we could not have expected to see any other issue, than the final Ruine and Destruction of this Kingdom, and thy Church amongst us.

   O our God! how gracious hast thou been unto us all, and to many of us even against our own wills! How much better hast thou provided for us, than we our selves could, or would have done, hadst thou left us in the Hand of our own foolish Counsels? Into thy blessed Hands, O God, we entirely surrender, and give up our selves, and whatever concerns us; beseeching thee to be still the same gracious God to us, and to our posterity after us.

   And the better to prepare and qualifie us for the continuance of thy Care, and good Providence; Enable us by thy Grace to live like a People, whom thou hast so often, and so wonderfully Redeemed; not following the Dictates of our own unruly Lusts or Passions, nor listning any longer to those that go about with Lies, and slander the Footsteps of thine Anointed; but studying every one to be quiet, and to do our own Business, fearing God, and honouring our King, and loving one another, and hereby adorning our most holy Profession; that so being delivered from our Enemies, and from the Hands of all that hate us, we may serve thee without fear in Holiness and Righteousness before thee all the days of our life, to the glory of thy Name, which is exalted far above all Blessing and Praise, through Jesus Christ our Lord. *Amen.*

[The BCP collect for the fifth Sunday after Trinity]

EVENING PRAYER

The Hymn, Not unto us, O Lord, *&c., appointed at Morning Prayer in stead of* Venite exultemus, *shall now also be used before the Psalms.*

[Ps. 118, 144]
[First lesson: 2 Sam. 22]
[Cantate Domino]
[Second lesson: 2 Pet. 2]
[Deus misereatur]

In stead of the Collect for the Day, shall the Thanksgiving, For peace and deliverance from our enemies*, be used, as in the Morning Prayer.*

Immediately before the Prayer of St Chrysostom *shall these Collects be used, viz. The Thanksgiving,* For restoring publick peace at home, *(as in Morning Prayer.)*

A Prayer for our Enemies.
Father of Mercies, and lover of Souls *[as 1683–EIr]*

[The BCP collect for the fifth Sunday after Trinity]

1686–E   Thanksgiving services for the Christian capture of Buda from the Ottomans

Sunday 12 September 1686 (St George's Chapel, Windsor, Westminster Abbey and St Mary-le-Bow, London)

From mid-June 1686, Habsburg imperial armies (including a small number of officers from the British Isles) besieged the Ottoman forces holding Buda, finally capturing the city on 2 September. James II gave the task of composing thanksgiving prayers to Bishops Crewe of Durham and Sprat of Rochester, two of the commissioners appointed to exercise the powers of the bishopric of London following the suspension of Bishop Compton on 6 September. It is unclear why Archbishop Sancroft was not involved in preparing the form. Unusually, the special service was only to be read in St George's Chapel, Windsor, Westminster Abbey (where Crewe and Sprat respectively were to preach) and St Mary-le-Bow, a peculiar of the archbishop of Canterbury in which the lord mayor normally worshipped. On this occasion, the mayor ordered the attendance of the City's livery men at the church.

Order: order by Sunderland, secretary of state, undated, in the form of prayer, sig. A4v.
Form of prayer: *A form of prayer and thanksgiving to almighty God, for the prosperity of the Christian arms against the Turks, and especially for taking the city of Buda: to be used publickly on Sunday the twelfth of September in his majesties free chappel of St. Georges Windsor, in the collegiate church of St. Peters Westminster, and in the parish-church of St. Mary le Bowe in the City of London. By his majesties special command* ([8] pp.; Wing C4124)*.
Additional sources: MS newsletter, 10 Sept. 1686, Harry Ransom HRC, University of Texas at Austin, Pforzheimer MS 103C, box 9; *CSPD, 1686–7*, p. 262; Morrice, III, 258; Evelyn, IV, 524.

ORDER

Order by Sunderland, secretary of state: undated
By His Majesties Command, SUNDERLAND P.

FORM OF PRAYER

MORNING PRAYER

The Morning Service shall be the same with the Common Office of the Day, Excepting these following Alterations.

[Opening sentences: Dan. 9:9–10]
[Ps. 2, 47, 62]
[First lesson: 2 Sam. 22]
[Te Deum]
[Second lesson: Heb. 11:24–35]
[Benedictus]

After the Collect for the Day, let this follow.

    O eternal God our heavenly Father, whose Name is the God of Hosts, who art the only giver of all Victory; We yield thee our hearty Praise and Thanksgiving for the late signal Deliverance, and glorious Success thou hast vouchsafed to those thy faithful Servants, who have not been ashamed to confess the Faith of Christ Crucified, but have manfully fought under his Banner. We adore and bless thy Divine Goodness, that thou didst not give them over as a prey to cruel and bloudthirsty men; but hast taught their Hands to War, and their Fingers to Fight, and hast shewed them a marvellous great kindness in a strong City. We humbly pray that these, and all other thy benefits, may raise in Us, and in the whole Church of God, a Spirit of Holy Joy, and Christian Charity, a Spirit of fervent Zeal for thy Name and glory, and a stedfast faith and perseverance in thy pure and undefiled Religion, through Jesus Christ Our Lord and Saviour. *Amen.*

LITANY

In the end of the Litany after the Collect [We humbly beseech thee, &c.] *Let the Collect be used (for Peace and deliverance from our Enemies.)*
[The BCP thanksgiving for peace and deliverance from our enemies]

COMMUNION

[Epistle: 1 John 4:1–8]
[Gospel: Matt. 28:18–20]

After the Prayer (for the whole state of Christ's Church) Let these following Prayers be used.

Almighty and everliving God, who art glorious in Holiness, fearful in praises, doing Wonders, who by miraculous Ways and Means, hast raised thy Houshold, the Church, building it on the Foundation of the Apostles and Prophets, Jesus Christ himself being the chief Corner Stone, who hast promised to be with it always even unto the end of the world, so that the Gates of Hell shall never be able to prevail against it; Who by so many marvellous Acts of thy Providence hast graciously made good this thy Promise in all Ages, particularly at this time didst not give over thine Heritage to Confusion, but hast blessed the Armies engaged in this Christian War, crowning them with Victory and Honour. We meekly beseech thee, O Lord, that we and the whole Christian World may make a right use of these thy undeserved Mercies. To this end we pray thee to keep and maintain all Christian Kings, Princes and Governours, in Peace, Amity and Concord, that being strengthned by thy Grace and Power, with united Hearts and Hands, in defence of thy Cause and Truth, they may wax valiant in Battle, see their desires on their Enemies, and put to flight the Armies of the Aliens. Preserve, O Lord, thy most holy Faith in those Kingdoms and Nations, where it is already planted, restore it to its antient Purity and Brightness where it lies in obscurity, oppressed by *Turkish* Tyranny, and their abominable Superstition. Enlarge its Borders into all Lands, that all the Ends of the Earth may see the Salvation of Our God. Grant this O Lord, for the sake of Our only Mediatour and Advocate Jesus Christ our Lord. *Amen.*

[The third BCP collect for Good Friday; the collect for the fifth Sunday after Trinity]

[The blessing]

1688–EIr1   Thanksgiving days for the pregnancy of Queen Mary

Sunday 15 January 1688 (London, Westminster and ten miles around); Sunday 29 January 1688 (elsewhere in England and Wales); Sunday 19 February 1688 (Dublin, suburbs and adjoining liberties); Sunday 26 February 1688 (elsewhere in Ireland)

The news that Queen Mary was pregnant, announced officially in the proclamation for this thanksgiving, was a boon for James's pro-catholic policy, and a shock to the king's critics, many of whom doubted whether the queen really was pregnant. Whereas James I and Charles I had issued single thanksgiving prayers when their queens became pregnant, James II decided to order a full thanksgiving day. The king initially ordered that the thanksgiving in the London area should be observed on Tuesday 10 January. Concerns that the occasion would be widely boycotted led him to change the date to the following Sunday, and the issuing of the proclamation was delayed by several days. The form of prayer was written by Bishops Crewe of Durham, Sprat of Rochester and White of Peterborough, the commissioners exercising the powers of the bishopric of London. As with 1686–E, Archbishop Sancroft was not involved. The thanksgiving was observed with bonfires and bells in various places, but several sources suggest that there was less public enthusiasm than on previous thanksgiving days. The earl of Clarendon noted that, while St James's Piccadilly was well attended, 'there were not above two or three in the church who brought the form of prayer with them'. The Irish proclamation was similar to that issued in England. The English form of prayer was also used, with one small change to the special collect. Presumably, the lord deputy acted on instructions from the English court (see 1685–EIr), though no correspondence has been found. In the colonies the authorities ordered thanksgivings in Connecticut, Jamaica, Massachusetts, New York and Nevis, but, as on earlier occasions, there is no evidence of an order having been sent from London.

Orders: ENGLAND AND WALES: royal proclamation, 23 Dec. 1687, Wing J313* [also Wing J314: Edinburgh reprint]; IRELAND: proclamation by the lord deputy and council, 8 Feb. 1688, Wing I841*.
Forms of prayer: ENGLAND AND WALES: *A form, or order, of thanksgiving, and prayer, to be used in London, and ten miles round it, on Sunday the 15th. of this instant January, and throughout England on Sunday the 29th. of the same month, by all parsons, vicars, and curates, in their respective parish churches, and chapels, in behalf of the king, the queen, and the royal family, upon occasion of the queen's being with child. By his majesties special command* ([8] pp.; Wing C4182)* [other impression, Wing C4182A]; IRELAND: *A form or order of thanksgiving, and prayer* ([8] pp.; Wing C4194Z; Pierpoint Morgan Library, New York, 17615.2).
Form of prayer (other edition): Holyroodhouse, [Peter Bruce], Wing C4182B.
Additional sources: Privy council register, PC2/72, fos. 560, 564–5; *CSPD, 1687–9*, p. 139; MS newsletter, 23 Dec. 1687, Harry Ransom HRC, University of Texas at Austin, Pforzheimer MS 103C, box 10; Newdigate newsletters, 29 Dec., 31 Dec. 1687, 3 Jan. 1688, Folger Shakespeare Library, Washington, DC, MS L.c. 1901–3; Mostyn newsletters, 27 Dec. 1687, 3 Jan., 10 Jan., 12 Jan., 17 Jan., 19 Jan. 1688, University of Wales, Bangor, MS 9092, fos. 145, 147–8, 150–2; HMC, *Rutland*, II, 117; Luttrell, I, 426; *The Portledge papers, being extracts from the letters of Richard Lapthorne ... to Richard Coffin*, ed. R. J. Kerr and I. C. Duncan (1928), p. 23; Morrice, IV, 204, 213, 223; Evelyn, IV, 567; Wood, III, 255; *The correspondence of Henry Hyde, earl of Clarendon, and of his brother Laurence Hyde, earl of Rochester*, ed. S. W. Singer (2 vols., 1828), II, 156; *A form or order of thanksgiving and prayer* (1720; ESTC 006308473) [reprint of the form of prayer]; *Council books of the corporation of Waterford*, ed. Pender, p. 281; *CSPC*, XII, 523, 525, 537; *The public records of the colony of Connecticut* (15 vols., Hartford, CT, 1850–90), III, 443–4; W. DeLoss Love, *The fast and thanksgiving days of New England* (Boston, 1895), p. 232.

ORDERS

England and Wales: royal proclamation, 23 December 1687

It having pleased Almighty God (who in signal manner hath blessed His Majesty and this Kingdom under His Majesties Government, with great Prosperity, Peace and Plenty) to give His Majesty also apparent hopes and good assurance of having Issue by His Royal Consort the Queen, who (through Gods great Goodness) is now with Child: And forasmuch as Increase of Issue of the Royal Family is a Publick Blessing, and (under God) a great Security of Peace and Happiness to this Kingdom: His Majesty therefore hath thought fit (at the humble request, and by the Advice of His Privy Council) to Appoint a time, upon this occasion, to render Publick and Hearty Thanks, throughout the Kingdom, for this great Blessing already begun, and to offer up Prayers to Almighty God for the continuance thereof: And His

Majesty doth accordingly Appoint, Command and Require, That upon the Fifteenth day of *January* next, within the Cities of *London* and *Westminster*, and Ten Miles thereabout, and upon the Nine and twentieth day of the same Month, in all other Places throughout this Kingdom, Publick Thanks, and Solemn Prayers be offered up to Almighty God upon the Occasion aforesaid: And for this purpose His Majesty hath signified His Royal Pleasure to the Right Reverend Fathers in God *Nathaniel* Lord Bishop of *Duresme*, *Thomas* Lord Bishop of *Rochester*, and *Thomas* Lord Bishop of *Peterborough* (being his Majesties Commissioners Constituted for Exercising the Episcopal Jurisdiction within the Diocess of *London*) forthwith to prepare a Form of Prayer and Religious Service, which may be suitable to this occasion; Which Form of Prayer and Service His Majesty will cause to be Printed and Published, and by the Right Reverend the Bishops Sent and Distributed throughout their several and respective Dioceses, to be observed and used in the Churches and Chappels of this Kingdom upon the several and respective days before mentioned: And lastly, His Majesty doth Charge and Command all His loving Subjects to take notice hereof, and to demean themselves in all things accordingly.

Ireland: proclamation by the lord deputy and council: 8 February 1688
Whereas it hath pleased Almighty God (who in signal manner hath Blessed His Majesty and His Kingdoms with great Prosperity *[as England and Wales above*: Peace and Plenty) ... and (under God) a*]* great Security of Peace and Happiness to these Kingdoms.

We have therefore thought fit to appoint a Time, upon this Occasion, to Render Publick and Hearty Thanks Through-out the Kingdom, for this Great Blessing already Begun, and to Offer up Prayers to Almighty God for the Continuance thereof. And We do hereby Appoint, that upon the nineteenth Day of this Instant *February*, within the City and Suburbs of *Dublin*, and Liberties adjoyning, and upon the six and Twentieth day of the same Month in all other places throughout this Kingdom publick Thanks and Solmn Prayers be offered up to Almighty God upon the occasion aforesaid, We willingly and strictly Commanding all persons within this Kingdom, with all sobriety, reverence and thankfullness to perform this duty upon the several and respective days before mentioned and to observe the same as becomes so Solmn an occasion, And that the same Form of Prayer with Thanksgiving prepared in *England*, for that occasion (which we have ordered to be Printed here and sent to the several Bishops to be distributed throughout their several Dioceses) be on the said days made use of in the several *Churches* and *Chappels* in this Kingdom.

FORMS OF PRAYER

England and Wales

This Service shall be the same with the usual Office for the Days above named, except where it is hereafter otherwise Appointed.

MORNING PRAYER

At the beginning of Morning Prayer, the Minister shall Read these Sentences following.

[1 Tim. 2:1–3; Matt. 7:12]

*In the Place of [*Venite Exultemus*] shall be used this following Hymn.*
O Sing unto the Lord a new Song, Sing unto the Lord all the whole Earth. (Ps. 96:1)
Sing unto the Lord, and Praise His Name by Telling His Salvation from Day to Day. (Ps. 96:2)
For the Lord is Great, and cannot worthily be Praised, He is more to be feared than all Gods. (Ps. 96:4)
Glory and Worship are before him, Power and Honour are in his Sanctuary. (Ps. 96:6)
Ascribe unto the Lord, O ye Kindreds of the People, Ascribe unto the Lord, Worship and Power. (Ps. 96:7)
Ascribe unto the Lord, the Honour due unto His Name, Bring Presents, and Come into His Courts. (Ps. 96:8)
God standeth in the Congregation of Princes, He is Judge among the Gods. (Ps. 82:1)
There is no King saved by the Multitude of an Host, neither is any Mighty Man Delivered by much strength. (Ps. 33:15)
But the Eye of the Lord is upon them that fear him, and upon them that Put their Trust in His Mercy. (Ps. 33:17)
Let all those that seek Thee, be Joyful and Glad in Thee, and let such as Love thy Salvation, say alway, the Lord be Praised. (Ps. 40:15)
O Think upon thy Congregation, whom Thou hast Redeemed, and Purchased of Old. (Ps. 74:2)
Think upon the Tribe of thine Inheritance, and Mount Sion wherein Thou hast Dwelt. (Ps. 74:3)
Thou, O God, hast sent forth Strength for Us, stablish, O Lord, what Thou hast wrought in Us. (Ps. 68:28)
So We thy People, and Sheep of thy Pasture, shall Give Thee Thanks for ever, and be shewing forth thy Praise from Generation to Generation. (Ps. 79:14)
Glory be to the Father, &c.
As it was in the beginning, &c.

[Ps. 21, 127, 128, 132]
[First lesson: Gen. 17:1–17]
[Second lesson: Heb. 11]

[Then as BCP from the Apostles' creed to the suffrages after the Lord's prayer, which are those used as at morning prayer]
Priest: O Lord shew thy mercy upon us.
[As BCP until]
Priest: O Lord, save the King.
Answer: *And evermore mightily Defend Him.*
Priest: Prevent Him with the Blessings of Goodness.
Answer: *And make Him Glad with the Joy of thy Countenance.*
Priest: O Lord, save Thy Servant the Queen.
Answer: *And make Her a Joyful Mother of Children.*
Priest: Endue thy Ministers with righteousness.
[As BCP]

The first Collect instead of that for the Day.

O Almighty God, the Fountain of all Life, by whose only Gift it Cometh, that Mankind is Encreased; Blessed be that Good Providence, which has Vouchsafed Vs fresh Hopes of Royal Issue by our Gracious Queen *Mary*; Strengthen Her, we beseech Thee, and Perfect what thou hast Begun. Command thy Holy Angels to Watch over Her Continually, and Defend Her from all Dangers, and evil Accidents, That what she has Conceiv'd may be happily brought forth, to the Joy of our Sovereign Lord the King, the farther Establishment of His Crown, the Happiness, and Welfare of the whole Kingdom, and the Glory of thy Great Name. Which We humbly Beg of thy Gracious Goodness, through Jesus Christ our Lord. *Amen.*

LITANY

At the end of the Litany, immediately after [We humbly beseech Thee, &c.] this following Prayer is to be used.

Almighty and Everliving God, We most humbly Acknowledge, That in Thee alone We Live, Move, and have our Being; and that Children, and the Fruit of the Womb are a Gift and Heritage that cometh only of Thee. We therefore devoutly beseech Thee to Preserve and Protect our most Gracious Sovereign Lord King *James*, and so Bless Him, that He may see His Children's Children, and Peace upon *Israel*. We Pray Thee also for his Royal Consort Queen *Mary*. Make her, O Lord, as a Fruitful Vine upon the Walls of his House, and his Children like Olive branches round about his Table. Encrease and Multiply the whole Royal Family, That the King's Seed may Endure for Ever, and his Throne be as the Sun before Thee. So We thy People shall Remember, and Praise thy Name from one Generation to another, though Jesus Christ our Lord. *Amen.*

COMMUNION

In the Communion Service next after the Commandments, the first Collect shall be the same, as in Morning Prayer, O Almighty God, the Fountain of all Life, &c. Then shall follow one of the two Collects for the King.

[Epistle: 1 Thess. 5:14–26]
[Gospel: Matt. 5:3–13]

After the Prayer for the Church Militant, shall follow this Prayer.

O almighty God the Blessed and only Potentate, by whose Appointment and Blessing Kings Reign, and Kingdoms are Establish't in Peace: We become Humble Suitors to thy Divine Majesty in Behalf of our Dread Sovereign Lord King *JAMES*, That Thou wouldst Defend his Person in Safety, and Prosper his Reign with Honourable Successes, and make his Name Glorious in the maintenance of Truth, Righteousness and Charity; That under the happy influence of his Government, We may all lead Quiet and Peaceable Lives, in all Godliness, and Honesty. We Acknowledge, with thankful Hearts, the great Mercy Thou hast bestow'd upon Him, and his Royal Consort, and the whole Realm, in the apparent Hopes of farther Issue. Let the Prayers of thy People Prevail, that our Hopes be not Cut off, nor our Expectations Disappointed. Let Thy Watchful Providence Overshadow our Gracious Queen, Preserve her Health, Support her Spirit, and Grant her an Easie, and Happy Deliverance. And do Thou so Graciously Bless and Multiply the whole Royal Family, That the Ages to come may evermore Rejoyce under the Government of our Sovereign, and his Posterity; Which we earnestly Crave of thy great Mercy, through Jesus Christ our only Lord, and Saviour. *Amen.*

Ireland

MORNING PRAYER

[As England and Wales above, until]

[In place of the collect for the day]
   O Almighty God, the Fountain of all Life *[as England and Wales above*: by whose only Gift … Establishment of His Crown,*]* the Happiness, and Welfare of these Kingdoms, and the Glory *[as England and Wales above*: of thy Great Name … *Amen]*.

[Then all as England and Wales, above]

1688–S1   Thanksgiving days for the pregnancy of Queen Mary

Sunday 29 January 1688 (Edinburgh diocese); Sunday 19 February 1688 (elsewhere in Scotland)

Reports of the queen's pregnancy (see 1688–EIr1) had arrived in Scotland by early January 1688. Following the English example, the Scottish privy council responded by appointing a thanksgiving day, by means of an act of council rather than a royal proclamation. In Edinburgh, the thanksgiving's date was perhaps chosen so that it was followed immediately by 30 January, the anniversary of Charles I's execution. Many episcopalians revered the martyred king, although 30 January was not officially observed in Scotland (see AC–30 Jan.). James VII's second declaration of indulgence, issued in June 1687, had permitted presbyterians to worship in meeting houses. In response, large numbers of the laity in southern Scotland abandoned worship in the established church. Because the order for this thanksgiving did not require special prayers in meeting houses, the occasion could essentially be ignored by these presbyterians. In Edinburgh, bonfires and bells marked the occasion, on the orders of the burgh council. The catholic printer at Holyroodhouse, Peter Bruce, reprinted the proclamation and form of prayer for 1688–EIr1, probably to serve as propaganda for the king, rather than in the belief that the proclamation had authority in Scotland, or that the form would be used by Scottish episcopalians (see also 1688–EIr2 and 1688–EIr3).

Order: act of the privy council, Edinburgh, 17 Jan. 1688, Wing S1453* [also in Wodrow, *History*, IV, 438–9].
Additional sources: Wodrow, *History*, IV, 438–9; Luttrell, I, 429; Lauder, *Historical notices*, II, 846, 850; Mostyn newsletter, 24 Jan. 1688, University of Wales, Bangor, MS 9092, fo. 153; *Edin. recs., 1681 to 1689*, pp. 229–30; *Alford exercise*, p. 367; *Inverness and Dingwall records*, p. 130.

ORDER

Act of the privy council: 17 January 1688

Since it hath pleased Almighty GOD, the Fountain of all Life, by whom Kings Reign and Kingdomes are established, to grant unto the Kings most excellent *Majesty*, fresh hopes of Royal Issue, by his most Serene Consort, Our Gracious Queen *Mary*, who (through the great Goodness and Blessing of God) is now with Child; And considering that the multiplying of the Branches of the Royal Family (especially Issuing from our present Sacred Soveraign, *James* the Seventh, under whose Auspitious, Wise and Clement Government, We enjoy so much Prosperity, Peace and Plenty) Is a most Desireable Blessing, a Native Support and Strengthning of the Crown, and by just Consequence a publick Blessing to this Kingdom, Tending to the further Security of the Peace and Happiness thereof: His *Majesty* Therefore (At the Humble and Earnest Desire, and by the Advice of his Privy Council) Hath thought fit upon this important Occasion, to set apart, and appoint a time, for rendering Devout and Solemn Thanks to GOD, for this great Mercy and Blessing, and for offering Publick and Hearty Prayers, to his Divine *Majesty*, To Blesse and Preserve the Sacred Person of our Dread Soveraign Lord, the King, to Prosper his Reign with Honourable and Glorious Successes, and to Prolong his Life, that he may see his Childrens Children, and his Throne may be as the Sun; As also that he may Blesse, Preserve and Strengthen, His Royal Consort the Queens *Majesty*, and make perfect his Work begun for Her, may Save and Defend Her from all Dangers and evil Accidents, that what She hath conceived, may be Preserved and Happily brought forth, to the Joy of our Soveraign Lord, the King, the further Security of his Crown, and the Happiness and Establishment of this Kingdom.

    For this end, His *Majesty*, with Advice foresaid, Doth Appoint and Ordain, that the foresaid Thanks-giving and Prayers, be Devoutly and Solemnly performed, in all the Paroch-Churches within the City and Diocese of *Edinburgh* upon the twenty ninth day of *January* instant, and in all the other Churches, within this Kingdom, upon the ninteenth day of *February* next. And His *Majesty* accordingly Requires and Commands, the most Reverend, and right Reverend, the Arch-Bishops and Bishops, to take care, that in all the Paroch-Churches, within their respective Dioceses, these Prayers and Thanksgivings be accordingly Celebrate, by all the Ministers and Presbyters under their Jurisdiction, and that they cause intimation be made hereof, by reading of the same, from the Pulpits in the several Paroch-Churches, the Lords-day, Immediatly preceeding the saids Solemn days of publick Thanksgiving, *respectivè*, And finally, His *Majesty* Charges and Commands all his Loving Subjects heartily, to joyn and concur in these Religious and Dutiful Performances, as they would shew their Piety and Loyalty, in praying for the Life of the King, the Encrease of his Royal Issue, the further Security of the Crown, and the Estbalishment of Peace, and Happiness in this His Ancient Kingdom. And that these Presents may be made publick and known, His *Majesty* Ordains His Lyon King at Armes, and his Brethren Heraulds, the Macers of the Privy Council, and Pursevants, to pass to the Mercat Cross of *Edinburgh*, and other places needful, and there, by open Proclamation, and with all accustomed Solemnities on extraordinary Occasions, make publication of the Premisses, that none may pretend ignorance.

1688–EIr2   Thanksgiving days for the birth of Prince James

Sunday 17 June 1688 (London, Westminster and ten miles around); Sunday 1 July 1688 (elsewhere in England and Wales; Dublin, suburbs and adjoining liberties); Sunday 8 July 1688 (elsewhere in Ireland); various dates (colonies)

The birth of James Francis Edward, on the morning of 10 June 1688, was quickly followed by official measures to encourage popular rejoicing, including this thanksgiving, appointed on the same day. Unlike the practice during the reigns of James I and Charles I, when individual prayers were issued after royal births, James II ordered a full thanksgiving day. With its instruction to Bishop Sprat of Rochester to compose the form of prayer, the proclamation illustrated how far episcopal support for James had contracted, even since the appointment of 1688–EIr1. Of the authors of the form for that occasion, White of Peterborough was in prison as one of the seven petitioning bishops, and Crewe of Durham had become less close to the king. The thanksgiving was observed lavishly, with wine in London conduits, bonfires and illuminations in Oxford, and volleys of cannon fire from naval vessels in the English Channel. Nevertheless, several sources suggest a public mood of anxiety or even defiance. In London, according to Morrice, many congregations (most notably at St Giles and Lincoln's Inn) refused to say the responses in the special prayers for the day. The thanksgiving in Ireland was presumably appointed on the instructions of the court in England. The form of prayer was identical to that issued in England and Wales. The meeting of the privy council on 10 June that approved the proclamation for the thanksgiving in England and Wales also wrote to Lord Deputy Tyrconnel instructing him to issue a similar proclamation in Ireland. The form of prayer published there was identical to that issued in England. Moreover, in an action that further emphasized the significance attached to the birth by the king and his supporters, for the first time formal privy council orders were sent to the 'Governors of his Majesty's Plantations' and of Jersey and Guernsey. Evidence for observance of the thanksgivings subsequently ordered in America, which in some colonies took place after William of Orange had landed in England, is mixed. In puritan Boston Samuel Sewall noted that the minister was hardly wholeheartedly enthusiastic when he prayed that the birth 'might be a Blessing', but in Maryland, where the catholic Lord Baltimore was proprietor, the general assembly passed an act for an anniversary day of thanksgiving to he held annually on 10 June.

Orders: ENGLAND AND WALES: royal proclamation, 10 June 1688, Wing J257*; IRELAND: proclamation by the lord deputy and council, 23 June 1688, Wing I842*; COLONIES: circular letter from the lords of the privy council to the proprietors and governors of the colonies, 10 June 1688, TNA, PRO, CO 324/5/32–3.
Forms of prayer: ENGLAND AND WALES: *A form of prayer with thanksgiving for the safe delivery of the queen, and happy birth of the young prince. To be used on Sunday next, being the seventeenth day of this instant June, in all churches and chappels, within the cities of London and Westminster, and ten miles distance; and upon the first day of July next, in all other places throughout this kingdom of England, dominion of Wales, and town of Berwick upon Tweed. By his majesties special command* ([8] pp.; Wing C4168)* [other impression, ESTC 006130373]; IRELAND: *A form of prayer with thanksgiving for the safe delivery of the queen, and happy birth of the young prince. To be used on Sunday the first of July, in the city of Dublin, and the liberties thereof; and upon the 8th day of the same month in all other places throughout this kingdom of Ireland* ([8] pp.; Wing C4169A; Marsh's Library, Dublin).
Form of prayer (other edition): Holyroodhouse, P[eter] B[ruce], Wing C4169.
Additional sources: *CSPD, 1687–9*, p. 211; Mostyn newsletters, 12 June, 19 June 1688, University of Wales, Bangor, MS 9094, fos. 29, 34; *London Gazette*, 2361 (2–5 July 1688), 2366 (19–23 July 1688); *Portledge papers*, ed. Kerr and Duncan, p. 36; Evelyn, IV, 588–9; Wood, III, 270–2; Luttrell, I, 443–4;

The correspondence of Henry Hyde, ed. Singer, II, 178; Morrice, IV, 285; privy council register, PC2/72, fos. 685–8; *CSPC*, XII, 559, 565, 584, 586–7, 591, 592, 593, 594, 596, 597, 603, 606–7, 622; *CSPC*, XIII, 4; *Pennsylvania archives: series 1* (12 vols., Harrisburg, PA, 1852–6), I, 106; Hutchinson, *History of Massachusetts*, II, 332; Robert Toppan, *Edward Randolph; including his letters and official papers* (7 vols., Boston, MA, 1898–1909), II, 75, VI, 263–5; *Documents relating to the colonial history of the state of New York* (10 vols., Albany, 1853–8), III, 554; *The diary of Samuel Sewall* (3 vols., Boston, MA, 1879–82), I, 223, 226; *Proceedings of the council of Maryland 1687/8–1693*, ed. W. H. Browne (Baltimore, 1890), pp. 44, 58–9; *Proceedings and acts of the general assembly of Maryland April 1684 – June 1692*, ed. W. H. Browne (Baltimore, 1894), pp. 152, 185–6, 209; *Executive journals of the council of Virginia*, I, 100; *Minutes of the provincial council of Pennsylvania* (16 vols., Harrisburg, PA, 1851–3), I, 229.
Printed sermon: Turner, St Thomas, Southwark (Wing T3318).

ORDERS

England and Wales: royal proclamation, 10 June 1688

It having pleased Almighty God of his great and continued Mercy to His Majesty and His Kingdoms, to Bless Him and His Royal Consort the Queen with a Son, and these His Kingdoms and Dominions with a Prince, His Majesty this day in Council hath thought fit to appoint a time of Publick Thanksgiving to Almighty God throughout this Kingdom for so great a Blessing: And His Majesty doth accordingly Appoint and Command, That upon *Sunday* next, being the Seventeenth day of this instant *June*, within the Cities of *London* and *Westminster* and Ten Miles distance, and upon the First day of *July* next in all other Places throughout this Kingdom of *England*, Dominion of *Wales*, and Town of *Berwick* upon *Tweed*, be had and Solemnized a Publick Thanksgiving to Almighty God for so great a Blessing vouchsafed to His Majesty and these His Kingdoms; And for this purpose His Majesty hath signified His Royal Pleasure to the Right Reverend Father in God *Thomas* Lord Bishop of *Rochester* forthwith to prepare a Form of Religious Service and Publick Thanksgiving, which may be suitable to this occasion; Which Form of Service and Publick Thanksgiving His Majesty will cause to be Printed and Published, and to be distributed throughout the several and respective Dioceses of this Kingdom, to be observed and used in the Churches and Chappels of this Kingdom and Dominion aforesaid, upon the several and respective days beforementioned.

Ireland: proclamation by the lord deputy and council, 23 June 1688

Whereas it hath pleased Almighty God of His Great and Continued Mercy to His Majesty and His Kingdoms to Bless Him and His Royal Consort, the Queen, with a Son; and These His Kingdoms and Dominions with a Prince. And forasmuch as increase of Issue of the Royal Family, and particularly the Birth of a Young Prince, is a Publick Blessing, and, under God, a Great Security of Peace and Happiness to His Majesty's Kingdoms, for which all His Majesty's Subjects are Obliged to make Solemn Acknowledgments to The Almighty God.

We have therefore thought fit to appoint a Time, upon this Occasion, for Publick Thanksgiving in all the Churches and Chapels throughout this Kingdom to Almighty God for so Great a Blessing. We do therefore Appoint, That upon Sunday the first Day of *July* next, within the City and Suburbs of *Dublin*, and the Liberties adjoyning; And upon Sunday the eighth Day of the Month of *July* aforesaid, in all other Places throughout the Kingdom, be had and solemnized a Publick Thanksgiving for so Great a Blessing vouchsafed to His Majesty and His Kingdoms. We willing and strictly Commanding all Persons within this Realm, with all Sobriety, Reverence and Thankfulness to perform this Duty upon the several and respective Days before mentioned, and to Observe the same as becomes so solemn an Occasion.

Colonies: circular letter from the lords of the privy council to the proprietors and governors of the colonies, 10 June 1688

After our very hearty Commendacons, It having pleased almighty God about ten of the Clock this Morning to bless his Majesty and His Royall Consort the Queen with the Birth of a Hopefull Son, and His Majestys Kingdomes and Dominions with a Prince His Majesty hath Commanded us to signifie the same unto you, and to pray and require you to Cause notice thereof to be forthwith given by Proclamation, throughout His Majestys Plantacon under your Government And thereby to appoint such Dayes as well for a solemn Thanksgiving to almighty God for this inestimable Blessing, as for such other Expressions of publick Rejoycings suitable to this great Occasion, as you shall judge fitt. And so not doubting of your ready Compliance herewith, wee bid you very heartily Farewell.

FORMS OF PRAYER

England and Wales; Ireland

This Service shall be the same with the usual Office for the Days above named, except where it is hereafter otherwise appointed.

MORNING PRAYER

At the beginning of Morning Prayer the Minister shall read these Sentences following. [Ps. 50:14; Ps. 54:6]

*In the place of [*Venite Exultemus*] shall be used this following Hymn.*
O Give thanks unto the Lord, and call upon his Name: tell the people what things he hath done. (Ps. 105:1)
O let your songs be of him, and praise him: let your talking be of all his wondrous works. (Ps. 105:2)
Give the Lord the honour due unto his Name: worship the Lord with holy worship. (Ps. 29:2)
One generation shall praise thy works unto another: and declare thy power. (Ps. 145:4)
For thou, Lord, hast made me glad through thy works: I will rejoyce in giving praise, for the operations of thy hands. (Ps. 92:4)
I will sing of the Lord because he hath dealt so lovingly with me: yea, I will praise the Name of the Lord most High. (Ps. 13:6)
The Lord is my strength: he is the wholsome defence of his Anointed. (Ps. 28:9)
Great prosperity giveth he unto his King: and sheweth loving kindness to David his Anointed, and to his seed for evermore. (Ps. 18:51)
O that men would therefore praise the Lord for his goodness: and declare the wonders he doth for the children of men. (Ps. 107:21)
That they would offer unto him the sacrifice of thanksgiving: and tell out his works with gladness. (Ps. 107:22)

That they would exalt him also in the congregation of the People: and praise him in the seat of the Elders. (Ps. 107:32)
For his merciful kindness is ever more and more towards us: and the truth of the Lord endureth for ever. (Ps. 117:2)
Glory be to the Father, &c.
As it was in the beginning, &c.

[Ps. 72, 89]
[First lesson: Isa. 12]
[Second lesson: Matt. 22:15–46]

[Then as BCP to the Lord's prayer]

Priest: O Lord shew thy mercy upon us.
[As BCP until]
Priest: O Lord, save the King.
Answer: *And let his seed be mighty upon earth.*
Priest: Let him evermore rejoyce in thy strength.
Answer: *And be exceeding glad in thy salvation.*
Priest: O Lord, save the Queen.
Answer: *And make her as a fruitful Vine.*
Priest: Endue thy Ministers with righteousness.
[As BCP]

The first Collect instead of that for the day.
O Almighty and everlasting Lord God of heaven and earth, who madest the World and all that is therein, and givest to all men life and breath and all things; We devoutly offer our most hearty thanks to thy Divine Majesty, that thou hast given our Dread Sovereign his hearts desire, and hast not denied us the request of our lips, in blessing him and our Gracious Queen with a Son, and all his Subjects with a Prince. Stablish the thing, O God, that thou hast wrought among us. Grant the Princely Infant health, strength, and long life, that he may grow up to live in thy fear, and to thy glory, and to excell in all virtues becoming his high Birth, and the Royal Dignity to which thou hast ordained him. O prepare thy loving mercy and faithfulness, that they may ever preserve him, for the honour of thy Name, and the establishment of the peace, security and happiness of these Nations from generation to generation, and this we beg for Jesus Christ his sake our only Mediatour and Redeemer. *Amen.*

LITANY

At the end of the Litany, immediately after [We humbly beseech thee] this following Prayer is to be used.
O most powerful and glorious God, who art wonderful in all the mysterious acts of thy Providence, and adorable in the various distributions of thy justice and mercy to the children of men; We meekly humble our selves, and fall low before the footstool of thy grace, rendring thee all worship and thanks, that, although for our manifold sins most justly provoking thee, thou in thy wrath hast heretofore taken from us so many of the Royal Progeny, yet in the midst of judgment thou hast remembred mercy, and according to thy continual goodness hast revived our hopes, and begun

to repair our former losses, by renewing fruitfulness to the Queen, and giving birth
to a Royal Prince. We beseech thee, O Lord, give the King and all his People, such
a due sense of this thy mercy, that our devout and thankful acceptance, and right
use of it, may divert thy judgments for the future, and incline thee to bestow more
such publick blessings upon us. So we who are thy people will reioyce evermore,
in every thing giving thanks unto thee, through our only Mediatour and Advocate
Jesus Christ our Lord. *Amen.*

COMMUNION

*In the Communion-Service next after the Commandments, the first Collect shall be
the same as in the Morning Prayer,* [O Almighty and Everlasting Lord God of heaven
and earth, &c.]

Then shall follow one of the two Collects for the King.

[Epistle: Col. 3:12–18]
[Gospel: Luke 1:57–67]

After the Prayer for the Church Militant, shall follow this Prayer.

    O Lord our Governour, whose Name is excellent in all the World, and who art
king for ever and ever: We praise and bless thy Divine Goodness, for all the marvellous Protections, and signal Favours, thou hast vouchsafed thy Servant our Gracious
King *JAMES*: particularly that after thou hadst preserved him from the dangers of
War, from the rage of the Sea, and from the madness of the People, thou didst in
thy due time bring him to great honour, by settling him on the Throne of his Ancestors, and hast now enlarged thy Blessings towards him, by this happy increase of
the Royal Issue: We most humbly beseech Thee, to continue and multiply these thy
mercies to Him and Us: That thou would'st give him Sons to grow up as the young
plants, and that his daughters may be as the polish'd Corners of the Temple. Bless,
O Lord, the whole Royal Family, with the blessings of the Heavens above, with the
blessings of the Deep beneath, with the blessings of the Breasts and of the Womb:
That when the King's days shall be fulfilled, and he shall sleep with his Fathers in
Peace and Glory, his Seed may be set up after him, and his House and Kingdom
may be establish'd for ever before Thee. Grant this, O Lord, for Jesus Christ his
sake our only Saviour. *Amen.*

1688–S2   Thanksgiving days for the birth of Prince James

Thursday 21 June 1688 (Edinburgh diocese and Lothian); Thursday 28 June 1688 (elsewhere in Scotland)

News of the birth of the prince of Wales, on 10 June 1688, arrived at Edinburgh
on 13 June. The absence from the city of the chancellor, the earl of Perth, delayed
the appointment of this thanksgiving until the following day, when a bonfire was
lit at Holyroodhouse. Like 1688–S1, the thanksgiving was appointed by means of
an act of the privy council, rather than a royal proclamation. On the broadside act,

the names of the councillors present were listed, presumably as an expression of loyalty. As with 1688–S1, presbyterian meeting houses were not enjoined to observe the thanksgiving. Nevertheless, the council instructed burgh authorities to mark the occasion. Music, food and wine were provided in Aberdeen, 'curious fyreworks at the North-Loch syde' in Edinburgh (Lauder, *Historical notices*, II, 870). The crown paid for a bonfire and wine at Holyroodhouse.

Order: act of the privy council, Edinburgh, 14 June 1688, Wing S1454* [also in Wodrow, *History*, IV, 441].

Additional sources: Wodrow, *History*, IV, 441; *Aber. recs., 1643–1747*, p. 309; *RPC*, 3rd ser., XIII, xlviii; Lauder, *Historical notices*, II, 869–70; *Alford exercise*, pp. 393–4; *Inverness and Dingwall records*, p. 134.

ORDER

Act of the privy council: 14 June 1688

It having pleased the Almighty GOD, by whom Kings Reign, to bless His Sacred *Majesty*, our August and Glorious Monarch, and in Him us his dutiful and happy Subjects, with the Birth of the most Serene and High-Born-Prince, the *Prince* and *Stewart* of *Scotland*, &c. by His Royal Consort, Our Gracious Queen *Mary*. And these glad News being intimated to us, by a most welcome Letter under His Royal Hand, VVe in acknowledgment of this great Blessing, do in the first place thank the great King of Heaven for so extraordinary a mercy, fitted to unite all our Hearts, and prevent all our Jealousies: Not doubting but that all His *Majesties* Loyal Subjects will express their solemn and sincere Joy, upon so signal an Occasion, and that they will put up their ardent Prayers to the Almighty, to whom they owe this hopeful Prince, for prolonging His Life, in which they ought to be concerned, as in their chief Earthly Blessing, next to that of His Royal Parents, whom GOD preserve. And for this end, VVe the Lords of His *Majesties* Privy Council do by His *Majesties* special VVarrant, Appoint and Ordain, that a Solemn and Publick Thanksgiving be kept and observed in all the Churches of this His *Majesties* Antient Kingdom, on the respective Days after-specified, *viz.* Those in the Diocess of *Edinburgh*, and the three *Lothians*, on *Thursday* the 21 day of *June* instant; and in all the other Paroch-Churches of the Kingdom on the *Thursday* thereafter, being the 28. of the same Moneth. And VVe, by warrant foresaid, do accordingly Require and Command the most Reverend, and the right Reverend, the Arch-bishops and Bishops, to take care that Intimation be made hereof, by the Ministers Reading the same from their Pulpits, the Lords-day immediatly preceeding the said days of Thanksgiving and Solemnity *respectivè*, and that in all the Paroch-Churches within their Diocesses, the said Thanksgiving be accordingly Celebrated, and VVe Require and Command the Magistrats of all Burghs-Royal, that they cause the said Thanksgiving and Solemnity be observed with all suitable marks of Joy and Congratulation within their respective Burghs. And Ordain the Lyon King at Arms, and his Brethren Heraulds, Macers of Council, and Pursevants, forthwith to pass to the Mercat-Cross of *Edinburgh*, and make Publication of these Presents.

1688–EIr3   Prayers during a threatened invasion by William of Orange

Daily [from 11 October] 1688 (England and Wales); daily [from 22 October] 1688 (Ireland)

In the summer of 1688, William of Orange amassed forces in preparation for an invasion of England. James II came to recognize the threat by mid-September. He attempted to renew his relations with the Anglican hierarchy, and at a meeting with some of the bishops on 8 October, requested that they prepare prayers in response to the feared invasion. James may also have envisaged appointing a fast day. Sancroft's draft was submitted to the king on 10 October and ordered to be printed on the following day. It was rumoured that the bishops had been instructed to describe the prince of Orange as an 'invader', but, while prayers for 'Repentance' and 'Peace and Unity' were included alongside one for the king, there was no condemnation of the invasion. It is not clear how widely the form was distributed and used, though Humphrey Humphreys offered to send Thomas Mostyn a Welsh translation. The English form was sent to Dublin, presumably with instructions for its use in Irish churches. It was reprinted by an order of the lord deputy, dated 22 October, which was included at the end of the form. On 11 December, immediately after James's flight, there was a meeting of 'a Great Number of the Clergy at the Deanery of St Pauls' to discuss an address to the prince of Orange and the continued reading of the prayers. Edward Stillingfleet and Thomas Tenison were deputed to take 'direction' from Sancroft, but the archbishop was reluctant to offer a lead, merely noting, when pressed, that, according to their title, the prayers were 'to be used *during* the present invasion'. This intimation was communicated to the London clergy on the evening of 12 December. Two forms of prayer in support of William's expedition, purportedly translated from Dutch, were published, presumably by the prince's supporters.

Orders: ENGLAND AND WALES: order by Sunderland, secretary of state, 11 Oct. 1688, in the form of prayer, 3; IRELAND: order by William Ellis, secretary to the lord deputy, 22 Oct. 1688, in the form of prayer, [4].
Forms of prayer: ENGLAND AND WALES: *Prayers to be used in all cathedral, collegiate, and parochial churches, and chapels, within this kingdom, during this time of publick apprehensions from the danger of invasion, and to be added to the daily office both morning and evening, immediately after the prayers for the king, and for the royal family* ([4] pp.; Wing C4188J)* [other impressions, ESTC 006146235, 006090541]; IRELAND: *Prayers to be used in all cathedral, collegiate, and parochial churches, and chapels, within this kingdom, during this time of publick apprehensions from the danger of invasion, and to be added to the daily office both morning and evening, immediately after the prayers for the king, and for the royal family* ([4] pp.; Wing C4188L; Marsh's Library, Dublin).
Form of prayer (other edition): Holyroodhouse, P[eter] B[ruce], Wing C4188K.
Additional sources: *CSPD, 1687–9*, p. 309; John Gutch, *Collectanea curiosa* (2 vols., Oxford, 1781), I, 414–18; Evelyn, IV, 600–1; HMC, *Seventh rep., app.*, p. 417; Humphrey Humphreys to Thomas Mostyn, 26 Nov. 1688, University of Wales, Bangor, MS 9070, fo. 46; Tanner 28, fos. 193–4; Robert Beddard, 'Observations of a London clergyman on the revolution of 1688–9: being an excerpt from the autobiography of Dr William Wake', *The Guildhall Miscellany*, II, 9 (1967), p. 415; *A form of prayer, &c. translated from the Dutch* ([London], [1688]; Wing F1569] [also Exeter edition, Wing F1570]; *The prince of Orange's letter to the English-fleet, and the form of prayer used in the Dutch-fleet, translated from the Dutch* ([London], [1688]; Wing W2351).

ORDERS

England and Wales: order by Sunderland, secretary of state, 11 October 1688
His Majesties Pleasure is, That these Prayers be forthwith Printed.

Ireland: order by William Ellis, secretary to the lord deputy, 22 October 1688
His Excellency the Lord Deputy's pleasure is, That these Prayers be forthwith Printed.

FORMS OF PRAYER

England and Wales; Ireland

[After the BCP prayer for the royal family at morning and evening prayer]
For Repentance.

Almighty God and most merciful Father; We miserable Sinners do here humbly acknowledge before Thee, That we are unworthy of the least of all thy Mercies. We confess, O Lord, in the bitterness of our Souls, that we have grievously sinned against Thee; that all Orders of Men amongst us, have transgressed thy righteous Laws; that we have hitherto rendred both thy Mercies and thy Judgments ineffectual to our Amendment. It is of thy meer Mercy, O Lord, that we are not consumed; for which our Souls do magnifie and bless thy Name. O God, who hast hitherto spar'd us, to the end, that thy Goodness might lead us to Repentance; let it be thy good pleasure, to give unto us all that godly sorrow, which worketh Repentance to Salvation, not to be repented of; that thou mayest turn from thy heavy displeasure against us; and mayest rejoyce over us to do us good, through the Merits and Mediation of Jesus Christ our Lord and only Saviour. *Amen.*

For the King.

O Almighty God, the blessed and only Potentate, We offer up our humble Supplications and Prayers to thy Divine Goodness, beseeching thee in this time of Danger to save and protect our most gracious King; Give thy Holy Angels Charge over Him; Preserve His Royal Person in Health and Safety; Inspire him with Wisdom and Justice in all His Counsels; Prosper all His Undertakings for thy Honour and Service with good Success; Fill His Princely Heart with a Fatherly Care of all his People, and give all his Subjects grace always to bear Faith and true Allegiance to His Majesty, that both King and People joyning together to promote thy Glory, and conscientiously discharging their Duties in their several Stations, may all give Thee Thanks and Praise for thy most mighty Protection, and for all other thy great Mercies vouchsafed to Us, through Jesus Christ thy Son, our Saviour. *Amen.*

For Peace, and Unity.

O Lord God, our only hope in time of need; Save and Deliver us we humbly beseech Thee from all those Dangers that threaten us; Give Peace in our days, O Lord, if it be thy will, and prevent the Effusion of Christian bloud in our Land; Reconcile all our Dissentions, and heal all our Breaches: Preserve that Holy Religion we profess, together with our Laws and Ancient Government; Unite us all in unfeigned and universal Charity one towards another, and in one and the same Holy Worship and Communion; That with one heart and one mouth we may glorifie thy Holy Name, and shew forth thy praise from Generation to Generation: And this we beg for the sake of Jesus thy Beloved, in whom thou art well pleased; to whom with Thee and the Holy Ghost, be all honour and glory now, and evermore. *Amen.*

The Collect appointed for the fifth Sunday after Trinity, and that for the fifth after Epiphany, or either of them may here also be used.

PUBLICATIONS

Forthcoming Publications

The Parker Certificates. Ed. Ralph Houlbrooke, Helen Parish and Felicity Heal

The Correspondence and Papers of Archbishop Richard Neile. Ed. Andrew Foster

The Correspondence of Archbishop Laud. Ed. Kenneth Fincham and Nicholas Cranfield

The Diary of John Bargrave, 1644–1645. Ed. Michael Brennan, Jas' Elsner and Judith Maltby

The 1669 Return of Nonconformist Conventicles. Ed. David Wykes

The Sermons of John Sharp. Ed. Françoise Deconinck-Brossard

The Correspondence of Francis Blackburne (1705–1787). Ed. G. M. Ditchfield

The Letters and Papers of William Paley. Ed. Neil Hitchin

The Correspondence, Diaries and Personal Memoranda of Charles Simeon. Ed. Andrew Atherstone

The Diary of an Oxford Parson: The Reverend John Hill, Vice-Principal of St Edmund Hall, Oxford, 1805–1808, 1820–1855. Ed. Grayson Carter

The Journal of Daniel Wilson, Bishop of Calcutta, 1845–1857. Ed. Andrew Atherstone

The Correspondence of Archbishop Lang with Bishop Wilfrid Parker. Ed. Garth Turner

Suggestions for publications should be addressed to Professor Stephen Taylor, General Editor, Church of England Record Society, Department of History, Durham University, 43 North Bailey, Durham, DH1 3EX, s.j.c.taylor@durham.ac.uk.

Membership of the Church of England Record Society is open to all who are interested in the history of the Church of England. Enquiries should be addressed to the Honorary Treasurer, Dr Sarah Mortimer, Christ Church, Oxford OX1 1DP.